FEMINIST FRONTIERS IV

LAUREL RICHARDSON
The Ohio State University

VERTA TAYLOR
The Ohio State University

NANCY WHITTIER
Smith College

The McGraw-Hill Companies, Inc.
New York   St. Louis   San Francisco   Auckland   Bogotá   Caracas   Lisbon
London   Madrid   Mexico City   Milan   Montreal   New Delhi
San Juan   Singapore   Sydney   Tokyo   Toronto

McGraw-Hill

A Division of The McGraw·Hill Companies

To our mothers,
Rose Foreman Richardson,
Alice F. Houston,
and Sally A. Kennedy;
and to our sisters,
Jessica Richardson Phillips,
Betty Jo Hudson,
and Sarah Whittier

FEMINIST FRONTIERS IV

2 3 4 5 6 7 8 9 0 FGR FGR 9 0 9 8 7

ISBN 0-07-052379-7

This book was set in Times New Roman by The Clarinda Company.
The editors were Jill S. Gordon and Katherine Blake;
the production supervisor was Kathryn Porzio.
The cover was designed by Armen Kojoyian.
Project Supervisor was done by The Total Book.
Quebecor Printing/Fairfield was printer and binder.

Library of Congress Cataloging–in–Publication Data
Feminist frontiers IV / [compiled by] Laurel Richardson, Verta Taylor,
    Nancy Whittier.
        p.   cm.
    Includes bibliographical references.
    ISBN 0-07-052379-7.—ISBN 0-07-052380-0   (Test Bank)
    1. Feminism—United States.   2. Women—United States.
3. Sex role—United States.   4. Women—Cross-cultural studies.
I. Richardson, Laurel.   II. Taylor, Verta A.   III. Whittier, Nancy,
(date)
HQ1426.F472   1997
305.42′0973—dc20   96-20823

ABOUT THE AUTHORS

LAUREL RICHARDSON is Professor Emerita of Sociology and Graduate Faculty of Women's Studies at The Ohio State University. She received her B.A. from the University of Chicago, where she was a Ford Fellow and a University Honors Fellow, and her Ph.D. from the University of Colorado, where she held a University Graduate Fellowship and a National Science Foundation Dissertation Fellowship. She has been the recipient of many grants and fellowships, including support from the National Institute of Education, the National Institute of Mental Health, the National Endowment for the Humanities, and various state and local awards. In 1970, she introduced the first Women's Studies course at Ohio State University, and has taught and written extensively about gender and feminist theory since then.

Professor Richardson is the author of *The Dynamics of Sex and Gender* (three editions), *Gender and University Teaching, Writing Strategies,* and *The New Other Woman,* which has been translated into Japanese, Portuguese, and German. In addition, her work has appeared in many journals, including the *Chicago Review, American Sociological Review, Social Forces, Gender & Society, Journal of Contemporary Ethnography, Qualitative Sociology, Social Psychology, Symbolic Interaction, Sociological Theory, Qualitative Inquiry,* and *Sociological Quarterly.* She is a frequent presenter on topics of gender, qualitative methods, and feminist-poststructuralist theory at national and international meetings. She has served on the editorial boards of *The National Women's Studies Journal, Gender & Society, Journal of Contemporary Ethnography, Sociological Quarterly,* and *Qualitative Inquiry.* She has just completed a book, *Fields of Play: Explorations in Time, Voice, Frame, and Text,* in which she places recent papers into autobiographical contexts, applying a feminist sociological critique to academic life.

VERTA TAYLOR is Associate Professor of Sociology and a member of the Graduate Faculty of the Center for Women's Studies at The Ohio State University, where she teaches courses on gender, women's studies, and social movements. She has won numerous teaching awards at Ohio State, including several graduate teaching awards in sociology, a University Distinguished Teaching Award, and a multicultural teaching award. In 1995 she was co-recipient of the Sociologists for Women in Society's Mentoring Award at the Annual Meetings of the American Sociological Association, and was voted Chair-Elect of the Section on Sex and Gender of the American Sociological Association.

Professor Taylor is the coauthor (with Leila J. Rupp) of *Survival in the Doldrums: The American Women's Rights Movement, 1945 to the 1960s,* which received scholarly research awards from the Collective Behavior and Social Movement Section of the American Sociological Association and the North Central Sociological Association. Her most recent book, *Rock-a-by Baby: Feminism, Self-Help and Postpartum Depression,* centers on the transformation of feminism in modern women's self-help and sets forth a framework for analyzing the intersections of gender and social movements. Her writings have appeared in numerous scholarly collections and in journals such as *The American Sociological Review, Social Problems, Signs, Gender & Society, Journal of Marriage and the Family, Mobilization,* and *Sociological Focus.* She has served as investigator of grants for the National Science Foundation, the National Institute of Mental Health, the National Endowment for the Humanities, and the Ohio Department of Mental Health. In addition, she is a member of the editorial boards of *Social Problems, Teaching Sociology, Gender & Society, Mobilization,* and the *Encyclopedia of Homosexuality Volume on Lesbianism*; an associate editor of the University of Minnesota Press book series "Social Movements, Protest, and Societies in Contention"; and has served on the editorial boards of *Mass Emergencies* and the *National Women's Studies*

Association Journal. In addition to her continuing research on women's movements and lesbian communities, Professor Taylor lectures frequently at national and international meetings on feminism and social movements.

NANCY WHITTIER is Assistant Professor of Sociology and a member of the Women's Studies Advisory Committee at Smith College. She teaches courses on gender, social movements, and research methods. She received her Ph.D. from The Ohio State University, where she held a University Fellowship and a Presidential Dissertation Fellowship.

Professor Whittier is the author of *Feminist Generations: The Persistence of the Radical Women's Movement*, which traces the evolution of radical feminism over the past 25 years and examines intergenerational differences within the women's movement. Her work on the women's movement, social movement culture and collective identity, and activist generations has appeared in several scholarly collections and journals. She serves on the editorial board of *Gender & Society*. She is currently working on a study of feminist child abuse prevention movements and their opponents.

C O N T E N T S

PART THREE:

SOCIAL ORGANIZATION OF GENDER

SECTION FIVE: Work

SECTION SIX: Families   261

SECTION SEVEN: Intimacy and Sexuality   307

SECTION EIGHT: Bodies and Medicine   351

SECTION NINE: Violence against Women   393

PART FOUR:

SOCIAL CHANGE   441

SECTION TEN: Global Politics and the State   445

SECTION ELEVEN: Social Protest and the Feminist Movement

P R E F A C E

The first edition of *Feminist Frontiers* was conceived in the late 1970s, at a time when many women inside and outside academia were beginning to recognize and challenge male domination. At the time of its publication, only a handful of books and anthologies written for classroom use presented a feminist perspective on women's status. The evolution of this book through four editions reflects both the successes of the women's movement and the development of feminist scholarship over the past two decades. Women's studies courses have blossomed and spread to campuses in even the most conservative regions of the country. Feminist scholars in the meantime have refined and enlarged our understanding of how gender inequality operates and how it intersects with other systems of domination based on race, ethnicity, nationality, class, and sexuality. There is no doubt that the situation of women has changed since the publication of the first edition of *Feminist Frontiers.* Gender inequality has not, however, disappeared.

With pride and excitement we write this preface to *Feminist Frontiers IV.* We are proud to be part of the continuing women's movement which struggles to reform the structure and culture of male dominance; and we are excited by the burgeoning of knowledge about diversity and differences among women. We feel fortunate to be writing, teaching, and learning at a time when feminist thought and research are flourishing and deepening. It is simultaneously a time to enjoy the bounty of feminist scholarship and to sow new feminist seeds. This fourth edition of *Feminist Frontiers* includes a new coeditor, Nancy Whittier. We are proud that this book is the collective effort of two established feminist scholars, Verta Taylor and Laurel Richardson, and a member of the new generation of feminist scholars, Nancy Whittier. We have enjoyed this collaboration across feminist generations, and we think it has enriched the book.

Feminist thought seeks to transform, in fundamental and profound ways, all the old patriarchal ways of seeing, defining, and understanding our experiences and the social world. Feminists view the accomplishment of this transformation as a global activity that must take account of differences and diversity. The articles in *Feminist Frontiers IV* underscore the pervasive cultural, racial, ethnic, sexual, and other differences that interact with gender. The experience of being a woman is not the same for different groups.

We developed this book for use as the major or supplementary text in courses on the sociology of women, women's studies, gender studies, or sex roles. In addition, because the book offers a general framework for analyzing women's status, it can be used as a supplementary text in introductory sociology courses and in courses on social problems, foundations of society, comparative studies, and American studies. Although we have retained some of the articles from previous editions of *Feminist Frontiers,* particularly writings that have become feminist classics, approximately half of the readings are new to this edition. We have selected readings that continue to emphasize the diversity of women's experiences and multicultural perspectives, while strengthening several sections and bringing in the most current issues in feminist scholarship.

Feminist Frontiers IV is organized into four parts, each introduced by a sociological-feminist analysis. Part One, "Introduction," begins with a section representing the diversity of women's experiences and gender systems, and contains a new second section, "Feminist Perspectives," which presents engaging and accessible feminist theoretical approaches. Part Two, "Learning Gender," has two sections, "Language, Images, and Culture" and "Socialization." The five sections of Part Three, "Social Organization of Gender," provide readings on work, families, intimacy and sexuality, bodies and medicine, and violence against women. Part Four, "Social Change," includes articles on politics and the state and on social protest and the feminist movement.

The new edition has an expanded focus on conceptualizing gender, with a new section on Feminist Perspectives that combines new work on gender categories, the social construction of gender, transsexualism, and black feminism, with feminist classics. We have also strengthened the sections on Language, Images, and Culture; Bodies and Medicine; Politics and the State; and Social Protest and the Feminist Movement by adding many new selections that reflect the growing body of research in these areas, on topics including women's music, hate radio, eating disorders, breast cancer, welfare policy toward single mothers, social policy regarding people with AIDS, women elected officials, and the experiences of employees at abortion clinics. In addition, all the sections have been updated, with new selections on topics such as adolescent girls' sense of self, comparable worth, sexual harassment, rape as a war crime, and lesbian mothers. We have added numerous new boxed inserts that keep the text lively and raise important issues that are not dealt with in the regular selections. Although analyses of women's experiences remain the core of the book, we have added selected articles and boxed inserts dealing with the construction of masculinity and men's resistance to the structure and culture of male dominance.

As we set about the task of selecting articles for this edition, we found an abundance of excellent pieces. We used the following criteria for choosing what to include: First, we wanted each selection to be engagingly written and accessible in style and language to readers from different disciplinary backgrounds. Second, as a testament to the tremendous growth in depth and understanding of feminist scholarship, we sought selections exploring a wide range of theoretical and substantive issues. Third, we wanted the anthology to reflect a diversity of racial, ethnic, generational, sexual, and cultural experiences. Fourth, we sought to capture the cross-disciplinary nature of gender research. The result is a collection that links well-written and significant articles within a general feminist sociological perspective.

We gratefully acknowledge the support, skill, and help of many people. We extend thanks to contributing authors, not only for writing the selected pieces but also for allowing us to reprint them here. At McGraw-Hill, we especially thank our publisher, Phil Butcher, for believing in and supporting this project; Jill Gordon, our sponsoring editor, for her encouragement and help in shaping the book; and Kathy Blake, associate editor, for shepherding the book through its development. We also thank Kate Scheinman of The Total Book for overseeing the final manuscript through editing and production, and Fred Courtright, permissions editor. Amber Ault was instrumental in shaping some section introductions for the previous edition of the book; we appreciate her contributions. Nicole Raeburn provided invaluable research assistance as we selected articles for this edition. Melissa Briggs, Eszter Hargittai, Aungela Price, and Molly Wallace provided clerical support and feedback from students' perspectives. In addition, Mary Margaret Fonow and Claire Robertson have given us valuable feedback on their teaching experiences with earlier editions of *Feminist Frontiers*. Finally, we express our appreciation to students in our sociology of women, sex and gender, and women's studies classes at Ohio State University and Smith College, who have contributed to the development of this anthology by their thoughtful responses to proposed articles.

The following scholars served as reviewers for *Feminist Frontiers IV*, and we thank them for their expert and generous comments: Lisa Brush, University of Pittsburgh; Naomi Gerstel, University of Massachusetts; Elizabeth Higginbotham, University of Memphis; Valerie Jenness, Washington State University; Michael Kimmel, State University of New York-Stony Brook; Judith Lorber, City University of New York Graduate Center; Debra Minkoff, Yale University; Sarah Projansky, University of California-Davis; Brenda Phillips, Texas Woman's University; Jennifer Reed, California State University-San Bernadino; and Shirley Yee, University of Washington.

Special thanks go to those close to us who inspired both the work and the authors. Ernest Lockridge has been steadfast in his belief in and support for the project. Leila Rupp critically reviewed the entire collection at every stage of the revision, and offered the friendship and support needed to carry out the project. Kate Weigand provided feedback and insight into the collection's organization and offered consistent encouragement and companionship. Jonah Weigand-Whittier is a constant source of inspiration as we seek to reconstruct gender. To them and to the many others who touched our lives positively, we express our gratitude.

Finally, we are full coeditors; our names are listed in alphabetical order.

Laurel Richardson
Verta Taylor
Nancy Whittier

P A R T   O N E

Introduction

What does it mean to be a woman? Thinking about women's experiences is a complicated task because women have as many differences from each other as commonalities. On the one hand, women everywhere suffer restrictions, oppression, and discrimination because they are living in patriarchal societies. Yet gender is not the sole influence on any woman's life. Differences of race, ethnicity, class, sexuality, age, nation, region, and religion shape women's experiences. Moreover, these differences intersect with each other. Lesbians of different ages, social classes, races, and religions, for example, have different experiences.

The experience of being a woman may be quite different for distinct groups of women. For a white, upper-class, heterosexual, American woman, for example, femininity might entail being economically dependent on her husband, perfecting a delicate and refined physical appearance, and achieving social influence through child-raising and volunteer work. Womanhood for a middle-class African-American woman might mean providing financial support for her children, holding influential and respected positions within her church and community, yet being stereotyped by the dominant white culture as sexually promiscuous or unintelligent. For a Cambodian immigrant to the United States, being a woman might mean seeing herself as secondary to her husband, yet enjoying support and influence within networks of other women. In short, gender is defined in various ways for different groups. Gender definitions bring with them a distinct set of restrictions and disadvantages for women in each group, as well as privileges and sources of power or resistance.

As if matters were not complex enough, feminist scholars also recognize that individuals have unique constellations of experiences: We each have our own story to tell. Each of us has multiple alliances and identifications with groups that shift through time and social context. The religious identity of childhood may be shunted aside during young adulthood, for example, only to be reclaimed again in later years. Self-definitions as heterosexual may give way later in life to new identities as lesbian or bisexual. As biracial or bicultural or mixed-religion daughters, we might identify with either parent's heritage or that of both. Large social forces such as sexism, racism, heterosexism, and class inequality shape our biographies, but it is as individuals that we experience and make sense of our lives. Individuals do not easily attribute our experiences to class, race, or gender as *separate* or *separable* enties. We rarely see our own biographies as sociohistorically situated.

The task of feminist scholarship, and of this volume, is to illuminate the social and structural roots of women's experiences, while simultaneously recognizing the complicated and unique factors that shape each woman's life. Feminist research builds upon and links two levels of analysis: *structure* and *biography*. The *structural* level looks at social institutions and cultural practices which create and sustain gender inequalities and links those inequalities to other systems of oppression such as racism, ageism, and homophobia. The *biographical* level honors each woman's expression of her own experience. It makes available individual self-representation and personal voice. Because feminist scholarship links structural understandings with individual biography, we learn how difference and commonality are structurally induced and personally experienced. We can see how larger social forces affect our own and others' lives.

Feminist research is not just about analyzing the ways that social structures shape and restrict the lives of women. Of course, documenting the inequalities faced by various groups of women and examining the ways that women have been oppressed and victimized based on gender are important tasks for scholars. Such experiences—discrimination in hiring and pay, sexual violence, and legal subordination, for example—are undeniably central to gender. Yet feminist scholarship also emphasizes the sources of power that women find—how women define themselves, influence their social contexts, and resist the restrictions they face. The articles in this volume view women not simply as passive victims of patriarchal social structures, but as actors who exercise agency despite social constraints. By documenting the influence of social structures and highlighting women's agency, feminist scholarship leads us to rethink the structural changes necessary to meet the needs of actual women.

Given the issues of diversity and difference, the resulting difficulty of analyzing women (or men) as a group, and the need simultaneously to document women's oppression and to recognize women's resistance, how do feminist researchers approach their work? Not surprisingly, there is considerable variation and debate among feminist scholars about theoretical explanations of gender and approaches to research. Nevertheless, feminist approaches have some identifiable commonalities. Building upon and adding to Judith Cook and Mary Margaret Fonow's analysis of feminist methodology, we will discuss five central "feminist ways of knowing."

1. *Acknowledging the pervasive influence of gender.* Gender and gender asymmetry are basic features of social life. Women, their worlds, and their subjective experiences, including their relationships to men and to gender inequality, are the focus. Claims about "human" behavior based on research on men are subject to critique. Indeed, the entire academic enterprise is scrutinized: How do claims to scientific and scholarly objectivity disguise male bias? How do the social conditions and practices of doing research reinforce gender inequities? Feminist scholars ask how research is conducted, how it is analyzed, and how the researchers, social settings, and financial support for research affect or bias the conclusions.

2. *Uncovering the links between gender and other asymmetric systems.* Feminist researchers understand systems of oppression as interlocking: Race, class, ethnicity, sexual orientation, and other systems of domination affect how one experiences gender. Therefore, although gender asymmetry is a basic fact of social life, it is experienced differently by women situated differently in society. These differences in women's experiences are not to be ignored or dismissed, but uncovered. Just as feminist researchers challenge knowledge claims based on research on men, they question knowledge about "women" based on research on white, middle-class women. In a self-reflexive manner, feminists question how their own scholarly practices and social locations (such as in a predominantly white academic department) bias their research and lead to false generalities.

3. *Focusing on consciousness-raising.* Consciousness-raising refers to the experience of recognizing through contact with other women (reading, research, discussion) that one's own experiences and problems are shared by others, and thus are a result of structural forces rather than personal failings. Feminist research alters the consciousness of researchers. As members of a society, feminist researchers have incorporated cultural understandings about women; as feminists, they have analyzed official ideologies and practices to reveal their implications for women's oppression. They have, therefore, as Liz Stanley and Sue Wise put it, "double vision": They see women's lives simultaneously through the old lens of patriarchy and the new lens of feminism. Having double vision helps

feminist researchers to recognize the diversity of responses to oppression and the contradictions between consciousness and action. Much feminist research looks at crisis points and transitions in women's lives, such as divorce, rape, coming out, pregnancy, menopause, sexual harassment, and career shifts. These transitions rupture the taken-for-granted world; at such times the "normalcy" of patriarchy is revealed to women, giving them an opportunity to rethink their lives.

4. *Rethinking the relationship between the researcher and the researched.* Scientific research assumes that there is a separation between the "researched" and the "researcher" and that this separation produces "objective" and "valid" knowledge. Feminist researchers challenge this tenet. Treating women as "objects" of research contravenes feminist goals for equality by elevating the researcher and her agenda above the researched and her agenda. One of the major questions of feminist thought is how to do research that empowers both the researcher and the researched. How do we create social research practices that reduce the power of the researcher to collect, categorize, and name the experiences of other women? For some, the solution has been to write about their own lives; some acknowledge directly how their own biases affect their work on other women; some study groups of which they are a part; and still others do "participatory" or "action" research in which the researcher and the researched determine together the topics, methods, goals, and political action to follow from the project, so that the scholar is a participant in the project, but not its leader.

These are not only pragmatic or theoretical concerns. For contemporary feminist researchers these are important *ethical* questions. What right does a scholar have to study and write about another woman's life? For what audiences should she write? What do you do if, through your interviewing, for example, you have raised the consciousness of a woman but cannot change her life circumstances? How can feminist scholars use the skills and privileges of academic practice to improve the life opportunities of other women? Feminist research is thus characterized by a constant critique of the morality of its labors.

5. *Emphasizing empowerment and transformation.* Ultimately, feminist researchers are concerned not only with understanding the structures of gender, but also with how their research can be used to improve the lives of women through individual empowerment or social change. For example, a study of battered women might be based on interviews with women in battered women's shelters and tell the stories of individual women and the effects that the shelter movement has had on their lives. The results may be disseminated through different media with the hope of reaching other women caught in abusive relationships. The topics for feminist research are legion because the sites in need of transformation—such as work, the family, sexual socialization, education, health care, and politics—are everywhere. Therefore, the opportunities for empowering women—and oneself—through research are, also, everywhere.

We invite you to engage in reading, thinking about, and doing feminist research. We encourage you to discuss your ideas, to debate the issues this volume raises with your friends and classmates, to disagree with the authors here when necessary, and to come to your own conclusions. We hope that through this engagement, you will discover how gender has shaped your life and how gender intersects with the other systems of inequality that affect you. We hope that you will share your understandings with others, becoming a researcher yourself and a theorist of your own and others' lives so that you might help empower us all and transform society.

SECTION ONE
Diversity and Difference

Conducting research about women has been the focus of feminist scholars from the 1960s to the present. In recent years, researchers have looked especially closely at the differences and commonalities among women and have also begun to examine how men's lives are shaped by cultural expectations of masculinity. Scholars are interested in learning about the rich complexities of women's lives and in discovering ways of knowing that stand true to women's experiences and also offer the prospect of effecting positive change. Women everywhere live with a ubiquitous "monotone" of male advantage, in all its manifestations. Yet differences among women arise from factors like race, ethnicity, class, sexual orientation, age, geographical region, and religion. Further, not all men possess the same advantages or social power; men of subordinate racial or ethnic groups, classes, or sexual orientations may have power relative to women in their own group, but are subordinate in some ways to other men and to women in more powerful groups.

Recognizing that women are not a homogeneous group raises questions about the basis of comparison and the grounds for affiliation among women. Can we even speak of "women" as a meaningful category, or is the diversity among women too great for any generalization? The readings in this section grapple with these questions from various points of view. The authors discuss points of similarity and difference among women, and illustrate the vast range of meanings that gender has for women—and men—in different groups.

One source of commonality that has attracted and shaped feminist understanding is the idea of *oppression*. As a concept, oppression has had a long history in contemporary feminist scholarship. What does it mean? Why is it important to think about? The first selection, "Oppression," answers these questions and raises some others. In that article, Marilyn Frye defines oppression as "living one's life confined and shaped by forces and barriers which are not accidental or occasional and hence avoidable, but are systematically related to each other in such a way as to catch one between and among them and restrict or penalize motion in any direction." There are, then, multiple sources of interrelated oppressions, making it difficult for people to recognize how the systems of oppression impinge on their lives or the lives of others. Knowing about the larger social forces, however, helps one to understand the shape of one's life and the difference between "suffering" and "suffering from oppression."

Whereas Frye emphasizes the structure of oppression which constricts all women, the remaining readings in this section pay particular attention to the distinctions among women's experiences. Rosalinda Méndez González discusses the history of the western United States from the point of view of women of various classes and ethnicities, in "Distinctions in Western Women's Experience: Ethnicity, Class, and Social Change." She suggests that the traditional history of westward expansion across the frontier is the story of only one group of women, the "pioneer" settlers of European descent. Considering the lives of

Indian, Mexican, and Chinese women means reconstructing our understanding of the development of the West. This article illustrates the task of contemporary feminist researchers: to examine the experiences of diverse groups of women, consider the impact of class and race inequalities, and rethink the biased assumptions and histories that scholars have long taken for granted.

Paula Gunn Allen, similarly, suggests that assumptions about what it means to be a woman in Anglo-European culture do not hold in American Indian culture. In "Where I Come From Is Like This," she draws on her bicultural experiences to explore the incongruity of the images of women embedded in Anglo and American Indian cultures. The images of Indian women she grew up with are images of "practicality, strength, reasonableness, intelligence, wit, and competence," in contrast to non-Indian ideas about women as "passive and weak." Again, we see the difficulty of generalizing about women's experiences.

Connell suggests that just as gender varies for different groups of women, men are not an undifferentiated group either. He argues that society as a whole has defined a "hegemonic masculinity" that prescribes a particular model of male behavior and serves to maintain male dominance. Yet subcultures define different masculinities, such as that constructed by gay men. Fundamental to hegemonic masculinity is dominance over both women and other men. Women, on the other hand, are expected to "perform" what Connell calls "emphasized femininity," displaying their subordination to men.

The difficulties of sensitively and accurately analyzing how systems of oppression affect a person's life are amplified in the final two articles. In "The Master's Tools Will Never Dismantle the Master's House," Audre Lorde argues that feminists must critically examine their own use of patriarchal concepts in their analyses of women's lives. Will the "regular" methods of scholarship and science be adequate to the task of understanding the diversity among women? Will new tools be necessary? Lorde argues that encouraging women to relate to each other at the points of their differences promotes growth, creativity, and social change. In "Something about the Subject Makes It Hard to Name," Gloria Yamato returns to the question of oppression. Adding to Frye's argument, Yamato emphasizes how oppression affects the actions, outlook, and self-image of oppressed people themselves. It is important to combat "internalized racism," she suggests, as well as to work against external racist acts and beliefs. Women, both Lorde and Yamato propose, gain more in celebrating their differences than in trying to erase them. What do the articles in this section suggest about the kinds of differences and commonalities that exist among women and men of different races, classes, sexualities, and cultures?

Oppression

MARILYN FRYE

It is a fundamental claim of feminism that women are oppressed. The word 'oppression' is a strong word. It repels and attracts. It is dangerous and dangerously fashionable and endangered. It is much misused, and sometimes not innocently.

The statement that women are oppressed is frequently met with the claim that men are oppressed too. We hear that oppressing is oppressive to those who oppress as well as to those they oppress. Some men cite as evidence of their oppression their much-advertised inability to cry. It is tough, we are told, to be masculine. When the stresses and frustrations of being a man are cited as evidence that oppressors are oppressed by their oppressing; the word 'oppression' is being stretched to meaninglessness; it is treated as though its scope includes any and all human experience of limitation or suffering, no matter the cause, degree or consequence. Once such usage has been put over on us, then if ever we deny that any person or group is oppressed, we seem to imply that we think they never suffer and have no feelings. We are accused of insensitivity; even of bigotry. For women, such accusation is particularly intimidating, since sensitivity is one of the few virtues that has been assigned to us. If we are found insensitive, we may fear we have no redeeming traits at all and perhaps are not real women. Thus are we silenced before we begin: the name of our situation drained of meaning and our guilt mechanisms tripped.

But this is nonsense. Human beings can be miserable without being oppressed, and it is perfectly consistent to deny that a person or group is oppressed without denying that they have feelings or that they suffer. . . .

The root of the word 'oppression' is the element 'press'. *The press of the crowd; pressed into military service; to press a pair of pants; printing press; press the button.* Presses are used to mold things or flatten them or reduce them in bulk, sometimes to reduce them by squeezing out the gasses or liquids in them. Something pressed is something caught between or among forces and barriers which are so related to each other that jointly they restrain, restrict or prevent the thing's motion or mobility. Mold. Immobilize. Reduce.

The mundane experience of the oppressed provides another clue. One of the most characteristic and ubiquitous features of the world as experienced by oppressed people is the double bind—situations in which options are reduced to a very few and all of them expose one to penalty, censure or deprivation. For example, it is often a requirement upon oppressed people that we smile and be cheerful. If we comply, we signal our docility and our acquiescence in our situation. We need not, then, be taken note of. We acquiesce in being made invisible, in our occupying no space. We participate in our own erasure. On the other hand, anything but the sunniest countenance exposes us to being perceived as mean, bitter, angry or dangerous. This means, at the least, that we may be found "difficult" or unpleasant to work with, which is enough to cost one one's livelihood; at worst, being seen as mean, bitter, angry or dangerous has been known to result in rape, arrest, beating and murder. One can only choose to risk one's preferred form and rate of annihilation.

Another example: It is common in the United States that women, especially younger women, are in a bind where neither sexual activity nor sexual inactivity is all right. If she is heterosexually active, a woman is open to censure and punishment for being loose, unprincipled or a whore. The "punishment" comes in the form of criticism, snide and embarrassing remarks, being treated as an easy lay by men, scorn from her more restrained female friends. She may have to lie and hide her behavior from her parents. She must juggle the risks of unwanted pregnancy and dangerous contraceptives. On the other hand, if she refrains from heterosexual activity, she is fairly constantly harassed by men who try to persuade her into it and pressure her to "relax" and "let her hair down"; she is threatened with labels like "frigid," "uptight," "man-hater," "bitch" and "cocktease." The same parents who would be disapproving of her sexual activity may be worried by her inactivity because it suggests she is not or will not be popular, or is not sexually normal. She may be charged with lesbianism. If a woman is raped, then if she has been heterosexually active she is subject to the presumption that she liked it (since her activity is presumed to show that she likes sex), and if she has not been heterosexually active, she is subject to the presumption that she liked it (since she is supposedly "repressed and frustrated"). Both heterosexual activity and heterosexual nonactivity are likely to be taken as proof that you wanted to be raped, and hence, of course, weren't *really* raped at all. You can't win. You are caught in a bind, caught between systematically related pressures.

Women are caught like this, too, by networks of forces and barriers that expose one to penalty, loss or contempt whether one works outside the home or not, is on welfare or not, bears children or not, raises children or not, marries or not, stays married or not, is heterosexual, lesbian, both or neither. Economic necessity; confinement to racial and/or sexual job ghettos; sexual harassment; sex discrimination; pressures of competing expectations and judgments about *women, wives* and *mothers* (in the society at large, in racial and ethnic subcultures and in one's own mind); dependence (full or partial) on husbands, parents or the state; commitment to political ideas; loyalties to racial or ethnic or other "minority" groups; the demands of self-respect and responsibilities to others. Each of these factors exists in complex tension with every other, penalizing or prohibiting all of the apparently available options. And nipping at one's heels, always, is the endless pack of little things. If one dresses one way, one is subject to the assumption that one is advertising one's sexual availability; if one dresses another way, one appears to "not care about oneself" or to be "unfeminine." If one uses "strong language," one invites categorization as a whore or slut; if one does not, one invites categorization as a "lady"—one too delicately constituted to cope with robust speech or the realities to which it presumably refers.

The experience of oppressed people is that the living of one's life is confined and shaped by forces and barriers which are not accidental or occasional and hence avoidable, but are systematically related to each other in such a way as to catch one between and among them and restrict or penalize motion in any direction. It is the experience of being caged in: all avenues, in every direction, are blocked or booby trapped.

Cages. Consider a birdcage. If you look very closely at just one wire in the cage, you cannot see the other wires. If your conception of what is before you is determined by this myopic focus, you could look at that one wire, up and down the length of it, and be unable to see why a bird would not just fly around the wire any time it wanted to go somewhere. Furthermore, even if, one day at a time, you myopically inspected each wire, you still could not see why a bird would have trouble going past the wires to get anywhere. There is no physical property of any one wire, *nothing* that the closest scrutiny could discover, that will reveal how a bird could be inhibited or harmed by it except in the most accidental way. It is only when you step back, stop looking at the wires one by one, microscopically, and take a macroscopic view of the whole cage, that you can see why the bird does not go anywhere; and then you will see it in a moment. It will require no great subtlety of mental powers. It is perfectly *obvious* that the bird is surrounded by a network of systematically related barriers, no one of which would be the least hindrance to its flight, but which, by their relations to each other, are as confining as the solid walls of a dungeon.

It is now possible to grasp one of the reasons why oppression can be hard to see and recognize: one can study the elements of an oppressive structure with great care and some good will without seeing the structure as a whole, and hence without seeing or being able to understand that one is looking at a cage and that there are people there who are caged, whose motion and mobility are restricted, whose lives are shaped and reduced.

The arresting of vision at a microscopic level yields such common confusion as that about the male door-opening ritual. This ritual, which is remarkably widespread across classes and races, puzzles many people, some of whom do and some of whom do not find it offensive. Look at the scene of the two people approaching a door. The male steps slightly ahead and opens the door. The male holds the door open while the female glides through. Then the male goes through. The door closes after them. "Now how," one innocently asks, "can those crazy womenslibbers say that is oppressive? The guy *removed* a barrier to the lady's smooth and unruffled progress." But each repetition of this ritual has a place in a pattern, in fact in several patterns. One has to shift the level of one's perception in order to see the whole picture.

The door-opening pretends to be a helpful service, but the helpfulness is false. This can be seen by noting that it will be done whether or not it makes any practical sense. Infirm men and men burdened with packages will open doors for able-bodied women who are free of physical burdens. Men will impose themselves awkwardly and jostle everyone in order to get to the door first. The act is not determined by convenience or grace. Furthermore, these very numerous acts of unneeded or even noisome "help" occur in counterpoint to a pattern of men not being helpful in many practical ways in which women might welcome help. What *women* experience is a world in which gallant princes charming commonly make a fuss about being helpful and providing small services when help and services are of little or no use, but in which there are rarely ingenious and adroit princes at hand when substantial assistance is really wanted either in mundane affairs or in situations of threat, assault or terror. There is no help with the (his) laundry; no help typing a report at 4:00 a.m.; no help in mediating disputes among relatives or children. There is nothing but advice that women should stay indoors after dark, be chaperoned by a man, or when it comes down to it, "lie back and enjoy it."

The gallant gestures have no practical meaning. Their meaning is symbolic. The door-opening and similar services provided are services which really are needed by people who are for one reason or another incapacitated—unwell, burdened with parcels, etc. So the message is that women are incapable. The detachment of the acts from the concrete realities of what women need and do not need is a vehicle for the message that women's actual needs and interests are unimportant or irrelevant. Finally, these gestures imitate the behavior of servants toward masters and thus mock women, who are in most respects the servants and caretakers of men. The message of the false helpfulness of male gallantry is female dependence, the invisibility or insignificance of women, and contempt for women.

One cannot see the meanings of these rituals if one's focus is riveted upon the individual event in all its particularity, including the particularity of the individual man's present conscious intentions and motives and the individual woman's conscious perception of the event in the moment. It seems sometimes that people take a deliberately myopic view and fill their eyes with things seen microscopically in order not to see macroscopically. At any rate, whether it is deliberate or not, people can and do fail to see the oppression of women because they fail to see macroscopically and hence fail to see the various elements of the situation as systematically related in larger schemes.

As the cageness of the birdcage is a macroscopic phenomenon, the oppressiveness of the situations in which women live our various and different lives is a macroscopic phenomenon. Neither can be *seen* from a microscopic perspective. But when you look macroscopically you can see it—a network of forces and barriers which are systematically related and which conspire to the immobilization, reduction and molding of women and the lives we live.

R E A D I N G   2

Distinctions in Western Women's Experience: Ethnicity, Class, and Social Change

ROSALINDA MÉNDEZ GONZÁLEZ

The issues of ethnicity, class, and social change as they relate to women in western history and to historical reevaluation derive in part from the social-change movements of the 1950s and 1960s. Until then academic research had

Rosalinda Méndez González, "Distinctions in Western Women's Experience: Ethnicity, Class, and Social Change" from *The Women's West*, edited by Susan Armitage and Elizabeth Jameson. Copyright © 1987 by the University of Oklahoma Press. Reprinted with the permission of the publishers.

tended to neglect the experiences of minorities, women, and the laboring classes or to justify their subordinate social condition. Then the civil rights, feminist, and nationalist movements raised challenges to these approaches.

The new research born of the rebellions of those exciting years sought to uncover and document the historical facts of the neglected groups; to critique the existing myths, stereotypes, and paradigms that veiled or rationalized the inequalities and the historical contributions of the affected social groups; and to examine and expose the structures of domination and subordination in our society.

At first, these investigations took a rigidly protective stance toward their subjects. Black or Chicano nationalist analyses tended to question all traditional assumptions and to defend all that was black or brown; women's analyses attacked institutions and ideologies as patriarchal without distinction as to class or ethnic inequalities; radicals imbued with class analysis criticized imperialism abroad and class structures at home without considering the ramifications of sex or ethnic discrimination. Those who sought to integrate the analyses of the various forms of social inequality were at first in the minority.

By the 1970s the diverse groups had successfully documented the importance of their subjects' contributions to historical development and demonstrated the existence of social structures of domination over each group. An effort began then to integrate this analysis and to arrive at a more complex, fundamental explanation of the interconnections among these distinct social-historical experiences.

The process of including women's history, black history, Indian, Chicano, Asian, immigrant, and labor histories in the chronicles of United States history has been a first step toward an integrated history. Now we are confronted with the next step of jointly interpreting our interrelated histories. This requires going beyond the empirical combination of facts, names, and dates to the conceptual problem of seeking an explanation of how the diverse experiences were daily woven by individual human beings into a single and common historical reality.

In outlining the factors involved in these interconnected experiences, we must be careful to search for both the subjective, cultural conditions that motivated the individual woman's experiences and perceptions, and the objective, political-economic conditions that shaped the experiences of each social group.

The use of diaries, personal testimonies, oral histories, and literature have proved to be effective for uncovering the first set of conditions: women's personal or subjective experiences. But there are shortcomings to this approach. Women of the poor, slave, or laboring classes do not tend to leave diaries. Different methods and different questions have to be posed if one is to recapture the personal experiences of Indian, Hispanic, black, Asian, and poor white women of the laboring classes.

To find a conceptual interpretation of these diverse personal experiences, we must address the objective conditions of western life. This involves first challenging the traditional Turnerian interpretation of western history as

the "frontier" period. The evolution of the West spans hundreds of years of Indian society before the American frontier. It is important to understand Indian social relations and the role of women before the Europeans imposed a class society.

Four centuries of Spanish conquest and settlement left a legacy of cultural development and social relations which is still in force today as, for example, in the legislation of western states.[1] Then, overlapping the three decades of Mexican rule over large parts of the West, comes the relatively brief period of United States conquest, the "frontier" period which has so absorbed myopic western historians. Finally, it is important to keep in mind that western history also comprises the twentieth century development of women in the West.[2]

THE QUESTION OF CLASS

In studying western history since European penetration, one of the most obvious but often ignored conditions is the existence of social classes.[3] A class system was first introduced in the sixteenth century by the conquering Spaniards into the area that is now the southwestern United States.

Acknowledging the class character of Spanish and Mexican society in the Southwest penetrates the mist of generalizations which inaccurately assume classless homogeneity. Albert Camarillo's study of the Chicano communities in Santa Barbara and Los Angeles, California, delineates the four classes that comprised Mexican society: the elite rich "Californios," wealthy land-owning ranchers whose holdings averaged 25,000 acres; the middle class of small property owners and ranchers; the majority class of artisans and laborers living in humble dwellings; and the Indian population which was converted into laborers for the missions and menial servants for the wealthy Californios.[4]

In this society, what would it mean to talk about the life cycles of women? Certainly women's lives would appear different within the same household, where the wealthy Californios lived with their slave-like Indian female servants. Historian Elinor Burkett encountered this problem when she set out to study the relations of class, race, and sex in Spanish colonial South America. In feminist studies, Burkett notes, we often assume that:

sex is as important a force in the historical process as class. Thus, we deal with the domestic squabbles of the aristocracy and the survival trials of the black female in the same conference without feeling uncomfortable; frequently forget that the position of the one is maintained only through the exploitation of the other and that such a relationship leaves little concrete room for sisterhood.[5]

If western historians raised these questions they might uncover in verbal records the gulf between the experiences of women of different classes. For example, the following black lullaby from the southern United States laments a black mother's inability to be with her newborn child through early motherhood and nursing because she had to tend to the baby of her mistress.[6]

All the Pretty Little Horses

Hushaby, don't you cry.
Go to sleepy, little baby.
When you wake, you shall have cake,
And all the pretty little horses.
Blacks and bays, dapples and grays,
Coach and six-a little horses.
Way down yonder in the meadow,
There's a poor little lambie;
The bees and the butterflies pickin' out his eyes,
The poor little thing cries, "Mammy."
Hushaby, don't you cry,
Go to sleepy, little baby.

The evidence of working class women's experience is there, but the prevailing orientations of studying history, even women's history, steer us toward elite or educated women and their written records; then from this limited and class-biased evidence generalizations are drawn and applied to all women.[7]

In fact, if one looks at history through the eyes of the majority of women, the poor and the laboring classes, a very different picture of society emerges; the picture is far more complete, for elite eyes take *their* world as the standard and assume that all society exists, or should exist, in their image.

But to see through the eyes of the women on the bottom, is to see not only the lives of the vast majority, but also to look upward through all levels of society; the flaws and contradictions of the upper classes and of the social structure they maintain become exposed from this perspective. The elite class perspective tends to be biased, myopic, and class-centered; the majority laboring class perspective tends to be more critical and encompassing.

WESTWARD EXPANSION

A second major historical consideration in studying the objective conditions that shaped women's experiences is the process of United States "westward expansion" which ultimately resulted in the appropriation of Indian, French, Spanish, and Mexican territories by the United States and the subordination of local ethnic groups as dispossessed cultural or national "minorities."

The process of westward expansion brings into play a host of major economic, political, and social developments. In a historical and economic sense the conquest of the West can be interpreted as corresponding to the similar process undergone by the western European countries in the sixteenth, seventeenth, and eighteenth centuries; known as the original or "primitive" accumulation of land and resources, this process constituted the preliminary stage for the development of industrial capitalist society.[8] In what sense is the conquest of the West a primitive accumulation?[9] And what is the significance of this process for women's experiences in the West?

Frederick Jackson Turner wrote that "the existence of an area of free land, its continuous recession, and the advance of American settlement westward, explain American development." Yet in the process of westward expansion the leading political actors clearly recognized the true character of that expansion: not an acquisition of an unclaimed territory free for the taking, not the expansion of "free land," but a military and political conquest of an already inhabited territory.[10]

Without the United States Army, in fact, the West could never have been "taken" by the settlers and pioneers. What effect did the army, both in the conquest and in its subsequent preservation, have on women in the West? What effect did it have on creating, altering, or maintaining class, ethnic, or racial divisions? Indian reservations in California were inevitably placed next to army posts and outposts.[11] What impact did the army have on Indian women who survived the devastating wars of extermination against their people?

The railroads were also instrumental in the penetration of the West. The building of the railroads was a key to expansion, not just as a means of military transportation but more fundamentally because of what lay behind the conquest: the penetration of the West by eastern capital. Linking the West Coast to the East Coast not only opened up the ports and raw materials of the West for exploitation by eastern bankers, industrialists, and land speculators but, far beyond that, opened up the Asian subcontinent for exploitation in such a way that it placed the United States at the crossroads of international commerce between the Far East and western Europe. Thus, the military conquest of the

Indian and Mexican West and the construction of the transcontinental railroads opened up both a national market and an international empire for giant eastern capitalists.[12]

The building of the transcontinental railroads affected women of diverse ethnic and class backgrounds in a variety of ways; the full effects remain to be studied. We know, for example, that the railroads, after the military, provided one of the most effective ways of destroying American Indian people's subsistence on the Plains, by establishing the policy of paying sharpshooters to kill the buffalo.

The railroads stimulated mass immigration from Europe into the United States and mass migration into the West and Southwest. The construction of the railroads was accomplished by exploiting immigrant laborers: the Chinese, Japanese, and Mexicans on the West Coast, the Irish and European immigrants on the East Coast.[13]

Yet the treatment of European immigrant laborers was qualitatively different, in a political sense, from that of the Asian and Mexican immigrants.[14] Chinese laborers, for example, were brought in as bound labor, as "coolies," a politically unfree form of contract labor. They were forbidden to bring their wives or families. This restriction had a negative and long-lasting impact on the development of Chinese communities in the West, and it led to the importation of Chinese women in the most brutal form of "white slave traffic," an experience quite distinct from that of European immigrant women in the East.[15]

The importation of Mexican labor by the railroads has also left a deep legacy. As with the placement of Indian reservations next to Army forts, maps show that the *colonias* or Mexican settlements in the first half of the twentieth century were invariably located along the railroad routes, since whole Mexican families were imported by the companies to clear, lay, and maintain the tracks. The railroad companies would segregate their work force along ethnic lines and establish Mexican colonies of boxcar residences in certain places along the track; thus, the phrase "the wrong side of the tracks" came to be applied to Mexican barrios.[16] In the growing search for roots among Chicanas and Chicanos, the oral histories and family records that are surfacing reveal, in instance after instance, the ties to the railroads among our parents, grandparents, and great-grandparents.[17]

Today many Chicano barrios are still alongside the "wrong side of the tracks." They developed on the original sites of the old railroad-track Mexican colonies; in cities throughout the Southwest from California to Texas, these barrios are still distinguished by adobe houses, unpaved dirt streets, lack of sidewalks, often in direct proximity to walled, modern, Anglo middle-class housing tracts with multitiered, air-conditioned, carpeted homes.

PROPERTY, PATRIARCHY, AND THE NUCLEAR FAMILY

What did the settlement of the land itself mean for women of different classes and ethnicity? Much of the preliminary analysis on women in the West focuses on pioneer women, and their lives are studied through the diaries or literature they left behind. But the majority of women in the nineteenth-century West neither read nor wrote English. Barbara Mayer Wertheimer points out that the ordinary American could not pack up and head West. "It took capital, about $1,500, to outfit a wagon, buy supplies, and tide the family over until the land began to produce. This was an impossible sum for most working-class families to come by."[18]

Without detracting from the courage and endurance of these pioneer women, we have to ask what the takeover and settlement of western lands really represents for the majority of Indian, Mexican, and immigrant women in the West. A more comprehensive answer has to be found by studying first what western conquest and settlement represented in American economic and historical development. The West was not really developed by individual pioneering men and women seeking land. Rather, the West was made economically exploitable by federal intervention in the form of massive land grants to railroads, mining companies, timber companies, and land speculators, and by virtue of federal legislation and funding that subsidized these private profit-making ventures and speculators at public expense.[19]

Industrial and financial magnates did not operate simply out of greed for lucrative profits; they were driven by the economic necessity for expansion, which is at the heart of this system of competition and property. When the United States broke away from England in 1783, capitalist expansion was faced with three obstacles: the plantation slave economy of the South which held onto a bound labor force, raw materials, and productive lands; the Indian tribes and nations which had been pushed together into the West; and the Mexican Northwest.

These barriers could only be overcome by the usurpation and appropriation that have characterized the birth of capitalism wherever it has appeared. This process essentially involves breaking up the existing economic system (e.g., feudalism, tribal societies, peasant communities), concentrating land and wealth in the hands of a few entrepreneurs, and uprooting the native peoples from their land and mode of living to provide a source of wage labor.

A bloody Civil War was launched to remove the first obstacle. Wars against the Indians removed the second, and an unprovoked war against Mexico eliminated the third obstacle. After the defeat of the slave plantation economy,

Indian tribal societies, and Mexican feudalism in the Southwest, the United States engaged in accelerated expansion and conquest of western territories. This process involved plunder, massacres, swindling, and bribery. It succeeded in imposing capitalist private property and, equally important, individualism and the patriarchal nuclear family which is so necessary to sustain this form of property.

Various methods were used to impose this system of property and family in the West. In the accumulation of Indian lands, force was not the only technique applied. Andrew Jackson and subsequent presidents attempted to deprive the Indians of their lands by refusing to deal with them as tribes or to negotiate treaties with them as nations. Instead the government forced the Indians, through bribery, treachery, and legislation, to deal with the government as individuals; this policy set them up against each other with the incentive of immediate cash payment to individuals selling plots of land. By forcing the foreign system of private property onto them, the government was attempting to destroy the fundamental communal basis of Indian tribes.

The General Allotment Act, or Dawes Act, of 1883 sought to push the Indians out of the way of western penetration and open up their lands to exploitation, by alloting parcels of tribal land to individuals. The bill was condemned by Senator Henry Teller of Colorado as "a bill to despoil the Indians of their lands and to make them vagabonds on the face of the earth," yet Congress passed it with the justification that "Indians needed to become competitive." Senator Henry Dawes, principal proponent of the measure, argued that Indians "needed to become selfish."[20]

Two centuries earlier the French colonizers in Canada had been amazed at the egalitarianism and freedom among the women and men of the Montagnais tribe, at their disdain for formal authority and domination, and at the respect and independence between husbands and wives. Yet the Jesuit policy of colonization sought to "give authority to one of them to rule the others," and to teach them "to elect and obey 'Captains,' inducing them to give up their children for schooling, and above all, attempting to introduce the principle of binding monogamy and wifely fidelity and obedience to male authority."[21]

In a similar manner the United States recognized that to break down Indian resistance it was necessary to undermine the tribal and clan social organization of the Indians and to enforce upon them the individual nuclear family, with the husband the authority figure over the women and children. This attempt had the multiple purposes of forcing the Indians to alienate their communal tribal lands, breaking their economic and social clan organization, transforming

them into individualist and competitive capitalist farmers, and providing the nuclear family institution through which the ideology of private property, individualism, and dominant-subordinate relations could be passed on.

Other American people—the small farmers, European immigrants, and settlers—also were subject to official policies promoting individualism in the process of westward expansion. The Homestead Act of 1862, which preceded the Dawes Act by almost three decades, forced individuals and individual families to settle independently; no land was made available for whole communities. On the other hand, huge tracts of land were made available only to the big companies penetrating the West: the railroads, banks, land speculators, and mining companies. While the individual homesteaders were told, "The government bets 160 acres against the entry fee of $14 that the settler can't live on the land for five years without starving to death,"[22] the financial and industrial giants were granted all the land they wanted; the government even provided capital for the infrastructural construction they needed to operate and extract their private profits.

The fostering of private property, individualism, and the nuclear family in the West thus resulted on the one hand in the breakup of the population into individual, isolated, competitive miniscule units:—nuclear families; and the concentration of wealth and power in the hands of an increasingly smaller elite on the other—monopolies. For monopolization to take place, it was necessary to fragment the population through the imposition of private property.

The United States government promoted this process in the West. Neither the government's nor the monopolies' intention, however, was to perpetuate small-scale production and independence. Rather, they brought people in to clear the land, develop the resources, and make the area productive and, when this was done, usurped this settled population from their small plots and transformed them into the wage-labor force needed in the West. Both stages were accomplished by fostering private property, individual ownership of land, and the privatization of the nuclear family.

EXPLOITATION OF WOMEN'S DOMESTIC LABOR

The patriarchal nuclear family was important, not just as a means of preserving and transferring private property and the values associated with it, but also, for the families of the laboring classes, as a means of privately producing through the domestic labor of women the goods and services necessary to sustain the agricultural or industrial labor force needed by capitalist enterprises.[23]

Among Mexican immigrant families in the early twentieth-century Southwest, women's domestic labor was exploited indirectly by large employers as a means of subsidizing the payment of discriminatory and substandard wages to their Mexican workers.[24] This policy was refined by the monopolies engaged in developing the Southwest; these companies in the extractive, infrastructural, and agricultural industries first imported Mexican immigrants in large numbers at the turn of the century.[25]

The monopolistic pattern of southwestern land ownership and industry in many places retained vestiges of the feudal system, such as tenant or sharecropping systems in agriculture or debt peonage in company mining towns. These practices retarded the assimilation of Mexican immigrants into the working class, and had the effect of perpetuating the bondage of the wife and children under the patriarchal family. Patriarchal family relations were particularly strong in rural areas. Women who were hired as agricultural laborers to pick cotton were never paid their own wages; rather, these were paid to the father, husband, or brother. Because of this system of "family wages," feudal relations in the countryside were not easily broken down, and wage labor did not offer women the economic independence that weakened patriarchal relations as did urban or industrial employment.[26]

Even in urban areas, Mexican families found themselves segregated and living in boxcars or makeshift housing. Mario Garcia, in a study of Mexican families in El Paso, Texas, at the turn of the century, documented how their reduced standard of living provided a justification for the payment of wages far below the "American standard." Mexican families were forced to live "75 percent cheaper than Americans" by a series of economic and political mechanisms. Racial discrimination and starvation wages confined Mexicans to the worst slums, with overcrowded, inferior housing in adobes or shacks. These settlements were denied public services (water, paved streets, electricity, sewers) because the Anglo property owners refused to pay taxes to provide them and because the city, in turn, argued that Mexican residents were not property owners and taxpayers, and therefore not entitled to services.[27]

Given this living situation, the domestic labor of women and children was particularly arduous. They hauled water long distances from the river in buckets, hand-ground corn for hours, gathered and chopped wood for fuel, to make up for the lack of adequate wages and public services.

This extreme exploitation of family labor and the intense immiseration of the laboring communities caused high infant-mortality rates, infectious diseases, and malnourishment, while providing the justification for lower wages. It also provided a pool of severely underpaid Mexican female servants whose dusk-to-dawn exploitation in the homes of Anglo-American families freed the women of these families to seek outside employment and enter the industrial world. The economic advancement of many Anglo-American women in the Southwest was carried out on the backs of Mexican-American women, as it was in the South on the backs of black women, and the immediate beneficiaries were the banks and monopolies dominating the South and West.

THE QUESTION OF RESEARCH AND SOCIAL CHANGE

My discussion has not centered on individual heroines of different ethnic or class backgrounds nor on the important subject of women's struggles to change the conditions of ethnic, class, racial, or sex discrimination. I have sought to demonstrate the necessity of taking into consideration the larger, more fundamental political-economic forces in the development of the West, which must be studied if one is to understand the experiences of *all* women.

The forces that had come to dominate the West at the end of the nineteenth century have continued to shape the experiences of women in the twentieth century, the more so as economic concentration and its influence through the growth of government power has expanded. In 1962, the wealthiest 10 percent of the United States population controlled close to 70 percent of all personal wealth, while the other 90 percent of the population shared a little over 30 percent.[28] Even this small share of the pie was unevenly divided. Poverty in the United States was concentrated in the South and West, and among blacks and Mexican-Americans. In 1960, for example, official figures showed that in the Southwest 35 percent of the Spanish-surnamed families and 42 percent of non-white families were living in poverty. Among Anglo families, only 16 percent were listed in poverty, and yet this represented a very large number, since Anglos comprised 66 percent of all poor in the Southwest.[29]

Today we know that poverty and unemployment have worsened, that two out of every three persons in poverty are women, and that black women and Chicanas are among those most affected. This situation continues as the "minority" peoples of the Southwest are rapidly becoming the majority.

The trend toward greater inequality is growing. Richard M. Cyert, president of Pittsburgh's Carnegie-Mellon University, which houses the most advanced research and experimentation center in the robotics fields, recently stated, "I don't think there's any question that we're moving toward a society where income distribution will be even more unequal than it is at present and where unemployment is going to be even greater than it is now."[30]

The issue of inequality confronts anyone seeking to develop a historically accurate, comprehensive analysis that integrates the experiences of the majority of poor and working-class women, the experiences of black, Chicana, Indian, Asian, and immigrant women. We have been dealing with the divisions among us: while these divisions of race and class have existed, we also have to deal with the fundamental unity among us.

Our task is to discover both the causes of the artificial, socially created divisions that have kept us apart and ways to make our fundamental unity a reality. If we are concerned with social change, if our research is to involve a commitment to shedding light on the historical roots of contemporary problems and inequalities so that these

inequalities can be abolished, then our research will have to address the issues of inequality, exploitation, and the related political question of democracy. For the history of the West, as the history of the United States, is a history of exploitation of the labor, land, and resources of diverse groups of peoples: Indians, indentured servants, black slaves, farmers, the working class, immigrants, and, not least, the exploitation of women in the home.

For this reason it is also a history of the unfolding struggle over democratic rights and against the powerful minority of anti-democratic forces who have sought to monopolize political power to ensure their economic concentration. This struggle for democracy has involved the Indians' struggle for their land and sovereignty; the struggle of immigrants, of blacks, of Chicanos; working-class and socialist struggles; and, integral to all of these, women's struggle for equality and political emancipation.

ACKNOWLEDGMENTS

Special thanks to Nancy Paige Fernandez, of the Program in Comparative Culture at the University of California at Irvine, for her thoughtful critique of my first draft, and to Lisa Rubens, Lyn Reese, Deanne Thompson, and all the other women at the Women's West Conference whose warm encouragement and extensive discussions and comments enlightened my analysis and understanding.

NOTES

1. E.g., community-property laws for married couples in many southern and western states (especially in former Spanish and French territories); and the Texas "cuckoo law," which allowed a husband to kill his wife's lover if he caught them "in the act." On community property consult Barbara Allen Babcock et al., *Sex Discrimination and the Law* (Boston: Little, Brown, 1975), pp. 604–13. On the Texas "cuckoo law" see "The 'Equal Shooting Rights,'" *Texas Observer,* 16 Mar. 1965; and "Origins of the Cuckoo Law," 2 Apr. 1965. The latter article observes, "Like so many of our especially Texan legal institutions (our homestead law, our venue statute, the independent executor, our adoption law, and our community property system), our legal attitude toward the cuckold's right to take vengeance for an affront to his conjugal honor is Spanish in origin." More accurately, they are feudal in origin.

2. If we include the twentieth century, certain "academic" problems are resolved, such as that there were few black women in "the West" narrowly defined as the frontier period. If we define the

West more fully, the presence of black women emerges as a real issue. How, for example, did the development of Jim Crow in the South in the early twentieth century under the sponsorship of the large propertied and monied interests affect women when Jim Crow was imposed on black, Mexican, and Asian communities in the West?

3. Louis M. Hacker, in "Sections—or Classes?" *The Nation* 137, no. 355 (26 July 1933): 108–10 leveled a sharp critique at the Turnerian thesis of a unique and democratic frontier environment in the West. See also Barry D. Karl, "Frederick Jackson Turner: The Moral Dilemma of Professionalization," *Reviews in American History* 3 (March 1975): 1–7.

4. Albert Camarillo, *Chicanos in a Changing Society: From Mexican Pueblos to American Barrios in Santa Barbara and Southern California, 1848–1930* (Cambridge, Mass.: Harvard University Press, 1979). Other studies of sixteenth- to nineteenth-century Mexican families or women include Leonard Pitt, *The Decline of the Californios: A Social History of the Spanish-*

Speaking Californians, 1846–1890 (Berkeley: University of California Press, 1971); Richard Griswold del Castillo, *The Los Angeles Barrio, 1850–1890: A Social History* (Berkeley: University of California Press, 1979); Richard Griswold del Castillo, *La Familia: Chicano Families in the Urban Southwest, 1848 to the Present* (Notre Dame, Ind.: University of Notre Dame Press, 1984); Frances Leon Swadesh, *Los Primeros Pobladores, Hispanic Americans of the Ute Frontier* (Notre Dame, Ind.: University of Notre Dame Press, 1974); Ramon A. Gutierrez, *Marriage, Sex, and the Family: Social Change in Colonial New Mexico, 1690–1846* (Ph.D. diss., University of Wisconsin, Madison, 1980); Ramon A. Gutierrez, "From Honor to Love: Transformation of the Meaning of Sexuality in Colonial New Mexico," in Raymond T. Smith, ed., *Love, Honor, and Economic Fate: Interpreting Kinship Ideology and Practice in Latin America* (Chapel Hill: University of North Carolina Press, 1983); Ramon A. Gutierrez, "Marriage and Seduction in Colonial New Mexico," in Adelaida del Castillo, ed., *Mexicana/Chicana Women's History,* Chicana Studies Research Center (forthcoming); Gloria E. Miranda, *"Gente De Razon* Marriage Patterns in Spanish and Mexican California: A Case Study of Santa Barbara and Los Angeles," *Southern California Quarterly* 39 no. 1 (March 1957): 149–66; Jane Dysart, "Mexican Women in San Antonio, 1830–1860: The Assimilation Process," Western *Historical Quarterly* 7 no. 4 (October 1976): 365–75; Fray Angelico Chavez, "Dona Tules, Her Fame and Her Funeral," *Palacio* 57 (August 1950): 227–34; Marcela Lucero Trujillo, "The Spanish Surnamed Woman of Yester Year," in José Otero and Evelio Echevarria, eds., *Hispanic Colorado* (Fort Collins, Colo.: Centennial Publications, 1977); Daniel J. Garr, "A Rare and Desolate Lane: Population and Race in Hispanic California," *Western Historical Quarterly* 6, no. 2 (April, 1975): 133–48. A masterful bibliography on the "Borderlands," containing hundreds of references for further research, is Charles C. Cumberland, *The United States–Mexican Border: A Selective Guide to the Literature of the Region,* published by *Rural Sociology* as vol. 25, no. 2 (June 1970): 230 pp. The work includes references to Spanish-Indian relations in the region.

5. Elinor C. Burkett, "In Dubious Sisterhood: Race and Class in Spanish Colonial South America," *Latin American Perspectives* 4 nos. 1–2 (Winter–Spring, 1977): 18–26.

6. "All the Pretty Little Horses," in Middleton Harris et al., *The Black Book* (New York: Random House, 1974), p. 65. The book is a photographic documentary history of the black experience in the United States, including documents and graphics of blacks in the West.

7. For example, Barbara Welter's "The Cult of True Womanhood: 1820–1860," *American Quarterly* 18, no. 2 (1966): 151–74, reprinted in Michael Gordon, ed., *The American Family in Socio-Historical Perspective* (New York: St. Martin's Press, 1973). Welter assumes an upper-class, native WASP homogeneity of all women in America: "It was a fearful obligation, a solemn responsibility, which the nineteenth century *American woman* had—to uphold the pillars of the temple with her frail *white hand"* (p. 225, emphasis added). Her article provides no discussion of property or of women and the family's relation to property. In her only (indirect) reference to the economic character of

American society and its class divisions, she blithely passes by without acknowledging these contradictions: "America was a land of precarious fortunes. . . . the woman who had servants today, might tomorrow, because of a depression or panic, be forced to do her own work. . . . she was to be the same cheerful consoler of her husband in their cottage as in their mansion" (p. 238).

In fact, this section contains the only references to the existence of other classes of women: ". . . the value of a wife in case of business reverses . . . of course she had a little help from 'faithful Dinah' who absolutely refused to leave her beloved mistress" (pp. 238–239). Welter cites quotations linking the Cult of True Womanhood to a certain order of society ("that a stable order of society depended upon her maintaining her traditional place in it" [p. 242]), yet she never questions that order, never examines that society and why its maintenance depended on women's domestic subordination.

8. Cf. Leo Huberman, *Man's Worldly Goods: The Story of the Wealth of Nations* (New York: Monthly Review Press, 1936); Maurice Dobb, *Studies in the Development of Capitalism* (New York: International Publishers, 1947). An incisive presentation of primitive accumulation and its devastating impact on peasant families in Europe is found in Karl Marx, *Capital*, vol. 1, part 8 "The So-Called Primitive Accumulation."

9. Raul A. Fernandez, in *The United States–New Mexico Border: A Politico-Economic Profile* (Notre Dame, Ind.: University of Notre Dame Press, 1977), presents an analysis of the complex character of this process in the Southwest. Ray Allen Billington's classic *Westward Expansion* traces the historical facts of the process of westward expansion, though from the perspective of Frederick Jackson Turner's "frontier thesis."

10. Both Jefferson Davis and Captain Randolph B. Marcy compared the conquest of the West with the French imperialist conquest of Algeria, and both argued that the United States Army should apply the French tactics in that conquest to the conquest of the Indians in the West. Walter Prescott Webb, *The Great Plains* (Lincoln: University of Nebraska Press, ca. 1931), pp. 194, 195, 196.

11. Lynwood Carranco, *Genocide and Vendetta: The Round Valley Wars in Northern California* (Norman: University of Oklahoma Press, 1981). An excellent survey of government-Indian relations is found in D'Arcy McNichols, *Native American Tribalism: Indian Survivals and Renewals* (published for the Institute of Race Relations, London, by Oxford University Press, 1973). Indian women's resistance in the face of both the Spanish and United States conquests is presented in Victoria Brady, Sarah Crome, and Lyn Reese's "Resist and Survive, Aspects of Native Women of California," (MS Sarah Crome, Institute for the Study of Social Change, University of California, Berkeley, Calif.)

12. For a very explicit account of the connections between this internal conquest and the creation of a foreign empire by the United States, see Scott Nearing, *The American Empire* (New York: Rand School of Social Science, 1921). See also Leo Huberman, *We, the People* (New York, London: Harper Brothers, 1947).

13. A good overview of immigration in the United States is found in Barbara Kaye Greenleaf, *America Fever: The Story of American Immigration* (New York: New American Library, 1974).

14. Rosalinda M. González, "Capital Accumulation and Mexican Immigration to the United States" (Ph.D. diss., University of California at Irvine, 1981) offers a political-economic analysis of the discriminatory treatment of Asian and Mexican immigrants that differs from the traditional explanations in terms of racism.

15. Dorothy Gray, "Minority Women in the West, Juanita, Biddy Mason, Donaldina Cameron," in *Women of the West* (Millbrae, Calif.: Les Femmes Publishing, 1976), pp. 62–75; *Asian Women* (Berkeley: University of California, Dwinelle Hall, 1971); Ruthanne Lum McCunn, *An Illustrated History of the Chinese in America* (San Francisco: Design Enterprises, 1979).

16. Case studies of these barrios and their twentieth-century development appear in Arthur J. Rubel, *Across the Tracks: Mexican-Americans in a Texas City* (Austin: University of Texas Press, 1966); and Ricardo Romo, *East Los Angeles, History of a Barrio* (Austin: University of Texas Press, 1983). The historical development of the Chicano people is examined in Carey McWilliams's classic *North from Mexico: The Spanish Speaking People of the United States* (New York: Greenwood Press, 1968); Rodolfo Acuna, *Occupied America: A History of Chicanos* (New York: Harper & Row, 1981); and the excellent bilingual pictorial history by Chicano Communications Center, *450 Years of Chicano History in Pictures* (South Pasadena, Calif.: Bilingual Educations Services, n.d.). A case study of how monopoly-motivated reforms of the Progressive Era were applied to Mexican immigrant communities at the turn of the century is found in Gilbert G. Gonzalez, *Progressive Education: A Marxist Interpretation* (Minneapolis: Marxist Educational Press, 1982). A historical analysis of Chicanas is presented in Martha P. Cotera, *Diosa y Hembra: The History and Heritage of Chicanas in the U.S.* (Austin, Tex.: Information Systems Development, 1976).

17. See, e.g., the beautiful and poignant description in Jose Lona's "Biographical Sketch of the Life of an Immigrant Woman," in Maria Linda Apodaca, "The Chicana Woman: An Historical Materialist Analysis," *Latin American Perspectives* 4, nos. 1–2: pp. 70–89. The Institute of Oral History at the University of Texas at El Paso has a growing collection of over 500 taped interviews, many of which relate to the railroads.

18. Barbara Mayer Wertheimer, *We Were There: The Story of Working Women in America* (New York: Pantheon Books, 1977), p. 249. Lillian Schlissel, in *Women's Diaries of the Westward Journey* (New York: Schocken Books, 1982), pointed out that most of the western pioneers were landowners and that their parents had also been landowners, "a class of 'peasant proprietors' " (pp. 10–11).

19. See, e.g., Gabriel Kolko, *Railroads and Regulation* (Westport, Conn.: Greenwood Press, 1976); Robert Wiebe, *The Search for Order, 1877–1920* (New York: Hill and Wang, 1968); James Weinstein, *The Corporate Idea in the Liberal State, 1900–1918* (Boston: Beacon Press, 1968); Matthew Josephson, *The Robber Barons* (New York: Harcourt Brace, 1934); and Matthew Josephson, *The Money Lords* (New York: Weybright and Talley, 1972).

20. McNichols, *Native American Tribalism*. For a brief description of the negative effects on tribal solidarity from the imposition of individualism and the nuclear family on Indian society, see the first two chapters of Keith Basso's *The Cibecue Apache* (New York: Holt, Rinehart and Winston, 1970).

21. Eleanor Leacock, "Women in Development: Anthropological Facts and Fictions," *Latin American Perspectives* 4, nos. 1–2.

22. Sheryll and Gene Pattersen-Black, *Western Women in History and Literature* (Crawford, Neb.: Cottonwood Press, 1978), p. 5.

23. An important article by Joan Jensen, "Cloth, Bread, and Boarders: Women's Household Production for the Market," *The Review of Radical Political Economics* 12, no. 2 (Summer 1980): 14–24, examines women's household production from the late-eighteenth to early-twentieth centuries. Jensen concludes that it increased the economic productivity of the family through women's provision of services and the home production of produce for domestic consumption and for local and regional markets. In rural areas the domestic labor of women allowed men to increase production of cash crops for urban markets without increasing food costs. "Low food costs combined with taking in boarders allowed the males of American urban families to work for lower wages than they might have required had women not contributed to the family income."

24. Rosalinda M. González, "Mexican Immigrants in the United States: Cultural Conflict and Class Transformation," *Labor History,* forthcoming; and Rosalinda M. González, "Chicanas and Mexican Immigrant Families, 1920–1940" in Joan Jensen and Lois Scharf, eds., *Decades of Discontent: The Women's Movement, 1920–1940* (Westport, Conn.: Greenwood Press, 1983).

25. Many of the leading entrepreneurs in western expansion also had their stakes in foreign conquest. In the Southwest, for example, Adolph Spreckles, who built his fortune in California and Hawaii sugar plantations, merged with Henry C. Havemeyer, the eastern sugar king, to form the sugar trust, which was obtaining concessions in Mexico to grant it complete monopolization. Spreckles was a close friend of the Southern Pacific Railroad, which under the leadership of Henry Huntington and subsequently under William Harriman was gobbling up railroads in the United States and Mexico and absorbing steamship lines and ports. John Kenneth Turner, *Barbarous Mexico* (Austin: University of Texas Press, 1969); Carey McWilliams, *Factories in the Field* (Santa Barbara, Calif.: Peregrine Publishers, 1971).

26. Ruth Allen, *The Labor of Women in the Production of Cotton* (Austin, Tex.: University of Texas Press, 1931).

27. Mario T. Garcia, *Desert Immigrants: The Mexicans of El Paso, 1880–1920* (New Haven, Conn.: Yale University Press, 1981).

28. Institute for Labor Education and Research, *What's Wrong with the U.S. Economy?* (Boston: South End Press, 1982), pp. xi, 32.

29. Leo Grebler et al., in "A Preview of Socioeconomic Conditions," *The Mexican American People* (New York: The Free Press, 1970), pp. 13–34.

30. Donald Dewey, "Robots Reach Out," *United* (August 1983): 92–99.

Where I Come From Is Like This

PAULA GUNN ALLEN

I

Modern American Indian women, like their non-Indian sisters, are deeply engaged in the struggle to redefine themselves. In their struggle they must reconcile traditional tribal definitions of women with industrial and postindustrial non-Indian definitions. Yet while these definitions seem to be more or less mutually exclusive, Indian women must somehow harmonize and integrate both in their own lives.

An American Indian woman is primarily defined by her tribal identity. In her eyes, her destiny is necessarily that of her people, and her sense of herself as a woman is first and foremost prescribed by her tribe. The definitions of woman's roles are as diverse as tribal cultures in the Americas. In some she is devalued, in others she wields considerable power. In some she is a familial/clan adjunct, in some she is as close to autonomous as her economic circumstances and psychological traits permit. But in no tribal definitions is she perceived in the same way as are women in western industrial and postindustrial cultures.

In the west, few images of women form part of the cultural mythos, and these are largely sexually charged. Among Christians, the madonna is the female prototype, and she is portrayed as essentially passive: her contribution is simply that of birthing. Little else is attributed to her and she certainly possesses few of the characteristics that are attributed to mythic figures among Indian tribes. This image is countered (rather than balanced) by the witch-goddess/whore characteristics designed to reinforce cultural beliefs about women, as well as western adversarial and dualistic perceptions of reality.

The tribes see women variously, but they do not question the power of femininity. Sometimes they see women as fearful, sometimes peaceful, sometimes omnipotent and omniscient, but they never portray women as mindless, helpless, simple, or oppressed. And while the women in a given tribe, clan, or band may be all these things, the individual woman is provided with a variety of images of women from the interconnected supernatural, natural, and social worlds she lives in.

As a half-breed American Indian woman, I cast about in my mind for negative images of Indian women, and I find none that are directed to Indian women alone. The negative images I do have are of Indians in general and in fact are more often of males than of females. All these images come to me from non-Indian sources, and they are always balanced by a positive image. My ideas of womanhood, passed on largely by my mother and grandmothers, Laguna Pueblo women, are about practicality, strength, reasonableness, intelligence, wit, and competence. I also remember vividly the women who came to my father's store, the women who held me and sang to me, the women at Feast Day, at Grab Days, the women in the kitchen of my Cubero home, the women I grew up with; none of them appeared weak or helpless, none of them presented herself tentatively. I remember a certain reserve on those lovely brown faces; I remember the direct gaze of eyes framed by bright-colored shawls draped over their heads and cascading down their backs. I remember the clean cotton dresses and carefully pressed hand-embroidered aprons they always wore; I remember laughter and good food, especially the sweet bread and the oven bread they gave us. Nowhere in my mind is there a foolish woman, a dumb woman, a vain woman, or a plastic woman, though the Indian women I have known have shown a wide range of personal style and demeanor.

My memory includes the Navajo woman who was badly beaten by her Sioux husband; but I also remember that my grandmother abandoned her Sioux husband long ago. I recall the stories about the Laguna woman beaten regularly by her husband in the presence of her children so that the children would not believe in the strength and power of femininity. And I remember the women who drank, who got into fights with other women and with the men, and who often won those battles. I have memories of tired women, partying women, stubborn women, sullen women, amicable women, selfish women, shy women, and aggressive women. Most of all I remember the women who laugh and scold and sit uncomplaining in the long sun on feast days and who cook wonderful food on wood stoves, in beehive mud ovens, and over open fires outdoors.

Among the images of women that come to me from various tribes as well as my own are White Buffalo Woman, who came to the Lakota long ago and brought them the religion of the Sacred Pipe which they still practice; Tinotzin the goddess who came to Juan Diego to remind him that she still walked the hills of her people and sent him with her message, her demand and her proof to the Catholic bishop in the city nearby. And from Laguna I take the images of Yellow Woman, Coyote Woman, Grandmother Spider (Spider Old Woman), who brought the light, who gave us weaving and medicine, who gave us life. Among the Keres she is known as Thought Woman who created us all and who keeps us in creation even now. I remember Iyatiku, Earth Woman, Corn Woman, who guides and counsels the people to peace and who welcomes us home when we cast off this coil of flesh as huskers cast off the leaves that wrap the corn. I remember Iyatiku's sister, Sun Woman, who held metals and cattle, pigs and sheep, highways and engines and so many things in her bundle, who went away to the east saying that one day she would return.

II

Since the coming of the Anglo-Europeans beginning in the fifteenth century, the fragile web of identity that long held tribal people secure has gradually been weakened and torn. But the oral tradition has prevented the complete destruction of the web, the ultimate disruption of tribal ways. The oral tradition is vital; it heals itself and the tribal web by adapting to the flow of the present while never relinquishing its connection to the past. Its adaptability has always been required, as many generations have experienced. Certainly the modern American Indian woman bears slight resemblance to her forebears—at least on superficial examination—but she is still a tribal woman in her deepest

being. Her tribal sense of relationship to all that is continues to flourish. And though she is at times beset by her knowledge of the enormous gap between the life she lives and the life she was raised to live, and while she adapts her mind and being to the circumstances of her present life, she does so in tribal ways, mending the tears in the web of being from which she takes her existence as she goes.

My mother told me stories all the time, though I often did not recognize them as that. My mother told me stories about cooking and childbearing; she told me stories about menstruation and pregnancy; she told me stories about gods and heroes, about fairies and elves, about goddesses and spirits; she told me stories about the land and the sky, about cats and dogs, about snakes and spiders; she told me stories about climbing trees and exploring the mesas; she told me stories about going to dances and getting married; she told me stories about dressing and undressing, about sleeping and waking; she told me stories about herself, about her mother, about her grandmother. She told me stories about grieving and laughing, about thinking and doing; she told me stories about school and about people; about darning and mending; she told me stories about turquoise and about gold; she told me European stories and Laguna stories; she told me Catholic stories and Presbyterian stories; she told me city stories and country stories; she told me political stories and religious stories. She told me stories about living and stories about dying. And in all of those stories she told me who I was, who I was supposed to be, whom I came from, and who would follow me. In this way she taught me the meaning of the words she said, that all life is a circle and everything has a place within it. That's what she said and what she showed me in the things she did and the way she lives.

Of course, through my formal, white, Christian education, I discovered that other people had stories of their own—about women, about Indians, about fact, about reality—and I was amazed by a number of startling suppositions that others made about tribal customs and beliefs. According to the un-Indian, non-Indian view, for instance, Indians barred menstruating women from ceremonies and indeed segregated them from the rest of the people, consigning them to some space specially designed for them. This showed that Indians considered menstruating women unclean and not fit to enjoy the company of decent (non-menstruating) people, that is, men. I was surprised and confused to hear this because my mother had taught me that white people had strange attitudes toward menstruation: they thought something was bad about it, that it meant you were sick, cursed, sinful, and weak and that you had to be

AIN'T I A WOMAN?

SOJOURNER TRUTH

Well, children, where there is so much racket there must be something out of kilter. I think that 'twixt the negroes of the South and the women of the North, all talking about rights, the white men will be in a fix pretty soon. But what's all this here talking about?

That man over there says that women need to be helped into carriages, and lifted over ditches, and to have the best place everywhere. Nobody ever helps me into carriages, or over mud-puddles, or gives me any best place! An ain't I a woman? Look at me! Look at my arm! I have ploughed and planted, and gathered into barns, and no man could head me! And ain't I a woman? I could work as much and eat as much as a man—when I could get it-and bear the lash as well! And ain't I a woman? I have borne thirteen children, and seen them most all sold

Sojourner Truth, excerpt from "Ain't I a Woman?" as found in *Women, Children, and Society: Popular Readings in Women's Studies*, edited by Mary Margaret Fonow and Cathy Rakowski (New York: Simon & Schuster Custom Publishing, 1994).

off to slavery, and when I cried out with my mother's grief, none but Jesus heard me! And ain't I a woman?

Then they talk about this thing in the head; what's this they call it?[Intellect, someone whispers.] That's it, honey. What's that got to do with women's rights or negro's rights? If my cup won't hold but a pint, and yours holds a quart, wouldn't you be mean not to let me have my little half-measure full?

Then that little man in black there, he says women can't have as much rights as men, 'cause Christ wasn't a woman! Where did your Christ come from? Where did your Christ come from? From God and a woman! Man had nothing to do with Him.

If the first woman God ever made was strong enough to turn the world upside down all alone, these women together ought to be able to turn it back, and get it right side up again! And now they is asking to do it, the .men better let them.

Obliged to you for hearing me, and now old Sojourner ain't got nothing more to say.

---

very careful during that time. She taught me that menstruation was a normal occurrence, that I could go swimming or hiking or whatever else I wanted to do during my period. She actively scorned women who took to their beds, who were incapacitated by cramps, who "got the blues."

As I struggled to reconcile these very contradictory interpretations of American Indians' traditional beliefs concerning menstruation, I realized that the menstrual taboos were about power, not about sin or filth. My conclusion was later borne out by some tribes' own explanations, which, as you may well imagine, came as quite a relief to me.

The truth of the matter as many Indians see it is that women who are at the peak of their fecundity are believed to possess power that throws male power totally out of kilter. They emit such force that, in their presence, any male-owned or -dominated ritual or sacred object cannot do its usual task. For instance, the Lakota say that a menstruating woman anywhere near a yuwipi man, who is a special sort of psychic, spirit-empowered healer, for a day or so before

he is to do his ceremony will effectively disempower him. Conversely, among many if not most tribes, important ceremonies cannot be held without the presence of women. Sometimes the ritual woman who empowers the ceremony must be unmarried and virginal so that the power she channels is unalloyed, unweakened by sexual arousal and penetration by a male. Other ceremonies require tumescent women, others the presence of mature women who have borne children, and still others depend for empowerment on postmenopausal women. Women may be segregated from the company of the whole band or village on certain occasions, but on certain occasions men are also segregated. In short, each ritual depends on a certain balance of power, and the positions of women within the phases of womanhood are used by tribal people to empower certain rites. This does not derive from a male-dominant view; it is not a ritual observance imposed on women by men. It derives from a tribal view of reality that distinguishes tribal people from feudal and industrial people.

Among the tribes, the occult power of women, inextricably bound to our hormonal life, is thought to be very great; many hold that we possess innately the blood-given power to kill—with a glance, with a step, or with a judicious mixing of menstrual blood into somebody's soup. Medicine women among the Pomo of California cannot practice until they are sufficiently mature; when they are immature, their power is diffuse and is likely to interfere with their practice until time and experience have it under control. So women of the tribes are not especially inclined to see themselves as poor helpless victims of male domination. Even in those tribes where something akin to male domination was present, women are perceived as powerful, socially, physically, and metaphysically. In times past, as in times present, women carried enormous burdens with aplomb. We were far indeed from the "weaker sex," the designation that white aristocratic sisters unhappily earned for us all.

I remember my mother moving furniture all over the house when she wanted it changed. She didn't wait for my father to come home and help—she just went ahead and moved the piano, a huge upright from the old days, the couch, the refrigerator. Nobody had told her she was too weak to do such things. In imitation of her, I would delight in loading trucks at my father's store with cases of pop or fifty-pound sacks of flour. Even when I was quite small I could do it, and it gave me a belief in my own physical strength that advancing middle age can't quite erase. My mother used to tell me about the Acoma Pueblo women she had seen as a child carrying huge ollas (water pots) on their heads as they wound their way up the tortuous stairwell carved into the face of the "Sky City" mesa, a feat I tried to imitate with books and tin buckets. ("Sky City" is the term used by the Chamber of Commerce for the mother village of Acoma, which is situated atop a high sandstone table mountain.) I was never very successful, but even the attempt reminded me that I was supposed to be strong and balanced to be a proper girl.

Of course, my mother's Laguna people are Keres Indian, reputed to be the last extreme mother-right people on earth. So it is no wonder that I got notably nonwhite notions about the natural strength and prowess of women. Indeed, it is only when I am trying to get non-Indian approval, recognition, or acknowledgment that my "weak sister" emotional and intellectual ploys get the better of my tribal woman's good sense. At such times I forget that I just moved the piano or just wrote a competent paper or just completed a financial transaction satisfactorily or have supported myself and my children for most of my adult life.

Nor is my contradictory behavior atypical. Most Indian women I know are in the same bicultural bind: we vacillate between being dependent and strong, self-reliant and powerless, strongly motivated and hopelessly insecure. We resolve the dilemma in various ways: some of us party all the time; some of us drink to excess; some of us travel and move around a lot; some of us land good jobs and then quit them; some of us engage in violent exchanges; some of us blow our brains out. We act in these destructive ways because we suffer from the societal conflicts caused by having to identify with two hopelessly opposed cultural definitions of women. Through this destructive dissonance we are unhappy prey to the self-disparagement common to, indeed demanded of, Indians living in the United States today. Our situation is caused by the exigencies of a history of invasion, conquest, and colonization whose searing marks are probably ineradicable. A popular bumper sticker on many Indian cars proclaims: "If You're Indian You're In," to which I always find myself adding under my breath, "Trouble."

III

No Indian can grow to any age without being informed that her people were "savages" who interfered with the march of progress pursued by respectable, loving, civilized white people. We are the villains of the scenario when we are mentioned at all. We are absent from much of white history except when we are calmly, rationally, succinctly, and systematically dehumanized. On the few occasions we are noticed in any way other than as howling, bloodthirsty beings, we are acclaimed for our noble quaintness. In this definition, we are exotic curios. Our ancient arts and customs are used to draw tourist money to state coffers, into the pocketbooks and bank accounts of scholars, and into support of the American-in-Disneyland promoters' dream.

As a Roman Catholic child I was treated to bloody tales of how the savage Indians martyred the hapless priests and missionaries who went among them in an attempt to lead them to the one true path. By the time I was through high school I had the idea that Indians were people who had benefited mightily from the advanced knowledge and superior morality of the Anglo-Europeans. At least I had, perforce, that idea to lay beside the other one that derived from my daily experience of Indian life, an idea less dehumanizing and more accurate because it came from my mother and the other Indian people who raised me. That idea was that Indians are a people who don't tell lies, who care for their children and their old people. You never see an Indian orphan, they said. You always know when you're old that someone will take care of you—one of your children will. Then they'd list the old folks who were being taken care of by this child or that. No child is ever considered illegitimate among the Indians, they said. If a girl gets pregnant, the baby is still part of the family, and the mother is too. That's what they said, and they showed me real people who lived according to those principles.

Of course the ravages of colonization have taken their toll; there are orphans in Indian country now, and abandoned, brutalized old folks; there are even illegitimate children, though the very concept still strikes me as absurd. There are battered children and neglected children, and there are battered wives and women who have been raped by Indian men. Proximity to the "civilizing" effects of white Christians has not improved the moral quality of life in Indian country, though each group, Indian and white, explains the situation differently. Nor is there much yet in the oral tradition that can enable us to adapt to these inhuman changes. But a force is growing in that direction, and it is helping Indian women reclaim their lives. Their power, their sense of direction and of self will soon be visible. It is the force of the women who speak and work and write, and it is formidable.

Through all the centuries of war and death and cultural and psychic destruction have endured the women who raise the children and tend the fires, who pass along the tales and the traditions, who weep and bury the dead, who are the dead, and who never forget. There are always the women, who make pots and weave baskets, who fashion clothes and cheer their children on at powwow, who make fry bread and piki bread, and corn soup and chili stew, who dance and sing and remember and hold within their hearts the dream of their ancient peoples—that one day the woman who thinks will speak to us again, and everywhere there will be peace. Meanwhile we tell the stories and write the books and trade tales of anger and woe and stories of fun and scandal and laugh over all manner of things that happen every day. We watch and we wait.

My great-grandmother told my mother: Never forget you are Indian. And my mother told me the same thing. This, then, is how I have gone about remembering, so that my children will remember too.

Hegemonic Masculinity and Emphasized Femininity

R. W. CONNELL

There is an ordering of versions of femininity and masculinity at the level of the whole society, in some ways analogous to the patterns of face-to-face relationship within institutions. The possibilities of variation, of course, are vastly greater. The sheer complexity of relationships involving millions of people guarantees that ethnic differences and generational differences as well as class patterns come into play. But in key respects the organization of gender on the very large scale must be more skeletal and simplified than the human relationships in face-to-face milieux. The forms of femininity and masculinity constituted at this level are stylized and impoverished. Their interrelation is centered on a single structural fact, the global dominance of men over women.

This structural fact provides the main basis for relationships among men that define a hegemonic form of masculinity in the society as a whole. 'Hegemonic masculinity' is always constructed in relation to various subordinated masculinites as well as in relation to women. The interplay between different forms of masculinity is an important part of how a patriarchal social order works.

R. W. Connell, "Hegemonic Masculinity and Emphasized Femininity" from *Gender and Power: Society, the Person and Sexual Politics.* Copyright © 1987 by R. W. Connell. Reprinted with the permission of Stanford University Press.

There is no femininity that is hegemonic in the sense that the dominant form of masculinity is hegemonic among men. This is not a new observation. Viola Klein's historical study of conceptions of 'the feminine character' noted wryly how little the leading theorists could agree on what it was: 'we find not only contradiction on particular points but a bewildering variety of traits considered characteristic of women by the various authorities'. More recently the French analyst Luce Irigaray, in a celebrated essay 'This Sex Which Is Not One', has emphasized the absence of any clear-cut definition for women's eroticism and imagination in a patriarchal society.

At the level of mass social relations, however, forms of femininity are defined clearly enough. It is the global subordination of women to men that provides an essential basis for differentiation. One form is defined around compliance with this subordination and is oriented to accommodating the interests and desires of men. I will call this 'emphasized femininity'. Others are defined centrally by strategies of resistance or forms of non-compliance. Others again are defined by complex strategic combinations of compliance, resistance and co-operation. The interplay among them is a major part of the dynamics of change in the gender order as a whole.

The rest of this section will examine more closely the cases of hegemonic masculinity and emphasized femininity, making brief comments on subordinated and marginalized forms.

In the concept of hegemonic masculinity, 'hegemony' means (as in Gramsci's analyses of class relations in Italy from which the term is borrowed) a social ascendancy achieved in a play of social forces that extends beyond contests of brute power into the organization of private life and cultural processes. Ascendancy of one group of men over another achieved at the point of a gun, or by the threat of unemployment, is not hegemony. Ascendancy which is embedded in religious doctrine and practice, mass media content, wage structures, the design of housing, welfare/taxation policies and so forth, is.

Two common misunderstandings of the concept should be cleared up immediately. First, though 'hegemony' does not refer to ascendancy based on force, it is not incompatible with ascendancy based on force. Indeed it is common for the two to go together. Physical or economic violence backs up a dominant cultural pattern (for example beating up 'perverts'), or ideologies justify the holders of physical power ('law and order'). The connection between hegemonic masculinity and patriarchal violence is close, though not simple.

Second, 'hegemony' does not mean total cultural dominance, the obliteration of alternatives. It means ascendancy achieved within a balance of forces, that is, a state of play. Other patterns and groups are subordinated rather than eliminated. If we do not recognize this it would be impossible to account for the everyday contestation that actually occurs in social life, let alone for historical changes in definitions of gender patterns on the grand scale.

Hegemonic masculinity, then, is very different from the notion of a general 'male sex role', though the concept allows us to formulate more precisely some of the sound points made in the sex-role literature. First, the cultural ideal (or ideals) of masculinity need not correspond at all closely to the actual personalities of the majority of men. Indeed the winning of hegemony often involves the creation of models of masculinity which are quite specifically fantasy figures, such as the film characters played by Humphrey Bogart, John Wayne and Sylvester Stallone. Or real models may be publicized who are so remote from everyday achievement that they have the effect of an unattainable ideal, like the Australian Rules footballer Ron Barassi or the boxer Muhammed Ali.

As we move from face-to-face settings to structures involving millions of people, the easily symbolized aspects of interaction become more prominent. Hegemonic masculinity is very public. In a society of mass communications it is tempting to think that it exists only as publicity. Hence the focus on media images and media discussions of masculinity in the 'Books About Men' of the 1970s and 1980s, from Warren Farrell's *The Liberated Man* to Barbara Ehrenreich's *The Hearts of Men*.

To focus on the media images alone would be a mistake. They need not correspond to the actual characters of the men who hold most social power—in contemporary societies the corporate and state elites. Indeed a ruling class may allow a good deal of sexual dissent. A minor but dramatic instance is the tolerance for homosexuality that the British diplomat Guy Burgess could assume from other men of his class during his career as a Soviet spy. The public face of hegemonic masculinity is not necessarily what powerful men are, but what sustains their power and what large numbers of men are motivated to support. The notion of 'hegemony' generally implies a large measure of consent. Few men are Bogarts or Stallones, many collaborate in sustaining those images.

There are various reasons for complicity, and a thorough study of them would go far to illuminate the whole system of sexual politics. Fantasy gratification is one—nicely satirized in Woody Allen's Bogart take-off, *Play it Again, Sam.*

Displaced aggression might be another—and the popularity of very violent movies from *Dirty Harry* to *Rambo* suggest that a great deal of this is floating around. But it seems likely that the major reason is that most men benefit from the subordination of women, and hegemonic masculinity is the cultural expression of this ascendancy.

This needs careful formulation. It does not imply that hegemonic masculinity means being particularly nasty to women. Women may feel as oppressed by non-hegemonic masculinities, may even find the hegemonic pattern more familiar and manageable. There is likely to be a kind of 'fit' between hegemonic masculinity and emphasized femininity. What it does imply is the maintenance of practices that institutionalize men's dominance over women. In this sense hegemonic masculinity must embody a successful collective strategy in relation to women. Given the complexity of gender relations no simple or uniform strategy is possible: a 'mix' is necessary. So hegemonic masculinity can contain at the same time, quite consistently, openings towards domesticity and openings towards violence, towards misogyny and towards heterosexual attraction.

Hegemonic masculinity is constructed in relation to women and to subordinated masculinities. These other masculinities need not be as clearly defined—indeed, achieving hegemony may consist precisely in preventing alternatives gaining cultural definition and recognition as alternatives, confining them to ghettos, to privacy, to unconsciousness.

The most important feature of contemporary hegemonic masculinity is that it is heterosexual, being closely connected to the institution of marriage; and a key form of subordinated masculinity is homosexual. This subordination involves both direct interactions and a kind of ideological warfare. Some of the interactions were described in chapter 1: police and legal harassment, street violence, economic discrimination. These transactions are tied together by the contempt for homosexuality and homosexual men that is part of the ideological package of hegemonic masculinity. The AIDS scare has been marked less by sympathy for gays as its main victims than by hostility to them as the bearers of a new threat. The key point of media concern is whether the 'gay plague' will spread to 'innocent', i.e., straight, victims.

In other cases of subordinated masculinity the condition is temporary. Cynthia Cockburn's splendid study of printing workers in London portrays a version of hegemonic masculinity that involved ascendancy over young men as well as over women. The workers recalled their apprenticeships in terms of drudgery and humiliation, a ritual of induction into trade and masculinity at the same time. But once they were in, they were 'brothers'.

Several general points about masculinity also apply to the analysis of femininity at the mass level. These patterns too are historical: relationships change, new forms of femininity emerge and others disappear. The ideological representations of femininity draw on, but do not necessarily correspond to, actual femininities as they are lived. What most women support is not necessarily what they are.

There is however a fundamental difference. All forms of femininity in this society are constructed in the context of the overall subordination of women to men. For this reason there is no femininity that holds among women the position held by hegemonic masculinity among men.

This fundamental asymmetry has two main aspects. First, the concentration of social power in the hands of men leaves limited scope for women to construct institutionalized power relationships over other women. It does happen on a face-to-face basis, notably in mother–daughter relationships. Institutionalized power hierarchies have also existed in contexts like the girls' schools pictured in *Mädchen in Uniform* and *Frost in May*. But the note of domination that is so important in relations between kinds of masculinity is muted. The much lower level of violence between women than violence between men is a fair indication of this. Second, the organization of a hegemonic form around dominance over the other sex is absent from the social construction of femininity. Power, authority, aggression, technology are not thematized in femininity at large as they are in masculinity. Equally important, no pressure is set up to negate or subordinate other forms of femininity in the way hegemonic masculinity must negate other masculinities. It is likely therefore that actual femininities in our society are more diverse than actual masculinities.

The dominance structure which the construction of femininity cannot avoid is the global dominance of heterosexual men. The process is likely to polarize around compliance or resistance to this dominance.

The option of compliance is central to the pattern of femininity which is given most cultural and ideological support at present, called here 'emphasized femininity'. This is the translation to the large scale of patterns already discussed in particular institutions and milieux, such as the display of sociability rather than technical competence, fragility in mating scenes, compliance with men's desire for titillation and ego-stroking in office relationships, acceptance of marriage and childcare as a response to labour-market discrimination against women. At the mass level these are organized around themes of sexual receptivity in relation to younger women and motherhood in relation to older women.

Like hegemonic masculinity, emphasized femininity as a cultural construction is very public, though its content is specifically linked with the private realm of the home and the bedroom. Indeed it is promoted in mass media and marketing with an insistence and on a scale far beyond that found for any form of masculinity. The articles and advertisements in mass-circulation women's magazines, the 'women's pages' of mass-circulation newspapers and the soap operas and 'games' of daytime television, are familiar cases. Most of this promotion, it might be noted, is organized, financed and supervised by men.

To call this pattern 'emphasized femininity' is also to make a point about how the cultural package is used in interpersonal relationships. This kind of femininity is performed, and performed especially to men. There is a great deal of folklore about how to sustain the performance. It is a major concern of women's magazines from *Women's Weekly* to *Vogue*. It is even taken up and turned into highly ambivalent comedy by Hollywood *(How to Marry a Millionaire; Tootsie)*. Marilyn Monroe was both archetype and satirist of emphasized femininity. Marabel Morgan's 'total woman', an image that somehow mixes sexpot and Jesus Christ, uses the same tactics and has the same ambivalences.

Femininity organized as an adaptation to men's power, and emphasizing compliance, nurturance and empathy as womanly virtues, is not in much of a state to establish hegemony over other kinds of femininity. There is a familiar paradox about antifeminist women's groups like 'Women Who Want to be Women' who exalt the *Kinder, Kirche und Küche* version of femininity: they can only become politically active by subverting their own prescriptions. They must rely heavily on religious ideology and on political backing from conservative men. The relations they establish with other kinds of femininity are not so much domination as attempted marginalization.

Central to the maintenance of emphasized femininity is practice that prevents other models of femininity gaining cultural articulation. When feminist historiography describes women's experience as 'hidden from history', in Sheila Rowbotham's phrase, it is responding partly to this fact. Conventional historiography recognizes, indeed presupposes, conventional femininity. What is hidden from it is the experience of spinsters, lesbians, unionists, prostitutes, madwomen, rebels and maiden aunts, manual workers, midwives and witches. And what is involved in radical sexual politics, in one of its dimensions, is precisely a reassertion and recovery of marginalized forms of femininity in the experience of groups like these.

NOTE

Quotation from Klein (1946) p. 164. On Burgess's remarkable immunity see Seale and McConville (1978). The concepts discussed in this section are both important and underdeveloped; my argument is more tentative than usual here. The mother–daughter relationship might modify the argument about femininity significantly.

The Master's Tools Will Never Dismantle the Master's House

AUDRE LORDE

I agreed to take part in a New York University Institute for the Humanities conference a year ago, with the understanding that I would be commenting upon papers dealing with the role of difference within the lives of american [*sic*] women: difference of race, sexuality, class, and age. The absence of these considerations weakens any feminist discussion of the personal and the political.

It is a particular academic arrogance to assume any discussion of feminist theory without examining our many differences, and without a significant input from poor women, Black and Third World women, and lesbians. And yet, I stand here as a Black lesbian feminist, having been invited to comment within the only panel at this conference where the input of Black feminists and lesbians is represented. What this says about the vision of this conference is sad, in a country where racism, sexism, and homophobia are inseparable. To read this program is to assume that lesbian and Black women have nothing to say about existentialism, the erotic, women's culture and silence, developing feminist theory, or heterosexuality and power. And what does it mean in personal and political terms when even the two Black women who did present here were literally found at the last hour? What does it mean when the tools of a racist patriarchy are used to examine the fruits of that same patriarchy? It means that only the most narrow perimeters of change are possible and allowable.

The absence of any consideration of lesbian consciousness or the consciousness of Third World women leaves a serious gap within this conference and within the papers presented here. For example, in a paper on material relationships between women, I was conscious of an either/or model of nurturing which totally dismissed my knowledge as a Black lesbian. In this paper there was no examination of mutuality between women, no systems of shared support, no interdependence as exists between lesbians and women-identified women. Yet it is only in the patriarchal model of nurturance that women "who attempt to emancipate themselves pay perhaps too high a price for the results," as this paper states.

For women, the need and desire to nurture each other is not pathological but redemptive, and it is within that knowledge that our real power is rediscovered. It is this real connection which is so feared by a patriarchal world. Only within a patriarchal structure is maternity the only social power open to women.

Interdependency between women is the way to a freedom which allows the *I* to *be*, not in order to be used, but in order to be creative. This is a difference between the passive *be* and the active *being*.

Advocating the mere tolerance of difference between women is the grossest reformism. It is a total denial of the creative function of difference in our lives. Difference must be not merely tolerated, but seen as a fund of necessary polarities between which our creativity can spark like a dialectic. Only then does the necessity for interdependency become unthreatening. Only within that interdependency of different strengths, acknowledged and equal, can the power to seek new ways of being in the world generate, as well as the courage and sustenance to act where there are no charters.

Within the interdependence of mutual (nondominant) differences lies that security which enables us to descend into the chaos of knowledge and return with true visions of our future, along with the concomitant power to effect those changes which can bring that future into being. Difference is that raw and powerful connection from which our personal power is forged.

As women, we have been taught either to ignore our differences, or to view them as causes for separation and suspicion rather than as forces for change. Without community there is no liberation, only the most vulnerable and temporary armistice between an individual and her oppression. But community must not mean a shedding of our differences, nor the pathetic pretense that these differences do not exist.

Those of us who stand outside the circle of this society's definition of acceptable women; those of us who have been forged in the crucibles of difference—those of us who are poor, who are lesbians, who are Black, who are older— know that *survival is not an academic skill.* It is learning how to stand alone, unpopular and sometimes reviled, and how to make common cause with those others identified as outside the structures in order to define and seek a world in which we can all flourish. It is learning how to take our differences and make them strengths. *For the master's tools will never dismantle the master's house.* They may allow us temporarily to beat him at his own game, but they will never enable us to bring about genuine change. And this fact is only threatening to those women who still define the master's house as their only source of support.

Poor women and women of Color know there is a difference between the daily manifestations of marital slavery and prostitution because it is our daughters who line 42nd Street. If white american [*sic*] feminist theory need not deal with the differences between us, and the resulting difference in our oppressions, then how do you deal with the fact that the women who clean your houses and tend your children while you attend conferences on feminist theory are, for the most part, poor women and women of Color? What is the theory behind racist feminism?

In a world of possibility for us all, our personal visions help lay the groundwork for political action. The failure of academic feminists to recognize difference as a crucial strength is a failure to reach beyond the first patriarchal les-

son. In our world, divide and conquer must become define and empower.

Why weren't other women of Color found to participate in this conference? Why were two phone calls to me considered a consultation? Am I the only possible source of names of Black feminists? And although the Black panelist's paper ends on an important and powerful connection of love between women, what about interracial cooperation between feminists who don't love each other?

In academic feminist circles, the answer to these questions is often, "We did not know who to ask." But that is the same evasion of responsibility, the same copout, that keeps Black women's art out of women's exhibitions, Black women's work out of most feminist publications except for the occasional "Special Third World Women's Issue," and Black women's texts off your reading lists. But as Adrienne Rich pointed out in a recent talk, white feminists have educated themselves about such an enormous amount over the past ten years, how come you haven't also educated yourselves about Black women and the differences between us—white and Black—when it is key to our survival as a movement?

Women of today are still being called upon to stretch across the gap of male ignorance and to educate men as to our existence and our needs. This is an old and primary tool of all oppressors to keep the oppressed occupied with the master's concerns. Now we hear that it is the task of women of Color to educate white women—in the face of tremendous resistance—as to our existence, our differences, our relative roles in our joint survival. This is a diversion of energies and a tragic repetition of racist patriarchal thought.

Simone de Beauvoir once said: "It is in the knowledge of the genuine conditions of our lives that we must draw our strength to live and our reasons for acting."

Racism and homophobia are real conditions of all our lives in this place and time. *I urge each one of us here to reach down into that deep place of knowledge inside herself and touch that terror and loathing of any difference that lives there. See whose face it wears.* Then the personal as the political can begin to illuminate all our choices.

Something about the Subject Makes It Hard to Name

GLORIA YAMATO

Racism—simple enough in structure, yet difficult to eliminate. Racism—pervasive in the U.S. culture to the point that it deeply affects all the local town folk and spills over, negatively influencing the fortunes of folk around the world. Racism is pervasive to the point that we take many of its manifestations for granted, believing "that's life." Many believe that racism can be dealt with effectively in one hellifying workshop, or one hour-long heated discussion. Many actually believe this monster, racism, that has had at least a few hundred years to take root, grow, invade our space and develop subtle variations . . . this mind-funk that distorts thought and action, can be merely wished away. I've run into folks who really think that we can beat this devil, kick this habit, be healed of this disease in a snap. In a sincere blink of a well-intentioned eye, presto—poof—racism disappears. "I've dealt with my racism . . . (envision a laying on of hands) . . . Hallelujah! Now I can go to the beach." Well, fine. Go to the beach. In fact, why don't we all go to the beach and continue to work on the sucker over there? Cuz you can't even shave a little piece off this thing called racism in a day, or a weekend, or a workshop.

When I speak of *oppression,* I'm talking about the systematic, institutionalized mistreatment of one group of people by another for whatever reason. The oppressors are purported to have an innate ability to access economic resources, information, respect, etc., while the oppressed are believed to have a corresponding negative innate abil-

ity. The flip side of oppression is *internalized oppression.* Members of the target group are emotionally, physically, and spiritually battered to the point that they begin to actually believe that their oppression is deserved, is their lot in life, is natural and right, and that it doesn't even exist. The oppression begins to feel comfortable, familiar enough that when mean ol' Massa lay down de whip, we got's to pick up and whack ourselves and each other. Like a virus, it's hard to beat racism, because by the time you come up with a cure it's mutated to a "new cure-resistant" form. One shot just won't get it. Racism must be attacked from many angles.

The forms of racism that I pick up on these days are 1) aware/blatant racism, 2) aware/covert racism, 3) unaware/unintentional racism, and 4) unaware/self-righteous racism. I can't say that I prefer any one form of racism over the others, because they all look like an itch needing a scratch. I've heard it said (and understandably so) that the aware/blatant form of racism is preferable if one must suffer it. Outright racists will, without apology or confusion, tell us that because of our color we don't appeal to them. If we so choose, we can attempt to get the hell out of their way before we get the sweat knocked out of us. Growing up, aware/covert racism is what I heard many of my elders bemoaning "up north," after having escaped the overt racism "down south." Apartments were suddenly no longer vacant or rents were outrageously high, when black, brown, red, or yellow persons went to inquire about them. Job vacancies were suddenly filled, or we were fired for very vague reasons. It still happens, though the perpetrators really take care to cover their tracks these days. They don't want to get gummed to death or slobbered on by the toothless laws that supposedly protect us from such inequities.

Unaware/unintentional racism drives usually tranquil white liberals wild when they get called on it, and confirms the suspicions of many people of color who feel that white folks are just plain crazy. It has led white people to believe that it's just fine to ask if they can touch my hair (while reaching). They then exclaim over how soft it is, how it does not scratch their hand. It has led whites to assume that bending over backwards and speaking to me in high-pitched (terrified), condescending tones would make up for all the racist wrongs that distort our lives. This type of racism has led whites right to my doorstep, talking 'bout, "We're sorry/we love you and want to make things right," which is fine, and further, "We're gonna give you the opportunity to fix it while we sleep. Just tell us what you need. 'Bye!!"—which *ain't* fine. With the best of intentions, the best of educations, and the greatest generosity of heart, whites, operating on the misinformation fed to them from day one, will behave in ways that are racist, will perpetuate racism by being "nice" the way we're taught to be nice. You can just "nice" somebody to death with naïveté and lack of awareness of privilege. Then there's guilt and the desire to end racism and how the two get all tangled up to the point that people, morbidly fascinated with their guilt, are immobilized. Rather than deal with ending racism, they sit and ponder their guilt and hope nobody notices how awful they are. Meanwhile, racism picks up momentum and keeps on keepin' on.

Now, the newest form of racism that I'm hip to is unaware/self-righteous racism. The "good white" racist attempts to shame Blacks into being blacker, scorns Japanese-Americans who don't speak Japanese, and knows more about the Chicano/a community than the folks who make up the community. They assign themselves as the "good whites," as opposed to the "bad whites," and are often so busy telling people of color what the issues in the Black, Asian, Indian, Latino/a communities should be that they don't have time to deal with their errant sisters and brothers in the white community. Which means that people of color are still left to deal with what the "good whites" don't want to . . . racism.

Internalized racism is what really gets in my way as a Black woman. It influences the way I see or don't see myself, limits what I expect of myself or others like me. It results in my acceptance of mistreatment, leads me to believe that being treated with less than absolute respect, at least this once, is to be expected because I am Black, because I am not white. "Because I am *(you fill in the color),*" you think, "life is going to be hard." The fact is life may be hard, but the color of your skin is not the cause of the hardship. The color of your skin may be used as an excuse to mistreat you, but there is no reason or logic involved in the mistreatment. If it seems that your color is

the reason, if it seems that your ethnic heritage is the cause of the woe, it's because you've been deliberately beaten down by agents of a greedy system until you swallowed the garbage. That is the internalization of racism.

Racism is the systematic, institutionalized mistreatment of one group of people by another based on racial heritage. Like every other oppression, racism can be internalized. People of color come to believe misinformation about their particular ethnic group and thus believe that their mistreatment is justified. With that basic vocabulary, let's take a look at how the whole thing works together. Meet "the Ism Family," racism, classism, ageism, adultism, elitism, sexism, heterosexism, physicalism, etc. All these ism's are systemic, that is, not only are these parasites feeding off our lives, they are also dependent on one another for foundation. Racism is supported and reinforced by classism, which is given a foothold and a boost by adultism, which also feeds sexism, which is validated by heterosexism, and so it goes on. You cannot have the "ism" functioning without first effectively installing its flip-side, the internalized version of the ism. Like twins, as one particular form of the ism grows in potency, there is a corresponding increasing in its internalized form within the population. Before oppression becomes a specific ism like racism, usually all hell breaks loose. War. People fight attempts to enslave them, or to subvert their will, or to take what they consider theirs, whether that is territory or dignity. It's true that the various elements of racism, while repugnant, would not be able to do very much damage, but for one generally overlooked key piece: power/privilege.

While in one sense we all have power, we have to look at the fact that, in our society, people are stratified into various classes and some of these classes have more privilege than others. The owning class has enough power and privilege to not have to give a good whinney what the rest of the folks have on their minds. The power and privilege of the owning class provides the ability to pay off enough of the working class and offer that paid-off group, the middle class, just enough privilege to make it agreeable to do various and sundry oppressive things to other workingclass and outright disenfranchised folk, keeping the lid on explosive inequities, at least for a minute. If you're at the bottom of this heap, and you believe the line that says you're there because that's all you're worth, it is at least some small solace to believe that there are others more worthless than you, because of their gender, race, sexual preference-. . . whatever. The specific form of power that runs the show here is the power to intimidate. The power to take away the most lives the quickest, and back it up with legal and "divine" sanction, is the very bottom line. It makes the difference between who's holding the racism end of the stick and who's getting beat with it (or beating others as vulnerable as they are) on the internalized racism end of the stick. What I am saying is, while people of color are welcome to tear up their own neighborhoods and each other, everybody knows that you cannot do that to white folks without hell to pay. People of color can be prejudiced against one another and whites but do not have an ice-cube's chance in hell of passing laws that will get whites sent to relocation camps "for their own protection and the security of the nation." People who have not thought about or refuse to acknowledge this imbalance of power/privilege often want to talk about the racism of people of color. But then that is one of the ways racism is able to continue to function. You look for someone to blame and you blame the victim, who will nine times out of ten accept the blame out of habit.

So, what can we do? Acknowledge racism for a start, even though and especially when we've struggled to be kind and fair, or struggled to rise above it all. It is hard to acknowledge the fact that racism circumscribes and pervades our lives. Racism must be dealt with on two levels, personal and societal, emotional and institutional. It is possible—and most effective—to do both at the same time. We must reclaim whatever delight we have lost in our own ethnic heritage or heritages. This so-called melting pot has only succeeded in turning us into fast food-gobbling "generics" (as in generic "white folks" who were once Irish, Polish, Russian, English, etc., and "black folks," who were once Ashanti, Bambara, Baule, Yoruba, etc.). Find or create safe places to actually *feel* what we've been forced to repress each time we were a victim of, witness to or perpetrator of racism, so that we do not continue, like puppets, to act out the past in the present and future. Challenge oppres-

sion. Take a stand against it. When you are aware of something oppressive going down, stop the show. At least call it. We become so numbed to racism that we don't even think twice about it, unless it is immediately life-threatening.

Whites who want to be allies to people of color: You can educate yourselves via research and observation rather than rigidly, arrogantly relying solely on interrogating people of color. Do not expect that people of color should teach you how to behave non-oppressively. Do not give into the pull to be lazy. Think, hard. Do not blame people of color for your frustration about racism, but do appreciate the fact that people of color will often help you get in touch with that frustration. Assume that your effort to be a good friend is appreciated, but don't expect or accept gratitude from people of color. Work on racism for your sake, not "their" sake. Assume that you are needed and capable of being a good ally. Know that you'll make mistakes and commit yourself to correcting them and continuing on as an ally, no matter what. Don't give up.

People of color, working through internalized racism: Remember always that you and others like you are completely worthy of respect, completely capable of achieving whatever you take a notion to do. Remember that the term "people of color" refers to a variety of ethnic and cultural backgrounds. These various groups have been oppressed in a variety of ways. Educate yourself about the ways different peoples have been oppressed and how they've resisted that oppression. Expect and insist that whites are capable of being good allies against racism. Don't give up. Resist the pull to give out the "people of color seal of approval" to aspiring white allies. A moment of appreciation is fine, but more than that tends to be less than helpful. Celebrate yourself. Celebrate yourself. Celebrate the inevitable end of racism.

Feminist Perspectives

Feminist scholars generally distinguish between *sex*, or the biological or innate characteristics of males and females, and *gender*, or the social statuses and meanings assigned to women and men. Gender is one of the most important social distinctions. Societies define men and women as separate and distinct categories, and gender or sex-based stratification is ubiquitous. An individual's gender is one of the first things we notice about her or him, and our own gender is central to our sense of who we are. Not only individuals are viewed in gendered terms, but also behaviors (aggression, nurturing), traits (strong, delicate), and even objects (pink or blue clothes). Feminist scholars seek to understand how societies construct the meaning of being a woman or a man and how gender affects individual identities, the ways people interact with each other, and inequality.

Explanations of gender inequality fall into two basic schools of thought: the essentialist and the social constructionist. The essentialist position holds that the behaviors of men and women are rooted in biological and genetic factors, including differences in hormonal patterns, physical size, aggressiveness, the propensity to "bond" with members of the same sex, and the capacity to bear children. Whether they view such differences as innate or as a natural outgrowth of human evolution, essentialists contend that sex-based inequality and the natural superiority of the male are inevitable, immutable, and necessary for the survival of the species. For the essentialist, the sexual division of labor in human societies is rooted in the sexual determination to be found in all species, from ants to deer to felines to primates.

The second school of thought, the social constructionist approach, bases its position on a growing body of historical and anthropological research that points to wide variations in gender behavior and in the sexual division of labor among human societies throughout time. Social constructionists contend that the diversity of cultural adaptations to biological differences in the sexes is so great that biological factors cannot sufficiently explain universal male dominance. They argue that one of the reasons the superiority of males appears to be inevitable is that in societies of various types cultural ideas or beliefs have arisen to justify and perpetuate sex-based stratification systems that entitle men to greater power, prestige, and wealth than women. While such ideologies do not cause gender inequality, they certainly justify it as natural.

In " 'Night to His Day': The Social Construction of Gender," Judith Lorber outlines a social constructionist approach. She defines gender as a social institution that rests on the "socially constructed statuses" of "man" and "woman." Even the apparently dimorphic physical characteristics of the two sexes, Lorber argues, are socially interpreted and emphasized. How does the social institution of gender create *sameness* among members of each gender, and *difference* between women and men? How are the genders ranked in a hierarchy that privileges men over women?

Judith Shapiro expands on how differences between women and men are created by examining the case of transsexuals. In "Transsexualism: Reflections on the Persistence of Gender and the

Mutability of Sex," she argues that transsexuals' attempts to become women or men entail displaying conventional markers of masculinity or femininity as well as surgical alteration of the body. Comparing transsexualism in several cultures, Shapiro suggests that transsexualism reflects a society's larger gender stratification system. What does transsexualism tell us about the relationship of gender, or the cultural differentiation between women and men, to sex, or the biological and embodied differences between males and females?

Whereas Shapiro emphasizes interaction and the presentation of self, the next article builds on Marxist feminist analyses to construct a *structural* explanation of gender inequality. Evelyn Nakano Glenn emphasizes the structural roots of gender and racial stratification in her analysis of paid reproductive work, "From Servitude to Service Work: Historical Continuities in the Racial Division of Paid Reproductive Labor." Reproductive labor, which is the paid or unpaid work necessary to sustain and reproduce the population, includes child-raising, food preparation, housecleaning, and the like, and historically has been assigned to women. Glenn argues that reproductive labor also has been stratified by race, with women of color assigned to perform domestic work for white women and given the dirtiest and most demeaning tasks. Categories of race and gender, Glenn argues, are thus overlapping, and are constructed in part by women's different positions in the labor force. The article illustrates a structuralist theory on the intersections of gender and race in its examination of the connections between the labor women perform and women's positions in the social hierarchy.

Adrienne Rich's classic article, "Compulsory Heterosexuality and Lesbian Existence," argues that one of the primary means of perpetuating male dominance is what she conceptualizes as the social institution of heterosexuality. Rich originally wrote this article partly in response to heterosexual feminists who did not see lesbian struggles as connected to the feminist struggle for women's liberation. Rich argues that the two struggles are inextricably linked, because the requirement that women be heterosexual penalizes all women. The article forces us to consider heterosexuality as a cultural ideology and social institution that proscribes and devalues all forms of female friendship and community as it perpetuates women's subordination to men.

Making a black woman's standpoint visible is the goal of Patricia Hill Collins's article, "The Social Construction of Black Feminist Thought." Hill Collins posits that African-American women's political and economic experiences have allowed them to develop a particular analysis of racism and sexism in the United States, as well as specific strategies of resistance. Hill Collins's analysis challenges the notions that oppressed groups are not conscious of their oppression and are somehow less capable than their oppressors of understanding the relations of ruling. It also challenges the idea that there can be one "feminist theory" or "feminist perspective," because individuals' positions in the social structure give rise to distinct standpoints, or perspectives on the world. Hill Collins thus suggests that an inclusive feminist vision will arise only from the patchwork of many distinct standpoints; it will be based on diversity among women, rather than seek to transcend or cover up such variations.

"Night to His Day": The Social Construction of Gender

JUDITH LORBER

Talking about gender for most people is the equivalent of fish talking about water. Gender is so much the routine ground of everyday activities that questioning its taken-for-granted assumptions and presuppositions is like thinking about whether the sun will come up.[1] Gender is so pervasive that in our society we assume it is bred into our genes. Most people find it hard to believe that gender is constantly created and re-created out of human interaction, out of social life, and is the texture and order of that social life. Yet gender, like culture, is a human production that depends on everyone constantly "doing gender" (West and Zimmerman 1987).

And everyone "does gender" without thinking about it. Today, on the subway, I saw a well-dressed man with a year-old child in a stroller. Yesterday, on a bus, I saw a man with a tiny baby in a carrier on his chest. Seeing men taking care of small children in public is increasingly common—at least in New York City. But both men were quite obviously stared at—and smiled at, approvingly. Everyone was doing gender—the men who were changing the role of fathers and the other passengers, who were applauding them silently. But there was more gendering going on that probably fewer people noticed. The baby was wearing a white crocheted cap and white clothes. You couldn't tell if it was a boy or a girl. The child in the stroller was wearing a dark blue T-shirt and dark print pants. As they started to leave the train, the father put a Yankee baseball cap on the child's head. Ah, a boy, I thought. Then I noticed the gleam of tiny earrings in the child's ears, and as they got off, I saw the little flowered sneakers and lace-trimmed socks. Not a boy after all. Gender done.

Gender is such a familiar part of daily life that it usually takes a deliberate disruption of our expectations of how women and men are supposed to act to pay attention to how it is produced. Gender signs and signals are so ubiquitous that we usually fail to note them—unless they are missing or ambiguous. Then we are uncomfortable until we have successfully placed the other person in a gender status; otherwise, we feel socially dislocated. In our society, in addition to man and woman, the status can be *transvestite* (a person who dresses in opposite-gender clothes) and *transsexual* (a person who has had sex-change surgery). Transvestites and transsexuals carefully construct their gender status by dressing, speaking, walking, gesturing in the ways prescribed for women or men—whichever they want to be taken for—and so does any "normal" person.

For the individual, gender construction starts with assignment to a sex category on the basis of what the genitalia look like at birth.[2] Then babies are dressed or adorned in a way that displays the category because parents don't want to be constantly asked whether their baby is a girl or a boy. A sex category becomes a gender status through naming, dress, and the use of other gender markers. Once a child's gender is evident, others treat those in one gender differently from those in the other, and the children respond to the different treatment by feeling different and behaving differently. As soon as they can talk, they start to refer to themselves as members of their gender. Sex doesn't come into play again until puberty, but by that time, sexual feelings and desires and practices have been shaped by gendered norms and expectations. Adolescent boys and girls approach and avoid each other in an elaborately scripted and gendered mating dance. Parenting is gendered, with different expectations for mothers and for fathers, and people of different genders work at different kinds of jobs. The work adults do as mothers and fathers and as low-level workers and high-level bosses, shapes women's and men's life experiences, and these experiences produce different feelings, consciousness, relationships, skills—ways of being that we call feminine or masculine.[3] All of these processes constitute the social construction of gender.

Gendered roles change—today fathers are taking care of little children, girls and boys are wearing unisex clothing and getting the same education, women and men are working at the same jobs. Although many traditional social groups are quite strict about maintaining gender differences, in other social groups they seem to be blurring. Then why the one-year-old's earrings? Why is it still so important to mark a child as a girl or a boy, to make sure she is not taken for a boy or he for a girl? What would happen if they were? They would, quite literally, have changed places in their social world.

To explain why gendering is done from birth, constantly and by everyone, we have to look not only at the way individuals experience gender but at gender as a social institution. As a social institution, gender is one of the major ways that human beings organize their lives. Human society depends on a predictable division of labor, a designated allocation of scarce goods, assigned responsibility for children and others who cannot care for themselves, common values and their systematic transmission to new members, legitimate leadership, music, art, stories, games, and other symbolic productions. One way of choosing people for the different tasks of society is on the basis of their talents, motivations, and competence—their demonstrated achievements. The other way is on the basis of gender, race, ethnicity—ascribed membership in a category of people. Although societies vary in the extent to which they use one or the other of these ways of allocating people to work and to carry out other responsibilities, every society uses gender and age grades. Every society classifies people as "girl and boy children," "girls and boys ready to be married," and "fully adult women and men," constructs similarities among them and differences between them, and assigns them to different roles and responsibilities. Personality characteristics, feelings, motivations, and ambitions flow from these different life experiences so that the members of these different groups become different kinds of people. The process of gendering and its outcome are legitimated by religion, law, science, and the society's entire set of values.

In order to understand gender as a social institution, it is important to distinguish human action from animal behavior. Animals feed themselves and their young until their young can feed themselves. Humans have to produce not only food but shelter and clothing. They also, if the group is going to continue as a social group, have to teach the children how their particular group does these tasks. In the process, humans reproduce gender, family, kinship, and a division of labor—social institutions that do not exist among animals. Primate social groups have been referred to as families, and their mating patterns as monogamy, adultery, and harems. Primate behavior has been used to prove the universality of sex differences—as built into our evolutionary inheritance (Haraway 1978). But animals' sex differences are not at all the same as humans' gender differences; animals' bonding is not kinship; animals' mating is not ordered by marriage; and animals' dominance hierarchies are not the equivalent of human stratification systems. Animals group on sex and age, relational categories that are physiologically, not socially, different. Humans create gender and age-group categories that are socially, and not necessarily physiologically, different.[4]

For animals, physiological maturity means being able to impregnate or conceive; its markers are coming into heat (estrus) and sexual attraction. For humans, puberty means being available for marriage; it is marked by rites that demonstrate this marital eligibility. Although the onset of physiological puberty is signaled by secondary sex characteristics (menstruation, breast development, sperm ejaculation, pubic and underarm hair), the onset of social adulthood is ritualized by the coming-out party or desert walkabout or bar mitzvah or graduation from college or first successful hunt or dreaming or inheritance of property. Humans have rituals that mark the passage from childhood into puberty and puberty into full adult status, as well as for marriage, childbirth, and death; animals do not (van Gennep 1960). To the extent that infants and the dead are differentiated by whether they are male or female, there are different birth rituals for girls and boys, and different funeral rituals for men and women (Biersack 1984, 132–33). Rituals of puberty, marriage, and becoming a parent are gendered, creating a "woman," a "man," a "bride," a "groom," a "mother," a "father." Animals have no equivalents for these statuses.

Among animals, siblings mate and so do parents and children; humans have incest taboos and rules that encourage or forbid mating between members of different kin groups (Lévi-Strauss 1956, [1949] 1969). Any animal of the same species may feed another's young (or may not, depending on the species). Humans designate responsibility for particular children by kinship; humans frequently limit responsibility for children to the members of their kinship group or make them into members of their kinship group with adoption rituals.

Animals have dominance hierarchies based on size or on successful threat gestures and signals. These hierarchies are usually sexed, and in some species, moving to the top of the hierarchy physically changes the sex (Austad 1986). Humans have stratification patterns based on control of surplus food, ownership of property, legitimate demands on others' work and sexual services, enforced determinations of who marries whom, and approved use of violence. If a woman replaces a man at the top of a stratification hierarchy, her social status may be that of a man, but her sex does not change.

Mating, feeding, and nurturant behavior in animals is determined by instinct and imitative learning and ordered by physiological sex and age (Lancaster 1974). In humans, these behaviors are taught and symbolically reinforced and ordered by socially constructed gender and age grades. Social gender and age statuses sometimes ignore or override physiological sex and age completely. Male and female animals (unless they physiologically change) are not interchangeable; infant animals cannot take the place of adult animals. Human females can become husbands and fathers, and human males can become wives and mothers, without sex-change surgery (Blackwood 1984). Human infants can reign as kings or queens.

Western society's values legitimate gendering by claiming that it all comes from physiology—female and male procreative differences. But gender and sex are not equivalent, and gender as a social construction does not flow automatically from genitalia and reproductive organs, the main physiological differences of females and males. In the construction of ascribed social statuses, physiological differences such as sex, stage of development, color of skin, and size are crude markers. They are not the source of the social statuses of gender, age grade, and race. *Social statuses* are carefully constructed through prescribed processes of teaching, learning, emulation, and enforcement. Whatever genes, hormones, and biological evolution contribute to human social institutions is materially as well as qualitatively transformed by social practices. Every social institution has a material base, but culture and social practices transform that base into something with qualitatively different patterns and constraints. The economy is much more than producing food and goods and distributing them to eaters and users; family and kinship are not the equivalent of having sex and procreating; morals and religions cannot be equated with the fears and ecstasies of the brain; language goes far beyond the sounds produced by tongue and larynx. No one eats "money" or "credit"; the concepts of "god" and "angels" are the subjects of theological disquisi-

tions; not only words but objects, such as their flag, "speak" to the citizens of a country.

Similarly, gender cannot be equated with biological and physiological differences between human females and males. The building blocks of gender are *socially constructed statuses.* Western societies have only two genders, "man" and "woman." Some societies have three genders—men, women, and *berdaches* or *hijras* or *xaniths*. Berdaches, hijras, and xaniths are biological males who behave, dress, work, and are treated in most respects as social women; they are therefore not men, nor are they female women; they are, in our language, "male women."[5] There are African and American Indian societies that have a gender status called *manly hearted women*—biological females who work, marry, and parent as men; their social status is "female men" (Amadiume 1987; Blackwood 1984). They do not have to behave or dress as men to have the social responsibilities and prerogatives of husbands and fathers; what makes them men is enough wealth to buy a wife.

Modern Western societies' *transsexuals* and *transvestites* are the nearest equivalent of these crossover genders, but they are not institutionalized as third genders (Bolin 1987). Transsexuals are biological males and females who have sex-change operations to alter their genitalia. They do so in order to bring their physical anatomy in congruence with the way they want to live and with their own sense of gender identity. They do not become a third gender; they change genders. Transvestites are males who live as women and females who live as men but do not intend to have sex-change surgery. Their dress, appearance, and mannerisms fall within the range of what is expected from members of the opposite gender, so that they "pass." They also change genders, sometimes temporarily, some for most of their lives. Transvestite women have fought in wars as men soldiers as recently as the nineteenth century; some married women, and others went back to being women and married men once the war was over.[6] Some were discovered when their wounds were treated; others not until they died. In order to work as a jazz musician, a man's occupation, Billy Tipton, a woman, lived most of her life as a man. She died recently at seventy-four, leaving a wife and three adopted sons for whom she was husband and father, and musicians with whom she had played and traveled, for whom she was "one of the boys" (*New York Times* 1989).[7] There have been many other such occurrences of women passing as men to do more prestigious or lucrative men's work (Matthaci 1982, 192–93).[8]

Genders, therefore, are not attached to a biological substratum. Gender boundaries are breachable, and individual and socially organized shifts from one gender to another call attention to "cultural, social, or aesthetic dissonances" (Garber 1992, 16). These odd or deviant or third genders show us what we ordinarily take for granted—that people have to learn to be women and men. Men who cross-dress for performances or for pleasure often learn from women's magazines how to "do femininity" convincingly (Garber 1992, 41–51). Because transvestism is direct evidence of how gender is constructed, Marjorie Garber claims it has "extraordinary power . . . to disrupt, expose, and challenge, putting in question the very notion of the 'original' and of stable identity" (1992, 16).

GENDER BENDING

It is difficult to see how gender is constructed because we take it for granted that it's all biology, or hormones, or human nature. The differences between women and men seem to be self-evident, and we think they would occur no matter what society did. But in actuality, human females and males are physiologically more similar in appearance than are the two sexes of many species of animals and are more alike than different in traits and behavior (C. F. Epstein 1988). Without the deliberate use of gendered clothing, hairstyles, jewelry, and cosmetics, women and men would look far more alike.[9] Even societies that do not cover women's breasts have gender-identifying clothing, scarification, jewelry, and hairstyles.

The ease with which many transvestite women pass as men and transvestite men as women is corroborated by the common gender misidentification in Westernized societies of people in jeans, T-shirts, and sneakers. Men with long hair may be addressed as "miss," and women with short hair are often taken for men unless they offset the potential ambiguity with deliberate gender markers (Devor 1987, 1989). Jan Morris, in *Conundrum,* an autobiographical account of events just before and just after a sex-change operation, described how easy it was to shift back and forth from being a man to being a woman when testing how it would feel to change gender status. During this time, Morris still had a penis and wore more or less unisex clothing; the context alone made the man and the woman:

> Sometimes the arena of my ambivalence was uncomfortably small. At the Travellers' Club, for example, I was obviously known as a man of sorts—women were only allowed on the premises at all during a few hours of the day, and even then were hidden away as far as

possible in lesser rooms or alcoves. But I had another club, only a few hundred yards away, where I was known only as a woman, and often I went directly from one to the other, imperceptibly changing roles on the way—"Cheerio, sir," the porter would say at one club, and "Hello, madam," the porter would greet me at the other. (1975, 132)

Gender shifts are actually a common phenomenon in public roles as well. Queen Elizabeth II of England bore children, but when she went to Saudi Arabia on a state visit, she was considered an honorary man so that she could confer and dine with the men who were heads of a state that forbids unrelated men and women to have face-to-unveiled-face contact. In contemporary Egypt, lower-class women who run restaurants or shops dress in men's clothing and engage in unfeminine aggressive behavior, and middle-class educated women of professional or managerial status can take positions of authority (Rugh 1986, 131). In these situations, there is an important status change: These women are treated by the others in the situation as if they are men. From their own point of view, they are still women. From the social perspective, however, they are men.[10]

In many cultures, gender bending is prevalent in theater or dance—the Japanese kabuki are men actors who play both women and men; in Shakespeare's theater company, there were no actresses—Juliet and Lady Macbeth were played by boys. Shakespeare's comedies are full of witty comments on gender shifts. Women characters frequently masquerade as young men, and other women characters fall in love with them; the boys playing these masquerading women, meanwhile, are acting out pining for the love of men characters.[11] In *As You Like It,* when Rosalind justifies her protective crossdressing, Shakespeare also comments on manliness:

> *Were it not better,*
> *Because that I am more than common tall,*
> *That I did suit me all points like a man:*
> *A gallant curtle-axe upon my thigh,*
> *A boar-spear in my hand, and in my heart*
> *Lie there what hidden women's fear there will,*
> *We'll have a swashing and martial outside,*
> *As many other mannish cowards have*
> *That do outface it with their semblances.*   *(I, i, 115–22)*

Shakespeare's audience could appreciate the double subtext: Rosalind, a woman character, was a boy dressed in girl's clothing who then dressed as a boy; like bravery, masculinity and femininity can be put on and taken off with changes of costume and role (Howard 1988, 435).[12]

M Butterfly is a modern play of gender ambiguities, which David Hwang (1989) based on a real person. Shi Peipu, a male Chinese opera singer who sang women's roles, was a spy as a man and the lover as a woman of a Frenchman, Gallimard, a diplomat (Bernstein 1986). The relationship lasted twenty years, and Shi Peipu even pretended to be the mother of a child by Gallimard. "She" also pretended to be too shy to undress completely. As "Butterfly," Shi Peipu portrayed a fantasy Oriental woman who made the lover a "real man" (Kondo 1990b). In Gallimard's words, the fantasy was "of slender women in chong sams and kimonos who die for the love of unworthy foreign devils. Who are born and raised to be perfect women. Who take whatever punishment we give them, and bounce back, strengthened by love, unconditionally" (D. H. Hwang 1989, 91). When the fantasy woman betrayed him by turning out to be the more powerful "real man," Gallimard assumed the role of Butterfly and, dressed in a geisha's robes, killed himself: "because 'man' and 'woman' are oppositionally defined terms, reversals . . . are possible" (Kondo 1990b, 18).[13]

But despite the ease with which gender boundaries can be traversed in work, in social relationships, and in cultural productions, gender statuses remain. Transvestites and transsexuals do not challenge the social construction of gender. Their goal is to be feminine women and masculine men (Kando 1973). Those who do not want to change their anatomy but do want to change their gender behavior fare less well in establishing their social identity. The women Holly Devor called "gender blenders" wore their hair short, dressed in unisex pants, shirts, and comfortable shoes, and did not wear jewelry or makeup. They described their everyday dress as women's clothing: One said, "I wore jeans all the time, but I didn't wear men's clothes" (Devor 1989, 100). Their gender identity was women, but because they refused to "do femininity," they were constantly taken for men (1987, 1989, 107–42). Devor said of them: "The most common area of complaint was with public washrooms. They repeatedly spoke of the humiliation of being challenged or ejected from women's washrooms. Similarly, they found public change rooms to be dangerous territory and the buying of undergarments to be a difficult feat to accomplish" (1987, 29). In an ultimate ironic twist, some of these women said "they would feel like transvestites if they were to wear dresses, and two women said that they had been called transvestites when they had done so" (1987, 31). They resolved the ambiguity of their gender status by

identifying as women in private and passing as men in public to avoid harassment on the street, to get men's jobs, and, if they were lesbians, to make it easier to display affection publicly with their lovers (Devor 1989, 107–42). Sometimes they even used men's bathrooms. When they had gender-neutral names, like Leslie, they could avoid the bureaucratic hassles that arose when they had to present their passports or other proof of identity, but because most had names associated with women, their appearance and their cards of identity were not conventionally congruent, and their gender status was in constant jeopardy.[14] When they could, they found it easier to pass as men than to try to change the stereotyped notions of what women should look like.

Paradoxically, then, bending gender rules and passing between genders does not erode but rather preserves gender boundaries. In societies with only two genders, the gender dichotomy is not disturbed by transvestites, because others feel that a transvestite is only transitorily ambiguous—is "really a man or woman underneath." After sex-change surgery, transsexuals end up in a conventional gender status—a "man" or a "woman" with the appropriate genitals (Eichler 1989). When women dress as men for business reasons, they are indicating that in that situation, they want to be treated the way men are treated; when they dress as women, they want to be treated as women:

> By their male dress, female entrepreneurs signal their desire to suspend the expectations of accepted feminine conduct without losing respect and reputation. By wearing what is "unattractive" they signify that they are not intending to display their physical charms while engaging in public activity. Their loud, aggressive banter contrasts with the modest demeanor that attracts men. . . . Overt signalling of a suspension of the rules preserves normal conduct from eroding expectations. (Rugh 1986, 131)

FOR INDIVIDUALS, GENDER MEANS SAMENESS

Although the possible combinations of genitalia, body shapes, clothing, mannerisms, sexuality, and roles could produce infinite varieties in human beings, the social institution of gender depends on the production and maintenance of a limited number of gender statuses and of making the members of these statuses similar to each other. Individuals are born sexed but not gendered, and they have to be taught to be masculine or feminine.[15] As Simone de

Beauvoir said: "One is not born, but rather becomes, a woman . . . ; it is civilization as a whole that produces this creature . . . which is described as feminine." (1952, 267).

Children learn to walk, talk, and gesture the way their social group says girls and boys should. Ray Birdwhistell, in his analysis of body motion as human communication, calls these learned gender displays *tertiary sex characteristics* and argues that they are needed to distinguish genders because humans are a weakly dimorphic species—their only sex markers are genitalia (1970, 39–46). Clothing, paradoxically, often hides the sex but displays the gender.

In early childhood, humans develop gendered personality structures and sexual orientations through their interactions with parents of the same and opposite gender. As adolescents, they conduct their sexual behavior according to gendered scripts. Schools, parents, peers, and the mass media guide young people into gendered work and family roles. As adults, they take on a gendered social status in their society's stratification system. Gender is thus both ascribed and achieved (West and Zimmerman 1987).

The achievement of gender was most dramatically revealed in a case of an accidental transsexual—a baby boy whose penis was destroyed in the course of a botched circumcision when he was seven months old (Money and Ehrhardt 1972, 118–23). The child's sex category was changed to "female," and a vagina was surgically constructed when the child was seventeen months old. The parents were advised that they could successfully raise the child, one of identical twins, as a girl. Physicians assured them that the child was too young to have formed a gender identity. Children's sense of which gender they belong to usually develops around the age of three, at the time that they start to group objects and recognize that the people around them also fit into categories—big, little; pink-skinned, brown-skinned; boys, girls. Three has also been the age when children's appearance is ritually gendered, usually by cutting a boy's hair or dressing him in distinctively masculine clothing. In Victorian times, English boys wore dresses up to the age of three, when they were put into short pants (Garber 1992, 1–2).

The parents of the accidental transsexual bent over backward to feminize the child—and succeeded. Frilly dresses, hair ribbons, and jewelry created a pride in looks, neatness, and "daintiness." More significant, the child's dominance was also feminized:

> The girl had many tomboyish traits, such as abundant physical energy, a high level of activity, stubbornness, and being often the dominant one in a girls' group. Her mother tried to modify her tomboyishness: ". . . I teach her to be more polite and quiet. I always wanted those virtues. I never did manage, but I'm going to try to manage them to—my daughter—to be more quiet and lady-like." From the beginning the girl had been the dominant twin. By the age of three, her dominance over her brother was, as her mother described it, that of a mother hen. The boy in turn took up for his sister, if anyone threatened her. (Money and Ehrhardt 1972, 122)

This child was not a tomboy because of male genes or hormones; according to her mother, she herself had also been a tomboy. What the mother had learned poorly while growing up as a "natural" female she insisted that her physically reconstructed son-daughter learn well. For both mother and child, the social construction of gender overrode any possibly inborn traits.

People go along with the imposition of gender norms because the weight of morality as well as immediate social pressure enforces them. Consider how many instructions for properly gendered behavior are packed into this mother's admonition to her daughter: "This is how to hem a dress when you see the hem coming down and so to prevent yourself from looking like the slut I know you are so bent on becoming" (Kincaid 1978).

Gender norms are inscribed in the way people move, gesture, and even eat. In one African society, men were supposed to eat with their "whole mouth, wholeheartedly, and not, like women, just with the lips, that is halfheartedly, with reservation and restraint" (Bourdieu [1980] 1990, 70). Men and women in this society learned to walk in ways that proclaimed their different positions in the society:

> The manly man . . . stands up straight into the face of the person he approaches, or wishes to welcome. Ever on the alert, because ever threatened, he misses nothing of what happens around him. . . . Conversely, a well brought-up woman . . . is expected to walk with a slight stoop, avoiding every misplaced movement of her body, her head or her arms, looking down, keeping her eyes on the spot where she will next put her foot, especially if she happens to have to walk past the men's assembly. (70)

Many cultures go beyond clothing, gestures, and demeanor in gendering children. They inscribe gender directly into bodies. In traditional Chinese society, mothers bound their daughters' feet into three-inch stumps to enhance their sexual attractiveness. Jewish fathers circumcise their infant sons to show their covenant with God. Women in African societies remove the clitoris of prepubescent girls, scrape their labia, and make the lips grow together to preserve their chastity and ensure their marriageability. In Western societies, women augment their breast size with silicone and reconstruct their faces with cosmetic surgery to conform to cultural ideals of feminine beauty. Hanna Papanek (1990) notes that these practices reinforce the sense of superiority or inferiority in the adults who carry them out as well as in the children on whom they are done: The genitals of Jewish fathers and sons are physical and psychological evidence of their common dominant religious and familial status; the genitals of African mothers and daughters are physical and psychological evidence of their joint subordination.[16]

Sandra Bem (1981, 1983) argues that because gender is a powerful "schema" that orders the cognitive world, one must wage a constant, active battle for a child not to fall into typical gendered attitudes and behavior. In 1972, *Ms. Magazine* published Lois Gould's fantasy of how to raise a child free of gender-typing. The experiment calls for hiding the child's anatomy from all eyes except the parents' and treating the child as neither a girl nor a boy. The child, called X, gets to do all the things boys *and* girls do. The experiment is so successful that all the children in X's class at school want to look and behave like X. At the end of the story, the creators of the experiment are asked what will happen when X grows up. The scientists' answer is that by then it will be quite clear what X is, implying that its hormones will kick in and it will be revealed as a female or male. That ambiguous, and somewhat contradictory, ending lets Gould off the hook; neither she nor we have any idea what someone brought up totally androgynously would be like sexually or socially as an adult. The hormonal input will not create gender or sexuality but will only establish secondary sex characteristics; breasts, beards, and menstruation alone do not produce social manhood or womanhood. Indeed, it is at puberty, when sex characteristics become evident, that most societies put pubescent children through their most important rites of passage, the rituals that officially mark them as fully gendered—that is, ready to marry and become adults.

Most parents create a gendered world for their newborn by naming, birth announcements, and dress. Children's relationships with same-gendered and different-gendered caretakers structure their self-identifications and personalities. Through cognitive development, children extract and apply to their own actions the appropriate behavior for those who belong in their own gender, as well as race, religion, ethnic group, and social class, rejecting what is not appropriate. If their social categories are highly valued, they value themselves highly; if their social categories are low status, they lose self-esteem (Chodorow 1974). Many feminist parents who want to raise androgynous children

soon lose their children to the pull of gendered norms (T. Gordon 1990, 87–90). My son attended a carefully nonsexist elementary school, which didn't even have girls' and boys' bathrooms. When he was seven or eight years old, I attended a class play about "squares" and "circles" and their need for each other and noticed that all the girl squares and circles wore makeup, but none of the boy squares and circles did. I asked the teacher about it after the play, and she said, "Bobby said he was not going to wear makeup, and he is a powerful child, so none of the boys would either." In a long discussion about conformity, my son confronted me with the question of who the conformists were, the boys who followed their leader or the girls who listened to the woman teacher. In actuality, they both were, because they both followed same-gender leaders and acted in gender-appropriate ways. (Actors may wear makeup, but real boys don't.)

For human beings there is no essential femaleness or maleness, femininity or masculinity, womanhood or manhood, but once gender is ascribed, the social order constructs and holds individuals to strongly gendered norms and expectations. Individuals may vary on many of the components of gender and may shift genders temporarily or permanently, but they must fit into the limited number of gender statuses their society recognizes. In the process, they re-create their society's version of women and men: "If we do gender appropriately, we simultaneously sustain, reproduce, and render legitimate the institutional arrangements. . . . If we fail to do gender appropriately, we as individuals—not the institutional arrangements—may be called to account (for our character, motives, and predispositions)" (West and Zimmerman 1987, 146).

> The gendered practices of everyday life reproduce a society's view of how women and men should act (Bourdieu [1980] 1990). Gendered social arrangements are justified by religion and cultural productions and backed by law, but the most powerful means of sustaining the moral hegemony of the dominant gender ideology is that the process is made invisible; any possible alternatives are virtually unthinkable (Foucault 1972; Gramsci 1971).[17]

FOR SOCIETY, GENDER MEANS DIFFERENCE

The pervasiveness of gender as a way of structuring social life demands that gender statuses be clearly differentiated. Varied talents, sexual preferences, identities, personalities, interests, and ways of interacting fragment the individual's bodily and social experiences. Nonetheless, these are organized in Western cultures into two and only two socially and legally recognized gender statuses, "man" and "woman."[18] In the social construction of gender, it does not matter what men and women actually do; it does not even matter if they do exactly the same thing. The social institution of gender insists only that what they do is *perceived* as different.

If men and women are doing the same tasks, they are usually spatially segregated to maintain gender separation, and often the tasks are given different job titles as well, such as executive secretary and administrative assistant (Reskin 1988). If the differences between women and men begin to blur, society's "sameness taboo" goes into action (G. Rubin 1975, 178). At a rock and roll dance at West Point in 1976, the year women were admitted to the prestigious military academy for the first time, the school's administrators "were reportedly perturbed by the sight of mirror-image couples dancing in short hair and dress gray trousers," and a rule was established that women cadets could dance at these events only if they wore skirts (Barkalow and Raab 1990, 53).[19] Women recruits in the U.S. Marine Corps are required to wear makeup—at a minimum, lipstick and eye shadow—and they have to take classes in makeup, hair care, poise, and etiquette. This feminization is part of a deliberate policy of making them clearly distinguishable from men Marines. Christine Williams quotes a twenty-five-year-old woman drill instructor as saying: "A lot of the recruits who come here don't wear makeup; they're tomboyish or athletic. A lot of them have the preconceived idea that going into the military means they can still be a tomboy. They don't realize that you are a *Woman* Marine" (1989, 76–77).[20]

If gender differences were genetic, physiological, or hormonal, gender bending and gender ambiguity would occur only in hermaphrodites, who are born with chromosomes and genitalia that are not clearly female or male. Since gender differences are socially constructed, all men and all women can enact the behavior of the other, because they know the other's social script: "'Man' and 'woman' are at once empty and overflowing categories. Empty because they have no ultimate, transcendental meaning. Overflowing because even when they appear to be fixed, they still contain within them alternative, denied, or suppressed definitions." (J. W. Scott 1988, 49). Nonetheless, though individuals may be able to shift gender statuses, the gender boundaries have to hold, or the whole gendered social order will come crashing down.

Paradoxically, it is the social importance of gender statuses and their external markers—clothing, mannerisms, and spatial segregation—that makes gender bending or gender crossing possible—or even necessary. The social viability of differentiated gender statuses produces the need or desire to shift statuses. Without gender differentiation, transvestism and transsexuality would be meaningless. You couldn't dress in the opposite gender's clothing if all clothing were unisex. There would be no need to reconstruct genitalia to match identity if interests and life-styles were not gendered. There would be no need for women to pass as men to do certain kinds of work if jobs were not typed as "women's work" and "men's work." Women would not have to dress as men in public life in order to give orders or aggressively bargain with customers.

Gender boundaries are preserved when transsexuals create congruous autobiographies of always having felt like what they are now. The transvestite's story also "recuperates social and sexual norms" (Garber 1992, 69). In the transvestite's normalized narrative, he or she "is 'compelled' by social and economic forces to disguise himself or herself in order to get a job, escape repression, or gain artistic or political 'freedom'" (Garber 1992, 70). The "true identity," when revealed, causes amazement over how easily and successfully the person passed as a member of the opposite gender, not a suspicion that gender itself is something of a put-on.

GENDER RANKING

Most societies rank genders according to prestige and power and construct them to be unequal, so that moving from one to another also means moving up or down the social scale. Among some North American Indian cultures, the hierarchy was male men, male women, female men, female women. Women produced significant durable goods (basketry, textiles, pottery, decorated leather goods), which could be traded. Women also controlled what they produced and any profit or wealth they earned. Since women's occupational realm could lead to prosperity and prestige, it was fair game for young men—but only if they became women in gender status. Similarly, women in other societies who amassed a great deal of wealth were allowed to become men—"manly hearts." According to Harriet Whitehead (1981):

Both reactions reveal an unwillingness or inability to distinguish the sources of prestige—wealth, skill, personal efficacy (among other things)—from masculinity. Rather there is the innuendo that if a person performing female tasks can attain excellence, prosperity, or social power, it must be because that person is, at some level, a man. . . . A woman who could succeed at doing the things men did was honored as a man would be. . . . What seems to have been more disturbing to the culture—which means, for all intents and purposes, to the men—was the possibility that women, within their own department, might be onto a good thing. It was into this unsettling breach that the berdache institution was hurled. In their social aspect, women were complimented by the berdache's imitation. In their anatomic aspect, they were subtly insulted by his vaunted superiority. (108)

In American society, men-to-women transsexuals tend to earn less after surgery if they change occupations; women-to-men transsexuals tend to increase their income (Bolin 1988, 153–60; Brody 1979). Men who go into women's fields, like nursing, have less prestige than women who go into men's fields, like physics. Janice Raymond, a radical feminist, feels that transsexual men-to-women have advantages over female women because they were not socialized to be subordinate or oppressed throughout life. She says:

We know that we are women who are born with female chromosomes and anatomy, and that whether or not we were socialized to be so-called normal women, patriarchy has treated and will treat us like women. Transsexuals have not had this same history. No man can have the history of being born and located in this culture as a woman. He can have the history of *wishing* to be a woman and of *acting* like a woman, but this gender experience is that of a transsexual, not of a woman. Surgery may confer the artifacts of outward and inward female organs but it cannot confer the history of being born a woman in this society. (1979, 114)

Because women who become men rise in the world and men who become women fall, Elaine Showalter (1987) was very critical of the movie *Tootsie,* in which Dustin Hoffman plays an actor who passes as a woman in order to be able to get work. "Dorothy" becomes a feminist "woman of the year" for standing up for women's rights not to be demeaned or sexually harassed. Showalter feels that the message of the movie is double-edged: "Dorothy's 'feminist' speeches . . . are less a response to the oppression of women than an instinctive situational male reaction to being treated like a woman. The implication is that women must be taught by men how to win their rights. . . . It says that feminist ideas are much less threatening when they come from a man" (123). Like Raymond, Showalter feels that being or having

been a man gives a transsexual man-to-woman or a man cross-dressed as a woman a social advantage over those whose gender status was always "woman."[21] The implication here is that there is an experiential superiority that doesn't disappear with the gender shift.

For one transsexual man-to-woman, however, the experience of living as a woman changed his/her whole personality. As James, Morris had been a soldier, foreign correspondent, and mountain climber; as Jan, Morris is a successful travel writer. But socially, James was far superior to Jan, and so Jan developed the "learned helplessness" that is supposed to characterize women in Western society:

We are told that the social gap between the sexes is narrowing, but I can only report that having, in the second half of the twentieth century, experienced life in both roles, there seems to me no aspect of existence, no moment of the day, no contact, no arrangement, no response, which is not different for men and for women. The very tone of voice in which I was now addressed, the very posture of the person next in the queue, the very feel in the air when I entered a room or sat at a restaurant table, constantly emphasized my change of status.

And if other's responses shifted, so did my own. The more I was treated as woman, the more woman I became. I adapted willy-nilly. If I was assumed to be incompetent at reversing cars, or opening bottles, oddly incompetent I found myself becoming. If a case was thought too heavy for me, inexplicably I found it so myself. . . . Women treated me with a frankness which, while it was one of the happiest discoveries of my metamorphosis, did imply membership of a camp, a faction, or at least a school of thought; so I found myself gravitating always towards the female, whether in sharing a railway compartment or supporting a political cause. Men treated me more and more as junior, . . . and so, addressed every day of my life as an inferior, involuntarily, month by month I accepted the condition. I discovered that even now men prefer women to be less informed, less able, less talkative, and certainly less self-centered than they are themselves; so I generally obliged them. (1975, 165–66)[22]

COMPONENTS OF GENDER

By now, it should be clear that gender is not a unitary essence but has many components as a social institution and as an individual status.[23]

As a social institution, gender is composed of:

Gender statuses, the socially recognized genders in a society and the norms and expectations for their enactment behaviorally, gesturally, linguistically, emotionally, and physically. How gender statuses are evaluated depends on historical development in any particular society.

Gendered division of labor, the assignment of productive and domestic work to members of different gender statuses. The work assigned to those of different gender statuses strengthens the society's evaluation of those statuses—the higher the status, the more prestigious and valued the work and the greater its rewards.

Gendered kinship, the family rights and responsibilities for each gender status. Kinship statuses reflect and reinforce the prestige and power differences of the different genders.

Gendered sexual scripts, the normative patterns of sexual desire and sexual behavior, as prescribed for the different gender statuses. Members of the dominant gender have more sexual prerogatives; members of a subordinate gender may be sexually exploited.

Gendered personalities, the combinations of traits patterned by gender norms of how members of different gender statuses are supposed to feel and behave. Social expectations of others in face-to-face interaction constantly bolster these norms.

Gendered social control, the formal and informal approval and reward of conforming behavior and the stigmatization, social isolation, punishment, and medical treatment of nonconforming behavior.

Gender ideology, the justification of gender statuses, particularly, their differential evaluation. The dominant ideology tends to suppress criticism by making these evaluations seem natural.

Gender imagery, the cultural representations of gender and embodiment of gender in symbolic language and artistic productions that reproduce and legitimate gender statuses. Culture is one of the main supports of the dominant gender ideology.

For an individual, gender is composed of:

Sex category to which the infant is assigned at birth based on appearance of genitalia. With prenatal testing and sex-typing, categorization is prenatal. Sex category may be changed later through surgery or reinspection of ambiguous genitalia.

Gender identity, the individual's sense of gendered self as a worker and family member.

Gendered marital and procreative status, fulfillment or nonfulfillment of allowed or disallowed mating, impregnation, childbearing, kinship roles.

Gendered sexual orientation, socially and individually patterned sexual desires, feelings, practices, and identification.

Gendered personality, internalized patterns of socially normative emotions as organized by family structure and parenting.

Gendered processes, the social practices of learning, being taught, picking up cues, enacting behavior already learned to be gender-appropriate (or inappropriate, if rebelling, testing), developing a gender identity, "doing gender" as a member of a gender status in relationships with gendered others, acting deferent or dominant.

Gender beliefs, incorporation of or resistance to gender ideology.

Gender display, presentation of self as a certain kind of gendered person through dress, cosmetics, adornments, and permanent and reversible body markers.

For an individual, all the social components are supposed to be consistent and congruent with perceived physiology. The actual combination of genes and genitalia, prenatal, adolescent, and adult hormonal input, and procreative capacity may or may not be congruous with each other and with sex-category assignment, gender identity, gendered sexual orientation and procreative status, gender display, personality, and work and family roles. At any one time, an individual's identity is a combination of the major ascribed statuses of gender, race, ethnicity, religion, and social class, and the individual's achieved statuses, such as education level, occupation or profession, marital status, parenthood, prestige, authority, and wealth. The ascribed statuses substantially limit or create opportunities for individual achievements and also diminish or enhance the luster of those achievements.

GENDER AS PROCESS, STRATIFICATION, AND STRUCTURE

As a social institution, gender is a process of creating distinguishable social statuses for the assignment of rights and responsibilities. As part of a stratification system that ranks these statuses unequally, gender is a major building block in the social structures built on these unequal statuses.

As a *process,* gender creates the social differences that define "woman" and "man." In social interaction throughout their lives, individuals learn what is expected, see what is expected, act and react in expected ways, and thus simultaneously construct and maintain the gender order: "The very injunction to be a given gender takes place through discursive routes: to be a good mother, to be a heterosexually desirable object, to be a fit worker, in sum, to signify a multiplicity of guarantees in response to a variety of different demands all at once" (J. Butler 1990, 145). Members of a social group neither make up gender as they go along nor exactly replicate in rote fashion what was done before. In almost every encounter, human beings produce gender, behaving in the ways they learned were appropriate for their gender status, or resisting or rebelling against these norms. Resistance and rebellion have altered gender norms, but so far they have rarely eroded the statuses.

Gendered patterns of interaction acquire additional layers of gendered sexuality, parenting, and work behaviors in childhood, adolescence, and adulthood. Gendered norms and expectations are enforced through informal sanctions of gender-inappropriate behavior by peers and by formal punishment or threat of punishment by those in authority should behavior deviate too far from socially imposed standards for women and men.

Everyday gendered interactions build gender into the family, the work process, and other organizations and institutions, which in turn reinforce gender expectations for individuals.[24] Because gender is a process, there is room not only for modification and variation by individuals and small groups but also for institutionalized change (J. W. Scott 1988, 7).

As part of a *stratification* system, gender ranks men above women of the same race and class. Women and men could be different but equal. In practice, the process of creating difference depends to a great extent on differential evaluation. As Nancy Jay (1981) says: "That which is defined, separated out, isolated from all else is A and pure. Not-A is necessarily impure, a random catchall, to which nothing is external except A and the principle of order that separates it from Not-A" (45). From the individual's point of view, whichever gender is A, the other is Not-A; gender boundaries tell the individual who is like him or her, and all the rest are unlike. From society's point of view, however, one gender is usually the touchstone, the normal, the dominant, and the other is different, deviant, and subordinate. In Western society, "man" is A, "wo-man" is Not-A. (Consider what a society would be like where woman was A and man Not-A.)

The further dichotomization by race and class constructs the gradations of a heterogeneous society's stratification scheme. Thus, in the United States, white is A, African American is Not-A; middle class is A, working class is Not-A, and "African-American women occupy a position whereby the inferior half of a series of these dichotomies converge" (P. H. Collins 1990, 70). The dominant categories are the hegemonic ideals, taken so for granted as the way things should be that white is not ordinarily thought of as a race, middle class as a class, or men as a gender. The characteristics of these categories define the Other as that which lacks the valuable qualities the dominants exhibit.

In a gender-stratified society, what men do is usually valued more highly than what women do because men do it, even when their activities are very similar or the same. In different regions of southern India, for example, harvesting rice is men's work, shared work, or women's work: "Wherever a task is done by women it is considered easy, and where it is done by [men] it is considered difficult" (Mencher 1988, 104). A gathering and hunting society's survival usually depends on the nuts, grubs, and small animals brought in by the women's foraging trips, but when the men's hunt is successful, it is the occasion for a celebration. Conversely, because they are the superior group, white men do not have to do the "dirty work," such as housework; the most inferior group does it, usually poor women of color (Palmer 1989).

Freudian psychoanalytic theory claims that boys must reject their mothers and deny the feminine in themselves in order to become men: "For boys the major goal is the achievement of personal masculine identification with their father and sense of secure masculine self, achieved through superego formation and disparagement of women" (Chodorow 1978, 165). Masculinity may be the outcome of boys' intrapsychic struggles to separate their identity from that of their mothers, but the proofs of masculinity are culturally shaped and usually ritualistic and symbolic (Gilmore 1990).

The Marxist feminist explanation for gender inequality is that by demeaning women's abilities and keeping them from learning valuable technological skills, bosses preserve them as a cheap and exploitable reserve army of labor. Unionized men who could be easily replaced by women collude in this process because it allows them to monopolize the better paid, more interesting, and more autonomous jobs: "Two factors emerge as helping men maintain their separation from women and their control of technological occupations. One is the active gendering of jobs and people. The second is the continual creation of sub-divisions in the work processes, and levels in work hierarchies, into which men can move in order to keep their distance from women" (Cockburn 1985, 13).

Societies vary in the extent of the inequality in social status of their women and men members, but where there is inequality, the status "woman" (and its attendant behavior and role allocations) is usually held in lesser esteem than the status "man." Since gender is also intertwined with a society's other constructed statuses of differential evaluation—race, religion, occupation, class, country of origin, and so on—men and women members of the favored groups command more power, more prestige, and more property than the members of the disfavored groups. Within many social groups, however, men are advantaged over women. The more economic resources, such as education and job opportunities, are available to a group, the more they tend to be monopolized by men. In poorer groups that have few resources (such as working-class African Americans in the United States), women and men are more nearly equal, and the women may even outstrip the men in education and occupational status (Almquist 1987).

As a *structure,* gender divides work in the home and in economic production, legitimates those in authority, and organizes sexuality and emotional life (Connell 1987, 91–142). As primary parents, women significantly influence children's psychological development and emotional attachments, in the process reproducing gender. Emergent sexuality is shaped by heterosexual, homosexual, bisexual, and sadomasochistic patterns that are gendered—different for girls and boys, and for women and men—so that sexual statuses reflect gender statuses.

When gender is a major component of structured inequality, the devalued genders have less power, prestige, and economic rewards than the valued genders. In countries that discourage gender discrimination, many major roles are still gendered; women still do most of the domestic labor and child rearing, even while doing full-time paid work; women and men are segregated on the job and each does work considered "appropriate"; women's work is usually paid less than men's work. Men dominate the positions of authority and leadership in government, the military, and the law; cultural productions, religions, and sports reflect men's interests.

In societies that create the greatest gender difference, such as Saudi Arabia, women are kept out of sight behind walls or veils, have no civil rights, and often create a cultural and emotional world of their own (Bernard 1981). But even in societies with less rigid gender boundaries, women and men spend much of their time with people of their own gender because of the way work and family are organized.

This spatial separation of women and men reinforces gendered differentness, identity, and ways of thinking and behaving (Coser 1986).

Gender inequality—the devaluation of "women" and the social domination of "men"—has social functions and a social history. It is not the result of sex, procreation, physiology, anatomy, hormones, or genetic predispositions. It is produced and maintained by identifiable social processes and built into the general social structure and individual identities deliberately and purposefully. The social order as we know it in Western societies is organized around racial ethnic, class, and gender inequality. I contend, therefore, that the continuing purpose of gender as a modern social institution is to construct women as a group to be the subordinates of men as a group. The life of everyone placed in the status "woman" is "night to his day—that has forever been the fantasy. Black to his white. Shut out of his system's space, she is the repressed that ensures the system's functioning" (Cixous and Clément [1975] 1986, 67).

THE PARADOX OF HUMAN NATURE

To say that sex, sexuality, and gender are all socially constructed is not to minimize their social power. These categorical imperatives govern our lives in the most profound and pervasive ways, through the social experiences and social practices of what Dorothy Smith calls the "everyday/everynight world" (1990, 31–57). The paradox of human nature is that it is *always* a manifestation of cultural meanings, social relationships, and power politics; "not biology, but culture, becomes destiny" (J. Butler 1990, 8). Gendered people emerge not from physiology or sexual orientation but from the exigencies of the social order, mostly, from the need for a reliable division of the work of food production and the social (not physical) reproduction of new members. The moral imperatives of religion and cultural representations guard the boundary lines among genders and ensure that what is demanded, what is permitted, and what is tabooed for the people in each gender is well known and followed by most (C. Davies 1982). Political power, control of scarce resources, and, if necessary, violence uphold the gendered social order in the face of resistance and rebellion. Most people, however, voluntarily go along with their society's prescriptions for those of their gender status, because the norms and expectations get built into their sense of worth and identity as a certain kind of human being, and because they believe their society's way is the natural way. These beliefs emerge from the imagery that pervades the way we think, the way we see and hear and speak, the way we fantasize, and the way we feel.

There is no core or bedrock human nature below these endlessly looping processes of the social production of sex and gender, self and other, identity and psyche, each of which is a "complex cultural construction" (J. Butler 1990, 36). *For humans, the social is the natural.* Therefore, "in its feminist senses, gender cannot mean simply the cultural appropriation of biological sexual difference. Sexual difference is itself a fundamental—and scientifically contested—construction. Both 'sex' and 'gender' are woven of multiple, asymmetrical strands of difference, charged with multifaceted dramatic narratives of domination and struggle" (Haraway 1990, 140).

NOTES

1. Gender is, in Erving Goffman's words, an aspect of *Felicity's Condition:* "any arrangement which leads us to judge an individual's . . . acts not to be a manifestation of strangeness. Behind Felicity's Condition is our sense of what it is to be sane" (1983, 27). Also see Bem 1993; Frye 1983, 17–40; Goffman 1977.

2. In cases of ambiguity in countries with modern medicine, surgery is usually performed to make the genitalia more clearly male or female.

3. See J. Butler 1990 for an analysis of how doing gender *is* gender identity.

4. Douglas 1973; MacCormack 1980; Ortner 1974; Ortner and Whitehead 1981; Yanagisako and Collier 1987. On the social construction of childhood, see Ariès 1962; Zelizer 1985.

5. On the hijras of India, see Nanda 1990; on the xaniths of Oman, Wikan 1982, 168–86; on the American Indian berdaches, W. L. Williams 1986. Other societies that have similar institutionalized third-gender men are the Koniag of Alaska, the Tanala of Madagascar, the Mesakin of Nuba, and the Chukchee of Siberia (Wikan 1982, 170).

6. Durova 1989; Freeman and Bond 1992; Wheelwright 1989.

7. Gender segregation of work in popular music still has not changed very much, according to Groce and Cooper 1989, despite considerable androgyny in some very popular figures. See Garber 1992 on the androgyny. She discusses Tipton on pp. 67–70.

8. In the nineteenth century, not only did these women get men's wages, but they also "had male privileges and could do all manner of things other women could not: open a bank account, write checks, own property, go anywhere unaccompanied, vote in elections" (Faderman 1991, 44).

9. When unisex clothing and men wearing long hair came into vogue in the United States in the mid-1960s, beards and mustaches for men also came into style again as gender identifications.

10. For other accounts of women being treated as men in Islamic countries, as well as accounts of women and men crossdressing in these countries, see Garber 1992, 304–52.

11. Dollimore 1986; Garber 1992, 32–40; Greenblatt 1987, 66–93; Howard 1988. For Renaissance accounts of sexual relations with women and men of ambiguous sex, see Laqueur 1990a, 134–39. For modern accounts of women passing as men that other women find sexually attractive, see Devor 1989, 136–37; Wheelwright 1989, 53–59.

12. Females who passed as men soldiers had to "do masculinity," not just dress in a uniform (Wheelwright, 1989, 50–78). On the triple entendres and gender resonances of Rosalind-type characters, see Garber 1992, 71–77.

13. Also see Garber 1992, 234–66.

14. Bolin describes how many documents have to be changed by transsexuals to provide a legitimizing "paper trail" (1988, 145–47). Note that only members of the same social group know which names are women's and which men's in their culture, but many documents list "sex."

15. For an account of how a potential man-to-woman transsexual learned to be feminine, see Garfinkel 1967, 116–85, 285–88. For a gloss on this account that points out how, throughout his encounters with Agnes, Garfinkel failed to see how he himself was constructing his own masculinity, see Rogers 1992.

16. Paige and Paige (1981, 147–49) argue that circumcision ceremonies indicate a father's loyalty to his lineage elders—"visible public evidence that the head of a family unit of their lineage is willing to trust others with his and his family's most valuable political asset, his son's penis" (147). On female circumcision, see El Dareer 1982; Lightfoot-Klein 1987; van der Kwaak 1992; Walker 1992. There is a form of female circumcision that removes only the prepuce of the clitoris and is similar to male circumcision, but most forms of female circumcision are far more extensive, mutilating, and spiritually and psychologically shocking than the usual form of male circumcision. However, among the Australian aborigines, boys' penises are slit and kept open, so that they urinate and bleed the way women do (Bettelheim 1962, 165–206).

17. The concepts of moral hegemony, the effects of everyday activities (praxis) on thought and personality, and the necessity of consciousness of these processes before political change can occur are all based on Marx's analysis of class relations.

18. Other societies recognize more than two categories, but usually no more than three or four (Jacobs and Roberts 1989).

19. Carol Barkalow's book has a photograph of eleven first-year West Pointers in a math class, who are dressed in regulation pants, shirts, and sweaters, with short haircuts. The caption challenges the reader to locate the only woman in the room.

20. The taboo on males and females looking alike reflects the U.S. military's homophobia (Bérubé 1989). If you can't tell those with a penis from those with a vagina, how are you going to deter-

mine whether their sexual interest is heterosexual or homosexual unless you watch them having sexual relations?

21. Garber feels that *Tootsie* is not about feminism but about transvestism and its possibilities for disturbing the gender order (1992, 5–9).

22. See Bolin 1988, 149–50, for transsexual men-to-women's discovery of the dangers of rape and sexual harassment. Devor's "gender blenders" went in the opposite direction. Because they found that it was an advantage to be taken for men, they did not

deliberately cross-dress, but they did not feminize themselves either (1989, 126–40).

23. See West and Zimmerman 1987 for a similar set of gender components.

24. On the "logic of practice," or how the experience of gender is embedded in the norms of everyday interaction and the structure of formal organizations, see Acker 1990; Bourdieu [1980] 1990; Connell 1987; Smith 1987a.

REFERENCES

Almquist, Elizabeth M. 1987. Labor market gendered inequality in minority groups. *Gender & Society* 1:400–14.

Amadiume, Ifi. 1987. *Male daughters, female husbands: Gender and sex in an African society* London: Zed Books.

Austad, Steven N. 1986. Changing sex nature's way. *International Wildlife,* May-June, 29.

Barkalow, Carol, with Andrea Raab. 1990. *In the men's house.* New York: Poseidon Press.

Bem, Sandra Lipsitz. 1981. Gender schema theory: A cognitive account of sex typing. *Psychological Review* 88:354–64.

———. 1983. Gender schema theory and its implications for child development: Raising gender-aschematic children in a gender-schematic society. *Signs* 8:598–616.

Bernard, Jessie. 1981. *The female world.* New York: Free Press.

Bernstein, Richard. 1986. France jails 2 in odd case of espionage. *New York Times,* 11 May.

Biersack, Aletta. 1984. Paiela "women-men": The reflexive foundations of gender ideology. *American Ethnologist* 11:118–38.

Birdwhistell, Ray L. 1970. *Kinesics and context: Essays on body motion communications.* Philadelphia: University of Pennsylvania Press.

Blackwood, Evelyn. 1984. Sexuality and gender in certain Native American tribes: The case of cross-gender females. *Signs* 10:27–42.

Bolin, Anne. 1987. Transsexualism and the limits of traditional analysis. *American Behavioral Scientist* 31:41–65.

———. 1988. *In search of Eve: Transsexual rites of passage.* South Hadley, Mass.: Bergin & Garvey.

Bourdieu, Pierre. [1980] 1990. *The logic of practice.* Stanford, Calif.: Stanford University Press.

Brody, Jane E. 1979. Benefits of transsexual surgery disputed as leading hospital halts the procedure. *New York Times,* 2 October.

Butler, Judith. 1990. *Gender trouble: Feminism and the subversion of identity.* New York and London: Routledge.

Chodorow, Nancy. 1974. Family structure and feminine personality. In Rosaldo and Lamphere.

———. 1978. *The reproduction of mothering.* Berkeley: University of California Press.

Cixous, Hélène, and Catherine Clément. [1975] 1986. *The newly born woman,* translated by Betsy Wing. Minneapolis: University of Minnesota Press.

Cockburn, Cynthia. 1985. *Machinery of dominance: Women, men and technical know-how.* London: Pluto Press.

Collins, Patricia Hill. 1990. *Black feminist thought: Knowledge, consciousness, and the politics of empowerment.* Boston: Unwin Hyman.

Connell, R. [Robert] W. 1987. *Gender and power: Society, the person, and sexual politics.* Stanford, Calif.: Stanford University Press.

Coser, Rose Laub. 1986. Cognitive structure and the use of social space. *Sociological Forum* 1:1–26.

Davies, Christie. 1982. Sexual taboos and social boundaries. *American Journal of Sociology* 87:1032–63.

De Beauvoir, Simone. 1953. *The second sex,* translated by H. M. Parshley. New York: Knopf.

Devor, Holly. 1987. Gender blending females: Women and sometimes men. *American Behavioral Scientist* 31:12–40.

———. 1989. *Gender blending: Confronting the limits of duality.* Bloomington: Indiana University Press.

Eichler, Margrit. 1989. Sex change operations: The last bulwark of the double standard. In Richardson and Taylor.

Epstein, Cynthia Fuchs, 1988. *Deceptive distinctions: Sex, gender and the social order.* New Haven: Yale University Press.

Foucault, Michel. 1972. *The archeology of knowledge and the discourse on language,* translated by A. M. Sheridan Smith. New York: Pantheon.

Garber, Marjorie. 1992. *Vested interests: Cross-dressing and cultural anxiety.* New York and London: Routledge.

Gilmore, David D. 1990. *Manhood in the making: Cultural concepts of masculinity.* New Haven: Yale University Press.

Gordon, Tuula. 1990. *Feminist mothers.* New York: New York University Press.

Gramsci, Antonio. 1971. *Selections from the prison notebooks,* translated and edited by Quintin Hoare and Geoffrey Nowell Smith. New York: International Publishers.

Haraway, Donna. 1978. Animal sociology and a natural economy of the body politic. Part I: A political physiology of dominance. *Signs* 4:21–36.

———. 1990. Investment strategies for the evolving portfolio of primate females. In Jacobus, Keller, and Shuttleworth.

Howard, Jean E. 1988. Crossdressing, the theater, and gender struggle in early modern England. *Shakespeare Quarterly* 39:418–41.

Hwang, David Henry. 1989. *M Butterfly.* New York: New American Library.

Jay, Nancy. 1981. Gender and dichotomy. *Feminist Studies* 7:38–56.

Kando, Thomas. 1973. *Sex change: The achievement of gender identity among feminized transsexuals.* Springfield, Ill.: Charles C. Thomas.

Kincaid, Jamaica. 1978. Girl. *The New Yorker,* 26 June.

Kondo, Dorinne K. 1990a. *Crafting selves: Power, gender, and discourses of identity in a Japanese workplace.* Chicago: University of Chicago Press.

———. 1990b. *M. Butterfly:* Orientalism, gender, and a critique of essentialist identity. *Cultural Critique,* no. 16 (Fall):5–29.

Lancaster, Jane Beckman. 1974. *Primate behavior and the emergence of human culture.* New York: Holt, Rinehart and Winston.

Lévi-Strauss, Claude. 1956. The family. In *Man, culture, and society,* edited by Harry L. Shapiro, New York: Oxford.

———. [1949] 1969. *The elementary structures of kinship,* translated by J. H. Bell and J. R. von Sturmer. Boston: Beacon Press.

Matthaei, Julie A. 1982. *An economic history of women's work in America.* New York: Schocken.

Mencher, Joan. 1988. Women's work and poverty: Women's contribution to household maintenance in South India. In Dwyer and Bruce.

Money, John, and Anke A. Ehrhardt. 1972. *Man & woman, boy & girl.* Baltimore, Md.: Johns Hopkins University Press.

Morris, Jan. 1975. *Conundrum.* New York: Signet.

New York Times. 1989. Musician's death at 74 reveals he was a woman. 2 February.

Palmer, Phyllis. 1989. *Domesticity and dirt: Housewives and domestic servants in the United States, 1920–1945.* Philadelphia: Temple University Press.

Papanek, Hanna. 1979. Family status production: The "work" and "non-work" of women. *Signs* 4:775–81.

Raymond, Janice G. 1979. *The transsexual empire: The making of the she-male.* Boston: Beacon Press.

Reskin, Barbara F. 1988. Bringing the men back in: Sex differentiation and the devaluation of women's work. *Gender & Society* 2:58–81.

Rubin, Gayle. 1975. The traffic in women: Notes on the political economy of sex. In *Toward an anthropology of women,* edited by Rayna R[app] Reiter. New York: Monthly Review Press.

Rugh, Andrea B. 1986. *Reveal and conceal: Dress in contemporary Egypt.* Syracuse, N.Y.: Syracuse University Press.

Scott, Joan Wallach. 1988. *Gender and the politics of history.* New York: Columbia University Press.

Showalter, Elaine. 1987. Critical cross-dressing: Male feminists and the woman of the year. In *Men in feminism,* edited by Alice Jardine and Paul Smith. New York: Methuen.

Smith, Dorothy E. 1990. *The conceptual practices of power: A feminist sociology of knowledge.* Toronto: University of Toronto Press.

Van Gennep, Arnold. 1960. *The rites of passage,* translated by Monika B. Vizedom and Gabrielle L. Caffee. Chicago: University of Chicago Press.

West, Candace, and Don Zimmerman. 1987. Doing gender. *Gender & Society* 1:125–51.

Wheelright, Julie. 1989. Amazons and military maids: Women who cross-dressed in pursuit of life, liberty and happiness. London: Pandora Press.

Whitehead, Ann. 1981. "I'm hungry, Mum": The politics of domestic budgeting. In Young, Wolkowitz, and McCullagh.

Williams, Christine L. 1989. *Gender differences at work: Women and men in nontraditional occupations.* Berkeley: University of California Press.

Transsexualism: Reflections on the Persistence of Gender and the Mutability of Sex

JUDITH SHAPIRO

There is a story about two small children in a museum standing in front of a painting of Adam and Eve. One child asks the other, "Which is the man and which is the lady?" The other child answers, "I can't tell—they don't have any clothes on." A story to delight those favoring the social constructionist view of gender. An even better story would be one in which the body itself becomes a set of clothes that can be put on.

All societies differentiate among their members on the basis of what we can identify as "gender." All gender systems rely, albeit in differing ways, on bodily sex differences between females and males. How can we understand the grounding of gender in sex as at once a necessity and an illusion?

Powerful cultural mechanisms operate to ensure that boys will be boys and girls will be girls. Such mechanisms appear to include turning some of the girls into boys and some of the boys into girls.

The purpose of this paper is to take transsexualism as a point of departure for examining the paradoxical relationship between sex and gender. In its suspension of the usual anatomical recruitment rule to gender category membership, transsexualism raises questions about what it means to consider sex as the "basis" for systems of gender difference. At the same time, the ability of traditional gender systems to absorb, or even require, such forms of gender-crossing as transsexualism leads us to a more sophisticated appreciation of the power of gender as a principle of social

and cultural order. While transsexualism reveals that a society's gender system is a trick done with mirrors, those mirrors are the walls of our species' very real and only home.

DEFINING TRANSSEXUALISM

The term "transsexual," as understood in its Euro-American context, is used in the following related senses: most broadly, to designate those who feel that their true gender is at variance with their biological sex; more specifically, to designate those who are attempting to "pass" as members of the opposite sex; and, most specifically, to designate those who have either had sex change surgery or are undergoing medical treatment with a view toward changing their sex anatomically.[1]

Male to female transformation appears to be far more frequent than the reverse.[2] There is also a general tendency in the literature for male to female transsexualism to function as an unmarked form, that is, for it to stand for the phenomenon in general.[3] Studies of transsexualism are overwhelmingly focused on men who have become women—an interesting twist on androcentric bias in research.

Transsexualism first captured the popular imagination both nationally and internationally with Christine Jorgensen's much publicized "sex-change operation" in Denmark in 1952. Her subsequent career can be seen as a prototype of the transsexual as celebrity, subsequent examples being Jan Morris (formerly James Morris, correspondent to the London *Times* and journalist who covered the first expedition to Mount Everest in 1953), and Renée Richards (tennis star and successful ophthalmologist, born Richard Raskind, the son of two Jewish doctors from New York). All three have written widely-read autobiographies (Jorgensen 1967,

Morris 1974, Richards 1983), which are valuable sources of ethnographic information on the place of gender in the construction of personal identity.

In the course of the 1960s, transsexualism became a focus of medical/psychiatric attention and the contested ground of competing therapies, from the psychoanalytic to the behaviorist to the surgical. Up until the mid-60s, the American medical establishment had taken a generally negative view of sex change surgery; with a few exceptions, those seeking operations generally had to go abroad to obtain it—the Mecca being Casablanca and the clinic of Dr. Georges Burou.[4] Through the efforts of a small number of physician advocates like the endocrinologist Harry Benjamin,[5] who is credited with propagating the use of "transsexualism" as a diagnostic category and who urged greater understanding and tolerance of the transsexual condition, gender clinics were established at some major American hospitals and sex change surgery became one of the forms of available therapy.

The turn to sex change surgery followed upon the apparent ineffectiveness of all forms of psychological therapy in dealing with transsexualism.[6] As two sociologists writing about transsexualism in 1978 noted, "[g]enitals have turned out to be easier to change than gender identity . . .[w]hat we have witnessed in the last 10 years is the triumph of the surgeons over the psychotherapists in the race to restore gender to an unambiguous reality" (Kessler and McKenna 1978: 120).

Prominent early contributors to the biomedical and psychological literature on transsexualism include, along with Benjamin, John Money, Robert Stoller, and Richard Green.[7] These researchers and clinicians, who accomplished a transfer in the frame of reference for transsexualism from the moral to the medical, generally viewed themselves as part of a movement to foster more enlightened, liberal and scientific attitudes toward sexuality. At the same time, their work reflects a highly traditional attitude toward gender, an issue that will be explored more fully below.

In the medical literature, the transsexual condition has commonly been designated by the term "gender dysphoria syndrome."[8] In fact, transsexuals usually claim to have a quite definite sense of their gender; it is their physical sex that is experienced as the problem.[9] The term "sexual dysphoria" was thus at one point suggested as being more appropriate (Prince 1973). And yet, the concept of biological "sex" is not without its own problems; the more we learn about it, the more complicated things become, since we might be talking about chromosomal (or genetic) sex, anatomical (or morphological) sex, genital (or gonadal)

sex, germinal sex, and hormonal sex.[10] Perhaps the most satisfactory formulation is that transsexuals are people who experience a conflict between their gender assignment, made at birth on the basis of anatomical appearance, and their sense of gender identity.[11]

This, however, opens up the question of what is meant by "gender identity." According to the literature of developmental psychology, a core gender identity is something that is established early and is relatively impervious to change. It designates the experience of belonging clearly and unambiguously to one—and only one—of the two categories, male and female.[12] Given such a notion of gender identity, transsexualism can be diagnosed as a form of crossed wiring. Whatever the reason for it, even if we cannot ultimately specify what causes it,[13] individuals can simply be recategorized, which has the considerable advantage of leaving the two-category system intact. The problem with this approach, as we shall see below, is that one cannot take at face value transsexuals' own accounts of a fixed and unchanging (albeit sex-crossed) gender identity, given the immense pressure on them to produce the kinds of life histories that will get them what they want from the medico-psychiatric establishment. To take the problem one step further, the project of autobiographical reconstruction in which transsexuals are engaged, although more focused and motivated from the one that all of us pursue, is not entirely different in kind. We must all repress information that creates problems for culturally canonical narratives of identity and the self, and consistency in gender attribution is very much a part of this.

Transsexualism as a diagnostic category is defined in relation to such other categories as transvestism and homosexuality. Transsexualism is generally distinguished from transvestism understood as cross-dressing that does not call into question a person's basic sense of gender identity. In cases in which cross-dressing becomes increasingly central to a person's life and comes to reflect a desire to assume the opposite gender role, transvestism and transsexualism can be seen as developmental stages in a gender-crossing career.[14] In recent years, the term "transgenderist" has come to be used to designate a career of gender-crossing, which may or may not be directed toward an ultimate physical sex change.

The way in which transsexualism is seen as being related, or not related, to homosexuality is a particularly interesting question, since it leads into general issues concerning the relationship between gender and sexual orientation, and how each enters into the construction of personal and social identity. The literature indicates that most transsexuals consider themselves to be heterosexual. A male to female transsexual who feels herself to be a woman wants to be able to have sex with a man as a woman, not as a male homosexual.[15] There are also homosexual transsexuals—for example, male to female lesbian feminist transsexuals, who caused a great deal of havoc in the separatist wing of the women's movement in the late 70s.

When I have shared my work and thoughts on transsexualism with colleagues, either at seminars or in informal conversations, I have frequently encountered the argument that transsexualism is a form of disguised homosexuality. Psychiatrists and psychologists are particularly apt to make the argument that men who believe themselves to be women are seeking an appropriate way to have other men as objects of desire while avoiding the stigma of homosexuality. It is hard to know whether such arguments reflect the homophobia of the person presenting them or a response to the level of homophobia found in society. In either event, they seem to indicate a certain obliviousness to the difficulties of life as a transsexual.

Some gays and lesbians view transsexuals as homosexuals who have found a particularly desperate and insidious way of staying in the closet. Transsexuals, for their part, often express negative attitudes toward homosexuals.[16] While it might be argued that transsexuals' hostility toward homosexuality is a form of denial, the same argument can be made (and often is made) about nontranssexual heterosexuals. Although denial of homosexuality may play a role in the transsexualism of particular individuals, the general argument that transsexualism is an epiphenomenon of homosexuality is neither convincing nor logically parsimonious. In the context of the analysis of transsexualism developed here, it can be understood as reflecting a fundamentalist approach to the relationship between sex and gender, that is, an inability to see an anatomical male as anything other than a man and an anatomical female as anything other than a woman.

TRANSSEXUALISM AND THE CONSERVATION OF GENDER

Transsexualism has attracted a considerable amount of attention from sociologists, in particular those of the ethnomethodological persuasion, who have seen it as a privileged vantage point from which to observe the social construction of reality—in this case, gender reality. Transsexuals shed a self-reflective light on what we are all engaged in as we perform our gender roles. Because transsexuals have to work at establishing their credentials as men or women in a relatively self-conscious way, whereas the rest of us are

under the illusion that we are just doing what comes naturally, they bring to the surface many of the tacit understandings that guide the creation and maintenance of gender differences in ongoing social life. Sociological studies of transsexualism thus belong not only to the literature on deviance, as one might expect, but are at the core of the sociological study of gender.

One of the major findings of the sociological literature on transsexualism is the degree of conservatism in transsexuals' views about masculinity and femininity. While transsexuals may be deviants in terms of cultural norms about how one arrives at being a man or a woman, they are, for the most part, highly conformist about what to do once you get there. The following summary characterization is representative of those commonly found in the literature:

> . . . many transsexuals said they viewed themselves as passive, nurturing, emotional, intuitive, and the like. Very often, many expressed a preference for female dress and make-up. Others saw their feminine identification in terms of feminine occupations: housework, secretarial, and stewardess work. Some expressed feminine identification in terms of marriage and motherhood—wanting to "meet the right man," "have him take care of me," "adopt kids," and "bring them up." One expressed very definite views on child-rearing that were quite ironic in this context: "I would definitely teach my kids that boys should be boys and girls should be girls". (Raymond 1979: 78)[17]

Many transsexuals are, in fact, "more royalist than the king" in matters of gender. The sociologist Thomas Kando, who worked with a group of transsexuals who had undergone sex change surgery at the University of Minnesota in 1968–1969, reported test and questionnaire results showing that transsexuals were more conservative about sex role norms than both men and women (or, to be precise, than nontranssexual men and women), women being the least conservative. Male to female transsexuals tested higher in femininity than women. Most of the transsexuals in Kando's sample held stereotypical women's jobs and seemed, on the average, to be "better adjusted" to the female role than women were. As Kando noted, "[transsexuals] are, in many of their everyday activities, attitudes, habits, and emphases what our culture expects women to be, only more so" (Kando 1973: 22–27).[18]

The gender conservatism of transsexuals is encouraged and reinforced by the medical establishment on which they are dependent for therapy. The conservatism of the doctors is in turn reinforced by their need to feel justified in undertaking as momentous a procedure as sex change surgery. In order to be convinced that such surgery is more likely to help than to harm, they feel the need to engage in close preoperative monitoring of the candidate's behavior, attitudes, and feelings. This is particularly important, since some of those who present themselves as candidates for surgery would not be appropriately diagnosed as transsexuals.[19] The gender identity clinics operated in conjunction with programs of sex change surgery provide the context of determining whether such surgery is indeed the most appropriate form of therapy for a particular individual, and also provide therapists and surgeons with an opportunity to judge how successful an applicant for surgery is likely to be at playing the desired gender role.

Given the preponderance of male to female transsexuals, it is interesting to keep in mind that the professional community in which this transformation is effected is largely male. It has been male surgeons' and psychiatrists' expectations about femininity that have had to be satisfied if a sex change operation is to be performed. There are reports in the literature of doctors using their own responses to a patient—that is, whether or not the doctor is attracted to the patient—to gauge the suitability of sex change surgery (Kessler and McKenna 1978: 118). Physical attractiveness seems to have provided the major basis for an optimistic prognosis in male to female sex change.

But looks aren't everything. Members of the medical establishment have also felt the need to socialize male to female transsexuals into their future roles in a gender-stratified economy. In the following excerpt from an "advice" column, published in the December 1963 issue of *Sexology Magazine,* Harry Benjamin, who had been outlining all the obstacles that lie before those seeking sex change surgery, from the physical rigors of the operation and related medical procedures themselves to the difficulties of learning to behave like a woman in matters of dress, make-up, body movement, speech style, etc., moved on to the bottom line:

> Finally, but highly important, how do you know you can make a living as a woman? Have you ever worked as a woman before? I assume that so far, you have only held a man's job and have drawn a man's salary. Now you have to learn something entirely new. Could you do that? Could you get along with smaller earnings? (Benjamin 1966: 109)[20]

Thus, while transsexualism may strike most people as being far out, it is clearly at the same time fairly far in. Thomas Kando put it as follows:

> Unlike various liberated groups, transsexuals are reactionary, moving back toward the core-culture rather than away from it. They are the Uncle Toms of the sexual revolution. With these individuals, the dialectic of social change comes full circle and the position of greatest deviance becomes that of the greatest conformity. (Kando 1973: 145)

Those who have been involved in the political struggle to transform the gender system and do away with its hierarchies have been particularly distrustful of transsexuals. Dwight Billings and Thomas Urban, in their socialist critique of transsexualism, noted the way in which "the medical profession has indirectly tamed and transformed a potential wildcat strike at the gender factory" (Billings and Urban 1982: 278). Janice Raymond, the author of a radical feminist critique of transsexualism that will be discussed further below, diagnosed transsexuals as gender revolutionaries manqué, carriers of a potentially subversive message who instead serve the interests of the patriarchal establishment (Raymond 1979: 36, 124). She viewed female to male transsexuals, who in her opinion should rightly have become lesbian feminists, as "castrated women," who have cut themselves off from their authentic source of female power. She compared them to the so-called "token woman" who becomes acceptable to the male establishment by aping men (Raymond 1979: xxiv). Raymond contemplated transsexualism with all the frustration and disgust of a missionary watching prime converts backslide into paganism and witchcraft.

PASSING

The efforts of transsexuals to achieve normal gender status involve them in what is generally referred to as "passing." Since the term "passing" carries the connotation of being accepted for something one is not, it is important to consider the complexities that arise when this term is applied to what transsexuals are doing.

First of all, transsexuals commonly believe that it is when they are trying to play the role of their anatomical sex, as opposed to their subjectively experienced gender, that they are trying to pass as something they are not. The way they frequently put this is to say that they feel they are "masquerading" as a man or a woman.[21]

At the same time, transsexuals must work hard at passing in their new gender status, however more authentic they may themselves believe it to be. They have, after all, come to that status in a way that is less than culturally legitimate.

They may also continue to have gender-inappropriate physical attributes, as well as behavioral habits acquired from years spent in the opposite gender role. Some transsexuals are, of course, more successful at passing than others, much of this depending on secondary sexual characteristics. Physical repairs are possible in certain areas: corrective surgery to reduce the size of an "Adam's Apple," electrolysis to remove facial and body hair.[22] Voice pitch cannot be changed, but transsexuals often seek speech therapy to help them achieve habits in conformity with their new gender.

The obstacles to successful passing provide an important context for the gender conservatism of transsexuals, discussed above. The strategies transsexuals use for passing in everyday life involve outward physical appearance, the more private body (which must be revealed in some contexts, for example, doctors' offices or communal dressing rooms), general conversation in a variety of social settings, and the construction of a suitable retrospective biography.[23] One aspect of biographical revision that transsexuals engage in, both for social purposes and for reasons of personal identity, is a recategorization of kinship ties they carry with them from the period before their sex change, particularly those associated with marriage. Jan Morris, for example, recategorized herself as a sister-in-law to her wife and an aunt to the children she fathered (Morris 1974: 122). A male to female transsexual in Thomas Kando's study reported the following conversation with a daughter:

". . . as far as Paula [the daughter] is concerned, what brought it to a head is, I was praying for a way to advise her, and then she called me one time and asked me 'Are we going to get together, because remember, 15th is Father's Day.' And I said, 'Paula, of course I love you very much, but I do have to tell you that I can no longer accept Father's Day gifts. If you wish to continue relations with me I could be your special Aunt Vanessa or something like that, but please don't remind me of that situation and certainly don't bring me any male clothing under any circumstances." (Kando 1973: 71)

The way in which transsexuals go about establishing their gender in social interactions reminds us that the basis on which we are assigned a gender in the first place (that is, anatomical sex) is not what creates the reality of gender in ongoing social life. Moreover, the strategies used by transsexuals to establish their gender socially are the same when they are playing the role associated with their original anatomical sex and when they are playing the role associated with their new achieved sex (Kessler and McKenna

1978: 127). In neither case is this accomplished by flashing. Transsexuals make explicit for us the usually tacit processes of gender attribution. As Harold Garfinkel put it, the transsexual reveals the extent to which the normally sexed person is a "contingent practical accomplishment" (Garfinkel 1967: 181).[24] In other words, they make us realize that we are all passing.

While establishing your gender credentials is a more demanding and riskier project if you are a transsexual, gender is not what could be called a sinecure for any of us. Fortunately, we receive a great deal of help from those around us who order their perceptions and interpretations according to the expectation that people should fall into one of two gender categories and remain there. The literature on transsexualism gives repeated examples of how slips and infelicities pass unnoticed as people discount incongruous information (see, for example, Kessler and McKenna 1978: 137–138).[25]

In this project of passing and being helped to pass, transsexuals sustain what the ethnomethodologist Harold Garfinkel called the "natural attitude" with respect to gender, which is made up of the assumptions that there are only two genders, that one's gender is invariant and permanent, that genitals are essential signs of gender, that there are no exceptions, that gender dichotomy and gender membership are "natural" (Garfinkel 1967: 122–128). At the same time, transsexuals reveal to the more detached and skeptical observer the ways in which such a natural attitude is socially and culturally achieved.

If transsexuals are commonly successful in passing as members of their gender of choice, the question arises as to how they are viewed when their particular circumstances become known. Are transsexuals accepted by nontranssexuals as "women" and as "men"?

Available research indicates that their status is problematic. The claims transsexuals make for the authenticity of their gender status are not convincing to most nontranssexuals. Transsexuals themselves are, in fact, ambivalent about the issue, sometimes saying they are "real" men and women and sometimes not. (See, for example, Kando 1973: 28–30.) Questions about the gender authenticity of transsexuals provide an occasion for culturally revealing negotiation around the definition of gender, transsexuals and nontranssexuals each gravitating toward definitions that work best to validate, or privilege, their own membership.

One transsexual who has argued forcefully and publicly for her status as a woman is Renée Richards, whose particular motivation came from her desire to pursue her career in tennis. Appealing to biology selectively, but in accordance with cultural definitions of gender, she considered that her female genitals settled the matter beyond question. That being the case, she felt that the chromosome tests administered by the various major tennis associations were an inappropriate and unfair barrier to her acceptance for women's tournament play. In fact, she asserted that of all players in women's tennis, her sex was least in question given all the publicity about it (Richards 1983: 320–321, 343). Clearly, the domain of physical sex differences leaves room for maneuver in finding a biological charter for gender. We can probably expect an increasing tendency to think of "real" biological sex in terms of chromosomes, although chromosomes clearly do not serve as the basis for determining sex, and hence gender, in ordinary practice.[26]

A particularly interesting case of negotiating the gender status of transsexuals came out of one segment of the feminist community in the late 1970s. In a book entitled *The Transsexual Empire,* Janice Raymond presented a critique of transsexualism motivated primarily by a felt need to exclude male to female transsexuals from the category of women, and, more specifically, to address the vexing issue of male to female lesbian feminist transsexuals. Her approach was to draw a picture of these transsexuals as men in ultimate drag, intruding on a world in which women have chosen to dedicate themselves socially and sexually to one another—a scenario reminiscent of *The Invasion of the Body Snatchers.*[27]

In denying womanhood to transsexuals, Raymond insisted on the physical limits of what can be accomplished through sex change operations and emphasized that male to female transsexuals can't, after all, have babies and don't have two X chromosomes (Raymond 1979: 10, 188). In the following representative passage from her argument, we see a once-a-man-always-a-man line of reasoning that slides between a definition of womanhood based on historical/ biographical experience and one defined biologically in terms of sex:

We know that we are women who are born with female chromosomes and anatomy, and that whether or not we were socialized to be so-called normal women, patriarchy has treated us and will treat us like women. Transsexuals have not had this same history. (Raymond 1979: 114)

To this argument, which apparently relies on the notion that chromosomes are destiny, is added an etherealized essentialism in which the defining attributes of womanhood that attract the male to female transsexual transcend the physical plane:

[T]he creative power that is associated with female biology is not envied primarily because it is able to give birth physically but because it is multidimensional, bearing culture, harmony, and true inventiveness. (Raymond 1979: 107)

If this had been intended simply as an ethnographic description of transsexual motivation, it would have captured well the desires and wishes expressed by many transsexuals. It is more accurately seen, however, as being itself ethnographic data on the feminine mystique that has characterized much feminist writing over the past couple of decades, in which there has been a somewhat unprincipled marriage of convenience between a social constructionist view of gender and an essentialist view of womanhood.

If asking what gender transsexuals "really" belong to begs a number of fundamental questions, an alternative that seems to capture their distinctive place in a particular cultural scheme of things is to think of them as "naturalized" women and men. Such a formulation can evoke multiple meanings of "naturalization": (1) a status acquired in the way foreigners acquire citizenship,[28] (2) a change in gender that entails a change in the body, which we associate with the domain of nature, and (3) a recognition of the transsexuals' own experience of sex change as validating what they believe to be their true nature.

TRANSSEXUAL EMBODIMENT

In order to achieve the sense of a unified gender that forms an essential part of the more general sense of a unified self, the transsexual must acquire an appropriate body. Jan Morris, for example, who flirted with mystic visions of transcending the body altogether,[29] expressed what was ultimately her dominant desire to be properly embodied with a particularly fierce vividness:

. . . if I were trapped in that cage again [a man's body] nothing would keep me from my goal, however fearful its prospect, however hopeless the odds. I would search the earth for surgeons, I would bribe barbers or abortionists, I would take knife and do it myself, without fear, without qualms, without a second thought. (Morris 1974: 169)

To those who might be tempted to diagnose the transsexual's focus on the genitals as obsessive or fetishistic (see, for example, Raymond 1979: 122), the response is that transsexuals are, in fact, simply conforming to their culture's criteria for gender assignment. Transsexuals' fixation on having the right genitals is clearly less pathological than if they were to insist that they were women with penises or men with vaginas (Kessler and McKenna 1978: 123).

Transsexuals can make use of the mind/body dualism when arguing for the primacy of their gender identity over their original anatomical sex, while at the same time insisting on the need to acquire the right kind of body. Consider, for example, the following arguments by a female to male transsexual:

> "Your body is just something that holds you together; it's part of you; it's an important part—but your mind is strong; it is your will; your mind is everything. I mean as far as everything you want to be. If you had the body, the hands to play baseball, and it just wasn't in your mind, and it wasn't what you enjoyed, you might go and be a doctor. When all this was going on, I thought of God: Am I doing wrong? God created me as a girl, so maybe I should be. But I couldn't be, and which is more important, your mind or your body? God created my mind too. . . ." (cited in Stoller 1968: 200)

This same person considered it self-evident that her sexual organs should be changed from female to male. Similarly, Jan Morris, whose desperation for physical sex change surgery has just been seen, at the same time identified gender with the soul and insisted upon the incorporeal nature of her quest:

> To me gender is not physical at all, but is altogether insubstantial. It is the soul perhaps . . . It is the essentialness of oneself, the psyche, the fragment of unity. (Morris 1974: 25)

> . . . that my conundrum might simply be a matter of penis or vagina, testicle or womb, seems to me still a contradiction in terms, for it concerned not my apparatus, but my *self*. (Morris 1974: 22; italics in original)

The bodily outcome of sex change surgery is itself somewhat makeshift. As Dr. Georges Burou put it: "'I don't change men into women. I transform male genitals into genitals that have a female aspect. All the rest is in the patient's mind'" (cited in Raymond 1979: 10). In a famous case study analyzed by the sociologist Harold

Garfinkel in *Studies in Ethnomethodology,* his informant, Agnes, admitted that her artificial vagina was inferior to one provided by nature. Her feeling about this reflected not only considerations of physical practicality, but also what we might call cultural metaphysics. At the same time, though, it was a vagina to which she felt legitimately and morally entitled, given that she was "really" a woman. Agnes spoke of her penis and testicles as if they were some unfortunate, pathological growth, a kind of tumor; getting rid of them was like removing a wart (Garfinkel 1967: 126–127, 181–182).

The relationship of the transsexed body to the "naturally" sexed body calls attention to notions of nature as being associated, on the one hand, with "reality" and, on the other, as something to be manipulated and controlled by science. In this sense, transsexualism is located at the intersection of bio-material fundamentalism and voluntaristic transcendence. Sex change surgery, for its part, belongs to the domain of heroic medicine,[30] destined, however, to be left behind as science marches on. The prospects of such things as recombinant DNA technology already permit us to look ahead to a time when these operations would be viewed as a crude and primitive approach to transforming our natural endowments. The futuristic possibilities of transsexualism are invoked in the following passage by a defensive male to female transsexual seeking to assert her superiority over what are here called "Gennys," or genetic females:

> Free from the chains of menstruation and child-bearing, transsexual women are obviously far superior to Gennys in many ways . . . Genetic women are becoming quite obsolete, which is obvious, and the future belongs to transsexual women. We know this, and perhaps some of you suspect it. All you will have left is your "ability" to bear children, and in a world which will groan to feed 6 billion by the year 2000, that's a negative asset. (cited in Raymond 1979: xvii)

If, on the other hand, we step back from the entire enterprise of physical sex change, as many critics of the transsexual phenomenon have done, we might see the most technologically sophisticated strategy imaginable as a crude and primitive approach to issues of personal and social identity. Though the analogy cannot be pushed too far, addressing gender issues through sex change surgery is a bit like turning to dermatologists to solve the race problem.

TRANSSEXUALISM IN CROSS-CULTURAL PERSPECTIVE

It is instructive to compare Euro-American transsexualism with forms of institutionalized gender crossing found in other societies. I have selected three such examples from very different cultural settings. Their juxtaposition to one another and to Euro-American transsexualism throws into relief certain culturally distinctive characteristics of the gender systems of which each is a part; at the same time, they all illustrate the same basic paradox—or, to use Morris' term, conundrum—at the heart of the relationship between sex and gender.

THE *BERDACHE* IN NORTH AMERICA

The best-known case of institutionalized gender crossing in the ethnographic literature is the so-called *berdache* found in a number of societies indigenous to North America. The term itself, which seems to come ultimately from Persian via Arabic, Italian, and French (Forgey 1975: 2) and not from any Native American language, has come to be used in the North Americanist literature as a general designation for individuals who take on gender roles in opposition to their anatomical sex by adopting the dress and performing the activities of members of the other group.[31] As in the case of Euro-American transsexualism, gender crossing in North American Indian societies is most commonly male to female; cases of girls or women who take on male behavior, dress, or activities are relatively rare.[32] The significance of such asymmetries in gender crossing will be discussed below.

Information on the *berdache* is uneven in quality and quite sparse in the case of some groups. It is also difficult to gauge how the colonial situation affected both the practices themselves and the quality of the information that outsiders were able to obtain about them. There seems to have been a great deal of variation in patterns of gender crossing from one society to another, and sometimes within a society as well. In some cases, the parents decided that a child of one sex would serve as a substitute for a child of the other. More commonly, children were allowed to take on attributes of the gender opposite to their anatomical sex if their general inclinations and preferred activities pointed in that direction. Some *berdache* were reported to have sexual relations with persons of the same sex; others seem not to have done so. As we can see from the discussion of trans-sexualism, it is not clear what it would mean to designate the *berdache's* same-sex sexual activity as "homosexual," particularly in the absence of fuller data from each society in question.

The defining feature of the *berdache* status seems generally to have been adopting the dress and assuming the day-to-day activities of the opposite sex. In a comparative analysis of the *berdache,* the anthropologist Harriet White-head has argued that the institution is to be understood in the context of certain distinguishing features of North American Indian cultures, notably, an ethic of individual destiny that could make itself known in a variety of ways and was often the outcome of a visionary encounter with a supernatural being. Whitehead also argued that the institution of the *berdache* reflects a social system in which the division of labor is at the forefront of gender definition (Whitehead 1981: 99–103).

We do not know enough about North American Indian concepts of gender to understand how the gender of the *berdache* was construed in the various societies in which the institution was found. Should we be thinking about the *berdache* in terms of a basic two-gender system with the possibility of individuals transferring from one to the other? Or is it more appropriate to think of the *berdache* as constituting a distinct third gender, a special status with cultural functions and meanings of its own?[33] How might different societies have varied in this regard? Was the *berdache* in some societies believed to have actually "become" a member of the opposite gender? If so, what does this say about how such societies might differ from our own in terms of the distinctive criteria of gender? Might a change in activities and demeanor suffice for legitimate gender transformation?[34] While we may not be able to answer these questions satisfactorily, an encounter with the North American berdache at least provokes us to ask them.

THE *XANITH* IN OMAN

In Oman, where men and women lead lives that are highly segregated from one another, there is a form of gender crossing in which men who adopt a distinctive form of dress and comportment can move in the world of women.[35] They may, for example, socialize freely with women who are not their relatives and may see unrelated women unveiled. The *xanith* engages in various forms of women's work, including cooking and paid domestic service. At the same time, *xanith* retain many jural privileges of male status. They may move about publicly in a way that women cannot. Their dress is not exactly the same as that of women, but is distinctive and can be seen as something in between male and female garb. While accepted as women for many purposes, they do not "pass."

The Omani status of *xanith* is coterminous with that of the male homosexual prostitute. The anthropologist who has provided the ethnographic information on this cultural practice, Unni Wikan, has argued that the *xanith* provides a means for Omani men to engage in premarital and extramarital sex without compromising the virtue of Omani women and the rights of the men who have responsibility over them.[36] Insofar as the *xanith*'s partner retains the active role in the sexual act, the partner's own masculine gender status is not in question. According to Wikan, the differential gender categorization of *xanith* and "men" indicates that the sex act takes priority over the sexual organs for purposes of establishing gender status.

Individuals may move in and out of the *xanith* status, and once a man has given it up by marrying and proving his sexual potency with his bride, he is fully accepted as a man. This presents a contrast with Euro-American transsexualism, in which the cultural current moves individuals toward an experience of essential and unchanging gender that is an intrinsic part of an essential and chronologically continuous self.

The two cases also offer interesting contrasts with respect to the relationship between sexual orientation and gender identity. Debate around the relationship between transsexualism and homosexuality in the Euro-American case reflects, on the one hand, their possible separability and, on the other, the way in which gender status is validated or challenged by considerations of sexual orientation; it also reflects the way in which both gender and sexual orientation are essentially defining of personhood and identity. Omani transgenderism involves a closer link between sexual orientation and gender status while at the same [time] reflecting the possibilities for change in these aspects of social identity over the course of a person's—or, rather, a male person's—life.

WOMAN-WOMAN MARRIAGE IN AFRICA

In a number of societies in Africa, it has traditionally been possible for a woman to take another woman as a wife, and to acquire rights both to the domestic services of the wife and to any offspring she produces. This practice of 'woman-woman marriage,' as it has come to be called,

while showing certain variations from one culture to another, at the same time reveals some basic similarities about the African societies in which it is found.[37] In general, woman-woman marriage operates within a system in which marriages are established through exchanges of wealth; in which they are relationships not so much between individuals as between kin groups; in which a major concern is the perpetuation of kin groups defined through descent; and in which paternity is achieved through payment of bridewealth rather than through sexual activity. The relationship between the female husband and her wife is not a sexual one. The wife has a lover or lovers, sometimes selected by the female husband and sometimes of the wife's own choosing.

Women who become husbands and fathers may do so by standing in for men of their lineage, for example, when there is no male to serve as an appropriate heir. In these cases, it seems that descent group membership is a sufficiently important aspect of social identity to override differences of role usually associated with gender. Insofar as marriages are established through exchanges of wealth, women can acquire wives if they have access to property over which they can exercise control. In societies in which women occupy positions of political leadership, they can take wives in order to form alliances with other kin groups in much the same way as men do. In some ethnographic reports, the role of female husband and father is said to be limited to barren women who have no children of their own through marriage to a male husband. In other cases, women combine their roles as wife and mother in one marriage with their roles as husband and father in another.

The question raised by woman-woman marriage for our present purposes is how the assumption of husbandhood and fatherhood affects a woman's gender status. When women become husbands and fathers, are they engaged in what would appropriately be termed gender crossing? The answer seems to be no in some cases and yes in others.

Among the Lovedu of South Africa, for example, the role of husband and father seems open to women as women. Lovedu women who acquire wives generally do so because they are entitled to a daughter-in-law from their brother's household and may themselves have no son, or no willing son, to serve as the husband. The woman may thus take her brother's daughter to be her own wife instead; in this case, the female husband is seen as being like a mother-in-law. Woman-woman marriage in Lovedu society is also linked to the ability of women to occupy various important political offices and to control the wealth they earn after they marry. The queen who traditionally ruled

Lovedu society customarily received wives given to solicit political favors; some of these wives were, in turn, given away in marriage by the queen in her own strategies of alliance formation (Krige 1974: 15–22).

Among the Nandi of Western Kenya, on the other hand, a woman who becomes a husband and father is reclassified as a man. The Nandi female husband is commonly a woman of relatively advanced years who has failed to produce a male heir. The need for such an heir is tied to a "house property complex," in which each of a man's co-wives is endowed with a share of her husband's property, which will be passed on to her son or sons to manage (Oboler 1980: 69, 73). A Nandi woman may acquire a wife to produce the needed heir, while she herself takes on the interim management of her house's share of her husband's estate. When a Nandi woman takes a wife, she must cease engaging in sexual relations with her husband, since this would both compromise her reclassification as a man and, should she conceive by some chance, raise problems of succession and inheritance. Female husbands are supposed to give up women's work. The ethnographer who has described woman-woman marriage among the Nandi, Regina Oboler, noted that in the past they were expected to adopt male dress and adornment, although this was no longer the case during the period of her fieldwork (Oboler 1980: 74, 85).

According to Oboler, the Nandi reclassify the female husband as a man because she is assuming economic and managerial responsibilities that Nandi see as the exclusive preserve of men:

> It is an ideological assertion which masks the fact that the female husband is an anomaly: she is a woman who of necessity behaves as no woman in her culture should. Her situation forces her to assume male behavior in certain areas that are crucial to the cultural definition of the differences between the sexes. These areas have to do with the management and transmission of the family estate. (Oboler 1980: 83)

The role played by the Nandi female husband is not something simply open to both women and men, nor is it apparently sufficient for the Nandi to think of the female husband as a woman taking on a man's responsibilities. Instead, the Nandi prefer to say that the female husband "is" a man.

In fact, it would seem more accurate to say that the female husband is a man in some contexts, but not in others. It is when matters of property and heirship are at issue that Nandi are most insistent about the female husband

being a man (Oboler 1980: 70). Although the ideology of the female-husband-as-man takes on a life of its own, leading the Nandi to assert that female husbands behave as men in all areas of social life, this is not actually the case. In many contexts, the female husband continues to behave more as a woman than as a man. Behaviors designated by Nandi as "masculine" in the case of female husbands are often not, in fact, gender-specific; others are characteristic of older women in general. It is also the case that the female husband whose own husband is still living continues in the role of wife to him, and mother to any children of the marriage. Thus, while the Nandi may generally characterize the female husband as a man, her manhood seems to be focused around the more specific project of maintaining the link between gender, control over property, and inheritance.

What all of these forms of gender crossing have in common, their considerable differences notwithstanding, is that they call into question systems of gender differentiation and at the same time support them. They pose an implicit, or in the Euro-American case explicit, challenge to the usual basis for sorting individuals into gender categories while operating to maintain culturally traditional distinctions between women and men.

We can see how this works more clearly if we consider the following two issues: 1) the significance of asymmetries in the directionality of culturally patterned forms of gender change, and 2) the paradoxical relationship between gender and sex.

ASYMMETRIES OF GENDER CROSSING

The cases of gender crossing presented here show various kinds of asymmetries. Two cases are unidirectional: the Omani *xanith* has no female to male counterpart; woman-woman marriage in African society has no comparable male-male form. The two others, Euro-American transsexualism and the North American *berdache,* are bidirectional, but show a skewed distribution with a greater frequency of male to female transformation. The reasons for these asymmetries are, in part, specific to the meanings and functions of gender in the respective societies at issue. However, they are also understandable in terms of gender hierarchy itself and the social dominance of men.

In order to see this, let us consider how asymmetry in Euro-American transsexualism can be understood. Among the factors cited in the literature are: the greater difficulty and cost of female to male sex change surgery, and its less satisfactory results; the greater propensity of men for the kind of experimentation, risk, and initiative involved in sex change surgery; the apparently greater propensity of males for sexual deviance in general; the dominant role of the mother in the rearing of children of both sexes; the relationship of transsexualism to other cultural institutions in which envious men are trying to appropriate the powers of women (for example, the dominance of men in the field of obstetrics and gynecology)—in this case, taking the ultimate step of becoming women themselves.[38]

Some authorities on transsexualism have remarked upon the apparently paradoxical relationship between the high ratio of male to female transsexuals and the results of survey research showing that it is more common for girls to say they want to be boys than the reverse, more common for adult women than for adult men to say they would rather have been born the opposite sex (see, for example, Benjamin 1966: 147; Pauly 1969: 60). This, taken together with society's greater permissiveness toward girls acting like boys than toward boys acting like girls, has been seen as a puzzle to be solved—often by recourse to biological or psychiatric speculation. A possible Freudian twist on all of this, given a view of women as castrated beings longing for possession of the penis, is that all women are transsexuals,[39] which either makes one wonder why more of them do not seek sex change surgery or makes one appreciate their success in finding symbolic substitutes.

The key to understanding the skewed Euro-American pattern of gender crossing would seem to lie in an understanding of the asymmetrical, hierarchical nature of our gender categories, and the extent to which masculinity is the unmarked category and femininity the marked category. That is, our notions of what a man should be like are linked to our notions of what a person, in general, should be like. This is an important factor in the differential tolerance for cross-gender behavior in women and in men. Women wanting to be like men can be seen as engaging in an understandable project of upward mobility. Insofar as becoming more like a man is becoming more like a person, the implications for gender reclassification are less radical than movement away from the unmarked, generic human standard.[40] When we encounter cases of female to male gender reclassification, as in some versions of African woman-woman marriage, these are perhaps best looked at in terms of social promotion to a superior status. In fact, the Nandi speak of it in just these terms (Oboler 1980: 74, 86).[41] By the same token, the absence of female to male gender crossing in a society like Oman reflects a lack of comparable opportunities for the upward mobility of women into the status of men.

Male to female transgenderists, for their part, would seem to be engaged in a willful act of downward mobility. When Renée Richards told a friend about her plans for a sex change operation, the friend said, "Anyone who voluntarily wants to become a forty-year-old woman, I take my hat off to" (Richards 1983: 308). Jan Morris was quite sensitive to the privileges she was losing in giving up her manhood. She remarked upon the shock of suddenly being condescended to and being assumed to be incompetent in a variety of areas: "[A]ddressed every day of my life as an inferior, involuntarily, month by month I accepted the condition" (Morris 1974: 149). At the same time, both Richards and Morris clearly felt that the compensations of womanhood more than made up for the drawbacks.

In the context of these considerations, we might see cultural discomfort with male to female transsexualism in Euro-American society as reflecting the fact that those who intentionally move down in the system are more threatening to its values than those seeking to move up. The latter may constitute a threat to the group concerned with maintaining its privileges, but the former constitute a threat to the principles on which the hierarchy itself is based. The greater cultural tolerance for male to female gender crossing in native North American societies may, in this light, be interpreted as an index of a less stratified relationship between men and women.

THE PARADOX OF SEX AND GENDER

The terms "sex" and "gender" are generally used to distinguish a set of biological differences from a system of social, cultural, and psychological ones. The culturally structured system of differences we designate by the term "gender" bears some relationship to the biological difference between women and men, but is not reducible to it. In other words, the relationship between sex and gender is at once a motivated and an arbitrary one. It is motivated insofar as there must be reasons for the cross-culturally universal use of sex as a principle in systems of social differentiation; it is arbitrary, or conventional, insofar as gender differences are not directly derivative of natural, biological facts, but rather vary from one culture to another in the way in which they order experience and action. In any society, the meaning of gender is constituted in the context of a variety of domains—political, economic, etc.—that extend beyond what we think of as gender per se, and certainly beyond what we understand by the term "sex" in its various senses.[42] Gender is a classic example of what the sociologist Marcel Mauss called a "total social fact":

> In these *total* social phenomena, as we propose to call them, all kinds of institutions find simultaneous expression: religious, legal, moral, and economic. In addition, the phenomena have their aesthetic aspect. . . . (Mauss [1925] 1954: 2)

We recognize "gender" as a cross-culturally distinct category of social difference by virtue of some relationship that it has to physical sex differences. When we inquire into what motivates the relationship between sex and gender, however, confusions may arise as to what kinds of connections we are talking about, given the multiple meanings of the term "sex." Is "sex" being used to designate general morphological differences between males and females? Is it being used to focus on reproductive capacities and roles more specifically? Is erotic activity what we have in mind? Are we using the term in a shifting sense, sometimes talking about all of the above and sometimes only some of it? The other major question is, of course, the extent to which our own culturally specific folk beliefs about biology saturate our view of gender and provide us with the illusory truths we hold to be self-evident.[43]

Just as the comparative study of gender differences shows how little of the specific content of such differences can be predicted by sex in any sense of the term, so the study of gender crossing shows us the robustness of gender systems in their transcendence of the usual rule of recruitment by sex. While sex differences may serve to "ground" a society's system of gender differences, the ground seems in some ways to be less firm than what it is supporting.[44]

Euro-American transsexualism presents us with the particular paradox of ascribed gender and achieved sex. While some may think of transsexuals as individuals exercising the right to "choose" their gender identity, freeing themselves from what is for most people a physically-determined fate, this identity is usually experienced by transsexuals themselves as something that is in no way subject to their own will. For transsexuals, gender is destiny and anatomy is achieved.[45]

This reversal of the Euro-American folk ontology of sex and gender was experienced by Jan Morris in terms she took from C. S. Lewis:

> Gender is a reality, and a more fundamental reality than sex. Sex is, in fact, merely the adaptation to organic life of a fundamental polarity which divides all created beings. Female sex is simply one of the things that have feminine gender; there are many others, and Masculine and Feminine meet us on planes of reality where male and female would be simply meaningless. (cited in Morris 1974: 25)

In sum, what we seem to see in systems of institutionalized gender-crossing is the maintenance of a society's gender system through the detachment of gender from the very principle that provides its apparent foundation.

NOTES

1. An earlier draft of this paper was written during a sabbatical semester at the Stanford Center for Advanced Study in the Behavioral Sciences, in the spring of 1989. I am using the term "sex change surgery" in this paper, although much of the current literature favors the term "sex reassignment surgery", or even "gender reassignment surgery." Each of these labels carries its own conceptual and analytical presuppositions, and none is completely satisfactory. My own choice is intended to be as neutral as possible; the theoretical orientation I am taking to transsexualism will emerge in the course of the discussion, as will my uses of the terms "sex" and "gender."

2. The population reported on in one important early study showed a ratio of 8:1 (Benjamin 1966: 147). The overall ratios presented in subsequent literature are lower, but still have tended to run 4:1 or 3:1 (Raymond 1979: 24). It should be noted that researchers frequently remark upon the difficulty of getting good statistical data on transsexualism and sex change surgery.

3. The following passage is an example: "Initially, many psychiatrists assumed that individuals seeking[sex change] surgery were psychotic, and they opposed the procedure in principle . . . However, as experience with patients seeking sex change accumulated, it became clear that there was a group of men characterized by extreme, lifelong feminine orientation and absence of a sense of maleness for whom sex change was followed by greatly improved emotional and social adjustment" (Newman and Stoller 1974: 437; note the elision from "individuals" to "men").

4. Dr. Burou's clinic is described by Jan Morris, who went there for her own surgery (Morris 1974: 135–144). Renée Richards

also traveled there, but twice developed cold feet at the clinic door (Richards 1983: 246–247, 252). Garber's essay in Chapter 9 of this volume, which takes an "Orientalist" perspective on transsexualism, opens with observations on how Casablanca was viewed by Jan Morris. An engagingly bizarre fictionalized account of Burou's clinic can be found in a novel by the Brazilian author Moacyr Scliar in which the protagonists, born as centaurs, go to Morocco to have operations to turn themselves into "normal" human beings (Scliar 1980).

5. See Benjamin 1966, for his most comprehensive discussion of transsexualism. Jan Morris and Renée Richards both describe the hormone treatment they received from Benjamin (Morris 1974: 48–9, 105; Richards 1983: 161ff.).

6. Renée Richards describes her two unsuccessful experiences with psychoanalysis, which together lasted over nine years (Richards 1983: 99ff., 120 ff.). She gives a particularly uncomplimentary and bitter portrait of her second analyst, a prominent member of the New York psychoanalytic community (see, e.g., 161, 362–3).

7. Major influential works include Stoller 1968, 1974; Green and Money 1969.

8. The adoption of this term as an instance of the "politics of renaming" has been discussed by Dwight Billings and Thomas Urban as a part of their critique of transsexualism as a symptom of the alienation and commodification of sex and gender in capitalist society (Billings and Urban 1982).

9. See, for example, Jan Morris: "It became fashionable later to talk of my condition as 'gender confusion,' but I think it a philistine misnomer: I have had no doubt about my gender since that moment of self-realization[which Morris claims came at the age of three or four]" (Morris 1974: 25).

10. For one discussion of these various dimensions of sex, see Benjamin 1966, 5–9.

11. This is the formulation adopted by Suzanne Kessler and Wendy McKenna in their sociological study of transsexualism (Kessler and McKenna 1978: 13).

12. Billings and Urban (1982) discuss the way in which concepts of core gender identity and its imperviousness to change have figured in the analysis and treatment of transsexualism.

13. Attempts by psychologists, psychiatrists and other medical researchers to identify the causes of transsexualism include some that look to biological or constitutional factors and others that emphasize early socialization and the constellation of family relations, with a developing consensus that both nature and nurture are probably at issue. In other words, it is not known why some people become transsexuals and others don't. Renée Richards, herself a doctor and well aware of the various debates in the medical literature, began her autobiography by raising the question of causes, noting that even if it should ultimately be discovered that transsexualism is biochemically determined, her own family experience offered an embarrassingly stereotyped picture of how transsexualism can be explained by an abnormal and gender-confused family situation (Richards 1983: 2). For the major clinical attempt to find causes for transsexualism in family dynamics, and in the

mother-son relationship most particularly, see Stoller 1968. Medico-psychiatric debate about the causes of transsexualism has obvious similarities with debate about the causes of homosexuality; the two have intersected at various points.

14. For a developmental approach to transvestism and transsexualism, see Doctor 1988.

15. See, for example, Renée Richards' accounts of the encounters she had with male homosexuals while she was still a man, in which the parties were clearly at cross purposes (Richard 1983: 77, 294–6).

16. For examples of negative attitudes toward homosexuality among transsexuals, see Jan Morris' autobiography (Morris 1974: 24, 62, 169) and the case studies reported in Kando 1973. Robert Stoller devotes a chapter of *Sex and Gender* (Vol. I) to a discussion of the transsexual's denial of homosexuality (Stoller 1968: 141–153). He also provides data from a female to male transsexual who became disgusted with a female lover she had during adolescence while she was still anatomically female; the other girl's interest in her genitals was experienced as unwelcome lesbianism (202–203).

17. Renée Richards expressed her relief that her own transsexualism did not in any way affect her son's clear masculine identity (Richards 1983: 370). It is important to keep in mind that the motivation for such sentiments is not simply gender conservatism, but also the desire to spare one's children the kind of suffering one has experienced oneself.

18. In the years since studies such as this one were carried out, more has come to be known about diversity among transsexuals. Patterns of transsexualism have also been affected by the kinds of social changes that have affected the lives of women and men generally. Stone's paper in this volume contributes to an understanding of such change, as well as providing the kind of insider perspectives that did not make their way into most of the scientific and scholarly literature. Stone makes the argument that transsexuals should come out of the closet and cease disappearing into the two-gender system.

19. See, for example, Newman and Stoller 1974 for case studies in which sex change surgery would have been a grave mistake; these include a fetishistic cross-dresser who combined the desire to wear women's clothes with an underlying attachment to his masculinity; a male homosexual who thought he could hold on to his bisexual lover if he became a "real woman"; and a schizophrenic who came seeking sex change surgery after having had a revelation that Jesus Christ was really a woman and that he himself was a reincarnation of Mary Magdalen.

20. Of the 51 transsexuals in Benjamin's study, the only 2 who were reported as having failed to adjust to their new, postoperative situation were male to female transsexuals who experienced a dislocating downward mobility in income and occupational status (Benjamin 1966: 122–124). The major problem that Renée Richards encountered in trying to obtain sex change surgery in the United States was that the doctors she consulted, Harry Benjamin among them, were fearful of destroying Richard Raskind's medical career (Richards 1983: 165, 178–179, 210).

21. See, for example, Benjamin 1966: 202, 242; Stoller 1968: 202; Kessler and McKenna 1978: 126–7. Jan Morris described the

experience of being in the 9th Queens Royal Lancers as akin to that of an anthropologist moving among an exotic tribe while being taken for a native (Morris 1974: 31–32).

22. For descriptions of the experience of undergoing both electrolysis and corrective surgery to the "Adam's Apple," see Richards 1983: 176–178 and 211–213.

23. These various dimensions of passing are discussed by Kessler and McKenna (1978: 127–135).

24. See also Kessler and McKenna 1978: 16–17, for a discussion of this point.

25. In this connection, we might think of the famous case dramatized in the play "M. Butterfly," in which a French diplomat carried on an affair for twenty years with a Chinese opera star who turned out not only to be a spy, but also to be a man, having deceived the diplomat on this point for the entire period of their relationship. Dorinne Kondo has provided an elegant analysis of the case and of the play by David Henry Hwang (Kondo 1990). She discusses how the opera star's ability to pass as a woman rested on his lover's propensity to interpret his behavior in terms of stereotypes involving both gender and race: the fact that the diplomat was never able to see the opera star unclothed, even in their most intimate moments, was interpreted as a sign of the "shame" and "modesty" appropriate to Asian women.

26. Stoller described an attempt on the part of a group of researchers in the late 1950s to arrive at a mathematical formula for determining gender by weighing the various components of somatic and psychological sex (Stoller 1968: 232).

27. An analysis of transsexualism shaped in response and opposition to Raymond's is presented in Stone's paper in this volume. There has, in fact, been division of opinion in the feminist community about male to female transsexuals, with some feminists adopting the liberal position that women, as a disadvantaged minority, should not be discriminating against transsexuals. Renée Richards appealed to such sentiments when she made a point of noting the support she had received over the years from members of minority groups (Richards 1983: 317, 324–325).

28. When I presented an earlier version of this paper at the University of California at Santa Cruz in 1989, one feminist member of the audience responded to this formulation by suggesting that male to female transsexuals be seen as "defectors" from the male status (that is, as people seeking asylum from an oppressive regime). She opposed those, who, like Raymond, reject male to female transsexuals as "women," maintaining instead that the feminist goal should be for all men to become women—without, of course, having to go through sex change surgery.

29. Such a vision of disembodiment was expressed in the context of a mysterious encounter Morris had with a holy man in the course of one of his solitary rambles during the Everest expedition (Morris 1974: 87–88).

30. Billings and Urban call attention to the fact that doctors view sex change surgery as a technical tour de force (1982: 269).

31. Forgey 1975, Whitehead 1981, Kessler and McKenna 1978 (21–41), and Williams 1986 provide comparative overviews and theoretical discussions of the *berdache* in Native American soci-

eties. A case study of two *berdache,* one Zuni and one Navajo, is presented in Roscoe 1988. For a critique of the historical anachronism of some analyses of the *berdache,* particularly those that come from a contemporary Euro-American gay male perspective, see Gutierrez 1989. The North American *berdache* has often been compared with similar patterns of institutionalized gender crossing among Siberian tribal peoples.

32. One such case of female to male gender crossing in Native North American is that of the "manly-hearted woman" among the Piegan (Lewis 1941).

33. Will Roscoe, who has provided case studies of Zuni and Navajo *berdache,* argues that they are to be seen as occupying a special and intermediate status between women and men, which draws its power from the very combination of gender attributes (Roscoe 1988). An example of such a status in an area other than North America is the *waneng aryem ser* ("sacred woman") among the Bimin-Kuskusman of Papua New Guinea, as described by Fitz John Porter Poole (1981). This role of ritual leadership, which is filled by a post-menopausal woman who is no longer married or sexually active, is intentionally ambiguous with respect to gender and is intended to evoke primordial, hermaphroditic ancestors (Poole 1981: 117).

34. These points are discussed in Kessler and McKenna 1978: 21–24, 38.

35. The material on the Omani *xanith* presented here comes from Wikan 1977. Wikan's essay provoked some criticism and interchange in the pages of the journal *Man* (sic), where it was published; the kinds of points that were raised there are taken into account in this presentation of Wikan's description and analysis. Garber's essay in this volume also includes a consideration of Omani gender-crossing and the debate around Wikan's work.

36. While there are in fact women prostitutes in Oman, it is interesting to note that the term for them is a modified form of the term *xanith* (Wikan 1977: 311, 319).

37. General and comparative discussions of woman-woman marriage can be found in Krige 1974 and O'Brien 1977. Krige's study is of particular value, since it combines a general discussion with case studies from several different societies and a detailed analysis of woman-woman marriage among the Lovedu, where Krige did fieldwork. Another excellent case study is Oboler's discussion of the female husband among the Nandi, in which particular attention is given to the gender status of the female husband (Oboler 1980). Krige offers information on how social change has affected the institution of woman-woman marriage. I use the notorious ethnographic present here, given the generality of the patterns I am addressing and their persistence over time. I should note, however, that the usage is problematic and that changes have no doubt occurred in the time since the research drawn upon here was carried out.

38. For examples of these various explanations, see Raymond 1979: 26; Pauly 1969: 60; Stoller 1968: 263–264. Raymond, who sees transsexualism as the usurpation by men of women's bodies, also sees the male surgeon in a sex change operation as usurping the reproductive powers of women; she claims that "[t]ranssexual-

ism can be viewed as one more androcentric interventionist procedure. Along with male-controlled cloning, test-tube fertilization, and sex selection technology, it tends to wrest from women those powers inherent to female biology" (Raymond 1979: 29). It is interesting to note here the distance traveled from the work of such feminists as Shulamith Firestone who were looking to medical technology to free women from servitude to their role in biological reproduction (Firestone 1970: 191–202).

39. Robert Stoller pointed out that Freud's view of femininity made all women transsexuals (Stoller 1968: 58–59).

40. We can see this kind of asymmetry in political revolutions that have sexual equality as one of their goals; the attempt to achieve such equality is generally a matter of trying to turn women into the social equivalents of men. A particularly clear example was the kibbutz movement in Israel, with its focus on "the problem of the woman." (There was never any comparable consideration of "the problem of the man.") Women had to be given the opportunity to work in agricultural production, in developing industries, and in the army. There was, however, no comparable effort to get men into the kitchens and laundries (Talmon 1974; Tiger and Shepher 1975; Shapiro 1976).

41. Female to male gender crossing as a form of upward mobility is also discussed in Castelli's article in this volume.

42. The way in which gender intersects with other axes of social inequality—including how it articulates with race and class differences, how it operates in societies with caste systems—has become a major focus of work on gender in recent years. Attention has also increasingly been given to the way in which gender oppo-

sitions structure and are structured by a variety of cultural symbolic domains, some familiar Euro-American examples being nature and culture, reason and emotion, domestic and public, individualism and social responsibility (see Shapiro 1988). Sex/gender difference provides a particularly powerful model for generating binary oppositions.

43. For a general discussion of this issue, see Yanagisako and Collier 1987. For a more ethnographically focused analysis of how the cultural preoccupations of Western anthropologists in matters of sex, procreation, and gender have skewed their understanding both of their own culture and others, see Delaney 1986. The attempt to liberate the study of gender from the thrall of our own bio-ideology has led some anthropologists to argue that the concept of gender should be unhooked from sex altogether (Yanagisako and Collier 1987). Elsewhere (Shapiro ms. 1989), I have argued that this is an impossible project; without reference to biological sex, the concept of gender dissolves altogether. Moreover, what has motivated the study of gender is an inquiry into the relationship between sex and culture, which, after all, includes an exploration of the limits of that relationship.

44. Jones and Stallybrass, in chapter 4 in this volume, also explore the illusory nature of the "grounding" of gender differences in a foundational definition of male and female.

45. Stoller has emphasized the extent to which the transsexual's sense of gender identity is beyond his or her control (Stoller 1968: 260, 268–269, 271). See Garfinkel 1967: 133–137 for a more theoretically elaborate discussion of the concepts of ascription and achievement as they apply to the transsexual experience.

REFERENCES

Benjamin, Harry. *The Transsexual Phenomenon.* New York: Julian Press, 1966.

Billings, Dwight B. and Thomas Urban. "The Socio-Medical Construction of Transsexualism: An Interpretation and Critique" *Social Problems* 29 (3), 266–282, 1982.

Delaney, Carol. "The Meaning of Paternity and the Virgin Birth Debate." *Man* 21(3): 494–513, 1986.

Docter, Richard F. *Transvestites and Transsexuals: Toward a Theory of Cross-Gender Behavior.* New York: Plenum, 1988.

Firestone, Shulamith. *The Dialectic of Sex: The Case for Feminist Revolution.* New York: Bantham Books, 1970.

Forgey, Donald G. "The Institution of Berdache Among the North American Plains Indians." *The Journal of Sex Research* 11(1): 1–15, 1975.

Garfinkel, Harold. *Studies in Ethnomethodology.* Englewood Cliffs, New Jersey: Prentice-Hall, 1967.

Green, Richard and John Money (eds.). *Transsexualism and Sex Reassignment.* Baltimore: The John Hopkins University Press, 1969.

Gutierrez, Ramon. "Must We Deracinate Indians to Find Gay Roots?" *Out/Look* 1(4): 61–67, 1989.

Jorgensen, Christine. *Christine Jorgensen: A Personal Biography.* Introduction by Harry Benjamin, M.D. New York: Paul S. Eriksson, Inc., 1967.

Kando, Thomas. *Sex Change: The Achievement of Gender Identity Among Feminized Transsexuals.* Springfield, Illinois: Charles C. Thomas Publisher, 1973.

Kessler, Suzanne J., and Wendy McKenna. *Gender: An Ethnomethodological Approach.* New York: John Wiley & Sons, 1978.

Kondo, Dorinne. "M. Butterfly: Orientalism, Gender, and a Critique of Essentialized Identity," *Cultural Critique* 16, Fall 1990: 5–29.

Krige, Eileen Jensen. "Woman-Marriage, With Special Reference to the Lovedu—Its Significance for the Definition of Marriage." *Africa* 44: 11–37, 1974.

Lewis, O. "Manly-Hearted Women among the North Piegan," *American Anthropologist,* 43: 173–187, 1941.

Mauss, Marcel. *The Gift: Forms and Functions of Exchange in Archaic Societies.* Translated by Ian Cunnison. Illinois: The Free Press, (1925) 1954.

Morris, Jan. *Conundrum.* New York: Harcourt, Brace, Jovanovich, 1974.

Newman, Lawrence E., and Robert J. Stoller. "Nontranssexual Men Who Seek Sex Reassignment." *American Journal of Psychiatry* 131(4): 437–41, 1974.

Oboler, Regina Smith. "Is the Female Husband a Man? Woman/Woman Marriage Among the Nandi of Kenya." *Ethnology* 19(1): 69–88, 1980.

O'Brien, Denise. "Female Husbands in Southern Bantu Societies." In Alice Schlegel, ed., *Sexual Stratification: A Cross-Cultural View,* 109–26, New York, 1977.

Pauly, Ira B. "Adult Manifestations of Female Transsexualism." In John Money, and Richard Green, eds., *Transsexualism and Sex Reassignment,* 59–87, Baltimore: John Hopkins University Press, 1969.

Prince, V. "Sex vs. Gender." In D. Laub, and D. Gandy, eds., *Proceedings of the Second Interdisciplinary Symposium on Gender Dysphoria Syndrome,* Stanford: Stanford University Medical Center, 1973.

Raymond, Janice. G. *The Transsexual Empire: The Making of the She-Male.* Boston: Beacon Press, 1979.

Richards, Renée, and John Ames. *Second Serve: The Renée Richards Story.* New York: Stein and Day, 1983.

Roscoe, Will. "We 'Wha and Klah: The American Indian Berdache as Artist and Priest." *American Indian Quarterly,* 12(2), Spring 1988: 127–50.

Scliar, Moacyr. *O Centauro no Jardim.* Rio de Janeiro: Editora Nova Fronteira, 1980.

Shapiro, Judith. "Determinants of Sex Role Differentiation: The Kibbutz Case." *Reviews in Anthropology* 3(6): 682–692, 1976.

———"Gender Totemism." In Richard R. Randolph, David M. Schneider, and May N. Diaz, eds., *Dialectics and Gender: Anthropological Approaches.* 1–19, Boulder: Westview Press, 1988.

———"The Concept of Gender." ms., 1989.

Stoller, Robert. *Sex and Gender,* Vol I. New York: Science House, 1968; Vol II *(The Transsexual Experiment).* London: Hogarth Press, 1975.

Talmon, Yonina. *Family and Community in the Kibbutz.* Cambridge: Harvard University Press, 1972.

Tiger, Lionel and Joseph Shepher. *Women in the Kibbutz.* New York: Harcourt, Brace, Jovanovich, 1975.

Whitehead, Harriet. "The Bow and the Burden Strap: A New Look at Institutionalized Homosexuality in Native North America." In Sherry B. Ortner and Harriet Whitehead, eds., *Sexual Meanings: The Cultural Construction of Gender and Sexuality,* 80–115. Cambridge: Cambridge University Press, 1981.

Wikan, Unni. "Man Becomes Woman: Transsexualism in Oman as a Key to Gender Roles." *Man* 12: 304–319, 1977.

Williams, W. *The Spirit and the Flesh: Sexual Diversity in American Indian Culture.* Boston: Beacon Press, 1986.

Yanagisako, Sylvia Junko, and Jane Fishburne Collier. "Toward a Unified Analysis of Gender and Kindship." In Jane Fishburne Collier, and Sylvia Junko Yanagisako, eds., *Gender and Kinship.* Stanford: Stanford University Press, 1987.

From Servitude to Service Work: Historical Continuities in the Racial Division of Paid Reproductive Labor

EVELYN NAKANO GLENN

Recent scholarship on African American, Latina, Asian American, and Native American women reveals the complex interaction of race and gender oppression in their lives. These studies expose the inadequacy of additive models that treat gender and race as separate and discrete systems of hierarchy (Collins 1986; King 1988; Brown 1989). In an additive model, white women are viewed solely in terms of gender, while women of color are thought to be "doubly" subordinated by the cumulative effects of gender plus race. Yet achieving a more adequate framework, one that captures the interlocking, interactive nature of these systems, has been extraordinarily difficult. Historically, race and gender have developed as separate topics of inquiry, each with its own literature and concepts. Thus features of social life considered central in understanding one system have been overlooked in analyses of the other.

One domain that has been explored extensively in analyses of gender but ignored in studies of race is social reproduction. The term *social reproduction* is used by feminist scholars to refer to the array of activities and relationships involved in maintaining people both on a daily basis and intergenerationally. Reproductive labor includes activities such as purchasing household goods, preparing and serving food, laundering and repairing clothing, maintaining furnishings and appliances, socializing children, providing care and emotional support for adults, and maintaining kin and community ties.

Marxist feminists place the gendered construction of reproductive labor at the center of women's oppression. They point out that this labor is performed disproportionately by women and is essential to the industrial economy. Yet because it takes place mostly outside the market, it is invisible, not recognized as real work. Men benefit directly and indirectly from this arrangement—directly in that they contribute less labor in the home while enjoying the services women provide as wives and mothers and indirectly in that, freed of domestic labor, they can concentrate their efforts in paid employment and attain primacy in that area. Thus the sexual division of reproductive labor in the home interacts with and reinforces sexual division in the labor market.[1] These analyses draw attention to the dialectics of production and reproduction and male privilege in both realms. When they represent gender as the sole basis for assigning reproductive labor, however, they imply that all women have the same relationship to it and that it is therefore a universal female experience.[2]

In the meantime, theories of racial hierarchy do not include any analysis of reproductive labor. Perhaps because, consciously or unconsciously, they are male centered, they focus exclusively on the paid labor market and especially on male-dominated areas of production.[3] In the 1970s several writers seeking to explain the historic subordination of peoples of color pointed to dualism in the labor market—its division into distinct markets for white workers and for racial-ethnic workers—as a major vehicle for maintaining white domination (Blauner 1972; Barrera 1979).[4]

Evelyn Nakano Glenn, "From Servitude to Service Work: Historical Continuities in the Racial Division of Paid Reproductive Labor," *Signs: Journal of Women in Culture and Society* 18, no. 1 (1992). Copyright © 1991 by The University of Chicago. Reprinted with the permission of the author and The University of Chicago Press.

According to these formulations, the labor system has been organized to ensure that racial-ethnic workers are relegated to a lower tier of low-wage, dead-end, marginal jobs; institutional barriers, including restrictions on legal and political rights, prevent their moving out of that tier and competing with Euro-American workers for better jobs. These theories draw attention to the material advantages whites gain from the racial division of labor. However, they either take for granted or ignore women's unpaid household labor and fail to consider whether this work might also be "racially divided."

In short, the racial division of reproductive labor has been a missing piece of the picture in both literatures. This piece, I would contend, is key to the distinct exploitation of women of color and is a source of both hierarchy and interdependence among white women and women of color. It is thus essential to the development of an integrated model of race and gender, one that treats them as interlocking, rather than additive, systems.

In this article I present a historical analysis of the simultaneous race and gender construction of reproductive labor in the United States, based on comparative study of women's work in the South, the Southwest, and the Far West. I argue that reproductive labor has divided along racial as well as gender lines and that the specific characteristics of the division have varied regionally and changed over time as capitalism has reorganized reproductive labor, shifting parts of it from the household to the market. In the first half of the century racial-ethnic women were employed as servants to perform reproductive labor in white households, relieving white middle-class women of onerous aspects of that work; in the second half of the century, with the expansion of commodified services (services turned into commercial products or activities), racial-ethnic women are disproportionately employed as service workers in institutional settings to carry out lower-level "public" reproductive labor, while cleaner white collar supervisory and lower professional positions are filled by white women.

I will examine the ways race and gender were constructed around the division of labor by sketching changes in the organization of reproductive labor since the early nineteenth century, presenting a case study of domestic service among African American women in the South, Mexican American women in the Southwest, and Japanese American women in California and Hawaii. . . . Race and gender emerge as socially constructed, interlocking systems that shape the material conditions, identities, and consciousnesses of all women.

HISTORICAL CHANGES IN THE ORGANIZATION OF REPRODUCTION

The concept of reproductive labor originated in Karl Marx's remark that every system of production involves both the production of the necessities of life and the reproduction of the tools and labor power necessary for production (Marx and Engels 1969, 31). Recent elaborations of the concept grow out of Engels's dictum that the "determining force in history is, in the last resort, the production and reproduction of immediate life." This has, he noted, "a two-fold character, on the one hand the production of subsistence and on the other the production of human beings themselves" (Engels 1972, 71). Although often equated with domestic labor or defined narrowly as referring to the renewal of labor power, the term *social reproduction* has come to be more broadly conceived, particularly by social historians, to refer to the creation and recreation of people as cultural and social, as well as physical, beings (Ryan 1981, 15). Thus, it involves mental, emotional, and manual labor (Brenner and Laslett 1986, 117). This labor can be organized in myriad ways—in and out of the household, as paid or unpaid work, creating exchange value or only use value—and these ways are not mutually exclusive. An example is the preparation of food, which can be done by a family member as unwaged work in the household, by a servant as waged work in the household, or by a short-order cook in a fast-food restaurant as waged work that generates profit for the employer. These forms exist contemporaneously.

Prior to industrialization, however, both production and reproduction were organized almost exclusively at the household level. Women were responsible for most of what might be designated as reproduction, but they were simultaneously engaged in the production of foodstuffs, clothing, shoes, candles, soap, and other goods consumed by the household. With industrialization, production of these basic goods gradually was taken over by capitalist industry. Reproduction, however, remained largely the responsibility of individual households. The ideological separation between men's "productive" labor and women's non-market-based activity that had evolved at the end of the eighteenth century was elaborated in the early decades of the nineteenth . An idealized division of labor arose in which men's work was to follow production outside the home, while women's work was to remain centered in the household (Boydston 1990, esp. 46–48). Household work continued to include the production of many goods consumed by members (Smuts 1959, 11–13; Kessler-Harris 1981), but as an expanding range of outside-manufactured goods became available, household work became increasingly focused on reproduction.[5] This idealized division of labor was largely illusory for working-class households, including immigrant and racial-ethnic families, in which men seldom earned a family wage; in these households women and children were forced into income-earning activities in and out of the home (Kessler-Harris, 1982).

In the second half of the twentieth century, with goods production almost completely incorporated into the market, reproduction has become the next major target for commodification. Aside from the tendency of capital to expand into new areas for profit making, the very conditions of life brought about by large-scale commodity production have increased the need for commercial services. As household members spend more of their waking hours employed outside the home, they have less time and inclination to provide for one another's social and emotional needs. With the growth of a more geographically mobile and urbanized society, individuals and households have become increasingly cut off from larger kinship circles, neighbors, and traditional communities. Thus, as Harry Braverman notes, "The population no longer relies upon social organization in the form of family, friends, neighbors, community, elders, children, but with few exceptions must go to the market and only to the market, not only for food, clothing, and shelter, but also for recreation, amusement, security, for the care of the young, the old, the sick, the handicapped. In time not only the material and service needs but even the emotional patterns of life are channeled through the market" (Braverman 1974, 276). Conditions of capitalist urbanism also have enlarged the population of those requiring daily care and support: elderly and very young people, mentally and physically disabled people, criminals, and other people incapable of fending for themselves. Because the care of such dependents becomes difficult for the "stripped-down" nuclear family or the atomized community to bear, more of it becomes relegated to institutions outside the family.[6]

The final phase in this process is what Braverman calls the "product cycle," which "invents new products and services, some of which become indispensable as the conditions of modern life change and destroy alternatives" (Braverman 1974, 281). In many areas (e.g., health care), we no longer have choices outside the market. New services and products also alter the definition of an acceptable standard of living. Dependence on the market is further reinforced by what happened earlier with goods production, namely, an "atrophy of competence," so that individuals no longer know how to do what they formerly did for themselves.

As a result of these tendencies, an increasing range of services has been removed wholly or partially from the household and converted into paid services yielding profits. Today, activities such as preparing and serving food (in restaurants and fast-food establishments), caring for handicapped and elderly people (in nursing homes), caring for children (in child-care centers), and providing emotional support, amusement, and companionship (in counseling offices, recreation centers, and health clubs) have become part of the cash nexus. In addition, whether impelled by a need to maintain social control or in response to pressure exerted by worker and community organizations, the state has stepped in to assume minimal responsibility for some reproductive tasks, such as child protection and welfare programs.[7] Whether supplied by corporations or the state, these services are labor-intensive. Thus, a large army of low-wage workers, mostly women and disproportionately women of color, must be recruited to supply the labor.

Still, despite vastly expanded commodification and institutionalization, much reproduction remains organized at the household level. Sometimes an activity is too labor-intensive to be very profitable. Sometimes households or individuals in them have resisted commodification. The limited commodification of child care, for example, involves both elements. The extent of commercialization in different areas of life is uneven, and the variation in its extent is the outcome of political and economic struggles (Brenner and Laslett 1986, 121; Laslett and Brenner 1989, 384). What is consistent across forms, whether commodified or not, is that reproductive labor is constructed as "female." The gendered organization of reproduction is widely recognized. Less obvious, but equally characteristic, is its racial construction: historically, racial-ethnic women have been assigned a distinct place in the organization of reproductive labor.

Elsewhere I have talked about the reproductive labor racial-ethnic women have carried out for their own families; this labor was intensified as the women struggled to maintain family life and indigenous cultures in the face of cultural assaults, ghettoization, and a labor system that relegated men and women to low-wage, seasonal, and hazardous employment (Glenn 1985; 1986, 86–108; Dill 1988). . . .

DOMESTIC SERVICE AS THE RACIAL DIVISION OF REPRODUCTIVE LABOR

Both the demand for household help and the number of women employed as servants expanded rapidly in the latter half of the nineteenth century (Chaplin 1978). This expansion paralleled the rise of industrial capital and the elaboration of middle-class women's reproductive responsibilities. Rising standards of cleanliness, larger and more ornately furnished homes, the sentimentalization of the home as a "haven in a heartless world" (Lasch 1977), and the new emphasis on childhood and the mother's role in nurturing children all served to enlarge middle-class women's responsibilities for reproduction at a time when technology had done little to reduce the sheer physical drudgery of housework.[8]

By all accounts middle-class women did not challenge the gender-based division of labor or the enlargement of their reproductive responsibilities. Indeed, middle-class women—as readers and writers of literature; as members and leaders of clubs, charitable organizations, associations, reform movements, and religious revivals; and as supporters of the cause of abolition—helped to elaborate the domestic code (Brenner and Laslett 1986).[9] Feminists seeking an expanded public role for women argued that the same nurturant and moral qualities that made women centers of the home should be brought to bear in public service. In the domestic sphere, instead of questioning the inequitable gender division of labor, they sought to slough off the more burdensome tasks onto more oppressed groups of women.[10]

Phyllis Palmer observes that at least through the first half of the twentieth century, "most white middle class women could hire another woman—a recent immigrant, a working class woman, a woman of color, or all three—to perform much of the hard labor of household tasks" (Palmer 1987, 182–83). Domestics were employed to clean house, launder and iron clothes, scrub floors, and care for infants and children. They relieved their mistresses of the heavier and dirtier domestic chores.[11] White middle-class women were thereby freed for supervisory tasks and for cultural, leisure, and volunteer activity or, more rarely during this period, for a career.[12]

Palmer suggests that the use of domestic servants also helped resolve certain contradictions created by the domestic code. She notes that the early twentieth-century housewife confronted inconsistent expectations of middle-class womanhood: domesticity and "feminine virtue." Domesticity—defined as creating a warm, clean, and attractive home for husband and children—required hard physical labor and meant contending with dirt. The virtuous woman, however, was defined in terms of spirituality, refinement, and the denial of the physical body. Additionally, in the 1920s and 1930s there emerged a new ideal of the modern wife as an intelligent and attractive companion. If the heavy parts of household work could be transferred to paid help, the middle-class housewife could fulfill her domestic

duties, yet distance herself from the physical labor and dirt and also have time for personal development (Palmer 1990, 127–51).

Who was to perform the "dirty work" varied by region. In the Northeast, European immigrant women, particularly those who were Irish and German, constituted the majority of domestic servants from the mid-nineteenth century to World War I (Katzman 1978, 65–70). In regions where there was a large concentration of people of color, subordinate-race women formed a more or less permanent servant stratum. Despite differences in the composition of the populations and the mix of industries in the regions, there were important similarities in the situation of Mexicans in the Southwest, African Americans in the South, and Japanese people in northern California and Hawaii. Each of these groups was placed in a separate legal category from whites, excluded from rights and protections accorded full citizens. This severely limited their ability to organize, compete for jobs, and acquire capital (Glenn 1985). The racial division of private reproductive work mirrored this racial dualism in the legal, political, and economic systems.

In the South, African American women constituted the main and almost exclusive servant caste. Except in times of extreme economic crisis, whites and Blacks did not compete for domestic jobs. Until the First World War 90 percent of all nonagriculturally employed Black women in the South were employed as domestics. Even at the national level, servants and laundresses accounted for close to half (48.4 percent) of nonagriculturally employed Black women in 1930.[13]

In the Southwest, especially in the states with the highest proportions of Mexicans in the population—Texas, Colorado, and New Mexico—Chicanas were disproportionately concentrated in domestic service.[14] In El Paso nearly half of all Chicanas in the labor market were employed as servants or laundresses in the early decades of the century (Garcia 1981, 76). In Denver, according to Sarah Deutsch, perhaps half of all households had at least one female member employed as a domestic at some time, and if a woman became a widow, she was almost certain to take in laundry (Deutsch 1987a, 147). Nationally, 39.1 percent of nonagriculturally employed Chicanas were servants or laundresses in 1930.[15]

In the Far West—especially in California and Hawaii, with their large populations of Asian immigrants—an unfavorable sex ratio made female labor scarce in the late nineteenth and early twentieth centuries. In contrast to the rest of the nation, the majority of domestic servants in California and Hawaii were men: in California until 1880

(Katzman 1978, 55) and in Hawaii as late as 1920 (Lind 1951, table 1). The men were Asian—Chinese and later Japanese. Chinese houseboys and cooks were familiar figures in late nineteenth-century San Francisco; so too were Japanese male retainers in early twentieth-century Honolulu. After 1907 Japanese women began to immigrate in substantial numbers, and they inherited the mantle of service in both California and Hawaii. In the pre-World War II years, close to half of all immigrant and native-born Japanese American women in the San Francisco Bay area and in Honolulu were employed as servants or laundresses (U.S. Bureau of the Census 1932, table 8; Glenn 1986, 76–79). Nationally, excluding Hawaii, 25.4 percent of non-agricultural Japanese American women workers were listed as servants in 1930.[16]

In areas where racial dualism prevailed, being served by members of the subordinate group was a prerequisite of membership in the dominant group. According to Elizabeth Rae Tyson, an Anglo woman who grew up in El Paso in the early years of the century, "almost every Anglo-American family had at least one, sometimes two or three servants: a maid and laundress, and perhaps a nursemaid or yardman. The maid came in after breakfast and cleaned up the breakfast dishes, and very likely last night's supper dishes as well; did the routine cleaning, washing and ironing, and after the family dinner in the middle of the day, washed dishes again, and then went home to perform similar services in her own home" (Garcia 1980, 327). In southwest cities, Mexican American girls were trained at an early age to do domestic work and girls as young as nine or ten were hired to clean house.[17]

In Hawaii, where the major social division was between the haole (Caucasian) planter class and the largely Asian plantation worker class, haole residents were required to employ one or more Chinese or Japanese servants to demonstrate their status and their social distance from those less privileged. Andrew Lind notes that "the literature on Hawaii, especially during the second half of the nineteenth century, is full of references to the open-handed hospitality of Island residents, dispensed by the ever-present maids and houseboys" (Lind 1951, 73). A public school teacher who arrived in Honolulu in 1925 was placed in a teacher's cottage with four other mainland teachers. She discovered a maid had already been hired by the principal: "A maid! None of us had ever had a maid. We were all used to doing our own work. Furthermore, we were all in debt and did not feel that we wanted to spend even four dollars a month on a maid. Our principal was quite insistent. Everyone on the plantation had a maid. It was, therefore, the thing to do" (Lind 1951, 76).

In the South, virtually every middle-class housewife employed at least one African American woman to do cleaning and child care in her home. Southern household workers told one writer that in the old days, "if you worked for a family, your daughter was expected to, too" (Tucker 1988, 98). Daughters of Black domestics were sometimes inducted as children into service to baby-sit, wash diapers, and help clean (Clark-Lewis 1987, 200–201).[18] White-skin privilege transcended class lines, and it was not uncommon for working-class whites to hire Black women for housework (Anderson and Bowman 1953). In the 1930s white women tobacco workers in Durham, North Carolina, could mitigate the effects of the "double day"—household labor on top of paid labor—by employing Black women to work in their homes for about one-third of their own wages (Janiewski 1983, 93). Black women tobacco workers were too poorly paid to have this option and had to rely on the help of overworked husbands, older children, Black women too old to be employed, neighbors, or kin.

Where more than one group was available for service, a differentiated hierarchy of race, color, and culture emerged. White and racial-ethnic domestics were hired for different tasks. In her study of women workers in Atlanta, New Orleans, and San Antonio during the 1920s and 1930s, Julia Kirk Blackwelder reported that "anglo women in the employ of private households were nearly always reported as housekeepers, while Blacks and Chicanas were reported as laundresses, cooks or servants" (Blackwelder 1978, 349).[19]

In the Southwest, where Anglos considered Mexican or "Spanish" culture inferior, Anglos displayed considerable ambivalence about employing Mexicans for child care. Although a modern-day example, this statement by an El Paso businessman illustrates the contradictions in Anglo attitudes. The man told an interviewer that he and his wife were putting off parenthood because "the major dilemma would be what to do with the child. We don't really like the idea of leaving the baby at home with a maid . . . for the simple reason if the maid is Mexican, the child may assume that the other person is its mother. Nothing wrong with Mexicans, they'd just assume that this other person is its mother. There have been all sorts of cases where the infants learned Spanish before they learned English. There've been incidents of the Mexican maid stealing the child and taking it over to Mexico and selling it" (Ruíz 1987b, 71).

In border towns, the Mexican group was further stratified by English-speaking ability, place of nativity, and immigrant status, with non-English-speaking women residing south of the border occupying the lowest rung. In Laredo and El Paso, Mexican American factory operatives often employed Mexican women who crossed the border daily or weekly to do domestic work for a fraction of a U.S. operative's wages (Hield 1984, 95; Ruíz 1987a, 64).

The Race and Gender Construction of Domestic Service

Despite their preference for European immigrant domestics, employers could not easily retain their services. Most European immigrant women left service upon marriage, and their daughters moved into the expanding manufacturing, clerical, and sales occupations during the 1910s and twenties.[20] With the flow of immigration slowed to a trickle during World War I, there were few new recruits from Europe. In the 1920s, domestic service became increasingly the specialty of minority-race women (Palmer 1990, 12). Women of color were advantageous employees in one respect: they could be compelled more easily to remain in service. There is considerable evidence that middle-class whites acted to ensure the domestic labor supply by tracking racial-ethnic women into domestic service and blocking their entry into other fields. Urban school systems in the Southwest tracked Chicana students into homemaking courses designed to prepare them for domestic service. The El Paso school board established a segregated school system in the 1880s that remained in place for the next thirty years; education for Mexican children emphasized manual and domestic skills that would prepare them to work at an early age. In 1909 the Women's Civic Improvement League, an Anglo organization, advocated domestic training for older Mexican girls. Their rationale is explained by Mario Garcia: "According to the league the housegirls for the entire city came from the Mexican settlement and if they could be taught housekeeping, cooking and sewing, every American family would benefit. The Mexican girls would likewise profit since their services would improve and hence be in greater demand" (Garcia 1981, 113).

The education of Chicanas in the Denver school system was similarly directed toward preparing students for domestic service and handicrafts. Sarah Deutsch found that Anglo women there persisted in viewing Chicanas and other "inferior-race" women as dependent, slovenly, and ignorant. Thus, they argued, training Mexican girls for domestic service not only would solve "one phase of women's work we seem to be incapable of handling" but it would simultaneously help raise the (Mexican) community by improving women's standard of living, elevating their morals, and facilitating Americanization (Deutsch 1987b, 736). One Anglo writer, in an article published in 1917

titled "Problems and Progress among Mexicans in Our Own Southwest," claimed, "When trained there is no better servant than the gentle, quiet Mexicana girl" (Romero 1988a, 16).

In Hawaii, with its plantation economy, Japanese and Chinese women were coerced into service for their husbands' or fathers' employers. According to Lind, prior to World War II:

It has been a usual practice for a department head or a member of the managerial staff of the plantation to indicate to members of his work group that his household is in need of domestic help and to expect them to provide a wife or daughter to fill the need. Under the conditions which have prevailed in the past, the worker has felt obligated to make a member of his own family available for such service, if required, since his own position and advancement depend upon keeping the goodwill of his boss. Not infrequently, girls have been prevented from pursuing a high school or college education because someone on the supervisory staff has needed a servant and it has seemed inadvisable for the family to disregard the claim.[Lind 1951, 77]

Economic coercion also could take bureaucratic forms, especially for women in desperate straits. During the Depression, local officials of the federal Works Project Administration (WPA) and the National Youth Administration (NYA), programs set up by the Roosevelt administration to help the unemployed find work, tried to direct Chicanas and Blacks to domestic service jobs exclusively (Blackwelder 1984, 120–22; Deutsch 1987a, 182–83). In Colorado, local officials of the WPA and NYA advocated household training projects for Chicanas. George Bickel, assistant state director of the WPA for Colorado, wrote: "The average Spanish-American girl on the NYA program looks forward to little save a life devoted to motherhood often under the most miserable circumstances" (Deutsch 1987a, 183). Given such an outlook, it made sense to provide training in domestic skills.

Young Chicanas disliked domestic service so much that slots in the programs went begging. Older women, especially single mothers struggling to support their families, could not afford to refuse what was offered. The cruel dilemma that such women faced was poignantly expressed in one woman's letter to President Roosevelt:

My name is Lula Gordon. I am a Negro woman. I am on the relief. I have three children. I have no husband and no job. I have worked hard ever since I was old enough. I am willing to do any kind of work because I have to support myself and my children. I was under the impression that the government or the W.P.A. would give the Physical [*sic*] fit relief clients work. I have been praying for that time to come. A lady, Elizabeth Ramsie, almost in my condition, told me she was going to try to get some work. I went with her. We went to the Court House here in San Antonio, we talked to a Mrs. Beckmon. Mrs. Beckmon told me to phone a Mrs. Coyle because she wanted some one to clean house and cook for ($5) five dollars a week. Mrs. Beckmon said if I did not take the job in the Private home I would be cut off from everything all together. I told her I was afraid to accept the job in the private home because I have registered for a government job and when it opens up I want to take it. She said that she was taking people off of the relief and I have to take the job in the private home or none. . . . I need work and I will do anything the government gives me to do. . . . Will you please give me some work. [Blackwelder 1984, 68–69]

Japanese American women were similarly compelled to accept domestic service jobs when they left the internment camps in which they were imprisoned during World War II. To leave the camps they had to have a job and a residence, and many women were forced to take positions as live-in servants in various parts of the country. When women from the San Francisco Bay area returned there after the camps were closed, agencies set up to assist the returnees directed them to domestic service jobs. Because they had lost their homes and possessions and had no savings, returnees had to take whatever jobs were offered them. Some became live-in servants to secure housing, which was in short supply after the war. In many cases domestic employment became a lifelong career (Glenn 1986).

In Hawaii the Japanese were not interned, but there nonetheless developed a "maid shortage" as war-related employment expanded. Accustomed to cheap and abundant household help, haole employers became increasingly agitated about being deprived of the services of their "mamasans." The suspicion that many able-bodied former maids were staying at home idle because their husbands or fathers had lucrative defense jobs was taken seriously enough to prompt an investigation by a university researcher.[21]

Housewives told their nisei maids it was the maids' patriotic duty to remain on the job. A student working as a live-in domestic during the war was dumbfounded by her mistress's response when she notified her she was leaving to take a room in the dormitory at the university. Her cultured and educated mistress, whom the student had heretofore admired, exclaimed with annoyance: "'I think especially in war time, the University should close down the dormitory.' Although she didn't say it in words, I sensed the implication that she believed all the (Japanese) girls should be placed in different homes, making it easier for the haole woman."[22] The student noted with some bitterness that although her employer told her that working as a maid was the way for her to do "your bit for the war effort," she and other haole women did not, in turn, consider giving up the "conveniences and luxuries of pre-war Hawaii" as their bit for the war.[23]

The dominant group ideology in all these cases was that women of color—African American women, Chicanas, and Japanese American women—were particularly suited for service. These racial justifications ranged from the argument that Black and Mexican women were incapable of governing their own lives and thus were dependent on whites—making white employment of them an act of benevolence—to the argument that Asian servants were naturally quiet, subordinate, and accustomed to a lower standard of living. Whatever the specific content of the racial characterizations, it defined the proper place of these groups as in service: they belonged there, just as it was the dominant group's place to be served.

David Katzman notes that "ethnic stereotyping was the stock in trade of all employers of servants, and it is difficult at times to figure out whether blacks and immigrants were held in contempt because they were servants or whether urban servants were denigrated because most of the servants were blacks and immigrants" (Katzman 1978, 221). Even though racial stereotypes undoubtedly preceded their entry into domestic work, it is also the case that domestics were forced to enact the role of the inferior. Judith Rollins and Mary Romero describe a variety of rituals that affirmed the subordination and dependence of the domestic; for example, employers addressed household workers by their first names and required them to enter by the back door, eat in the kitchen, and wear uniforms. Domestics understood they were not to initiate conversation but were to remain standing or visibly engaged in work whenever the employer was in the room. They also had to accept with gratitude "gifts" of discarded clothing and leftover food (Rollins 1985, chap. 5; Romero 1987).

For their part, racial-ethnic women were acutely aware that they were trapped in domestic service by racism and not by lack of skills or intelligence. In their study of Black life in prewar Chicago, St. Clair Drake and Horace Cayton found that education did not provide African Americans with an entree into white collar work. They noted, "Colored girls are often bitter in their comments about a society which condemns them to the 'white folks' kitchen'" (Drake and Cayton 1962, 246). Thirty-five years later, Anna May Madison minced no words when she declared to anthropologist John Gwaltney: "Now, I don't do nothing for white women or men that they couldn't do for themselves. They don't do anything I couldn't learn to do every bit as well as they do it. But, you see, that goes right back to the life that you have to live. If that was the life I had been raised up in, I could be President or any other thing I got a chance to be" (Gwaltney 1980, 173).

Chicana domestics interviewed by Mary Romero in Colorado seemed at one level to accept the dominant culture's evaluation of their capabilities. Several said their options were limited by lack of education and training. However, they also realized they were restricted just because they were Mexican. Sixty-eight-year-old Mrs. Portillo told Romero: "There was a lot of discrimination, and Spanish people got just regular housework or laundry work. There was so much discrimination that Spanish people couldn't get jobs outside of washing dishes—things like that" (Romero 1988b, 86).

Similarly, many Japanese domestics reported that their choices were constrained because of language difficulties and lack of education, but they, too, recognized that color was decisive. Some nisei domestics had taken typing and business courses and some had college degrees, yet they had to settle for "school girl" jobs after completing their schooling. Mrs. Morita, who grew up in San Francisco and was graduated from high school in the 1930s, bluntly summarized her options: "In those days there was no two ways about it. If you were Japanese, you either worked in an art store ('oriental curios' shop) where they sell those little junks, or you worked as a domestic. . . . There was no Japanese girl working in an American firm" (Glenn 1986, 122).

Hanna Nelson, another of Gwaltney's informants, took the analysis one step further; she recognized the coercion that kept African American women in domestic service. She saw this arrangement as one that allowed white women to exploit Black women economically and emotionally and exposed Black women to sexual assaults by white men, often with white women's complicity. She says, "I am a woman sixty-one years old and I was born into this world with some talent. But I have done the work that my grandmother's mother did. It is not through any failing of mine that this is so. The whites took my mother's milk by force,

and I have lived to hear a human creature of my sex try to force me by threat of hunger to give my milk to an able man. I have grown to womanhood in a world where the saner you are, the madder you are made to appear" (Gwaltney 1980, 7).

Race and Gender Consciousness

Hanna Nelson displays a consciousness of the politics of race and gender not found among white employers. Employers' and employees' fundamentally different positions within the division of reproductive labor gave them different interests and perspectives. Phyllis Palmer describes the problems the YWCA and other reform groups encountered when they attempted to establish voluntary standards and working hours for live-in domestics in the 1930s. White housewives invariably argued against any "rigid" limitation of hours; they insisted on provisions for emergencies that would override any hour limits. Housewives saw their own responsibilities as limitless, and apparently felt there was no justification for boundaries on domestics' responsibilities. They did not acknowledge the fundamental difference in their positions: they themselves gained status and privileges from their relationships with their husbands—relationships that depended on the performance of wifely duties. They expected domestics to devote long hours and hard work to help them succeed as wives, without, however, commensurate privileges and status. To challenge the inequitable gender division of labor was too difficult and threatening, so white housewives pushed the dilemma onto other women, holding them to the same high standards by which they themselves were imprisoned (Kaplan 1987; Palmer 1990).

Some domestic workers were highly conscious of their mistresses' subordination to their husbands and condemned their unwillingness to challenge their husbands' authority. Mabel Johns, a sixty-four-year-old widow, told Gwaltney:

I work for a woman who has a good husband; the devil is good to her, anyway. Now that woman could be a good person if she didn't think she could just do everything and have everything. In this world whatsoever you get you will pay for. Now she is a grown woman, but she won't know that simple thing. I don't think there's anything wrong with her mind, but she is greedy and she don't believe in admitting that she is greedy. Now you may say what you willormay [sic] about people being good to you, but there just ain' a living soul in this world that thinks more of you than you do of yourself. . . . She's a grown woman, but she have to keep accounts and her husband tells her whether or not he will let her do thus-and-so or buy this or that.[Gwaltney 1980, 167]

Black domestics are also conscious that a white woman's status comes from her relationship to a white man, that she gains privileges from the relationship that blinds her to her own oppression, and that she therefore willingly participates in and gains advantages from the oppression of racial-ethnic women. Nancy White puts the matter powerfully when she says,

My mother used to say that the black woman is the white man's mule and the white woman is his dog. Now, she said that to say this: we do the heavy work and get beat whether we do it well or not. But the white woman is closer to the master and he pats them on the head and lets them sleep in the house, but he ain' gon' treat neither one like he was dealing with a person. Now, if I was to tell a white woman that, the first thing she would do is to call you a nigger and then she'd be real nice to her husband so he would come out here and beat you for telling his wife the truth.[Gwaltney 1980, 148]

Rather than challenge the inequity in the relationship with their husbands, white women pushed the burden onto women with even less power. They could justify this only by denying the domestic worker's womanhood, by ignoring the employee's family ties and responsibilities. Susan Tucker found that southern white women talked about their servants with affection and expressed gratitude that they shared work with the servant that they would otherwise have to do alone. Yet the sense of commonality based on gender that the women expressed turned out to be one-way. Domestic workers knew that employers did not want to know much about their home situations (Kaplan 1987, 96; Tucker 1988). Mostly, the employers did not want domestics' personal needs to interfere with serving them. One domestic wrote that her employer berated her when she asked for a few hours off to pay her bills and take care of pressing business (Palmer 1990, 74). Of relations between white mistresses and Black domestics in the period from 1870 to 1920, Katzman says that in extreme cases "even the shared roles of motherhood could be denied." A Black child nurse reported in 1912 that she worked fourteen to sixteen hours a day caring for her mistress's four children. Describing her existence as a "treadmill life," she reported that she was allowed to go home "only once in every two weeks, every other Sunday afternoon—even then I'm not permitted to stay all night. I see my own children only when they happen to see me on the streets when I am out with the children[of her mistress], or when my children come to the yard to see me, which isn't often, because my white folks don't like to see their servants' children hanging around their premises."[24]

While this case may be extreme, Tucker reports, on the basis of extensive interviews with southern African American domestics, that even among live-out workers in the 1960s,

White women were also not noted for asking about childcare arrangements. All whites, said one black woman, "assume you have a mother, or an older daughter to keep your child, so it's all right to leave your kids." Stories of white employers not believing the children of domestics were sick, but hearing this as an excuse not to work, were also common. Stories, too, of white women who did not inquire of a domestic's family—even when that domestic went on extended trips with the family—were not uncommon. And work on Christmas morning and other holidays for black mothers was not considered by white employers as unfair. Indeed, work on these days was seen as particularly important to the job.[Tucker 1988, 99]

The irony is, of course, that domestics saw their responsibilities as mothers as the central core of their identity. The Japanese American women I interviewed, the Chicana day workers Romero interviewed, and the African American domestics Bonnie Thornton Dill interviewed all emphasized the primacy of their role as mothers (Dill 1980; Glenn 1986; Romero 1988b). As a Japanese immigrant single parent expressed it, "My children come first. I'm working to upgrade my children." Another domestic, Mrs. Hiraoka, confided she hated household work but would keep working until her daughter graduated from optometry school.[25] Romero's day workers arranged their work hours to fit around their children's school hours so that they could be there when needed. For domestics, then, working had meaning precisely because it enabled them to provide for their children.

Perhaps the most universal theme in domestic workers' statements is that they are working so their own daughters will not have to go into domestic service and confront the same dilemmas of leaving their babies to work. A Japanese American domestic noted, "I tell my daughters all the time, 'As long as you get a steady job, stay in school. I want you to get a good job, not like me.' That's what I always tell my daughters: make sure you're not stuck."[26]

In a similar vein, Pearl Runner told Dill, "My main goal was I didn't want them to follow in my footsteps as far as working" (Dill 1980, 109). Domestic workers wanted to protect their daughters from both the hardships and the dangers that working in white homes posed. A Black domestic told Drake and Cayton of her hopes for her daughters: "I hope they may be able to escape a life as a domestic worker, for I know too well the things that make a girl desperate on these jobs" (Drake and Cayton 1962, 246).

When they succeed in helping their children do better than they themselves did, domestics may consider that the hardships were worthwhile. Looking back, Mrs. Runner is able to say, "I really feel that with all the struggling that I went through, I feel happy and proud that I was able to keep helping my children, that they listened and that they all went to high school. So when I look back, I really feel proud, even though at times the work was very hard and I came home very tired. But now, I feel proud about it. They all got their education" (Dill 1980, 113). Domestics thus have to grapple with yet another contradiction. They must confront, acknowledge, and convey the undesirable nature of the work they do to their children, as an object lesson and an admonition, and at the same time maintain their children's respect and their own sense of personal worth and dignity (Dill 1980, 110). When they successfully manage that contradiction, they refute their white employers' belief that "you are your work" (Gwaltney 1980, 174). . . .

CONCLUSIONS AND IMPLICATIONS

This article began with the observation that the racial division of reproductive labor has been overlooked in the separate literatures on race and gender. The distinct exploitation of women of color and an important source of difference among women have thereby been ignored. How, though, does a historical analysis of the racial division of reproductive labor illuminate the lives of women of color and white women? What are its implications for concerted political action? In order to tackle these questions, we need to address a broader question, namely, how does the analysis advance our understanding of race and gender? Does it take us beyond the additive models I have criticized?

The Social Construction of Race and Gender

Tracing how race and gender have been fashioned in one area of women's work helps us understand them as socially constructed systems of relationships—including symbols, normative beliefs, and practices—organized around perceived differences. This understanding is an important counter to the universalizing tendencies in feminist thought. When feminists perceive reproductive labor only as gendered, they imply that domestic labor is identical for all women and that it therefore can be the basis of a common identity of womanhood. By not recognizing the different relationships women have had to such supposedly universal female experiences as motherhood and domesticity, they risk essentializing gender—treating it as static, fixed, eternal, and natural. They fail to take seriously a basic premise of feminist thought, that gender is a social construct.

If race and gender are socially constructed systems, then they must arise at specific moments in particular circumstances and change as these circumstances change. We can study their appearance, variation, and modification over time. I have suggested that one vantage point for looking at their development in the United States is in the changing division of labor in local economies. A key site for the emergence of concepts of gendered and racialized labor has been in regions characterized by dual labor systems.

As subordinate-race women within dual labor systems, African American, Mexican American, and Japanese American women were drawn into domestic service by a combination of economic need, restricted opportunities, and educational and employment tracking mechanisms. Once they were in service, their association with "degraded" labor affirmed their supposed natural inferiority. Although ideologies of "race" and "racial difference" justifying the dual labor system already were in place, specific ideas about racial-ethnic womanhood were invented and enacted in everyday interactions between mistresses and workers. Thus ideologies of race and gender were created and verified in daily life (Fields 1982).

Two fundamental elements in the construction of racial-ethnic womanhood were the notion of inherent traits that suited the women for service and the denial of the women's identities as wives and mothers in their own right. Employers accepted a cult of domesticity that purported to elevate the status of women as mothers and homemakers, yet they made demands on domestics that hampered them from carrying out these responsibilities in their own households. How could employers maintain such seemingly inconsistent orientations? Racial ideology was critical in resolving the contradiction: it explained why women of color were suited for degrading work. Racial characterizations effectively neutralized the racial-ethnic woman's womanhood, allowing the mistress to be "unaware" of the domestic's relationship to her own children and household. The exploitation of racial-ethnic women's physical, emotional, and mental work for the benefit of white households thus could be rendered invisible in consciousness if not in reality.

With the shift of reproductive labor from household to market, face-to-face hierarchy has been replaced by structural hierarchy. In institutional settings, stratification is built into organizational structures, including lines of authority, job descriptions, rules, and spatial and temporal segregation. Distance between higher and lower orders is ensured by structural segregation. Indeed, much routine service work is organized to be out of sight: it takes place behind institutional walls where outsiders rarely penetrate (e.g., nursing homes, chronic care facilities), in back rooms (e.g., restaurant kitchens), or at night or other times when occupants are gone (e.g., in office buildings and hotels). Workers may appreciate this time and space segregation because it allows them some autonomy and freedom from demeaning interactions. It also makes them and their work invisible, however. In this situation, more privileged women do not have to acknowledge the workers or to confront the contradiction between shared womanhood and inequality by race and class. Racial ideology is not necessary to explain or justify exploitation, not for lack of racism, but because the justification for inequality does not have to be elaborated in specifically racial terms: instead it can be cast in terms of differences in training, skill, or education.[27]

Because they are socially constructed, race and gender systems are subject to contestation and struggle. Racial-ethnic women continually have challenged the devaluation of their womanhood. Domestics often did so covertly. They learned to dissemble, consciously "putting on an act" while inwardly rejecting their employers' premises and maintaining a separate identity rooted in their families and communities. . . . In domestic service, women have transcended the limitations of their work by focusing on longer-term goals, such as their children's future.

Beyond Additive Models: Race and Gender as Interlocking Systems

As the foregoing examples show, race and gender constructs are inextricably intertwined. Each develops in the context of the other; they cannot be separated. This is important because when we see reproductive labor only as gendered, we extract gender from its context, which includes other interacting systems of power. If we begin with gender separated out, then we have to put race and class back in when we consider women of color and working-class women. We thus end up with an additive model in which white women have only gender and women of color have gender plus race.

The interlock is evident in the case study of domestic workers. In the traditional middle-class household, the availability of cheap female domestic labor buttressed white male privilege by perpetuating the concept of reproductive labor as women's work, sustaining the illusion of a protected private sphere for women and displacing conflict away from husband and wife to struggles between housewife and domestic.

The racial division of labor also bolstered the gender division of labor indirectly by offering white women a slightly more privileged position in exchange for accepting domesticity. Expanding on Judith Rollins's notion that white housewives gained an elevated self-identity by casting Black domestics as inferior contrast figures, Phyllis Palmer suggests the dependent position of the middle-class housewife made a contrasting figure necessary. A dualistic conception of women as "good" and "bad," long a part of western cultural tradition, provided ready-made categories for casting white and racial-ethnic women as oppositional figures (Davidoff 1979; Palmer 1990, 11, 137–39). The racial division of reproductive labor served to channel and recast these dualistic conceptions into racialized gender constructs. By providing them an acceptable self-image, racial constructs gave white housewives a stake in a system that ultimately oppressed them.

The racial division of labor similarly protects white male privilege in institutional settings. White men, after all, still dominate in professional and higher management positions where they benefit from the paid and unpaid services of women. And as in domestic service, conflict between men and women is redirected into clashes among women. . . . In both household and institutional settings, white professional and managerial men are the group most insulated from dirty work and contact with those who do it. White women are frequently the mediators who have to negotiate between white male superiors and racial-ethnic subordinates. Thus race and gender dynamics are played out in a three-way relationship involving white men, white women, and women of color.

Beyond Difference: Race and Gender as Relational Constructs

Focusing on the racial division of reproductive labor also uncovers the relational nature of race and gender. By "relational" I mean that each is made up of categories (e.g., male/female, Anglo/Latino) that are positioned, and therefore gain meaning, in relation to each other (Barrett 1987). Power, status, and privilege are axes along which categories are positioned. Thus, to represent race and gender as relationally constructed is to assert that the experiences of white women and women of color are not just different but connected in systematic ways.

The interdependence is easier to see in the domestic work setting because the two groups of women confront one another face-to-face. That the higher standard of living of one woman is made possible by, and also helps to perpetuate, the other's lower standard of living is clearly evident. In institutional service work the relationship between those who do the dirty work and those who benefit from it is mediated and buffered by institutional structures, so the dependence of one group on the other for its standard of living is not apparent. Nonetheless, interdependence exists, even if white women do not come into actual contact with women of color.[28]

The notion of relationality also recognizes that white and racial-ethnic women have different standpoints by virtue of their divergent positions. This is an important corrective to feminist theories of gendered thought that posit universal female modes of thinking growing out of common experiences such as domesticity and motherhood. When they portray reproductive labor only as gendered, they assume there is only one standpoint—that of white women. Hence, the activities and experiences of middle-class women become generic "female" experiences and activities, and those of other groups become variant, deviant, or specialized.

In line with recent works on African American, Asian American, and Latina feminist thought, we see that taking the standpoint of women of color gives us a different and more critical perspective on race and gender systems (Garcia 1989; Anzaldúa 1990; Collins 1990.) Domestic workers in particular—because they directly confront the contradictions in their lives and those of their mistresses—develop an acute consciousness of the interlocking nature of race and gender oppression.

Perhaps a less obvious point is that understanding race and gender as relational systems also illuminates the lives of white American women. White womanhood has been constructed not in isolation but in relation to that of women of color. Therefore, race is integral to white women's gender identities. In addition, seeing variation in racial division of labor across time in different regions gives us a more variegated picture of white middle-class womanhood. White women's lives have been lived in many circumstances; their "gender" has been constructed in relation to varying others, not just to Black women. Conceptualizing white womanhood as monolithically defined in opposition to men or to Black women ignores complexity and variation in the experiences of white women.

Implications for Feminist Politics

Understanding race and gender as relational, interlocking, socially constructed systems affects how we strategize for change. If race and gender are socially constructed rather than being "real" referents in the material world, then they can be deconstructed and challenged. Feminists have made considerable strides in deconstructing gender; we now need to focus on deconstructing gender and race simultaneously. An initial step in this process is to expose the structures that support the present division of labor and the constructions of race and gender around it.

Seeing race and gender as interlocking systems, however, alerts us to sources of inertia and resistance to change. The discussion of how the racial division of labor reinforced the gender division of labor makes clear that tackling gender hierarchy requires simultaneously addressing race hierarchy. As long as the gender division of labor remains intact, it will be in the short-term interest of white women to support or at least overlook the racial division of labor because it ensures that the very worst labor is performed by someone else. Yet, as long as white women support the racial division of labor, they will have less impetus to struggle to change the gender division of labor. This quandary is apparent in cities such as Los Angeles, which have witnessed a large influx of immigrant women fleeing violence and poverty in Latin America, Southeast Asia, and the Caribbean. These women form a large reserve army of low-wage labor for both domestic service and institutional service work. Anglo women who ordinarily would not be able to afford servants are employing illegal immigrants as maids at below-minimum wages (McConoway 1987). Not only does this practice diffuse pressure for a more equitable sharing of household work but it also recreates race and gender ideologies that justify the subordination of women of color. Having a Latino or Black maid picking up and cleaning after them teaches Anglo children that some people exist primarily to do work that Anglos do not want to do for themselves.

Acknowledging the relational nature of race and gender and therefore the interdependence between groups means that we recognize conflicting interests among women. Two examples illustrate the divergence. With the move into the labor force of all races and classes of women, it is tempting to think that we can find unity around the common problems of "working women." With that in mind, feminist policymakers have called for expanding services to assist employed mothers in such areas as child care and elderly care. We need to ask, Who is going to do the work? Who will benefit from increased services? The historical record suggests that it will be women of color, many of them new immigrants, who will do the work and that it will be women of color, many of them new immigrants, who will do the work and that it will be middle-class women who will receive the services. Not so coincidentally, public officials seeking to reduce welfare costs are promulgating regulations requiring women on public assistance to work. The needs of employed middle-class women and women on welfare might thus be thought to coincide: the needs of the former for services might be met by employing the latter to provide the services. The divergence in interest becomes apparent, however, when we consider that employment in service jobs at current wage levels guarantees that their occupants will remain poor. However, raising their wages so that they can actually support themselves and their children at a decent level would mean many middle-class women could not afford these services.

A second example of an issue that at first blush appears to bridge race and ethnic lines is the continuing earnings disparity between men and women. Because occupational segregation, the concentration of women in low-paying, female-dominated occupations, stands as the major obstacle to wage equity, some feminist policymakers have embraced the concept of comparable worth (Hartmann 1985; Acker 1989). This strategy calls for equalizing pay for "male" and "female" jobs requiring similar levels of skill and responsibility, even if differing in content. Comparable worth accepts the validity of a job hierarchy and differential pay based on "real" differences in skills and responsibility. Thus, for example, it attacks the differential between nurses and pharmacists but leaves intact the differential between nurses and nurse's aides. Yet the division between "skilled" and "unskilled" jobs is exactly where the racial division typically falls. To address the problems of women of color service workers would require a fundamental attack on the concept of a hierarchy of worth; it would call for flattening the wage differentials between highest- and lowest-paid ranks. A claim would have to be made for the right of all workers to a living wage, regardless of skill or responsibility.

These examples suggest that forging a political agenda that addresses the universal needs of women is highly problematic not just because women's priorities differ but because gains for some groups may require a corresponding loss of advantage and privilege for others. As the history of the racial division of reproductive labor reveals, conflict and contestation among women over definitions of womanhood, over work, and over the conditions of family life are part of our legacy as well as the current reality. This does not mean we give up the goal of concerted struggle. It means we give up trying falsely to harmonize women's interests. Appreciating the ways race and gender division of labor creates both hierarchy and interdependence may be a better way to reach an understanding of the interconnectedness of women's lives.

ACKNOWLEDGMENTS

Work on this project was made possible by a Title F leave from the State University of New York at Binghamton and a visiting scholar appointment at the Murray Research Center at Radcliffe College. Discussions with Elsa Barkley Brown, Gary Glenn, Carole Turbin, and Barrie Thorne contributed immeasurably to the ideas developed here. My thanks to Joyce Chinen for directing me to archival materials in Hawaii. I am also grateful to members of the Women and Work Group and to Norma Alarcon, Gary Dymski, Antonia Glenn, Margaret Guilette, Terence Hopkins, Eileen McDonagh, JoAnne Preston, Mary Ryan, and four anonymous *Signs* reviewers for their suggestions.

NOTES

1. For various formulations, see Benston (1969), Secombe (1974), Barrett (1980), Fox (1980), and Sokoloff (1980).

2. Recently, white feminists have begun to pay attention to scholarship by and about racial-ethnic women and to recognize racial stratification in the labor market and other public arenas. My point here is that they still assume that women's relationship to domestic labor is universal; thus they have not been concerned with explicating differences across race, ethnic, and class groups in women's relationship to that labor.

3. See, e.g., Reisler (1976), which, despite its title, is exclusively about male Mexican labor.

4. I use the term *racial-ethnic* to refer collectively to groups that have been socially constructed and constituted as racially as well as culturally distinct from European Americans and placed in separate legal statuses from "free whites" (c.f. Omi and Winant 1986). Historically, African Americans, Latinos, Asian Americans, and Native Americans were so constructed. Similarly, I have capitalized the word *Black* throughout this article to signify the racial-ethnic construction of that category.

5. Capitalism, however, changed the nature of reproductive labor, which became more and more devoted to consumption activities, i.e., using wages to acquire necessities in the market and then processing these commodities to make them usable (see Weinbaum and Bridges 1976; and Luxton 1980).

6. This is not to deny that family members, especially women, still provide the bulk of care of dependents, but to point out that there has been a marked increase in institutionalized care in the second half of the twentieth century.

7. For a discussion of varying views on the relative importance of control versus agency in shaping state welfare policy, see Gordon (1990). Piven and Cloward note that programs have been created only when poor people have mobilized and are intended to defuse pressure for more radical change (1971, 66). In their *Poor People's Movements* (Piven and Cloward 1979), they document the role of working-class struggles to win concessions from the state. For a feminist social control perspective, see Abramovitz (1988).

8. These developments are discussed in Degler (1980), Strasser (1982), Cowan (1983), and Dudden (1983, esp. 240–42).

9. See also Blair (1980); Epstein (1981); Ryan (1981); Dudden (1983); and Brenner and Laslett (1986).

10. See, e.g., Kaplan (1987).

11. Phyllis Palmer, in her *Domesticity and Dirt,* found evidence that mistresses and servants agreed on what were the least desirable tasks—washing clothes, washing dishes, and taking care of children on evenings and weekends—and that domestics were more likely to perform the least desirable tasks (1990, 70).

12. It may be worth mentioning the importance of unpaid cultural and charitable activities in perpetuating middle-class privilege and power. Middle-class reformers often aimed to mold the poor in ways that mirrored middle-class values but without actually altering their subordinate position. See, e.g., Sanchez (1990) for discussion of efforts of Anglo reformers to train Chicanas in domestic skills.

13. U.S. Bureau of the Census 1933, chap. 3, "Color and Nativity of Gainful Workers," tables 2, 4, 6. For discussion of the concentration of African American women in domestic service, see Glenn (1985).

14. I use the terms *Chicano, Chicana,* and *Mexican American* to refer to both native-born and immigrant Mexican people/women in the United States.

15. U.S. Bureau of the Census 1933.

16. Ibid.

17. For personal accounts of Chicano children being inducted into domestic service, see Ruiz (1987a) and interview of Josephine Turietta in Elsasser, MacKenzie, and Tixier y Vigil (1980, 28–35).

18. See also life history accounts of Black domestics, such as that of Bolden (1976) and of Anna Mae Dickson by Wendy Watriss (Watriss 1984).

19. Blackwelder also found that domestics themselves were attuned to the racial-ethnic hierarchy among them. When advertising for jobs, women who did not identify themselves as Black overwhelmingly requested "housekeeping" or "governess" positions, whereas Blacks advertised for "cooking," "laundering," or just plain "domestic work."

20. This is not to say that daughters of European immigrants experienced great social mobility and soon attained affluence. The nondomestic jobs they took were usually low paying and the conditions of work often deplorable. Nonetheless, white native-born and immigrant women clearly preferred the relative freedom of industrial, office, or shop employment to the constraints of domestic service (see Katzman 1978, 71–72).

21. Document Ma 24, Romanzo Adams Social Research Laboratory papers. I used these records when they were lodged in the sociology department; they are currently being cataloged by the university archives and a finding aid is in process.

22. Ibid., document Ma 15, 5.

23. Ibid.

24. "More Slavery at the South: A Negro Nurse," from the *Independent* (1912), in Katzman and Tuttle (1982, 176–85, 179).

25. From an interview conducted by the author in the San Francisco Bay area in 1977.

26. Ibid.

27. That is, the concentration of minority workers in lower-level jobs can be attributed to their lack of "human capital"—qualifications—needed for certain jobs.

28. Elsa Barkley Brown pointed this out to me in a personal communication.

REFERENCES

Abramovitz, Mimi. 1988. *Regulating the Lives of Women: Social Welfare Policy from Colonial Times to the Present.* Boston: South End Press.

Acker, Joan. 1989. *Doing Comparable Worth: Gender, Class, and Pay Equity.* Philadelphia: Temple University Press.

Adams, Romanzo. Social Research Laboratory papers. University of Hawaii Archives, Manoa.

American Nurses' Association. 1965. *Health Occupations Supportive to Nursing.* New York: American Nurses' Association.

Anderson, C. Arnold, and Mary Jean Bowman. 1953. "The Vanishing Servant and the Contemporary Status System of the American South." *American Journal of Sociology* 59:215–30.

Anzaldúa, Gloria. 1990. *Making Face, Making Soul—Haciendo Caras: Creative Critical Perspectives by Women of Color.* San Francisco: Aunt Lute Foundation.

Barrera, Mario. 1979. *Race and Class in the Southwest: A Theory of Racial Inequality.* Notre Dame, Ind., and London: University of Notre Dame Press.

Barrett, Michèle. 1980. *Women's Oppression Today: Problems in Marxist Feminist Analysis.* London: Verso.

———. 1987. "The Concept of 'Difference.'" *Feminist Review* 26(July):29–41.

Benson, Susan Porter. 1986. *Counter Cultures: Saleswomen, Customers, and Managers in American Department Stores, 1890–1940.* Urbana and Chicago: University of Illinois Press.

Benston, Margaret. 1969. "The Political Economy of Women's Liberation." *Monthly Review* 21(September):13–27.

Blackwelder, Julia Kirk. 1978. "Women in the Work Force: Atlanta, New Orleans, and San Antonio, 1930 to 1940." *Journal of Urban History* 4(3):331–58, 349.

———. 1984. *Women of the Depression: Caste and Culture in San Antonio, 1929–1939.* College Station: Texas A&M University Press.

Blair, Karen. 1980. *The Clubwoman as Feminist: True Womanhood Redefined, 1868–1914.* New York: Holmes & Meier.

Blauner, Robert. 1972. *Racial Oppression in America.* Berkeley: University of California Press.

Bolden, Dorothy. 1976. "Forty-two Years a Maid: Starting at Nine in Atlanta." In *Nobody Speaks for Me! Self-Portraits of American Working Class Women,* ed. Nancy Seifer. New York: Simon & Schuster.

Boydston, Jeanne. 1990. *Home and Work: Housework, Wages, and the Ideology of Labor in the Early Republic.* New York: Oxford University Press.

Braverman, Harry. 1974. *Labor and Monopoly Capital: The Degradation of Labor in the Twentieth Century.* New York and London: Monthly Review Press.

Brenner, Johanna, and Barbara Laslett. 1986. "Social Reproduction and the Family." In *Sociology, from Crisis to Science?* Vol. 2, *The Social Reproduction of Organization and Culture,* ed. Ulf Himmelstrand, 116–31. London: Sage.

Brown, Elsa Barkley. 1989. "Womanist Consciousness: Maggie Lena Walker and the Independent Order of Saint Luke." *Signs: Journal of Women in Culture and Society* 14(3):610–33.

Cannings, Kathleen, and William Lazonik. 1975. "The Development of the Nursing Labor Force in the United States: A Basic Analysis." *International Journal of Health Sciences* 5(2): 185–216.

Carnegie, Mary Elizabeth. 1986. *The Path We Tread: Blacks in Nursing, 1854–1954.* Philadelphia: Lippincott.

Chaplin, David. 1978. "Domestic Service and Industrialization." *Comparative Studies in Sociology* 1:97–127.

Clark-Lewis, Elizabeth. 1987. "This Work Had an End: African American Domestic Workers in Washington, D.C., 1910–1940." In *"To Toil the Livelong Day": America's Women at Work, 1780–1980,* ed. Carole Groneman and Mary Beth Norton. Ithaca, N.Y.: Cornell University Press.

Coleman, Barbara. 1989. "States Grapple with New Law." *AARP News Bulletin,* 30(2):4–5.

Collins, Patricia Hill. 1986. "Learning from the Outsider Within: The Sociological Significance of Black Feminist Thought." *Social Problems* 33(6):14–32.

———. 1990. *Black Feminist Thought: Knowledge, Consciousness, and the Politics of Empowerment.* New York: Allen & Unwin.

Cowan, Ruth Schwartz. 1983. *More Work for Mother: The Ironies of Household Technology from the Open Hearth to the Microwave.* New York: Basic.

Davidoff, Lenore. 1979. "Class and Gender in Victorian England: The Diaries of Arthur J. Munby and Hannah Cullwick." *Feminist Studies* 5(Spring):86–114.

Degler, Carl N. 1980. *At Odds: Women and the Family in America from the Revolution to the Present.* New York: Oxford University Press.

Deming, Dorothy. 1947. *The Practical Nurse.* New York: Commonwealth Fund.

Deutsch, Sarah. 1987a. *No Separate Refuge: Culture, Class, and Gender on an Anglo-Hispanic Frontier in the American Southwest, 1880–1940.* New York: Oxford University Press.

———. 1987b. "Women and Intercultural Relations: The Case of Hispanic New Mexico and Colorado." *Signs* 12(4):719–39.

Diamond, Timothy. 1988. "Social Policy and Everyday Life in Nursing Homes: A Critical Ethnography." In *The Worth of Women's Work: A Qualitative Synthesis,* ed. Anne Statham, Eleanor M. Miller, and Hans O. Mauksch. Albany, N.Y.: SUNY Press.

Dill, Bonnie Thornton. 1980. "The Means to Put My Children Through: Childrearing Goals and Strategies among Black Female Domestic Servants." In *The Black Woman,* ed. La Frances Rodgers-Rose. Beverly Hills and London: Sage.

———. 1988. "Our Mothers' Grief: Racial Ethnic Women and the Maintenance of Families." *Journal of Family History* 12(4):415–31.

Drake, St. Clair, and Horace Cayton. (1945) 1962. *Black Metropolis: A Study of Negro Life in a Northern City,* vol. 1. New York: Harper Torchbook.

Dudden, Faye E. 1983. *Serving Women: Household Service in Nineteenth Century America.* Middletown, Conn.: Wesleyan University Press.

Elsasser, Nan, Kyle MacKenzie, and Yvonne Tixier y Vigil. 1980. *Las Mujeres: Conversations from a Hispanic Community.* Old Westbury, N.Y.: Feminist Press.

Engels, Friedrich. 1972. *The Origins of the Family, Private Property and the State.* New York: International Publishers.

Epstein, Barbara. 1981. *The Politics of Domesticity: Women, Evangelism, and Temperance in Nineteenth Century America.* Middletown, Conn.: Wesleyan University Press.

Fields, Barbara. 1982. "Ideology and Race in American History." In *Region, Race, and Reconstruction: Essays in Honor of C. Vann Woodward,* ed. J. Morgan Kousser and James M. McPherson. New York: Oxford University Press.

Fink, Leon, and Brian Greenberg. 1979. "Organizing Montefiore: Labor Militancy Meets a Progressive Health Care Empire." In *Health Care in America: Essays in Social History,* ed. Susan Reverby and David Rosner. Philadelphia: Temple University Press.

Fox, Bonnie, ed. 1980. *Hidden in the Household: Women's Domestic Labour under Capitalism.* Toronto: Women's Press.

Gamarinikow, Eva. 1978. "Sexual Division of Labour: The Case of Nursing." In *Feminism and Materialism: Women and Modes of Production,* ed. Annette Kuhn and Ann-Marie Wolpe, 96–123. London: Routledge & Kegan Paul.

Game, Ann, and Rosemary Pringle. 1983. *Gender at Work.* Sydney: Allen & Unwin.

Garcia, Alma. 1989. "The Development of Chicana Feminist Discourse, 1970–1980." *Gender and Society* 3(2):217–38.

Garcia, Mario T. 1980. "The Chicana in American History: The Mexican Women of El Paso, 1880–1920: A Case Study." *Pacific Historical Review* 49(2):315–39.

———. 1981. *Desert Immigrants: The Mexicans of El Paso, 1880–1920.* New Haven, Conn.: Yale University Press.

Glazer, Nona. 1988. "Overlooked, Overworked: Women's Unpaid and Paid Work in the Health Services' 'Cost Crisis,'" *International Journal of Health Services* 18(2):119–37.

Glenn, Evelyn Nakano. 1985. "Racial Ethnic Women's Labor: The Intersection of Race, Gender and Class Oppression." *Review of Radical Political Economy* 17(3):86–108.

———. 1986. *Issei, Nisei, Warbride: Three Generations of Japanese American Women in Domestic Service.* Philadelphia: Temple University Press.

Gordon, Linda. 1990. "The New Feminist Scholarship on the Welfare State." In *Women, the State, and Welfare,* ed. Linda Gordon, 9–35. Madison: University of Wisconsin Press.

Gwaltney, John, ed. 1980. *Drylongso: A Self-Portrait of Black America.* New York: Random House.

Hartmann, Heidi I., ed. 1985. *Comparable Worth: New Directions for Research.* Washington, D.C.: National Academy Press.

Hield, Melissa. 1984. "Women in the Texas ILGWU, 1933–50." In *Speaking for Ourselves: Women of the South,* ed. Maxine Alexander, 87–97. New York, Pantheon.

Hine, Darlene Clark, ed. 1985. *Black Women in the Nursing Profession: A Documentary History.* New York: Pathfinder.

———. 1989. *Black Women in White: Racial Conflict and Cooperation in the Nursing Profession, 1890–1950.* Bloomington: Indiana University Press.

Janiewski, Delores. 1983. "Flawed Victories: The Experiences of Black and White Women Workers in Durham during the 1930s." In *Decades of Discontent: The Women's Movement, 1920–1940,* ed. Lois Scharf and Joan M. Jensen, 85–112. Westport, Conn., and London: Greenwood.

Kaplan, Elaine Bell. 1987. "'I Don't Do No Windows': Competition between the Domestic Worker and the Housewife." In *Competition: A Feminist Taboo?"* ed. Valerie Miner and Helen E. Longino. New York: Feminist Press at CUNY.

Katzman, David M. 1978. *Seven Days a Week: Women and Domestic Service in Industrializing America.* New York: Oxford University Press.

Katzman, David M., and William M. Tuttle, Jr., eds. 1982. *Plain Folk: The Life Stories of Undistinguished Americans.* Urbana and Chicago: University of Illinois Press.

Kessler-Harris, Alice. 1981. *Women Have Always Worked: A Historical Overview.* Old Westbury, N.Y.: Feminist Press.

———. 1982. *Out to Work: A History of Wage-earning Women in the United States.* New York: Oxford University Press.

King, Deborah K. 1988. "Multiple Jeopardy, Multiple Consciousness: The Context of a Black Feminist Ideology." *Signs* 14(1):42–72.

Lamphere, Louise. 1987. *From Working Daughters to Working Mothers: Immigrant Women in a New England Industrial Community.* Ithaca, N.Y.: Cornell University Press.

Lasch, Christopher. 1977. *Haven in a Heartless World: The Family Besieged.* New York: Basic.

Laslett, Barbara, and Johanna Brenner. 1989. "Gender and Social Reproduction: Historical Perspectives." *Annual Review of Sociology* 15:381–404.

Lind, Andrew. 1951. "The Changing Position of Domestic Service in Hawaii." *Social Process in Hawaii* 15:71–87.

Luxton, Meg. 1980. *More than a Labour of Love: Three Generations of Women's Work in the Home.* Toronto: Women's Press.

McConoway, Mary Jo. 1987. "The Intimate Experiment." *Los Angeles Times Magazine,* February 19, 18–23, 37–38.

Marx, Karl, and Friedrich Engels. 1969. *Selected Works,* vol. 1. Moscow: Progress.

Mellor, Earl F. 1987. "Workers at the Minimum Wage or Less: Who They Are and the Jobs They Hold." *Monthly Labor Review,* July, 34–38.

Omi Michael, and Howard Winant. 1986. *Racial Formation in the United States.* New York: Routledge.

Palmer, Phyllis. 1987. "Housewife and Household Worker: Employer-Employee Relations in the Home, 1928–1941." In *"To Toil the Livelong Day": America's Women at Work,*

1780–1980, ed. Carole Groneman and Mary Beth Norton, 179–95. Ithaca, N.Y.: Cornell University Press.

———. 1990. *Domesticity and Dirt: Housewives and Domestic Servants in the United States, 1920–1945.* Philadelphia: Temple University Press.

Piven, Frances Fox, and Richard A. Cloward. 1971. *Regulating the Poor: The Functions of Public Welfare.* New York: Pantheon.

———. 1979. *Poor People's Movements: Why They Succeed, How They Fail.* New York: Pantheon.

Reisler, Mark. 1976. *By the Sweat of Their Brow: Mexican Immigrant Labor in the United States, 1900–1940.* Westport, Conn.: Greenwood.

Reverby, Susan M. 1979. "From Aide to Organizer: The Oral History of Lillian Roberts." In *Women of America: A History,* ed. Carol Ruth Berkin and Mary Beth Norton. Boston: Houghton Mifflin.

———. 1987. *Ordered to Care: The Dilemma of American Nursing, 1850–1945.* Cambridge: Cambridge University Press.

Rollins, Judith. 1985. *Between Women: Domestics and Their Employers.* Philadelphia: Temple University Press.

Romero, Mary. 1987. "Chicanas Modernize Domestic Service." Unpublished manuscript.

———. 1988a. "Day Work in the Suburbs: The Work Experience of Chicana Private Housekeepers." In *The Worth of Women's Work: A Qualitative Synthesis,* ed. Anne Statham, Eleanor M. Miller, and Hans O. Mauksch, 77–92. Albany: SUNY Press.

———. 1988b. "Renegotiating Race, Class and Gender Hierarchies in the Everyday Interactions between Chicana Private Household Workers and Employers." Paper presented at the 1988 meetings of the Society for the Study of Social Problems, Atlanta.

Rose, Hilary. 1986. "Women's Work: Women's Knowledge." In *What Is Feminism?* ed. Juliet Mitchell and Ann Oakley, 161–83. Oxford: Basil Blackwell.

Ruíz, Vicki L. 1987a. "By the Day or the Week: Mexicana Domestic Workers in El Paso." In *Women on the U.S.-Mexico Border: Responses to Change,* ed. Vicki L. Ruíz and Susan Tiano, 61–76. Boston: Allen & Unwin.

———. 1987b. "Oral History and La Mujer: The Rosa Guerrero Story." In *Women on the U.S.-Mexico Border: Responses to Change,* ed. Vicki L. Ruíz and Susan Tiano, 219–32. Boston: Allen & Unwin.

Ryan, Mary P. 1981. *Cradle of the Middle Class: The Family in Oneida County, New York, 1790–1865.* Cambridge: Cambridge University Press.

Sacks, Karen Brodkin. 1988. *Caring by the Hour: Women, Work, and Organizing at Duke Medical Center.* Urbana and Chicago: University of Illinois Press.

Sacks, Karen Brodkin, and Dorothy Remy, eds. 1984. *My Troubles Are Going to Have Trouble with Me: Everyday Trials and Triumphs of Women Workers.* New Brunswick, N.J.: Rutgers University Press.

Sanchez, George J. 1990. "'Go after the Women': Americanization and the Mexican Immigrant Woman, 1915–1929." In *Unequal Sisters: A Multicultural Reader in Women's History,* ed. Ellen Carol DuBois and Vicki L. Ruiz, 250–63. New York: Routledge.

Secombe, Wally. 1974. "The Housewife and Her Labour under Capitalism." *New Left Review* 83(January–February):3–24.

Sekcenski, Edward S. 1981. "The Health Services Industry: A Decade of Expansion." *Monthly Labor Review* (May):10–16.

Silvestri, George T., and John M. Lukasiewicz. 1987. "A Look at Occupational Employment Trends to the Year 2000." *Monthly Labor Review* (September): 46–63.

Smuts, Robert W. 1959. *Women and Work in America.* New York: Schocken.

Sokoloff, Natalie J. 1980. *Between Money and Love: The Dialectics of Women's Home and Market Work.* New York: Praeger.

Starr, Paul. 1982. *The Social Transformation of American Medicine.* New York: Basic.

Strasser, Susan. 1982. *Never Done: A History of American Housework.* New York: Pantheon.

Tucker, Susan. 1988. "The Black Domestic in the South: Her Legacy as Mother and Mother Surrogate." In *Southern Women,* ed. Carolyn Matheny Dillman, 93–102. New York: Hemisphere.

U.S. Bureau of the Census. 1932. *Fifteenth Census of the United States: 1930, Outlying Territories and Possessions.* Washington, D.C.: Government Printing Office.

———. 1933. *Fifteenth Census of the United States: 1930, Population.* Vol. 5, *General Report on Occupations.* Washington, D.C.: Government Printing Office.

———. 1984. *Census of the Population, 1980.* Vol. 1, *Characteristics of the Population.* Washington, D.C.: Government Printing Office.

U.S. Department of Labor. 1987a. *Industry Wage Survey: Hospitals, August 1985.* Bureau of Labor Statistics Bulletin 2273. Washington, D.C.: Government Printing Office.

———. 1987b. *Industry Wage Survey: Nursing and Personal Care Facilities, September 1985.* Bureau of Labor Statistics Bulletin 2275. Washington, D.C.: Government Printing Office.

———. 1989. *Employment and Earnings, January 1989.* Bureau of Labor Statistics Bulletin. Washington, D.C.: Government Printing Office.

Wagner, David. 1980. "The Proletarianization of Nursing in the United States, 1932–1945." *International Journal of Health Services* 10(2):271–89.

Watriss, Wendy. 1984. "It's Something Inside You." In *Speaking for Ourselves: Women of the South,* ed. Maxine Alexander. New York: Pantheon.

Weinbaum, Batya, and Amy Bridges. 1976. "The Other Side of the Paycheck." *Monthly Review* 28:88–103.

Compulsory Heterosexuality and Lesbian Existence

ADRIENNE RICH

FOREWORD

I want to say a little about the way "Compulsory Heterosexuality" was originally conceived and the context in which we are now living. It was written in part to challenge the erasure of lesbian existence from so much of scholarly feminist literature, an erasure which I felt (and feel) to be not just antilesbian but antifeminist in its consequences, and to distort the experience of heterosexual women as well. It was not written to widen divisions but to encourage heterosexual feminists to examine heterosexuality as a political institution which disempowers women—and to change it. I also hoped that other lesbians would feel the depth and breadth of woman identification and woman bonding that has run like a continuous though stifled theme through the heterosexual experience, and that this would become increasingly a politically activating impulse, not simply a validation of personal lives. I wanted the essay to suggest new kinds of criticism, to incite new questions in classrooms and academic journals, and to sketch, at least, some bridge over the gap between *lesbian* and *feminist*. I wanted, at the very least, for feminists to find it less possible to read, write, or teach from a perspective of unexamined heterocentricity.

Within the three years since I wrote "Compulsory Heterosexuality"—with this energy of hope and desire—the pressures to conform in a society increasingly conservative in mood have become more intense. The New Right's messages to women have been, precisely, that we are the emotional and sexual property of men, and that the autonomy and equality of women threaten family, religion, and state. The institutions by which women have traditionally been controlled—patriarchal motherhood, economic exploitation, the nuclear family, compulsory heterosexuality—are being strengthened by legislation, religious fiat, media imagery, and efforts at censorship. In a worsening economy, the single mother trying to support her children confronts the feminization of poverty which Joyce Miller of the National Coalition of Labor Union Women has named one of the major issues of the 1980s. The lesbian, unless in disguise, faces discrimination in hiring and harassment and violence in the street. Even within feminist-inspired institutions such as battered-women's shelters and Women's Studies programs, open lesbians are fired and others warned to stay in the closet. The retreat into sameness—assimilation for those who can manage it—is the most passive and debilitating of responses to political repression, economic insecurity, and a renewed open season on difference.

I want to note that documentation of male violence against women—within the home especially—has been accumulating rapidly in this period (see note 9). At the same time, in the realm of literature which depicts woman bonding and woman identification as essential for female survival, a steady stream of writing and criticism has been coming from women of color in general and lesbians of color in particular—the latter group being even more profoundly erased in academic feminist scholarship by the double bias of racism and homophobia.[1]

There has recently been an intensified debate on female sexuality among feminists and lesbians, with lines often furiously and bitterly drawn, with *sadomasochism* and *pornography* as key words, which are variously defined according to who is talking. The depth of women's rage and fear regarding sexuality and its relation to power and pain is real, even when the dialogue sounds simplistic, self-righteous, or like parallel monologues.

Because of all these developments, there are parts of this essay that I would word differently, qualify, or expand if I were writing it today. But I continue to think that het-erosexual feminists will draw political strength for change from taking a critical stance toward the ideology which *demands* heterosexuality, and that lesbians cannot assume that we are untouched by that ideology and the institutions founded upon it. There is nothing about such a critique that requires us to think of ourselves as victims, as having been brainwashed or totally powerless. Coercion and compulsion are among the conditions in which women have learned to recognize our strength. Resistance is a major theme in this essay and in the study of women's lives, if we know what we are looking for.

I

Biologically men have only one innate orientation—a sexual one that draws them to women—while women have two innate orientations, sexual toward men and reproductive toward their young.[2]

I was a woman terribly vulnerable, critical, using femaleness as a sort of standard or yardstick to measure and discard men. Yes—something like that. I was an Anna who invited defeat from men without ever being conscious of it. (But I am conscious of it. And being conscious of it means I shall leave it all behind me and become—but what?) I was stuck fast in an emotion common to women of our time, that can turn them bit-ter, or Lesbian, or solitary. Yes, that Anna during that time was . . .

[Another blank line across the page:][3]

The bias of compulsory heterosexuality, through which lesbian experience is perceived on a scale ranging from deviant to abhorrent or simply rendered invisible, could be illustrated from many texts other than the two just preced-ing. The assumption made by Rossi, that women are "innately" sexually oriented only toward men, and that made by Lessing, that the lesbian is simply acting out of her bitterness toward men, are by no means theirs alone; these assumptions are widely current in literature and in the social sciences.

I am concerned here with two other matters as well: first, how and why women's choice of women as passionate comrades, life partners, co-workers, lovers, community has been crushed, invalidated, forced into hiding and disguise; and second, the virtual or total neglect of lesbian existence in a wide range of writings, including feminist scholarship.

Obviously there is a connection here. I believe that much feminist theory and criticism is stranded on this shoal.

My organizing impulse is the belief that it is not enough for feminist thought that specifically lesbian texts exist. Any theory of cultural/political creation that treats lesbian existence as a marginal or less "natural" phenomenon, as mere "sexual preference," or as the mirror image of either heterosexual or male homosexual relations is profoundly weakened thereby, whatever its other contributions. Feminist theory can no longer afford merely to voice a tol-eration of "lesbianism" as an "alternative life style" or make token allusion to lesbians. A feminist critique of com-pulsory heterosexual orientation for women is long over-due. In this exploratory paper, I shall try to show why.

I will begin by way of examples, briefly discussing four books that have appeared in the last few years, written from different viewpoints and political orientations, but all pre-senting themselves, and favorably reviewed, as feminist.[4] All take as a basic assumption that the social relations of the sexes are disordered and extremely problematic, if not disabling, for women; all seek paths toward change. I have learned more from some of these books than from others, but on this I am clear: each one might have been more accurate, more powerful, more truly a force for change had the author dealt with lesbian existence as a reality and as a source of knowledge and power available to women, or with the institution of heterosexuality itself as a beachhead of male dominance.[5] In none of them is the question ever raised as to whether, in a different context or other things being equal, women would *choose* heterosexual coupling and marriage; heterosexuality is presumed the "sexual pref-erence" of "most women," either implicitly or explicitly. In none of these books, which concern themselves with moth-ering, sex roles, relationships, and societal prescriptions for women, is compulsory heterosexuality ever examined as an institution powerfully affecting all these, or the idea of "preference" or "innate orientation" even indirectly ques-tioned.

In *For Her Own Good: 150 Years of the Experts' Advice to Women* by Barbara Ehrenreich and Deirdre English, the authors' superb pamphlets *Witches, Midwives and Nurses: A History of Women Healers and Complaints and Dis-orders: The Sexual Politics of Sickness* are developed into a provocative and complex study. Their thesis in this book is that the advice given to American women by male health professionals, particularly in the areas of marital sex, maternity, and child care, has echoed the dictates of the economic marketplace and the role capitalism has needed women to play in production and/or reproduction. Women have become the consumer victims of various cures, thera- pies, and normative judgments in different periods (includ- ing the prescription to middle-class women to embody and preserve the sacredness of the home—the "scientific" romanticization of the home itself). None of the "experts" advice has been either particularly scientific or women-ori- ented; it has reflected male needs, male fantasies about women, and male interest in controlling women—particu- larly in the realms of sexuality and motherhood—fused with the requirements of industrial capitalism. So much of this book is so devastatingly informative and is written with such lucid feminist wit that I kept waiting as I read for the basic proscription against lesbianism to be examined. It never was.

This can hardly be for lack of information. Jonathan Katz's *Gay American History*[6] tells us that as early as 1656 the New Haven Colony prescribed the death penalty for lesbians. Katz provides many suggestive and informative documents on the "treatment" (or torture) of lesbians by the medical profession in the nineteenth and twentieth cen- turies. Recent work by the historian Nancy Sahli docu- ments the crackdown on intense female friendships among college women at the turn of the present century.[7] The ironic title *For Her Own Good* might have referred first and foremost to the economic imperative to heterosexuality and marriage and to the sanctions imposed against single women and widows—both of whom have been and still are viewed as deviant. Yet, in this often enlightening Marxist- feminist overview of male prescriptions for female sanity and health, the economics of prescriptive heterosexuality go unexamined.[8]

Of the three psychoanalytically based books, one, Jean Baker Miller's *Toward a New Psychology of Women,* is written as if lesbians simply do not exist, even as marginal beings. Given Miller's title, I find this astonishing. How- ever, the favorable reviews the book has received in femi- nist journals, including *Signs* and *Spokeswoman,* suggest that Miller's heterocentric assumptions are widely shared. In *The Mermaid and the Minotaur: Sexual Arrangements and the Human Malaise,* Dorothy Dinnerstein makes an impassioned argument for the sharing of parenting between women and men and for an end to what she perceives as the male/female symbiosis of "gender arrangements," which she feels are leading the species further and further into violence and self-extinction. Apart from other problems that I have with this book (including her silence on the institutional and random terrorism men have practiced on women—and children—throughout history,[9] and her obses- sion with psychology to the neglect of economic and other

material realities that help to create psychological reality), I find Dinnerstein's view of the relations between women and men as "a collaboration to keep history mad" utterly ahistorical. She means by this a collaboration to perpetuate social relations which are hostile, exploitative, and destruc- tive to life itself. She sees women and men as equal part- ners in the making of "sexual arrangements," seemingly unaware of the repeated struggles of women to resist oppression (their own and that of others) and to change their condition. She ignores, specifically, the history of women who—as witches, *femmes seules,* marriage resisters, spinsters, autonomous widows, and/or lesbians—have man- aged on varying levels *not* to collaborate. It is this history, precisely, from which feminists have so much to learn and on which there is overall such blanketing silence. Dinnerstein acknowledges at the end of her book that "female separatism," though "on a large scale and in the long run wildly impractical," has something to teach us: "Separate, women could in principle set out to learn from scratch—undeflected by the opportunities to evade this task that men's presence has so far offered—what intact self- creative humanness is."[10] Phrases like "intact self-creative humanness" obscure the question of what the many forms of female separatism have actually been addressing. The fact is that women in every culture and throughout history *have* undertaken the task of independent, nonheterosexual, woman-connected existence, to the extent made possible by their context, often in the belief that they were the "only ones" ever to have done so. They have undertaken it even though few women have been in an economic position to resist marriage altogether, and even though attacks against unmarried women have ranged from aspersion and mock- ery to deliberate gynocide, including the burning and tor- turing of millions of widows and spinsters during the witch persecutions of the 15th, 16th, and 17th centuries in Europe.

Nancy Chodorow does come close to the edge of an acknowledgment of lesbian existence. Like Dinnerstein, Chodorow believes that the fact that women, and women only, are responsible for child care in the sexual division of labor has led to an entire social organization of gender inequality, and that men as well as women must become primary carers for children if that inequality is to change. In the process of examining, from a psychoanalytic perspec- tive, how mothering by women affects the psychological development of girl and boy children, she offers documen- tation that men are "emotionally secondary" in women's lives, that "women have a richer, ongoing inner world to fall back on . . . men do not become as emotionally important to women as women do to men."[11] This would carry into the late 20th century Smith-Rosenberg's findings about 18th- and 19th-century women's emotional focus on women. "Emotionally important" can, of course, refer to anger as well as to love, or to that intense mixture of the two often found in women's relationships with women— one aspect of what I have come to call the "double life of women" (see below). Chodorow concludes that because women have women as mothers, "the mother remains a primary internal object [*sic*] to the girl, so that heterosexual relationships are on the model of a nonexclusive, second relationship for her, whereas for the boy they re-create an exclusive, primary relationship." According to Chodorow, women "have learned to deny the limitations of masculine lovers for both psychological and practical reasons."[12]

But the practical reasons (like witch burnings, male control of law, theology, and science, or economic nonviability within the sexual division of labor) are glossed over. Chodorow's account barely glances at the constraints and sanctions which historically have enforced or ensured the coupling of women with men and obstructed or penalized women's coupling or allying in independent groups with other women. She dismisses lesbian existence with the comment that "lesbian relationships do tend to re-create mother–daughter emotions and connections, but most women are heterosexual" (implied: more mature, having developed beyond the mother–daughter connection?). She then adds: "This heterosexual preference and taboos on homosexuality, in addition to objective economic dependence on men, make the option of primary sexual bonds with other women unlikely—though more prevalent in recent years."[13] The significance of that qualification seems irresistible, but Chodorow does not explore it further. Is she saying that lesbian existence has become more *visible* in recent years (in certain groups), that economic and other pressures have changed (under capitalism, socialism, or both), and that consequently more women are rejecting the heterosexual "choice"? She argues that women want children because their heterosexual relationships lack richness and intensity, that in having a child a woman seeks to re-create her own intense relationship with her mother. It seems to me that on the basis of her own findings, Chodorow leads us implicitly to conclude that heterosexuality is *not* a "preference" for women, that, for one thing, it fragments the erotic from the emotional in a way that women find impoverishing and painful. Yet her book participates in mandating it. Neglecting the covert socializations and the overt forces which have channeled women into marriage and heterosexual romance, pressures ranging from

the selling of daughters to the silences of literature to the images of the television screen, she, like Dinnerstein, is stuck with trying to reform a manmade institution—compulsory heterosexuality—as if, despite profound emotional impulses and complementarities drawing women toward women, there is a mystical/biological heterosexual inclination, a "preference" or "choice" which draws women toward men.

Moreover, it is understood that this "preference" does not need to be explained unless through the tortuous theory of the female Oedipus complex or the necessity for species reproduction. It is lesbian sexuality which (usually, and incorrectly, "included" under male homosexuality) is seen as requiring explanation. This assumption of female heterosexuality seems to me in itself remarkable: it is an enormous assumption to have glided so silently into the foundations of our thought.

The extension of this assumption is the frequently heard assertion that in a world of genuine equality, where men are nonoppressive and nurturing, everyone would be bisexual. Such a notion blurs and sentimentalizes the actualities within which women have experienced sexuality; it is a liberal leap across the tasks and struggles of here and now, the continuing process of sexual definition which will generate its own possibilities and choices. (It also assumes that women who have chosen women have done so simply because men are oppressive and emotionally unavailable, which still fails to account for women who continue to pursue relationships with oppressive and/or emotionally unsatisfying men.) I am suggesting that heterosexuality, like motherhood, needs to be recognized and studied as a *political institution*—even, or especially, by those individuals who feel they are, in their personal experience, the precursors of a new social relation between the sexes.

II

If women are the earliest sources of emotional caring and physical nurture for both female and male children, it would seem logical, from a feminist perspective at least, to pose the following questions: whether the search for love and tenderness in both sexes does not originally lead toward women; *why in fact women would ever redirect that search;* why species survival, the means of impregnation, and emotional/erotic relationships should ever have become so rigidly identified with each other; and why such violent strictures should be found necessary to enforce women's total emotional, erotic loyalty and subservience to men. I doubt that enough feminist scholars and theorists have taken the pains to acknowledge the societal forces which wrench women's emotional and erotic energies away from themselves and other women and from woman-identified values. These forces, as I shall try to show, range from literal physical enslavement to the disguising and distorting of possible options.

I do not assume that mothering by women is a "sufficient cause" of lesbian existence. But the issue of mothering by women has been much in the air of late, usually accompanied by the view that increased parenting by men would minimize antagonism between the sexes and equalize the sexual imbalance of power of males over females. These discussions are carried on without reference to compulsory heterosexuality as a phenomenon, let alone as an ideology. I do not wish to psychologize here but rather to identify sources of male power. I believe large numbers of men could, in fact, undertake child care on a large scale without radically altering the balance of male power in a male-identified society.

In her essay "The Origin of the Family," Kathleen Gough lists eight characteristics of male power in archaic and contemporary societies which I would like to use as a framework: "men's ability to deny women sexuality or to force it upon them; to command or exploit their labor to control their produce; to control or rob them of their children; to confine them physically and prevent their movement; to use them as objects in male transactions; to cramp their creativeness; or to withhold from them large areas of the society's knowledge and cultural attainments."[14] (Gough does not perceive these power characteristics as specifically enforcing heterosexuality, only as producing sexual inequality.) Below, Gough's words appear in italics; the elaboration of each of her categories, in brackets, is my own.

Characteristics of male power include *the power of men*

1. *to deny women* [their own] *sexuality*—[by means of clitoridectomy and infibulation; chastity belts; punishment, including death, for female adultery; punishment, including death, for lesbian sexuality; psychoanalytic denial of the clitoris; strictures against masturbation; denial of maternal and postmenopausal sensuality; unnecessary hysterectomy; pseudo-lesbian images in the media and literature; closing of archives and destruction of documents relating to lesbian existence]

2. or to force it [male sexuality] upon them—[by means of rape (including marital rape) and wife beating; father–daughter, brother–sister incest; the socialization of women to feel that male sexual "drive" amounts to a right;[15] idealization of heterosexual romance in art, litera-

ture, the media, advertising, etc.; child marriage; arranged marriage; prostitution; the harem; psychoanalytic doctrines of frigidity and vaginal orgasm; pornographic depictions of women responding pleasurably to sexual violence and humiliation (a subliminal message being that sadistic heterosexuality is more "normal" than sensuality between women)]

3. *to command or exploit their labor to control their produce*—[by means of the institutions of marriage and motherhood as unpaid production; the horizontal segregation of women in paid employment; the decoy of the upwardly mobile token woman; male control of abortion, contraception, sterilization, and childbirth; pimping; female infanticide, which robs mothers of daughters and contributes to generalized devaluation of women]

4. *to control or rob them of their children*—[by means of father right and "legal kidnaping";[16] enforced sterilization; systematized infanticide; seizure of children from lesbian mothers by the courts; the malpractice of male obstetrics; use of the mother as "token torturer"[17] in genital mutilation or in binding the daughter's feet (or mind) to fit her for marriage]

5. *to confine them physically and prevent their movement*—[by means of rape as terrorism, keeping women off the streets; purdah; foot binding; atrophying of women's athletic capabilities, high heels and "feminine" dress codes in fashion; the veil; sexual harassment on the streets; horizontal segregation of women in employment; prescriptions for "full-time" mothering at home; enforced economic dependence of wives]

6. *to use them as objects in male transactions*—[use of women as "gifts"; bride price; pimping; arranged marriage; use of women as entertainers to facilitate male deals—e.g., wife–hostess, cocktail waitress required to dress for male sexual titillation, call girls, "bunnies," geisha, *kisaeng* prostitutes, secretaries]

7. *to cramp their creativeness*—[witch persecutions as campaigns against midwives and female healers, and as pogrom against independent, "unassimilated" women;[18] definition of male pursuits as more valuable than female within any culture, so that cultural values become the embodiment of male subjectivity; restriction of female self-fulfillment to marriage and motherhood; sexual exploitation of women by male artists and teachers; the social and economic dis-ruption of women's creative aspirations;[19] erasure of female tradition][20]

8. *to withhold from them large areas of the society's knowledge and cultural attainments*—[by means of noneducation of females; the "Great Silence" regarding women

and particularly lesbian existence in history and culture;[21] sex-role tracking which deflects women from science, technology, and other "masculine" pursuits; male social/professional bonding which excludes women; discrimination against women in the professions]

These are some of the methods by which male power is manifested and maintained. Looking at the schema, what surely impresses itself is the fact that we are confronting not a simple maintenance of inequality and property possession, but a pervasive cluster of forces, ranging from physical brutality to control of consciousness, which suggests that an enormous potential counterforce is having to be restrained.

Some of the forms by which male power manifests itself are more easily recognizable as enforcing heterosexuality on women than are others. Yet each one I have listed adds to the cluster of forces within which women have been convinced that marriage and sexual orientation toward men are inevitable—even if unsatisfying or oppressive—components of their lives. The chastity belt; child marriage; erasure of lesbian existence (except as exotic and perverse) in art, literature, film; idealization of heterosexual romance and marriage—these are some fairly obvious forms of compulsion, the first two exemplifying physical force, the second two control of consciousness. While clitoridectomy has been assailed by feminists as a form of woman torture,[22] Kathleen Barry first pointed out that it is not simply a way of turning the young girl into a "marriageable" woman through brutal surgery. It intends that women in the intimate proximity of polygynous marriage will not form sexual relationships with each other, that—from a male, genital-fetishist perspective—female erotic connections, even in a sex-segregated situation, will be literally excised.[23]

The function of pornography as an influence on consciousness is a major public issue of our time, when a multibillion-dollar industry has the power to disseminate increasingly sadistic, women-degrading visual images. But even so-called soft-core pornography and advertising depict women as objects of sexual appetite devoid of emotional context, without individual meaning or personality—essentially as a sexual commodity to be consumed by males. (So-called lesbian pornography, created for the male voyeuristic eye, is equally devoid of emotional context or individual personality.) The most pernicious message relayed by pornography is that women are natural sexual prey to men and love it, that sexuality and violence are congruent, and that for women sex is essentially masochistic, humiliation pleasurable, physical abuse erotic. But along

with this message comes another, not always recognized: that enforced submission and the use of cruelty, if played out in heterosexual pairing, is sexually "normal," while sensuality between women, including erotic mutuality and respect, is "queer," "sick," and either pornographic in itself or not very exciting compared with the sexuality of whips and bondage.[24] Pornography does not simply create a climate in which sex and violence are interchangeable; *it widens the range of behavior considered acceptable from men in heterosexual intercourse*—behavior which reiteratively strips women of their autonomy, dignity, and sexual potential, including the potential of loving and being loved by women in mutuality and integrity.

In her brilliant study *Sexual Harassment of Working Women: A Case of Sex Discrimination,* Catharine A. MacKinnon delineates the intersection of compulsory heterosexuality and economics. Under capitalism, women are horizontally segregated by gender and occupy a structurally inferior position in the workplace. This is hardly news, but MacKinnon raises the question why, even if capitalism "requires some collection of individuals to occupy low-status, low-paying positions . . . such persons must be biologically female," and goes on to point out that "the fact that male employers often do not hire qualified women, *even when they could pay them less than men,* suggests that more than the profit motive is implicated" [emphasis added].[25] She cites a wealth of material documenting the fact that women are not only segregated in low-paying service jobs (as secretaries, domestics, nurses, typists, telephone operators, child-care workers, waitresses), but that "sexualization of the woman" is part of the job. Central and intrinsic to the economic realities of women's lives is the requirement that women will "market sexual attractiveness to men, who tend to hold the economic power and position to enforce their predilections." And MacKinnon documents that "sexual harassment perpetuates the interlocked structure by which women have been kept sexually in thrall to men at the bottom of the labor market. Two forces of American society converge: men's control over women's sexuality and capital's control over employees' work lives."[26] Thus, women in the workplace are at the mercy of sex as power in a vicious circle. Economically disadvantaged, women—whether waitresses or professors—endure sexual harassment to keep their jobs and learn to behave in a complaisantly and ingratiatingly heterosexual manner because they discover this is their true qualification for employment, whatever the job description. And, MacKinnon notes, the woman who too decisively resists sexual overtures in the workplace is accused of being "dried up" and sexless, or lesbian. This raises a specific difference between the experiences of lesbians and homosexual men. A lesbian, closeted on her job because of heterosexist prejudice, is not simply forced into denying the truth of her outside relationships or private life. Her job depends on her pretending to be not merely heterosexual, but a heterosexual *woman* in terms of dressing and playing the feminine, deferential role required of "real" women.

MacKinnon raises radical questions as to the qualitative differences between sexual harassment, rape, and ordinary heterosexual intercourse. ("As one accused rapist put it, he hadn't used 'any more force than is usual for males during the preliminaries.'") She criticizes Susan Brownmiller[27] for separating rape from the mainstream of daily life and for her unexamined premise that "rape is violence, intercourse is sexuality," removing rape from the sexual sphere altogether. Most crucially she argues that "taking rape from the realm of 'the sexual,' placing it in the realm of 'the violent,' allows one to be against it without raising any questions about the extent to which the institution of heterosexuality has defined force as a normal part of 'the preliminaries.'"[28] "Never is it asked whether, under conditions of male supremacy, the notion of 'consent' has any meaning."[29]

The fact is that the workplace, among other social institutions, is a place where women have learned to accept male violation of their psychic and physical boundaries as the price of survival; where women have been educated—no less than by romantic literature or by pornography—to perceive themselves as sexual prey. A woman seeking to escape such casual violations along with economic disadvantage may well turn to marriage as a form of hoped-for protection, while bringing into marriage neither social nor economic power, thus entering that institution also from a disadvantaged position. MacKinnon finally asks:

> What if inequality is built into the social conceptions of male and female sexuality, of masculinity and femininity, of sexiness and heterosexual attractiveness? Incidents of sexual harassment suggest that male sexual desire itself may be aroused by female vulnerability. . . . Men feel they can take advantage, so they want to, so they do. Examination of sexual harassment, precisely because the episodes appear commonplace, forces one to confront the fact that sexual intercourse normally occurs between economic (as well as physical) unequals . . . the apparent legal requirement that violations of women's sexuality appear out of the ordinary before they will be punished helps prevent women from defining the ordinary conditions of their own consent.[30]

Given the nature and extent of heterosexual pressures—the daily "eroticization of women's subordination," as MacKinnon phrases it[31]—I question the more or less psychoanalytic perspective (suggested by such writers as Karen Horney, H. R. Hayes, Wolfgang Lederer, and, most recently, Dorothy Dinnerstein) that the male need to control women sexually results from some primal male "fear of women" and of women's sexual insatiability. It seems more probable that men really fear not that they will have women's sexual appetites forced on them or that women want to smother and devour them, but that women could be indifferent to them altogether, that men could be allowed sexual and emotional—therefore economic—access to women *only* on women's terms, otherwise being left on the periphery of the matrix.

The means of assuring male sexual access to women have recently received searching investigation by Kathleen Barry.[32] She documents extensive and appalling evidence for the existence, on a very large scale, of international female slavery, the institution once known as "white slavery" but which in fact has involved, and at this very moment involves, women of every race and class. In the theoretical analysis derived from her research, Barry makes the connection between all enforced conditions under which women live subject to men: prostitution, marital rape, father–daughter and brother–sister incest, wife beating, pornography, bride price, the selling of daughters, purdah, and genital mutilation. She sees the rape paradigm—where the victim of sexual assault is held responsible for her own victimization—as leading to the rationalization and acceptance of other forms of enslavement where the woman is presumed to have "chosen" her fate, to embrace it passively, or to have courted it perversely through rash or unchaste behavior. On the contrary, Barry maintains, "female sexual slavery is present in ALL situations where women or girls cannot change the conditions of their existence; where regardless of how they got into those conditions, e.g., social pressure, economic hardship, misplaced trust or the longing for affection, they cannot get out; and where they are subject to sexual violence and exploitation."[33] She provides a spectrum of concrete examples, not only as to the existence of a widespread international traffic in women, but also as to how this operates—whether in the form of a Minnesota pipeline" funneling blonde, blue-eyed midwestern runaways to Times Square, or the purchasing of young women out of rural poverty in Latin America or Southeast Asia, or the providing of *maisons d'abattage* for migrant workers in the eighteenth arrondissement of Paris. Instead of "blaming the victim" or trying to diagnose her presumed pathology, Barry turns her floodlight on the pathology of sex colonization itself, the ideology of "cultural sadism" represented by the pornography industry and by the overall identification of women primarily as "sexual beings whose responsibility is the sexual service of men."[34]

Barry delineates what she names a "sexual domination perspective" through whose lens sexual abuse and terrorism of women by men has been rendered almost invisible by treating it as natural and inevitable. From its point of view, women are expendable as long as the sexual and emotional needs of the male can be satisfied. To replace this perspective of domination with a universal standard of basic freedom for women from gender-specific violence, from constraints on movement, and from male right of sexual and emotional access is the political purpose of her book. Like Mary Daly in *Gyn/Ecology,* Barry rejects structuralist and other cultural-relativist rationalizations for sexual torture and antiwoman violence. In her opening chapter, she asks of her readers that they refuse all handy escapes into ignorance and denial. "The only way we can come out of hiding, break through our paralyzing defenses, is to know it all—the full extent of sexual violence and domination of women. . . . In *knowing,* in facing directly, we can learn to chart our course out of this oppression, by envisioning and creating a world which will preclude sexual slavery."[35]

"Until we name the practice, give conceptual definition and form to it, illustrate its life over time and in space, those who are its most obvious victims will also not be able to name it or define their experience."

But women are all, in different ways and to different degrees, its victims; and part of the problem with naming and conceptualizing female sexual slavery is, as Barry clearly sees, compulsory heterosexuality.[36] Compulsory heterosexuality simplifies the task of the procurer and pimp in worldwide prostitution rings and "eros centers," while, in the privacy of the home, it leads the daughter to "accept" incest/rape by her father, the mother to deny that it is happening, the battered wife to stay on with an abusive husband. "Befriending or love" is a major tactic of the procurer, whose job it is to turn the runaway or the confused young girl over to the pimp for seasoning. The ideology of heterosexual romance, beamed at her from childhood out of fairy tales, television, films, advertising, popular songs, wedding pageantry, is a tool ready to the procurer's hand and one which he does not hesitate to use, as Barry documents. Early female indoctrination in "love" as an emotion may be largely a Western concept; but a more universal ideology concerns the primacy and uncontrollability of the male sexual drive. This is one of many insights offered by Barry's work:

> As sexual power is learned by adolescent boys through the social experience of their sex drive, so do girls learn that the locus of sexual power is male. Given the importance placed on the male sex drive in the socialization of girls as well as boys, early adolescence is probably the first significant phase of male identification in a girl's life and development. . . . As a young girl becomes aware of her own increasing sexual feelings . . . she turns away from her heretofore primary relationships with girlfriends. As they become secondary to her, recede in importance in her life, her own identity also assumes a secondary role and she grows into male identification.[37]

We still need to ask why some women never, even temporarily, turn away from "heretofore primary relationships" with other females. And why does male identification—the casting of one's social, political, and intellectual allegiances with men—exist among lifelong sexual lesbians? Barry's hypothesis throws us among new questions, but it clarifies the diversity of forms in which compulsory heterosexuality presents itself. In the mystique of the overpowering, all-conquering male sex drive, the penis-with-a-life-of-its-own, is rooted the law of male sex right to women, which justifies prostitution as a universal cultural assumption on the one hand, while defending sexual slavery within the family on the basis of "family privacy and cultural uniqueness" on the other.[38] The adolescent male sex drive, which, as both young women and men are taught, once triggered cannot take responsibility for itself or take no for an answer, becomes, according to Barry, the norm and rationale for adult male sexual behavior: a condition of *arrested sexual development.* Women learn to accept as natural the inevitability of this "drive" because they receive it as dogma. Hence, marital rape; hence, the Japanese wife resignedly packing her husband's suitcase for a weekend in the *kisaeng* brothels of Taiwan; hence, the psychological as well as economic imbalance of power between husband and wife, male employer and female worker, father and daughter, male professor and female student.

The effect of male identification means

> internalizing the values of the colonizer and actively participating in carrying out the colonization of one's self and one's sex. . . . Male identification is the act whereby women place men above women, including

themselves, in credibility, status, and importance in most situations, regardless of the comparative quality the women may bring to the situation. . . . Interaction with women is seen as a lesser form of relating on every level.[39]

What deserves further exploration is the doublethink many women engage in and from which no woman is permanently and utterly free: However woman-to-woman relationships, female support networks, a female and feminist value system are relied on and cherished, indoctrination in male credibility and status can still create synapses in thought, denials of feeling, wishful thinking, a profound sexual and intellectual confusion.[40] I quote here from a letter I received the day I was writing this passage: "I have had very bad relationships with men—I am now in the midst of a very painful separation. I am trying to find my strength through women—without my friends, I would not survive." How many times a day do women speak words like these or think them or write them, and how often does the synapse reassert itself?

Barry summarizes her findings:

Considering the arrested sexual development that is understood to be normal in the male population, and considering the numbers of men who are pimps, procurers, members of slavery gangs, corrupt officials participating in this traffic, owners, operators, employees of brothels and lodging and entertainment facilities, pornography purveyors, associated with prostitution, wife beaters, child molesters, incest perpetrators, johns (tricks) and rapists, one cannot but be momentarily stunned by the enormous male population engaging in female sexual slavery. The huge number of men engaged in these practices should be cause for declaration of an international emergency, a crisis in sexual violence. But what should be cause for alarm is instead accepted as normal sexual intercourse.[41]

Susan Cavin, in a rich and provocative, if highly speculative, dissertation, suggests that patriarchy becomes possible when the original female band, which includes children but ejects adolescent males, becomes invaded and outnumbered by males; that not patriarchal marriage, but the rape of the mother by the son, becomes the first act of male domination. The entering wedge, or leverage, which allows this to happen is not just a simple change in sex ratios; it is also the mother-child bond, manipulated by adolescent males in order to remain within the matrix past the age of exclusion. Maternal affection is used to establish male right of sexual access, which, however, must ever after be held by force (or through control of consciousness) since the original deep adult bonding is that of woman for woman.[42] I find this hypothesis extremely suggestive, since one form of false consciousness which serves compulsory heterosexuality is the maintenance of a mother–son relationship between women and men, including the demand that women provide maternal solace, nonjudgmental nurturing, and compassion for their harassers, rapists, and batterers (as well as for men who passively vampirize them).

But whatever its origins, when we look hard and clearly at the extent and elaboration of measures designed to keep women within a male sexual purlieu, it becomes an inescapable question whether the issue feminists have to address is not simple "gender inequality" nor the domination of culture by males nor mere "taboos against homosexuality," but the enforcement of heterosexuality for women as a means of assuring male right of physical, economic, and emotional access.[43] One of many means of enforcement is, of course, the rendering invisible of the lesbian possibility, an engulfed continent which rises fragmentedly into view from time to time only to become submerged again. Feminist research and theory that contribute to lesbian invisibility or marginality are actually working against the liberation and empowerment of women as a group.[44]

The assumption that "most women are innately heterosexual" stands as a theoretical and political stumbling block for feminism. It remains a tenable assumption partly because lesbian existence has been written out of history or catalogued under disease, partly because it has been treated as exceptional rather than intrinsic, partly because to acknowledge that for women heterosexuality may not be a "preference" at all but something that has had to be imposed, managed, organized, propagandized, and maintained by force is an immense step to take if you consider yourself freely and "innately" heterosexual. Yet the failure to examine heterosexuality as an institution is like failing to admit that the economic system called capitalism or the caste system of racism is maintained by a variety of forces, including both physical violence and false consciousness. To take the step of questioning heterosexuality as a "preference" or "choice" for women—and to do the intellectual and emotional work that follows—will call for a special quality of courage in heterosexually identified feminists, but I think the rewards will be great: a freeing-up of thinking, the exploring of new paths, the shattering of another great silence, new clarity in personal relationships.

III

I have chosen to use the terms *lesbian existence* and *lesbian continuum* because the word *lesbianism* has a clinical and limiting ring. *Lesbian existence* suggests both the fact of the historical presence of lesbians and our continuing creation of the meaning of that existence. I mean the term *lesbian continuum* to include a range—through each woman's life and throughout history—of woman-identified experience, not simply the fact that a woman has had or consciously desired genital sexual experience with another woman. If we expand it to embrace many more forms of primary intensity between and among women, including the sharing of a rich inner life, the bonding against male tyranny, the giving and receiving of practical and political support, if we can also hear it in such associations as *marriage resistance* and the "haggard" behavior identified by Mary Daly (obsolete meanings: "intractable," "willful," "wanton," and "unchaste," "a woman reluctant to yield to wooing"),[45] we begin to grasp breadths of female history and psychology which have lain out of reach as a consequence of limited, mostly clinical, definitions of *lesbianism.*

Lesbian existence comprises both the breaking of a taboo and the rejection of a compulsory way of life. It is also a direct or indirect attack on male right of access to women. But it is more than these, although we may first begin to perceive it as a form of naysaying to patriarchy, an act of resistance. It has, of course, included isolation, self-hatred, breakdown, alcoholism, suicide, and intrawoman violence; we romanticize at our peril what it means to love and act against the grain, and under heavy penalties; and lesbian existence has been lived (unlike, say, Jewish or Catholic existence) without access to any knowledge of a tradition, a continuity, a social underpinning. The destruction of records and memorabilia and letters documenting the realities of lesbian existence must be taken very seriously as a means of keeping heterosexuality compulsory for women, since what has been kept from our knowledge is joy, sensuality, courage, and community, as well as guilt, self-betrayal, and pain.[46]

Lesbians have historically been deprived of a political existence through "inclusion" as female versions of male homosexuality. To equate lesbian existence with male homosexuality because each is stigmatized is to erase female reality once again. Part of the history of lesbian existence is, obviously, to be found where lesbians, lacking a coherent female community, have shared a kind of social life and common cause with homosexual men. But there are differences: women's lack of economic and cultural privi-

lege relative to men; qualitative differences in female and male relationships—for example, the patterns of anonymous sex among male homosexuals, and the pronounced ageism in male homosexual standards of sexual attractiveness. I perceive the lesbian experience as being, like motherhood, a profoundly *female* experience, with particular oppressions, meanings, and potentialities we cannot comprehend as long as we simply bracket it with other sexually stigmatized existences. Just as the term *parenting* serves to conceal the particular and significant reality of being a parent who is actually a mother, the term *gay* may serve the purpose of blurring the very outlines we need to discern, which are of crucial value for feminism and for the freedom of women as a group.[47]

As the term *lesbian* has been held to limiting, clinical associations in its patriarchal definition, female friendship and comradeship have been set apart from the erotic, thus limiting the erotic itself. But as we deepen and broaden the range of what we define as lesbian existence, as we delineate a lesbian continuum, we begin to discover the erotic in female terms: as that which is unconfined to any single part of the body or solely to the body itself; as an energy not only diffuse but, as Audre Lorde has described it, omnipresent in "the sharing of joy, whether physical, emotional, psychic," and in the sharing of work; as the empowering joy which "makes us less willing to accept powerlessness, or those other supplied states of being which are not native to me, such as resignation, despair, self-effacement, depression, self-denial."[48] In another context, writing of women and work, I quoted the autobiographical passage in which the poet H. D. described how her friend Bryher supported her in persisting with the visionary experience which was to shape her mature work:

> I knew that this experience, this writing-on-the-wall before me, could not be shared with anyone except the girl who stood so bravely there beside me. This girl said without hesitation, "Go on." It was she really who had the detachment and integrity of the Pythoness of Delphi. But it was I, battered and dissociated . . . who was seeing the pictures, and who was reading the writing or granted the inner vision. Or perhaps, in some sense, we were "seeing" it together, for without her, admittedly, I could not have gone on.[49]

If we consider the possibility that all women—from the infant suckling at her mother's breast, to the grown woman experiencing orgasmic sensations while suckling her own child, perhaps recalling her mother's milk smell in her own, to two women, like Virginia Woolf's Chloe and Olivia, who share a laboratory,[50] to the woman dying at ninety, touched and handled by women—exist on a lesbian continuum, we can see ourselves as moving in and out of this continuum, whether we identify ourselves as lesbian or not.

We can then connect aspects of woman identification as diverse as the impudent, intimate girl friendships of eight or nine year olds and the banding together of those women of the 12th and 15th centuries known as Beguines who "shared houses, rented to one another, bequeathed houses to their room-mates . . . in cheap subdivided houses in the artisans' area of town," who "practiced Christian virtue on their own, dressing and living simply and not associating with men," who earned their livings as spinsters, bakers, nurses, or ran schools for young girls, and who managed—until the Church forced them to disperse—to live independent both of marriage and of conventual restrictions.[51] It allows us to connect these women with the more celebrated "Lesbians" of the women's school around Sappho of the 7th century B.C., with the secret sororities and economic networks reported among African women, and with the Chinese marriage-resistance sisterhoods—communities of women who refused marriage or who, if married, often refused to consummate their marriages and soon left their husbands, the only women in China who were not footbound and who, Agnes Smedley tells us, welcomed the births of daughters and organized successful women's strikes in the silk mills.[52] It allows us to connect and compare disparate individual instances of marriage resistance: for example, the strategies available to Emily Dickinson, a 19th-century white woman genius, with the strategies available to Zora Neale Hurston, a 20th-century Black woman genius. Dickinson never married, had tenuous intellectual friendships with men, lived self-convented in her genteel father's house in Amherst, and wrote a lifetime of passionate letters to her sister-in-law Sue Gilbert and a smaller group of such letters to her friend Kate Scott Anthon. Hurston married twice but soon left each husband, scrambled her way from Florida to Harlem to Columbia University to Haiti and finally back to Florida, moved in and out of white patronage and poverty, professional success, and failure; her survival relationships were all with women, beginning with her mother. Both of these women in their vastly different circumstances were marriage resisters, committed to their own work and selfhood, and were later characterized as "apolitical." Both were drawn to men of intellectual quality; for both of them women provided the ongoing fascination and sustenance of life.

If we think of heterosexuality as *the* natural emotional and sensual inclination for women, lives such as these are seen as deviant, as pathological, or as emotionally and sensually deprived. Or, in more recent and permissive jargon, they are banalized as "life styles." And the work of such women, whether merely the daily work of individual or collective survival and resistance or the work of the writer, the activist, the reformer, the anthropologist, or the artist—the work of self-creation—is undervalued, or seen as the bitter fruit of "penis envy" or the sublimation of repressed eroticism or the meaningless rant of a "man-hater." But when we turn the lens of vision and consider the degree to which and the methods whereby heterosexual "preference" has actually been imposed on women, not only can we understand differently the meaning of individual lives and work, but we can begin to recognize a central fact of women's history: that women have always resisted male tyranny. A feminism of action, often though not always without a theory, has constantly re-emerged in every culture and in every period. We can then begin to study women's struggle against powerlessness, women's radical rebellion, not just in male-defined "concrete revolutionary situations"[53] but in all the situations male ideologies have not perceived as revolutionary—for example, the refusal of some women to produce children, aided at great risk by other women,[54] the refusal to produce a higher standard of living and leisure for men (Leghorn and Parker show how both are part of women's unacknowledged, unpaid, and ununionized economic contribution). We can no longer have patience with Dinnerstein's view that women have simply collaborated with men in the "sexual arrangements" of history. We begin to observe behavior, both in history and in individual biography, that has hitherto been invisible or misnamed, behavior which often constitutes, given the limits of the counterforce exerted in a given time and place, radical rebellion. And we can connect these rebellions and the necessity for them with the physical passion of woman for woman which is central to lesbian existence: the erotic sensuality which has been, precisely, the most violently erased fact of female experience.

Heterosexuality has been both forcibly and subliminally imposed on women. Yet everywhere women have resisted it, often at the cost of physical torture, imprisonment, psychosurgery, social ostracism, and extreme poverty. "Compulsory heterosexuality" was named as one of the "crimes against women" by the Brussels International Tribunal Crimes against Women in 1976. Two pieces of testimony from two very different cultures reflect the degree to which persecution of lesbians is a global practice here and now. A report from Norway relates:

A lesbian in Oslo was in a heterosexual marriage that didn't work, so she started taking tranquillizers and ended up at the health sanatorium for treatment and rehabilitation. . . . The moment she said in family group therapy that she believed she was a lesbian, the doctor told her she was not. He knew from "looking into her eyes," he said. She had the eyes of a woman who wanted sexual intercourse with her husband. So she was subjected to so-called "couch therapy." She was put into a comfortably heated room, naked, on a bed, and for an hour her husband was to . . . try to excite her sexually. . . . The idea was that the touching was always to end with sexual intercourse. She felt stronger and stronger aversion. She threw up and sometimes ran out of the room to avoid this "treatment." The more strongly she asserted that she was a lesbian, the more violent the forced heterosexual intercourse became. This treatment went on for about six months. She escaped from the hospital, but she was brought back. Again she escaped. She has not been there since. In the end she realized that she had been subjected to forcible rape for six months.

And from Mozambique:

I am condemned to a life of exile because I will not deny that I am a lesbian, that my primary commitments are, and will always be to other women. In the new Mozambique, lesbianism is considered a left-over from colonialism and decadent Western civilization. Lesbians are sent to rehabilitation camps to learn through self-criticism the correct line about themselves. . . . If I am forced to denounce my own love for women, if I therefore denounce myself, I could go back to Mozambique and join forces in the exciting and hard struggle of rebuilding a nation, including the struggle for the emancipation of Mozambiquan women. As it is, I either risk the rehabilitation camps, or remain in exile.[55]

Nor can it be assumed that women like those in Carroll Smith-Rosenberg's study, who married, stayed married, yet dwelt in a profoundly female emotional and passional world, "preferred" or "chose" heterosexuality. Women have married because it was necessary, in order to survive economically, in order to have children who would not suffer economic deprivation or social ostracism, in order to remain respectable, in order to do what was expected of women, because coming out of "abnormal" childhoods they wanted to feel "normal" and because heterosexual romance has been represented as the great female adventure, duty,

and fulfillment. We may faithfully or ambivalently have obeyed the institution, but our feelings—and our sensuality—have not been tamed or contained within it. There is no statistical documentation of the numbers of lesbians who have remained in heterosexual marriages for most of their lives. But in a letter to the early lesbian publication *The Ladder,* the playwright Lorraine Hansberry had this to say:

I suspect that the problem of the married woman who would prefer emotional-physical relationships with other women is proportionally much higher than a similar statistic for men. (A statistic surely no one will ever really have.) This because the estate of women being what it is, how could we ever begin to guess the numbers of women who are not prepared to risk a life alien to what they have been taught all their lives to believe was their "natural" destiny—AND—their only expectation for ECONOMIC security. It seems to be that this is why the question has an immensity that it does not have for male homosexuals. . . . A woman of strength and honesty may, if she chooses, sever her marriage and marry a new male mate and society will be upset that the divorce rate is rising so—but there are few places in the United States, in any event, where she will be anything remotely akin to an "outcast." Obviously this is not true for a woman who would end her marriage to take up life with another woman.[56]

This *double life*—this apparent acquiescence to an institution founded on male interest and prerogative—has been characteristic of female experience: in motherhood and in many kinds of heterosexual behavior, including the rituals of courtship; the pretense of asexuality by the 19th-century wife; the simulation of orgasm by the prostitute, the courtesan, the 20th-century "sexually liberated" woman.

Meridel LeSueur's documentary novel of the depression, *The Girl,* is arresting as a study of female double life. The protagonist, a waitress in a St. Paul working-class speakeasy, feels herself passionately attracted to the young man Butch, but her survival relationships are with Clara, an older waitress and prostitute, with Belle, whose husband owns the bar, and with Amelia, a union activist. For Clara and Belle and the unnamed protagonist, sex with men is in one sense an escape from the bedrock misery of daily life, a flare of intensity in the gray, relentless, often brutal web of day-to-day existence:

It was like he was a magnet pulling me. It was exciting and powerful and frightening. He was after me too and when he found me I would run, or be petrified, just standing in front of him like a zany. And he told me not to be wandering with Clara to the Marigold where we danced with strangers. He said he would knock the shit out of me. Which made me shake and tremble, but it was better than being a husk full of suffering and not knowing why.[57]

Throughout the novel the theme of double life emerges; Belle reminisces about her marriage to the bootlegger Hoinck:

You know, when I had that black eye and said I hit it on the cupboard, well he did it the bastard, and then he says don't tell anybody. . . . He's nuts, that's what he is, nuts, and I don't see why I live with him, why I put up with him a minute on this earth. But listen kid, she said, I'm telling you something. She looked at me and her face was wonderful. She said, Jesus Christ, Goddam him I love him that's why I'm hooked like this all my life, Goddam him I love him.[58]

After the protagonist has her first sex with Butch, her women friends care for her bleeding, give her whiskey, and compare notes.

My luck, the first time and I got into trouble. He gave me a little money and I come to St. Paul where for ten bucks they'd stick a huge vet's needle into you and you start it and then you were on your own. . . . I never had no child. I've just had Hoinck to mother, and a hell of a child he is.[59]

Later they made me go back to Clara's room to lie down. . . . Clara lay down beside me and put her arms around me and wanted me to tell her about it but she wanted to tell about herself. She said she started it when she was twelve with a bunch of boys in an old shed. She said nobody had paid any attention to her before and she became very popular.. . . They like it so much, she said, why shouldn't you give it to them and get presents and attention? I never cared anything for it and neither did my mama. But it's the only thing you got that's valuable.[60]

Sex is thus equated with attention from the male, who is charismatic though brutal, infantile, or unreliable. Yet it is the women who make life endurable for each other, give physical affection without causing pain, share, advise, and stick by each other. (*I am trying to find my strength through women—without my friends, I could not survive.*) LeSueur's *The Girl* parallels Toni Morrison's remarkable *Sula,* another revelation of female double life:

Nel was the one person who had wanted nothing from her, who had accepted all aspects of her. . . . Nel was one of the reasons Sula had drifted back to Medallion. . . . The men . . . had merged into one large personality: the same language of love, the same entertainments of love, the same cooling of love. Whenever she introduced her private thoughts into their rubbings and goings, they hooded their eyes. They taught her nothing but love tricks, shared nothing but worry, gave nothing but money. She had been looking all along for a friend, and it took her a while to discover that a lover was not a comrade and could never be—for a woman.

But Sula's last thought at the second of her death is "Wait'll I tell Nel." And after Sula's death, Nel looks back on her own life:

"All that time, all that time, I thought I was missing Jude." And the loss pressed down on her chest and came up into her throat. "We was girls together," she said as though explaining something. "O Lord, Sula," she cried, "Girl, girl, girlgirlgirl!" It was a fine cry—loud and long—but it had no bottom and it had no top, just circles and circles of sorrow.[61]

The Girl and *Sula* are both novels which examine what I am calling the lesbian continuum, in contrast to the shallow or sensational "lesbian scenes" in recent commercial fiction.[62] Each shows us woman identification untarnished (till the end of LeSueur's novel) by romanticism; each depicts the competition of heterosexual compulsion for women's attention, the diffusion and frustration of female bonding that might, in a more conscious form, reintegrate love and power.

IV

Woman identification is a source of energy, a potential springhead of female power, curtailed and contained under the institution of heterosexuality. The denial of reality and visibility to women's passion for women, women's choice of women as allies, life companions, and community, the forcing of such relationships into dissimulation and their disintegration under intense pressure have meant an incalculable loss to the power of all women *to change the social relations of the sexes, to liberate ourselves and each other.* The lie of compulsory female heterosexuality today afflicts not just feminist scholarship but every profession, every reference work, every curriculum, every organizing attempt, every relationship or conversation over which it hovers. It creates, specifically, a profound falseness, hypocrisy, and hysteria in the heterosexual dialogue, for every heterosexual relationship is lived in the queasy strobe light of that lie. However we choose to identify ourselves, however we find ourselves labeled, it flickers across and distorts our lives.[63]

The lie keeps numberless women psychologically trapped, trying to fit mind, spirit, and sexuality into a prescribed script because they cannot look beyond the parameters of the acceptable. It pulls on the energy of such women even as it drains the energy of "closeted" lesbians—the energy exhausted in the double life. The lesbian trapped in the "closet," the woman imprisoned in prescriptive ideas of the "normal" share the pain of blocked options, broken connections, lost access to self-definition freely and powerfully assumed.

The lie is many-layered. In Western tradition, one layer—the romantic—asserts that women are inevitably, even if rashly and tragically, drawn to men; that even when that attraction is suicidal (e.g., *Tristan and Isolde,* Kate Chopin's *The Awakening*), it is still an organic imperative. In the tradition of the social sciences it asserts that primary love between the sexes is "normal"; that women *need* men as social and economic protectors, for adult sexuality, and for psychological completion; that the heterosexually constituted family is the basic social unit, that women who do not attach their primary intensity to men must be, in functional terms, condemned to an even more devastating outsiderhood than their outsiderhood as women. Small wonder that lesbians are reported to be a more hidden population than male homosexuals. The Black lesbian-feminist critic Lorraine Bethel, writing on Zora Neale Hurston, remarks that for a Black woman—already twice an outsider—to choose to assume still another "hated identity" is problematic indeed. Yet the lesbian continuum has been a life line for Black women both in Africa and the United States.

Black women have a long tradition of bonding together . . . in a Black/women's community that has been a source of vital survival information, psychic and emotional support for us. We have a distinct Black woman-identified folk culture based on our experiences as Black women in this society; symbols, language and modes of expression that are specific to the realities of our lives. . . . Because Black women were rarely among those Blacks and females who gained access to literary and other acknowledged forms of artistic expression, this Black female bonding and Black woman-identification has often been hidden and unrecorded except in the individual lives of Black women through our own memories of our particular Black female tradition.[64]

Another layer of the lie is the frequently encountered implication that women turn to women out of hatred for men. Profound skepticism, caution, and righteous paranoia about men may indeed be part of any healthy woman's response to the misogyny of male-dominated culture, to the forms assumed by "normal" male sexuality, and to *the failure even of "sensitive" or "political" men to perceive or find these troubling.* Lesbian existence is also represented as mere refuge from male abuses, rather than as an electric and empowering charge between women. One of the most frequently quoted literary passages on lesbian relationship is that in which Colette's Renée, in *The Vagabond,* describes "the melancholy and touching image of two weak creatures who have perhaps found shelter in each other's arms, there to sleep and weep, safe from man who is often cruel, and there to taste *better than any pleasure, the bitter happiness of feeling themselves akin, frail and forgotten* [emphasis added]."[65] Colette is often considered a lesbian writer. Her popular reputation has, I think, much to do with the fact that she writes about lesbian existence as if for a male audience; her earliest "lesbian" novels, the Claudine series, were written under compulsion for her husband and published under both their names. At all events, except for her writings on her mother, Colette is a less reliable source on the lesbian continuum than, I would think, Charlotte Brontë, who understood that while women may, indeed must, be one another's allies, mentors, and comforters in the female struggle for survival, there is quite extraneous delight in each other's company and attraction to each others' minds and character, which attend a recognition of each others' strengths.

By the same token, we can say that there is a *nascent* feminist political content in the act of choosing a woman lover or life partner in the face of institutionalized heterosexuality.[66] But for lesbian existence to realize this political content in an ultimately liberating form, the erotic choice must deepen and expand into conscious woman identification—into lesbian feminism.

The work that lies ahead, of unearthing and describing what I call here "lesbian existence," is potentially liberating for all women. It is work that must assuredly move beyond the limits of white and middle-class Western Women's Studies to examine women's lives, work, and groupings within every racial, ethnic, and political structure. There are differences, moreover, between "lesbian existence" and the "lesbian continuum," differences we can discern even in the movement of our own lives. The lesbian continuum, I suggest, needs delineation in light of the "double life" of women, not only women self-described as heterosexual but also of self-described lesbians. We need a far more exhaustive account of the forms the double life has assumed. Historians need to ask at every point how heterosexuality as institution has been organized and maintained through the female wage scale, the enforcement of middle-class women's "leisure," the glamorization of so-called sexual liberation, the withholding of education from women, the imagery of "high art" and popular culture, the mystification of the "personal" sphere, and much else. We need an economics which comprehends the institution of heterosexuality, with its doubled workload for women and its sexual divisions of labor, as the most idealized of economic relations.

The question inevitably will arise: Are we then to condemn all heterosexual relationships, including those which are least oppressive? I believe this question, though often heartfelt, is the wrong question here. We have been stalled in a maze of false dichotomies which prevents our apprehending the institution as a whole: "good" versus "bad" marriages; "marriage for love" versus arranged marriage; "liberated" sex versus prostitution; heterosexual intercourse versus rape; *Liebeschmerz* versus humiliation and dependency. Within the institution exist, of course, qualitative differences of experience; but the absence of choice remains the great unacknowledged reality, and in the absence of choice, women will remain dependent upon the chance or luck of particular relationships and will have no collective power to determine the meaning and place of sexuality in their lives. As we address the institution itself, moreover, we begin to perceive a history of female resistance which has never fully understood itself because it has been so fragmented, miscalled, erased. It will require a courageous grasp of the politics and economics, as well as the cultural propaganda, of heterosexuality to carry us beyond individual cases or diversified group situations into the complex kind of overview needed to undo the power men everywhere wield over women, power which has become a model for every other form of exploitation and illegitimate control.

AFTERWORD

In 1980, Ann Snitow, Christine Stansell, and Sharon Thompson, three Marxist-feminist activists and scholars, sent out a call for papers for an anthology on the politics of

sexuality. Having just finished writing "Compulsory Heterosexuality" for *Signs,* I sent them that manuscript and asked them to consider it. Their anthology, *Powers of Desire,* was published by the Monthly Review Press New Feminist Library in 1983 and included my paper. During the intervening period, the four of us were in correspondence, but I was able to take only limited advantage of this dialogue due to ill health and resulting surgery. With their permission, I reprint here excerpts from that correspondence as a way of indicating that my essay should be read as one contribution to a long exploration in progress, not as my own "last word" on sexual politics. I also refer interested readers to *Powers of Desire* itself.

Dear Adrienne,

. . . In one of our first letters, we told you that we were finding parameters of left-wing/feminist sexual discourse to be far broader than we imagined. Since then, we have perceived what we believe to be a crisis in the feminist movement about sex, an intensifying debate (although not always an explicit one), and a questioning of assumptions once taken for granted. While we fear the link between sex and violence, as do Women Against Pornography, we wish we better understood its sources in ourselves as well as in men. In the Reagan era, we can hardly afford to romanticize any old norm of a virtuous and moral sexuality.

In your piece, you are asking the question, what would women choose in a world where patriarchy and capitalism did *not* rule? We agree with you that heterosexuality is an institution created between these grind stones, but we don't conclude, therefore, that it is entirely a male creation. You only allow for female historical agency insofar as women exist on the lesbian continuum while we would argue that women's history, like men's history, is created out of a dialectic of necessity and choice.

All three of us (hence one lesbian, two heterosexual women) had questions about your use of the term "false consciousness" for women's heterosexuality. In general, we think the false-consciousness model can blind us to the necessities and desires that comprise the lives of the oppressed. It can also lead to the too easy denial of others' experience when that experience is different from our own. We posit, rather, a complex social model in which all erotic life is a continuum, one which therefore includes relations with men.

Which brings us to this metaphor of the continuum. We know you are a poet, not an historian, and we look forward to reading your metaphors all our lives—and standing straighter as feminists, as women, for having read them. But the metaphor of the lesbian continuum is open to all kinds of misunderstandings, and these sometimes have odd political effects. For example, Sharon reports that at a recent meeting around the abortion-rights struggle, the notions of continuum arose in the discussion several times and underwent divisive transformation. Overall, the notion that two ways of being existed on the same continuum was interpreted to mean that those two ways were the *same*. The sense of range and gradation that your description evokes disappeared. Lesbianism and female friendship became exactly the same thing. Similarly, heterosexuality and rape became the same. In one of several versions of the continuum that evolved, a slope was added, like so:

Lesbianism

          Sex with men,
          no penetration

                    Sex with men,
                       penetration

                                    Rape

This sloped continuum brought its proponents to the following conclusion: An appropriate, workable abortion-rights strategy is to inform all women that heterosexual penetration is rape, whatever their subjective experiences to the contrary. All women will immediately recognize the truth of this and opt for the alternative of nonpenetration. The abortion-rights struggle will thus be simplified into a struggle against coercive sex and its consequences (since no enlightened woman would voluntarily undergo penetration unless her object was procreation—a peculiarly Catholic-sounding view).

The proponents of this strategy were young women who have worked hard in the abortion-rights movement for the past two or more years. They are inexperienced but they are dedicated. For this reason, we take their reading of your work seriously. We don't think, however, that it comes solely, or even at all, from the work itself. As likely a source is the tendency to dichotomize that has plagued the women's movement. The source of that tendency is harder to trace.

In that regard, the hints in "Compulsory" about the double life of women intrigue us. You define the double life as "the apparent acquiescence to an institution founded on male interest and prerogative." But that definition doesn't really explain your other references—to, for instance, the "intense mixture" of love and anger in lesbian relationships and to the peril of romanticizing what it means "to love and

act against the grain." We think these comments raise extremely important issues for feminists right now; the problem of division and anger among us needs airing and analysis. Is this, by any chance, the theme of a piece you have in the works?

. . . We would still love it if we could have a meeting with you in the next few months. Any chance? . . . Greetings and support from us—in all your undertakings.

                        We send love,
                        Sharon, Chris, and Ann

New York City
April 19, 1981

Dear Ann, Chris, and Sharon,

. . . It's good to be back in touch with you, you who have been so unfailingly patient, generous, and persistent. Above all, it's important to me that you know that ill health, not a withdrawal because of political differences, delayed my writing back to you. . . .

"False consciousness" can, I agree, be used as a term of dismissal for any thinking we don't like to adhere to. But, as I tried to illustrate in some detail, there is a real, identifiable system of heterosexual propaganda, of defining women as existing for the sexual use of men, which goes beyond "sex role" or "gender" stereotyping or "sexist imagery" to include a vast number of verbal and nonverbal messages. And this I call "control of consciousness." The possibility of a woman who does not exist sexually for men—the lesbian possibility—is buried, erased, occluded, distorted, misnamed, and driven underground. The feminist books—Chodorow, Dinnerstein, Ehrenreich and English, and others—which I discuss at the beginning of my essay contribute to this invalidation and era-sure, and as such are part of the problem.

My essay is founded on the belief that we all think from within the limits of certain solipsisms—usually linked with privilege, racial, cultural, and economic as well as sexual—which present themselves as "the universal," "the way things are," "all women," etc., etc. I wrote it equally out of the belief that in becoming conscious of our solipsisms we have certain kinds of choices, that we can and must re-educate ourselves. I never have maintained that heterosexual feminists are walking about in a state of "brainwashed" false consciousness. Nor have such phrases as "sleeping with the enemy" seemed to me either profound or useful. *Homophobia* is too diffuse a term and does not go very far in helping us identify and talk about the sexual solipsism of heterosexual feminism. In this paper I was trying to ask heterosexual feminists to examine their experience of heterosexuality critically and antagonistically, to critique the institution of which they are a part, to struggle with the norm and its implications for women's freedom, to become more open to the considerable resources offered by the lesbian-feminist perspective, to refuse to settle for the personal privilege and solution of the individual "good relationship" within the institution of heterosexuality.

As regards "female historical agency," I wanted, precisely, to suggest that the victim model is insufficient; that there *is* a history of female agency and choice which has actually challenged aspects of male supremacy; that, like male supremacy, these can be found in many different cultures. . . . It's not that I think all female agency has been solely and avowedly lesbian. But by erasing lesbian existence from female history, from theory, from literary criticism . . . from feminist approaches to economic structure, ideas about "the family," etc., an enormous amount of female agency is kept unavailable, hence unusable. I wanted to demonstrate that that kind of obliteration continues to be acceptable in seriously regarded feminist texts. What surprised me in the responses to my essay, including your notes, is how almost every aspect of it has been considered, except this—to me—central one. I was taking a position which was neither lesbian/separatist in the sense of dismissing heterosexual women nor a "gay civil rights" plea for . . . openness to lesbianism as an "option" or an "alternate life style." I was urging that lesbian *existence* has been an unrecognized and unaffirmed claiming by women of their sexuality, thus a pattern of resistance, thus also a kind of borderline position from which to analyze and challenge the relationship of heterosexuality to male supremacy. And that lesbian existence, when recognized, demands a conscious restructuring of feminist analysis and criticism, not just a token reference or two.

I certainly agree with you that the term *lesbian continuum* can be misused. It was, in the example you report of the abortion-rights meeting, though I would think anyone who had read my work from *Of Woman Born* onward would know that my position on abortion and sterilization abuse is more complicated than that. My own problem with the phrase is that it can be, is, used by women who have not yet begun to examine the privileges and solipsisms of heterosexuality, as a safe way to describe their felt connections with women, without having to share in the risks and threats of lesbian existence. What I had thought to delineate rather complexly as a continuum has begun to sound more like "life-style shopping." *Lesbian continuum*—the phrase—came from a desire to allow for the greatest possible varia-

tion of female-identified experience, while paying a different kind of respect to *lesbian existence*—the traces and knowledge of women who have made their primary erotic and emotional choices for women. If I were writing the paper today, I would still want to make this distinction, but would put more caveats around *lesbian continuum.* I fully agree with you that Smith-Rosenberg's "female world" is not a social ideal, enclosed as it is within prescriptive middle-class heterosexuality and marriage.

My own essay could have been stronger had it drawn on more of the literature by Black women toward which Toni Morrison's *Sula* inevitably pointed me. In reading a great deal more of Black women's fiction I began to perceive a different set of valences from those found in white women's fiction for the most part: a different quest for the woman hero, a different relationship both to sexuality with men and to female loyalty and bonding. . . .

You comment briefly on your reactions to some of the radical-feminist works I cited in my first footnote.[67] I am myself critical of some of them even as I found them vitally useful. What most of them share is a taking seriously of misogyny—of organized, institutionalized, normalized hostility and violence against women. I feel no "hierarchy of oppressions" is needed in order for us to take misogyny as seriously as we take racism, anti-Semitism, imperialism. To take misogyny seriously needn't mean that we perceive women merely as victims, without responsibilities or choices; it does mean recognizing the "necessity" in that "dialectic of necessity and choice"—identifying, describing, refusing to turn aside our eyes. I think that some of the apparent reductiveness, or even obsessiveness, of some white radical-feminist theory derives from racial and/or class solipsism, but also from the immense effort of trying to render women hating visible amid so much denial. . . .

Finally, as to poetry and history: I want both in my life; I need to see through both. If metaphor can be misconstrued, history can also lead to misconstrual when it obliterates acts of resistance or rebellion, wipes out transformational models, or sentimentalizes power relationships. I know you know this. I believe we are all trying to think and write out of our best consciences, our most open consciousness. I expect that quality in this book which you are editing, and look forward with anticipation to the thinking—and the actions—toward which it may take us.

In sisterhood,
Adrienne

Montague, Massachusetts
November 1981

NOTES

1. See, for example, Paula Gunn Allen, *The Sacred Hoop: Recovering the Feminine in American Indian Traditions* (Boston: Beacon, 1986); Beth Brant, ed., *A Gathering of Spirit: Writing and Art by North American Indian Women* (Montpelier, Vt.: Sinister Wisdom Books, 1984); Gloria Anzaldúa and Cherríe Moraga, eds., *This Bridge Called My Back: Writings by Radical Women of Color* (Watertown, Mass.: Persephone, 1981; distributed by Kitchen Table/Women of Color Press, Albany, N.Y.); J. R. Roberts, *Black Lesbians: An Annotated Bibliography* (Tallahassee, Fla.: Naiad, 1981); Barbara Smith, ed., *Home Girls: A Black Feminist Anthology* (Albany, N.Y.: Kitchen Table/Women of Color Press, 1984). As Lorraine Bethel and Barbara Smith pointed out in *Conditions 5: The Black Women's Issue* (1980), a great deal of fiction by Black women depicts primary relationships between women. I would like to cite here the work of Ama Ata Aidoo, Toni Cade Bambara, Buchi Emecheta, Bessie Head, Zora Neale Hurston, Alice Walker. Donna Allegra, Red Jordan Arobateau, Audre Lorde, Ann Allen Shockley, among others, write directly as Black lesbians. For fiction by other lesbians of color, see Elly Bulkin, ed., *Lesbian Fiction: An Anthology* (Watertown, Mass.: Persephone, 1981).

See also, for accounts of contemporary Jewish-lesbian existence, Evelyn Torton Beck, ed., *Nice Jewish Girls: A Lesbian Anthology* (Watertown, Mass.: Persephone, 1982; distributed by Crossing Press, Trumansburg, N.Y. 14886); Alice Bloch, *Lifetime Guarantee* (Watertown, Mass.: Persephone, 1982); and Melanie Kaye-Kantrowitz and Irena Klepfisz, eds., *The Tribe of Dina: A Jewish Women's Anthology* (Montpelier, Vt.: Sinister Wisdom Books, 1986).

The earliest formulation that I know of heterosexuality as an institution was in the lesbian-feminist paper *The Furies,* founded in 1971. For a collection of articles from that paper, see Nancy Myron and Charlotte Bunch, eds., *Lesbianism and the Women's Movement* (Oakland, Calif.: Diana Press, 1975; distributed by Crossing Press, Trumansburg, N.Y. 14886).

2. Alice Rossi, "Children and Work in the Lives of Women," paper delivered at the University of Arizona, Tucson, February 1976.

3. Doris Lessing, *The Golden Notebook,* 1962 (New York: Bantam, 1977), p. 480.

4. Nancy Chodorow, *The Reproduction of Mothering* (Berkeley: University of California Press, 1978); Dorothy Dinnerstein, *The Mermaid and the Minotaur: Sexual Arrangements and the Human Malaise* (New York: Harper & Row, 1976); Barbara Ehrenreich and Deirdre English, *For Her Own Good: 150 Years of the Experts' Advice to Women* (Garden City, N.Y.: Doubleday, Anchor, 1978); Jean Baker Miller, *Toward a New Psychology of Women* (Boston: Beacon, 1976).

5. I could have chosen many other serious and influential recent books, including anthologies, which would illustrate the same point: e.g., *Our Bodies, Ourselves,* the Boston Women's Health Book Collective's best seller (New York: Simon and Schuster, 1976), which devotes a separate (and inadequate) chapter to lesbians, but whose message is that heterosexuality is most women's life preference; Berenice Carroll, ed., *Liberating Women's History: Theoretical and Critical Essays* (Urbana: University of Illinois Press, 1976), which does not include even a token essay on the lesbian presence in history, though an essay by Linda Gordon, Persis Hunt, et al. notes the use by male historians of "sexual deviance" as a category to discredit and dismiss Anna Howard Shaw, Jane Addams, and other feminists ("Historical Phallacies: Sexism in American Historical Writing"); and Renate Bridenthal and Claudia Koonz, eds., *Becoming Visible: Women in European History* (Boston: Houghton Mifflin, 1977), which contains three mentions of male homosexuality but no materials that I have been able to locate on lesbians. Gerda Lerner, ed., *The Female Experience: An American Documentary* (Indianapolis: Bobbs-Merrill, 1977), contains an abridgment of two lesbian-feminist–position papers from the contemporary movement but no other documentation of lesbian existence. Lerner does note in her preface, however, how the charge of deviance has been used to fragment women and discourage women's resistance. Linda Gordon, in *Woman's Body, Woman's Right: A Social History of Birth Control in America* (New York: Viking, Grossman, 1976), notes accurately that "it is not that feminism has produced more lesbians. There have always been many lesbians, despite the high levels of repression; and most lesbians experience their sexual preference as innate" (p. 410).

[A. R., 1986: I am glad to update the first annotation in this footnote. *"The New" Our Bodies, Ourselves* (New York: Simon and Schuster, 1984) contains an expanded chapter on "Loving Women: Lesbian Life and Relationships" and furthermore emphasizes *choices* for women throughout—in terms of sexuality, health care, family, politics, etc.]

6. Jonathan Katz, ed., *Gay American History: Lesbians and Gay Men in the U.S.A.* (New York: Thomas Y. Crowell, 1976).

7. Nancy Sahli, "Smashing Women's Relationships before the Fall," *Chrysalis: A Magazine of Women's Culture* 8 (1979): 17–27.

8. This is a book which I have publicly endorsed. I would still do so, though with the above caveat. It is only since beginning to write this article that I fully appreciated how enormous is the unasked question in Ehrenreich and English's book.

9. See, for example, Kathleen Barry, *Female Sexual Slavery* (Englewood Cliffs, N.J.: Prentice-Hall, 1979); Mary Daly, *Gyn/Ecology: The Metaethics of Radical Feminism* (Boston: Beacon, 1978); Susan Griffin, *Woman and Nature: The Roaring inside Her* (New York: Harper & Row, 1978); Diana Russell and Nicole van de Ven, eds., *Proceedings of the International Tribunal of Crimes against Women* (Millbrae, Calif.: Les Femmes, 1976); and Susan Brownmiller, *Against Our Will: Men, Women and Rape* (New York: Simon and Schuster, 1975); *Aegis: Magazine on Ending Violence against Women* (Feminist Alliance against Rape, P.O. Box 21033, Washington, D.C. 20009).

[A. R., 1986: Work on both incest and on woman battering has appeared in the 1980s which I did not cite in the essay. See Florence Rush, *The Best-kept Secret* (New York: McGraw-Hill, 1980); Louise Armstrong, *Kiss Daddy Goodnight: A Speakout on Incest* (New York: Pocket Books, 1979); Sandra Butler, *Conspiracy of Silence: The Trauma of Incest* (San Francisco: New Glide, 1978); F. Delacoste and F. Newman, eds., *Fight Back!: Feminist Resistance to Male Violence* (Minneapolis: Cleis Press, 1981); Judy Freespirit, *Daddy's Girl: An Incest Survivor's Story* (Langlois, Ore.: Diaspora Distribution, 1982); Judith Herman, *Father-Daughter Incest* (Cambridge, Mass.: Harvard University Press, 1981); Toni McNaron and Yarrow Morgan, eds., *Voices in the Night: Women Speaking about Incest* (Minneapolis: Cleis Press, 1982); and Betsy Warrior's richly informative, multipurpose compilation of essays, statistics, listings, and facts, the *Battered Women's Directory* (formerly entitled *Working on Wife Abuse*), 8th ed. (Cambridge, Mass.: 1982).]

10. Dinnerstein, p. 272.

11. Chodorow, pp. 197–198.

12. Ibid., pp. 198–199.

13. Ibid., p. 200.

14. Kathleen Gough, "The Origin of the Family," in *Toward an Anthropology of Women,* ed. Rayna [Rapp] Reiter (New York: Monthly Review Press, 1975), pp. 69–70.

15. Barry, pp. 216–219.

16. Anna Demeter, *Legal Kidnapping* (Boston: Beacon, 1977), pp. xx, 126–128.

17. Daly, pp. 139–141, 163–165.

18. Barbara Ehrenreich and Deirdre English, *Witches, Midwives and Nurses: A History of Women Healers* (Old Westbury, N.Y.: Feminist Press, 1973); Andrea Dworkin, *Woman Hating* (New York: Dutton, 1974), pp. 118–154; Daly, pp. 178–222.

19. See Virginia Woolf, *A Room of One's Own* (London: Hogarth, 1929), and ibid., *Three Guineas* (New York: Harcourt Brace, [1938] 1966); Tillie Olsen, *Silences* (Boston: Delacorte, 1978); Michelle Cliff, "The Resonance of Interruption" *Chrysalis: A Magazine of Women's Culture* 8 (1979): 29–37.

20. Mary Daly, *Beyond God the Father* (Boston: Beacon, 1973), pp. 347–351; Olsen, pp. 22–46.

21. Daly, *Beyond God the Father,* p. 93.

22. Fran P. Hosken, "The Violence of Power: Genital Mutilation of Females," *Heresies: A Feminist Journal of Art and Politics* 6 (1979): 28–35; Russell and van de Ven, pp. 194–195.

[A. R., 1986: See especially "Circumcision of Girls," in Nawal El Saadawi, *The Hidden Face of Eve: Women in the Arab World* (Boston: Beacon, 1982), pp. 33–43.]

23. Barry, pp. 163–164.

24. The issue of "lesbian sadomasochism" needs to be examined in terms of dominant cultures' teachings about the relation of sex and violence. I believe this to be another example of the "double life" of women.

25. Catharine A. MacKinnon, *Sexual Harassment of Working Women: A Case of Sex Discrimination* (New Haven, Conn.: Yale University Press, 1979), pp. 15–16.

26. Ibid., p. 174.

27. Brownmiller, *Against Our Will.*

28. MacKinnon, p. 219. Susan Schecter writes: "The push for heterosexual union at whatever cost is so intense that . . . it has become a cultural force of its own that creates battering. The ideology of romantic love and its jealous possession of the partner as property provide the masquerade for what can become severe abuse" (*Aegis: Magazine on Ending Violence against Women* [July–August 1979]: 50–51).

29. MacKinnon, p. 298.

30. Ibid., p. 220.

31. Ibid., p. 221.

32. Barry, *Female Sexual Slavery.*

[A. R., 1986: See also Kathleen Barry, Charlotte Bunch, and Shirley Castley, eds., *International Feminism: Networking against Female Sexual Slavery* (New York: International Women's Tribune Center, 1984).]

33. Barry, p. 33.

34. Ibid., p. 103.

35. Ibid., p. 5.

36. Ibid., p. 100.

[A. R., 1986: This statement has been taken as claiming that "all women are victims" purely and simply, or that "all heterosexuality equals sexual slavery." I would say, rather, that all women are affected, though differently, by dehumanizing attitudes and practices directed at women as a group.]

37. Ibid., p. 218.

38. Ibid., p. 140.

39. Ibid., p. 172.

40. Elsewhere I have suggested that male identification has been a powerful source of white women's racism and that it has often been women already seen as "disloyal" to male codes and systems who have actively battled against it (Adrienne Rich, "Disloyal to Civilization: Feminism, Racism, Gynephobia," in *On Lies, Secrets, and Silence: Selected Prose, 1966–1978* [New York: W. W. Norton, 1979]).

41. Barry, p. 220.

42. Susan Cavin, "Lesbian Origins" (Ph.D. diss., Rutgers University, 1978), unpublished, ch. 6.

[A. R., 1986: This dissertation was recently published as *Lesbian Origins* (San Francisco: Ism Press, 1986).]

43. For my perception of heterosexuality as an economic institution I am indebted to Lisa Leghorn and Katherine Parker, who allowed me to read the unpublished manuscript of their book *Woman's Worth: Sexual Economics and the World of Women* (London and Boston: Routledge & Kegan Paul, 1981).

44. I would suggest that lesbian existence has been most recognized and tolerated where it has resembled a "deviant" version of heterosexuality—e.g., where lesbians have, like Stein and Toklas, played heterosexual roles (or seemed to in public) and have been chiefly identified with male culture. See also Claude E. Schaeffer, "The Kuterai Female Berdache: Courier, Guide, Prophetess and Warrior," *Ethnohistory* 12, no. 3 (Summer 1965): 193–236. (Berdache: "an individual of a definite physiological sex [m. or f.]

who assumes the role and status of the opposite sex and who is viewed by the community as being of one sex physiologically but as having assumed the role and status of the opposite sex" [Schaeffer, p. 231].) Lesbian existence has also been relegated to an upper-class phenomenon, an elite decadence (as in the fascination with Paris salon lesbians such as Renée Vivien and Natalie Clifford Barney), to the obscuring of such "common women" as Judy Grahn depicts in her *The Work of a Common Woman* (Oakland, Calif.: Diana Press, 1978) and *True to Life Adventure Stories* (Oakland, Calif.: Diana Press, 1978).

45. Daly, *Gyn/Ecology,* p. 15.

46. "In a hostile world in which women are not supposed to survive except in relation with and in service to men, entire communities of women were simply erased. History tends to bury what it seeks to reject" (Blanche W. Cook, "'Women Alone Stir My Imagination': Lesbianism and the Cultural Tradition," *Signs: Journal of Women in Culture and Society* 4, no. 4 [Summer 1970]: 719–720). The Lesbian Herstory Archives in New York City is one attempt to preserve contemporary documents on lesbian existence—a project of enormous value and meaning, working against the continuing censorship and obliteration of relationships, networks, communities in other archives and elsewhere in the culture.

47. [A. R., 1986: The shared historical and spiritual "crossover" functions of lesbians and gay men in cultures past and present are traced by Judy Grahn in *Another Mother Tongue: Gay Words, Gay Worlds* (Boston: Beacon, 1984). I now think we have much to learn both from the uniquely female aspects of lesbian existence and from the complex "gay" identity we share with gay men.]

48. Audre Lorde, "Uses of the Erotic: The Erotic as Power," in *Sister Outsider* (Trumansburg, N.Y.: Crossing Press, 1984).

49. Adrienne Rich, "Conditions for Work: The Common World of Women," in *On Lies, Secrets, and Silence,* p. 209; H. D., *Tribute to Freud* (Oxford: Carcanet, 1971), pp. 50–54.

50. Woolf, *A Room of One's Own,* p. 126.

51. Gracia Clark, "The Beguines: A Mediaeval Women's Community," *Quest: A Feminist Quarterly* 1, no. 4 (1975): 73–80.

52. See Denise Paulmé, ed., *Women of Tropical Africa* (Berkeley: University of California Press, 1963), pp. 7, 266–267. Some of these sororities are described as "a kind of defensive syndicate against the male element," their aims being "to offer concerted resistance to an oppressive patriarchate," "independence in relation to one's husband and with regard to motherhood, mutual aid, satisfaction of personal revenge." See also Audre Lorde, "Scratching the Surface: Some Notes on Barriers to Women and Loving" in *Sister Outsider,* pp. 45–52; Marjorie Topley, "Marriage Resistance in Rural Kwangtung," in *Women in Chinese Society,* ed. M. Wolf and R. Witke (Stanford, Calif.: Stanford University Press, 1978), pp. 67–89; Agnes Smedley, *Portraits of Chinese Women in Revolution,* ed. J. MacKinnon and S. MacKinnon (Old Westbury, N.Y.: Feminist Press, 1976), pp. 103–110.

53. See Rosalind Petchesky, "Dissolving the Hyphen: A Report on Marxist-Feminist Groups 1–5," in *Capitalist Patriarchy and the Case for Socialist Feminism,* ed. Zillah Eisenstein (New York: Monthly Review Press, 1979), p. 387.

54. [A. R., 1986: See Angela Davis, *Women, Race and Class* (New York: Random House, 1981), p. 102; Orlando Patterson, *Slavery and Social Death: A Comparative Study* (Cambridge: Harvard University Press, 1982), p. 133.]

55. Russell and van de Ven, pp. 42–43, 56–57.

56. I am indebted to Jonathan Katz's *Gay American History* for bringing to my attention Hansberry's letters to *The Ladder* and to Barbara Grier for supplying me with copies of relevant pages from *The Ladder,* quoted here by permission of Barbara Grier. See also the reprinted series of *The Ladder,* ed. Jonathan Katz et al. (New York: Arno, 1975), and Deirdre Carmody, "Letters by Eleanor Roosevelt Detail Friendship with Lorena Hickok." *New York Times* (October 21, 1979).

57. Meridel LeSueur, *The Girl* (Cambridge, Mass.: West End Press, 1978), pp. 10–11. LeSueur describes, in an afterword, how this book was drawn from the writings and oral narrations of women in the Workers Alliance who met as a writers' group during the depression.

58. Ibid., p. 20.

59. Ibid., pp. 53–54.

60. Ibid., p. 55.

61. Toni Morrison, *Sula* (New York: Bantam, 1973), pp. 103–104, 149. I am indebted to Lorraine Bethel's essay "'This Infinity of Conscious Pain': Zora Neale Hurston and the Black Female Literary Tradition," in *All the Women Are White, All the Blacks Are Men, but Some of Us Are Brave: Black Women's Studies,* ed. Gloria T. Hull, Patricia Bell Scott, and Barbara Smith (Old Westbury, N.Y.: Feminist Press, 1982).

62. See Maureen Brady and Judith McDaniel, "Lesbians in the Mainstream: The Image of Lesbians in Recent Commercial Fiction," *Conditions* 6 (1979): 82–105.

63. See Russell and van de Ven, p. 40: "Few heterosexual women realize their lack of free choice about their sexuality, and few realize how and why compulsory heterosexuality is also a crime against them."

64. Bethel, "'This Infinity of Conscious Pain.'"

65. Dinnerstein, the most recent writer to quote this passage, adds ominously: "But what has to be added to her account is that these 'women enlaced' are sheltering each other not just from what men want to do to them, but also from what they want to do to each other" (Dinnerstein, p. 103). The fact is, however, that woman-to-woman violence is a minute grain in the universe of male-against-female violence perpetuated and rationalized in every social institution.

66. Conversation with Blanche W. Cook, New York City, March 1979.

67. See note 9, above.

The Social Construction of Black Feminist Thought

PATRICIA HILL COLLINS

Sojourner Truth, Anna Julia Cooper, Ida Wells Barnett, and Fannie Lou Hamer are but a few names from a growing list of distinguished African-American women activists. Although their sustained resistance to Black women's victimization within interlocking systems of race, gender, and class oppression is well known, these women did not act alone.[1] Their actions were nurtured by the support of countless, ordinary African-American women who, through strategies of everyday resistance, created a powerful foundation for this more visible Black feminist activist tradition.[2] Such support has been essential to the shape and goals of Black feminist thought.

The long-term and widely shared resistance among African-American women can only have been sustained by an enduring and shared standpoint among Black women about the meaning of oppression and the actions that Black women can and should take to resist it. Efforts to identify the central concepts of this Black women's standpoint figure prominently in the works of contemporary Black feminist intellectuals.[3] Moreover, political and epistemological issues influence the social construction of Black feminist thought. Like other subordinate groups, African-American women not only have developed distinctive interpretations of Black women's oppression but have done so by using alternative ways of producing and validating knowledge itself. . . .

THE CONTOURS OF AN AFROCENTRIC FEMINIST EPISTEMOLOGY

Africanist analyses of the Black experience generally agree on the fundamental elements of an Afrocentric standpoint.

Patricia Hill Collins, "The Social Construction of Black Feminist Thought," *Signs: Journal of Women in Culture and Society* 14, no.4 (1989): 745–773 (excerpted). Copyright © 1989 by The University of Chicago. Reprinted with the permission of the author and The University of Chicago Press.

In spite of varying histories, Black societies reflect elements of a core African value system that existed prior to and independently of racial oppression.[4] Moreover, as a result of colonialism, imperialism, slavery, apartheid, and other systems of racial domination, Blacks share a common experience of oppression. These similarities in material conditions have fostered shared Afrocentric values that permeate the family structure, religious institutions, culture, and community life of Blacks in varying parts of Africa, the Caribbean, South America, and North America.[5] This Afrocentric consciousness permeates the shared history of people of African descent through the framework of a distinctive Afrocentric epistemology.[6]

Feminist scholars advance a similar argument. They assert that women share a history of patriarchal oppression through the political economy of the material conditions of sexuality and reproduction.[7] These shared material conditions are thought to transcend divisions among women created by race, social class, religion, sexual orientation, and ethnicity and to form the basis of a women's standpoint with its corresponding feminist consciousness and epistemology.[8]

Since Black women have access to both the Afrocentric and the feminist standpoints, an alternative epistemology used to rearticulate a Black women's standpoint reflects elements of both traditions.[9] The search for the distinguishing features of an alter-native epistemology used by African-American women reveals that values and ideas that Africanist scholars identify as being characteristically "Black" often bear remarkable resemblance to similar ideas claimed by feminist scholars as being characteristically "female."[10] This similarity suggests that the material conditions of oppression can vary dramatically and yet generate some uniformity in the epistemologies of subordinate groups. Thus, the significance of an Afrocentric feminist epistemology may lie in its enrichment of our understanding of how subordinate groups create knowledge that enables them to resist oppression.

The parallels between the two conceptual schemes raise a question: Is the worldview of women of African descent more intensely infused with the overlapping feminine/Afrocentric standpoints than is the case for either African-American men or white women?[11] While an Afrocentric feminist epistemology reflects elements of epistemologies used by Blacks as a group and women as a group, it also paradoxically demonstrates features that may be unique to Black women. On certain dimensions, Black women may more closely resemble Black men, on others, white women, and on still others, Black women may stand apart from both groups. Black feminist sociologist Deborah K. King describes this phenomenon as a "both/or" orientation, the act of being simultaneously a member of a group and yet standing apart from it. She suggests that multiple realities among Black women yield a "multiple consciousness in Black women's politics" and that this state of belonging yet not belonging forms an integral part of Black women's oppositional consciousness.[12] Bonnie Thornton Dill's analysis of how Black women live with contradictions, a situation she labels the "dialectics of Black womanhood," parallels King's assertions that this "both/or" orientation is central to an Afrocentric feminist consciousness.[13] Rather than emphasizing how a Black women's standpoint and its accompanying epistemology are different than those in Afrocentric and feminist analyses, I use Black women's experiences as a point of contact between the two.

Viewing an Afrocentric feminist epistemology in this way challenges analyses claiming that Black women have a more accurate view of oppression than do other groups. Such approaches suggest that oppression can be quantified and compared and that adding layers of oppression produces a potentially clearer standpoint. While it is tempting to claim that Black women are more oppressed than everyone else and therefore have the best standpoint from which to understand the mechanisms, processes, and effects of oppression, this simply may not be the case.[14]

African-American women do not uniformly share an Afrocentric feminist epistemology since social class introduces variations among Black women in seeing, valuing, and using Afrocentric feminist perspectives. While a Black women's standpoint and its accompanying epistemology stem from Black women's consciousness of race and gender oppression, they are not simply the result of combining Afrocentric and female values—standpoints are rooted in real material conditions structured by social class.[15]

Concrete Experience as a Criterion of Meaning

Carolyn Chase, a thirty-one-year-old inner city Black woman, notes, "My aunt used to say, 'A heap see, but a few know.'"[16] This saying depicts two types of knowing, knowledge and wisdom, and taps the first dimension of an Afrocentric feminist epistemology. Living life as Black women requires wisdom since knowledge about the dynamics of race, gender, and class subordination has been essential to Black women's survival. African-American women give such wisdom high credence in assessing knowledge.

Allusions to these two types of knowing pervade the words of a range of African-American women. In explaining the tenacity of racism, Zilpha Elaw, a preacher of the mid-1800s, noted: "The pride of a white skin is a bauble of great value with many in some parts of the United States, who readily sacrifice their intelligence to their prejudices, and possess more knowledge than wisdom."[17] In describing differences separating African-American and white women, Nancy White invokes a similar rule: "When you come right down to it, white women just *think* they are free. Black women *know* they ain't free."[18] Geneva Smitherman, a college professor specializing in African-American linguistics, suggests that "from a black perspective, written documents are limited in what they can teach about life and survival in the world. Blacks are quick to ridicule 'educated fools,' . . . they have 'book learning' but no 'mother wit,' knowledge, but not wisdom."[19] Mabel Lincoln eloquently summarizes the distinction between knowledge and wisdom: "To black people like me, a fool is funny—you know, people who love to break bad, people you can't tell anything to, folks that would take a shotgun to a roach."[20]

Black women need wisdom to know how to deal with the "educated fools" who would "take a shotgun to a roach." As members of a subordinate group, Black women cannot afford to be fools of any type, for their devalued status denies them the protections that white skin, maleness, and wealth confer. This distinction between knowledge and wisdom, and the use of experience as the cutting edge dividing them, has been key to Black women's survival. In the context of race, gender, and class oppression, the distinction is essential since knowledge without wisdom is adequate for the powerful, but wisdom is essential to the survival of the subordinate.

For ordinary African-American women, those individuals who have lived through the experiences about which they claim to be experts are more believable and credible than those who have merely read or thought about such experiences. Thus, concrete experience as a criterion for credibility frequently is invoked by Black women when making knowledge claims. For instance, Hannah Nelson describes the importance that personal experience has for her: "Our speech is most directly personal, and every black person assumes that every other black person has a right to a personal opinion. In speaking of grave matters, your personal experience is considered very good evidence. With us, distant statistics are certainly not as important as the actual experience of a sober person."[21] Similarly, Ruth Shays uses her concrete experiences to challenge the idea that formal education is the only route to knowledge: "I am the kind of person who doesn't have a lot of education, but both my mother and my father had good common sense. Now, I think that's all you need. I might not know how to use thirty-four words where three would do, but that does not mean that I don't know what I'm talking about . . . I know what I'm talking about because I'm talking about myself. I'm talking about what I have lived."[22] Implicit in Shays's self-assessment is a critique of the type of knowledge that obscures the truth, the "thirty-four words" that cover up a truth that can be expressed in three.

Even after substantial mastery of white masculinist epistemologies, many Black women scholars invoke their own concrete experiences and those of other Black women in selecting topics for investigation and methodologies used. For example, Elsa Barkley Brown subtitles her essay on Black women's history, "how my mother taught me to be an historian in spite of my academic training."[23] Similarly, Joyce Ladner maintains that growing up as a Black woman in the South gave her special insights in conducting her study of Black adolescent women.[24]

Henry Mitchell and Nicholas Lewter claim that experience as a criterion of meaning with practical images as its symbolic vehicles is a fundamental epistemological tenet in African-American thought-systems.[25] Stories, narratives, and Bible principles are selected for their applicability to the lived experiences of African-Americans and become symbolic representations of a whole wealth of experience. For example, Bible tales are told for their value to common life, so their interpretation involves no need for scientific historical verification. The narrative method requires that the story be "told, not torn apart in analysis, and trusted as core belief, not admired as science."[26] Any biblical story contains more than characters and a plot—it presents key ethical issues salient in African-American life.

June Jordan's essay about her mother's suicide exemplifies the multiple levels of meaning that can occur when concrete experiences are used as a criterion of meaning. Jordan describes her mother, a woman who literally died trying to stand up, and the effect that her mother's death had on her own work:

I think all of this is really about women and work. Certainly this is all about me as a woman and my life work. I mean I am not sure my mother's suicide was something extraordinary. Perhaps most women must deal with a similar inheritance, the legacy of a woman whose death you cannot possibly pinpoint because she died so many, many times and because, even before she became your mother, the life of that woman was taken. . . . I came too late to help my mother to her feet. By way of everlasting thanks to all of the women who have helped me to stay alive I am working never to be late again.[27]

While Jordan has knowledge about the concrete act of her mother's death, she also strives for wisdom concerning the meaning of that death.

Some feminist scholars offer a similar claim that women, as a group, are more likely than men to use concrete knowledge in assessing knowledge claims. For example, a substantial number of the 135 women in a study of women's cognitive development were "connected knowers" and were drawn to the sort of knowledge that emerges from first-hand observation. Such women felt that since knowledge comes from experience, the best way of understanding another person's ideas was to try to share the experiences that led the person to form those ideas. At the heart of the procedures used by connected knowers is the capacity for empathy.[28]

In valuing the concrete, African-American women may be invoking not only an Afrocentric tradition, but a women's tradition as well. Some feminist theorists suggest that women are socialized in complex relational nexuses where contextual rules take priority over abstract principles in governing behavior. This socialization process is thought to stimulate characteristic ways of knowing.[29] For example, Canadian sociologist Dorothy Smith maintains that two modes of knowing exist, one located in the body and the space it occupies and the other passing beyond it. She asserts that women, through their child-rearing and nurturing activities, mediate these two modes and use the concrete experiences of their daily lives to assess more abstract knowledge claims.[30]

WOMANIST

ALICE WALKER

Womanist   1. From *womanish.*   (Opp. of "girl-ish," i.e., frivolous, irresponsible, not serious.) A black feminist or feminist of color. From the black folk expression of mothers to female children, "You acting womanish," i.e., like a woman. Usually referring to out-rageous, audacious, courageous or *willful* behavior. Wanting to know more and in greater depth than is con-sidered "good" for one. Interested in grown-up doings. Acting grown up. Being grown up. Interchangeable with another black folk expression: "You trying to be grown." Responsible. In charge. *Serious.*

.   .   .

2. *Also:*   A woman who loves other women, sexu-ally and/or nonsexually. Appreciates and prefers women's culture, women's emotional flexibility (values tears as natural counterbalance of laughter), and

Alice Walker, "Womanist" from *In Search of Our Mothers' Gardens: Womanist Prose.* Copyright © 1983 by Alice Walker. Reprinted with the permission of Harcourt Brace & Company.

women's strength. Sometimes loves individual men, sexually and/or nonsexually. Committed to survival and wholeness of entire people, male *and* female. Not a separatist, except periodically, for health. Traditionally universalist, as in: "Mama, why are we brown, pink, and yellow, and our cousins are white, beige, and black?" Ans.: "Well, you know the colored race is just like a flower garden, with every color flower repre-sented." Traditionally capable, as in: "Mama, I'm walking to Canada and I'm taking you and a bunch of other slaves with me." Reply: "It wouldn't be the first time."

.   .   .

3.   Loves music. Loves dance. Loves the moon. *Loves* the Spirit. Loves love and food and roundness. Loves struggle. *Loves* the Folk. Loves herself. *Regardless.*

.   .   .

4.   Womanist is to feminist as purple to lavender.

Amanda King, a young Black mother, describes how she used the concrete to assess the abstract and points out how difficult mediating these two modes of knowing can be:

The leaders of the ROC [a labor union] lost their jobs too, but it just seemed like they were used to losing their jobs. . . . This was like a lifelong thing for them, to get out there and protest. They were like, what do you call them—intellectuals. . . . You got the ones that go to the university that are supposed to make all the speeches, they're the ones that are supposed to lead, you know, put this little revolution together, and then you got the little ones . . . that go to the factory everyday, they be the ones that have to fight. I had a child and I thought I don't have the time to be running around with these people. . . . I mean I understand some of that stuff they were talking about, like the bourgeoisie, the rich and the poor and all that, but I had surviving on my mind for me and my kid.[31]

For King, abstract ideals of class solidarity were mediated by the concrete experience of motherhood and the connect-edness it involved.

In traditional African-American communities, Black women find considerable institutional support for valuing concrete experience. Black extended families and Black churches are two key institutions where Black women experts with concrete knowledge of what it takes to be self-defined Black women share their knowledge with their younger, less experienced sisters. This relationship of sisterhood among Black women can be seen as a model for a whole series of relationships that African-American women have with each other, whether it is networks among women in extended fami-lies, among women in the Black church, or among women in the African-American community at large.[32]

Since the Black church and the Black family are both woman-centered and Afrocentric institutions, African-American women traditionally have found considerable institutional support for this dimension of an Afrocentric feminist epistemology in ways that are unique to them. While white women may value the concrete, it is questionable whether white families, particularly middle-class nuclear ones, and white community institutions provide comparable types of support. Similarly, while Black men are supported by Afrocentric institutions, they cannot participate in Black women's sisterhood. In terms of Black women's relationships with one another then, African-American women may indeed find it easier than others to recognize connectedness as a primary way of knowing, simply because they are encouraged to do so by Black women's tradition of sisterhood.

The Use of Dialogue in Assessing Knowledge Claims

For Black women, new knowledge claims are rarely worked out in isolation from other individuals and are usually developed through dialogues with other members of a community. A primary epistemological assumption underlying the use of dialogue in assessing knowledge claims is that connectedness rather than separation is an essential component of the knowledge-validation process.[33]

The use of dialogue has deep roots in an African-based oral tradition and in African-American culture.[34] Ruth Shays describes the importance of dialogue in the knowledge-validation process of enslaved African-Americans: "They would find a lie if it took them a year . . . the foreparents found the truth because they listened and they made people tell their part many times. Most often you can hear a lie. . . . Those old people was everywhere and knew the truth of many disputes. They believed that a liar should suffer the pain of his lies, and they had all kinds of ways of bringing liars to judgement."[35]

The widespread use of the call and response discourse mode among African-Americans exemplifies the importance placed on dialogue. Composed of spontaneous verbal and nonverbal interaction between speaker and listener in which all of the speaker's statements or "calls" are punctuated by expressions or "responses" from the listener, this Black discourse mode pervades African-American culture. The fundamental requirement of this interactive network is active participation of all individuals.[36] For ideas to be tested and validated, everyone in the group must participate. To refuse to join in, especially if one really disagrees with what has been said is seen as "cheating."[37]

June Jordan's analysis of Black English points to the significance of this dimension of an alternative epistemology.

Our language is a system constructed by people constantly needing to insist that we exist. . . . Our language devolves from a culture that abhors all abstraction, or anything tending to obscure or delete the fact of the human being who is here and now/the truth of the person who is speaking or listening. Consequently, *there is no passive voice construction possible in Black English.* For example, you cannot say, "Black English is being eliminated." You must say, instead, "White people eliminating Black English." The assumption of the presence of life governs all of Black English . . . every sentence assumes the living and active participation of at least two human beings, the speaker and the listener.[38]

Many Black women intellectuals invoke the relationships and connectedness provided by use of dialogue. When asked why she chose the themes she did, novelist Gayle Jones replied: "I was . . . interested . . . in oral traditions of storytelling—Afro-American and others, in which there is always the consciousness and importance of the hearer."[39] In describing the difference in the way male and female writers select significant events and relationships, Jones points out that "with many women writers, relationships within family, community, between men and women, and among women—from slave narratives by black women writers on—are treated as complex and significant relationships, whereas with many men the significant relationships are those that involve confrontations—relationships outside the family and community."[40] Alice Walker's reaction to Zora Neale Hurston's book, *Mules and Men,* is another example of the use of dialogue in assessing knowledge claims. In *Mules and Men,* Hurston chose not to become a detached observer of the stories and folktales she collected but instead, through extensive dialogues with the people in the communities she studied, placed herself at the center of her analysis. Using a similar process, Walker tests the truth of Hurston's knowledge claims: "When I read *Mules and Men* I was delighted. Here was this perfect book! The 'perfection' of which I immediately tested on my relatives, who are such typical Black Americans they are useful for every sort of political, cultural, or economic survey. Very regular people from the South, rapidly forgetting their Southern cultural inheritance in the suburbs and ghettos of Boston and New York, they sat around reading the book themselves, listening to me read the book, listening to each other read the book, and a kind of paradise was regained."[41]

Their centrality in Black churches and Black extended families provides Black women with a high degree of support from Black institutions for invoking dialogue as a dimension of an Afrocentric feminist epistemology. However, when African-American women use dialogues in assessing knowledge claims, they might be invoking a particularly female way of knowing as well. Feminist scholars contend that males and females are socialized within their families to seek different types of autonomy, the former based on separation, the latter seeking connectedness, and that this variation in types of autonomy parallels the characteristic differences between male and female ways of knowing.[42] For instance, in contrast to the visual metaphors (such as equating knowledge with illumination, knowing with seeing, and truth with light) that scientists and philosophers typically use, women tend to ground their epistemological premises in metaphors suggesting speaking and listening.[43]

While there are significant differences between the roles Black women play in their families and those played by middle-class white women, Black women clearly are affected by general cultural norms prescribing certain familial roles for women. Thus, in terms of the role of dialogue in an Afrocentric feminist epistemology, Black women may again experience a convergence of the values of the African-American community and woman-centered values.

The Ethic of Caring

"Ole white preachers used to talk wid dey tongues widdout sayin' nothin', but Jesus told us slaves to talk wid our hearts."[44] These words of an ex-slave suggest that ideas cannot be divorced from the individuals who create and share them. This theme of "talking with the heart" taps another dimension of an alternative epistemology used by African-American women, the ethic of caring. Just as the ex-slave used the wisdom in his heart to reject the ideas of the preachers who talked "wid dey tongues widdout sayin' nothin'," the ethic of caring suggests that personal expressiveness, emotions, and empathy are central to the knowledge-validation process.

One of three interrelated components making up the ethic of caring is the emphasis placed on individual uniqueness. Rooted in a tradition of African humanism, each individual is thought to be a unique expression of a common spirit, power, or energy expressed by all life.[45] This belief in individual uniqueness is illustrated by the value placed on personal expressiveness in African-American communities.[46] Johnetta Ray, an inner city resident, describes this Afrocentric emphasis on individual uniqueness: "No matter

how hard we try, I don't think black people will ever develop much of a herd instinct. We are profound individualists with a passion for self-expression."[47]

A second component of the ethic of caring concerns the appropriateness of emotions in dialogues. Emotion indicates that a speaker believes in the validity of an argument.[48] Consider Ntozake Shange's description of one of the goals of her work: "Our [Western] society allows people to be absolutely neurotic and totally out of touch with their feelings and everyone else's feelings, and yet be very respectable. This, to me, is a travesty. . . . I'm trying to change the idea of seeing emotions and intellect as distinct faculties."[49] Shange's words echo those of the ex-slave. Both see the denigration of emotion as problematic, and both suggest that expressiveness should be reclaimed and valued.

A third component of the ethic of caring involves developing the capacity for empathy. Harriet Jones, a sixteen-year-old Black woman, explains why she chose to open up to her interviewer: "Some things in my life are so hard for me to bear, and it makes me feel better to know that you feel sorry about those things and would change them if you could."[50]

These three components of the ethic of caring—the value placed on individual expressiveness, the appropriateness of emotions, and the capacity for empathy—pervade African-American culture. One of the best examples of the interactive nature of the importance of dialogue and the ethic of caring in assessing knowledge claims occurs in the use of the call and response discourse mode in traditional Black church services. In such services, both the minister and the congregation routinely use voice rhythm and vocal inflection to convey meaning. The sound of what is being said is just as important as the words themselves in what is, in a sense, a dialogue between reason and emotions. As a result, it is nearly impossible to filter out the strictly linguistic-cognitive abstract meaning from the sociocultural psycho-emotive meaning.[51] While the ideas presented by a speaker must have validity, that is, agree with the general body of knowledge shared by the Black congregation, the group also appraises the way knowledge claims are presented.

There is growing evidence that the ethic of caring may be part of women's experience as well. Certain dimensions of women's ways of knowing bear striking resemblance to Afrocentric expressions of the ethic of caring. Belenky, Clinchy, Goldberger, and Tarule point out that two contrasting epistemological orientations characterize knowing—one, an epistemology of separation based on impersonal procedures for establishing truth, and the other, an epistemology of connection in which truth emerges through care. While these ways of knowing are not gender specific, disproportionate numbers of women rely on connected knowing.[52]

The parallels between Afrocentric expressions of the ethic of caring and those advanced by feminist scholars are noteworthy. The emphasis placed on expressiveness and emotion in African-American communities bears marked resemblance to feminist perspectives on the importance of personality in connected knowing. Separate knowers try to subtract the personality of an individual from his or her ideas because they see personality as biasing those ideas. In contrast, connected knowers see personality as adding to an individual's ideas, and they feel that the personality of each group member enriches a group's understanding.[53] Similarly, the significance of individual uniqueness, personal expressiveness, and empathy in African-American communities resembles the importance that some feminist analyses place on women's "inner voice."[54]

The convergence of Afrocentric and feminist values in the ethic-of-care dimension of an alternative epistemology seems particularly acute. While white women may have access to a women's tradition valuing emotion and expressiveness, few white social institutions except the family validate this way of knowing. In contrast, Black women have long had the support of the Black church, an institution with deep roots in the African past and a philosophy that accepts and encourages expressiveness and an ethic of caring. While Black men share in this Afrocentric tradition, they must resolve the contradictions that distinguish abstract, unemotional Western masculinity from an Afrocentric ethic of caring. The differences among race/gender groups thus hinge on differences in their access to institutional supports valuing one type of knowing over another. Although Black women may be denigrated within white-male-controlled academic institutions, other institutions, such as Black families and churches, which encourage the expression of Black female power, seem to do so by way of their support for an Afrocentric feminist epistemology.

The Ethic of Personal Accountability

An ethic of personal accountability is the final dimension of an alternative epistemology. Not only must individuals develop their knowledge claims through dialogue and present those knowledge claims in a style proving their concern for their ideas, people are expected to be accountable for their knowledge claims. Zilpha Elaw's description of slavery reflects this notion that every idea has an owner and that the owner's identity matters: "Oh, the abominations of

slavery! . . . every case of slavery, however lenient its inflictions and mitigated its atrocities, indicates an oppressor, the oppressed, and oppression."[55] For Elaw, abstract definitions of slavery mesh with the concrete identities of its perpetrators and its victims. Blacks "consider it essential for individuals to have personal positions on issues and assume full responsibility for arguing their validity."[56]

Assessments of an individual's knowledge claims simultaneously evaluate an individual's character, values, and ethics. African-Americans reject Eurocentric masculinist beliefs that probing into an individual's personal viewpoint is outside the boundaries of discussion. Rather, all views expressed and actions taken are thought to derive from a central set of core beliefs that cannot be other than personal.[57] From this perspective, knowledge claims made by individuals respected for their moral and ethical values will carry more weight than those offered by less respected figures.[58]

An example drawn from an undergraduate course composed entirely of Black women, which I taught, might help clarify the uniqueness of this portion of the knowledge-validation process. During one class discussion, I assigned the students the task of critiquing an analysis of Black feminism advanced by a prominent Black male scholar. Instead of dissecting the rationality of the author's thesis, my students demanded facts about the author's personal biography. They were especially interested in concrete details of his life such as his relationships with Black women, his marital status, and his social class background. By requesting data on dimensions of his personal life routinely excluded in positivist approaches to knowledge validation, they were invoking concrete experience as a criterion of meaning. They used this information to assess whether he really cared about his topic and invoked this ethic of caring in advancing their knowledge claims about his work. Furthermore, they refused to evaluate the rationality of his written ideas without some indication of his personal credibility as an ethical human being. The entire exchange could only have occurred as a dialogue among members of a class that had established a solid enough community to invoke an alternative epistemology in assessing knowledge claims.[59]

The ethic of personal accountability is clearly an Afrocentric value, but is it feminist as well? While limited by its attention to middle-class, white women, Carol Gilligan's work suggests that there is a female model for moral development where women are more inclined to link morality to responsibility, relationships, and the ability to maintain social ties.[60] If this is the case, then African-American women again experience a convergence of values from Afrocentric and female institutions.

The use of an Afrocentric feminist epistemology in traditional Black church services illustrates the inter-active nature of all four dimensions and also serves as a metaphor for the distinguishing features of an Afrocentric feminist way of knowing. The services represent more than dialogues between the rationality used in examining biblical texts/stories and the emotion inherent in the use of reason for this purpose. The rationale for such dialogues addresses the task of examining concrete experiences for the presence of an ethic of caring. Neither emotion nor ethics is subordinated to reason. Instead, emotion, ethics, and reason are used as interconnected, essential components in assessing knowledge claims. In an Afrocentric feminist epistemology, values lie at the heart of the knowledge-validation process such that inquiry always has an ethical aim. . . .

ACKNOWLEDGMENTS

Special thanks go out to the following people for reading various drafts of this manuscript: Evelyn Nakano Glenn, Lynn Weber Cannon, and participants in the 1986 Research Institute, Center for Research on Women, Memphis State University; Elsa Barkley Brown, Deborah K. King, Elizabeth V. Spelman, and Angelene Jamison-Hall; and four anonymous reviewers at *Signs*.

NOTES

1. For analyses of how interlocking systems of oppression affect Black women, see Frances Beale, "Double Jeopardy: To Be Black and Female," in *The Black Woman,* ed. Toni Cade (New York: Signet, 1970); Angela Y. Davis, *Women, Race and Class* (New York: Random House, 1981); Bonnie Thornton Dill, "Race, Class, and Gender: Prospects for an All-Inclusive Sisterhood," *Feminist Studies* 9, no. 1 (1983): 131–50; bell hooks, *Ain't I a Woman? Black Women and Feminism* (Boston: South End Press, 1981); Diane Lewis, "A Response to Inequality: Black Women, Racism, and Sexism," *Signs: Journal of Women in Culture and Society* 3, no. 2 (Winter 1977): 339–61; Pauli Murray, "The Liberation of Black Women," in *Voices of the New Feminism,* ed. Mary Lou Thompson (Boston: Beacon, 1970), 87–102; and the introduction in Filomina Chioma Steady, *The Black Woman Cross-Culturally* (Cambridge, Mass.: Schenkman, 1981), 7–41.

2. See the introduction in Steady for an overview of Black women's strengths. This strength-resiliency perspective has greatly influenced empirical work on African-American women. See, e.g., Joyce Ladner's study of low-income Black adolescent girls, *Tomorrow's Tomorrow* (New York: Doubleday, 1971); and Lena Wright Myers's work on Black women's self-concept, *Black Women: Do They Cope Better?* (Englewood Cliffs, N.J.: Prentice-Hall, 1980). For discussions of Black women's resistance, see Elizabeth Fox-Genovese, "Strategies and Forms of Resistance: Focus on Slave Women in the United States," in *In Resistance: Studies in African, Caribbean and Afro-American History,* ed. Gary Y. Okihiro (Amherst, Mass.: University of Massachusetts Press, 1986), 143–65; and Rosalyn Terborg-Penn, "Black Women in Resistance: A Cross-Cultural Perspective," in Okihiro, ed., 188–209. For a comprehensive discussion of everyday resistance, see James C. Scott, *Weapons of the Weak: Everyday Forms of Peasant Resistance* (New Haven, Conn.: Yale University Press, 1985).

3. See Patricia Hill Collins's analysis of the substantive content of Black feminist thought in "Learning from the Outsider Within: The Sociological Significance of Black Feminist Thought," *Social Problems* 33, no. 6 (1986): 14–32.

4. For detailed discussions of the Afrocentric worldview, see John S. Mbiti, *African Religions and Philosophy* (London: Heinemann, 1969); Dominique Zahan, *The Religion, Spirituality, and Thought of Traditional Africa* (Chicago: University of Chicago Press, 1979); and Mechal Sobel, *Trabelin' On: The Slave Journey to an Afro-Baptist Faith* (Westport, Conn.: Greenwood Press, 1979), 1–76.

5. For representative works applying these concepts to African-American culture, see Niara Sudarkasa, "Interpreting the African Heritage in Afro-American Family Organization," in *Black Families,* ed. Harriette Pipes McAdoo (Beverly Hills, Calif.: Sage, 1981); Henry H. Mitchell and Nicholas Cooper Lewter, *Soul Theology: The Heart of American Black Culture* (San Francisco: Harper & Row, 1986); Robert Farris Thompson, *Flash of the Spirit: African and Afro-American Art and Philosophy* (New York: Vintage, 1983); and Ortiz M. Walton, "Comparative Analysis of the African and the Western Aesthetics," in *The Black Aesthetic,* ed. Addison Gayle (Garden City, N.Y.: Doubleday, 1971), 154–64.

6. One of the best discussions of an Afrocentric epistemology is offered by James E. Turner, "Foreword: Africana Studies and Epistemology; a Discourse in the Sociology of Knowledge," in *The*

Next Decade: Theoretical and Research Issues in Africana Studies, ed. James E. Turner (Ithaca, N.Y.: Cornell University Africana Studies and Research Center, 1984), v–xxv. See also Vernon Dixon, "World Views and Research Methodology," summarized in Sandra Harding, *The Science Question in Feminism* (Ithaca, N.Y.: Cornell University Press, 1986), 170.

7. See Hester Eisenstein, *Contemporary Feminist Thought* (Boston: G. K. Hall, 1983). Nancy Hartsock's *Money, Sex, and Power* (Boston: Northeastern University Press, 1983), 145–209, offers a particularly insightful analysis of women's oppression.

8. For discussions of feminist consciousness, see Dorothy Smith, "A Sociology for Women," in *The Prism of Sex: Essays in the Sociology of Knowledge,* ed. Julia A. Sherman and Evelyn T. Beck (Madison: University of Wisconsin Press, 1979); and Michelle Z. Rosaldo, "Women, Culture, and Society: A Theoretical Overview," in *Woman, Culture, and Society,* ed. Michelle Z. Rosaldo and Louise Lamphere (Stanford, Calif.: Stanford University Press, 1974), 17–42. Feminist epistemologies are surveyed by Alison M. Jaggar, *Feminist Politics and Human Nature* (Totowa, N.J.: Rowan & Allanheld, 1983).

9. One significant difference between Afrocentric and feminist standpoints is that much of what is termed women's culture is, unlike African-American culture, created in the context of and produced by oppression. Those who argue for a women's culture are electing to value, rather than denigrate, those traits associated with females in white patriarchal societies. While this choice is important, it is not the same as identifying an independent, historic culture associated with a society. I am indebted to Deborah K. King for this point.

10. Critiques of the Eurocentric masculinist knowledge-validation process by both Africanist and feminist scholars illustrate this point. What one group labels "white" and "Eurocentric," the other describes as "male-dominated" and "masculinist." Although he does not emphasize its patriarchal and racist features, Morris Berman's *The Reenchantment of the World* (New York: Bantam, 1981) provides a historical discussion of Western thought. Afrocentric analyses of this same process can be found in Molefi Kete Asante, "International/Intercultural Relations," in *Contemporary Black Thought,* ed. Molefi Kete Asante and Abdulai S. Vandi (Beverly Hills, Calif.: Sage, 1980), 43–58; and Dona Richards, "European Mythology: The Ideology of 'Progress,'" in Asante and Vandi, eds., 59–79. For feminist analyses, see Hartsock, *Money, Sex, and Power.* Harding also discusses this similarity (see chap. 7, "Other 'Others' and Fractured Identities: Issues for Epistemologists," 163–96).

11. Harding, 166.

12. Deborah K. King, "Race, Class, and Gender Salience in Black Women's Womanist Consciousness" (Dartmouth College, Department of Sociology, Hanover, N.H., 1987, typescript).

13. Bonnie Thornton Dill, "The Dialectics of Black Womanhood," *Signs* 4, no. 3 (Spring 1979): 543–55.

14. One implication of standpoint approaches is that the more subordinate the group, the purer the vision of the oppressed group. This is an outcome of the origins of standpoint approaches in Marxist social theory, itself a dualistic analysis of social structure.

Because such approaches rely on quantifying and ranking human oppressions—familiar tenets of positivist approaches—they are rejected by Blacks and feminists alike. See Harding (n. 6 above) for a discussion of this point. See also Elizabeth V. Spelman's discussion of the fallacy of additive oppression in "Theories of Race and Gender: The Erasure of Black Women," *Quest* 5, no. 4 (1982): 36–62.

15. Class differences among Black women may be marked. For example, see Paula Giddings's analysis in *When and Where I Enter: The Impact of Black Women on Race and Sex in America* (New York: William Morrow, 1984) of the role of social class in shaping Black women's political activism; or Elizabeth Higginbotham's study of the effects of social class in Black women's college attendance in "Race and Class Barriers to Black Women's College Attendance," *Journal of Ethnic Studies* 13, no. 1 (1985): 89–107. Those African-American women who have experienced the greatest degree of convergence of race, class, and gender oppression may be in a better position to recognize and use an alternative epistemology.

16. John Langston Gwaltney, *Drylongso: A Self-Portrait of Black America* (New York: Vintage, 1980), 83.

17. William L. Andrews, *Sisters of the Spirit: Three Black Women's Autobiographies of the Nineteenth Century* (Bloomington: Indiana University Press, 1986), 85.

18. Gwaltney, 147.

19. Geneva Smitherman, *Talkin and Testifyin: The Language of Black America* (Detroit: Wayne State University Press, 1986), 76.

20. Gwaltney, 68.

21. Ibid., 7.

22. Ibid., 27, 33.

23. Elsa Barkley Brown, "Hearing Our Mothers' Lives" (paper presented at the Fifteenth Anniversary Faculty Lecture Series, African-American and African Studies, Emory University, Atlanta, 1986).

24. Ladner (n. 2 above).

25. Mitchell and Lewter (n. 5 above). The use of the narrative approach in African-American theology exemplifies an inductive system of logic alternately called "folk wisdom" or a survival-based, need-oriented method of assessing knowledge claims.

26. Ibid., 8.

27. June Jordan, *On Call: Political Essays* (Boston: South End Press, 1985), 26.

28. Mary Belenky, Blythe Clinchy, Nancy Goldberger, and Jill Tarule, *Women's Ways of Knowing* (New York: Basic, 1986), 113.

29. Hartsock, *Money, Sex and Power* (n. 7 above), 237; and Nancy Chodorow, *The Reproduction of Mothering* (Berkeley and Los Angeles: University of California Press, 1978).

30. Dorothy Smith, *The Everyday World as Problematic* (Boston: Northeastern University Press, 1987).

31. Victoria Byerly, *Hard Times Cotton Mill Girls: Personal Histories of Womanhood and Poverty in the South* (New York: ILR Press, 1986), 198.

32. For Black women's centrality in the family, see Steady (n. 1 above): Ladner (n. 2 above); Brown (n. 23 above); and McAdoo, ed. (n. 5 above). See Cheryl Townsend Gilkes, " 'Together and in

Harness:' Women's Traditions in the Sanctified Church," *Signs* 10, no. 4 (Summer 1985): 678–99, for Black women in the church; and chap. 4 of Deborah Gray White, *Ar'n't I a Woman? Female Slaves in the Plantation South* (New York: Norton, 1985). See also Gloria Joseph, "Black Mothers and Daughters: Their Roles and Functions in American Society," in *Common Differences: Conflicts in Black and White Feminist Perspectives,* ed. Gloria Joseph and Jill Lewis (Garden City, N.Y.: Anchor, 1981), 75–126. Even though Black women play essential roles in Black families and Black churches, these institutions are not free from sexism.

33. As Belenky et al. note, "Unlike the eye, the ear requires closeness between subject and object. Unlike seeing, speaking and listening suggest dialogue and interaction" (18).

34. Thomas Kochman, *Black and White: Styles in Conflict* (Chicago: University of Chicago Press, 1981); and Smitherman (n. 19 above).

35. Gwaltney (n. 16 above), 32.

36. Smitherman, 108.

37. Kochman, 28.

38. Jordan (n. 27 above), 129.

39. Claudia Tate, *Black Women Writers at Work* (New York: Continuum, 1983), 91.

40. Ibid., 92.

41. Alice Walker, *In Search of Our Mothers' Gardens* (New York: Harcourt Brace Jovanovich, 1974), 84.

42. Evelyn Fox Keller, *Reflections on Gender and Science* (New Haven, Conn.: Yale University Press, 1985); Chodorow (n. 29 above).

43. Belenky et al. (n. 28 above), 16.

44. Thomas Webber, *Deep Like the Rivers* (New York: Norton, 1978), 127.

45. In her discussion of the West African Sacred Cosmos, Mechal Sobel (n. 4 above) notes that Nyam, a root word in many West African languages, connotes an enduring spirit, power, or energy possessed by all life. In spite of the pervasiveness of this key concept in African humanism, its definition remains elusive. She points out, "Every individual analyzing the various Sacred Cosmos of West Africa has recognized the reality of this force, but no one has yet adequately translated this concept into Western terms" (13).

46. For discussions of personal expressiveness in African-American culture, see Smitherman (n. 19 above); Kochman (n. 34 above), esp. chap. 9; and Mitchell and Lewter (n. 5 above).

47. Gwaltney (n. 16 above), 228.

48. For feminist analyses of the subordination of emotion in Western culture, see Arlie Russell Hochschild, "The Sociology of Feeling and Emotion: Selected Possibilities," in *Another Voice: Feminist Perspectives on Social Life and Social Science,* ed. Marcia Millman and Rosabeth Kanter (Garden City, N.Y.: Anchor, 1975), 280–307; and Chodorow.

49. Tate (n. 39 above), 156.

50. Gwaltney, 11.

51. Smitherman, 135 and 137.

52. Belenky et al. (n. 28 above), 100–130.

53. Ibid., 119.

54. See ibid., 52–75, for a discussion of inner voice and its role in women's cognitive styles. Regarding empathy, Belenky et al. note: "Connected knowers begin with an interest in the facts of other people's lives, but they gradually shift the focus to other people's ways of thinking. . . . It is the form rather than the content of knowing that is central. . . . Connected learners learn through empathy" (115).

55. Andrews (n. 17 above), 98.

56. Kochman (n. 34 above), 20 and 25.

57. Ibid, 23.

58. The sizable proportion of ministers among Black political leaders illustrates the importance of ethics in African-American communities.

59. Belenky et al. discuss a similar situation. They note, "People could critique each other's work in this class and accept each other's criticisms because members of the group shared a similar experience. . . . Authority in connected knowing rests not on power or status or certification but on commonality of experience" (118).

60. Carol Gilligan, *In a Different Voice* (Cambridge, Mass.: Harvard University Press, 1982). Carol Stack critiques Gilligan's model by arguing that African-Americans invoke a similar model of moral development to that used by women (see "The Culture of Gender: Women and Men of Color," *Signs* 11, no. 2 [Winter 1986]: 321–24). Another difficulty with Gilligan's work concerns the homogeneity of the subjects whom she studied.

P A R T   T W O

Learning Gender

Everyone is born into a *culture*—a set of shared ideas about the nature of reality, standards of right and wrong, and what is good and desirable versus bad and undesirable. These ideas are manifested in behaviors and artifacts. As totally dependent infants we are *socialized*—taught the rules, roles, and relationships of the social world we will inherit. We exchange our infant hedonism for love, protection, and the attention of others; in the process, we learn to think, act, and feel as we are "supposed to."

One of the earliest and most deeply seated ideas to which we are socialized is that of gender identity: the idea that "I am a boy" or "I am a girl." Because the culture has strong ideas about what boys and girls are like, we learn to identify our gender identity (our "boyness" or "girlness") with behaviors that are sex-assigned in our culture. Thus, for example, a girl who plays with dolls is viewed as behaving in an appropriate and "feminine" manner and a boy who plays with trucks as acting appropriately "masculine." Sometimes consciously and sometimes unconsciously, children are categorized, differentially responded to and regarded, and encouraged to adopt behaviors and attitudes on the basis of their sex. We raise, in effect, two different kinds of children: boys and girls.

Parents (or surrogate parents) are strong socializing influences, and they provide the first and most deeply experienced socialization experiences. Despite claims to the contrary, American parents treat their infant girls and boys differently. Boys have "boy toys," "boy names," "boy room decor," and are played with in more "boylike" ways than girls. Even if parents monitor their actions in the hope of preventing sexism from affecting their child, their endeavors cannot succeed, because *other* socializing influences bear down on the child.

One of the primary socializing influences is *language.* In learning to talk we acquire the thought patterns and communication styles of our culture. Those patterns and styles in all languages perpetuate and reinforce differentiation by sex and sex stereotyping, although the kind of stereotyping may vary from culture to culture. A "gendered" person is thus created through different linguistic and cultural contexts. All languages teach deep-seated ideas about men and women. They do it "naturally": as one learns a language, one learns the viewpoint of one's culture. In the English language, for example, the generic *man* is supposed to include males and females, as well as people of all races and ethnicities; but in linguistic practice it does not. People other than white and male are linguistically tagged in writing and in speech. For example, occupational categories are sex-tagged if the person's sex or race does not fit cultural stereotypes about who will be in those occupations. Consider: doctor/woman doctor/black woman doctor; nurse/male nurse/Asian male nurse. What is being taught is the centricity of "white men" in a socially prescribed system of inequity.

As societies become more complex, increasingly the mass media have become centralized agents for the transmission of dominant cultural beliefs. Movements toward cultural heterogeneity are thwarted through the homogenizing effects of television, in particular. The media present sex stereotypes in their purest and simplest forms. Whether the program is about African-American families, Latino families, white families, or talking animals, the sex-stereotyping messages are endlessly repetitive. Children in the United States spend more time watching television than they spend in school or interacting with parents or peers. Moreover, they believe that what they see on television is an accurate representation of how the world is and should be organized. White middle-class male dominance is the repetitive theme.

The socialization effected by the family, language, and the mass media is supplemented by the educational system. Educational institutions are formally charged with teaching the young. While teaching them reading, writing, and arithmetic, however, the schools also imbue them with sexist values. They do so through the pattern of staffing (male principals and custodians, female teachers and food servers), curriculum materials, the sex segregation of sports and activities, and differential *expectations* of boys and girls. No child can avoid this socialization experience.

Through powerful social institutions, then, children learn a culture. The culture they learn is one that views manhood as superior to womanhood; it is a system that differentially assigns behaviors and attitudes to males and females. Subcultures that promote values and beliefs different from the mainstream do exist, and individuals do not necessarily internalize every message from the dominant culture. Nevertheless, traditional cultural views of gender are ubiquitous and powerful.

Socialization—whether through the home, the school, language, or the mass media—creates and sustains gender differences. Boys are taught that they will inherit the privileges and prestige of manhood, while girls are taught that they are less socially valuable than boys. Both are expected to view their status as right, moral, and appropriate. Moreover, socialization never ends. As adults we continue to be resocialized by the books we read, the movies we see, and the people we spend time with.

The readings in this part of *Feminist Frontiers IV* illustrate and explain different aspects of cultural constructions of gender and the socialization process and provide the reader with conceptual frameworks and perspectives for understanding the implications of gender.

SECTION THREE

Language, Images, and Culture

Language—both verbal and nonverbal—affects the way we view ourselves and our relationships to each other and to the world around us. Language reflects and perpetuates the values of a society. The English language teaches that men and masculine values, behaviors, and goals are more important than women and their values, behaviors, and goals. In addition to images of gender created by language, images in various media surround us with cultural messages about the power differences between women and men. This section explores images of women and men expressed in language and mass media.

Laurel Richardson's "Gender Stereotyping in the English Language" demonstrates the major ways in which sexism pervades the structure and standard usage of modern American English. Her analysis reveals differential expectations of men and women embedded in the language; offers insights on how we internalize and reinforce gender differences as we read, write, and speak English or hear it spoken; and implicitly raises questions about the relationships between language and social life, including connections between linguistic and social change. What are some examples of nonsexist language? How do you think that using nonsexist language affects people's attitudes about women?

Embedded in language are ideas about beauty and sexuality. In many societies, standards of beauty and eroticism require women's bodies to conform to unrealistic and distorted ideals. Kamy Cunningham describes one such ideal in American culture: the Barbie doll. In "Barbie Doll Culture and the American Waistland," Cunningham analyses the pervasiveness of the thin-waisted, big-breasted Barbie image and its effects on her and other women. Beauty, she suggests, is too often defined as an artificial plastic emptiness, and being beautiful is the ultimate measure of a woman's value. Do you agree with Cunningham? How important do you think being stereotypically attractive is for college women? Is beauty of a higher priority than academic success?

Such male-defined standards and ideals are indeed pervasive. But, as Cynthia Lont suggests in "Women's Music: No Longer a Small Private Party," alternate images of women are making inroads into popular culture. Lesbian-feminist activists built a strong network of performers, audiences, and distributors for explicitly feminist and lesbian music during the 1970s and 1980s. Lont argues that this oppositional culture aimed to bring about social change by presenting images of women as strong, independent, and self-defined and by constructing a new value system. In the 1990s, feminist and lesbian performers have become successful in mainstream markets and record labels. Lont explores the pitfalls and benefits of "going mainstream" for feminist music. Has the music you listen to been influenced by feminist values? What images of women and men are imbedded in your favorite songs?

Patricia J. Williams, in "Hate Radio," reminds us that despite the gains of women's music, the mass media remain deeply sexist and racist. Williams describes her shock at the blatant bigotry expressed by such talk radio hosts as Rush Limbaugh and Howard Stern, and examines some of the social roots and implications of their radio programs. The mass media, she argues, can be a powerful force for hate, reinforcing bigoted beliefs among the powerful and fear and marginality among the oppressed.

We cannot emphasize too strongly the importance of language and media images in the construction of our understandings about women's positions in society. We are continuously exposed to ideas of women as subordinate to men. Moreover, since the language we have acquired and the images we use are so deeply rooted and inseparable, it is very difficult for us to break from them, to see and describe the world and our experiences in nonsexist ways. Yet women and other subordinate groups *do* attempt to construct alternate systems of meaning and draw strength from cultures of resistance. The power to define has a major influence on our perceptions of ourselves and others.

Gender Stereotyping in the English Language

LAUREL RICHARDSON

Everyone in our society, regardless of class, ethnicity, sex, age, or race, is exposed to the same language, the language of the dominant culture. Analysis of verbal language can tell us a great deal about a people's fears, prejudices, anxieties, and interests. A rich vocabulary on a particular subject indicates societal interests or obsessions (e.g., the extensive vocabulary about cars in America). And different words for the same subject (such as *freedom fighter* and *terrorist, passed away* and *croaked, make love* and *ball*) show that there is a range of attitudes and feelings in the society toward that subject.

It should not be surprising, then, to find differential attitudes and feelings about men and women rooted in the English language. Although the English language has not been completely analyzed, six general propositions concerning these attitudes and feelings about males and females can be made.

First, in terms of grammatical and semantic structure, women do not have a fully autonomous, independent existence; they are part of man. The language is not divided into male and female with distinct conjugations and declensions, as many other languages are. Rather, *women* are included under the generic *man.* Grammar books specify that the pronoun *he* can be used generically to mean *he* or *she.* Further, *man,* when used as an indefinite pronoun, grammatically refers to both men and women. So, for example, when we read *man* in the following phrases we are to interpret it as applying to both men and women: "man the oars," "one small step for man, one giant step for

mankind," "man, that's tough," "man overboard," "man the toolmaker," "alienated man," "garbageman." Our rules of etiquette complete the grammatical presumption of inclusivity. When two persons are pronounced "man and wife," Miss Susan Jones changes her entire name to Mrs. Robert Gordon (Vanderbilt, 1972). In each of these correct usages, women are a part of man; they do not exist autonomously. The exclusion of women is well expressed in Mary Daly's ear-jarring slogan "the sisterhood of man" (1973:7–21).

However, there is some question as to whether the theory that *man* means everybody is carried out in practice (see Bendix, 1979; Martyna, 1980). For example, an eight-year-old interrupts her reading of "The Story of the Cavemen" to ask how we got here without cavewomen. A ten-year-old thinks it is dumb to have a woman post*man.* A beginning anthropology student believes (incorrectly) that all shamans ("witch doctors") are males because her textbook and professor use the referential pronoun *he.*

But beginning language learners are not the only ones who visualize males when they see the word *man.* Research has consistently demonstrated that when the generic *man* is used, people visualize men, not women (Schneider & Hacker, 1973; DeStefano, 1976; Martyna, 1978; Hamilton & Henley, 1982). DeStefano, for example, reports that college students choose silhouettes of males for sentences with the word *man* or *men* in them. Similarly, the presumably generic *he* elicits images of men rather than women. The finding is so persistent that linguists doubt whether there actually is a semantic generic in English (MacKay, 1983).

Man, then, suggests not humanity but rather male images. Moreover, over one's lifetime, an educated American will be exposed to the prescriptive *he* more than a million times (MacKay, 1983). One consequence is the exclusion of women in the visualization, imagination, and thought of males and females. Most likely this linguistic practice perpetuates in men their feelings of dominance over and

Laurel Richardson, "Gender Stereotyping in the English Language" adapted from *The Dynamics of Sex and Gender: A Sociological Perspective, Third Edition* (New York: Harper & Row, 1987). Copyright © 1981 by Houghton Mifflin Company. Copyright © 1987 by Harper & Row, Publishers, Inc. Reprinted with the permission of the author.

A MONUMENTAL OVERSIGHT

EDITORIAL STAFF, WOMEN RIGHT NOW, *GLAMOUR MAGAZINE*

A few weeks after **Betsy Gotbaum** . . . became New York City's parks and recreation commissioner (the first female to hold the position), someone asked her how many statues of women were in the city's parks. "I said I wasn't sure, but I'd find out," Gotbaum says. What she found was that *there isn't a single statue of an American woman in New York City.* In fact, of the Park Department's 417 monuments considered significant in terms of size, subject or artist, only three depict individual and identifiable females: Joan of Arc, Alice in Wonderland and Mother Goose. "I counted Mother Goose because she's a mother and I was trying to make sure I was getting everybody in," says Gotbaum. "But I was also making a point."

Part of the problem is that most of the monuments and statues in New York City were erected between 1876 and 1917. "Before the women's movement, women were not considered on a par with men in terms of their accomplishments," Gotbaum says. "There's a visual domination of males in our society."

Procuring more statues of women won't be easy, but Gotbaum's a fighter—and she's already getting results. "The owner of an art gallery read about what our department is trying to do and donated a statue of Gertrude Stein," she says. "It's going to go into Bryant Park, next to the public library, within the next few months." Also in the works are a plaque dedicated to Emma Lazarus (the writer of the Statue of Liberty sonnet) and the Eleanor Roosevelt Memorial, a landscape that will include a bronze sculpture and panels of quotes from the first lady.

"Maybe if women read about what we're doing here in New York, they'll be inspired to do it in their cities," says Gotbaum. "I'd love to get a whole movement going."

responsibility for women, feelings that interfere with the development of equality in relationships.

Second, in actual practice, our pronoun usage perpetuates different personality attributes and career aspirations for men and women. Nurses, secretaries, and elementary school teachers are almost invariably referred to as *she;* doctors, engineers, electricians, and presidents as *he.* In one classroom, students referred to an unidentified child as *he* but shifted to *she* when discussing the child's parent. In a faculty discussion of the problems of acquiring new staff, all architects, engineers, security officers, faculty, and computer programmers were referred to as *he;* secretaries and file clerks were referred to as *she.* Martyna (1978) has noted that speakers consistently use *he* when the referent has a high-status occupation (e.g., doctor, lawyer, judge) but shift to *she* when the occupations have lower status (e.g., nurse, secretary).

Even our choice of sex ascription to nonhuman objects subtly reinforces different personalities for males and females. It seems as though the small (e.g., kittens), the graceful (e.g., poetry), the unpredictable (e.g., the fates), the nurturant (e.g., the church, the school), and that which is owned and/or controlled by men (e.g., boats, cars, governments, nations) represent the feminine, whereas that which is a controlling forceful power in and of itself (e.g., God, Satan, tiger) primarily represents the masculine. Even athletic teams are not immune. In one college, the men's teams are called the Bearcats and the women's teams the Bearkittens.

Some of you may wonder whether it matters that the female is linguistically included in the male. The inclusion of women under the pseudogeneric *man* and the prescriptive *he,* however, is not a trivial issue. Language has tremendous power to shape attitudes and influence behavior. Indeed, MacKay (1983) argues that the prescriptive *he* "has all the characteristics of a highly effective propaganda technique": frequent repetition, early age of acquisition (before age 6), covertness (*he* is not thought of as propaganda), use by high-prestige sources (including university texts and professors), and indirectness (presented as though it were a matter of common knowledge). As a result, the prescriptive affects females' sense of life options and feelings of well-being. For example, Adamsky (1981) found that women's sense of power and importance was enhanced when the prescriptive *he* was replaced by *she*.

Awareness of the impact of the generic *man* and prescriptive *he* has generated considerable activity to change the language. One change, approved by the Modern Language Association, is to replace the prescriptive *he* with the plural *they*—as was accepted practice before the 18th century. Another is the use of *he or she*. Although it sounds awkward at first, the *he or she* designation is increasingly being used in the media and among people who have recognized the power of the pronoun to perpetuate sex stereotyping. When a professor, for example, talks about "the lawyer" as "he or she," a speech pattern that counteracts sex stereotyping is modeled. This drive to neutralize the impact of pronouns is evidenced further in the renaming of occupations: a policeman is now a police officer, a postman is a mail carrier, a stewardess is a flight attendant.

Third, linguistic practice defines females as immature, incompetent, and incapable and males as mature, complete, and competent. Because the words *man* and *woman* tend to connote sexual and human maturity, common speech, organizational titles, public addresses, and bathroom doors frequently designate the women in question as *ladies*. Simply contrast the different connotations of *lady* and *woman* in the following common phrases:

Luck, be a lady (woman) tonight.
Barbara's a little lady (woman).
Ladies' (Women's) Air Corps.

In the first two examples, the use of *lady* desexualizes the contextual meaning of *woman*. So trivializing is the use of *lady* in the last phrase that the second is wholly anomalous. The male equivalent, *lord,* is never used; and its synonym, *gentleman,* is used infrequently. When *gentleman* is used, the assumption seems to be that certain culturally condoned aspects of masculinity (e.g., aggressivity, activity, and strength) should be set aside in the interests of maturity and order, as in the following phrases:

A gentlemen's (men's) agreement.
A duel between gentlemen (men).
He's a real gentleman (man).

Rather than feeling constrained to set aside the stereotypes associated with *man,* males frequently find the opposite

process occurring. The contextual connotation of *man* places a strain on males to be continuously sexually and socially potent, as the following examples reveal:

I was not a man (gentleman) with her tonight.
This is a man's (gentleman's) job.
Be a man (gentleman).

Whether males, therefore, feel competent or anxious, valuable or worthless in particular contexts is influenced by the demands placed on them by the expectations of the language.

Not only are men infrequently labeled *gentlemen,* but they are infrequently labeled *boys*. The term *boy* is reserved for young males, bellhops, car attendants, and as a putdown to those males judged inferior. *Boy* connotes immaturity and powerlessness. Only occasionally do males "have a night out with the boys." They do not talk "boy talk" at the office. Rarely does our language legitimize carefreeness in males. Rather, they are expected, linguistically, to adopt the responsibilities of manhood.

On the other hand, women of all ages may be called *girls*. Grown females "play bridge with the girls" and indulge in "girl talk." They are encouraged to remain childlike, and the implication is that they are basically immature and without power. Men can become men, linguistically, putting aside the immaturity of childhood; indeed, for them to retain the openness and playfulness of boyhood is linguistically difficult.

Further, the presumed incompetence and immaturity of women are evidenced by the linguistic company they keep. Women are categorized with children ("women and children first"), the infirm ("the blind, the lame, the women"), and the incompetent ("women, convicts, and idiots"). The use of these categorical designations is not accidental happenstance; "rather these selectional groupings are powerful forces behind the actual expressions of language and are based on distinctions which are not regarded as trivial by the speakers of the language" (Key, 1975:82). A total language analysis of categorical groupings is not available, yet it seems likely that women tend to be included in groupings that designate incompleteness, ineptitude, and immaturity. On the other hand, it is difficult for us to conceive of the word *man* in any categorical grouping other than one that extends beyond humanity, such as "Man, apes, and angels" or "Man and Superman." That is, men do exist as an independent category capable of autonomy; women are grouped with the stigmatized, the immature, and the foolish. Moreover, when men are in human groupings, males are invari-

DIFFERENT WORDS, DIFFERENT WORLDS

DEBORAH TANNEN

Intimacy is key in a world of connection where individuals negotiate complex networks of friendship, minimize differences, try to reach consensus, and avoid the appearance of superiority, which would highlight differences. In a world of status, *independence* is key, because a primary means of establishing status is to tell others what to do, and taking orders is a marker of low status. Though all humans need both intimacy and independence, women tend to focus on the first and men on the second. It is as if their life-blood ran in different directions.

These differences can give women and men differing views of the same situation, as they did in the case of a couple I will call Linda and Josh. When Josh's old high-school chum called him at work and announced he'd be in town on business the following month, Josh invited him to stay for the weekend. That evening he informed Linda that they were going to have a houseguest, and that he and his chum would go out together the first night to shoot the breeze like old times. Linda was upset. She was going to be away on business the week before, and the Friday night when Josh would be out with his chum would be her first night home. But what upset her the most was that Josh had made these plans on his own and informed her of them, rather than discussing them with her before extending the invitation.

Linda would never make plans, for a weekend or an evening, without first checking with Josh. She can't understand why he doesn't show her the same courtesy and consideration that she shows him. But when she protests, Josh says, "I can't say to my friend, 'I have to ask my wife for permission'!"

Deborah Tannen, "Different Words, Different Worlds" (editors' title) from *You Just Don't Understand: Women and Men in Conversation.* Copyright © 1990 by Deborah Tannen, Ph.D. Reprinted with the permission of William Morrow & Company, Inc.

To Josh, checking with his wife means seeking permission, which implies that he is not independent, not free to act on his own. It would make him feel like a child or an underling. To Linda, checking with her husband has nothing to do with permission. She assumes that spouses discuss their plans with each other because their lives are intertwined, so the actions of one have consequences for the other. Not only does Linda not mind telling someone, "I have to check with Josh"; quite the contrary—she likes it. It makes her feel good to know and show that she is involved with someone, that her life is bound up with someone else's.

Linda and Josh both felt more upset by this incident, and others like it, than seemed warranted, because it cut to the core of their primary concerns. Linda was hurt because she sensed a failure of closeness in their relationship: He didn't care about her as much as she cared about him. And he was hurt because he felt she was trying to control him and limit his freedom.

A similar conflict exists between Louise and Howie, another couple, about spending money. Louise would never buy anything costing more than a hundred dollars without discussing it with Howie, but he goes out and buys whatever he wants and feels they can afford, like a table saw or a new power mower. Louise is disturbed, not because she disapproves of the purchases, but because she feels he is acting as if she were not in the picture.

Many women feel it is natural to consult with their partners at every turn, while many men automatically make more decisions without consulting their partners. This may reflect a broad difference in conceptions of decision making. Women expect decisions to be discussed first and made by consensus. They appreciate the discussion itself as evidence of involvement and communication. But many men feel oppressed by lengthy discussions about what they see as minor decisions, and they feel hemmed in if they can't just act without talking first. When women try to initiate a freewheeling discussion by asking, "What do you think?" men often think they are being asked to decide. . . .

Because men and women are regarding the landscape from contrasting vantage points, the same scene can appear very different to them, and they often have opposite interpretations of the same action. . . .

A colleague mentioned that he got a letter from a production editor working on his new book, instructing him to let her know if he planned to be away from his permanent address at any time in the next six months, when his book would be in production. He commented that he hadn't realized how like a parole officer a production editor could be. His response to this letter surprised me, because I have received similar letters from publishers, and my response is totally different: I like them, because it makes me feel important to know that my whereabouts matter. When I mentioned this difference to my colleague, he was puzzled and amused, as I was by his reaction. Though he could understand my point of view intellectually, emotionally he could not imagine how one could not feel framed as both controlled and inferior in rank by being told to report one's movements to someone. And though I could understand his perspective intellectually, it simply held no emotional resonance for me.

In a similar spirit, my colleague remarked that he had read a journal article written by a woman who thanked her husband in the acknowledgments section of her paper for helpful discussion of the topic. When my colleague first read this acknowledgment, he thought the author must be incompetent, or at least insecure: Why did she have to consult her husband about her own work? Why couldn't she stand on her own two feet? After hearing my explanation that women value evidence of connection, he reframed the acknowledgment and concluded that the author probably valued her husband's involvement in her work and made reference to it with the pride that comes of believing one has evidence of a balanced relationship.

If my colleague's reaction is typical, imagine how often women who think they are displaying a positive quality—connection—are misjudged by men who perceive them as revealing a lack of independence, which the men regard as synonymous with incompetence and insecurity. . . .

If women speak and hear a language of connection and intimacy, while men speak and hear a language of status and independence, then communication between men and women can be like cross-cultural communication, prey to a clash of conversational styles. Instead of different dialects, it has been said they speak different genderlects. . . .

Although each style is valid on its own terms, misunderstandings arise because the styles are different. Taking a cross-cultural approach to male-female conversations makes it possible to explain why dissatisfactions are justified without accusing anyone of being wrong or crazy.

Learning about style differences won't make them go away, but it can banish mutual mystification and blame. Being able to understand why our partners, friends, and even strangers behave the way they do is a comfort, even if we still don't see things the same way. It makes the world into more familiar territory. And having others understand why we talk and act as we do protects us from the pain of their puzzlement and criticism.

In discussing her novel *The Temple of My Familiar*, Alice Walker explained that a woman in the novel falls in love with a man because she sees in him "a giant ear." Walker went on to remark that although people may think they are falling in love because of sexual attraction or some other force, "really what we're looking for is someone to be able to hear us."

We all want, above all, to be heard—but not merely to be heard. We want to be understood—heard for what we think we are saying, for what we know we meant. With increased understanding of the ways women and men use language should come a decrease in frequency of the complaint "You just don't understand."

ably first on the list ("men and women," "he and she," "man and wife"). This order is not accidental but was prescribed in the 16th century to honor the worthier party.

Fourth, in practice women are defined in terms of their sexual desirability (to men); men are defined in terms of their sexual prowess (over women). Most slang words in reference to women refer to their sexual desirability to men (e.g., *dog, fox, broad, ass, chick*). Slang about men refers to their sexual prowess over women (e.g., *dude, stud, hunk*). The fewer examples given for men is not an oversight. An analysis of sexual slang, for example, listed more than 1,000 words and phrases that derogate women sexually but found "nowhere near this multitude for describing men" (Kramarae, 1975:72). Farmer and Henley (cited in Schulz, 1975) list 500 synonyms for *prostitute,* for example, and only 65 for *whoremonger.* Stanley (1977) reports 220 terms for a sexually promiscuous woman and only 22 for a sexually promiscuous man. Shuster (1973) reports that the passive verb form is used in reference to women's sexual experiences (e.g., *to be laid, to be had, to be taken*), whereas the active tense is used in reference to the male's sexual experience (e.g., *lay, take, have*). Being sexually attractive to males is culturally condoned for women and being sexually powerful is approved for males. In this regard, the slang of the street is certainly not countercultural; rather it perpetuates and reinforces different expectations in females and males as sexual objects and performers.

Further, we find sexual connotations associated with neutral words applied to women. A few examples should suffice. A male academician questioned the title of a new course, asserting it was "too suggestive." The title? "The Position of Women in the Social Order." A male tramp is simply a hobo, but a female tramp is a slut. And consider the difference in connotation of the following expressions:

It's easy.
He's easy.
She's easy.

In the first, we assume something is "easy to do"; in the second, we might assume a professor is an "easy grader" or a man is "easygoing." But when we read "she's easy," the connotation is "she's an easy lay."

In the world of slang, men are defined by their sexual prowess. In the world of slang and proper speech, women are defined as sexual objects. The rule in practice seems to be: If in doubt, assume that *any* reference to a women has a sexual connotation. For both genders, the constant bombardment of prescribed sexuality is bound to have real consequences.

Fifth, women are defined in terms of their relations to men; men are defined in terms of their relations to the world at large. A good example is seen in the words *master* and *mistress.* Originally these words had the same meaning—"a person who holds power over servants." With the demise of the feudal system, however, these words took on different meanings. The masculine variant metaphorically refers to power over something; as in "He is the master of his trade"; the feminine variant metaphorically (although probably not in actuality) refers to power over a man sexually, as in "She is Tom's mistress." Men are defined in terms of their power in the occupational world, women in terms of their sexual power over men.

The existence of two contractions for Mistress (*Miss* and *Mrs.*) and but one for Mister (*Mr.*) underscores the cultural concern and linguistic practice: women are defined in relation to men. Even a divorced woman is defined in terms of her no-longer-existing relation to a man (she is still *Mrs. Man's Name*). But apparently the divorced state is not relevant enough to the man or to the society to require a label. A divorced woman is a *divorcee,* but what do you call a divorced man? The recent preference of many women to be called *Ms.* is an attempt to provide for women an equivalency title that is not dependent on marital status.

Sixth, a historical pattern can be seen in the meanings that come to be attached to words that originally were neutral: those that apply to women acquire obscene and/or debased connotations but no such pattern of derogation holds for neutral words referring to men. The processes of *pejoration* (the acquiring of an obscene or debased connotation) and *amelioration* (the reacquiring of a neutral or positive connotation) in the English language in regard to terms for males and females have been studied extensively by Muriel Schulz (1975).

Leveling is the least derogative form of pejoration. Through leveling, titles that originally referred to an elite class of persons come to include a wider class of persons. Such democratic leveling is more common for female designates than for males. For example, contrast the following: *lord–lady (lady); baronet–dame (dame); governor–governess (governess).*

Most frequently what happens to words designating women as they become pejorated, however, is that they come to denote or connote sexual wantonness. *Sir* and *mister,* for example, remain titles of courtesy, but at some time *madam, miss,* and *mistress* have come to designate, respectively, a brothelkeeper, a prostitute, and an unmarried sexual partner of a male (Schulz, 1975:66).

Names for domestic helpers, if they are females, are frequently derogated. *Hussy,* for example, originally meant "housewife." *Laundress, needlewoman, spinster* ("tender of the spinning wheel"), and *nurse* all referred to domestic occupations within the home, and all at some point became slang expressions for prostitute or mistress.

Even kinship terms referring to women become denigrated. During the 17th century, *mother* was used to mean "a bawd"; more recently *mother* (*mothuh f——*) has become a common derogatory epithet (Cameron, 1974). Probably at some point in history every kinship term for females has been derogated (Schulz, 1975:66).

Terms of endearment for women also seem to follow a downward path. Such pet names as Tart, Dolly, Kitty, Polly, Mopsy, Biddy, and Jill all eventually became sexually derogatory (Schulz, 1975:67). *Whore* comes from the same Latin root as *care* and once meant "a lover of either sex."

Indeed, even the most neutral categorical designations— *girl, female, woman, lady*—at some point in their history have been used to connote sexual immorality. *Girl* originally meant "a child of either sex"; through the process of semantic degeneration it eventually meant "a prostitute." Although *girl* has lost this meaning, *girlie* still retains sexual connotations. *Woman* connoted "a mistress" in the early 19th century; *female* was a degrading epithet in the latter part of the 19th century; and when *lady* was introduced as a euphemism, it too became deprecatory. "Even so neutral a term as *person,* when it was used as substitute for *woman,* suffered [vulgarization]" (Mencken, 1963: 350, quoted in Schulz, 1975:71).

Whether one looks at elite titles, occupational roles, kinship relationships, endearments, or age-sex categorical designations, the pattern is clear. Terms referring to females are pejorated—"become negative in the middle instances and abusive in the extremes" (Schulz, 1975:69). Such semantic derogation, however, is not evidenced for male referents. *Lord, baronet, father, brother, nephew, footman, bowman, boy, lad, fellow, gentleman, man, male,* and so on "have failed to undergo the derogation found in the history of their corresponding feminine designations" (Schulz, 1975:67). Interestingly, the male word, rather than undergoing derogation, frequently is replaced by a female referent when the speaker wants to debase a male. A weak man, for example, is referred to as a *sissy* (diminutive of *sister*), and an army recruit during basic training is called a *pussy.* And when one is swearing at a male, he is referred to as a *bastard* or a *son-of-a-bitch*— both appellations that impugn the dignity of a man's mother.

In summary, these verbal practices are consistent with the gender stereotypes that we encounter in everyday life. Women are thought to be a part of man, nonautonomous, dependent, relegated to roles that require few skills, characteristically incompetent and immature, sexual objects, best defined in terms of their relations to men. Males are visible, autonomous and independent, responsible for the protection and containment of women, expected to occupy positions on the basis of their high achievement or physical power, assumed to be sexually potent, and defined primarily by their relations to the world of work. The use of the language perpetuates the stereotypes for both genders and limits the options available for self-definition.

REFERENCES

Adamsky, C. 1981. "Changes in pronominal usage in a classroom situation." *Psychology of Women Quarterly* 5:773–79.

Bendix, J. 1979. "Linguistic models as political symbols: Gender and the generic 'he' in English." In J. Orasanu, M. Slater, and L. L. Adler, eds., *Language, sex and gender: Does la différence make a difference?* pp. 23–42. New York: New Academy of Science Annuals.

Cameron, P. 1974. "Frequency and kinds of words in various social settings, or What the hell's going on?" In M. Truzzi, ed., *Sociology for pleasure,* pp. 31–37. Englewood Cliffs, N.J.: Prentice-Hall.

Daly, M. 1973. *Beyond God the father.* Boston: Beacon Press.

DeStefano, J. S. 1976. Personal communication. Columbus: Ohio State University.

Hamilton, N., & Henley, N. 1982. "Detrimental consequences of the generic masculine usage." Paper presented to the Western Psychological Association meetings, Sacramento.

Key, M. R. 1975. *Male/female language.* Metuchen, N.J.: Scarecrow Press.

Kramarae, Cheris. 1975. "Woman's speech: Separate but unequal?" In Barrie Thorne and Nancy Henley, eds., *Language and sex: Difference and dominance,* pp. 43–56. Rowley, Mass.: Newbury House.

MacKay, D. G. 1983. "Prescriptive grammar and the pronoun problem." In B. Thorne, C. Kramarae, and N. Henley, eds., *Language, gender, and society,* pp. 38–53. Rowley, Mass.: Newbury House.

Martyna, W. 1978. "What does 'he' mean? Use of the generic masculine." *Journal of Communication* 28:131–38.

Martyna, W. 1980. "Beyond the 'he/man' approach: The case for nonsexist language." *Signs* 5:482–93.

Mencken, H. L. 1963. *The American language.* 4th ed. with supplements. Abr. and ed. R. I. McDavis. New York: Knopf.

Schneider, J., & Hacker, S. 1973. "Sex role imagery in the use of the generic 'man' in introductory texts: A case in the sociology of sociology." *American Sociologist* 8:12–18.

Schulz, M. R. 1975. "The semantic derogation of women." In B. Thorne and N. Henley, eds., *Language and sex: Difference and dominance,* pp. 64–75. Rowley, Mass.: Newbury House.

Shuster, Janet. 1973. "Grammatical forms marked for male and female in English." Unpublished paper. Chicago: University of Chicago.

Stanley, J. P. 1977. "Paradigmatic woman: The prostitute." In D. L. Shores, ed., *Papers in language variation.* Birmingham: University of Alabama Press.

Vanderbilt, A. 1972. *Amy Vanderbilt's etiquette.* Garden City, N.Y.: Doubleday.

R E A D I N G   1 3

Barbie Doll Culture and the American Waistland

KAMY CUNNINGHAM

A Waistland is a land where, if you're a woman, you have to have a tiny waist in order to not feel like something the cat drug out of the garbage bin. I remember at age ten gazing at my first Barbie, the sloe-eyed version with painted toenails in its zebra-striped suit, and deciding, well, I guess this pneumatic creature (I already had a pretty sophisticated vocabulary back then) with the long, horsey legs and Scarlett O'Hara waist was what I was supposed to grow up to look like.

Doesn't every little, and big, American girl want to look like Barbie? And doesn't she want to *be* Barbie, wholesome and popular and perky? In short, a plastic doll.

Barbie beckons us little, and big, girls, but toward what? And if it's toward beauty, what sort of beauty is this, with its tiny waist?

During a moment of epiphany in the middle of a television commercial the other night (most people just go to the bathroom), I speculated that it might be the beauty of the Heartland of America, cholesterol free and patriotically waving tubs of margarine called Promise.

Kamy Cunningham, "Barbie Doll Culture and the American Waistland," *Symbolic Interaction* 16, no. 1 (1993). Copyright © 1993 by JAI Press, Inc. Reprinted with the permission of the publisher.

The show between the commercials was the Ms. Teenage America Pageant followed, a couple of days later, by a grown-up beauty contest, the Supermodel of the Year. The teenage hopefuls were all ruffles and tans and soufflés of clichés, each determined to be herself and not succumb to peer pressure and to work with the handicapped, the learning disabled, the old, and the terminally ill because, of course, the most wonderful thing in life is to help others and be the best you can be.

Their supermodel counterparts were slinky, and slid along the stage like skinny eels, in that funny model posture, pelvis jutting forward, small bosoms receding onto the terrace of the breastbone, that makes a woman look like a limp piece of spaghetti about to fall over—backwards.

Barbie combines the prototypes of the two pageants—she's all ruffles and cuteness *and* all experienced slinkiness. A recent version, the Fashion Play Barbie, is a good illustration of what I mean. Clad in a Frederick's of Hollywood wisp of lingerie and topped by luxuriant platinum tresses, the doll has lavender eyes, both willing and innocent, that look out of a face cutely dimpled and empty of feminine guile, yet somehow eerily seductive.

In her own plastic person, Barbie carries the Virgin/Whore paradox to an even more tensile extreme than does, say, a

Marilyn Monroe, or a Madonna. Marilyn combined helpless, yielding child with voluptuous, knowing woman in a caricature of the two that was almost obscene. Madonna—shrewd, ruthless, experienced, slightly perverse—is a walking, strutting contradiction to the name of the Virgin she has appropriated.

Slip off that wisp of lingerie, barely clinging to those fulsome curves, and a naked Barbie doll is a sexy thing. Pouty bosom, that tiny waist so oft spoke of, flared hips, lissome legs. Squeeze her and knead her and she has a rubbery life of her own. Cup her, King Kong fashion, and feel the points of the breasts press into your palm. Run your hand down the full 11-1/2" and experience cool, clean silk feel of plastic. Wholesome and seductive.

Is this beauty? Egyptian woman painted their eyelids a heavy charcoal black. Medieval paintings show that women with small tulip breasts and big, ovenrounded bellies were desirable. Rubens and Titian and Ingres thought that women layered like lily-white, hothouse marshmallows were best. In some cultures the male is the heavily painted and artificial one. Like an obscene, opalescent peacock or an aquamarine bird of paradise with blue dragons curling around his arms, in sinuous indigo, he gyrates in front of the womenfolk, hoping (and hopping) to be "pretty" enough to be picked.

The question is not really one of beauty, of course, but of the oppressive equation of beauty, however we define it, with worth. Surface so dominates essence in America that the equation has gotten out of hand. The reason is obvious. We are bombarded by images of Barbie doll women. On a recent *Smithsonian World*, a popular culture critic called advertising "one of the predominate art forms of our time." Advertising is so dominate, the show goes on to say, that "its messages are the only ones being heard." "America is about selling" and "we accept the marketplace as the arbiter of values."

Ads create the symbols of our culture; they suggest that the Johnson's make-me-your-baby-powder woman is the only acceptable version of the feminine.

When I was ten years old, I didn't know that I was longing for a Rubenesque or a Titianesque, rather than a Barbiesque, visual model. I didn't know at the time that she was influencing and reinforcing impossible cultural norms of physical beauty, norms that I would never be able to even approximate. I didn't know that most men want Barbie doll women, the ones with long blonde hair, innocent baby-blue (or baby-lavender) eyes, substantial Cosmocover melons, tiny waists, flat tummies, taut bottoms, and long graceful legs. (And absurdly small feet:

Barbie doesn't even have to wear heels in order to be "hobbled"—it's built into those ridiculous concubine feet.) I didn't know that to be considered desirable, I would have to be a centerfold, zipped into my nakedness like a shrimp in its casing.

If I had known all of this, I would probably have thrown myself off Hoover Dam and never reached age eleven.

There are some other things wrong with Barbie too. She's a simulacrum of a human being, a sad grotesquerie: her creators gave her breasts but no nipples, flared hips but no womb, seductively spread legs but no vagina. No milk, no sucklings, no procreation. A twilight zone creature, as strange as her life-sized counterpart—the department store mannequin with the sterility of a lavender sheen on its cadaverous, blue-grey cheeks—she is an emblem of frustration and unfulfillment.

In Las Vegas, at Caesars Palace, an enormous figurehead of Cleopatra juts out over the casino. With her huge bronze breasts that dangle above your head and her ample but shapely girth, she looks as if she could have mothered the whole human race. Instead, taut in every disappointed muscle, she strains out into nothing, gazing at this sterile indoor cosmos of star-spangled chandeliers.

Las Vegas showgirls look manufactured—identical lanky clones carrying ten pounds of feathers above eyes so mascared no eyes are there. Ads across the country misrepresent them as voluptuous; actually, by some ironic twist, they're all tiny-bosomed because big breasts bounce around on the stage with the least step or jiggle. All the girls would look like cumbersome, milkheavy cows. Go to a Las Vegas show and the sensation is eerie: two-hundred identical breasts with tiny peppermint nipples point your way, like the pink noses of puppies. Beneath the nipples, identical Rockettes' legs. Large breasts might be an improvement: the hilarity would relieve the manufactured look of the women.

The "simply irresistible" clone women, of Pepsi commercial and MTV fame, produce a similar shuddering sensation. Painted over with that lavender sheen of the mannequin, with big, hard, dark eyes, and starved cheeks, their faces look like those of boxed dolls—identical and inexpressive. Only their bodies are alive, in a mechanical way, as they move. Their eyes are dead. Some even wear goggles, blinders that make them look like horses in harness. They have been zapped of all their vitality, by being turned into mindless doll-like clones. Dead dolls, vampire women. Plastic. Manufactured. Artificial. Unreal. No room for the appealing flaws and living warmth of "real" women, those whose Rubenesque curves might spread a little and whose

THE BEAUTY MYTH

NAOMI WOLF

. . . Beauty pornography looks like this: The perfected woman lies prone, pressing down her pelvis. Her back arches, her mouth is open, her eyes shut, her nipples erect; there is a fine spray of moisture over her golden skin. The position is female superior; the stage of arousal, the plateau phase just preceding orgasm. On the next page, a version of her, mouth open, eyes shut, is about to tongue the pink tip of a lipstick cylinder. On the page after, another version kneels in the sand on all fours, her buttocks in the air, her face pressed into a towel, mouth open, eyes shut. The reader is looking through an ordinary women's magazine. In an ad for Reebok shoes, the woman sees a naked female torso, eyes averted. In an ad for Lily of France lingerie, she sees a naked female torso, eyes shut; for Opium perfume, a naked woman, back and buttocks bare, falls facedown from the edge of a bed; for Triton showers, a naked woman, back arched, flings her arms upward; for Jogbra sports bras, a naked female torso is cut off at the neck. In these images, where the face is visible, it is expressionless in a rictus of ecstasy. The reader understands from them that she will have to look like that if she wants to feel like that.

Beauty sadomasochism is different: In an ad for Obsession perfume, a well-muscled man drapes the naked, lifeless body of a woman over his shoulder. In an ad for Hermès perfume, a blond woman trussed in black leather is hanging upside down, screaming, her wrists looped in chains, mouth bound. In an ad for Fuji cassettes, a female robot with a playmate's body, but made of steel, floats with her genitals exposed, her ankles bolted and her face a steel mask with slits for the eyes and mouth. In an ad for Erno Laszlo skin care products, a woman sits up and begs, her wrists clasped together with a leather leash that is also tied to her dog, who is sitting up in the same posture and begging. In an American ad for Newport cigarettes, two men tackle one woman and pull another by the hair; both women are screaming. In another Newport ad, a man forces a woman's head down to get her distended mouth around a length of spurting hose gripped in his fist; her eyes are terrified. In an ad for Saab automobiles, a shot up a fashion model's thighs is captioned, "Don't worry. It's ugly underneath." In a fashion layout in *The Observer* (London), five men in black menace a model, whose face is in shock, with scissors and hot iron rods. In *Tatler* and *Harper's and Queen,* "designer rape sequences (women beaten, bound and abducted, but immaculately turned out and artistically photographed)" appear. In Chris von Wangenheim's *Vogue* layout, Doberman pinschers attack a model. Geoffrey Beene's metallic sandals are displayed against a background of S and M accessories. The woman learns from these images that no matter how assertive she may be in the world, her private submission to control is what makes her desirable. . . .

Sexual "explicitness" is not the issue. We could use a lot more of that, if explicit meant honest and revealing;

Titianesque arms might have a bit of the soft sway of the basset hound. Warm arms, motherly arms.

Barbie, with all of her accessories (thousands of little outfits, and dozens of pieces of pink plastic furniture, and Hollywood hot tubs and sleek racing cars) brings in three quarters of a billion dollars a year for Mattel. Every two seconds someone somewhere in the world buys a Barbie. Numerically, there are 2.5 Barbies for every household in America.

She is obviously a powerful cultural icon, but what is her iconography? What text is she illustrating? The text of woman as manufactured cadaver? Woman robbed of any insides because she has to be all outside?

Barbie's living clone, Vanna White, Goddess of the Empty Woman, seems to be illustrating a depressing blankness (note the name *White*). Vanna's message is that if you look like her and dress beautifully and smile warmly and turn letters with great skill and remain forever, mentally and emotionally, on the level of an untroubled child, then you will be valued and given lots of money. Turning letters counts for far more, apparently, than turning a phrase.

if there were a full spectrum of erotic images of uncoerced real women and real men in contexts of sexual trust, beauty pornography could theoretically hurt no one. Defenders of pornography base their position on the idea of freedom of speech, casting pornographic imagery as language. Using their own argument, something striking emerges about the representation of women's bodies: The representation is heavily censored. Because we see many versions of the naked Iron Maiden, we are asked to believe that our culture promotes the display of female sexuality. It actually shows almost none. It censors representations of women's bodies, so that only the official versions are visible. Rather than seeing images *of* female desire or that cater *to* female desire, we see mock-ups of living mannequins, made to contort and grimace, immobilized and uncomfortable under hot lights, professional set-pieces that reveal little about female sexuality. In the United States and Great Britain, which have no tradition of public nakedness, women rarely—and almost never outside a competitive context—see what other *women* look like naked; we see only identical humanoid products based loosely on women's bodies. . . .

. . . Leaving aside the issue of what violent sexual imagery does, it is still apparent that there is an officially enforced double standard for men's and women's nakedness in mainstream culture that bolsters power inequities.

The practice of displaying breasts, for example, in contexts in which the display of penises would be unthinkable, is portrayed as trivial because breasts are not "as naked" as penises or vaginas; and the idea of half exposing men in a similar way is moot because men don't have body parts comparable to breasts. But if we think about how women's genitals are physically concealed, unlike men's, and how women's breasts are physically exposed, unlike men's, it can be seen differently: women's breasts, then correspond to men's penises as the vulnerable "sexual flower" on the body, so that to display the former and conceal the latter makes women's bodies vulnerable while men's are protected. Cross-culturally, unequal nakedness almost always expresses power relations: In modern jails, male prisoners are stripped in front of clothed prison guards; in the antebellum South, young black male slaves were naked while serving the clothed white masters at table. To live in a culture in which women are routinely naked where men aren't is to learn inequality in little ways all day long. So even if we agree that sexual imagery is in fact a language, it is clearly one that is already heavily edited to protect men's sexual—and hence social-confidence while undermining that of women. . . .

When they discuss[their bodies], women lean forward, their voices lower. They tell their terrible secret. It's my breasts, they say. My hips. It's my thighs. I hate my stomach. This is not aesthetic distaste, but deep sexual shame. The parts of the body vary. But what each woman who describes it shares is the conviction that *that* is what the pornography of beauty most fetishizes. Breasts, thighs, buttocks, bellies: the most sexually central parts of women, whose "ugliness" therefore becomes an obsession. Those are the parts most often battered by abusive men. The parts that sex murderers most often mutilate. The parts most often defiled by violent pornography. The parts that beauty surgeons most often cut open. The parts that bear and nurse children and feel sexual. A misogynist culture has succeeded in making women hate what misogynists hate. . . .

Rarely, in the history of womankind mankind, has so little been so richly rewarded.

One night, on *Wheel of Fortunate,* she gushed, in a see-Spot-run vocabulary, over an "island paradise" vacation she'd just taken that was "simply wonderful" and "so great." (Her narrative, childishly adjectival and without a story line, had not quite reached the level of sophistication of the "cow jumped over the moon.") I feel resentful that Vanna and her ilk (all those manufactured mannequins and cadaverous clones) can pile up fortunes by selling their bodies and that I can't make anything by selling my mind.

But, to temper my tirade (a bit), I feel a little sorry for her (and them). And happy for me, a little. In a world where you have to sell something to survive, maybe it's better to have a mind to market than a transient body.

Perhaps, decades from now, I may be able to entertain myself with books and thoughts after all the centerfolds have sagged and the Vannas have died away from their own untroubled boredom.

R E A D I N G   1 4

Women's Music: No Longer a Small Private Party

CYNTHIA M. LONT

We never wanted to be perceived as women's music. We don't want to be found only in the specialty bin at the record stores. We want to be in your face.

—*Gretchen Phillips of 2 Nice Girls[1]*

This chapter has two intentions, neither primary. First, I want to document the history of women's music. While some musicologists and cultural critics have listened to women's music, and/or know something about it, few have a firm understanding of its cultural basis. Unlike other subcultural music forms, women's music has received little attention in either mainstream or music industry media. Such "symbolic annihilation"[2] of women's music is not surprising. That is the norm concerning women and their inclusion in the media. With rare exceptions (Cris Williamson on the front cover of *Ms.* or Holly Near on the "Today Show"), women's music performers have been blatantly absent from mainstream and other subcultures' press. If the media pay no attention to you (whether it be good or bad press) you don't exist. In the case of women's music, the media's silence is mostly due to the music's foundation in the lesbian community.

My second intention is to detail the relationship between the 1970s and 1980s phenomena of women's music and the new wave of women performers who've become popular in the late '80s and '90s: Tracy Chapman, Michelle Shocked, k.d. lang, and others. Do these performers represent the cooptation of women's music by major labels that now realize the buying power of feminist and lesbian audiences (for example, Michelle Shocked's *Campfire Tapes,* an album originally recorded on a Walkman, sold 30,000 copies to the women's community in England)? Are the more "androgynous" artists (we don't say "lesbian" on major labels) now acceptable to fans who have tired of the stereotyped male fantasies of female pop singers, or is this another quickly passing trend in the music business?

I don't view optimistically the acceptance of women in the mainstream, since economics plays an enormous role; nor do I believe that there is such a large number of new female artists that feminists should be unconcerned with the 99.9 percent of female performers who continue to portray their lives as less than complete without males. Yet an incredible energy does derive from women's music that has cut a narrow path through the sexism at the heart of popular music. The question remains whether the message of women's music has been heard by enough people to result in more changes than just the acceptance of a few women performers in mainstream music.

WOMEN'S MUSIC

Women's music was originally defined as music by women, for women, about women, and financially controlled by women.[3] By this definition, a song written by women, about women, and for women would not be considered a part of women's music if it were recorded on a major label. This alternative music industry was originally called lesbian music because many felt the music was started by lesbians for lesbians. Others believed the music was started by heterosexual feminists and taken over by lesbian-feminists when they broke away from the women's liberation movement in the early 1970s.

The term women's music stuck because it was less threatening, both to the dominant social order and to women's music performers and audiences. Women were less likely to be harassed for listening to or performing "women's music" than "lesbian music." Prior to the late '60s, the supportive gay movement and resulting gay pride were nonexistent. Thus the term women's music shielded lesbians not only from the harsh criticism of the dominant social order but from their own internal criticism.

Knowledge of women's music became a key into the lesbian community. If a woman mentioned certain performers in women's music such as Cris Williamson or Meg Christian, it identified her as a lesbian, while talking about one's interest in the music of Joan Baez or Joni Mitchell was not a clear indication that one was a lesbian or lesbian-identified.

The term women's music refers to more than music. The individuals and groups that produced the music were a tangible example of the power of women organized apart from the dominant culture. Lesbian-feminists could take enormous pride knowing that women (read "lesbians") were responsible for the record (performers, musicians, engineers, cover artists); for distribution to the local feminist (read lesbian) bookstore; and for the promotional tours to rural areas, university towns, and small cities. The lesbian-feminist movement was made visible in concert halls and coffeehouses.

THE POLITICAL AND (SUB)CULTURAL FOUNDATION OF WOMEN'S MUSIC

Women's music didn't burst into being via one critical political and cultural moment. Instead, the explosion of disturbances from within the political left and a blatant disregard for women throughout the social order created the "space" for diverse women to form the women's music industry.

Women who began women's music labels, and later, distributors of women's music primarily came from the ranks of politically left (counter-culture, student, and Civil Rights) groups which ignored women's skills and talents, and invalidated women's experiences. Lesbian organizers entered women's music from the women's liberation movement, many from the National Organization for Women, (which denied the existence of lesbians within its ranks until 1971) or from the Gay Liberation Front (which focused on gay men and their needs).

The existence of women's music (the lyrics, the music, and its support structure) directly opposed the patriarchal culture in which mainstream popular music existed.

Mainstream music was based on the experiences of males, subsuming women's experiences within men's experiences or ignoring women's experiences completely. The "symbolic annihilation" of women and women's autonomous experiences within popular music was the impetus for women's music.

The absence of positive women's images within popular music paralleled a lack of opportunities for female performers.[4] In the late 1960s and early 1970s, mainstream labels signed only a few women's bands, including Fanny, Bertha, Deadly Nightshade, and Goldie and the Gingerbreads. Fanny, one of the first all-women's bands on a major record label, "served notice to the rock world that women could do more than simply sing—that women could also write and play rock passionately."[5] While these bands showed that women could play, their lyrics were no more women-centered than those of other rock music.

The women's liberation movement nurtured feminist audiences who wanted their lives portrayed as more than sexual objects for males. For the feminist music listener of the early 1970s, finding selections which didn't rock one's sensibilities was not an easy task. Even the seemingly "independent" women (Tina Turner and Linda Ronstadt) were pouring out their guts for male approval. A feminist record collection was quite limited; a lesbian collection was non-existent.

The intersection of women performers seeking a place to play women-centered music, political organizers seeking a cooperative work environment, and feminists and lesbians seeking music to reaffirm their lifestyles and experiences created the energy and space for women's music to thrive.

EARLY HISTORY OF WOMEN'S MUSIC

Perhaps at no other time in history could women's music have developed. Following the example of Black Liberation, women increasingly organized apart from men in the late '60s and early '70s. Lesbians faced with discrimination within feminist groups argued vehemently over whether to completely withdraw from male and straight society. "Separatism" was a tactic which focused women's energy and would give an enormous boost to the growth and development of women's music.

The first record performed and recorded by an "out" lesbian artist was Maxine Feldman's "Angry Athis," a 45-rpm single with explicitly lesbian lyrics by an "out" performer, produced by lesbians.

> *I hate not being able*
> *To hold my lover's hand*
> *'Cept under some dimly lit table*
> *Afraid of being who I am*
> *I hate to tell lies*
> *Live in the shadow of fear*
> *We've run half our lives*
> *From that damn word queer*[6]

Like Feldman, lesbian and straight feminists were singing their politics across the country and they began to record.

In 1973, Alix Dobkin, a lesbian separatist, formed a musical group, Lavender Jane, with flutist Kay Gardner and bass player Patches Attom. Financial and emotional support from the lesbian community encouraged Lavender Jane to record an album. Dobkin located a lesbian sound engineer and, soon thereafter, *Lavender Jane Loves Women* was available. Dobkin stated on the album cover:

> For a dozen years I tried to "make it" in the music business—as a solo artist, demo artist, in groups, as a songwriter, a commercial writer and even in coffeehouse management. So many times I came so close, and felt great frustration and disappointment. Always there was this rough element of mine—an abrasive edge—an imperfection. Record and publishing executives, independent producers, managers, agents, P.R. men and assorted hustlers could never quite polish me into a neat commercial package. Lucky for me.[7]

Lavender Jane cost $3,300 for the first 1,000 copies, all of which sold in three months with no formal distribution system other than mail order and a few lesbian-feminist bookstores.

At the same time, an independent label, Rounder Records, produced *Mountain Movin' Day* by an all-straight women band, The Chicago Women's Liberation Rock Band. This band sang rock songs and pantomimed the way men perform rock, demonstrating the underlying sexist nature of the actions.

Although these recordings were important, there was little organization to the production, distribution, and promotion of women's music. In 1973, a group of politically active women (some from the disbanded Furies collective) were searching for a way to implement their lesbian-feminist politics. After meeting two performers, Meg Christian and Cris Williamson, and seeing the need for and interest in music by lesbian-feminists, they formed Olivia Records. With the exception of the short-lived Women's Music Network in New York City (1973–1976), this was the first collective attempt at an organization committed to the production, distribution, and promotion of women's music.

Olivia Records' first 45 rpm (Meg Christian's rendition of "Lady" by Carole King/Gerry Goffin and Cris Williamson's "If It Weren't For the Music") sold 5,000 copies through mail order. This enabled Olivia to produce their first album, Meg Christian's *I Know You Know.* The first year, 10,000 to 12,000 copies were sold. *I Know You Know* was followed by Cris Williamson's *The Changer and the Changed,* "one of the all-time best selling albums on any independent label—in or out of women's music."[8] Over ten years later, "Sweet Woman," one of the songs on *Changer,* continues as one of top five all-time favorite women's music songs (1987–88) in *Hot Wire's* Readers' Choice Awards.

In a few short years, the women's music industry expanded drastically and changed steadily. In 1975, Kay Gardner included classical music on her first album, *Mooncircles,* recorded on her own label, Wide Woman/Urana. Margie Adam, with Barbara Price, created her own label, Pleiades, and Holly Near and friends restructured Redwood Records. The first women of color to record on a women's music label, Sweet Honey in the Rock, had a strong feminist following in 1978 when they recorded the album *B'lieve I'll Run On . . . See What the End's Gonna Be* on Redwood Records. Their contemporary and traditional songs of black experience made new connections between black audiences and the predominantly white women's music audiences.

Women's music "resistance" against the dominant culture followed the example of the hippies' political strategy: cultural revolution. Rather than directly confronting patriarchy, women's music for the most part ignored it, and by its very existence, created an alternative culture. Women's music dared to emphasize the experiences of women in a culture that ignored, devalued, or subsumed women's experiences within males' experiences. Males and the dominant culture weren't portrayed negatively in women's music, they just weren't included. Instead, women's music created a space and form in which women's autonomy and, in particular, lesbian lifestyles were encouraged. Women's music portrayed women's cultures, separate and safe from patriarchal domination. Women's music portrayed women's interactions with one another, something completely counter to the dominant culture's understanding of important relationships.

By 1978, women's music labels covered over a dozen albums. Although the most well-known performers—Adam, Christian, Near, and Williamson—continued in light folk/rock style, women's music labels included other genres: new age, country, jazz, blues, etc. As the number of records grew, so did the need for a distribution network. Olivia early on recognized this need and sought volunteers to distribute their records. Women's music grew so rapidly that these volunteers formed a network called WILD (Women's Independent Labels Distributors), which distributed other women's music labels' albums. There was little competition among distributors as parts of the country were evenly assigned to WILD members, distributing women's music to individuals, feminist bookstores, and audiences at concerts and festivals. Also in 1978, Roadwork Inc., a national booking company, formed to help women's music performers book tours.

Women's music festivals showcased new women's music talent. Women's music fans from small towns came to hear their favorite artists, buy albums they couldn't obtain at home, and, in many cases, spend time in women-only space. The Michigan Womyn's Music Festival, the largest and one of the most well-known festivals, started in 1976, and continues to attract 8,000 women annually. For four days, women "live in a woman-only, idyllic world of sunny days warming bare breasts and starry nights with the full moon shining through the trees and over the stage."[9]

PROFIT VERSUS POLITICS

The integration of politics and profit continually plagued women's music. Many felt there was no place for a discussion of profit within the confines of a politically charged organization. Alix Dobkin called the combining of good business with feminist ideals, "living with contradictions."[10] What one woman felt was a good business decision, another saw as a bad political move.

Based on a political model of social change, rather than a capitalist model of profit, women's music never intended to compete with or become part of mainstream music. Those involved in women's music wanted political change, not profit-sharing. Ginny Berson of the Olivia collective said they had two goals—to create an alternative economic institution which would employ women in a non-oppressive situation and to "be in a position to affect large numbers of women."[11]

As with most movements, money was a problem. Money for a record was donated or collected from the women's community and, after production and manufacturing, little was left for the artists or the company. While major labels spent $75,000 in 1977 to produce an album, Olivia spent $7,500.

Record-making continued, but women's music labels were always on the brink of bankruptcy. Holly Near's lesbian-identified album, *Imagine My Surprise* (Redwood Records) sold 100,000 copies, a success by women's music standards. Yet Redwood was $75,000 in debt.

The pressure on women's music performers was immense. At first, there were few performers and many stops on a tour. Everyone knew the importance of touring the small rural communities as well as the urban centers. In general, performers stayed at people's homes, were paid very little, and traveled as cheaply as they could. Producers worried about economic solvency. Women's music concerts, at first held in church basements or in university spaces, had poor or absent sound systems and a mostly volunteer production staff. Over the years, performers expected more than expenses, production crews expected to be paid, and the audience demanded better space and sound. Producers felt that performers and workers deserved the best sound, location, and payment, which meant an increase in concert ticket prices. In other words, most everyone concerned with the production of women's music needed more money.

THE MOVE TO CROSS-OVER OR MAINSTREAM

By the 1980s, the women's music market was saturated. While released albums increased, the audience to purchase them did not. The record industry, in general, saw a decrease in records sales. In order to survive, every level of women's music (musicians, labels, distributors, engineers, and producers) played with two options—a move toward mainstream audiences or crossing over to other political audiences.

Initially, Redwood Records sought a more mainstream audience. The resulting album, entitled *Fire in the Rain* (1981), included a commercial, slick look and sound. June Millington, one of the original members of Fanny, played electric guitar and provided direction for the album. Holly Near's voice, though kept intact, was backed up by a group of musicians more accustomed to playing mainstream music. Redwood pushed for radio airplay with one single and hired an industry professional to "work" the record. The result was sales of 30,000 copies in the first month and television appearances of Near on the "Today Show" and "Sesame Street."

Olivia Records also moved toward mainstream audiences, creating Second Wave, a subsidiary label which over the years "released less feminist-identified music and broke with its [Olivia's] commitment to use only female musi-

WOMEN RAP BACK

MICHELE WALLACE

Like many black feminists, I look on sexism in rap as a necessary evil. In a society plagued by poverty and illiteracy, where young black men are as likely to be in prison as in college, rap is a welcome articulation of the economic and social frustrations of black youth.

It offers the release of creative expression and historical continuity; it draws on precedents as diverse as jazz, reggae, calypso, Afro-Cuban, African and heavy-metal, and its lyrics include rudimentary forms of political, economic, and social analysis.

But though there are exceptions, like raps advocating world peace (The W.I.S.E. Guyz's "Time for Peace") and opposing drug use (Ice T's "I'm Your Pusher"), rap lyrics can be brutal, raw, and, where women are the subject, glaringly sexist.

Though styles vary—from that of the X-rated Ice T to the sybaritic Kwamé to the hyperpolitics of Public

Michele Wallace, "Women Rap Back," *Ms.* 1, no. 3 (November–December 1990). Copyright © 1990 by Lang Communications. Reprinted with the permission of *Ms.*

Enemy—what seems universal is how little male rappers respect sexual intimacy and how little regard they have for the humanity of the black woman.

At present there is only a small platform for black women to address the problems of sexism in rap and in their community. For a black feminist to chastise misogyny in rap publicly would be viewed as divisive and counterproductive. The charge is hardly new. Such a reaction greeted Ntozake Shange's play *For Colored Girls Who Have Considered Suicide When the Rainbow Is Enuf,* my own essays, *Black Macho and the Myth of the Superwoman,* and Alice Walker's novel *The Color Purple,* all of which were perceived as being critical of black men.

Rap is rooted not only in the blaxploitation films of the 1960s but also in an equally sexist tradition of black comedy. In the use of four-letter words and explicit sexual references, both Richard Pryor and Eddie Murphy, who themselves drew upon the earlier examples of Redd Foxx, Pigment Markham, and Moms Mabley, are conscious reference points for the 2 Live

cians."[12] Margie Adam summed up the early 1980s: "While reading in the feminist press that women's music was dying, I was reading in the mainstream press that several other artists were trying to distance themselves from the label 'women's music.'"[13]

As women's music peaked, problems arose. Women's music audiences expected more from women's music performers than they did from their mainstream counterparts. Performers burned out from too many tours and too many demands on their time. Meg Christian left Olivia Records and women's music in 1984. Meg Christian had given 15 years to women's music. She was among the most popular, if not *the* most popular, artist in women's music. Of the four "big cheeseburgers" (Adam, Christian, Near, and Williamson), Meg most gave of herself, and was in many ways the "ideal" lesbian performer. She was an "out" lesbian, her songs blatantly lesbian, and her rapport with an audience unprecedented—and then she was gone.

Margie Adam also left women's music. In retrospect, she expressed a political concern that as women artists began to move away from women's music "as an artistic and political principle . . . the possibility for radical change with our music was proportionately lessened. The power of this women-loving organizing tool began to dissipate."[14]

Olivia continued recording Cris Williamson, but her music differed greatly not only in style but in its representation of lesbianism—it was subtle, and much more accepted by mainstream audiences. According to Judy Dlugacz, co-founder and president of Olivia:

Church groups connect and want to play Cris Williamson's music, and nuns want to take their vows to "Song of the Soul," one of Cris' classics. Girl Scout troops sing our music at the camps, and we are really looking into that homegrown type of thing because I think that is where our purpose lies.[15]

Crew. Black comedy, in turn, draws on an oral tradition in which black men trade "toasts," stories in which dangerous badmen and trickster figures like Stackolee and Dolomite sexually exploit women and promote violence among men.

Rap remains almost completely dominated by black males and this mind-set. Although women have been involved in rap since at least the mid-1980s, record companies have only recently begun to promote them. And as women rappers like Salt-N-Pepa, Monie Love, M.C. Lyte, L.A. Star, and Queen Latifah slowly gain more visibility, rap's sexism may emerge as a subject for scrutiny. Indeed, the answer may lie with women, expressing in lyrics and videos the tensions between the sexes in the black community.

Today's women rappers range from a high ground that refuses to challenge male rap on its own level (Queen Latifah) to those who subscribe to the same sexual high jinks as male rappers (Oaktown 3.5.7.). M.C. Hammer launched Oaktown 3.5.7., made up of his former backup dancers. These female rappers manifest the worst-case scenario: their skimpy, skintight leopard costumes in the video of "Wild and Loose (We Like It)" suggest an exotic animalistic sexuality. Clearly, their bodies are more important than rapping. And in a field in which writing one's own rap is crucial, their lyrics are written by their former boss, M.C. Hammer.

Most women rappers constitute the middle ground: they talk of romance, narcissism, and parties. On the other hand, Salt-N-Pepa on "Shake Your Thang" uses the structure of the 1969 Isley Brothers song "It's Your Thing" to insert a protofeminist rap response: "Don't try to tell me how to party. It's my dance and it's my body." M.C. Lyte, in a dialogue with Positive K on "I'm Not Havin' It," comes down hard on the notion that women can't say no, and criticizes the shallowness of the male rap.

Queen Latifah introduces her video "Ladies First," performed with the English rapper Monie Love, with photographs of black political heroines like Winnie Mandela, Sojourner Truth, Harriet Tubman, and Angela Davis. With a sound that resembles scat as much as rap, Queen Latifah chants "Stereotypes they got to go" against a backdrop of newsreel footage of the apartheid struggle in South Africa. The politically sophisticated Queen Latifah seems worlds apart from the adolescent, buffoonish sex orientation of most rap. In general, women rappers seem so much more grown up.

Can they inspire a more beneficent attitude toward sex in rap?

What won't subvert rap's sexism is the actions of men; what will is women speaking in their own voice.

While Olivia moved toward mainstream, Redwood significantly changed its direction and built coalitions with other political and social change audiences. *Speed of Light* (1982) became the clearest declaration of Near's and Redwood's future direction. Afrikan Dreamland and Near close with the following reggae-tinged plea for political unity:

> One man fights the KKK
> But he hates the queers
> One woman fights for ecology
> It's equal rights she fears
> Some folks know that war is hell
> But then they put down the blind
> I think there must be a common ground
> But it's mighty hard to find
> Hang on, don't give up the ship
> Hang on, don't let the anchor slip

> We are all sailors and we're in mutiny
> The safety of this journey depends on Unity.[16]

Coalition-building or crossing over continues through both Near's and Redwood's albums. Near's records include collaborations with activists Ronnie Gilbert of the Weavers, Trapezoid and John McCutcheon, Inti-Illimani, Arlo Guthrie, and Pete Seeger. Near records songs by well-known political artists Phil Ochs, Malvina Reynolds, and Bernice Johnson Reagon, while Redwood Records produces or distributes artists known for their international politics: Ronnie Gilbert, Inti-Illimani, Judy Small, Guardabarranco, Salvador Bustos, and Victor Jara. Continued support for women's music includes albums by Linda Tillery, Ferron, Hunter Davis, Nancy Vogl, and Betsy Rose.

Labels were not the only component of women's music feeling the need to look elsewhere for larger audiences. Some distributors left women's music for larger salaries and better benefits. WILD included other independent labels' recordings, distributing records to political bookstores as well as feminist bookstores. As early as 1985, Sue Brown of Ladyslipper, a major distributor of women's music in the east, saw money as the big challenge. "There are few, if any feminist businesses for which cash flow and lack of capital are not constant concerns."[17] Many distributors opened up their catalogs to non-women's music. Ladyslipper broadened its catalog to include women artists who would not normally fall within women's music (Bonnie Raitt, Judy Mowatt, and the Roches). Gay and anti-sexist music by men was also included.

Boston recording engineer Karen Kane exemplifies the impact of a move from women's music. "Although in the mid-70s, women's music kept me going," she stated, "I wouldn't want to do just women's music projects in 1986—there are simply not enough people like that with the money to make the albums."[18]

THE COOPTATION OF WOMEN'S MUSIC?

Though mainstream female performers from Tina Turner to Laurie Anderson chipped away at the stale stereotyped male image of the female performer, the mainstream success of Suzanne Vega's song "Luka" (*Billboard's* number three hit), created avenues for a new breed of pop women. The economic success of Vega turned major labels' attention to other "serious women" performers. "In the record business new trends are not motivated by good taste or guilty consciences," stated *Musician Magazine's* editor Bill Flanagan, "Someone thinks that serious women can sell records. . ."[19]

Yet Vega and other mainstream artists before her did not open up these frontiers for other women performers without a lot of help. Women's music performers sang about "real women" and their needs for 20 years. In fact, many of the new performers, such as Tracy Chapman, Phranc, Ferron, Melissa Etheridge, and Michele Shocked, got their first boost from women's music audiences. Other performers, like k.d. lang, resemble the lesbian images women's music has always portrayed. That women's music performers were not widely known was in part due to the lack of a feminist movement preceding them. Women's labels also couldn't compete with mainstream labels' marketing, which can put a half million dollars in print and media promotions and another half in radio promotion for an artist. Holly Near believes that "if we [Redwood] had been able to put a million dollars behind Ferron, she'd be a major star."[20]

So, why do performers stay with women's music labels even when mainstream labels are interested? In truth, many don't, and therein lies the conflict between the '70s and '80s generation. Older artists argue that newer performers gained access to the pop charts through the groundwork laid by women's music.[21] What, if any, repayment do the new performers owe? The women's music community varies in its response. Holly Near acknowledges that access to mainstream success is not blocked for women the way it was 15 years ago, but also points out that women pop performers "couldn't have done it without us."[22] Near and others are pleased when women performers move to major labels because one of women's music goals is to get political messages out to as many people as possible. Near describes their relationship as a parent to a child: "We feel pride that we laid the groundwork that allowed them to go on."[23]

Others' reactions are less supportive. Women's music supporters resent the mainstream press portrayals of the new women performers as if they appeared out of thin air. In fact, this music has been available through women's music labels for well over 20 years, but now no credit is given to those who worked in women's music singing about the same issues for which Tracy Chapman is being heralded. Cris Williamson explains,

> There I am, hacking with my machete, making my way through the jungle and I look behind me and Tracy's striding down the path. Part of me is a bit jealous of that success. And in my rational mind I say, Cris, this is why you did it.[24]

Another issue is the new performers' lack of gender specificity regarding their sexuality. Although Chapman, and others, have made their way into mainstream, their lesbian connections (i.e. the women's music festivals and audiences which supported them) are intentionally ignored in their promotional material and in conversations, unless they are talking to the gay and lesbian press. While gender-neutral songs are acceptable, songs with lesbians lyrics are not. Jo-Lynne Worley of Redwood Records noted that while the majors' interest was strong in Teresa Trull's album, *A Step Away,* the album "was not pursued further . . . because of her specific lesbian lyrics."[25] Through subtle self-presentation, new performers present themselves as objects of female as well as male desire. The argument continues: Should those in the mainstream come out and possibly lose other audiences or be more subtle in their lesbian identity to seek a broader audience? Veterans of women's music believe their lesbianism is an important part of their politics and should be presented. Other women seem less convinced.

WHAT YOUNG LESBIANS WANT IS 2 NICE GIRLS

In the 1990s, young lesbians, both performers and fans, reject much of the politics of women's music. Lesbian musician Phranc found herself spending more time arguing politics than getting the message out in the big world, and changing attitudes and raising consciousness in the process. "It just seemed very isolated."[26] Likewise 2 Nice Girls didn't want to be in the ghetto of the women's music bin: "we want to be in your face."[27] Many young lesbians want their lifestyles to be included in the mainstream. Performers like Tracy Chapman and k.d. lang may not state that they are lesbians but they present an unmistakable image, while 2 Nice Girls and Phranc leave no doubt about their sexuality. Kathy Korniloff of 2 Nice Girls explains that although they love the early albums of Christian's and Near's, the entire women's scene is a "pre-punk experience . . . we've grown up in the post-punk world and our music is a reflection of that."[28]

Some would argue that Phranc and 2 Nice Girls are the future of lesbian music. "Indeed, because the band [2 Nice Girls] is willing, both personally and in their music, to state that they are queer, they have fast become role models in a community continually starved for them."[29] Phranc's record, *I Enjoy Being a Girl,* includes a description of Phranc as a "little daughter of bilitis," and her record company, Island Records, promotes her as a "basic all-American Jewish Lesbian folksinger."[30] While acknowledging Phranc's lesbian audience, the label seeks out cross-over groups—college and independent music audiences—to gain more mainstream acceptance.

Another argument for artist cross-over efforts is that acceptance of a few out-lesbians (Phranc and 2 Nice Girls) can be a way in which to inoculate the mainstream audience against reacting negatively to the potent political messages imbedded in lesbian music. Expose the audience (especially that which is less politically reactionary) to a little of the music; get them to form a non-threatened reaction to it; then when exposed to more radical music, the reaction will be mild.

WHAT'S LEFT FOR WOMEN'S MUSIC?

We've made the world safe for androgyny in the charts, but a few women musicians in the forefront is not what we wanted.[31]

—*Deidre McCalla*

Have women's music goals been attained through the success of such performers as Tracy Chapman? Not really. Consider the reasons women's music began. In part, it was the desire to get their message to women, but another goal was to get women into the production side of the business: engineering, recording, as musicians, distributors, etc. Few such in-roads exist. As one reads about the new breed, one also reads about their managers, men; the musicians with whom they work, men; the distributors of their albums, men. From this perspective, little has changed. In addition, we shouldn't overemphasize the women who have now made it. First, you can count on your fingers the number who are successful in the mainstream. Compared to male performers and male-identified women, it is a small percentage. It is also too soon to determine that the inclusion of feminist and lesbian musicians into mainstream is a lasting trend. Popularity in pop is notoriously short-lived for most artists. Economics determines whether the concept of "intelligent women's music" continues with new performers signed or present contracts extended. We should remember that a few women in the 1970s also sang some songs of social significance. In the 1980s, they were quickly replaced.

When new women performers attain success in mainstream music, why do others stay in women's music? For some, like Holly Near, it relates to control. She controls her music, her schedule, her political agenda. Of course, performers who sign with mainstream labels seek more control as they gain more commercial success, but they rarely get it. Phranc gets her way most of the time, but during a 1989 tour to England and Scotland, she was unable to, along with her regular shows, do women-only or gay and lesbian shows. "I really didn't have a choice this time. I had to play ball with the boys."[32]

There is also a lot of pressure and a different definition of success with a mainstream label. "If an artist at Redwood sells 100,000 records, they get a party, . . . whereas a 100,000 record sales won't get the attention of the Big Guys, certainly you can get dropped from a major label if that's all you sell."[33] Many women prefer the lesser pressure.

Performers also get more personal attention with the women's music labels. There isn't a huge machine to work within. And performers can have a life-long career with a company such as Olivia or Redwood but on a major label might be "a star for only a moment."[34]

Does all this mean that women's music will continue to keep a very narrow role within the lesbian-feminist movement? It's already obvious that women's music has changed as economics and politics have changed. The movement toward mainstream or other politically left groups seems to broaden women's music. The days of complete separateness from other subcultural groups is over. While women-only music festivals continue to attract increasing numbers of women with each succeeding year, and there are artists who continue to perform for women-only audiences, the majority of the women's music performers are forced to change or leave. The second wave of women's music (including Chapman, lang, Phranc, and all the newer performers) brings to the forefront some mainstream acceptance and some of its own radical lesbians. Anyone who thinks women's music is dead hasn't seen what it has become. Holly Near says it doesn't look like it did in the 1970s.

It looks like Faith Nolan going into prisons and youth institutions and singing about class and drugs and health and homophobia, it look like Ronnie Gilbert going down and listening to women sing in picket lines. It's Tracy Chapman and it's K.T. Oslin singing to working class straight women about feminist issues in songs like "Ladies of the Eighties."[35]

NOTES

1. Arlene Stein, "Androgyny Goes Pop: But Is It Lesbian Music?" *Out/look.* Spring 1991. p. 31.

2. Gaye Tuchman, A.K. Daniels, J. Benet, *Hearth and Home: Images of Women in the Mass Media.* New York: Oxford University Press, 1978.

3. Toni Armstrong, Jr., "An Endangered Species: Women's Music By, For, and About Women," *Hot Wire: The Journal of Women's Music and Culture,* 5. September 1989. p. 17. See also Cynthia M. Lont, *Between Rock and a Hard Place: Subcultural Persistence and Women's Music,* Ph.D. Thesis. University of Iowa, 1984.

4. Steve Chapple and Reebee Garofalo, *Rock and Roll is Here to Pay: The History and Politics of the Music Industry.* Chicago: Nelson Hall, 1980.

5. Laura Post, "The Institute for the Musical Arts." *Hot Wire: Journal of Women's Music and Culture,* 5. September 1989. p. 47.

6. Maxine Feldman, "Angry Athis." Athis Music Publishers BMF, 1969, 1972. Used with permission.

7. Alix Dobkin, *Lavender Jane Loves Women.* Project 1, 1975. Insert.

8. Laura Post, "Olivia Record Artist Profiles." *Hot Wire: Journal of Women's Music and Culture,* 4. July 1988. p. 32.

9. Maida Tilchen, "Lesbians and Women's Music," in Trudy Darty and Sandee Potter, *Women-Identified-Women.* Palo Alto, CA: Mayfield Publishers, 1984. pp. 287–303.

10. Maida Tilchen, "Women's Music: Politics for Sale?" *Gay Community News.* June Supplement 1982. p. 2.

11. Jorjet Harper and Toni Armstrong, Jr., "Meg Departs." *Hot Wire: Journal of Women's Music and Culture,* 5. January 1989. p. 21.

12. Stein, Spring 1991. p. 29.

13. Toni Armstrong, Jr. "Welcome Back Margie Adam." *Hot Wire: Journal of Women's Music and Culture.* January 1992. p. 2.

14. Ibid.

15. Sheila Rene, "No Madonnas: Olivia Records, the Premiere Women's Music Label, Celebrates 15 years in the Trenches." *Indie Special.* 1989. p. 53.

16. Holly Near, *Speed of Light.* Redwood Records, 1982.

17. Susanna J. Sturgis, "Ladyslipper: Meeting the Challenges of Feminist Business." *Hot Wire: Journal of Women's Music and Culture.* May 1985. p. 38.

18. Susan Wilson, "Women's Music: Then and Now." *The Boston Sunday Globe.* March 9, 1986. p. 68.

19. Susan Wilson, "Talkin' 'bout Revolution For Women in Pop?" *The Boston Sunday Globe.* November 20, 1988. p. 101.

20. Sandy Carter, "Redwood Records: Slippin and Sliding." *Z Magazine.* May 1989. p. 65.

21. Noelle Hanrahan, "A New Wave of Women on Vinyl." *Coming Up!* August 1988. p. 45.

22. Scott Alarik, "Does Women's Music Have Any Place Left To Go?" *The Boston Sunday Globe.* November 12, 1989. p. B7.

23. Carter, *Z Magazine,* 1989. p. 64.

24. Wilson, 1988. p. 96.

25. Hanrahan, 1988. p. 45.

26. Confabulation, "Hi, Phranc. This is Alix Calling." *Hot Wire: The Journal of Women's Music and Culture.* January 1990. p. 17.

27. Stein, 1991. p. 31.

28. Larry Kelp, "Getting in Tune with the Times." *The Tribune Calendar.* July 9, 1989. p. 24.

29. Rachel Pepper, "The Winning Duo . . . er . . . Threesome." *Outweek.* September 19, 1990. p. 39.

30. Confabulation, 1990. p. 17.

31. Stein, 1991. p. 32.

32. Confabulation, 1990. p. 16–17.

33. Carter, *Z Magazine.* 1989. p. 64.

34. Carter, *Z Magazine.* 1989. p. 65.

35. Alarik, 1989. p. B7.

Hate Radio: Why We Need to Tune In to Limbaugh and Stern

PATRICIA J. WILLIAMS

Three years ago I stood at my sink, washing the dishes and listening to the radio. I was tuned to rock and roll so I could avoid thinking about the big news from the day before—George Bush had just nominated Clarence Thomas to replace Thurgood Marshall on the Supreme Court. I was squeezing a dot of lemon Joy into each of the wineglasses when I realized that two smoothly radio-cultured voices, a man's and a woman's, had replaced the music.

"I think it's a stroke of genius on the president's part," said the female voice.

"Yeah," said the male voice. "Then those blacks, those African Americans, those Negroes—hey 'Negro' is good enough for Thurgood Marshall—whatever, they can't make up their minds [what] they want to be called. I'm gonna call them Blafricans. Black Africans. Yeah, I like it. Blafricans. Then they can get all upset because now the president appointed a Blafrican."

"Yeah, well, that's the way those liberals think. It's just crazy."

"And then after they turn down his nomination the president can say he tried to please 'em, and then he can appoint someone with some intelligence."

Back then, this conversation seemed so horrendously unusual, so singularly hateful, that I picked up a pencil and wrote it down. I was certain that a firestorm of protest was going to engulf the station and purge those radio mouths with the good clean soap of social outrage.

I am so naive. When I finally turned on the radio and rolled my dial to where everyone else had been tuned while I was busy watching Cosby reruns, it took me a while to understand that there's a firestorm all right, but not of protest. In the two and a half years since Thomas has assumed his post on the Supreme Court, the underlying assumptions of the conversation I heard as uniquely outrageous have become commonplace, popularly expressed, and louder in volume. I hear the style of that snide polemicism everywhere, among acquaintances, on the street, on television in toned-down versions. It is a crude demagoguery that makes me heartsick. I feel more and more surrounded by that point of view, the assumptions of being without intelligence, the coded epithets, the "Blafrican"-like stand-ins for "nigger," the mocking angry glee, the endless tirades filled with non-specific, nonempirically based slurs against "these people" or "those minorities" or "feminazis" or "liberals" or "scumbags" or "pansies" or "jerks" or "sleazeballs" or "loonies" or "animals" or "foreigners."

At the same time I am not so naive as to suppose that this is something new. In clearheaded moments I realize I am not listening to the radio anymore, I am listening to a large segment of white America think aloud in ever louder resurgent thoughts that have generations of historical precedent. It's as though the radio has split open like an egg, Morton Downey, Jr.'s clones and Joe McCarthy's ghost spilling out, broken yolks, a great collective of sometimes clever, sometimes small, but uniformly threatened brains—they have all come gushing out. Just as they were about to pass into oblivion, Jack Benny and his humble black sidekick Rochester get resurrected in the ungainly bodies of Howard Stern and his faithful black henchwoman, Robin Quivers. The culture of Amos and Andy has been revived and reassembled in Bob Grant's radio minstrelry and radio newcomer Daryl Gates's sanctimonious imprecations on behalf of decent white people. And in striking imitation of Jesse Helms's nearly forgotten days as a radio host, the far Right has found its undisputed king in the personage of Rush Limbaugh—a polished demagogue with a weekly radio audience of at least 20 million, a television show that vies for ratings with the likes of Jay Leno, a newsletter with a circulation of 380,000, and two best-selling books whose combined sales are closing in on six million copies.

From Churchill to Hitler to the old Soviet Union, it's clear that radio and television have the power to change the course of history, to proselytize, and to coalesce not merely the good and the noble, but the very worst in human nature as well. Likewise, when Orson Welles made his famous radio broadcast "witnessing" the landing of a spaceship full of hostile Martians, the United States ought to have learned a lesson about the power of radio to appeal to mass instincts and incite mass hysteria. Radio remains a particularly powerful medium even today, its visual emptiness in a world of six trillion flashing images allowing one of the few remaining playgrounds for the aural subconscious. Perhaps its power is attributable to our need for an oral tradition after all, some conveying of stories, feelings, myths of ancestors, epics of alienation, and the need to rejoin ancestral roots, even ignorant bigoted roots. Perhaps the visual quiescence of radio is related to the popularity of E-mail or electronic networking. Only the voice is made manifest, unmasked worlds that cannot—or dare not?—be seen. Just yet. Nostalgia crystallizing into a dangerous future. The preconscious voice erupting into the expressed, the prime time.

What comes out of the modern radio mouth could be the *Iliad,* the *Rubaiyat,* the griot's song of our times. If indeed radio is a vessel for the American "Song of Songs," then what does it mean that a manic, adolescent Howard Stern is so popular among radio listeners, that Rush Limbaugh's wittily smooth sadism has gone the way of prime time television, and that both vie for the number one slot on all the best-selling book lists? What to make of the stories being told by our modern radio evangelists and their tragic unloved chorus of callers? Is it really just a collapsing economy that spawns this drama of grown people sitting around scaring themselves to death with fantasies of black feminist Mexican able-bodied gay soldiers earning $100,000 a year on welfare who are so criminally depraved that Hillary Clinton or the Antichrist-of-the-moment had no choice but to invite them onto the government payroll so they can run the country? The panicky exaggeration

reminds me of a child's fear . . . *And then, and then, a huge lion jumped out of the shadows and was about to gobble me up, and I can't ever sleep again for a whole week.*

As I spin the dial on my radio, I can't help thinking that this stuff must be related to that most poignant of fiber-optic phenomena, phone sex. Aural Sex. Radio Racism with a touch of S & M. High-priest hosts with the power and run-amok ego to discipline listeners, to smack with the verbal back of the hand, to smash the button that shuts you up once and for all. "Idiot!" shouts New York City radio demagogue Bob Grant and then the sound of droning telephone emptiness, the voice of dissent dumping out some trapdoor in aural space.

As I listened to a range of such programs what struck me as the most unifying theme was not merely the specific intolerance on such hot topics as race and gender, but much more general contempt for the world, a verbal stoning of anything different. It is like some unusually violent game of "Simon Says," this mockery and shouting down of callers, this roar of incantations, the insistence on agreement.

But, ah, if you *will* but only agree, what sweet and safe reward, what soft enfolding by a stern and angry radio god. And as an added bonus, the invisible shield of an AM community, a family of fans who are Exactly Like You, to whom you can express, in anonymity, all the filthy stuff you imagine "them" doing to you. The comfort and relief of being able to ejaculate, to those who understand, about the dark imagined excess overtaking, robbing, needing to be held down and taught a good lesson, needing to put it in its place before a ravenous demon enervates all that is true and good and pure in this life.

The audience for this genre of radio flagellation is mostly young, white, and male. Two thirds of Rush Limbaugh's audience is male. According to *Time* magazine, 75 percent of Howard Stern's listeners are white men. Most of the callers have spent their lives walling themselves off from any real experience with blacks, feminists, lesbians, or gays. In this regard, it is probably true, as former Secretary of Education William Bennett says, that Rush Limbaugh "tells his audience that what you believe inside, you can talk about in the marketplace." Unfortunately, what's "inside" is then mistaken for what's "outside," treated as empirical and political reality. The *National Review* extols Limbaugh's conservative leadership as no less than that of Ronald Reagan, and the Republican party provides Limbaugh with books to discuss, stories, angles, and public support. "People were afraid of censure by gay activists, feminists, environmentalists—now they are not because Rush takes them on," says Bennett.

U.S. history has been marked by cycles in which brands of this or that hatred come into fashion and go out, are unleashed and then restrained. If racism, homophobia, jingoism, and woman-hating have been features of national life in pretty much all of modern history, it rather begs the question to spend a lot of time wondering if right-wing radio is a symptom or a cause. For the last 400 years, prevailing attitudes in the West have considered African Americans less intelligent. Recent statistics show that 53 percent of the people in the U.S. agree that blacks and Latinos are less intelligent than whites, and a majority believe that blacks are lazy, violent, welfare-dependent, and unpatriotic.

I think that what has made life more or less tolerable for "out" groups have been those moments in history when those "inside" feelings were relatively restrained. In fact, if I could believe that right-wing radio were only about idiosyncratic, singular, rough-hewn individuals thinking those inside thoughts, I'd be much more inclined to agree with Columbia University media expert Everette Dennis, who says that Stern's and Limbaugh's popularity represents the "triumph of the individual" or with *Time* magazine's bottom line that "the fact that either is seriously considered a threat . . . is more worrisome than Stern or Limbaugh will ever be." If what I were hearing had even a tad more to do with real oppressions, with real white *and* black levels of joblessness and homelessness, or with the real problems of real white men, then I wouldn't have bothered to slog my way through hours of Howard Stern's miserable obsessions.

Yet at the heart of my anxiety is the worry that Stern, Limbaugh, Grant, et al. represent the very antithesis of individualism's triumph. As the *National Review* said of Limbaugh's ascent, "It was a feat not only of the loudest voice but also of a keen political brain to round up, as Rush did, the media herd and drive them into the conservative corral." When asked about his political aspirations, Bob Grant gloated to the Washington *Post,* "I think I would make a rather good dictator."

The polemics of right-wing radio are putting nothing less than hate onto the airwaves, into the marketplace, electing it to office, teaching it in schools, and exalting it as freedom. What worries me is the increasing-to-constant commerce of retribution, control, and lashing out, fed not by fact but fantasy. What worries me is the reemergence, more powerfully than at any time since the institution of Jim Crow, of a sociocentered self that excludes "the likes of," well, me for example, from the civic circle, and that would rob me of my worth and claim and identity as a citizen. As the *Economist* rightly observes, "Mr. Limbaugh takes mass market—white, mainly male, middle-class, ordinary America—and talks to it as an endangered minority."

I worry about this identity whose external reference is a set of beliefs, ethics, and practices that excludes, restricts, and acts in the world on me, or mine, as the perceived if not real enemy. I am acutely aware of losing *my* mythic individualism to the surface shapes of my mythic group fearsomeness as black, as female, as left wing. "I" merge not fluidly but irretrievably into a category of "them." I become a suspect self, a moving target of loathsome properties, not merely different but dangerous. And that worries me a lot.

What happens in my life with all this translated license, this permission to be uncivil? What happens to the social space that was supposedly at the sweet mountaintop of the civil rights movement's trail? Can I get a seat on the bus without having to be reminded that I *should* be standing? Did the civil rights movement guarantee us nothing more than to use public accommodations while surrounded by raving lunatic bigots? "They didn't beat this idiot [Rodney King] enough," says Howard Stern.

Not long ago I had the misfortune to hail a taxicab in which the driver was listening to Howard Stern undress some woman. After some blocks, I had to get out. I was, frankly, afraid to ask the driver to turn it off—not because I was afraid of "censoring" him, which seems to be the only thing people will talk about anymore, but because the driver was stripping me too, as he leered through the rearview mirror. "Something the matter?" he demanded, as I asked him to pull over and let me out well short of my destination. (I'll spare you the full story of what happened from there—trying to get another cab, as the cabbies stopped for all the white businessmen who so much as scratched their heads near the curb; a nice young white man, seeing my plight, giving me his cab, having to thank him, he hero, me saved-but-humiliated, cabdriver pissed and surly. I fight my way to my destination, finally arriving in bad mood, militant black woman, cranky feminazi.)

When Yeltsin blared rock music at his opponents holed up in the parliament building in Moscow, the imitation of the U.S. Marines trying to torture Manual Noriega in Panama, all I could think of was that it must be like being trapped in a crowded subway car when all the portable stereos are turned to Bob Grant or Howard Stern. With Howard Stern's voice a tinny, screeching backdrop, with all the faces growing dreamily mean as though some superficially evil hallucinogen were gushing into their bloodstreams, I'd start begging to surrender.

Surrender to what? Surrender to the laissez-faire desegregation that is the metaphoric significance of the hundreds of "Rush rooms" that have cropped up in restaurants around the country; rooms broadcasting Limbaugh's words, rooms for your listening pleasure, rooms where bigots can capture the purity of a Rush-only lunch counter, rooms where all those unpleasant others just "choose" not to eat? Surrender to the naughty luxury of a room in which a Ku Klux Klan meeting could take place in orderly, First Amendment fashion? Everyone's "free" to come in (and a few of you outsiders do), but most of the understandable nonconformists are gently repulsed away. It's a high-tech world of enhanced choice. Whites choose mostly to sit in the Rush room. Feminists, blacks, lesbians, and gays "choose" to sit elsewhere. No need to buy black votes, you just pay them not to vote; no need to insist on white-only schools, you just sell the desirability of black-only schools. Just sit back and watch it work, like those invisible shock shields that keep dogs cowering in their backyards.

How real is the driving perception behind all the Sturm und Drang of this genre of radio-harangue—the perception that white men are an oppressed minority, with no power and no opportunity in the land that they made great? While it is true that power and opportunity are shrinking for all but the very wealthy in this country (and would that Limbaugh would take that issue on), the fact remains that white men are still this country's most privileged citizens and market actors. To give just a small example, according to the *Wall Street Journal,* blacks were the only racial group to suffer a net job loss during the 1990–91 economic downturn at the companies reporting to the Equal Employment Opportunity Commission. Whites, Latinos, and Asians, meanwhile, gained thousands of jobs. While whites gained 71,144 jobs at these companies, Latinos gained 60,040, Asians gained 55,104, and blacks lost 59,479. If every black were hired in the United States tomorrow, the numbers would not be sufficient to account for white men's expanding balloon of fear that they have been specifically dispossessed by African Americans.

Given deep patterns of social segregation and general ignorance of history, particularly racial history, media remain the principal source of most Americans' knowledge of each other. Media can provoke violence or induce passivity. In San Francisco, for example, a radio show on KMEL called "Street Soldiers" has taken this power as a responsibility with great consequence: "Unquestionably," writes Ken Auletta in the *New Yorker,* "the show has helped avert violence. When a Samoan teenager was slain, apparently by Filipino gang members, in a drive-by shooting, the phones lit up with calls from Samoans wanting to tell [the host] they would not rest until they had exacted revenge. Threats filled the air for a couple of weeks. Then the dead Samoan's father called in, and, in a poignant exchange, the father said he couldn't tolerate the thought of more young men senselessly slaughtered. There would be no retaliation, he vowed. And there was none." In contrast, we must wonder at the phenomenon of the very powerful leadership of the Republican party, from Ronald Reagan to Robert Dole to William Bennett, giving advice, counsel, and friendship to Rush Limbaugh's passionate divisiveness.

The outright denial of the material crisis at every level of U.S. society, most urgently in black inner-city neighborhoods but facing us all, is a kind of political circus, dissembling as it feeds the frustrations of the moment. We as a nation can no longer afford to deal with such crises by *imagining* an excess of bodies, of babies, of job-stealers, of welfare mothers, of overreaching immigrants, of too-powerful (Jewish, in whispers) liberal Hollywood, of lesbians and gays, of gang members ("gangsters" remain white, and no matter what the atrocity, less vilified than "gang members," who are black), of Arab terrorists, and uppity women. The reality of our social poverty far exceeds these scapegoats. This right-wing backlash resembles, in form if not substance, phenomena like anti-Semitism in Poland: there aren't but a handful of Jews left in that whole country, but the giant balloon of heated anti-Semitism flourishes apace, Jews blamed for the world's evils.

The overwhelming response to right-wing excesses in the United States has been to seek an odd sort of comfort in the fact that the First Amendment is working so well that you can't suppress this sort of thing. Look what's happened in Eastern Europe. Granted. So let's not talk about censorship or the First Amendment for the next ten minutes. But in Western Europe, where fascism is rising at an appalling rate, suppression is hardly the problem. In Eastern and Western Europe as well as the United States, we must begin to think just a little bit about the fiercely coalescing power of media to spark mistrust, to fan it into forest fires of fear and revenge. We must begin to think about the levels of national and social complacence in the face of such resolute ignorance. We must ask ourselves what the expected result is, not of censorship or suppression, but of so much encouragement, so much support, so much investment in the fashionability of hate. What future is it that we are designing with the devotion of such tremendous resources to the disgraceful propaganda of bigotry?

R E A D I N G 1 6

En rapport, In Opposition: Cobrando cuentas a las nuestras

GLORIA ANZALDÚA

WATCH FOR FALLING ROCKS

The first time I drove from El Paso to San Diego, I saw a sign that read *Watch for Falling Rocks*. And though I watched and waited for rocks to roll down the steep cliff walls and attack my car and me, I never saw any falling rocks. Today, one of the things I'm most afraid of are the rocks we throw at each other. And the resultant guilt we carry like a corpse strapped to our backs for having thrown rocks. We colored women have memories like elephants. The slightest hurt is recorded deep within. We do not forget the injury done to us and we do not forget the injury we have done another. For unfortunately we do not have hides like elephants. Our vulnerability is measured by our capacity for openness, intimacy. And we all know that our own kind is driven through shame or self-hatred to poke at all our open wounds. And we know they know exactly where the hidden wounds are.

> *I keep track of all distinctions. Between past and present. Pain and pleasure. Living and surviving. Resistance and capitulation. Will and circumstances. Between life and death. Yes. I am scrupulously accurate. I have become a keeper of accounts.*
>
> *Irena Klepfisz[1]*

One of the changes that I've seen since *This Bridge Called My Back* was published[2] is that we no longer allow white women to efface us or suppress us. Now we do it to each other. We have taken over the missionary's "let's civilize the savage role," fixating on the "wrongness" and moral or political inferiority of some of our sisters, insisting on a profound difference between oneself and the *Other*. We have been indoctrinated into adopting the old imperialist ways of conquering and dominating, adopting a way of confrontation based on differences while standing on the ground of ethnic superiority.

In the "dominant" phase of colonialism, European colonizers exercise direct control of the colonized, destroy the native legal and cultural systems, and negate non-European civilizations in order to ruthlessly exploit the resources of the subjugated with the excuse of attempting to "civilize" them. Before the end of this phase, the natives internalize Western culture. By the time we reach the "neocolonialist" phase, we've accepted the white colonizers' system of values, attitudes, morality, and modes of production.[3] It is not by chance that in the more rural towns of Texas Chicano neighborhoods are called *colonias* rather than *barrios*.

There have always been those of us who have "cooperated" with the colonizers. It's not that we have been "won" over by the dominant culture, but that it has exploited pre-existing power relations of subordination and subjugation within our native societies.[4] The great White ripoff and they are still cashing in. Like our exploiters who fixate on the inferiority of the natives, we fixate on the fucked-upness of our sisters. Like them we try to impose our version of "the ways things should be"; we try to impose one's self on the *Other* by making her the recipient of one's negative elements, usually the same elements that the Anglo projected on us. Like them, we project our self-hatred on her; we stereotype her; we make her generic.

JUST HOW ETHNIC ARE YOU?

One of the reasons for this hostility among us is the forced cultural penetration, the rape of the colored by the white, with the colonizers depositing their perspective, their language, their values in our bodies. External oppression is paralleled with our internalization of that oppression. And our acting out from that oppression. They have us doing to those within our own ranks what they have done and continue to do to us—*Othering* people. That is, isolating them, pushing them out of the herd, ostracizing them. The internalization of negative images of ourselves, our self-hatred, poor self-esteem, makes our own people the *Other*. We shun the white-looking Indian, the "high yellow" Black woman, the Asian with the white lover, the Native woman who brings her white girl friend to the Pow Wow, the Chicana who doesn't speak Spanish, the academic, the uneducated. Her difference makes her a person we can't trust. *Para que sea "legal,"* she must pass the ethnic legitimacy test we have devised. And it is exactly our internalized whiteness that desperately wants boundary lines (this part of me is Mexican, this Indian) marked out and woe to any sister or any part of us that steps out of our assigned places, woe to anyone who doesn't measure up to our standards of ethnicity. *Si no cualifica,* if she fails to pass the test, *le aventamos mierda en la cara, le aventamos piedras, la aventamos.* We throw shit in her face, we throw rocks, we kick her out. *Como gallos de pelea nos atacamos unas a las otras—mexicanas de nacimiento contra* the born-again *mexicanas.* Like fighting cocks, razor blades strapped to our fingers, we slash out at each other. We have turned our anger against ourselves. And our anger is immense. *Es un acido que corroe.*

INTERNAL AFFAIRS

o las que niegan a su gente

> *Tu traición yo la llevo aquá muy dentro,*
> *la llevo dentro de mi alma*
> *dentro de mi corazón.*
> *Tu traicón.*
>
> *Cornelio Reyna*[5]

I get so tired of constantly struggling with my sisters. The more we have in common, including love, the greater the heartache between us, the more we hurt each other. It's excruciatingly painful, this constant snarling at our own shadows. Anything can set the conflict in motion: the lover getting more recognition by the community, the friend getting a job with higher status, a break-up. As one of my friends said, "We can't fucking get along."

So we find ourselves *entreguerras,*[6] a kind of civil war among intimates, an in-class, in-race, in-house fighting, a war with strategies, tactics that are our coping mechanisms, that once were our survival skills and which we now use upon one another,[7] producing intimate terrorism—a modern form of *las guerras floridas,* the war of flowers that the Aztecs practiced in order to gain captives for the sacrifices. Only now we are each other's victims, we offer the *Other* to our politically correct altar.

El deniego. The hate we once cast at our oppressors we now fling at women of our own race. Reactionary— we have gone to the other extreme—denial of our own. We struggle for power, compete, vie for control. Like kin, we are there for each other, but like kin we come to blows. And the differences between us and this new *Other* are not racial but ideological, not metaphysical but psychological. *Nos negamos a si mismas y el deniego nos causa daño.*

BREAKING OUT OF THE FRAME

> *I'm standing at the sea end of the truncated Berkeley pier. A boat had plowed into the black posts gouging out a few hundred feet of structure, cutting the pier in two. I stare at the sea, surging silver-plated, between me and the lopped-off corrugated arm, the wind whipping my hair. I look down, my head and shoulders, a shadow on the sea. Yemaya pours strings of light over my dull jade, flickering body, bubbles pop out of my ears. I feel the tension easing and, for the first time in months, the litany of work yet to do, of deadlines, that sings incessantly in my head, blows away with the wind.*
>
> > *Oh, Yemaya, I shall speak the words*
> > *you lap against the pier.*
>
> *But as I turn away I see in the distance a ship's fin fast approaching. I see fish heads lying listless in the sun, smell the stench of pollution in the waters.*

From where I stand, *queridas carnalas*—in a feminist position—I see, through a critical lens with variable focus, that we must not drain our energy breaking down the male/white frame (the whole of Western culture) but turn to our own kind and change our terms of reference. As long as we see the world and our experiences through white eyes—in a dominant/subordinate way—we're trapped in the tar and pitch of the old manipulative and strive-for-power ways.

Even those of us who don't want to buy in get sucked into the vortex of the dominant culture's fixed oppositions, the duality of superiority and inferiority, of subject and object. Some of us, to get out of the internalized neocolonial phase, make for the fringes, the Borderlands. And though we have not broken out of the white frame, we at least see it for what it is. Questioning the values of the dominant culture which imposes fundamental difference on those of the "wrong" side of the good/bad dichotomy is the first step. Responding to the *Other* not as irrevocably different is the second step. By highlighting similarities, downplaying divergences, that is, by *rapprochement* between self and *Other* it is possible to build a syncretic relationship. At the basis of such a relationship lies an understanding of the effects of colonization and its resultant pathologies.

We have our work cut out for us. Nothing is more difficult than identifying emotionally with a cultural alterity, with the *Other. Alter:* to make different; to castrate. *Altercate:* to dispute angrily. *Alter ego:* another self or another aspect of oneself. *Alter idem:* another of the same kind. Nothing is harder than identifying with an interracial identity, with a mestizo identity. One has to leave the permanent boundaries of a fixed self, literally "leave" oneself and see oneself through the eyes of the *Other.* Cultural identity is "nothing more nor less than the mean between selfhood and otherness. . . ."[8] Nothing scares the Chicana more than a quasi Chicana; nothing disturbs a Mexican more than an acculturated Chicana; nothing agitates a Chicana more than a Latina who lumps her with the *norteamericanas.* It is easier to retreat to the safety of difference behind racial, cultural and class borders. Because our awareness of the *Other* as object often swamps our awareness of ourselves as subject, it is hard to maintain a fine balance between cultural ethnicity and the continuing survival of that culture, between traditional culture and an evolving hybrid culture. How much must remain the same, how much must change.

For most of us our ethnicity is still the issue. Ours continues to be a struggle of identity—not against a white background so much as against a colored background. *Ya no estamos afuera o atras del marco de la pintura*—we no longer stand outside nor behind the frame of the painting. We are both the foreground, the background and the figures predominating. Whites are not the central figure, they are not even in the frame, though the frame of reference is still white, male and heterosexual. But the white is still there, invisible, under our skin—we have subsumed the white.

El desengaño/DISILLUSIONMENT

And yes I have some criticism, some self-criticism. And no I will not make everything nice. There is shit among us we need to sift through. Who knows, there may be some fertilizer in it. I've seen collaborative efforts between us end in verbal abuse, cruelty and trauma. I've seen collectives fall apart, dumping their ideals by the wayside and treating each other worse than they'd treat a rabid dog. My momma said, "Never tell other people our business, never divulge family secrets." Chicano dirt you do not air out in front of white folks, nor lesbian dirty laundry in front of heterosexuals. The cultural things stay with la Raza. Colored feminists must present a united front in front of white and other groups. But the fact is we are not united. (I've come to suspect that unity is another Anglo invention like their one sole god and the myth of the monopole.[9]) We are not going to cut through *la mierda* by sweeping the dirt under the rug.

We have a responsibility to each other, certain commitments. The leap into self-affirmation goes hand in hand with being critical of self. Many of us walk around with reactionary, self-righteous attitudes. We preach certain political behaviors and theories and we do fine with writing about them. Though we want others to live their lives by them, we do not live them. When we are called on it, we go into a self-defensive mode and denial just like whites did when we started asking them to be accountable for their race and class biases.

Las opuestas/THOSE IN OPPOSITION

In us, intra- and cross-cultural hostilities surface in not so subtle put-downs. *Las no comprometidas, las que negan a sus gente. Fruncemos las caras y negamos toda responsabilidad.* Where some of us racially mixed people are stuck in now is denial and its damaging effects. Denial of the white aspects that we've been forced to acquire, denial of our sisters who for one reason or another cannot "pass" as 100% ethnic—as if such a thing exists. Racial purity, like language purity, is a fallacy. Denying the reality of who we are destroys the basis needed from which to talk honestly and deeply about the issues between us. We cannot make any real connections because we are not touching each other. So we sit facing each other and before the words escape our mouths the real issues are blanked in our consciousness, erased before they register because it hurts too much to talk about them, because it makes us vulnerable to the hurt the *carnala* may dish out, because we've been wounded too deeply and too often in the past. So we sit, a paper face before another paper face—two people who suddenly cease to be real. *La no compasiva con la complaciente, lo incomunicado atorado en sus gargantas.*

We, the new Inquisitors, swept along with the "swing to the right" of the growing religious and political intolerance, crusade against racial heretics, mow down with the sickle of righteous anger our dissenting sisters. The issue (in all aspects of life) has always been when to resist changes and when to be open to them. Right now, this rigidity will break us.

Recobrando / RECOVERING

Una luz fria y cenicienta bañada en la plata palida del amanecer entra a mi escritorio and I think about the critical stages we feminists of color are going through, chiefly that of learning to live with each other as carnalas, parientes, amantes, as kin, as friends, as lovers. Looking back on the road that we've walked on during the last decade, I see many emotional, psychological, spiritual, political gains—primarily developing an understanding and acceptance of the spirituality of our root ethnic cultures. This has given us the ground from which to see that our spiritual lives are not split from our daily acts. En recobrando our affinity with nature and her forces (deities), we have "recovered" our ancient identity, digging it out like dark clay, pressing it to our current identity, molding past and present, inner and outer. Our clay-streaked faces acquiring again images of our ethnic self and self-respect taken from us by the colonizadores. And if we've suffered losses, if often in the process we have momentarily "misplaced" our *carnala*-hood, our sisterhood, there beside us always are the women, las mujeres. And that is enough to keep us going.

By grounding in the earth of our native spiritual identity, we can build up our personal and tribal identity. We can reach out for the clarity we need. Burning sage and sweetgrass by itself won't cut it, but it can be a basis from which we act.

And yes, we are elephants with long memories, but scrutinizing the past with binocular vision and training it on the juncture of past with present, and identifying the options on hand and mapping out future roads will ensure us survival.

So if we won't forget past grievances, let us forgive. Carrying the ghosts of past grievances *no vale la pena.* It is not worth the grief. It keeps us from ourselves and each other; it keeps us from new relationships. We need to cultivate other ways of coping. I'd like to think that the in-fighting that we presently find ourselves doing is only a stage in the continuum of our growth, an offshoot of the conflict that the process of biculturation spawns, a phase of the internal colonization process, one that will soon cease to hold sway over our lives. I'd like to see it as a skin we will shed as we are born into the 21st century.

And now in these times of the turning of the century, of harmonic conversion, of the end of *El Quinto Sol* (as the ancient Aztecs named our present age), it is time we began to get out of the state of opposition and into *rapprochment,* time to get our heads, words, ways out of white territory. It is time that we broke out of the invisible white frame and stood on the ground of our own ethnic being.

NOTES

1. Irena Klepfisz, *Keeper of Accounts* (Montpelier, VT: Sinister Wisdom, 1982), 85.

2. According to Chela Sandoval, the publication of *Bridge* marked the end of the second wave of the women's movement in its previous form. *U.S. Third World Feminist Criticism: The Theory and Method of Oppositional Consciousness,* a dissertation in process.

3. Abdul R. JanMohamed, "The Economy of Manichean Allegory: The Function of Racial Difference in Colonialist Literature," *"Race," Writing, and Difference,* ed. Henry Louis Gates, Jr. (Chicago: University of Chicago Press, 1985), 80–81.

4. JanMohamed, 81.

5. A Chicano from Texas who sings and plays *bajo-sexto* in his *música norteña/conjunto. "Tu Traición"* is from the album *15 Exitasos,* Reyna Records, 1981.

6. *Entreguerras, entremundos/Inner Wars Among the Worlds* is the title of a forthcoming book of narratives/novel.

7. Sarah Hoagland, "Lesbian Ethics: Intimacy & Self-Understanding," *Bay Area Women's News,* May/June 1987, vol. 1, no. 2, 7.

8. Nadine Gordimer is quoted in JanMohamed's essay, 88.

9. Physicists are searching for a single law of physics under which all other laws will fall.

Socialization

We are born into cultures that have definite ideas about men and women and their appropriate attitudes, values, and behaviors. Dominant American culture values men's behaviors, occupations, and attitudes more highly than those associated with women. It assumes that what men do is right and normal. Women are judged in accordance with how well they conform to the male standard. This way of thinking is known as *androcentrism*.

Learning about our culture begins in the family. We learn about gender not only from what our parents say but also from what they do. Some theorists argue that women's mothering role has consequences for both the development of gender-related personality differences and the unequal social status of women and men. Nancy Chodorow, in "Family Structure and Feminine Personality," proposes that because women do the mothering, men are socioculturally superior but psychologically defensive and insecure. Women's secondary social value is somewhat countered, however, by their gains in psychological strength and security. Elizabeth Spelman, however, takes issue with Chodorow's basic assumptions, pointing out that a theoretical explanation of how individuals acquire *gender* cannot be detached from a discussion of how individuals of different races and classes acquire different definitions of gender. In short, Spelman contends that there can be no universal theory of gender identity. Do you think Chodorow's theory is useful despite its lack of explicit attention to differences of race and class?

Because the culture differentiates not only along the basis of gender but on the bases of race, ethnicity, and class as well, our socialization experiences differ along these lines. What an African-American mother, for example, needs to teach her sons and daughters to enable them to survive in a white-male-dominated society is different from what a white mother has to teach her children. These kinds of racial differences, in turn, are compounded by differences in class status.

In "'The Means to Put My Children Through': Child-Rearing Goals and Strategies among Black Female Domestic Servants," Bonnie Thornton Dill writes about the complexity of race and gender issues by focusing on the experiences of African-American women domestic workers. Contrasting the race and class advantages available to white employers' children with the goals domestic workers held for their own children, Dill outlines the reactions and responses of black female servants who cared for white children to provide income but who reared their own children to enter the middle class. What differences are apparent between the child-raising patterns that Dill describes and the model that Chodorow proposed?

The family provides an environment in which interactions establish deep-seated ideas about gender and gender-appropriate behavior. Today many parents claim that they raise their boys and girls without gender bias, but considerable evidence indicates that such claims have little validity. Letty Cottin Pogrebin, in "The Secret Fear That Keeps Us from Raising Free Children," discusses a common but unfounded fear of many parents: that if their children are allowed sex-role freedom they may grow up to be gay or lesbian. This fear, Pogrebin argues, helps ensure that parents socialize their sons and daughters into traditional gender roles.

Gender socialization is carried out in schools as well as homes. By the time children are in school, they not only have been socialized into their gender but also are able to negotiate how and in which situations gender will be socially salient. Barrie Thorne, in "Girls and Boys Together . . . But Mostly Apart: Gender Arrangements in Elementary Schools," argues for this more complex idea of gender as socially constructed and context specific. In her observations of social relations among children in elementary school, she finds that the organization of one's sex and gender depends on the particular situation, and that children socialize each other.

As a result of gender socialization, by adolescence many girls experience a loss of self-confidence and self-definition, as Carol Gilligan describes in "Women's Psychological Development: Implications for Psychotherapy." The adolescent girls Gilligan interviewed feel a daunting social pressure to deny their own perceptions as they struggle between asserting their own identities and conforming to societal definitions of womanhood. They are caught between their desire to forge genuine relationships in which they can be themselves and the growing disconnection between what they know to be true and how they are expected to behave. Each forges her own path through the obstacles of gender socialization, resisting some prescriptions for femininity, accepting others, and seeking to make sense of her experiences through her relationships with others.

Throughout these readings we come to understand that families, schools, and peers continuously socialize and resocialize us into our culture. We invite you to reflect upon your own socialization experiences. How have the members of your family, the teachers and staff in your school, and your friends, coworkers, and classmates influenced your ideas about sex and gender? Reciprocally, how have you influenced theirs?

READING 17

Family Structure and Feminine Personality

NANCY CHODOROW

I propose here[1] a model to account for the reproduction within each generation of certain general and nearly universal differences that characterize masculine and feminine personality and roles. My perspective is largely psychoanalytic. Cross-cultural and social-psychological evidence suggests that an argument drawn solely from the universality of biological sex differences is unconvincing.[2] At the same time, explanations based on patterns of deliberate socialization (the most prevalent kind of anthropological, sociological, and social-psychological explanation) are in themselves insufficient to account for the extent to which psychological and value commitments to sex differences are so emotionally laden and tenaciously maintained, for the way gender identity and expectations about sex roles and gender consistency are so deeply central to a person's consistent sense of self.

This paper suggests that a crucial differentiating experience in male and female development arises out of the fact that women, universally, are largely responsible for early child care and for (at least) later female socialization. This points to the central importance of the mother–daughter relationship for women, and to a focus on the conscious and unconscious effects of early involvement with a female for children of both sexes. The fact that males and females experience this social environment differently as they grow up accounts for the development of basic sex differences in personality. In particular, certain features of the mother–daughter relationship are internalized universally as basic elements of feminine ego structure (although not necessarily what we normally mean by "femininity").

Specifically, I shall propose that, in any given society, feminine personality comes to define itself in relation and connection to other people more than masculine personality does. (In psychoanalytic terms, women are less individuated than men; they have more flexible ego boundaries.)[3] Moreover, issues of dependency are handled and experienced differently by men and women. For boys and men, both individuation and dependency issues become tied up with the sense of masculinity, or masculine identity. For girls and women, by contrast, issues of femininity, or feminine identity, are not problematic in the same way. The structural situation of child rearing, reinforced by female and male role training, produces these differences, which are replicated and reproduced in the sexual sociology of adult life.

The paper is also a beginning attempt to rectify certain gaps in the social-scientific literature, and a contribution to the reformulation of psychological anthropology. Most traditional accounts of family and socialization tend to emphasize only role training, and not unconscious features of personality. Those few that rely on Freudian theory have abstracted a behaviorist methodology from this theory, concentrating on isolated "significant" behaviors like weaning and toilet training. The paper advocates instead a focus on the ongoing interpersonal relationships in which these various behaviors are given meaning.[4]

More empirically, most social-scientific accounts of socialization, child development, and the mother–child relationship refer implicitly or explicitly only to the development and socialization of boys and to the mother–son relationship. There is a striking lack of systematic description about the mother–daughter relationship, and a basic theoretical discontinuity between, on the one hand, theories about female development, which tend to stress the development of "feminine" qualities in relation to and comparison with men, and on the other hand, theories about women's ultimate mothering role. This final lack is particularly crucial, because women's motherhood and mothering role seem to be the most important features in accounting for the universal secondary status of women (Chodorow, 1971; Ortner, Rosaldo, this volume). The present paper describes the development of psychological qualities in women that are central to the perpetuation of this role.

In a formulation of this preliminary nature, there is not a great body of consistent evidence to draw upon. Available evidence is presented that illuminates aspects of the theory—for the most part psychoanalytic and social-psychological accounts based almost entirely on highly industrialized Western society. Because aspects of family structure are discussed that are universal, however, I think it is worth considering the theory as a general model. In any case, this is in some sense a programmatic appeal to people doing research. It points to certain issues that might be especially important in investigations of child development and family relationships, and suggests that researchers look explicitly at female vs. male development, and that they consider seriously mother–daughter relationships even if these are not of obvious "structural importance" in a traditional anthropological view of that society.

THE DEVELOPMENT OF GENDER PERSONALITY

According to psychoanalytic theory,[5] personality is a result of a boy's or girl's social-relational experiences from earliest infancy. Personality development is not the result of conscious parental intention. The nature and quality of the social relationships that the child experiences are appropriated, internalized, and organized by her/him and come to constitute her/his personality. What is internalized from an ongoing relationship continues independent of that original relationship and is generalized and set up as a permanent feature of the personality. The conscious self is usually not aware of many of the features of personality, or of its total structural organization. At the same time, these are important determinants of any person's behavior, both that which is culturally expected and that which is idiosyncratic or unique to the individual. The conscious aspects of personality, like a person's general self-concept and, importantly, her/his gender identity, require and depend upon the consistency and stability of its unconscious organization. In what follows I shall describe how contrasting male and female experiences lead to differences in the way the developing masculine or feminine psyche resolves certain relational issues.

Separation and Individuation (Preoedipal Development)

All children begin life in a state of "infantile dependence" (Fairbairn, 1952) upon an adult or adults, in most cases their mother. This state consists first in the persistence of primary identification with the mother: the child does not differentiate herself/himself from her/his mother but experiences a sense of oneness with her. (It is important to distinguish this from later forms of identification, from "secondary identification," which presuppose at least some degree of experienced separateness by the person who identifies.) Second, it includes an oral-incorporative mode of relationship to the world, leading, because of the infant's total helplessness, to a strong attachment to and dependence upon whoever nurses and carries her/him.

Both aspects of this state are continuous with the child's prenatal experience of being emotionally and physically part of the mother's body and of the exchange of body material through the placenta. That this relationship continues with the natural mother in most societies stems from the fact that women lactate. For convenience, and not because of biological necessity, this has usually meant that mothers, and females in general, tend to take all care of babies. It is probable that the mother's continuing to have major responsibility for the feeding and care of the child (so that the child interacts almost entirely with her) extends and intensifies her/his period of primary identification with her more than if, for instance, someone else were to take major or total care of the child. A child's earliest experience, then, is usually of identity with and attachment to a single mother, and always with women.

For both boys and girls, the first few years are preoccupied with issues of separation and individuation. This includes breaking or attenuating the primary identification with the mother and beginning to develop an individuated sense of self, and mitigating the totally dependent oral attitude and attachment to the mother. I would suggest that, contrary to the traditional psychoanalytic model, the preoedipal experience is likely to differ for boys and girls. Specifically, the experience of mothering for a woman involves a double identification (Klein & Rivière, 1937). A woman identifies with her own mother and, through identification with her child, she (re)experiences herself as a cared-for child. The particular nature of this double identification for the individual mother is closely bound up with her relationship to her own mother. As Deutsch expresses it, "In relation to her own child, woman repeats her own mother–child history" (1944:205). Given that she was a female child, and that identification with her mother and mothering are so bound up with her being a woman, we might expect that a woman's identification with a girl child might be stronger; that a mother, who is, after all, a person who is a woman and not simply the performer of a formally defined role, would tend to treat infants of different sexes in different ways.

There is some suggestive sociological evidence that this is the case. Mothers in a women's group in Cambridge, Massachusetts (see note 1), say that they identified more with their girl children than with boy children. The perception and treatment of girl vs. boy children in high-caste, extremely patriarchal, patrilocal communities in India are in the same vein. Families express preference for boy children and celebrate when sons are born. At the same time, Rajput mothers in North India are "as likely as not" (Minturn & Hitchcock, 1963) to like girl babies better than boy babies once they are born, and they and Havik Brahmins in South India (Harper, 1969) treat their daughters with greater affection and leniency than their sons. People in both groups say that this is out of sympathy for the future plight of their daughters, who will have to leave their natal family for a strange and usually oppressive postmarital household. From the time of their daughters' birth, then, mothers in these communities identify anticipatorily, by reexperiencing their own past, with the experiences of separation that their daughters will go through. They develop a particular attachment to their daughters because of this and by imposing their own reaction to the issue of separation on this new external situation.

It seems, then, that a mother is more likely to identify with a daughter than with a son, to experience her daughter (or parts of her daughter's life) as herself. Fliess's description (1961) of his neurotic patients who were the children of ambulatory psychotic mothers presents the problem in its psychopathological extreme. The example is interesting, because, although Fliess claims to be writing about people defined only by the fact that their problems were tied to a particular kind of relationship to their mothers, an overwhelmingly large proportion of the cases he presents are women. It seems, then, that this sort of disturbed mother inflicts her pathology predominantly on daughters. The mothers Fliess describes did not allow their daughters to perceive themselves as separate people, but simply acted as if their daughters were narcissistic extensions or doubles of themselves, extensions to whom were attributed the mothers' bodily feelings and who became physical vehicles for their mothers' achievement of autoerotic gratification. The daughters were bound into a mutually dependent "hyper-symbiotic" relationship. These mothers, then, perpetuate a mutual relationship with their daughters of both primary identification and infantile dependence.

A son's case is different. Cultural evidence suggests that insofar as a mother treats her son differently, it is usually by emphasizing his masculinity in opposition to herself and by pushing him to assume, or acquiescing in his assumption of, a sexually toned male-role relation to her. Whiting (1959) and Whiting et al. (1958) suggest that mothers in societies with mother–child sleeping arrangements and postpartum sex taboos may be seductive toward infant sons. Slater (1968) describes the socialization of precarious masculinity in Greek males of the classical period through their mothers' alternation of sexual praise and seductive behavior with hostile deflation and ridicule. This kind of behavior contributes to the son's differentiation from his mother and to the formation of ego boundaries (I will later discuss certain problems that result from this).

Neither form of attitude or treatment is what we would call "good mothering." However, evidence of differentiation of a pathological nature in the mother's behavior toward girls and boys does highlight tendencies in "normal" behavior. It seems likely that from their children's earliest childhood, mothers and women tend to identify more with daughters and to help them to differentiate less, and that processes of separation and individuation are made more difficult for girls. On the other hand, a mother tends to identify less with her son, and to push him toward differentiation and the taking on of a male role unsuitable to his age, and undesirable at any age in his relationship to her.

For boys and girls, the quality of the preoedipal relationship to the mother differs. This, as well as differences in development during the oedipal period, accounts for the persisting importance of preoedipal issues in female development and personality that many psychoanalytic writers describe.[6] Even before the establishment of gender identity, gender personality differentiation begins.

Gender Identity (Oedipal Crisis and Resolution)

There is only a slight suggestion in the psychological and sociological literature that preoedipal development differs for boys and girls. The pattern becomes explicit at the next developmental level. All theoretical and empirical accounts agree that after about age three (the beginning of the "oedipal" period, which focuses on the attainment of a stable gender identity) male and female development becomes radically different. It is at this stage that the father, and men in general, begin to become important in the child's primary object world. It is, of course, particularly difficult to generalize about the attainment of gender identity and sex-role assumption, since there is such wide variety in the sexual sociology of different societies. However, to the extent that in all societies women's life tends to be more private and domestic, and men's more public and social . . . we can make general statements about this kind of development.

In what follows, I shall be talking about the development of gender personality and gender identity in the tradition of psychoanalytic theory. Cognitive psychologists have established that by the age of three, boys and girls have an irreversible conception of what their gender is (see Kohlberg, 1966). I do not dispute these findings. It remains true that children (and adults) may know definitely that they are boys (men) or girls (women), and at the same time experience conflicts or uncertainty about "masculinity" or "femininity," about what these identities require in behavioral or emotional terms, etc. I am discussing the development of "gender identity" in this latter sense.

A boy's masculine gender identification must come to replace his early primary identification with his mother. This masculine identification is usually based on identification with a boy's father or other salient adult males. However, a boy's father is relatively more remote than his mother. He rarely plays a major care-taking role even at this period in his son's life. In most societies, his work and social life take place farther from the home than do those of his wife. He is, then, often relatively inaccessible to his son, and performs his male role activities away from where the son spends most of his life. As a result, a boy's male gender identification often becomes a "positional" identification, with aspects of his father's clearly or not-so-clearly defined male role, rather than a more generalized "personal" identification—a diffuse identification with his father's personality, values, and behavioral traits—that could grow out of a real relationship to his father.[7]

Mitscherlich (1963), in his discussion of Western advanced capitalist society, provides a useful insight into the problem of male development. The father, because his work takes him outside of the home most of the time, and because his active presence in the family has progressively decreased, has become an "invisible father." For the boy, the tie between affective relations and masculine gender identification and role learning (between libidinal and ego development) is relatively attenuated. He identifies with a fantasied masculine role, because the reality constraint that contact with his father would provide is missing. In all societies characterized by some sex segregation (even

those in which a son will eventually lead the same sort of life as his father), much of a boy's masculine identification must be of this sort, that is, with aspects of his father's role, or what he fantasies to be a male role, rather than with his father as a person involved in a relationship to him.

There is another important aspect to this situation, which explains the psychological dynamics of the universal social and cultural devaluation and subordination of women.[8] A boy, in his attempt to gain an elusive masculine identification, often comes to define this masculinity largely in negative terms, as that which is not feminine or involved with women. There is an internal and external aspect to this. Internally, the boy tries to reject his mother and deny his attachment to her and the strong dependence upon her that he still feels. He also tries to deny the deep personal identification with her that has developed during his early years. He does this by repressing whatever he takes to be feminine inside himself, and, importantly, by denigrating and devaluing whatever he considers to be feminine in the outside world. As a societal member, he also appropriates to himself and defines as superior particular social activities and cultural (moral, religious, and creative) spheres—possibly, in fact, "society" and "culture" themselves.[9]

Freud's description of the boy's oedipal crisis speaks to the issues of rejection of the feminine and identification with the father. As his early attachment to his mother takes on phallic-sexual overtones, and his father enters the picture as an obvious rival (who, in the son's fantasy, has apparent power to kill or castrate his son), the boy must radically deny and repress his attachment to his mother and replace it with an identification with his loved and admired, but also potentially punitive, therefore feared, father. He internalizes a superego.[10]

To summarize, four components of the attainment of masculine gender identity are important. First, masculinity becomes and remains a problematic issue for a boy. Second, it involves denial of attachment or relationship, particularly of what the boy takes to be dependence or need for another, and differentiation of himself from another. Third, it involves the repression and devaluation of femininity on both psychological and cultural levels. Finally, identification with his father does not usually develop in the context of a satisfactory affective relationship, but consists in the attempt to internalize and learn components of a not immediately apprehensible role.

The development of a girl's gender identity contrasts with that of a boy. Most important, femininity and female role activities are immediately apprehensible in the world of her daily life. Her final role identification is with her mother and women, that is, with the person or people with whom she also has her earliest relationship of infantile dependence. The development of her gender identity does not involve a rejection of this early identification, however. Rather, her later identification with her mother is embedded in and influenced by their ongoing relationship of both primary identification and preoedipal attachment. Because her mother is around, and she has had a genuine relationship to her as a person, a girl's gender and gender-role identification are mediated by and depend upon real affective relations. Identification with her mother is not positional—the narrow learning of particular role behaviors—but rather a personal identification with her mother's general traits of character and values. Feminine identification is based not on fantasied or externally defined characteristics and negative identification, but on the gradual learning of a way of being familiar in everyday life, and exemplified by the person (or kind of people—women) with whom she has been most involved. It is continuous with her early childhood identifications and attachments.

The major discontinuity in the development of a girl's sense of gender identity, and one that has led Freud and other early psychoanalysts to see female development as exceedingly difficult and tortuous, is that at some point she must transfer her primary sexual object choice from her mother and females to her father and males, if she is to attain her expected heterosexual adulthood. Briefly, Freud considers that all children feel that mothers give some cause for complaint and unhappiness: they give too little milk; they have a second child; they arouse and then forbid their child's sexual gratification in the process of caring for her/him. A girl receives a final blow, however: her discovery that she lacks a penis. She blames this lack on her mother, rejects her mother, and turns to her father in reaction.

Problems in this account have been discussed extensively in the general literature that has grown out of the women's movement, and within the psychoanalytic tradition itself. These concern Freud's misogyny and his obvious assumption that males possess physiological superiority, and that a woman's personality is inevitably determined by her lack of a penis.[11] The psychoanalytic account is not completely unsatisfactory, however. A more detailed consideration of several theorists[12] reveals important features of female development, especially about the mother–daughter relationship, and at the same time contradicts or mitigates the absoluteness of the more general Freudian outline.

These psychoanalysts emphasize how, in contrast to males, the female oedipal crisis is not resolved in the same absolute way. A girl cannot and does not completely reject her mother in favor of men, but continues her relationship of dependence upon and attachment to her. In addition, the strength and quality of her relationship to her father is completely dependent upon the strength and quality of her relationship to her mother. Deutsch suggests that a girl wavers in a "bisexual triangle" throughout her childhood and into puberty, normally making a very tentative resolution in favor of her father, but in such a way that issues of separation from and attachment to her mother remain important throughout a woman's life (1944:205):

> It is erroneous to say that the little girl gives up her first mother relation in favor of the father. She only gradually draws him into the alliance, develops from the mother–child exclusiveness toward the triangular parent–child relationship and continues the latter, just as she does the former, although in a weaker and less elemental form, all her life. Only the principal part changes: now the mother, now the father plays it. The ineradicability of affective constellations manifests itself in later repetitions.

We might suggest from this that a girl's internalized and external object-relations become and remain more complex, and at the same time more defining of her, than those of a boy. Psychoanalytic preoccupation with constitutionally based libidinal development, and with a normative male model of development, has obscured this fact. Most women are genitally heterosexual. At the same time, their lives always involve other sorts of equally deep and primary relationships, especially with their children, and, importantly, with other women. In these spheres also, even more than in the area of heterosexual relations, a girl imposes the sort of object-relations she has internalized in her preoedipal and later relationship to her mother.

Men are also for the most part genitally heterosexual. This grows directly out of their early primary attachment to their mother. We know, however, that in many societies their heterosexual relationships are not embedded in close personal relationship but simply in relations of dominance and power. Furthermore, they do not have the extended personal relations women have. They are not so connected to children, and their relationships with other men tend to be based not on particularistic connection or affective ties, but rather on abstract, universalistic role expectations.

Building on the psychoanalytic assumption that unique individual experiences contribute to the formation of individual personality, culture and personality theory has held that early experiences common to members of a particular society contribute to the formation of "typical" personalities organized around and preoccupied with certain issues: "Prevailing patterns of child-rearing must result in similar internalized situations in the unconscious of the majority of individuals in a culture, and these will be externalized back into the culture again to perpetuate it from generation to generation" (Guntrip, 1961:378). In a similar vein, I have tried to show that to the extent males and females, respectively, experience similar interpersonal environments as they grow up, masculine and feminine personality will develop differently.

I have relied on a theory which suggests that features of adult personality and behavior are determined, but which is not biologically determinist. Culturally expected personality and behavior are not simply "taught," however. Rather, certain features of social structure, supported by cultural beliefs, values, and perceptions, are internalized through the family and the child's early social object-relationships. This largely unconscious organization is the context in which role training and purposive socialization take place.

SEX-ROLE LEARNING AND ITS SOCIAL CONTEXT

Sex-role training and social interaction in childhood build upon and reinforce the largely unconscious development I have described. In most societies (ours is a complicated exception) a girl is usually with her mother and other female relatives in an interpersonal situation that facilitates continuous and early role learning and emphasizes the mother–daughter identification and particularistic, diffuse, affective relationships be-tween women. A boy, to a greater or lesser extent, is also with women for a large part of his childhood, which prevents continuous or easy masculine role identification. His development is characterized by discontinuity.

Ariès (1962:61), in his discussion of the changing concept of childhood in modern capitalist society, makes a distinction that seems to have more general applicability. Boys, he suggests, became "children" while girls remained "little women." "The idea of childhood profited the boys first of all, while the girls persisted much longer in the traditional way of life which confused them with the adults: we shall have cause to notice more than once this delay on the part of the women in adopting the visible forms of the essentially masculine civilization of modern times." This took place first in the middle classes, as a situation developed in which boys needed special schooling in order to prepare for their future work and could not begin to do this kind of work in childhood. Girls (and working-class boys) could still learn work more directly from their parents, and could begin to participate in the adult economy at an earlier age. Rapid economic change and development have exacer-

bated the lack of male generational role continuity. Few fathers now have either the opportunity or the ability to pass on a profession or skill to their sons.

Sex-role development of girls in modern society is more complex. On the one hand, they go to school to prepare for life in a technologically and socially complex society. On the other, there is a sense in which this schooling is a pseudo-training. It is not meant to interfere with the much more important training to be "feminine" and a wife and mother, which is embedded in the girl's unconscious development and which her mother teaches her in a family context where she is clearly the salient parent.

This dichotomy is not unique to modern industrial society. Even if special, segregated schooling is not necessary for adult male work (and many male initiation rites remain a form of segregated role training), boys still participate in more activities that characterize them as a category apart from adult life. Their activities grow out of the boy's need to fill time until he can begin to take on an adult male role. Boys may withdraw into isolation and self-involved play or join together in a group that remains more or less unconnected with either the adult world of work and activity or the familial world.

Jay (1969) describes this sort of situation in rural Modjokuto, Java. Girls, after the age of five or so, begin gradually to help their mothers in their work and spend time with their mothers. Boys at this early age begin to form bands of age mates who roam and play about the city, relating neither to adult men nor to their mothers and sisters. Boys, then, enter a temporary group based on universalistic membership criteria, while girls continue to participate in particularistic role relations in a group characterized by continuity and relative permanence.

The content of boys' and girls' role training tends in the same direction as the context of this training and its results. Barry, Bacon, and Child, in their well-known study (1957), demonstrate that the socialization of boys tends to be oriented toward achievement and self-reliance and that of girls toward nurturance and responsibility. Girls are thus pressured to be involved with and connected to others, boys to deny this involvement and connection.

ADULT GENDER PERSONALITY AND SEX ROLE

A variety of conceptualizations of female and male personality all focus on distinctions around the same issue, and provide alternative confirmation of the developmental model I have proposed. Bakan (1966:15) claims that male personality is preoccupied with the "agentic," and female personality with the "communal." His expanded definition of the two concepts is illuminating:

> I have adopted the terms "agency" and "communion" to characterize two fundamental modalities in the existence of living forms, agency for the existence of an organism as an individual and communion for the participation of the individual in some larger organism of which the individual is a part. Agency manifests itself in self-protection, self-assertion, and self-expansion; communion manifests itself in the sense of being at one with other organisms. Agency manifests itself in the formation of separations; communion in the lack of separations. Agency manifests itself in isolation, alienation, and aloneness; communion in contact, openness, and union. Agency manifests itself in the urge to master; communion in noncontractual cooperation. Agency manifests itself in the repression of thought, feeling, and impulse; communion in the lack and removal of repression.

Gutmann (1965) contrasts the socialization of male personalities in "allocentric" milieux (milieux in which the individual is part of a larger social organization and system of social bonds) with that of female personalities in "autocentric" milieux (in which the individual herself/himself is a focus of events and ties).[13] Gutmann suggests that this leads to a number of systematic differences in ego functioning. Female ego qualities, growing out of participation in autocentric milieux, include more flexible ego boundaries (i.e., less insistent self–other distinctions), present orientation rather than future orientation, and relatively greater subjectivity and less detached objectivity.[14]

Carlson (1971) confirms both characterizations. Her tests of Gutmann's claims lead her to conclude that "males represent experiences of self, others, space, and time in individualistic, objective, and distant ways, while females represent experiences in relatively interpersonal, subjective, immediate ways" (p. 270). With reference to Bakan, she claims that men's descriptions of affective experience tend to be in agentic terms and women's in terms of communion, and that an examination of abstracts of a large number of social-psychological articles on sex differences yields an overwhelming confirmation of the agency/communion hypothesis.

Cohen (1969) contrasts the development of "analytic" and "relational" cognitive style, the former characterized by a stimulus-centered, parts-specific orientation to reality, the latter centered on the self and responding to the global characteristics of a stimulus in reference to its total context. Although focusing primarily on class differences in cognitive style, she also points out that girls are more likely to mix the two types of functioning (and also to exhibit internal conflict about this). Especially, they are likely to exhibit at the same time both high field dependence and highly developed analytic skills in other areas. She suggests that boys and girls participate in different sorts of interactional subgroups in their families: boys experience their family more as a formally organized primary group; girls experience theirs as a group characterized by shared and less clearly delineated functions. She concludes (p. 836): "Since embedded responses covered the gamut from abstract categories, through language behaviors, to expressions of embeddedness in their social environments, it is possible that embeddedness may be a distinctive characteristic of female sex-role learning in this society regardless of social class, native ability, ethnic differences, and the cognitive impact of the school."

Preliminary consideration suggests a correspondence between the production of feminine personalities organized around "communal" and "autocentric" issues and characterized by flexible ego boundaries, less detached objectivity, and relational cognitive style, on the one hand, and important aspects of feminine as opposed to masculine social roles, on the other.

Most generally, I would suggest that a quality of embeddedness in social interaction and personal relationships characterizes women's life relative to men's. From childhood, daughters are likely to participate in an intergenerational world with their mother, and often with their aunts and grandmothers, whereas boys are on their own or participate in a single-generation world of age mates. In adult life, women's interaction with other women in most societies is kin-based and cuts across generational lines. Their roles tend to be particularistic, and to involve diffuse relationships and responsibilities rather than specific ones. Women in most societies are *defined* relationally (as someone's wife, mother, daughter, daughter-in-law; even a nun becomes the bride of Christ). Men's association (although it too may be kin-based and intergenerational) is much more likely than women's to cut across kinship units, to be restricted to a single generation, and to be recruited according to universalistic criteria and involve relationships and responsibilities defined by their specificity.

In these three settings, the mother–daughter tie and other female kin relations remain important from a woman's childhood through her old age. Daughters stay closer to home in both childhood and adulthood, and remain involved in particularistic role relations. Sons and men are more likely to feel uncomfortable at home, and to spend work and play time away from the house. Male activities and spheres emphasize universalistic, distancing qualities: men in Java are the bearers and transmitters of high culture and formal relationships; men in East London spend much of their time in alienated work settings; Atjehnese boys spend their time in school, and their fathers trade in distant places.

Mother–daughter ties in these three societies, described as extremely close, seem to be composed of companionship and mutual cooperation, and to be positively valued by both mother and daughter. The ethnographies do not imply that women are weighed down by the burden of their relationships or by overwhelming guilt and responsibility. On the contrary, they seem to have developed a strong sense of self and self-worth, which continues to grow as they get older and take on their maternal role. The implication is that "ego strength" is not completely dependent on the firmness of the ego's boundaries.

Guntrip's distinction between "immature" and "mature" dependence clarifies the difference between mother–daughter relationships and women's psyche in the Western middle class and in the matrifocal societies described. Women in the Western middle class are caught up to some extent in issues of infantile dependence, while the women in matrifocal societies remain in definite connection with others, but in relationships characterized by mature dependence. As Guntrip describes it (1961:291): *"Mature dependence* is characterized by full differentiation of ego and object (emergence from primary identification) and therewith a capacity for valuing the object for its own sake and for giving as well as receiving; a condition which should be described not as independence but as mature dependence." This kind of mature dependence is also to be distinguished from the kind of forced independence and denial of need for relationship that I have suggested characterizes masculine personality, and that reflects continuing conflict about infantile dependence (Guntrip, 1961:293; my italics): "Maturity is not equated with independence though it includes a certain capacity for independence. . . . The independence of the mature person is simply that he does not collapse when he has to stand alone. It is not an independence of needs for other persons with whom to have relationship: *that would not be desired by the mature."*

Depending on its social setting, women's sense of relation and connection and their embeddedness in social life provide them with a kind of security that men lack. The quality of a mother's relationship to her children and maternal self-esteem, on the one hand, and the nature of a daughter's developing identification with her mother, on the other, make crucial differences in female development.

Women's kin role, and in particular the mother role, is central and positively valued in Atjeh, Java, and East London. Women gain status and prestige as they get older; their major role is not fulfilled in early motherhood. At the same time, women may be important contributors to the family's economic support, as in Java and East London, and in all three societies they have control over real economic resources. All these factors give women a sense of self-esteem independent of their relationship to their children. Finally, strong relationships exist between women in these societies, expressed in mutual cooperation and frequent contact. A mother, then, when her children are young, is likely to spend much of her time in the company of other women, not simply isolated with her children.

These social facts have important positive effects on female psychological development. (It must be emphasized that all the ethnographies indicate that these same social facts make male development difficult and contribute to psychological insecurity and lack of ease in interpersonal relationships in men.) A mother is not invested in keeping her daughter from individuating and becoming less dependent. She has other ongoing contacts and relationships that help fulfill her psychological and social needs. In addition, the people surrounding a mother while a child is growing up become mediators between mother and daughter, by providing a daughter with alternative models for personal identification and objects of attachment, which contribute to her differentiation from her mother. Finally, a daughter's identification with her mother in this kind of setting is with a strong woman with clear control over important spheres of life, whose sense of self-esteem can reflect this. Acceptance of her gender identity involves positive valuation of herself, and not an admission of inferiority. In psychoanalytic terms, we might say it involves identification with a preoedipal, active, caring mother. Bibring points to clinical findings supporting this interpretation: "We find in the analysis of the women who grew up in this 'matriarchal' setting the rejection of the feminine role less frequently than among female patients coming from the patriarchal family culture" (1953:281).

There is another important aspect of the situation in these societies. The continuing structural and practical importance of the mother–daughter tie not only ensures that a daughter develops a positive personal and role identification with her mother, but also re-quires that the close psychological tie between mother and daughter become firmly grounded in real role expectations. These provide a certain constraint and limitation upon the relationship, as well as an avenue for its expression through common spheres of interest based in the external social world.

All these societal features contrast with the situation of the Western middle-class woman. Kinship relations in the middle class are less important. Kin are not likely to live near each other, and, insofar as husbands are able to provide adequate financial support for their families, there is no need for a network of mutual aid among related wives. As the middle-class woman gets older and becomes a grandmother, she cannot look forward to increased status and prestige in her new role.

The Western middle-class housewife does not have an important economic role in her family. The work she does and the responsibilities that go with it (household management, cooking, entertaining, etc.) do not seem to be really necessary to the economic support of her family (they are crucial contributions to the maintenance and reproduction of her family's class position, but this is not generally recognized as important either by the woman herself or by the society's ideology). If she works outside the home, neither she nor the rest of society is apt to consider this work to be important to her self-definition in the way that her housewife role is.

Child care, on the other hand, is considered to be her crucially important responsibility. Our post-Freudian society in fact assigns to parents (and especially to the mother)[16] nearly total responsibility for how children turn out. A middle-class mother's daily life is not centrally involved in relations with other women. She is isolated with her children for most of her workday. It is not surprising, then, that she is likely to invest a lot of anxious energy and guilt in her concern for her children and to look to them for her own self-affirmation, or that her self-esteem, dependent on the lives of others than herself, is shaky. Her life situation leads her to an overinvolvement in her children's lives.

A mother in this situation keeps her daughter from differentiation and from lessening her infantile dependence. (She also perpetuates her son's dependence, but in this case society and his father are more likely to interfere in order to assure that, behaviorally, at least, he doesn't *act* dependent.) And there are no other people around to mediate in the mother–daughter relationship. Insofar as the father is actively involved in a relationship with his daughter and his daughter develops some identification with him, this helps her individuation, but the formation of ego autonomy through identification with and idealization of her father may be at the expense of her positive sense of feminine self. Unlike the situation in matrifocal families, the continuing closeness of the mother–daughter relationship is expressed only on a psychological, interpersonal level. External role expectations do not ground or limit it.

It is difficult, then, for daughters in a Western middle-class family to develop self-esteem. Most psychoanalytic and social theorists[17] claim that the mother inevitably represents to her daughter (and son) regression, passivity, dependence, and lack of orientation to reality, whereas the father represents progression, activity, independence, and reality orientation.[18] Given the value implications of this dichotomy, there are advantages for the son in giving up his mother and identifying with his father. For the daughter, feminine gender identification means identification with a devalued, passive mother, and personal maternal identification is with a mother whose own self-esteem is low. Conscious rejection of her oedipal maternal identification, however, remains an unconscious rejection and devaluation of herself, because of her continuing pre-oedipal identification and boundary confusion with her mother.

Cultural devaluation is not the central issue, however. Even in patrilineal, patrilocal societies in which women's status is very low, women do not necessarily translate this cultural devaluation into low self-esteem, nor do girls have to develop difficult boundary problems with their mother. In the Moslem Moroccan family, for example, a large amount of sex segregation and sex antagonism gives women a separate (domestic) sphere in which they have a real productive role and control, and also a life situation in which any young mother is in the company of other women.[19] Women do not need to invest all their psychic energy in their children, and their self-esteem is not dependent on their relationship to their children. In this and other patrilineal, patrilocal societies, what resentment women do have at their oppressive situation is more often expressed toward their sons, whereas daughters are seen as allies against oppression. Conversely, a daughter develops relationships of attachment to and identification with other adult women. Loosening her tie to her mother therefore does not entail the rejection of all women. The close tie that remains between mother and daughter is based not simply on mutual overinvolvement but often on mutual understanding of their oppression.

CONCLUSION

Women's universal mothering role has effects both on the development of masculine and feminine personality and on the relative status of the sexes. This paper has described the development of relational personality in women and of personalities preoccupied with the denial of relation in men. In its comparison of different societies it has suggested that men, while guaranteeing to themselves sociocultural superiority over women, always remain psychologically defensive and insecure. Women, by contrast, although always of secondary social and cultural status, may in favorable circumstances gain psychological security and a firm sense of worth and importance in spite of this.

Social and psychological oppression, then, is perpetuated in the structure of personality. The paper enables us to suggest what social arrangements contribute (and could contribute) to social equality between men and women and their relative freedom from certain sorts of psychological conflict. Daughters and sons must be able to develop a personal identification with more than one adult, and preferably one embedded in a role relationship that gives it a social context of expression and provides some limitation upon it. Most important, boys need to grow up around men who take a major role in child care, and girls around women who, in addition to their child-care responsibilities, have a valued role and recognized spheres of legitimate control. These arrangements could help to ensure that children of both sexes develop a sufficiently individuated and strong sense of self, as well as a positively valued and secure gender identity that does not bog down either in ego-boundary confusion, low self-esteem, and overwhelming relatedness to others or in compulsive denial of any connection to others or dependence upon them.

NOTES

1. My understanding of mother–daughter relationships and their effect on feminine psychology grows out of my participation beginning in 1971 in a women's group that discusses mother–daughter relationships in particular and family relationships in general. All the women in this group have contributed to this understanding. An excellent dissertation by Marcia Millman (1972) first suggested to me the importance of boundary issues for women and became a major organizational focus for my subsequent work. Discussions with Nancy Jay, Michelle Rosaldo, Philip Slater, Barrie Thorne, Susan Weisskopf, and Beatrice Whiting have been central to the development of the ideas presented here. I am grateful to George Goethals, Edward Payne, and Mal Slavin for their comments and suggestions about earlier versions of this paper.

2. Margaret Mead provides the most widely read and earliest argument for this viewpoint (cf., e.g., 1935 and 1949); see also Chodorow (1971) for another discussion of the same issue.

3. Unfortunately, the language that describes personality structure is itself embedded with value judgment. The implication in most studies is that it is always better to have firmer ego boundaries, that "ego strength" depends on the degree of individuation. Gutmann, who recognizes the linguistic problem, even suggests that "so-called ego pathology may have adaptive implications for women" (1965:231). The argument can be made that extremes in either direction are harmful. Complete lack of ego boundaries is clearly pathological, but so also, as critics of contemporary Western men point out (cf., e.g., Bakan, 1966, and Slater, 1970), is individuation gone wild, what Bakan calls "agency unmitigated by communion," which he takes to characterize, among other things, both capitalism based on the Protestant ethic and aggressive masculin-

ity. With some explicit exceptions that I will specify in context, I am using the concepts solely in the descriptive sense.

4. Slater (1968) provides one example of such an investigation. LeVine's recent work on psychoanalytic anthropology (1971a, b) proposes a methodology that will enable social scientists to study personality development in this way.

5. Particularly as interpreted by object-relations theorists (e.g., Fairbairn, 1952, and Guntrip, 1961) and, with some similarity, by Parsons (1964) and Parsons and Bales (1955).

6. See, e.g., Brunswick, 1940; Deutsch, 1932, 1944; Fliess, 1948; Freud, 1931; Jones, 1927; and Lampl-de Groot, 1927.

7. The important distinction between "positional" and "personal" identification comes from Slater, 1961, and Winch, 1962.

8. For more extensive arguments concerning this, see, e.g., Burton & Whiting (1961), Chodorow (1971), and Slater (1968).

9. The processes by which individual personal experiences and psychological factors contribute to or are translated into social and cultural facts, and, more generally, the circularity of explanations in terms of socialization, are clearly very complicated. A discussion of these issues, however, is not within the scope of this paper.

10. The question of the universality of the oedipus complex as Freud describes it is beyond the scope of this paper. Bakan (1966, 1968) points out that in the original Oedipus myth, it was the father who first tried to kill his son, and that the theme of paternal infanticide is central to the entire Old Testament. He suggests that for a variety of reasons, fathers probably have hostile and aggressive fantasies and feelings about their children (sons). This more general account, along with a variety of psychological and anthropological data, convinces me that we must take seriously the notion

that members of both generations may have conflicts over the inevitable replacement of the elder generation by the younger, and that children probably feel both guilt and (rightly) some helplessness in this situation.

11. These views are most extreme and explicit in two papers (Freud, 1925, 1933) and warrant the criticism that has been directed at them. Although the issue of penis envy in women is not central to this paper, it is central to Freud's theory of female development. Therefore I think it worthwhile to mention three accounts that avoid Freud's ideological mistakes while allowing that his clinical observations of penis envy might be correct.

Thompson (1943) suggests that penis envy is a symbolic expression of women's culturally devalued and underprivileged position in our patriarchal society; that possession of a penis symbolizes the possession of power and privilege. Bettelheim (1954) suggests that members of either sex envy the sexual functions of the other, and that women are more likely to express this envy overtly, because, since men are culturally superior, such envy is considered "natural." Balint (1954) does not rely on the fact of men's cultural superiority, but suggests that a little girl develops penis envy when she realizes that her mother loves people with penises, i.e., her father, and thinks that possession of a penis will help her in her rivalry for her mother's attentions.

12. See, e.g., Brunswick, 1940; Deutsch, 1925, 1930, 1932, 1944; Freedman, 1961; Freud, 1931; Jones, 1927.

13. Following Cohen (1969), I would suggest that the external structural features of these settings (in the family or in school, for instance) are often similar or the same for boys and girls. The different kind and amount of adult male and female participation in these settings accounts for their being experienced by children of different sexes as different sorts of milieux.

14. Gutmann points out that all these qualities are supposed to indicate lack of adequate ego strength, and suggests that we ought to evaluate ego strength in terms of the specific demands of different people's (e.g., women's as opposed to men's) daily lives. Bakan goes even further and suggests that modern male ego qualities are a pathological extreme. Neither account is completely adequate. Gutmann does not consider the possibility (for which we have good evidence) that the everyday demands of an autocentric milieu are unreasonable: although women's ego qualities may be "functional" for their participation in these milieux, they do not necessarily contribute to the psychological strength of the women themselves. Bakan, in his (legitimate) preoccupation with the lack of connection and compulsive independence that characterize Western masculine success, fails to recognize the equally clear danger (which, I will suggest, is more likely to affect women) of communion unmitigated by agency—of personality and behavior with no sense of autonomous control or independence at all.

I think this is part of a more general social-scientific mistake, growing out of the tendency to equate social structure and society with male social organization and activities within a society. This is exemplified, for instance, in Erikson's idealistic conception of maternal qualities in women (1965) and, less obviously, in the contrast between Durkheim's extensive treatment of "anomic" suicide (1897) and his relegation of "fatalistic" suicide to a single footnote (p. 276).

15. This ethnography and a reading of it that focuses on strong female kin relations (Siegel, 1969) were brought to my attention by Tanner (1971).

16. See Slater (1970) for an extended discussion of the implications of this.

17. See, e.g., Deutsch, 1944, *passim;* Erikson, 1964:162; Klein & Rivière, 1937:18; Parsons, 1964, *passim;* Parsons & Bales, 1955, *passim.*

18. Their argument derives from the universal fact that a child must outgrow her/his primary identification with and total dependence upon the mother. The present paper argues that the value implications of this dichotomy grow out of the particular circumstances of our society and its devaluation of relational qualities. Allied to this is the suggestion that it does not need to be, and often is not, relationship to the father that breaks the early maternal relationship.

19. Personal communication from Fatima Mernissi, based on her experience growing up in Morocco and her sociological fieldwork there.

REFERENCES

Ariès, P. 1962. *Centuries of childhood: A social history of family life.* New York.

Bakan, D. 1966. *The duality of human existence: Isolation and communion in Western man.* Boston.

———. 1968. *Disease, pain, and sacrifice: Toward a psychology of suffering.* Boston.

Balint, A. 1954. *The early years of life: A psychoanalytic study.* New York.

Barry, H., Bacon, M., & Child, I. 1957. "A cross-cultural survey of some sex differences in socialization." *Journal of Abnormal and Social Psychology* 55:327–32.

Bettelheim, B. 1954. *Symbolic wounds: Puberty rites and the envious male.* New York.

Bibring, G. 1953. "On the 'passing of the Oedipus complex' in a matriarchal family setting." In R. Lowenstein, ed., *Drives, affects and behavior: Essays in honor of Marie Bonaparte,* pp. 278–84. New York.

Brunswick, R. 1940. "The preoedipal phase of the libido development." In R. Fliess, ed., pp. 231–53.

Burton, R., & Whiting, J. 1961. "The absent father and cross-sex identity." *Merrill-Palmer Quarterly of Behavior and Development* 7 (2):85–95.

GENDER IN THE CONTEXT OF RACE AND CLASS: NOTES ON CHODOROW'S "REPRODUCTION OF MOTHERING"

ELIZABETH V. SPELMAN

. . . Much of feminist theory has proceeded on the assumption that gender is indeed a variable of human identity independent of other variables such as race and class, that whether one is a woman is unaffected by what class or race one is.[1] Feminists have also assumed that sexism is distinctly different from racism and classism, that whether and how one is subject to sexism is unaffected by whether and how one is subject to racism or classism.

The work of Nancy Chodorow has seemed to provide feminist theory with a strong foundation for these arguments. It has explicitly and implicitly been used to justify the assumption that there is nothing problematic about trying to examine gender independently of other variables such as race, class, and ethnicity. Though Chodorow's writings have received sometimes scathing criticism from feminists, more often they have been seen by feminist scholars in many different disciplines as providing a particularly rich understanding of gender.[2] Indeed, Chodorow offers what appears to be a very promising account of the relations between gender identity and other important aspects of identity such as race and class. For while she treats gender as separable from race and class, she goes on to suggest ways in which the sexist oppression intimately connected to gender differences is related to racism and classism.

. . . While Chodorow's work is very compelling, it ought to be highly problematic for any version of feminism that demands more than lip service to the significance of race and class, racism and classism, in the lives of the women on whom Chodorow focuses. The problem, as I see it, is not that feminists have taken Chodorow seriously, but that we have not taken her seriously enough. Her account points to a more complicated understanding of gender and the process of becoming gendered than she herself develops. She tells us to look at the social context of mothering in order to understand the effect of mothering on the acquisition of gender identity in children; but if we follow her advice, rather than her own practice, we are led to see that gender identity is not neatly separable from other aspects of identity such as race and class. They couldn't be if, as Chodorow insists, the acquisition of gender occurs in and helps perpetuate the "hierarchical and differentiated social worlds" we inhabit. . . . It is a general principle of feminist inquiry to be sceptical about any account of human relations that fails to mention gender or consider the possible effects of gender differences: for in a world in which there is sexism, obscuring the workings of gender is likely to involve—whether intentionally or not—obscuring the workings of sexism. We thus ought to be sceptical about any account of gender relations that fails to mention race and class or to consider the possible effects of race and class differences on gender: for in a world in which there is racism and classism, obscuring the workings of race and class is likely to involve—whether intentionally or not—obscuring the workings of racism and classism.

NOTES

[1] Notice how different this is from saying that whether one is *female* is unaffected by what race or class one is.

[2] Among the philosophers and political theorists who have incorporated Chodorow's work into their own analyses are Jane Flax, "Political Philosophy and the Patriarchal Unconscious: A Psychoanalytic Perspective on Epistemology and Metaphysics," Nancy C. M. Hartsock, "The Feminist Standpoint: Developing the Ground for a Specifically Feminist Historical Materialism," Naomi Scheman, "Individualism and the Objects of Psychology," and Sandra Harding, "Why Has the Sex/Gender System Become Visible Only Now?"—all in *Dis-*

covering Reality, ed. Harding and Hintikka. See also Isaac D. Balbus, *Marxism and Domination* (Princeton: Princeton University Press, 1982). Chodorow's work also has been incorporated into the literary criticism of Judith Kegan Gardiner, "On Female Identity and Writing by Women," *Critical Inquiry* 8, no. 2 (1981): 347–61, and of Elizabeth Abel, "(E)Merging Identities: The Dynamics of Female Friendship in Contemporary Fiction by Women," *Signs* 6, no. 3 (1981): 413–35. Students of psychoanalysis such as Jessica Benjamin and Evelyn Fox Keller have found Chodorow's work helpful in explaining their own positions, Benjamin in "Master

For this reason alone we may have a lot to learn from the following questions about any account of gender relations that presupposes or otherwise insists on the separability of gender, race, and class: Why does it seem possible or necessary to separate them? Whatever the motivations for doing so, does it serve the interests of some people and not others? Does methodology ever express race or class privilege—for example, do any of the methodological reasons that might be given for trying to investigate gender in isolation from race and class in fact serve certain race or class interests?

These questions are not rhetorical. For very good and very important reasons, feminists have insisted on asking how gender affects or is affected by every branch of human inquiry (even those such as the physical sciences, which seem to have no openings for such questions). And with very good reason we have been annoyed by the absence of reference to gender in inquiries about race or class, racism and classism. Perhaps it seems the best response, to such a state of affairs, first to focus on gender and sexism and then to go on to think about how gender and sexism are related to race and racism, class and classism. Hence the appeal of the work of Nancy Chodorow and the variations on it by others. But however logically, methodologically, and politically sound such inquiry seems, it obscures the ways in which race and class identity may be intertwined with gender identity. Moreover, since in a racist and classist society the racial and class identity of those who are subject to racism and classism are not obscured, all it can really mask is the racial and class identity of white middle-class women. It is because white middle-class women have something at stake in not having their racial and class identity made and kept visible that we must question accepted feminist positions on gender identity.

If feminism is essentially about gender, and gender is taken to be neatly separable from race and class, then race and class don't need to be talked about except in some peripheral way. And if race and class are peripheral to women's identities as women, then racism and classism can't be of central concern to feminism. Hence the racism and classism some women face and other women help perpetuate can't find a place in feminist theory unless we keep in mind the race and class of all women (not just the race and class of those who are the victims of racism and classism). I have suggested here that one way to keep them in mind is to ask about the extent to which gender identity exists in concert with these other aspects of identity. This is quite different from saying either (1) we need to talk about race and class instead of gender or (2) we need to talk about race and class in addition to gender. Some feminists may be concerned that focus on race and class will deflect attention away from gender and from what women have in common and thus from what gives feminist inquiry its distinctive cast. This presupposes not only that we ought not spend too much time on what we don't have in common but that we have gender in common. But do we have gender identity in common? In one sense, of course, yes: all women are women. But in another sense, no: not if gender is a social construction and females become not simply women but particular kinds of women. If I am justified in thinking that what it means for me to be a woman must be exactly the same as what it means for you to be a woman (since we both are women), I needn't bother to find out anything from you or about you in order to find out what it means for you to be a woman: I can simply deduce what it means from my own case. On the other hand, if the meaning of what we apparently have in common (being women) depends in some ways on the meaning of what we don't have in common (for example, our different racial or class identities), then far from distracting us from issues of gender, attention to race and class in fact helps us to understand gender. In this sense it is only if we pay attention to how we differ that we come to an understanding of what we have in common.[3]

and Slave: The Fantasy of Erotic Domination," in *Powers of Desire: The Politics of Sexuality,* ed. Ann Snitow, Christine Stansell, and Sharon Thompson (New York: Monthly Review Press, 1983), 280–99; Keller in "Gender and Science," *Psychoanalysis and Contemporary Thought* 2, no. 3 (1978): 409–33. Chodorow's work has also influenced the far-reaching work of Carol Gilligan, *In a Different Voice* (Cambridge: Harvard University Press, 1982). Chodorow's book and earlier articles were the subject of a critical symposium in *Signs 6,* no. 3 (1981), with comments from Judith Lorber, Rose Laub Coser, Alice S. Rossi, and a response from Chodorow. Iris Young recently has expressed doubts about the wisdom of Flax's, Hartsock's, and Harding's use of Chodorow, in "Is Male Gender Identity the Cause of Male Domination?" in *Mothering: Essays in Feminist Theory,* ed. Joyce Trebilcot (Totowa, N.J.: Rowman and Allanheld, 1983). In the *Mothering* volume also appears Pauline Bart's highly critical review of Chodorow's book, a review first found in *off our backs* 11, no. 1 (1981). Adrienne Rich has pointed out the heterosexist bias in *The Reproduction of Mothering* in "Compulsory Heterosexuality and Lesbian Existence," *Signs 5,* no. 4 (1980): 631–60. As discussed below, Gloria Joseph has addressed the fact of the absence of a discussion of race and racism in accounts like Chodorow's.

[3]Thanks to Helen Longino, Monica Jakuc, and Marilyn Schuster for helpful comments on a very early draft of this chapter.

Carlson, R. 1971. "Sex differences in ego functioning: Exploratory studies of agency and communion." *Journal of Consulting and Clinical Psychology* 37:267–77.

Chodorow, N. 1971. "Being and doing. A cross-cultural examination of the socialization of males and females." In V. Gornick & B. Moran, eds., *Woman in sexist society: Studies in power and powerlessness.* New York.

Cohen, R. 1969. "Conceptual styles, culture conflict, and nonverbal tests of intelligence." *American Anthropologist* 71:828–56.

Deutsch, H. 1925. "The psychology of woman in relation to the functions of reproduction." In R. Fliess, ed., pp. 165–79.

———. 1930. "The significance of masochism in the mental life of women." In R. Fliess, ed., pp. 195–207.

———. 1932. "On female homosexuality." In R. Fliess, ed., pp. 208–30.

———. 1944, 1945. *Psychology of women.* Vols. I & II. New York.

Durkheim, E. 1897. *Suicide.* New York, 1968.

Erikson, E. 1964. *Insight and responsibility.* New York.

———. 1965. "Womanhood and the inner space." In R. Lifton, ed., *The woman in America.* Cambridge, Mass.

Fairbairn, W. 1952. *An object-relations theory of the personality.* New York.

Fliess, R. 1948. "Female and preoedipal sexuality: A historical survey." In R. Fliess, ed., pp. 159–64.

———. 1961. *Ego and body ego: Contributions to their psychoanalytic psychology.* New York, 1970.

Fliess, R., ed. 1969. *The psychoanalytic reader: An anthology of essential papers with critical introductions.* New York. Originally published in 1948.

Freedman, D. 1961. "On women who hate their husbands." In H. Ruitenbeek, ed., pp. 221–37.

Freud, S. 1925. "Some psychological consequences of the anatomical distinction between the sexes." In J. Strachey, ed., *The standard edition of the complete psychological works of Sigmund Freud,* Vol. XIX, pp. 248–58. London.

———. 1931. "Female sexuality." In H. Ruitenbeek, ed., pp. 88–105.

———. 1933. "Femininity." In *New introductory lectures in psychoanalysis,* pp. 112–35. New York, 1961.

Geertz, H. 1961. *The Javanese family: A study of kinship and socialization.* New York.

Guntrip, H. 1961. *Personality structure and human interaction: The developing synthesis of psycho-dynamic theory.* New York.

Gutmann, D. 1965. "Women and the conception of ego strength." *Merrill-Palmer Quarterly of Behavior and Development* 2:229–40.

Harper, E. 1969. "Fear and the status of women." *Southwestern Journal of Anthropology* 25:81–95.

Jay, R. 1969. *Javanese villagers: Social relations in rural Modjokuto.* Cambridge, Mass.

Jones, E. 1927. "The early development of female sexuality." In H. Ruitenbeek, ed., pp. 21–35.

Klein, M., & Rivière, J. 1937. *Love, hate and reparation.* New York, 1964.

Kohlberg, L. 1966. "A cognitive-developmental analysis of children's sex-role concepts and attitudes." In E. Maccoby, ed., *The development of sex differences,* pp. 82–173. Stanford, Calif.

Komarovsky, M. 1962. *Blue-collar marriage,* New York, 1967.

Lampl-de Groot, J. 1927. "The evolution of the Oedipus complex in women." In R. Fliess, ed., pp. 180–94.

LeVine, R. 1971a. "The psychoanalytic study of lives in natural social settings." *Human Development* 14:100–109.

———. 1971b. "Re-thinking psychoanalytic anthropology." Paper presented at the Institute on Psychoanalytic Anthropology, 70th Annual Meeting of the American Anthropological Association, New York.

Mead, M. 1935. *Sex and temperament in three primitive societies.* New York, 1963.

———. 1949. *Male and female: A study of sexes in a changing world.* New York, 1968.

Millman, M. 1972. "Tragedy and exchange: Metaphoric understandings of interpersonal relationships." Ph.D. dissertation, Department of Sociology, Brandeis University.

Minturn, L., & Hitchcock, J. 1963. "The Rajputs of Khalapur, India." In B. Whiting, ed., *Six cultures: Studies in child rearing.* New York.

Mitscherlich, A. 1963. *Society without the father.* New York, 1970.

Parsons, T., 1964. *Social structure and personality.* New York.

Parsons, T., & Bales, R. 1955. *Family, socialization and interaction process.* New York.

Ruitenbeek, H., ed. 1966. *Psychoanalysis and female sexuality.* New Haven.

Siegel, J. 1969. *The rope of God.* Berkeley, Calif.

Slater, P. 1961. "Toward a dualistic theory of identification." *Merrill-Palmer Quarterly of Behavior and Development* 7:113–26.

———. 1968. *The glory of Hera: Greek mythology and the Greek family.* Boston.

———. 1970. *The pursuit of loneliness: American culture at the breaking point.* Boston.

Tanner, N. 1971. "Matrifocality in Indonesia and among Black Americans." Paper presented at the 70th Annual Meeting of the American Anthropological Association, New York.

Tax, M. 1970. *Woman and her mind: The story of daily life.* Boston.

Thompson, C. 1943. "'Penis envy' in women." In H. Ruitenbeek, ed., pp. 246–51.

Whiting, J. 1959. "Sorcery, sin and the superego: A cross-cultural study of some mechanisms of social control." In C. Ford, ed., *Cross-cultural approaches: Readings in comparative research,* pp. 147–68. New Haven, 1967.

Whiting, J., Kluckhohn, R., & Anthony, A. 1958. "The function of male initiation rites at puberty." In E. Maccoby, T. Newcomb, & E. Hartley, eds., *Readings in social psychology,* pp. 359–70. New York.

Winch, R. 1962. *Identification and its familial determinants.* New York.

Young, M., & Willmott, P. 1957. *Family and kinship in East London.* London, 1966.

"The Means to Put My Children Through": Child-Rearing Goals and Strategies among Black Female Domestic Servants

BONNIE THORNTON DILL

This essay explores the family and child-rearing strategies presented by a small group of Afro-American women who held jobs as household workers while raising their children. The data are drawn from a study of the relationship of work and family among American-born women of African descent who were private household workers (domestic servants) for most of their working lives.

The primary method of data collection was life histories, collected through open-ended, in-depth interviews with 26 women living in the northeastern United States. All participants were between 60 and 80 years old. A word of caution in reading this essay: The conclusions are not meant to apply to all Black female domestic servants, but represent only my interpretation of the experiences of these 26 women.

The life history method is particularly useful in studying Black female domestic workers whose stories and experiences have largely been distorted or ignored in the social science literature.* According to Denzin (1970:220), the

method "presents the experiences and definitions held by one person, group or organization as that person, group or organization interprets those experiences." As such, it provides a means of exploring the processes whereby people construct, endure, and create meaning in both the interactional and structural aspects of their lives. It aids in the identification and definition of concepts appropriate to a sociological understanding of the subject's experience, and moves toward building theory that is grounded in imagery and meanings relevant to the subject. Collected through in-depth interviews, life histories are active processes of rendering meaning to one's life—its conflicts, ambiguities, crises, successes, and significant interpersonal relationships. Subjects are not merely asked to "report" but rather to reconstruct and interpret their choices, situations and experiences.* The study of Black Americans cries out for such a sensitized approach to their lives.

The child-rearing goals and strategies adopted by the women who participated in this study are particularly revealing of the relationship of work and family. As working mothers, they were concerned with providing safe and secure care for their children while they were away from home. As working-class people, seeking to advance their children beyond their own occupational achievements, they confronted the problem of guiding them toward goals that were outside of their own personal experience. These issues, as well as others, take on a particular form for women who were household workers primarily because of the nature of their work.

*There is a very limited body of literature directly focused upon Black women in domestic service in the United States. Many of these studies are confined to the Southern experience. Among the most important containing data on Black women in northern cities are Haynes (1923), Eaton (1967), and Chaplin (1964). Some discussion of the subject was also found in community studies, particularly those conducted before World War II (Drake & Cayton, 1945; Ovington, 1969). Labor studies provided a third source of data (among these were Green & Woodson, 1930, and Haynes, 1912).

*This discussion is largely drawn from a paper by Dill and Joselin (1977).

Unlike many other occupations, domestic work brings together, in a closed and intimate sphere of human interaction, people whose paths would never cross were they to conduct their lives within the socio-economic boundaries to which they were ascribed. These intimate interactions across the barriers of income, ethnicity, religion, and race occur within a sphere of life that is private and has little public exposure—the family.

As household workers, these women often become vital participants in the daily lives of two separate families: their employer's and their own. In fact, they have often been described as being "like one of the family" (Childress, 1956), and yet the barriers between them and their employers are real and immutable ones. In addition, working-class Black women employed by middle- and upper-class white families observe and experience vast differences in the material quality of life in the two homes. With regard to child-rearing, employers could provide luxuries and experiences for their children that were well beyond the financial means of the employee.

This essay, therefore, presents some of the ways in which the women talked about their reactions and responses to the discrepancies in life chances between those of their children and those of their employers. To some extent, these discrepancies became the lens through which we viewed their goals for their children and their child-rearing practices. At the same time, the contrast in objective conditions provides a background against which the women's perceptions of similarities between themselves and their employers are made more interesting.

The data from this study indicate that the relationship between the employee's family life and her work was shaped by four basic factors. First, there was the structure of the work. Whether she worked full-time or part-time and lived in, lived out, or did day work determined the extent to which she became involved in the employer's day-to-day life. It also determined the amount of time she had to share with her own family. Second were the tasks and duties she was assigned. With regard to her own child-rearing goals and strategies, the intermingling of employer and employee lifestyles occurred most frequently among those women who took care of the employer's children. It is through their discussion of these activities that the similarities and differences between the two families are most sharply revealed. A third factor is the degree of employer–employee intimacy. An employee who cared for the employer's children was more likely to have an intimate relationship with her employing family, but not always. Though the employer–employee relationship in domestic service is

characterized as a personalized one when compared with other work relationships, this does not presume intimacy between the two parties; that is, a reciprocal exchange of interests and concerns. Among the women who participated in this study, those who did not share much of their own life with their employers appeared to minimize the interaction of work and family. Finally were the employee's goals for her children. Those women who felt that their employers could aid them in achieving the educational or other goals they had set for their children were more likely to encourage an intermingling of these two parts of their lives.

On domestic work and upward mobility:

Strangely enough, I never intended for my children to have to work for anybody in the capacity that I worked. Never. And I never allowed my children to do any babysitting or anything of the sort. I figured it's enough for the mother to do it and in this day and time you don't have to do that. . . . So they never knew anything about going out to work or anything. They went to school.

Given the low social status of the occupation, the ambivalent and defensive feelings many of the women expressed about their work and the eagerness with which women left the occupation when other opportunities were opened to them, it is not at all surprising that most of the women in this study said they did not want their children to work in domestic service. Their hopes were centered upon "better" jobs for their children: jobs with more status, income, security, and comfort. Pearl Runner* recalled her goals for her children:

My main goal was I didn't want them to follow in my footsteps as far as working. I always wanted them to please go to school and get a good job because it's important. That was really my main object.

Lena Hudson explained her own similar feelings this way:

They had a better chance than I had, and they shouldn't look back at what I was doing. They had a better chance and a better education than I had, so look out for something better than I was doing. And they did. I haven't had a one that had to do any housework or anything like that. So I think that's good.

* The names used for the participants in the study are fictitious.

The notion of a better chance is a dominant one in the women's discussions of their goals for their children. They portray themselves as struggling to give their children the skills and training they did not have; and as praying that opportunities which had not been open to them would be open to their children. In their life histories, the women describe many of the obstacles they encountered in this quest. Nevertheless, there are dilemmas which, though not discussed explicitly, are implicit in their narratives and a natural outgrowth of their aspirations.

First of these is the task of guiding children toward a future over which they had little control and toward occupational objectives with which they had no direct experience. Closely tied to this problem was their need to communicate the undesirability of household work and at the same time maintain their personal dignity despite the occupation. While these two problems are not exceptional for working-class parents in an upwardly mobile society, they were mediated for Black domestic workers through the attitudes toward household work held by members of the Black communities in which the women lived and raised their children.

Had domestic work not been the primary occupation of Black women and had racial and sexual barriers not been so clearly identifiable as the reason for their concentration in this field of employment, these problems might have been viewed more personally and the women's histories might have been more self-deprecating than in fact they were. This particular set of circumstances would suggest that the women at least had the option of directing their anger and frustration about their situation outward upon the society rather than turning it inward upon themselves. Drake and Cayton (1945) confirm this argument in their analysis of domestic work, saying that "colored girls are often bitter in their comments about a society which condemns them to the 'white folks' kitchen" (p. 246). In addition, attitudes in the Black community toward domestic service work mediated some of the more negative attitudes which were prevalent in the wider society. Thus, the community could potentially become an important support in the child-rearing process, reinforcing the idea that while domestic service was low-status work, the people who did it were not necessarily low-status people.

The data in this study do not include the attitudes of the children of domestic servants toward their mothers' occupation. To my knowledge, there has been no systematic study of this issue. However, some biographies and community studies have provided insight into the range of feelings children express. Drake and Cayton (1945), for example,

cite one woman who described her daughter as being "bitter against what she calls the American social system." DuBois talks about feeling an instinctive hatred toward the occupation (1920:110). I have had employers tell me that their domestics' children hated their children because the employer's kids got the best of their mother's time. I have also heard Black professionals speak with a mixture of pride, anger, and embarrassment about the fact that their mother worked "in the white folks' kitchen" so that they could get an education. Clearly, these issues deserve further study.

Throughout these histories, the women identified education as the primary means through which mobility could be achieved. As with many working-class people, education was seen as a primary strategy for upward mobility; a means to a better-paying and more prestigious job. Most of the women who participated in this study had not completed high school (the mean years of schooling completed for the group was 9.2 years). They reasoned that their limited education in combination with racial discrimination had hindered their own chances for upward mobility. Zenobia King explained her attitudes toward education in this way:

> In my home in Virginia, education, I don't think, was stressed. The best you could do was be a school teacher. It wasn't something people impressed upon you you could get. I had an aunt and cousin who were trained nurses and the best they could do was nursing somebody at home or something. They couldn't get a job in a hospital. . . . I didn't pay education any mind really until I came to New York. I'd gotten to a certain stage in domestic work in the country and I didn't see the need for it. When I came, I could see opportunities that I could have had if I had a degree. People said it's too bad I didn't have a diploma.

From Mrs. King's perspective and from those of some of the other women, education for a Black woman in the South before World War II did not seem to offer any tangible rewards. She communicates the idea that an education was not only unnecessary but could perhaps have been a source of even greater frustration and dissatisfaction. This idea was reemphasized by other women who talked about college-educated women they knew who could find no work other than domestic work. In fact, both Queenie Watkins and Corrinne Raines discussed their experiences as trained teachers who could not find suitable jobs and thus took work in domestic service. Nevertheless, Corrinne

Raines maintained her belief in education as a means of upward mobility, a belief that was rooted in her family of orientation. She said:

> I am the 12th child [and was] born on a farm. My father was—at that day, you would call him a successful farmer. He was a man who was eager for his children to get an education. Some of the older ones had gotten out of school and were working and they were able to help the younger ones. That's how he was able to give his children as much education as he gave them, because the older ones helped him out.

Given this mixed experience with education and social mobility, it might be expected that many of the women would have expressed reservations about the value of an education for their children's mobility. However, this was not the case. Most of them, reflecting on their goals for their children, expressed sentiments similar to Pearl Runner's:

> This is the reason why I told them to get an education. . . . If they want to go to college it was fine because the higher you go the better jobs you get. They understood that because I always taught that into them. Please try to get an education so you can get a good job 'cause it was hard for colored girls to get jobs, period. They had to have an education.

Mrs. Runner's statement is important because it contains the rudiments of an explanation for why she and other women stressed education in the face of discriminatory practices that frequently discounted even their best efforts. Opallou Tucker elaborates on this theme and provides a somewhat more detailed explanation:

> It's [domestic work] all right if you want to do it and if you can't do anything else, but it's not necessary now. If you prepare yourself for something that's better, the doors are open now. I know years ago there was no such thing as a Black typist. I remember girls who were taking typing when I was going to school. They were never able to get a job at it. So it really [was] for their own personal use. My third child, and a niece, after they got up some size, started taking typing. And things began to open up after she got grown up. But in my day and time you could have been the greatest typist in the world, but you would never have gotten a job. It's fine to prepare yourself so that when opportunity knocks, you'll be able to catch up.

In these statements, Mrs. Runner and Mrs. Tucker convey a complex and subtle understanding of the interaction of racism and opportunity. They recognize the former as a real and tangible barrier, but they do not give in to it. They describe themselves as having taught their children to be prepared. Education was seen as a means of equipping one-self for whatever breaks might occur in the nation's patterns of racial exclusion. Thus, key to their aspirations for their children was the hope and belief that opportunities would eventually open and permit their children to make full use of the skills and knowledge they encouraged them to attain.

Nevertheless, maintaining these hopes could not have been as easy and unproblematic as hindsight makes it seem. The fact that many of the women who expressed this strong commitment to education at the time of the interview had seen their children complete a number of years of schooling and enter jobs which would never have been open to them when they were young was clearly a source of pride and satisfaction which could only have strengthened their beliefs. Thus, as they recalled their goals and aspirations for their children, they tended to speak with a sense of self-affirmation about their choices; confidence that may not have been present years earlier. As Mrs. Runner expressed,

> I tell you I feel really proud and I really feel that with all the struggling that I went through, I feel happy and proud that I was able to keep helping my children, that they listened and that they all went to high school. So when I look back, I really feel proud, even though at times the work was very hard and I came home very tired. But now, I feel proud about it. They all got their education.

Perhaps reflective of their understanding of the complex interaction of racism and opportunity, most of the women described limited and general educational objectives for their children. Although a few women said they had wanted their children to go to college and one sent her son to a private high school with the help of scholarships, most women saw high school graduation as the concrete, realizable objective which they could help their children attain. Willie Lee Murray's story brings out a theme that was recurrent in several other histories:

> My children did not go to college. I could not afford to send them to college. And they told me, my younger one especially, he said: Mommy, I don't want to go to college at your expense. When I go to college, I'll go on

my own. I would not think of you workin' all your days—sometimes you go sick and I don't know how you gonna get back. You put us through school and you gave us a beautiful life. We'll get to college on our own.

Mrs. Murray seems to indicate that while she would have liked her children to go to college, she limited her goals and concentrated her energies upon their completing high school.

In addition to limited educational objectives, most of the women did not describe themselves as having had a specific career objective in mind for their children. They encouraged the children to get an education in order to get a better job. Precisely what those jobs would be was left open, to be resolved through the interaction of their son or daughter's own luck, skill, perseverance, and the overall position of the job market vis-à-vis Black entrants.

Closely related to the goals the women expressed about their children's future position in society were their goals relative to their child's development as a person. Concern that their children grow up to be good, decent, law-abiding citizens was a dominant theme in these discussions. Most of the women in the study described their employers as having very specific career goals for their children, usually goals that would have the children following their parents' professional footsteps. In characterizing the differences between their goals and those of their employers, the women stressed the differences in economic resources. Johnnie Boatwright was quite explicit on this point:

> There was a lot of things they [employers] did that I wanted to do for mine, but I just couldn't afford it. . . . Like sending them to school. Then they could hire somebody; child slow, they could hire a tutor for the child. I wish I could have been able to do what they done. And then too, they sent them to camps, nice camps, not any camp but one they'd pick out. . . . So that's what I wished I could had did for him [her son]. . . . See whether it was right or wrong, mines I couldn't do it because I didn't have the money to do it. I wasn't able to do it. So that's the way it was. I did what I could and that was better than nothing.

In light of these discrepancies in resources, personal development was an important and realizable goal which may have been an adaptive response to the barriers which constricted the women's range of choices. This was an area over which the women had greater influence and potential control. It was also an area in which they probably received considerable community support, since values in the Black community, as pointed out above, attribute status to success along personal and family dimensions in addition to the basic ones of occupation, education, and income.

While Mrs. Boatwright conveys a sense of resignation and defeat in discussing her inability to do for her son what the employers did for theirs, Pearl Runner is more optimistic and positive about what she was able to do for her children.

> Their money may be a little more, but I felt my goal was just as important as long as they [the children] got their education. They [employers] had the money to do lots more than I did, but I felt that if I kept working, my goals was just as important. I felt my children were just as important.

Feelings like those expressed by both Mrs. Runner and Mrs. Boatwright are reflected throughout the data in the women's comparisons of their aspirations and expectations for their children's future with those of their employers. However, it also seems apparent that their intimate participation in families in which the husbands were doctors, lawyers, stockbrokers, college professors, writers, and housewives provided considerable support for their more limited educational objectives. While not everyone had the specific experience of Lena Hudson, whose employer provided an allowance for her daughter which permitted the girl to stay in high school, the model of the employer's life with regard to the kinds of things they were able to give their children was a forceful one and is repeatedly reflected in the women's discussions of their child-rearing goals.

When asked: "What do you think were the goals that the Wallises [her employers] had for their children? What did they want for their children? What did they want them to become in life?" Lena Hudson replied:

> Well, for *their* children, I imagine they wanted them to become like they were, educators or something that like. What they had in mind for *my* children, they saw in me that I wasn't able to make all of that mark. But raised my children in the best method I could. Because I wouldn't have the means to put *my* children through like they could for *their* children. And they see I wasn't the worst person in the world, and they saw I meant *some* good to my family, you see, so I think that was the standard with them and my family.

Her answers provide insight into the personal and social relationship between the two families and into her recognition of the points of connectedness and distance between them. The way in which she chose to answer the question reflects her feelings about working for the Wallis family and how that helped her accomplish the goals which she had set for her own family.

MRS. HUDSON: And in the meantime, they owned a big place up in Connecticut. And they would take my children, and she, the madam, would do for my children just what she did for theirs.

INTERVIEWER: What kinds of things do you think your children learned from that, from the time that they spent with them?

MRS. HUDSON: Well, I think what they learnt from them, to try to live a decent life themselves, and try to make the best out of their life and the best out of the education they had. So I think that's what they got from them.

INTERVIEWER: What would you say you liked most about the work that you did?

MRS. HUDSON: Well, what I liked most about it, the things that I weren't able to go to school to do for my children. I could kinda pattern from the families that I worked for, that I could give my children the best of my abilities. And I think that's the thing I got from them, though they [her children] couldn't become professors, but they could be good in whatever they did.

The warm personal relationship between the two families was based not only on the direct assistance which the Wallises gave Mrs. Hudson, but also on the ways in which she was able to utilize her position in their family to support and sustain her personal goals. Thus, we can understand why she saw work as an ability rather than a burden. Work was a means for attaining her goals; it provided her with the money she needed to be an independent person, and it exposed her and her children to "good" things—values and a style of life which she considered important. To some extent, Lena Hudson found the same things in her work that she found in her church; reinforcement for the standards which she held for her children and for herself.

The women who stressed education for their children and saw their children attain it were most frequently women like Mrs. Hudson who were closely tied to one or two employing families for a long period of time. For the most part, they were the women who had careers in domestic service. However, ties with employers were not crucial even within this small group, because some women said they had received very little support from their employers along these lines. Several women, as indicated above, pointed to a strong emphasis upon education in their families of orientation. Additionally, education as a means of up-ward mobility is a fundamental element in American social ideology. It appears, therefore, that the importance of the employer–employee relationship was in the support and reinforcement these middle-class families' goals, aspirations, and style of life provided the women. The amount of support varied, of course, with the particular relationship the employee had with her employer's family and the degree of the employer's interest in and commitment to the employee's personal life. On the spectrum presented by the women in this study, Mrs. Hudson's relationship with the Wallis family would be at one end; the relationship between Georgia Sims and the family for whom she worked longest at the other. The following segment of the interview with Mrs. Sims is a good example of a minimally interactive employer–employee relationship:

INTERVIEWER: What were your goals for your children?

MRS. SIMS: Well, to be decent, law-abiding men. That's all.

INTERVIEWER: Do you think there were any similarities between your goals for your children and the goals your employers, the Peters, had for their children?

MRS. SIMS: Oh, sure! Oh, yes, because I mean you must remember, they had the money; now I didn't have it. Oh, definitely there was different goals between us. [*Note:* Mrs. Sims obviously understood the question to be about *differences* rather than similarities, so the question was asked again.]

INTERVIEWER: Do you think there were any things that were alike in terms of your goals for your children and their goals for their children?

MRS. SIMS: No. Nothing.

INTERVIEWER: Nothing at all?

MRS. SIMS: No.

INTERVIEWER: What kinds of goals did they have for their children?

MRS. SIMS: Oh, I mean education, going on to be, you know, upstanding citizens, and they had the jobs— My children couldn't get up, I mean when they become 20, 21, they couldn't get up and go out and say, well, I'm gonna get an office job, I'm gonna get this kind of job. No. The best thing they could do is go and be a porter in the subway.

Mrs. Sims was very detached from her occupation. She was not a career household worker. In fact, she described herself as having had very limited contact with her employers, arriving when they were all on their way to work and school and often departing before they returned home. She said that she had no specific child-care duties. Thus, her description of the employers' goals for their children is probably more of a projection on her part than it is based on discussion or direct participation in the employers' life.

Two types of child-rearing goals have been identified thus far: goals regarding the child's future position in the society and goals regarding his or her personal development. In addition to these two types of goals, the women aspired to provide their children with some accoutrements of a middle-class lifestyle. Their discussion of these desires often reflects the discrepancies between their lives and those of their employers. Jewell Prieleau describes her employer's children as follows:

Her children always dress nice. Whenever her daughter was going to music school or anyplace, I had to take her in a taxi. Whenever she finish, she had to be picked up. I had to go get her.

In describing her own grandchildren, she said:

I went to three nice department stores and I opened up credit for them so I could send them to school looking nice. I got up early in the morning and sent them off to school. After school I would pick them up in a taxi and bring them here [the job].

Mrs. Prieleau is not the only woman in this study who talked about going into debt to give her children some of the material things that she never had and that were part of her image of a "better life" for her children. Willa Murray told the following story:

I remember when my sons wanted that record player. I said I'm gonna get a record player; I'm gonna do days work. But I had to get AC current for this record player. I called up this lady [her employer] and I said, I'm goin' to Household Finance this morning. If they call you for a reference would you give me some reference. She said, sure. I sat down and the man said come in. He said, Miz Murray, do you have a co-signer. I said, no. He said, well what's your collateral? I said something about the furniture. He said, do you work? I said, yeah, I do days work. He said, days work? You don't have a steady job? I said yes sir, days work. He said, who do you work for? I told him. He said, we'll see what we can do. He

gave the hundred and fifty dollars. I came home, phone the electric company, told them they could send the man to put the current in.

In these statements and some of the ones quoted earlier, we begin to see how the employer's style of life influenced these women. However, it cannot be assumed that the women's desires were merely an outgrowth of the employer–employee relationship. The material products which they sought are so widely available in the culture that they are considered general symbols of upward mobility. Upward mobility for their children was the basic goal of most of the women who participated in this study. It was a goal which seems to have existed prior to and apart from their work situation and the values of their employers. Nevertheless, in some cases the women found reinforcement for and regeneration of these goals within the work situation, just as they found supports within their community and family lives.

RAISING THE "WHITE FOLKS" CHILDREN

The women's discussion of child-rearing strategies, particularly such issues as discipline, exemplify both the class and cultural differences between employer and employee. For private household workers, these differences are expressed within a relationship of inequality. The data collected in this study permitted an examination of employer parent–child interactions as it was perceived and constructed by the household workers. This has benefits as well as liabilities. As outsiders whose child-rearing practices and lifestyle differed from those of the employers, the women in this study provide a particularly revealing picture of parent–child relationships in the employing family. However, they were not mere observers of the process; they participated in it and thereby restructured it. The women's insights, therefore, offer a unique critical perspective that is found only in subordinates' characterizations of their superiors. However, as participants in the process, their observations are limited to the time frame in which they were present and make it virtually impossible to assess the women's impact on the process. Nevertheless, their stories about their own role in rearing the employer's children provide considerable understanding of how they saw their work and, more importantly, how their work affected their own style of parenting. Willa Murray's comments illuminate this:

Throughout, the people that I worked for taught their children that they can talk back. They would let them [the children] say anything they wanted to say to them. I noticed a lot of times they [the children] would talk back or something and they [the parents] would be hurt. They would say to me, I wish they [the children] wouldn't. I wish they were more like your children. They allowed them to do so much. But they taught them a lot of things. I know one thing, I think I got a lot of things from them. . . . I think I've learnt a lot about [how to do] with my children by letting them do and telling them—like the whites would tell them—that I trust you. I think a lot of Black mothers when we come along, they didn't trust us. They were telling us what we were gonna do. . . . But I think they [whites] talk to their children about what's in life, what's for them, what not to do. And they let them talk, they tell them all the things that we didn't tell our children. We're beginning to tell our children. . . . The alternative is that I told my children straight, that if a boy and a girl have sexual intercourse—I learned that from the white people—and you don't have anything to protect it, that girl will get a baby. So my children were looking out for that. I learned that from my people. I listened to what they tell [their children].

Talk between parents and children is a dominant theme of Mrs. Murray's comments. She is critical of her employers for permitting their children to "talk back" to them; to question their instructions, to respond impertinently or otherwise mock or demean the parents' authority. Yet, talking *with* the children, reasoning with them, explaining things and hearing their thoughts and opinions on various matters, is behavior which she admired enough to try to emulate. Telling the children that you "trust them" places greater emphasis upon self-direction than upon following orders. Clearly, the line between letting the children talk and permitting them to "talk back" is a difficult one to draw, yet Mrs. Murray draws it in transferring her work-learned behavior to her own child-rearing circumstances.

It should not be surprising that there would be behavioral characteristics which employers would admire in employee children, just as there were traits which Mrs. Murray and others admired in their employers' interactions with their children. In fact, it is striking that each would admire aspects of the other and seek to incorporate them within their own lives while the circumstances that generated those particular patterns were quite different. Nevertheless, reorienting the parent–child relationship in the employer's family was frequently described as a regular part of the worker's child-care activity. In fact, the women's discussions of their experiences in caring for their employers' children are variations upon the stories of resistance which characterized their establishing themselves in the employer–employee relationship. Queenie Watkins' description of the following child-care incident provides a good example:

One morning I was feeding Stevie oatmeal and I was eating oatmeal. His uncle, the little girl and I were all sitting at the table together eating. He said, I don't want this and I'm gonna spit it out. I said, you better not, Stevie. With that he just let it all come into my face. I took myself a big mouthful and let it go right back in his face. He screamed, and his uncle said, what did you do that for? I said, you fight fire with fire. My psychology is to let a child know he can't do to you what you can't do to him. The mother came running. I said, this ends my work here but she said, just wash Stevie's face. I said, I'm not gonna wash it; let him wash it himself—he wasn't two years old. Finally, I said, I'll take him and wash his face but who's gonna wash my face? His mother started to laugh and said, you're some character. And you know what, he never did that again. He ate his food and I never had to chastise Stevie about anything after that.

Zenobia King told a slightly different story about the way in which she inserted her values into the parent–child relationship of an employing family:

One time the daughter went out and she stayed all day. She didn't tell her mother where she was. And when she came back, her mother jumped on her in a really bad way. She told her she wished she had died out there, etc., etc., and her daughter said if her mother had loved her she would have asked where she was going. So, I separated them. I sent the daughter to one room and the mother to the other and talked to both of them and I brought them back together.

In both of these stories, as in others in this genre, the women see themselves as the instructor of both the children and the parents. They characterize themselves as helping the parent learn how to parent while simultaneously setting rules and regulations as to the kind of treatment they should expect from the children. Queenie Watkins' philosophy of fighting fire with fire was reiterated by Oneida Harris in describing her relations with one of the children whom she cared for:

He was nine years old and he rate me the worst maid they'd ever had because I wouldn't take any of his foolishness. If he kicked me in the shins, I'd kick him back. . . . I said he hasn't any bringing up, and if I stay here he's gonna listen. I said to his mother, if you don't want me, tell me tomorrow and I'll go. So anyway, the next day he would bring me up a little bit; she's the next-to-the-worst maid we ever had. Each week I came up till I was the best one.

As in the stories of resistance, both Queenie Watkins and Oneida Harris depict themselves as setting guidelines for respect from the children in the same way respect was established in the employer–employee relationship. The additional dimension of instructing parents in the ways of handling their children was another recurrent theme in the life histories.

Through these and other similar anecdotes which the women used to describe their participation in caring for their employers' children, they communicate a perception of their employers as uncomfortable in exercising the power associated with the parenting role. To a large degree, they depict their employers as either inconsistent and afraid of their children or ignorant of child-rearing strategies that would develop obedience and respect. The women see this as their forte; in many instances they describe themselves as exercising power on behalf of the parents and teaching the children to obey them and respect their parents. In so doing, they also present themselves as teaching the parents. Willa Murray is keenly aware of the paradoxical nature of this situation when she says: "Now I'm the maid, not the mistress." In the maid–mistress relationship, the latter gives instructions which the former carries out. In a sense, Willa Murray's story presents a role reversal, one which she finds both surprising and amusing but also appropriate. It is akin to the anecdote in which she described herself telling her employers that they had more education than she did but their behavior was not intelligent. These presentations suggest that despite stereotypic conceptions of the maid–mistress relationship, women in these roles could gain considerable power and influence within a family, particularly where they had worked for a number of years and had considerable responsibility.

The household worker's impact on the parent–child relationship is only one aspect of their child-care role. The other, equally important, aspect of this role is their relationship with the children they cared for and the fact, implicit in our earlier discussion, that they describe themselves as surrogate mothers for these children:

There's a long time she [the child] use to thought I was her mamma. She would ask me why is my skin white and yours brown, you my mamma? I tell her I'm not your mamma and I see the hurt coming in her eye. You know like she didn't want me to say that. I said there's your mamma in there, I'm just your nurse. She said no, you my mamma. [Mattie Washington]

I took care of the children. In fact, the children would call me when they had a problem or something, before they would call her [their mother]. [Zenobia King]

He [the boy] looked at me as a mother. When he went away to school he just would not come home if I wasn't there. And even when he was at home, if he was out playing with the boys he'd come in, his mother, grandmother and father would be sitting around, he'd say, where is everybody? His mother would look around and say well if you mean Oneida, I think she's upstairs. Upstairs he'd come. And they couldn't get that. It was sad, you see. They give him everything in the world but love. [Oneida Harris]

I was more like a mother to them, and you see she didn't have to take too much time as a mother should to know her children. They were more used to me because I put them to bed. The only time she would actually be with them was like when I'm off Thursday and on Sundays. They would go out sometime, but actually I was really the mother because I raised them from little. [Pearl Runner]

Without exception, the women in this study who had child-care responsibilities talked about themselves as being "like a mother" to the employers' children. Their explanations of the development of this kind of relationship tended to follow those of Oneida Harris and Pearl Runner: their employers were frequently unavailable and spent less time with the children than they did. Because they interacted with the children on a daily basis and often had responsibility for their care, discipline, play, and meals, their role was a vital and important one in the eyes of both child and parent. This explains, in part, some of their power in affecting the parent–child relationship, as discussed above. The fact that the women had such an important and pivotal role in the development of the employer's children and at the same time held a job in which they could be replaced gave the entire relationship of parent, child, and housekeeper a particularly intense quality. For the most part, workers developed their strongest emotional ties to the children in the employing family.

Because the women saw themselves as surrogate mothers, the children whom they cared for could easily become their surrogate children. This is particularly apparent when we compare their comments and discussions about their own and their employers' children. One of the most prevalent patterns was to talk with pride and satisfaction about the accomplishments of their surrogate children. In general, the women would talk about how frequently they heard from these children and whether they got cards, letters, or money at Mothers' Day or Christmas. In addition, they would describe the (now grown) children's occupation and family and, if they had pictures available, they would show them to me. This type of commentary provided an interesting parallel to their discussions of their own children. But even more important, it was designed to communicate the closeness that they felt existed between them and the children they had raised; closeness which was maintained over a number of years even after the children were grown.

Surrogate mothering, as pointed out in Opallou Tucker's case study, had the prospect of tying the worker into the emotional life of the employing family. For the women who lived outside the employer's household and were actively engaged in rearing their own children and caring for their own families, as were most of the women in this study, the prospect was minimized. However, for a woman like Mattie Washington, who lived in for most of the 30 years that she worked for one family, the potential for becoming enveloped in their life, at the expense of her own, was much greater.

In most instances, the women described themselves as caretakers, playmates, disciplinarians, confidantes, and friends of the employer's children. Nevertheless, it is clear from their discussions that in most cases the real ties of affection between themselves and their employer came through the children.

The children, therefore, provided the ties that bound the women to their employers as well as the mark of their difference. The role of surrogate mother allowed the women to cross these barriers and, for a fleeting moment, express their love and concern for a child without regard to the obstacles that lay ahead. Also, because most young children readily return love that is freely given and are open and accepting of people without regard to status factors that have meaning for their parents, the workers probably felt that they were treated with greater equality and more genuine acceptance by the children of the household.

REFERENCES

Chaplin, D. 1964. "Domestic service and the Negro." In A. Shostak and W. Gamberg, eds., *Blue Collar World*. Englewood Cliffs, N.J.: Prentice-Hall.

Childress, A. 1956. *Like one of the family*. Brooklyn: Independence Publishers.

Denzin, N. K. 1970. *The research act*. Chicago: AVC.

Dill, B. T., & Joselin, D. 1977. "The limit of quantitative methods: The need of life histories." Paper presented at the Society for the Study of Social Problems Annual Meetings, Chicago.

Drake, S. C., & Cayton, H. 1945. *Black metropolis*. New York: Harper & Row.

DuBois, W. E. B. 1920. *Darkwater*. New York: Harcourt Brace.

Eaton, I. 1967. "Negro domestic service in Seventh Ward Philadelphia." In W. E. B. DuBois, *The Philadelphia Negro*. New York: Schocken.

Greene, L. J., & Woodson, C. G. 1930. *The Negro wage earner*. Washington, D.C.: Association for the Study of Negro Life and History.

Haynes, G. 1912. *The Negro at work in New York City: A study in economic progress*. New York: Longmans.

Haynes, G. 1923. "Negroes in domestic service in the United States." *Journal of Negro History* 8:384–442.

Ovington, M. W. 1969. *Half a man*. New York: Schocken.

The Secret Fear That Keeps Us from Raising Free Children

LETTY COTTIN POGREBIN

In the 19th century when women of all races began their drive for the vote, what was the argument most often used against them?

That voting was a masculine concern, and that therefore women who attempted it would become (or already were) "mannish," "unwomanly," and "unnatural." In short, sexually suspect.

In the 20th century when young men objected to the rationale for the American military presence in Vietnam, what was the argument most used to discredit their protest?

That refusing a masculine enterprise like war made them "like a woman," "soft," "scared," and therefore sexually suspect.

It's time we faced head-on the most powerful argument that authoritarian forces in any society use to keep people—male or female—in line: the idea that you are not born with gender but must earn it, and thus the threat that if you don't follow orders you will not be a "real man" or "real woman."

Even those of us who have long since stopped worrying about this conformity for ourselves may find that our own deepest conditioning takes over in the emotional landscape inhabited by our children and our feelings about child-rearing. It is this conditioning that the right wing plays on to prevent change, no matter how life-enhancing. And it is these fears that sometimes inhibit pro-child attitudes in the most well-intentioned parents; the fear

1. that sex roles determine sexuality;
2. that specific ingredients *make* a child homosexual; and
3. that homosexuality is one of the worst things that can happen.

ASSUMPTION I: SEX ROLES DETERMINE SEXUALITY

It was inevitable that the cult of sex differences would lead us to the familiar romantic bromide—*opposites attract.* Most people truly believe that the more "masculine" you are, the more you'll love and be loved by females, and the more "feminine" you are, the more you'll love and be loved by males.

If you believe this quid pro quo, you will systematically raise your daughters and sons differently so that they become magnets for their "opposites," and you will fear that resistance to stereotyped sex roles might distort their behavior in bed as adults.

Clever, this patriarchy. In return for conformity, it promises a "normal" sex life for our children. But it can't deliver on that promise, because all available evidence proves that *sex role does not determine sexual orientation.*

During the last decade thousands of homosexual men and women have "come out" from behind their "straight" disguises, and we discovered that except for choice of sex partner, they look and act so much the same as everyone else that as sexologist Dr. Wainright Churchill put it, "they may not be identified as homosexuals even by experts." Most female and male homosexuals have tried heterosexual intercourse; many have been married and have children; and sometimes they are remarkable only for being so *unlike* the "gay" stereotype.

Take a quintessential "man's man," David Kopay—six feet one, 205 pounds, 10-year veteran of pro football. "I was the typical jock," writes Kopay in his autobiography (*The David Kopay Story;* Bantam). "I was tough. I was successful. And all the time I knew I preferred sex with men."

And great beauties, such as Maria Schneider, the sex bomb of *Last Tango in Paris;* "feminine-looking" women, married women, mothers of many children have, for centuries, had lesbian love affairs with one another, disproving the opposites-attract theory with a vengeance, and reminding us again that sex roles do not determine sexuality.

ASSUMPTION 2: SPECIFIC INGREDIENTS *MAKE* A CHILD HOMOSEXUAL

Although no one knows what causes homosexuality, there is no shortage of theories on the subject. Sociobiologists and other behavioral scientists pursue the idea that "genetic loading" can create a predisposition toward homosexuality, a theory that will remain farfetched until researchers find many sets of identical twins both members of which became homosexual although reared separately.

Proponents of *hormone theory* have tried to find a definitive connection between testosterone level and homosexual orientation. However, various biochemical studies of the last decade show directly contradictory results, and even when hormonal differences are found, no one knows whether hormones cause the homosexuality, or the homosexual activities cause the hormone production.

The biochemical "explorers," like the geneticists, perpetuate the idea that homosexuals are a different species with a hormonal disturbance that chemistry might "cure." So far, attempts to alter sexual orientation with doses of hormones have only succeeded in increasing the *amount* of sex drive, not in changing its direction.

The *conditioned-response theory* holds that sexual orientation depends not on biology or "instincts" but on learning from experience, from the same reward-and-punishment process as any other acquired behavior, and from sexual trigger mechanisms, such as pictures, music, or certain memories, that set off homosexual or heterosexual responses the way the bell set off Pavlov's dog salivating.

The conditioning theory, logical as far as it goes, leads us down several blind alleys. Why might one child experience a certain kind of stroking as pleasurable when a same-sex friend does it but *more* pleasurable when a friend of the other sex does it, while another child feels the reverse? Why do some children "learn to" overcome the effects of a frightening early sexual experience, while others may be hurt by it forever, and still others "learn" to merge pain with pleasure?

Doesn't cultural pressure itself "teach" children to avoid a particular sexual response, no matter what the body has learned to like? Otherwise, how do millions of adolescents move from masturbation to homosexual experimentation— often the *only* interpersonal sexual pleasure they have known—to heterosexuality?

Perhaps the conditioned-response theory can explain the man who has felt homosexual since childhood, but how does it account for the woman who, after 20 years as an orgasmic, exclusive heterosexual, had a lesbian encounter and found she didn't have to "learn" to like it?

One research psychiatrist reminds us that we don't yet understand the basic mechanism of sexual arousal in the human central nervous system, and until we do, questions about homosexual or heterosexual arousal are entirely premature.

Psychoanalytic theory, the most steadfast and intimidating of all the causation theories, is the one that "blames" homosexuality on the family. To challenge it, we must begin at the beginning.

In 1905, Sigmund Freud declared that human beings are innately *bisexual* at birth and their early psychosexual experiences tip the scales one way or the other.

To ensure a heterosexual outcome, the child is supposed to identify with the same-sex parent, to "kill them off," so to speak, as an object of sexual interest. For example, a girl's psychodynamic is "I become like Mother, therefore I no longer desire Mother; I desire Father, but I can't have him so I desire those who are like him."

If instead the girl identifies with the other-sex parent ("I become like Father"), he is killed off as object choice ("therefore I do not desire Father"), and the girl will be a lesbian ("I desire Mother or those who are like her"). For the boy, obviously, the same psychodynamic is true in reverse.

According to this theory, female homosexuality derived mainly from too much *hostility* toward the mother for passing on her inferior genital equipment. The lesbian girl identifies with the Father and compensates for her hatred of the inferior mother by loving women, while rejecting "femininity" (meaning passivity, masochism, inferiority) for herself.

Male homosexuality derives mainly from too much *attachment* to the mother, i.e., a Momma's Boy can't be a woman's man.

Although many contemporary psychologists now believe otherwise, and despite the fact that Freud's views are unsupported by objective evidence, it is his ideas that millions of lay people have accepted—the view that human beings grow "healthy" by the Oedipal resolution: fearing and thus respecting one parent (Dad) and disdaining the other (Mom). Since our parents stand as our first models of male and female, this primal fear and disdain tends to form a paradigm for lifelong sexual enmity, suspicion, betrayal, and rejection.

Father is supposed to represent reality and Mother is associated with infant dependency. In order to gain their independence, both girls and boys must form an alliance with Father against Mother. Politically, this translates to male supremacy ("alliance with Father") and cultural misogyny ("against Mother"). Psychologically, the message is conform or you might turn out "queer."

The hitch is, as we've noted, that sex role and sexual orientation have been shown to be totally unrelated. Modern practitioners may know this, but since they have not loudly and publicly revised psychoanalytic theories on homosexuality, they are in effect supporting the old lies. What's more, their silence leaves unchallenged these contradictions within psychoanalytic theory itself:

- A human *instinct,* by definition, should be the same for everyone, everywhere; yet in societies where sex stereotypes do not exist, the supposedly instinctual Oedipal psychodrama doesn't exist either.
- If the castration complex, the fear of losing the penis, is the founding element of "masculinity," how is it that Dr. Robert Stoller, professor of psychiatry at UCLA Medical School, found boys who were born without penises believed themselves boys anyway?
- How do we account for millions of children who become heterosexual though raised in father-absent homes? How do these mothers arouse fear and respect in the boy and the requisite penis envy in the girl?
- Why do batteries of psychological tests *fail to show any significant difference* between lesbians and heterosexuals on the psychological criteria that are supposed to "cause" female homosexuality?
- How can one say that male homosexuals identify with Mother and take on "feminine" ways, when mothers of homosexuals are supposedly "masculine," dominant, and aggressive?
- If a woman's compensation for her missing penis is a baby boy, then of course she'll overprotect her son as a hedge against a *second* castration—losing him. It's a cruel tautology to posit motherhood in these terms and, at the same time, to hold Mother responsible for

overprotection of the one treasure she's supposedly spent her whole life seeking.

- Could it be that girls and women envy the *privileges* that accrue to people whose distinguishing feature happens to be the penis, without envying the penis?
- Freud declared the "vaginal orgasm" to be the diploma of heterosexual maturity, yet in *Human Sexual Response,* William Masters and Virginia Johnson have proved the clitoris to be the physiological source of all female orgasms. Why require a girl to unlearn clitoral pleasure when in every other instance Freud believed that "urges dissipate when they become satisfied"? Is it because the clitoral orgasm is active, not receptive; because it doesn't require a penis and it doesn't result in procreation? Was the promotion of the "vaginal orgasm" patriarchy's way of keeping females passive, male-connected, and frequently pregnant?

We could devote pages and pages to poking holes in psychoanalytic theory, but these final points should do the trick: studies show that the classic "homosexual-inducing" family produces plenty of "straight" children; other kinds of families raise both heterosexual and homosexual siblings under the same roof; and totally "straight" family constellations rear homosexual kids.

And so, all speculations have been found wanting, and we are left with one indisputable fact: *no one knows what causes homosexuality.*

ASSUMPTION 3: HOMOSEXUALITY IS ONE OF THE WORST THINGS THAT CAN HAPPEN TO ANYONE

Studies show that the majority of American people want homosexuality "cured." Yet the facts—when this volatile subject can be viewed factually—prove that homosexuality is neither uncommon, abnormal, nor harmful to its practitioners or anyone else.

When the "naturalness" of heterosexuality is claimed via examples in the animal kingdom, one can point to recorded observations of homosexuality among seagulls, cows, mares, sows, primates, and many other mammals. But more important, among humans, "there is probably no culture from which homosexuality has not been reported," according to Drs. Clellan Ford and Frank Beach in *Patterns of Sexual Behavior* (Harper). And no matter what moral or legal prohibitions have been devised through the ages, none has ever eliminated homosexuality. In fact, the incidence of

BALLET! TOUCHÉ!

SUSAN EISENBERG

"You don't really want to do that fluffbottom stuff, do you? Why don't we find you a class in modern or jazz?" *Slight humor. Sarcasm held in check. I had probably slid through. But then I went too far.* "You sure you don't want to sign up for Little League again?"

"Baseball just isn't me, Mom." And we were back to ballet. Last year she'd insisted on baseball and played outfield in a red jersey with the name of a local barroom on the back. There were supposedly four girls on the team of sixteen. But at most practices and games, she was the *only* girl, though her coach always swore that the other girls hadn't dropped out and would definitely be there the next time.

Her statement that baseball really wasn't her didn't convince me. I thought it was probably the way her male teammates kicked each other in the shins while waiting their turn at catching grounders. But whenever I asked, she assured me their behavior was no problem. "They never kick me, Mom. They ignore me." Fourteen years in union construction, often as the only woman on the job site, I didn't find that reassuring.

Seeing that extra bit of room between her and her teammates when they sat on the bench, or watching her

warm up alone, rarely invited to join in the casual games of toss before the coach pulled all the kids together for practice, was more unnerving than I'd expected. Watching my daughter face the isolation of crossing gender boundaries—all the armor I'd built up as an electrician in the construction industry dissolved. I felt my hysteria going ballistic.

Sure, there had been some improvement: when I was growing up *no* girls played Little League. However, opening Little League to girls, like including women in the construction industry, has to mean more than allowing a few females past the gate. I'd spent years arguing for the need to move beyond tokenism in the workplace, to change the industry to *include* women. I knew those three other girls would never show. My daughter was the token girl.

Two tradeswomen friends who'd been teaching Zoe how to throw and catch and knew I needed handholding, came to her first game. A base hit her first time up at bat! When she struck out, I cried. She was committed and stuck it through the whole season, every game. Each time she came up to bat, the infield moved forward and all the adults held their breath for her.

"But what's wrong with ballet?" she wanted to know.

I went through my long list, beginning first with the fact that in ballet women present themselves as frail, needing to be lifted by a man. "I'll look for something else," I told her.

homosexuality is greater in countries that forbid it than in those that don't. With all the fluctuations of public morality, many sources confirm that 10 percent of the entire population consider themselves exclusively homosexual at any given place and time.

Aside from choosing to love members of their own sex, lesbians and homosexual males have been found no different from heterosexuals in gender identity or self-esteem, in drinking, drug use, suicide rates, relationships with parents and friends, and general life satisfaction. One study actually found lower rates of depression among les-

bians; another study measured higher competence and intellectual efficiency; still another found more lesbians (87 percent) than heterosexual women (18 percent) experienced orgasm "almost always"; and two important recent reports revealed that homosexuals seem clearly far *less* likely than heterosexuals to commit child abuse or other sexual crimes. In short, many homosexuals "could very well serve as models of social comportment and psychological maturity." And yet, parents feel obliged to protect their children from it.

Why?

About a month later Zoe came home from school: "I'm going to take ballet and you don't have to pay for anything or drive me," and waved a flyer at me about CityDance, a program involving the Boston Ballet and the Boston public schools.

"They're auditioning all the third graders at your school, Zoe," I explained after reading the notice, already planning how to cushion her disappointment. "They're not going to pick very many kids."

She looked me dead in the eye. "I want this." She was determined. "I'm going to be chosen." And she was right.

On Friday mornings a bus drives her and a dozen other students back and forth from their school to the Ballet's education center. They've been given leotards, shoes, and professional training. And for every performance at the Wang Center—an enormous old theater recently renovated, complete with gilded angels and concession stands that serve champagne—they each receive a pair of free tickets.

I've now accompanied my daughter to a full season of three-hour-long ballet performances, including *Cinderella* and *Romeo and Juliet*. She sits transfixed—literally at the edge of her chair. I usually take at least one nap, though the naps have grown shorter for each ballet. Afterwards, we talk about costumes, the performance, and sometimes about female bodies and behavior.

In the almost one-hundred-year history of my union local, Zoe was the first child born to a journeyman electrician. Zoe grew up assuming it was absolutely normal for women to be electricians, painters and carpenters. She was surprised and disappointed when she discovered men could be plumbers, too.

Once when she was five and a baby-sitter couldn't come, I had to bring her with me to morning referral at my union hall. She looked up from the coloring books I'd brought, scanned the room packed with men and asked, "Where are the other women?" I realized that I'd never told her that the tradeswomen she saw at our house were a rarity on union job-sites. Since that time I've been more honest with her—and myself—about the emotional cost of going where you're not fully welcome, and tried to convey the importance of including that price in weighing decisions.

For Zoe, baseball was not joyous. It could have been; she liked baseball. But to fight for her place in that world, she'd have to love it. And she didn't. She loves ballet.

Watching her live out that passion and assert her place within an adult world has been . . . a thrill. I say this as a mother, and as a feminist. I insisted, though, on three simple ground rules:

1. School work has to come first.
2. On Friday mornings, when I brush her hair into a bun, assisted by several dozen bobby pins, I must be shown the same respect as adults at the ballet and be called Ms. Susan.
3. Before leaping into my arms from across the room, she must warn me.

"Poke right here," she commands, pointing to her thigh. She grins as my finger meets the firm wall of muscle. "Does that make you feel better?"

It does.

In a word, *homophobia*—fear and intolerance of homosexuality. Despite the facts just enumerated, millions still believe homosexuality *is* the worst thing. In one study, nearly half of the college students questioned labeled it more deviant than murder and drug addiction. Others reveal their homophobia by sitting an average of 10 inches further away from an interviewer of the same sex wearing a "gay and proud" button than from an interviewer wearing no button. Another group said they wouldn't be able to form a close friendship with a gay person.

In a society that works as hard as ours does to convince everyone that Boys are Better, homosexual taunts whether "sissy" or "faggot," say *nonboy*. In pure form, the worst insult one boy can scream at another is "You girl!" That curse is the coming home to roost of the cult of sex differences. Indeed, sexism and homophobia go hand in hand. The homophobic male *needs* sharp sex-role boundaries to help him avoid transgressing to the "other side." His terror is that he is not different enough from the "opposite" sex, and that his "masculine" facade may not always protect him from the "femininity" within himself that he learned as a boy to hate and repress. Among men, homophobia is rooted in contempt for everything female.

A homophobic man cannot love a woman with abandon, for he might reveal his vulnerability; he cannot adore and nurture his children because being around babies is "sissy" and child care is "women's work." According to his perverse logic, making women pregnant is "masculine," but making children happy is a betrayal of manhood. One man complained that his child wouldn't shake hands and was getting too old for father–son kissing. How old was "too old"? Three.

Homophobia, the malevolent enforcer of sex-role behavior, is the enemy of children because it doesn't care about children, it cares about conformity, differences, and divisions.

If women seem to be less threatened by homosexuality than men and less obsessed with latent homosexual impulses, it's because the process of "becoming" a woman is considered less arduous for the female and less important to society than the process of "proving" one's manhood. "Masculinity" once won is not to be lost. But a girl needn't guard against losing that which is of little value.

Like male homosexuals, the lesbian doesn't need the other sex for physical gratification. But the lesbian's crime goes beyond sex: she doesn't need men at all. Accordingly, despite the relative unimportance of female sexuality, lesbianism is seen as a hostile alternative to heterosexual marriage, family, and patriarchal survival.

Before children have the vaguest idea about who or what is a homosexual, they learn that homosexuality is something frightening, horrid, and nasty. They become homophobic long before they understand what it is they fear. They learn that "What are you, a sissy?" is the fastest way to coerce a boy into self-destructive exploits.

While homophobia cannot prevent homosexuality, its power to destroy female assertiveness and male sensitivity is boundless. For children who, for whatever reason, would have been homosexual no matter what, homophobia only adds external cruelty to their internal feelings of alienation. And for those who become the taunters, the ones who mock and harass "queers," homophobia is a clue to a disturbed sense of self.

It's all so painful. And so unnecessary. Eliminate sex-role stereotypes and you eliminate homophobia. Eliminate homophobia and you eliminate the power of words to wound and the power of stigma to mold a person into something she or he was never meant to be. So here's my best advice on the subject: *Don't worry about how to raise a heterosexual child; worry about how not to be a homophobic parent.*

READING 20

Girls and Boys Together . . . But Mostly Apart: Gender Arrangements in Elementary Schools

BARRIE THORNE

Throughout the years of elementary school, children's friendships and casual encounters are strongly separated by

Barrie Thorne, "Girls and Boys Together . . . But Mostly Apart: Gender Arrangements in Elementary Schools" from *Relationships and Development,* edited by Willard W. Hartup and Zick Rubin (Hillsdale, N. J.: Lawrence Erlbaum Associates, 1986). Volume sponsored by the Social Science Research Council. Copyright © 1986 by Lawrence Erlbaum Associates. Reprinted with the permission of the author and publisher.

sex. Sex segregation among children which starts in preschool and is well established by middle childhood, has been amply documented in studies of children's groups and friendships (e.g., Eder & Hallinan, 1978; Schofield, 1981) and is immediately visible in elementary school settings. When children choose seats in classrooms or the cafeteria, or get into line, they frequently arrange themselves in same-sex clusters. At lunchtime, they talk matter-of-factly about "girls' tables" and "boys' tables." Playgrounds have gendered turfs, with some areas and activities, such as large playing fields and basketball courts, controlled mainly by boys, and others—smaller enclaves like jungle-gym areas and concrete spaces for hopscotch or jumprope—more often controlled by girls. Sex segregation is so common in elementary schools that it is meaningful to speak of separate girls' and boys' worlds.

Studies of gender and children's social relations have mostly followed this "two worlds" model, separately describing and comparing the subcultures of girls and boys (e.g., Lever, 1976; Maltz & Borker, 1983). In brief summary: Boys tend to interact in larger, more age-heterogeneous groups (Lever, 1976; Waldrop & Halverson, 1975; Eder & Hallinan, 1978). They engage in more rough and tumble play and physical fighting (Maccoby & Jacklin, 1974). Organized sports are both a central activity and a major metaphor in boys' subcultures; they use the language of "teams" even when not engaged in sports, and they often construct interaction in the form of contests. The shifting hierarchies of boys' groups (Savin-Williams, 1976) are evident in their more frequent use of direct commands, insults, and challenges (Goodwin, 1980).

Fewer studies have been done of girls' groups (Foot, Chapman, & Smith, 1980; McRobbie & Garber, 1975), and—perhaps because categories for description and analysis have come more from male than female experience—researchers have had difficulty seeing and analyzing girls' social relations. Recent work has begun to correct this skew. In middle childhood, girls' worlds are less public than those of boys; girls more often interact in private places and in smaller groups or friendship pairs (Eder & Hallinan, 1978; Waldrop & Halverson, 1975). Their play is more cooperative and turn-taking (Lever, 1976). Girls have more intense and exclusive friendships, which take shape around keeping and telling secrets, shifting alliances, and indirect ways of expressing disagreement (Goodwin, 1980; Lever, 1976; Maltz & Borker, 1983). Instead of direct commands, girls more often use directives which merge speaker and hearer, e.g., "let's" or "we gotta" (Goodwin, 1980).

Although much can be learned by comparing the social organization and subcultures of boys' and of girls' groups, the separate worlds approach has eclipsed full, contextual understanding of gender and social relations among children. The separate worlds model essentially involves a search for group sex differences, and shares the limitations of individual sex difference research. Differences tend to be exaggerated and similarities ignored, with little theoretical attention to the integration of similarity and difference (Unger, 1979). Statistical findings of difference are often portrayed as dichotomous, neglecting the considerable individual variation that exists; for example, not all boys fight, and some have intense and exclusive friendships. The sex difference approach tends to abstract gender from its social context, to assume that males and females are qualitatively and permanently different (with differences perhaps unfolding through separate developmental lines). These assumptions mask the possibility that gender arrangements and patterns of similarity and difference may vary by situation, race, social class, region, or subculture.

Sex segregation is far from total, and is a more complex and dynamic process than the portrayal of separate worlds reveals. Erving Goffman (1977) has observed that sex segregation has a "with-then-apart" structure; the sexes segregate periodically, with separate spaces, rituals, groups, but they also come together and are, in crucial ways, part of the same world. This is certainly true in the social environment of elementary schools. Although girls and boys do interact as boundaried collectivities—an image suggested by the separate worlds approach—there are other occasions when they work or play in relaxed and integrated ways. Gender is less central to the organization and meaning of some situations than others. In short, sex segregation is not static, but is a variable and complicated process.

To gain an understanding of gender which can encompass both the "with" and the "apart" of sex segregation, analysis should start not with the individual, nor with a search for sex differences, but with social relationships. Gender should be conceptualized as a system of relationships rather than as an immutable and dichotomous given. Taking this approach, I have organized my research on gender and children's social relations around questions like the following: How and when does gender enter into group formation? In a given situation, how is gender made more or less salient or infused with particular meanings? By what rituals, processes, and forms of social organization and conflict do "with-then-apart" rhythms get enacted? How are these processes affected by the organization of institutions (e.g., different types of schools, neighborhoods, or summer camps), varied settings (e.g., the constraints and possibilities governing interaction on playgrounds vs. classrooms), and particular encounters?

METHODS AND SOURCES OF DATA

This study is based on two periods of participant observation. In 1976–1977 I observed for 8 months in a largely working-class elementary school in California, a school with 8% Black and 12% Chicana/o students. In 1980 I did fieldwork for 3 months in a Michigan elementary school of similar size (around 400 students), social class, and racial composition. I observed in several classrooms—a kindergarten, a second grade, and a combined fourth-fifth grade—and in school hallways, cafeterias, and playgrounds. I set out to follow the round of the school day as children experience it, recording their interactions with one another, and with adults, in varied settings.

Participant observation involves gaining access to everyday, "naturalistic" settings and taking systematic notes over an extended period of time. Rather than starting with preset categories for recording, or with fixed hypotheses for testing, participant observers record detail in ways which maximize opportunities for discovery. Through continuous interaction between observation and analysis, "grounded theory" is developed (Glaser & Strauss, 1967).

The distinctive logic and discipline of this mode of inquiry emerges from: (1) theoretical sampling—being relatively systematic in the choice of where and whom to observe in order to maximize knowledge relevant to categories and analysis which are being developed; and (2) comparing all relevant data on a given point in order to modify emerging propositions to take account of discrepant cases (Katz, 1983). Participant observation is a flexible, open-ended and inductive method, designed to understand behavior within, rather than stripped from, social context. It provides richly detailed information which is anchored in everyday meanings and experience.

DAILY PROCESSES OF SEX SEGREGATION

Sex segregation should be understood not as a given, but as the result of deliberate activity. The outcome is dramatically visible when there are separate girls' and boys' tables in school lunchrooms, or sex-separated groups on playgrounds. But in the same lunchroom one can also find tables where girls and boys eat and talk together, and in some playground activities the sexes mix. By what processes do girls and boys separate into gender-defined and relatively boundaried collectivities? And in what contexts, and through what processes, do boys and girls interact in less gender-divided ways?

In the school settings I observed, much segregation happened with no mention of gender. Gender was implicit in the contours of friendship, shared interest, and perceived risk which came into play when children chose companions—in their prior planning, invitations, seeking of access, saving of places, denials of entry, and allowing or protesting of "cuts" by those who violated the rules for lining up. Sometimes children formed mixed-sex groups for play, eating, talking, working on a classroom project, or moving through space. When adults or children explicitly invoked gender—and this was nearly always in ways which separated girls and boys—boundaries were heightened and mixed-sex interaction became an explicit arena of risk.

In the schools I studied, the physical space and curricula were not formally divided by sex, as they have been in the history of elementary schooling (a history evident in separate entrances to old school buildings, where the words "Boys" and "Girls" are permanently etched in concrete). Nevertheless, gender was a visible marker in the adult-organized school day. In both schools, when the public address system sounded, the principal inevitably opened with: "Boys and girls . . . ," and in addressing clusters of children, teachers and aides regularly used gender terms ("Heads down, girls"; "The girls are ready and the boys aren't"). These forms of address made gender visible and salient, conveying an assumption that the sexes are separate social groups.

Teachers and aides sometimes drew upon gender as a basis for sorting children and organizing activities. Gender is an embodied and visual social category which roughly divides the population in half, and the separation of girls and boys permeates the history and lore of schools and playgrounds. In both schools— although through awareness of Title IX, many teachers had changed this practice— one could see separate girls' and boys' lines moving, like caterpillars, through the school halls. In the fourth–fifth-grade classroom the teacher frequently pitted girls against boys for spelling and math contests. On the playground in the Michigan school, aides regarded the space close to the building as girls' territory, and the playing fields "out there" as boys' territory. They sometimes shooed children of the other sex away from those spaces, especially boys who ventured near the girls' area and seemed to have teasing in mind.

In organizing their activities, both within and apart from the surveillance of adults, children also explicitly invoked gender. During my fieldwork in the Michigan school, I kept daily records of who sat where in the lunchroom. The amount of sex segregation varied: it was least at the first-grade tables and almost total among sixth-graders. There was also variation from classroom to classroom within a given age, and from day to day. Actions like the following heightened the gender divide: In the lunchroom, when the two second-grade tables were filling, a high-status boy walked by the inside table, which had a scattering of both boys and girls, and said loudly, "Oooo, too many girls," as he headed for a seat at the far table. The boys at the inside table picked up their trays and moved, and no other boys sat at the inside table, which the pronouncement had effectively made taboo. In the end, that day (which was not the case every day), girls and boys ate at separate tables.

Eating and walking are not sex-typed activities, yet in forming groups in lunchrooms and hallways children often separated by sex. Sex segregation assumed added dimensions on the playground, where spaces, equipment, and activities were infused with gender meanings. My inventories of activities and groupings on the playground showed similar patterns in both schools: boys controlled the large fixed spaces designated for team sports (baseball diamonds, grassy fields used for football or soccer); girls more often played closer to the building, doing tricks on the monkey bars (which, for sixth-graders, became an area for sitting and talking) and using cement areas for jumprope, hopscotch, and group games like four-square. (Lever, 1976, provides a good analysis of sex-divided play.) Girls and boys most often played together in kickball, and in group (rather than team) games like four-square, dodgeball, and handball. When children used gender to exclude others from play, they often drew upon beliefs connecting boys to some activities and girls to others: A first-grade boy avidly watched an all-female game of jumprope. When the girls began to shift positions, he recognized a means of access to the play and he offered, "I'll swing it." A girl responded, "No way, you don't know how to do it, to swing it. You gotta be a girl." He left without protest. Although children sometimes ignored pronouncements about what each sex could or could not do, I never heard them directly challenge such claims.

When children had explicitly defined an activity or a group as gendered, those who crossed the boundary—especially boys who moved into female-marked space—risked being teased. ("Look! Mike's in the girls' line!"; "That's a girl over there," a girl said loudly, pointing to a boy sitting at an otherwise all-female table in the lunchroom.) Children, and occasionally adults, used teasing—especially the tease of "liking" someone of the other sex, or of "being" that sex by virtue of being in their midst—to police gender boundaries. Much of the teasing drew upon heterosexual romantic definitions, making cross-sex interaction risky, and increasing social distance between boys and girls.

RELATIONSHIPS BETWEEN THE SEXES

Because I have emphasized the "apart" and ignored the occasions of "with," this analysis of sex segregation falsely implies that there is little contact between girls and boys in daily school life. In fact, relationships between girls and boys—which should be studied as fully as, and in connection with, same-sex relationships—are of several kinds:

1. "Borderwork," or forms of cross-sex interaction which are based upon and reaffirm boundaries and asymmetries between girls' and boys' groups.
2. Interactions which are infused with heterosexual meanings.
3. Occasions where individuals cross gender boundaries to participate in the world of the other sex.
4. Situations where gender is muted in salience, with girls and boys interacting in more relaxed ways.

Borderwork

In elementary school settings boys' and girls' groups are sometimes spatially set apart. Same-sex groups sometimes claim fixed territories such as the basketball court, the bars, or specific lunchroom tables. However, in the crowded, multifocused, and adult-controlled environment of the school, groups form and disperse at a rapid rate and can never stay totally apart. Contact between girls and boys sometimes lessens sex segregation, but gender-defined groups also come together in ways which emphasize their boundaries.

"Borderwork" refers to interaction across, yet based upon and even strengthening gender boundaries. I have drawn this notion from Fredrik Barth's (1969) analysis of social relations which are maintained across ethnic boundaries without diminishing dichotomized ethnic status.* His focus is on more macro, ecological arrangements; mine is on face-to-face behavior. But the insight is similar: groups may interact in ways which strengthen their borders, and the maintenance of ethnic (or gender) groups can best be understood by examining the boundary that defines the groups, "not the cultural stuff that it encloses" (Barth, 1969:15). In elementary schools there are several types of borderwork: contests or games where gender-defined teams compete; cross-sex rituals of chasing and pollution; and group invasions. These interactions are asymmetrical, challenging the separate-but-parallel model of "two worlds."

*I am grateful to Frederick Erickson for suggesting the relevance of Barth's analysis.

Contests   Boys and girls are sometimes pitted against each other in classroom competitions and playground games. The fourth–fifth-grade classroom had a boys' side and a girls' side, an arrangement that reemerged each time the teacher asked children to choose their own desks. Although there was some within-sex shuffling, the result was always a spatial moiety system—boys on the left, girls on the right—with the exception of one girl (the "tomboy" whom I'll describe later), who twice chose a desk with the boys and once with the girls. Drawing upon and reinforcing the children's self-segregation, the teacher often pitted the boys against the girls in spelling and math competitions, events marked by cross-sex antagonism and within-sex solidarity. The teacher introduced a math game; she would write addition and subtraction problems on the board, and a member of each team would race to be the first to write the correct answer. She wrote two score-keeping columns on the board: "Beastly Boys". . . "Gossipy Girls." The boys yelled out, as several girls laughed, "Noisy girls! Gruesome girls!" The girls sat in a row on top of their desks; sometimes they moved collectively, pushing their hips or whispering "Pass it on." The boys stood along the wall, some reclining against desks. When members of either group came back victorious from the front of the room, they would do the "giving five" hand-slapping ritual with their team members.

On the playground a team of girls occasionally played a team of boys, usually in kickball or team two-square. Sometimes these games proceeded matter-of-factly, but if gender became the explicit basis of team solidarity, the interaction changed, becoming more antagonistic and unstable. Two fifth-grade girls played against two fifth-grade boys in a team game of two-square. The game proceeded at an even pace until an argument ensued about whether the ball was out or on the line. Karen, who had hit the ball, became annoyed, flashed her middle finger at the other team, and called to a passing girl to join their side. The boys then called out to other boys, and cheered as several arrived to play. "We got five and you got three!" Jack yelled. The game continued, with the girls yelling, "Bratty boys! Sissy boys!" and the boys making noises—"Weee haw," "Ha-ha-ha"—as they played.

Chasing   Cross-sex chasing dramatically affirms boundaries between girls and boys. The basic elements of chase and elude, capture and rescue (Sutton-Smith, 1971) are found in various kinds of tag with formal rules, and in informal episodes of chasing which punctuate life on playgrounds. These episodes begin with a provocation (taunts like "You can't get me!" or "Slobber monster!"; bodily pokes or the grabbing of possessions). A provocation may be ignored, or responded to by chasing. Chaser and chased may then alternate roles. In an ethnographic study of chase sequences on a school playground, Christine Finnan (1982) observes that chases vary in number of chasers to chased (e.g., one chasing one or five chasing two); form of provocation (a taunt or a poke); outcome (an episode may end when the chased outdistances the chaser, or with a brief touch, being wrestled to the ground, or the recapturing of a hat or a ball); and in use of space (there may or may not be safety zones).

Like Finnan (1982) and Sluckin (1981), who studied a playground in England, I found that chasing has a gendered structure. Boys frequently chase one another, an activity which often ends in wrestling and mock fights. When girls chase girls, they are usually less physically aggressive; they less often, for example, wrestle one another to the ground.

Cross-sex chasing is set apart by special names—"girls chase the boys"; "boys chase the girls"; "the chase"; "chasers"; "chase and kiss"; "kiss chase"; "kissers and chasers"; "kiss or kill"—and by children's animated talk about the activity. The names vary by region and school, but contain both gender and sexual meanings (this form of play is mentioned, but only briefly analyzed, in Finnan, 1982; Sluckin, 1981; Parrott, 1972; and Borman, 1979).

In "boys chase the girls" and "girls chase the boys" (the names most frequently used in both the California and Michigan schools) boys and girls become, by definition, separate teams. Gender terms override individual identities, especially for the other team ("Help, a girl's chasin' me!"; "C'mon, Sarah, let's get that boy"; "Tony, help save me from the girls"). Individuals may also grab someone of their sex and turn them over to the opposing team: Ryan grabbed Billy from behind, wrestling him to the ground. "Hey, girls, get 'im," Ryan called.

Boys more often mix episodes of cross-sex with same-sex chasing. Girls more often have safety zones, places like the girls' restroom or an area by the school wall, where they retreat to rest and talk (sometimes in animated postmortems) before new episodes of cross-sex chasing begin.

Early in the fall in the Michigan school, where chasing was especially prevalent, I watched a second-grade boy teach a kindergarten girl how to chase. He slowly ran backwards, beckoning her to pursue him, as he called, "Help, a girl's after me." In the early grades chasing mixes with fantasy play, e.g., a first-grade boy who played "sea monster," his arms outflung and his voice growling, as he chased a group of girls. By third grade, stylized gestures—exaggerated stalking motions, screams (which only girls do), and karate kicks—accompany scenes of chasing.

Names like "chase and kiss" mark the sexual meanings of cross-sex chasing, a theme I return to later. The threat of kissing—most often girls threatening to kiss boys—is a ritualized form of provocation. Cross-sex chasing among sixth-graders involves elaborate patterns of touch and touch avoidance, which adults see as sexual. The principal told the sixth-graders in the Michigan school that they were not to play "pom-pom," a complicated chasing game, because it entailed "inappropriate touch."

Rituals of Pollution Cross-sex chasing is sometimes entwined with rituals of pollution, as in "cooties," where specific individuals or groups are treated as contaminating or carrying "germs." Children have rituals for transfering cooties (usually touching someone else and shouting, "You've got cooties!"), for immunization (e.g., writing "CV" for "cootie vaccination" on their arms), and for eliminating cooties (e.g., saying "no gives" or using "cootie catchers" made of folded paper) (described in Knapp & Knapp, 1976). While girls may give cooties to girls, boys do not generally give cooties to one another (Samuelson, 1980).

In cross-sex play, either girls or boys may be defined as having cooties, which they transfer through chasing and touching. Girls give cooties to boys more often than vice versa. In Michigan, one version of cooties is called "girl stain"; the fourth-graders whom Karkau (1973) describes used the phrase "girl touch." "Cootie queens" or "cootie girls" (there are no "kings" or "boys") are female pariahs, the ultimate school un-touchables, seen as contaminating not only by virtue of gender, but also through some added stigma such as being overweight or poor.* That girls are seen as more polluting than boys is a significant asymmetry, which echoes cross-cultural patterns, although in other cultures female pollution is generally connected to menstruation, and not applied to prepubertal girls.

Invasions Playground invasions are another asymmetric form of borderwork. On a few occasions I saw girls invade and disrupt an all-male game, most memorably a group of tall sixth-grade girls who ran onto the playing field and grabbed a football which was in play. The boys were surprised and frustrated, and, unusual for boys this old, finally

*Sue Samuelson (1980) reports that in a racially mixed playground in Fresno, California, Mexican-American but not Anglo children gave cooties. Racial as well as sexual inequality may be expressed through these forms.

tattled to the aide. But in the majority of cases, boys disrupt girls' activities rather than vice versa. Boys grab the ball from girls playing four-square, stick feet into a jumprope and stop an ongoing game, and dash through the area of the bars where girls are taking turns performing, sending the rings flying. Sometimes boys ask to join a girls' game and then, after a short period of seemingly earnest play, disrupt the game. Two second-grade boys begged to "twirl" the jumprope for a group of second-grade girls who had been jumping for some time. The girls agreed, and the boys began to twirl. Soon, without announcement, the boys changed from "seashells, cockle bells" to "hot peppers" (spinning the rope very fast), and tangled the jumper in the rope. The boys ran away laughing.

Boys disrupt girls' play so often that girls have developed almost ritualized responses: they guard their ongoing play, chase boys away, and tattle to the aides. In a playground cycle which enhances sex segregation, aides who try to spot potential trouble before it occurs sometimes shoo boys away from areas where girls are playing. Aides do not anticipate trouble from girls who seek to join groups of boys, with the exception of girls intent on provoking a chase sequence. And indeed, if they seek access to a boys' game, girls usually play with boys in earnest rather than breaking up the game.

A close look at the organization of borderwork—or boundaried interactions between the sexes—shows that the worlds of boys and girls may be separate, but they are not parallel, nor are they equal. The worlds of girls and boys articulate in several asymmetric ways:

1. On the playground, boys control as much as ten times more space than girls, when one adds up the area of large playing fields and compares it with the much smaller areas where girls predominate. Girls, who play closer to the building, are more often watched over and protected by the adult aides.

2. Boys invade all-female games and scenes of play much more than girls invade boys. This, and boys' greater control of space, correspond with other findings about the organization of gender, and inequality, in our society: compared with men and boys, women and girls take up less space, and their space and talk are more often violated and interrupted (Greif, 1982; Henley, 1977; West & Zimmerman, 1983).

3. Although individual boys are occasionally treated as contaminating (e.g., a third-grade boy who both boys and girls said was "stinky" and "smelled like pee"), girls are more often defined as polluting. This pattern ties to themes that I discuss later: it is more taboo for a boy to play with

(as opposed to invade) girls, and girls are more sexually defined than boys.

A look at the boundaries between the separated worlds of girls and boys illuminates within-sex hierarchies of status and control. For example, in the sex-divided seating in the fourth–fifth-grade classroom, several boys recurringly sat near "female space": their desks were at the gender divide in the classroom, and they were more likely than other boys to sit at a predominantly female table in the lunchroom. These boys—two nonbilingual Chicanos and an overweight "loner" boy who was afraid of sports—were at the bottom of the male hierarchy. Gender is sometimes used as a metaphor for male hierarchies; the inferior status of boys at the bottom is conveyed by calling them "girls." Seven boys and one girl were playing basketball. Two younger boys came over and asked to play. While the girl silently stood, fully accepted in the company of players, one of the older boys disparagingly said to the younger boys, "You girls can't play."*

In contrast, the girls who more often travel in the boys' world, sitting with groups of boys in the lunchroom or playing basketball, soccer, and baseball with them, are not stigmatized. Some have fairly high status with other girls. The worlds of girls and boys are asymmetrically arranged, and spatial patterns map out interacting forms of inequality.

Heterosexual Meanings

The organization and meanings of gender (the social categories "woman/man," "girl/boy") and of sexuality vary cross-culturally (Ortner & Whitehead, 1981)—and, in our society, across the life course. Harriet Whitehead (1981) observed that in our (Western) gender system, and that of many traditional North American Indian cultures, one's choice of a sexual object, occupation, and dress and demeanor are closely associated with gender. However, the "center of gravity" differs in the two gender systems. For Indians, occupational pursuits provide the primary imagery of gender; dress and demeanor are secondary, and sexuality is least important. In our system, at least for adults, the order is reversed: heterosexuality is central to our definitions of "man" and "woman" ("masculinity/femininity") and the relationships that obtain between them, whereas occupation and dress/demeanor are secondary.

*This incident was recorded by Margaret Blume, who, for an undergraduate research project in 1982, observed in the California school where I earlier did fieldwork. Her observations and insights enhanced my own, and I would like to thank her for letting me cite this excerpt.

Whereas erotic orientation and gender are closely linked in our definitions of adults, we define children as relatively asexual. Activities and dress/demeanor are more important than sexuality in the cultural meanings of "girl" and "boy." Children are less heterosexually defined than adults, and we have nonsexual imagery for relations between girls and boys. However, both children and adults sometimes use heterosexual language—"crushes," "like," "goin' with," "girlfriends," and "boyfriends"—to define cross-sex relationships. This language increases through the years of elementary school; the shift to adolescence consolidates a gender system organized around the institution of heterosexuality.

In everyday life in the schools, heterosexual and romantic meanings infuse some ritualized forms of interaction between groups of boys and girls (e.g., "chase and kiss") and help maintain sex segregation. "Jimmy likes Beth" or "Beth likes Jimmy" is a major form of teasing, which a child risks in choosing to sit by or walk with someone of the other sex. The structure of teasing and children's sparse vocabulary for relationships between girls and boys are evident in the following conversation which I had with a group of third-grade girls in the lunchroom. Susan asked me what I was doing, and I said I was observing the things children do and play. Nicole volunteered, "I like running, boys chase all the girls. See Tim over there? Judy chases him all around the school. She likes him." Judy, sitting across the table, quickly responded, "I hate him. I like him for a friend." "Tim loves Judy," Nicole said in a loud, sing-song voice.

In the younger grades, the culture and lore of girls contains more heterosexual romantic themes than that of boys. In Michigan, the first-grade girls often jumped rope to a rhyme which began: "Down in the valley where the green grass grows, there sat Cindy [name of jumper], as sweet as a rose. She sat, she sat, she sat so sweet. Along came Jason, and kissed her on the cheek. First comes love, then comes marriage, then along comes Cindy with a baby carriage." Before a girl took her turn at jumping, the chanters asked her, "Who do you want to be your boyfriend?" The jumper always proffered a name, which was accepted matter-of-factly. In chasing, a girl's kiss carried greater threat than a boy's kiss; "girl touch," when defined as contaminating, had sexual connotations. In short, starting at an early age, girls are more sexually defined than boys.

Through the years of elementary school, and increasing with age, the idiom of heterosexuality helps maintain the gender divide. Cross-sex interactions, especially when children initiate them, are fraught with the risk of being teased about "liking" someone of the other sex. I learned of several close cross-sex friendships, formed and maintained in neighborhoods and church, which went underground during the school day.

By the fifth grade a few children began to affirm, rather than avoid, the charge of having a girlfriend or a boyfriend; they introduced the heterosexual courtship rituals of adolescence. In the lunchroom in the Michigan school, as the tables were forming, a high-status fifth-grade boy called out from his seat at the table: "I want Trish to sit by me." Trish came over, and almost like a king and queen, they sat at the gender divide—a row of girls down the table on her side, a row of boys on his. In this situation, which inverted earlier forms, it was not a loss but a gain in status to publicly choose a companion of the other sex. By affirming his choice, the boy became unteasable (note the familiar asymmetry of heterosexual courtship rituals: the male initiates). This incident signals a temporal shift in arrangements of sex and gender.

Traveling in the World of the Other Sex

Contests, invasions, chasing, and heterosexually defined encounters are based upon and reaffirm boundaries between girls and boys. In another type of cross-sex interaction, individuals (or sometimes pairs) cross gender boundaries, seeking acceptance in a group of the other sex. Nearly all the cases I saw of this were tomboys—girls who played organized sports and frequently sat with boys in the cafeteria or classroom. If these girls were skilled at activities central in the boys' world, especially games like soccer, baseball, and basketball, they were pretty much accepted as participants.

Being a tomboy is a matter of degree. Some girls seek access to boys' groups but are excluded; other girls limit their "crossing" to specific sports. Only a few—such as the tomboy I mentioned earlier, who chose a seat with the boys in the sex-divided fourth–fifth grade—participate fully in the boys' world. That particular girl was skilled at the various organized sports which boys played in different seasons of the year. She was also adept at physical fighting and at using the forms of arguing, insult, teasing, naming, and sports-talk of the boys' subculture. She was the only Black child in her classroom, in a school with only 8% Black students; overall that token status, along with unusual athletic and verbal skills, may have contributed to her ability to move back and forth across the gender divide. Her unique position in the children's world was widely recognized in the school. Several times, the teacher said to me, "She thinks she's a boy."

I observed only one boy in the upper grades (a fourth-grader) who regularly played with all-female groups, as opposed to "playing at" girls' games and seeking to disrupt them. He frequently played jumprope and took turns with girls doing tricks on the bars, using the small gestures—for example, a helpful push on the heel of a girl who needed momentum to turn her body around the bar—which mark skillful and earnest participation. Although I never saw him play in other than an earnest spirit, the girls often chased him away from their games, and both girls and boys teased him. The fact that girls seek and have more access to boys' worlds than vice versa, and the fact that girls who travel with the other sex are less stigmatized for it, are obvious asymmetries, tied to the asymmetries previously discussed.

Relaxed Cross-Sex Interactions

Relationships between boys and girls are not always marked by strong boundaries, heterosexual definitions, or interacting on the terms and turfs of the other sex. On some occasions girls and boys interact in relatively comfortable ways. Gender is not strongly salient nor explicitly invoked, and girls and boys are not organized into boundaried collectivities. These "with" occasions have been neglected by those studying gender and children's relationships, who have emphasized either the model of separate worlds (with little attention to their articulation) or heterosexual forms of contact.

Occasions when boys and girls interact without strain, when gender wanes rather than waxes in importance, frequently have one or more of the following characteristics:

1. The situations are organized around an absorbing task, such as a group art project or creating a radio show, which encourages cooperation and lessens attention to gender. This pattern accords with other studies finding that cooperative activities reduce group antagonism (e.g., Sherif & Sherif, 1953, who studied divisions between boys in a summer camp; and Aronson et al., 1978, who used cooperative activities to lessen racial divisions in a classroom).

2. Gender is less prominent when children are not responsible for the formation of the group. Mixed-sex play is less frequent in games like football, which require the choosing of teams, and more frequent in games like handball or dodgeball, which individuals can join simply by getting into a line or a circle. When adults organize mixed-sex encounters—which they frequently do in the classroom and in physical education periods on the playground—they

legitimize cross-sex contact. This removes the risk of being teased for choosing to be with the other sex.

3. There is more extensive and relaxed cross-sex interaction when principles of grouping other than gender are explicitly invoked—for example, counting off to form teams for spelling or kickball, dividing lines by hot lunch or cold lunch, or organizing a work group on the basis of interests or reading ability.

4. Girls and boys may interact more readily in less public and crowded settings. Neighborhood play, depending on demography, is more often sex and age integrated than play at school, partly because with fewer numbers, one may have to resort to an array of social categories to find play partners or to constitute a game. And in less crowded environments there are fewer potential witnesses to "make something of it" if girls and boys play together.

Relaxed interactions between girls and boys often depend on adults to set up and legitimize the contact.* Perhaps because of this contingency—and the other, distancing patterns which permeate relations between girls and boys—the easeful moments of interaction rarely build to close friendship. Schofield (1981) makes a similar observation about gender and racial barriers to friendship in a junior high school.

IMPLICATIONS FOR DEVELOPMENT

I have located social relations within an essentially spatial framework, emphasizing the organization of children's play, work, and other activities within specific settings and in one type of institution, the school. In contrast, frameworks of child development rely upon temporal metaphors, using images of growth and transformation over time. Taken alone, both spatial and temporal frameworks have shortcomings; fitted together, they may be mutually correcting.

Those interested in gender and development have relied upon conceptualizations of "sex-role socialization" and "sex differences." Sexuality and gender, I have argued, are more situated and fluid than these individualist and intrinsic models imply. Sex and gender are differently organized and defined across situations, even within the same institution. This situational variation (e.g., in the extent to which an encounter heightens or lessens gender boundaries, or is

infused with sexual meanings) shapes and constrains individual behavior. Features which a developmental perspective might attribute to individuals and understand as relatively internal attributes unfolding over time may, in fact, be highly dependent on context. For example, children's avoidance of cross-sex friendship may be attributed to individual gender development in middle childhood. But attention to varied situations may show that this avoidance is contingent on group size, activity, adult behavior, collective meanings, and the risk of being teased.

A focus on social organization and situation draws attention to children's experiences in the present. This helps correct a model like "sex-role socialization" which casts the present under the shadow of the future, or presumed "endpoints" (Speier, 1976). A situated analysis of arrangements of sex and gender among those of different ages may point to crucial disjunctions in the life course. In the fourth and fifth grades, culturally defined heterosexual rituals ("goin' with") begin to suppress the presence and visibility of other types of interaction between girls and boys, such as nonsexualized and comfortable interaction and traveling in the world of the other sex. As "boyfriend/girlfriend" definitions spread, the fifth-grade tomboy I described had to work to sustain "buddy" relationships with boys. Adult women who were tomboys often speak of early adolescence as a painful time when they were pushed away from participation in boys' activities. Other adult women speak of the loss of intense, even erotic ties with other girls when they entered puberty and the rituals of dating, that is, when they became absorbed into the situation of heterosexuality (Rich, 1980). When Lever (1976) describes best-friend relationships among fifth-grade girls as preparation for dating, she imposes heterosexual ideologies onto a present which should be understood on its own terms.

As heterosexual encounters assume more importance, they may alter relations in same-sex groups. For example, Schofield (1981) reports that for sixth- and seventh-grade children in a middle school, the popularity of girls with other girls was affected by their popularity with boys, while boys' status with other boys did not depend on their relations with girls. This is an asymmetry familiar from the adult world; men's relationships with one another are defined through varied activities (occupations, sports), while relationships among women—and their public status—are more influenced by their connections to individual men.

A full understanding of gender and social relations should encompass cross-sex as well as within-sex interactions. "Borderwork" helps maintain separate, gender-linked

---

*Note that in daily school life, depending on the individual and the situation, teachers and aides sometimes lessened and at other times heightened sex segregation.

subcultures, which, as those interested in development have begun to suggest, may result in different milieux for learning. Daniel Maltz and Ruth Borker (1983), for example, argue that because of different interactions within girls' and boys' groups, the sexes learn different rules for creating and interpreting friendly conversation, rules which carry into adulthood and help account for miscommunication between men and women. Carol Gilligan (1982) fits research on the different worlds of girls and boys into a theory of sex differences in moral development. Girls develop a style of reasoning, she argues, which is more personal and relational; boys develop a style which is more positional, based on separateness. Eleanor Maccoby (1982), also following the insight that because of sex segregation, girls and boys grow up in different environments, suggests implications for gender-differentiated prosocial and antisocial behavior.

This separate worlds approach, as I have illustrated, also has limitations. The occasions when the sexes are together should also be studied, and understood as contexts for experience and learning. For example, asymmetries in cross-sex relationships convey a series of messages: that boys are more entitled to space and to the nonreciprocal right of interrupting or invading the activities of the other sex; that girls are more in need of adult protection, lower in status, more defined by sexuality, and may even be polluting. Different types of cross-sex interaction—relaxed, boundaried, sexualized, or taking place on the terms of the other sex—provide different contexts for development.

By mapping the array of relationships between and within the sexes, one adds complexity to the overly static and dichotomous imagery of separate worlds. Individual experiences vary, with implications for development. Some children prefer same-sex groupings; some are more likely to cross the gender boundary and participate in the world of the other sex; some children (e.g., girls and boys who frequently play "chase and kiss") invoke heterosexual meanings, while others avoid them.

Finally, after charting the terrain of relationships, one can trace their development over time. For example, age variation in the content and form of borderwork, or of cross- and same-sex touch, may be related to differing cognitive, social, emotional, or physical capacities, as well as to age-associated cultural forms. I earlier mentioned temporal shifts in the organization of cross-sex chasing, from mixing with fantasy play in the early grades to more elaborately ritualized and sexualized forms by the sixth grade. There also appear to be temporal changes in same- and cross-sex touch. In kindergarten, girls and boys touch one another more freely than in fourth grade, when children avoid relaxed cross-sex touch and instead use pokes, pushes, and other forms of mock violence, even when the touch clearly expresses affection. This touch taboo is obviously related to the risk of seeming to *like* someone of the other sex. In fourth grade, same-sex touch begins to signal sexual meanings among boys as well as between boys and girls. Younger boys touch one another freely in cuddling (arm around shoulder) as well as mock-violence ways. By fourth grade, when homophobic taunts like "fag" become more common among boys, cuddling touch begins to disappear for boys, but less for girls.

Overall, I am calling for more complexity in our conceptualizations of gender and of children's social relationships. Our challenge is to retain the temporal sweep, looking at individual and group lives as they unfold over time, while also attending to social structure and context and to the full variety of experiences in the present.

ACKNOWLEDGMENTS

I would like to thank Jane Atkinson, Nancy Chodorow, Arlene Daniels, Peter Lyman, Zick Rubin, Malcolm Spector, Avril Thorne, and Margery Wolf for comments on an earlier version of this paper. Conversations with Zella Luria enriched this work.

REFERENCES

Aronson, E., et al. 1978. The jigsaw classroom. Beverly Hills, Calif.: Sage.

Barth, F., ed. 1969. *Ethnic groups and boundaries.* Boston: Little, Brown.

Borman, K. M. 1979. "Children's interactions in playgrounds," *Theory into Practice* 18:251–57.

Eder, D., & Hallinan, M. T. 1978. "Sex differences in children's friendships." *American Sociological Review* 43:237–50.

Finnan, C. R. 1982. "The ethnography of children's spontaneous play." In G. Spindler, ed., *Doing the ethnography of schooling,* pp. 358–80. New York: Holt, Rinehart & Winston.

Foot, H. C.; Chapman, A. J.; & Smith, J. R. 1980. "Introduction." *Friendship and social relations in children,* pp. 1–14. New York: Wiley.

Gilligan, C. 1982. *In a different voice: Psychological theory and women's development.* Cambridge: Harvard University Press.

Glaser, B. G., & Strauss, A. L. 1967. *The discovery of grounded theory.* Chicago: Aldine.

Goffman, E. 1977. "The arrangement between the sexes." *Theory and Society* 4:301–36.

Goodwin, M. H. 1980. "Directive-response speech sequences in girls' and boys' task activities." In S. McConnell-Ginet, R. Borker, & N. Furman, eds., *Women and language in literature and society,* pp. 157–73. New York: Praeger.

Greif, E. B. 1982. "Sex differences in parent-child conversations." *Women's Studies International Quarterly* 3:253–58.

Henley, N. 1977. *Body politics: Power, sex, and nonverbal communication.* Englewood Cliffs, N.J.: Prentice-Hall.

Karkau, K. 1973. *Sexism in the fourth grade.* Pittsburgh: KNOW, Inc. (pamphlet).

Katz, J. 1983. "A theory of qualitative methodology: The social system of analytic fieldwork." In R. M. Emerson, ed., *Contemporary field research,* pp. 127–48. Boston: Little, Brown.

Knapp, M., & Knapp, H. 1976. *One potato, two potato: The secret education of American children.* New York: W. W. Norton.

Lever, J. 1976. "Sex differences in the games children play." *Social Problems* 23:478–87.

Maccoby, E. 1982. "Social groupings in childhood: Their relationship to prosocial and antisocial behavior in boys and girls." Paper presented at conference on The Development of Prosocial and Antisocial Behavior, Voss, Norway.

Maccoby, E., & Jacklin, C. 1974. *The psychology of sex differences.* Stanford, Calif.: Stanford University Press.

McRobbie, A., & Garber, J. 1975. "Girls and subcultures." In S. Hall & T. Jefferson, eds., *Resistance through rituals,* pp. 209–23. London: Hutchinson.

Maltz, D. N., & Borker, R. A. 1983. "A cultural approach to male–female miscommunication." In J. J. Gumperz, ed., *Language and social identity,* pp. 195–216. New York: Cambridge University Press.

Ortner, S. B., & Whitehead, H. 1981. *Sexual meanings.* New York: Cambridge University Press.

Parrott, S. 1972. "Games children play: Ethnography of a second-grade recess." In J. P. Spradley & D. W. McCurdy, eds., *The cultural experience,* pp. 206–19. Chicago: Science Research Associates.

Rich, A. 1980. "Compulsory heterosexuality and lesbian existence." *Signs,* 5:631–60.

Samuelson, S. 1980. "The cooties complex." *Western Folklore* 39:198–210.

Savin-Williams, R. C. 1976. "An ethological study of dominance formation and maintenance in a group of human adolescents." *Child Development* 47:972–79.

Schofield, J. W. 1981. "Complementary and conflicting identities: Images and interaction in an interracial school." In S. R. Asher & J. M. Gottman, eds., *The development of children's friendships,* pp. 53–90. New York: Cambridge University Press.

Sherif, M., & Sherif, C. 1953. *Groups in harmony and tension.* New York: Harper.

Sluckin, A. 1981. *Growing up in the playground.* London: Routledge & Kegan Paul.

Speier, M. 1976. "The adult ideological viewpoint in studies of childhood." In A. Skolnick, ed., *Rethinking childhood,* pp. 168–86. Boston: Little, Brown.

Sutton-Smith, B. 1971. "A syntax for play and games." In R. E. Herron and B. Sutton-Smith, eds., *Child's play,* pp. 298–307. New York: Wiley.

Unger, R. K. 1979. "Toward a redefinition of sex and gender." *American Psychologist* 34:1085–94.

Waldrop, M. F., & Halverson, C. F. 1975. "Intensive and extensive peer behavior: Longitudinal and cross-sectional analysis." *Child Development* 46:19–26.

West, C., & Zimmerman, D. H. 1983. "Small insults: A study of interruptions in cross-sex conversations between unacquainted persons." In B. Thorne, C. Kramarae, & N. Henley, eds., *Language, gender, and society.* Rowley, Mass.: Newbury House.

Whitehead, H. 1981. "The bow and the burden strap: A new look at institutionalized homosexuality in Native America." In S. B. Ortner & H. Whitehead, eds., *Sexual meanings,* pp. 80–115. New York: Cambridge University Press.

Women's Psychological Development: Implications for Psychotherapy[1]

CAROL GILLIGAN

REVISION

. . . I am in a room filled with thirteen-year-old girls—the eighth grade of the Laurel School in Cleveland. Portraits of women hang on the walls, looking down decorously at the sprawl of girls, backpacks, sweaters. The five-year study of girls' development which these girls have been part of has ended, and I want to know how they want to be involved, now that we are writing about this work and presenting it in public.[2] A consensus silently forms and Zoe speaks: "We want you to tell them everything we said, and we want our names in the book." We begin to talk about the details, and Paula raises her hand. "When we were in fourth grade, we were stupid," she says. I say it would never have occurred to me to use the word "stupid" to describe them as fourth graders, since what impressed me most when they were nine was how much they knew. "I mean," Paula corrects herself, "when we were in fourth grade, we were honest."

Adrienne Rich (1979) writes about re-vision as an act of survival for women:

> Until we can understand the assumptions in which we are drenched we cannot know ourselves. And this drive to self-knowledge, for women, is more than a search for identity: it is part of our refusal of the self-destructiveness of male-dominated society. (p. 35)

Writing as revision—the subject of Rich's essay—becomes an act of political resistance, offering writers in particular

"the challenge and promise of a whole new psychic geography to be explored."

But an exploration of the landscape of women's psychology reveals a resistance of a different sort: a revision which covers over the world of girls' childhood, as girls, coming-of-age, name the relational life they have lived, often most intensely with their mothers, as "false," or "illogical," or "stupid." This act of revision washes away the grounds of girls' feelings and thoughts and undermines the transformatory potential which lies in women's development by leaving girls-turning-into-women with the sense that their feelings are groundless, their thoughts are about nothing real, what they experienced never happened, or at the time they could not understand it.

As girls at adolescence revise the story of their childhood, however, they draw attention to a relational crisis which is at the center of women's development—a crisis which has generally been seen retrospectively.[3] In conversations between girls and women, this relational struggle tends to stir when the subject turns to knowing and not knowing. I begin with examples taken from different school settings. . . .

* * *

It is early in the morning in the middle of winter, and I am sitting with Sheila in a quiet room in the coeducational school she is attending. Outside the window, light spreads across fields of snow. Inside it is dim; we have lit a lamp and I begin with my first question. "Looking back over the past year, what stands out for you?" It is the third year of the study, and Sheila, now sixteen, says that all her relationships have changed. They "used to be stable and long-lasting, and they are very unstable now." She dates this upheaval to the betrayal of a confidence by a girl she had thought her best friend. Since then, she has "gotten very close and in insane arguments with people, and so relationships go to more extremes: hot and extremely cold. . . . I have come together and grown apart with a lot of people."

Reflecting on these changes, Sheila says that she does not "really like myself enough to look out for myself." Stirred by the sadness of this statement, I ask, "Do you really feel that way?" She says, "Yeah. I mean I do look out for myself, but I care about other people I think, more than I care about myself. I don't know." And with this string of self-portraying statements—"I mean I do . . . but I care . . . I think . . . I care . . . I don't know"— Sheila unravels a relational crisis which leaves her feeling disconnected from others, out of touch with the world, and essentially all alone.

Asked about a time when she felt down on herself, Sheila says, "the last five years"—since she was eleven. And she has developed an intricate strategy for protection, taking herself out of relationship for the sake of "relationships" with people whom she feels do not know or value her. Lori Stern writes about Sheila as exemplifying girls' puzzling tendency to disavow themselves (see Gilligan, Rogers, & Tolman, 1991). Extending Stern's analysis, I wish to focus on Sheila's experience of relational impasse—the logic of which Sheila lays out clearly in the course of the following dialogue between us. Sheila describes an internal conversation between a voice which asks her, "What do you want in relationships?" and another voice which essentially cuts off the question and functions as a kind of internalized back-seat driver. I begin with this voice:

SHEILA: There is always that little part jumping up in the back saying, "Hey me, hey me, you are not worthwhile."

CAROL: And why not?

SHEILA: Because people have shown it. Because my relationships have proven that.

CAROL: How can they show that? How can other people know?

SHEILA: Other people say, "It has to be true because you are stupid. You don't know it yourself, you are not even worthwhile to know the truth." Other people must know it.

CAROL: Do you believe that?

SHEILA: In a way.

CAROL: And in another way?

SHEILA: In another way, I think I must be smarter because I haven't let them in.

CAROL: Ah, so if you haven't let them in, then they can't know.

SHEILA: I am safe, right?

CAROL: But if you let them in all the way?

SHEILA: Then it's not safe. Then if I do something, then I know it's me.

CAROL: I see. This way you could always say they don't know the real you.

SHEILA: Uh-huh. Sane, isn't it?

CAROL: It's a very good hedge. But at the cost [of what you have said you want]. It precludes . . . what you have called "honesty in relationships."

As I question the seemingly unquestionable voice which Sheila heeds but does not believe or agree with, Sheila describes her feelings of helplessness in the face of others whom she has in fact outsmarted, keeping herself safe but at the cost of sacrificing the relationships she wanted.

The previous year, Sheila had created a powerful image of relational crisis in describing her relationship with her boyfriend. Her striking and witty description of standing helplessly in a relationship which is sinking captures her own situation and also the feelings of other girls and women who, like Sheila, are reluctant to say what they clearly know is happening:

> It is like two people standing in a boat that they both know is sinking. I don't want to say anything to you because it will upset you, and you don't want to say anything to me because it will upset you. And we are both standing here in water up to about our ankles, watching it rise, and I don't want to say anything to you, you know.

Girls often use the phrase "I don't know" to cover knowledge which they believe may be dangerous, and the phrase "you know," correspondingly to discover what it is possible for them to know and still be connected with other people.

* * *

I am sitting with Rosie in the teachers' lounge—a small room on the second floor of her school.[5] A coffee pot, unplugged, sits on the wooden desk, and wooden cross-panes mark off the daylight into even squares. Rosie is fifteen, and she says, "I am confused." She knows the disparities between the way she is and the way her mother wants to see her ("as close to the perfect child") and she also knows the differences between the way she sees her mother and the way her mother wants to be seen by Rosie. Caught between viewpoints, she becomes confused in describing herself:

> When I am describing myself, I am confused. Just really trying to sort everything out and figure out what exactly my viewpoints are. Putting things in order and deciding how to think about things.

Rosie knows she is not the perfect girl whom her ambitious and successful Latina mother imagines—the girl who "gets straight A's and has a social life but still gets home exactly on the dot, on time, and does everything her parents say, and keeps her room neat." I ask, "Are there girls like that?" Rosie says, "Perhaps, saints." "Do saints have sex," I wonder aloud, thinking of Rosie whose mother has just discovered that she is having sex with her boyfriend. And Rosie begins, "I don't know," but then fills in what has been her solution: "If they want, as long as they don't get caught, as long as nobody knows."

Yet Rosie intensely wants to be known by her mother. Once her mother knows about her sexuality, Rosie says, "I hunted her down and made her talk to me, and it wasn't like a battle or anything. I just wanted to see what she had to say." But Rosie's viewpoints are so radically disruptive of the order of her mother's household that Rosie may wonder whether, by changing her own viewpoint or perhaps arranging things differently, she might be able to repair what otherwise seems an irreparable division: between staying in touch with herself thereby knowing what she is seeing and feeling ("I looked at her little study and bedroom, and they are a mess too") and staying in connection with her mother's way of seeing herself and Rosie. "So," Rosie concludes, "I don't know."

A PERSISTENT OBSERVATION

Beginning in the nineteenth century, psychiatrists and psychologists have consistently marked adolescence as a particularly difficult time in women's development—a time when girls "are more liable to suffer" (Henry Maudsley, 1879, cited in Showalter, 1985, p. 130). And among the girls who suffer in adolescence are those who seem most psychologically vital. Elaine Showalter quotes the following passage from Josef Breuer as illustrative:

Adolescents who are later to become hysterical are for the most part lively, gifted, and full of intellectual interests before they fall ill. Their energy of will is often remarkable. They include girls who get out of bed at night so as secretly to carry out some study that their parents have forbidden for fear of their overworking. The capacity for forming sound judgments is certainly not more abundant in them than in other people; but it is rare to find in them simple, dull intellectual inertia or stupidity. (p. 158)

Michelle Fine (1986), studying high school drop outs at the end of the twentieth century, notes that the girls who drop out of inner-city schools—at the time they drop out—are among the least depressed and the brightest. Lively, intelligent, and willful girls at both ends of the century and the social class spectrum thus find themselves in trouble at adolescence.

Anne Petersen (1988), reviewing the literature on adolescence, pulls together a series of findings which provide further evidence that girls are likely to experience psychological problems at this time. Adolescence witnesses a marked increase in episodes of depression, eating disorders, poor body image, suicidal thoughts and gestures, and a fall in girls' sense of self-worth. Petersen's review extends the impressions of clinicians across the century that girls at adolescence experience a kind of psychic constraint or narrowing (Freud, 1905, 1933; Horney, 1926; Miller, 1984; Thompson, 1964) and suffer from a range of depressive symptoms, dissociative processes, and "as if" phenomena (Demitrack et al., 1990; Deutsch, 1944; Rutter, 1986).

Epidemiological studies offer further evidence. Elder and Caspi (1990) report that when families are under stress—whether from marital conflict, economic hardship, or fathers going off to war—the children who are most psychologically at risk are boys in childhood and girls at adolescence. Block (1990) reports a sudden drop in girls' resiliency around the age of eleven, with no corresponding finding for boys. Seligman (1991) finds that "girls, at least up to puberty, are more noticeably optimistic than boys," (p. 125) and concludes that "whatever causes the huge difference in depression in adulthood, with women twice as vulnerable as men, it does not have its roots in childhood. Something must happen at or shortly after puberty that causes a flip-flop—and hits girls very hard indeed" (pp. 149-150). And a recent national survey (Greenberg-Lake Analysis Group, 1991) finds that white girls tend to experience a drop in feelings of self-worth around the age of eleven, Latinas experience a more precipitous drop a few years later—around the beginning of high school—and black girls tend to sustain their feelings of self-worth but at the expense, perhaps, of dissociating themselves from school and disagreeing publicly with their teachers.

Taken together, this evidence suggests that girls face a psychological crisis at the time of adolescence—a crisis to which some girls respond by devaluing themselves and feeling themselves to be worthless, while others disagree publicly and dissociate themselves from institutions which devalue them—in this case, the schools. Both solutions, however, are costly for girls. Yet despite this remarkable convergence of clinical observation, developmental findings, and epidemiological data, pointing repeatedly to a striking asymmetry between girls' and boys' development—and one which has clear implications for preventing suffering and fostering development—this persistent observation of difference has, until recently, remained unexplored and unexplained theoretically (see Brown & Gilligan, 1990b; Gilligan, 1990a; Gilligan, Brown, & Rogers, 1990; Rogers, 1990).

GIRLS

Sounds, touching memory, filtering through theory, collecting, like water slowly filling a basin and then suddenly overflowing or rain falling steadily onto the afternoon streets of childhood—girls' voices, shouting, screaming, whispering, speaking, singing, running up and down the octaves of feelings. And the silence. Faces calm, eyes steady, ears open, girls sitting in a circle and then suddenly rising—like a flock of birds. Taking off and then settling, as if by prearrangement. And yet, nothing has been said, nothing is spoken. Only girls' faces and bodies taking in, registering the tides of daily living, following the drifts of thoughts and feelings, picking up the currents of relationship. I wade in.

It is Tuesday afternoon in the beginning of November—just after Halloween. The Theater, Writing, and Outing Club is meeting for the second year—part of a project designed by three women to learn from girls about girls' experience in the time when childhood turns into adolescence and to offer girls in return our help in sustaining and strengthening their voices, their resistance, their courage and their relationships.[6] Ten girls, ages ten and eleven—three African-American, five European-American, one Asian-American, one with a parent from India—and three women (Annie Rogers and myself—European-American psychologists, and Normi Noel, a Canadian-born actor, the-

ater director and voice teacher) stream into the science room of the public school which the girls are attending. The girls have decided this year to teach us what they know.

Two girls stand side-by-side in the center of the clearing we have created. Two other girls—"their thoughts"—stand behind them. The drama begins. One girl says that she wants to play with the other; the other clearly does not want to. As the two girls face into this relational impasse, their "thoughts" articulate the stream of their consciousness—a brilliant rendering of each girls' thoughts and feelings in response to what is happening between them. Finally, the thoughts take over, and speaking now directly to one another, set into motion feelings and thoughts which initially seemed fixed, unchangeable and settled, and in doing so begin to work out the relational problem.

What girls know about relationships and feelings unfolded steadily through our weekly meetings in the second year of the group. The immediate grasp of psychological processes, the keeping of a watchful eye and open ear constantly tuned to the relational surround which we had observed in girls and heard in interview settings (Brown & Gilligan, 1990b; Gilligan, Brown, & Rogers, 1990), now was dramatized directly for us by girls who seemed to want to leave no question in our minds about the strength of their voices and the depths of their knowing and the intensity of their desire for honest relationships between us. The week Normi introduced neutral masks from Greek theater by demonstrating how a face can mask feelings, each girl, going around one by one in a circle, turned her face into a mask and then named the feelings in the mask and the feelings which the mask was hiding. The feelings masked were feeling "ordinary, nothing special" (covered over by a mask that was "snooty") and feeling angry, not wanting to be with someone, hating someone, being bored (covered over by masks that were "nice," "smiling" and "interested"). "But Normi," eleven year old Joan says at the end of the exercise, "people always mask their feelings."

Girls' facility in turning their faces into the faces of nice, smiling and interested girls was coupled by their ear for false voices—especially the false voices of women in false relationships. On Halloween, when Annie and I brought pieces of costumes, including angel wings for "someone too good to be true," the girls, putting on the wings, instantly raised their voices to the high-pitched breathiness of good-woman conversation, dramatizing both the persona of the too-good-to-be-true woman and the mechanism of disconnection—the use of voice to cover rather than to convey thoughts and feelings and thus to close rather than to open a channel of connection between people. Separating their voices from the well of feelings and thoughts which lies deep in the body, girls did precise imitations of women's greeting rituals and social gestures and in doing so revealed how well they know the timbre and pitch of false female friendships.

Daily, girls take in evidence from the human world around them—the world which is open for psychological observation all day long, every day, "for free." And in this way, girls often see what is not supposed to be seen and hear what supposedly was unspoken. Like anthropologists, they pick up the culture; like sociologists, they observe race, class and sex differences; like psychologists, they come to know what is happening beneath the surface; like naturalists, they collect their observations, laying them out, sorting them out, discussing them between themselves in an ongoing conversation about relationships and people which goes on, on and off, for much of the day, every day. . . . This relational capacity may well underlie the psychological resiliency which girls show throughout childhood—an ability to tune themselves into the relational world, to connect with different people. . . .

It was surprising to discover the readiness with which younger girls—seven and eight-year-olds—tell people how they feel, mark relational violations, and openly respond to what is happening in relationships, even when their response leads them to experience painful feelings or cause others to be upset.[8] This relational honesty is vividly caught in Lyn Mikel Brown's (1989) example of Diane, an eight-year-old whistle-blower in the relational world. When Diane is asked about a time when someone was not being listened to, she speaks of her experience at dinner when her brother and sister interrupt her and "steal [her] mother's attention." Diane's solution is to bring a whistle to dinner and to blow the whistle when she is interrupted. Mother, brother, and sister, she reports, suddenly stopped talking and turned to her, at which point she said, "in a normal voice, 'that's much nicer.'" Karin, her classmate, walks out of the room on the second day when the teacher ignores her hand and calls on others "to do all the hard problems." Karin (see Brown, 1989; Brown & Gilligan, 1990b) knows that people seeing her in the hall will think that she is in trouble, but she also knows "I wasn't in trouble. I just couldn't take it. So I guess I just left." Asked if her teacher knows why she left, Karin makes a fine distinction between knowing and listening, saying "She wouldn't listen to me, but I told her, so I guess she knows."

Girls' willingness to voice painful relational realities is rawly evident as eight-year-old Jesse, in Brown's description (see Gilligan, Rogers, & Tolman, 1991) tells of the time when she went to play with a friend and the friend had another friend over and they would not play with Jesse. Jesse told her friend that she wasn't having any fun "just sitting there" and that she would go home if they did not play with her, at which point her friend, she reports, said "Just go home." In contrast, Tanya, at thirteen, reveals the treachery which flows from not speaking about painful relational realities. She and another friend backed out of a plan to go to camp with a third girl who was, Tanya says, "supposedly my best friend." When the girl discovers what has happened and asks if she can go to the other camp with them, Tanya says to her, "If you want to; it's up to you," while being perfectly clear that "I didn't want her to come." Tanya feels trapped because "I can't say so. . . . I can't say anything to her. Because she'll be hurt, so I have no idea what to do."

Victoria, at eleven, in the face of such relational treachery, opts for radical isolation—"independence from everyone." Describing her withdrawal from relationships in an effort to stay with her own experience, she is unequivocal in her judgment that what she is doing is harmful: "I try to build, it's kind of bad really to do it, but I try to build a little shield."

* * *

Learning from girls what girls are doing at the time they reach adolescence, I mark the places that are both familiar to me and surprising. And notice the sensations which bring back memories, like the feeling of moving without hesitation and the sound of a voice speaking directly without qualification—the open sounds of voices coming directly from the center of girls' bodies. Picking up from girls the feeling of moving freely in a girl's body, I find myself running with girls as I remember running in childhood.

And listening to girls' voices, I also begin to listen with girls to the voices which they are taking in. Opening their ears to the world, listening in, eavesdropping on the daily conversations, girls take in voices which silence their relational knowledge. And as their experience and their bodies change with adolescence, girls are more apt to discount the experiences of their childhood or to place a cover over their childhood world so that it remains intact. Yet, closing the door on their childhood, girls are in danger of knocking out what are in effect the T-cells of their psychological immune system—their seemingly effortless ability to tune into the relational world. Voices which intentionally or unintentionally interfere with girls' knowing, or encourage girls to silence themselves, keep girls from picking up or bringing out into the open a series of relational violations which they are acutely keyed into, such as not being listened to, being ignored, being left out, being insulted, being criticized, being spoken about meanly, being humiliated or made fun of, being whispered about, being talked about behind one's back, being betrayed by a friend, or being physically overpowered or hurt.

Tanya, at sixteen, writes a letter to Lyn Mikel Brown—the director of the Harvard-Laurel Project—about her feelings in response to a paper which Lyn and I had written (a paper which she and Lyn had discussed together at some length) (see Brown & Gilligan, 1990a, 1990b). She speaks of "a voice inside" her which "has been muffled." She explains, "The voice that stands up for what I believe in has been buried deep inside of me." Tanya wants to be in honest relationship with people. And yet, taking in what she is hearing about perfect girls whom people seem to love and admire, Tanya finds herself paying attention to voices which impede her relational desires. "I do not want the image of a 'perfect girl' to hinder myself from being a truly effective human being," she writes. "Yet, I still want to be nice, and I never want to cause any problem.". . .

"Cover up," girls are told as they reach adolescence, daily, in innumerable ways. Cover your body, cover your feelings, cover your relationships, cover your knowing, cover your voice, and perhaps above all, cover desire (see also Debold & Tolman, 1991; Gilligan, Rogers, & Tolman, 1991). And the wall that keeps memory from seeping through these covers may be the wall with the sign which labels body, feelings, relationships, knowing, voice and desire as bad.

A THEORY OF DEVELOPMENT

If psychological health consists, most simply, of staying in relationship with oneself, with others, and with the world, then psychological problems signify relational crises: losing touch with one's thoughts and feelings, being isolated from others, cut off from reality. The zen of development which makes human growth such a fascinating journey is that relationships which are the channels of growth are also the avenues through which people are psychically wounded. Vulnerability—the opening to experience which is at the heart of development—thus always carries with it the risk of being seriously hurt or diminished, and this play of opening and closing, embodiment and disembodiment, is reflected in the two meanings of the word "courage" (see Rogers, 1990).

The evidence that boys are more likely than girls to suffer psychologically in early childhood whereas girls are more at risk for developing psychological difficulties in adolescence calls for explanation and implies a revision—a new way of speaking about psychological development. This difference, I will suggest, also contains a hope for transformation.

Learning from girls about the relational crisis which girls experience as they approach adolescence—a place where development seems impassable—I offer as a working thesis that adolescence is a comparable time in women's psychological development to early childhood for men. It precipitates a relational crisis which poses an impasse in psychological development, a place where for the sake of relationship (with other people and with the world), one must take oneself out of relationship. Because this separation of self from relationship is psychologically untenable and also essentially confusing (if one is not in one's relationships, then the word "relationships" loses meaning), this division must be resisted and some compromise arrived at.

Freud (1899/1900) suggested as much for boys when he spoke about the "oedipus complex" as a turning point in boys' early childhood and also as the foundation for neurotic suffering and for civilization. The pressure girls are under as they reach adolescence and girls' experience of severe relational crisis similarly marks a turning point or watershed in girls' development. But girls' relationship to the culture is different, and also girls at adolescence are at a very different point in their own development than boys in early childhood—with far more experience of relationships and also perhaps with less incentive to give up relationship as the cost, ironically, of entering society. Consequently, women's psychological development—as others have observed (see Miller, 1986)—is profoundly transformational.

The relational crisis of boys' early childhood and of girls' adolescence is marked by a struggle to stay in relationship—a healthy resistance to disconnections which are psychologically wounding (from the body, from feelings, from relationships, from reality). This struggle takes a variety of forms, but at its center is a resistance to loss—to giving up the reality of relationships for idealizations or, as it is sometimes called, identifications. As young boys are pressured to take on images of heroes, or superheroes, as the grail which inform their quest to inherit their birthright or their manhood, so girls are pressed at adolescence to take on images of perfection as the model of the pure or perfectly good woman: the woman whom everyone will promote and value and want to be with (see Gilligan, 1990a; Brown & Gilligan, 1990b; Jack, 1991).

Children's healthy resistance to disconnection—the intense human desire for relationship which now is generally taken as foundational of psychic life—thus tends to lead children into a political struggle. Boys in early childhood resist leaving the comforts and pleasures, as well as the discomforts and pains, of their relational life: They want to stay with the people who have been with them. And girls at adolescence resist leaving the rich relational tapestry of their childhood. This resistance calls into question the prevailing order of social relationships and calls forth counter-pressures to enforce that order in the name, currently, of psychological health, as well as for the sake of civilization.

Thus at the time of early childhood for boys, when masculinity seems in question, and in early adolescence for girls, when femininity seems on the line, a healthy resistance to disconnections which turns into a political struggle comes under pressure to turn into a psychological resistance—that is, a resistance to knowing what is happening and an impulse to cover the struggle.

Here, the differences observed over the century between the times of seemingly heightened vulnerability or openness to growth and wounding in boys' and girls' lives contains a promise of transformation. If girls can sustain in adolescence a resistance which is more easily overwhelmed in boys' childhood, then women's psychological development will change the prevailing order of relationships. Compared with boys, whose desires for relationship, although strongly felt, tend to be less articulate, more inchoate, more laced with early loss and terror, girls' desires for relationship, leavened through years of childhood experience, tend to be hardier, more easily spoken, better known, more finely textured or differentiated and consequently less frightening although no less painful. Girls' healthy resistance to disconnection which springs up at the edge of adolescence as girls approach a culture of relationships which has been built largely by men thus calls into question what has been accepted as the canonical story of human development: the story which takes separation for granted, the story which seems logical, the story which rejects the possibility of honest or genuine, relationship. . . .

IMPLICATIONS FOR PSYCHOTHERAPY

In my dream, I am wearing my glasses over my contact lenses. I am literally seeing double, although I do not realize this in the dream. I sit with a woman and remorsefully realize that I have wanted too much in the relationship— that I cannot possibly have what I want. She says, "I cannot offer you myself," and the logic of her statement feels overwhelming. And then—still in the dream—I take off my glasses and suddenly say, "No," because I suddenly know that this is not it—this remorseful wanting of what cannot be given. "No," I say, and then go on to speak the truth of my experience in the relationship. With this, my head suddenly swivels, like an owl's head turning 180 degrees around, and I feel—in the dream—a strong jolt, like a shock, and overwhelmingly dizzy, as if I am seeing double. Only after I wake up do I realize that when I felt dizzy was when I was seeing straight, and that in the dream when I felt I was seeing clearly, I was literally seeing double— wearing two sets of lenses which made it impossible to see straight.

I dream this dream on the first night of the second year of the Theater, Writing, and Outing Club which Annie Rogers, Normi Noel and I have formed with eight girls from the Atrium School. We are in New Hampshire, near Mount Sunapee for the weekend. And I realize the next morning that this work with girls is seeping deeply into my dream life, leading me to re-vision—to a new seeing and naming of my experience; taking me back to the time of adolescence, the time, I realize, when straight-seeing became shocking, surprising really in the manner Nina describes in speaking about the girl in her story; angering and yet, at bottom, somehow more sorrowful. The time when relationships flowed—albeit through some rocky places; the time before voice and vision doubled.

Adolescent girls offer a key to understanding women's psychological development. And they offer some suggestions for preventing and treating psychological suffering. To catch girls in the moment of their revision—at the time just before or around adolescence—is to see a world disappearing: a rich world of relationships which seems so powerful in part because it feels so ordinary. To see this world disappearing while girls are saying that nothing is being lost or at least nothing of value, and to hear one story of love begin to cover and eclipse another until, like the moon in the sun's shadow, the under story glowing faintly red, is to ask the question which is at the heart of therapy and prevention: is this loss necessary, is this suffering and psychic diminution inevitable—a question which ties in with girls' healthy resistance and girls' courage (also see Rogers, 1990).

Then the central paradox of women's—and men's— psychological development becomes opened for re-examination: the taking of oneself out of relationship for the sake of relationships. And the incoherence at the center of this sentence—the dizzying black spot where the word "relationship" loses or changes meaning—then becomes the focus of a new question: what would it mean not to give up relationship?

Heads swirl, dizziness descends, threatening blackness, a voice whispers "take cover." As in speaking with Gail or Sheila or Rosie, I am asking myself the question which leads into the underground: the healthy resistance to disconnection which becomes a political resistance or struggle, which then is under pressure to turn into a psychological resistance: a seeing double, a not knowing.

Because women and girls who resist disconnections are likely to find themselves in therapy—for having gotten themselves into some combination of political and psychological trouble—therapists are in a key position to strengthen healthy resistance and courage, to help women recover lost voices and tell lost stories, and to provide safe houses for the underground. Tuning themselves into the voices of girls in the time before the re-vision, therapists can be good company for women as they return through the passages—going backward now—from a psychological resistance which takes the form of not knowing and covers a series of disconnections, to a political resistance which exposes false relationships and brings relational violations out into the open, to a healthy resistance to disconnection which grants immunity to psychological illness—the resistance which is rooted in wanting and having honest relationships.

NOTES

1. I am most grateful for the support and encouragement of Joan Lipsitz and the Lilly Endowment, the late Lawrence Cremin and the Spencer Foundation, and Wendy Puriefoy and the Boston Foundation. The work described in this paper would not have been possible without grants from the Geraldine Rockefeller Dodge Foundation, the Joseph S. Klingenstein Foundation, the Cleveland Foundation, the Gund Foundation, and Mrs. Marilyn Brachman Hoffman. Lyn Mikel Brown, the director of the Harvard-Laurel Project, and Annie Rogers, the director of the "Strengthening Healthy Resistance and Courage in Girls" project have contributed centrally to my understanding of girls' voices and my thinking about women's psychological development. I wish to thank Lyn and Annie, the other members of the Harvard Project on the Psychology of Women and the Development of Girls—Elizabeth Debold, Judy Dorney, Barbara Miller, Mark Tappan, Jill Taylor, Deborah Tolman and Janie Ward, Sarah Hanson—the project assistant, and all of the girls who have joined with us in this work and taught us about girls' experience.

2. The Harvard Project on the Psychology of Women and the Development of Girls began in the early 1980s to explore a series of questions about women's psychological development by joining women and girls, research and clinical practices, psychology and politics. Over the course of the decade, the Project has conducted a variety of studies, retreats and prevention projects at a range of locations designed to ensure the inclusion of different voices—from girls at Emma Willard School for girls (1981-84); to girls and boys in Boys' and Girls' Clubs in three ethnically different Boston neighborhoods and coeducational public and private schools in and around the city (1984-90); to girls ages six to seventeen at the Laurel School in Cleveland—a project that expanded to include women who as teachers, psychologists, and mothers were involved in teaching girls (1985-90); and beginning in 1989, to more intensive work involving women from the Harvard Project and girls from the Atrium School in Watertown, Massachusetts and from a public school in the vicinity of Boston, as well as other women who as mothers, teachers, psychotherapists, ministers and policy makers have become involved with us in this project.

3. For the relational crisis in women's psychological development, see Gilligan, 1982, and Miller, 1986, 1988. See also Belenky et al. (1986), Gilligan, Lyons, & Hanmer (1990), and the Stone Center Working Papers Series. For a retrospective view of the crisis in girls' lives at adolescence, see Hancock (1990).

* * *

5. For a fuller discussion of Rosie, see Gilligan, 1990a.

6. The Theater, Writing, and Outing Club is a central part of the project, "Strengthening Healthy Resistance and Courage in Girls." This prevention project is designed to help girls sustain their knowledge of relationships and the clarity of their voices into adolescence through theater and writing exercises created to strengthen and expand the range of girls' voices and girls' relationships and outings designed to encourage girls' active responses to the natural and cultural worlds. The project works centrally through developing healthy relationships between girls and women.

7. My analysis of Diane, Karin, Jesse and Victoria draws heavily on Lyn Mikel Brown's work on girls' narratives of relationships (Brown, 1989, in press, this volume; see also Brown & Gilligan, 1990b).

8. In writing about Nina, I draw on conversations with Annie Rogers with whom I read Nina's interviews, as well as on the insights of Kathryn Geismar, Amy Grillo, Sarah Ingersoll, Kate O'Neill, and Heather Thompson—members of the research group on the "Strengthening Healthy Resistance and Courage in Girls" project.

REFERENCES

Belenky, M., Clinchy, B., Goldberger, N., & Tarule, J. (1986). *Women's ways of knowing: the development of self, voice, and mind.* New York: Basic Books.

Block, J. (1990, October). Ego resilience through time: Antecedents and ramifications. In *Resilience and Psychological health.* Symposium of the Boston Psychoanalytic Society, Boston, MA.

Brown, L. M. (1989). *Narratives of relationship: The development of a care voice in girls ages 7 to 16.* Unpublished doctoral dissertation, Harvard University Graduate School of Education, Cambridge, MA.

Brown, L. M. (in press). A problem of vision: The development of voice and relational knowledge in girls ages 7 to 16. *Women's Studies Quarterly.*

Brown, L. M. (1991). Telling a girl's life. *Women & Therapy.*

Brown, L. M., & Gilligan, C. (1990a, August). Listening for self and relational voices: A responsive/resisting reader's guide. In M. Franklin (Chair), *Literary theory as a guide to psychological analysis.* Symposium conducted at the annual meeting of the American Psychological Association, Boston, MA.

Brown, L. M., & Gilligan, C. (1990b). Meeting at the crossroads: The psychology of women and the development of girls. Manuscript submitted for publication.

Debold, E. (1991). The body at play. *Women & Therapy.*

Debold, E., & Tolman, D. (1991, January). Made in whose image? Paper presented at the Ms. Foundation's Fourth Annual Women Managing Wealth Conference, New York.

Demitrack, M., Putnam, F., Brewerton, T., Brandt, H., & Gold, P. (1990). Relation of clinical variables to dissociative phenomena in eating disorders. *The American Journal of Psychiatry,* 147(9), 1184–1188.

Deutsch, H. (1944). *Psychology of women,* Vol. I. New York: Grune & Stratton.

Elder, G., & Caspi, A. (1990). Studying lives in a changing society: Sociological and personological explorations. In A. Rabin, R. Zucker, R. Emmons, & S. Frank (Eds.), *Studying persons and lives* (pp. 226–228). New York: Springer.

Fine, M. (1986). Why urban adolescents drop into and out of public high school. *Teachers College Record,* 87(3), 393–409.

Freud, S. (1899/1900). The interpretation of dreams. In J. Strachey (Ed. and Trans.), *The standard edition of the complete psychological works of Sigmund Freud* (Vols. IV & V). London: Hogarth Press.

Freud, S. (1933). New introductory lectures on psychoanalysis (Lecture XXXIII: Femininity). In J. Strachey (Ed. and Trans.), *The standard edition of the complete psychological works of Sigmund Freud* (Vol. XXII). London: The Hogarth Press.

Freud, S. (1905). Three essays on the theory of sexuality. In J. Strachey (Ed. and Trans.), *The standard edition of the complete psychological works of Sigmund Freud* (Vol. VII). London: The Hogarth Press.

Gilligan, C. (1982). *In a different voice: Psychological theory and women's development.* Cambridge, MA: Harvard University Press.

Gilligan, C. (1990a). Joining the resistance: Psychology, politics, girls and women. *Michigan Quarterly Review, 29*(4), 501–536.

Gilligan, C. (1990b). Teaching Shakespeare's sister: Notes from the underground of female adolescence. In C. Gilligan, N. Lyons, & T. Hanmer (Eds.), *Making connections: The relational worlds of adolescent girls at Emma Willard School* (pp. 6–29). Cambridge, MA: Harvard University Press.

Gilligan, C., Brown, L. M., & Rogers, A. (1990). Psyche embedded: A place for body, relationships, and culture in personality theory. In A. Rabin, R. Zucker, R. Emmons, & S. Frank (Eds.), *Studying persons and lives* (pp. 86–147). New York: Springer.

Gilligan, C., Lyons, N., & Hanmer, T. (Eds.). (1990). *Making connections: The relational worlds of adolescent girls at Emma Willard School.* Cambridge, MA: Harvard University Press.

Gilligan, C., Rogers, A. G., and Tolman, D. L. (Eds.) (1991). *Women, Girls, and Psychotherapy.* New York: Haworth Press.

Greenberg-Lake Analysis Group Inc. (1991, January). Shortchanging girls, shortchanging America: A nationwide poll to assess self esteem, educational experiences, interest in math and science, and career aspirations of girls and boys ages 9-15. (Available from The American Association of University Women, 515 Second Street NE, Washington, DC 20002).

Hancock, E. (1989). *The girl within: A groundbreaking new approach to female identity.* New York: Fawcett Columbia.

Horney, K. (1926). The flight from womanhood. *International Journal of Psychoanalysis, 7,* 324–339.

Jack, D. (1991). *Silencing the self: depression and women.* Cambridge, MA: Harvard University Press.

Kincaid, J. (1985). *Annie John.* New York: Farrar Straus Giroux.

Kingston, M. H. (1977). *The Woman Warrior.* New York: Alfred A. Knopf.

Miller, J. B. (1984). The development of women's sense of self. *Work in Progress, No. 12.* Wellesley, MA: Stone Center Working Papers Series.

Miller, J. B. (1986). *Toward a New Psychology of Women* (second edition). Boston: Beacon.

Miller, J. B. (1988). Connections, disconnections and violations. *Work in Progress, No. 33.* Wellesley, MA: Stone Center Working Papers Series.

Petersen, A. (1988). Adolescent development. *Annual Review of Psychology, 39,* 583–607.

Rich, A. (1979). *On lies, secrets, and silence: Selected prose, 1966-1978.* New York: Norton.

Rogers, A. (1990). The development of courage in girls and women. Unpublished manuscript, Harvard University, Project on the Psychology of Women and the Development of Girls, Cambridge, MA.

Rogers, A. (1991). A feminist poetics of psychotherapy. *Women & Therapy.*

Rutter, M. (1986). The developmental psychopathology of depression: Issues and perspectives. In M. Rutter, C. Izzard, & P. Read (Eds.), *Depression in young people: Developmental and clinical perspectives.* New York: Guilford Press.

Seligman, M. E. P. (1991). *Learned optimism.* New York: Random House.

Showalter, E. (1985). *The Female Malady.* New York: Penguin.

Stern, Lori. (1991). Disavowing the self in female adolescence. *Women & Therapy.*

Stone Center Working Papers Series. *Work in Progress.* Wellesley, MA: Wellesley College.

Thompson, C. (1964). *Interpersonal psychoanalysis.* New York: Basic.

Tolman, D. (1991). Adolescent girls, women and sexuality: Discerning dilemmas of desire. *Women & Therapy.*

P A R T   T H R E E

Social Organization of Gender

The processes of gender socialization that begin in early childhood work to prepare us for participation in society as men and women. Socialization alone, however, cannot account for the differences in power and prestige apparent between men and women in almost all societies. Because most people in contemporary societies have experiences that lead them to question the beliefs inherent in their socialization, childhood socialization cannot ensure that adults will conform to the patterns of belief and behavior dictated by the social groups to which they belong. Gender encompasses more than the socialized differences between individual women and men. As Judith Lorber pointed out in Section Two, gender also affects the way that social institutions—from the family to medicine to politics—are structured. Key to feminist analyses is an understanding of the role of a society's *institutions* in perpetuating gender inequality.

Like other forms of social inequality, *gender inequality* can be regarded as including the unequal distribution of rights to control three kinds of valued commodities. First, inequality entails differential access to power, defined as the ability to carry out one's will despite opposition. Second, differential access to the sources of prestige—defined as the ability to command respect, honor, and deference—constitutes part of structural inequalities. Third, differential access to wealth, or economic and material resources, is an aspect of inequality. Those who have access to any of these resources—power, wealth, or prestige—occupy a position from which they are likely to achieve access to the others and thereby reinforce their status over those who have less. In the case of gender-stratified social systems, men's greater access to wealth, power, and prestige enhances their opportunities to exploit women and decreases women's ability to resist.

Of course, not all men have equal access to wealth, power, or prestige. Men of subordinate racial or ethnic groups, working-class and poor men, and many gay or elderly men are also excluded from socially sanctioned sources of prestige, power, and wealth. Women, too, vary in their degree of access to power, prestige, and wealth; white or upper-class women receive benefits from their class and race even while they are penalized for their gender. Patricia Hill Collins suggests that we think of gender as one system of domination, which interacts with other systems of domination such as racism, class inequality, and heterosexism (Collins, 1990). The task of feminist scholars is to trace the intersections of gender with other systems of domination, examining the varied ways that gender inequality is expressed and reinforced in social institutions.

Institutions that express and enhance male dominance appear in a variety of forms. Economic and legal systems; political, educational, medical, religious, and familial institutions; public media; and the institutions of science and technology in male-dominated societies reinforce the ideology of women's inferiority and preserve men's greater access to power, wealth, and prestige. How? Fundamentally, the control of these institutions usually rests in the hands of men, and social scientists understand that dominant groups tend to behave in ways that enhance their own power. Beyond the individuals who wield power, the *structures* of institutions are gendered in that they privilege men and those traits labeled masculine and penalize women and the traits labeled feminine. Such institutions engage in practices that discriminate against women, exclude women's perspectives, and perpetuate the idea that male dominance is natural.

In addition, these institutions establish various kinds of rewards and punishments which encourage women to behave in submissive ways, and such behavior perpetuates the idea that women should submit. For example, as Adrienne Rich pointed out in Section Two, a complex social system in the United States exerts strong pressures on women to marry heterosexually: Families train daughters to be wives and mothers; high school events require opposite-sex dates; college fraternities and sororities promote heterosexual coupling; widespread violence against women encourages them, ironically, to seek male protection; and men's higher incomes mean that heterosexual marriage tends to improve a woman's standard of living. A woman's failure to marry constitutes a violation of social prescriptions and often leaves her economically disadvantaged and socially suspect. On the other hand, despite women's increasing participation in the paid labor force, heterosexual marriage still usually allows the burden of domestic labor to fall disproportionately on women, a dynamic that helps maintain the inequality between men and women in the work world.

It is important to reiterate that gender stratification is not the only form of inequality affecting women's lives and the structure of social institutions. Social institutions that disadvantage racial or ethnic groups, older people, the disabled, the poor, or particular religious or class-based groups also discriminate against both women and men who belong to those groups. Understanding women's oppression as a function of the social organization of gender necessitates understanding the convergence of sexism and other forms of subordination.

The following articles present examinations of how particular institutions express, construct, and maintain gender inequality. They analyze the ways that women's subordination is maintained in work, families, intimacy and sexuality, medical treatment of bodies, and violence against women. The articles do not simply document women's submission, however; they also examine the ways that women in various groups resist oppression and attempt to exercise control over their choices and their lives. To what extent are women able to resist, and to what extent are they controlled by gendered social institutions?

REFERENCE

Collins, Patricia Hill. 1990. *Black Feminist Thought.* New York: Routledge.

SECTION FIVE

Work

"Work for pay" influences many aspects of our lives: our economic prosperity, our social status, our relationships with family members and friends, our health, and even our access to health care. Our work experiences influence how we come to view others, ourselves, and the social world around us. Reciprocally, how we are situated in society often influences the kinds of work we do and our compensation for that work. In traditional societies, division of labor based on sex and age did not necessarily correspond to differences in the importance assigned to different tasks: "women's work" might be considered just as socially valuable as "men's work." In societies like ours, however, social divisions of labor based on gender, race, and age reflect and perpetuate power differences among groups.

This section begins with Alice Kessler-Harris's examination of the historical justifications of pay inequities between women and men. In "The Wage Conceived: Value and Need as Measures of a Woman's Worth," we begin to understand the ideological bases of the differential economic rewards available to men and women, and the implications of both gender ideologies and economic practices for women's participation in society.

Inequities between women and men in earnings often exist because the genders are concentrated in different occupations. Those jobs performed by women are valued less, primarily because they draw on traditionally feminine skills which are seen as innate abilities rather than acquired skills. Barbara F. Reskin's article, "Bringing the Men Back In: Sex Differentiation and the Devaluation of Women's Work," examines the political nature of sex segregation in the labor force. Reskin argues that two commonly posed solutions to the persistent problem of sex segregation—comparable worth and integrating women into traditionally male occupations—will not succeed because the men who retain a vested interest in maintaining male power ultimately define the terms of such reform efforts.

The remaining articles in this section offer focused examinations of the work experiences of particular groups of women. Beverly W. Jones traces the interplay of race, class, and gender in "Race, Sex, and Class: Female Tobacco Workers in Durham, North Carolina, 1920–1940, and the Development of Female Consciousness." Jones describes a tobacco company's relegation of black women to unhealthy working conditions because of race, and to the lowest-paying jobs because of sex. In response to their oppression, black women tobacco workers developed a class identity, and from it emerged a sisterhood of struggle, support, dignity, and resistance.

Robin Leidner examines the construction of gender identity in two common contemporary occupations: fast food service, a job performed primarily by women, and insurance sales, a job performed primarily by men. Leidner shows how workers and managers in both jobs interpreted the skills and tasks required as best suited for either women (in the case of fast food) or men (in insurance sales). Workers, Leidner suggests, are not just doing their jobs. They are also constructing and reaffirming cultural definitions of gender and their own gender identities.

In "Boundary Lines: Labeling Sexual Harassment in Restaurants," Patti Giuffre and Christine Williams discuss how waiters and waitresses interpret sexual interactions at work. Sexual banter and joking, they suggest, is common and workers do not always define it as harassment. Workers are most likely to see sexual interaction as harassment when it occurs across the lines of race or sexual orientation—especially when men of color harass white women or when gay men harass heterosexual men. Giuffre and Williams call attention to the ways that race and sexual orientation, as well as gender, are important in individuals' inter-pretations of sexual harassment. By doing so, they also illustrate how women come to define certain types of sexual behavior on the job as acceptable or inevitable.

As these articles demonstrate, women's ethnici-ties, ages, and class backgrounds affect both the structural opportunities available to them in the labor force and their interpretations of these expe-riences. What experiences, if any, do working women *share* by virtue of their gender?

R E A D I N G 2 2

The Wage Conceived:
Value and Need as Measures of a Woman's Worth

ALICE KESSLER-HARRIS

When a person complains that a certain wage rate is unduly low, he may be making that judgment in the light of what he thinks is due the kind of person *performing that work, e.g. a married man. Others may regard the same rate as not unreasonable in view of the kind of* work *it is.*

— *Henry A. Landsberger*[1]

In 1915 New York State's Factory Investigating Commission asked some seventy-five prominent individuals—economists, social reformers, businessmen, and publicists among them—what factors determined the rate of wages. The answers varied. Some suggested that workers' organizations were most important; others believed the size of a business's profits could enhance or restrain the wages of employees. Another key factor was the standard of living anticipated by workers. But the majority of those interviewed believed the efficiency of the worker and the supply of labor constituted by far the two most powerful determinants of wages.[2] These traditional explanations for wage rates would have found favor with the proponents of the economic theory then popular.

Widely accepted wage theory at the turn of the century was rooted in, though not limited to, the law of supply and demand. If that phrase, as economic historian Arnold Tolles implies, does not do economists justice, it does, at least, convey the economists' belief "that the reward for every kind of human effort is controlled by some kind of impersonal and irresistible force, similar to the force of gravity."[3]

Theory held that wages would rise or fall in response to employers' fluctuating willingness to pay. That willingness in turn was predicated on what employers thought they could earn from labor as well as on how much labor was available at different wage rates. Thus, in theory, the demand for labor (measured by the additional revenue labor could produce) and the supply (which took into account the differences in education and training of the worker) together determined the wage.[4]

Despite the apparent certainty of economists such as Professor Roy Blakely of Cornell who testified before the commission that "wages tend to approximate the value of what they produce,"[5] the theory left room for a substantial degree of subjective judgment on the part of employers as to the value of particular workers. A critical part of the chemical mix that determined the wages of workers in general involved something intangible called "custom." If a male worker was paid according to some formula that reflected the value of what he produced and the difficulty of replacing him, he was also paid according to what he and other workers thought he was worth. Custom, or tradition, played an acknowledged but uncalculated role in regulating the wage. But custom and tradition were gendered. They influenced male and female wages in different ways. And especially in the female wage, they played a far larger role than we have earlier been willing to concede. The women's wage, at least for the early twentieth century, rested in large measure on conceptions of what women needed.

The distinction alerts us to the rich possibilities contained in the wage conceived as a social rather than as a theoretical construct. If the wage is, as most economists readily acknowledge, simultaneously a set of ideas about how people can and should live and a marker of social status, then it contains within it a set of social messages and a system of meanings that influence the way women and men behave. We are all familiar with the capacity of these social meanings to reduce the wages of recent immigrants, of African-Americans, and of other groups. But, partly because it is so apparently natural, the capacity of the wage to speak to issues of gender is less clear. Yet the language with which the women's wage is conceived throws into relief the same process that exists for men. The wage frames gendered messages; it encourages or inhibits certain forms of behavior; it can reveal a system of meaning that shapes the expectations of men and women and anticipates their struggles over power; it participates in the negotiations that influence the relationships of the sexes inside and outside the family. In all these capacities, the wage functions as a terrain of contest over visions of fairness and justice. This essay will attempt to illustrate some of these processes in the early twentieth century.

The structure of wages that emerged in the course of industrialization in the late nineteenth century reflected a long tradition that revolved around what has become known as the family wage—the sum necessary to sustain family members. That sum had been earned by several family members for most of the history of capitalism. Family income was typically pooled and then redistributed by one family member. But the dream of a family wage that could be earned by a male breadwinner alone had long been an object of struggle among organized working people who thought of it as a mechanism for regulating family life and allowing women to work in their own homes.[6] Ideally, and sometimes in practice, the family wage was a male wage, a wage that went to a male breadwinner.[7]

What then of a woman's wage? It reflected not what was but what ought to be. That men ought to be able to support wives and daughters implied that women need not engage in such support. They ought to be performing home duties. Thus, if a woman earned wages, the normal expectation was that she did so to supplement those of other family wage earners. Theoretically, at least, the decision as to who would and would not earn was regulated by the family unit. The wage belonged to her family. Until the third quarter of the nineteenth century, U.S. law and practice reflected these assumptions. Typically, a woman's wage was legally the property of her husband or father. The average wage of women workers was little more than half of the male wage. And even the most skilled women rarely earned as much as two-thirds of the average paid to unskilled men. If a woman lived independently, her wage was normally not sufficient to support her. Nor was it intended to do so.

The nineteenth century fight for a family wage was thus simultaneously a fight for a social order in which men

could support their families and receive the services of women; and women, dependent on men, could stay out of the labor force. Historians have debated the advantages and disadvantages of this mode of thinking, but for our purposes it is important to note only that the family wage reflected popular thinking—a sense of what was right and just.[8] Widely supported by working class men and women at the end of the nineteenth century, it rested on what seemed to many to be a desirable view of social order.

Its incarnation in the form of the living wage more clearly isolated the female role. Though the content of a living wage varied, like the family wage, it was imbued with gendered expectations. John Ryan, the Catholic priest who was the United States' most prolific exponent of the living wage, for example, asserted the laborer's right to a "decent and reasonable" life that meant to him "the right to exercise one's primary faculties, supply one's essential needs, and develop one's personality."[9] Others were somewhat more specific. British economist William Smart thought the living wage ought to pay for "a well-drained dwelling, with several rooms, warm clothing with some changes of under-clothing, pure water, a plentiful supply of cereal food with a moderate allowance of meat and milk and a little tea, etc., some education, and some recreation, and lastly sufficient freedom for his wife from other work to enable her to perform properly her maternal and her household duties."[10] John Mitchell, head of the United Mine Workers union, was somewhat more ambitious. The wage, he thought, ought to be enough to purchase "the American standard of living." This included, but was not limited to, "a comfortable house of at least six rooms," which contained a bathroom, good sanitary plumbing, parlor, dining room, kitchen, sleeping rooms, carpets, pictures, books, and furniture.[11]

For Ryan, as for other proponents of the living wage, the "love and companionship of a person of the opposite sex"[12] was an essential element of what a living wage should purchase. The bottom line, according to Ryan, was the laborer's capacity "to live in a manner consistent with the dignity of a human being."[13] The *Shoe Workers' Journal* proposed that "everything necessary to the life of *a normal man* be included in the living wage: the right to marriage, the right to have children and to educate them."[14]

As the family wage held the promise of female home-making, the living wage, which explicitly incorporated wife and children, excluded the possibility that female dignity could inhere either in a woman's ability to earn wages or in her capacity to support a family. Because the living wage idealized a world in which men had the privilege of caring for women and children, it implicitly refused women that privilege. And, because it assumed female dependency, to imagine female independence impugned male roles and male egos. Ground rules for female wage earners required only self-support, and even that was estimated at the most minimal level. Champions of the living wage for women counted among her necessities food, clothing, rent, health, savings, and a small miscellaneous fund.[15] Nothing in the arguments for a female living wage vitiates the harsh dictum of John Stuart Mill. The wages of single women, asserted that famous economist, "must be equal to their support, but need not be more than equal to it; the minimum in their case is the pittance absolutely required for the sustenance of one human being."[16] "Women who are forced to provide their own sustenance have a right," echoed Ryan, "to what is a living wage *for them*." Their compensation, he argued, with apparent generosity, "should be sufficient to enable them to live decently."[17]

At the time Ryan wrote, women constituted close to 25 percent of the industrial work force. More than one-third of wage-earning women in urban areas lived independently of their families, and three-quarters of those living at home helped to support other family members. False conceptions of women who needed only to support themselves did a particular disservice to Black women, who were eight times as likely to earn wages as white women. For Black women racial discrimination and its attendant poverty meant that more that one-third of those who were married would continue to earn wages, and virtually all of those who earned wages participated in family support.[18] Yet the real needs of these women were rarely acknowledged. Nor did the brief, dismissive commentary on "a woman's living wage" mention recreation or comfort or human dignity or the capacity to care for others.

Ryan readily conceded that men without families to support and/or with other means of support were entitled to draw a living wage because "they perform as much labor as their less fortunate fellows."[19] His proposals generously allocated a living wage to men who never intended to marry because "rights are to be interpreted according to the average conditions of human life."[20] But the same generosity was not evident in notions of the living wage for women workers. Rather, it seemed fair to reduce women to the lowest levels of bestiality. Advocates of the living wage confidently explained that women's "standard of physical comfort, in other words, their standard of life" was lower than that of men." While her ideals were "naturally higher than those of men," her physical wants are simpler. The living wage for a woman is lower than the living wage for a man because it is possible for her as a result of her tradi-

tional drudgery and forced tolerance of pain and suffering to keep alive upon less."[21] Women, with a single set of exceptions, were to be paid only according to their most minimal needs. Only to women who were employed in the same jobs as men did Ryan concede the need for equal pay because, he argued, "when women receive less pay than men, the latter are gradually driven out of the occupation."[22]

Ryan failed to acknowledge that in attributing to women "average conditions" that reflected social myth rather than reality he undermined his own cause. While his vision and that of most living wage advocates came from a desire to protect the home, not from antagonism to the pitiable condition of those women who worked for wages, his proposals left the home vulnerable. "The welfare of the whole family," he noted, "and that of society likewise, renders it imperative that the wife and mother should not engage in any labor except that of the household. When she works for hire, she can neither care properly for her own health, rear her children aright, nor make her home what it should be for her husband, her children, herself."[23] Theoretically, that might have been true; but in practice, by reducing women's potential capacity to earn adequate incomes, he diminished their ability to support themselves and their homes.

Without negating the good intentions of Ryan and others on behalf of the family and without imposing anachronistic judgments about their desire to protect the family and to place family needs ahead of women's individual rights, one can still see that the consequences of their rhetoric for women who earned wages were no mere abstractions. They assumed a hard and concrete reality, for example, in discussions of the minimum wage for women that took place between about 1911 and 1913. To alleviate the plight of women workers, social reformers attempted to pass legislation that would force employers to pay a wage sufficient to meet a woman's minimal needs. Between 1912 and 1923, thirteen states and the District of Columbia passed such legislation in one form or another. Each statute was preceded by a preamble that declared the legislators' intentions to offer protection that ranged from providing a sum "adequate for maintenance" to ensuring enough to "maintain the worker in health" and guaranteeing her "moral well-being." Whatever the language of the preamble, and whatever the mechanism by which the wage was ultimately to be decided, the minimum was invariably rooted in what was determined to be a "living" wage for women workers.[24] But the discussion required some estimate of what a living wage might be. Elizabeth Beardsley Butler who surveyed working women in Pittsburgh in 1907 suggested that a woman could "not live decently and be self supporting" at a wage of less than $7 a week. Three years later Louise Bosworth estimated the living wage of Boston's women ranged from $9 to $11 a week—the first amount would keep a woman from dying of cold or hunger; the second provided the possibility of efficiency at work and some minimal recreation.[25] The question, said social pundit Thomas Russell, was whether "it is to be an amount that shall provide only the bare necessaries of life or shall it include some provision for comforts, recreation and the future?"[26]

The budgets drawn up by experts generally opted only for the necessities. Arrived at after extensive surveys to uncover the actual expenditures of "working girls," and heavily reliant on language and imagery that reduced women to perpetual girlhood, they included almost nothing beyond the barest sustenance.[27] A typical survey was undertaken by Sue Ainslee Clark in 1908 and published by Clark and Edith Wyatt in the pages of *McClure's* magazine in 1910.[28] The authors focused on the effortful struggle to make ends meet, turning survival itself into a praiseworthy feat. They exuded sympathy for the girl who "ate no breakfast," whose "luncheon consisted of coffee and rolls for ten cents," and who, as "she had no convenient place for doing her own laundry, . . . paid 21 cents a week to have it done. Her regular weekly expenditure was as follows: lodging, 42 cents; board, $1.40; washing, 21 cents; clothing and all other expenses, $1.97: total, $4."[29] Such estimates encouraged social investigators to define precisely how much a female wage earner might spend for everything from undergarments to gifts.

The debate over the minimum wage revealed what this outward order dictated: to live alone required the strictest exercise of thrift, self-discipline, and restraint. The budgets warned fiercely against expectations of joy, spontaneity, pleasure, or recreation. Even the carfare that might provide access to a walk in the country was rigidly restricted. The wage prescribed a spartan life-style, sufficient, it was hoped, to preserve morality for those destined to earn but not so generous as to tempt those in families to live outside them. It limited fantasy to the price of survival and held open the door of ambition only to a meagre independence. Its effects are grimly reflected in a series of snippets selected by and published in *Harper's Bazar* in 1908 under the title "The Girl Who Comes to the City."[30]

Offering to pay $5 for each one it used, the magazine solicited brief essays "written by those girl readers who have gone through the experience of coming to the city, and either succeeding or failing there during the last ten years."[31] Success, in these pieces, is measured in small and treasured doses. Mere survival emerges as a potent source of satisfaction. In a period when most experts estimated a living wage at around $9 a week, a pay envelope that amounted to $10 a week could yield happiness. A $2 a week raise, accompanied by a kind boss, and perhaps the chance to improve oneself by reading occasionally at work seemed to be the height of ambition.[32] At the top of the wage scale, a bookkeeper could aspire to $65 a month, enough to ensure a small cash balance in the bank if one limited social excursions to one night a week and carefully selected clothes from among sale items.[33] The stories reveal justified pride and accomplishment in the ability to sustain oneself. But they also tell us something of the limits imposed on women's aspirations. "I had," boasted one contributor about the period before she returned home, "made both ends meet financially for five months and I had saved a modest sum for the purchase of a winter suit."[34] Even women who needed help in the form of occasional contributions of clothing felt they had managed very nicely.

And yet, in practice, survival was the best, not the worst, that the wage embodied. The estimates made by well-intentioned reformers and the efforts of the most well-meaning women were compromised by the refusal of most employers to concede a woman's need even to support herself. Evidence for this is part of the folklore of the female labor market before World War II and has frequently been recorded by historians.[35] The *Harper's Bazar* series is no exception. There, as elsewhere, women recalled how difficult it was to ask for reasonable compensation. A stenographer described how a lawyer had refused to pay more because "he expected young women had friends who helped them out." A budding news reporter was told by a potential employer that his "rule is never to employ a woman who must depend entirely upon my salaries."[36]

The aspirations of young women thus fell victim to the self-confirming myths that enforced their dependence. Nineteenth century British economist William Smart described the process succinctly. Part of the reason a woman's wage is low, he suggested, was "because she does not require a high wage, whether it be because her father partly supports her, or because her maintenance does not cost so much."[37] Employers routinely acted upon this myth. "We try to employ girls who are members of families," a box manufacturer told social investigator and economist Elizabeth Butler, "for we don't pay the girls a living wage in this trade."[38] Historian Joanne Meyerowitz summed up the prevailing attitude this way: "Employers assumed that all working women lived in families where working males provided them with partial support. It profited employers to use this idealized version of the family economy to determine women's wages."[39]

For all the elaborate theory justifying low wages, the bottom line turned out almost always to be the employer's sense of what was acceptable. Men, as Elizabeth Butler noted, came into occupations at a wage paid for the job. Women came into them at a wage deemed appropriate for female workers—not, that is to say, at the customary wage level of the occupation but "at a level analogous to that paid women generally in other occupations."[40] New York City social worker Mary Alden Hopkins told the Factory Investigating Commission that the sex of the employee was one of the most important influences on women's wages. "In laundry work, factory work, some mercantile establishments and home work, efficiency has little and often no effect upon wages," she declared.[41] The hardest woman's job, in her judgment, was the lowest paid, and an increase in worker productivity and employer profits led less often to rewarding workers than to discharging high-paid workers in favor of those who could be paid for less. The young Scott Nearing summarized the process this way: "Noone even pretends that there is a definite relation between the values produced by the workers and the wage which he secures."[42] Samuel Gompers would have agreed: "Everyone knows that there is little connection between the value of services and wages paid; the employer pays no more than he must."[43]

While from the economist's perspective this may be a gross oversimplification, employers, workers, and observers all accepted the critical importance of custom in the wage structure. A vice-president of the Pullman Company, speaking before the commission that investigated the great strike of 1894, acknowledged as much. Piece rates, he said, were based on the company's estimates of a "reasonable wage for ten hours . . . for a competent workman." If the company discovered "that at the piece price fixed the known less competent and less industrious workmen are regularly making an unreasonable day's wage, it becomes apparent that the piece price allotted is too large."[44] At issue here was what was "reasonable" and "unreasonable," not the productivity or efficiency of the worker. In this context, that part of the content of custom should rest on the sex of the worker appears to be merely natural. An official of International Harvester, testifying before an Illinois investigating commission in 1912, described his company's efforts to set a minimum wage for female employees. His company's desire, he claimed, "was to establish a minimum that would be fair and reasonable." But the constraints of

what was deemed reasonable were established as much by the nature and characteristics of the worker as by the company's financial spread sheets. "The girls affected by lower wages," he said in mitigation, "are mostly of foreign birth. They are not required to dress up for their employment. Many of those to whom we will pay $8 could not earn a dollar downtown."[45] Presumably, the same kind of reasoning led to paying Black women less than white women. Although occupational segregation accounts for most of the wage differential between Black and white women, Black women who worked on the same kinds of jobs routinely received one dollar a week less.

Nor was the weight of custom in setting wages a hidden dimension. Rather, the comments of employers and others reveal it to have been quite conscious and available. Several respondents to the Factory Investigating Commission's survey noted its influence in setting wage rates, pointing out that wages could not be set without reference to such factors as the "needs of the individual and family," the influence of "local or trade union conditions," and the differential requirements of "pin-money workers." Edward Page, an officer of the Merchants' Association of New York, thought that the "customary or habitual rate of wages which prevails in the group to which the workingman belongs and which is usual in the industry under consideration . . . is by far the most important factor in the determination of wages."[46] On their face these factors were gender neutral. But since each embodied deeply rooted aspects of gendered expectations, the wage both reflected and perpetuated gendered behavior.

If the role of custom in fixing wages is not surprising, and we can take for granted that sex played a part, then we need ask only to what degree the sex of the worker influenced custom. When it came to women, one might argue that custom played not the smallest but the largest part in determining the wage. William Smart placed the factors that determined the wages of women in the category of "wants." The wage scale in a modern industrial economy, he suggested, was typically determined by "what a worker does." But for a woman "what the worker is" was the gauge of wages. The difference made him uneasy. "If a male worker," he asked, "is supposed to get a high wage when he produces much, a low wage when he produces little, why should a woman's wage be determined by another principle? We cannot hunt with the individualist hounds and run with the socialist hare."[47]

Yet women's wages at the turn of the century clung stubbornly to what Smart would have called her "wants" rather than to either the value of the product or the level of the worker's productivity. For if custom was inscribed into the wage and the wage was conceived male, what women earned was not in the same sense as males a "wage." In the minds of employers and of male workers, the wage was to be paid to those who supported families.[48] If part of its function was to reflect the value of the product made, another and equally important part was to make a statement about the value of the worker who made the product. As long as female workers were not—could not be—male workers, their wages could not hope to touch those of their male peers.

We can guess that employers thought of it that way by their responses to questions about how much they paid women. Louise Bosworth cited the case of a woman who told her employer, "We cannot live on what we earn," and was asked in response, "Then what wages can you live on?"[49] The same paternalistic assumptions appear among employers who testified before the commission that investigated Illinois's white slave traffic in 1912. The employers interviewed reported unhesitatingly that they paid their male and female workers on the basis of what they estimated each needed. Julius Rosenwald, head of Sears, Roebuck and Company, then a mail-order house, told an investigative commission that "the concern made it a point not to hire girls not living at home at less than $8 a week."[50] A Montgomery Ward vice-president echoed the sentiment: "We claim that all our employees without homes are on a self-supporting basis, and if we discover they are not we will put them there in an hour."[51] One department store executive described how his store asked all job applicants to sign a form "giving their estimate of necessary expenses in addition to family particulars. The girls who are not receiving sufficient to live on come to us. There are many instances of such receiving an increase." No one ever investigated the accuracy of the application forms, and even the commission chair was dubious as to who the procedure protected. A girl might readily lie about home support, he noted, "to assure herself of a job."[52] But at bottom, this was less the issue than the prevailing assumption that "girls" could and should be paid at a minimum that relied on family subsidy rather than on what their labor was worth.

If employers and popular opinion are any guide, and the question of what appeared to be reasonable lay at the heart of the wage structure, then all wages—not only those of women—contained a greater proportion of wants than most of us have recognized. Women's wages, then, are only uniquely vulnerable in the sense that they participate in

popular definitions of gender that denigrate the needs of one sex. The wage simultaneously framed job-related expectation in the light of existing gender roles and shaped gender experiences to avoid disappointment in view of the prevailing wage structure. More than exploitation of women, or paternalism towards them, the wage reflected a rather severe set of injunctions about how men and women were to live. These injunctions could be widely negated only at the peril of social order. Thus, part of the function of the female wage was to ensure attachment to family. The male wage, in contrast, provided incentives to individual achievement. It promoted geographical mobility and sometimes hinted at the possibility of social mobility as well. The female wage allowed women to survive; the male wage suggested a contribution to national economic well-being. These messages affirmed existing values and integrated all the parties into a set of understandings that located the relationships of working men and women to each other.

Some of these messages are powerful. Existing wage fund theory posited a limited sum available for all wages. It reduced the incentive to provide a higher wage for women by suggesting that their gain would come at the cost of male raises and therefore threaten the family's well-being. Smart put it this way: "Women's wages are, after all, part and parcel of the one share in the distribution of income which falls to labor."[53] What followed from that, of course, was that raising women's wages would merely reduce those of the men in their class by a similar proportion, leaving families in the same place economically and depriving them of maternal care to boot. Samuel Gompers translated this into a warning to members of the American Federation of Labor: "In industries where the wives and children toil, the man is often idle because he has been supplanted, or because the aggregate wages of the family are no higher than the wages of the adult man—the husband and father of the family."[54]

If women's wage gains could come only at the cost of the family, then their low wages affirmed and supported existing family life. As the renowned economist Alfred Marshall put it, a higher wage for women might be "a great gain in so far as it tends to develop their faculties, but an injury in so far as it tempts them to neglect their duty of building up a true home, and of investing their efforts in the personal capital of their children's character and abilities."[55] To Marshall the clear social choice implicit in the wage payment was between individual achievement and family well-being. His statement affirms the use of wages to preserve what is desirable to him: that all women are or will be married, that marriage is a normal state, that women will be continuously supported by men with sufficient wages, and that under these circumstances a wage that might be translated into an incentive not to marry or remain within families poses a challenge. Moreover, Marshall's view reflected the prevailing belief that a man was entitled to a wife to serve him and their home. It contained the assumption that a female who did not have a husband had erred. The differential female wage thus carried a moral injunction, a warning to women to follow the natural order.

The absence, by choice or necessity, of a family of her own did not excuse a woman from adherence to familial duties or morals, nor did it impel a more generous attitude toward wages. In fact, the level of the wage, which signaled an affirmation of family life, simultaneously threw out a challenge to preserve morality. In a March 1913 letter to the *New York Herald,* the head of Illinois's vice commission commented that "our investigations . . . show conclusively that thousands of good girls are going wrong every year merely because they can not live upon the wages paid them by employers."[56] But this was not necessarily an invitation to raise wages. Since not to live within a family was itself immoral, and the wage was seen as primarily a contribution to family life, a higher wage would only contribute to immorality. An ongoing debate over the fine line between a wage high enough to tempt women into supporting themselves and one so low that it could push the unwary into prostitution placed the wage in thrall to morality. Social worker Jeannette Gilder found herself in the awkward position of testifying against a pay raise for working women because "it seems to me to be paying a pretty poor compliment to the young women of this country to suggest that their virtue hangs upon such a slender thread that its price can be fixed somewhere between $6 and $8 a week."[57] And yet those who insisted that a low wage was an invitation to prostitution dominated the debate.

The wage also transmitted messages about the work force. Employers feared that a rise in women's wages would trigger a demand for higher wages for men. As the wage captured social restrictions on female aspirations at work, so it conveyed the male potential for advancement, promotion, loyalty, and persistence. Contemporaries understood this well. When Elizabeth Butler remarked that "boys are often preferred to girls . . . because they can be relied on to learn the trade and women cannot,"[58] she captured the notion that implicit in the wage is the assumption that a man's wage is an investment in the future, while a woman's wage assumes only that the work at hand will be done. Economist Francis Walker said this in a different way. If a man marries, he "becomes a better and more notable workman on that account." In contrast, if a woman marries, "it is most probable that she will . . . be a less desirable laborer than she was before."[59] Yet these statements promote the self-fulfilling function they simultaneously reflect. Lacking a man's wage, women were not normally given the opportunity to demonstrate that they too could be an investment in the future. Such experiments would be dangerous. Not only would a higher wage for women convey an inaccurate estimate of the potential occupational mobility of females, but it might inhibit the employer's capacity to use wages to construct the work force to his liking.

Finally, the wage made a familiar statement about female personality. Holding the stereotypical male as the norm, it claimed recompense for the costs of translating female qualities into the marketplace. Francis Walker exaggerated but caught the point when he insisted that the wage reflected women's character traits as well as their domestic orientation. It took account, he noted, of personalities that were "intensely sensitive to opinion, [and] shrink from the familiar utterances of blame." Coldness and indifference alone, he thought, were often sufficient to repress women's "impulses to activity."[60] These qualities of character exacted supervisory costs of the employer that were recaptured in the lower pay of women. As Charles Cheney, a South Manchester, Connecticut, manufacturer, put it, part of the reason women were paid less than men was because "they are sensitive and require extraordinarily tactful and kindly treatment and much personal consideration."[61]

Restrictive as the messages thrown out by a woman's wage were clearly intended to be, they were by no means the only messages that reached women. The very existence of a wage, the possibility of earning income evoked a contrary set of images: images that derived some support from the promise of American success. The same wage that evoked a struggle to survive and placed a lid on social mobility, the same wage that obscured women's visions of independence and citizenship had the capacity to conjure contrary images as well. It could even point the way to potential equality for women. These tensions are visible in the huge strikes that wracked the garment industry beginning in 1909–10, in the energy of young female labor leaders, and in the quest of more affluent women for lives that combined career and motherhood. Such events indicate that the notion of wages rooted in wants existed in a contested sphere—tempered by a broader ideology of individualism. They lead us to wonder about the role played by a woman's wage in a period of changing wants and rising levels of personal ambition.

The wage that in some measure helped to affirm and construct gendered expectations in the period before World
War I continued to play that role afterward. But the dramatic social changes that came during and after the war,
particularly the rise of a consumer culture, created their
own pressures on the structure of gender. Because for most
people the wage offered access to consumption, it mediated
some of the tensions in gender roles that emerged in the
1920s. While public perception of a woman's wage
remained conceptually "needs-based," continuing to limit
female expectations, it quickly became clear that changing
needs demanded some concessions to women's individual
aspirations. These mixed messages contributed to arguments among women about who deserved a wage.[62]

In the statistical tables, the war appears as a small blip
in the history of working women. New entrants into the
labor force were relatively few, and the teens ended with
little apparent increase in the numbers of women who
earned wages. But the big surprise lay in the numbers of
women who switched jobs. About half a million women, it
seemed, chose to move into men's jobs. The *New York
Times* commented on these figures with surprise: "The
world of men woke up and took a second look at the world
of women during the World War. It is still looking." And, it
continued, "the Great War has in many cases been responsible for a change of premise as well as job."[63]

The primary explanation for these job shifts seems to
have been the attraction of the male wage. Historian
Maurine Greenwald estimates, for example, that women
who became streetcar conductors immediately increased
their wages by about one-third over those they had earned
in traditional female jobs.[64] Daniel Nelson, who has
explored the transformation of the factory, notes that after
1915 "the wages offered by machinery and munitions makers" drew an increasing number of women who had worked
in traditional women's fields.[65] Though women's productivity was frequently acknowledged to be as high as that of the
men they replaced, women were not, on principle, offered
the same wage. A twenty-six city survey by the New York
State Industrial Commission at the end of the war revealed
that less than 10 percent of the women who replaced men
received pay equal to that of the men who had preceded
them. The commission reported that "in many cases the
production of women was equal to that of men, in others it
was greater, and in still others, less. The wages paid had little, if anything, to do with productive efficiency."[66] Since
women who were paid less than men still earned far more
than they could have at women's jobs, few of those who
benefited from wartime opportunities complained. But the

pressure of a dual wage structure on male wages posed a
problem. Fearing a breakdown of social order, men and
women began to call for a wage paid for the job—or equal
pay. This slogan, as we will see later, was designed primarily to reduce pressure on men's wages.

Though most of the wartime job shifts proved to be temporary, they signaled an incipient dissatisfaction among
some wage-earning women over the issue of wages—a dissatisfaction that could no longer be contained by rationalizations over social role. These struggles frequently pitted
women who earned wages against those who did not, revealing something about contested definitions of womanhood
among white women. For example, when female streetcar
conductors in several large cities waged largely futile battles
to hang on to their high-paying jobs, they were fighting not
only the men who wanted their jobs back but a conception of
womanliness that restricted access to outdoor work. And the
female printers in New York State who successfully struggled to exempt themselves from legislation that precluded
their working during the lucrative night hours simultaneously attacked rigid conceptions of family life.

Such campaigns were opposed by clear signals from
government and corporations to women not to expect too
much. The Women's Bureau of the Department of Labor
offers a case in point. In 1920, when the bureau was created, it received a meagre $75,000 lump-sum appropriation
and distributed it as effectively as it could. In 1922 a House
proviso "stipulated that no salary in the Women's Bureau
should be more than $1800, except three at $2000, and the
director's and assistant director's salaries which have been
fixed by statute." If effected, the proviso, as the Women's
Bureau pointed out, would have left it with "no staff of
technically trained, experienced people to direct and super-
vise its work." But more important, the bureau noted that
other agencies of the government paid their male employees with the same qualifications "very much higher salaries
than any that have even been suggested by the Women's
Bureau—twice as much in many instances."[67]

Such policies were routine in industry. In the electrical
industry of the 1920s, Ronald Schatz reports that "corporations maintained separate pay scales for men and women.
Male wage keysheets began where female keysheets left
off; the least skilled male workers earned more than the
most capable female employee."[68] Still, the point for
women was that even this low pay exceeded that of such
traditionally female jobs as laundry work and waiting on
tables. "For this reason, many young women preferred jobs
in electrical factories." When the Ford Motor Company
instituted a $5 day for its male employees after the war, it

deliberately omitted women workers. According to Vice-President James Couzens, women "are not considered such economic factors as men."[69]

Corporations carefully distinguished between the kinds of social welfare programs offered as extensions of cash wages to women and men. General Electric and Westinghouse offered men programs that stressed financial and job security such as a 5 percent bonus every six months after five years of service; a pension after twenty years, and group life insurance and paid vacations after ten years of service. Women, for whom longevity was not encouraged and for whom it was thought not to matter, got programs that emphasized sociability such as "dances, cooking classes, secretarial instruction, picnics, clubs, and summer camps."[70]

The not-so-subtle relationship between policy and practice is beautifully illustrated in the self-confirming apparatus in effect at the General Electric company where President Gerard Swope defended his policies on the grounds that "our theory was that women did not recognize the responsibilities of life and were hoping to get married soon and would leave us, and therefore, this insurance premium deduction from the pay would not appeal to them."[71] As historian Ronald Schatz notes, because GE compelled women to quit if they married, women rarely acquired enough seniority to obtain pensions or vacations with pay. Women's aspirations could not be entirely stilled by these measures. The Ford Motor Company, according to historian Stephen Meyer III, "considered all women, regardless of their family stakes, as youths: that is as single men under twenty-two without dependents, and therefore ineligible for Ford profits." Yet "as the result of criticism from women's rights advocates, the company eventually allowed some women, who were the heads of households, to participate in its welfare plan."[72]

One result of such policies and an instrument in their perpetuation as well was that women carefully rationalized their increasing work force participation and defended themselves by comparing their wages only to those of other women. The model was familiar. The numerous investigating commissions of the prewar period had already asserted the injustice of paying women as much as men. Thus, investigators exploring the feasibility of a higher wage for women raised such issues as what, for instance, a firm would "have to pay a man with a family if it paid $2 a day to girls with no one but themselves to support?"[73] This does not seem to have inhibited women's desire for higher incomes. But it seems to have channeled their grievances away from men who earned far more than they and toward

women instead. Among Western Electric workers interviewed in the late 1920s, a typical female who complained about wages tended to be distressed not at her absolute wage but at how it compared with those of other women. As one female employee complained, "the girl next to me, her job pays $39.80 per hundred, and mine pays $28.80 and I work just as hard as she does. I don't see how they figure that out. She makes ten cents more on every one she makes."[74]

These powerful and sometimes explicit barriers extended across race lines and to the social wages offered by modern corporations. In their presence Black women were paid less than white women for the same or similar jobs. Employers utilized them to sanction distinctions in the amenities they offered to Black and white women. An early survey of the tobacco industry in Virginia reflects the value of such circumscribed comparisons. "Tuesday and Friday," the report noted matter of factly, "the white girls have 15 minutes extra in order to dance, but the 15 minutes is paid for by the firm."[75]

What kept the "wage" pot bubbling, then, was not women's desire to achieve male pay but their urge to satisfy more concrete wants. As mass production jobs and clerical work opened up to white women, some factory jobs became available to Black women. New, relatively well-paying jobs and rising real wages for both men and women contributed to the advent of the consumer society and helped to create a new definition of wants that drew on a prevailing individualism from which women could hardly be excluded. Marketing techniques, installment buying, and the increasing value placed on consumption replaced thrift and postponed gratification as appropriate spirits of the time. New definitions of wants attracted new groups of women to the work force and suggested new rationales for staying there.

The changing population of female workers challenged perceptions of a wage that spoke to simpler needs. To women for whom the prewar women's wage had offered little apart from the despair of poverty, the wage now stretched to encompass the hope of individual achievement measured by material goals. Defined in prewar practice as the minimum required to sustain a single woman partially supported by her family, the postwar wage at least suggested the capacity to earn a living.[76] Ronald Edsforth, who studied auto workers in the 1920s, notes that government investigators discovered among the women working in auto factories in the 1920s a "genuinely modern level of individual materialism . . . guiding . . . life-shaping decisions." They concluded that "jobs in the auto factories were most

NOTES

1. Henry A. Landsberger, *Hawthorne Revisited: Management and the Worker, Its Critics, and the Developments in Human Relations in Industry* (Ithaca, N.Y.: Cornell University, 1958), 19.

2. New York State, *Factory Investigating Commission,* Fourth Report (Albany: S.B. Lyon Co., 1915), vol. 1, app. 3, passim. (Hereinafter referred to as FIC.)

3. N. Arnold Tolles, *Origins of Modern Wage Theories* (Englewood Cliffs, N.J.: Prentice-Hall, 1964), 8.

4. This theory, known as marginal productivity theory, was predicated on the assumption of perfect competition and emphasized the demands of employers in calculating the wage. Its classic exposition is John Bates Clark, *The Distribution of Wealth* (New York: Macmillan, 1899).

5. FIC, Fourth Report, vol. 4, 435.

6. In the United States, organized workers agitated for the idea beginning in the 1830s.

7. Melton McLaurin, *Paternalism and Protest: Southern Cotton Mill Workers and Organized Labor, 1875–1905* (Westport, Conn.: Greenwood Press, 1971), 23, describes how the notion of a family wage that rested on the labor of all family members could contribute to expectations of female and child labor. In southern textile mills, "mill management argued that the total annual income of a mill family was far greater than that of a farm family. Thus the 'family wage' was used as a cover for the low wages paid individuals" (23). But this is not the usual understanding. See Martha May, "The Historical Problem of the Family Wage: The Ford Motor Company and the Five Dollar Day," *Feminist Studies,* 8 (Summer 1982), 394–424.

8. For access to the opposing positions, see Jane Humphries, "The Working Class Family, Women's Liberation, and Class Struggle: The Case of Nineteenth Century British History," *Review of Radical Political Economics,* 9 (Fall 1977), 25–41; Michelle Barrett and Mary McIntosh, "The Family Wage: Some Problems for Socialists and Feminists," *Capital and Class,* 11 (1980), 51–72; and Hilary Land, "The Family Wage," *Feminist Review,* 6 (1980), 55–78.

9. John A. Ryan, *A Living Wage: Its Ethical and Economic Aspects* (New York: Macmillan, 1906), 117.

10. William Smart, *Studies in Economics* (London: Macmillan, 1985), 34. Smart added that "in addition perhaps some consumption of alcohol and tobacco, and some indulgence in fashionable dress are, in many places, so habitual that they may be said to be 'conventionally necessary'"(34).

11. Cited by Ryan, *Living Wage,* 130, from the *American Federationist,* 1898.

12. Ryan, *Living Wage,* 117.

13. Ibid., vii.

14. Italics mine. Quoted in May, "Historical Problem of the Family Wage," 402. Samuel Gompers believed the worker's living wage should "be sufficient to sustain himself and those dependent upon him in a manner to maintain his self-respect, to educate his children, supply his household with literature, with opportunities to spend a portion of his life with his family." In Samuel Gompers, "A Minimum Living Wage," *American Federationist,* 5 (April 1898), 26.

15. See, for example, the list compiled by F. Spencer Baldwin in Louise Bosworth, *The Living Wage of Women Workers* (New York: Longmans Green and Co., 1911), 7; see also Elizabeth Beardsley Butler, *Women and the Trades: Pittsburgh, 1907–1908* (Pittsburgh: University of Pittsburgh Press, 1984 [1909]), 346–47.

16. J. Laurence Laughlin, ed., *Principles of Political Economy by John Stuart Mill* (New York: D. Appleton and Company, 1885), 214.

17. Italics mine. Ryan, *Living Wage,* 107.

18. Lynn Y. Wiener, *From Working Girl to Working Mother: The Female Labor Force in the United States, 1820–1980* (Chapel Hill: University of North Carolina, 1985), 19, 26, 84.

19. Ryan, *Living Wage,* 107.

20. Ibid., 120.

21. Kellogg Durland, "Labor Day Symposium," *American Federationist* 12 (September 1905), 619.

22. Ryan, *Living Wage,* 107.

23. Ibid., 133.

24. Dorothy W. Douglas, *American Minimum Wage Laws at Work* (New York: National Consumers' League, 1920), 14.

25. Butler, *Women and the Trades,* 346; Bosworth, *Living Wage of Women Workers,* 9. The Women's Bureau estimated that the minimums in effect from 1913 to 1915 ranged from $8.50 to $10.74. See Bulletin no. 61, *The Development of Minimum Wage Laws in the United States: 1912–1927* (Washington, D.C.: Government Printing Office, 1928).

26. Thomas Herbert Russell, *The Girl's Fight for a Living: How to Protect Working Women from Dangers Due to Low Wages* (Chicago: M.A. Donahue, 1913), 108.

27. Elizabeth Brandeis, "Labor Legislation," vol. 3 of John Commons, *History of Labor in the United States* (New York: Macmillan, 1935), 524–25, makes the point that these budgets were calculated in one of two ways: on the basis of actual expenditures (a problem because women had to live on what they earned, however small) or on the basis of theoretical budgets (a problem because employer-members of boards resisted the inclusion of such items as recreation, "party dress," etc.). They were then "modified" by estimates of prevailing wages, consideration of the amounts of the proposed increases, and possible consequences for business conditions.

28. Sue Ainslee Clark and Edith Wyatt, "Working-Girls' Budgets: A Series of Articles Based upon Individual Stories of Self-Supporting Girls," *McClure's,* 35 (October 1910). Additional articles appeared in *McClure's* in vol. 36 in November and December 1910 and February 1911. They were published in book form under the title, *Making Both Ends Meet: The Income and Outlay of New York Working-Girls* (New York: Macmillan, 1911). The classic study is that of Louise Bosworth, cited above.

29. Clark and Wyatt, "Working-Girls' Budgets," *McClure's,* 35 (October 1910), 604. See the discussion of these budgets in

Wiener, *From Working Girl to Working Mother,* 75–77; and Joanne Meyerowitz, *Women Adrift: Independent Wage Earners in Chicago, 1880–1930* (Chicago: University of Chicago Press, 1988), 33–35.

30. The magazine advertised for contributions in January 1908 and published from four to six contributions from February 1908 to January 1909. In September 1908 it announced that it was flooded with contributions and would no longer accept any more. There is no way of knowing how heavily these were edited, so they have been used here only to extract a broad gauge of opinion.

31. "The Girl Who Comes to the City," *Harper's Bazaar,* 42 (January 1908), 54.

32. "The Girl Who Comes to the City," 42 (October 1908), 1005; 42 (July 1908), 694.

33. "The Girl Who Comes to the City," 42 (August 1908), 776. The maximum achieved by any of these women was the $100 a month earned by a Washington D.C., civil servant (42[November 1908], 1141). That sum was sufficient for a single woman not only to live reasonably well but to save and invest some of her income. It was rarely achieved by women.

34. "The Girl Who Comes to the City," 42 (November 1908), 1141; see also October 1908, 1007.

35. See, for example, Alice Kessler-Harris, *Out to Work: A History of Wage Earning Women in the United States* (New York: Oxford, 1982), 99–101; Meyerowitz, *Women Adrift,* 34–36.

36. "The Girl Who Comes to the City," 42 (March 1908), 277; 42 (May 1908), 500. The widespread nature of this assumption is apparent in "Women's Wages," *Nation,* 108 (February 22, 1919), 270–71: "The employer of women today is in a large proportion of cases heavily subsidized; for there is a considerable gap between the $9 a week that is paid to a girl and her actual cost of maintenance. Who makes up the difference? In the employer's mind it is usually the girl's family—which is often mythical."

37. Smart, *Studies in Economics,* 115.

38. Butler, *Women and the Trades,* 346.

39. Meyerowitz, *Women Adrift,* 33.

40. Butler, *Women and the Trades,* 344.

41. FIC, Fourth Report, vol. 4, app. 3, 450.

42. Scott Nearing, "The Adequacy of American Wages," *Annals of the American Academy of Political and Social Sciences,* 59 (May 1915), 2.

43. "Women's Wages and Morality," *American Federationist,* 20 (June 1913), 467.

44. Smart, *Studies in Economics,* 125.

45. Russell, *Girl's Fight for a Living,* 21. On pay differences by race, see Meyerowitz, *Women Adrift,* 36; and Dolores Janiewski, *Sisterhood Denied: Race, Gender and Class in a New South Community* (Philadelphia: Temple University Press, 1985), 110–13.

46. FIC, Fourth Report, vol. 2, app. 3, 468; Don D. Lescohier, then a Minnesota statistician and later to become an eminent gatherer of labor statistics, commented at the same hearings that "custom . . . plays a far larger part in holding wages stationary than we have been accustomed to think" (ibid., 459).

47. Smart, *Studies in Economics,* 116. The radical Scott Nearing, in a minority opinion, held that the male wage was not determined by another principle at all. He protested industry's lack of attention to social relations: "The man with a family is brought into active competition with the man who has no family obligations. The native-born head of a household must accept labor terms which are satisfactory to the foreign-born single man. Industry does not inquire into a worker's social obligations" (Nearing, "Adequacy of American Wages," 123).

48. Which is not, of course, to imply that all males who earned wages were paid enough to support families. See Janiewski, *Sisterhood Denied,* for illustrations of wages in the southern tobacco and textile industries that required the labor of three or more people to sustain a family.

49. Bosworth, *Living Wage,* 4.

50. Russell, *Girl's Fight for a Living,* 73.

51. Ibid., 108.

52. Ibid., 83.

53. Smart, *Studies in Economics,* 107.

54. Samuel Gompers, "Woman's Work, Rights and Progress," *American Federationist,* 20 (August 1913), 625.

55. Alfred Marshall, *Principles of Economics,* 8th ed. (New York: Macmillan, 1953), 685.

56. Quoted in Russell, *Girl's Fight for a Living,* 16; and see "Women's Wages and Morality," 465.

57. Russell, *Girl's Fight for a Living,* 38; cf. also the testimony of Ida Tarbell in ibid., 39.

58. Butler, *Women and the Trades,* 342–43.

59. Frances Amasa Walker, *The Wages Question: A Treatise on Wages and the Wages Class* (New York: Henry Holt and Company, 1876), 374.

60. Ibid., 378.

61. Quoted in Marjorie Shuler, "Industrial Women Confer," *Woman Citizen,* 8 (January 27, 1923), 25.

62. Such arguments were prefigured in the late nineteenth century by assertions that the greedy were taking jobs from the needy. See Kessler-Harris, *Out to Work,* 99ff.

63. "Women as Wage Earners," *New York Times,* January 28, 1923, 26.

64. Maurine Greenwald, *Women, War, and Work: The Impact of World War One on Women in the United States* (Westport, Conn.: Greenwood Press, 1980), 155. Greenwald notes that a female janitor who might have made $35 a month earned $75–80 a month as a conductor.

65. Daniel Nelson, *Managers and Workers: Origins of the New Factory System in the United States* (Madison: University of Wisconsin Press, 1975), 145.

66. Quoted in "Women and Wages," *The Woman Citizen,* 4 (June 7, 1919), 8. The article went on to report that one plant had "reckoned women's production as 20 per cent greater than that of the men preceding them. But this did not prevent the same plant from cutting down the women's pay one-third."

67. Typescript, "Memoranda Regarding Women's Bureau," in National Archives, Record Group 86, Box 4, File: WTUL Action

on Policies. The bureau lost this battle. As a result, its professional staff tended to work more out of loyalty and commitment than for monetary gain. See Judith Sealander, *As Minority Becomes Majority: Federal Reaction to the Phenomenon of Women in the Work Force, 1920–1963* (Westport, Conn.: Greenwood Press, 1983), chap. 3, for the early days of the Women's Bureau.

68. Ronald W. Schatz, *The Electrical Workers: A History of Labor at General Electric and Westinghouse, 1923–60* (Urbana: University of Illinois Press, 1983), 32.

69. Quoted in Stephen Meyer III, *The Five Dollar Day: Labor Management and Social Control in the Ford Motor Company, 1908–1921* (Albany: State University of New York Press, 1981), 140.

70. Schatz, *Electrical Workers,* 20–21.

71. Quoted in Schatz, *Electrical Workers,* 21; Nelson, *Managers and Workers,* 118, confirms that the wage as welfare differed for men and women: "Manufacturers who employed large numbers of women usually emphasized measures to make the factory more habitable. Lunchrooms, restrooms, landscaping and other decorative features conveyed the idea of a home away from home. At the same time, the classes in domestic economy and child rearing, social clubs, outings and dances (women only) assured the worker that she need not sacrifice her femininity when she entered the male world of the factory. But, because the female operative was (or was thought to be) a secondary wage earner and probably a transient, she was not offered pensions, savings programs and insurance plans."

72. Meyer, *Five Dollar Day,* 140; implicit in the Ford policy was a quite conscious attempt to circumscribe the roles and self-perceptions of men as well as of women. Meyer quotes a Ford policy manual from the 1920s to the effect that "if a man wants to remain a profit sharer, his wife should stay at home and assume the obligations she undertook when married" (141). See the commentary on this issue in "Housework Wages," *The Woman Citizen,* 4 (October 4, 1919), 449.

73. Russell, *Girl's Fight for a Living,* 101; the same investigator asked an employer, "If you raised a little girl from $3 to $8 would a man getting $15 feel aggrieved?" (112)—a question that loads the dice by imagining women as no more than children.

74. Microfilm records, Western Electric Plant, Hawthorne Works, Operating Branch M., interviews, Reel 6, July 8, 1929. Records of individuals are not identified or tagged beyond the branch where the interviews were taken. The growing sense of entitlement to comparable wages was captured by an experienced female worker who declared herself satisfied with her work "because it was more interesting and I could make my rate" but nevertheless complained that "I don't see why they didn't raise me anyway like they did the other girls, every half year or every year."

In ibid., July 9, 1929. This phenomenon was not specific to women alone. F. J. Roethlisberger and William Dickson, analyzing the Western Electric research, commented, "The results of the interviewing program show very clearly that the worker was quite as much concerned with these differentials, that is the relation of his wages to that of other workmen as with the absolute amount of his wages." See *Management and the Worker: An Account of a Research Program Conducted by the Western Electric Company, Hawthorne Works, Chicago* (Cambridge, Mass.: Harvard University Press, 1946), 543. But nothing in the interviews indicates that women compared their wages with those of men, nor did men with those of women.

75. Mary Schaill and Ethel Best to Mary Anderson, November 5, 1919, Virginia Survey, Bulletin no. 10, National Archives, Record Group 86: Records of the Women's Bureau, Box 2.

76. Pauline Newman, veteran trade unionist, challenged old notions of a living wage in "The 'Equal Rights' Amendment," *American Federationist,* 45 (August 1938), 815. She wrote, "It is not a wage which affords an opportunity for intellectual development; it is not a wage which allows for spiritual growth; it is not a wage on which wage-earning women can enjoy the finer things of life."

77. Ronald Edsforth, *Class Conflict and Cultural Consensus: The Making of a Mass Consumer Society in Flint, Michigan* (New Brunswick, N.J.: Rutgers University Press, 1987), 95.

78. Daniel T. Rodgers, *The Work Ethic in Industrial America: 1850–1920* (Chicago: University of Chicago Press, 1974), 196.

79. Theresa Wolfson, *The Woman Worker and the Trade Unions* (New York: International Publishers, 1926), 42.

80. Microfilm records, Western Electric Plant, Hawthorne Works, Operating Branch M., interviews, Reel 6, July 8, 1929.

81. Wolfson, *Woman Worker,* 42–43.

82. Microfilm records, Western Electric Plant, Hawthorne Works, Operating Branch M., interviews, Reel 6, Folder 1, Box 14, July 1, 1929.

83. Mary Anderson, "Industrial Standards for Women," *American Federationist,* 32 (July 1925), 565.

84. Jacquelyn Dowd Hall et al., *Like a Family: The Making of a Southern Cotton Mill World* (Chapel Hill: University of North Carolina Press, 1987), 255–56.

85. See interviews with Ada Mae Wilson, Mary Ethel Shockley, Ina Wrenn, and Gertrude Shuping in Southern Oral History Project Collection, Martin Wilson Library, University of North Carolina, Chapel Hill. Used with the kind help of Jacquelyn Dowd Hall.

86. The quotation is from FIC, Fourth Report, vol. 4, 440. The percentage of married black women working and supporting families was far higher than that for white women.

87. Shuler, "Industrial Women Confer," 12.

Bringing the Men Back In: Sex Differentiation and the Devaluation of Women's Work

BARBARA F. RESKIN

One of the most enduring manifestations of sex inequality in industrial and postindustrial societies is the wage gap.[1] In 1986, as in 1957, among full-time workers in the United States, men earned 50 percent more per hour than did women. This disparity translated to $8,000 a year in median earnings, an all-time high bonus for being male. Most sociologists agree that the major cause of the wage gap is the segregation of women and men into different kinds of work (Reskin and Hartmann 1986). Whether or not women freely choose the occupations in which they are concentrated, the outcome is the same: the more proportionately female an occupation, the lower its average wages (Treiman and Hartmann 1981). The high level of job segregation (Bielby and Baron 1984) means that the 1963 law stipulating equal pay for equal work did little to reduce the wage gap.[2]

This "causal model"—that the segregation of women and men into different occupations causes the wage gap—implies two possible remedies. One is to equalize men and women on the causal variable—occupation—by ensuring women's access to traditionally male occupations. The other is to replace occupation with a causal variable on which women and men differ less, by instituting comparable-worth pay policies that compensate workers for the "worth" of their job regardless of its sex composition.

I contend, however, that the preceding explanation of the wage gap is incorrect because it omits variables responsible for the difference between women and men in their distribu-tion across occupations. If a causal model is incorrect, the remedies it implies may be ineffective. Lieberson's (1985, p. 185) critique of causal analysis as it is commonly practiced explicates the problem by distinguishing between *superficial* (or surface) causes that *appear to* give rise to a particular outcome and *basic* causes that *actually* produce the outcome. For example, he cites the belief that the black-white income gap is due to educational differences and thus can be reduced by reducing the educational disparity. As Lieberson pointed out, this analysis misses the fact that "the dominant group . . . uses its dominance to advance its own position" (p. 166), so that eliminating race differences in education is unlikely to reduce racial inequality in income because whites will find another way to maintain their income advantage. In other words, what appear in this example to be both the outcome variable (the black-white income gap) and the imputed causal variable (the black-white educational dispar-ity) may stem from the same basic cause (whites' attempt to maintain their economic advantage). If so, then if the dispar-ity in education were eliminated, some other factor would arise to produce the same economic consequence (Lieberson 1985, p. 164).

Dominant groups remain privileged because they write the rules, and the rules they write "enable them *to continue to write the rules*" (Lieberson 1985, p. 167; emphasis added). As a result, they can change the rules to thwart challenges to their position. Consider the following exam-ple. Because Asian American students tend to outscore occidentals on standard admissions tests, they are increas-ingly overrepresented in some university programs. Some universities have allegedly responded by imposing quotas for Asian students (Hechinger 1987, p. C1) or weighing more heavily admissions criteria on which they believe Asian Americans do less well.[3]

Barbara F. Reskin, "Bringing the Men Back In: Sex Differentiation and the Devaluation of Women's Work," *Gender & Society* 2, no. 1 (March 1988). Copyright © 1988 by Sociologists for Women and Society. Reprinted with the permission of Sage Publications, Inc.

How can one tell whether a variable is a superficial or a basic cause of some outcome? Lieberson offered a straightforward test: Does a change in that variable lead to a change in the outcome? Applying this rule to the prevailing causal theory of the wage gap, we find that between 1970 and 1980 the index of occupational sex segregation declined by 10 percent (Beller 1984), but the wage gap for full-time workers declined by just under 2 percent (computed from data in Blau and Ferber 1986, p. 171). Although its meaning may be equivocal,[4] this finding is consistent with other evidence that attributing the wage gap to job segregation misses its basic cause: men's propensity to maintain their privileges. This claim is neither novel nor specific to men. Marxist and conflict theory have long recognized that dominant groups act to preserve their position (Collins 1975). Like other dominant groups, men are reluctant to give up their advantages (Goode 1982). To avoid having to do so, they construct "rules" for distributing rewards that guarantee them the lion's share (see also Epstein 1985, p. 30). In the past, men cited their need as household heads for a "family wage" (May 1982) and designated women as secondary earners. Today, when millions of women who head households would benefit from such a rule, occupation has supplanted it as the principle for assigning wages.

Neoclassical economic theory holds that the market is the mechanism through which wages are set, but markets are merely systems of rules (Marshall and Paulin n.d., p. 15) that dominant groups establish for their own purposes. When other groups, such as labor unions, amassed enough power, they modified the "market" principle.[5] Steinberg (1987) observed that when consulted in making comparable-worth adjustments, male-dominated unions tended to support management over changes that would raise women's salaries (see also Simmons, Freedman, Dunkle, and Blau 1975, pp. 115–36; Hartmann 1976).

In sum, the basic cause of the income gap is not sex segregation but men's desire to preserve their advantaged position and their ability to do so by establishing rules to distribute valued resources in their favor.[6] Figure 1 represents this more complete causal model. Note that currently segregation is a superficial cause of the income gap, in part through "crowding" (Bergmann 1974), but that some other distributional system such as comparable-worth pay could replace it with the same effect.

With respect to income, this model implies that men will resist efforts to close the wage gap. Resistance will include opposing equalizing women's access to jobs

FIGURE I   Heuristic model of the wage gap

because integration would equalize women and men on the current superficial cause of the wage gap—occupation. Men may also try to preserve job segregation because it is a central mechanism through which they retain their dominance in other spheres, and because many people learn to prefer the company of others like them. My theory also implies that men will resist efforts to replace occupation with alternative principles for assigning pay that would mitigate segregation's effect on women's wages (as pay equity purports to do).

Before I offer evidence for these claims, let us examine how dominant groups in general and men in particular maintain their privileged position. I formulate my analysis with reference to dominant groups to emphasize that the processes I discuss are not specific to sex classes. It also follows that, were women the dominant sex, the claims I make about men's behavior should hold for women.

DIFFERENTIATION, DEVALUATION, AND HIERARCHY

Differentiation—the practice of distinguishing categories based on some attribute—is the fundamental process in hierarchical systems, a logical necessity for differential evaluation and differential rewards. But differentiation involves much more than merely acting on a preexisting difference. In a hierarchical context, differentiation assumes, amplifies, and even creates psychological and behavioral differences in order to ensure that the subordinate group differs from the dominant group (Epstein 1985, p. 36; Jagger 1983, pp. 109–10; MacKinnon 1987, p. 38; West and Zimmerman 1987, p. 137), "because the systematically differential delivery of benefits and deprivations require[s] making no mistake about who was who" (MacKinnon 1987, p. 40) and because "differences are inequality's post hoc excuse" (MacKinnon 1987, p. 8).

Differentiated status characteristics influence evaluations of people's behavior and their overall worth (Berger, Cohen, and Zelditch 1972; Pugh and Wahrman 1983). In hierarchical systems in which differentiation takes the form of an Aristotelian dichotomy, individuals are classified as either A ("the subject") or Not-A ("the other"). But these two classes are not construed as natural opposites that both have positive qualities; instead, A's characteristics are valued as normal or good and Not-A's as without value or negative (de Beauvoir 1953, p. xvi; Jay 1981).

The official response to the influx of south- and central-eastern European immigrants to the United States early in this century, when people assumed that each European country represented a distinct biological race (Lieberson 1980, p. 24), illustrates differentiation's central role in dominance systems. A congressionally mandated immigration commission concluded that "innate, ineradicable race distinctions separated groups of men from one another" and agreed on the

necessity of classifying these races to know which were most worthy of survival. The immediate problem was to ascertain "whether there may not be certain races that are inferior to other races . . . to discover some test to show whether some may be better fitted for American citizenship than others." (Lieberson 1980, pp. 2–26)

Thus differentiation in all its forms supports dominance systems by demonstrating that superordinate and subordinate groups differ in essential ways and that such differences are natural and even desirable.

"Sex Differentiation" versus "Gender Differentiation": A Note on Terminology

Scholars speak of both "sex" and "gender" differentiation: the former when biological sex or the "sex category" into which people are placed at birth (West and Zimmerman 1987, p. 127) is the *basis for* classification and differential treatment; the latter to refer to the *result* of that differential treatment. In order to emphasize that the initial biological difference (mediated through sex category) is the basis for differential treatment, I use the terms *sex differentiation* and

sex segregation. This usage should not obscure the fact that the process of converting sex category into gender is a social one or that most differences that are assumed to distinguish the sexes are socially created. I agree with Kessler and McKenna (1978) that the "gender attribution process" assumes dimorphism and seeks evidence of it to justify classifying people as male and female and treating them unequally. This article examines how and why those differences are produced.

Sex Differentiation and Devaluation

Probably no system of social differentiation is as extensive as that based on sex category. Its prevalence led anthropologist Gayle Rubin to claim that there is "a taboo against the sameness of men and women, a taboo dividing the sexes into two mutually exclusive categories, a taboo which exacerbates the biological differences between the sexes and thereby *creates* gender" (1975, p. 178). Moreover, although femaleness is not always devalued, its deviation from maleness in a culture that reserves virtues for men has meant the devaluation of women (Jay 1981). Bleier's research on biological scientists' study of sex differences illustrates this point: the "search for the truth about differences, [implies] that difference means *different from the white male norm and, therefore, inferior*" (1987, p. 2; emphasis added). In consequence, men's activities are typically valued above women's, regardless of their content or importance for group survival (Goode 1964; Mead 1949; Schur 1983, pp. 35–48), and both sexes come to devalue women's efforts (Major, McFarlin, and Gagnon 1984). Thus it should be no surprise that women's occupations pay less at least partly *because* women do them (Treiman and Hartmann 1981).

In short, differentiation is the sine qua non of dominance systems. Because of its importance, it is achieved through myriad ways:

To go for a walk with one's eyes open is enough to demonstrate that humanity is divided into two classes of individuals whose clothes, faces, bodies, smiles, gaits, interests and occupations are manifestly different. (de Beauvoir 1953, p. xiv)

We differentiate groups in their location, appearance, and behavior, and in the tasks they do. Now let us turn to how these mechanisms operate to differentiate women and men.

THE MOMMY TEST

BARBARA EHRENREICH

My, my, girls, what's all the fuss over the new "mommy test"? Hundreds of eager young female job seekers have written to me in the last few weeks alone, confident of being able to pass the drug test, the polygraph test, Exxon's new breathalyzer test—but panicked over the mommy test. Well, the first thing you have to grasp if you hope to enter the ranks of management is that corporations have a perfect *right* to separate the thieves from the decent folk, the straights from the druggies, and, of course, the women from the mommies.

For starters, you should know that thousands of U.S. women, even those afflicted with regular ovulatory cycles and patent fallopian tubes, have been taking—and *passing*—the mommy test for decades. In fact, it used to be almost the first question (just after "Can you type?") in the standard female job interview: "Are you now, or have you ever, contemplated marriage, motherhood, or the violent overthrow of the U.S. government?"

Today, thanks to women's lib, you won't be out on the street even if you fail. All right, there are disadvantages to the mommy track: mandatory milk and cookies at ten, quiet time at three, and so forth. But many women are happy to get a paycheck of any kind, even if it is a gift certificate to Toys 'R' Us. And if you *still* want to be on the fast track, with the grown-ups and the men, here are a few simple tips for acing the mommy test:

1. Be prepared for tricky psychological questions, such as: Would you rather (a) spend six straight hours in a windowless conference room with a group of arrogant, boorish men fighting over their spread sheets, or (b) scrape congealed pabulum off a linoleum floor? (The answer, surprisingly, is *a.*) Or try this one: Would you rather (a) feed apple juice to a hungry baby, or (b) figure out how to boost profits by diluting the company's baby apple-juice product with wastewater from the local nuclear power plant? But you get the idea. . . .
2. Bring proof of infertility: your uterus in a mason jar, for example. Alternatively, tell the interviewer that you already had a child, but—and at this point you stare pensively into space—it didn't work out. . . .
3. Your interviewer will no doubt have framed photos of his own wife and children displayed prominently on his desk. Do not be misled; this is *part of the test*. Be sure to display appropriate levels of disgust and commiseration. You might ask, in a pitying tone, "Oh, did you marry a *mommy*?"
4. If you actually are a mommy, and have small children of your own who, for some reason, are still living with you, the case is almost hopeless. Unless you

PHYSICAL SEGREGATION

Dominant groups differentiate subordinate groups by physically isolating them—in ghettos, nurseries, segregated living quarters, and so on. Physical segregation fosters unequal treatment, because physically separate people can be treated differently and because it spares members of the dominant group the knowledge of the disparity and hides it from the subordinate group. Although women and men are integrated in some spheres, physical separation continues to differentiate them (e.g., see Goffman 1977, p. 316).

Cohn's (1985) vivid account of women's physical segregation in the British Foreign Office in the nineteenth century illustrates the extent to which organizations have gone to separate the sexes. The Foreign Office hid its first female typists in an attic, but it failed to rescind the requirement that workers collect their pay on the ground floor. When payday came, managers evacuated the corridors, shut all the doors, and then sent the women running down the attic stairs to get their checks and back up again. Only after they were out of sight were the corridors reopened to men.

can prove that, as a result of some bioengineering feat or error on their birth certificates, you are actually their daddy and hence have no day-to-day responsibility for their care.

But the key thing is *attitude*. If you go for your job interview in a hostile, self-pitying mood, if you're convinced that the mommy test is an example of discrimination or prejudice, believe me, it will show. And there isn't prejudice against mommies today, not really. They're no longer subject to the extreme residential segregation imposed in the fifties, when mommies were required to live in special suburban compounds, far from the great centers of commerce. Today, you'll find them living just about everywhere, even in jaunty little cardboard structures within walking distance of Wall Street.

Today it is no longer necessary (as it was for poor Nancy Reagan) for a woman who aspires to public recognition to renounce all knowledge of, and contact with, her children. We even have a special day devoted to the distribution of flowers on the graves of dead mothers, as well as to those mothers who, for some reason, still linger on.

However, even if we acknowledge all the tremendous contributions mothers have made—and there were mommies at Plymouth Rock, at Gettysburg, possibly even at the Republican National Convention—we must admit that they have, as a race, shown remarkably little aptitude for the fine points of corporate management. When have you ever seen a get-rich-quick book titled *Leveraged Buyouts: A Mother's Secrets,* or *Swimming with the Sharks: A Mommy's Guide to Eating the Competition (And Finishing Every Last Bite)*?

But the bottom line (not to be confused, gals, with the mark left by overly tight Pampers!) is: Even if you respect mommies, like mommies, and are aware of the enormous diversity among them, would you really want to work with one? This is the question that thousands of top U.S. male managers have had to face: Would you want to be at a $100 power lunch and risk being told to polish your plate? Hence the mommy track. It just makes *sense* to segregate them in special offices equipped with extra umbrellas, sweaters, raincoats, and toothbrushes—for their own sake as much as anything.

Personally, I think the mommy track may be just the first step in a new wave of corporate cost cutting. There's a new approach based on the experience of a brilliant young fast-track executive who got pregnant unbeknownst to herself and handily delivered in the ladies' room during a break in the third-quarter sales conference. The baby was raised on phenobarbital and take-out food until it outgrew the lower right-hand desk drawer, at which point our fast tracker hired a baby-sitter—to take over her corporate responsibilities!

For the truth is, all you eager young job seekers, that no one knows for sure what the management of top U.S. corporations does all day or well into the night. Sitting at desks has been observed. Sitting at meetings has been observed. Initialing memos has been observed. Could a woman—even a mommy—do all this? Certainly, and with time left over for an actual job of some sort. So the question that our corporate leaders must ultimately face is: What does our vast army of pin-striped managers do anyway, and could it be done by a reliable baby-sitter?

This account raises the question of *why* managers segregate working men and women. What licentiousness did the Foreign Office fear would occur in integrated hallways? Contemporary answers are markedly similar to turn-of-the-century fears. Compare the scenario expressed in a 1923 editorial in the *Journal of Accountancy* ("any attempt at heterogeneous personnel [in after-hours auditing of banks] would hamper progress and lead to infinite embarrassment" [p. 151]) with recent reactions to the prospect of women integrating police patrol cars, coal mines, and merchant marine vessels (e.g., Martin 1980). At or just below the surface lies the specter of sexual liaisons. For years, McDonald's founder Ray Kroc forbade franchisees to hire women counter workers because they would attract "the wrong type" of customers (Luxenburg 1985). The U.S. Army ended sex-integrated basic training to "facilitate toughening goals" (National Organization for Women 1982), and the Air Force reevaluated whether women could serve on two-person Minuteman missile-silo teams because "it could lead to stress" (*New York Times* 1984).

My thesis offers a more parsimonious alternative to these ad hoc explanations—men resist allowing women and men to work together *as equals* because doing so undermines differentiation and hence male dominance.

BEHAVIORAL DIFFERENTIATION

People's behavior is differentiated on their status-group membership in far too many ways for me to review the differences adequately here. I concentrate in this section on differentiation of behaviors that occur in the workplace: task differentiation and social differentiation.

Task differentiation assigns work according to group membership. It was expressed in the extreme in traditional Hindu society in which caste virtually determined life work. Task assignment based on sex category—the sexual division of labor—both prescribes and proscribes assorted tasks to each sex, and modern societies still assign men and women different roles in domestic work (Pleck 1985), labor-market work (Reskin and Hartmann 1986), and emotional and interpersonal work (Fishman 1982; Hochschild 1983).[7] Task differentiation generally assigns to lower-status groups the least desirable, most poorly rewarded work: menial, tedious, and degraded tasks, such as cleaning, disposing of waste, and caring for the dying.[8] This practice symbolizes and legitimates the subordinate group's low status, while making it appear to have an affinity for these undesirable tasks. As an added benefit, members of the dominant group don't have to do them! Important to discussions of the wage gap, because modern law and custom permit unequal pay for different work, task differentiation justifies paying the subordinate group lower wages, thereby ensuring their economic inferiority. Women's assignment to child care, viewed as unskilled work in our society, illustrates these patterns. Women are said to have a "natural talent" for it and similar work; men are relieved from doing it; society obtains free or cheap child care; and women are handicapped in competing with men. As researchers have shown, sex-based task differentiation of both nonmarket and market work legitimates women's lower pay, hinders women's ability to succeed in traditionally male enterprises, and, in general, reinforces men's hegemony (Coverman 1983).

Social differentiation is achieved through norms that set dominant and subordinate groups apart in their appearance (sumptuary rules) or behavior (etiquette rules [van den Berghe 1960]). When applied to sex, Goffman's (1976) concept of "gender display" encompasses both. Sumptuary rules require certain modes of dress, diet, or life-style of members of subordinate groups as emblems of their inferior status, and reserve other modes to distinguish the dominant group. For example, Rollins (1985) discovered that white female employers preferred black domestic employees to dress shabbily to exaggerate their economic inferiority. Sex-specific sumptuary rules are epitomized in norms that dictate divergent dress styles that often exaggerate physical sex differences and sometimes even incapacitate women (Roberts 1977).[9] An extreme example is the *burqua* fundamentalist Muslim women wear as a symbol of their status and as a portable system of segregation (Papanek 1973).

Etiquette rules support differentiation by requiring subordinate group members to display ritualized deference toward dominants. Relations between enlistees and officers (van den Berghe 1960) or female domestic workers and their employers (Rollins 1985) illustrate their role. Although typically it is the subordinate group that must defer, gender etiquette that requires middle- and upper-class men to display deference to women of the same classes preserves differentiation by highlighting women's differentness. Women who do not express gratitude or who refuse to accept the deference are faced with hostility, shattering the fiction that women hold the preferred position.

Physical segregation, behavioral differentiation, social separation, and even hierarchy are functional alternatives for satisfying the need for differentiation in domination systems. For example, when their physical integration with the dominant group means that a subordinate group's status differences might otherwise be invisible, special dress is usually required of them, as servants are required to wear uniforms. Physical separation can even compensate for the absence of hierarchy, a point acknowledged in the black folk saying that southern whites don't care how close blacks get if they don't get too high, and northern whites don't care how high blacks get if they don't get too close (Lukas 1985).

This substitutability explains why men will tolerate women in predominantly male work settings if they work in "women's" jobs and accept women doing "men's" jobs in traditionally female settings, but resist women doing traditionally male jobs in male work settings (e.g., Schroedel 1985). Physical proximity per se is not threatening as long as another form of differentiation sets women apart. But the absence of *any* form of differentiation precludes devaluation and unequal rewards and hence threatens the sex-gender hierarchy. Because of the centrality of differentiation in domination systems, dominant groups have a considerable stake in maintaining it.

DOMINANTS' RESPONSE TO CHALLENGES

Dominants respond to subordinates' challenges by citing the group differences that supposedly warrant differential treatment (Jackman and Muha 1984). Serious challenges often give rise to attempts to demonstrate biological differences scientifically.

The nineteenth-century antislavery and women's rights movements led reputable scientists to try to prove that women's and blacks' brains were underdeveloped (Bleier 1987). The Great Migration to the United States in the first two decades of this century fueled a eugenics movement that purported to establish scientifically the inferiority of south- and central-eastern Europeans (Lieberson 1980, pp. 25–26). The civil rights movement of the 1960s stimulated renewed efforts to establish racial differences in intelligence. And we are once again witnessing a spate of allegedly scientific research seeking a biological basis for presumed sex differences in cognitive ability and, specifically, for boys' higher average scores on math questions in some standardized tests. As Bleier pointed out, "The implication if not purposes of [such] research is to demonstrate that the structure of society faithfully reflects the natural order of things" (1987, p. 11; see also Epstein 1985, pp. 32, 35, for a similar pattern in the social sciences). According to Bleier, reputable journals have published studies that violate accepted standards of proof, and the scientific press has given dubious findings considerable attention (as in the news story in *Science* that asked, "Is There a Male Math Gene?"). Although subsequently these studies have been discredited, the debate serves its purpose by focusing attention on how groups differ.[10]

MEN'S RESPONSE TO OCCUPATIONAL INTEGRATION

An influx of women into male spheres threatens the differentiation of men and women, and men resist (Goode 1982). One response is to bar women's entry. Women have had to turn to the courts to win entry into Little League sports, college dining clubs, private professional clubs, and the Rotary (Anderson 1987; Association of American Colleges 1985, p. 11; Schafran 1981). Recently, University of North Carolina trustees decried the fact that women are now a majority of UNC students, and some proposed changing the weights for certain admission criteria to

restore the male majority (Greene 1987).[11] Twice since a shortage of male recruits forced the army to lift its quota on women, it has reduced the number of jobs open to women (Becraft 1987, p. 3).

Numerous studies have documented men's resistance to women entering "their" jobs (e.g., see Hartmann 1976 on cigar makers; Schroedel 1985 on a cross-section of trades). Sometimes the resistance is simply exclusion; at other times it is subtle barriers that block women's advancement or open harassment (Reskin 1978). Now that more women hold managerial jobs, one hears of "a glass ceiling" that bars middle-management women from top-level positions (e.g., Hymowitz and Schellhardt 1986), and Kanter (1987) claimed that organizations are changing the rules of what one must do to reach the top in order to make it more difficult for women to succeed.

My thesis implies that men will respond to women's challenge in the workplace by emphasizing how they differ from men. Especially common are reminders of women's "natural" roles as wife, mother, or sexual partner. Witness the recent—and subsequently disputed-claims that women who postponed marriage and childbearing to establish their careers had a negligible chance of finding husbands and were running the risk that their "biological clocks" would prevent pregnancy, and accounts of women dropping out of middle management to spend more time with their children.[12]

Men who cannot bar women from "male" jobs can still preserve differentiation in other spheres. Their attempts to do so may explain why so few husbands of wage-working women share housework (Pleck 1985, p. 146), as well as elucidating Wharton and Baron's (1987) finding that among men working in sex-integrated jobs, those whose wives were employed were more dissatisfied than unmarried men or men married to homemakers.

Another response to women's challenge is to weaken the mechanisms that have helped women advance in the workplace. Since 1980, the Reagan administration has sought to undermine equal-opportunity programs and affirmative-action regulations, and the campaign has partly succeeded. Efforts to dilute or eliminate Equal Employment Opportunity (EEO) programs are advanced by claims that sex inequality has disappeared (or that men now experience "reverse discrimination"). For example, the *New York Times* (Greer 1987, pp. C1, 10) recently described the Department of Commerce announcement that women now compose the majority in professional occupations as a "historic milestone," adding that "the barriers have fallen."

THE ILLUSION OF OCCUPATIONAL INTEGRATION

If male resistance is so pervasive, how can we explain the drop in the index of occupational sex segregation in the 1970s and women's disproportionate gains in a modest number of male-dominated occupations (Rytina and Bianchi 1984)? In order to answer this question, Patricia Roos and I embarked on a study of the changing sex composition of occupations (Reskin and Roos forthcoming). The results of our case studies of a dozen traditionally male occupations in which women made disproportionate statistical gains during the 1970s cast doubt on whether many women can advance economically through job integration.

The case studies revealed two general patterns. First, within many occupations nominally being integrated, men and women remain highly segregated, with men concentrated in the highest-status and best-paying jobs. For example, although women's representation in baking grew from 25 percent in 1970 to 41 percent in 1980, men continue to dominate production baking. The increase in women bakers is due almost wholly to their concentration in proliferating "in-store" bakeries (Steiger 1987). Although women now make up the majority of residential real estate salespersons, men still monopolize commercial sales (Thomas and Reskin 1987).

The second pattern shows that women often gained access to these occupations after changes in work content and declines in autonomy or rewards made the work less attractive to men (Cockburn 1986, p. 76). In some occupations, the growth of functions already socially labeled as "women's work" (e.g., clerical, communications, or emotional work) spurred the change. For example, computerization and the ensuing clericalization prompted women's entry into typesetting and composing (Roos 1986) and insurance adjusting and examining (Phipps 1986). An increasing emphasis on communicating and interpersonal or emotional work contributed to women's gains in insurance sales (Thomas 1987), insurance adjusting and examining (Phipps 1987), systems analysis (Donato 1986), public relations (Donato 1987), and bank and financial management (Bird 1987).

Brief summaries of our findings for two occupations illustrate these processes.[13] First, women's disproportionate gains in pharmacy have been largely confined to the retail sector (male pharmacists work disproportionately in research and management) and occurred after retail pharmacists lost professional status and entrepreneurial opportunities. After drug manufacturers took over the compounding of drugs, pharmacists increasingly resembled retail sales clerks; their primary duties became dispensing and record keeping. As chain and discount-store pharmacies supplanted independently owned pharmacies, retail pharmacy no longer offered a chance to own one's own business, reducing another traditional attraction for men. The resulting shortages of male pharmacy graduates eased women's access to training programs and retail jobs (Phipps 1987).

Second, book editing illustrates how declining autonomy and occupational prestige contributed to feminization of an occupation. For most of this century, the cultural image of publishing attracted bright young men and women despite very low wages. But during the 1970s, multinational conglomerates entered book publishing, with profound results. Their emphasis on the bottom line robbed publishing of its cultural aura, and the search for blockbusters brought a greater role for marketing people in acquisition decisions, thereby eroding editorial autonomy. As a result, editing could no longer compete effectively for talented men who could choose from better opportunities. Because women's occupational choices are more limited than men's, editing still attracted them, and the occupation's sex composition shifted accordingly (Reskin 1987).

In sum, although sex integration appears to have occurred in the 1970s among census-designated detailed occupations (Beller 1984), our findings indicate that within these occupations, women are segregated into certain specialties or work settings and that they gained entry because various changes made the occupations less attractive to men. The nominal integration that occurred in the 1970s often masks within-occupation segregation or presages resegregation of traditionally male occupations as women's work. In short, the workplace is still overwhelmingly differentiated by sex. Moreover, our preliminary results suggest that real incomes in the occupations we are studying declined during the 1970s; so reducing segregation at the occupational level appears to have been relatively ineffective in reducing the wage gap—and certainly not the remedy many experts predicted. This brings us to the other possible remedy for the wage gap—comparable worth.

IMPLICATIONS FOR COMPARABLE WORTH

The comparable-worth movement calls for equal pay for work of equal worth. Worth is usually determined by job-evaluation studies that measure the skill, effort, and responsibility required, but in practice, assessing worth often turns on how to conceptualize and measure skill.

Although some objective criteria exist for assessing skill (e.g., how long it takes a worker to learn the job [see Spenner 1985, pp. 132–136]), typically the designation of work as skilled is socially negotiated. Workers are most likely to win it when they control social resources that permit them to press their claims, such as a monopoly over a labor supply or authority based on their personal characteristics such as education, training, or sex (Phillips and Taylor 1980). As a result, the evaluation of "skill" is shaped by and confounded with workers' sex (Dex 1985, p. 100).

Groups use the same power that enabled them to define their work as skilled to restrict competition by excluding women (among others) from training for and practicing their trade or profession (Dex 1985, p. 103; see also Hartmann 1976), as Millicent Fawcett recognized almost a hundred years ago when she declared, "Equal pay for equal work is a fraud for women." Because men use their power to keep women "from obtaining equal skills, their work [cannot be] equal" (Hartmann 1976, p. 157). Roos's (1986) case history of the effect of technological change on women's employment in typesetting illustrates these points. When a Linotype machine was developed that "female typists could operate," the International Typographical Union (ITU) used its labor monopoly to force employers to agree to hire as operators only skilled printers who knew *all* aspects of the trade. By denying women access to apprenticeships or other channels to become fully skilled and limiting the job of operating the Linotype to highly skilled printers, the ITU effectively barred women from the new Linotype jobs. In short, the ITU used its monopoly power both to restrict women's access to skills and credentials and to define its members as "uniquely skilled" to operate the Linotype.

Excluded from occupations male workers define as skilled, women are often unable, for several reasons, to press the claim that work in traditionally female occupations is skilled. First, as I have shown, the devaluation of women's work leads whatever work women do to be seen as unskilled. Second, women's powerlessness prevents their successfully defining their work—caring for children, entering data, assembling microelectronic circuits—as skilled. Third, because many female-dominated occupations require workers to acquire skills before employment, skill acquisition is less visible and hence unlikely to be socially credited. Fourth, the scarcity of apprenticeship pro-

grams for women's jobs and women's exclusion from other programs denies women a credential society recognizes as denoting skill (Reskin and Hartmann 1986). Finally, "much of women's work involves recognizing and responding to subtle cues" (Feldberg 1984, p. 321), but the notion of "women's intuition" permits men to define such skills as inborn and hence not meriting compensation. Thus women are both kept from acquiring socially valued skills and not credited for those they do acquire (Steinberg 1984–85). As a result, the sex of the majority of workers in an occupation influences whether or not their work is classified as skilled (Feldberg 1984; Gregory 1987).

In view of these patterns, how effective can comparable worth be in reducing the wage gap? As with the Equal Pay Act, implementing it has symbolic value. Moreover, it would bar employers from underpaying women relative to their job-evaluation scores, the practice alleged in *AFSCME v. Washington State* (1985). But setting salaries according to an occupation's worth will reduce the wage gap only to the extent that (1) women have access to tasks that society values, (2) evaluators do not take workers' sex into account in determining a job's worth, and (3) implementers do not sacrifice equity to other political agendas.

Neither of the first two conditions holds. As I have shown, men already dominate jobs society deems skilled. Moreover, the tendency to devalue women's work is embedded in job-evaluation techniques that define job worth (Steinberg 1984–85); so such techniques may yield biased evaluations of traditionally female jobs and lower their job-evaluation scores (Treiman and Hartmann 1981; Marshall and Paulin n.d., p. 5). Beyond these difficulties is the problem of good-faith implementation. Acker (1987), Brenner (1987), and Steinberg (1987) have documented the problems in implementing comparable-worth pay adjustments. According to Steinberg (p. 8), New York State's proposed compensation model *negatively* values working with difficult clients, work performed in historically female and minority jobs (in other words, workers lose pay for doing it!), and Massachusetts plans to establish separate comparable-worth plans across sex-segregated bargaining units. For these reasons, the magnitude of comparable-worth adjustments have been about half of what experts expected—only 5 percent to 15 percent of salaries (Steinberg 1987).

Moreover, to the extent that equity adjustments significantly raise salaries in women's jobs, men can use their power to monopolize them. It is no accident that the men who integrated the female semiprofessions moved rapidly to the top (Grimm and Stern 1974). The recent experience of athletic directors provides an additional illustration. Title IX required college athletic programs to eliminate disparities in resources between women's and men's programs, including salaries. Within ten years the proportion of coaches for women's programs who were male grew from 10 percent to 50 percent (Alfano 1985). Finally, men as the primary implementers of job evaluation have a second line of defense—they can and do subvert the process of job evaluation.

CONCLUSION

Integrating men's jobs and implementing comparable-worth programs have helped some women economically and, more fully implemented, would help others. But neither strategy can be broadly effective because both are premised on a flawed causal model of the pay gap that assigns primary responsibility to job segregation. A theory that purports to explain unequal outcomes without examining the dominant group's stake in maintaining them is incomplete. Like other dominant groups, men make rules that preserve their privileges. With respect to earnings, the current rule—that one's job or occupation determines one's pay—has maintained white men's economic advantage because men and women and whites and nonwhites are differently distributed across jobs.[14]

Changing the allocation principle from occupation to job worth would help nonwhites and women if occupation were the pay gap's *basic* cause. But it is not. As long as a dominant group wants to subordinate others' interests to its own and is able to do so, the outcome—distributing more income to men than women—is, in a sense, its own cause, and tinkering with superficial causes will not substantially alter the outcome. Either the rule that one's occupation determines one's wages exists *because* men and women hold different occupations, or men and women hold different occupations because we allocate wages according to one's occupation. Obviously the dominant group will resist attempts to change the rules. In *Lemons v. City and County of Denver* (1980), the court called comparable worth "pregnant with the possibility of disrupting the entire economic system" (Steinberg 1987). "Disrupting the entire white-male dominance system" would have been closer to the mark.

If men's desire to preserve their privileges is the basic cause of the wage gap, then how can we bring about change? The beneficiaries of hierarchical reward systems yield their privileges only when failing to yield is more costly than yielding. Increasing the costs men pay to maintain the status quo or rewarding men for dividing resources more equitably may reduce their resistance.

As individuals, many men will gain economically if their partners earn higher wages. Of course, these men stand to lose whatever advantages come from outearning one's partner (Hartmann 1976; Kollock, Blumstein, and Schwartz 1985). But more important than individual adjustments are those achieved through organizations that have the power to impose rewards and penalties. Firms that recognize their economic stake in treating women equitably (or can be pressed by women employees or EEO agencies to act as if they do) can be an important source of pressure on male employees. Employers have effectively used various incentives to overcome resistance to affirmative action (e.g., rewarding supervisors for treating women fairly [Shaeffer and Lynton 1979; Walshok 1981]). Employers are most likely to use such mechanisms if they believe that regulatory agencies are enforcing equal-opportunity rules (Reskin and Hartmann 1986). We can attack men's resistance through political pressure on employers, the regulatory agencies that monitor them, and branches of government that establish and fund such agencies.

Analyses of sex inequality in the 1980s implicitly advance a no-fault concept of institutionalized discrimination rather than fixing any responsibility on men. But men *are* the dominant group, the makers and the beneficiaries of the rules. Of course, most men do not consciously oppose equality for women (Kluegel and Smith 1986) or try to thwart women's progress. When men and women work together, both can gain, as occurred when the largely male blue-collar union supported the striking Yale clerical and technical workers (Ladd-Taylor 1985; see also Glazer 1987). But as a rule, this silent majority avoids the fray, leaving the field to those who do resist to act on behalf of all men (Bergmann and Darity 1981). It is time to bring men back into our theories of economic inequality. To do so does not imply that women are passive agents. The gains we have made in the last two decades in the struggle for economic equality—redefining the kinds of work women can do, reshaping young people's aspirations, and amassing popular support for pay equity despite opponents' attempt to write it off as a "loony tune" idea—stand as testimony to the contrary. Just as the causal model I propose views the dominant group's self-interest as the source of unequal outcomes, so too does it see subordinate groups as the agents of change.

ACKNOWLEDGMENTS

Author's note: This article is a revised version of the Cheryl Allyn Miller Lecture on Women and Social Change, presented at Loyola University on May 1, 1987. I am grateful to Sociologists for Women in Society and the friends and family of Cheryl Allyn Miller who prompted me to develop these ideas. The present version owes a great deal to Judith Lorber and Ronnie Steinberg for their extensive comments. I also wish to thank James Baron, Cynthia Epstein, Lowell Hargens, Mary Jackman, Kathleen Much, Deborah Rhode, Patricia Roos, and an anonymous reviewer for their helpful suggestions, but I ask readers to remember that I did not always take their advice and that they will not necessarily agree with my final conclusions. This article was partly prepared while I was a Fellow at the Center for Advanced Study in the Behavioral Sciences, where I was supported in part by a grant from the John D. and Catherine T. MacArthur Foundation. Grants from the National Science Foundation (SES-85-12452) and the Rockefeller Foundation Program on the Long-Term Implications of Changing Gender Roles supported the larger study that contributed to my developing these ideas.

NOTES

1. Women's incomes are not depressed uniformly. Women of color continue to earn less than white women, particularly when their hours of work are controlled. As I indicate below, the same general social processes that subordinate women as a group—differentiation and devaluation—operate to preserve the advantages of white men *and women.*

2. Workplace segregation occurs across occupations and, within occupations, across jobs. For convenience, I speak primarily of occupational segregation because most segregation and income data are for occupations, but my remarks apply as well to jobs.

3. My informant said his campus now weighs the admissions essay more heavily for this reason.

4. For example, Smith and Ward (1984) attributed the wage gap's failure to narrow to the influx of less-experienced women into the labor force during the 1970s.

5. Some employers do reward productivity, as neoclassical economists predict, but for the most part, wages are attached to occupations—the proximate cause of workers' wages.

6. Of course, only a subset of men—predominantly upper-class whites—actually make rules, and the rules they make protect class- and race- as well as sex-based interests.

7. A full explanation of the specific forces that produce the sexual division of labor is beyond the scope of this article, but social-control systems, including gender ideology, "custom," socialization, and myriad institutionalized structures, shape the preferences of wives and husbands, workers and employers, women and men (Reskin and Hartmann 1986). These preferences in turn are played out in concert with institutional arrangements (training programs, personnel practices, child-care facilities, informal organization) to give rise to the task differentiation we observe in the home and workplace.

8. This is not to say that all tasks assigned to subordinate groups are unimportant or undesirable. Many, such as reproducing, socializing the young, and burying the dead, are essential. Others are more intrinsically pleasant (e.g., office work) than the work some dominant-group members do (which has led economists to argue that men's wages are higher than women's partly to compensate them for doing less desirable jobs [Filer 1985]).

9. This perspective elucidates the importance that the media attached to the wearing, spurning, and burning of bras in the early 1970s. Shedding or burning these symbols of women's sex (and hence their status) constituted insubordination.

10. For example, at the 1987 meetings of the American Educational Research Association, 25 sessions reported research on sex differences in interest or achievement in math and science (Holden 1987, p. 660).

11. Trustee John Pope remarked, "Any time you get over 50 percent, it's becoming more and more a girls' school . . . and I don't think favoritism should be given to the females" (Greene 1987). It apparently did not strike him as favoritism when the rules produced a male majority.

12. The return in the late 1970s of feminine dress styles following the entry of large numbers of women into professional and managerial jobs is probably not coincidental. Although caution is in order in drawing conclusions about changing dress styles, a quick trip through a department store should persuade readers that dresses and skirts have supplanted pants for women (see Reskin and Roos 1987). Although fashion is ostensibly a woman's choice, most women are aware of the sanctions that await those who fail to dress appropriately.

13. Limited space forces me to condense sharply the causes of women's disproportional gains in these occupations. For a full account, see the complete studies.

14. It also serves the interest of the economically dominant classes by legitimating a wide disparity in income. Comparable-worth pay would largely preserve that disparity, in keeping with the class interests of its middle-class proponents and its implementers (Brenner 1987).

REFERENCES

Acker, Joan. 1987. "Sex Bias in Job Evaluation: A Comparable-Worth Issue." Pp. 183–96 in *Ingredients for Women's Employment Policy,* edited by Christine Bose and Glenna Spitze. Albany: SUNY University Press.

AFSCME v. State of Washington. 1985. 770 F.2d 1401. 9th Circuit.

Alfano, Peter. 1985. "Signs of Problems Amid the Progress." *New York Times* (December 14):25, 28.

Anderson, Susan Heller. 1987. "Men's Clubs Pressed to Open Doors for Women." *New York Times* (February 1).

Association of American Colleges. 1985. "Princeton's All-Male Eating Clubs Eat Crow." *Project on the Status and Education of Women* (Fall):11.

Becraft, Carolyn. 1987. "Women in the Military." Pp. 203–7 in *The American Woman: A Report in Depth,* edited by Sara Rix. New York: W. W. Norton.

Beller, Andrea. 1984. "Trends in Occupational Segregation by Sex and Race." Pp. 11–26 in *Sex Segregation in the Workplace: Trends, Explanations, Remedies,* edited by Barbara F. Reskin. Washington, DC: National Academy Press.

Berger, Joseph, Bernard P. Cohen, and Morris Zelditch. 1972. "Status Characteristics and Social Interaction." *American Sociological Review* 37:241–55.

Bergmann, Barbara R. 1974. "Occupational Segregation, Wages and Profits When Employers Discriminate by Race or Sex." *Eastern Economic Journal* 1:103–10.

Bergmann, Barbara R. and William Darity. 1981. "Social Relations, Productivity, and Employer Discrimination." *Monthly Labor Review* 104:47–9.

Bielby, William T. and James N. Baron. 1984. "A Woman's Place Is with Other Women." Pp. 27–55 in *Sex Segregation in the Workplace: Trends, Explanations, Remedies,* edited by Barbara F. Reskin. Washington, DC: National Academy Press.

Bird, Chloe. 1987. "Changing Sex Composition of Bank and Financial Managers." Unpublished manuscript. University of Illinois, Urbana.

Blau, Francine D. and Marianne A. Ferber. 1986. *The Economics of Women, Men and Work.* Englewood Cliffs, NJ: Prentice-Hall.

Bleier, Ruth. 1987. "Gender Ideology: The Medical and Scientific Construction of Women." Lecture presented at the University of Illinois, Urbana.

Brenner, Johanna. 1987. "Feminist Political Discourses: Radical vs. Liberal Approaches to the Feminization of Poverty and Comparable Worth." *Gender & Society* 1:447–65.

Cockburn, Cynthia. 1986. "The Relations of Technology: Implications for Theories of Sex and Class." Pp. 74–85 in *Gender and Stratification,* edited by Rosemary Crompton and Michael Mann. Cambridge, England: Polity Press.

Cohn, Samuel. 1985. *The Process of Occupational Sex Typing.* Philadelphia: Temple University Press.

Collins, Randall. 1975. *Conflict Sociology.* New York: Academic Press.

Coverman, Shelley. 1983. "Gender, Domestic Labor Time, and Wage Inequality." *American Sociological Review* 48:623–37.

de Beauvoir, Simone. 1953. *The Second Sex.* New York: Knopf.

Dex, Shirley. 1985. *The Sexual Division of Work.* New York: St. Martin's Press.

Donato, Katharine M. 1986. "Women in Systems Analysis." Paper presented at Annual Meetings, American Sociological Association, New York.

———. 1987. "Keepers of the Corporate Image: Women in Public Relations." Paper presented at Annual Meetings, American Sociological Association, Chicago.

Epstein, Cynthia F. 1985. "Ideal Roles and Real Roles or the Fallacy of the Misplaced Dichotomy." *Research in Social Stratification and Mobility* 4:29–51.

Feldberg, Roslyn L. 1984. "Comparable Worth: Toward Theory and Practice in the U.S." *Signs: Journal of Women in Culture and Society* 10:311–28.

Filer, Randall K. 1985. "Male-Female Wage Differences: The Importance of Compensating Differentials." *Industrial & Labor Relations Review* 38:426–37.

Fishman, Pamela. 1982. "Interaction: The Work Women Do." Pp. 170–80 in *Women and Work,* edited by Rachel Kahn-Hut and Arlene Kaplan Daniels. New York: Oxford University Press.

Glazer, Nona Y. 1987. "Where Are the Women? The Absence of Women as Social Agents in Theories of Occupational Sex Segregation." Paper presented at Annual Meetings, American Sociological Association, Chicago.

Goffman, Erving. 1976. "Gender Display." *Studies in the Anthropology of Visual Communication* 3:69–77.

———. 1977. "The Arrangement Between the Sexes." *Theory and Society* 4:301–31.

Goode, William C. 1964. *The Family.* Englewood Cliffs, NJ: Prentice-Hall.

———. 1982. "Why Men Resist." Pp. 121–50 in *Rethinking the Family,* edited by Barrie Thorne with Marilyn Yalom. New York: Longman.

Greene, Elizabeth. 1987. "Too Many Women? That's The Problem at Chapel Hill, Say Some Trustees." *Chronicle of Higher Education* (January 28):27–8.

Greer, William R. 1987. "In Professions, Women Now a Majority." *New York Times* (March 19):C1, 10.

Gregory, R. G. 1987. Lecture, Labor and Industrial Relations Institute, University of Illinois, Urbana.

Grimm, James W. and Robert N. Stern. 1974. "Sex Roles and Internal Labor Market Structures: The Female Semi-Professions." *Social Problems* 21:690–705.

Hartmann, Heidi. 1976. "Capitalism, Patriarchy, and Job Segregation by Sex." *Signs: Journal of Women in Culture and Society* 1, (Part 2):137–69.

Hechinger, Fred M. 1987. "The Trouble with Quotas." *New York Times* (February 10):C1.

Hochschild, Arlie. 1983. *The Managed Heart.* Berkeley, CA: University of California Press.

Holden, Constance. 1987. "Female Math Anxiety on the Wane." *Science* 236:660–61.

Hymowitz, Carol and Timothy D. Schellhardt. 1986. "The Glass Ceiling." *The Wall Street Journal* (March 24):Section 4, 1.

Jackman, Mary and Michael Muha. 1984. "Education and Intergroup Attitudes." *American Sociological Review* 49: 751–69.

Jagger, Allison M. 1983. *Feminist Politics and Human Nature.* Totowa, NJ: Rowman & Allanheld.

Jay, Nancy. 1981. "Gender and Dichotomy." *Feminist Studies* 7:38–56.

Journal of Accountancy. 1984. "J of A Revisited: Women in Accountancy." 158:151–2.

Kanter, Rosabeth Moss. 1987. "Men and Women of the Change Master Corporation (1977–1987 and Beyond): Dilemmas and Consequences of Innovations of Organizational Structure." Paper presented at Annual Meetings, Academy of Management, New Orleans.

Kessler, Suzanne and Wendy McKenna. 1978. *Gender: An Ethnomethodological Approach.* New York: John Wiley.

Kluegel, James R. and Eliot R. Smith. 1986. *Beliefs about Inequality.* New York: Aldine de Gruyter.

Kollock, Peter, Philip Blumstein, and Pepper Schwartz. 1985. "Sex and Power in Interaction." *American Sociological Review* 50:34–46.

Ladd-Taylor, Molly. 1985. "Women Workers and the Yale Strike." *Feminist Studies* 11:464–89.

Lemon v. City and County of Denver. 1980. 620 F.2d 228. 10th Circuit.

Lieberson, Stanley. 1980. *A Piece of the Pie.* Berkeley: University of California Press.

———. 1985. *Making It Count.* Berkeley: University of California Press.

Lukas, J. Anthony. 1985. *Common Ground.* New York: Knopf.

Luxenberg, Stan. 1985. *Roadside Empires.* New York: Viking.

MacKinnon, Catharine. 1987. *Feminism Unmodified.* Cambridge, MA: Harvard University Press.

Major, Brenda, Dean B. McFarlin, and Diana Gagnon. 1984. "Overworked and Underpaid: On the Nature of Gender Differences in Personal Entitlement." *Journal of Personality and Social Psychology* 47:1399–1412.

Marshall, Ray and Beth Paulin. N.D. "Some Practical Aspects of Comparable Worth." Unpublished manuscript.

Martin, Susan E. 1980. *Breaking and Entering.* Berkeley: University of California Press.

May, Martha. 1982. "Historical Problems of the Family Wage: The Ford Motor Company and the Five Dollar Day." *Feminist Studies* 8:395–424.

Mead, Margaret. 1949. *Male and Female.* New York: Morrow.

National Organization for Women. 1982. *NOW Times,* July.

New York Times. 1984. "Air Force Studies Male-Female Missile Crews." December 12.

———. 1987. "Dispute on Sex Ratio Troubles Women at North Carolina University." March 22.

Papanek, Hanna. 1973. "Purdah: Separate Worlds and Symbolic Shelter." *Comparative Studies in Society and History* 15:289–325.

Phillips, Anne and Barbara Taylor. 1980. "Sex and Skill." *Feminist Review* 6:79–88.

Phipps, Polly. 1986. "Occupational Resegregation: A Case Study of Insurance Adjusters, Examiners and Investigators." Paper presented at Annual Meetings, American Sociological Association, New York.

———. 1987. "Women in Pharmacy: Industrial and Occupational Change." Paper presented at Annual Meetings, American Sociological Association, Chicago.

Pleck, Joseph H. 1985. *Working Wives, Working Husbands.* Beverly Hills, CA: Sage.

Pugh, M.D. and Ralph Wahrman. 1983. "Neutralizing Sexism in Mixed-Sex Groups: Do Women Have to Be Better than Men?" *American Journal of Sociology* 88:746–62.

Reskin, Barbara F. 1978. "Sex Differentiation and the Social Organization of Science." *Sociological Inquiry* 48:6–36.

———. 1987. "Culture, Commerce and Gender: The Changing Sex Composition of Book Editors." Unpublished manuscript.

———. and Heidi I. Hartmann. 1986. *Women's Work, Men's Work, Sex Segregation on the Job.* Washington, DC: National Academy Press.

Reskin, Barbara F. and Patricia A. Roos. 1987. "Sex Segregation and Status Hierarchies." Pp. 1–21 in *Ingredients for Women's Employment Policy,* edited by Christine Bose and Glenna Spitze. Albany: SUNY University Press.

———. Forthcoming. *Gendered Work and Occupational Change.*

Roberts, Helene E. 1977. "The Exquisite Slave: The Role of Clothes in the Making of the Victorian Woman." *Signs: Journal of Women in Culture and Society* 2:554–69.

Rollins, Judith. 1985. *Between Women.* Philadelphia: Temple University Press.

Roos, Patricia A. 1986. "Women in the Composing Room: Technology and Organization as the Determinants of Social Change." Paper presented at Annual Meetings, American Sociological Association, New York.

Rubin, Gayle. 1975. "The Traffic in Women: Notes on the 'Political Economy' of Sex." Pp. 157–210 in *Toward an Anthropology of Women,* edited by Rayna R. Reiter. New York: Monthly Review Press.

Rytina, Nancy F. and Suzanne M. Bianchi. 1984. "Occupational Reclassification and Changes in Distribution by Gender." *Monthly Labor Review* 107:11–17.

Schafran, Lynn Hecht. 1981. *Removing Financial Support from Private Clubs that Discriminate Against Women.* New York: Women and Foundations Corporate Philanthropy.

Schroedel, Jean Reith. 1985. *Alone in a Crowd.* Philadelphia: Temple University Press.

Schur, Edwin M. 1983. *Labeling Women Deviant.* New York: Random House.

Shaeffer, Ruth Gilbert and Edith F. Lynton. 1975. *Corporate Experience in Improving Women's Job Opportunities.* Report no. 755. New York: The Conference Board.

Simmons, Adele, Ann Freedman, Margaret Dunkle, and Francine Blau. 1975. *Exploitation from 9 to 5.* Lexington, MA: Lexington.

Smith, James P. and Michael Ward. 1984. *Women's Wages and Work in the Twentieth Century.* R-3119 NICHD. Santa Monica, CA: Rand Corporation.

Spenner, Kenneth I. 1985. "The Upgrading and Downgrading of Occupations: Issues, Evidence, and Implications for Education." *Review of Educational Research 55* (Summer):125–54.

Steiger, Thomas. 1987. "Female Employment Gains and Sex Segregation: The Case of Bakers." Paper presented at Annual Meetings, American Sociological Association, Chicago.

Steinberg, Ronnie J. 1984–85. "Identifying Wage Discrimination and Implementing Pay Equity Adjustments." In *Comparable Worth: Issues for the 80s.* Vol. 1. Washington, DC: U.S. Commission on Civil Rights.

———. 1987. "Radical Challenges in a Liberal World: The Mixed Successes of Comparable Worth." *Gender & Society* 1:466–75.

Thomas, Barbara J. 1987. "Changing Sex Composition of Insurance Agents." Unpublished manuscript.

———. and Barbara F. Reskin. 1987. "Occupational Change and Sex Integration in Real Estate Sales." Paper presented at the Annual Meetings, American Sociological Association, Chicago.

Treiman, Donald J. and Heidi Hartmann. 1981. *Women, Work and Wages.* Washington, DC: National Academy Press.

van den Berghe, Pierre. 1960. "Distance Mechanisms of Stratification." *Sociology and Social Research* 44:155–64.

Walshok, Mary Lindenstein. 1981. "Some Innovations in Industrial Apprenticeship at General Motors." Pp. 173–82 in *Apprenticeship Research: Emerging Findings and Future Trends* edited by Vernon M. Briggs, Jr., and Felician Foltman. Ithaca: New York State School of Industrial Relations.

West, Candace and Don H. Zimmerman. 1987. "Doing Gender." *Gender & Society* 1:125–51.

Wharton, Amy and James Baron. 1987. "The Impact of Gender Segregation on Men at Work." *American Sociological Review* 52:574–87.

R E A D I N G   2 4

Race, Sex, and Class: Black Female Tobacco Workers in Durham, North Carolina, 1920–1940, and the Development of Female Consciousness

BEVERLY W. JONES

This article examines how race, sex, and class affected the lives and consciousness of black female tobacco workers in Durham, North Carolina, and how they conceptualized work and its meaning in their lives. The research was based

Beverly W. Jones, "Race, Sex, and Class: Black Female Tobacco Workers in Durham, North Carolina, 1920–1940, and the Development of Female Consciousness," *Feminist Studies* 10, no. 3 (Fall 1984). Copyright © 1984 by Feminist Studies, Inc. Reprinted with the permission of Feminist Studies, Inc., c/o Women's Studies Program, University of Maryland, College Park, MD 20742.

on 15 interviews. The interviewees fall into three broad age categories: five were born before 1908, seven between 1908 and 1916, and three between 1916 and 1930. All were born in the rural South. The majority migrated to Durham in the 1920s, subsequently entering the labor force.

Historically, black labor of both females and males has been critical to the tobacco manufacturing industry. As cigarette manufacture became mechanized, blacks were hired as stemmers, sorters, hangers, and pullers. These "dirty" jobs were seen as an extension of field labor and therefore as "Negro work" for which whites would not compete.[1]

TABLE I TOBACCO INDUSTRY EMPLOYMENT BY RACE AND GENDER

DURHAM COUNTY: 1930			
White		Negro	
Male	Female	Male	Female
2,511	2,932	1,336	1,979
NORTH CAROLINA: 1940			
White		Negro	
Male	Female	Male	Female
6,517	3,175	5,899	5,898

SOURCE : U.S. Bureau of the Census, *Population: 1930* (Washington, D.C.: GPO, 1930), vol. 3, pt. 2, pp. 355, 378; *Labor Force: 1940* (Washington, D.C.: GPO, 1940), vol. 3, pt. 4, p. 566.

The rapidly expanding number of tobacco factories employed the thousands of black females and males migrating from the rural South. The pull of better paying jobs and the push of falling farm prices, perennial pests, and hazardous weather induced a substantial number of black sharecroppers, renters, and landowners to seek refuge in Durham.

Charlie Necoda Mack, the father of three future female tobacco workers, remembered the difficulties of making an adequate living out of farming in Manning, South Carolina. "I was a big cotton farmer; I made nine bales of cotton one year. Next year I made, I think, one or two, and the next year I didn't make none. I left in July, I had to leave. I borrowed money to get up here—Durham. I had six children and I know no jobs available. Well, then I came up here in July in 1922 and got a job at the factory. And by Christmas I had all my children with clothes and everything." Unlike the Mack family, who were pushed out of South Carolina, others were pulled into the city. Dora Miller, after marrying in 1925, left Apex, North Carolina, because she heard of the "better paying jobs in Durham." Mary Dove, at age 10 and accompanied by her family, left Roxboro, North Carolina, because a "Duke agent told us that a job in the factory at Liggett Myers was waiting for my daddy." Rosetta Branch, age eighteen and single, left Wilmington, North Carolina, because her mother had died, and "there were no other kinfolks."[2]

Thus, Durham's gainfully employed black population swelled from 6,869 in 1910 to 12,402 in 1930. (The city's total black population in 1930 was 23,481.) According to the census, the number of black female tobacco workers in 1930 was 1,979 out of a total black female population of

12,388. (See table 1.) Durham and Winston-Salem tobacco factories employed more black females than other cities: one-half of the number of women employed in tobacco factories in 1930 in these cities were black compared with the 19.7 in Petersburg and Richmond in Virginia.[3]

Upon disembarking at the central train station, the newly arrived southern migrants were immediately faced with race restrictions. Rigidly segregated communities were the dominant feature of Durham's black life. Many of the migrants settled in the dilapidated housing in the larger communities of East End and Hayti, a bustling commercial district of black businesses, and in the smaller areas of Buggy Bottom and Hickstown. Almost all black workers rented either from the company and white landlords or from black real estate agents. The comments of Annie Barbee, the daughter of Necoda Mack, reflect her first impressions of Durham.

We were renting in the southern part of Durham—the Negro section—on Popular Street, second house from the corner, across the railroad tracks. The house was small, two rooms, but somehow we managed. The street was not paved and when it rained it got muddy and in the fall, the wind blew all the dust into your eyes and face. There were no private family bathrooms. But it was an exciting life. See, in the country things were so dull—no movie houses. . . . Up here people were always fighting and going on all the time.[4]

Despite the exploitive living conditions described by Barbee, urban employment did have some liberating consequences for rural daughters.

Race restricted the black population to segregated neighborhoods and also determined the kinds of jobs black females could get. Black female tobacco workers also faced discrimination as poor people and as females. Although class and sex restraints punctuated the lives of white female tobacco workers, their impact was reinforced by management policies. Although white females' wages were a fraction of white males' and inadequate to support a family, black females' wages were even lower. According to some black female tobacco workers, the wage inequity led many white women to consider black women inferior. This in turn led to an atmosphere of mistrust between black and white females. Management strengthened racial and class inequities in hiring practices, working conditions, and spatial organization of the factory, and therefore impeded the formation of gender bonds among working-class women.

Black females were usually hired as if they were on an auction block. "Foremen lined us up against the walls," one worker stated, "and chose the sturdy robust ones." Mary Dove recalled that she had "to hold up one leg at a time and then bend each backwards and forwards."[5] Once hired, black and white women were separated on different floors at the American Tobacco Company and in entirely different buildings at the Liggett & Myers Tobacco Company. In the 1920s and 1930s, according to a report by the Women's Bureau (the federal agency created in 1920), and confirmed by my interviews, 98 percent of these black females were confined to the prefabrication department, where they performed the "dirty" jobs—sorting, cleaning, and stemming tobacco.[6] White females had the "cleaner" jobs in the manufacturing and packing department as they caught, inspected, and packed the tobacco. However, both jobs were defined by the sex division of labor—jobs to be performed by women. Black men moved between the areas pushing 500-pound hogsheads of tobacco while white men worked as inspectors, safeguarding the sanctity of class and sex segregation.[7]

Reflecting on these blatant differences in working conditions, some 50 years later many black women expressed anger at the injustice. Annie Barbee recalled: "You're over here doing all the nasty dirty work. And over there on the cigarette side white women over there wore white uniforms. . . . You're over here handling all the old sweaty tobacco. There is a large difference. It ain't right!" Rosetta Branch spoke of her experience with anger. "They did not treat us Black folks right. They worked us like dogs. Put us in separate buildings . . . thinking maybe we were going to hurt those white women. Dirty work, dirty work we had to do. Them white women think they something working doing the lighter jobs."[8] These comments reflect both the effectiveness of management policies to aggravate racial and sexual differences in order to preclude any possible bonds of gender, but also illustrate the unhealthy working conditions to which black women were exposed.

In fact, the interviews indicate that the health of some black women suffered in the factories. Pansy Cheatham, another daughter of Necoda Mack, maintained that the Georgia leaf tobacco "was so dusty that I had to go to the tub every night after work. There was only one window and it got so hot that some women just fainted. The heat and smell was quite potent." Mary Dove recounted one of her fainting spells. "You know on the floor there was a salt dispenser, because it would get so hot. I did not feel so well when I came to work but I had to work. After about two hours standing on my feet, I got so dizzy—I fell out. My clothes was soaking wet from my head to my feet. When I woke up I was in the dispensary."[9]

Blanche Scott and another worker were forced to quit for health reasons. Scott, who began working for Liggett & Myers in 1919, quit four years later. "When I left the factory, it became difficult for me to breathe. The dust and fumes of the burly tobacco made me cough. The burly tobacco from Georgia had chicken feathers and even manure in it. Sometimes I would put an orange in my mouth to keep from throwing up. I knew some women who died of TB." The other worker had miscarried twice. Pregnant again, she decided not to return to the American Tobacco Company. "I felt that all that standing while I stemmed tobacco," she stated, "was the reason I lost my two children." Some women found momentary relief from the dust by retreating outside the confines of the factory complex to breathe the fresh air while sitting under trees or on the sidewalk during lunch.[10]

These comments on the poor, unhealthy working conditions were verified by research on Durham's death records between 1911 and 1930. In many instances, the records were imprecise and failed to provide information about race and occupation. Of the 105 certificates that identified black women as tobacco workers who died between 1911 and 1920, 48 (about 46 percent) died of tuberculosis, sometimes listed as phthisis and consumption. Of the 134 recorded deaths of black female tobacco workers between 1920 and 1930, 86 (64.5 percent) died of tuberculosis. Because tuberculosis is caused by a bacillus that can be transmitted by a tubercular person through the cough, it is likely that poorly ventilated rooms and incessant coughing by workers, possibly by a carrier, made some workers susceptible to the disease, although deplorable living conditions for workers cannot be dismissed as a contributing factor.[11]

As studies have found in other cities, black females in Durham were more likely to work than white females.[12] Black females also earned lower wages than white females. In the early 1900s, wages for black tobacco workers, both female and male, ranked the lowest in the nation. In 1930, 45.5 percent of native-born white women in Durham were gainfully employed—27.7 percent in tobacco. While 44 percent of black women were working, 36.2 percent were employed in tobacco. From 1920 to 1930, Durham's white female tobacco workers averaged about 29 cents per hour, while black female hand stemmers earned about 11.9 cents an hour. However, black men, as well as black women who stemmed tobacco by machine, averaged about 27 cents an hour, still less than white women.[13]

Wage differentials continued and worsened throughout the 1930s. By the eve of the New Deal, a Women's Bureau survey reported figures for North Carolina which revealed an even higher wage discrepancy. White women working in the making and packing departments reported a median weekly wage of $15.35. Wages ranged from $14.10 earned as catchers to $20.50 on older packing machines. On the newest packing machines, the median wage was $18.15. Black women, working in the leaf department, reported a median weekly wage of $7.95. Hand stemmers earned a median wage of $6.50.[14]

The low wage was itself demeaning to black female workers. But the inadequate wages also forced many into the labor force at an early age. Black women thus worked for a longer part of their lives, and henceforth were more vulnerable to diseases and other health problems. Blanche Scott, for example, began working at the age of twelve. "Since my mother stayed so sick, I had to go to work. I worked at Liggett Myers after school got out. I attended West End School. I'd normally get out at 1:30 and worked from two o'clock to 6 P.M. I was just twelve years old. In the summer, they're let children come and work all day until four o'clock." Pansy Cheatham began working at age thirteen. "My father talked to the foreman," she stated. "I worked because my sisters Mae and Annie worked; I stemmed tobacco by hand. But Papa did collect the money and use it for food and clothing." Cheatham's statement would indicate that at the top of the gender hierarchy of the black family was the father, who controlled the daughter's wages.[15]

Many women saw their employment as a means of "helping out the family." Better stated in the words of Margaret Turner, "that's what a family is all about, when we—the children—can help out our parents."[16] Out of the fifteen interviewees, the ten women who entered the work force at an early age all conceptualized the central meaning of their work in relation to their families.

By the late 1920s and early 1930s, the enforcement of the Child Labor Law of 1917 arrested the practice of employing children under the age of sixteen. "They began to ask for your birth certificate," one worker stated. A study done by Hugh Penn Brinton substantiated the decrease of child labor employment in Durham's factories. Brinton found that from 1919 to 1930 the percentage of black laboring-class households sending children into the labor force had decreased from 35 to 14 percent.[17]

However, the legislation against child labor did not force the wages up for black tobacco workers, and the constant low earning power of both female and male breadwinners continued to affect the lives of black female workers psychologically. Many women submitted to the demands of the foreman and other company officials. Viewed as short-term cheap labor, some females submitted to physical and

verbal harassment, because in many instances defiance would have certainly resulted in the loss of jobs. Dora Miller asserted that "since the foreman knew you needed the job, you obeyed all of his demands without question. He called you dirty names and used foul language but you took it." Mary Dove recalled what it was like to work under one "of the toughest bosses." "Our foreman was a one-eyed fella named George Hill. He was tight! He was out of South Carolina, and he was tight. I mean tight! He'd get on top of them machines—they had a machine that altered the tobacco—he'd get on top of that machine and watch you, see if you was working all right and holler down and curse. Holler down and say, 'GD . . . get to work! GD . . . go to work there you ain't doin' nothing.' Janie Mae Lyons remembered one who walked in on her while she "was in the sitting position on the stool" and told her "that if you ain't finished then you can pack up and leave. I was so embarrassed and that's what I did."[18]

Lyons's departure from the factory represented a form of militancy—a definitive stance against further harassment. Other women resisted verbally. Annie Barbee publicly castigated "women who allowed the foreman to fumble their behind" and further stated that if "one did that to me he would be six feet under." She indicated no one ever did. One worker resisted "by playing the fool." "The foreman thought I was crazy and left me alone."[19]

Constantly resisting physical and verbal abuse and trying to maintain their jobs, the workers were further threatened by increased mechanization. "I don't think it is right," one woman stated, "to put them machines to take away from us poor people." "Because of the strain we work under," another maintained, "they don't care nothing for us." One woman recalled crying at the machines because she could not quit in the face of high unemployment. "With them machines you have to thread the tobacco in. Them machines run so fast that after you put in one leaf you got to be ready to thread the other. If you can't keep pace the foreman will fire you right on the spot. Sometimes I get so nervous but I keep on going."[20]

The increased mechanization of the tobacco factories resulting in physical hardships of female workers can to some degree be attributed to Franklin D. Roosevelt's National Industrial Recovery Acts of 1933 and 1934. On the one hand, President Roosevelt's New Deal measures fostered economic stability for many black families by establishing standard minimum wages and maximum hours. On the other hand, this standardization exacerbated the job insecurity of black workers by indirectly catalyzing many companies to maximize profits by replacing hand labor with technology. During the latter part of the 1930s, Liggett & Myers closed its green leaf department, which had employed the majority of black women.[21]

The long-term insecurities of their jobs led black female stemmers to organize Local 194. The limited success of the union was reflected in the decline of its membership of two thousand in January 1935 to less than two hundred by May 1935. Black female union members found little support from either Local 208, black controlled, or Local 176, white controlled. In the eyes of the male unionists, the temporary nature of women's jobs excluded them from any serious consideration by the locals.[22] Conscious of their auxiliary position and the lack of support from male-led unions, black females chose not to support the April 16, 1939, strike at Liggett & Myers. Reporting for work on that day, they were turned away as management had no other recourse but to close the factory. Dora Miller recalled that the black stemmery workers "were never involved in the strike because demands for wage increases did not include us."[23] On April 26, 1939, the company capitulated. The contract indeed reaffirmed Miller's assessment because the stemmery workers were not mentioned.[24]

The factory policies of hiring, wages, working conditions, and spatial segregation, inherently reinforced by racism, the "cult of true white womanhood," and the inadvertent effect of New Deal governmental measures, all came together to touch the lives of black women tobacco workers with sex, race, and class exploitation. These practices further dissipated any possible gender bonds between black women and white women workers. As a race, black female tobacco workers were confined to unhealthy segregated areas either in separate buildings or on separate floors. As a working class, they were paid inadequate wages. As a sex, they were relegated to the worst, lowest paid, black women's jobs.

Black females conceptualized work as a means of "helping out the family." Denied self-respect and dignity in the factory, black female tobacco workers felt a need to validate themselves in other spheres. Victimized by their working conditions, female tobacco workers looked to the home as a preferred if not powerful arena. The home became the inner world that countered the factory control over their physical well-being. The duality of their lives—workers of production and nurturers of the family—could be assessed as a form of double jeopardy. But it was their role as nurturers, despite the hardship of work, that provided them with a sense of purpose and "joy." As Pansy Cheatham described her daily routine, "I get up at 5:30 A.M. I feed, clothe, and kiss my children. They stay with my sister while I work. At 7 A.M. I am on the job. A half-hour for lunch at about 12 noon. At 4 P.M. I quit work. At home about 4:30, then I cook, sometimes mend and wash clothes before I retire. About 11:30 I go to bed with joy in my heart for my children are safe and I love them so."[25]

Black females who worked together in the tobacco factories also had the positive experience of creating networks of solidarity. Viewing their plight as one, black females referred to one another as "sisters." This sisterhood was displayed in the collection of money during sickness and death and celebration of birthdays. The networks established in the factory overlapped into the community and church. Many of these workers belonged to the same churches—Mount Vernon, Mount Gilead, and White Rock Baptist churches—and functioned as leaders of the usher boards, missionary circles, and Sunday School programs. These bonds were enhanced in the community by the development of clubs. These church groups and females' clubs overlapped the factory support networks and functioned in similar ways.

Finally, the resistance to the physical and verbal abuse that was a constant in the work lives of black women fostered among some a sense of autonomy, strength, and self-respect. Annie Barbee was one of those women. The assertiveness, dignity, and strength she developed through work became an intricate part of her private life. At age 40 and pregnant, she decided to obtain private medical assistance despite her husband's resistance. "When you know things ain't right God gave you a head and some sense. That's my body. I knew I wasn't going to Duke Clinic. And I was working and making my own money, I went where I wanted to go. You see, being married don't mean that your husband controls your life. That was my life and I was carrying his child, it's true, but I was going to look after myself."[26]

Although the work experience of black women tobacco workers was one of racial, sex, and class oppression, the early entrance into the labor force, the resistance to exploitation, and the longevity of work created a consciousness that fostered a sense of strength and dignity among some women in this working class. Management tactics of wage inequity, hiring practices, and racial-sexual division of labor pitted black women against white women economically as workers, and made the formation of gender bonds across race lines all but impossible. Yet among black women, the linkages of sisterhood engendered a consciousness of female strength, if not feminism.

ACKNOWLEDGMENTS

I am deeply grateful to North Carolina Central University for a Faculty Research Grant and for the excellent editorial comments of the *Feminist Studies* editors.

NOTES

1. For discussion of the historical involvement of black labor in tobacco manufacturing, see Joseph C. Robert, *The Tobacco Kingdom* (Durham, N.C.: Duke University Press, 1938).

2. Author's interviews with Charlie Necoda Mack, 22 May 1979; Dora Miller, 6 June 1979; Mary Dove, 7 July 1979; Rosetta Branch, 15 August 1981; all on file in the Southern Oral History Program, University of North Carolina, Chapel Hill, hereafter cited as SOHP/UNC.

3. The 1940 labor force figures do not include information for Durham County. U.S. Bureau of the Census, *Population: 1930* (Washington, D.C.: GPO, 1930), 3:341. In 1900, the major tobacco industries in the South were the American Tobacco Company and Liggett & Myers in Durham; R. J.Reynolds in Winston-Salem; and P. Lorillard in Richmond, Virginia.

4. Annie Barbee, interview, 28 May 1979, SOHP/UNC.

5. Mary Dove, interviews, 7 July 1971 and 30 May 1981.

6. Women's Bureau, *The Effects of Changing Conditions in the Cigar and Cigarette Industries,* Bulletin no. 110 (Washington, D.C.: GPO, 1932), 774–75. The Women's Bureau was established by Congress in 1920 under the aegis of the United States Department of Labor. Its purpose was to gather information and to provide advice to working women.

7. Mary Dove, interviews, 7 July 1971, 15 and 28 August 1981.

8. Annie Barbee and Rosetta Branch, interviews.

9. Pansy Cheatham, interview, 9 July 1979, SOHP/UNC; Mary Dove, interview, 7 July 1971.

10. Blanche Scott, interviews, 11 July 1979 (SOHP/UNC), 8 and 15 June, 1981; Mary Dove, Annie Barbee interviews.

11. Death certificates, 1911–1930, Durham County Health Department, Vital Records, Durham, North Carolina. I was also interested in the correlation of working conditions and female-related maladies such as stillbirths, miscarriages, and uterine disorders. Further perusal of death certificates of stillbirths was less valuable for there were no indications of mothers' occupations. Even hospital statistics lacked occupational data. This area of inquiry as it relates to the health of black female workers and working conditions needs further research. Further questions that will have to be explored include: Was there a higher percentage of female tobacco workers dying of tuberculosis than non-female tobacco workers? How long were stricken female workers employed in the factory? How much weight must be given to the working environment over that of home environs? Despite the lack of solid data on these questions, the interviews and death records clearly indicate that racial division of labor negatively impacted upon the health of many black female tobacco workers.

12. Elizabeth H. Pleck, "A Mother's Wage: Income Earning among Married Italian and Black Women, 1896–1911," in *The American Family in Social-Historical Perspective,* 2d ed, ed. Michael Gordon (New York: St. Martin's Press, 1978), 490–510; "Culture, Class, and Family Life among Low-Income Urban Negroes," in *Employment, Race, and Poverty,* ed. Arthur M. Ross and Herbert Hill (New York: Harcourt Brace & World, 1967), 149–72; "The Kindred of Veola Jackson: Residence and Family Organization of an Urban Black American Family," in *Afro-American Anthropology: Contemporary Perspectives,* ed. Norman E. Whitten, Jr., and John F. Szwed (New York: Free Press, 1970), chap. 16.

13. U.S. Bureau of the Census, *Population: 1930,* vols. 3 and 4; U.S. Department of Labor, Women's Bureau, *Hours and Earning in Tobacco Stemmeries,* Bulletin no. 127 (Washington, D.C.: GPO, 1934).

14. Women's Bureau, *Effects of Changing Conditions,* 172–75.

15. Blanche Scott and Pansy Cheatham, interviews.

16. Margaret Turner, interview with author, 25 September 1979, SOHP/UNC.

17. Interview, 8 June 1981; Hugh Penn Brinton, "The Negro in Durham: A Study in Adjustment to Town Life" (Ph.D. diss., University of North Carolina, Chapel Hill, 1930).

18. Dora Miller and Mary Dove, interviews; Janie Mae Lyons, interview with author, 4 August 1981.

19. Annie Barbee, interviews 28 May 1979, 10 July 1981.

20. Interviews, 4 and 15 June 1981.

21. For the best discussions of the National Industrial Recovery Act's impact on blacks, see Raymond Wolters, *Negroes and the Great Depression: The Problem of Economic Recovery,* ed. Stanley E. Kutler (Westport, Conn.: Greenwood, 1970); and Bernard Sternsher, ed., *The Negro in the Depression and War: Prelude to Revolution, 1930–45* (Chicago: Quadrangle, 1969). Also see Dolores Janiewski, "From Field to Factory: Race, Class, and Sex and the Woman Worker in Durham, 1880–1940" (Ph.D. diss., Duke University, 1979).

22. *Durham* (N.C.) *Morning Herald,* 17, 18 April 1939, p. 1; Janiewski.

23. Dora Miller, interview.

24. For terms of contract, see *Durham Morning Herald* and *Durham Sun,* 27 April 1939, pp. 1, 2; Janiewski.

25. Pansy Cheatham, interview.

26. Annie Barbee, interview.

Serving Hamburgers and Selling Insurance: Gender, Work, and Identity in Interactive Service Jobs

ROBIN LEIDNER

All workers look for ways to reconcile the work they do with an identity they can accept, either by interpreting the work positively or by discounting the importance of the work as a basis of identity. Hughes, emphasizing the active process of interpretation, recommended examining the "social and social-psychological arrangements and devices by which men [sic] make their work tolerable, or even make it glorious to themselves and others" ([1951] 1984, 342). If the work cannot be construed as glorious, or even honorable, workers will look for ways to distance themselves from their jobs, assuring themselves that the work they are doing does not reflect their true worth. One of the most important determinants of the meaning of a type of work, as well as of how the work is conducted and rewarded, is its association with a particular gender. Acceptance by a worker of the identity implied by a job is therefore determined in part by the degree to which the job can be interpreted as allowing the worker to enact gender in a way that is satisfying.

Much contemporary theory and research on gender shares an emphasis on its active and continual construction through social interaction (Garfinkel 1967; Goffman 1977; Kessler and McKenna 1978; West and Zimmerman 1987). West and Zimmerman argue that "participants in interaction organize their various and manifold activities to reflect or express gender, and they are disposed to perceive the behavior of others in a similar light" (1987, 127). One of the most striking aspects of the social construction of gen-

der is that its successful accomplishment creates the impression that gender differences in personality, interests, character, appearance, manner, and competence are natural—that is, that they are not social constructions at all. Gender segregation of work reinforces this appearance of naturalness. When jobholders are all of one gender, it appears that people of that gender must be especially well suited to the work, even if at other times and places, the other gender does the same work. Thus Milkman's analysis of industrial work during World War II demonstrates "how idioms of sex-typing can be flexibly applied to whatever jobs women and men happen to be doing" (1987, 50).

In this article, I will argue that jobholders and their audiences may make this interpretation even under the most unlikely conditions: when the work might easily be interpreted as more suitable for the other gender, and when many aspects of the workers' presentations of self are closely dictated by superiors and are clearly not spontaneous expressions of the workers' characters, interests, or personalities. My analysis of the flexibility of interpretations of gender-appropriate work draws on research on the routinization of jobs that involve direct interaction with customers or clients—what I call "interactive service work" (see Leidner 1988). These sorts of jobs merit attention, since service work is increasingly central to the U.S. economy: The service sector is expected to continue to provide most new jobs through the year 2000 (Personick 1987; Silvestri and Lukasiewic 1987).

Interactive service jobs have several distinctive features that make them especially revealing for investigation of the interrelation of work, gender, and identity. These jobs differ from other types of work in that the distinctions among product, work process, and worker are blurred or nonexistent, since the quality of the interaction may itself be part of

Robin Leidner, "Serving Hamburgers and Selling Insurance: Gender, Work, and Identity in Interactive Service Jobs," *Gender & Society* 5, no. 2 (June 1991). Copyright © 1991 by Sociologists for Women in Society. Reprinted with the permission of Sage Publications.

the service offered (Hochschild 1983). In many kinds of interactive service work, workers' identities are therefore not incidental to the work but are an integral part of it. Interactive jobs make use of workers' looks, personalities, and emotions, as well as their physical and intellectual capacities, sometimes forcing them to manipulate their identities more self-consciously than do workers in other kinds of jobs. The types of relations with service recipients structured by the jobs may also force workers to revise taken-for-granted moral precepts about personal interaction. Workers who feel that they owe others sincerity, individual consideration, nonmanipulativeness, or simply full attention may find that they cannot be the sort of people they want to be and still do their jobs adequately (Hochschild 1983). While a variety of distancing strategies and rationalizations are possible (Rollins 1985), it may be difficult for interactive service workers to separate themselves from the identities implied by their jobs (Leidner 1988).

When interactive work is routinized, workers' interactions are directly controlled by employers, who may use scripting, uniforms, rules about proper demeanor and appearance, and even far-reaching attempts at psychological reorientation to standardize service encounters. The interactions are expressly designed to achieve a certain tone (friendliness, urgency) and a certain end (a sale, a favorable impression, a decision). Analysis of how employers try to combine the proper interactive elements to achieve the desired effects can make visible the processes by which meaning, control, and identity are ordinarily created through interaction in all kinds of settings. Workers' and service recipients' acceptance or rejection of the terms of the standardized interactions and their efforts to tailor the prescribed roles and routines to suit their own purposes are similarly revealing about the extent to which people sustain beliefs about who they are through how they treat others and are treated by them.

Gender is necessarily implicated in the design and enactment of service interactions. In order to construct routines for interactions, especially scripts, employers make many assumptions about what customers like, what motivates them, and what they consider normal interactive behavior. Some of the assumptions employers make concern how men and women should behave. Once these assumptions about proper gender behavior are built into workers' routines, service recipients may have to accept them in order to fit smoothly into the service interaction. My research on the routinization of service jobs was inspired in part by my astonishment at one such script: I

learned that employees of Gloria Marshall Figure Salons were expected to ask their customers, "Have you and your husband discussed your figure needs?" (Lally-Benedetto 1985). The expectation that workers could toss out the term *figure needs* as if it were everyday speech was startling in itself, but I was especially intrigued by the layers of assumptions the question implied about the natures of women and men and the power relations between them.

As this example illustrates, scripts can embody assumptions about proper gendered behavior in fairly obvious ways. To do such jobs as intended, workers must "do gender" in a particular way (Berk 1985b; West and Zimmerman 1987). Even where the gender component is less obvious, workers in all kinds of jobs need to consider how their work relates to their own identities, including their gender identities. Whether workers take pride in the work itself or see it as stigmatizing, whether they work harder than is required or put in the least effort they can get away with, and whether they identify themselves with the job or seek self-definition elsewhere are related not just to job tasks and working conditions but to the extent that the jobs can be interpreted as honorable, worthwhile, and suitable for persons of their gender (Ouellet 1986).

This process of interpretation may be unusually salient and unusually open to analysis in routinized interactive service work. In such jobs, a convincing performance is important, and so employers are concerned about the degree to which workers enact their roles with conviction. The employers may therefore participate in reconciling workers' selves with the identities demanded by the work by providing positive interpretations of the work role or psychic strategies for dealing with its potentially unpleasant or demeaning aspects. In short, employers of interactive service workers may be unusually open in their attempts to channel workers' attitudes and manipulate workers' identities.

Gender is more salient in some service jobs than others, of course. There are routinized interactive service jobs for which the gender of employees and customers is not particularly relevant to how the jobs were constructed or how the interactions are carried out—telephone interviewing, for example, is apparently gender neutral and is done by men and women. However, the gender of workers is not irrelevant in these jobs, since respondents may react differently to men and women interviewers. Similarly, while airplane flight attendant is a job currently held by men as well as women, Hochschild found that men flight attendants were more likely to have their authority respected and less likely to be subjected to emotional outbursts from passengers than were their women co-workers (Hochschild 1983). At the other extreme are jobs that are gender segregated and that would be virtually incomprehensible without extensive assumptions about how both workers and customers enact gender. The Gloria Marshall salon workers' job assumed that both workers and customers would be women. The script used by Playboy Bunnies, who were trained to respond to being molested by saying, "Please, sir, you are not allowed to touch the Bunnies" (Steinem 1983, 48), took for granted a male customer (see also Spradley and Mann 1975). Both scripts dictated "common understandings" about what men and women are like and how power is distributed between them.

I studied two jobs that fall between these extremes; they are neither gender neutral nor entirely saturated with assumptions about gender. I conducted fieldwork at McDonald's and at Combined Insurance Company of America. At McDonald's, my research centered on the food servers who dealt directly with the public (*window crew,* in McDonald's parlance), and at Combined Insurance, I studied life insurance agents. These jobs were not strictly gender segregated, but they were held predominantly by either men or women, influencing how workers, employers, and customers thought about the jobs. Most, but not all, of McDonald's window crew were young women, and almost all of Combined Insurance's agents were men. Their gender attributes were not essential to their jobs. In fact, both jobs can be gender typed in the opposite direction—in its early years, McDonald's hired only men (Boas and Chain 1976), and in Japan, door-to-door insurance sales is a woman's job (*Life Insurance Business in Japan, 1987/88*).

Workers in both jobs tried to make sense of de facto job segregation by gender, interpreting their jobs as congruent with proper gender enactment. Examination of these two jobs and of how workers thought about them highlights a central paradox in the construction of gender: The considerable flexibility of notions of proper gender enactment does not undermine the appearance of inevitability and naturalness that continues to support the division of labor by gender. Although the work of the insurance agents required many of the same kinds of interactive behavior as the McDonald's job, including behavior that would ordinarily be considered feminine, the agents were able to interpret the work as suitable only for men. They did so by emphasizing aspects of their job that required "manly" attributes and by thinking about their interactive work in terms of control rather than deference. Their interpretation suggests not only the plasticity of gender idioms but the asymmetry of those idioms: Defining work as masculine has a different

meaning for men workers than defining work as feminine has for women workers.

Because interactive service work by definition involves nonemployees in the work process, the implications of the gender constructions of the routines extend beyond the workers. When service jobs are done predominantly by men or predominantly by women, the gender segregation provides confirming "evidence" to the public that men and women have different natures and capabilities. This appearance is especially ironic when employers, treating their workers' selves as fairly malleable, reshape the self-presentations and interactional styles of the service workers. A brief account of my fieldwork and of the routinization of the two jobs precedes further discussion of how work, gender, and identity are enmeshed in these jobs.

ROUTINIZED INTERACTIONS

My data were gathered from participant observation and interviewing. I attended classes at McDonald's management training center, Hamburger University, in June 1986, and spoke with "professors" and trainees there. I conducted research at a local McDonald's franchise from May through November 1986, going through orientation and window-crew training, working on the window, interviewing window workers and managers, and hanging around the crew room to observe and talk with workers. At Combined Insurance, I went through the two-week training for life insurance agents in January 1987. Between January and March, I interviewed trainees and managers and spent one-and-a-half weeks in the field with a sales team, observing sales calls and talking to agents. Since insurance agents must be licensed and bonded, I did not actually sell insurance myself. I also conducted follow-up interviews with Combined Insurance managers in the summer of 1989. The workers and managers with whom I worked at both companies were aware that I was conducting research.

These two jobs were similar in a number of ways. Both were filled, by and large, with young, inexperienced workers, and both had extremely high rates of employee turnover. Neither job is held in high esteem by the public, which affected both customers' treatment of workers and the workers' willingness to embrace their roles (see Zelizer 1979, on the low prestige of life insurance agents). The companies, however, took training very seriously, and they carried the routinization of service interactions very far indeed. McDonald's and Combined Insurance each tried to exercise extensive control over their workers' presentation of themselves. However, they went about this task differently and placed different sorts of demands on their workers' psyches. The differences largely have to do with the kinds of relations that the companies established between workers and customers and are related to the gender typing of the work.

McDonald's

McDonald's has been a model of standardization for many kinds of service businesses, and its success, based upon the replication of standard procedures, has been truly phenomenal. The goal is to provide the same quality of food and service every day at every McDonald's, and the company tries to leave nothing to chance. Individual franchisees have considerable leeway in some matters, including labor practices, but they are held to strict standards when it comes to the McDonald's basics of QSC—quality, service, and cleanliness.

At the McDonald's where I worked, all of the workers were hired at the minimum wage of $3.35. There were no fringe benefits and no guarantee of hours of work. As is typical at McDonald's, most men worked on the grill, and most women worked serving customers—about three-quarters of the window workers were women. About 80 percent of the restaurant's employees were Black, though Blacks were a minority of the city's population. Few of the workers were older than their early 20s, but most were out of high school—65 percent of my sample were 18 or over. The clientele, in contrast, was quite diverse in class, race, age, and gender.

The window workers were taught their jobs in a few hours and were fully trained in a couple of days. The job involved carrying out the "Six Steps of Window Service," an unvarying routine for taking and delivering orders. The modern cash registers used at this McDonald's made it unnecessary for window workers to remember prices or to know how to calculate change. The machines also reminded workers to "suggestive sell": For example, if someone ordered a Big Mac, french fries, and a shake, the cash register's buttons for apple pies, ice cream, and cookies would light up, to remind the worker to suggest dessert. (Garson [1988] provides a scathing view of McDonald's routinization and computerization.) These workers were closely supervised, not only by McDonald's managers, but also by customers, whose constant presence exerted pressure to be diligent and speedy.

The workers wore uniforms provided by McDonald's and were supposed to look clean-cut and wholesome—for instance, a young man with a pierced ear had to wear a Band-Aid on his earlobe. The lack of control workers had over their self-presentations was brought home clearly when a special promotion of Shanghai McNuggets began, and window workers were forced to wear big Chinese peasant hats made of Styrofoam, which most felt made them look ridiculous.

Workers were told to be themselves on the job, but they were also told to be cheerful and polite at all times. Crew people were often reprimanded for not smiling. Almost all of the workers I interviewed said that most customers were pleasant to deal with, but the minority of rude or unreasonable customers had a disproportionate impact. Enduring customers' behavior, no matter how obnoxious, was a basic part of the job. Unfortunately for the workers, they completely lacked what Hochschild calls a "status shield" (1983, 163). Some customers who might have managed to be polite to higher-status workers seemed to have no compunction at all about snarling at McDonald's employees. The window crew could not escape from angry customers by leaving, and they were not allowed to argue or make smartalecky remarks. Their only legitimate responses to rudeness or angry outbursts from customers were to control their anger, apologize, try to correct the problem, and in extreme cases, ask a manager to handle it.

The major task for the workers was to serve, and their major psychic task was to control or suppress the self. Workers were required to be nice to one person after another in a way that was necessarily unindividualized and to keep their tempers no matter how they were treated. What McDonald's demanded of its workers was a stripped-down interactive style, with some *pseudo-gemeinschaft* thrown in. The workers were supposed to be efficient, courteous, and friendly, but in short bursts and within a very narrow range. While they were told to be themselves, there was obviously not much range for self-expression.

Combined Insurance

Combined Insurance placed very different sorts of demands on its workers. The company's business is based on door-to-door sales in rural areas and small towns, and its profits depend on a high volume of sales of relatively inexpensive policies. Combined Insurance was founded in the 1920s by W. Clement Stone, and its agents still use many of the sales and self-conditioning techniques that he developed when he started out in the business-*The Success System That Never Fails* (Stone 1962). Almost all of the company's life insurance agents are men, most are white, and most are young—

all of the members of the sales team I studied were in their early twenties. The prospects I called on with the agents were all white, about equally men and women, and quite varied in age.

The agents' initial training was more extensive than the McDonald's workers', involving two weeks of lectures, script memorization, and role playing. During sales school, trainees were taught what to say and do in almost hilarious detail. They memorized scripts for the basic sales presentations, for Rebuttals 1 through 5, corresponding to Objections 1 through 5, and for Interruption-stoppers. They were taught exactly how to stand while waiting for a door to be opened, how to position themselves and the potential customers (known as "prospects"), when to make and break eye contact, how to deliver the Standard Joke, and so on. A lot of class time was spent chanting the scripts in unison and rehearsing proper body movements, as well as in practicing responses to be used in various sales situations.

The trainer underlined the possibility of success through standardization with stories of foreign-born agents who succeeded even before they could speak English—they allegedly learned their sales presentations phonetically. It might seem that the message of these stories was that a parrot could succeed in this job, but in fact, the trainer argued that personal characteristics were vitally important to success, and the most important of these was a Positive Mental Attitude—what Stone called PMA. While McDonald's merely instructed workers to smile and behave pleasantly to customers, Combined Insurance tried to affect its employees' psyches quite fundamentally—to inculcate optimism, determination, enthusiasm, and confidence and to destroy habits of negative thinking. The trainees were taught that through proper self-conditioning, they could learn to suppress negative thoughts altogether. The message for agents was somewhat paradoxical: You should do everything exactly the way we tell you to, but success depends on your strength of character.[1]

While McDonald's workers' main task was to serve people who had already chosen to do business with McDonald's, Combined Insurance's agents had to sell, to take prospects and turn them into customers. The agents' job was to establish rapport quickly with the people they called on (by "warming up the prospect"), to go through the basic sales presentation, to counter any objections raised by the prospects, and to persuade them to buy as much life insurance as possible. Naturally, most of the people they called on were strongly motivated to prevent them from going through this sequence, so their task was not easy. Since the agents' incomes were entirely based on commission, and their desire to handle their interactions successfully was of course very great, the detailed instructions for proper behavior provided by the company did not seem to strike them as ludicrous or intrusive.

Because the agents worked on their own, rather than in a central workplace, and because their interactions with customers could be much longer and cover a broader range than those of McDonald's workers, the agents were called on to use much more of their selves than the window workers were. They had to motivate themselves and keep up their enthusiasm, and they had to respond appropriately to a wide variety of situations, adjusting their behavior to suit the problems presented by each prospect. Although their basic routine was unvaried, they needed to be chameleon-like to a certain extent and adapt to circumstances. They were, like the McDonald's workers, required to control themselves, but their focus was always on controlling the prospect and the interaction. Virtually every detail of their routines was designed to help them do just that.

DOING GENDER WHILE DOING THE JOB

Although their jobs were largely segregated by gender, McDonald's and Combined Insurance workers interacted with both men and women as customers or prospects. Neither company suggested significantly different approaches to men and women service recipients; the Combined Insurance trainer recommended slightly varied techniques for persuading men and women to buy policies without first consulting their spouses. While the gender of the service recipient might well have influenced how the workers experienced their interactions, I did not find consistent patterns of variation in workers' behavior along this dimension.

At McDonald's, most of the window crew took the division of labor by gender for granted and did not seem to feel any need to account for it. Since there were no differences in the pay or prestige of window and grill work, and since there were exceptions to the pattern of gender segregation, few workers considered the division of labor by gender unfair.[2] When I asked the workers why they thought that there were more women than men working the window, about two-thirds of the 23 respondents said that they did not know, with about half offering a guess based on stereotypes about proper gender roles, whether or not they thought the stereotype was justified. About one-quarter of the sample, however, stated explicitly that they disapproved of the division of labor by gender, and three women said that they had asked a manager about it. The store's manager told me that women were typically assigned to start work on the window because "more females have an aversion to grill." Two of the window workers, however (both Black men), thought that men might have an aversion to window because that job required swallowing one's pride and accepting abuse calmly:

THEO: [More women than men work window] because women are afraid of getting burned [on the grill], and men are afraid of getting aggravated and going over the counter and smacking someone.

ALPHONSE: I found the men who work here on window have a real quick temper. You know, all of them. And women can take a lot more. They deal with a lot of things, you know.

Although I never heard the masculinity of the few male window workers impugned, it was commonly taken for granted that men were naturally more explosive than women and would find it more difficult to accept abuse without answering back. The male window workers were usually able to reconcile themselves to swallowing insults, as the women were, either by dissociating themselves from their role or by telling themselves that by keeping their tempers they were proving themselves superior to the rude customers. Refusing to become riled when provoked is consistent with "the cool pose," which Majors says Black men use to "fight to preserve their dignity, pride, respect and masculinity" by enacting an imperviousness to hurt (1989, 86). Thus, while the job did not allow workers to try to get the better of opponents, its demands were not seen as irreconcilable with enacting masculinity. However, no workers argued that men's capacity to tolerate abuse made them especially well-suited to the job, and the Black men quoted above made the opposite argument. Moreover, the job requirements of smiling and otherwise demonstrating deference are not in keeping with the cool pose. Those committed to that stance might well find such behavior demeaning, especially in interactions with white customers or those of higher status.

Other explanations given by workers of the predominance of women on window crew included assertions that women were more interested in dealing with people, that women "were more presentable" and looked better on window, that their nimble fingers suited them to working the registers, and that customers were more likely to find them trustworthy. Several of the workers who offered such stereotyped responses indicated that they did not believe

that the stereotypes were sufficient justification for the predominance of women on the window crew.

It might easily have been argued that men were unsuited to work on the grill—cooking, after all, is usually considered women's work. As the work was understood at McDonald's, however, cooking presented no challenge to masculinity. Serving customers, which involved adopting an ingratiating manner, taking orders from anyone who chose to give them, and holding one's tongue when insulted, was more difficult to conceive as congruent with the proper enactment of manliness. Thus, while the crew people did not argue that window work was especially expressive of femininity, most found it unremarkable that women predominated in that job.

The work of Combined Insurance's agents, in contrast, was defined as properly manly, even though the job presented interactive imperatives that are generally identified with femininity, along with some stereotypically masculine elements. The life insurance sales force was almost entirely composed of men, and the agents on the sales team I observed felt strongly that women would be unlikely to succeed in the job.[3] Moreover, the 22-year-old manager of this sales team told me bluntly (without my having raised the question) that he "would never hire a woman."[4] Since some aspects of the agents' job required skills that are not generally considered manly, the agents' understanding of the job as demanding masculine attributes meant that these skills had to be reinterpreted or de-emphasized.

Like many other kinds of interactive service jobs, including McDonald's window work, insurance sales requires that workers adopt an attitude of congeniality and eagerness to please. This in itself may strike some men as incompatible with the proper enactment of gender, as suggested by the cool pose, which associates masculinity with toughness and detachment (Majors 1989, 84). In *America's Working Man,* Halle records that a few of the chemical workers he studied did not support Jimmy Carter's presidential candidacy because they "suspected that a man who smiled all the time might be a homosexual" (1984, 246). To them, behavior that is transparently intended to please others, to encourage liking, is not considered masculine. Toughness, gruffness, and pride are taken-for-granted elements of masculinity to many blue-collar men (Gray 1987; Willis 1977), and Combined's agents come largely from blue-collar or agricultural backgrounds. For such men, deferential behavior and forced amiability are often associated with servility, and occasions that call for these attitudes—dealings with superiors, for instance—may feel humiliating. Such behavior is not easy to reconcile with the autonomy and assertiveness that are considered central to "acting like a man." The rebellious working class "lads" Willis studied were therefore concerned to find jobs with "an essentially masculine ethos," jobs "where you would not be expected to be subservient" (1977, 96). Sennett and Cobb, drawing on their interviews with blue-collar men, interpret the low prestige ratings of many service jobs relative to blue-collar jobs as a response to the perceived dependence of service workers on other people, whose shifting demands they must meet (1972, 236).

Thus the glad-handing insincerity required of many sorts of businessmen may seem effete and demeaning to working-class men. The job of salesman, which is on the lower end of the white-collar hierarchy, would seem especially degrading from this point of view. Since success is largely dependent on ingratiating oneself with customers, playing up to others is an essential part of the agent's job, rather than just a demand of the social milieu. Salesmen must swallow insults, treat even social inferiors with deference, and keep smiling.

These aspects of the sales job were quite pronounced for Combined Insurance's life agents. The warming-up-the-prospect phase of the routine called for agents to figure out what topics might interest the prospects and display a flattering enthusiasm for those topics and for the prospects' accomplishments. Agents had to be willing to disguise their true feelings and to seem to accept the prospect's view of the world in order to ingratiate themselves. It was crucial that they not lose their tempers with prospects but remain polite and respectful at all times. Like most salespeople, they had to try to change prospective customers' minds while never seeming to argue with them and to stay pleasant even when rudely dismissed.

The skills required for establishing and maintaining rapport—drawing people out, bolstering their egos, displaying interest in their interests, and carefully monitoring one's own behavior so as not to offend—are usually considered womanly arts. In analyses of a small sample of conversations, Fishman (1978) found that women had to do much more interactive work than men simply to sustain dialogues; men largely took for granted that their conversational attempts would succeed in engaging their partner's interest. Judging only by these interactive demands of insurance sales work, it would seem that women are especially well suited to be agents. We might even expect that the association of ingratiating conversational tactics with women would lead men to view the extensive interactive work required of salespeople as degrading, since it requires that they assume the role of the interactive inferior who

must constantly negotiate permission to proceed. Given the additional attack on personal autonomy implicit in Combined Insurance's programming of employees to follow scripts, it would seem to be difficult for men to combine successful enactment of the role of Combined Insurance agent with the successful enactment of gender.

On the contrary, Combined Insurance's trainers and agents interpreted the agent's job as demanding manly attributes. They assigned a heroic character to the job, framing interactions with customers as contests of will. To succeed, they emphasized, required determination, aggressiveness, persistence, and stoicism. These claims were accurate, but qualities in which women excel, including sensitivity to nuance and verbal dexterity, were also important for success. While the sales training did include tips on building such skills, determination and aggressiveness were treated as the decisive factors for career success. It was through this need for toughness that the work was constructed as manly.[5]

Of course it was quite true that considerable determination, self-motivation, and persistence were required to do this job. The agents had to make numerous sales calls every day, despite the knowledge that many people would be far from glad to see them. They had to keep making calls, even after meeting with repeated rejection and sometimes hostility. And in sales interactions, they had to stick to their objectives even when prospects displayed reluctance to continue the conversation, as most did. Some agents and managers believed that women were unlikely to meet these job demands because they are too sensitive, too unaggressive, and not able to withstand repeated rejection. Josh, one of the agents, claimed, "Most girls don't have what it takes. They don't have that killer instinct." Josh had, however, recruited a woman he knew to join Combined's sales force. "She does have [the killer instinct], if I can bring it out," he said. Ralph, the sales manager, also acknowledged that there might be some exceptional women who could do the job. He amended his statement that he would never hire a woman by saying, "Only if she had a kind of bitchy attitude." "A biker woman" is the kind he meant, he said, "someone hard-core." Obviously, he did not believe it was possible to combine the traits necessary for success as an agent with femininity.[6]

One manager attributed women's assumed deficiencies not to their nature but to economics, arguing that women whose husbands provided an income were unlikely to have the requisite "burning need" to succeed that financial necessity provides. An obvious factor that would prevent most mothers from taking the job—at least one week a month was spent away from home—was not mentioned by any agents in explaining the dearth of women agents, though two managers did mention it. Two agents told me that they "wouldn't want their wives doing this" because of the unpleasant or potentially dangerous places agents must sometimes visit.

This emphasis on aggression, domination, and danger is only one possible construction of sales work. Biggart (1989) and Connelly and Rhoton (1988) discuss in detail the very different ways that direct sales organizations that rely on a female labor force characterize sales work. These organizations, some of which are hugely successful, emphasize nurturance, helpfulness, and service both in relations with customers and among salespeople. Combined Insurance's training also encouraged agents to think of themselves as providing a service to prospective customers, largely in order to overcome trainees' reluctance to impose on others, and some of the agents I spoke with did use the service ideology to counter demeaning images of insurance sales as high-pressure hucksterism. For the most part, however, the agents emphasized the more "manly" dimensions of the work, though there is ample evidence that women can succeed in life insurance sales. For example, Thomas (1990) notes that after the Equitable Life Assurance Society made a commitment to recruiting and supporting women agents, the company's saleswomen outperformed salesmen in sales and commissions.

While most agents would not feel the need, on a daily basis, to construct an explanation for why there were so few women selling life insurance for their company, they did need to construct an interpretation of their work as honorable and fitting for a man if they were to maintain their positive attitudes and do well at their jobs, which required much more self-motivation than did McDonald's jobs. The element of competition, the battle of wills implicit in their interactions with customers, seemed to be a major factor that allowed the agents to interpret their work as manly. Virtually every step of the interaction was understood as a challenge to be met—getting in the door, making the prospect relax and warm up, being allowed to start the presentation, getting through the presentation despite interruptions, overcoming prospects' objections and actually making the sale, and perhaps even increasing the size of the sale. Since many prospects did their best to prevent the agents from continuing, going through these steps did not simply represent following a prescribed routine; it was experienced by agents as proof of their skill and victories of their wills. Each sales call seemed an uphill battle, as the interactions took place on the prospects' turf and prospects always had the option of telling the agent to leave.

The spirit of jousting was especially clear in some of the techniques taught for closing sales. As the trainer explained "The Assumptive Close," the agents were supposed to "challenge customers"; it was up to the prospects to object if they did not want to go along with the sales. The routine allowed agents to limit the customers' options without seeming to do so, to let prospects believe that they were making decisions while the agents remained in control of the interaction. The pattern bears some resemblance to the seduction of an initially unwilling partner, and the satisfaction that the agents took in "winning" such encounters is perhaps similar to the satisfaction some men take in thinking of sexual encounters as conquests. The agents seemed to approach sales interactions with men in much the same spirit as those with women, however, though they often adjusted their presentation of self to suit a particular prospect's gender, age, and manner—subtly flirtatious, respectfully deferential, or efficient and businesslike.

This sort of manipulation of interactions required a peculiar combination of sensitivity to other people and callousness. The agent had to figure out which approach would work best at any given moment and avoid seeming cold or aggressive but still disregard the customers' stated wishes. The required mix of deference and ruthlessness was well illustrated in an exchange that took place during a sales-team training session. The agents were discussing how to deal with interruptions during a presentation: One of their superiors had advised ignoring them altogether, but the "training module" stated that it was insulting to fail to acknowledge a prospect's comment. When the sales manager instructed, "You have to let them know that you heard them," one of the agents finished the sentence for him: "and that you don't give a shit."

All kinds of interactive service workers—including McDonald's window crew—try to exercise control over their interactions with customers, though not all of them are given organizational resources to help them do so (see, e.g., Whyte 1962, on waitresses, and Benson 1986, on department store saleswomen). Women who can successfully dominate interactions at work might well take pleasure in doing so, as did Combined's life insurance agents. However, it is unlikely that these women's capacity to control other people would be taken as evidence that the work was womanly, unless it were reinterpreted in less aggressive terms, such as "skill in dealing with people."

If following a script could be given a manly cast when it involved asserting one's will through controlling an interaction, it was more difficult to do so when the interactions did not go the agents' way. Refusals were such a routine part of the job, however, that agents could accept most of them as inevitable, not a result of lack of skill or determination. In sales school, the trainers emphasized that not everyone was going to buy—some people really do not need or cannot afford the product; some are just close-minded and would not listen to any salesperson. A greater challenge to the agent's definition of himself was presented by customers who were actively hostile. Some people were angry at being interrupted; some had a grievance against the company; some became furious if they felt that they were being manipulated. In any case, it was not unusual for agents to meet with loud insults, condescending sneers, and slammed doors. To accept this sort of treatment passively could certainly be seen as unmanly. However, the agents were expected to keep their cool, refrain from rudeness, and leave graciously. Some agents did tell me, with glee, of instances when they shouted obscenities once they got out the door, in response to particularly outrageous treatment from a customer. For the most part, however, passive acceptance of ill-treatment was reconciled with manly honor by defining it as maintaining one's control and one's positive attitude, a strategy similar to that used by male and female McDonald's workers. In this view, screaming back at a customer would not be considered standing up for yourself but letting the customer get the better of you, "letting them blow your attitude." Agents proved themselves to be above combative and insulting customers by maintaining their dignity and holding on to their self-concepts as winners, not by sinking to the customers' level.

Other attributes of the job, not directly connected with job routinization, also contributed to the salesmen's ability to define their jobs as compatible with properly enacting gender. The most important of these were the sense of independence agents felt and their belief that they could earn as much as they were worth. Within the limits of their work assignments, agents could set their own schedules, behave as they chose, and work only as hard as they felt like. Because of the importance of self-motivation to success, those who did well could feel justifiably proud, and those lacking in motivation could appreciate the freedom from pressure. The agents thus felt that their jobs provided some of the benefits of self-employment. They could live with the knowledge that many people looked down on them, put up with insults, endure futile days of failure, and still maintain a sense that their work was compatible with manliness and social honor, as long as there was the possibility of "making it big."

DISCUSSION

Until the 1970s, most sociological work concerning the connection between workers' genders and their jobs mirrored the commonsense view that men and women hold different sorts of jobs because of differing physical capacities, psychological orientations, and family responsibilities. Moss Kanter (1977) reversed the traditional argument that women's traits determine the sorts of jobs they hold, claiming instead that the structural features of most women's jobs determine characteristic attitudinal and behavioral responses, which are then interpreted as reflecting women's natures. She focused on power, opportunity, and numbers of like individuals in the workplace as the factors determining workers' responses to jobs. In her analysis, preexisting gender segregation leads workers, managers, and observers to believe incorrectly that gender explains how workers respond to their jobs. As Fenstermaker Berk (1985b) has argued, Moss Kanter understated the distinctive properties of gender and minimized the extent to which gender assumptions are built into jobs by work organizations (see also Acker 1990).

More recently, analysts have called attention to the ways that occupations are gendered—they are designed and evolve in particular ways because of the gender of typical incumbents (Cockburn 1985; Reverby 1987). Moreover, theorists have argued that gender is not simply imported into the workplace: Gender itself is constructed in part through work (Beechey 1988; Berk 1985a, 1985b). This argument applies both to the gender identities of individual workers and to cultural understandings of women's and men's natures and capacities and is supported by the cases of McDonald's and Combined Insurance.

Just how jobs are gendered and how doing these jobs affects workers' gender identities remain to be clarified, however. Cockburn describes the gendering of jobs and people as a two-way process: "People have a gender and their gender rubs off on the jobs they mainly do. The jobs in turn have a gender character which rubs off on the people who do them" (1985, 169). While acknowledging that the gender designation of jobs, tools, fields of knowledge, and activities may shift over time, she treats these designations as cultural givens. For example, Cockburn writes (1985, 70):

> An 18th-century man no doubt felt effeminate using a spinning wheel, though he would have felt comfortable enough repairing one. Today it is difficult to get a teenage lad to use a floor mop or a typewriter because they contradict his own gender identity.

Cockburn correctly perceives the relevance of work tasks to the workers' gender identity, but overstates the rigidity of the gender typing of those tasks: At McDonald's, mopping has largely become low-status men's work. I argue that despite the existence of culturally shaped gender designations of work activities, employers and workers retain the flexibility to reinterpret them in ways that support jobholders' gender identities. However, the gender designation of work is likely to have different kinds of significance for women and men.

Workers at both McDonald's and Combined Insurance were expected to adjust their moods and demeanors to the demands of their jobs and to learn to handle customers in ways that might be very different from their ordinary styles of interaction. To some extent, workers in both jobs had to take on the role of interactive inferior, adjusting themselves to the styles and apparent preferences of their customers. They were supposed to paste on smiles when they did not feel like smiling and to behave cheerfully and deferentially to people of every status and with every attitude. The workers were not permitted to respond to rudeness in kind but had to try to remain pleasant even in the face of insult.

This sort of behavior is usually associated with femininity, but in fact the two jobs were interpreted quite differently. At McDonald's, many workers and managers considered it natural, even self-evident, that women were best suited to deal with customers. At Combined Insurance, women were generally seen as ill equipped to handle such work. The insurance agents were able to define their job as masculine by emphasizing those aspects of the work that require "manly" traits (control and self-direction) and by reinterpreting some of the more "feminine" job requirements in ways that were not degrading. McDonald's workers' superiors emphasized that the crew's role was to serve, and attempts by window workers to assert their wills in interactions with customers were strongly discouraged. Combined Insurance's agents, on the other hand, were taught that their job was to establish and maintain control in interactions with prospects. They were told that they control their own destinies and were urged to cultivate the qualities of aggressiveness, persistence, and belief in themselves. While success might require that they take on a deferential manner, it was seen as a matter of skill in manipulating situations, not as servility, and therefore was not taken to be inconsistent with manliness. Similarly, accepting abuse calmly was interpreted as a refusal to let someone else dictate the terms of the interaction, not as a loss of control. This conceptualization of the work as an arena for enacting masculinity allowed the agents to accept working conditions that might otherwise have been seen as unacceptably frustrating and demeaning.

When Hughes called attention to the "social and social-psychological arrangements and devices by which men make their work tolerable, or even make it glorious to themselves and others," he apparently meant "men" to include men and women. In fact, the case of Combined Insurance's agents suggests that defining a job as "men's work" is precisely how some men make their work tolerable or even glorious. Willis (1977) and Ouellet (1986) have shown how ideas about masculinity can transform what otherwise might be considered negative job features—danger, hard physical labor, dirt—into badges of honor. In other circumstances, work that seems "glorious" on its own merits—because it is understood to be important, highly skilled, responsible, powerful—is defined as masculine (see, e.g., Cockburn 1985). Identifying work as manly, then, can compensate male workers for hardships, but it also justifies privilege.

Some working-class boys and men insist that only jobs that are physically demanding, exhausting, or dangerous can be considered manly (cf. Halle 1984; Willis 1977), but in fact, the gender designation of particular job tasks is quite plastic, a matter of interpretation in which jobholders, employers, and customers may participate. The actual features of the work do not rigidly determine its gender designation. Nevertheless, the association of a job with manliness serves to elevate the work itself and allows men to construe success on the job as proof of masculinity. The importance of manly work for constructing and maintaining masculine identity may explain some of the resistance of men working in gender-segregated occupations to women co-workers; they tend to define their work not just as particularly appropriate for men but as work that women would not be able to do (Cockburn 1983, 1985; Halle 1984; Swerdlow 1989; Willis 1977). The experiences of women entering previously male-dominated occupations bear out this interpretation. For example, Schroedel (1985, 20-21) quotes a female pipe fitter:

> You see it is just very hard for them to work with me because they're really into proving their masculinity and being tough. And when a woman comes on a job that can work, get something done as fast and efficiently, as well as they can, it really affects them. Somehow if a woman can do it, it ain't that masculine, not that tough.

The Combined Insurance agents sustained the belief that women could not handle their job, even though the work required some skills and qualities typically associated with women.

Interpreting work as womanly has a different meaning for women than interpreting work as manly has for men.

Certain jobs, including nursing and elementary-school teaching, are understood to require some positively valued "female" traits, such as nurturance or sensitivity, and the identification of the work with femininity significantly determines how the work is organized (Melosh 1982; Reverby 1987). Even when the work is seen as expressive of feminine capacities, however, it is not seen as offering proof of female identity in quite the same way that manly work supports male identity, because adult female identity has not traditionally been regarded as something that is achieved through paid work. In other words, while women in traditionally female-defined jobs might well take pleasure in doing work that supports their self-identification as feminine, they are unlikely to think of such work as a necessary part of their gender identity. Thus men and women respond differently to challenges to gender segregation of work. Williams (1989) found that women nurses did not feel threatened when men joined their ranks, though male marines much preferred to keep women out of the corps. Furthermore, while male nurses were concerned to differentiate their activities from those of their women co-workers, female marines did not feel that doing quintessentially masculine work was a challenge to their femininity.

Williams draws on the work of Chodorow (1978) to provide a psychoanalytic explanation for male workers' concern with defining their work as masculine and with maintaining gender segregation at work. She argues that because men, whose original identification is with a female caretaker, must achieve masculinity by distancing themselves from femininity, they are psychologically threatened when one proof of their masculinity is challenged by evidence that women can do the work they have defined as manly. Women, who need not alter their original identification with a female caretaker, have no corresponding need to prove their femininity: "What one *does* has little bearing on how feminine one is" (Williams 1989, 140; emphasis in original). Whether or not the psychoanalytic explanation is valid, Williams persuasively demonstrates that gendered jobs have different meanings for men and women.

The different cultural valuation of behavior labeled masculine and feminine also contributes to the different meanings that enacting gender at work has for women and men. While the constant "doing" of gender is mandatory for everyone, many theorists have noted that the effects of this demand are asymmetrical, since doing masculinity generally means asserting dominance, while doing femininity often means enacting submission (Acker 1990; Berk 1985a). Frye claims (1983, 33) that the female "cannot move or speak without engaging in self-deprecation. The male cannot move or speak without engaging in self-

aggrandizement." Thus many men value the opportunity to do work that supports cultural understandings of masculinity and their own sense of manliness, but we cannot assume that job features that allow or require gender-appropriate behavior will necessarily be welcomed by women workers in the same way. In some cases, women may appreciate the opportunity to enact such "womanly" attributes as nurturance, helpfulness, or sexiness at work, because that behavior affirms their gender identity. On the other hand, servility may be congruent with femininity, but we would hardly expect female McDonald's workers to take the same pleasures in enacting it at work that Combined's agents take in asserting control.

Job features that allow or require gender-appropriate behaviors are not necessarily welcomed, then, but work routines that prevent workers from enacting gender in ways that they are comfortable with are resented and may contribute to workers' decisions to limit their investments of energy, effort, and self-definition in their jobs. Job features that allow gender enactment in ways workers find gratifying, on the other hand, may make up for deficiencies in more objective job benefits. In any case, the variation in the interpretations of similar job demands at McDonald's and Combined Insurance demonstrates that the actual features of the jobs do not themselves determine whether the work will be defined as most appropriate for men or women. Rather, these job features are resources for interpretation that can be drawn on by workers, their superiors, and other audiences.

Despite this flexibility in the interpretation of gender appropriateness, in these two work settings the association of the work with either women or men was made to seem natural—an expression of the essential natures of women and men. Even though the workers' behavior was largely dictated by routines they had no part in creating, and even where the job drew on traits associated with both femininity and masculinity, job segregation by gender was interpreted largely as an outgrowth of inherent gender differences in attitudes and behavior. In trying to make sense of the fact of gender segregation, many of the workers and managers I spoke with drew on taken-for-granted beliefs about the qualities and preferences of women and men. The prevalence of either men or women in a job became evidence that the job demanded specifically masculine or feminine qualities and that the jobholders must be best suited for the work. For the public, as well as for employers and workers, gender segregation of service jobs contributes to the general perception that differences in men's and women's social positions are straightforward reflections of differences in their natures and capabilities.

ACKNOWLEDGMENTS

This article is the 1989 winner of the American Sociological Association Sex and Gender Section Dissertation Paper Award.

I would like to thank Carol A. Heimer, Arthur L. Stinchcombe, Arlene Kaplan Daniels, Sam Kaplan, Judith Lorber, and the Gender & Society reviewers for their help and suggestions.

NOTES

1. Combined Insurance has recently made changes in its life insurance products and sales techniques. Agents are now taught a more interactive sales routine ("needs selling") for a policy that can be tailored to suit customers' circumstances, allowing the agents somewhat greater flexibility. The company's largest division, which sells accident insurance, continues to follow Stone's original techniques closely. Positive Mental Attitude training is still stressed for all agents.

2. The job of "host," however, was viewed as less prestigious by some workers. That polite job title referred to those whose main responsibilities were to empty the trash and keep the lobby, windows, bathrooms, and dining areas clean. When one woman took this job, I heard two women window workers express their disapproval; they felt that "girls" should not have to do the dirty work of handling garbage.

3. I learned, in fact, that the two other women in my training class had lasted, respectively, only one day and three weeks in the field. Managers interviewed in 1989 reported that the number of women agents had increased since the new selling system was introduced, though women were still a small minority of the sales force. Reduced travel demands were one reason given for the job's increasing attractiveness to women. See also note 5.

4. The higher-level managers I interviewed did not endorse these discriminatory views, and some commented on the many successful women in the insurance industry. See Thomas (1990) for a discussion of the growth of women's employment in insurance sales. She shows that by 1980, women were 25 percent of U.S. insurance agents.

5. Some managers believe that the new needs-selling approach is better suited to women agents because it requires a less domineering stance and allows women to draw on their understanding of families' needs.

6. Similarly, Williams (1989, 32) reports a backlash against women in the military among male soldiers during World War II. She argues that military men claimed that women soldiers must be unfeminine because the men did not want to accept the alternative explanation for the women's presence—that military service is not inherently masculine.

REFERENCES

Acker, Joan. 1990. Hierarchies, jobs, bodies: A theory of gendered organizations. *Gender & Society* 4:139–58.

Beechey, Veronica. 1988. Rethinking the definition of work: Gender and work. In *Feminization of the labor force: Paradoxes and promises,* edited by Jane Jenson, Elisabeth Hagen, and Ceallaigh Reddy. New York: Oxford University Press.

Benson, Susan Porter. 1986. *Counter cultures: Saleswomen, managers, and customers in American department stores, 1890–1940.* Urbana: University of Illinois Press.

Berk, Sarah Fenstermaker. 1985a. *The gender factory: The apportionment of work in American households.* New York: Plenum.

———. 1985b. Women's work and the production of gender. Paper presented at the annual meeting of the American Sociological Association, Washington, DC.

Biggart, Nicole. 1989. *Charismatic capitalism: Direct selling organizations in America.* Chicago: University of Chicago Press.

Boas, Max, and Steve Chain. 1976. *Big Mac: The unauthorized story of McDonald's.* New York: Mentor, New American Library.

Chodorow, Nancy. 1978. *The reproduction of mothering: Psychoanalysis and the sociology of gender.* Berkeley: University of California Press.

Cockburn, Cynthia. 1983. *Brothers: Male dominance and technological change.* London: Pluto.

———. 1985. *Machinery of dominance: Women, men and technical know-how.* London: Pluto.

Connelly, Maureen, and Patricia Rhoton. 1988. Women in direct sales: A comparison of Mary Kay and Amway sales workers. In *The worth of women's work: A qualitative synthesis,* edited by Anne Statham, Eleanor M. Miller, and Hans O. Mauksch. Albany: State University of New York Press.

Fishman, Pamela M. 1978. Interaction: The work women do. *Social Problems* 25:397–406.

Frye, Marilyn. 1983. Sexism. In *The politics of reality*. Trumansberg, NY: Crossing Press.

Garfinkel, Harold. 1967. *Studies in ethnomethodology*. Englewood Cliffs, NJ: Prentice-Hall.

Garson, Barbara. 1988. *The electronic sweatshop*. New York: Simon & Schuster.

Goffman, Erving. 1977. The arrangements between the sexes. *Theory and Society* 4:301–31.

Gray, Stan. 1987. Sharing the shop floor. In *Beyond patriarchy: Essays by men on pleasure, power, and change*, edited by Michael Kaufman. Toronto: Oxford University Press.

Halle, David. 1984. *America's working man*. Chicago: University of Chicago Press.

Hochschild, Arlie Russell. 1983. *The managed heart: Commercialization of human feeling*. Berkeley: University of California Press.

Hughes, Everett C. [1951] 1984. Work and self. In *The sociological eye*. New Brunswick, NJ: Transaction.

Kanter, Rosabeth Moss. 1977. *Men and women of the corporation*. New York: Basic Books.

Kessler, Suzanne J., and Wendy McKenna. 1978. *Gender: An ethnomethodological approach*. Chicago: University of Chicago Press.

Lally-Benedetto, Corinne. 1985. Women and the tone of the body: An analysis of a figure salon. Paper presented at the annual meeting of the Midwest Sociological Society, St. Louis, MO.

Leidner, Robin. 1988. Working on people: The routinization of interactive service work. Ph.D. diss., Northwestern University, Evanston, IL.

Life insurance business in Japan, 1987/88. Tokyo: Life Assurance Association of Japan.

Majors, Richard. 1989. Cool pose: The proud signature of Black survival. In *Men's lives*, edited by Michael S. Kimmel and Michael A. Messner. New York: Macmillan.

Melosh, Barbara. 1982. *"The physician's hand": Work culture and conflict in American nursing*. Philadelphia: Temple University Press.

Milkman, Ruth. 1987. *Gender at work: The dynamics of job segregation by sex during World War II*. Urbana: University of Illinois Press.

Ouellet, Lawrence J. 1986. Work, commitment, and effort: Truck drivers and trucking in small, non-union, West coast trucking companies. Ph.D. diss., Northwestern University, Evanston, IL.

Personick, Valerie A. 1987. Industry output and employment through the end of the century. *Monthly Labor Review* 10 (September): 30–45.

Reverby, Susan M. 1987. *Ordered to care: The dilemma of American nursing, 1850–1945*. Cambridge: Cambridge University Press.

Rollins, Judith. 1985. *Between women: Domestics and their employers*. Philadelphia: Temple University Press.

Schroedel, Jean Reith. 1985. *Alone in a crowd: Women in the trades tell their stories*. Philadelphia: Temple University Press.

Sennett, Richard, and Jonathan Cobb. 1972. *The hidden injuries of class*. New York: Knopf.

Silvestri, George T., and John M. Lukasiewic. 1987. A look at occupational employment trends to the year 2000. *Monthly Labor Review* 10 (September): 46–63.

Spradley, James P., and Brenda J. Mann. 1975. *The cocktail waitress: Woman's work in a man's world*. New York: Wiley.

Steinem, Gloria. 1983. I was a Playboy bunny. In *Outrageous acts and everyday rebellions*. New York: Holt, Rinehart & Winston.

Stone, W. Clement. 1962. *The success system that never fails*. Englewood Cliffs, NJ: Prentice-Hall.

Swerdlow, Marian. 1989. Men's accommodations to women entering a nontraditional occupation: A case of rapid transit operatives. *Gender & Society* 3:373–87.

Thomas, Barbara J. 1990. Women's gains in insurance sales: Increased supply, uncertain demand. In *Job queues, gender queues: Women's movement into male occupations*, edited by Barbara Reskin and Patricia Roos. Philadelphia: Temple University Press.

West, Candace, and Don Zimmerman. 1987. Doing gender. *Gender & Society* 1:125–51.

Whyte, William F. 1962. When workers and customers meet. In *Man, work, and society*, edited by Sigmund Nosow and William H. Form. New York: Basic Books.

Williams, Christine. 1989. *Gender differences at work: Women and men in nontraditional occupations*. Berkeley: University of California Press.

Willis, Paul. 1977. *Learning to labor: How working class kids get working class jobs*. New York: Columbia University Press.

Zelizer, Viviana A. Rotman. 1979. *Morals and markets: The development of life insurance in the United States*. New York: Columbia University Press.

Boundary Lines: Labeling Sexual Harassment in Restaurants

PATTI A. GIUFFRE and CHRISTINE L. WILLIAMS

Sexual harassment occurs when submission to or rejection of sexual advances is a term of employment, is used as a basis for making employment decisions, or if the advances create a hostile or offensive work environment (Konrad and Gutek 1986). Sexual harassment can cover a range of behaviors, from leering to rape (Ellis, Barak, and Pinto 1991; Pryor 1987; Reilly et al. 1992; Schneider 1982). Researchers estimate that as many as 70 percent of employed women have experienced behaviors that may legally constitute sexual harassment (MacKinnon 1979; Powell 1986); however, a far lower percentage of women claim to have experienced sexual harassment. Paludi and Barickman write that "the great majority of women who are abused by behavior that fits legal definitions of sexual harassment—and who are traumatized by the experience—do not label what has happened to them 'sexual harassment' " (1991, 68).

Why do most women fail to label their experiences as sexual harassment? Part of the problem is that many still do not recognize that sexual harassment is an actionable offense. Sexual harassment was first described in 1976 (MacKinnon 1979), but it was not until 1986 that the U.S. Supreme Court included sexual harassment in the category of gender discrimination, thereby making it illegal (Paludi and Barickman 1991); consequently, women may not yet identify their experiences as sexual harassment because a substantial degree of awareness about its illegality has yet to be developed.

Patti A. Giuffre and Christine L. Williams, "Boundary Lines: Labeling Sexual Harassment in Restaurants," *Gender & Society* 8, no. 3 (September 1994). Copyright © 1994 by Sociologists for Women in Society. Reprinted with the permission of the authors and Sage Publications, Inc.

Many victims of sexual harassment may also be reluctant to come forward with complaints, fearing that they will not be believed, or that their charges will not be taken seriously (Jensen and Gutek 1982). As the Anita Hill-Clarence Thomas hearings demonstrated, women who are victims of sexual harassment often become the accused when they bring charges against their assailant.

There is another issue at stake in explaining the gap between experiencing and labeling behaviors "sexual harassment": many men and women experience some sexual behaviors in the workplace as pleasurable. Research on sexual harassment suggests that men are more likely than women to enjoy sexual interactions at work (Gutek 1985; Konrad and Gutek 1986; Reilly et al. 1992), but even some women experience sexual overtures at work as pleasurable (Pringle 1988). This attitude may be especially strong in organizations that use and exploit the bodies and sexuality of the workers (Cockburn 1991). Workers in many jobs are hired on the basis of their attractiveness and solicitousness—including not only sex industry workers, but also service sector workers such as receptionists, airline attendants, and servers in trendy restaurants. According to Cockburn (1991), this sexual exploitation is not completely forced: many people find this dimension of their jobs appealing and reinforcing to their own sense of identity and pleasure; consequently, some men and women resist efforts to expunge all sexuality from their places of work.

This is not to claim that all sexual behavior in the workplace is acceptable, even to some people. The point is that it is difficult to label behavior as sexual harassment because it forces people to draw a line between illicit and "legitimate" forms of sexuality at work—a process fraught with ambiguity. Whether a particular interaction is identified as

247

harassment will depend on the intention of the harasser and the interpretation of the interchange by the victim, and both of these perspectives will be highly influenced by work-place culture and the social context of the specific event.

This article examines how one group of employees—restaurant workers—distinguishes between sexual harassment and other forms of sexual interaction in the workplace. We conducted an in-depth interview study of waitpeople and found that complex double standards are often used in labeling behavior as sexual harassment: identical behaviors are labeled sexual harassment in some contexts and not others. Many respondents claimed that they *enjoyed* sexual interactions involving co-workers of the same race/ethnicity, sexual orientation, and class/status backgrounds. Those who were offended by such interactions nevertheless dismissed them as natural or inevitable parts of restaurant culture.[1] When the same behavior occurred in contexts that upset these hegemonic heterosexual norms—in particular, when the episode involved interactions between gay and heterosexual men, or men and women of different racial/ethnic backgrounds—people seemed willing to apply the label sexual harassment.

We argue that identifying behaviors that occur only in counterhegemonic contexts as sexual harassment can potentially obscure and legitimate more insidious forms of domination and exploitation. As Pringle points out, "Men control women through direct use of power, but also through definitions of pleasure—which is less likely to provoke resistance" (1988, 95). Most women, she writes, actively seek out what Rich (1980) termed "compulsory heterosexuality" and find pleasure in it. The fact that men and women may enjoy certain sexual interactions in the workplace does not mean they take place outside of oppressive social relationships, nor does it imply that these routine interactions have no negative consequences for women. We argue that the practice of labeling as "sexual harassment" only those behaviors that challenge the dominant definition of acceptable sexual activity maintains and supports men's institutionalized right of sexual access and power over women.

METHODS

The occupation of waiting tables was selected to study the social definition of sexual harassment because many restaurants have a blatantly sexualized workplace culture (Cobble 1991; Paules 1991). According to a report published in a magazine that caters to restaurant owners, "Restaurants . . . are about as informal a workplace as there is, so much so as

to actually encourage—or at the very least tolerate—sexual banter" (Anders 1993, 48). Unremitting sexual banter and innuendo, as well as physical jostling, create an environment of "compulsory jocularity" in many restaurants (Pringle 1988, 93). Sexual attractiveness and flirtation are often institutionalized parts of a waitperson's job description; consequently, individual employees are often forced to draw the line for themselves to distinguish legitimate and illegitimate expressions of sexuality, making this occupation an excellent context for examining how people determine what constitutes sexual harassment. In contrast, many more sexual behaviors may be labeled sexual harassment in less highly sexualized work environments.[2]

Eighteen in-depth interviews were conducted with male and female wait staff who work in restaurants in Austin, Texas. Respondents were selected from restaurants that employ equal proportions of men and women on their wait staffs. Overall, restaurant work is highly sex segregated: women make up about 82 percent of all waitpeople (U.S. Department of Labor 1989), and it is common for restaurants to be staffed only by either waitresses or waiters, with men predominating in the higher-priced restaurants (Cobble 1991; Hall 1993; Paules 1991). We decided to focus only on waitpeople who work in mixed-sex groups for two reasons. First, focusing on waitpeople working on integrated staffs enables us to examine sexual harassment between coworkers who occupy the same position in an organizational hierarchy. Co-worker sexual harassment is perhaps the most common form of sexual harassment (Pryor 1987; Schneider 1982); yet most case studies of sexual harassment have examined either unequal hierarchical relationships (e.g., boss-secretary harassment) or harassment in highly skewed gender groupings (e.g., women who work in nontraditional occupations) (Benson and Thomson 1982; Carothers and Crull 1984; Gruber and Bjorn 1982). This study is designed to investigate sexual harassment in unequal hierarchical relationships, as well as harassment between organizationally equal co-workers.

Second, equal proportions of men and women in an occupation implies a high degree of male-female interaction (Gutek 1985). Waitpeople are in constant contact with each other, help each other when the restaurant is busy, and informally socialize during slack periods. In contrast, men and women have much more limited interactions in highly sex-segregated restaurants and indeed, in most work environments. The high degree of interaction among the wait staff provides ample opportunity for sexual harassment between men and women to occur and, concomitantly, less opportunity for same-sex sexual harassment to occur.

The sample was generated using "snowball" techniques and by going to area restaurants and asking waitpeople to volunteer for the study. The sample includes eight men and ten women. Four respondents are Latina/o, two African American, and twelve white. Four respondents are gay or lesbian; one is bisexual; thirteen are heterosexual. (The gay men and lesbians in the sample are all "out" at their respective restaurants.) Fourteen respondents are single; three are married; one is divorced. Respondents' ages range from 22 to 37.

Interviews lasted approximately one hour, and they were tape-recorded and transcribed for this analysis. All interviews were conducted by the first author, who has over eight years' experience waiting tables. Respondents were asked about their experiences working in restaurants; relationships with managers, customers, and other co-workers; and their personal experiences of sexual harassment. Because interviews were conducted in the fall of 1991, when the issue was prominent in the media because of the Hill-Thomas hearings, most respondents had thought a lot about this topic.

FINDINGS

Respondents agreed that sexual banter is very common in the restaurant: staff members talk and joke about sex constantly. With only one exception, respondents described their restaurants as highly sexualized. This means that 17 of the 18 respondents said that sexual joking, touching, and fondling were common, everyday occurrences in their restaurants. For example, when asked if he and other waitpeople ever joke about sex, one waiter replied, "about 90 percent of [the jokes] are about sex." According to a waitress, "at work . . . [we're] used to patting and touching and hugging." Another waiter said, "I do not go through a shift without someone . . . pinching my nipples or poking me in the butt or grabbing my crotch. . . . It's just what we do at work."

These informal behaviors are tantamount to "doing heterosexuality," a process analogous to "doing gender" (West and Zimmerman 1987).[3] By engaging in these public flirtations and open discussions of sex, men and women reproduce the dominant cultural norms of heterosexuality and lend an air of legitimacy—if not inevitability—to heterosexual relationships. In other words, heterosexuality is normalized and naturalized through its ritualistic public display. Indeed, although most respondents described their workplaces as highly sexualized, several dismissed the constant sexual innuendo and behaviors as "just joking," and nothing to get upset about. Several respondents claimed that this is simply "the way it is in the restaurant business," or "just the way men are."

With only one exception, the men and women interviewed maintained that they enjoyed this aspect of their work. Heterosexuality may be normative, and in these contexts, even compulsory, yet many men and women find pleasure in its expression. Many women—as well as men—actively reproduce hegemonic sexuality and apparently enjoy its ritual expression; however, in a few instances, sexual conduct was labeled as sexual harassment. Seven women and three men said they had experienced sexual harassment in restaurant work. Of these, two women and one man described two different experiences of sexual harassment, and two women described three experiences. Table 1 describes the characteristics of each of the respondents and their experiences of sexual harassment.

We analyzed these 17 accounts of sexual harassment to find out what, if anything, these experiences shared in common. With the exception of two episodes (discussed later), the experiences that were labeled "sexual harassment" were not distinguished by any specific words or behaviors, nor were they distinguished by their degree of severity. Identical behaviors were considered acceptable if they were perpetrated by some people, but considered offensive if perpetrated by others. In other words, sexual behavior in the workplace was interpreted differently depending on the context of the interaction. In general, respondents labeled their experiences sexual harassment only if the offending behavior occurred in one of three social contexts: (1) if perpetrated by someone in a more powerful position, such as a manager; (2) if perpetrated by someone of a different race/ethnicity; or (3) if perpetrated by someone of a different sexual orientation.

Our findings do not imply that sexual harassment did not occur outside of these three contexts. Instead, they simply indicate that our respondents *labeled* behavior as "sexual harassment" when it occurred in these particular social contexts. We will discuss each of these contexts and speculate on the reasons why they were singled out by our respondents.

Powerful Position

In the restaurant, managers and owners are the highest in the hierarchy of workers. Generally, they are the only ones who can hire or fire waitpeople. Three of the women and one of the men interviewed said they had been sexually

TABLE I   DESCRIPTION OF RESPONDENTS AND THEIR REPORTED EXPERIENCES OF SEXUAL HARASSMENT AT WORK

Pseudonym	Age	Race[a]	SO[b]	MS[c]	Years in Restaurant[d]	Sexualized Environment[e]	Sexually Harassed[f]
Kate	23	W	H	S	1	yes	yes (1)
Beth	26	W	H	S	5	yes	yes (1)
Ann	29	W	H	S	1*	yes	yes (2)
Cathy	29	W	H	S	8 mos.*	yes	yes (3)
Carla	22	W	H	M	5 mos.*	yes	yes (3)
Diana	32	L	H	M	6	no	no
Maxine	30	L	H	M	4	yes	no
Laura	27	W	B	S	2*	yes	yes (1)
Brenda	23	W	L	S	3	yes	yes (2)
Lynn	37	B	L	D	5*	yes	no
Jake	22	W	H	S	1	yes	yes (1)
Al	23	W	H	S	3	yes	no
Frank	29	W	H	S	8	yes	yes (1)
John	31	W	H	S	2	yes	no
Trent	23	W	G	S	1*	yes	no
Rick	24	B	H	S	1.5	yes	yes (2)
David	25	L	H	S	5	yes	no
Don	24	L	G	S	1*	yes	no

a. Race: B = Black, L = Latina/o, W = White.
b. SO = sexual orientation: B = bisexual, G = gay, H = heterosexual, L = lesbian.
c. MS = marital status: D = divorced, M = married, S = single.
d. Years in restaurant refers to length of time employed in current restaurant. An asterisk indicates that respondent has worked in other restaurants.
e. Whether or not the respondent claimed sexual banter and touching were common occurrences in their restaurant.
f. Responded yes or no to the question: "Have you ever been sexually harassed in the restaurant?" Number in parentheses refers to number of incidents described in the interview.

harassed by their restaurants' managers or owners. In addition, several others who did not personally experience harassment said they had witnessed managers or owners sexually harassing other waitpeople. This finding is consistent with other research indicating people are more likely to think that sexual harassment has occurred when the perpetrator is in a more powerful position (e.g., Ellis et al. 1991).

Carla describes being sexually harassed by her manager:

One evening, [my manager] grabbed my body, not in a private place, just grabbed my body, period. He gave me

like a bear hug from behind a total of four times in one night. By the end of the night I was livid. I was trying to avoid him. Then when he'd do it, I'd just ignore the conversation or the joke or whatever and walk away.

She claimed that her co-workers often give each other massages and joke about sex, but she did not label any of their behaviors sexual harassment. In fact, all four individuals who experienced sexual harassment from their managers described very similar types of behavior from their co-workers, which they did not define as sexual harassment. For example, Cathy said that she and the other waitpeople talk and joke about sex constantly: "Everybody stands around and talks about sex a lot . . . Isn't that weird? You know, it's something about working in restaurants and, yeah, so we'll all sit around and talk about sex." She said that talking with her co-workers about sex does not constitute sexual harassment because it is "only joking." She does, however, view her male manager as a sexual harasser:

> My employer is very sexist. I would call that sexual harassment. Very much of a male chauvinist pig. He kind of started [saying] stuff like, "You can't really wear those shorts because they're not flattering to your figure. . . . But I like the way you wear those jeans. They look real good. They're tight." It's like, you know [I want to say to him], "You're the owner, you're in power. That's evident. You know, you need to find a better way to tell me these things." We've gotten to a point now where we'll joke around now, but it's never ever sexual, ever. I won't allow that with him.

Cathy acknowledges that her manager may legitimately dictate her appearance at work, but only if he does so in professional—and not personal—terms. She wants him "to find a better way to tell me these things," implying that he is not completely out-of-line in suggesting that she wear tight pants. He "crosses the line" when he personalizes his directive, by saying to Cathy "*I like* the way you wear those jeans." This is offensive to Cathy because it is framed as the manager's personal prerogative, not the institutional requirements of the job.

Ann described a similar experience of sexual harassment from a restaurant owner:

> Yeah, there's been a couple of times when a manager has made me feel real uncomfortable and I just removed myself from the situation. . . . Like if there's something I really want him to hear or something I think is really important there's no touching. Like, "Don't touch me while I'm talking to you." You know, because I take that as very patronizing. I actually blew up at one of the owners once because I was having a rough day and he came up behind me and he was rubbing my back, like up and down my back and saying, you know, "Oh, is Ann having a bad day?" or something like that and I shook him off of me and I said, "You do not need to touch me to talk to me."

Ann distinguishes between legitimate and illegitimate touching: if the issue being discussed is "really impor-

tant"—that is, involving her job status—she insists there be no touching. In these specific situations, a back rub is interpreted as patronizing and offensive because the manager is using his powerful position for his *personal* sexual enjoyment.

One of the men in the sample, Frank, also experienced sexual harassment from a manager:

> I was in the bathroom and [the manager] came up next to me and my tennis shoes were spray-painted silver so he knew it was me in there and he said something about, "Oh, what do you have in your hand there?" I was on the other side of a wall and he said, "Mind if I hold it for a while?" or something like that, you know. I just pretended like I didn't hear it.

Frank also described various sexual behaviors among the waitstaff, including fondling, "joking about bodily functions," and "making bikinis out of tortillas." He said, "I mean, it's like, what we do at work. . . . There's no holds barred. I don't find it offensive. I'm used to it by now. I'm guilty of it myself." Evidently, he defines sexual behaviors as "sexual harassment" only when perpetrated by someone in a position of power over him.[4]

Two of the women in the sample also described sexual harassment from customers. We place these experiences in the category of "powerful position" because customers do have limited economic power over the waitperson insofar as they control the tip (Crull 1987). Cathy said that male customers often ask her to "sit on my lap" and provide them with other sexual favors. Brenda, a lesbian, described a similar experience of sexual harassment from women customers:

> One time I had this table of lesbians and they were being real vulgar towards me. Real sexual. This woman kind of tripped me as I was walking by and said, "Hurry back." I mean, gay people can tell when other people are gay. I felt harassed.

In these examples of harassment by customers, the line is drawn using a similar logic as in the examples of harassment by managers. These customers acted as though the waitresses were providing table service to satisfy the customers' private desires, instead of working to fulfill their job descriptions. In other words, the customers' demands were couched in personal—and not professional—terms, making the waitresses feel sexually harassed.

It is not difficult to understand why waitpeople singled out sexual behaviors from managers, owners, and customers as sexual harassment. Subjection to sexual advances by someone with economic power comes closest to the quid pro quo form of sexual harassment, wherein employees are given the option to either "put out or get out." Studies have found that this type of sexual harassment is viewed as the most threatening and unambiguous sort (Ellis et al. 1991; Fitzgerald 1990; Gruber and Bjorn 1982).

But even in this context, lines are drawn between legitimate and illegitimate sexual behavior in the workplace. As Cathy's comments make clear, some people accept the employers' prerogative to exploit the workers' sexuality, by dictating appropriate "sexy" dress, for example. Like airline attendants, waitresses are expected to be friendly, helpful, and sexually available to the male customers (Cobble 1991). Because this expectation is embedded in restaurant culture, it becomes difficult for workers to separate sexual harassment from the more or less accepted forms of sexual exploitation that are routine features of their jobs. Consequently, some women are reluctant to label blatantly offensive behaviors as sexual harassment. For example, Maxine, who claims that she has never experienced sexual harassment, said that customers often "talk dirty" to her:

> I remember one day, about four or five years ago when I was working as a cocktail waitress, this guy asked me for a "Slow Comfortable Screw" [the name of a drink]. I didn't know what it was. I didn't know if he was making a move or something. I just looked at him. He said, "You know what it is, right?" I said, "I bet the bartender knows!" (laughs). . . . There's another one, "Sex on the Beach." And there's another one called a "Screaming Orgasm." Do you believe that?

Maxine is subject to a sexualized work environment that she finds offensive; hence her experience could fit the legal definition of sexual harassment. But because sexy drink names are an institutionalized part of restaurant culture, Maxine neither complains about it nor labels it sexual harassment: Once it becomes clear that a "Slow Comfortable Screw" is a legitimate and recognized restaurant demand, she accepts it (albeit reluctantly) as part of her job description. In other words, the fact that the offensive behavior is institutionalized seems to make it beyond reproach in her eyes. This finding is consistent with others' findings that those who work in highly sexualized environments may be less likely to label offensive behavior "sexual harassment" (Gutek 1985; Konrad and Gutek 1986).

Only in specific contexts do workers appear to define offensive words and acts of a sexual nature as sexual harassment—even when initiated by someone in a more powerful position. The interviews suggest that workers use this label to describe their experiences only when their bosses or their customers couch their requests for sexual attentions in explicitly personal terms. This way of defining sexual harassment may obscure and legitimize more institutionalized—and hence more insidious—forms of sexual exploitation at work.

Race/Ethnicity

The restaurants in our sample, like most restaurants in the United States, have racially segregated staffs (Howe 1977). In the restaurants where our respondents are employed, men of color are concentrated in two positions: the kitchen cooks and bus personnel (formerly called busboys). Five of the white women in the sample reported experiencing sexual harassment from Latino men who worked in these positions. For example, when asked if she had ever experienced sexual harassment, Beth said:

> Yes, but it was not with the people . . . it was not, you know, the people that I work with in the front of the house. It was with the kitchen. There are boundaries or lines that I draw with the people I work with. In the kitchen, the lines are quite different. Plus, it's a Mexican staff. It's a very different attitude. They tend to want to touch you more and, at times, I can put up with a little bit of it but . . . because I will give them a hard time too but I won't touch them. I won't touch their butt or anything like that.

> [Interviewer: So sometimes they cross the line?]

> It's only happened to me a couple of times. One guy, like, patted me on the butt and I went off. I lost my shit. I went off on him. I said, "No. Bad. Wrong. I can't speak Spanish to you but, you know, this is it." I told the kitchen manager who is a guy and he's not . . . the head kitchen manager is not Hispanic. . . . I've had to do that over the years only a couple of times with those guys.

Beth reported that the waitpeople joke about sex and touch each other constantly, but she does not consider their behavior sexual harassment. Like many of the other men and women in the sample, Beth said she feels comfortable engaging in this sexual banter and play with the other waitpeople (who were predominantly white), but not with the Mexican men in the kitchen.

Part of the reason for singling out the behaviors of the cooks as sexual harassment may involve status differences between waitpeople and cooks. Studies have suggested that people may label behaviors as sexual harassment when they are perpetrated by people in lower status organizational positions (Grauerholz 1989; McKinney 1990); however, it is difficult to generalize about the relative status of cooks and waitpeople because of the varied and often complex organizational hierarchies of restaurants (Paules 1991, 107–10). If the cook is a chef, as in higher-priced restaurants, he or she may actually have more status than waitpeople, and indeed may have the formal power to hire and fire the waitstaff. In the restaurants where our respondents worked, the kitchen cooks did not wield this sort of formal control, but they could exert some informal power over the waitstaff by slowing down food orders or making the orders look and/or taste bad. Because bad food can decrease the waitperson's tip, the cooks can thereby control the waitperson's income; hence servers are forced to negotiate and to some extent placate the wishes and desires of cooks to perform their jobs. The willingness of several respondents to label the cooks' behavior as sexual harassment may reflect their perception that the cooks' informal demands had become unreasonable. In such cases, subjection to the offensive behaviors is a term of employment, which is quid pro quo sexual harassment. As mentioned previously, this type of sexual harassment is the most likely to be so labeled and identified.

Because each recounted case of sexual harassment occurring between individuals of different occupational statuses involved a minority man sexually harassing a white woman, the racial context seems equally important. For example, Ann also said that she and the other waiters and waitresses joke about sex and touch each other "on the butt" all the time, and when asked if she had ever experienced sexual harassment, she said,

> I had some problems at [a previous restaurant] but it was a communication problem. A lot of the guys in the kitchen did not speak English. They would see the waiters hugging on us, kissing us and pinching our rears and stuff. They would try to do it and I couldn't tell them, "No. You don't understand this. It's like we do it because we have a mutual understanding but I'm not comfortable with you doing it." So that was really hard and a lot of times what I'd have to do is just sucker punch them in the chest and just use a lot of cuss words

and they knew that I was serious. And there again, I felt real weird about that because they're just doing what they see go on everyday.

Kate, Carla, and Brenda described very similar racial double standards. Kate complained about a Mexican busser who constantly touched her:

> This is not somebody that I talk to on a friendly basis. We don't sit there and laugh and joke and stuff. So, when he touches me, all I know is he is just touching me and there is no context about it. With other people, if they said something or they touched me, it would be funny or . . . we have a relationship. This person and I and all the other people do not. So that is sexual harassment.

And according to Brenda:

> The kitchen can be kind of sexist. They really make me angry. They're not as bad as they used to be because they got warned. They're mostly Mexican, not even Mexican-American. Most of them, they're just starting to learn English.
>
> [Interviewer: What do they do to you?]
>
> Well, I speak Spanish, so I know. They're not as sexual to me because I think they know I don't like it. Some of the other girls will come through and they will touch them like here [points to the lower part of her waist]. . . . I've had some pretty bad arguments with the kitchen.
>
> [Interviewer: Would you call that sexual harassment?]
>
> Yes. I think some of the girls just don't know better to say something. I think it happens a lot with the kitchen guys. Like sometimes, they will take a relleno in their hands like it's a penis. Sick!

Each of these women identified the sexual advances of the minority men in their restaurants as sexual harassment, but not the identical behaviors of their white male co-workers; moreover, they all recognize that they draw boundary lines differently for Anglo men and Mexican men: each of them willingly participates in "doing heterosexuality" only in racially homogamous contexts. These women called the behavior of the Mexican cooks "sexual harassment" in part because they did not "have a relationship" with these men, nor was it conceivable to them that they *could* have a relationship with them, given cultural and language barriers—and, probably, racist attitudes as well. The white men, on the other hand, can "hug, kiss, and pinch rears" of the white women because they have a "mutual understanding"—implying reciprocity and the possibility of intimacy.

The importance of this perception of relationship potential in the assessment of sexual harassment is especially clear in the cases of the two married women in the sample, Diana and Maxine. Both of these women said that they had never experienced sexual harassment. Diana, who works in a family-owned and -operated restaurant, claimed that her restaurant is not a sexualized work environment. Although people occasionally make double entendre jokes relating to sex, according to Diana, "there's no contact whatsoever like someone pinching your butt or something." She said that she has never experienced sexual harassment:

> Everybody here knows I'm married so they're not going to get fresh with me because they know that it's not going to go anywhere, you know so . . . and vice versa. You know, we know the guys' wives. They come in here to eat. It's respect all the way. I don't think they could handle it if they saw us going around hugging them. You know what I mean? It's not right.

Similarly, Maxine, who is Colombian, said she avoids the problem of sexual harassment in her workplace because she is married:

> The cooks don't offend me because they know I speak Spanish and they know how to talk with me because I set my boundaries and they know that. . . . I just don't joke with them more than I should. They all know that I'm married, first of all, so that's a no-no for all of them. My brother used to be a manager in that restaurant so he probably took care of everything. I never had any problems anyway in any other jobs because, like I said, I set my boundaries. I don't let them get too close to me.

> [Interviewer: You mean physically?]

> Not physically only. Just talking. If they want to talk about, "Do you go dancing? Where do you go dancing?" Like I just change the subject because it's none of their business and I don't really care to talk about that with them . . . not because I consider them to be on the lower levels than me or something but just because if you start talking with them that way then you are just

giving them hope or something. I think that's true for most of the guys here, not just talking about the cooks. . . . I do get offended and they know that so sometimes they apologize.

Both Maxine and Diana said that they are protected from sexual harassment because they are married. In effect, they use their marital status to negotiate their interactions with their co-workers and to ward off unwanted sexual advances. Furthermore, because they do not view their co-workers as potential relationship "interests," they conscientiously refuse to participate in any sexual banter in the restaurant.

The fact that both women speak Spanish fluently may mean that they can communicate their boundaries unambiguously to those who only speak Spanish (unlike the female respondents in the sample who only speak English). For these two women, sexual harassment from co-workers is not an issue. Diana, who is Latina, talks about "respect all around" in her restaurant; Maxine claims the cooks (who are Mexican) aren't the ones who offend her. Their comments seem to reflect more mutual respect and humanity toward their Latino co-workers than the comments of the white waitresses. On the other hand, at least from Maxine's vantage point, racial harassment is a bigger problem in her workplace than is sexual harassment. When asked if she ever felt excluded from any groups at work, she said:

> Yeah, sometimes. How can I explain this? Sometimes, I mean, I don't know if they do it on purpose or they don't but they joke around you about being Spanish. . . . Sometimes it hurts. Like they say, "What are you doing here? Why don't you go back home?"

Racial harassment—like sexual harassment—is a means used by a dominant group to maintain its dominance over a subordinated group. Maxine feels that, because she is married, she is protected from sexual harassment (although, as we have seen, she is subject to a sexualized workplace that is offensive to her); however, she does experience racial harassment where she works, and she feels vulnerable to this because she is one of very few nonwhites working at her restaurant.

One of the waiters in the sample claimed that he had experienced sexual harassment from female co-workers, and race may have also been a factor in this situation. When Rick (who is African American) was asked if he had ever been sexually harassed, he recounted his experiences with some white waitresses:

> Yes. There are a couple of girls there, waitpeople, who will pinch my rear.
>
> [Interviewer: Do you find it offensive?]
>
> No (laughs) because I'm male. . . . But it is a form of sexual harassment.
>
> [Interviewer: Do you ever tell them to stop?]
>
> If I'm really busy, if I'm in the weeds, and they want to touch me, I'll get mad. I'll tell them to stop. There's a certain time and place for everything.

Rick is reluctant about labeling this interaction "sexual harassment" because "it doesn't bother me unless I'm, like, busy or something like that." In those cases where he is busy, he feels that his female co-workers are subverting his work by pinching him. Because of the race difference, he may experience their behaviors as an expression of racial dominance, which probably influences his willingness to label the behavior as sexual harassment.

In sum, the interviews suggest that the perception and labeling of interactions as "sexual harassment" may be influenced by the racial context of the interaction. If the victim perceives the harasser as expressing a potentially reciprocal relationship interest, they may be less likely to label their experience sexual harassment. In cases where the harasser and victim have a different race/ethnicity and class background, the possibility of a relationship may be precluded because of racism, making these cases more likely to be labeled "sexual harassment."

This finding suggests that the practices associated with "doing heterosexuality" are profoundly racist. The white women in the sample showed a great reluctance to label unwanted sexual behavior sexual harassment when it was perpetrated by a potential (or real) relationship interest—that is, a white male co-worker. In contrast, minority men are socially constructed as potential harassers of white women: any expression of sexual interest may be more readily perceived as nonreciprocal and unwanted. The assumption of racial homogamy in heterosexual relationships thus may protect white men from charges of sexual harassment of white women. This would help to explain why so many white women in the sample labeled behaviors perpetrated by Mexican men as sexual harassment, but not the identical behaviors perpetrated by white men.

Sexual Orientation

There has been very little research on sexual harassment that addresses the sexual orientation of the harasser and victim (exceptions include Reilly et al. 1992; Schneider 1982, 1984). Surveys of sexual harassment typically include questions about marital status but not about sexual orientation (e.g., Fain and Anderton 1987; Gruber and Bjorn 1982; Powell 1986). In this study, sexual orientation was an important part of heterosexual men's perceptions of sexual harassment. Of the four episodes of sexual harassment reported by the men in the study, three involved openly gay men sexually harassing straight men. One case involved a male manager harassing a male waiter (Frank's experience, described earlier). The other two cases involved co-workers. Jake said that he had been sexually harassed by a waiter:

> Someone has come on to me that I didn't want to come on to me. . . . He was another waiter [male]. It was laughs and jokes the whole way until things got a little too much and it was like, "Hey, this is how it is. Back off. Keep your hands off my ass." . . . Once it reached the point where I felt kind of threatened and bothered by it.

Rick described being sexually harassed by a gay baker in his restaurant:

> There was a baker that we had who was really, really gay. . . . He was very straightforward and blunt. He would tell you, in detail, his sexual experiences and tell you that he wanted to do them with you. . . . I knew he was kidding but he was serious. I mean, if he had a chance he would do these things.

In each of these cases, the men expressed some confusion about the intentions of their harassers—"I knew he was kidding but he was serious." Their inability to read the intentions of the gay men provoked them to label these episodes sexual harassment. Each man did not perceive the sexual interchange as reciprocal, nor did he view the harasser as a potential relationship interest. Interestingly, however, all three of the men who described harassment from gay men claimed that sexual banter and play with other *straight* men did not trouble them. Jake, for example, said that "when men get together, they talk sex," regardless of whether there are women around. He acceded, "people find me offensive, as a matter of fact," because he gets "pretty raunchy" talking and joking about sex. Only when this talk was initiated by a gay man did Jake label it as sexual harassment.

Johnson (1988) argues that talking and joking about sex is a common means of establishing intimacy among heterosexual men and maintaining a masculine identity. Homosexuality is perceived as a direct challenge and threat to the achievement of masculinity and consequently, "the male homosexual is derided by other males because he is not a real man, and in male logic if one is not a real man, one is a woman" (p. 124). In Johnson's view, this dynamic not only sustains masculine identity, it also shores up male dominance over women; thus, for some straight men, talking about sex with other straight men is a form of reasserting masculinity and male dominance, whereas talking about sex with gay men threatens the very basis for their masculine privilege. For this reason they may interpret the sex talk and conduct of gay men as a form of sexual harassment.

In certain restaurants, gay men may in fact intentionally hassle straight men as an explicit strategy to undermine their privileged position in society. For example, Trent (who is openly gay) realizes that heterosexual men are uncomfortable with his sexuality, and he intentionally draws attention to his sexuality in order to bother them:

[Interviewer: Homosexuality gets on whose nerves?]

The straight people's nerves. . . . I know also that we consciously push it just because, we know, "Okay. We know this is hard for you to get used to but tough luck. I've had my whole life trying to live in this straight world and if you don't like this, tough shit." I don't mean like we're shitty to them on purpose but it's like, "I've had to worry about being accepted by straight people all my life. The shoe's on the other foot now. If you don't like it, sorry."

[Interviewer: Do you get along well with most of the waitpeople?]

I think I get along with straight women. I get along with gay men. I get along with gay women usually. If there's ever going to be a problem between me and somebody it will be between me and a straight man.

Trent's efforts to "push" his sexuality could easily be experienced as sexual harassment by straight men who have limited experience negotiating unwanted sexual advances. The three men who reported being sexually harassed by gay men seemed genuinely confused about the intentions of their harassers, and threatened by the possibility that they would actually be subjected to and harmed by unwanted sexual advances. But it is important to point out that Trent works in a restaurant owned by lesbians, which empowers him to confront his straight male co-workers. Not all restaurants provide the sort of atmosphere that makes this type of engagement possible; indeed, some restaurants have policies explicitly banning the hiring of gays and lesbians. Clearly, not all gay men would be able to push their sexuality without suffering severe retaliation (e.g., loss of job, physical attacks).

In contrast to the reports of the straight men in this study, none of the women interviewed reported sexual harassment from their gay or lesbian co-workers. Although Maxine was worried when she found out that one of her co-workers was lesbian, she claims that this fact no longer troubles her:

Six months ago I found out that there was a lesbian girl working there. It kind of freaked me out for a while. I was kind of aware of everything that she did towards me. I was conscious if she walked by me and accidently brushed up against me. She's cool. She doesn't bother me. She never touches my butt or anything like that. The gay guys do that to the [straight] guys but they know they're just kidding around. The [straight] guys do that to the [straight] girls, but they don't care. They know that they're not supposed to do that with me. If they do it, I stop and look at them and they apologize and they don't do it anymore. So they stay out of my way because I'm a meanie (laughs).

Some heterosexual women claimed they feel *more* comfortable working with gay men and lesbians. For example, Kate prefers working with gay men rather than heterosexual men or women. She claims that she often jokes about sex with her gay co-workers, yet she does not view them as potential harassers. Instead, she feels that her working conditions are more comfortable and more fun because she works with gay men. Similarly, Cathy prefers working with gay men over straight men because "gay men are a lot like women in that they're very sensitive to other people's space." Cathy also works with lesbians, and she claims that she has never felt sexually harassed by them.

The gays and lesbians in the study did not report any sexual harassment from their gay and lesbian co-workers. Laura, who is bisexual, said she preferred to work with gays and lesbians instead of heterosexuals because they are "more relaxed" about sex. Brenda said she feels comfortable working around all of her male and female colleagues—regardless of their sexual orientation:

> The guys I work with [don't threaten me]. We always run by each other and pat each other on the butt. It's no big deal. Like with my girlfriend [who works at the same restaurant], all the cocktailers and hostesses love us. They don't care that we're gay. We're not a threat. We all kind of flirt but it's not sexual. A lesbian is not going to sexually harass another woman unless they're pretty gross anyway. It has nothing to do with their sexuality; it has to do with the person. You can't generalize and say that gays and lesbians are the best to work with or anything because it depends on the person.

Brenda enjoys flirtatious interactions with both men and women at her restaurant, but distinguishes these behaviors from sexual harassment. Likewise, Lynn, who is a lesbian, enjoys the relaxed sexual atmosphere at her workplace. When asked if she ever joked about sex in her workplace, she said:

> Yes! (laughs) All the time! All the time—everybody has something that they want to talk about on sex and it's got to be funny. We have gays. We have lesbians. We have straights. We have people who are real Christian-oriented. But we all jump in there and we all talk about it. It gets real funny at times. . . . I've patted a few butts . . . and I've been patted back by men, and by the women, too! (laughs).

Don and Trent, who are both gay, also said that they had never been sexually harassed in their restaurants, even though both described their restaurants as highly sexualized.

In sum, our interviews suggest that sexual orientation is an important factor in understanding each individual's experience of sexual harassment and his or her willingness to label interactions as sexual harassment. In particular, straight men may perceive gay men as potential harassers. Three of our straight male respondents claimed to enjoy the sexual banter that commonly occurs among straight men, and between heterosexual men and women, but singled out the sexual advances of gay men as sexual harassment. Their contacts with gay men may be the only context where they feel vulnerable to unwanted sexual encounters. Their sense of not being in control of the situation may make them more willing to label these episodes sexual harassment.

Our findings about sexual orientation are less suggestive regarding women. None of the women (straight, lesbian, or bisexual) reported sexual harassment from other female co-workers or from gay men. In fact, all but one of the women's reported cases of sexual harassment involved a heterosexual man. One of the two lesbians in the sample (Brenda) did experience sexual harassment from a group of lesbian customers (described earlier), but she claimed that sexual orientation is *not* key to her defining the situation as harassment. Other studies have shown that lesbian and bisexual women are routinely subjected to sexual harassment in the workplace (Schneider 1982, 1984); however, more research is needed to elaborate the social contexts and the specific definitions of harassment among lesbians.

The Exceptions

Two cases of sexual harassment were related by respondents that do not fit in the categories we have thus far described. These were the only incidents of sexual harassment reported between co-workers of the same race: in both cases, the sexual harasser is a white man, and the victim, a white woman. Laura—who is bisexual—was sexually harassed at a previous restaurant by a cook:

> This guy was just constantly badgering me about going out with him. He like grabbed me and took me in the walk-in one time. It was a real big deal. He got fired over it too. . . . I was in the back doing something and he said, "I need to talk to you," and I said, "We have nothing to talk about." He like took me and threw me against the wall in the back. . . . I ran out and told the manager, "Oh my God. He just hit me," and he saw the expression on my face. The manager went back there . . . and then he got fired.

This episode of sexual harassment involved violence, unlike the other reported cases. The threat of violence was also present in the other exception, a case described by Carla. When asked if she had ever been sexually harassed, she said,

> I experienced two men, in wait jobs, that were vulgar or offensive and one was a cook and I think he was a rapist. He had the kind of attitude where he would rape a woman. I mean, that's the kind of attitude he had. He would say totally, totally inappropriate [sexual] things.

These were the only two recounted episodes of sexual harassment between "equal" co-workers that involved white men and women, and both involved violence or the threat of violence.[5]

Schneider (1982, 1991) found the greatest degree of consensus about labeling behavior sexual harassment when that behavior involves violence. A victim of sexual harassment may be more likely to be believed when there is evidence of assault (a situation that is analogous to acquaintance rape). The assumption of reciprocity among homogamous couples may protect assailants with similar characteristics to their victims (e.g., class background, sexual orientation, race/ethnicity, age)—*unless* there is clear evidence of physical abuse. Defining only those incidents that involve violence as sexual harassment obscures—and perhaps even legitimatizes—the more common occurrences that do not involve violence, making it all the more difficult to eradicate sexual harassment from the workplace.

DISCUSSION AND CONCLUSION

We have argued that sexual harassment is hard to identify, and thus difficult to eradicate from the workplace, in part because our hegemonic definition of sexuality defines certain contexts of sexual interaction as legitimate. The interviews with waitpeople in Austin, Texas, indicate that how people currently identify sexual harassment singles out only a narrow range of interactions, thus disguising and ignoring a good deal of sexual domination and exploitation that take place at work.

Most of the respondents in this study work in highly sexualized atmospheres where sexual banter and touching frequently occur. There are institutionalized policies and practices in the workplace that encourage—or at the very least tolerate—a continual display and performance of heterosexuality. Many people apparently accept this ritual display as being a normal or natural feature of their work; some even enjoy this behavior. In the in-depth interviews, respondents labeled such experiences as sexual harassment in only three contexts: when perpetrated by someone who took advantage of their powerful position for personal sexual gain; when the perpetrator was of a different race/ethnicity than the victim—typically a minority man harassing a white woman; and when the perpetrator was of a different sexual orientation than the victim—typically a gay man harassing a straight man. In only two cases did respondents label experiences involving co-workers of the same race and sexual orientation as sexual harassment—and both episodes involved violence or the threat of violence.

These findings are based on a very small sample in a unique working environment, and hence it is not clear whether they are generalizable to other work settings. In less sexualized working environments, individuals may be more likely to label all offensive sexual advances as sexual harassment, whereas in more highly sexualized environments (such as topless clubs or striptease bars), fewer sexual advances may be labeled sexual harassment. Our findings do suggest that researchers should pay closer attention to the interaction context of sexual harassment, taking into account not only gender but also the race, occupational status, and sexual orientation of the assailant and the victim.

Of course, it should not matter who is perpetrating the sexually harassing behavior: sexual harassment should not be tolerated under any circumstances. But if members of oppressed groups (racial/ethnic minority men and gay men) are selectively charged with sexual harassment, whereas members of the most privileged groups are exonerated and excused (except in cases where institutionalized power or violence are used), then the patriarchal order is left intact. This is very similar to the problem of rape prosecution: minority men are the most likely assailants to be arrested and prosecuted, particularly when they attack white women (LaFree 1989). Straight white men who sexually assault women (in the context of marriage, dating, or even work) may escape prosecution because of hegemonic definitions of "acceptable" or "legitimate" sexual expression. Likewise, as we have witnessed in the current debate on gays in the military, straight men's fears of sexual harassment justify the exclusion of gay men and lesbians, whereas sexual harassment perpetrated by straight men against both straight and lesbian women is tolerated and even endorsed by the military establishment, as in the Tailhook investigation (Britton and Williams, forthcoming). By singling out these contexts for the label "sexual harassment," only marginalized men will be prosecuted, and the existing power structure that guarantees privileged men's sexual access to women will remain intact.

Sexual interactions involving men and women of the same race and sexual orientation have a hegemonic status in our society, making sexual harassment difficult to identify and eradicate. Our interviews suggest that many men and women are active participants in the sexualized culture of the workplace, even though ample evidence indicates that women who work in these environments suffer negative repercussions to their careers because of it (Jaschik and Fretz 1991; Paludi and Barickman 1991; Reilly et al. 1992; Schneider 1982). This is how cultural hegemony works—by getting under our skins and defining what is and is not pleasurable to us, despite our material or emotional interests.

Our findings raise difficult issues about women's complicity with oppressive sexual relationships. Some women obviously experience pleasure and enjoyment from public forms of sexual engagement with men; clearly, many would resist any attempt to eradicate all sexuality from work—an impossible goal at any rate. Yet, it is also clear that the sexual "pleasure" many women seek out and enjoy at work is structured by patriarchal, racist, and heterosexist norms. Heterosexual, racially homogamous relationships are privileged in our society: they are institutionalized in organizational policies and job descriptions, embedded in ritualistic workplace practices, and accepted as legitimate, normal, or inevitable elements of workplace culture. This study suggests that only those sexual interactions that violate these policies, practices, and beliefs are resisted and condemned with the label "sexual harassment."

We have argued that this dominant social construction of pleasure protects the most privileged groups in society from charges of sexual harassment and may be used to oppress and exclude the least powerful groups. Currently, people seem to consider the gender, race, status, and sexual orientation of the assailant when deciding to label behaviors as sexual harassment. Unless we acknowledge the complex double standards people use in "drawing the line," then sexual domination and exploitation will undoubtedly remain the normative experience of women in the workforce.

NOTES

1. It could be the case that those who find this behavior extremely offensive are likely to leave restaurant work. In other words, the sample is clearly biased in that it includes only those who are currently employed in a restaurant and presumably feel more comfortable with the level of sexualized behavior than those who have left restaurant work.

2. It is difficult, if not impossible, to specify which occupations are less highly sexualized than waiting tables. Most occupations probably are sexualized in one way or another; however, specific workplaces may be more or less sexualized in terms of institutionalized job descriptions and employee tolerance of sexual banter. For example, Pringle (1988) describes some offices as coolly professional—with minimal sexual joking and play—whereas others are characterized by "compulsory jocularity." Likewise, some restaurants may deemphasize sexual flirtation between waitpeople and customers, and restrain informal interactions among the staff (one respondent in our sample worked at such a restaurant).

3. We thank Margaret Andersen for drawing our attention to this fruitful analogy.

4. It is also probably significant that this episode of harassment involved a gay man and a heterosexual man. This context of sexual harassment is discussed later in this article.

5. It is true that both cases involved cooks sexually harassing waitresses. We could have placed these cases in the "powerful position" category, but did not because in these particular instances, the cooks did not possess institutionalized power over the waitpeople. In other words, in these particular cases, the cook and waitress had equal organizational status in the restaurant.

REFERENCES

Anders, K. T. 1993. Bad sex: Who's harassing whom in restaurants? *Restaurant Business,* 20 January, pp. 46–54.

Benson, Donna J., and Gregg E. Thomson. 1982. Sexual harassment on a university campus: The confluence of authority relations, sexual interest and gender stratification. *Social Problems* 29:236–51.

Britton, Dana M., and Christine L. Williams. Forthcoming. Don't ask, don't tell, don't pursue: Military policy and the construction of heterosexual masculinity. *Journal of Homosexuality.*

Carothers, Suzanne C., and Peggy Crull. 1984. Contrasting sexual harassment in female- and male-dominated occupations. In *My troubles are going to have trouble with me: Everyday trials and triumphs of women workers,* edited by K. B. Sacks and D. Remy. New Brunswick, NJ: Rutgers University Press.

Cobble, Dorothy Sue. 1991. *Dishing it out: Waitresses and their unions in the twentieth century.* Urbana: University of Illinois Press.

Cockburn, Cynthia. 1991. *In the way of women.* Ithaca, NY: I.L.R. Press.

Crull, Peggy. 1987. Searching for the causes of sexual harassment: An examination of two prototypes. In *Hidden aspects of women's work,* edited by Christine Bose, Roslyn Feldberg, and Natalie Sokoloff. New York: Praeger.

Ellis, Shmuel, Azy Barak, and Adaya Pinto. 1991. Moderating effects of personal cognitions on experienced and perceived sexual harassment of women at the workplace. *Journal of Applied Social Psychology* 21:1320–37.

Fain, Terri C., and Douglas L. Anderton. 1987. Sexual harassment: Organizational context and diffuse status. *Sex Roles* 17:291–311.

Fitzgerald, Louise F. 1990. Sexual harassment: The definition and measurement of a construct. In *Ivory power: Sexual harassment on campus,* edited by Michele M. Paludi. Albany: State University of New York Press.

Grauerholz, Elizabeth. 1989. Sexual harassment of women professors by students: Exploring the dynamics of power,
authority, and gender in a university setting. *Sex Roles*
21:789–801.

Gruber, James E., and Lars Bjorn. 1982. Blue-collar blues: The
sexual harassment of women auto workers. *Work and
Occupations* 9:271–98.

Gutek, Barbara A. 1985. *Sex and the workplace.* San Francisco:
Jossey-Bass.

Hall, Elaine J. 1993. Waitering/waitressing: Engendering the work
of table servers. *Gender & Society* 7:329–46.

Howe, Louise Kapp. 1977. *Pink collar workers: Inside the world
of women's work.* New York: Avon.

Jaschik, Mollie L., and Bruce R. Fretz. 1991. Women's perceptions
and labeling of sexual harassment. *Sex Roles* 25:19–23.

Jensen, Inger W., and Barbara A. Gutek. 1982. Attributions and
assignment of responsibility in sexual harassment. *Journal of
Social Issues* 38:122–36.

Johnson, Miriam. 1988. *Strong mothers, weak wives.* Berkeley:
University of California Press.

Konrad, Alison M., and Barbara A. Gutek. 1986. Impact of work
experiences on attitudes toward sexual harassment.
Administrative Science Quarterly 31:422–38.

LaFree, Gary D. 1989. *Rape and criminal justice: The social construction of sexual assault.* Belmont, CA: Wadsworth.

MacKinnon, Catherine A. 1979. *Sexual harassment of working
women: A case of sex discrimination.* New Haven, CT: Yale
University Press.

McKinney, Kathleen. 1990. Sexual harassment of university faculty by colleagues and students. *Sex Roles* 23:421–38.

Paludi, Michele, and Richard B. Barickman. 1991. *Academic and
workplace sexual harassment.* Albany: State University of New
York Press.

Paules, Greta Foff. 1991. *Dishing it out: Power and resistance
among waitresses in a New Jersey restaurant.* Philadelphia:
Temple University Press.

Powell, Gary N. 1986. Effects of sex role identity and sex on definitions of sexual harassment. *Sex Roles* 14:9–19.

Pringle, Rosemary. 1988. *Secretaries talk: Sexuality, power and
work.* London: Verso.

Pryor, John B. 1987. Sexual harassment proclivities in men. *Sex
Roles* 17:269–90.

Reilly, Mary Ellen, Bernice Lott, Donna Caldwell, and Luisa
DeLuca. 1992. Tolerance for sexual harassment related to self-
reported sexual victimization. *Gender & Society* 6:122–38.

Rich, Adrienne. 1980. Compulsory heterosexuality and lesbian
existence. *Signs* 5:631–60.

Schneider, Beth E. 1982. Consciousness about sexual harassment
among heterosexual and lesbian women workers. *Journal of
Social Issues* 38:75–98.

———. 1984. The office affair: Myth and reality for heterosexual
and lesbian women workers. *Sociological Perspectives*
27:443–64.

———. 1991. Put up and shut up: Workplace sexual assaults.
Gender & Society 5:533–48.

U.S. Department of Labor, Bureau of Labor Statistics. 1989,
January. *Employment and earnings.* Washington, DC:
Government Printing Office.

West, Candace, and Don H. Zimmerman. 1987. Doing gender.
Gender & Society 1:125–51.

SECTION SIX

Families

Families are a fundamental social unit. In families we develop a sense of ourselves as individuals and as members of a primary group. We internalize messages about our position in our communities, nations, and the world. We are taught systems of belief, usually consistent with the society in which we live, about appropriate roles for particular kinds of people. For example, we learn to think differently about men and women, elders and children, and people of various races, classes, and social statuses. We also learn how we are expected to treat the people we encounter in the world around us.

It is within families that members of a society first develop ideas and feelings about themselves as gendered individuals. The socialization we receive contains strong messages about the appropriate attitudes and behaviors for males and females. Families usually expect their members to assume interpersonal roles considered appropriate for people of one gender or the other. Yet families come in many forms, even within one society. The normative family structure of a married mother and father with children no longer represents the majority of families. Instead, a family may be a single parent with children, a couple with no children, lesbian or gay parents and their children, or even a group of people who decide to share a household. As a result, individuals' experiences in families vary widely.

Feminist scholars examine the family as a major source of the reproduction of sexism in society. Researchers ask questions about how the organization of family life supports women's oppression in society through its ideologies, economics, distribution of domestic tasks, and intimate relations. Reciprocally, researchers examine the impact of demographic, technological, economic, and political structures on women's power and positions in their families. At the same time, feminist researchers also examine families as a source of women's strength and resistance. Alternative family forms are one way that women restructure their family lives; in addition, families may provide a source of resistance to other forms of oppression, such as racism or class inequality. Feminist family studies make central considerations of the ways that race, ethnicity, sexuality, and class influence our family experiences. In contrast, earlier generalizations about "the family" glossed over important differences in the ways people organize their domestic and interpersonal lives and, in fact, tended to present one kind of familial organization pattern as "normal" and desirable while presenting others as "deviant" and dysfunctional.

In the first selection in Section Six, Arlie Hochschild examines the conflicts between family and paid work for heterosexual couples. Hochschild observed and interviewed heterosexual couples in order to understand how changing gender ideologies and women's increasing participation in the paid work force have affected domestic life. According to this research, women's participation in the paid labor force does little to diminish families' perceptions of domestic responsibilities as "women's work." As a result, heterosexual couples adopt various strategies for mediating the tensions

261

between rhetoric about "equal partnerships" and the reality of unequal burdens. In "The Second Shift: Working Parents and the Revolution at Home," Hochschild describes the social meanings assigned to household labor by different families, as well as what those meanings tell us about women's lives and social status.

The ways that heterosexual women balance work and family vary according to class, ethnicity, culture, and nationality. Segura analyzes how Chicana and Mexicana immigrant mothers view their lives as employed mothers in "Working at Motherhood: Chicana and Mexicana Immigrant Mothers and Employment." She finds that many Mexicana immigrants in the study viewed working for pay as an important part of motherhood because the income helped support their families. Many Chicana mothers, in contrast, had been socialized with the American notion of a separation between spheres of work and family and therefore expressed more ambivalence about combining employment and mothering. The article illustrates how the meaning and practice of motherhood are culturally constructed and thus vary among different groups of women.

For single mothers, the meaning of motherhood depends largely on cultural attitudes of stigma or support. Rickie Solinger, in "Race and 'Value': Black and White Illegitimate Babies, 1945–1965," traces changing views of unwed mothers and their offspring following World War II. Unmarried white mothers were pressured to put their "desirable" babies up for adoption during this period. Black women, in contrast, were denigrated by dominant discourse as sexually irresponsible, yet received more community support for keeping and raising their children than did white women. Solinger's article illustrates how ideologies about gender and race structure how categories of women and various family structures are viewed in public discourse. How are these ideologies toward unmarried white and black women who have babies apparent today in public policy debates over welfare and teen pregnancy?

Ellen Lewin also shows how different groups of women reinterpret the meaning of motherhood. She examines how lesbian mothers interpret their dual identities, in "Negotiating Lesbian Motherhood: The Dialectics of Resistance and Accommodation." Lesbian mothers, both those who have children from previous heterosexual relationships and those who choose to have children as lesbians, resist narrow formulations of women's mothering role and challenge stereotypes about lesbians. Yet because the identities "lesbian" and "mother" are culturally defined as mutually exclusive, lesbian mothers have difficulty juggling the two identities.

For most women, these articles suggest, family relationships are a complicated mixture of accommodation and resistance to gender oppression. How do women accept traditional definitions of their family roles? How do they make choices about the relationship of paid employment to mothering? How do they gain power and fulfillment through family relationships, and how are these relationships constrictive?

READING 27

The Second Shift:
Working Parents and the Revolution at Home

ARLIE HOCHSCHILD

She is not the same woman in each magazine advertisement, but she is the same idea. She has that working-mother look as she strides forward, briefcase in one hand, smiling child in the other. Literally and figuratively, she is moving ahead. Her hair, if long, tosses behind her; if it is short, it sweeps back at the sides, suggesting mobility and progress. There is nothing shy or passive about her. She is confident, active, "liberated." She wears a dark tailored suit, but with a silk bow or colorful frill that says, "I'm really feminine underneath." She has made it in a man's world without sacrificing her femininity. And she has done this on her own. By some personal miracle, this image suggests, she has managed to combine what 150 years of industrialization have split wide apart—child and job, frill and suit, female culture and male.

When I showed a photograph of a supermom like this to the working mothers I talked to . . . many responded with an outright laugh. One daycare worker and mother of two, ages three and five, threw back her head: "Ha! They've got to be *kidding* about her. Look at me, hair a mess, nails jagged, twenty pounds overweight. Mornings, I'm getting my kids dressed, the dog fed, the lunches made, the shopping list done. That lady's got a maid." Even working mothers who did have maids couldn't imagine combining work and family in such a carefree way. "Do you know what a baby *does* to your life, the two o'clock feedings, the four o'clock feedings?" Another mother of two said: "They don't show it, but she's whistling"—she imitated a whistling woman, eyes to the sky—"so she can't hear the din." They envied the apparent ease of the woman with the flying hair, but she didn't remind them of anyone they knew.

The women I interviewed—lawyers, corporate executives, word processors, garment pattern cutters, daycare workers—and most of their husbands, too—felt differently about some issues: how right it is for a mother of young children to work a full-time job, or how much a husband should be responsible for the home. But they all agreed that it was hard to work two full-time jobs and raise young children.

How well do couples do it? The more women work outside the home, the more central this question. The number of women in paid work has risen steadily since before the turn of the century, but since 1950 the rise has been staggering. In 1950, 30 percent of American women were in the labor force; in 1986, it was 55 percent. In 1950, 28 percent of married women with children between six and seventeen worked outside the home; in 1986, it had risen to 68 percent. In 1950, 23 percent of married women with children under six worked. By 1986, it had grown to 54 percent. We don't know how many women with children under the age of one worked outside the home in 1950; it was so rare that the Bureau of Labor kept no statistics on it. Today half of such women do. Two-thirds of all mothers are now in the labor force; in fact, more mothers have paid jobs (or are actively looking for one) than nonmothers. Because of this change in women, two-job families now make up 58 percent of all married couples with children.[1]

Since an increasing number of working women have small children, we might expect an increase in part-time work. But actually, 67 percent of the mothers who work have full-time jobs—that is, thirty-five hours or more weekly. That proportion is what it was in 1959.

If more mothers of young children are stepping into full-time jobs outside the home, and if most couples can't afford household help, how much more are fathers doing at home? As I began exploring this question I found many studies on the hours working men and women devote to housework and childcare. One national random sample of 1,243 working parents in forty-four American cities, conducted in 1965–66 by Alexander Szalai and his coworkers, for example, found that working women averaged three hours a day on housework while men averaged 17 minutes; women spent fifty minutes a day of time exclusively with their children; men spent twelve minutes. On the other side of the coin, working fathers watched television an hour longer than their working wives, and slept a half hour longer each night. A comparison of this American sample with eleven other industrial countries in Eastern and Western Europe revealed the same difference between working women and working men in those countries as well.[2] In a 1983 study of white middle-class families in greater Boston, Grace Baruch and R. C. Barnett found that working men married to working women spent only three-quarters of an hour longer each week with their kindergarten-aged children than did men married to housewives.[3]

Szalai's landmark study documented the now familiar but still alarming story of the working woman's "double day," but it left me wondering how men and women actually felt about all this. He and his coworkers studied how people used time, but not, say, how a father felt about his twelve minutes with his child, or how his wife felt about it. Szalai's study revealed the visible surface of what I discovered to be a set of deeply emotional issues: What should a man and woman contribute to the family? How appreciated does each feel? How does each respond to subtle changes in the balance of marital power? How does each develop an unconscious "gender strategy" for coping with the work at home, with marriage, and, indeed, with life itself? These were the underlying issues.

But I began with the measurable issue of time. Adding together the time it takes to do a paid job and to do housework and childcare, I averaged estimates from the major studies on time use done in the 1960s and 1970s, and discovered that women worked roughly fifteen hours longer each week than men. Over a year, they worked an *extra month of twenty-four-hour days a year*. Over a dozen years, it was an extra year of twenty-four-hour days. Most women without children spend much more time than men on housework; with children, they devote more time to both housework and childcare. Just as there is a wage gap between men and women in the workplace, there is a "leisure gap" between

them at home. Most women work one shift at the office or factory and a "second shift" at home.

Studies show that working mothers have higher self-esteem and get less depressed than housewives, but compared to their husbands, they're more tired and get sick more often. In Peggy Thoits's 1985 analysis of two large-scale surveys, each of about a thousand men and women, people were asked how often in the preceding week they'd experienced each of twenty-three symptoms of anxiety (such as dizziness or hallucinations). According to the researchers' criteria, working mothers were more likely than any other group to be "anxious."

In light of these studies, the image of the woman with the flying hair seems like an upbeat "cover" for a grim reality, like those pictures of Soviet tractor drivers smiling radiantly into the distance as they think about the ten-year plan. The Szalai study was conducted in 1965–66. I wanted to know whether the leisure gap he found in 1965 persists, or whether it has disappeared. Since most married couples work two jobs, since more will in the future, since most wives in these couples work the extra month a year, I wanted to understand what the wife's extra month a year meant for each person, and what it does for love and marriage in an age of high divorce.

MY RESEARCH

With my research associates Anne Machung and Elaine Kaplan, I interviewed fifty couples very intensively, and I observed in a dozen homes. We first began interviewing artisans, students, and professionals in Berkeley, California, in the late 1970s. This was at the height of the women's movement, and many of these couples were earnestly and self-consciously struggling to modernize the ground rules of their marriages. Enjoying flexible job schedules and intense cultural support to do so, many succeeded. Since their circumstances were unusual they became our "comparison group" as we sought other couples more typical of mainstream America. In 1980 we located more typical couples by sending a questionnaire on work and family life to every thirteenth name—from top to bottom—of the personnel roster of a large, urban manufacturing company. At the end of the questionnaire, we asked members of working couples raising children under six and working full time jobs if they would be willing to talk to us in greater depth. Interviewed from 1980 through 1988, these couples, their neighbors and friends, their children's teachers, daycare workers and baby-sitters, form the heart of this [analysis] .

THE GAME OF THE NAME

NEIL A. F. POPOVIĆ

The name thing. Seven years ago, when Susan and I decided to get married, we realized that we were going to have to deal with it *somehow*. The idea of her taking my family surname, Friedman, seemed absurd: both of us have always had serious problems with that sexist tradition—it smells too much of the days when a wife was her husband's property. Then we ruled out keeping our own names: we decided we wanted to share a single name as a symbol of our union. Hyphenation struck us as unwieldy and, after a few generations, unmanageable. Should we create a new hybrid name? No, we decided, that would mean no historical continuity at all.

Then, logically, came the idea of my taking Susan's surname, Popović. Sure, it seemed a bit bold, but it fit all our requirements, and more important, it gave us the chance to turn a bit of sexism on its head, to do some "affirmative action" toward a more equal society. Such a simple solution! Or so we thought.

When we told my family about my name change, they seemed to accept it—although my father called a week before the wedding with cold feet. Again, we talked it all through, and he decided to support us.

Next, my mother called. She asked me what would become of "Friedman," which struck me as odd. She knew as well as I did that my two brothers (one of whom has a wife with his name) could easily carry on the family name. And, ironically, she herself had taken on Friedman only to end up—more than 20 years later—divorced and desperate to establish a credit record in her own name. She knew better than I the kind of nonidentity society bestows on married women. But, as she later said, she was concerned that I was setting myself up for a lot of hassles. As usual, Mom was right.

Hassle number one was the DMV. When Susan went down to the California Department of Motor Vehicles to get a driver's license with her married name (we both added my family name as a second middle name), they quickly obliged. But when I made my way to the same office with the same request, the guy behind the counter

responded with a curt "No can do." A short tirade about state-sponsored sexism eventually persuaded him to change my name—unfortunately to "Neil Anthony Friedmanpopović." It took yet another long line and a six-week wait before I got a correct license.

The U.S. Passport Agency gave me trouble-free service, I must admit, but the Internal Revenue Service just could not cope. When they discovered that my Social Security number did not match my name, I got a letter instructing me to visit a local Social Security office. After waiting the customary 45 minutes in line, I asked for a card with my new name. The feds said no.

"We just can't do it," said the civil servant.

"Do you mean to tell me that when a woman takes her husband's name you won't issue her a new card?"

"Of course not. We do that all the time."

"What's the difference?"

"All right, then, let me see two pieces of photo ID with the new name." He thought he'd trumped me, but I had an ace up my sleeve: along with my hard-won driver's license, I produced a federal court ID card (I was working for a judge at the time). Proof that I was a fellow fed had an almost magical effect. Twenty minutes and several phone calls later, they found it in their rules—if not in their hearts—to accommodate me. But what would have happened if I had just been Joe Citizen?

Then there were the kids' birth certificates. When our first child was born in 1990, the form had spaces for the father's first, middle, and "family" names—no slot for a married name. The mother's section asked only for Susan's "maiden name," a tacit assumption that she had changed her name to mine. By the time our second child was born, the form was slightly different, but it still didn't allow my married name. As a result, both of our kids have inaccurate birth certificates.

So, all things considered, has this name change been worth all the hassles? Hell yes! I'd do it again—although I hope never to have the occasion. You see, even if taking my wife's name is just a tiny blip on the radar screen of social evolution, it is still a thought-provoking act. And it's a great conversation-starter: when people hear about what we did—and the kind of resistance we faced—it tends to make them think.

Neil A. F. Popović, "The Game of the Name," *Ms.* (November/December 1994). Copyright © 1994 by Lang Communications, Inc. Reprinted with the permission of *Ms.*

When we called them, a number of baby-sitters replied as one woman did, "You're interviewing us? Good. We're human too." Or another, "I'm glad you consider what we do work. A lot of people don't." As it turned out, many daycare workers were themselves juggling two jobs and small children, and so we talked to them about that, too.

We also talked with other men and women who were not part of two-job couples; divorced parents who were war-weary veterans of two-job marriages, and traditional couples, to see how much of the strain we were seeing was unique to two-job couples.

I also watched daily life in a dozen homes during a weekday evening, during the week-end, and during the months that followed, when I was invited on outings, to dinner, or just to talk. I found myself waiting on the front doorstep as weary parents and hungry children tumbled out of the family car. I shopped with them, visited friends, watched television, ate with them, walked through parks, and came along when they dropped their children at daycare, often staying on at the baby-sitter's house after parents waved good-bye. In their homes, I sat on the living-room floor and drew pictures and played house with the children. I watched as parents gave them baths, read bedtime stories, and said good night. Most couples tried to bring me into the family scene, inviting me to eat with them and talk. I responded if they spoke to me, from time to time asked questions, but I rarely initiated conversations. I tried to become as unobtrusive as a family dog. Often I would base myself in the living room, quietly taking notes. Sometimes I would follow a wife upstairs or down, accompany a child on her way out to "help Dad" fix the car, or watch television with the other watchers. Sometimes I would break out of my peculiar role to join in the jokes they often made about acting like the "model" two-job couple. Or perhaps the joking was a subtle part of my role, to put them at ease so they could act more naturally. For a period of two to five years, I phoned or visited these couples to keep in touch even as I moved on to study the daily lives of other working couples—black, Chicano, white, from every social class and walk of life.

I asked who did how much of a wide variety of household tasks. I asked who cooks? Vacuums? Makes the beds? Sews? Cares for plants? Sends Christmas or Hanukkah cards? I also asked: Who washes the car? Repairs household appliances? Does the taxes? Tends the yard? I asked who did most household planning, who noticed such things as when a child's fingernails need clipping, cared more how the house looked or about the change in a child's mood.

INSIDE THE EXTRA MONTH A YEAR

The women I interviewed seemed to be far more deeply torn between the demands of work and family than were their husbands. They talked with more animation and at greater length than their husbands about the abiding conflict between them. Busy as they were, women more often brightened at the idea of yet another interviewing session. They felt the second shift was *their* issue and most of their husbands agreed. When I telephoned one husband to arrange an interview with him, explaining that I wanted to ask him about how he managed work and family life, he replied genially, "Oh, this will *really* interest my *wife.*"

It was a woman who first proposed to me the metaphor, borrowed from industrial life, of the "second shift." She strongly resisted the *idea* that homemaking was a "shift." Her family was her life and she didn't want it reduced to a job. But as she put it, "You're on duty at work. You come home, and you're on duty. Then you go back to work and you're on duty." After eight hours of adjusting insurance claims, she came home to put on the rice for dinner, care for her children, and wash laundry. Despite herself her home life *felt* like a second shift. That was the real story and that was the real problem.

Men who shared the load at home seemed just as pressed for time as their wives, and as torn between the demands of career and small children. . . . But the majority of men did not share the load at home. Some refused outright. Others refused more passively, often offering a loving shoulder to lean on, an understanding ear as their working wife faced the conflict they both saw as hers. At first it seemed to me that the problem of the second shift was hers. But I came to realize that those husbands who helped very little at home were often indirectly just as deeply affected as their wives by the need to do that work, through the resentment their wives feel toward them, and through their need to steel themselves against that resentment. Evan Holt, a warehouse furniture salesman . . . did very little housework and played with his four-year-old son, Joey, at his convenience. Juggling the demands of work with family at first seemed a problem for his wife. But Evan himself suffered enormously from the side effects of "her" problem. His wife did the second shift, but she resented it keenly, and half-consciously expressed her frustration and rage by losing interest in sex and becoming overly absorbed with Joey. One way or another, most men I talked with do suffer the severe repercussions of what I think is a transitional phase in American family life.

One reason women take a deeper interest than men in the problems of juggling work with family life is that even when husbands happily shared the hours of work, their wives felt more *responsible* for home and children. More women kept track of doctors' appointments and arranged for playmates to come over. More mothers than fathers worried about the tail on a child's Halloween costume or a birthday present for a school friend. They were more likely to think about their children while at work and to check in by phone with the baby-sitter.

Partly because of this, more women felt torn between one sense of urgency and another, between the need to soothe a child's fear of being left at daycare, and the need to show the boss she's "serious" at work. More women than men questioned how good they were as parents, or if they did not, they questioned why they weren't questioning it. More often than men, women alternated between living in their ambition and standing apart from it.

As masses of women have moved into the economy, families have been hit by a "speed-up" in work and family life. There is no more time in the day than there was when wives stayed home, but there is twice as much to get done. It is mainly women who absorb this "speed-up." Twenty percent of the men in my study shared housework equally. Seventy percent of men did a substantial amount (less than half but more than a third), and 10 percent did less than a third. Even when couples share more equitably in the work at home, women do two-thirds of the *daily* jobs at home, like cooking and cleaning up—jobs that fix them into a rigid routine. Most women cook dinner and most men change the oil in the family car. But, as one mother pointed out, dinner needs to be prepared every evening around six o'clock, whereas the car oil needs to be changed every six months, any day around that time, any time that day. Women do more childcare than men, and men repair more household appliances. A child needs to be tended daily while the repair of household appliances can often wait "until I have time." Men thus have more control over *when* they make their contributions than women do. They may be very busy with family chores but, like the executive who tells his secretary to "hold my calls," the man has more control over his time. The job of the working mother, like that of the secretary, is usually to "take the calls."

Another reason women may feel more strained than men is that women more often do two things at once—for example, write checks and return phone calls, vacuum and keep an eye on a three-year-old, fold laundry and think out the shopping list. Men more often cook dinner *or* take a child to the park. Indeed, women more often juggle three spheres—job, children, and housework—while most men

juggle two—job and children. For women, two activities compete with their time with children, not just one.

Beyond doing more at home, women also devote *proportionately more* of their time at home to housework and proportionately less of it to childcare. Of all the time men spend working at home, more of it goes to childcare. That is, working wives spend relatively more time "mothering the house"; husbands spend more time "mothering" the children. Since most parents prefer to tend to their children than clean house, men do more of what they'd rather do. More men than women take their children on "fun" outings to the park, the zoo, the movies. Women spend more time on maintenance, feeding and bathing children, enjoyable activities to be sure, but often less leisurely or "special" than going to the zoo. Men also do fewer of the "undesirable" household chores: fewer men than women wash toilets and scrub the bathroom.

As a result, women tend to talk more intently about being overtired, sick, and "emotionally drained." Many women I could not tear away from the topic of sleep. They talked about how much they could "get by on" . . . six and a half, seven, seven and a half, less, more. They talked about who they knew who needed more or less. Some apologized for how much sleep they needed—"I'm afraid I need eight hours of sleep"—as if eight was "too much." They talked about the effect of a change in baby-sitter, the birth of a second child, or a business trip on their child's pattern of sleep. They talked about how to avoid fully waking up when a child called them at night, and how to get back to sleep. These women talked about sleep the way a hungry person talks about food.

All in all, if in this period of American history, the two-job family is suffering from a speed up of work and family life, working mothers are its primary victims. It is ironic, then, that often it falls to women to be the "time and motion expert" of family life. Watching inside homes, I noticed it was often the mother who rushed children, saying, "Hurry up! It's time to go," "Finish your cereal now," "You can do that later," "Let's go!" When a bath is crammed into a slot between 7:45 and 8:00 it was often the mother who called out, "Let's see who can take their bath the quickest!" Often a younger child will rush out, scurrying to be first in bed, while the older and wiser one stalls, resistant, sometimes resentful: "Mother is always rushing us." Sadly enough, women are more often the lightning rods for family aggressions aroused by the speed-up of work and family life. They are the "villains" in a process of which they are also the primary victims. More than the longer hours, the sleeplessness, and feeling torn, this is the saddest cost to women of the extra month a year. . . .

NOTES

1. U.S. Bureau of Labor Statistics, *Employment and Earnings, Characteristics of Families: First Quarter* (Washington, D.C.: U.S. Department of Labor, 1988).

2. Alexander Szalai, ed., *The Use of Time: Daily Activities of Urban and Suburban Populations in Twelve Countries* (The Hague: Mouton, 1972), p. 668, Table B. Another study found that men spent a longer time than women eating meals (Shelley Coverman, "Gender, Domestic Labor Time and Wage Inequality," *American Sociological Review* 48 [1983]:626). With regard to sleep, the pattern differs for men and women. The higher the social class of a man, the more sleep he's likely to get. The higher the class of a woman, the less sleep she's likely to get. (Upper-white-collar men average 7.6 hours sleep a night. Lower-white-

collar, skilled and unskilled men all averaged 7.3 hours. Upper-white-collar women average 7.1 hours of sleep; lower-white-collar workers average 7.4; skilled workers 7.0 and unskilled workers 8.1.) Working wives seem to meet the demands of high-pressure careers by reducing sleep, whereas working husbands don't. . . .

3. Grace K. Baruch and Rosalind Barnett, "Correlates of Fathers' Participation in Family Work: A Technical Report," Working Paper no. 106 (Wellesley, Mass.: Wellesley College Center for Research on Women, 1983), pp. 80–81. Also see Kathryn E. Walker and Margaret E. Woods, *Time Use: A Measure of Household Production of Goods and Services* (Washington, D.C.: American Home Economics Association, 1976).

R E A D I N G   2 8

Working at Motherhood: Chicana and Mexican Immigrant Mothers and Employment[1]

DENISE A. SEGURA

In North American society, women are expected to bear and assume primary responsibility for raising their children. This socially constructed form of motherhood encourages women to stay at home during their children's early or formative years, and asserts activities that take married mothers out of the home (for instance, paid employment) are less important or "secondary" to their domestic duties.[2] Motherhood as a social construction rests on the ideological position that women's biological abilities to bear and suckle children are "natural," and therefore fundamental to women's "fulfillment." This position, however, fails to appreciate that motherhood is a culturally formed structure whose meanings can vary and are subject to change.

Despite the ideological impetus to mother at home, over half of all women with children work for wages.[3] The growing incongruence between social ideology and individual behaviors has prompted some researchers to suggest that traditional gender role expectations are changing (for example, greater acceptance of women working outside the home).[4] The profuse literature on the "ambivalence" and "guilt" employed mothers often feel when they work outside the home, however, reminds us that changes in expectations are neither absolute nor uncontested.

Some analysts argue that the ambivalence felt by many employed mothers stems from their discomfort in deviating from a socially constructed "idealized mother," who stays home to care for her family.[5] This image of motherhood, popularized in the media, schoolbooks, and public policy, implies that the family and the economy constitute two separate spheres, private and public. Dubois and Ruiz argue, however, that the notion of a private-public dichotomy largely rests on the experiences of white, leisured women, and lacks immediate relevance to less privileged women (for instance, immigrant women, women of color), who have historically been important economic actors both inside and outside the home.[6] The view that the relationship between motherhood and employment varies by class, race, and/or culture raises several important questions. Do the ideology of motherhood and the "ambivalence" of employed mothers depicted within American sociology and feminist scholarship pertain to women of Mexican descent in the United States? Among these women, what is the relation between the ideological constructs of motherhood and employment? Is motherhood mutually exclusive from employment among Mexican-heritage women from different social locations?

In this chapter I explore these questions using qualitative data gathered from thirty women of Mexican descent in the United States—both native-born Chicanas (including two Mexico-born women raised since preschool years in the U.S.) and resident immigrant Mexicanas.[7] I illustrate that notions of motherhood for Chicanas and Mexicanas are embedded in different ideological constructs operating within two systems of patriarchy. Contrary to the expectations of acculturation models, I find that Mexicanas frame motherhood in ways that foster a more consistent labor market presence than do Chicanas. I argue that this distinction—typically bypassed in the sociological literature on motherhood, women and work, or Chicano Studies—is rooted in their dissimilar social locations—that is, the "social spaces" they engage within the social structure created by the intersection of class, race, gender, and culture.[8]

I propose that Mexicanas, raised in a world where economic and household work often merged, do not dichotomize social life into public and private spheres, but appear to view employment as one workable domain of motherhood. Hence, the more recent the time of emigration, the less ambivalence Mexicanas express regarding employment. Chicanas, on the other hand, raised in a society that celebrates the expressive functions of the family and obscures its productive economic functions, express higher adherence to the ideology of stay-at-home motherhood, and correspondingly more ambivalence toward full-time employment—even when they work.

These differences between Mexicanas and Chicanas challenge current research on Mexican-origin women that treats them as a single analytic category (for instance, "Hispanic") as well as research on contemporary views of motherhood that fails to appreciate diversity among women. My examination of the intersection of motherhood and employment among Mexican immigrant women also reinforces emerging research focusing on women's own economic and social motivations to emigrate to the U.S. (rather than the behest of husbands and/or fathers).[9]

My analysis begins with a brief review of relevant research on the relationship between motherhood and employment. Then I explore this relationship in greater detail, using in-depth interview data. I conclude by discussing the need to recast current conceptualizations of the dilemma between motherhood and employment to reflect women's different social locations.

THEORETICAL CONCERNS

The theoretical concerns that inform this research on Chicana/Mexicana employment integrate feminist analyses of the hegemonic power of patriarchy over work and motherhood with a critique of rational choice models and other models that overemphasize modernity and acculturation. In much of the literature on women and work, familial roles tend to be portrayed as important constraints on both women's labor market entry and mobility. Differences among women related to immigrant status, however, challenge this view.

Within rational choice models, motherhood represents a prominent social force behind women's job decisions. Becker and Polachek, for example, argue that women's "preference" to mother is maximized in jobs that exact fewer penalties for interrupted employment, such as part-time, seasonal, or clerical work.[10] According to this view, women's pursuit of their rational self-interest reinforces their occupational segregation within low-paying jobs (for example, clerical work) and underrepresentation in higher-paying, male-dominated jobs that typically require significant employer investments (for example, specialized training). Employers may be reluctant to "invest" in or train women workers who, they perceive, may leave a job at any time for familial reasons.[11] This perspective views motherhood as a major impediment to employment and mobility. But it fails to consider that the organization of production has developed in ways that make motherhood an impediment. Many feminist scholars view this particular development as consistent with the hegemonic power of patriarchy.

Distinct from rational choice models, feminist scholarship directs attention away from individual preferences to consider how patriarchy (male domination/female subordination) shapes the organization of production resulting in the economic, political, and social subordination of women to men.[12] While many economists fail to consider the power of ideological constructs such as "family" and "motherhood" in shaping behavior among women, employers, and the organization of production itself, many feminist scholars focus on these power dynamics.

Within feminist analyses, motherhood as an ideology obscures and legitimizes women's social subordination because it conceals particular interests within the rubric of a universal prerogative (reproduction). The social construction of motherhood serves the interest of capital by providing essential childbearing, child care, and housework at a minimal cost to the state, and sustains women as a potential reservoir of labor power, or a "reserve army of labor."[13] The strength of the ideology of motherhood is such that women continue to try to reconcile the "competing urgencies"[14] of motherhood and employment despite the lack of supportive structures at work or within the family.

Because employers view women as mothers (or future mothers), they encounter discrimination in job entry and advancement.[15] Because women are viewed as mothers, they also work a "second shift" at home.[16] The conflict between market work and family work has caused considerable ambivalence within women. Berg, for example, notes that one of the dominant themes in analyzing women and work is the "guilt" of employed mothers based on "espousing something different" from their own mothers.[17]

The notion Berg describes of "conflict" or "guilt" rests on several suppositions. The first assumption is that motherhood is a unilaterally oppressive state; the second, that employed mothers feel guilt; and the third, that today's employed mothers do not have working mothers (which partially explains their "guilt feelings"). Inasmuch as large numbers of working-class, immigrant, and racial ethnic women have long traditions of working in the formal and informal economic sectors, such assumptions are suspect.

Research on women of Mexican descent and employment indicates their labor force participation is lower than that of other women when they have young children.[18] Moreover, Chicanas and Mexicanas are occupationally segregated in the lowest-paying of female-dominated jobs.[19] Explanations for their unique employment situation range from analyses of labor market structures and employer discrimination[20] to deficient individual characteristics (for instance, education, job skills)[21] and cultural differences.[22]

Analyses of Chicana/Mexicana employment that utilize a cultural framework typically explain the women's lower labor force participation, higher fertility, lower levels of education, and higher levels of unemployment as part of an ethnic or cultural tradition.[23] That is, as this line of argument goes, Chicano/Mexican culture emphasizes a strong allegiance to an idealized form of motherhood and a patriarchal ideology that frowns upon working wives and mothers and does not encourage girls to pursue higher education or employment options. These attitudes are supposed to vary by generation, with immigrant women (from Mexico) holding the most conservative attitudes.[24]

There are two major flaws in the research on Chicana/Mexicana employment, however. First, inconsistency in distinguishing between native-born and resident immigrant women characterizes much of this literature. Second, overreliance on linear acculturation persists. Both procedures imply either that Chicanas and Mexicanas are very similar, or that they lie on a sort of "cultural continuum," with Mexican immigrants at one end holding more conservative behaviors and attitudes grounded in traditional (often rural) Mexican culture, and U.S.-born Chicanos holding an amalgamation of cultural traditions from Mexico and the United States.[25] In terms of motherhood and employment, therefore, Mexicanas should have more "traditional" ideas about motherhood than U.S.-born Chicanas. Since the traditional ideology of motherhood typically refers to women staying home to "mother" children rather than going outside the home to work, Mexicanas theoretically should not be as willing to work as Chicanas or North American women in general—unless there is severe economic need. This formulation, while logical, reflects an underlying emphasis on modernity—or the view that "traditional" Mexican culture lags behind North American culture in developing behaviors and attitudes conducive to participating fully in modern society.[26] Inasmuch as conventional North American views of motherhood typically idealize labor market exit to care for children, embracing this prototype may be more conducive to maintaining patriarchal privilege (female economic subordination to men) than facilitating economic progress generally. In this sense, conceptualizations of motherhood that affirm its economic character may be better accommodating to women's market participation in the U.S.

The following section discusses the distinct views of motherhood articulated by Chicanas and Mexicanas and their impact on employment attitudes and behaviors. In contrast to the notion that exposure to North American values enhances women's incentives to work, proportionately more Chicanas than Mexicanas express ambivalence toward paid employment when they have children at home. I analyze these differences among a selected sample of clerical, service, and operative workers.

METHOD AND SAMPLE

This paper is based on in-depth interviews with thirty Mexican origin women—thirteen Chicanas and seventeen Mexicanas—who had participated in the 1978 to 79 or 1980 to 81 cohorts of an adult education and employment training program in the greater San Francisco Bay Area.[27] All thirty respondents had been involved in a conjugal relationship (either legal marriage or informal cohabitation with a male partner) at some point in their lives before I interviewed them in 1985, and had at least one child under eighteen years of age. At the time of their interviews, six Chicanas and fourteen Mexicanas were married; seven Chicanas and three Mexicanas were single parents.

On the average, the married Chicanas have 1.2 children at home; the Mexicanas report 3.5 children. Both Chicana and Mexicana single mothers average 1.6 children. The children of the Chicanas tend to be preschool age or in elementary school. The children of the Mexicanas exhibit a greater age range (from infant to late adolescence), reflecting their earlier marriages and slightly older average age.

With respect to other relevant characteristics, all but two Mexicanas and five Chicanas had either a high school diploma or its equivalent (GED). The average age was 27.4 years for the Chicanas; and thirty-three years for the Mexicanas.[28] Upon leaving the employment training program, all the women secured employment. At the time of their interviews, about half of the Chicanas (n = 7); and three-fourths of the Mexicanas were employed (n = 12). Only two out of the seven (twenty-eight percent) employed Chicanas worked full-time (thirty-five or more hours per week) whereas nine out of the twelve (seventy-five percent) employed Mexicanas worked full-time. Most of the Chicanas found clerical or service jobs (for example, teacher assistants); most of the Mexicanas labored in operative jobs or in the service sector (for example, hotel maids), with a small minority employed as clerical workers.

I gathered in-depth life and work histories from the women to ascertain:

1. What factors motivated them to enter, exit, and stay employed in their specific occupations;
2. whether familial roles or ideology influenced their employment consistency; and
3. whether other barriers limited their job attachment and mobility.

My examination of the relationship between motherhood and employment forms part of a larger study of labor market stratification and occupational mobility among Chicana and Mexican immigrant women.[29]

MOTHERHOOD AND EMPLOYMENT

Nearly all of the respondents, both Chicana and Mexicana, employed and nonemployed, speak of motherhood as their most important social role. They differ sharply in their employment behaviors and views regarding the relationship between motherhood and market work. Women fall into four major groups. The first group consists of five *Involuntary Nonemployed Mothers* who are not employed but care full-time for their children. All of these women want to be employed at least part time. They either cannot secure the job they want and/or they feel pressured to be at home mothering full-time.

The second group consists of six *Voluntary Nonemployed Mothers* who are not employed but remain out of the labor force by *choice*. They feel committed to staying at home to care for preschool and/or elementary school age children.

The third category, *Ambivalent Employed Mothers,* includes eleven employed women. They have either preschool or elementary school age children. Women in this group believe that employment interferes with motherhood, and feel "guilty" when they work outside the home. Despite these feelings, they are employed at least part-time.

The fourth group, *Nonambivalent Employed Mothers* includes eight employed women. What distinguishes these women from the previous group is their view that employment and motherhood seem compatible social dynamics irrespective of the age of their children. All eight women are Mexicanas. Some of these women believe employment could be problematic, however, *if* a family member could not care for their children or be at home for the children when they arrived from school.

Chicanas tend to fall in the second and third categories, whereas Mexicanas predominate in the first and fourth groups. Three reasons emerged as critical in explaining this difference:

1. the economic situations of their families;
2. labor market structure (four-fifths of the nonemployed Mexicanas were involuntarily unemployed); and
3. women's conceptualizations of motherhood, in particular, their expressed *need* to mother.

Age of the women and number of children did not fall into any discernible pattern, therefore I did not engage them in depth within my analysis.

First, I consider the situation of the *Voluntary Non-employed Mothers,* including three married Chicanas, one single-parent Mexicana and one single-parent Chicana. All but one woman exited the labor market involuntarily (for reasons such as layoffs or disability). All five women remain out of the labor force by choice. Among them, the expressed need to mother appears strong—overriding all other concerns. They view motherhood as mutually exclusive from employment. Lydia, a married Chicana with a small toddler, articulates this perspective:

Right now, since we've had the baby, I feel, well he [her husband] feels the same way, that I want to spend this time with her and watch her grow up. See, because when I was small my grandmother raised me so I felt this *loss* [her emphasis] when my grandmother died. And I've never gotten that *real love,* that mother love from my mother. We have a friendship, but we don't have that "motherly love." I want my daughter to know that I'm here, especially at her age, it's very important for them to know that when they cry that mama's there. Even if it's not a painful cry, it's still important for them to know that mommy's there. She's my number one—she's all my attention . . . so working-wise, it's up to [her husband] right now.

Susana, a Chicana single parent with a five-year-old child said:

I'm the type of person that has always wanted to have a family. I think it was more like I didn't have a family-type home when I was growing up. I didn't have a mother and a father and the kids all together in the same household all happy. I didn't have that. And that's what I want more than anything! I want to be different from my mother, who has worked hard and is successful in her job. I don't want to be successful in the same way.

Lydia, Susana, and the other voluntarily unemployed Chicanas adamantly assert that motherhood requires staying home with their children. Susana said: "A good mother is there for her children all the time when they are little and when they come home from school." All the Chicanas in this category believe that motherhood means staying home with children—even if it means going on welfare (AFDC). This finding is similar to other accounts of working-class women.[30]

The sense shared among this group of women that motherhood and employment are irreconcilable, especially when children are of preschool age, is related to their social locations. A small minority of the Chicanas had been raised by nonemployed mothers (n = 3). They feel they should stay at home with their children as long as it's economically feasible. Most of the Chicanas, however, resemble Lydia and Susana, who had been raised by employed mothers. Although these women recognize that their mothers had worked out of economic need, they believe they did not receive sufficient love and care from their mothers. Throughout their interviews, this group of Chicanas expressed hostility and resentment against their employed mothers for leaving them with other caretakers. These feelings contribute to their decisions to stay at home with their children, and/or their sense of "guilt" when they are employed. Their hostility and guilt defies psychoanalytic theories that speculate that the cycle of gender construction locking women into "exclusive mothering" roles can be broken if the primary caretaker (the mother) undertakes more diverse roles.[31] Rather, Chicanas appear to value current conceptionalizations of motherhood that prioritize the expressive work of the mother as distinct from her economic activities.

This group of Chicanas seems to be pursuing the social construction of motherhood that is idealized within their ethnic community, their churches, and society at large.[32] Among Chicanos and Mexicanos the image of *la madre* as self-sacrificing and holy is a powerful standard against which women often compare themselves.[33] The Chicana informants also seem to accept the notion that women's primary duty is to provide for the emotional welfare of the children, and that economic activities which take them outside the home are secondary. Women's desire to enact the socially constructed motherhood ideal was further strengthened by their conviction that many of their current problems (for instance, low levels of education, feelings of inadequacy, single parenthood) are related to growing up in families that did not conform to the stay-at-home mother/father-as-provider configuration. Their evaluation of the close relationship between motherhood and economic or emotional well-being of offspring parallels popular emphasis on the primacy of individual efforts and the family environment to emotional vigor and achievement (Parsons and Bales 1955; Bradley and Caldwell 1984; Caspi and Elder 1988; Parcel and Menaghan 1990).[34]

Informants in this group speak to a complex dimension of mothering and gender construction in the Chicano/Mexicano communities. These women reject their employed mothers' organization of family life. As children, most had been cared for by other family members, and now feel closer to their grandmothers or other female relatives than to their own biological mothers. This causes them considerable pain—pain they want to spare their own children. Many, like Susana, do not want to be "successful" in the tradition of their own employed mothers. Insofar as "success" means leaving their children with other caretakers, it contradicts their conceptualization of motherhood. Rather, they frame "success" in more affective terms: having children who are happy and doing well in school. This does not suggest that Chicanas disagree with the notion that having a good job or a lucrative career denotes "success." They simply feel that successful careers could and should be deferred until their children are older (for instance, in the upper grades of elementary school) and doing well academically and emotionally.

Only one married Mexicana, Belen, articulated views similar to those of the Chicanas. Belen left the labor market in 1979 to give birth and care for her newborn child. It is important to note that she has a gainfully employed husband who does not believe mothers should work outside the home. Belen, who has two children and was expecting a third when I interviewed her, said:

> I wanted to work or go back to school after having my first son, but my husband didn't want me to. He said, "no one can take care of your child the way you can." He did not want me to work. And I did not feel right having someone else care for my son. So I decided to wait until my children were older.

Belens' words underscore an important dynamic that impacted on both Mexicana and Chicana conceptualizations of motherhood: spousal employment and private patriarchy. Specifically, husbands working in full-time, year-round jobs with earnings greater than those of their wives, tended to pressure women to mother full-time. Women who succumb to this pressure become economically dependent on their husbands and reaffirm male authority in the organization of the family. These particular women tend to consider motherhood and employment in similar ways. This suggests that the form the social construction of motherhood takes involves women's economic relationship to men as well as length of time in the U.S.

Four Mexicanas and one Chicana were involuntarily nonemployed. They had been laid off from their jobs or were on temporary disability leave. Three women (two Mexicanas/one Chicana) were seeking employment; the other two were in the last stages of pregnancy but intended to look for a job as soon as possible after their child's birth.

All five women reported feeling "good" about being home with their children, but wanted to rejoin the labor force as soon as possible. Ideologically these women view motherhood and employment as reconcilable social dynamics. As Isabel, an unemployed production worker, married with eight children, said:

> I believe that women always work more. We who are mothers work to maintain the family by working outside, but also inside the house caring for the children.

Isabel voiced a sentiment held by all of the informants— that women work hard at motherhood. Since emigrating to the U.S. about a decade ago, Isabel had been employed nearly continuously, with only short leaves for childbearing. Isabel and nearly all of the Mexicanas described growing up in environments where women, men, and children were important economic actors. In this regard they are similar to the *Nonambivalent Employed Mothers*—all of whom are also Mexicanas. They tended not to dichotomize social life in the same way as the *Voluntary Nonemployed Chicanas* and *Ambivalent Employed* informants.

Although all of the Chicanas believe that staying home best fulfills their mother roles, slightly fewer than half actually stay out of the labor market to care for their young children. The rest of the Chicanas are employed and struggling to reconcile motherhood with employment. I refer to these women as *Ambivalent Employed Mothers*. They express guilt about working and assert they *would not work* if they did not have to for economic reasons. Seven of these women are Chicanas; four are Mexicanas.

To try and alleviate their guilt and help meet their families' economic goals, most of the Chicanas work in part-time jobs. This option permits them to be home when their children arrive from school. Despite this, they feel guilty and unhappy about working. As Jenny, a married Chicana with two children, ages two and four, who is employed part-time, said:

> Sure, I feel guilty. I *should* [her emphasis] be with them [her children] while they're little. He [her husband] really feels that I should be with my kids all the time. And it's true.

Despite their guilt, most of the women in this group remain employed because their jobs offer them the means to provide for family economic betterment—a goal that transcends staying home with their children. However, women's utilization of economic rationales for working sometimes served as a smoke screen for individualistic desires to "do something outside the home" and to establish a degree of autonomy. Several women, for example, stated that they enjoyed having their "own money." When I asked these women to elaborate, they typically retreated to a familistic stance. That is, much of *her* money is used *for the family* (for example, child care, family presents, clothing). When money is used *for the woman* (make-up, going out with the girls) it is often justified as necessary for her emotional well-being, which in turn helps her to be a good wife and mother.

The Mexicana mothers who are employed express their ambivalence somewhat differently from the Chicanas. One Mexicana works full-time; the other three are employed part-time. Angela, a Mexicana married with one child and employed full-time as a seamstress, told me with glistening eyes:

Always I have had to work. I had to leave my son with the baby-sitter since he was six months old. It was difficult. Each baby-sitter has their own way of caring for children which isn't like yours. I know the baby-sitter wouldn't give him the food I left. He always had on dirty diapers and was starving when I would pick him up. But there wasn't any other recourse. I had to work. I would just clean him and feed him when I got home.

Angela's "guilt" stemmed from her inability to find good, affordable child care. Unlike most of the Mexicanas, who had extensive family networks, Angela and her husband had few relatives to rely on in the U.S. Unlike the Chicana informants, Angela did not want to exit the labor market to care for her child. Her desire is reinforced by economic need; her husband is irregularly employed.[35] For the other three Mexicanas in this group, guilt as an employed mother appears to have developed with stable spousal employment. That is, the idea of feeling guilty about full-time employment emerged *after* husbands became employed in secure, well-paying jobs and "reminded" them of the importance of stay-at-home, full-time motherhood. Lourdes, who was married with eight children and working as a part-time hotel maid said:

I was offered a job at a——factory, working from eleven at night to seven in the morning. But I had a baby and so I wasn't able to work. I would have liked to take the job because it paid $8.25 an hour. I couldn't though, because of my baby. And my husband didn't want me to work at night. He said, "If we both work at night, who will take care of the children? So I didn't take the job.

To thwart potential guilt over full-time employment and to ease marital tension (if she had taken this job she would have earned more money than her husband), Lourdes declined this high-paying job. When her child turned two, she opted to work part-time as a hotel maid. Lourdes, and the other Mexicanas employed part-time, told me that they *would* work full-time *if* their husbands supported their preferences. Mexicanas' ambivalence, then, is related to unease about their children's child care situations, as well as to anger at being held accountable to a narrow construction of motherhood enforced by their husbands.

All *Ambivalent Employed Mothers* report worrying about their children while at work. While this does not necessarily impair their job performance, it adds another psychological or emotional burden on their shoulders. This burden affects their ability to work full-time (overtime is especially problematic) or seek the means (especially schooling) to advance in their jobs.

Women seem particularly troubled when they have to work on weekends. This robs them of precious family time. As Elena, a Chicana single parent with two children, ages nine and three, who works part-time as a hotel maid, said:

Yes, I work on weekends. And my kids, you know how kids are—they don't like it. And it's hard. But I hope to find a job soon where the schedule is fixed and I won't have to work on weekends—because that time should be for my kids.

There is a clear sense among the women I interviewed that a boundary between *time for the family* and *market time* should exist. During times when this boundary folds, women experience both internal conflict (within the woman herself) and external conflict (among family members). They regard jobs that overlap on family time with disfavor and unhappiness. When economic reasons compel women to work during what they view as family time, they usually try to find as quickly as possible a different job that allows them to better meet their mother roles.

Interestingly, the Chicanas appear less flexible in reconciling the boundaries of family time and market time than the Mexicanas. That is, Chicanas overwhelmingly "choose" part-time employment to limit the amount of spillover time from employment on motherhood and family activities. Mexicanas, on the other hand, overwhelmingly work full time (n = 9) and attempt to do both familial caretaking and market work as completely as possible.

This leads us to consider the fourth category I call *Nonambivalent Employed Mothers*. This category consists of Mexicana immigrants, both married and single-parent (six and two women, respectively). Mexicanas in this group do not describe motherhood as a *need* requiring a separate sphere for optimal realization. Rather, they refer to motherhood as one function of womanhood compatible with employment insofar as employment allows them to provide for their family's economic subsistence or betterment. As Pilar, a married Mexicana with four children, employed full-time as a line supervisor in a factory, said: "I work to help my children. That's what a mother should do." This group of Mexicanas does not express *guilt* over leaving their children in the care of others so much as *regret* over the limited amount of time they could spend with them. As Norma, a Mexicana full-time clerical worker, who is married with two children ages three and five, said:

> I don't feel guilty for leaving my children because if I didn't work they might not have the things they have now. . . . Perhaps if I had to stay at home I would feel guilty and frustrated. I'm not the type that can stay home twenty-four hours a day. I don't think that would help my children any because I would feel pressured at being cooped up *[encerrada]* at home. And that way I wouldn't have the same desire to play with my daughters. But now, with the time we have together, we do things that we want to, like run in the park, because there's so little time.

All of the Mexicanas in this group articulate views similar to Norma's. Their greater comfort with the demands of market and family work emanates from their social locations. All of the Mexicanas come from poor or working-class families, where motherhood embraced both economic and affective features. Their activities were not viewed as equal to those of men, however, and ideologically women saw themselves as *helping* the family rather than *providing* for it.

Few Mexicanas reported that their mothers were wage-laborers (n = 3), but rather, described a range of economic activities they remembered women doing "for the family."[36] Mexicanas from rural villages (n = 7) recounted how their mothers had worked on the land and made assorted products or food to sell in local marketplaces. Mexicanas from urban areas (n = 5) also discussed how their mothers had been economically active. Whether rural or urban,

Mexicanas averred that their mothers had taught them to "help" the family as soon as possible. As Norma said:

> My mother said: "it's one thing for a woman to lie around the house but it's a different thing for the work that needs to be done. As the saying goes, work is never done; the work does you in *[el trabajo acaba con uno; uno nunca acaba con el trabajo]*.

Lourdes and two other Mexicanas cleaned houses with their mothers after school. Other mothers sold clothes to neighbors, cooked and sold food, or did assorted services for pay (for example, giving penicillin shots to neighbors). The Mexicanas do not view these activities as "separate" or less important than the emotional nurturing of children and family. Rather, they appreciate both the economic and the expressive as important facets of motherhood.

Although the Mexicanas had been raised in worlds where women were important economic actors, this did not signify gender equality. On the contrary, male privilege, or patriarchy, characterizes the organization of the family, the economy, and the polity in both rural and urban Mexican society.[37] In the present study, Mexicanas indicated that men wielded greater authority in the family, the community and the state than women. Mexicanas also tended to uphold male privilege in the family by viewing both domestic work and women's employment as "less important" than the work done by men. As Adela, a married Mexicana with four children, said: "Men are much stronger and do much more difficult work than women." Mexicanas also tended to defer to husbands as the "head" of the family—a position they told me was both "natural" and "holy."[38]

WORKING AT MOTHERHOOD

The differences presented here between the Chicanas and Mexicanas regarding motherhood and employment stem from their distinct social locations. Raised in rural or working-class families in Mexico, the Mexicanas described childhoods where they and their mothers actively contributed to the economic subsistence of their families by planting crops, harvesting, selling homemade goods, and cleaning houses. Their situations resonate with what some researchers term a family economy, where all family members work at productive tasks differentiated mainly by age and sex.[39] In this type of structure, there is less distinction between economic life and domestic life. Motherhood in this context is both economic and expressive, embracing both employment as well as childrearing.

The family economy the Mexicanas experienced differs from the family organization that characterizes most of the Chicanas' childhoods. The Chicanas come from a world that idealizes a male wage earner as the main economic "provider," with women primarily as consumers, and only secondarily as economic actors.[40] Women in this context are mothers first, wage earners second. Families that challenge this structure are often discredited, or perceived as dysfunctional and the source of many social problems.[41] The ambivalence Chicanas recurrently voice stems from their belief in what Kanter calls "the myth of separate worlds."[42] They seek to realize the popular notion or stereotype that family is a separate structure—a haven in a heartless world. Their attachment to this ideal is underscored by a harsh critique of their own employed mothers and themselves *when* they work full-time. Motherhood framed within this context appears irreconcilable with employment.

There are other facets to the differences between Chicanas and Mexicanas. The Mexicanas, as immigrant women, came to the United States with a vision of improving the life chances of their families and themselves. This finding intersects with research on "selective immigration." That is, that Mexican immigrants tend to possess higher levels of education than the national average in Mexico, and a wide range of behavioral characteristics (for instance, high achievement orientation) conducive to success in the U.S.[43]

The Mexicanas emigrated hoping to work—hence their high attachment to employment, even in physically demanding, often demeaning jobs. Mexican and Chicano husbands support their wives' desires to work *so long as* this employment does not challenge the patriarchal structure of the family. In other words, so long as the Mexicanas: (1) articulate high attachment to motherhood *and* family caretaker roles, (2) frame their employment in terms of family economic goals, and (3) do not ask men to do equal amounts of housework or childcare, they encounter little resistance from husbands or other male family members.

When Mexican and Chicano husbands secure good jobs, however, they begin pressuring wives to quit working or to work only part-time. In this way, Mexican and Chicano men actively pursue continuity of their superordinate position within the family. This suggests that the way motherhood is conceptualized in both the Mexican and Chicano communities, particularly with respect to employment, is wedded to male privilege, or patriarchy. Ironically then,

Mexicanas' sense of employment's continuity with motherhood enhances their job attachment but does not challenge a patriarchal family structure or ethos.

Similarly, Chicanas' preference for an idealized form of motherhood does not challenge male privilege in their community. Their desire to stay at home to mother exercised a particularly strong influence on the employment behavior of single-parent Chicanas and women with husbands employed in relatively good jobs. This preference reflects an adherence both to an idealized, middle-class life-style that glorifies women's domestic roles, as well as to maintenance of a patriarchal family order. Chicanas feel they should stay at home to try and provide their children with the mothering they believe children should have—mothering that many of them had not experienced. Chicanas also feel compelled by husbands and the larger community to maintain the status of men as "good providers." Men earning wages adequate to provide for their families' needs usually urged their wives to leave the labor market. While the concept of the good provider continues to be highly valued in our society, it also serves as a rationale that upholds male privilege ideologically and materially, and reinforces the myth of separate spheres that emanates from the organization of the family and the economy.

CONCLUSION

By illustrating how Chicanas and Mexicanas differ in their conceptualizations and organization of the motherhood and employment nexus, this study demonstrates how motherhood is a culturally formed structure with various meanings and subtexts. The vitality of these differences among a group who share a common historical origin and many cultural attributes underscores the need for frameworks that analyze diversity among all groups of women. Most essential to such an undertaking is a critique of the privileging of the "separate spheres" concept in analyses of women and work.

The present study provides additional coherence to recent contentions that the private-public dichotomy lacks immediate relevance to less privileged women (for instance, Chicana and Mexican immigrant women). In the process of illustrating how Chicanas and Mexicanas organized the interplay between motherhood and employment, it became clear that a more useful way of understanding this intersection might be to problematize motherhood itself. Considering motherhood from the vantage point of women's diverse social locations revealed considerable heterogeneity in how one might speak of it. For example, motherhood has an economic component for both groups of women, but it is most strongly expressed by Mexicana immigrants. The flavor of the expressive, however, flows easily across both groups of women, and for the Mexicanas embraces the economic. What this suggests is that the dichotomy of the separate spheres lacks relevance to Chicanas and Mexicanas, and other women whose social origins make economic work necessary for survival.

This leads us to consider the relative place and function of the ideology of motherhood prevalent in our society. Motherhood constructed to privilege the woman who stays at home serves a myriad of functions. It pushes women to dichotomize their lives rather than develop a sense of fluidity across roles, responsibilities, and preferences. Idealized, stay-at-home motherhood eludes most American women with children. As an ideology, however, it tells them what "should be," rendering them failures *as women* when they enter the labor market. Hence the feelings of ambivalence that characterized employed mother's lives for the most part—except those who had not yet internalized these standards. The present research provided examples of such women, along with the understanding that other women from different social locations may demonstrate distinct ways of organizing the motherhood-employment nexus as well.

Feminist analyses of women and work emphasize the role of patriarchy to maintain male privilege and domina-tion economically and ideologically. It is important to recognize that male privilege is not experienced equally by all men, and that patriarchy itself can be expressed in different ways. The present study found that notions of motherhood among Mexicanas and Chicanas are embedded in different ideological constructs operating within two systems of patriarchy. For Mexicanas, patriarchy takes the form of a corporate family model, with all members contributing to the common good. For Chicanas, the patriarchal structure centers more closely around a public-private dichotomy that idealizes men as economic providers, and women primarily as caretakers-consumers.

The finding that women from more "traditional" backgrounds (such as rural Mexico) are likely to approach full-time employment with less ambivalence than more "American" women (such as the Chicanas) rebuts linear acculturation models that assume a negative relationship between ideologies (such as motherhood) constructed within "traditional" Mexican society, and employment. It also complements findings on the negative relationship between greater length of time in the U.S. and high aspirations among Mexicans.[44] This suggests that employment problems (for example, underemployment, unemployment) are related less to "traditional" cultural configurations than to labor market structure and employment policies. Understanding the intersections between employment policy, social ideology, and private need is a necessary step toward expanding possibilities for women in our society.

NOTES

1. This article is a revised version of "Ambivalence or Continuity?: Motherhood and Employment among Chicanas and Mexican Immigrant Women," *AZTLAN, International Journal of Chicano Studies Research* (1992). I would like to thank Maxine Baca Zinn, Evelyn Nakano Glenn, Arlie Hochschild, Beatriz Pesquera, and Vicki Ruiz for their constructive feedback and criticism of earlier drafts of this paper. A special thanks goes to Jon Cruz for his assistance in titling this paper. Any remaining errors or inconsistencies are my own responsibility. This research was supported in part by a 1986–87 University of California President's Postdoctoral Fellowship.

2. Betsy Wearing, *The Ideology of Motherhood, A Study of Sydney Suburban Mothers* (Sydney: George Allen and Unwin, 1984); Barbara J. Berg, *The Crisis of the Working Mother, Resolving the Conflict Between Family and Work* (New York: Summit Books, 1986); Nancy Folbre "The Pauperization of Motherhood: Patriarchy and Public Policy in the United States," *Review of Radical Political Economics* 16 (1984). The view that mothers should not work outside the home typically pertains to married women. Current state welfare policies (e.g., Aid to Families with Dependent Children [AFDC], workfare) indicate that single, unmarried mothers belong in the labor force, not at home caring for their children full-time. See Naomi Gerstel and Harriet Engel Gross, "Introduction," in N. Gerstel and H. E. Gross, eds., *Families and Work* (Philadelphia: Temple University Press, 1987), pp. 1–12; Deborah K. Zinn and Rosemary C. Sarri, Turning Back the Clock on Public Welfare," in *Signs: Journal of Women in Culture and Society* 10 (1984), pp. 355–370; Nancy Folbre "The Pauperization of Motherhood; Nancy A. Naples, "A Socialist Feminist Analysis of the Family Support Act of 1988," AFFILIA 6 (1991), pp. 23–38.

3. Allyson Sherman Grossman, "More than Half of All Children Have Working Mothers," Special Labor Force Reports—Summaries, *Monthly Labor Review* (February, 1982), pp. 41–43; Howard Hayghe, "Working Mothers Reach Record Number in 1984,"

Monthly Labor Review 107 (December, 1984), pp. 31–34; U.S. Bureau of The Census "Fertility of American Women: June 1990," *Current Population Report,* Series P–20, No. 454, (Washington D.C.: United States Government Printing Office, 1991). In June 1990, over half (53.1 percent) of women between the ages of 18–44 who had had a child in the last year were in the labor force. This proportion varied by race: 54.9 percent of white women, 46.9 percent of Black women, and 44.4 percent of Latinas were in the labor force. See U.S. Bureau of the Census (1991), p. 5.

4. Simon and Landis report that a 1986 Gallup Poll indicates that support for married women to work outside the home is considerably greater than 1938 levels: 76 percent of women and 78 percent of men approve (1989: 270). Comparable 1938 levels are 25 percent and 19 percent, respectively of women and men. The 1985 Roper Poll finds the American public adhering to the view that a husband's career supersedes that of his wife: 72 percent of women and 62 percent of men agree that a wife should quit her job and relocate if her husband is offered a good job in another city (189: 272). In the reverse situation, 20 percent of women and 22 percent of men believe a husband should quit his job and relocate with his wife (1989: 272). Simon and Landis conclude: "The Women's Movement has not radicalized the American woman: she is still prepared to put marriage and children ahead of her career and to allow her husband's status to determine the family's position in society" (1989: 269). Rita J. Simon and Jean M. Landis, "Women's and Men's Attitudes About a Woman's Place and Role," *Public Opinion Quarterly* (1989), 53: 265–276.

5. Arlie Hochschild with Anne Machung, *The Second Shift, Working Parents and the Revolution at Home* (New York: Viking Penguin Books, 1989); Kathleen Gerson, *Hard Choices* (Berkeley, California: University of California Press, 1985); Barbara J. Berg, *The Crisis of the Working Mother, Resolving the Conflict Between Family and Work* (New York: Summit Books, 1986). The concept of "separate spheres" is approached in a variety of ways and often critiqued. See Michele Barrett, *Women's Oppression Today, Problems in Marxist Feminist Analysis* (London, Verso Press, 1980); Nona Glazer "Servants to capital: Unpaid domestic labor and paid work," *Review of Radical Economics* 16 (1984), pp. 61–87. Zaretsky contends that distinct family and market spheres arose with the development of industrial capitalism: "men and women came to see the family as separate from the economy, and personal life as a separate sphere of life divorced from the larger economy." See Eli Zaretsky, *Capitalism, The Family and Personal Life* (New York: Harper Colophon Books, 1976), p. 78. This stance is substantially different from that of early radical feminist approaches, including Firestone, who argued that the separation antedates history. See Shulamith Firestone, *The Dialectic of Sex* (New York: Bantam Books, 1970). Other scholars assert that the relations of production and reproduction are intertwined and virtually inseparable. See Heidi Hartmann, "Capitalism, Patriarchy and Job Segregation by Sex," in Martha Blaxall and Barbara Reagan, eds., *Women and the Work Place* (Chicago, Illinois: University of Chicago Press, 1976), pp. 137–169.

6. Hood argues that the "ideal" of stay-at-home motherhood and male provider has historically been an unrealistic standard for families outside the middle and upper classes. She points out that early surveys of urban workers indicate between 40% and 50% of all families supplemented their income with the earnings of wives and children. See Jane C. Hood, "The Provider Role: Its Meaning and Measurement," *Journal of Marriage and the Family* 48 (May, 1986), pp. 349–359.

7. It should be noted that native-born status is not an essential requirement for the ethnic label, "Chicana/o." There are numerous identifiers used by people of Mexican descent, including: Chicana/o, Mexican, Mexican-American, Mexicana/o, Latina/o, and Hispanic. Often people of Mexican descent use two or three of the above labels, depending on the social situation (e.g., "Mexican-American" in the family or "Chicana/o" at school). See John A. Garcia, "Yo Soy Mexicano . . . : Self-identity and Sociodemographic Correlates," *Social Science Quarterly* 62 (March, 1981), pp. 88–98; Susan E. Keefe and Amado M. Padilla, *Chicano Ethnicity* (Albuquerque, NM: University of New Mexico Press, 1987). My designation of study informants as either "Chicana" or "Mexicana" represents an analytic separation that facilitates demonstrating the heterogeneity among this group.

8. Patricia Zavella, "Reflections on Diversity among Chicanos," *Frontiers* 2 (1991), p. 75.

9. See Rosalia Solorzano-Torres, "Female Mexican Immigrants in San Diego County," in V. L. Ruiz and S. Tiano, eds., *Women on the U.S.-Mexico Border: Responses to Change* (Boston: Allen and Unwin, 1987), pp. 41–59; Reynaldo Baca and Bryan Dexter, "Mexican Women, Migration and Sex Roles," *Migration Today* 13 (1985), pp. 14–18; Sylvia Guendelman and Auristela Perez-Itriago, "Double Lives: The Changing Role of Women in Seasonal Migration," *Women's Studies* 13 (1987), pp. 249–271.

10. Gary S. Becker, "Human Capital, Effort, and the Sexual Division of Labor," *Journal of Labor Economics* 3 (1985 Supplement), pp. S33–S58; Gary S. Becker, *A Treatise on the Family* (Cambridge, MA: Harvard University Press, 1981); Solomon W. Polachek, "Occupational Self-Selection: A Human Capital Approach to Sex Differences in Occupational Structure," *Review of Economics and Statistics* 63 (1981), pp. 60–69; S. Polachek "Occupational Segregation Among Women: Theory, Evidence, and a Prognosis" in C. B. Lloyd, E. S. Andrews and C. L. Gilroy, eds., *Women in the Labor Market* (New York: Columbia University Press, 1981), pp. 137–157; S. Polachek, "Discontinuous Labor Force Participation and Its Effect on Women's Market Earnings," in C. Lloyd, ed., *Sex Discrimination and the Division of Labor* (New York: Columbia University Press, 1975), pp. 90–122. Becker's classic treatise, *Human Capital,* uses the following example borrowed from G. Stigler, "The Economics of Information," *Journal of Political Economy* (June 1961): "Women spend less time in the labor force than men and, therefore, have less incentive to have less incentive than residents of the area to invest in knowledge of specific consumption activities." See Gary S. Becker, *Human Capital* (Chicago: University of Chicago Press, 1975), p. 74.

11. Some institutional economists argue that "statistical discrimination" is one critical labor market dynamic that often impedes women and minorities. See Kenneth Arrow, "Economic Dimensions of Occupational Segregation: Comment I," *Signs: Journal of Women in Culture and Society* 1 (1987), pp. 233–237; Edmund Phelps, "The Statistical Theory of Racism and Sexism," in A. H. Amsden, ed., *The Economics of Women and Work* (New York: St. Martin's Press, 1980), pp. 206–210. This perspective suggests that prospective employers often lack detailed information about individual applicants and therefore utilize statistical averages and normative views of the relevant group(s) to which the applicant belongs in their hiring decisions (e.g., college-educated men tend to be successful and committed employees; all women are potential mothers; or women tend to exit the labor force for childbearing).

Bielby and Baron pose an important critique to the underlying rationale of statistical discrimination. They argue that utilizing perceptions of group differences between the sexes is "neither as rational nor as efficient as the economists believe." That is, utilizing stereotypical notions of "men's work" and "women's work" is often costly to employers and therefore irrational. This suggests that sex segregation is imbedded in organizational policies which reflect and reinforce "belief systems that are also rather inert." See William T. Bielby and James N. Baron, "Undoing Discrimination: Job Integration and Comparable Worth," in C. Bose and G. Spitze, eds., *Ingredients for Women's Employment Policy* (New York: State University of New York Press, 1987), p. 216, pp. 221–222.

12. Annette Kuhn, "Structure of Patriarchy and Capital in the Family," in A. Kuhn and Annemarie Wolfe, eds., *Feminism and Materialism: Women and Modes of Production* (London: Routledge and Kegan Paul, 1978); Heidi Hartmann, "Capitalism, Patriarchy, and Job Segregation by Sex," in Martha Blaxall and Barbara Reagan, eds., *Women and the Work Place* (Chicago, Illinois: University of Chicago Press, 1976), pp. 137–169; H. Hartmann, "The Family as the Locus of Gender, Class, and Political Struggle: The Example of Housework," *Signs: Journal of Women in Culture and Society* 6 (1981), pp. 366–394; Michele Barrett *Women's Oppression Today, Problems in Marxist Feminist Analysis* (London: Verso Press, 1980).

13. Lourdes Beneria and Martha Roldan, *The Crossroads of Class and Gender, Industrial Homework, Subcontracting, and Household Dynamics in Mexico City* (Chicago: The University of Chicago Press, 1987); L. Beneria and Gita Sen, "Accumulation, Reproduction, and Women's Role in Economic Development: Boserup Revisited," in E. Leacock and H. I. Safa, eds., *Women's Work: Development and Division of Labor by Gender* (Massachusetts: Bergin and Garvey Publishers, 1986), pp. 141–157; Dorothy Smith, "Women's Inequality and the Family," in N. Gerstel and H. E. Gross, eds., *Families and Work* (Philadelphia: Temple University Press, 1987), pp. 23–54.

14. This phrase was coined by Arlie R. Hochschild and quoted in Lillian B. Rubin, *Intimate Strangers, Men and Women Together* (New York: Harper and Row, 1983).

15. Rosabeth Moss Kanter, *Men and Women in the Corporation* (New York: Basic Books, 1977). Bielby and Baron note: "employers expect certain behaviors from women (e.g., high turnover) and therefore assign them to routine tasks and dead-end jobs. Women respond by exhibiting the very behavior employers expect, thereby reinforcing the stereotype." Bielby and Baron, "Undoing Discrimination: Job Integration and Comparable Worth," p. 221.

16. Arlie Hochschild with Anne Machung, *The Second Shift, Working Parents and the Revolution of Home* (New York: Viking Penguin Books, 1989).

17. Barbara J. Berg, *The Crisis of the Working Mother, Resolving the Conflict Between Family and Work* (New York: Summit Books, 1986), p. 42.

18. Howard Hayghe, "Working Mothers Reach Record Number in 1984," *Monthly Labor Review* 107 (December, 1984), pp. 31–34; U.S. Bureau of the Census, "Fertility of American Women: June 1990" in Current Population Report, Series P-20, No. 454 (Washington D.C.: United States Government Printing Office, 1991); U.S. Bureau of Census Report, "Fertility of American Women: June 1986" in Current Population Report, Series P-20. No. 421 (Washington, D.C.: United States Printing Press). In June 1986 (the year closest to the year I interviewed the respondents where I found relevant data), 49.8 percent of all women with newborn children were in the labor force. Women demonstrated differences in this behavior: 49.7 percent of white women, 51.1 percent of Black women, and 40.6 percent of Latinas with newborn children were in the labor force. See U.S. Bureau of the Census "Fertility of American Women: June 1986" (1987), p. 5.

19. Bonnie Thornton Dill, Lynn Weber Cannon, and Reeve Vanneman, "Pay Equity: An Issue of Race, Ethnicity and Sex" (Washington D.C.: National Commission on Pay Equity, February, 1987); Julianne Malveaux and Phyllis Wallace, "Minority Women in the Workplace," in K. S. Koziara, M. Moskow, and L. Dewey Tanner, eds., *Women and Work: Industrial Relations Research Association Research Volume* (Washington D.C.: Bureau of National Affairs, 1987), pp. 265–298; Vicki L. Ruiz, " 'And Miles to go. . . .': Mexican Women and Work, 1930–1985" in L. Schlissel, V. L. Ruiz, and J. Monk, eds., *Western Women, Their Land, Their Lives* (Albuquerque: University of New Mexico Press, 1988), pp. 117–136.

20. Mario Barrera, *Race and Class in the Southwest: A Theory of Racial Inequality* (Notre Dame, IN: University of Notre Dame Press, 1979); Tomas Almaguer, "Class, Race, and Chicano Oppression," in *Socialist Revolution* 5 (1975), pp. 71–99; Denise Segura, "Labor Market Stratification: The Chicana Experience," *Berkeley Journal of Sociology* 29 (1984), pp. 57–91.

21. Marta Tienda and P. Guhleman, "The Occupational Position of Employed Hispanic Women," in G. J. Borjas and M. Tienda, eds., *Hispanics in the U.S. Economy* (New York: Academic Press, 1985), pp. 243–273.

22. Edgar J. Kranau, Vicki Green, and Gloria Valencia-Weber, "Acculturation and the Hispanic Woman: Attitudes Towards Women, Sex-Role Attribution, Sex-Role Behavior, and Demographics," *Hispanic Journal of Behavioral Sciences* 4 (1982), pp. 21–40;

Alfredo Mirande and Evangelina Enriquez, *La Chicana, The Mexican American Woman* (Chicago: The University of Chicago Press, 1979).

23. Kranau, Green, and Valencia-Weber, "Acculturation and the Hispanic Woman," pp. 21–40; Alfredo Mirande, *The Chicano Experience: An Alternative Perspective* (Notre Dame: University of Notre Dame Press, 1985).

24. Vilma Ortiz and Rosemary Santana Cooney, "Sex-Role Attitudes and Labor Force Participation among Young Hispanic Females and Non-Hispanic White Females," *Social Science Quarterly* 65 (June, 1984), pp. 392–400.

25. Susan E. Keefe and Amado M. Padilla, *Chicano Ethnicity* (Albuquerque, NM: University of New Mexico Press, 1987); Richard H. Mendoza, "Acculturation and Sociocultural Variability," in J. L. Martinez Jr. and R. H. Mendoza, eds., *Chicano Psychology,* Second Edition (New York: Academic Press, 1984), pp. 61–75.

26. Maxine Baca Zinn, "Mexican-American Women in the Social Sciences," *Signs: Journal of Women in Culture and Society* 8 (1982), pp. 259–272. M. Baca Zinn, "Employment and Education of Mexican-American Women: The Interplay of Modernity and Ethnicity in Eight Families," *Harvard Educational Review* 50 (February 1980), pp. 47–62. M. Baca Zinn, "Chicano Family Research: Conceptual Distortions and Alternative Directions," *Journal of Ethnic Studies* 7 (1979) pp. 59–71.

27. For additional information on the methods and sample selection, I refer the reader to Denise A. Segura, "Chicanas and Mexican Immigrant Women in the Labor Market: A Study of Occupational Mobility and Stratification," unpublished Ph.D. dissertation, Department of Sociology, University of California, Berkeley (1986).

28. The ages of the Chicanas range from 23 to 42 years. The Mexicanas reported ages from 24 to 45. The age profile indicates that most of the women were in peak childbearing years.

29. Denise A. Segura, "Chicanas and Mexican Immigrant Women in the Labor Market."

30. For an example, see Betsy Wearing, *The Ideology of Motherhood, A Study of Sydney Suburban Mothers* (Sydney: George Allen and Unwin, 1984).

31. For an example, see Nancy Chodorow, *The Reproduction of Mothering* (Berkeley: University of California Press, 1979).

32. Manuel Ramirez III and Alfredo Castaneda, *Cultural Democracy, Bicognitive Development, and Education* (New York: Academic Press, 1974); Robert F. Peck and Rogelio Diaz-Guerrero, "Two Core-Culture Patterns and the Diffusion of Values Across Their Borders," *International Journal of Psychology* 2 (1967), pp. 272–282; Javier I. Escobat and E. T. Randolph, "The Hispanic and Social Networks," in R. M. Becerra, M. Karno, and J. I. Escobar, eds., *Mental Health and Hispanic Americans: Clinical Perspectives* (New York: Grune and Stratton, 1982).

33. Alfredo Mirande and Evangelina Enriquez, *La Chicana, The Mexican American Woman* (Chicago: The University of Chicago Press, 1979); Margarita Melville, "Introduction" and "Matrascence" in M. B. Melville, ed., *Twice a Minority: Mexican*

American Women (St. Louis: The C.V. Mosby Co., 1980), pp. 1–16; Gloria Anzaldua, *Borderlands, La Frontera: The New Mestiza* (San Francisco: Spinsters/Aunt Lute Book Co., 1987); Linda C. Fox, "Obedience and Rebellion: Re-Vision of Chicana Myths of Motherhood," *Women's Studies Quarterly* (Winter, 1983), pp. 20–22.

34. Talcott Parsons and Robert Bales, *Family, Socialization, and Interaction Processes* (New York: Free Press, 1955); Robert H. Bradley and Bettye M. Caldwell, "The Relation of Infants' Home Environments to Achievement Test Performance in First Grade: A Follow-up Study," *Child Development* 55 (1984), pp. 803–809; Toby L. Parcel and Elizabeth G. Menaghan, "Maternal Working Conditions and Child Verbal Facility: Studying the Intergenerational Transmission of Inequality from Mothers to Young Children," *Social Psychology Quarterly* 53 (1990), pp. 132–147; Avshalom Caspi and Glen H. Elder, "Emergent Family Patterns: The Intergenerational Construction of Problem Behavior and Relationships," in R. Hinde and J. Stevenson Hinde, eds., *Understanding Family Dynamics* (New York: Oxford University Press, 1988).

35. For a full discussion of the interplay between economic goals and economic status of the respondents and their employment decisions, I refer the reader to Denise Segura, "The Interplay of Familism and Patriarchy on Employment among Chicana and Mexican Immigrant Women," in the *Renato Rosaldo Lecture Series Monograph* 5 (Tucson, AZ: The University of Arizona, Center for Mexican American Studies, 1989), pp. 35–53.

36. Two of the Mexicanas reported that their mothers had died while they were toddlers and therefore were unable to discuss their economic roles.

37. Patricia M. Fernandez-Kelly, "Mexican Border Industrialization, Female Labor-Force Participation and Migration," in J. Nash and M. P. Fernandez-Kelly, eds., *Women, Men, and the International Division of Labor* (Albany: State University of New York Press, 1983), pp. 205–223; Sylvia Guendelman and Auristela Perez-Itriago, "Double Lives: The Changing Role of Women in Seasonal Migration," *Women's Studies* 13 (1987), pp. 249–271; Reynaldo Baca and Dexter Bryan, "Mexican Women, Migration and Sex Roles," *Migration Today* 13 (1985), pp. 14–18.

38. Research indicates religious involvement plays an important role in gender beliefs. See Ross K. Baker, Laurily K. Epstein, and Rodney O. Forth, "Matters of Life and Death: Social, Political, Religious Correlates of Attitudes on Abortion," *American Politics Quarterly* 9 (1981), pp. 89–102; Charles E. Peek and Sharon Brown, "Sex Prejudice among White Protestants: Like or Unlike Ethnic Prejudice?" *Social Forces* 59 (1980), pp. 169–185. Of particular interest for the present study is that involvement in fundamentalist Christian churches is positively related to adherence to traditional gender role ideology. See Clyde Wilcox and Elizabeth Adell Cook, "Evangelical Women and Feminism: Some Additional Evidence," *Women and Politics* 9 (1989), pp. 27–49; Clyde Wilcox, "Religious Attitudes and Anti-Feminism: An Analysis of the Ohio Moral Majority," *Women and Politics* 48 (1987), pp. 1041–1051. Half of the Mexicanas (and all but two Chicanas)

adhered to the Roman Catholic religion; half belonged to various fundamentalist Christian churches (e.g., Assembly of God). Two Chicanas belonged to other Protestant denominations. I noticed that the women who belonged to the Assembly of God tended to both work full-time in the labor market and voice the strongest convictions of male authority in the family. During their interviews many of the women brought out the Bible and showed me the biblical passages that authorized husbands to "rule" the family. Catholic women also voiced traditional beliefs regarding family structure but did not invoke God.

39. Frances Rothstein, "Women and Men in the Family Economy: An Analysis of the Relations Between the Sexes in Three Peasant Communities," *Anthropological Quarterly* 56 (1983), pp. 10–23. Ruth Schwartz Cowan, "Women's Work, Housework, and History: The Historical Roots of Inequality in Work-Force Participation," in N. Gerstel and H. E. Gross, eds., *Families and Work* (Philadelphia: Temple University, 1987), pp. 164–177. Louise A. Tilly and Joan W. Scott, *Women, Work, and Family* (New York: Holt, Rinehart, and Winston, 1978).

40. Jessie Bernard, "The Rise and Fall of the Good Provider Role," *American Psychologist* 36 (1981), pp. 1–12; J. Bernard, *The Future of Motherhood* (New York: Penguin Books, 1974); Jane C. Hood, "The Provider Role: Its Meaning and Measurement," *Journal of Marriage and the Family* 48 (May, 1986), pp. 349–359.

41. Lorraine O. Walker and Mary Ann Best, "Well-Being of Mothers with Infant Children: A Preliminary Comparison of Employed Women and Homemakers," *Women and Health* 17 (1991), pp. 71–88; William J. Doherty and Richard H. Needle, "Psychological Adjustment and Substance Use Among Adolescents Before and After a Parental Divorce," *Child Development* 62 (1991), pp. 328–337; Eugene E. Clark and William Ramsey, "The Importance of Family and Network of Other Relationships in Children's Success in School," *International Journal of Sociology of the Family* 20 (1990), pp. 237–254.

42. Rosabeth Moss Kanter, *Men and Women of the Corporation* (New York: Basic Books, 1977).

43. John M. Chavez and Raymond Buriel, "Reinforcing Children's Effort: A Comparison of Immigrant, Native-Born Mexican American and Euro-American Mothers," *Hispanic Journal of Behavioral Sciences* 8 (1986), pp. 127–142. Raymond Buriel, "Integration with Traditional Mexican-American Culture and Sociocultural Adjustment" in J. L. Martinez, Jr. and R. H. Mendoza, eds., *Chicano Psychology,* Second Edition (New York: Academic Press, 1984), pp. 95–130; Leo R. Chavez, "Households, Migration and Labor Market Participation: The Adaptation of Mexicans to Life in the United States," *Urban Anthropology* 14 (1985), pp. 301–346.

44. Raymond Buriel, "Integration with Traditional Mexican-American Culture and Sociocultural Adjustment," in J. L. Martinez, Jr. and R. H. Mendoza, eds., *Chicano Psychology,* Second Edition (New York: Academic Press, 1984), pp. 95–130. In their analysis of differences in educational goals among Mexican-Americans, Buriel and his associates found that: "third generation Mexican Americans felt less capable of fulfilling their educational objectives." See Raymond Buriel, Silverio Caldaza, and Richard Vasquez, "The Relationship of Traditional Mexican American Culture to Adjustment and Delinquency among Three Generations of Mexican American Adolescents," *Hispanic Journal of Behavioral Sciences* 4 (1982), p. 50. Similar findings were reported by Nielsen and Fernandez: "we find that students whose families have been in the U.S. longer have *lower* [their emphasis] aspirations than recent immigrants." See Francois Nielsen and Roberto M. Fernandez, *Hispanic Students in American High Schools: Background Characteristics and Achievement* (Washington D.C.: United States Government Printing Office, 1981), p. 76.

In their analysis of Hispanic employment, Bean and his associates reported an unexpected finding—that English-proficient Mexican women exhibit a greater "constraining influence of fertility" on their employment vis-à-vis Spanish-speaking women. They speculate that more acculturated Mexican women may have "a greater desire for children of higher quality," and therefore "be more likely to devote time to the informal socialization and education of young children." They wonder "why this should hold true for English-speaking but not Spanish-speaking women." See Frank D. Bean, C. Gray Swicegood, and Allan G. King, "Role Incompatibility and the Relationship Between Fertility and Labor Supply Among Hispanic Women" in G. J. Borjas and M. Tienda, eds., *Hispanics in the U.S. Economy* (New York: Academic Press, 1985), p. 241.

Race and "Value": Black and White Illegitimate Babies, 1945–1965

RICKIE SOLINGER

There are two histories of single pregnancy in the post-World War II era, one for Black women and one for white. But for girls and women of both races, being single and pregnant has revealed that, either publicly or privately, their fertility can become a weapon used by others to keep such females vulnerable, defenseless, dependent and, without male protection, in danger. One aspect of single pregnancy that sharply and powerfully illustrates both the common vulnerability of unwed mothers and the racially distinct treatment they have received is the question of what an unmarried girl or woman can or will do with her illegitimate child.

Throughout my study of unwed pregnancy in the pre-*Roe v. Wade* era,[1] racially distinct ideas about the "value" of the illegitimate baby surface again and again as central to an unmarried mother's fate. In short, after World War II, the white bastard child was no longer the child nobody wanted. The Black illegitimate baby became the child white politicians and taxpayers loved to hate. The central argument of this essay is that the "value" of illegitimate babies has been quite different in different historical eras, and that in the United States during the mid-twentieth century, the emergence of racially specific attitudes toward illegitimate babies, including ideas about what to do with them, fundamentally shaped the experiences of single mothers.

Social, cultural, and economic imperatives converged in the postwar era in such a way as to sanction very narrow

and rigid, but different, options for Black and white unwed mothers, no matter what their personal preferences. Black single mothers were expected to keep their babies, as most unwed mothers, Black and white, had done throughout the history of the United States. Unmarried white mothers, for the first time in this country's history, were urged to put their babies up for adoption. These racially specific prescriptions exacerbated racism and racial antagonism in postwar America, and have influenced the politics of female fertility into our own time.

During the Progressive era of the late nineteenth and early twentieth centuries up through the 1930s, social commentators and social service professionals typically considered an illegitimate baby a "child of sin," the product of a mentally deficient mother.[2] As such, this child was tainted and undesirable. The girl or woman, Black or white, who gave birth to it was expected by family, by the community, and by the state to bring it up. Commentators assumed that others rarely wanted a child who stood to inherit the sinful character—the mental and moral weaknesses—of its parent. Before World War II, state laws and institutional regulations supported this mandate, not so much because there were others vying for the babies, but so as to ensure that the mothers would not abandon the infants. State legislators in Minnesota and elsewhere required mothers seeking care in maternity homes to breast-feed their babies for three months and more, long enough to establish unseverable bonds between infant and mother.[3]

Prewar experts stressed that the biology of illegitimacy stamped the baby permanently with marks of mental and moral deficiency, and affirmed that moral conditions were embedded in and revealed by these biological events.[4] Likewise, the unwed mother's pregnancy both revealed her innate biological and moral shortcomings, and condemned her, through the illicit conception and birth, to carry the permanent stain of biological and moral ruin. The biological experience she underwent was tied to her moral status in a fixed, direct, and inexorable relationship. Equally important, her motherhood was immutable. While the deficiencies, the stain, and her ruination violated her biological integrity, as well as her social and moral standing in the community, the unwed mother's maternal relation to the child was not compromised. That was also fixed directly and inexorably by the biological facts of conception and birth.

These attitudes reflected, in part, the importance of bridal virginity and marital conception in mainstream American culture. They also reflected early twentieth-century ideas among moral and medical authorities regarding the strong link between physical, mental, and moral degeneracy and the degeneracy of sex. Until the 1940s, illegitimacy usually carried one meaning; cultural, racial, or psychological determinants which admitted group or individual variability were not sought to explain its occurrence. In this prewar period, social, religious, and educational leaders rarely called for the rehabilitation of unwed mothers or suggested that there were steps they could take to restore their marriageability and their place in the community. What was lost could not be regained; what was acquired could not be cast off. Consequently, most unwed mothers did not have choices to make in that era about the disposition of the bastard child.

WHITE UNWED MOTHERS AND THEIR BABIES: THE POSTWAR ADOPTION MANDATE

After the war, state-imposed breast-feeding regulations and institutional policies asserting the immutability of the white unwed mother's relationship to her illegitimate baby became harder to sustain in the face of a complex and changing set of social conditions. First, the demographic facts of single pregnancy were changing. White birth control and abortion remained illegal and hard to obtain. More girls and women were participating in nonmarital, heterosexual intercourse; thus more of them became pregnant and carried babies to term.[5] As nonmarital sex and pregnancy became more common (and then very common during the later postwar period), it became increasingly difficult to sequester, punish, and insist on the permanent ruination of ever larger numbers of girls and women. This was particularly the case since many of these single pregnant females were members of the growing proportion of the population

that considered itself middle class. As a result, it became increasingly difficult for parents and the new service professionals, themselves members of the middle class, to sanction treating "our daughters" as permanently ruined.

In addition, a strain of postwar optimism emerged that rejected the view that the individual, white, unwed mother was at the mercy of harmful environmental or other forces having the power to determine her fate. The modern expert offered the alternative claim that illegitimacy reflected an emotional and psychological, not environmental or biological disorder. It was, in general, a symptom of individual, treatable neuroses. Reliance on the psychological explanation redeemed both American society and the individual female. Moreover, by moving the governing imperative from the body (biology) to the mind (psychology), all of the fixed relationships previously defining white illegitimacy became mutable, indeterminate, even deniable.

Psychological explanations transformed the white unwed mother from a genetically tainted unfortunate into a maladjusted woman who could be cured. While there was no solvent that could remove the biological stain of illegitimacy, the neuroses that fostered illegitimacy could respond to treatment. The white out-of-wedlock child, therefore, was no longer a flawed by-product of innate immorality and low intelligence.[6] The child's innocence was restored and its adoptability established. At the same time, psychologists argued that white unwed mothers, despite their deviant behavior, could be rehabilitated, and that a successful cure rested in large measure on the relinquishment of the child.[7] The white unwed mother no longer had an immutable relationship to her baby.

In postwar America, the social conditions of motherhood, along with notions about the psychological status of the unwed mother, became more important than biology in defining white motherhood. Specifically, for the first time, it took more than a baby to make a white girl or woman into a mother. Without a preceding marriage, a white female could not achieve true motherhood. Leontine Young, the prominent authority on social casework theory in the area of unwed mothers, cautioned in 1954, "The caseworker has to clarify for herself the differences between the feelings of the normal [married] woman for her baby and the fantasy use of the child by the neurotic unmarried mother."[8] Accepting these new imperatives, social authorities insisted on the centrality of the male to female adult roles, thereby offsetting postwar concerns that women were aggressively undermining male prerogatives in the United States. Experts explained that the unwed mother who came to terms with the baby's existence, symbolically or concretely, and relinquished the child, enhanced her ability to "function [in the future] as a healthy wife and mother."[9]

Release from the biological imperative represented a major reform in the treatment of the many white unwed mothers who desperately desired a way out of trouble, a way to undo their life-changing mistake. The rising rate and numbers of white single pregnancy, particularly among unmarried, middle-class women, would have created an ever larger number of ruined girls and women if unwed mothers continued to have no option but to keep their illegitimate children. In a postwar society that increasingly privileged couples, marriage, children, families, and conformity, this prospect would not have been a happy one. The option of placing an illegitimate child for adoption became, in a sense, an unplanned but fortuitous safety valve for thousands of white girls and women who became unwed mothers but—thanks to the sanctioning of adoption—could go on to become properly married wives and mothers soon thereafter.

This arrangement could only work if there was a sizable population of white couples who wanted to adopt infants, and who didn't mind if the babies had been born to unwed mothers. In the postwar period, this condition was met in part because the postwar family imperative put new pressures on infertile couples who in the past would have remained childless. A social scientist in the mid-1950s referred to illegitimate babies as "the silver lining in a dark cloud":

> Over one in ten of all marriages are involuntarily childless. Since most of these couples desire to adopt a baby, illegitimacy is a blessing to [them]. Curiously, from their standpoint there are not enough illegitimate births because most of these couples must wait one or two or three years in order to adopt a baby, and some are never able to have one because there is not enough for all who want them.[10]

In the early 1950s a leading social work theorist, using what was becoming a popular metaphor, worried about "the tendency growing out of the demand for babies to regard unmarried mothers as breeding machines . . . [by people intent] upon securing babies for quick adoptions."[11]

Through adoption, then, the unwed mother could put the mistake—both the baby *qua* baby, and the proof of nonmarital sexual experience—behind her. Her parents were not stuck with a ruined daughter and a bastard grandchild for life. And the baby could be brought up in a normative family, by a couple prejudged to possess all the attributes and resources necessary for successful parenthood.

Some unmarried pregnant girls considered abortion the best way to efface their mistake, but the possibility in the mid-1950s of getting a safe, legal, hospital abortion was slim, in fact, slimmer than it had been in the prewar decades. If a girl or woman knew about hospital abortions, she might appeal to a hospital abortion committee, a (male) panel of the director of obstetrics/gynecology, and the chiefs of medicine, surgery, neuropsychiatry and pediatrics. In hospitals, including Mt. Sinai in New York, which set up an abortion committee in 1952, the panel of doctors met once a week and considered cases of women who could bring letters from two specialists diagnosing them as psychologically impaired and unfit to be mothers.[12]

By the early 1950s, doctors claimed that new procedures and medications had eliminated the need for almost all medically indicated abortions.[13] That left only psychiatric grounds, which might have seemed promising for girls and women desperate not to have a child.[14] After all, psychiatric explanations were in vogue, and white unwed mothers were categorically diagnosed as deeply neurotic, or worse. There was, however, a catch. These abortion committees had been set up to begin with because their very existence was meant to reduce requests for "therapeutic" abortions, which they did.[15] It was, in fact, a matter of pride and competition among hospitals to have the highest ratio of births to abortions on record.[16] But even though psychiatric illness was the only remaining acceptable basis for request, many doctors did not believe in these grounds. A professor of obstetrics in a large university hospital said, "We haven't done a therapeutic abortion for psychiatric reasons in ten years. . . . We don't recognize psychiatric indications."[17] So an unwed pregnant girl or woman could be diagnosed and certified as disturbed, probably at considerable cost, but she couldn't convince the panel that she was sick enough. The committee may have, in fact, agreed with the outside specialists that the abortion petitioner was psychotic, but the panel often claimed the problem was temporary, with sanity recoverable upon delivery.[18]

The doctors were apparently not concerned with questions about when life begins. They were very concerned with what they took to be their responsibility to protect and preserve the links between femininity, maternity, and marriage. One doctor spoke for many of his colleagues when he complained of the "clever, scheming women, simply trying to hoodwink the psychiatrist and obstetrician" in their appeals for permission for abortions.[19] The mere request, in fact, was taken, according to another doctor, "as proof [of the petitioner's] inability and failure to live through the destiny of being a woman."[20] If such permission were granted, one claimed, the woman "will become an unpleasant person to live with and possibly lose her glamour as a wife. She will gradually lose conviction in playing a female role."[21] An angry committee member, refusing to grant permission to one woman, asserted, "Now that she has had her fun, she wants us to launder her dirty underwear. From my standpoint, she can sweat this one out."[22]

For many doctors, however, condemning the petitioner to sweat it out was not sufficient punishment. In the mid-1950s, in Maryland, a doctor would almost never agree to perform a therapeutic abortion unless he sterilized the woman at the same time.[23] The records of a large, Midwestern, general hospital showed that between 1941 and 1950, seventy-five percent of the abortions performed there were accompanied by sterilization.[24] The bottom line was that, if you were single and pregnant (and without rich or influential parents who might, for example, make a significant philanthropic gesture to the hospital), your chances with the abortion committee were pretty bleak. Thousands of unhappily pregnant women each year got illegal abortions, but for thousands of others, financially, morally, or otherwise unable to arrange for the operation, adoption seemed their only choice.

Service agencies, however, found the task of implementing the adoption mandate complicated. Many who worked with white unwed mothers in maternity homes, adoption agencies, or public welfare offices in this period had to braid unmatched strands into a coherent plan. Agency workers were deeply uneasy about separating babies from the one individual who until recently had been historically and culturally designated as best suited, no matter what her marital status, to care for her own baby. In addition, the community response to out-of-wedlock pregnancy and maternity in the United States had historically been punitive.[25] Keeping mother and child together was simultaneously in the child's best interest and the earned wages of sin for the unwed mother. Until the postwar era, most social workers had trained and practiced in this tradition.[26]

After World War II, social workers struggled to discard the two most basic assumptions that had previously guided their work with white unwed mothers. These girls and women were no longer considered the best mothers for their babies. And they would no longer be expected to pay for their illicit sexual experience and illegitimate pregnancy by living as ruined women and outcast mothers of bastard children. Social workers were now to offer them a plan which would protect them from lasting stigma and rehabilitate them for normative female roles. The psychological literature supporting definitions of unwed mothers as not-mothers, the interest of many white couples in obtaining newborn babies, and postwar concepts of family helped

social workers accept new ideas about the disposition of illegitimate white babies.

After the war, in all parts of the country, public agencies, national service organizations, and maternity homes allocated the resources and developed techniques for separating mother and child. Services became increasingly so streamlined that in many maternity homes, such as the Florence Crittenton Home in Houston, "Babies [went] directly from the hospital to children's [adoption] agencies."[27] Indeed, public and private agencies were functioning in an environment in which the separation of single mother and child was becoming the norm. In Minnesota, for example, in 1925 there were two hundred such separations; in 1949, one thousand; between 1949 and 1955, approximately seventeen hundred each year. Nationally, by 1955, ninety thousand babies born out of wedlock were being placed for adoption, an eighty percent increase since 1944.[28]

To meet the demand and to justify their own existence, agencies and individual operators not infrequently resorted to questionable tactics, including selling babies for profit. When the federal government undertook to investigate widespread coercive and profit-oriented adoption practices in the United States in the 1950s, the task was assigned to Senator Estes Kefauver's Subcommittee to Investigate Juvenile Delinquency. This committee was charged with redressing the problem of adoption for profit and assuring the "suitability of the home" for adoptable children, a criterion which could not, by definition, be met in homes headed by unmarried mothers.[29] While illegitimate pregnancy and babies had, in the past, been a private matter handled by family members, perhaps assisted by charity workers, by mid-century, these issues had become public concerns and public business.

The Kefauver committee and the organizations and individuals it investigated defined white unmarried mothers out of their motherhood. If not by law, then *de facto,* they were not parents. This judgment was in line with and supported various forms of state control over single, pregnant girls and women, and those who might become pregnant, including, of course, the state's formal and informal proscriptions against birth control for unmarried girls and women, its denial of access to safe, legal abortion, and its tolerance in many places of unsafe, illegal abortions. The state determined what types of agencies and individuals an unmarried mother could deal with in planning for her child, and either strongly suggested or legislated which ones were "morally wrong." These state prerogatives allowed some agencies and individuals to abuse and exploit childbearing, single, white women.

A very articulate, eighteen-year-old, unmarried mother from Minnesota wrote to her governor in August, 1950, illustrating how some public agencies took direct action to separate white babies from their mothers, even against the mother's will. She said that a welfare worker in her city told her she could not keep her baby, "that the baby should be brought up by both a mother and a father." Having gotten no satisfaction, she wrote in frustration and anger to President Truman:

> With tears in my eyes and sorrow in my heart I'm trying to defend the rights and privileges which every citizen in the United States is supposed to enjoy under our Constitution [but are] denied me and my baby. . . . The Welfare Department refuses to give me my baby without sufficient cause or explanation. . . . I have never done any wrong and just because I had a baby under such circumstances the welfare agency has no right to condemn me and to demand my child be placed [for adoption].[30]

A year earlier, a young man living in Sterling, Colorado, wrote to the Children's Bureau about a similar case. In this situation, a young man and a young deaf woman had conceived a baby out of wedlock, but planned to marry. When the man went to the Denver Welfare Department for assistance a few days before the baby was born, he found that the baby had already been targeted for adoption.

This case, in particular, demonstrates a couple of key assumptions underlying the behavior of some agency workers in matters of out-of-wedlock adoptions. The young mother was deaf. As a handicapped person and an unmarried girl, her maternity, as well as her child, was considered illegitimate, and could be rightfully terminated by the authorities. Physically defective women had curtailed rights as mothers, just as physically defective illegitimate babies had diminished opportunities to join the middle class. This case also suggests the very important notion that white babies were so valuable because in postwar America, they were born not only untainted but also *unclassed*. A poor, "white trash" teenager could have a white baby in Appalachia; it could be adopted by an upper-middle-class couple in Westport, Connecticut, and the baby would, in that transaction, become upper-middle-class also.

Finally, this case illustrates that agency workers believed that a successful separation often depended on an early and very quick transaction. This was noticed by contemporaries, including the authors of a state-certified report on adoption in Cook County, Illinois that warned about the problems that arose when "mothers come into court service division to sign a consent either on the day they are released from the hospital, or shortly thereafter [and] are physically and emotionally upset to the extent that they are not capable of making rational decisions."[31]

Courts also facilitated adoption abuse. A chief probation officer in the Richmond County, Alabama, Juvenile Court spent a great deal of her time finding and "freeing" white babies for adoption, using her position to legitimize these activities. One unwed mother told of her encounter with the officer, a Miss Hamilton. She said:

> Several hours after delivery [Miss Hamilton] informed me that my baby had been born dead. She told me that if I signed a paper she had, no one, my family or friends, would know about the situation, and that everything would be cleared up easily. She described the paper as being a consent authorizing the burial of the child. . . . I signed the paper without really looking at it, as I was in a very distressed and confused condition at the time.

This young woman went on to say that, "Two years later I was shocked to receive in the mail adoption papers from the Welfare Department in California since I was under the impression that the child was deceased."[32]

Illegalities and abuse existed in some mainstream institutions, but a great many of the worst abuses were committed by individual baby brokers—lawyers, doctors and non-professionals cashing in on the misfortune of unwed mothers. In postwar, consumerist America, institutions promoted services and attitudes to protect the out-of-wedlock child from market-driven deals, and to see that it was well placed. On the other hand, these same institutions were themselves behaving in market-oriented ways as they promoted a specific, socially beneficial product: the two-parent/two-plus child family. This double message justified the baby brokers' commoditylike treatment of unwed mothers and their babies. Charlton G. Blair, a lawyer who handled between thirty and sixty adoptions a year in the late 1950s, justified his operation by denying he ever "paid one red cent" to a prospective mother of an illegitimate child to persuade her to part with the baby. But in suggesting why the adopting parents were willing to pay up to fifteen hundred dollars for a child, which included the lawyer's seven hundred fifty-dollar fee, Blair defined his sense of the transaction very clearly: "If they're willing to pay three thousand dollars for an automobile these days, I don't see why they can't pay this much for a child."[33] A baby broker in Texarkana, Texas boasted to an employee that she had sold

993 illegitimate babies throughout the United States and that she wanted to make it one thousand before she died.[34]

A case which dramatically captures the plight of poor, white, unwed mothers was presented at the Kefauver hearings by Mary Grice, an investigative reporter for the *Wichita Beacon.* Grice testified about a woman, "Mrs. T.," who had been in the adoption business since 1951 or 1952. "Mrs. T." warehoused unwed, pregnant girls in the basement of her home. "She would have them on cots for prospective adoptive parents [who] would come in and she would take them downstairs, and she would point to the girls and say, 'Point out the girl that you want to be the mother of your child.' " Grice's investigation revealed that "Mrs. T." kept on average seven unmarried mothers in her basement at a time, and that she would oversee a number of the deliveries herself in the basement. According to Grice, between one hundred and fifty and one hundred and sixty-four adoptions each year of this sort were taking place in Sedgwick County, Kansas. "Mrs. T." often collaborated with Grace Schauner, a Wichita abortionist. Unmarried pregnant girls and women would first see Schauner, and if they decided not to have an abortion, they would be referred to "Mrs. T." who would "care for them and sell their infants after birth."[35]

"Mrs. T's" girls were the ones whose class, gender, and race combined to render them most vulnerable. Because they were poor, they did not have the information or other resources to resist baby-market operators. Because they were female (specifically, white females), their socially mandated shame precluded self-protection and motherhood. Because they were white, their babies had value. This combination of poverty, race and gender—in a context which defined white unwed mothers as not-mothers, and defined their babies as valuable—put some white, unwed mothers in a position of extreme vulnerability.

Again, there is no question that for many white unwed mothers, the opportunity to place their babies independently meant that they could get exactly what they needed when they needed it: money to live on, shelter, medical care, and assurances about the placement of the baby, all with no questions asked. These girls and women were often spared the delays, the layers of authority, the invasions of privacy, the permanent black mark engraved in the files of the welfare department, and they were spared the pressure to reveal the father's name, all of which characterized the bureaucratic agency approach.[36] Their experience demonstrated how difficult it was for institutions to perform simultaneously as agents of social control and as sources of humanitarian assistance for the needy and vulnerable.

The stories of unwed mothers abused by the baby market reveal how class, gender, and (white) race together created the possibilities to use these girls and women for profit. Cultural constructions of female sexuality and maternity in the postwar decades, and the sanctions against sexual and maternal nonconformity, sent unwed mothers with few resources into the anonymous marketplace which offered, simultaneously, protection and danger.

An intruder in the courtroom in Miami, Florida, where a section of the Kefauver hearings was held in November, 1955, expressed the frustration of some girls and women who felt they had lost control over the disposition of their illegitimate children. This woman stood up, unbidden, and lectured the men before her in a loud voice. She said,

> Excuse me. I am not leaving no court. . . . You have to carry these children nine months and then you have them taken away by the Catholic Charities, and then they throw you out and drag you all over the street. . . . I'm no drunk, I'm no whore. . . . I gave birth to two children and had them taken away from me. I don't sleep nights thinking about my children. What do you people care? Don't take my picture. You people have no feelings at all. That man [a judge testifying that there are plenty of services available for unwed mothers] is sitting there and lying—lying. These people just take other people's children away from them. All that he has said is a lie. My baby was born . . . and I haven't seen it since. . . . How would you like it? Year after year you have to go to the people . . . and ask them why you can't have your children.[37]

Clark Vincent, a sociologist who closely followed the treatment of white, unwed mothers in this era, offered the following vision of a world in the near future where the state would have unrestrained authority to determine who is a mother.

> If the demand for adoptable infants continues to exceed the supply; if more definitive research . . . substantiates that the majority of unwed mothers who keep their children lack the potential for "good motherhood"; and if there continues to be an emphasis through laws and courts on the "rights of the child" superseding the "rights of the parents"; then it is quite probable that in the near future unwed mothers will be "punished" by having their children taken away from them at birth. Such a policy would not be enacted nor labeled overtly

as "punishment." Rather it would be implemented under such pressures and labels as "scientific finding," "the best interests of the child," "rehabilitation goals for the unwed mother," and the "stability of the family and society."[38]

THE BLACK UNWED MOTHER AND HER CHILD: A TAXPAYERS' ISSUE

In postwar America, there was only one public intention for white, unwed mothers and their babies: separate them. Toward Black, single mothers and their babies, however, there were three broadly different public attitudes.[39] One attitude, often held by middle-of-the-road politicians, social service administrators, and practitioners, maintained that Blacks had babies out of wedlock because they were Negro, because they were ex-Africans and ex-slaves, irresponsible and immoral, but baby-loving. According to this attitude, the state and its institutions and agencies could essentially ignore breeding patterns, since Blacks would take care of their children themselves. And if Blacks did not, they were responsible for their own mess. Adopting Daniel Moynihan's famous phrase from this period, I call this public attitude toward Black illegitimacy *benign neglect.*

A second response to Black mothers and babies was *punitive.* The conservative, racist politicians who championed this position argued simply that the mothers were bad and should be punished. The babies were expendable because they were expensive and undesirable as citizens. Public policies could and should be used to punish Black unmarried mothers and their children in the form of legislation enabling states to cut them off from welfare benefits, and to sterilize or incarcerate "illegitimate mothers."[40]

I label the third way of seeing this group *benevolent reformist.* Employees at the United States Children's Bureau and many in the social work community who took this position maintained that Black girls and women who had children out of wedlock were just like whites who did the same. Both groups of females were equally disturbed and equally in need of help, particularly in need of social casework. Regarding the baby, benevolent reformers held that Black, unwed mothers should be accorded every opportunity to place the infant for adoption, just like whites.

Despite these different attitudes toward Black women and their babies, proponents of all three shared a great deal. First, they shared the belief that the Black, illegitimate baby was the product of pathology. This was the case whether it was a pathology grounded in race, as it was for the benign neglecters and the punishers, or in gender, as it was for the benevolent reformers. Second, all commentators agreed that the baby's existence justified a negative moral judgment about the mother and the mother-and-baby dyad. The Black illegitimate infant was proof of its mother's moral incapacities; its illegitimacy suggested its own probable tendencies toward depravity. Because of the eager market for white babies, this group was cleared of the charge of inherited moral taint, while Black babies were not. Indeed, proponents of each of the three perspectives agreed that the unwed, Black mother must, in almost every case, keep her baby. Where they differed was in explaining why this was so. The different answers reflected different strains of racism and carried quite different implications for public policies and practices regarding the Black, unmarried mother and her child.

The benign neglecters began to articulate their position at about the same time that the psychologists provided new explanations for white, single pregnancy. In tandem, these developments set Black and white, unwed mothers in different universes of cause and effect. According to these "experts," Black and white single mothers were different from each other in several ways. When Black, single girls and women had intercourse, it was a sexual, not a psychological act, and Black mothers had "natural affection" for their children, whatever their birth status. The white, unwed mother had only neurotic feelings for her out-of-wedlock child. The "unrestrained sexuality" of Black women, and their capacity to love the resulting illegitimate children, were perceived as inbred traits, and unchangeable parts of Black culture.

Thus, by becoming mothers, even unwed mothers, Black women were simply doing what came naturally. There was no reason for social service workers or policy-makers to interfere. It was also important in this regard that the operative concept of "culture" excised considerations of environment. Environment was not a primary factor in shaping female sexual behavior or the mother's relationship to her illegitimate baby. These were determined by "culture," an essentially biological construct. Therefore, since professionals could only have an impact on the immediate situation—and could not penetrate or rearrange Black "culture," it was doubly futile to consider interfering. The absence of services for these women and their children was justified in this way. Issues regarding Blacks and adoption were quickly dismissed by those who counselled neglect. Agencies claimed that Blacks didn't want to part with their babies, and, just as important, Black couples didn't want to adopt children.[41]

White policymakers and service providers often pointed to the Black grandmothers—willing, able, loving, and present—to justify their contentions that the Black family would take care of its own, and that no additional services were necessary. Yet when grandmothers rendered such service, policymakers labelled them "matriarchs" and blamed them for "faulty personality growth and for maladaptive functioning in children."[42] The mother was similarly placed in a double bind. She was denied services because she was black, an alleged cultural rather than a racial distinction, and then she was held responsible for the personal and social consequences.[43] The social service system was, in this way, excused from responsibility or obligation to Black, unwed mothers.

The punishers, both Southern Dixiecrats and Northern racists, drew in part on the "cultural" argument to target both the unwed mother and her baby. They held that Black culture was inherited, and that the baby would likely be as great a social liability as its mother. Moreover, they claimed that for a poor, Black woman to have a baby was an act of selfishness, as well as of pathology, and deserved punishment.[44] Once the public came to believe that Black illegitimacy was not an innocuous social fact, but carried a direct and heavy cost to white taxpayers, many whites sanctioned their political representatives to target Black, unwed mothers and their babies for attack.[45]

The willingness to attack was expressed, in part, by a special set of tropes which drew on the language and concepts of the marketplace. The "value" assigned to the illegitimate child-as-commodity became useful in classifying the violation of the Black, unwed mother in a consumer society. Repeatedly, Black, unmarried mothers were construed as "women whose business is having illegitimate children."[46] This illicit "occupation" was portrayed as violating basic consumerist principles, including good value in exchange for a good price, for a product which, in general, benefits society. Black, unmarried mothers, in contrast, were said to offer bad value (Black babies) at a high price (taxpayer-supported welfare grants) to the detriment of society, demographically and economically. The behavior of these women—most of whom did not receive Aid to Dependent Children grants for their illegitimate children[47]—was construed as meeting only the consumerist principle that everything can, potentially, be a commodity. These women were accused of treating their reproductive capacities and their children as commodities, with assigned monetary values. From this perspective, Black, unmarried

mothers were portrayed as "economic women," making calculated decisions for personal, financial gain.[48]

The precise economic principle most grossly violated by these women was, according to many, that they got something (ADC) for nothing (another Black baby); they were cheating the public with a bad sell. The fact that it was, overwhelmingly, a buyers' market for Black babies "proved" the valuelessness of these children, despite their expense to the taxpaying public.[49] White babies entered a healthy sellers' market, with up to ten couples competing for every one adoptable infant.[50]

Spokespeople for this point of view believed that Black, unmarried mothers should pay dearly for the bad bargain they foisted on society, especially on white taxpayers. But many felt that rather than paying for their sins, Black women were being paid, by ADC grants, an exchange which encouraged additional sexual and fiscal irresponsibility.[51] Thus, society was justified in punishing Black, unwed mothers. In addition, the Black unmarried woman, allegedly willing to trade on her reproductive function, willing to use her body and her child so cheaply, earned the state's equal willingness to regard her childbearing capacity cheaply, and take it away, for example, by sterilization legislation.

The ironic truth was that ADC benefits were such inadequate support (and employment and child care opportunities so meager or nonexistent) that government policies had the effect of causing, not responding to, the economic calculations a woman made that might lead to pregnancy. The average welfare payment per child, per month, was $27.29 with monthly averages less than half that amount in most Southern states.[52] The following encounter illustrates the relationship between illegitimacy and economics, from one woman's point of view.

> When the case analyst visited the family, the little girl came in with a new dress and shoes. The mother explained that it was the last day of school and the child had begged for new clothes like the other children had. She got them, but the mother's comment was, "I hope that dress does not cause me another baby."[53]

This mother's economic and sexual calculations were rooted in poverty and maternal concern, not in some desire to multiply inadequate stipends through additional pregnancies.

In Florida, the assumptions of welfare officials and legislators concerning the "business" intentions of Black, unwed mothers received a jolt in the early 1960s, when mothers withdrew from the ADC program rather than risk having their children taken away from them and sent, for example, to the homes of married relatives, under the state's "suitable home" law. This law aimed to punish illegitimate mothers who "persisted" in having babies, while saving taxpayers' money by reducing welfare rolls. "At least some [social workers] anticipated that among Negro families, the 'extended family pattern' would ease the pain of separation and rarely generate resistance to placement. But as one mother said, 'People give away puppies and kittens, but they don't give away their children.' "[54] In the face of the persistence of a slave owners' mentality among Florida's welfare professionals and politicians, and the commodization of children this view supported, Black women demonstrated their adherence to a value system which placed their children and their bodies outside of the economic nexus, as far as the government and the welfare system were concerned.[55]

The public's interest in casting Black, unwed mothers and their babies as consumer violators was reflected in opinion polls that suggested the American public wanted to withhold federal support, or food money, from illegitimate, Black babies.[56] Among dissenters were people who believed it was wrong "to deny food to children because of the sins of the parents."[57] Both groups, however, fell into a trap set by conservative politicians who found it politically profitable to associate Black illegitimacy in their constituent's minds with the rising costs of public welfare grants. The Aid to Dependent Children caseload increased in the postwar period for many reasons, including the basic increase in numbers of children and families, and the increase in households headed by women because of divorce, separation, desertion, *and* illegitimacy. Between 1953 and 1959, the number of families headed by women rose 12.8 percent, while the number of families rose only 8.3 percent.[58] While white sentiment was being whipped up to support punitive measures against Black "subsidized immorality,"[59] only about sixteen percent of nonwhite, unwed mothers were receiving ADC grants.[60] Adoption, which was not an option for most Blacks, was the most important factor in removing white children from would-be ADC families. Of unwed, white mothers who kept their children, thirty percent, or nearly twice as large a percentage as Blacks, were receiving Aid to Dependent Children grants in 1959.[61] Yet in the minds of large segments of the white public, Black, unwed mothers were being paid, in welfare coin, to have children. The "suitable home" laws which were originally designed, it was claimed, to protect the interests of children, were not instrumental in stopping those payments. The children in question represented low value to politicians leading the attacks on welfare costs. These were politicians who had no qualms about using Black, illegitimate children as pawns in their attempt to squash Black "disobedience" via morals charges.[62]

Led by Annie Lee Davis, a Black social worker at the United States Children's Bureau, many members of the social work community worked unceasingly to convert benign neglecters and punishers into benevolent reformers. Davis was a committed integrationist. She was dedicated to convincing the white social service establishment that Black, unmarried mothers needed and deserved the same services as their white counterparts. In 1948, Davis addressed this message to her colleagues: "Within minority groups, unmarried mothers suffer guilt and shame as in the majority group." She added, "I know there are those who will challenge this statement," but, she insisted, "In the process of adopting the cultural traits of the dominant group in America all groups are striving to be American."[63]

Davis insisted white public officials and social workers be brought to believe that Black, unwed mothers were psychologically and morally the equals of whites. Only then would Blacks be eligible for the best available services. Ironically, Davis believed that a key element of proof was to establish that Blacks were as interested in adoptive placements for their illegitimate babies as whites were urged to be. Her task was to convince her colleagues that lack of alternative options alone created the custom and the necessity that Blacks kept their illegitimate children.

Benevolent reformers typically took the position that it was unacceptable and potentially racist to assume that Blacks did not want every opportunity that whites had, including adoption. But it was extremely difficult for the reformers to suggest that some Black, single mothers wanted their children, and others did not. It was not simply unwed mothers and their babies at issue, it was the race. For the reformers, constructing an equivalency between Black and white unmarried mothers was the most promising and practical route to social services and social justice.

But even if a Black, single mother did consider placing her child for adoption, she knew that the likelihood that the agency would expeditiously approve a couple as adoptive parents was slim.[64] While a white, unwed mother could expect a rapid placement, the Black one knew that her child would be forced, in part because of agency practices, to spend months in foster homes or institutions before placement, if that was ever achieved. For example, adoption agencies frequently rejected Blacks who applied for babies, claiming they did not meet the agency's standards for adoptive parents. They also neglected to work with schools and hospitals in contact with Black, unwed mothers to improve referral services between these institutions and the agencies, because they feared recruiting Black babies when there might not be homes for them. In these ways the organizations that reformers depended on to provide services for Black, unwed mothers equal to those for whites, and to make it more possible for society to perceive these Blacks in the same way as they saw whites, did not hold up their end. The reformers had their integrationist vision, but the institutions of society would not cooperate, even when some Black, unwed mothers did.

In fact, the evidence from postwar Black communities suggests that the Black, unwed mother accepted responsibility for her baby as a matter of course,[65] even when she was sorry to have gotten pregnant.[66] A study in the mid-1960s cautioned the social work profession: "Social work wisdom is that Negroes keep because there is no place to give the baby up, but the study showed . . . that Negroes did not favor adoption, opportunities or their absence notwithstanding." Findings showed that the issue of disposition of the child was the only one that consistently yielded a difference between Black and white respondents, no matter whether they were the unwed mother, her parents, or professional staff. In fact, the Blacks revealed their determination to keep mother and child together and the whites their determination to effect separation, "no matter how [the investigator] varied the content of the questions."[67]

In the same period in Cincinnati, several researchers captured the comments of the mothers themselves. Some girls and women focused on the needs of the baby. One typical respondent claimed, "An innocent child should not be denied his mother's love." Joyce Ladner's subjects in another Midwestern city considered the illegitimate baby as "a child who had the right to be cared for and reared in the community of his parents without stigmatization."[68] Others in the Cincinnati study focused on the strength of their own needs, "I'd grieve myself to death if I let my baby go." A few predicted they would have had nervous breakdowns if they hadn't been allowed to keep their babies. A representative outlook drew on the sanctified status of motherhood: "The Lord suffered for you to have a baby. He will suffer for you to get food for the baby." Still others expressed themselves in forward-looking, practical terms, "You were less apt to have regrets if you kept the baby than if you let him go."[69]

For many Black, unwed mothers, the reasons to keep a baby were simply grounded in an immutable moral code of maternal responsibility. A young, Black woman said, "Giving a child away is not the sort of thing a good person would do"; and a teenager asserted, "My parents wouldn't

let me give up the baby for adoption."[70] Two Black women in Philadelphia subscribed to this morality. One said:

> I sure don't think much of giving babies up for adoption. The mother mightn't be able to give it the finest and best in the world, but she could find a way like I did. My mother had thirteen heads and it was during the Depression. . . . *She* didn't give us away.

The other commented, "If you have a child, bring it up. Take the responsibility. Hard or easy, it's yours."[71]

The central question for all of these Black, single mothers was how good a mother you were, not whether you were legally married.[72] The overriding stimulus in structuring the personal decisions of these girls and women was a "powerful drive toward family unity, even if the family is not the socially approved one of father, mother and children."[73] In a study of thirty poor, single, Black mothers, only two told the investigators that they would advise another woman in their situation to give the baby up, and both cited difficulties with the welfare office as their reason.[74] The author of the study referred to the "vehemence" of most Black, single mothers about their decision to keep the child.[75]

Helen Harris Perlman, recognizing the negative attitudes of social workers toward girls and women who failed to relinquish illegitimate babies, counselled her colleagues in the 1960s, "Even if more opportunities for adoption of Negro babies become possible, there is a strong probability that most Negro mothers—indeed, most unwed mothers—will want to keep their babies."[76]

CONCLUSION

A research team in North Carolina investigating illegitimacy concluded in the early 1960s that one major difference between white and Black unwed mothers was that the white girl generally felt that a "new maturity" had come with the experience of conceiving out of wedlock. The team claimed that this was not true for the Black subjects, and explained: "The white subculture demands learning from experience," so the white unwed mother must learn her lesson. The white girl "has probably been encouraged to look within herself for the reasons for her mistake because the white subculture stresses individual responsibility for error."[77]

These observations capture a great deal of the intentionality underlying the white culture's treatment of unwed mothers under the adoption mandate. For these girls and women, the "lesson" was twofold: no baby without a husband; and no one is to blame but yourself. Learning the lesson meant stepping on the road to maturity and womanhood. The illegitimate child was an encumbrance or an obstacle to following this route. The ability to relinquish was constructed as the first, most crucial step in the right direction.

Joyce Ladner, in her study of Black women in the 1960s, dealt with the same issue—the relationship between illegitimacy and maturity. She suggested a strikingly different finding:

> The adolescent Black girl who became pregnant out of wedlock changed her self-conception from one who was approaching maturity to one who had attained the status of womanhood. . . . Mothers were quick to say that their daughters had become grown, that they have "done as much as I have done."[78]

The road to maturity for Black, unwed mothers was unmediated. Maturity accompanied maternity, the baby's legal status notwithstanding.

Both Black and white women in the postwar era were subject to a definition of maturity that depended on motherhood. The most pervasive, public assumption about Black and white unwed mothers, however, was that their nonmarital childbearing did not constitute maternity in the culturally sanctioned sense. The treatment of these girls and women reinforced the notion that legitimation of sexuality and maternity were the province of the state and the community, and were not the rights of individual girls and women. In the case of white, unwed mothers, the community (including the mother herself, and her family) with government support, was encouraged to efface episodes of illicit sex and maternity. Outside of marriage neither the sex nor the resulting child had "reality" in the community or in the mother's life. They became simply momentary mental aberrations. In the case of Black, unwed mothers, sexuality was brute biology and childbearing its hideous result. The state, with the support of public institutions, could deface the Black, single mother's dignity, diminish her resources, threaten her right to keep her child, and even threaten her reproductive capacity.

In both cases, the policies and practices which structured the meanings of race and gender, sexuality, and motherhood for unwed mothers were tied to social issues—such as the postwar adoption market for white babies, and the white, taxpaying public's hostile identification of ADC as a program to support Black, unwed mothers and their unwanted babies—which used single, pregnant women as resources and scapegoats.

In the immediate pre-*Roe v. Wade* era, the uses of race combined with the uses of gender, sexuality, and maternity in ways that dealt Black and white unwed mothers quite different hands. According to social and cultural intentions for the white, unwed mother and her baby, relinquishment of the baby was meant to place all scent of taint behind them and thus restore good value to both. The Black, unwed mother and her child, triply devalued, had all their troubles before them.

NOTES

1. This essay is taken from a larger study, *"Wake Up Little Susie": Single Pregnancy and Race in the pre-*Roe v. Wade *Era* (New York: Routledge, 1992).

2. See, for example, Charlotte Lowe, "Intelligence and Social Background of the Unmarried Mother," *Mental Hygiene* 4 (October, 1927), pp. 783–794; and Henry C. Schumacher, M.D., "The Unmarried Mother: A Socio-Psychiatric Viewpoint," *Mental Hygiene* 4 (October, 1927), pp. 775–782.

3. Maryland passed such a law in 1919 and Wisconsin in 1922. It was claimed that these laws would reduce high infant mortality rates, although they were never shown to do so. Maternity home residents were targeted since this group was considered most likely, in its search for secrecy, to abandon its babies. See Elza Virginia Dahlgren, "Attitudes of a Group of Unmarried Mothers Toward the Minnesota Three Months Nursing Regulation and Its Application," M.A. thesis, University of Minnesota, 1940.

4. See, for example, Percy Kammerer, *The Unmarried Mother* (Boston: Little, Brown & Co., 1918) and Schumacher, "The Unmarried Mother."

5. Even though many studies published in this era claimed that rates of illicit coition were not rising in the postwar era, the fact that the illegitimacy rates and illegal abortion rates were higher than ever suggests otherwise. See, for example, Alfred C. Kinsey, Wardell B. Pomeroy, Clyde E. Martin, and Paul H. Gebhard, *Sexual Behavior in the Human Female* (Philadelphia: W. B. Saunders Company, 1953), chap. 8. Also see Phillips Cutright, "Illegitimacy in the United States: 1920–1968," in Charles F. Westoff and Robert Parke, Jr., eds., *Demographic and Social Aspects of Population Growth* (Washington, D.C.: Commission on Population Growth and the American Future), p. 384.

6. See Viviana A. Zelizer, *Pricing the Priceless Child: The Changing Social Value of Children* (New York: Basic Books, 1985) for an interesting discussion of related issues.

7. See, for example, Mary Lynch Crockett, "An Examination of Services to the Unmarried Mother in Relation to Age at Adoption Placement of the Baby," *Casework Papers, 1960* (New York: Columbia University Press, 1960), pp. 75–85.

8. Leontine Young, *Out of Wedlock* (New York: McGraw Hill, 1954), p. 216.

9. Janice P. Montague, "Acceptance or Denial—The Therapeutic Uses of the Mother/Baby Relationship," paper presented at the Florence Crittenton Association of America Northeast Conference, 1964.

10. Winston Ehrmann, "Illegitimacy in Florida II: Social and Psychological Aspects of Illegitimacy," *Eugenics Quarterly* 3 (December, 1956), p. 227.

11. Leontine Young, "Is Money Our Trouble?" paper presented at the National Conference on Social Work, 1953.

12. Mary Calderone, ed., *Abortion in the United States* (New York: Harper and Brothers, 1958), pp. 92–93, 139; Alan Guttmacher, "Therapeutic Abortion: The Doctor's Dilemma," *Journal of Mt. Sinai Hospital* 21 (1954), p. 111; Lewis Savel, "Adjudication of Therapeutic Abortion and Sterilization," in Edmund W. Overstreet, ed., *Therapeutic Abortion and Sterilization* (New York: Harper and Row, 1964), pp. 14–21.

13. Calderone, ed., *Abortion in the United States,* pp. 86–88.

14. See, for example, J. G. Moore and J. H. Randall, "Trends in Therapeutic Abortion: A Review of 137 Cases," *American Journal of Obstetrics and Gynecology* 63 (1952), p. 34.

15. Harry A. Pearce and Harold A. Ott, "Hospital Control of Sterilization and Therapeutic Abortion," *American Journal of Obstetrics and Gynecology* 60 (1950), p. 297; James M. Ingram, H.S.B. Treloar, G. Phillips Thomas, and Edward B. Rood, "Interruption of Pregnancy for Psychiatric Indications—A Suggested Method of Control," *Obstetrics and Gynecology* 29 (1967), pp. 251–55.

16. See, for example, Charles C. Dahlberg, "Abortion," in Ralph Slovenko, ed., *Sexual Behavior and the Law* (Springfield, IL.: Charles Thomas, 1965), p. 384.

17. Arthur Mandy, "Reflections of a Gynecologist," in Harold Rosen, ed., *Therapeutic Abortion* (New York: The Julian Press, 1954), p. 291.

18. Gregory Zillboorg, "The Clinical Issues of Postpartum Psychopathology Reactions," *American Journal of Obstetrics and Gynecology* 73 (1957), p. 305; Roy J. Heffernon and William Lynch, "What Is The Status of Therapeutic Abortion in Modern Obstetrics?" *American Journal of Obstetrics and Gynecology* 66 (1953), p. 337.

19. Nicholson J. Eastman, "Obstetric Forward," in Rosen, *Therapeutic Abortion,* p. xx.

20. Theodore Lidz, "Reflections of a Psychiatrist," in Rosen, *Therapeutic Abortion,* p. 279.

21. Flanders Dunbar, "Abortion and the Abortion Habit," in Rosen, *Therapeutic Abortion,* p. 27.

22. Mandy, "Reflections," p. 289.

23. Manfred Guttmacher, "The Legal Status of Therapeutic Abortion," in Rosen, *Therapeutic Abortion,* p. 183. Also see

Nanette Davis, *From Crime to Choice: The Transformation of Abortion in America* (Westport CT.: Greenwood Press, 1985), p. 73; Johan W. Eliot, Robert E. Hall, J. Robert Willson, and Carolyn Hauser, "The Obstetrician's View," in Robert E. Hall, ed., *Abortion in a Changing World,* Vol. 1 (New York: Columbia University Press, 1970), p. 93: Kenneth R. Niswander, "Medical Abortion Practice in the United States," in David T. Smith, ed., *Abortion and the Law* (Cleveland: The Press of Case Western Reserve University, 1967), p. 57.

24. David C. Wilson, "The Abortion Problem in the General Hospital," in Rosen, *Therapeutic Abortion,* pp. 190–1. Also see Myra Loth and H. Hesseltine, "Therapeutic Abortion at the Chicago Lying-In Hospital," *American Journal of Obstetrics and Gynecology* 72 (1956), pp. 304–311, which reported that 69.4% of their sample were sterilized along with abortion. Also relevant are Keith P. Russell, "Changing Indications for Therapeutic Abortion: Twenty Years Experience at Los Angeles County Hospital," *Journal of the American Medical Association* (January 10, 1953), pp. 108–111, which reported an abortion-sterilization rate of 75.6%; and Lewis E. Savel, "Adjudication of Therapeutic Abortion and Sterilization," *Clinical Obstetrics and Gynecology* 7 (1964), pp. 14–21.

25. See, for example, Michael W. Sedlak, "Young Women and the City: Adolescent Deviance and the Transformation of Educational Policy, 1870–1960," *History of Education Quarterly* 23 (1983), pp. 1–28.

26. See Lillian Ripple, "Social Work Standards of Unmarried Parenthood as Affected by Contemporary Treatment Formulations," Ph.D. Dissertation, University of Chicago, 1953.

27. *Directory of Maternity Homes* (Cleveland: National Association of Services for Unmarried Parents, 1960).

28. U.S. Congress, Senate Judiciary Committee, Subcommittee to Investigate Juvenile Delinquency, Interstate Adoption Practices, July 15–16, 1955, 84th Congress, 1st sess. (Washington, D.C.: Government Printing Office, 1955), p. 200.

29. U.S. Congress, Senate Judiciary Committee, Subcommittee to Investigate Juvenile Delinquency, Commercial Child Adoption Practices, May 16, 1956, 84th Congress, 2nd sess. (Washington, D.C.: Government Printing Office, 1956), p. 6.

30. Duluth, Minnesota to Governor Luther Youngdahl, August 2, 1950, and to President Truman, August 14, 1950 Box 457, File 7–4–3–3–4, Record Group 102, National Archives.

31. U.S. Congress, Commercial Child Adoption Practices, May 16, 1956, p. 86.

32. Ibid., p. 120.

33. *New York Times* (July 10, 1958).

34. U.S. Congress, Senate Committee on the Judiciary, Subcommittee to Investigate Juvenile Delinquency in the United States, 84th Congress, 2nd sess., Unpublished Hearing, May 11, 1956.

35. U.S. Congress, Senate Judiciary Committee, *Hearings Before the Subcommittee to Investigate Juvenile Delinquency, Interstate Adoption Practices,* Miami, Florida, November 14–15, 1955, 84th Congress, 1st sess. (Washington, D.C.: Government Printing Office, 1956), p. 54–56.

36. U.S. Congress, Interstate Adoption Practices, July 15–16, 1955, p. 206.

37. U.S. Congress, Interstate Adoption Practices, Miami, Florida, November 14–15, 1955, p. 245.

38. Clark Vincent, "Unwed Mothers and the Adoption Market: Psychological and Familial Factors," *Journal of Marriage and Family Living* 22 (May 1960), p. 118.

39. See Solinger, *"Wake Up Little Susie"* chap. 7 for a fuller discussion of these three public perspectives.

40. See Winifred Bell, *Aid to Dependent Children* (New York: Columbia University Press, 1965); and Julius Paul, "The Return of Punitive Sterilization Proposals," *Law and Society Review* 3 (August, 1968), pp. 77–106.

41. See, for example, Andrew Billingsley and Jeanne Giovannoni, *Children of the Storm* (New York: Harcourt, Brace and Jovanovich, Inc., 1972), p. 142.

42. Patricia Garland, "Illegitimacy—A Special Minority-Group Problem in Urban Areas," *Child Welfare* 45 (February 1966), p. 84.

43. Ibid.

44. See, for example, the editorial, "It Merits Discussion," Richmond News Leader, March 22, 1957.

45. During the period considered here, Black women in the South were among the first in the United States to receive publicly subsidized birth control, sterilization, and abortion services. See Thomas Shapiro, *Population Control Politics: Women, Sterilization and Reproductive Choice* (Philadelphia: Temple University Press, 1985); Gerald C. Wright, "Racism and the Availability of Family Planning Services in the United States," *Social Forces* 56 (June, 1978), pp. 1087–1098; and Martha C. Ward, *Poor Women, Powerful Men: America's Great Experiment in Family Planning* (Boulder: Westview Press, 1986).

46. See, for example, the *New York Times,* August 28, 1960, which quotes Louisiana Governor Jimmie H. Davis justifying the recent state legislation targeting "those who make it their business to produce illegitimate children."

47. See *Illegitimacy and Its Impact on the Aid to Dependent Children Program,* Bureau of Public Assistance, Social Security Administration, U.S. Department of Health, Education and Welfare (Washington, D.C.: Government Printing Office, 1960).

48. The *Atlanta Constitution,* January 25, 1951. The *Constitution* reported that the Georgia State Welfare Director, making an argument for denying Aid to Dependent Children grants to mothers with more than one illegitimate child, noted that "Seventy percent of all mothers with more than one illegitimate children are Negro. . . . Some of them, finding themselves tied down to one child are not adverse to adding others as a business proposition." A Philadelphia judge recommended in 1958 that mothers of three or more illegitimate children be jailed [because it is] apparent that childbearing has become a business venture to collect relief benefits." *New York Times,* March 4, 1958.

49. "A Study of Negro Adoptions," *Child Welfare* 38 (February, 1959), p. 33, quoting David Fanshel, *A Study in Negro Adoptions* (New York: Child Welfare League of America, 1957): "In moving from white to Negro adoptions we are moving from what economists would call a 'seller's market' . . . to a 'buyer's market.'"

50. See, for example, Lydia Hylton, "Trends in Adoption," *Child Welfare* 44 (February, 1966), pp. 377–386. Hylton cites the figures of 182 white applicants for every 100 white infants in the mid-1960s, although higher ratios were obtained earlier in the period of this study. In 1960, a government report claimed that in some communities, there were ten suitable applicants for every white infant, *Illegitimacy and Its Impact,* p. 28.

51. One of a number of readers responding irately to a *New York Times'* editorial in support of giving welfare grants to unmarried mothers, wrote to the *Times,* "As for your great concern for those careless women who make a career of illicit pregnancy, they should either bear the expense or be put where they can no longer indulge in their weaknesses." *New York Times,* July 7, 1961.

52. *New York Times,* August 9, 1959. In late 1958, average monthly family grants in the ADC program were $99.83 nationally, but in the South, ranged between $27.09 in Alabama and $67.73 in Texas. Bell, *Aid to Dependent Children,* p. 224.

53. Hazel McCalley, "The Community Looks at Illegitimacy," Florence Crittenton Association of America Papers, Box 3, folder: FCAA Annual 11th, 1960–61, Social Welfare History Archives, University of Minnesota (hereafter cited as SWHA). See *Facts, Fallacies and the Future—A Study of the ADC Program of Cook County, Illinois* (New York: Greenleigh Associates, 1960), p. 29, for a prominent, contemporary discussion concerning how small welfare grants to single mothers were directly responsible for increasing these women's financial and social dependence on men.

54. "Suitable Home Law," (Jacksonville: Florida Department of Public Welfare, 1962), pp. 25–26; quoted in Bell, *Aid to Dependent Children,* p. 132.

55. An excellent study of Black, single mothers' strategies in this era is Renee M. Berg, "A Study of a Group of Unmarried Mothers Receiving ADC," Doctor of Social Work dissertation, University of Pennsylvania School of Social Work, 1962.

56. A Gallup Poll conducted in 1960 found that only "one in ten [respondents] favored giving aid to further children born to unwed parents who have already produced an out of wedlock child." *St. Louis Post Dispatch,* August 8, 1961.

57. *Milwaukee Journal,* August 9, 1961.

58. *Illegitimacy and Its Impact,* p. 30.

59. *Buffalo Currier Express,* December 5, 1957.

60. *Illegitimacy and Its Impact,* p. 36.

61. Ibid.

62. See "The Current Attack on ADC in Louisiana," September 16, 1960, Florence Crittenton Association of America Papers, Box 3, folder: National Urban League, New York City, SWHA.

63. Annie Lee Davis, "Attitudes Toward Minority Groups: Their Effect on Services for Unmarried Mothers," paper presented at the National Conference on Social Work, 1948.

64. See Seaton W. Manning, "The Changing Negro Family: Implications for the Adoption of Children," *Child Welfare* 43 (November 1964), pp. 480–485; Elizabeth Herzog and Rose

Bernstein, "Why So Few Negro Adoptions?" *Children* 12 (January–February 1965), pp. 14–15; Billingsley and Giovannoni, *Children of the Storm;* Fanshel, *A Study in Negro Adoption;* Trudy Bradley, "An Exploration of Caseworkers' Perceptions of Adoptive Applicants," *Child Welfare* 45 (October, 1962), pp. 433–443.

65. Elizabeth Tuttle, "Serving the Unmarried Mother Who Keeps Her Child," *Social Welfare* 43 (October, 1962), p. 418.

66. See *Facts, Fallacies and Future,* pp. 19–20; 552 out of 619 mothers of illegitimate children in this study did not want another child but reported that they had no information about how to prevent conception.

67. Deborah Shapiro, "Attitudes, Values and Unmarried Motherhood," in *Unmarried Parenthood: Clues to Agency and Community Action* (New York: National Council on Illegitimacy, 1967), p. 60.

68. Joyce Ladner, *Tomorrow's Tomorrow: The Black Woman* (New York: Doubleday and Co., 1971), pp. 2, 8.

69. Ellery Reed and Ruth Latimer, *A Study of Unmarried Mothers Who Kept Their Babies* (Cincinnati: Social Welfare Research, Inc., 1963), p. 72.

70. Shapiro, "Attitudes, Values," p. 61.

71. Renee Berg, "Utilizing the Strengths of Unwed Mothers in the AFDC Program," *Child Welfare* 43 (July 1964), p. 337.

72. Ibid.

73. Berg, "A Study of a Group of Unwed Mothers Receiving ADC," p. 96.

74. Ibid., p. 93.

75. Ibid., p. 95.

76. Helen Harris Perlman, "Observations on Services and Research," in *Unmarried Parenthood: Clues to Agency and Community Action* (New York: National Council on Illegitimacy, 1967), p. 41.

77. Charles Bowerman, Donald Irish, and Hallowell Pope, *Unwed Motherhood: Personal and Social Consequences* (Chapel Hill: University of North Carolina, 1966), p. 261.

78. Ladner, *Tomorrow's Tomorrow,* pp. 214–215.

R E A D I N G   3 0

Negotiating Lesbian Motherhood: The Dialectics of Resistance and Accommodation[1]

ELLEN LEWIN

When I first began to assemble resources for a study of lesbian mothers in 1976, very few people were aware of the existence of such a category, and if they were, they usually saw it as an oxymoron. Lesbian mothers occasionally gained the attention of the general public when they were involved in custody cases that received publicity, but such notoriety was infrequent and typically fleeting. In fact, aside from those who had lesbian mothers in their social circles, even the wider lesbian population was aware of lesbian mothers mainly in connection with custody cases. In

Ellen Lewin, "Negotiating Lesbian Motherhood: The Dialectics of Resistance and Accommodation" from *Mothering: Ideology, Experience, and Agency,* edited by Evelyn Nakano Glenn, Grace Chang, and Linda Rennie Forcey. Copyright © 1994 by Routledge. Reprinted with the permission of Routledge, Chapman and Hall.

the early collections of articles on lesbian issues that emerged from the lesbian feminist movement, lesbian mothers were almost never mentioned except in connection with their vulnerability to custody litigation.[2] Mothers in these cases either lost custody of their children, or won custody only under highly compromised conditions, sometimes with the stipulation that the child have no contact with the mother's partner.[3]

Well-known custody cases in the 1970s demonstrated the likelihood that lesbian mothers would face considerable discrimination in court. The Mary Jo Risher case, in which a mother lost custody of her younger son after her teenaged son testified against her, was perhaps the best documented of these, particularly after the story was dramatized as a made-for-TV movie.[4] And the case of Sandy and Madeleine, two mothers who became lovers and subsequently had custody challenged by both ex-husbands, was extensively publicized in the lesbian community with the circulation of a film called "Sandy and Madeleine's Family." The case demonstrated that lesbian mothers' custody could be challenged repeatedly, even after a favorable ruling in court, at least until the children achieved majority. The film, originally produced for use in court, emphasized the strong religious values of the mothers, their involvement in wholesome activities with both sets of children, and the warmth and nurturance of the family environment they provided.[5]

All these images of lesbian mothers were defensive. When lesbian mothers found themselves in court, they necessarily had to convince the judge (and in the Risher case, the jury) that they were as good at being mothers as any other women, that they were, in fact, *good* in the sense of possessing the moral attributes of altruism and nurturance that are culturally demanded of mothers in North American cultures. In these formulations, mothers are assumed to be *naturally* equipped to place their children's interests ahead of their own, to be selfless in a way that precludes or overshadows their own sexuality;[6] such assumptions are at the heart of twentieth-century presumptions of maternal suitability for custody.[7] When mothers are lesbians, however, the courts, reflecting popular views of homosexuality as "unnatural," tend to view them as morally flawed, and thus as unfit parents. Their task in dealing with the legal system, therefore, is to demonstrate that they possess the "natural" attributes expected of mothers, and are thus worthy of receiving custody of their children. Maternal virtue, therefore, shifts from being a quality inherent to women to being a behavior one must actively demonstrate in order to pursue a claim to custody.[8]

While many lesbian mothers understood that the way to keep custody of their children was to show that they were "as good as" heterosexual mothers, they firmly believed that they would eventually be shown to be superior parents who were bringing new, nonsexist families into being. They viewed the two-parent, heterosexual, nuclear family as the arena in which the patriarchy inscribed gender expectations onto both women and men. If the power dynamics of that family form were largely responsible for the continuing devalued status of women, and for a variety of abusive practices, then a domestic arrangement based on presumably nongendered relations between two "equal" women partners would constitute a first step toward the better sort of world feminists dreamed of. Jeanne Vaughn, the coeditor of *Politics of the Heart: A Lesbian Parenting Anthology,* put it this way:

> We have an opportunity for radical social change beginning in our homes, change that requires rethinking our

views of family, of kinship, of work, of social organization. We need to develop some specifically lesbian-feminist theories of family. How would/did/could we mother our children without the institution of compulsory heterosexuality?[9]

The image many lesbian mothers conjured up was utopian, resembling the broad outlines of Charlotte Perkins Gilman's *Herland,* a fictional society of women in which motherhood and caring were elevated to the center of the inhabitants' lives. Without the need to serve and please powerful males, without the degradations of daily experience in a patriarchal society, Gilman's image suggests, women might be free to express their true, nurturant natures. They would reveal abilities unlikely to emerge in male-dominated society, and would focus on creative, constructive projects rather than on frivolities such as fancy dress and (hetero)sexuality.[10]

The popular images of mothers and families that dominated the lesbian community in the 1970s, then, focused on the ways in which being a mother and having a family could constitute a form of resistance to traditional, and thereby patriarchal, family forms. In particular, success at motherhood (as measured by how well one's child turned out) would demonstrate that children did not need the structure of a heterosexual family, and, most significantly, the regular contribution of a father, to develop normally. The achievement of lesbian mothers would both counteract the notion that lesbianism and motherhood are inherently contradictory and, in fact, redefine and desexualize what it means to be a lesbian.

At the same time, however, the complexities of living as a mother required lesbian mothers to reinstate the dichotomy of natural/unnatural and mother/nonmother that their redefinition of lesbianism sought to subvert. Negotiating the daily issues of being a mother and meeting obligations to one's children brought them into conflict both with the dominant heterosexist society and with lesbians who had not chosen motherhood.

FEMINIST VIEWS OF RESISTANCE

When many of us took up a feminist agenda in our scholarship, directing our attention to documenting the experience of women from their point of view, it seemed that we had no choice but to concentrate on describing a depressing history of victimization and oppression. As we examined the social and cultural lives of women, not only in familiar terrain, but also outside Western traditions, we found over and over again that women were confined to secondary social status, relegated to devalued cultural roles, and often brutalized and demeaned in their daily lives. The evidence of despair poured in, bolstered at every turn by the grim discoveries we continued to make about our own society and our own lives.[11]

In many instances, the best it seemed that we could offer to help remedy this situation was to produce astute, woman-centered descriptions of the conditions under which women's lives were lived, paired with analyses geared toward change. In many instances, feminist scholars directed their energies toward the documentation of women's point of view, focusing on ways to dissolve the hegemony of male-centered assumptions about the organization of social life and women's place in it. In anthropology, such work often proposed alternative views of traditionally patriarchal institutions.[12] But in other instances, feminist interpretations came to center on resistance, looking at how even clearly oppressed women might take action on their own behalf, either by directly sabotaging the instruments of male dominance, or by constituting their consciousness in a way that undermined their subordination.[13]

Feminist scholars have most commonly applied the concept of resistance to studies of women in the work force. Bonnie Thornton Dill's research on Black women household workers, for example, focuses on the way they manage their relationships with employers to enhance their own self-respect. She documents how these workers organized "strategies for gaining mastery over work that was socially defined as demeaning and . . . actively resisted the depersonalization of household work."[14]

Along similar lines, Aihwa Ong, writing about women factory workers in Malaysia, shows how labor practices introduced by capitalism lead to the reconstruction of meanings of gender and sexuality. In response to proletarianization, Malay women organize cultural responses to their changing status, most markedly in the form of episodes of spirit possession. "Spirit attacks," Ong tells us, "were indirect retaliations against coercion and demands for justice in personal terms within the industrial milieu."[15]

Notions of resistance have also informed studies of women outside the workplace. Emily Martin, for example, has contrasted women's ideas about their bodies and the ideology of mainstream medicine, describing instances in which women resist medical assumptions at variance with their own experience. She sees working-class women as most able to reject scientific metaphors of women's bodies, particularly those that focus on production and failed pro-

duction, perhaps because "they have less to gain from productive labor in the society."[16] Self-consciousness and verbal protest are taken as evidence of resistance in Martin's analysis, as are instances of sabotage or outright refusal to cooperate with medical instructions.

Louise Lamphere's study of immigrant factory workers in New England also looks carefully at resistance, but frames it as one of several strategies women can mount to cope with employers' efforts to control their lives. She views women "as active strategists, weighing possibilities and devising means to realize goals, and not as passive acceptors of their situations."[17] Lamphere cautions, however, against viewing all of women's actions on their own behalf as resistance. Rather, she emphasizes the importance of distinguishing between "strategies of resistance" and "strategies of accommodation," pointing out that some strategies may best be seen as adjustments that allow women to cope with their place in the labor market by diffusing employers' control of the workplace. Such strategies ought not to be viewed, Lamphere says, as resistance only, since they may not be based in purposeful opposition to the employer, and since they may only result in continuing exploitation of the workers, and, as such, constitute a kind of consent to existing relations of domination.[18]

Taking a different approach, Judith Butler has proposed that scholars reconsider their dependence on the concept of gender, arguing that gender, as a dualistic formulation, rests on the same asymmetry that feminists seek to overturn. She urges the adoption of strategies that would "disrupt the oppositional binary itself,"[19] and suggests that calling into question the "continuity and coherence" of gender identities, sabotaging the "intelligibility" of gender, would undermine the "regulatory aims" of gender as a cultural system.[20] Butler's claim seems to be that lesbianism, or other sexual stances at odds with normative heterosexuality, could constitute a kind of resistance to the very existence of gender. She locates gender continuities within the domain of sexuality, viewing "intelligible" genders . . . as those which in some sense institute and maintain relations of coherence and continuity among sex, gender, sexual practice, and desire."[21] The decisions one takes with regard to one's identity, then, and in particular, the extent to which they may be said to destabilize conventional expectations and representations, may constitute resistance not only to specific forms of oppression, but to the oppressive effects of gender as an ideological straitjacket.

All of these approaches to resistance reveal a commitment to render women as active subjects. While these scholars are reluctant to blame women for their subordination, neither are they willing to cast them as hapless victims of actions wholly beyond their control. Women are thus seen as capable of framing strategies for enhancing their situations, whether the battleground be material—as when women's resistance improves their working conditions—or symbolic—as when refusal to conform to common conventions of gender may be interpreted as constituting sabotage of the larger system.

This concern with subjectivity and agency raises significant questions for the study of women who seem to defy gender limitations in any aspect of their lives. Just as Butler has suggested that incongruent sexuality might be viewed as resistance, one might ask whether other "disorders" of sexuality and gender could also be viewed in this light. The question becomes particularly pressing when women themselves explain their behavior as subversive. We must then ask whether apparently conscious refusals by lesbian mothers, or any other group of women, to accept the strictures of gender are best understood as instances of resistance.

LESBIAN MOTHERS AND RESISTANCE TO HETEROSEXISM

By the time I was well into my research, at the end of the 1970s, the custody problems that had concerned me at the outset were no longer the only issues facing lesbian mothers. Pregnant women were starting to appear at lesbian social gatherings, at political meetings and concerts, sometimes alone and sometimes in the company of their lovers. These women were not, for the most part, new to lesbian life; most had never been married, and child custody fears did not figure prominently for them. They certainly had not become pregnant by accident. While some of the mothers and mothers-to-be had had romantic interludes with men, more explained how they had "made themselves pregnant" by arranging a sexual situation with a man, or by using some form of "insemination."[22]

The emphasis in these women's accounts of their experiences was on how they had to overcome their earlier fears that being lesbian would preclude motherhood. Lesbians reported that they had often thought of themselves as not being suitable mothers, having internalized images of homosexuals as self-serving, immature, or otherwise not capable of the kind of altruism basic to maternal performance.

Sarah Klein,[23] a lesbian who lives with her one-year-old daughter and her lover, explained the conflict as she perceived it:

I've always wanted to have a child. In terms of being real tied up with being gay, it was one of the reasons that for a long time I was hesitant to call myself a lesbian. I thought that automatically assumed you had nothing to do with children. . . . I felt, well, if you don't *say* you're a lesbian, you can still work with children, you can still have a kid, you can have relationships with men. But once I put this label on myself, [it would] all [be] over.

By having a child, Sarah repudiated the boundaries she had once associated with being a lesbian; she has claimed what she sees as her right to be a mother.

But other lesbians' accounts indicate that not all perceive themselves as having had a lifelong desire for motherhood. Among those who claim not to remember wanting children when they were younger was Kathy Lindstrom. She had a child by insemination when she was in her early 30s, but says that she never considered the possibility until a few years earlier. She could only explain her behavior as arising from some sort of "hormonal change."

It just kind of came over me. It wasn't really conscious at first. It was just a need.

Kathy's understanding of her desire to be a mother as something "hormonal," that is, natural, suggests an implicit assertion that this is something so deep and so essentially part of her that nothing, including her lesbianism, can undermine it. Her account indicates that she refuses to allow the associations others have with her status as a lesbian to interfere with her own perception of herself and her needs.

Other lesbian mothers view their urge to have a child as stemming from a desire to settle down, to achieve adulthood, and to counteract forces toward instability in their lives. Ruth Zimmerman, who had a five-year-old son from a relationship with a man she selected as a "good" father, had ended the relationship soon after she became pregnant.

I definitely felt like I was marking time, waiting for something. I wasn't raised to be a career woman. I was raised to feel like I was grown up and finished growing up and living a regular normal life when I was married and had kids. And I knew that the married part wasn't going to happen. I feel like I've known that for a long time.

Like Kathy, Ruth defined her progress as a human being, and as a woman, in terms that are strikingly conventional and recall traditional feminine socialization. While clearly accepting motherhood as a marker of adulthood and "living a normal life," Ruth tried to overcome the equally conventional limits placed on lesbians in order to have her child.

The notion that having a child signifies adulthood, the acceptance of social responsibility, and demonstrates that one has "settled down" appears in the accounts of many lesbian mothers. Most often, lesbian mothers speak of their lives before motherhood as empty and aimless, and see the birth of their children as having centered them emotionally. They frequently cite new interests in education, nutrition, and health, and reconciliations with family members with whom they had not been on good terms, as evidence of their new maturity. As Louise Green, a young lesbian mother who describes herself as a former hippie, explains: "I think [having my daughter] has turned my life into this really good thing."

Louise describes herself as living a marginal, disorganized existence until she finally decided that she would have a child. She did not consider using mainstream medicine to get pregnant, assuming that such resources would never be available to her, both for financial reasons and because she would be viewed with hostility by medical professionals. Instead, she went about asking men she met whether they would like to be sperm donors; she finally located a willing prospect and obtained a sperm sample from him. Louise never told this man her real name, and once she had conceived she left the area, concerned that he could somehow pose a threat to her relationship with her child.

Louise's account focuses on conception and birth as spiritual transitions to a higher and better existence. She became pregnant on her first attempt, which she explained as evidence that mystical forces "meant" for this to happen. She wanted very much to have a home delivery, but after a protracted and complicated labor, she was transferred to a hospital, where she finally gave birth with the aid of multiple technological interventions. Despite this interference with the kind of spiritual environment she had hoped to give birth in, Louise describes the entire experience in mystical terms.

> It was about the best thing I ever experienced. I was totally amazed. The labor was like I had died. . . . I had just died. The minute she came out, I was born again. It was like we'd just been born together.

Louise did not allow either her counterculture life-style or her status as a lesbian to interfere with the spiritual agenda she felt destined to complete. She says the mystical process she underwent in becoming a mother has permitted her to become more fully herself, to explore aspects of her being that would have remained hidden if she allowed lesbianism alone to define who she is.

> [After] I had [my daughter] I felt it was okay to do these things I've been wanting to do real bad. One of them is to paint my toenails red. I haven't done it yet, but I'm going to do it. I felt really okay about wearing perfume and I just got a permanent in my hair. . . . I feel like I'm robbing myself of some of the things I want to do by trying to fit this lesbian code. I feel like by my having this child, it has already thrown me out in the sidelines.

Louise has used the process of becoming a mother to construct her identity in a way that includes being a lesbian but also draws from other sources. She sees her need to do this as essential and intended, and has moved along her path with the assurance that she is realizing her destiny.

Not all lesbians become mothers as easily as Louise. On a purely practical level, of course, the obstacles to a lesbian becoming pregnant can be formidable. Even if she knows a man who is interested in such a venture, she might not contemplate a heterosexual liaison with enthusiasm and might be equally reluctant to ask him to donate sperm. Mainstream medicine may not seem like an option either, because of financial considerations, or because of fears that doctors will be unwilling to inseminate a lesbian or even a single woman—a realistic concern, of course.

Once one has defined oneself as a lesbian, the barriers to becoming a mother are so significant, in fact, that many of the formerly married lesbian mothers I interviewed explained that they had gone through with marriages (sometimes of long duration) because this seemed the only way to realize their dream of being mothers and being normal in the eyes of their families and communities.

Harriet Newman, an artist who lives with her two daughters in a rural area north of San Francisco, fell in love with another woman during her first year in college. Her parents discovered the affair and forced her to leave school and to see a psychiatrist. The experience convinced her that it would be safer "to be a regular person in the world." When she met a gay man who also wanted to live more conventionally, they married, and almost immediately had their two children.

> The main thing that made us decide to get married was that we very much wanted to part of the mainstream of life, instead of on the edges. We wanted to be substantial . . . part of the common experience.

For lesbians who become mothers through insemination or some other method,[24] then, conscious resistance to rigid formulations of "the lesbian" seems to be central to their intentions. Unwilling to deny their identity as lesbians, they also demand the right to define what that identity constitutes. The intrinsic benefits of motherhood—the opportunity to experience birth and child development—are experiences they do not want to forego. In particular, once the relatively simple technology of donor insemination became widely known, and given the haphazard controls exerted over access to sperm donations, lesbians have come to understand that they can, indeed, be mothers. Access to motherhood thus comes to be viewed as a "civil right" not dissimilar to equal opportunity in the job market, or other rights lesbians and gay men now demand with increasing insistence.

In some instances, women explained that their age made having a child imperative. Laura Bergeron, who had two sons from a relationship prior to coming out, decided to find a donor for a third child when she entered her late 30s.

> I really did want to have a girl, and I was getting older. . . . I was feeling that I didn't really want to have children past the appropriate childbearing age. I had been doing too much reading about retardation and mongoloids and everything else . . . so I put some ads [for donors] in the paper.

Annabel Jessop voices similar concerns, explaining that she decided to use artificial insemination to become pregnant even though she would have preferred being settled in a long-term relationship before embarking on motherhood.

> I decided that I wanted to have a kid, and that because I'm in my 30s my time was limited. I look at it as a life choice. There's only so many things you can do in your life, and this is one of the things I wanted to do, and it was time to do it. Waiting wasn't going to do any good. Professionally, I was together, I was as stable as I was every going to be financially, I had a little put away, and there was just no reason not to do it now.

Becoming a mother is central to being able to claim to an identity as a "good" woman, drawn from one's association with children. Mothers describe childhood as a time of innocence and discovery, and a mother can gain spiritual benefits through her contribution to a child's development. One lesbian mother explained:

> You get to have a lot of input in another human being's very formative years. That's real special to have that privilege of doing that, and you get to see them growing and developing and it's sort of like you put in the fertile

soil and . . . hopefully what will happen is that they grow and blossom and become wonderful. . . . I think it's definitely the most important thing that people do . . . to build the next generation.

As Louise Green's narrative indicated, lesbians often characterize their transformation into mothers as a spiritual journey, an experience that gives them access to special knowledge and that makes them worthier than they otherwise could have been. Regina Carter, whose daughter is six, put it this way:

> My kid has given me more knowledge than any other experience in my life. She's taught me more than all the teachings I've ever learned as far as education, and I mean that as far as academic education, spiritual education. Taught me things that no other person, place or thing could possibly teach me. And those are, you know, those things are without words.

Similarly, Bonnie Peters echoed these views when she told me that being a mother connected her with sources of honesty and worthiness.

> I've become more at peace with me [since having my daughter]. She's given me added strength; she's made me—it's like looking in the mirror in many ways; she's made me see myself for who I am. She's definitely given me self-worth. I've become, I think, a more honest person.

Motherhood, then, can draw a woman closer to basic truths, sensitizing her to the feelings of others and discovering a degree of altruism they had not perceived in themselves prior to having a child. It may provide the opportunity for a woman to make clear her involvement with a kind of authenticity, a naturalness, that brings her closer to profound, but ineffable, truths.

MANAGING LESBIAN MOTHERHOOD

While the accounts given by some lesbian mothers suggest that they have resisted the cultural opposition between "mother" and "lesbian" and demanded the right to be both, the ongoing management of being a lesbian mother may depend on separating these two statuses, thus intensifying their dichotomization. Lesbian mothers frequently speak of these two dimensions of their identities as competing or interfering with each other; conflicts with lesbians who are not mothers sometimes further solidify these divisions.

Tanya Petroff, who lives with her seven-year-old daughter in an East Bay city, speaks evocatively of how being a mother overshadows her identity as a lesbian.

> The mothering thing, the thing about being a mother seems to be more important to me than my sexual orientation. . . . I've had [lesbians] tell me that I had chosen a privileged position in having a child and if it was going to be difficult for me then it was too goddam bad.

For Tanya, the conflict is most acute when she is developing a new relationship with another woman. She must then make clear that she views herself and her daughter as an indivisible social unit that takes precedence over other attachments.

> I'm definitely part of a package deal. I come with my daughter and people who can't relate to both of us are not people I want to relate to for very long.

What this means in terms of other relationships is that Tanya sees other mothers, regardless of whether they are gay or straight, as the people with whom she has the most in common. Since relocating to the Bay Area from a town in the Midwest, Tanya has tended to minimize her contact with what she calls the "lesbian community" in favor of socializing with other mothers. She feels that she is better able to resist pressures to raise her daughter to be a "little amazon," an expectation she believes common to lesbians who are not mothers. Beyond this, Tanya feels that there are simply too many practical obstacles to meaningful friendships with women who are not mothers. Living alone and having a demanding job mean that Tanya has to plan ahead to arrange child care. People who don't have children are no help with this; she accounts for this by explaining that they are "single," meaning that they have no children. There is such a deep gulf between mothers and nonmothers, in her view, that there is simply no meaningful basis for understanding or trust.

> There is a difference between people who have children and people who don't have children. People who don't have children, to my way of thinking, are very selfish. . . . They needn't consider anyone other than themselves. They can do exactly what they want to do at any given time. And though I admire that, it's not possible

for me to do that and I guess for that reason most of my friends are single mothers, because it's hard for me to coordinate my needs and my time with someone who's in a completely different head set. "Why can't you get a sitter for the kid?"—that kind of thing. . . . I just prefer being with people who have some sense of what it's like to be me, and I understand where they are too.

Tanya's belief that she can only find truly supportive friends among those whose situations closely mirror her own with respect to single motherhood grows not only out of her very real need for material assistance, but also from the importance she places on having friends who affirm or validate her identity. The most essential aspect of her identity, by this account, is that of being a mother. It supersedes her sexual orientation, her ethnicity, her job.

For some lesbian mothers, difficult experiences with lovers parallel disappointments with the wider lesbian community. Leslie Addison, who lives alone with her twelve-year-old daughter, describes a long series of conflicts with lesbian community groups over support for mothers. While she can easily explain the failure of these women to be conscious about mothers as stemming from their being "single," she has had a harder time dealing with lovers and prospective lovers who do not understand or are unwilling to accommodate her needs as a mother. Shortly after her divorce, she began her first relationship with a woman with the expectation that a woman lover would naturally help her with her child, and be eager to participate in their family activities. Leslie found instead that her lover was reluctant to spend more than minimal amounts of time with her daughter, never offering to help with child care or domestic responsibilities. Ironically, when she was straight, she says that she could always get a boyfriend to baby-sit for her; as a lesbian, she finds that women usually refuse to do child care.

> That wasn't quite what I expected. I expected there would be more sharing between women of the child. But I found it's really not, because another woman has a role identity crisis. She can't be the mother, because you're already the mother. She can't be the father, because she's not the father, whereas the men sort of played that role. It was easier for them to fall into it. They could just play daddy, I could play momma, and everybody'd be happy.

The stark separation between "mother" and "lesbian" as elements of identity may be even more sharply drawn for women concerned with maintaining secrecy about their sexual orientation. In these instances, daily life is segregated into time when they are "mothers" and time when they are "lesbians," creating constant concern about information management and boundary maintenance. While some mothers who voice these concerns are motivated by fears about custody, others seem to be more worried by what they understand to be broad community standards. Segregation may seem the best way to protect children from being stigmatized, but in addition, lesbian mothers know that motherhood itself tends to preclude their being suspected of homosexuality. As one mother explained, "Of course, I have the mask. I have a child. I'm accepted [as heterosexual] because I have a child and that kind of protection."

Laura Bergeron, who had three children outside of marriage, is not only secretive about her lesbianism in her relations with the wider community, but she has not allowed her children to find out that she is a lesbian. Her lover, a married woman, is unwilling to do anything that might disrupt current arrangements, and Laura explains that her lover's situation is the major reason for her secrecy. But she is also concerned that the father of her two sons might try to get custody if he knew about her sexual orientation, despite the fact that he only agreed to help her get pregnant with the stipulation that he would never have any formal obligations to their children. And she fears that her civil service job would somehow be compromised as well were her sexual orientation known.

> There's just no way that we could ever be anything but heavily closeted. We have a lot of women's activities that go on here, but we don't mix the worlds. . . . That's why my children can't know. . . . I've set up my life so that it doesn't include my children.

Laura has made complicated arrangements for supervising her children before and after school and, in order to spend more time with her lover, has installed an intercom between the two houses that enables her to monitor her kids' activities. Meeting both her children's and her lover's needs means that she has little time for herself, and she sees most of her time with her children as mechanical. While she describes motherhood as separate from her "life," it is clear that managing the division between the two worlds creates a problem in organizing her identity.

For some women who maintain strict separation between their identities as mothers and as lesbians, the threat of custody litigation is more than an abstract fear. Theresa Baldocchi, whose son is nine years old, survived a protracted custody trial at the time she divorced her former husband, John. Her legal expenses and liability for debts incurred by John during their marriage left her virtually bankrupt, and it has taken years for her to solidify her financial situation. Theresa was not a lesbian at the time of the divorce, but John made allegations that she was. Now that she has come out, she is convinced that she must carefully separate her life as a mother and as a lesbian, lest her former husband decide to institute another custody case against her. Despite the fact that John has an extensive history of psychiatric hospitalization, and that she is a successful professional, she is sure that her chances of winning in such a trial would be slim.

> Now that I'm gay, I'd lose. There's just no way in the world I would win, after having had my fitness questioned when I was Lady Madonna, let alone now.

Theresa has decided that living in a middle-class suburban area and arranging her home in an impeccably conventional fashion help shield her from suspicion of being anything other than a typical "mom." The Bay Bridge, which she must cross each day between her home and San Francisco, where she works and socializes with her lesbian friends, symbolizes her strategy. She feels that each trip involves a palpable transition, as she prepares herself to meet the requirements of her destination—home or San Francisco. Most crucial for her strategy is not telling her son that she is a lesbian, since she feels it would be inappropriate to expect him to maintain her secret.

If Theresa was concerned only with managing information about her homosexuality, she would probably avoid seeing her former husband, and thus be able to relax, at least, at home. But Theresa firmly believes that being a good mother demands that she take every opportunity to maximize her son's contact with John, a model father in her eyes. Because John is not regularly employed, he has offered to take care of their son each day while Theresa is at work. This arrangement has meant both that Theresa does not have to obtain paid child care during these hours, and that her son has daily contact with his father. It also means that she has virtually no privacy. She must control the kinds of friends who visit her, and must make sure that nothing that might reveal her sexual orientation can be found in her home. Most poignantly, she must limit her lover's access to her home for fear that her presence would somehow make the situation transparent. She consigns her most reliable potential source of support to the background, leaving herself isolated and anxious much of the time.

In other instances, lesbian mothers may separate the two aspects of their lives in order to maintain fragile relationships with their families. Rita García, who lives in San Francisco with her eight-year-old son and her lover, Jill Hacker, has made arrangements with her family that she believes can be sustained only if she avoids mention of her partner and their relationship. She comes from a large and close Mexican-American family. When they first learned that she was a lesbian, shortly after her divorce, they were so angry, and so convinced that she was no longer a fit parent, that they briefly considered supporting her husband's claim for custody. Once the case finally came to trial, however, Rita's husband abandoned his interest in custody. The family learned, during these proceedings, that he had abused her on numerous occasions, once beating her so severely that she had to go to the hospital. They withdrew their support from her husband, but also refused to communicate with Rita.

Rita did not see her parents at all for over a year. When Rita's grandmother had surgery and demanded to see her favorite granddaughter, the family relented, and Rita became a central figure in the grandmother's nursing care. The crisis allowed her to be reintegrated into the family, and she began once again to be her mother's closest confidante. This rapprochement, however, was founded on an unspoken agreement that Rita not mention her lover or anything about her home life.

The situation had stabilized, with Rita spending a great deal of time with her parents. Her son attends a Catholic school in her parents' neighborhood, so she drops him off there each day on her way to work. Rita's mother makes him breakfast every morning, and after school he returns to his grandparents' house to play and do his homework. Before Rita picks him up in the evening, he usually eats dinner as well, which allows Rita to work overtime at her job. Whenever Rita and Jill have plans in the evening, he spends the night with his grandparents. Besides this kind of practical support, Rita depends on her father for help with her car and for advice about financial matters. She is close to her sister, and often exchanges overnight baby-sitting with her.

But Rita never mentions her lover to her family, and her parents have established a strict policy of never visiting her home. Jill is never invited to family events, spending Christmas and Thanksgiving with her own family. While her parents know that she is a lesbian, Rita has decided not to tell her son, reasoning that it might be difficult for him to manage his relations with his grandparents if he had to be secretive about this topic. Separating her identity as a les-

bian from her identity as a mother is consistent with her notion of being a good mother. Her son's welfare is enhanced by his ties to his grandparents, and Rita is able to provide better for him with the assistance they provide. Anything that might undermine that relationship would have the effect of harming her child, and that would make her a bad mother, undeserving, should the issue come up again, of being the custodial parent.

Other mothers explain the separation of motherhood from other dimensions of their lives, and the centrality of being a mother, to framing their identities more practically, citing the weighty and unrelenting obligations faced by parents. Peggy Lawrence, who lives with her lover, Sue Alexander, her ten-year-old daughter, and Sue's two sons, spoke at length about the effects of being a mother on her personal freedom. Being a mother means that she must be concerned about continuity and stability in ways that constrain her spontaneity, and earning money must be a priority no matter how oppressive her work. Peggy and Sue live in a neighborhood close to their children's school, and have chosen to live in San Francisco because they think their children will encounter less discrimination here as the children of lesbians than in the Midwest, where they would prefer to live. Peggy explains what being a mother means to her:

> Being a mother, to me—being a mother is more consuming than any other way that I could possibly imagine identifying myself . . . any other way that I identify myself is an identification of some part of my being a mother. I am a lesbian mother, I am a working mother—"mother" hardly ever modifies any other thing. Mother is always the primary—it's always some kind of mother, but it's never a mother-anything. Mother is—mother, for mothers, is always the thing that is more consuming.

But others understand motherhood to mean the uniquely intense feelings that exist between mother and child. Lisa Stark, who describes the weightiness of single parenthood as almost unbearable, has come to see her children as the reason she can continue to struggle with her obligations, paradoxically the explanation for both her suffering and her very survival.

> I've . . . never had to live for myself. The only reason I get up in the morning is to get them off to school. For me to trot off to work in order to earn the money to support them. I don't know what I'd do if I didn't have them. They're everything I've got. . . . I love them so much that it really is painful.

Having a child or being a mother may be said to create and reinforce meaningful ties with the world, and to make struggle worthwhile. While being a lesbian mother can be difficult, and may make a woman's life complicated and stressful, children offer significant intrinsic rewards—most importantly, a way to experience feelings of special intimacy, and to be connected to higher-order, spiritual values. Motherhood allows lesbians to be more like other women, at least with respect to the most defining feminine role expectation, but segregating these two dimensions of the self becomes the most efficient way to manage practical obligations, and intensifies the dichotomization of "lesbian" and "mother."

LESBIAN MOTHERHOOD: RESISTANCE OR ACCOMMODATION?

The goals motherhood allows lesbians to enhance are, of course, no different from those heterosexual women describe for themselves. Being a mother, in particular, becoming a mother, is perceived as a transformative experience, an accomplishment that puts other achievements in their proper perspective. It is also construed as an individual achievement, something a woman can "do" to make herself a mother, that is, to transform herself into an altruistic, spiritually-aware human being. In a culture that elevates what has been characterized as "mythic individualism" as a central value, individuals idealize autonomy, self-reliance, and the notion that one must "find oneself" and "make something" of oneself.[25]

> Clearly, the meaning of one's life for most Americans is to become one's own person, almost to give birth to oneself.[26]

Women in America have particular difficulty living up to this cultural ideal. Individualistic and assertive behaviors valued in men are discouraged in women. Dependency, particularly through marriage, is represented as a specifically feminine sort of success. I have discussed elsewhere the remarkable congruences I observed in accounts both lesbian and heterosexual women offered of their divorces, and the similarities between these stories and lesbians' coming-out narratives.[27] These narratives are constructed around themes of agency, independence, and individuality, and celebrate women's ability to define their own lives, to decide how to represent their identities, and to achieve adulthood and autonomy. Despite the fact that both divorce and coming out as a lesbian are popularly understood to be prob-

lematic, and, indeed, have historically been defined as stigmatized statuses, women represent them as odysseys of self-discovery leading to more authentic formulations of the self.

Accounts of becoming a mother, in similar fashion, focus on the power of the individual to construct herself as a mother, to negotiate the formation of her self and to bring something good into her life. For lesbians, particularly for lesbians who decided to become mothers once their identification as lesbians was firm, the process of becoming a mother demands agency. At the same time, to the extent that wanting to be a mother is perceived as a *natural* desire, one unmediated by culture or politics, then becoming a mother permits a lesbian to move into a more natural or normal status than she would otherwise achieve. In this sense, becoming a mother represents a sort of conformity with conventional gender expectations. At the same time, to the extent that becoming a mother means overcoming the equation of homosexuality with *unnaturalness,* then this transformation allows the lesbian mother to resist gendered constructions of sexuality. This act of resistance is paradoxically achieved through compliance with conventional expectations for women, so it may also be construed as a gesture of accommodation.

Placing motherhood at the center of one's identity often involves, as we have seen, simultaneously placing other aspects of the self, most notably lesbianism, at the margins. Demanding the right to be a mother suggests a repudiation of gender conventions that define "mother" and "lesbian" as inherently incompatible identities, the former natural and intrinsic to women, organized around altruism, the latter unnatural, and organized around self-indulgence. But living as a mother means making other choices, and these choices reinscribe the opposition between "mother" and "lesbian." Subversion of orderly gender expectations is hypothetical, at best, in the lives of many lesbian mothers, at the same time that knowledge of their existence can only be imagined by the wider public as a rebellion of the most fundamental sort.

The model I would suggest based on the accounts presented here is that lesbian mothers are neither resisters nor accommodators—or perhaps that they are both. A more accurate way of framing their narratives is that they are strategists, using the cultural resources offered by motherhood to achieve a particular set of goals. That these are the goals framed by past experience in a heterosexist and perhaps patriarchal society, and that these resources are culturally constrained and shaped by the exigencies of gender, does not simplify the analysis. While such women are often conscious resisters, others gladly organize their experience as a reconciliation with what they view as traditional values. At the same time that some outsiders may see their behavior as transgressive (and thereby label them resisters or subversives), others perceive lesbian motherhood (along with other indications of compliance with conventional behaviors, such as gay/lesbian marriage) as evidence that lesbians (and other "deviants") can be domesticated and tamed.[28]

The search for cultures of resistance continues to be a vital dimension of the feminist academic enterprise. At the same time that we cannot limit our analyses of women's lives to accounts of victimization, we cannot be complacent when we discover evidence of resistance and subversion. Either interpretation may fail to reveal the complex ways in which resistance and accommodation, subversion and compliance, are interwoven and interdependent, not distinct orientations, but mutually reinforcing aspects of a single strategy. Lesbian mothers are, in some sense, both lesbians and mothers, but they shape identity and renegotiate its meanings at every turn, reinventing themselves as they make their way in a difficult world.

NOTES

1. This paper draws on research conducted with the support of National Institute of Mental Health Grant MH-30890 and a grant from the Rockefeller Foundation Gender Roles Program. A more extensive treatment of this material appears in Ellen Lewin, *Lesbian Mothers: Accounts of Gender in American Culture* (Ithaca, N.Y.: Cornell University Press, 1993).

2. See, for example, Ginny Vida, ed., *Our Right to Love: A Lesbian Resource Book* (Englewood Cliffs, N.J.: Prentice-Hall, 1978).

3. Donna Hitchens, "Social Attitudes, Legal Standards, and Personal Trauma in Child Custody Cases," *Journal of Homosexuality,* vol. 5, (1979), pp. 89–95; Ellen Lewin, "Lesbianism and Motherhood: Implications for Child Custody," *Human Organization,* vol. 40, No. 1, (1981), pp. 6–14; Rhonda R. Rivera, "Our Strait-Laced Judges: The Legal Position of Homosexual Persons in the United States," *Hastings Law Journal* 30, (1979), p. 799.

4. Clifford Guy Gibson, *By Her Own Admission: A Lesbian Mother's Fight to Keep Her Son* (Garden City, N.Y.: Doubleday, 1977).

5. Sherrie Farrell, John Gordon Hill, and Peter M. Bruce, "Sandy and Madeleine's Family" (film) (San Francisco: Multi Media Resource Center, 1973).

6. Not only lesbians, but heterosexual mothers whose sexual activity comes to the attention of the authorities, may be vulnerable in cases where their custody is challenged. See Nancy D. Polikoff, "Gender and Child Custody Determinations: Exploding the Myths," in Irene Diamond, ed., *Families, Politics, and Public Policy: A Feminist Dialogue on Women and the State* (New York: Longman, 1983), pp. 183–202.

7. Nan Hunter and Nancy D. Polikoff, "Custody Rights of Lesbian Mothers: Legal Theory and Litigation Strategy," *Buffalo Law Review* 25, (1976), p. 691; Lewin, "Lesbianism and Motherhood."

8. Ellen Lewin, "Claims to Motherhood: Custody Disputes and Maternal Strategies," in Faye Ginsburg and Anna Lowenhaupt Tsing, eds., *Uncertain Terms: Negotiating Gender in American Culture* (Boston: Beacon Press, 1990), pp. 199–214.

9. Jeanne Vaughn, "A Question of Survival," in Sandra J. Pollack and Jeanne Vaughn, eds., *Politics of the Heart: A Lesbian Parenting Anthology* (Ithaca, N.Y.: Firebrand Books, 1987), p. 26.

10. Charlotte Perkins Gilman, *Herland* (1915, New York: Pantheon Books, 1979).

11. A number of works that have chronicled the second wave of feminism in the United States have noted that the treatment of agency and victimization has been a central issue in the framing of feminist theory. See, for example, Alice Echols, *Daring to be Bad: Radical Feminism in America, 1967–1975* (Minneapolis: University of Minnesota Press, 1989); Hester Eisenstein, *Contemporary Feminist Thought* (Boston: G. K. Hall, 1983); Alison M. Jaggar, *Feminist Politics and Human Nature* (Totowa, N.J.: Rowman & Allanheld, 1983). Central issues giving rise to these theories, particularly the essentialist stances taken by adherents of cultural feminism, were those of violence and abuse—rape, incest, battering, and the like.

12. See, for example, Jane Goodale, *Tiwi Wives: A Study of the Women of Melville Island, North Australia* (Seattle: University of Washington Press, 1971); Annette B. Weiner, *Women of Value, Men of Renown: New Perspectives in Trobriand Exchange* (Austin: University of Texas Press, 1976); Margery Wolf, *Women and the Family in Rural Taiwan* (Stanford: Stanford University Press, 1972).

13. Lila Abu-Lughod has reviewed the diverse forms an emphasis on resistance has taken in anthropology and in other disciplines in "The Romance of Resistance: Tracing Transformations of Power Through Bedouin Women," *American Ethnologist,* vol. 17, No. 1 (February 1990), pp. 41–55. Abu-Lughod urges us not to romanticize resistance, but to use its appearance "to teach us about the complex interworkings of historically changing structures of power."

Some scholars, notably James Scott, have suggested that interest in resistance has blossomed as scholars on the left have been forced to confront the failure of socialist revolutions. See *Weapons of the Weak: Everyday Forms of Peasant Resistance* (New Haven: Yale University Press, 1985).

14. Bonnie Thornton Dill, "Domestic Service and the Construction of Personal Dignity," in Ann Bookman and Sandra Morgen, eds., *Women and the Politics of Empowerment* (Philadelphia: Temple University Press, 1988), p. 33.

15. Aihwa Ong, *Spirits of Resistance and Capitalist Discipline: Factory Women in Malaysia* (Albany: State University of New York Press, 1987), p. 220.

16. Emily Martin, *The Woman in the Body: A Cultural Analysis of Reproduction* (Boston: Beacon Press, 1987), p. 110.

17. Louise Lamphere, *From Working Daughters to Working Mothers: Immigrant Women in a New England Industrial Community* (Ithaca, N.Y.: Cornell University Press, 1987), pp. 29–30.

18. Lamphere, *From Working Daughters to Working Mothers,* p. 30.

19. Judith Butler, *Gender Trouble: Feminism and the Subversion of Identity* (New York: Routledge, 1990), p. 27.

20. Butler, *Gender Trouble,* p. 17.

21. Ibid.

22. Although artificial insemination is often included among the "new" reproductive technologies such as *in vitro* fertilization, embryo transfer, and sex predetermination, there is actually nothing particularly new about the procedure. Originally developed for use in animal husbandry, artificial insemination by donor (AID) conceptions are estimated as accounting for thousands of births in the United States each year. See Martin Curie-Cohen, Lesleigh Luttrell, and Sander Shapiro, "Current Practice of Artificial Insemination by Donor in the United States," *New England Journal of Medicine* 300 (11) (1979), pp. 585–590.

The procedure itself introduces sperm into the vagina with a needle-less syringe at a time calculated to coincide with the woman's ovulation. Once methods for freezing sperm were perfected in 1949, the possibility of expanded use presented itself (both for animals and for humans), as sperm banks and various sorts of matching services came into existence; Gena Corea, *The Mother Machine: Reproductive Technologies from Artificial Insemination to Artificial Wombs* (New York: Harper and Row, 1985), p. 36. At present, there is only minimal government regulation of artificial insemination or of sperm banks. Sperm banks and access to medically supervised insemination are controlled almost exclusively by physicians, who act as gatekeepers in terms of who may have access to frozen sperm. This means both that medical screening of donors is far from consistent or reliable, and that physicians tend to use their personal values to determine who should have access to these services; Judith N. Lasker and Susan Borg, *In Search of Parenthood: Coping with Infertility and High-Tech Conception* (Boston: Beacon Press, 1987). Since frozen sperm can be expensive, unmarried women, as well as low-income patients may not have the same access to insemination as affluent couples; Curie-Cohen, Luttrell, and Shapiro, "Current Practice of Artificial Insemination"; Maureen McGuire and Nancy Alexander,

"Artificial Insemination of Single Women," *Fertility and Sterility* 43 (1985), pp. 182–184; Carson Strong and Jay Schinfeld, "The Single Woman and Artificial Insemination by Donor," *Journal of Reproductive Medicine* 29 (1984), pp. 293–299.

Despite these obstacles, the low-tech nature of artificial insemination and the possibility of mobilizing alternatives to physician-controlled sperm banks have meant that women, in fact, can easily retain control of the procedure. Women whose physicians may be unwilling to inseminate—whether they be single, low-income, or lesbian—can use their informal networks to carry out insemination outside conventional medical settings; Rona Achilles, "Donor insemination: The Future of a Public Secret," in Christine Overall, ed., *The Future of Human Reproduction* (Toronto: The Women's Press, 1989), pp. 105–119; Francie Hornstein, "Children by Donor Insemination: A New Choice for Lesbians," in Rita Arditti, Renate Duelli Klein, and Shelley Minden, eds., *Test-Tube Women: What Future for Motherhood?* (London: Pandora Press, 1984), pp. 373–381; Ellen Lewin, "By Design: Reproductive Strategies and the Meaning of Motherhood," in Hilary Homans, ed., *The Sexual Politics of Reproduction* (London: Gower, 1985), pp. 123–138.

In the late 1970s, this process was generally called "artificial insemination." Within a few years, however, mothers began to use alternate language, labelling the procedure either "donor insemination" or simply "insemination" in an effort to downplay the implication that there was anything intrinsically "unnatural" about getting pregnant in this way.

23. Names and some other details have been changed to preserve the anonymity of women whom I interviewed. For a detailed account of the methods used in this research, see Lewin, *Lesbian Mothers.*

24. Adoption, though difficult, was another approach used by lesbians who wished to become mothers. Because of the large number of two-parent families who wish to adopt, and the small number of healthy newborn babies available for adoption, single women (and men) are rarely considered prime candidates as adoptive parents. Their chances are, of course, even slighter if they are known to be lesbian or gay. Adoption is more in reach of these prospective parents if they can arrange a private adoption or if they are willing to adopt an older, disabled, abused, or minority/mixed-race child—those considered less desirable. See Editors of the Harvard Law Review, *Sexual Orientation and the Law* (Cambridge, MA: Harvard University Press, 1989).

25. Robert Bellah, et al., *Habits of the Heart: Individualism and Commitment in American Life* (Berkeley: University of California Press, 1985), p. 65.

26. Bellah, *Habits of the Heart,* p. 82.

27. Lewin, *Lesbian Mothers.*

28. See Ellen Lewin, *Lesbian Mothers,* and "On the Outside Looking In: The Politics of Lesbian Motherhood," in Faye Ginsburg and Rayna Rapp, eds., *Conceiving the New World Order: Local/Global Intersections in the Politics of Reproduction* (Berkeley: University of California Press, 1995, for a discussion of how the popular media has accommodated images of lesbian families and poses them in opposition to still-abnormal childless lesbians.

Intimacy and Sexuality

The processes of socialization encourage women to develop strong interpersonal skills in preparation for roles as wives, mothers, and keepers of the hearth, and for employment in professions associated with nurturance, like teaching and nursing. As a consequence, many women assign great importance and devote much energy to creating satisfying interpersonal relationships in the context of partnerships, families, and communities. Despite women's common interests in interpersonal relationships, the forms those relationships take vary widely. Situated in particular historical, social, and economic contexts, women's beliefs and practices concerning love, intimacy, and sexuality reflect broader social trends. In this section, readings offer glimpses of women's experiences with intimacy and sexuality in particular settings, pointing out that even ideas and feelings about such a seemingly personal matter as sexuality are *socially constructed*.

In the first reading, "The Approach–Avoidance Dance: Men, Women, and Intimacy," Lillian Rubin discusses the difficulties many heterosexual couples face in establishing intimate relationships. Tracing the disjuncture between women's emotional fluency and men's lack of access to their feelings, Rubin argues that this gender difference is rooted in early childhood experiences. Male socialization to conceal emotions, combined with the expectation that boys "sever" their emotional bond with their mothers in order to identify with their fathers, render emotional intimacy a discomfiting experience for men. Rubin draws on the theory of gender identification that Nancy Chodorow discussed in Section Four, in "Family Structure and Feminine Personality." Because of these gender differences, Rubin argues, men and women enter intimate relationships with different expectations and responses to conflict.

Whereas Rubin makes a general argument about gender differences in intimate relationships, Madeline Davis and Elizabeth Lapovsky Kennedy examine relationships within the context of a specific community. In "Oral History and the Study of Sexuality in the Lesbian Community: Buffalo, New York, 1940–1960," Davis and Kennedy document the sexual, social, and political evolution of a lesbian community. In the construction of that community, lesbians created sexual roles that validated women's sexuality and laid the groundwork for the feminist and gay liberation movements. By paying careful attention to the practices of participants in the Buffalo community during this time period, the reading underscores how groups construct and understand sexuality and intimacy in various ways according to the social context.

Leila Rupp provides another illustration of the various interpretations women develop of their intimate lives in "'Imagine My Surprise': Women's Relationships in Mid-Twentieth Century America." Women's relegation to the "private sphere," combined with changing expectations for how women conduct themselves in relationships, makes historical interpretation of women's intimate lives difficult for feminist scholars. Rupp explores the difficulty of labeling women's intimate relationships with other

women as lesbian relationships, given changing definitions of lesbianism, as well as the social creation of
a distinct lesbian identity. By allowing the letters and
other documents of mid-twentieth-century women
to speak for themselves, Rupp offers us insight on
our foremothers' lives and provides an example of a
woman-centered historical analysis. The article contrasts with Davis and Kennedy's account of the
Buffalo lesbian community: Although both groups of
women formed intimate relationships with other
women, the working-class lesbians of Davis and
Kennedy's study interpreted their relationships very
differently from Rupp's middle-class subjects.

The section's concluding article, "Doing Desire:
Adolescent Girls' Struggles for/with Sexuality," by
Deborah Tolman, examines how another group of
women understand their sexuality: adolescent girls.
Adolescents have been the site of considerable
recent public debate over sexuality, with many politicians suggesting that teenage sexual activity should

be discouraged. Yet, Tolman notes, adolescence is the
lifestage during which we begin to develop our sexual selves and form a sense of our intimate connections to others. Tolman examines how adolescent
girls construct desire, tracing the complex mix of
pleasure and desire with danger and fear, and highlighting differences of sexual orientation. As a result
of the cultural repression of women's sexuality,
Tolman argues, adolescent girls are "denied full
access to the power of their own desire."

Like family life, sexuality and intimate relationships are both a source of support and strength for
women and a location of women's oppression. What
do these readings suggest about how women find
sexuality and intimate relationships to be a means of
fulfillment and an expression of self-definition? In
contrast, how do the readings show sexuality to be
a means of the social control of women? In short,
how are women oppressed and how do they resist
in their intimate lives?

The Approach–Avoidance Dance: Men, Women, and Intimacy

LILLIAN B. RUBIN

> *For one human being to love another, that is perhaps the most difficult of all our tasks, the ultimate, the last test and proof, the work for which all other work is but preparation.*
>
> —*Rainer Maria Rilke*

Intimacy. We hunger for it, but we also fear it. We come close to a loved one, then we back off. A teacher I had once described this as the "go away a little closer" message. I call it the approach–avoidance dance.

The conventional wisdom says that women want intimacy, men resist it. And I have plenty of material that would *seem* to support that view. Whether in my research interviews, in my clinical hours, or in the ordinary course of my life, I hear the same story told repeatedly. "He doesn't talk to me," says a woman. "I don't know what she wants me to talk about," says a man. "I want to know what he's feeling," she tells me. "I'm not feeling anything," he insists. "Who can feel nothing?" she cries. "I can," he shouts. As the heat rises, so does the wall between them. Defensive and angry, they retreat—stalemated by their inability to understand each other.

Women complain to each other all the time about not being able to talk to their men about the things that matter most to them—about what they themselves are thinking and feeling, about what goes on in the hearts and minds of the men they're relating to. And men, less able to expose themselves and their conflicts—those within themselves or those with the women in their lives—either turn silent or take cover by holding women up to derision. It's one of the norms of male camaraderie to poke fun at women, to complain laughingly about the mystery of their minds, wonderingly about their ways. Even Freud did it when, in exasperation, he asked mockingly, "What do women want? Dear God, what do they want?"

But it's not a joke—not for the women, not for the men who like to pretend it is.

> The whole goddamn business of what you're calling intimacy bugs the hell out of me. I never know what you women mean when you talk about it. Karen complains that I don't talk to her, but it's not talk she wants, it's some other damn thing, only I don't know what the hell it is. Feelings, she keeps asking for. So what am I supposed to do if I don't have any to give her or to talk about just because she decides it's time to talk about feelings? Tell me, will you: maybe we can get some peace around here.

The expression of such conflicts would seem to validate the common understandings that suggest that women want and need intimacy more than men do—that the issue belongs to women alone; that, if left to themselves, men would not suffer it. But things are not always what they seem. And I wonder: "If men would renounce intimacy, what is their stake in relationships with women?"

Some would say that men need women to tend to their daily needs—to prepare their meals, clean their houses, wash their clothes, rear their children—so that they can be free to attend to life's larger problems. And, given the traditional structure of roles in the family, it has certainly worked that way most of the time. But, if that were all men seek, why is it that, even when they're not relating to women, so much of their lives is spent in search of a relationship with another, so much agony experienced when it's not available?

These are difficult issues to talk about—even to think about—because the subject of intimacy isn't just complicated, it's slippery as well. Ask yourself: What is intimacy? What words come to mind, what thoughts?

It's an idea that excites our imagination, a word that seems larger than life to most of us. It lures us, beckoning us with a power we're unable to resist. And, just because it's so seductive, it frightens us as well—seeming sometimes to be some mysterious force from outside ourselves that, if we let it, could sweep us away.

But what is it we fear?

Asked what intimacy is, most of us—men and women—struggle to say something sensible, something that we can connect with the real experience of our lives. "Intimacy is knowing there's someone who cares about the children as much as you do." "Intimacy is a history of shared experience. It's sitting there having a cup of coffee together and watching the eleven o'clock news." "It's knowing you care about the same things." "It's knowing she'll always understand." "It's him sitting in the hospital for hours at a time when I was sick." "It's knowing he cares when I'm hurting." "It's standing by me when I was out of work." "It's seeing each other at our worst." "It's sitting across the breakfast table." "It's talking when you're in the bathroom." "It's knowing we'll begin and end each day together."

These seem the obvious things—the things we expect when we commit our lives to one another in a marriage, when we decide to have children together. And they're not to be dismissed as inconsequential. They make up the daily experience of our lives together, setting the tone for a relationship in important and powerful ways. It's sharing such commonplace, everyday events that determines the temper and the texture of life, that keeps us living together even when other aspects of the relationship seem less than perfect. Knowing someone is there, is constant, and can be counted on in just the ways these thoughts express provides the background of emotional security and stability we look for when we enter a marriage. Certainly a marriage and the people in it will be tested and judged quite differently in an unusual situation or in a crisis. But how often does life present us with circumstances and events that are so out of the range of ordinary experience?

These ways in which a relationship feels intimate on a daily basis are only one part of what we mean by intimacy,

however—the part that's most obvious, the part that doesn't awaken our fears. At a lecture where I spoke of these issues recently, one man commented also, "Intimacy is putting aside the masks we wear in the rest of our lives." A murmur of assent ran through the audience of a hundred or so. Intuitively we say, "yes." Yet this is the very issue that also complicates our intimate relationships.

On the one hand, it's reassuring to be able to put away the public persona—to believe we can be loved for who we *really* are, that we can show our shadow side without fear, that our vulnerabilities will not be counted against us. "The most important thing is to feel I'm accepted just the way I am," people will say.

But there's another side. For, when we show ourselves thus without the masks, we also become anxious and fearful. "Is it possible that someone could love the *real* me?" we're likely to ask. Not the most promising question for the further development of intimacy, since it suggests that, whatever else another might do or feel, it's we who have trouble loving ourselves. Unfortunately, such misgivings are not usually experienced consciously. We're aware only that our discomfort has risen, that we feel a need to get away. For the person who has seen the "real me" is also the one who reflects back to us an image that's usually not wholly to our liking. We get angry at that, first at ourselves for not living up to our own expectations, then at the other, who becomes for us the mirror of our self-doubts—a displacement of hostility that serves intimacy poorly.

There's yet another level—one that's further below the surface of consciousness, therefore, one that's much more difficult for us to grasp, let alone to talk about. I'm referring to the differences in the ways in which women and men deal with their inner emotional lives—differences that create barriers between us that can be high indeed. It's here that we see how those early childhood experiences of separation and individuation—the psychological tasks that were required of us in order to separate from mother, to distinguish ourselves as autonomous persons, to internalize a firm sense of gender identity—take their toll on our intimate relationships.

Stop a woman in mid-sentence with the question, "What are you feeling right now?" and you might have to wait a bit while she reruns the mental tape to capture the moment just passed. But, more than likely, she'll be able to do it successfully. More than likely, she'll think for a while and come up with an answer.

The same is not true of a man. For him, a similar question usually will bring a sense of wonderment that one would even ask it, followed quickly by an uncomprehending and puzzled response. "What do you mean?" he'll ask. "I was just talking," he'll say.

I've seen it most clearly in the clinical setting where the task is to get to the feeling level—or, as one of my male patients said when he came into therapy, to "hook up the head and the gut." Repeatedly when therapy begins, I find myself having to teach a man how to monitor his internal states—how to attend to his thoughts and feelings, how to bring them into consciousness. In the early stages of our work, it's a common experience to say to a man, "How does that feel?," and to see a blank look come over his face. Over and over, I find myself listening as a man speaks with calm reason about a situation which I know must be fraught with pain. "How do you feel about that?" I'll ask. "I've just been telling you," he's likely to reply. "No," I'll say, "you've told me what happened, not how you *feel* about it." Frustrated, he might well respond, "You sound just like my wife."

It would be easy to write off such dialogues as the problems of men in therapy, of those who happen to be having some particular emotional difficulties. But it's not so, as any woman who has lived with a man will attest. Time and again women complain: "I can't get him to verbalize his feelings." "He talks, but it's always intellectualizing." "He's so closed off from what he's feeling, I don't know how he lives that way." "If there's one thing that will eventually ruin this marriage, it's the fact that he can't talk about what's going on inside him." "I have to work like hell to get anything out of him that resembles a feeling that's something besides anger. That I get plenty of—me and the kids, we all get his anger. Anything else is damn hard to come by with him." One woman talked eloquently about her husband's anguish over his inability to get problems in his work life resolved. When I asked how she knew about his pain, she answered:

I pull for it, I pull hard, and sometimes I can get something from him. But it'll be late at night in the dark— you know, when we're in bed and I can't look at him while he's talking and he doesn't have to look at me. Otherwise, he's just defensive and puts on what I call his bear act, where he makes his warning, go-away faces, and he can't be reached or penetrated at all.

To a woman, the world men live in seems a lonely one—a world in which their fears of exposing their sadness and pain, their anxiety about allowing their vulnerability to show, even to a woman they love, is so deeply rooted inside them that, most often, they can only allow it to happen "late at night in the dark."

Yet, if we listen to what men say, we will hear their insistence that they *do* speak of what's inside them, *do* share their thoughts and feelings with the women they love. "I tell her, but she's never satisfied," they complain. "No matter how much I say, it's never enough," they grumble.

From both sides, the complaints have merit. The problem lies not in what men don't say, however, but in what's not there—in what, quite simply, happens so far out of consciousness that it's not within their reach. For men have integrated all too well the lessons of their childhood—the experiences that taught them to repress and deny their inner thoughts, wishes, needs, and fears; indeed, not even to notice them. It's real, therefore, that the kind of inner thoughts and feelings that are readily accessible to a woman generally are unavailable to a man. When he says, "I don't know what I'm feeling," he isn't necessarily being intransigent and withholding. More than likely, he speaks the truth.

Partly that's a result of the ways in which boys are trained to camouflage their feelings under cover of an exterior of calm, strength, and rationality. Fears are not manly. Fantasies are not rational. Emotions, above all, are not for the strong, the sane, the adult. Women suffer them, not men—women, who are more like children with what seems like their never-ending preoccupation with their emotional life. But the training takes so well because of their early childhood experience when, as very young boys, they had to shift their identification from mother to father and sever themselves from their earliest emotional connection. Put the two together and it does seem like suffering to men to have to experience that emotional side of themselves, to have to give it voice.

This is the single most dispiriting dilemma of relations between women and men. He complains, "She's so emotional, there's no point in talking to her." She protests, "It's him you can't talk to, he's always so darned rational." He says, "Even when I tell her nothing's the matter, she won't quit." She says, "How can I believe him when I can see with my own eyes that something's wrong?" He says, "Okay, so something's wrong! What good will it do to tell her?" She cries, "What are we married for? What do you need me for, just to wash your socks?"

These differences in the psychology of women and men are born of a complex interaction between society and the individual. At the broadest social level is the rending of thought and feeling that is such a fundamental part of Western thought. Thought, defined as the ultimate good, has been assigned to men; feeling, considered at best a problem, has fallen to women.

So firmly fixed have these ideas been that, until recently, few thought to question them. For they were built into the structure of psychological thought as if they spoke to an eternal, natural, and scientific truth. Thus, even such a great and innovative thinker as Carl Jung wrote, "The woman is increasingly aware that love alone can give her her full stature, just as the man begins to discern that spirit alone can endow his life with its highest meaning. Fundamentally, therefore, both seek a psychic relation one to the other, because love needs the spirit, and the spirit love, for their fulfillment."*

For a woman, "love"; for a man, "spirit"—each expected to complete the other by bringing to the relationship the missing half. In German, the word that is translated here as spirit is *Geist*. But *The New Cassell's German Dictionary* shows that another primary meaning of *Geist* is "mind, intellect, intelligence, wit, imagination, sense of reason." And, given the context of these words, it seems reasonable that *Geist* for Jung referred to a man's highest essence—his mind. There's no ambiguity about a woman's calling, however. It's love.

Intuitively, women try to heal the split that these definitions of male and female have foisted upon us.

I can't stand that he's so damned unemotional and expects me to be the same. He lives in his head all the time, and he acts like anything that's emotional isn't worth dealing with.

Cognitively, even women often share the belief that the rational side, which seems to come so naturally to men, is the more mature, the more desirable.

I know I'm too emotional, and it causes problems between us. He can't stand it when I get emotional like that. It turns him right off.

Her husband agrees that she's "too emotional" and complains:

Sometimes she's like a child who's out to test her parents. I have to be careful when she's like that not to let her rile me up because otherwise all hell would break loose. You just can't reason with her when she gets like that.

It's the rational-man-hysterical-woman script, played out again and again by two people whose emotional reper- toire is so limited that they have few real options. As the interaction between them continues, she reaches for the strongest tools she has, the mode she's most comfortable and familiar with: She becomes progressively more emotional and expressive. He falls back on his best weapons: He becomes more rational, more determinedly reasonable. She cries for him to attend to her feelings, whatever they may be. He tells her coolly, with a kind of clenched-teeth reasonableness, that it's silly for her to feel that way, that she's just being emotional. And of course she is. But that dismissive word "just" is the last straw. She gets so upset that she does, in fact, seem hysterical. He gets so bewildered by the whole interaction that his only recourse is to build the wall of reason even higher. All of which makes things measurably worse for both of them.

The more I try to be cool and calm her the worse it gets. I swear, I can't figure her out. I'll keep trying to tell her not to get so excited, but there's nothing I can do. Anything I say just makes it worse. So then I try to keep quiet, but . . . wow, the explosion is like crazy, just nuts.

And by then it *is* a wild exchange that any outsider would agree was "just nuts." But it's not just her response that's off, it's his as well—their conflict resting in the fact that we equate the emotional with the nonrational.

This notion, shared by both women and men, is a product of the fact that they were born and reared in this culture. But there's also a difference between them in their capacity to apprehend the *logic* of emotions—a difference born in their early childhood experiences in the family, when boys had to repress so much of their emotional side and girls could permit theirs to flower. . . . It should be understood: Commitment itself is not a problem for a man; he's good at that. He can spend a lifetime living in the same family, working at the same job—even one he hates. And he's not without an inner emotional life. But when a relationship requires the sustained verbal expression of that inner life and the full range of feelings that accompany it, then it becomes burdensome for him. He can act out anger and frustration inside the family, it's true. But ask him to express his sadness, his fear, his dependency—all those feelings that would expose his vulnerability to himself or to another—and he's likely to close down as if under some compulsion to protect himself.

All requests for such intimacy are difficult for a man, but they become especially complex and troublesome in relations with women. It's another of those paradoxes. For, to the degree that it's possible for him to be emotionally

---

*Carl Gustav Jung, *Contributions to Analytical Psychology* (New York: Harcourt, Brace & Co., 1928), p. 185.

open with anyone, it is with a woman—a tribute to the power of the childhood experience with mother. Yet it's that same early experience and his need to repress it that raises his ambivalence and generates his resistance.

He moves close, wanting to share some part of himself with her, trying to do so, perhaps even yearning to experience again the bliss of the infant's connection with a woman. She responds, woman style—wanting to touch him just a little more deeply, to know what he's thinking, feeling, fearing, wanting. And the fear closes in—the fear of finding himself again in the grip of a powerful woman, of allowing her admittance only to be betrayed and abandoned once again, of being overwhelmed by denied desires.

So he withdraws.

It's not in consciousness that all this goes on. He knows, of course, that he's distinctly uncomfortable when pressed by a woman for more intimacy in the relationship, but he doesn't know why. And, very often, his behavior doesn't please him any more than it pleases her. But he can't seem to help it.

R E A D I N G   3 2

Oral History and the Study of Sexuality in the Lesbian Community: Buffalo, New York, 1940–1960

MADELINE DAVIS and ELIZABETH LAPOVSKY KENNEDY

We began a study of the history of the Buffalo lesbian community, 1940–1960, to determine that community's contribution to the emergence of the gay liberation movement of the 1960s.[1] Because this community centered around bars and was highly role defined, its members often have been stereotyped as low-life societal discards and pathetic imitators of heterosexuality. We suspected instead that these women were heroines who had shaped the development of gay pride in the twentieth century by forging a culture for survival and resistance under prejudicial conditions and by passing this sense of community on to newcomers; in our minds, these are indications of a movement in its prepolitical stages.[2] Our original research plan assumed the conceptual division between the public (social life and politics) and the private (intimate life and sex), which is deeply rooted in modern consciousness and which feminism has

only begun to question. Thus we began our study by looking at gay and lesbian bars—the public manifestations of gay life at the time[1]—and relegated sex to a position of less importance, viewing it as only incidentally relevant. As our research progressed we came to question the accuracy of this division. This article records the transformation in our thinking and explores the role of sexuality in the cultural and political development of the Buffalo lesbian community.

At first, our use of the traditional framework that separates the public and private spheres was fruitful.[3] Because the women who patronized the lesbian and gay bars of the past were predominantly working class and left no written records, we chose oral history as our method of study. Through the life stories of over forty narrators, we found that there were more bars in Buffalo during the forties and fifties than there are in that city today. Lesbians living all over the city came to socialize in these bars, which were located primarily in the downtown area. Some of these women were born and raised in Buffalo; others had migrated there in search of their kind. In addition, women from nearby cities, Rochester and Toronto, came to Buffalo bars on weekends. Most of the women who frequented these bars had full-time jobs. Many were factory workers, taxi drivers, bartenders, clerical workers, hospital technicians; a few were teachers or women who owned their own businesses.[4]

Our narrators documented, beyond our greatest expectations, the truth of our original hypothesis that this public bar community was a formative predecessor to the modern gay liberation movement. These bars not only were essential meeting places with distinctive cultures and mores, but they were also the central arena for the lesbian confrontation with a hostile world. Participants in bar life were engaged in constant, often violent, struggle for public space. Their dress code announced them as lesbians to their neighbors, to strangers on the streets, and of course to all who entered the bars. Although confrontation with the straight world was a constant during this period, its nature changed over time. In the forties, women braved ridicule and verbal abuse, but rarely physical conflict. One narrator of the forties conveys the tone: "There was a great difference in looks between a lesbian and her girl. You had to take a streetcar—very few people had cars. And people would stare and such."[5] In the fifties, with the increased visibility of the established gay community, the concomitant postwar rigidification of sex roles, and the political repression of the McCarthy era, the street dyke emerged. She was a full-time "queer," who frequented the bars even on week nights and was ready at any time to fight for her space and dignity. Many of our fifties' narrators were both aware and proud that their fighting contributed to a safer, more comfortable environment for lesbians today.

Things back then were horrible, and I think that because I fought like a man to survive I made it somehow easier for the kids coming out today. I did all their fighting for them. I'm not a rich person; I don't even have a lot of money; I don't even have a little money. I would have nothing to leave anybody in this world, but I have that that I can leave to the kids who are coming out now, who will come out into the future, that I left them a better place to come out into. And that's all I have to offer, to leave them. But I wouldn't deny it; even though I was getting my brains beaten up I would never stand up and say, "No, don't hit me, I'm not gay, I'm not gay." I wouldn't do that.

When we initially gathered this material on the growth and development of community life, we placed little emphasis on sexuality. In part we were swept away by the excitement of the material on bars, dress, and the creation of public space for lesbians. In addition, we were part of a lesbian feminist movement that opposed a definition of lesbianism based primarily on sex. Moreover, we were influenced by the popular assumption that sexuality is natural and unchanging and the related sexist assumption of women's sexual passivity—both of which imply that sexuality is not a valid subject for historical study. Only recently have historians turned their attention to sexuality, a topic that used to be of interest mainly to psychologists and the medical profession. Feminists have added impetus to this study by suggesting that women can desire and shape sexual experience. Finally, we were inhibited by the widespread social reluctance to converse frankly about sexual matters. Thus for various reasons, all stemming, at least indirectly, from modern society's powerful ideological division between the public and the private, we were indisposed to consider how important sexuality might have been to the women we were studying.

The strength of the oral history method is that it enables narrators to shape their history, even when their views contradict the assumptions of historians. As our work progressed, narrators volunteered information about their sexual and emotional lives, and often a shyly asked question would inspire lengthy, absorbing discourse. By proceeding in the direction in which these women steered us, we came to realize that sexuality and sexual identity were not incidental but were central to their lives and their community. Our narrators taught us that although securing public space was indeed important, it was strongly motivated by the need to provide a setting for the formation of intimate relationships. It is the nature of this community that it created public space for lesbians and gay men, while at the same time it organized sexuality and emotional relationships. Appreciation of this dynamic interconnection requires new ways of thinking about lesbian history.

What is an appropriate framework for studying the sexual component of a lesbian community's history and for revealing the role of sexuality in the evolution of twentieth-century lesbian and gay politics? So little research has been done in this area that our work is still exploratory and tentative. At present, we seek primarily to understand forms of lesbian sexual expression and to identify changes in sexual norms, experiences, and ideas during the 1940s and 1950s. We also look for the forces behind these changes in the evolving culture and politics of the lesbian community. Our goal has been to ascertain what part, if any, sexuality played in the developing politics of gay liberation. As an introduction to this discussion, we shall present our method of research because it has been crucial in our move to study sexuality, and so little has been written on the use of oral history for research on this topic.

USING ORAL HISTORY TO CONSTRUCT THE HISTORY OF THE BUFFALO LESBIAN COMMUNITY

The memories of our narrators are colorful, illuminating, and very moving. Our purpose, however, was not only to collect individual life stories, but also to use these as a basis for constructing the history of the community. To create from individual memories a historically valid analysis of this community presented a difficult challenge. The method we developed was slow and painstaking.[6] We treated each oral history as a historical document, taking into account the particular social position of each narrator and how that might affect her memories. We also considered how our own point of view influenced the kind of information we received and the way in which we interpreted a narrator's story. We juxtaposed all interviews with one another to identify patterns and contradictions and checked our developing understanding with other sources, such as newspaper accounts, legal cases, and labor statistics.

As mentioned earlier, we first focused on understanding and documenting lesbian bar life. From the many vibrant and humorous stories about adventures in bars and from the mountains of seemingly unrelated detail about how people spent their time, we began to identify a chronology of bars and to recognize distinctive social mores and forms of lesbian consciousness that were associated with different time periods and even with different bars. We checked and supplemented our analysis by research into newspaper accounts of bar raids and closings and actions of the State Liquor Authority. Contradictions frequently emerged in our material on bars, but, as we pursued them, we found they were rarely due to idiosyncratic or faulty memory on the part of our narrators but to the complexity of bar life. Often the differences could be resolved by taking into account the different social positions of our narrators or the kinds of questions we had asked to elicit the information we received. If conflicting views persisted, we tried to return to our narrators for clarification. Usually we found that we had misunderstood our narrators or that contradictions indeed existed in the community at the time. For instance, narrators consistently told us about the wonderful times in bars as well as how terrible they were. We came to understand that both of these conditions were part of the real experience of bar life.

When we turned our attention to sexuality and romance in this community, we were at first concerned that our method would not be adequate. Using memories to trace the evolution of sexual norms and expression is, at least superficially, more problematic than using them to document social life in bars. There are no concrete public events or institutions to which the memories can be linked. Thus, when a narrator talks about butch–fem sexuality in the forties, we must bear in mind the likelihood that she has modified her view and her practice of butch–fem sexuality in the fifties, sixties, seventies, and eighties. In contrast, when a narrator tells about bars in the forties, even though social life in bars might have changed over the last forty years, she can tie her memories to a concrete place like Ralph Martin's bar, which existed during a specific time period. Although not enough is known about historical memory to fully evaluate data derived from either type of narrative, our guess is that, at least for lesbian communities, they are equally valid.[7] The vividness of our narrators' stories suggests that the potential of oral history to generate full and rich documents about women's sexuality might be especially rich in the lesbian community. Perhaps lesbian memories about sexual ideals and experiences are not separated from the rest of life because the building of public communities is closely connected with the pursuit of intimate relationships. In addition, during this period, when gay oppression marked most lesbians' lives with fear of punishment and lack of acceptance, sexuality was one of the few areas in which many lesbians found satisfaction and pleasure. This was reinforced by the fact that, for lesbians, sexuality was not directly linked with the pain and/or danger of women's responsibility for childbearing and women's economic dependence on men. Therefore, memories of sexual experience might be more positive and more easily shared. But these ideas are tentative. An understanding of the nature of memory about sexuality must await further research.

The difficulty of tying memories about sexual or emotional life to public events does present special problems. We cannot identify specific dates for changes in sexual and emotional life, such as when sex became a public topic of conversation or when role-appropriate sex became a community concern. We can talk only of trends within the framework of decades. In addition, we are unable to find supplementary material to verify and spark our narrators' memories. There are no government documents or newspaper reports on lesbian sexuality. The best one can find are memoirs or fiction written about or by residents in other cities, and even these don't exist for participants in working-class communities of the forties.[8] In general, we have not found these problems to require significant revision of our method.

Our experience indicates that the number of people interviewed is critical to the success of our method, whether we are concerned with analyzing the history of bar life or of emotional and sexual life. We feel that between five and ten narrators' stories need to be juxtaposed in order to develop an analysis that is not changed dramatically by each new story. At the present time, our analysis of the white lesbian community of the fifties is based on oral histories from over fifteen narrators. In contrast, we have only five narrators who participated in the white community of the forties, four for the black community of the fifties, and one from the black community of the forties. Therefore, we emphasize the fifties in this article and have the greatest confidence in our analysis of that decade. Our discussion of the forties must be viewed as only tentative. Our material on the black community is not yet sufficient for separate treatment; so black and white narrators' memories are interspersed throughout the article. Ultimately, we hope to be able to write a history of each community.

SEXUALITY AS PART OF THE CULTURAL POLITICAL DEVELOPMENT OF THE BUFFALO LESBIAN COMMUNITY

Three features of lesbian sexuality during the forties and fifties suggest its integral connection with the lesbian community's cultural-political development. First, butch–fem roles created an authentic lesbian sexuality appropriate to the flourishing of an independent lesbian culture. Second, lesbians actively pursued rich and fulfilling sexual lives at a time when sexual subjectivity was not the norm for women. This behavior was not only consistent with the creation of a separate lesbian culture, but it also represented the roots of a personal and political feminism that characterized the gay liberation movement of the sixties. Third, although butch–fem roles and the pursuit of sexual autonomy remained constant throughout this period, sexual mores changed in relation to the evolving forms of resistance to oppression.

Most commentators on lesbian bar life in the forties and fifties have noted the prominence of butch–fem roles.[9] Our research corroborates this; we found that roles constituted a powerful code of behavior that shaped the way individuals handled themselves in daily life, including sexual expression. In addition, roles were the primary organizer for the lesbian stance toward the straight world as well as for building love relationships and for making friends.[10] To understand butch–fem roles in their full complexity is a fundamental issue for students of lesbian history; the particular concern of this article is the intricate connection between roles and sexuality. Members of the community, when explaining how one recognized a person's role, regularly referred to two underlying determinants: image, including dress and mannerism, and sexuality.[11] Some people went so far as to say that one never really knew a woman's role identity until one went to bed with her. "You can't tell butch–fem by people's dress. You couldn't even really tell in the fifties. I knew women with long hair, fem clothes, and found out they were butches. Actually I even knew one who wore men's clothes, haircuts and ties, who was a fem."

Today, butch–fem roles elicit deep emotional reactions from many heterosexuals and lesbians. The former are affronted by women assuming male prerogatives; the latter by lesbians adopting male-defined role models. The hostility is exemplified by the prevalent ugly stereotype of the butch–fem sexual dyad: the butch with her dildo or penis substitute, trying to imitate a man, and the simpering passive fem who is kept in her place by ignorance. This representation evokes pity for lesbians because women who so interact must certainly be sexually unfulfilled; one partner cannot achieve satisfaction because she lacks the "true" organ of pleasure, and the other is cheated because she is denied the complete experience of the "real thing." Our research counters the view that butch–fem roles are solely an imitation of sexist heterosexual society.

Inherent in butch–fem relationships was the presumption that the butch is the physically active partner and the leader in lovemaking. As one butch narrator explains, "I treat a woman as a woman, down to the basic fact it'd have to be my side doin' most of the doin'." Insofar as the butch was the doer and the fem was the desired one, butch–fem roles did indeed parallel the male/female roles in heterosexuality. Yet unlike the dynamics of many heterosexual relationships, the butch's foremost objective was to give sexual pleasure to a fem; it was in satisfying her fem that the butch received fulfillment. "If I could give her satisfaction to the highest, that's what gave me satisfaction." As for the fem, she not only knew what would give her physical pleasure, but she also knew that she was neither object nor receptacle for someone else's gratification. The essence of this emotional/sexual dynamic is captured by the ideal of the "stone butch," or untouchable butch, that prevailed during this period. A "stone butch" does all the "doin'" and does not ever allow her lover to reciprocate in kind. To be untouchable meant to gain pleasure from giving pleasure. Thus, although these women did draw on models in heterosexual society, they transformed those models into an authentically lesbian interaction. Through role-playing they developed distinctive and fulfilling expressions of women's sexual love for women.

The archetypal lesbian couple of the 1940s and 1950s, the "stone butch" and the fem, poses one of the most tantalizing puzzles of lesbian history and possibly of the history of sexuality in general.[12] In a culture that viewed women as sexually passive, butches developed a position as sexual aggressor, a major component of which was untouchability. However, the active or "masculine" partner was associated with the giving of sexual pleasure, a service usually assumed to be "feminine." Conversely, the fem, although the more passive partner, demanded and received sexual pleasure and in this sense might be considered the more self-concerned or even more "selfish" partner. These attributes of butch–fem sexual identity remove sexuality from the realm of the "natural," challenging the notion that sexual performance is a function of biology and affirming the view that sexual gratification is socially constructed.

Within this framework of butch–fem roles, individual lesbians actively pursued sexual pleasure. On the one hand, butch–fem roles limited sexual expression by imposing a definite structure. On the other hand, this structure ordered and gave a determinant shape to lesbian desire, which allowed individuals to know and find what they wanted. The restrictions of butch–fem sexuality, as well as the pathways it provided for satisfaction, are best captured and explored by examining what it meant for both butch and fem that the butch was the doer; how much leeway was there before the butch became fem, or the fem became butch?

Although there was complete agreement in the community that the butch was the leader in lovemaking, there was a great deal of controversy over the feasibility or necessity of being a "stone butch." In the forties, most butches lived up to the *ideal* of "the untouchable." One fem, who was in a relationship with an untouchable butch at that time, had tried to challenge her partner's behavior but met only with resistance. Her butch's whole group—those who hung out at Ralph Martin's—were the same. "Because I asked her one time, I said, 'Do you think that you might be just the only one?' 'Oh no,' she said. 'I know I'm not, you know, that I've discussed with . . . different people.' [There were] no exceptions, which I thought was ODD, but, I thought, well, you know. This is how it is."

In the fifties, the "stone butch" became a publicly discussed model for appropriate sexual behavior, and it was a standard that young butches felt they had to achieve to be a "real" or "true" butch. In contrast to the forties, a fifties' fem, who was out in the community, would not have had to ask her butch friend why she was untouchable, and if there were others like her. She would have known it was the expected behavior for butches. Today our narrators disagree over whether it was, in fact, possible to maintain the ideal and they are unclear about the degree of latitude allowed in the forties or fifties before a butch harmed her reputation. Some butches claim that they were absolutely untouchable; that was how they were, and that's how they enjoyed sex. When we confronted one of our narrators, who referred to herself as an "untouchable," with the opinion of another narrator, who maintained that "stone butches" had never really existed, she replied, "No, that's not true. I'm an 'untouchable.' I've tried to have my lover make love to me, but I just couldn't stand it. . . . I really think there's something physical about that." Like many of our butch narrators, this woman has always been spontaneously orgasmic; that is, her excitement level peaks to orgasm while making love to another woman. Another "stone butch" explains: "I wanted to satisfy them [women], and I wanted to make love—I love to make love. I still think that's the greatest thing in life. But I don't want them to touch me. I feel like that spoils the whole thing—I am the way I am. And I figure if a girl is attracted to me, she's attracted to me because of what I am."

Other butches who consider themselves, and have the reputation of being, untouchable claim that it is, as a general matter, impossible to be completely untouchable. One, when asked if she were really untouchable, replied, "Of course not. How would any woman stay with me if I was? It doesn't make any sense. . . . I don't believe there was ever such a class—other than what they told each other." This woman preferred not to be touched, but she did allow mutual lovemaking from time to time during her long-term relationships. A first time in bed, however:

> There's no way in hell that you would touch me . . . if you mean untouchable like that. But if I'm living with a woman, I'd have to be a liar if I said that she hadn't touched me. But I can say that I don't care for it to happen. And the only reason it does happen is because she wants it. It's not like something I desire or want. But there's no such thing as an untouchable butch—and I'm the finest in Buffalo and I'm telling you straight—and don't let them jive you around it—no way.

This narrator's distinction between her behavior on a first night and her behavior in long-term relationships appeared to be accepted practice. The fact that some—albeit little—mutuality was allowed over the period of a long relationship did not affect one's reputation as an untouchable butch, nor did it counter the presumption of the butch as the doer.

This standard of untouchability was so powerful in shaping the behavior of fifties' butches that many never experienced their fems making love to them. By the seventies, however, when we began our interviewing, norms had changed enough so that our butch narrators had had opportunities to experience various forms of sexual expression. Still, many of them—in fact all of those quoted above on "stone butches"—remained untouchable. It was their personal style long after community standards changed. Today these women offer explanations for their preference that provide valuable clues about both the personal importance and the social "rightness" of untouchability as a community norm in the forties and fifties. Some women, as indicated in one of the above quotes, continue to view their discomfort with being touched as physical or biological. Others feel that if a fem were allowed the physical liberties usually associated with the butch role, distinctions would blur and the relationship would become confusing. "I feel that if we're in bed and she does the same thing to me that I do her, we're the same thing." Another narrator, reflecting on the fact that she always went to bed with her clothes on, suggests that "what it came to was being uncomfortable with the female body. You didn't want people you were with to realize the likeness between the two." Still other butches are hesitant about the vulnerability implicit in mutual lovemaking. "When the first girl wanted to make a mutual exchange sexually, . . . I didn't want to be in the position of being at somebody's disposal, or at their command that much—maybe that's still inside me. Maybe I never let loose enough."

But many untouchables of the fifties did try mutual lovemaking later on, and it came as a pleasant surprise when they found they enjoyed being touched. "For some reason . . . I used to get enough mental satisfaction by satisfying a woman . . . then it got to the point where this one woman said, 'Well, I'm just not gonna accept that,' and she started venturing, and at first I said, 'No, no,' and then I said, 'Well, why not?' and I got to enjoy it." This change was not easy for a woman who had spent many years as an "untouchable." At first she was very nervous and uncomfortable about mutual sex, but "after I started reaching physical climaxes instead of just mental, it went, that little restlessness about it. It just mellowed me right out, y'know." The social pressure of the times prevented some women from experiencing expanded forms of sexual expression they might have enjoyed, and it also put constraints upon some women who had learned mutual sex outside of a structured community. One of our narrators had begun her sex life with mutual relations and enjoyed it immensely, but in order to conform to the community standard for butches, adopted untouchability as her sexual posture. She accepted to this behavioral change willingly and saw it as a logical component of her role during this period.

How was a community able to monitor the sexual activities of its members, and how might people come to know if a butch "rolled over"—the community lingo for a butch who allowed fems to make love to her? The answer was simple: fems talked! A butch's reputation was based on her performance with fems.

Despite the fact that sexual performance could build or destroy a butch's reputation, some butches of the fifties completely ignored the standard of untouchability. Our narrators give two reasons for this. One reason is the opinion that a long-term relationship requires some degree of mutuality to survive. One butch, a respected leader of the community because of her principles, her affability, and her organizational skills, was not only "touchable" but also suspects that most of the butches she knew in the fifties were not "stone butches." "Once you get in bed or in your bedroom and the lights go out, when you get in between those sheets, I don't think there's any male or there's any female or butch or fem, and it's a fifty–fifty thing. And I think that any relationship . . . any true relationship that's gonna survive has got to be that way. You can't be a giver and can't be a taker. You've gotta both be givers and both gotta be takers." The second reason is the pleasure of being touched. Some women experienced this in the fifties and continued to follow the practice.

> When it came to sex [in the fifties] butches were untouchable, so to speak. They did all the lovemaking, but love was not made back to them. And after I found out how different it was, and how great it was, I said, "What was I missing?" I remember a friend of mine, that I had, who dressed like a man all her life . . . and I remember talking to [her] and saying to her, you know you've got to stop being an untouchable butch, and she just couldn't agree. And I remember one time reaching over and pinching her and I said, "Did you feel that?" and she said, "Yes," and I said, "It hurt, didn't it? Well, why aren't you willing to feel something that's good?"

We do not know if in the forties, as in the fifties, butches who preferred a degree of mutuality in lovemaking existed side by side with the ideal of untouchability because we have considerably less information on that decade. Therefore, we cannot judge whether there was in fact a development toward mutual sexuality, the dominant form of lesbian lovemaking of the sixties and seventies, or whether the "stone butch" prescribed ideal and mutual lovemaking couples existed side by side consistently throughout the forties and fifties.

Our information on fem sexuality is not as extensive as that on butch sexuality because we have been able to contact fewer fem narrators. Nevertheless, from the fems we have interviewed and from comments by butches who sought them out and loved them, we do have an indication that fems were not passive receivers of pleasure, but for the most part knew what they wanted and pursued it.[13] Many butches attributed their knowledge of sex to fems, who educated them by their sexual responsiveness as well as by their explicit directions in lovemaking.

As implied by our discussion of butch sexuality, many fems had difficulty accepting "untouchability." One fem narrator of the forties had a ten-year relationship with an untouchable butch, and the sexual restrictions were a source of discomfort for her. "It was very one-sided, you know, and . . . you never really got a chance to express your love. And I think this kind of suppressed . . . your feelings, your emotions. And I don't know whether that's healthy. I don't think so." But at the same time the majority of these fems appreciated being the center of attention; they derived a strong sense of self-fulfillment from seeking their own satisfaction and giving pleasure—by responding to their butches. "I've had some that I couldn't touch no parts of their bodies. It was all about me. Course I didn't mind! But every once in a while I felt like, well, hey, let me do something to you. I could NEVER understand that. 'Cause I lived with a girl. I couldn't touch any part of her, no part. But boy, did she make me feel good, so I said . . . All right with me . . . I don't mind laying down."

What emerges from our narrators' words is in fact a range of sexual desires that were built into the framework of role-defined sexuality. For butches of the period, we found those who preferred untouchability; those who learned it and liked it; those who learned it and adjusted to it for a time; those who preferred it, but sensed the need for some mutuality; and those who practiced mutuality regularly. For fems, we found those who accepted pleasure, thereby giving pleasure to their lovers; usually such women would aggressively seek what they wanted and instruct their lovers with both verbal and nonverbal cues. Some fems actively sought to make love to their butches and were

successful. And finally, we found some women who were not consistent in their roles, changing according to their partners. In the varied sex lives of these role-identified women of the past, we can find the roots of "personal-political" feminism. Women's concern with the ultimate satisfaction of other women is part of a strong sense of female and potentially feminist agency and may be the wellspring for the confidence, the goals, and the needs that shaped the later gay and lesbian feminist movement. Thus, when we develop our understanding of this community as a predecessor to the gay liberation movement, our analysis must include sexuality. For these lesbians actively sought, expanded, and shaped their sexual experience, a radical undertaking for women in the 1940s and 1950s.

Although butch–fem roles were the consistent framework for sexual expression, sexual mores changed and developed throughout this period; two contradictory trends emerged. First, the community became more open to the acceptance of new sexual practices, the discussion of sexual matters, and the learning about sex from friends as well as lovers. Second, the rules of butch–fem sexuality became more rigid, in that community concern for the role-appropriate behavior increased.

In the forties there were at least two social groups, focused in two prominent bars, Ralph Martin's and Winters. According to our narrators, the sexual mores of these two groups differed: the former group was somewhat conservative; the latter group was more experimental, presaging what were to become the accepted norms of the fifties. The lesbian patrons of Ralph Martin's did not discuss sex openly, and oral sex was disdained. "People didn't talk about sex. There was no intimate conversation. It was kind of hush, hush . . . I didn't know there were different ways." By way of contrast, this narrator recalls a visit to Winters, where other women were laughing about "sixty-nine." "I didn't get it. I went to [my partner] and said, 'Somebody says "sixty-nine" and everybody gets hysterical.'" Finally her partner learned what the laughter was all about. At that time our narrator would have mentioned such intimacies only with a lover. It wasn't until later that she got into bull sessions about such topics. Not surprisingly, this narrator does not recall having been taught about sex. She remembers being scared during her first lesbian experience, then found that she knew what to do "naturally." She had no early affairs with partners older than herself.

The Winters' patrons had a more open, experimental attitude toward sex; they discussed it unreservedly and accepted the practice of oral sex. These women threw parties in which women tried threesomes and daisy chains.

"People would try it and see how it worked out. But nothing really happened. One person would always get angry and leave, and they would end up with two." Even if their sexual adventures did not always turn out as planned, these women were unquestionably innovative for their time. Our narrator from the Winters' crowd reminisced that it was always a contrast to go home to the serene life of her religious family. She also raved about two fems who were her instructors in sexual matters, adding, "I was an apt pupil."

During the fifties the picture changed, and the mores of the Ralph Martin's group virtually disappeared. Sex came to be a conversation topic among all social groups. Oral sex became an accepted form of lovemaking, so that an individual who did not practice it was acting on personal preference rather than on ignorance or social proscription. In addition, most of our fifties' butch narrators recall having been teachers or students of sex. As in the Winters' group in the forties, an important teacher for the butch was the fem. "I had one girl who had been around who told me. I guess I really frustrated the hell out of her. And she took a piece of paper and drew me a picture and she said, 'Now you get this spot right here.' I felt like a jerk. I was embarrassed that she had to tell me this." According to our narrator, the lesson helped, and she explains that "I went on to greater and better things."

The fifties also saw the advent of a completely new practice—experienced butches teaching novice butches about sex. One narrator remembers that younger women frequently approached her with questions about sex: "There must be an X on my back. They just pick me out. . . ." She recalls one young butch who "had to know every single detail. She drove me crazy. Jesus Christ, y'know, just get down there and do it—y'get so aggravated." The woman who aggravated her gives the following account of learning about sex:

And I finally talked to a butch buddy of mine. . . . She was a real tough one. I asked her "What do you do when you make love to a woman?" And we sat up for hours and hours at a time. . . . "I feel sexually aroused by this woman, but if I take her to bed, what am I gonna do?" And she says, "Well, what do you feel like doing?" and I says "Well, the only thing I can think of doing is . . . all I want to do is touch her, but what is the full thing of it . . . you know." So when [she] told me I says, "Really," well there was this one thing in there, uh . . . I don't know if you want me to state it. Maybe I can . . . well, I won't . . . I'll put in terms that you can understand. Amongst other things, the oral gratification.

Well, that kind of floored me because I never expected something like that and I thought, well, who knows, I might like it.

She later describes her first sexual experience in which she was so scared that her friend had to shove her into the bedroom where the girl was waiting.

At the same time that attitudes toward discussions of and teachings about sexuality relaxed, the fifties' lesbian community became stricter in enforcing role-appropriate sexuality. Those who deviated from the pattern in the forties might have identified themselves as "lavender butch" and might have been labeled by others as "comme ci, comme ca." Although their divergence from the social norm would have been noticed and discussed, such women were not stigmatized. But the community of the fifties left little room to deviate. Those who did not consistently follow one role in bed were considered "ki-ki" (neither–nor), or more infrequently, "AC/DC," both pejorative terms imposed by the community. Such women were viewed as disruptive of the social order and not to be trusted. They not only elicited negative comments, but they also were often ostracized from social groups. From the perspective of the 1980s, in which mutuality in lovemaking is emphasized as a positive quality, it is important to clarify that "ki-ki" did not refer to an abandonment of role-defined sex but rather to a shifting of sexual posture depending upon one's bed partner. Therefore, it was grounded absolutely in role playing. One of our narrators in fact defined "ki-ki" as "double role playing."[14]

These contradictory trends in attitudes and norms of lesbian sexuality parallel changes in the heterosexual world. Movement toward open discussion of sex, the acceptance of oral sex, and the teaching about sex took place in the society at large, as exemplified by the publication of and the material contained in the Kinsey reports.[15] Similarly, the lesbian community's stringent enforcement of role-defined behavior in the fifties occurred in the context of straight society's postwar move toward a stricter sexual division of labor and the ideology that accompanied it.[16] These parallels indicate a close connection between the evolution of heterosexual and homosexual cultures, a topic that requires further research.[17] At this point, we wish to stress that drawing parallels with heterosexuality can only partially illuminate changes in lesbian sexual mores. As an integral part of lesbian life, lesbian sexuality undergoes transformations that correspond with changing forms of the community's resistance to oppression.

Two developments occurred in this prepolitical period that are fundamental for the later emergence of the lesbian and gay liberation movement of the sixties. The first development was the flourishing of a lesbian culture; the second was the evolving stance of public defiance. The community of the forties was just beginning to support places for public gatherings and socializing, and during this period lesbians were to be found in bars only on weekends. Narrators of the forties do not remember having role models or anyone willing to instruct them in the ways of gay life. The prevalent feeling was that gay life was hard, and if people wanted it, they had to find it for themselves. In the fifties, the number of lesbian bars increased, and lesbians could be found socializing there every night of the week. As bar culture became more elaborate and open, lesbians more freely exchanged information about all aspects of their social lives, including sexuality. Discussion of sex was one of the many dimensions of an increasingly complex culture. The strengthening of lesbian culture and the concomitant repression of gays in the fifties led the community to take a more public stance. This shift toward public confrontation subsequently generated enough sense of pride to counter the acknowledged detriments of gay life so that members of the community were willing to instruct newcomers both socially and sexually. Almost all our narrators who came out in the fifties remember a butch who served as a role model or remember acting as a role model themselves. Instruction about sexuality was part of a general education to community life that developed in the context of expanding community pride.

However, the community's growing public defiance was also related to its increased concern for enforcing role-appropriate behavior in the fifties. Butches were key in this process of fighting back. The butches alone, or the butch–fem couple, were always publicly visible as they walked down the street, announcing themselves to the world. To deal effectively with the hostility of the straight world, and to support one another in physical confrontations, the community developed, for butches in particular, rules of appropriate behavior and forms of organization and exerted pressure on butches to live up to these standards. Because roles organized intimate life, as well as the community's resistance to oppression, sexual performance was a vital part of these fifties' standards.

From the vantage point of the 1980s and twenty more years of lesbian and gay history, we know that just as evolving community politics created this tension between open discussion and teaching about sex and strict enforcement of role-appropriate sexual behavior, it also effected the resolution. Our research suggests that in the late sixties in Buffalo, with the development of the political activities of gay liberation, explicitly political organizations and tactics replaced butch–fem roles in leading the resistance to gay oppression. Because butch–fem roles were no longer the primary means for organizing the community's stance toward the straight world, the community no longer needed to enforce role-appropriate behavior.[18] This did not mean that butch–fem roles disappeared. As part of a long tradition of creating an authentic lesbian culture in an oppressive society, butch–fem roles remain, for many lesbians, an important code of personal behavior in matters of either appearance, sexuality, or both.

ACKNOWLEDGMENTS

This article is a revision of a paper originally presented at the "International Conference on Women's History and Oral History," Columbia University, New York, 18 November 1983. We want to thank Michael Frisch, Ellen DuBois, and Bobbi Prebis for reading the original version and offering us helpful comments. We also want to thank Rayna Rapp and Ronald Grele for their patience throughout the revision process.

NOTES

1. This research is part of the work of the Buffalo Women's Oral History Project, which was founded in 1978 with three goals: (1) to produce a comprehensive, written history of the lesbian community in Buffalo, New York, using as the major source oral histories of lesbians who came out prior to 1970; (2) to create and index an archive of oral history tapes, written interviews, and rele-

vant supplementary materials; and (3) to give this history back to the community from which it derives. Madeline Davis and Elizabeth (Liz) Kennedy are the directors of the project. Avra Michelson was an active member from 1978 to 1981 and had a very important influence on the development of the project. Wanda Edwards has been an active member of the project since 1981, particularly in regard to research on the black lesbian community and on racism in the white lesbian community.

2. This hypothesis was shaped by our personal contact with Buffalo lesbians who came out in the 1940s and 1950s, and by discussion with grass roots gay and lesbian history projects around the country, in particular, the San Francisco Lesbian and Gay History Project, the Boston Area Gay and Lesbian History Project, and the Lesbian Herstory Archives. Our approach is close to and has been influenced by the social constructionist tendency of lesbian and gay history. See in particular, Jonathan Katz, *Gay American History: Lesbians and Gay Men in the U.S.A.* (New York: Crowell, 1976); Gayle Rubin, Introduction to *A Woman Appeared to Me*, by Renée Vivien (Nevada: Naiad Press, 1976), iii-xxxvii; Jeffrey Weeks, *Coming Out: Homosexual Politics in Britain from the Nineteenth Century to the Present* (London: Quartet Books, 1977). We want to thank all these sources which have been inspirational to our work.

3. The Buffalo Women's Oral History Project has written two papers on bar life, both by Madeline Davis, Elizabeth (Liz) Kennedy, and Avra Michelson: "Buffalo Lesbian Bars in the Fifties," presented at the National Women's Studies Association, Bloomington, Indiana, May 1980, and "Buffalo Lesbian Bars: 1930–1960," presented at the Fifth Berkshire Conference on the History of Women, Vassar College, Poughkeepsie, N.Y., June 1981. Both papers are on file at the Lesbian Herstory Archives, P.O. Box 1258, New York, New York 10116.

4. We think that this community could accurately be designated as a working-class lesbian community, but this is not a concept many members of this community would use; therefore, we have decided to call it a public bar community.

5. All quotes are taken from the interviews conducted for this project between 1978 and 1984. The use of the phrase "lesbian and her girl" in this quote reflects some of our butch narrators' belief that the butch member of a couple was the lesbian and the fem member's identity was less clear.

6. A variety of sources were helpful for learning about issues and problems of oral history research. They include the Special Issue on Women's Oral History, *Frontiers* 2 (Summer 1977); Willa K. Baum, *Oral History for the Local Historical Society* (Nashville, Tenn.: American Association for State and Local History, 1975); Michael Frisch, "Oral History and *Hard Times*: A Review Essay," *Oral History Review* (1979): 70–80; Ronald Grele, ed., *Envelopes of Sound: Six Practitioners Discuss the Method, Theory, and Practice of Oral History and Oral Tradition* (Chicago: Precedent Publishing, 1975); Ronald Grele, "Can Anyone over Thirty Be Trusted: A Friendly Critique of Oral History," *Oral History Review* (1978): 36–44; "Generations: Women in the South," *Southern Exposure* 4 (Winter 1977); "No More Moanin'," *Southern*

Exposure 1 (Winter 1974); Peter Friedlander, *The Emergence of a UAW Local, 1936–1939* (Pittsburgh: University of Pittsburgh Press, 1975); William Lynwood Montell, *The Saga of Coe Ridge: A Study in Oral History* (Knoxville: University of Tennessee Press, 1970); Studs Terkel, *Hard Times: An Oral History of the Great Depression* (New York: Pantheon Books, 1970); Martin B. Duberman, *Black Mountain: An Exploration in Community* (Garden City, N.Y.: Doubleday, 1972); Sherna Gluck, ed., *From Parlor to Prison: Five American Suffragists Talk about Their Lives* (New York: Vintage, 1976); and Kathy Kahn, *Hillbilly Women* (New York: Doubleday, 1972).

7. For a helpful discussion of memory, see John A. Neuenschwander, "Remembrance of Things Past: Oral Historians and Long-Term Memory," *Oral History Review* (1978): 46–53; many sources cited in the previous note also have relevant discussions of memory; in particular, see Frisch; Grele, *Envelopes of Sound;* Friedlander; and Montell.

8. See for instance, Joan Nestle, "Esther's Story: 1960," *Common Lives/Lesbian Lives* 1 (Fall 1981):5–9; Joan Nestle, "Butch–Fem Relationships: Sexual Courage in the 1950s," *Heresies* 12 (1981): 21–24; Audre Lorde, "Tar Beach," *Conditions,* no. 5 (1979): 34–47 and Audre Lorde, "The Beginning," in *Lesbian Fiction,* ed. Elly Bulkin (Watertown, Mass.: Persephone Press, 1981), 225–74. Lesbian pulp fiction can also provide insight into the emotional and sexual life of this period; see, for instance, Ann Bannon's *I Am a Woman* (Greenwich, Conn.: Fawcett, 1959) and *Beebo Brinker* (Greenwich, Conn.: Fawcett, 1962).

9. See, for instance, Nestle, "Butch–Fem Relationships"; Lorde, "Tar Beach"; Del Martin and Phyllis Lyon, *Lesbian/Woman* (New York: Bantam, 1972); John D'Emilio, *Sexual Politics, Sexual Communities: The Making of a Homosexual Minority in the United States 1940–1970* (Chicago: University of Chicago Press, 1983).

10. For a full discussion of our research on butch–fem roles, see Madeline Davis and Elizabeth (Liz) Kennedy, "Butch–Fem Roles in the Buffalo Lesbian Community, 1940–1960" (paper presented at the Gay Academic Union Conference, Chicago, October 1982). This paper is on file at the Lesbian Herstory Archives.

11. These two main determinants of roles are quite different from what would usually be considered as indicators of sex roles in straight society; they do not include the sexual division of labor.

12. The origins of the "stone butch" and fem couple are beyond the scope of this paper. For an article that begins to approach these issues, see Esther Newton, "The Mythic Mannish Lesbian: Radclyffe Hall and the New Woman," *Signs* 9 (Summer 1984): 557–75.

13. Our understanding of the fem role has been enhanced by the following: Nestle's "Butch–Fem Relationships" and "Esther's Story"; Amber Hollibaugh and Cherrie Moraga, "What We're Rolling Around in Bed With: Sexual Silences in Feminism: A Conversation toward Ending Them," *Heresies* 12 (1981):58–62.

14. For indications that "ki-ki" was used nationally in the lesbian subculture, see Jonathan Katz, *Gay/Lesbian Almanac: A New Documentary* (New York: Harper & Row, 1983), 15, 626.

15. Alfred C. Kinsey, Wardell B. Pomeroy, and Clyde E. Martin, *Sexual Behavior in the Human Male* (Philadelphia: W. B. Saunders, 1948); and Alfred Kinsey et al., *Sexual Behavior in the Human Female* (Philadelphia: W. B. Saunders, 1953). Numerous sources document this trend; see, for instance, Ann Snitow, Christine Stansell, and Sharon Thompson, eds., *Powers of Desire: The Politics of Sexuality* (New York: Monthly Review Press, 1983), in particular, Introduction, sec. 2, "Sexual Revolutions," and sec. 3, "The Institution of Heterosexuality," 9–47, 115–71, 173–275; and Katz, *Gay/Lesbian Almanac*.

16. See Mary P. Ryan, *Womanhood in America: From Colonial Times to the Present* (New York: Franklin Watts, 1975).

17. A logical result of the social constructionist school of gay history is to consider that heterosexuality is also a social construction. Katz, in *Gay/Lesbian Almanac*, begins to explore this idea.

18. Although national homophile organizations began in the fifties, no such organizations developed in Buffalo until the formation of the Mattachine Society of the Niagara Frontier in 1969. But we do not think that the lack of early homophile organizations in this city made the bar community's use of roles as an organizer of its stance toward the straight world different from that of cities where homophile organizations existed. In general, these organizations, whether mixed or all women, did not draw from or affect bar communities. Martin and Lyon in chap. 8, "Lesbians United," *Lesbian/Woman* (238–79), present Daughters of Bilitis (DOB) as an alternative for those dissatisfied with bar life, not as an organization to coalesce the forces and strengths of the bar community. Gay liberation combined the political organization of DOB and the defiance and pride of bar life and therefore affected and involved both communities.

R E A D I N G 3 3

*"Imagine My Surprise": Women's Relationships in Mid-Twentieth Century America**

LEILA J. RUPP

When Carroll Smith-Rosenberg's article, "The Female World of Love and Ritual," appeared in the pages of *Signs*

Leila J. Rupp, " 'Imagine My Surprise': Women's Relationships in Mid-Twentieth Century America," *Frontiers: A Journal of Women Studies* 5, no. 3 (Fall 1980). Copyright © 1980 by Frontiers Editorial Collective. Reprinted with the permission of the publishers.

*Holly Near's song, "Imagine My Surprise," celebrates the discovery of women's relationships in the past. The song is recorded on the album, *Imagine My Surprise,* Redwood Records. I am grateful to Holly Near and Redwood Records for their permission to use the title here.

This is a revised version of an article originally published in *Frontiers: A Journal of Women Studies* 5 (Fall 1980). The original research was made possible by a fellowship from the Radcliffe Research Scholars Program. Additional research, funded by the National Endowment for the Humanities, was undertaken jointly with Verta Taylor for our book, *Survival in the Doldrums: The American Women's Rights Movement* (1987).

in 1975, it revolutionized the way in which women's historians look at nineteenth-century American society and even served notice on the historical profession at large that women's relationships would have to be taken into account in any consideration of Victorian society.[1] Since then we have learned more about relationships between women in the past, but we have not reached consensus on the issue of characterizing these relationships.

Debate within the women's movement has centered around the work of two writers. In 1980, Adrienne Rich published "Compulsory Heterosexuality and Lesbian Existence," in which she argued for the concept of a lesbian continuum based on solidarity among women and resistance to patriarchy rather than on identity or sexual behavior.[2] The next year, Lillian Faderman's *Surpassing the Love of Men,* which traced the history of women's relationships, suggested that the nineteenth-century phenomenon of romantic friendship involved a deep commitment and sensuality but not, ordinarily, genital sexuality.[3] As a result of the controversy that has swirled around these works, we have no simple answer to the question, asked of a variety of historical figures: Was she a lesbian?

Meanwhile, outside the feminist world, Smith-Rosenberg's work has increasingly been misused to deny the sexual aspect of relationships between prominent women in the past. In response, feminist scholars have reacted to such distortions by bestowing the label "lesbian" on women who would themselves not have used the term. The issue goes beyond labels, however, because the very nature of women's relationships is so complex. The problem of classification becomes particularly thorny in twentieth-century history with the establishment of a lesbian identity. I would like to consider here the issue of women's relationships in the twentieth century by reviewing the conflicting approaches to lesbian labeling, by tracing the continuity of romantic friendship into the mid-century, and, finally, by suggesting a conceptual approach that recognizes the complexity of women's relationships without denying the common bond shared by all women who have committed their lives to other women in the past.

Looking first at what Blanche Cook proclaimed "the historical denial of lesbianism," we find the most publicized and most egregious example in Doris Faber's *The Life of Lorena Hickok: E. R.'s Friend,* the story of the relationship of Eleanor Roosevelt and reporter Lorena Hickok.[4] Author Doris Faber presented page after page of evidence that delineated the growth and development of a love affair between the two women, yet she steadfastly maintained that a woman of Eleanor Roosevelt's "stature" could not have *acted* on the love that she expressed for Hickok. This attitude forced Faber to go to great lengths with the evidence before her. For example, she quoted a letter Roosevelt wrote to Hickok and asserted that it is "particularly susceptible to misinterpretation." Roosevelt's wish to "lie down beside you tonight and take you in my arms," Faber claimed, represented maternal—"albeit rather extravagantly" maternal—solicitude. For Faber, "there can be little doubt that the final sentence of the above letter does not mean what it appears to mean" (p. 176).

Faber's book received far more public attention than serious works of lesbian history because the idea of a famous and well-respected—even revered—woman engaging in lesbian acts was titillating. An article about the Hickok book was even carried in the *National Enquirer* which, for a change, probably presented the material more accurately, if more leeringly, than the respectable press.[5]

Faber's interpretation, unfortunately, is not an isolated one. She acknowledged an earlier book, *Miss Marks and Miss Woolley,* for reinforcing her own views "regarding the unfairness of using contemporary standards to characterize the behavior of women brought up under almost inconceivably different standards."[6] Anna Mary Wells, the author of the Marks and Woolley book, set out originally to write a biography of Mary Woolley, a president of Mount Holyoke, but almost abandoned the plan when she discovered the love letters of the two women. Ultimately Wells went ahead with a book about the relationship, but only after she decided, as she explained in the preface, that there was no physical relationship between them.

Another famous women's college president, M. Carey Thomas of Bryn Mawr, received the same sort of treatment in a book that appeared at the same time as the Hickok book, but to less fanfare.[7] The discovery of the Woolley-Marks letters sparked a mild panic among Mount Holyoke alumnae and no doubt created apprehension about what might lurk in Thomas's papers, which were about to be microfilmed and opened to the public.[8] But Marjorie Dobkin, editor of *The Making of a Feminist: Early Journals and Letters of M. Carey Thomas,* insisted that there was nothing to worry about. Thomas admittedly fell for women throughout her life. At fifteen, she wrote: "I think I must feel towards Anna for instance like a boy would, for I admire her so . . . and then I like to touch her and the other morning I woke up and she was asleep and I admired her hair so much that I kissed it. I never felt so much with anybody else." And at twenty: "One night we had stopped reading later than usual and obeying a sudden impulse I turned to her and asked, 'Do you love me?' She threw her arms around me and whispered, 'I love you passionately.' She did not go home that night and we talked and talked." At twenty-three, Thomas wrote to her mother: "If it were only possible for women to elect women as well as men for a 'life's love!' . . . It is possible but if families would only regard it in that light!" (pp. 72, 118, 229).

Thomas did in fact choose women for her "life's loves," but Dobkin, who found it "hard to understand why anyone should very much care" about personal and private behavior and considered the question of lesbianism "a relatively inconsequential matter," assured us that "physical contact" unquestionably played a part in Thomas's relationships with women, but, making a labored distinction, insisted that "sexuality" just as unquestionably did not (pp. 79, 86).

The authors of these three books were determined to give us an "acceptable" version of these prominent women's relationships in the past, and they seized gratefully on Smith-Rosenberg's work to do it. Likewise, Arthur Schlesinger, Jr., in *The New York Times Book Review,* found the question of whether Hickok and Roosevelt were "lovers in the physical sense" an "issue of stunning inconsequence," but cited Smith-Rosenberg's work to conclude that the two women were "children of the Victorian age" which accepted celibate love between women.[9]

As Blanche Cook pointed out in her review of Faber's book, however, it is absurd to pretend that the years 1932 to 1962 now belong to the nineteenth century.[10] Although it is vitally important not to impose modern concepts and standards on the past, we have gone entirely too far with the notion of an idyllic Victorian age in which chaste love between people of the same sex was possible and acceptable.

It is not surprising, in light of such denials of sexuality, that many feminist scholars have chosen to claim as lesbians all women who have loved women in the past. Blanche Cook has concluded firmly that "women who love women, who choose women to nurture and support and to create a living environment in which to work creatively and independently, are lesbians."[11] Cook named as lesbians Jane Addams, the founder of Hull House who lived for forty years with Mary Rozet Smith; Lillian Wald, also a settlement house pioneer, who left evidence of a series of intense relationships with women; and Jeannette Marks and Mary Woolley. All, Cook insisted, in the homophobic society in which we live, must be claimed as lesbians.

In the simplest terms, we are faced with a choice between labelling women lesbians who might have violently rejected the notion or glossing over the significance of women's relationships by considering them asexual and Victorian.[12] But what is problematic enough when we are dealing with a period in which the concept of lesbianism did not exist becomes even more troubling when we turn to the twentieth century.

What the research increasingly suggests is that two separate largely class-bound forms of relationships between women existed. We seem to have little trouble identifying the working-class phenomena—"crossing" women who dressed and worked as men and who married women, and lesbian communities that grew up around the bars and, eventually, in the military—as sexual and, therefore, lesbian. But what about the middle- and upper-class romantic friends? It is not a question of nineteenth-century romantic friends becoming lesbians in the twentieth century. Despite the sexualization of American society at the turn of the century and the concomitant "discovery of lesbianism," romantic friendship and "Boston marriage" continued to exist.[13] I would like to illustrate this continuity, and therefore the complexity of women's relationships in

historical perspective, with examples from the American women's rights movement in the late 1940s and 1950s.

I have found evidence of a variety of relationships in collections of women's papers and in the records of women's organizations from this period. I do not have enough information about many of these relationships to characterize them in any definitive way, nor can I even offer much information about some of the women. But we cannot afford to overlook whatever evidence women have left us, however fragmentary. Since my research focuses on feminist activities, the women I discuss here are by no means a representative group of women. The women's rights movement in the period after the Second World War was composed primarily of white, privileged women who maintained a preexisting commitment to feminism by creating an isolated and homogeneous feminist community.[14]

Within the women's rights movement were two distinct phenomena—couple relationships and intense devotion to a charismatic leader—that help clarify the problems that face us if we attempt to define these relationships in any cut-and-dried fashion. None of the women who lived in couple relationships and belonged to the women's rights movement in the post-1945 period would, as far as can be determined, have identified themselves as lesbians. They did, however, often live together in long-term committed relationships, which were accepted in the movement, and they did sometimes build a community with other women like themselves. Descriptions of a few relationships that come down to us in the sources provide some insight into their nature.

Jeannette Marks and Mary Woolley, subjects of the biography mentioned earlier, met at Wellesley College in 1895 when Marks began her college education and Woolley arrived at the college as a history instructor. Less than five years later they made "a mutual declaration of ardent and exclusive love" and "exchanged tokens, a ring and a jeweled pin, with pledges of lifelong fidelity."[15] They spent the rest of their lives together, including the many years at Mount Holyoke where Woolley served as president and Marks taught English. Mary Woolley worked in the American Association of University Women and the Women's International League for Peace and Freedom. Jeannette Marks committed herself to suffrage and, later, through the National Woman's Party, to the Equal Rights Amendment. It is clear from Mark's correspondence with women in the movement that their relationship was accepted as a primary commitment. Few letters to Marks in the 1940s fail to inquire about Woolley, whose serious illness clouded Mark's life and work. One married woman, who found herself forced to withdraw from Woman's Party work because of her husband's health, acknowledged in a letter to Marks the centrality of Marks's and Woolley's commitment when she compared her own reason for "pulling out" to "those that have bound you to Westport," the town in which the two women lived.[16] Mary Woolley died in 1947, and Jeannette Marks lived on until 1964, devoting herself to a biography of Woolley.

Lena Madesin Phillips, the founder of the International Federation of Business and Professional Women's Clubs, lived for some thirty years with Marjory Lacey-Baker, an actress whom she first met in 1919. In an unpublished autobiography included in Phillips's papers, she straightforwardly wrote about her lack of interest in men and marriage. As a young girl, she wrote that she "cared little for boys," and at the age of seven she wrote a composition for school that explained: "There are so many little girls in the school and the thing i [sic] like about it there are no boys in school. i [sic] like that about it."[17] She noted that she had never taken seriously the idea of getting married. "Only the first of the half dozen proposals of marriage which came my way had any sense of reality to me. They made no impression because I was wholly without desire or even interest in the matter." Phillips seemed unperturbed by possible Freudian and/or homophobic explanations of her attitudes and behavior. She explained unabashedly that she wanted to be a boy and suffered severe disappointment when she learned that, contrary to her father's stories, there was no factory in Indiana that made girls into boys. She mentioned in her autobiography the "crushes" she had on girls at the Jessamine Female Institute—nothing out of the ordinary for a young woman of her generation, but perhaps a surprising piece of information chosen for inclusion in the autobiography of a woman who continued to devote her emotional energies to women.

In 1919, Phillips attended a pageant in which Lacey-Baker performed and she inquired about the identity of the woman who had "[t]he most beautiful voice I ever heard."[18] Phillips "lost her heart to the sound of that voice," and the two women moved in together in the 1920s. In 1924, according to Lacey-Baker's notes for a biography of Phillips, the two women went different places for Easter; recording this caused Lacey-Baker to quote from *The Prophet:* "Love knows not its own depth until the hour of separation."[19] Phillips described Lacey-Baker in her voluminous correspondence as "my best friend," or noted that she "shares a home with me."[20] Phillips's friends and acquaintances regularly mentioned Lacey-Baker. One male correspondent, for example, commented that Phillips's "lady-friend" was "so lovely, and so devoted to you and

cares for you."[21] Phillips happily described the tranquillity of their life together to her many friends: "Marjory and I have had a lovely time, enjoying once more our home in summertime. . . . Marjory would join in the invitation of this letter and this loving greeting if she were around. Today she is busy with the cleaning woman, while I sit with the door closed working in my study."[22] "We have had a happy winter, with good health for both of us. We have a variety of interests and small obligations, but really enjoy most the quiet and comfort of Apple Acres."[23] "We read and talk and work."[24]

Madesin Phillips's papers suggest that she and Marjory Lacey-Baker lived in a world of politically active women friends. Phillips had devoted much of her energy to international work with women, and she kept in touch with European friends through her correspondence and through her regular trips to Europe accompanied by Lacey-Baker. Gordon Holmes, of the British Federation of Business and Professional Women, wrote regularly to "Madesin and Maggie." In a 1948 letter she teased Phillips by reporting that "two other of our oldest & closest Fed officers whom you know could get married but are refusing—as they are both more than middle-aged (never mind their looks) it suggests 50–60 is about the new dangerous age for women (look out for Maggie!)."[25] Phillips reported to Holmes on their social life: "With a new circle of friends around us here and a good many of our overseas members coming here for luncheon or tea with us the weeks slip by."[26] The integral relationship between Phillips's social life and her work in the movement is suggested by Lacey-Baker's analysis of Phillips's personal papers from the year 1924: "There is the usual crop of letters to LMP following the Convention [of the BPW] from newly-met members in hero-worshipping mood—most of whom went on to be her good friends over the years."[27] Lacey-Baker was a part of Phillips's movement world, and their relationship received acceptance and validation throughout the movement, both national and international.

The lifelong relationship between feminist biographer Alma Lutz and Marguerite Smith began when they roomed together at Vassar in the early years of the twentieth century. From 1918 until Smith's death in 1959, they shared a Boston apartment and a summer home, Highmeadow, in the Berkshires. Lutz and Smith, a librarian at the Protestant Zion Research Library in Brookline, Massachusetts, worked together in the National Woman's Party. Like Madesin Phillips, Lutz wrote to friends in the movement of their lives together: "We are very happy here in the country— each busy with her work and digging in the garden."[28] They traveled together, visiting Europe several times in the 1950s. Letters to one of them about feminist work invariably sent greetings or love to the other. When Smith died in 1959, Lutz struggled with her grief. She wrote to her acquaintance Florence Kitchelt, in response to condolences: "I am at Highmeadow trying to get my bearings. . . . You will understand how hard it is. . . . It has been a very difficult anxious time for me."[29] She thanked another friend for her note and added, "It's a hard adjustment to make, but one we all have to face in one way or another and I am remembering that I have much to be grateful for."[30] In December she wrote to one of her regular correspondents that she was carrying on but it was very lonely for her.[31]

The fact that Lutz and Smith seemed to have many friends who lived in couple relationships with other women suggests that they had built a community of women within the women's rights movement. Every year Mabel Vernon, a suffragist and worker for peace, and her friend and companion Consuelo Reyes, whom Vernon had met through her work with the Inter-American Commission of Women, spent the summer at Highmeadow. Vernon, one of Alice Paul's closest associates during the suffrage struggle, had met Reyes two weeks after her arrival in the United States from Costa Rica in 1942. They began to work together in Vernon's organization, People's Mandate, in 1943, and they shared a Washington apartment from 1951 until Vernon's death in 1975.[32] Reyes received recognition in Vernon's obituaries as her "devoted companion" or "nurse-companion."[33] Two other women who also maintained a life-long relationship, Alice Morgan Wright and Edith Goode, also kept in contact with Lutz, Smith, Vernon, and Reyes. Sometimes they visited Highmeadow in the summer.[34] Wright and Goode had met at Smith and were described as "always together" although they did not live together.[35] Like Lutz and Smith, they worked together in the National Woman's Party, where they had also presumably met Vernon. Both Wright and Goode devoted themselves to two causes, women's rights and humane treatment for animals. Wright described herself as having "fallen between two stools—animals and wimmin."[36] The two women traveled together and looked after each other as age began to take its toll.

These examples illustrate what the sources provide: the bare outlines of friendship networks made up of woman-committed women. Much of the evidence must be pieced together, and it is even scantier when the women did not live together. Alma Lutz's papers, for example, do not include any personal correspondence from the post-1945 period, so what we know about her relationship with Marguerite Smith comes from the papers of her correspondents. Sometimes a relationship surfaces only upon the death of one of the women. For example, Agnes Wells, chairman of the National Woman's Party in the late 1940s, explained to an acquaintance in the Party that her "friend of forty-one years and house-companion for twenty-eight years" had just died.[37] When Mabel Griswold, executive secretary of the Woman's Party, died in 1955, a family member suggested that the Party send the telegram of sympathy to Elsie Wood, the woman with whom Griswold had lived.[38] This kind of reference tells us little about the nature of the relationship involved, but we do get a sense of acceptance of couple relationships within the women's rights movement.

A second important phenomenon found in the women's rights movement—the charismatic leader who attracted intense devotion—also adds to our understanding of the complexity of women's relationships. Alice Paul, the founder and leading light of the National Woman's Party, inspired devotion that bordered on worship. One woman even addressed her as "My Beloved Deity."[39] But, contrary to both the ideal type of the charismatic leader and the portrait of Paul as it exists now in historical scholarship, Paul maintained close relationships with a number of women she had first met in the suffrage struggle.[40] Paul's correspondence in the National Woman's Party papers does not reveal much about the nature of her relationships, but it does make it clear that her friendships provided love and support for her work.

It is true that many of the expressions of love, admiration, and devotion addressed to Paul seem to have been one-sided, from awe-struck followers, but this is not the only side of the story. Paul maintained close friendships with a number of women discussed earlier who lived in couple relationships with other women. She had met Mabel Vernon when they attended Swarthmore College together, and they maintained contact throughout the years, despite Vernon's departure from the Woman's Party in the 1930s.[41] Of Alice Morgan Wright, she said that, when they first met, they ". . . just became sisters right away."[42] Jeannette Marks regularly sent her love to "dear Alice" until a conflict in the Woman's Party ruptured their relationship.[43] Other women, too, enjoyed a closer relationship than the formal work-related one for which Paul is so well known.

Paul obviously cared deeply, for example, for her old friend Nina Allender, the cartoonist of the suffrage movement. Allender, who lived alone in Chicago, wrote to Paul in 1947 of her memories of their long association: "No words can tell you what that [first] visit grew to mean to me & to my life. . . . I feel now as I did then—only more

IN PRAISE OF "BEST FRIENDS":
THE REVIVAL OF A FINE OLD INSTITUTION

BARBARA EHRENREICH

All the politicians, these days, are "profamily," but I've never heard of one who was "profriendship." This is too bad and possibly shortsighted. After all, most of us would never survive our families if we didn't have our friends.

I'm especially concerned about the fine old institution of "best friends." I realized that it was on shaky ground a few months ago, when the occasion arose to introduce my own best friend (we'll call her Joan) at a somewhat intimidating gathering. I got as far as saying, "I am very proud to introduce my best friend, Joan . . . " when suddenly I wasn't proud at all: I was blushing. "Best friend," I realized as soon as I heard the words out loud, sounds like something left over from sixth-grade cliques: the kind of thing where if Sandy saw you talking to Stephanie at recess, she might tell you after school that she wasn't going to be your best friend anymore, and so forth. Why couldn't I have just said "my good friend Joan" or something *grown-up* like that?

But Joan is not just any friend, or even a "good friend"; she is my best friend. We have celebrated each other's triumphs together, nursed each other through savage breakups with the various men in our lives, discussed the Great Issues of Our Time, and cackled insanely over things that were, objectively speaking, not even funny. We have quarreled and made up; we've lived in the same house and we've lived thousands of miles apart. We've learned to say hard things, like "You really upset me when . . . " and even "I love you." Yet, for all this, our relationship has no earthly weight or status. I can't even say the name for it without sounding profoundly silly.

Why is best friendship, particularly between women, so undervalued and unrecognized? Partly, no doubt,

because women themselves have always been so undervalued and unrecognized. In the Western tradition, male best friendships are the stuff of history and high drama. Reread Homer, for example, and you'll realize that Troy did not fall because Paris, that spoiled Trojan prince, loved Helen, but because Achilles so loved Patroclus. It was Patroclus' death, at the hands of the Trojans, that made Achilles snap out of his sulk long enough to slay the Trojans' greatest warrior and guarantee victory to the Greeks. Did Helen have a best friend, or any friend at all? We'll never know, because the only best friendships that have survived in history and legend are man-on-man: Alexander and Hephaestion, Orestes and Pylades, Heracles and Iolas.

Christianity did not improve the status of female friendship. "Every woman ought to be filled with shame at the thought that she is a woman," declaimed one of the early church fathers, Clement of Alexandria, and when two women got together, the shame presumably doubled. Male friendship was still supposed to be a breeding ground for all kinds of upstanding traits—honor, altruism, courage, faith, loyalty. Consider Arthur's friendship with Lancelot, which easily survived the latter's dalliance with Queen Guinevere. But when two women got together, the best you could hope for, apparently, was bitchiness, and the worst was witchcraft.

Yet, without the slightest encouragement from history, women have persisted in finding best friends. According to recent feminist scholarship, the 19th century seems to have been a heyday of female best friendship. In fact, feminism might never have gotten off the ground at all if it hadn't been for the enduring bond between Elizabeth Cady Stanton, the theoretician of the movement, and Susan B. Anthony, the movement's first great pragmatist.

And they are only the most famous best friends. According to Lillian Faderman's book *Surpassing the Love of Men*, there were thousands of anonymous female couples who wrote passionate letters to each other, exchanged promises and tokens of love, and suffered through the separations occasioned by marriage and migration. Feminist scholars have debated whether these great best friendships were actually lesbian, sexual relationships—a question that I find both deeply fascinating (if these were lesbian relationships, were the women involved conscious of what a bold and subversive step they had taken?) and somewhat beside the point. What matters is that these women honored their friendships, and sought ways to give them the kind of coherence and meaning that the larger society reserved only for marriage.

In the 20th century, female best friendship was largely eclipsed by the new ideal of the "companionate marriage." At least in the middle-class culture that celebrated "togetherness," your *husband* was now supposed to be your best friend, as well, of course, as being your lover, provider, coparent, housemate, and principal heir. My own theory (profamily politicians please take note) is that these expectations have done more damage to the institution of marriage than no-fault divorce and the sexual revolution combined. No man can be all things to even one woman. And the foolish idea that one could has left untold thousands of women not only divorced, but what is in the long run far worse—friendless.

Yet even feminism, when it came back to life in the early seventies, did not rehabilitate the institution of female best friendship. Lesbian relationships took priority, for the good and obvious reason that they had been not only neglected, but driven underground. But in our zeal to bring lesbian relationships safely out of the closet, we sometimes ended up shoving best friendships further out of sight. "Best friends?" a politically ever-so-correct friend once snapped at me, in reference to Joan, "why aren't you lovers?" In the same vein, the radical feminist theoretician Shulamith Firestone wrote that after the gender revolution, there would be no asexual friendships. The coming feminist Utopia, I realized sadly, was going to be a pretty lonely place for some of us.

Then, almost before we could get out of our jeans and into our corporate clone clothes, female friendship came back into fashion—but in the vastly attenuated form of "networking." Suddenly we are supposed to have dozens of women friends, hundreds if time and the phone bill allow, but each with a defined function: mentors, contacts, connections, allies, even pretty ones who might be able to introduce us, now and then, to their leftover boyfriends. The voluminous literature on corporate success for women is full of advice on friends: whom to avoid ("turkeys" and whiners), whom to cultivate (winners and potential clients), and how to tell when a friend is moving from the latter category into the former. This is an advance, because it means we are finally realizing that women are important enough to be valued friends and that friendship among women is valuable enough to write and talk about. But in the pushy new dress-for-success world, there's less room than ever for best friendships that last through thick and thin, through skidding as well as climbing.

Hence my campaign to save the institution of female best friendship. I am not asking you to vote for anyone, to pray to anyone, or even to send me money. I'm just suggesting that we all begin to give a little more space, and a little more respect, to the best friendships in our lives. To this end, I propose three rules:

1. Best friendships should be given social visibility. If you are inviting Pat over for dinner, you would naturally think of inviting her husband, Ed. Why not Pat's best friend, Jill? Well, you may be thinking, how childish! They don't have to go everywhere together. Of course they don't, but neither do Pat and Ed. In many settings, including your next dinner party or potluck, Pat and Jill may be the combination that makes the most sense and has the most fun.

2. Best friendships take time and nurturance, even when that means taking time and nurturance away from other major relationships. Everyone knows that marriages require "work." (A ghastly concept, that. "Working on a marriage" has always sounded to me like something on the order of lawn maintenance.) Friendships require effort, too, and best friendships require our very best efforts. It should be possible to say to husband Ed or whomever, "I'm sorry I can't spend the evening with you because I need to put in some quality time with Jill." He will be offended only if he is a slave to heterosexual couple-ism—in which case you shouldn't have married him in the first place.

3. Best friendship is more important than any work-related benefit that may accrue from it, and should be treated accordingly. Maybe your best friend will help

you get that promotion, transfer, or new contract. That's all well and good, but the real question is: Will that promotion, transfer, or whatever help your best friendship? If it's a transfer to San Diego and your best friend's in Cincinnati, it may not be worth it. For example, as a writer who has collaborated with many friends, including "Joan," I am often accosted by strangers exclaiming, "It's just amazing that you got through that book [article, or other project] together and you're still friends!" The truth is, in nine cases out of ten, that the friendship was always far more important than the book. If a project isn't going to strengthen my friendship—and might even threaten it—I'd rather not start.

When I was thinking through this column—out loud of course, with a very good friend on the phone—she sniffed, "So what exactly do you want—formal legalized friendships, with best-friend licenses and showers and property settlements in case you get in a fight over the sweaters you've been borrowing from each other for the past ten years?" No, of course not, because the beauty of best friendship, as opposed to, say, marriage, is that it's a totally grass-roots creative effort that requires no help at all from the powers-that-be. Besides, it would be too complicated. In contrast to marriage— and even to sixth-grade cliques—there's no rule that says you can have only one "best" friend.

intensely—I have never changed or doubted—but have grown more inspired as the years have gone by. . . . There is no use going into words. I believe them to be unnecessary between us."[44] Paul wrote that she thought of Allender often and sent her "devoted love."[45] She worried about Allender's loneliness and gently encouraged her to come to Washington to live at Belmont House, the Woman's Party headquarters, where she would be surrounded by loving friends who appreciated the work she had done for the women's movement.[46] Paul failed to persuade her to move, however. Two years later Paul responded to a request from Allender's niece for help with the cost of a nursing home with a hundred-dollar check and a promise to contact others who might be able to help.[47] But Allender died within a month at the age of eighty-five.

Paul does not seem to have formed an intimate relationship with any one woman, but she did live and work within a close-knit female world. When in Washington, she lived, at least some of the time, at Belmont House; when away she lived either alone or with her sister, Helen Paul, and later with her lifelong friend Elsie Hill. It is clear that Alice Paul's ties—whether to her sister or to close friends or to admirers—served as a bond that knit the Woman's Party together. That Paul and her network could also tear the movement asunder is obvious from the stormy history of the Woman's Party.[48]

Alice Paul is not the only example of a leader who inspired love and devotion among women in the movement. One senses from Marjory Lacey-Baker's comment, quoted above—that "newly met members in hero-worshipping mood" wrote to Lena Madesin Phillips after

every BPW convention—that Phillips too had a charismatic aura. But the best and most thoroughly documented example of a charismatic leader is Anna Lord Strauss of the League of Women Voters, an organization that in the post-1945 years distanced itself from women's rights.

Strauss, the great-granddaughter of Lucretia Mott, came from an old and wealthy family; she was prominent and respected, a staunch liberal who rejected the label of "feminist." She never married and her papers leave no evidence of intimate relationships outside her family. Yet Strauss was the object of some very strong feelings on the part of the women with whom she worked. She, like Alice Paul and Madesin Phillips, received numerous hero-worshipping letters from awe-struck followers. But in her case we also have evidence that some of her coworkers fell deeply in love with her. It is hard to know how the women discussed here would have interpreted their relationship with Strauss. The two women who expressed their feelings explicitly were both married women, and in one case Strauss obviously had a cordial relationship with the woman's husband and children. Yet there can be no question that this League officer fell in love with Strauss. She found Strauss "the finest human being I had ever known" and knowing her "the most beautiful and profound experience I have ever had."[49] Loving Strauss—she asked permission to say it— made the earth move and "the whole landscape of human affairs and nature" take on a new appearance.[50] Being with Strauss made "the tone and fiber" of her day different; although she could live without her, she could see no reason for having to prove it all the time.[51] She tried to "ration and control" her thoughts of Strauss, but it was small satisfaction.[52] When Strauss was recovering from an operation, this woman wrote: "I love you! I can't imagine the world without you. . . . I love you. I need you."[53]

Although our picture of this relationship is completely one-sided—for Strauss did not keep copies of most of her letters—it is clear that Strauss did not respond to such declarations of love. This woman urged Strauss to accept her and what she had to say without "the slightest sense of needing to be considerate of me because I feel as I do." She understood the "unilateral character" of her feelings, and insisted that she had more than she deserved by simply knowing Strauss at all.[54] But her hurt, and her growing suspicion that Strauss shunned intimacy, escaped on occasion. She asked: "And how would it hurt you to let someone tell you sometime how beautiful—how wonderful you are? Did you ever let anyone have a decent chance to try?"[55] She realized that loving someone did not always make things easier—that sometimes, in fact, it made life more of a struggle—but she believed that to withdraw from love was to withdraw from life. In what appears to have been a hastily written note, she expressed her understanding—an understanding that obviously gave her both pain and comfort—that Strauss was not perfect after all: "Way back there in the crow's nest (or at some such time) you decided not to become embroiled in any intimate human relationship, except those you were, by birth, committed to. I wonder. . . . There is something you haven't mastered. Something you've been afraid of after all."[56]

This woman's perception that Strauss avoided intimacy is confirmed elsewhere in Strauss's papers. One old friend was struck, in 1968, by Strauss's ability to "get your feelings out and down on paper!" She continued: "I know you so well that I consider this great progress in your own inner state of mental health. It is far from easy for you to express your feelings. . . ."[57] This aspect of Strauss's personality fits with the ideal type of the charismatic leader. The other case of a woman falling in love with Strauss that emerges clearly from her papers reinforces this picture. This woman, also a League officer, wrote in circuitous fashion of her intense pleasure at receiving Strauss's picture. In what was certainly a reference to lesbianism, she wrote that she hoped Strauss would not think that she was "one of those who had never outgrown the emotional extravaganzas of the adolescent." Before she got down to League business, she added:

But, Darling, as I softly close the door on all this—as I should and as I want to—and as I must since all our meetings are likely to be formal ones in a group—as I go back in the office correspondence to "Dear Miss Strauss" and "Sincerely Yours," . . . as I put myself as much as possible in the background at our March meeting in order to share you with the others who have not been with you as I have—as all these things happen, I want you to be very certain that what is merely under cover is still there—as it most surely will be—and that if all the hearts in the room could be exposed there'd be few, I'm certain, that would love you more than . . . [I].[58]

Apparently Strauss never responded to this letter, for a month later, this woman apologized for writing it: "I have had qualms, dear Anna, about that letter I wrote you. (You knew I would eventually of course!)." Continuing in a vein that reinforces the previously quoted perception of Strauss's inability to be intimate, she wrote of imagining the "recoil . . . embarrassment, self-consciousness and general discomfort" her letter must have provoked in such a "reserved person." She admitted that the kind of admiration she had expressed, "at least in certain classes of relationships (of which mine to you is one)—becomes a bit of moral wrongdoing."[59] She felt ashamed and asked forgiveness.

What is clear is that this was a momentous and significant relationship to at least one of the parties. Almost twenty years later, this woman wrote of her deep disappointment in missing Strauss's visit to her city. She had allowed herself to dream that she could persuade Strauss to stay with her awhile, even though she knew that others would have prior claims on Strauss's time. She wrote:

I have not seen you since that day in Atlantic City when you laid the gavel of the League of Women Voters down. . . . I do not look back on that moment of ending with any satisfaction for my own behavior, for I passed right by the platform on which you were still standing talking with one of the last persons left in the room and shyness at the thought of expressing my deep feeling about your going—and the fact that you were talking with someone else led me to pass on without even a glance in your direction as I remember though you made some move to speak to me! . . . But if I gave you a hurt it is now a very old one and forgotten, I'm sure—as well as understood.[60]

Whatever the interpretation these two women would have devised to explain their feelings for Strauss, it is clear that the widely shared devotion to this woman leader could sometimes grow into something more intense. Strauss's reserve and her inability to express her feelings may or may not have had anything to do with her own attitude toward intimate relationships between women. One tantalizing letter from a friend about to be married suggests that Strauss's decision not to marry had been made early: "I remember so well your answer when I pressed you, once, on why you had never married. . . . Well, it is very true, one does not marry unless one can see no other life."[61] A further fragment, consisting of entries in the diary of Doris Stevens—a leading suffragist who took a sharp swing to the right in the interwar period—suggests that at least some individuals suspected Strauss of lesbianism. Stevens, by this time a serious red-baiter and, from the evidence quoted here, a "queerbaiter" as well, apparently called a government official in 1953 to report that Strauss was "not a bit interested in men."[62] She seemed to be trying to discredit Strauss, far too liberal for her tastes, with a charge of "unorthodox morals."[63]

Stevens had her suspicions about other women as well. She recorded in her diary a conversation with a National Woman's Party member about Jeannette Marks and Mary Woolley, noting that the member, who had attended Wellesley with Marks, "Discreetly indicated there was 'talk.' "[64] At another point she reported a conversation with a different Woman's Party member who had grown disillusioned about Alice Paul. Stevens noted that her informant related "weird goings on at Wash. hedquts wherein it was clear she thought Paul a devotee of Lesbos & afflicted with Jeanne d'Arc identification."[65] Along the same lines, the daughter of a woman who had left the National Woman's Party complained that Alice Paul and another leader had sent her mother a telegram that "anybody with sense" would think "was from two people who were adolescent [*sic*] or from two who had imbied [*sic*] too much or else Lesbians to a Lesbian."[66]

Such comments suggest that the intensity of women's relationships and the existence and acceptance of couple relationships in women's organizations had the potential, particularly during the McCarthy years, to attract denunciation. Doris Stevens herself wrote to the viciously right-wing and anti-Semitic columnist Westbrook Pegler to "thank you for knowing I'm not a queerie" despite the fact that she considered herself a feminist.[67] Although the association between feminism and lesbianism was not new in the 1950s, the McCarthyite connection between political deviance and homosexuality seemed to fuel suspicion.[68] How real the threat was for women is suggested by two further incidents involving opposition to the appointment of women, both described in the memoirs of India Edwards, a top woman in the Truman administration.[69]

In 1948, opposition to tax court judge Marion Harron's reappointment to the bench arose from Harron's fellow judges, who cited her lack of judicial temperament and "unprovable charges of an ethical nature." Although Edwards did not specify the nature of the charges, we know from *The Life of Lorena Hickok* that Harron had written letters to "E. R.'s friend" that even Doris Faber had to admit were love letters. The other case that Edwards described left no doubt about what ethical and moral charges were involved. When Truman appointed Kathryn McHale, long-time executive director of the American Association of University Women, to the Subversive Activities Control Board, Senator Pat McCarran advised Truman to withdraw her name and threatened to hold public hearings during which "information would be brought out that she was a lesbian."

On the whole, though, the feminists who lived in couple relationships managed to do so respectably, despite the emergence of a lesbian culture and the occasional charges of lesbianism. This was because they worked independently or in professional jobs, had the money to buy homes together, and enjoyed enough status to be beyond reproach in the world in which they moved. Women who later identified as lesbians but did not attach an identity to their emotions and behaviors in the 1950s describe that period as one in which women might live together without raising any eyebrows, but it is important to remember that even the class privilege that protected couple relationships would not necessarily suffice if women sought to enter powerful male-dominated institutions.[70]

What exactly should we make of all this? In one way it is terribly frustrating to have such tantalizingly ambiguous glimpses into women's lives. In another way, it is exciting to find out so much about women's lives in the past. I think it is enormously important not to read into these relationships what we want to find, or what we think we should find. At the same time, we cannot dismiss what little evidence we have as insufficient when it is all we have; nor can we continue to contribute to the conspiracy of silence that urges us to ignore what is not perfectly straightforward. Thus, although it is tempting to try to speculate about the relationships I have described here in order to impose some analysis on them, I would rather simply lay them out, fragmentary as they are, in order to suggest a conceptual approach that recognizes the complexities of the issue.

It is clear, I think, that none of these relationships can be easily categorized. There were women who lived their entire adult lives in couple relationships with other women, and married women who fell in love with other women.

Were they lesbians? Probably they would be shocked to be identified in that way. Alice Paul, for example, spoke scornfully of *Ms.* magazine as "all about homosexuality and so on."[71] Another woman who lived in a couple relationship distinguished between the (respectable) women involved in the ERA struggle in the old days and the "lesbians and bra-burners" of the contemporary movement.[72] Sasha Lewis, in *Sunday's Women,* reported an incident we would do well to remember here. One of her informants, a lesbian, went to Florida to work against Anita Bryant and stayed with an older cousin who had lived for years in a marriagelike relationship with another woman. When Lewis's informant saw the way the two women lived—sharing everything, including a bedroom—she remarked about the danger of Bryant's campaign for their lives. They were aghast that she would think them lesbians, since, they said, they did not do anything sexual together.[73] If even women who chose to share beds with other women would reject the label "lesbian," what about the married women, or the women who avoided intimate relationships?

What is critical here, I would argue, is that these women lived at a time during which some women *did* identify as lesbians. The formation of a lesbian identity, from both an individual and historical perspective, is enormously significant. So far, most of the historical debate over the use of the term "lesbian" has focused on earlier periods.[74] Passionate love between women has existed, but it has not always been named. Since it *has* been named in the twentieth century, and since there *was* such a thing as a lesbian culture, we need to distinguish between women who identify as lesbians and/or who are part of a lesbian culture, where one exists, and a broader category of women-committed women who would not identify as lesbians but whose primary commitment, in emotional and practical terms, was to other women. There is an important difference between, on the one hand, butch-fem couples in the 1950s who committed what Joan Nestle has aptly called an act of "sexual courage" by openly proclaiming the erotic aspect of their relationships, and, on the other, couples like Eleanor Roosevelt and Lorena Hickok or Alma Lutz and Marguerite Smith.[75]

We know that identity and sexual behavior are not the same thing.[76] There are lesbians who have never had a sexual relationship with another woman and there are women who have had sexual experiences with women but do not identify as lesbians. This is not to suggest that there is no difference between women who loved each other and lived together but did not make love (although even that can be difficult to define, since sensuality and sexuality, "physical contact" and "sexual contact" have no distinct boundaries) and those who did. But sexual behavior—something about which we rarely have historical evidence anyway—is only one of a number of relevant factors in a relationship. Blanche Cook has said everything that needs to be said about the inevitable question of evidence: "Genital 'proofs' to confirm lesbianism are never required to confirm the heterosexuality of men and women who live together for twenty, or fifty, years." Cook reminds us of the publicized relationship of General Eisenhower and Kay Summersby during the Second World War: They "were passionately involved with each other. . . . They were inseparable. But they never 'consummated' their love in the acceptable, traditional, sexual manner. Now does that fact render Kay Summersby and Dwight David Eisenhower somehow less in love? Were they not heterosexual?"[77]

At this point, I think, the best we can do as historians is to describe carefully and sensitively what we do know about a woman's relationships, keeping in mind both the historical development of a lesbian identity (Did such a thing as a lesbian identity exist? Was there a lesbian culture?) and the individual process that we now identify as "coming out" (Did a woman feel attachment to another woman or women? Did she act on this feeling in some positive way? Did she recognize the existence of other women with the same commitment? Did she express solidarity with those women?). Using this approach allows us to make distinctions among women's relationships in the past—intimate friendships, supportive relationships growing out of common political work, couple relationships—without denying their significance or drawing fixed boundaries. We can recognize the importance of friendships among a group of women who, like Alma Lutz, Marguerite Smith, Mabel Vernon, Consuelo Reyes, Alice Morgan Wright, and Edith Goode built a community of women but did not identify it as a lesbian community. We can do justice to both the woman-committed woman who would angrily reject any suggestion of lesbianism and the self-identified lesbian without distorting their common experiences.

This approach does not solve all the problems of dealing with women's relationships in the past, but it is a beginning. The greatest problem remains the weakness of sources. Not only have women who loved women in the past been wisely reluctant to leave evidence of their relationships for the prying eyes of a homophobic society, but what evidence they did leave was often suppressed or destroyed.[78] Furthermore, as the three books discussed at the beginning show, even the evidence saved and brought to light can be savagely misinterpreted.

How do we know if a woman felt attachment, acted on it, recognized the existence of other women like her, or expressed solidarity? There is no easy answer to this, but it is revealing, I think, that both Doris Faber and Anna Mary Wells are fairly certain that Lorena Hickok and Jeannette Marks, respectively, did have "homosexual tendencies" (although Faber insists that even Hickok cannot fairly be placed in the "contemporary gay category"), even if the admirable figures in each book, Eleanor Roosevelt and Mary Woolley, certainly did not. That is, both of these authors, as hard as they try to deny lesbianism, find evidence that forces them to discuss it, and both cope by pinning the "blame" on the women they paint as unpleasant— fat, ugly, pathetic Lorena Hickok and nasty, tortured, arrogant Jeannette Marks.

So we present what evidence we have, being careful to follow Linda Gordon's advice and "listen quietly and intently" to the women who speak to us from the sources.[79] In the case of twentieth-century history, we may also have the opportunity to listen to women speak in the flesh. We may privately believe that all the evidence suggests that a woman was a lesbian, but what do we do if she insisted, either explicitly or implicitly, that she was not? That is why the process of coming out is so important to us as historians. In a world in which some women claimed a lesbian identity and built lesbian communities, the choice to reject that identification has a meaning of its own. It is imperative that we not deny the reality of any woman's historical experience by blurring the distinctions among different kinds of choices. At the same time, recognition of the common bond of commitment to women shared by diverse women throughout history strengthens our struggle against those who attempt to divide and defeat us.

NOTES

1. Carroll Smith-Rosenberg, "The Female World of Love and Ritual: Relations between Women in Nineteenth Century America," *Signs* 1 (1975): 1–29.

2. Adrienne Rich, "Compulsory Heterosexuality and Lesbian Existence," *Signs* 5 (1980): 631–60. See also Ann Ferguson, Jacquelyn N. Zita, and Kathryn Pyne Addelson, "On Compulsory Heterosexuality and Lesbian Existence: Defining the Issues," *Signs* 7 (1981): 158–99.

3. Lillian Faderman, *Surpassing the Love of Men: Romantic Friendship and Love between Women from the Renaissance to the Present* (New York: William Morrow, 1981). See also Faderman's *Scotch Verdict* (New York: Quill, 1983), a compelling re-creation of the trial of two Edinburgh school-teachers accused of having sex together (the model for Lillian Hellman's *The Children's Hour*). Faderman argues against a sexual component in the two women's relationship, suggesting that "for many women, what *ought* to be, in fact *was*" (p. 126).

For examples, of reviews that discussed the controversial nature of Faderman's argument, see the Muriel Haynes's review of *Surpassing the Love of Men* in *Ms.* 9 (June 1981): 36; and reviews of *Scotch Verdict* by Karla Jay in *Women's Review of Books* 1 (December 1983):9–10 and by Terry Castle in *Signs* 9 (1984): 717–20.

4. Blanche Wiesen Cook, "The Historical Denial of Lesbianism," *Radical History Review* 20 (1979): 60–65; Doris Faber, *The Life of Lorena Hickok: E.R.'s Friend* (New York: William Morrow, 1980).

5. Edward Sigall, "Eleanor Roosevelt's Secret Romance—the Untold Story," *National Enquirer,* November 13, 1979, pp. 20–21.

6. Anna Mary Wells, *Miss Marks and Miss Woolley* (Boston: Houghton Mifflin, 1978); Faber, *Lorena Hickok,* p. 354. Cook, "Historical Denial," is a review of the Wells book.

7. Marjorie Housepian Dobkin, *The Making of a Feminist: Early Journals and Letters of M. Carey Thomas* (Kent, Ohio: Kent State University Press, 1980).

8. *The New York Times,* August 21, 1976, p. 22.

9. Arthur Schlesinger, Jr., "Interesting Women," *The New York Times Book Review,* February 17, 1980, p. 31.

10. Cook, review of *The Life of Lorena Hickok, Feminist Studies* 6 (1980): 511–16.

11. Cook, "Female Support Networks and Political Activism: Lillian Wald, Crystal Eastman and Emma Goldman," *Chrysalis* 3 (1977): 48.

12. In a review of books on Frances Willard, Alice Paul, and Carrie Chapman Catt, Gerda Lerner criticized the denial of sexuality in relationships in which women shared their lives "in the manner of married couples." In an attempt to bridge the two approaches, Lerner suggested that perhaps Paul, Willard, Catt, along with Susan B. Anthony, Anna Dickinson, and Jane Addams, were "simply what Victorian 'lesbians' looked like." Gerda Lerner, "Where Biographers Fear to Tread," *Women's Review of Books* 11 (September 1987): 11–12.

13. On the significance of class, see Myriam Everard, "Lesbian History: A History of Change and Disparity," *Journal of Homosexuality* 12 (1986): 123–37 and "Lesbianism and Medical Practice in the Netherlands, 1897–1930," paper presented at the Berkshire Conference of Women Historians, Wellesley, Massachusetts, 1987. Not all the lesbian communities we know of prior

to the 1950s were working class, however. There were middle- and upper-class communities in Europe and, to a lesser extent, among American bohemians at the turn of the century. On "crossing" women, see Jonathan Katz, *Gay American History* (New York: Thomas Y. Crowell, 1976), and *Gay/Lesbian Almanac* (New York: Harper and Row, 1983). On the emergence of a lesbian community, see Madeline Davis and Elizabeth Lapovsky Kennedy, "Oral History and the Study of Sexuality in the Lesbian Community: Buffalo, New York, 1940–1960," in this volume; Joan Nestle, "Butch-Fem Relationships: Sexual Courage in the 1950's," *Heresies: The Sex Issue* 12 (1981): 21–24; Allan Bérubé, "Coming Out Under Fire," *Mother Jones* (February/March 1983): 23–45; and John D'Emilio, *Sexual Politics, Sexual Communities: The Making of a Homosexual Minority in the U.S. 1940–1970* (Chicago: University of Chicago Press, 1983).

On the "discovery of lesbianism," see Nancy Sahli, "Smashing: Women's Relationships Before the Fall," *Chrysalis* 8 (1979): 17–27; George Chauncey, Jr., "From Sexual Inversion to Homosexuality: Medicine and the Changing Conceptualization of Female Deviance," *Salmagundi* 58/59 (Fall 1982/Winter 1983): 114–46; Christina Simmons, "Women's Sexual Consciousness and Lesbian Identity, 1900–1940" (paper presented at the Berkshire Conference of Women Historians, Northhampton, Massachusetts, 1984); Esther Newton, "The Mythic Mannish Lesbian: Radclyffe Hall and the New Woman," in this volume.

14. See Leila J. Rupp and Verta Taylor, *Survival in the Doldrums: The American Women's Rights Movement, 1945 to the 1960s* (New York: Oxford University Press, 1987).

15. Wells, *Miss Marks and Miss Woolley,* p. 56.

16. Caroline Babcock to Jeannette Marks, February 12, 1947, Babcock papers, box 8 (105), Schlesinger Library, Radcliffe College, Cambridge, Massachusetts. I am grateful to the Schlesinger Library for permission to use the material quoted here.

17. "The Unfinished Autobiography of Lena Madesin Phillips," Phillips papers, Schlesinger Library.

18. "Chronological Records of Events and Activities for the Biography of Lena Madesin Phillips, 1881–1955," Phillips papers, Schlesinger Library.

19. "Chronological Records of Events and Activities for the Biography of Lena Madesin Phillips, 1881–1955," Phillips papers, Schlesinger Library.

20. Lena Madesin Phillips to Audrey Turner, January 21, 1948, Phillips papers, Schlesinger Library; Phillips to Olivia Rossetti Agresti, April 26, 1948, Phillips papers, Schlesinger Library.

21. Robert Heller to Phillips, September 26, 1948, Phillips papers, Schlesinger Library.

22. Phillips to Mary C. Kennedy, August 20, 1948, Phillips papers, Schlesinger Library.

23. Phillips to Gordon Holmes, March 28, 1949, Phillips papers, Schlesinger Library.

24. Phillips to [Ida Spitz], November 13, 1950, Phillips papers, Schlesinger Library.

25. Holmes to Madesin & Maggie, December 15, 1948, Phillips papers, Schlesinger Library.

26. Phillips to Holmes, March 28, 1949, Phillips papers, Schlesinger Library.

27. "Chronological Record of Events and Activities for the Biography of Lena Madesin Phillips, 1881–1955," Phillips papers, Schlesinger Library.

28. Alma Lutz to Florence Kitchelt, July 1, 1948, Kitchelt papers, box 6 (177), Schlesinger Library.

29. Lutz to Kitchelt, July 29, 1959, Kitchelt papers, box 7 (178), Schlesinger Library.

30. Lutz to Florence Armstrong, August 26, 1959, Armstrong papers, box 1 (17), Schlesinger Library.

31. Lutz to Rose Arnold Powell, December 14, 1959, Powell papers, box 3 (43), Schlesinger Library.

32. Mabel Vernon, "Speaker for Suffrage and Petitioner for Peace," an oral history conducted in 1972 and 1973 by Amelia R. Fry, Regional Oral History Office, University of California, 1976. Courtesy, the Bancroft Library.

33. Press release from Mabel Vernon Memorial Committee, Vernon, "Speaker for Suffrage"; obituary in the *Wilmington Morning News,* September 3, 1975, Vernon, "Speaker for Suffrage."

34. Alice Morgan Wright to Anita Pollitzer, July 9, 1946, National Woman's Party papers, reel 89. The National Woman's Party papers have been microfilmed and are distributed by the Microfilming Corporation of America. I am grateful to the National Woman's Party for permission to quote the material used here.

35. Alice Paul, "Conversations with Alice Paul: Woman Suffrage and the Equal Rights Amendment," an oral history conducted in 1972 and 1973 by Amelia R. Fry, Regional Oral History Office, University of California, 1976, p. 614. Courtesy, the Bancroft Library. Nora Stanton Barney to Alice Paul, n.d. [received May 10, 1945], National Woman's Party papers, reel 86.

36. Wright to Pollitzer, n.d. [July 1946], National Woman's Party papers, reel 89.

37. Agnes Wells to Pollitzer, August 24, 1946, National Woman's Party papers, reel 89.

38. Paul to Dorothy Griswold, February 2, 1955, National Woman's Party papers, reel 101.

39. Lavinia Dock to Paul, May 9, 1945, National Woman's Party papers, reel 86.

40. See, for example, Susan D. Becker, *The Origins of the Equal Rights Amendment: American Feminism Between the Wars* (Westport, Conn.: Greenwood Press, 1981), and Christine A. Lunardini, *From Equal Suffrage to Equal Rights: Alice Paul and the National Woman's Party, 1910–1928* (New York: New York University Press, 1986).

41. Vernon, "Speaker for Suffrage."

42. Paul, "Conversations," p. 197.

43. Jeannette Marks to Paul, March 25, 1945, National Woman's Party papers, reel 85; Marks to Paul, March 30, 1945, National Woman's Party papers, reel 85; Marks to Paul, April 27, 1945, National Woman's Party papers, reel 85.

44. Nina Allender to Paul, January 5, 1947, National Woman's Party papers, reel 90.

45. Paul to Allender, March 9, 1950, National Woman's Party papers, reel 96.

46. Paul to Allender, November 20, 1954, National Woman's Party papers, reel 100; Kay Boyle to Paul, December 5, 1954, National Woman's Party papers, reel 100; Paul to Nina, December 6, 1954, National Woman's Party papers, reel 100.

47. Boyle to Paul, February 13, 1957, National Woman's Party papers, reel 103; Paul to Boyle, March 5, 1957, National Woman's Party papers, reel 103.

48. See Leila J. Rupp, "The Women's Community in the National Woman's Party, 1945 to the 1960s," *Signs* 10 (1985): 715–40.

49. Letter to Anna Lord Strauss, December 22, 1945, Strauss papers, box 6 (118), Schlesinger Library. Because of the possibly sensitive nature of the material reported here, I am not using the names of the women involved.

50. Letter to Strauss, September 19, 1946, Strauss papers, box 6 (119), Schlesinger Library.

51. Letter to Strauss, May 9, 1947, Strauss papers, box 6 (121), Schlesinger Library.

52. Letter to Strauss, June 28, 1948, Strauss papers, box 6 (124), Schlesinger Library.

53. Letter to Strauss, February 26, 1951, Strauss papers, box 1 (15), Schlesinger Library.

54. Letter to Strauss, December 22, 1945, Strauss papers, box 6 (118), Schlesinger Library.

55. Letter to Strauss, May 9, 1947, Strauss papers, box 6 (121), Schlesinger Library.

56. "Stream of consciousness," March 10, 1948, Strauss papers, box 6 (124), Schlesinger Library.

57. Augusta Street to Strauss, n.d. [1968], Strauss papers, box 7 (135), Schlesinger Library.

58. Letter to Strauss, February 11, 1949, Strauss papers, box 6 (125), Schlesinger Library.

59. Letter to Strauss, March 3, 1949, Strauss papers, box 6 (125), Schlesinger Library.

60. Letter to Strauss, March 8, 1968, Strauss papers, box 7 (135), Schlesinger Library.

61. Lilian Lyndon to Strauss, April 23, 1950, Strauss papers, box 1 (14), Schlesinger Library.

62. Diary entries, August 30, 1953 and September 1, 1953, Doris Stevens papers, Schlesinger Library.

63. Diary entry, August 24, 1953, Doris Stevens papers, Schlesinger Library.

64. Diary entry, February 4, 1946, Doris Stevens papers, Schlesinger Library.

65. Diary entry, December 1, 1945, Doris Stevens papers, Schlesinger Library.

66. Katharine Callery to Stevens, Aug. 17, 1944, Stevens papers, Schlesinger Library.

67. Stevens to Westbrook Pegler, May 3, 1946, Stevens papers, Schlesinger Library.

68. See Margaret Jackson, "Sexual Liberation or Social Control? Some Aspects of the Relationship between Feminism and the Social Construction of Sexual Knowledge in the Early Twentieth Century," *Women's Studies International Forum* 6 (1983): 1–17; Carroll Smith-Rosenberg, "Discourses of Sexuality and Subjectivity: The New Woman, 1870–1936," in this volume; and John D'Emilio, "The Homosexual Menace: The Politics of Sexuality in Cold War America," unpublished paper presented at the Organization of American Historians Conference, Philadelphia, 1982.

69. India Edwards, *Pulling No Punches* (New York: Putnam's 1977), pp. 189–90.

70. Interviews by Leila J. Rupp and Verta Taylor; see Rupp and Taylor, *Survival in the Doldrums*.

71. Paul, "Conversations," pp. 195–96.

72. Interview conducted by Taylor and Rupp, December 10, 1979.

73. Sasha Gregory Lewis, *Sunday's Women: A Report on Lesbian Life Today* (Boston: Beacon Press, 1979), p. 94.

74. See, for an example, the discussion in Judith C. Brown, *Immodest Acts: The Life of a Lesbian Nun in Renaissance Italy* (New York: Oxford University Press, 1986), pp. 171–73.

75. Nestle, "Butch-Fem Relationships."

76. Much of the literature on lesbianism emphasizes this crucial distinction between identity and experience. See, for example, Barbara Ponse, *Identities in the Lesbian World: The Social Construction of Self* (Westport, Conn.: Greenwood Press, 1978); and E.M. Ettore, *Lesbians, Women and Society* (London: Routledge & Kegan Paul, 1980).

77. Cook, "Historical Denial," p. 64.

78. The Mount Holyoke administration closed the Marks-Woolley papers when Wells discovered the love letters, and the papers are only open to researchers now because an American Historical Association committee, which included Blanche Cook as one of its members, applied pressure to keep the papers open after Wells, to her credit, contacted them. Faber describes her unsuccessful attempts to persuade the archivists at the FDR Library to close the Lorena Hickok papers.

79. Linda Gordon, "What Should Women's Historians Do: Politics, Social Theory, and Women's History," *Marxist Perspectives* 3 (1978), 128–36.

Doing Desire: Adolescent Girls' Struggles for/with Sexuality

DEBORAH L. TOLMAN

In order to perpetuate itself, every oppression must corrupt or distort those various sources of power within the culture of the oppressed that can provide energy for change. For women, this has meant suppression of the erotic as a considered source of power and information within our lives.

(Lorde 1984, 53)

Recent research suggests that adolescence is the crucial moment in the development of psychological disempowerment for many women (e.g., Brown and Gilligan 1992; Gilligan 1990). As they enter adolescence, many girls may lose an ability to speak about what they know, see, feel, and experience evident in childhood as they come under cultural pressure to be "nice girls" and ultimately "good women" in adolescence. When their bodies take on women's contours, girls begin to be seen as sexual, and sexuality becomes an aspect of adolescent girls' lives; yet "nice" girls and "good" women are not supposed to be sexual outside of heterosexual, monogamous marriage (Tolman 1991). Many girls experience a "crisis of connection," a relational dilemma of how to be oneself and stay in relationships with others who may not want to know the truth of girls' experiences (Gilligan 1989). In studies of adolescent girls' development, many girls have demonstrated the ironic tendency to silence their own thoughts and feelings for the sake of relationships, when what they think and feel threatens to be disruptive

Deborah L. Tolman, "Doing Desire: Adolescent Girls' Struggles for/with Sexuality," *Gender & Society* 8, no. 3 (September 1994). Copyright © 1994 by Sociologists for Women in Society. Reprinted with the permission of Sage Publications, Inc.

(Brown and Gilligan 1992). At adolescence, the energy needed for resistance to crushing conventions of femininity often begins to get siphoned off for the purpose of maintaining cultural standards that stand between women and their empowerment. Focusing explicitly on embodied desire, Tolman and Debold (1993) observed similar patterns in the process of girls learning to look at, rather than experience, themselves to know themselves from the perspective of men, thereby losing touch with their own bodily feelings and desires. It is at this moment in their development that many women will start to experience and develop ways of responding to their own sexual feelings. Given these realities, what are adolescent girls' experiences of sexual desire? How do girls enter their sexual lives and learn to negotiate or respond to their sexuality?

Despite the real gains that feminism and the sexual revolution achieved in securing women's reproductive rights and increasing women's sexual liberation (Rubin 1990), the tactics of silencing and denigrating women's sexual desire are deeply entrenched in this patriarchal society (Brown 1991). The Madonna/whore dichotomy is alternately virulent and subtle in the cultures of adolescents (Lees 1986; Tolman 1992). Sex education curricula name male adolescent sexual desire; girls are taught to recognize and to keep a lid on the sexual desire of boys but not taught to acknowledge or even to recognize their own sexual feelings (Fine 1988; Tolman 1991). The few feminist empirical studies of girls' sexuality suggest that sexual desire is a complicated, important experience for adolescent girls about which little is known. In an ethnographic study, Fine noticed that adolescent girls' sexuality was acknowledged by adults in school, but in terms that denied the sexual subjectivity of girls; this "missing discourse of desire" was, however, not always absent from the ways girls themselves spoke about their sexual experiences

(Fine 1988). Rather than being "educated," girls' bodies are suppressed under surveillance and silenced in the schools (see also Lesko 1988). Although Fine ably conveys the existence of girls' discourse of desire, she does not articulate that discourse. Thompson collected 400 girls' narratives about sexuality, romance, contraception and pregnancy (Thompson 1984, 1990) in which girls' desire seems frequently absent or not relevant to the terms of their sexual relationships. The minority of girls who spoke of sexual pleasure voiced more sexual agency than girls whose experiences were devoid of pleasure. Within the context of girls' psychological development, Fine's and Thompson's work underscore the need to understand what girls' experiences of their sexual desire are like.

A psychological analysis of this experience for girls can contribute an understanding of both the possibilities and limits for sexual freedom for women in the current social climate. By identifying how the culture has become anchored in the interior of women's lives—an interior that is birthed through living in the exterior of material conditions and relationships—this approach can keep distinct women's psychological responses to sexual oppression and also the sources of that oppression. This distinction is necessary for avoiding the trap of blaming women for the ways our minds and bodies have become constrained.

METHODOLOGICAL DISCUSSION

Sample and Data Collection

To examine this subject, I interviewed 30 girls who were juniors in an urban and a suburban public high school ($n = 28$) or members of a gay and lesbian youth group ($n = 2$). They were 16.5 years old on average and randomly selected. The girls in the larger study are a heterogeneous group, representing different races and ethnic backgrounds (Black, including Haitian and African American; Latina, including Puerto Rican and Colombian; Euro-American, including Eastern and Western European), religions (Catholic, Jewish, and Protestant), and sexual experiences. With the exception of one Puerto Rican girl, all of the girls from the suburban school were Euro-American; the racial/ethnic diversity in the sample is represented by the urban school. Interviews with school personnel confirmed that the student population of the urban school was almost exclusively poor or working class and the students in the suburban school were middle and upper-middle class. This information is important in that my focus is on how girls'

social environments shape their understanding of their sexuality. The fact that girls who live in the urban area experience the visibility of and discourse about violence, danger and the consequences of unprotected sex, and that the suburban girls live in a community that offers a veneer of safety and stability, informs their experiences of sexuality. Awareness of these features of the social contexts in which these girls are developing is essential for listening to and understanding their narratives about sexual experiences.

The data were collected in one-on-one, semistructured clinical interviews (Brown and Gilligan 1992). This method of interviewing consists of following a structured interview protocol that does not direct specific probes but elicits narratives. The interviewer listens carefully to a girl, taking in her voice, and responding with questions that will enable the girl to clarify her story and know she is being heard. In these interviews, I asked girls direct questions about desire to elicit descriptions and narratives. Most of the young women wove their concerns about danger into the narratives they told.

Analytic Strategy

To analyze these narratives, I used the Listening Guide—an interpretive methodology that joins hermeneutics and feminist standpoint epistemology (Brown et al. 1991). It is a voice-centered, relational method by which a researcher becomes a listener, taking in the voice of a girl, developing an interpretation of her experience. Through multiple readings of the same text, this method makes audible the "polyphonic and complex" nature of voice and experience (Brown and Gilligan 1992, 15). Both speaker and listener are recognized as individuals who bring thoughts and feelings to the text, acknowledging the necessary subjectivity of both participants. Self-consciously embedded in a standpoint acknowledging that patriarchal culture silences and obscures women's experiences, the method is explicitly psychological and feminist in providing the listener with an organized way to respond to the coded or indirect language of girls and women, especially regarding topics such as sexuality that girls and women are not supposed to speak of. This method leaves a trail of evidence for the listener's interpretation, and thus leaves room for other interpretations by other listeners consistent with the epistemological stance that there is multiple meaning in such stories. I present *a* way to understand the stories these young women chose to tell me, our story as I have heard and understood it. Therefore, in the interpretations that follow I include my responses, those of an adult woman, to these girls' words, providing information about girls' experiences of sexual desire much like countertransference informs psychotherapy.

Adolescent Girls' Experiences of Sexual Desire

The first layer of the complexity of girls' experiences of their sexual desire was revealed initially in determining whether or not they felt sexual feelings. A majority of these girls (two-thirds) said unequivocally that they experienced sexual desire; in them I heard a clear and powerful way of speaking about the experience of feeling desire that was explicitly relational and also embodied. Only three of the girls said they did not experience sexual feelings, describing silent bodies and an absence of or intense confusion about romantic or sexual relationships. The remaining girls evidenced confusion or spoke in confusing ways about their own sexual feelings. Such confusion can be understood as a psychic solution to sexual feelings that arise in a culture that denigrates, suppresses, and heightens the dangers of girls' sexuality and in which contradictory messages about women's sexuality abound.

For the girls who said they experienced sexual desire, I turned my attention to how they said they responded to their sexual feelings. What characterized their responses was a sense of struggle; the question of "doing desire"—that is, what to do when they felt sexual desire—was not straightforward for any of them. While speaking of the power of their embodied feelings, the girls in this sample described the difficulties that their sexual feelings posed, being aware of both the potential for pleasure and the threat of danger that their desire holds for them. The struggle took different shapes for different girls, with some notable patterns emerging. Among the urban girls, the focus was on how to stay safe from bodily harm, in and out of the context of relational or social consequences, whereas among the suburban girls the most pronounced issue was how to maintain a sense of themselves as "good" and "normal" girls (Tolman 1992). In this article, I will offer portraits of three girls. By focusing on three girls in depth, I can balance an approach to "variance" with the kind of case study presentation that enables me to illustrate both similarities and differences in how girls in the larger sample spoke about their sexual feelings. These three girls represent different sexual preferences—one heterosexual, one bisexual, and one lesbian.[1] I have chosen to forefront the difference of sexual preference because it has been for some women a source of empowerment and a route to community; it has also been a source of divisiveness among feminists. Through this approach, I can illustrate

both the similarities and differences in their experiences of sexual desire, which are nested in their individual experiences as well as their social contexts. Although there are many other demarcations that differentiate these girls—social class, race, religion, sexual experience—and this is not the most pervasive difference in this sample,[2] sexual preference calls attention to the kinds of relationships in which girls are experiencing or exploring their sexual desire and which take meaning from gender arrangements and from both the presence and absence of institutionalization (Fine 1988; Friend 1993). Because any woman whose sexuality is not directly circumscribed by heterosexual, monogamous marriage is rendered deviant in our society, all adolescent girls bear suspicion regarding their sexuality, which sexual preference highlights. In addition, questions of identity are heightened at adolescence.

Rochelle Doing Desire

Rochelle is a tall, larger, African American girl who is heterosexual. Her small, sweet voice and shy smile are a startling contrast to her large body, clothed in white spandex the day of our interview. She lives in an urban area where violence is embedded in the fabric of everyday life. She speaks about her sexual experience with a detailed knowledge of how her sexuality is shaped, silenced, denigrated, and possible in relationships with young men. As a sophomore, she thought she "had to get a boyfriend" and became "eager" for a sexual relationship. As she describes her first experience of sexual intercourse, she describes a traditional framing of male-female relationships:

> I felt as though I had to conform to everything he said that, you know, things that a girl and a guy were supposed to do, so like, when the sex came, like, I did it without thinking, like, I wish I would have waited . . . we started kissing and all that stuff and it just happened. And when I got, went home, I was like, I was shocked, I was like, why did I do that? I wish I wouldn't a did it.

Did you want to do it?

> Not really. Not really. I just did it because, maybe because he wanted it, and I was always like tryin' to please him and like, he was real mean, mean to me, now that I think about it. I was like kind of stupid, cause like I did everything for him and he just treated me like I was nothing and I just thought I had just to stay with him because I needed a boyfriend so bad to make my life complete but like now it's different.

Rochelle's own sexual desire is absent in her story of defloration—in fact, she seems to be missing altogether. In a virtual caricature of dominant cultural conventions of femininity, Rochelle connects her disappearance at the moment of sex—"it just happened"—to her attempts to fulfill the cultural guidelines for how to "make [her] life complete." She has sex because "he wanted it," a response that holds no place for whether or not she feels desire. In reflecting on this arrangement, Rochelle now feels she was "stupid . . . to do everything for him" and in her current relationship, things are "different." As she explains: "I don't take as much as I did with the first guy, cause like, if he's doin' stuff that I don't like, I tell him, I'll go, I don't like this and I think you shouldn't do it and we compromise, you know. I don't think I can just let him treat me bad and stuff."

During the interview, I begin to notice that desire is not a main plot line in Rochelle's stories about her sexual experiences, especially in her intimate relationships. When I ask her about her experiences of sexual pleasure and sexual desire, she voices contradictions. On one hand, as the interview unfolds, she is more and more clear that she does not enjoy sex: "I don't like sex" quickly becomes "I hate sex . . . I don't really have pleasure." On the other hand, she explains that

> there are certain times when I really really really enjoy it, but then, that's like, not a majority of the times, it's only sometimes, once in a while . . . if I was to have sex once a month, then I would enjoy it . . . if I like go a long period of time without havin' it then, it's really good to me, cause it's like, I haven't had something for a long time and I miss it. It's like, say I don't eat cake a lot, but say, like every two months, I had some cake, then it would be real good to me, so that's like the same thing.

Rochelle conveys a careful knowledge of her body's hunger, her need for tension as an aspect of her sexual pleasure, but her voiced dislike of sex suggests that she does not feel she has much say over when and how she engages in sexual activity.

In describing her experiences with sexuality, I am overwhelmed at how frequently Rochelle says that she "was scared." She is keenly aware of the many consequences that feeling and responding to her sexual desire could have. She is scared of being talked about and getting an undeserved reputation: "I was always scared that if I did that (had sexual intercourse) I would be portrayed as, you know, something bad." Even having sex within the confines of a rela-

tionship, which has been described by some girls as a safe haven for their sexuality (Rubin 1990; Tolman 1992), makes her vulnerable; she "could've had a bad reputation, but luckily he wasn't like that"; he did not choose to tell other boys (who then tell girls) about their sexual activity. Thinking she had a sexually transmitted disease was scary. Because she had been faithful to her boyfriend, having such a disease would mean having to know that her boyfriend cheated on her and would also make her vulnerable to false accusations of promiscuity from him. Her concern about the kind of woman she may be taken for is embedded in her fear of using contraception: "When you get birth control pills, people automatically think you're having sex every night and that's not true." Being thought of as sexually insatiable or out of control is a fear that many girls voice (Tolman 1992); this may be intensified for African American girls, who are creating a sexual identity in a dominant cultural context that stereotypes Black women as alternately asexual and hypersexual (Spillers 1984).

Rochelle's history provides other sources of fear. After her boyfriend "flattened [her] face," when she realized she no longer wanted to be with him and broke off the relationship, she learned that her own desire may lead to male violence. Rochelle confided to me that she has had an abortion, suffering such intense sadness, guilt, and anxiety in the wake of it that, were she to become pregnant again, she would have the baby. For Rochelle, the risk of getting pregnant puts her education at risk, because she will have to sacrifice going to college. This goal is tied to security for her; she wants to "have something of my own before I get a husband, you know, so if he ever tries leavin' me, I have my own money." Given this wall of fears, I am not surprised when Rochelle describes a time when simply feeling desire made her "so scared that I started to cry." Feeling her constant and pervasive fear, I began to find it hard to imagine how she can feel any other feelings, including sexual ones.

I was thus caught off guard when I asked Rochelle directly if she has felt desire and she told me that she does experience sexual desire; however, she explained "most of the time, I'm by myself when I do." She launched, in breathless tones, into a story about an experience of her own sexual desire just the previous night:

> Last night, I had this crank call. . . . At first I thought it was my boyfriend, cause he likes to play around, you know. But I was sitting there talking, you know, and thinking of him and then I found out it's not him, it was so crazy weird, so I hang the phone up and he called back, he called back and called back. And then I couldn't

sleep, I just had this feeling that, I wanted to have sex so so bad. It was like three o'clock in the morning. And I didn't sleep the rest of the night. And like, I called my boyfriend and I was tellin' him, and he was like, what do you want me to do, Rochelle, I'm sleeping! [Laughs.] I was like, okay, okay, well I'll talk to you later, bye. And then, like, I don't know, I just wanted to, and like, I kept tossin' and turnin'. And I'm trying to think who it was, who was callin' me, cause like, it's always the same guy who always crank calls me, he says he knows me. It's kinda scary. . . . I can't sleep, I'm like, I just think about it, like, oh I wanna have sex so bad, you know, it's like a fever, drugs, something like that. Like last night, I don't know, I think if I woulda had the car and stuff, I probably woulda left the house. And went over to his house, you know. But I couldn't, cause I was babysitting.

When I told her that it sounds a little frightening but it sounds like there's something exciting about it, she smiled and leaned forward, exclaiming, "Yeah! It's like sorta arousing." I was struck by the intensity of her sexual feelings and also by the fact that she is alone and essentially assured of remaining alone due to the late hour and her responsibilities. By being alone, not subject to observation or physical, social, emotional, or material vulnerability, Rochelle experienced the turbulent feelings that are awakened by this call in her body. Rochelle's desire has not been obliterated by her fear; desire and fear both reverberate through her psyche. But she is not completely alone in this experience of desire, for her feelings occur in response to another person, whom she at first suspects is her boyfriend speaking from a safe distance, conveying the relational contours of her sexual desire. Her wish to bring her desire into her relationship, voiced in her response of calling her boyfriend, is in conflict with her fear of what might happen if she did pursue her wish—getting pregnant and having a baby, a consequence that Rochelle is desperate to avoid.

I am struck by her awareness of both the pleasure and danger in this experience and how she works the contradiction without dissociating from her own strong feelings. There is a brilliance and also a sadness in the logic her body and psyche have played out in the face of her experiences with sexuality and relationships. The psychological solution to the dilemma that desire means for her, of feeling sexual desire only when she cannot respond as she says she would like to, arises from her focus on these conflicts as personal experiences, which she suffers and solves privately. By identifying and solving the dilemma in this way,

Rochelle is diminished, as is the possibility of her developing a critique of these conflicts as not just personal problems but as social inequities that emerge in her personal relationships and on her body. Without this perspective, Rochelle is less likely to become empowered through her own desire to identify that the ways in which she must curtail herself and be curtailed by others are socially constructed, suspect, and in need of change.

Megan Doing Desire

Megan, a small, freckled, perky Euro-American, is dressed in baggy sweats, comfortable, unassuming, and counterpointed by her lively engagement in our interview.[3] She identifies herself as "being bisexual" and belongs to a gay youth group; she lives in a city in which wealth and housing projects coexist. Megan speaks of knowing she is feeling sexual desire for boys because she has "kind of just this feeling, you know? Just this feeling inside my body." She explains: "My vagina starts to kinda like act up and it kinda like quivers and stuff, and like I'll get like tingles and and, you can just feel your hormones (laughing) doing something weird, and you just, you get happy and you just get, you know, restimulated kind of and it's just, and Oh! Oh!" and "Your nerves feel good." Megan speaks about her sexual desire in two distinct ways, one for boys and one for girls. In our interview, she speaks most frequently about her sexual feelings in relation to boys. The power of her own desire and her doubt about her ability to control herself frighten her: "It scares me when I'm involved in a sexual situation and I just wanna go further and further and cause it just, and it scares me that, well, I have control, but if I even just let myself not have control, you know? . . . I'd have sex and I can't do that." Megan knows that girls who lose control over their desire like that can be called "sluts" and ostracized.

When asked to speak about an experience of sexual desire, Megan chooses to describe the safety of a heterosexual, monogamous relationship. She tells me how she feels when a boyfriend was "feeling me up"; not only is she aware of and articulate about his bodily reactions and her own, she narrates the relational synergy between her own desire and his:

I just wanted to go on, you know? Like I could feel his penis, you know, 'cause we'd kinda lied down you know, and, you just really get so into it and intense and, you just wanna, well you just kinda keep wanting to go on or something, but it just feels good. . . . His penis

THE MYTH OF THE PERFECT BODY

ROBERTA GALLER

A woman was experiencing severe abdominal pain. She was rushed to the emergency room and examined, then taken to the operating room, where an appendectomy was performed. After surgery, doctors concluded that her appendix was fine but that she had VD. It never occurred to them that this woman had a sexual life at all, because she was in a wheelchair.

I saw a woman who had cerebral palsy at a neuromuscular clinic. She was covered with bruises. After talking with her, it became clear that she was a battered wife. I brought her case to the attention of the medical director and social worker, both progressive practitioners who are knowledgeable about resources for battered women. They said, "But he supports her. Who else will take care of her? And besides, if she complains, the court might take custody of her children."

As a feminist and psychotherapist I am politically and professionally interested in the impact of body image on a woman's self-esteem and sense of sexuality. However, it is as a woman with a disability that I am personally involved with these issues. I had polio when I was 10 years old, and now with arthritis and some new aches and pains I feel in a rather exaggerated fashion other effects of aging, a progressive disability we all share to some degree.

Although I've been disabled since childhood, until the past few years I didn't know anyone else with a disability and in fact *avoided* knowing anyone with a disability. I had many of the same fears and anxieties

which many of you who are currently able-bodied might feel about close association with anyone with a disability. I had not opted for, but in fact rebelled against the prescribed role of dependence expected of women growing up when I did and which is still expected of disabled women. I became the "exceptional" woman, the "super-crip," noted for her independence. I refused to let my identity be shaped by my disability. I wanted to be known for *who* I am and not just by what I physically cannot do.

Although I was not particularly conscious of it at the time, I was additionally burdened with extensive conflicts about dependency and feelings of shame over my own imperfections and realistic limitations. So much of my image and definition of myself had been rooted in a denial of the impact of my disability. Unfortunately, my values and emphasis on independence involved an assumption that any form of help implied dependence and was therefore humiliating.

As the aging process accelerated the impact of my disability, it became more difficult to be stoic or heroic or ignore my increased need for help at times. This personal crisis coincided in time with the growing national political organization of disabled persons who were asserting their rights, demanding changes in public consciousness and social policy, and working to remove environmental and attitudinal barriers to the potential viability of their lives.

Disabled women also began a dialogue within the feminist community. On a personal level it has been through a slow process of disability consciousness-raising aided by newly-found "sisters in disability," as well as through profoundly moving discussions with close, non-disabled friends that we, through mutual support and self-disclosure, began to explore our feelings and to shed the shame and humiliation associated with needing help. We began to understand that to need help did not imply helplessness nor was it the opposite of independence. This increased appreciation of mutual interdependence as part of the human condition caused us to reexamine the feminist idea of autonomy versus dependence.

Feminists have long attacked the media image of "the Body Beautiful" as oppressive, exploitative, and objectifying. Even in our attempts to create alternatives, however, we develop standards which oppress some of us. The feminist ideal of autonomy does not take into account the realistic needs for help that disabled, aging—and, in fact, most—women have. The image of the physically strong "superwoman" is also out of reach for most of us.

As we began to develop disability consciousness, we recognized significant parallels to feminist consciousness. For example, it is clear that just as society creates an ideal of beauty which is oppressive for us all, it creates an ideal model of the physically perfect person who is not beset with weakness, loss, or pain. It is toward these distorted ideals of perfection in form and function that we all strive and with which we identify.

The disabled (and aging) woman poses a symbolic threat by reminding us how tenuous that model, "the myth of the perfect body," really is, and we might want to run from this thought. The disabled woman's body may not meet the standard of "perfection" in either image, form, or function. On the one hand, disabled women share the social stereotype of women in general as being weak and passive, and in fact are depicted as the epitome of the incompetent female. On the other hand, disabled women are not viewed as women at all, but portrayed as helpless, dependent children in need of protection. She is not seen as the sexy, but the sexless object, asexual, neutered, unbeautiful and unable to find a lover. This stigmatized view of the disabled woman reflects a perception of assumed inadequacy on the part of the non-disabled.

For instance, disabled women are often advised by professionals not to bear children, and are (within race and class groupings) more likely to be threatened by or be victims of involuntary sterilization. Concerns for reproductive freedom and child custody, as well as rape and domestic violence often exclude the disabled woman by assuming her to be an asexual creature. The perception that a disabled woman couldn't possibly get a man to care for or take care of her underlies the instances where professionals have urged disabled women who have been victims of brutal battery to stay with abusive males. Members of the helping professions often assume that no other men would want them.

Disability is often associated with sin, stigma and a kind of "untouchability." Anxiety, as well as a sense of vulnerability and dread, may cause others to respond to the "imperfections" of a disabled woman's body with terror, avoidance, pity and/or guilt. In a special *Off Our Backs* issue on disabled women, Jill Lessing postulated that it is "through fear and denial that attitudes of repulsion and oppression are acted out on disabled people in ways ranging from our solicitous good intentions to total invisibility and isolation."*

Even when the disabled woman is idealized for surmounting all obstacles, she is the recipient of a distancing admiration, which assumes her achievement to be necessary compensation for a lack of sexuality, intimacy, and love. The stereotype of the independent "super-crip," although embodying images of strength and courage, involves avoidance and denial of the realities of disability for both the observer and the disabled woman herself.

These discomforts may evoke a wish that disabled women remain invisible and that their sexuality be a hidden secret. However, disabled (and aging) women are coming out; we are beginning to examine our issues publicly, forcing other women to address not only the issues of disability but to reexamine their attitudes toward their own limitations and lack of perfection, toward oppressive myths, standards, and social conditions which affect us all. . . .

*Jill Lessing, "Denial and Disability," *Off Our Backs,* vol. xi, no. 5, May 1981, p. 21.

being on my leg made, you know, it hit a nerve or something, it did something because it just made me start to
get more horny or whatever, you know, it just made me
want to do more things and stuff. I don't know how, I
can't, it's hard for me to describe exactly how I felt, you
know like, (intake of breath) . . . when he gets more
excited then he starts to do more things and you can
kind of feel his pleasure and then you start to get more
excited.

With this young man, Megan knows her feelings of sexual
desire to be "intense," to have a momentum of their own,
and to be pleasurable. Using the concrete information of his
erection, she describes the relational contours of her own
embodied sexual desire, a desire that she is clear is her own
and located in her body but that also arises in response to
his excitement.

Although able to speak clearly in describing a specific
experience she has had with her desire, I hear confusion seep
into her voice when she notices that her feelings contradict
or challenge societal messages about girls and sexuality:

It's so confusing, 'cause you have to like say no, you
have to be the one to say no, but why should you be the
one to, cause I mean maybe you're enjoying it and you
shouldn't have to say no or anything. But if you don't,
maybe the guy'll just keep going and going, and you
can't do that, because then you would be a slut. There's
so [much] like, you know, stuff that you have to deal
with and I don't know, just I keep losing my thought.

Although she knows the logic offered by society—that she
must "say no" to keep him from "going and going," which
will make her "a slut"—Megan identifies what is missing
from that logic, that "maybe you're"—she, the girl—"the
one who is enjoying it." The fact that she may be experiencing sexual desire makes the scripted response—to
silence his body—dizzying. Because she does feel her own
desire and can identify the potential of her own pleasure,
Megan asks the next logical question, the question that can
lead to outrage, critique, and empowerment: "Why should
you have to be the one to [say no]?" But Megan also gives
voice to why sustaining the question is difficult; she knows
that if she does not conform, if she does not "say no"—both
to him and to herself—then she may be called a slut, which
could lead to denigration and isolation. Megan is caught in
the contradiction between the reality of her sexual feelings
in her body and the absence of her sexual feelings in the
cultural script for adolescent girls' sexuality. Her confusion

is an understandable response to this untenable and unfair
choice: a connection with herself, her body, and sexual
pleasure or a connection with the social world.

Megan is an avid reader of the dominant culture. Not
only has she observed the ways that messages about girls'
sexuality leave out or condemn her embodied feelings for
boys, she is also keenly aware of the pervasiveness of cultural norms and images that demand heterosexuality:

Every teen magazine you look at is like, guy this, how to
get a date, guys, guys, guys, guys, guys. So you're constantly faced with I have to have a boyfriend, I have to
have a boyfriend, you know, even if you don't have a
boyfriend, just [have] a fling, you know, you just want to
kiss a guy or something. I've had that mentality for so
long.

In this description of compulsory heterosexuality (Rich
1983), Megan captures the pressure she feels to have a
boyfriend and how she experiences the insistence of this
demand, which is ironically in conflict with the mandate to
say no when with a boy. She is aware of how her psyche
has been shaped into a "mentality" requiring any sexual or
relational interests to be heterosexual, which does not cor-
roborate how she feels. Compulsory heterosexuality comes
between Megan and her feelings, making her vulnerable to
a dissociation of her "feelings" under this pressure.

Although she calls herself bisexual, Megan does not
describe her sexual feelings for girls very much in this
interview. In fact, she becomes so confused that at one
point she says she is not sure if her feelings for girls are
sexual:

I mean, I'll see a girl I really really like, you know,
because I think she's so beautiful, and I might, I don't
know. I'm so confused. . . . But there's, you know, that
same mentality as me liking a guy if he's really cute,
I'm like, oh my God, you know, he's so cute. If I see a
woman that I like, a girl, it's just like wow, she's so
pretty, you know. See I can picture like hugging a girl; I
just can't picture the sex, or anything, so, there's something being blocked.

Megan links her confusion with her awareness of the
absence of images of lesbian sexuality in the spoken or
imagistic lexicon of the culture, counterpointing the pervasiveness of heterosexual imagery all around her. Megan
suggests that another reason that she might feel "confused"
about her feelings for girls is a lack of sexual experience.

Megan knows she is feeling sexual desire when she can identify feelings in her own body—when her "vagina acts up"—and these feelings occur for her in the context of a sexual relationship, when she can feel the other person's desire. Because she has never been in a situation with a girl that would allow this embodied sexual response, she posits a connection between her lack of sexual experience with girls and her confusion.

Yet she has been in a situation where she was "close to" a girl and narrates how she does not let her body speak:

> There was this one girl that I had kinda liked from school, and it was like really weird 'cause she's really popular and everything. And we were sitting next to each other during the movie and, kind of her leg was on my leg and I was like, wow, you know, and that was, I think that's like the first time that I've ever felt like sexual pleasure for a girl. But it's so impossible, I think I just like block it out, I mean, it could never happen. . . . I just can't know what I'm feeling. . . . I probably first mentally just say no, don't feel it, you know, maybe. But I never start to feel, I don't know. It's so confusing. 'Cause finally it's all right for me to like a girl, you know? Before it was like, you know, the two times that I really, that it was just really obvious that I liked them a lot, I had to keep saying no no no no, you know, I just would not let myself. I just hated myself for it, and this year now that I'm talking about it, now I can start to think about it.

Megan both narrates and interprets her dissociation from her embodied sexual feelings and describes the disciplinary stance of her mind over her body in how she "mentally" silences her body by saying "no," preempting her embodied response. Without her body's feelings, her embodied knowledge, Megan feels confused. If she runs interference with her own sexual feelings by silencing her body, making it impossible for her to feel her desire for girls, then she can avoid the problems she knows will inevitably arise if she feels sexual feelings she "can't know"—compulsory heterosexuality and homophobia combine to render this knowledge problematic for her. Fearing rejection, Megan keeps herself from feelings that could lead to disappointment, embarrassment, or frustration, leaving her safe in some ways, yet also psychologically vulnerable.

Echoing dominant cultural constructions of sexual desire, Megan links her desire for girls with feelings of fear: "I've had crushes on some girls . . . you can picture

yourself kissing a guy but then if you like a girl a lot and then you picture yourself kissing her, it's just like, I can't, you know, oh my God, no (laughs), you know it's like scary . . . it's society . . . you never would think of, you know, it's natural to kiss a girl." Megan's fear about her desire for girls is different from the fears associated with her desire for boys; whereas being too sexual with boys brings the stigma of being called a "slut," Megan fears "society" and being thought of as "unnatural" when it comes to her feelings for girls. Given what she knows about the heterosexual culture in which she is immersed—the pressure she feels to be interested in "guys" and also given what she knows about homophobia—there is an inherent logic in Megan's confused response to her feelings for girls.

Melissa Doing Desire

Melissa, dressed in a flowing gypsy skirt, white skin pale against the lively colors she wears, is clear about her sexual desire for girls, referring to herself as "lesbian"; she is also a member of a gay/lesbian youth group. In speaking of her desire, Melissa names not only powerful feelings of "being excited" and "wanting," but also more contained feelings; she has "like little crushes on like millions of people and I mean, it's enough for me." Living in a world defined as heterosexual, Melissa finds that "little crushes" have to suffice, given a lack of opportunity for sexual exploration or relationship: "I don't know very many people my age that are even bisexual or lesbians . . . so I pretty much stick to that, like, being hugely infatuated with straight people. Which can get a little touchy at times . . . realistically, I can't like get too ambitious, because that would just not be realistic."

At the forefront of how Melissa describes her desire is her awareness that her sexual feelings make her vulnerable to harm. Whereas the heterosexual girls in this study link their vulnerability to the outcomes of responding to their desire—pregnancy, disease, or getting a bad reputation—Melissa is aware that even the existence of her sexual desire for girls can lead to anger or violence if others know of it: "Well I'm really lucky that like nothing bad has happened or no one's gotten mad at me so far, that, by telling people about them, hasn't gotten me into more trouble than, it has, I mean, little things but not like, anything really awful. I think about that and I think it, sometimes, I mean, it could be more dangerous." In response to this threat of violence, Melissa attempts to restrain her own desire: "Whenever I start, I feel like I can't help looking at someone for more than a few seconds, and I keep, and I feel like I have to make myself not, stare at them or something." Another strategy is to express her desire covertly by being physically affectionate with other girls, a behavior that is common and acceptable; by keeping her sexuality secret, she can "hang all over [girls] and stuff and they wouldn't even think that I meant anything by it." I am not surprised that Melissa associates feeling sexual desire with frustration; she explains that she "find(s) it safer to just think about the person than what I wanna do, because if I think about that too much and I can't do it, then that'll just frustrate me," leading her to try to intervene in her feelings by "just think[ing] about the person" rather than about the more sexual things she "want(s) to do." In this way, Melissa may jeopardize her ability to know her sexual desire and, in focusing on containing what society has named improper feelings, minimize or exorcise her empowerment to expose that construction as problematic and unjust.

My questions about girls' sexual desire connect deeply with Melissa's own questions about herself; she is in her first intimate relationship, and this interview proves an opportunity to explore and clarify painful twinges of doubt that she had begun to have about it. This relationship began on the initiative of the other girl, with whom she had been very close, rather than out of any sexual feelings on Melissa's part. In fact, Melissa was surprised when her friend had expressed a sexual interest, because she had not "been thinking that" about this close friend. After a history of having to hold back her sexual desire, of feeling "frustrated" and being "hugely infatuated with straight people," rather than having the chance to explore her sexuality, Melissa's response to this potential relationship was that she "should take advantage of this situation." As the interview progresses, Melissa begins to question whether she is sexually attracted to this girl or "it's just sort of like I just wanted something like this for so long that I'm just taking advantage of the situation."

When I ask Melissa questions about the role of her body in her experience of sexual desire, her confusion at first intensifies:

Is that [your body] part of what feels like it might be missing?

(eight-second pause) It's not, well, sometimes, I mean I don't know how, what I feel all the time. It's hard like, because I mean I'm so confused about this. And it's hard like when it's actually happening to be like, ok, now how do I feel right now? How do I feel right now? How am I gonna feel about this? . . . I don't know, 'cause I don't know what to expect, and I haven't been

with anyone else so I don't know what's supposed to happen. So, I mean I'm pretty confused.

The way she speaks about monitoring her body suggests that she is searching for bodily feelings, making me wonder what, if anything, she felt. I discern what she does not say directly; that her body was silent in these sexual experiences. Her hunger for a relationship is palpable: "I really wanted someone really badly, I think, I was getting really sick of being by myself. . . . I would be like God, I really need someone." The desperation in her voice, and the sexual frustration she describes, suggest that her "want" and "need" are distinctly sexual as well as relational.

One reason that Melissa seems to be confused is that she felt a strong desire to be "mothered," her own mother having died last year. In trying to distinguish her different desires in this interview, Melissa began to distinguish erotic feelings from another kind of wanting she also experienced: she said that "it's more of like but I kind of feel like it's really more of like a maternal thing, that I really want her to take care of me and I just wanna touch someone and I just really like the feeling of just how I mean I like, when I'm with her and touching her and stuff. A lot, but it's not necessarily a sexual thing at this point." In contrast to her feelings for her girlfriend, Melissa describes feeling sexually attracted to another girl. In so doing, Melissa clarifies what is missing in these first sexual adventures, enabling her to know what had bothered her about her relationship with her girlfriend:

I don't really think I'm getting that much pleasure, from her, it's just, I mean it's almost like I'm getting experience, and I'm sort of having fun, it's not even that exciting, and that's why I think I don't really like her . . . because my friend asked me this the other day, well, I mean does it get, I mean when you're with her does it get really, I don't remember the word she used, but just really, like what was the word she used? But I guess she meant just like, exciting [laughing]. But it doesn't, to me. It's weird, because I can't really say that, I mean I can't think of like a time when I was really excited and it was like really, sexual pleasure, for me, because I don't think it's really like that. I mean not that I think that this isn't good because, I don't know, I mean, I like it, but I mean I think I have to, sort of realize that I'm not that much attracted to her, personally.

Wanting both a relationship and sexual pleasure, a chance to explore closeness and her sexual curiosity, and discovering that this relationship leaves out her sexual desire, Melissa laments her silent body: "I sort of expect or hope or whatever that there would be some kind of more excited feeling just from feeling sexually stimulated or whatever. I would hope that there would be more of a feeling than I've gotten so far." Knowing consciously what she "knows" about the absence of her sexual feelings in this relationship has left her with a relational conflict of large proportions for her: "I'm not that attracted to her and I don't know if I should tell her that. Or if I should just kind of pretend I am and try to . . . anyway" I ask her how she would go about doing that—pretending that she is. She replies, "I don't think I could pretend it for too long." Not being able to "pretend" to have feelings that she knows she wants as part of an intimate relationship, Melissa faces a dilemma of desire that may leave her feeling isolated and lonely or even fraudulent.

ADOLESCENT GIRLS' SEXUAL DESIRE AND THE POSSIBILITIES OF EMPOWERMENT

All of the girls in this study who said they felt sexual desire expressed conflict when describing their responses to their sexual feelings—conflict between their embodied sexual feelings and their perceptions of how those feelings are, in one way or another, anathema or problematic within the social and relational contexts of their lives. Their experiences of sexual desire are strong and pleasurable, yet they speak very often not of the power of desire but of how their desire may get them into trouble. These girls are beginning to voice the internalized oppression of their women's bodies; they knew and spoke about, in explicit or more indirect ways, the pressure they felt to silence their desire, to dissociate from those bodies in which they inescapably live. Larger societal forces of social control in the form of compulsory heterosexuality (Rich 1983), the policing of girls' bodies through school codes (Lesko 1988), and media images play a clear part in forcing this silence and dissociation. Specific relational dynamics, such as concern about a reputation that can easily be besmirched by other girls and by boys, fear of male violence in intimate relationships, and fear of violent repercussion of violating norms of heterosexuality are also audible in these girls' voices.

To be able to know their sexual feelings, to listen when their bodies speak about themselves and about their relationships, might enable these and other girls to identify and know more clearly the sources of oppression that press on their full personhood and their capacity for knowledge, joy, and connection. Living in the margins of a heterosexual society, the bisexual and lesbian girls voice an awareness of these forces as formative of the experiences of their bodies and relationships; the heterosexual girls are less clear and less critical about the ways that dominant constructions of their sexuality impinge on their embodied and relational worlds. Even when they are aware that societal ambivalence and fears are being played out on their minds and bodies, they do not speak of a need for collective action, or even the possibility of engaging in such activities. More often, they speak of the danger of speaking about desire at all. By dousing desire with fear and confusion, or simple, "uncomplicated" denial, silence, and dissociation, the girls in this study make individual psychological moves whereby they distance or disconnect themselves from discomfort and danger. Although disciplining their bodies and curbing their desire is a very logical and understandable way to stay physically, socially, and emotionally safe, it also heightens the chance that girls and women may lose track of the fact that an inequitable social system, and not a necessary situation, renders women's sexual desire a source of danger, rather than one of pleasure and power in their lives. In "not knowing" desire, girls and women are at risk for not knowing that there is nothing wrong with having sexual feelings and responding to them in ways that bring joy and agency.

Virtually every girl in the larger study told me that no woman had ever talked to her about sexual desire and pleasure "like this"—in depth, listening to her speak about her own experiences, responding when she asked questions about how to masturbate, how to have cunnilingus, what sex is like after marriage. In the words of Rubin: "The ethos of privacy and silence about our personal sexual experience makes it easy to rationalize the refusal to speak [to adolescents]" (1990, 83; Segal 1993). Thompson (1990) found that daughters of women who had talked with them about pleasure and desire told narratives about first intercourse that were informed by pleasure and agency. The recurrent strategy the girls in my study describe of keeping their desire under wraps as a way to protect themselves also keeps girls out of authentic relationships with other girls and women. It is within these relationships that the empowerment of women can develop and be nurtured through shared experiences of both oppression and power, in which collectively articulated critiques are carved out and voiced. Such knowledge of how a patriarchal society systematically keeps girls and women from their own desire can instigate demand and agency for social change. By not talking about sexual desire with each other or with women, a source for empowerment is lost. There is a symbiotic interplay between desire and empowerment: to be empowered to desire one needs a critical perspective, and that critical perspective will be extended and sustained through knowing and experiencing the possibilities of desire and healthy embodied living. Each of these girls illustrates the phenomenon observed in the larger study—the difficulty for girls in having or sustaining a critical perspective on the culture's silencing of their sexual desire. They are denied full access to the power of their own desire and to structural supports for that access.

Common threads of fear and joy, pleasure and danger, weave through the narratives about sexual desire in this study, exemplified by the three portraits. Girls have the right to be informed that gaining pleasure and a strong sense of self and power through their bodies does not make them bad or unworthy. The experiences of these and other adolescent girls illustrate why girls deserve to be educated about their sexual desire. Thompson concludes that "to take possession of sexuality in the wake of the anti-erotic sexist socialization that remains the majority experience, most teenage girls need an erotic education" (1990, 406). Girls need to be educated about the duality of their sexuality, to have safe contexts in which they can explore both danger and desire (Fine 1988) and to consider why their desire is so dangerous and how they can become active participants in their own redemption. Girls can be empowered to know and act on their own desire, a different educational direction than the simplistic strategies for avoiding boys' desire that they are offered. The "just say no" curriculum obscures the larger social inequities being played out on girls' bodies in heterosexual relationships and is not relevant for girls who feel sexual feelings for girls. Even adults who are willing or able to acknowledge that girls experience sexual feelings worry that knowing about their own sexual desire will place girls in danger (Segal 1993). But keeping girls in the dark about their power to choose based on their own feelings fails to keep them any safer from these dangers. Girls who trust their minds and bodies may experience a stronger sense of self, entitlement, and empowerment that could enhance their ability to make safe decisions. One approach to educating girls is for women to speak to them about the vicissitudes of sexual desire—which means that women must let themselves speak and know their own sexual feelings, as well as the pleasures and dangers associated with women's sexuality and the solutions that we have wrought to the dilemma of desire: how to balance the realities of pleasure and danger in women's sexuality.

Asking these girls to speak about sexual desire, and listening and responding to their answers and also to their questions, proved to be an effective way to interrupt the standard "dire consequences" discourse adults usually employ when speaking at all to girls about their sexuality. Knowing and speaking about the ways in which their sexuality continues to be unfairly constrained may interrupt the appearance of social equity that many adolescent girls (especially white, middle-class young women) naively and trustingly believe, thus leading them to reject feminism as unnecessary and mean-spirited and not relevant to their lives. As we know from the consciousness-raising activities that characterized the initial years of second-wave feminism, listening to the words of other girls and women can make it possible for girls to know and voice their experiences, their justified confusion and fears, their curiosities. Through such relationships, we help ourselves and each other to live in our different female bodies with an awareness of danger, but also with a desire to feel the power of the erotic, to fine-tune our bodies and our psyches to what Audre Lorde has called the "yes within ourselves" (Lorde 1984, 54).

NOTES

1. The bisexual girl and the lesbian girl were members of a gay/lesbian youth group and identify themselves using these categories. As is typical for members of privileged groups for whom membership is a given, the girls who feel sexual desire for boys and not for girls (about which they were asked explicitly) do not use the term "heterosexual" to describe themselves. Although I am aware of the debate surrounding the use of these categories and labels to delimit women's (and men's) experience, because my interpretive practice is informed by the ways society makes meaning of girls' sexuality, the categories that float in the culture as ways of describing the girls are relevant to my analysis. In addition, the bisexual and lesbian girls in this study are deeply aware of compulsory heterosexuality and its impact on their lives.

2. Of the 30 girls in this sample, 27 speak of a desire for boys and not for girls. This pattern was ascertained by who appeared in their desire narratives and also by their response to direct questions about sexual feelings for girls, designed explicitly to interrupt the hegemony of heterosexuality. Two of the 30 girls described sexual desire for both boys and girls and one girl described sexual desire for girls and not for boys.

3. Parts of this analysis appear in Tolman (1994).

REFERENCES

Brown, L. 1991. Telling a girl's life: Self authorization as a form of resistance. In *Women, girls and psychotherapy: Reframing resistance,* edited by C. Gilligan, A. Rogers, and D. Tolman. New York: Haworth.

Brown, L., E. Debold, M. Tappan, and C. Gilligan. 1991. Reading narratives of conflict for self and moral voice: A relational method. In *Handbook of moral behavior and development: Theory, research, and application,* edited by W. Kurtines and J. Gewirtz. Hillsdale, NJ: Lawrence Erlbaum.

Brown, L., and C. Gilligan. 1992. *Meeting at the crossroads: Women's psychology and girls' development.* Cambridge, MA: Harvard University Press.

Fine, Michelle. 1988. Sexuality, schooling and adolescent females: The missing discourse of desire. *Harvard Educational Review* 58:29–53.

Friend, Richard. 1993. Choices, not closets. In *Beyond silenced voices,* edited by M. Fine and L. Weis. New York: State University of New York Press.

Gilligan, Carol. 1989. Teaching Shakespeare's sister. In *Making connections: The relational world of adolescent girls at Emma Willard School,* edited by C. Gilligan, N. Lyons, and T. Hamner. Cambridge, MA: Harvard University Press.

———. 1990. Joining the resistance: Psychology, politics, girls and women. *Michigan Quarterly Review* 29:501–36.

Lees, Susan. 1986. *Losing out: Sexuality and adolescent girls.* London: Hutchinson.

Lesko, Nancy. 1988. The curriculum of the body: Lessons from a Catholic high school. In *Becoming feminine: The politics of popular culture,* edited by L. Roman. Philadelphia: Falmer.

Lorde, Audre. 1984. The uses of the erotic as power. In *Sister outsider: Essays and speeches.* Freedom, CA: Crossing Press.

Miller, Jean Baker. 1976. *Towards a new psychology of woman.* Boston: Beacon Press.

Rich, Adrienne. 1983. Compulsory heterosexuality and lesbian existence. In *Powers of desire: The politics of sexuality,* edited by A. Snitow, C. Stansell, and S. Thompson. New York: Monthly Review Press.

Rubin, Lillian. 1990. *Erotic wars: What happened to the sexual revolution?* New York: HarperCollins.

Segal, Lynne. 1993. Introduction. In *Sex exposed: Sexuality and the pornography debate,* edited by L. Segal and M. McIntosh. New Brunswick, NJ: Rutgers University Press.

Spillers, Hortense. 1984. Interstices: A small drama of words. In *Pleasure and danger: Exploring female sexuality,* edited by C. Vance. Boston: Routledge and Kegan Paul.

Thompson, Sharon. 1984. Search for tomorrow: On feminism and the reconstruction of teen romance. In *Pleasure and danger: Exploring female sexuality,* edited by C. Vance. Boston: Routledge and Kegan Paul.

———. 1990. Putting a big thing in a little hole: Teenage girls' accounts of sexual initiation. *Journal of Sex Research* 27:341–61.

Tolman, Deborah L. 1991. Adolescent girls, women and sexuality: Discerning dilemmas of desire. *Women girls and psychotherapy: Reframing resistance,* edited by C. Gilligan, A. Rogers, and D. Tolman. New York: Haworth.

———. 1992. Voicing the body: A psychological study of adolescent girls' sexual desire. Unpublished dissertation, Harvard University.

———. 1994. Daring to desire: Culture and the bodies of adolescent girls. In *Sexual cultures: Adolescents, communities and the construction of identity,* edited by J. Irvine. Philadelphia: Temple University Press.

Tolman, Deborah, and Elizabeth Debold. 1993. Conflicts of body and image: Female adolescents, desire, and the no-body. In *Feminist treatment and therapy of eating disorders,* edited by M. Katzman, P. Fallon, and S. Wooley. New York: Guilford.

S E C T I O N   E I G H T

Bodies and Medicine

It might seem that women's physical bodies and health are biological matters, rather than social. In fact, however, factors like access to health care, working conditions, and nutrition are all socially determined. In addition, cultural ideologies about women's bodies affect how we perceive our own bodies, as well as how social institutions regulate women's bodies and health. Women's bodies are *contested terrain,* the subject of struggle over political rights, reproductive control, and access to woman-defined health care and medical research. Much feminist scholarship and activism focuses on women's health issues. Women's rights to control their reproductive lives, to live and work in conditions not injurious to their health, and to receive safe, effective, and affordable medical care are central to women's welfare. Feminists have devoted considerable energy to changing public health policy on women's behalf and to increasing research funding to women's health issues during the last two decades.

In the 1970s a women's health movement developed in the United States as an outgrowth of the feminist and consumer health movements. Women's health advocates criticized and challenged the tendency of the existing medical establishment to view women as abnormal and inherently diseased simply because the female reproductive cycle deviates from the male. Women today across the world are asserting the right to control their own bodies by exposing and resisting the medical abuse of women in forms ranging from forced sterilization and sex selection against females to pharmaceutical experi-

mentation. Women are also increasing their control over their own health care by enhancing women's access to information and specialized training that allow them to more accurately assess their health care needs and make informed decisions about medical treatment.

This section explores the social construction of women's bodies, the role of medicine in the maintenance of gender inequality, and issues related to women's health, including what illness tells us about women's position in society.

In "Hormonal Hurricanes: Menstruation, Menopause, and Female Behavior," Anne Fausto-Sterling examines traditional research on menstruation and menopause and finds that it reflects a deep bias against women by advancing the view that women are "slaves of their reproductive physiologies." Reviewing recent feminist studies of premenstrual syndrome and menopause, Fausto-Sterling suggests other approaches to women's health issues. Her work forces us to realize that social contexts deeply affect medical interpretations of the female reproductive cycle.

Social contexts also shape and create health problems for women. Becky Waansgard Thompson examines the social roots of women's eating problems in "'A Way Outa No Way': Eating Problems among African-American, Latina, and White Women." Thompson argues that compulsive eating, compulsive dieting, anorexia, and bulimia are coping strategies that women employ in response to sexual abuse, poverty, heterosexism, racism, and "class injuries." Eating problems are thus not just about conforming to a norm of physical appearance, but are also a "serious response to injustices." Thompson's article illustrates how examining women's multiple oppressions—race, class, and sexuality as well as gender—can alter feminist analyses.

Angela Davis examines the ways that racism and class inequality have shaped the ideology and practice of motherhood and reproduction in the United States, in "Outcast Mothers and Surrogates: Racism and Reproductive Politics in the Nineties." Davis shows how motherhood and reproduction have been constructed differently for women of color and poor women than for white, middle-class women. She traces the historical view of enslaved African women as breeders and "surrogate mothers" to the children of white slave-owners and discusses how contemporary women of color and poor women are denigrated as single teen mothers, lack access to abortion, and remain subject to involuntary sterilization. Motherhood has been glorified,

on the other hand, for white, middle or upper-class women, and current infertility technologies continue to encourage women with the financial means to become biological mothers at any cost. In short, Davis illustrates how racism and class inequality affect the politics of reproduction.

The final article in this section, "The Politics of Breast Cancer," by Susan M. Love, M.D., documents women's attempts to increase funding for breast cancer research. Breast cancer remains largely a medical mystery, with little known about its causes, prevention, or effective treatment. Nevertheless, Love shows, it received little attention and few resources from the federal government until breast cancer survivors began intensive protest and lobbying efforts. These activists' success in raising money and affecting the direction of scientific research provides an illustration of women's resistance to their treatment by the male-dominated medical institution. Along these lines, how do the three earlier readings in this section illustrate women's resistance?

Hormonal Hurricanes:
Menstruation, Menopause, and Female Behavior

ANNE FAUSTO-STERLING

Woman is a pair of ovaries with a human being attached, whereas man is a human being furnished with a pair of testes.

—*Rudolf Virchow, M.D. (1821–1902)*

Estrogen is responsible for that strange mystical phenomenon, the feminine state of mind.

—*David Reuben, M.D., 1969*

In 1900, the president of the American Gynecological Association eloquently accounted for the female life cycle:

Many a young life is battered and forever crippled in the breakers of puberty; if it crosses these unharmed and is not dashed to pieces on the rock of childbirth, it may still ground on the ever-recurring shadows of menstruation and lastly upon the final bar of the menopause ere protection is found in the unruffled waters of the harbor beyond the reach of the sexual storms.[1]

Since then we have amassed an encyclopedia's worth of information about the existence of hormones, the function of menstruation, the regulation of ovulation, and the physiology of menopause. Yet many people, scientists and nonscientists alike, still believe that women function at the beck and call of their hormonal physiology. In 1970, for example, Dr. Edgar Berman, the personal physician of for-

mer Vice President Hubert Humphrey, responded to a female member of Congress:

Even a Congresswoman must defer to scientific truths . . . there just are physical and psychological inhibitants that limit a female's potential. . . . I would still rather have a male John F. Kennedy make the Cuban missile crisis decisions than a female of the same age who could possibly be subject to the curious mental aberrations of that age group.[2]

In a more grandiose mode, Professor Steven Goldberg, a university sociologist, writes that "men and women differ in their hormonal systems . . . every society demonstrates patriarchy, male dominance and male attainment. The thesis put forth here is that the hormonal renders the social inevitable."[3]

At the broadest political level, writers such as Berman and Goldberg raise questions about the competency of *any and all* females to work successfully in positions of leadership, while for women working in other types of jobs, the question is, Should they receive less pay or more restricted job opportunities simply because they menstruate or experience menopause? And further, do women in the throes of premenstrual frenzy frequently try to commit suicide? Do they really suffer from a "diminished responsibility" that should exempt them from legal sanctions when they beat their children or murder their boyfriends?[4] Is the health of large numbers of women threatened by inappropriate and even ignorant medical attention—medical diagnoses that miss real health problems, while resulting instead in the prescription of dangerous medication destined to create future disease?

The idea that women's reproductive systems direct their lives is ancient. But whether it was Plato, writing about the disruption caused by barren uteri wandering about the body,[5] Pliny, writing that a look from a menstruating woman will "dim the brightness of mirrors, blunt the edge of steel and take away the polish from ivory,"[6] or modern scientists writing about the changing levels of estrogen and progesterone, certain messages emerge quite clearly. Women, by nature emotionally erratic, cannot be trusted in positions of responsibility. Their dangerous, unpredictable furies warrant control by the medical profession,* while ironically, the same "dangerous" females also need protection because their reproductive systems, so necessary for the procreation of the race, are vulnerable to stress and hard work.

"The breakers of puberty," in fact, played a key role in a debate about higher education for women, a controversy that began in the last quarter of the nineteenth century and still echoes today in the halls of academe. Scientists of the late 1800s argued on physiological grounds that women and men should receive different types of education. Women, they believed, could not survive intact the rigors of higher education. Their reasons were threefold: first, the education of young women might cause serious damage to their reproductive systems. Energy devoted to scholastic work would deprive the reproductive organs of the necessary "flow of power," presenting particular problems for pubescent women, for whom the establishment of regular menstruation was of paramount importance. Physicians cited cases of women unable to bear children because they pursued a course of education designed for the more resilient young man.[7] In an interesting parallel to modern nature-nurture debates, proponents of higher education for women countered biological arguments with environmental ones. One anonymous author argued that, denied the privilege afforded their brothers of romping actively through the woods, women became fragile and nervous.[8]

Opponents of higher education for women also claimed that females were less intelligent than males, an assertion based partly on brain size itself but also on the overall size differences between men and women. They held that women cannot "consume so much food as men . . . [because] their average size remains so much smaller; so that the sum total of food converted into thought by women can never equal the sum total of food converted to thought by men. It follows, therefore, that *men will always think more than women*."[9] One respondent to this bit of scientific reasoning asked the thinking reader to examine the data: Aristotle and Napoleon were short, Newton, Spinoza, Shakespeare, and Comte delicate and of medium height, Descartes and Bacon sickly, "while unfortunately for a theory based upon superior digestion, Goethe and Carlyle were confirmed dyspeptics."[10] Finally, as if pubertal vulnerability and lower intelligence were not enough, it seemed to nineteenth-century scientists that menstruation rendered women "more or less sick and unfit for hard work" "for one quarter of each month during the best years of life."[11]

Although dated in some of the particulars, the turn-of-the-century scientific belief that women's reproductive functions make them unsuitable for higher education remains with us today. Some industries bar fertile women from certain positions because of workplace hazards that might cause birth defects, while simultaneously deeming equally vulnerable men fit for the job.* Some modern psychologists and biologists suggest that women perform more poorly than do men on mathematics tests because hormonal sex differences alter male and female brain structures; and many people believe women to be unfit for certain professions because they menstruate. Others argue that premenstrual changes cause schoolgirls to do poorly in their studies, to become slovenly and disobedient, and even to develop a "nymphomaniac urge [that] may be responsible for young girls running away from home . . . only to be found wandering in the park or following boys."[12]

If menstruation really casts such a dark shadow on women's lives, we ought certainly to know more about it—how it works, whether it can be controlled, and whether it indeed warrants the high level of concern expressed by some. Do women undergo emotional changes as they progress through the monthly ovulatory cycle? And if so do hormonal fluctuations bring on these ups and downs? If not—if a model of biological causation is appropriate—how else might we conceptualize what happens?

---

*In the nineteenth century, control took the form of sexual surgery such as ovariectomies and hysterectomies, while twentieth-century medicine prefers the use of hormone pills. The science of the 1980s has a more sophisticated approach to human physiology, but its political motives of control and management have changed little. For an account of medicine's attitudes toward women, see Barbara Ehrenreich and Deidre English, *For Her Own Good: 150 Years of Experts' Advice to Women* (New York: Doubleday, 1979); and G. J. Barker-Benfield, *The Horrors of the Half-Known Life* (New York: Harper & Row, 1977).

*The prohibited work usually carries a higher wage.

THE SHADOWS OF MENSTRUATION: A READER'S LITERATURE GUIDE

The Premenstrual Syndrome

SCIENCE UPDATE: PREMENSTRUAL STRAIN LINKED TO CRIME

—Providence Journal

ERRATIC FEMALE BEHAVIOR TIED TO PREMENSTRUAL SYNDROME

—Providence Journal

VIOLENCE BY WOMEN IS LINKED TO MENSTRUATION

—National Enquirer

Menstruation makes news, and the headlines summarize the message. According to Dr. Katharina Dalton, Premenstrual Syndrome (PMS) is a medical problem of enormous dimensions. Under the influence of the tidal hormonal flow, women batter their children and husbands, miss work, commit crimes, attempt suicide, and suffer from up to 150 different symptoms, including headaches, epilepsy, dizziness, asthma, hoarseness, nausea, constipation, bloating, increased appetite, low blood sugar, joint and muscle pains, heart palpitations, skin disorders, breast tenderness, glaucoma, and conjunctivitis.[13] Although the great concern expressed in the newspaper headlines just quoted may come from a single public relations source,[14] members of the medical profession seem eager to accept at face value the idea that "70 to 90% of the female population will admit to recurrent premenstrual symptoms and that 20 to 40% report some degree of mental or physical incapacitation."[15]

If all this is true, then we have on our hands nothing less than an overwhelming public health problem, one that deserves a considerable investment of national resources in order to develop understanding and treatment. If, on the other hand, the claims about premenstrual tension are cut from whole cloth, then the consequences are equally serious. Are there women in need of proper medical treatment who do not receive it? Do some receive dangerous medication to treat nonexistent physiological problems? How often are women refused work, given lower salaries, taken less seriously because of beliefs about hormonally induced erratic behavior? In the game of PMS the stakes are high.

The key issues surrounding PMS are so complex and interrelated that it is hard to know where to begin. There is,

as always, the question of evidence. To begin with we can look, in vain, for credible research that defines and analyzes PMS. Despite the publication of thousands of pages of allegedly scientific analyses, the most recent literature reviews simultaneously lament the lack of properly done studies and call for a consistent and acceptable research definition and methodology.[16] Intimately related to the question of evidence is that of conceptualization. Currently held theoretical views about the reproductive cycle are inadequate to the task of understanding the emotional ups and downs of people functioning in a complex world. Finally, lurking beneath all of the difficulties of research design, poor methods, and muddy thinking is the medical world's view of the naturally abnormal woman. Let's look at this last point first.

If you're a woman you can't win. Historically, females who complained to physicians about menstrual difficulties, pain during the menstrual flow, or physical or emotional changes associated with the premenstruum heard that they were neurotic. They imagined the pain and made up the tension because they recognized menstruation as a failure to become pregnant, to fulfill their true role as a woman.[17] With the advent of the women's health movement, however, women began to speak for themselves.[18] The pain is real, they said; our bodies change each month. The medical profession responded by finding biological/hormonal causes, proposing the need for doctor-supervised cures. A third voice, however, entered in: that of feminists worried about repercussions from the idea that women's natural functions represent a medical problem capable of preventing women from competing in the world outside the home. Although this multisided discussion continues, I currently operate on the premise that some women probably do require medical attention for incapacitating physical changes that occur in synchrony with their menstrual cycle. Yet in the absence of any reliable medical research into the problem it is impossible to diagnose true disease or to develop rational treatment. To start with, we must decide what is normal.

The tip-off to the medical viewpoint lies in its choice of language. What does it mean to say "70 to 90% of the female population will admit to recurrent premenstrual symptoms"?[19] The word *symptom* carries two rather different meanings. The first suggests a disease or an abnormality, a condition to be cured or rendered normal. Applying this connotation to a statistic suggesting 70 to 90 percent symptom formation leads one to conclude that the large majority of women are by their very nature diseased. The second meaning of *symptom* is that of a sign or signal. If the figure of 70 to 90 percent means nothing more than that most women recognize signs in their own bodies of an oncoming menstrual flow, the statistics are unremarkable. Consider then the following, written in 1974 by three scientists:

> It is estimated that from 25% to 100% of women experience some form of premenstrual or menstrual emotional disturbance. Eichner makes the discerning point that the few women who do not admit to premenstrual tension are basically unaware of it but one only has to talk to their husbands or co-workers to confirm its existence.[20]

Is it possible that up to 100 percent of all menstruating women regularly experience emotional disturbance? Compared to whom? Are males the unstated standard of emotional stability? If there is but a single definition of what is normal and men fit that definition, then women with "female complaints" must by definition be either crazy or in need of medical attention. A double bind indeed.

Some scientists explicitly articulate the idea of the naturally abnormal female. Professor Frank Beach, a pioneer in the field of animal psychology and its relationship to sexuality, suggests the following evolutionary account of menstruation. In primitive hunter-gatherer societies adult women were either pregnant or lactating, and since life spans were so short they died well before menopause; low-fat diets made it likely that they did not ovulate every month; they thus experienced no more than ten menstrual cycles. Given current life expectancies as well as the widespread use of birth control, modern women may experience a total of four hundred menstrual cycles. He concludes from this reasoning that "civilization has given women *a physiologically abnormal status* which may have important implications for the interpretation of psychological responses to periodic fluctuations in the secretion of ovarian hormones"—that is, to menstruation (emphasis added).[21] Thus the first problem we face in evaluating the literature on the premenstrual syndrome is figuring out how to deal with the underlying assumption that women have "a physiologically abnormal status."

Researchers who believe in PMS hold a wide variety of viewpoints (none of them supported by scientific data) about the basis of the problem. For example, Dr. Katharina Dalton, the most militant promoter of PMS, says that it results from a relative end-of-the-cycle deficiency in the hormone progesterone. Others cite deficiencies in vitamin B-6, fluid retention, and low blood sugar as possible causes. Suggested treatments range from hormone injection to the use of lithium, diuretics, megadoses of vitamins, and con-

TABLE I   ALLEGED CAUSES AND PROPOSED TREATMENTS OF PMS

Hypothesized Causes of Premenstrual Syndrome	Various PMS Treatments (used but not validated)
Estrogen excess	Oral contraceptives (combination estrogen and progesterone pills)
Progesterone deficiency	
Vitamin B deficiency	
Vitamin A deficiency	Estrogen alone
Hypoglycemia	Natural progesterone
Endogenous hormone allergy	Synthetic progestins
Psychosomatic	Valium or other tranquilizers
Fluid retention	Nutritional supplements
Dysfunction of the neurointermediate lobe of the pituitary	Minerals
	Lithium
	Diuretics
Prolactin metabolism	A prolactin inhibitor/ dopamine agonist
	Exercise
	Psychotherapy, relaxation, education, reassurance

SOURCES: Robert L. Reid and S. S. Yen, "Premenstrual Syndrome," *American Journal of Obstetrics and Gynecology* 139 (1981): 85–104; and Judith Abplanalp, "Premenstrual Syndrome: A Selective Review," *Women and Health* 8 (1983): 107–24.

trol of sugar in the diet[22] (see Table 1 for a complete list). Although some of these treatments are harmless, others are not. Progesterone injection causes cancer in animals. What will it do to humans? And a recent issue of *The New England Journal of Medicine* contains a report that large doses of vitamin B-6 damage the nerves, causing a loss of feeling in one's fingers and toes.[23] The wide variety of PMS "causes" and "cures" offered by the experts is confusing, to put it mildly. Just what *is* this syndrome that causes such controversy? How can a woman know if she has it?

With a case of the measles it's really quite simple. A fever and then spots serve as diagnostic signs. A woman said to have PMS, however, may or may not have any of a very large number of symptoms. Furthermore, PMS indicators such as headaches, depression, dizziness, loss or gain of appetite show up in everyone from time to time. Their mere presence cannot (as would measle spots) help one to diagnose the syndrome. In addition, whether any of these signals connote disease depends upon their severity. A slight headache may reflect nothing more than a lack of sleep, but repeated, severe headaches could indicate high blood pressure. As one researcher, Dr. Judith Abplanalp, succinctly put it: "There is no one set of symptoms which is considered to be the hallmark of or standard criterion for defining the premenstrual syndrome."[24] Dr. Katharina Dalton agrees but feels one can diagnose PMS quite simply by applying the term to "any symptoms or complaints which regularly come just before or during early menstruation but are absent at other times of the cycle."[25] Dalton contrasts this with men suffering from potential PMS "symptoms," because, she says, they experience them randomly during the month while women with the same physical indications acknowledge them only during the premenstruum.

PMS research usually bases itself on an ideal, regular, twenty-eight-day menstrual cycle. Researchers eliminate as subjects for study women with infrequent, shorter, or longer cycles. As a result, published investigations look at a skewed segment of the overall population. Even for those women with a regular cycle, however, a methodological problem remains because few researchers define the premenstrual period in the same way. Some studies look only at the day or two preceding the menstrual flow, others look at the week preceding, while workers such as Dalton cite cases that begin two weeks before menstruation and continue for one week after. Since so few investigations use exactly the same definition, research publications on PMS are difficult to compare with one another.[26] On this score if no other, the literature offers little useful insight, extensive as it is.

Although rarely stated, the assumption is that there is but *one* PMS. Dalton defines the problem so broadly that she and others may well lump together several phenomena of very different origins, a possibility heightened by the fact that investigators rarely assess the severity of the symptoms. Two women, one suffering from a few low days and the other from suicidal depression, may both be diagnosed as having PMS. Yet their difficulties could easily have different origins and ought certainly to receive different treatments. When investigators try carefully to define PMS, the number of people qualifying for study decreases dramatically. In one case a group used ten criteria (listed in Table 2) to define PMS only to find that no more than 20 percent of those who had volunteered for their research project met them.[27] In the absence of any clearly agreed-upon definition(s) of PMS, examinations of the topic should at least state clearly the methodology used; this would enable comparison between publications, and allow us to begin to accumulate some knowledge about the issues at hand (Table 2 lists suggested baseline information). At the moment the literature is filled with individual studies

TABLE 2   TOWARD A DEFINITION OF PREMENSTRUAL SYNDROME

Experimental criteria (rarely met in PMS studies):
Premenstrual symptoms for at least six preceding cycles
Moderate to severe physical and psychological symptoms
Symptoms *only* during the premenstrual period with marked relief at onset of menses
Age between 18 and 45 years
Not pregnant
Regular menses for six previous cycles
No psychiatric disorder; normal physical examination and laboratory test profile
No drugs for preceding four weeks
Will not receive anxiolytics, diuretics, hormones, or neuroleptic drugs during the study

Minimal descriptive information to be offered in published studies of PMS (rarely offered in the current literature):
Specification of the ways in which subjects were recruited
Age limitations
Contraception and medication information
Marital status
Parity
Race
Menstrual history data
Assessment instruments
Operational definition of PMS
Psychiatric history data
Assessment of current psychological state
Criteria for assessment of severity of symptoms
Criteria for defining ovulatory status of cycle
Cut-off criteria for "unacceptable" subjects

source: Judith Abplanalp, "Premenstrual Syndrome: A Selective Review," *Women and Health* 8 (1983): 107–24.

that permit neither replication nor comparison with one another—an appropriate state, perhaps, for an art gallery but not for a field with pretensions to the scientific.

Despite the problems of method and definition, the conviction remains that PMS constitutes a widespread disorder, a conviction that fortifies and is fortified by the idea that women's reproductive function, so different from that of "normal" men, places them in a naturally diseased state. For those who believe that 90 percent of all women suffer from a disease called PMS, it becomes a reasonable research strategy to look at the normally functioning menstrual cycle for clues about the cause and possible treatment. There are, in fact, many theories but no credible evidence about the origins of PMS. In Table 1 I've listed the

IF MEN COULD MENSTRUATE—

GLORIA STEINEM

A white minority of the world has spent centuries conning us into thinking that a white skin makes people superior—even though the only thing it really does is make them more subject to ultraviolet rays and to wrinkles. Male human beings have built whole cultures around the idea that penis-envy is "natural" to women—though having such an unprotected organ might be said to make men vulnerable, and the power to give birth makes womb-envy at least as logical.

In short, the characteristics of the powerful, whatever they may be, are thought to be better than the characteristics of the powerless—and logic has nothing to do with it.

What would happen, for instance, if suddenly, magically, men could menstruate and women could not?

The answer is clear—menstruation would become an enviable, boast-worthy, masculine event:

Men would brag about how long and how much.

Boys would mark the onset of menses, that longed-for proof of manhood, with religious ritual and stag parties.

Congress would fund a National Institute of Dysmenorrhea to help stamp out monthly discomforts.

Sanitary supplies would be federally funded and free. (Of course, some men would still pay for the prestige of commercial brands such as John Wayne Tampons, Muhammad Ali's Rope-a-dope Pads, Joe Namath Jock Shields—"For Those Light Bachelor Days," and Robert "Barretta" Blake Maxi-Pads.)

Military men, right-wing politicians, and religious fundamentalists would cite menstruation ("*men*struation") as proof that only men could serve in the Army ("you have to give blood to take blood"), occupy political office ("can women be aggressive without that steadfast cycle governed by the planet Mars?"), be priests and ministers ("how could a woman give her blood for our sins?"), or rabbis ("without the monthly loss of impurities, women remain unclean").

Male radicals, left-wing politicians, and mystics, however, would insist that women are equal, just different; and that any woman could enter their ranks if only

most frequently cited hypotheses, most of which involve in some manner the hormonal system that regulates menstruation. Some of the theories are ingenious and require a sophisticated knowledge of human physiology to comprehend. Nevertheless, the authors of one recent review quietly offer the following summary: "To date no one hypothesis has adequately explained the constellation of symptoms composing PMS."[28] In short, PMS is a disease in search of a definition and cause.

PMS also remains on the lookout for a treatment. That many have been tried is attested to in Table 1. The problem is that only rarely has the efficacy of these treatments been tested with the commonly accepted standard of a large-scale, double-blind study that includes placebos. In the few properly done studies "there is usually (1) a high placebo response and (2) the active agent is usually no better than a placebo."[29] In other words, women under treatment for PMS respond just as well to sugar pills as to medication

containing hormones or other drugs. Since it is probable that some women experience severe distress caused by malfunctions of their menstrual system, the genuinely concerned physician faces a dilemma. Should he or she offer treatment until the patient says she feels better even though the drug used may have dangerous side effects; or should a doctor refuse help for as long as we know of no scientifically validated treatment for the patient's symptoms? I have no satisfactory answer. But the crying need for some scientifically acceptable research on the subject stands out above all. If we continue to assume that menstruation is itself pathological, we cannot establish a baseline of health against which to define disease. If, instead, we accept in theory that a range of menstrual normality exists, we can then set about designing studies that define the healthy female reproductive cycle. Only when we have some feeling for *that* can we begin to help women who suffer from diseases of menstruation.

she were willing to self-inflict a major wound every month ("you *must* give blood for the revolution"), recognize the preeminence of menstrual issues, or subordinate her selfness to all men in their Cycle of Enlightenment.

Street guys would brag ("I'm a three-pad man") or answer praise from a buddy ("Man, you lookin' *good!* ") by giving fives and saying, "Yeah, man, I'm on the rag!"

TV shows would treat the subject at length. ("Happy Days": Richie and Potsie try to convince Fonzie that he is still "The Fonz," though he has missed two periods in a row.) So would newspapers. (SHARK SCARE THREATENS MENSTRUATING MEN. JUDGE CITES MONTHLY STRESS IN PARDONING RAPIST.) And movies. (Newman and Redford in "Blood Brothers"!)

Men would convince women that intercourse was *more* pleasurable at "that time of the month." Lesbians would be said to fear blood and therefore life itself—though probably only because they needed a good menstruating man.

Of course, male intellectuals would offer the most moral and logical arguments. How could a woman master any discipline that demanded a sense of time, space, mathematics, or measurement, for instance, without that in-built gift for measuring the cycles of the moon and planets—and thus for measuring anything at all? In the rarefied fields of philosophy and religion, could women compensate for missing the rhythm of the universe? Or for their lack of symbolic death-and-resurrection every month?

Liberal males in every field would try to be kind: the fact that "these people" have no gift for measuring life or connecting to the universe, the liberals would explain, should be punishment enough.

And how would women be trained to react? One can imagine traditional women agreeing to all these arguments with a staunch and smiling masochism. ("The ERA would force housewives to wound themselves every month": Phyllis Schlafly. "Your husband's blood is as sacred as that of Jesus—and so sexy, too!": Marabel Morgan.) Reformers and Queen Bees would try to imitate men, and *pretend* to have a monthly cycle. All feminists would explain endlessly that men, too, needed to be liberated from the false idea of Martian aggressiveness, just as women needed to escape the bonds of menses-envy. Radical feminists would add that the oppression of the nonmenstrual was the pattern for all other oppressions. ("Vampires were our first freedom fighters!") Cultural feminists would develop a bloodless imagery in art and literature. Socialist feminists would insist that only under capitalism would men be able to monopolize menstrual blood. . . . In fact, if men could menstruate, the power justifications could probably go on forever.

If we let them.

Many of those who reject the alarmist nature of the publicity surrounding PMS believe nevertheless that women undergo mood changes during their menstrual cycle. Indeed, most Western women would agree. But do studies of large segments of our population support this generality? And if so, what causes these ups and downs? In trying to answer these questions we confront another piece of the medical model of human behavior, the belief that biology is primary, that hormonal changes cause behavioral ones, but not vice versa. Most researchers use such a linear, unicausal model without thinking about it. Their framework is so much a part of their belief system that they forget to question it. Nevertheless it is the model from which they work, and failure to recognize and work skeptically with it often results in poorly conceived research combined with implausible interpretations of data. Although the paradigm of biological causation has until very recently dominated menstrual cycle research, it now faces serious and intellectually stimulating challenge from feminist experts in the field. . . .

MENOPAUSE: THE STORM BEFORE THE CALM

An unlikely specter haunts the world. It is the ghost of former womanhood . . . "unfortunate women abounding in the streets walking stiffly in twos and threes, seeing little and observing less. . . . The world appears [to them] as through a grey veil, and they live as docile, harmless creatures missing most of life's values." According to Dr. Robert Wilson and Thelma Wilson, though, one should not be fooled by their "vapid cow-like negative state" because "there is ample evidence that the course of history has been changed not only by the presence of estrogen, but by its absence. The untold misery of alcoholism, drug addiction, divorce and broken homes caused by these unstable estrogen-starved women cannot be presented in statistical form."[30]

Rather than releasing women from their monthly emotional slavery to the sex hormones, menopause involves them in new horrors. At the individual level one encounters the specter of sexual degeneration, described so vividly by Dr. David Reuben: "The vagina begins to shrivel, the breasts atrophy, sexual desire disappears. . . . Increased facial hair, deepening voice, obesity . . . coarsened features, enlargement of the clitoris, and gradual baldness complete the tragic picture. Not really a man but no longer a functional woman, these individuals live in the world of intersex."[31] At the demographic level writers express foreboding about women of the baby-boom generation, whose life span has increased from an average forty-eight years at the turn of the century to a projected eighty years in the year 2000.[32] Modern medicine, it seems, has played a cruel trick on women. One hundred years ago they didn't live long enough to face the hardships of menopause but today their increased longevity means they will live for twenty-five to thirty years beyond the time when they lose all possibility of reproducing. To quote Dr. Wilson again: "The unpalatable truth must be faced that all postmenopausal women are castrates."[33]

But what medicine has wrought, it can also rend asunder. Few publications have had so great an effect on the lives of so many women as have those of Dr. Robert A. Wilson, who pronounced menopause to be a disease of estrogen deficiency. At the same time in an influential popular form, in his book *Feminine Forever,* he offered a treatment: estrogen replacement therapy (ERT).[34] During the first seven months following publication in 1966, Wilson's book sold one hundred thousand copies and was excerpted in *Vogue* and *Look* magazines. It influenced thousands of physicians to prescribe estrogen to millions of women, many of whom had no clinical "symptoms" other than cessation of the menses. As one of his credentials Wilson lists himself as head of the Wilson Research Foundation, an outfit funded by Ayerst Labs, Searle, and Upjohn, all pharmaceutical giants interested in the large potential market for estrogen. (After all, no woman who lives long enough can avoid menopause.) As late as 1976 Ayerst also supported the Information Center on the Mature Woman, a public relations firm that promoted estrogen replacement therapy. By 1975 some six million women had started long-term treatment with Premarin (Ayerst Labs' brand name for estrogen), making it the fourth or fifth most popular drug in the United States. Even today, two million of the forty

million postmenopausal women in the United States contribute to the $70 million grossed each year from the sale of Premarin-brand estrogen.[35] The "disease of menopause" is not only a social problem: it's big business.[36]

The high sales of Premarin continue despite the publication in 1975 of an article linking estrogen treatment to uterine cancer.[37] Although in the wake of that publication many women stopped taking estrogen and many physicians became more cautious about prescribing it, the idea of hormone replacement therapy remains with us. At least three recent publications in medical journals seriously consider whether the benefits of estrogen might not outweigh the dangers.[38] The continuing flap over treatment for this so-called deficiency disease of the aging female forces one to ask just what *is* this terrible state called menopause? Are its effects so unbearable that one might prefer to increase, even ever so slightly, the risk of cancer rather than suffer the daily discomforts encountered during "the change of life"?

Ours is a culture that fears the elderly. Rather than venerate their years and listen to their wisdom, we segregate them in housing built for "their special needs," separated from the younger generations from which we draw hope for the future. At the same time we allow millions of old people to live on inadequate incomes, in fear that serious illness will leave them destitute. The happy, productive elderly remain invisible in our midst. (One must look to feminist publications such as *Our Bodies, Ourselves* to find women who express pleasure in their postmenopausal state.) Television ads portray only the arthritic, the toothless, the wrinkled, and the constipated. If estrogen really is the hormone of youth and its decline suggests the coming of old age, then its loss is a part of biology that our culture ill equips us to handle.

There is, of course, a history to our cultural attitudes toward the elderly woman and our views about menopause. In the nineteenth century physicians believed that at menopause a woman entered a period of depression and increased susceptibility to disease. The postmenopausal body might be racked with "dyspepsia, diarrhea . . . rheumatic pains, paralysis, apoplexy . . . hemorrhaging . . . tuberculosis . . . and diabetes," while emotionally the aging female risked becoming irritable, depressed, hysterical, melancholic, or even insane. The more a woman violated social laws (such as using birth control or promoting female suffrage), the more likely she would be to suffer a disease-ridden menopause.[39] In the twentieth century, psychologist Helene Deutsch wrote that at menopause "woman has ended her existence as a bearer of future life and has reached her natural end—her partial death—as a servant of the species."[40] Deutsch believed that during the post-menopausal years a woman's main psychological task was to accept the progressive biological withering she experienced. Other well-known psychologists have also accepted the idea that a woman's life purpose is mainly reproductive and that her postreproductive years are ones of inevitable decline. Even in recent times postmenopausal women have been "treated" with tranquilizers, hormones, electroshock, and lithium.[41]

But should women accept what many see as an inevitable emotional and biological decline? Should they believe, as Wilson does, that "from a practical point of view a man remains a man until the end," but that after menopause "we no longer have the 'whole woman'—only the 'part woman' "?[42] What is the real story of menopause?

The Change: Its Definition and Physiology

In 1976 under the auspices of the American Geriatric Society and the medical faculty of the University of Montpellier, the First International Congress on the Menopause convened in the south of France. In the volume that emerged from that conference, scientists and clinicians from around the world agreed on a standard definition of the words *menopause* and *climacteric.* "Menopause," they wrote, "indicates the final menstrual period and occurs during the climacteric. The climacteric is that phase in the aging process of women marking the transition from the reproductive stage of life to the non-reproductive stage."[43] By consensus, then, the word *menopause* has come to mean a specific event, the last menstruation, while *climacteric* implies a process occurring over a period of years.*

During the menstrual cycle the blood levels of a number of hormones rise and fall on a regular basis. At the end of one monthly cycle, the low levels of estrogen and progesterone trigger the pituitary gland to make follicle stimulating hormone (FSH) and luteinizing hormone (LH). The FSH influences the cells of the ovary to make large amounts of estrogen, and induces the growth and maturation of an oocyte. The LH, at just the right moment, induces ovulation and stimulates certain ovarian cells to form a

progesterone-secreting structure called a corpus luteum. When no pregnancy occurs the life of the corpus luteum is limited and, as it degenerates, the lowered level of steroid hormones calls forth a new round of follicle stimulating and luteinizing hormone synthesis, beginning the cycle once again. Although the ovary produces the lion's share of these steroid hormones, the cells of the adrenal gland also contribute and this contribution increases in significance after menopause.

What happens to the intricately balanced hormone cycle during the several years preceding menopause is little understood, although it seems likely that gradual changes occur in the balance between pituitary activity (FSH and LH production) and estrogen synthesis.[45] One thing, however, is clear: menopause does not mean the *absence* of estrogen, but rather a gradual lowering in the availability of *ovarian* estrogen. Table 3 summarizes some salient information about changes in steroid hormone levels during the menstrual cycle and after menopause. In looking at the high point of cycle synthesis and then comparing it to women who no longer menstruate, the most dramatic change is seen in the estrogenic hormone estradiol.* The other estrogenic hormones, as well as progesterone and testosterone, drop off to some extent but continue to be synthesized at a level comparable to that observed during the early phases of the menstrual cycle. Instead of concentrating on the notion of estrogen deficiency, however, it is more important to point out that (1) postmenopausally the body makes different kinds of estrogen; (2) the ovaries synthesize less and the adrenals more of these hormones; and (3) the monthly ups and downs of these hormones even out following menopause.

While estrogen levels begin to decline, the levels of FSH and LH start to increase. Changes in these hormones appear as early as eight years before menopause.[46] At the time of menopause and for several years afterward, these two hormones are found in very high concentrations compared to menstrual levels (FSH as many as fourteen times more concentrated than premenopausally, and LH more than three times more). Over a period of years such high levels are reduced to about half their peak value, leaving the postmenopausal woman with one-and-one-half times more LH and seven times more FSH circulating in her blood than when she menstruated regularly.

It is to all of these changes in hormone levels that the words *climacteric* and *menopause* refer. From these alter-

---

*There is also a male climacteric, which entails a gradual reduction in production of the hormone testosterone over the years as part of the male aging process. What part it plays in that process is poorly understood and seems frequently to be ignored by researchers, who prefer to contrast continuing male reproductive potency with the loss of childbearing ability in women.[44]

---

*Estrogens are really a family of structurally similar molecules. Their possibly different biological roles are not clearly delineated.

TABLE 3   HORMONE LEVELS AS A PERCENTAGE OF MID-MENSTRUAL-CYCLE HIGH POINT

Stage of Menstrual Cycle	TYPE OF ESTROGEN			Progesterone	Testosterone	Androstenedione
	Estrone	Estradiol	Estriol			
Premenopausal stage						
Early (menses)	20%	13%	67%	100%	55%	87%
Mid (ovulation)	100	100	—	—	100	100
Late (premenstrual)	49	50	100	—	82	—
Postmenopausal stage	17	3	50	50	23	39

SOURCE: Wulf H. Utian, *Menopause in Modern Perspectives* (New York: Appleton-Century-Crofts, 1980), 32.

ations Wilson and others have chosen to blame estrogen for the emotional deterioration they believe appears in post-menopausal women. Why they have focused on only one hormone from a complex system of hormonal changes is anybody's guess. I suspect, however, that the reasons are (at least) twofold. First, the normative biomedical disease model of female physiology looks for simple cause and effect. Most researchers, then, have simply assumed estrogen to be a "cause" and set out to measure its "effect." The model or framework out of which such investigators work precludes an interrelated analysis of all the different (and closely connected) hormonal changes going on during the climacteric. But why single out estrogen? Possibly because this hormone plays an important role in the menstrual cycle as well as in the development of "feminine" characteristics such as breasts and overall body contours. It is seen as the quintessential female hormone. So where could one better direct one's attention if, to begin with, one views menopause as the loss of true womanhood?

Physical changes do occur following menopause. Which, if any, of these are caused by changing hormone levels is another question. Menopause research comes equipped with its own unique experimental traps.[47] The most obvious is that a postmenopausal population is also an aging population. Do physical and emotional differences found in groups of postmenopausal women have to do with hormonal changes or with other aspects of aging? It is a difficult matter to sort out. Furthermore, many of the studies on menopause have been done on preselected populations, using women who volunteer because they experience classic menopausal "symptoms" such as the hot flash. Such investigations tell us nothing about average changes within the population as a whole. In the language of the social scientist, we have no baseline data, nothing to which we can compare menopausal women, no way to tell whether the complaint of a particular woman is typical, a cause for medical concern, or simply idiosyncratic.

Since the late 1970s feminist researchers have begun to provide us with much-needed information. Although their results confirm some beliefs long held by physicians, these newer investigators present them in a more sophisticated context. Dr. Madeleine Goodman and her colleagues designed a study in which they drew information from a large population of women ranging in age from thirty-five to sixty. All had undergone routine multiphasic screening at a health maintenance clinic, but none had come for problems concerning menopause. From the complete clinic records they selected a population of women who had not menstruated for at least one year and compared their health records with those who still menstruated, looking at thirty-five different variables, such as cramps, blood glucose levels, blood calcium, and hot flashes, to see if any of these symptoms correlated with those seen in postmenopausal women. The results are startling. They found that only 28 percent of Caucasian women and 24 percent of Japanese women identified as postmenopausal "reported traditional menopausal symptoms such as hot flashes, sweats, etc., while in nonmenopausal controls, 16% in Caucasians and 10% in Japanese also reported these same symptoms."[48] In other words, 75 percent of menopausal women in their sample reported no remarkable menopausal symptoms, a result in sharp contrast to earlier studies using women who identified themselves as menopausal.

In a similar exploration, researcher Karen Frey found evidence to support Goodman's results. She wrote that menopausal women "did not report significantly greater frequency of physical symptoms or concern about these symptoms than did pre- or post-menopausal women."[49] The studies of Goodman, Frey, and others[50] draw into serious question the notion that menopause is generally or necessarily associated with a set of disease symptoms. Yet at least three physical changes—hot flashes, vaginal dryness and irritation, and osteoporosis—and one emotional one—

depression—remain associated in the minds of many with the decreased estrogen levels of the climacteric. Goodman's work indicates that such changes may be far less widespread than previously believed, but if they are troublesome to 26 percent of all menopausal women they remain an appropriate subject for analysis.

We know only the immediate cause of hot flashes: a sudden expansion of the blood flow to the skin. The technical term to describe them, *vasomotor instability,* means only that nerve cells signal the widening of blood vessels allowing more blood into the body's periphery. A consensus has emerged on two things: (1) the high concentration of FSH and LH in blood probably causes hot flashes, although exactly how this happens remains unknown; and (2) estrogen treatment is the only currently available way to suppress the hot flashes. One hypothesis is that by means of a feedback mechanism, artificially raised blood levels of estrogen signal the brain to tell the pituitary to call off the FSH and LH. Although estrogen does stop the hot flashes, its effects are only temporary; remove the estrogen and the flashes return. Left alone, the body eventually adjusts to the changing levels of FSH and LH. Thus a premenopausal woman has two choices in dealing with hot flashes: she can either take estrogen as a permanent medication, a course Wilson refers to as embarking "on the great adventure of preserving or regaining your full femininity,"[51] or suffer some discomfort while nature takes its course. Since the longer one takes estrogen, the greater the danger of estrogen-linked cancer, many health-care workers recommend the latter.[52]

Some women experience postmenopausal vaginal dryness and irritation that can make sexual intercourse painful. Since the cells of the vaginal wall contain estrogen receptors, it is not surprising that estrogen applied locally or taken in pill form helps with this difficulty. Even locally applied, however, the estrogen enters into the bloodstream, presenting the same dangers as when taken in pill form. There are alternative treatments, though, for vaginal dryness. The Boston Women's Health Collective, for example, recommends the use of nonestrogen vaginal creams or jellies, which seem to be effective and are certainly safer. Continued sexual activity also helps—yet another example of the interaction between behavior and physiology.

Hot flashes and vaginal dryness are the *only* climacteric-associated changes for which estrogen unambiguously offers relief. Since significant numbers of women do not experience these changes and since for many of those that do the effects are relatively mild, the wisdom of ERT must be examined carefully and on an individual basis. Both men and women undergo certain changes as they age, but Wilson's cata-

strophic vision of postmenopausal women—those ghosts gliding by "unnoticed and, in turn, notic[ing] little"[53]—is such a far cry from reality that it is a source of amazement that serious medical writers continue to quote his work.

In contrast to hot flashes and vaginal dryness, osteoporosis, a brittleness of the bone which can in severe cases cripple, has a complex origin. Since this potentially life-threatening condition appears more frequently in older women than in older men, the hypothesis of a relationship with estrogen levels seemed plausible to many. But as one medical worker has said, a unified theory of the disease "is still non-existent, although sedentary life styles, genetic predisposition, hormonal imbalance, vitamin deficiencies, high-protein diets, and cigarette smoking all have been implicated."[54] Estrogen treatment seems to arrest the disease for a while, but may lose effectiveness after a few years.[55]

Even more than in connection with any physical changes, women have hit up against a medical double bind whenever they have complained of emotional problems during the years of climacteric. On the one hand physicians dismissed these complaints as the imagined ills of a hormone-deficient brain, while on the other they generalized the problem, arguing that middle-aged women are emotionally unreliable, unfit for positions of leadership and responsibility. Women had two choices: to complain and experience ridicule and/or improper medical treatment, or to suffer in silence. Hormonal changes during menopause were presumed to be the cause of psychiatric symptoms ranging from fatigue, dizziness, irritability, apprehension, and insomnia to severe headaches and psychotic depression. In recent years, however, these earlier accounts have been supplanted by a rather different consensus now emerging among responsible medical researchers.

To begin with, there are no data to support the idea that menopause has any relationship to serious depression in women. Postmenopausal women who experience psychosis have almost always had similar episodes premenopausally.[56] The notion of the hormonally depressed woman is a shibboleth that must be laid permanently to rest. Some studies have related irritability and insomnia to loss of sleep from nighttime hot flashes. Thus, for women who experience hot flashes, these emotional difficulties might, indirectly, relate to menopause. But the social, life history, and family contexts in which middle-aged women find themselves are more important links to emotional changes occurring during the years of the climacteric. And these, of course, have nothing whatsoever to do with hormones. Quite a number of studies suggest that the majority of women do not consider menopause a time of crisis. Nor do most women suffer from the so-called "empty nest syndrome" supposedly experienced when children leave home. On the contrary, investigation suggests that women without small children are less depressed and have higher incomes and an increased sense of well-being.[57] Such positive reactions depend upon work histories, individual upbringing, cultural background, and general state of health, among other things.

In a survey conducted for *Our Bodies, Ourselves,* one which in no sense represents a balanced cross section of U.S. women, the Boston Women's Health Collective recorded the reactions of more than two hundred menopausal or postmenopausal women, most of whom were suburban, married, and employed, to a series of questions about menopause. About two-thirds of them felt either positively or neutrally about a variety of changes they had undergone, while a whopping 90 percent felt okay or happy about the loss of childbearing ability![58] This result probably comes as no surprise to most women, but it flies in the face of the long-standing belief that women's lives and emotions are driven in greater part by their reproductive systems.

No good account of adult female development in the middle years exists. Levinson,[59] who studied adult men, presents a linear model of male development designed primarily around work experiences. In his analysis, the male climacteric plays only a secondary role. Feminist scholars Rosalind Barnett and Grace Baruch have described the difficulty of fitting women into Levinson's scheme: "It is hard to know how to think of women within this theory—a woman may not enter the world of work until her late thirties, she seldom has a mentor, and even women with life-long career commitments rarely are in a position to reassess their commitment pattern by age 40," as do the men in Levinson's study.[60]

Baruch and Barnett call for the development of a theory of women in their middle years, pointing out that an adequate one can emerge only when researchers set aside preconceived ideas about the central role of biology in adult female development and listen to what women themselves say. Paradoxically, in some sense we will remain unable to understand more about the role of biology in women's middle years until we have a more realistic *social* analysis of women's postadolescent psychological development. Such an analysis must, of course, take into account ethnic, racial, regional, and class differences among women, since once biology is jettisoned as a universal cause of female behavior, it no longer makes sense to lump all women into a single category.

Much remains to be understood about menopause. Which biological changes, for instance, result from ovarian degeneration and which from other aspects of aging? How does the aging process compare in men and women? What causes hot flashes and can we find safe ways to alleviate the discomfort they cause? Do other aspects of a woman's life affect the number and severity of menopausally related physical symptoms? What can we learn from studying the experience of menopause in other, especially non-Western cultures? A number of researchers have proposed effective ways of finding answers to these questions.[61] We need only time, research dollars, and an open mind to move forward.

CONCLUSION

The premise that women are by nature abnormal and inherently diseased dominates past research on menstruation and menopause. While appointing the male reproductive system as normal, this viewpoint calls abnormal any aspect of the female reproductive life cycle that deviates from the male's. At the same time such an analytical framework places the essence of a woman's existence in her reproductive system. Caught in her hormonal windstorm, she strives to attain normality but can do so only by rejecting her biological uniqueness, for that too is essentially deformed: a double bind indeed. Within such an intellectual structure no medical research of any worth to women's health can be done, for it is the blueprint itself that leads investigators to ask the wrong questions, look in the wrong places for answers, and then distort the interpretation of their results.

Reading through the morass of poorly done studies on menstruation and menopause, many of which express deep hatred and fear of women, can be a discouraging experience. One begins to wonder how it can be that within so vast a quantity of material so little quality exists. But at this very moment the field of menstrual-cycle research (including menopause) offers a powerful antidote to that disheartenment in the form of feminist researchers (both male and female) with excellent training and skills, working within a new analytical framework. Rejecting a strict medical model of female development, they understand that men and women have different reproductive cycles, *both* of which are normal. Not binary opposites, male and female physiologies have differences *and* similarities. These research pioneers know too that the human body functions in a social milieu and that it changes in response to that context. Biology is not a one-way determinant but a dynamic component of our existence. And, equally important, these new investigators have learned not only to *listen* to what women say about themselves but to *hear* as well. By and large, these researchers are not in the mainstream of medical and psychological research, but we can look forward to a time when the impact of their work will affect the field of menstrual-cycle research for the better and for many years to come.

NOTES

1. Carroll Smith-Rosenberg and Charles Rosenberg, "The Female Animal: Medical and Biological Views of Woman and Her Role in 19th Century America," *Journal of American History* 60(1973):336.

2. Edgar Berman, Letter to the Editor, *New York Times,* 26 July 1970.

3. Steven Goldberg, *The Inevitability of Patriarchy* (New York: William Morrow, 1973), 93.

4. Herbert Wray, "Premenstrual Changes," *Science News* 122(1982):380–81.

5. Ilza Veith, *Hysteria: The History of a Disease* (Chicago: University of Chicago Press, 1965).

6. Pliny the Elder, quoted in M. E. Ashley and Montagu, "Physiology and Origins of the Menstrual Prohibitions," *Quarterly Review of Biology* 15(1940):211.

7. Smith-Rosenberg and Rosenberg, "The Female Animal"; Henry Maudsley, "Sex in Mind and in Education," *Popular Science Monthly* 5(1874):200; and Joan Burstyn, "Education and Sex: The Medical Case Against Higher Education for Women in England 1870–1900," *Proceeds of the American Philosophical Society* 177(1973):7989.

8. Carroll Smith-Rosenberg, "The Hysterical Woman: Sex Roles and Role Conflict in 19th Century America," *Social Research* 39(1972):652–78.

9. M. A. Hardaker, "Science and the Woman Question," *Popular Science Monthly* 20(1881):583.

10. Nina Morais, "A Reply to Ms. Hardaker on: The Woman Question," *Popular Science Monthly* 21(1882):74–75.

11. Maudsley, "Sex in Mind and in Education," 211.

12. Katharina Dalton, *Once a Month* (Claremont, Calif.: Hunter House, 1983), 78.

13. Ibid.; Katharina Dalton, *The Premenstrual Syndrome* (London: William Heinemann Medical Books, 1972).

14. Andrea Eagan, "The Selling of Premenstrual Syndrome," *Ms.* Oct. 1983, 26–31.

15. Robert L. Reid and S. S. Yen, "Premenstrual Syndrome," *American Journal of Obstetrics and Gynecology* 139(1981):86.

16. J. Abplanalp, R. F. Haskett, and R. M. Rose, "The Premenstrual Syndrome," *Advances in Psychoneuroendocrinology* 3(1980):327–47.

17. Dalton, *Once a Month.*

18. Boston Women's Health Collective, *Our Bodies, Ourselves* (New York: Simon and Schuster, 1979).

19. Reid and Yen, "Premenstrual Syndrome," 86.

20. John O'Connor, M. Shelley Edward, and Lenore O. Stern, "Behavioral Rhythms Related to the Menstrual Cycle," in *Biorhythms and Human Reproduction,* ed. M. Fern et al. (New York: Wiley, 1974), 312.

21. Frank A. Beach, Preface to chapter 10, in *Human Sexuality in Four Perspectives* (Baltimore: Johns Hopkins University Press, 1977), 271.

22. M. B. Rosenthal, "Insights into the Premenstrual Syndrome," *Physician and Patient* (April 1983):46–53

23. Herbert Schaumberg et al., "Sensory Neuropathy from Pyridoxine Abuse," *New England Journal of Medicine* 309(1983):446–48.

24. Judith Abplanalp, "Premenstrual Syndrome: A Selective Review," *Women and Health* 8(1983):110.

25. Dalton, *Once a Month,* 12.

26. Abplanalp, Haskett, and Rose, "The Premenstrual Syndrome"; and Abplanalp, "Premenstrual Syndrome: A Selective Review."

27. Abplanalp, "Premenstrual Syndrome: A Selective Review."

28. Reid and Yen, "Premenstrual Syndrome," 97.

29. G. A. Sampson, "An Appraisal of the Role of Progesterone in the Therapy of Premenstrual Syndrome," in *The Premenstrual Syndrome,* ed. P. A. vanKeep and W. H. Utian (Lancaster, England: MTP Press Ltd. International Medical Publishers, 1981), 51–69; and Sampson, "Premenstrual Syndrome: A Double-Bind Controlled Trial of Progesterone and Placebo," *British Journal of Psychiatry* 135 (1979):209–15.

30. Robert A. Wilson and Thelma A. Wilson, "The Fate of the Nontreated Postmenopausal Woman: A Plea for the Maintenance of Adequate Estrogen from Puberty to the Grave," *Journal of the American Geriatric Society* 11(1963):352–56.

31. David Reuben, *Everything You Always Wanted to Know about Sex but Were Afraid to Ask* (New York: McKay, 1969), 292.

32. Wulf H. Utian, *Menopause in Modern Perspectives* (New York: Appleton-Century-Crofts, 1980).

33. Wilson and Wilson, "The Fate of the Nontreated Postmenopausal Woman," 347.

34. Robert A. Wilson, *Feminine Forever* (New York: M. Evans, 1966).

35. Marilyn Grossman and Pauline Bart, "The Politics of Menopause," in *The Menstrual Cycle,* vol. 1, ed. Dan, Graham, and Beecher.

36. Kathleen MacPherson, "Menopause as Disease: The Social Construction of a Metaphor," *Advances in Nursing Science* 3(1981):95–113; A. Johnson, "The Risks of Sex Hormones as Drugs," *Women and Health* 2(1977):8–11.

37. D. Smith et al., "Association of Exogenous Estrogen Endometrial Cancer," *New England Journal of Medicine* 293(1975):1164–67.

38. H. Judd et al., "Estrogen Replacement Therapy," *Obstetrics and Gynecology* 58(1981):267–75; M. Quigley, "Postmenopausal Hormone Replacement Therapy: Back to Estrogen Forever?" *Geriatric Medicine Today* 1(1982):78–85; and Thomas Skillman, "Estrogen Replacement: Its Risks and Benefits," *Consultant* (1982):115–27.

39. C. Smith-Rosenberg, "Puberty to Menopause: The Cycle of Femininity in 19th Century America," *Feminist Studies* 1(1973):65.

40. Helene Deutsch, *The Psychology of Women* (New York: Grune and Stratton, 1945), 458.

41. J. H. Osofsky and R. Seidenberg, "Is Female Menopausal Depression Inevitable?" *Obstetrics and Gynecology* 36(1970):611.

42. Wilson and Wilson, "The Fate of the Nontreated Postmenopausal Woman," 348.

43. P. A. vanKeep, R. B. Greenblatt, and M. Albeaux-Fernet, eds., *Consensus on Menopause Research* (Baltimore: University Park Press, 1976), 134.

44. Marcha Flint, "Male and Female Menopause: A Cultural Put-on," in *Changing Perspectives on Menopause,* ed. A. M. Voda, M. Dinnerstein, and S. O'Donnell (Austin: University of Texas Press, 1982).

45. Utian, *Menopause in Modern Perspectives.*

46. Ibid.

47. Madeleine Goodman, "Toward a Biology of Menopause," *Signs* 5(1980):739–53.

48. Madeleine Goodman, C. J. Stewart, and F. Gilbert, "Patterns of Menopause: A Study of Certain Medical and Physiological Variables among Caucasian and Japanese Women Living in Hawaii," *Journal of Gerontology* 32(1977):297.

49. Karen Frey, "Middle-Aged Women's Experience and Perceptions of Menopause," *Women and Health* 6(1981):31.

50. Eve Kahana, A. Kiyak, and J. Liang, "Menopause in the Context of Other Life Events," in *The Menstrual Cycle,* vol. 1, ed. Dan, Graham, and Beecher, 167–78.

51. Wilson, *Feminine Forever,* 134.

52. A. Voda and M. Eliasson, "Menopause: The Closure of Menstrual Life," *Women and Health* 8(1983):137–56.

53. Wilson and Wilson, "The Fate of the Nontreated Postmenopausal Woman," 356.

54. Louis Avioli, "Postmenopausal Osteoporosis: Prevention vs. Cure," *Federation Proceedings* 40(1981):2418.

55. Voda and Eliasson, "Menopause: The Closure of Menstrual Life."

56. G. Winokur and R. Cadoret, "The Irrelevance of the Menopause to Depressive Disease," in *Topics in Psychoendocrinology,* ed. E. J. Sachar (New York: Grune and Stratton, 1975).

57. Rosalind Barnett and Grace Baruch, "Women in the Middle Years: A Critique of Research and Theory," *Psychology of Women Quarterly* 3(1978):187–97.

58. Boston Women's Health Collective, *Our Bodies, Ourselves.*

59. D. Levinson et al., "Periods in the Adult Development of Men: Ages 18–45," *The Counseling Psychologist* 6(1976): 21–25.

60. Barnett and Baruch, "Women in the Middle Years," 189.

61. Ibid.; Goodman, "Toward a Biology of Menopause"; and Voda, Dinnerstein, and O'Donnell, eds., *Changing Perspectives on Menopause.*

R E A D I N G   3 6

"A Way Outa No Way": Eating Problems among African-American, Latina, and White Women

BECKY WANGSGAARD THOMPSON

Bulimia, anorexia, binging, and extensive dieting are among the many health issues women have been confronting in the last 20 years. Until recently, however, there has been almost no research about eating problems among African-American, Latina, Asian-American, or Native

American women, working-class women, or lesbians.[1] In fact, according to the normative epidemiological portrait, eating problems are largely a white, middle-, and upper-class heterosexual phenomenon. Further, while feminist research has documented how eating problems are fueled by sexism, there has been almost no attention to how other systems of oppression may also be implicated in the development of eating problems.

In this article, I reevaluate the portrayal of eating problems as issues of appearance based in the "culture of thinness." I propose that eating problems begin as ways women

Becky Wangsgaard Thompson, "'A Way Outa No Way': Eating Problems among African American, Latina, and White Women," *Gender & Society* 6, no. 4 (December 1992). Copyright © 1994 by Sociologists for Women in Society. Reprinted with the permission of the author.

cope with various traumas including sexual abuse, racism, classism, sexism, heterosexism, and poverty. Showing the interface between these traumas and the onset of eating problems explains why women may use eating to numb pain and cope with violations to their bodies. This theoretical shift also permits an understanding of the economic, political, social, educational, and cultural resources that women need to change their relationship to food and their bodies.

EXISTING RESEARCH ON EATING PROBLEMS

There are three theoretical models used to explain the epidemiology, etiology, and treatment of eating problems. The biomedical model offers important scientific research about possible physiological causes of eating problems and the physiological dangers of purging and starvation (Copeland 1985; Spack 1985). However, this model adopts medical treatment strategies that may disempower and traumatize women (Garner 1985; Orbach 1985). In addition, this model ignores many social, historical, and cultural factors that influence women's eating patterns. The psychological model identifies eating problems as "multidimensional disorders" that are influenced by biological, psychological, and cultural factors (Garfinkel and Garner 1982). While useful in its exploration of effective therapeutic treatments, this model, like the biomedical one, tends to neglect women of color, lesbians, and working-class women.

The third model, offered by feminists, asserts that eating problems are gendered. This model explains why the vast majority of people with eating problems are women, how gender socialization and sexism may relate to eating problems, and how masculine models of psychological development have shaped theoretical interpretations. Feminists offer the culture of thinness model as a key reason why eating problems predominate among women. According to this model, thinness is a culturally, socially, and economically enforced requirement for female beauty. This imperative makes women vulnerable to cycles of dieting, weight loss, and subsequent weight gain, which may lead to anorexia and bulimia (Chernin 1981; Orbach 1978, 1985; Smead 1984).

Feminists have rescued eating problems from the realm of individual psychopathology by showing how the difficulties are rooted in systematic and pervasive attempts to control women's body sizes and appetites. However, researchers have yet to give significant attention to how race, class, and sexuality influence women's understanding of their bodies and appetites. The handful of epidemiological studies that include African-American women and Latinas casts doubt on the accuracy of the normative epidemiological portrait. The studies suggest that this portrait reflects which particular populations of women have been studied rather than actual prevalence (Andersen and Hay 1985; Gray, Ford, and Kelly 1987; Hsu 1987; Nevo 1985; Silber 1986).

More important, this research shows that bias in research has consequences for women of color. Tomas Silber (1986) asserts that many well-trained professionals have either misdiagnosed or delayed their diagnoses of eating problems among African-American and Latina women due to stereotypical thinking that these problems are restricted to white women. As a consequence, when African-American women or Latinas are diagnosed, their eating problems tend to be more severe due to extended processes of starvation prior to intervention. In her autobiographical account of her eating problems, Retha Powers (1989), an African-American woman, describes being told not to worry about her eating problems since "fat is more acceptable in the Black community" (p. 78). Stereotypical perceptions held by her peers and teachers of the "maternal Black woman" and the "persistent mammy-brickhouse Black woman image" (p. 134) made it difficult for Powers to find people who took her problems with food seriously.

Recent work by African-American women reveals that eating problems often relate to women's struggles against a "simultaneity of oppression" (Clarke 1982; Naylor 1985; White 1991). Byllye Avery (1990), the founder of the National Black Women's Health Project, links the origins of eating problems among African-American women to the daily stress of being undervalued and overburdened at home and at work. In Evelyn C. White's (1990) anthology, *The Black Woman's Health Book: Speaking for Ourselves,* Georgiana Arnold (1990) links her eating problems partly to racism and racial isolation during childhood.

Recent feminist research also identifies factors that are related to eating problems among lesbians (Brown 1987; Dworkin 1989; Iazzetto 1989; Schoenfielder and Wieser 1983). In her clinical work, Brown (1987) found that lesbians who have internalized a high degree of homophobia are more likely to accept negative attitudes about fat than are lesbians who have examined their internalized homophobia. Autobiographical accounts by lesbians have also indicated that secrecy about eating problems among lesbians partly reflects their fear of being associated with a stigmatized illness ("What's Important" 1988).

Attention to African-American women, Latinas, and lesbians paves the way for further research that explores the possible interface between facing multiple oppressions and the development of eating problems. In this way, this study is part of a larger feminist and sociological research agenda that seeks to understand how race, class, gender, nationality, and sexuality inform women's experiences and influence theory production.

METHODOLOGY

I conducted 18 life history interviews and administered lengthy questionnaires to explore eating problems among African-American, Latina, and white women. I employed a snowball sample, a method in which potential respondents often first learn about the study from people who have already participated. This method was well suited for the study since it enabled women to get information about me and the interview process from people they already knew. Typically, I had much contact with the respondents prior to the interview. This was particularly important given the secrecy associated with this topic (Russell 1986; Silberstein, Striegel-Moore, and Rodin 1987), the necessity of women of color and lesbians to be discriminating about how their lives are studied, and the fact that I was conducting across-race research.

To create analytical notes and conceptual categories from the data, I adopted Glaser and Strauss's (1967) technique of theoretical sampling, which directs the researcher to collect, analyze, and test hypotheses during the sampling process (rather than imposing theoretical categories onto the data). After completing each interview transcription, I gave a copy to each woman who wanted one. After reading their interviews, some of the women clarified or made additions to the interview text.

Demographics of the Women in the Study

The 18 women I interviewed included 5 African-American women, 5 Latinas, and 8 white women. Of these women, 12 are lesbian and 6 are heterosexual. Five women are Jewish, 8 are Catholic, and 5 are Protestant. Three women grew up outside of the United States. The women represented a range of class backgrounds (both in terms of origin and current class status) and ranged in age from 19 to 46 years old (with a median age of 33.5 years).

The majority of the women reported having had a combination of eating problems (at least two of the following: bulimia, compulsive eating, anorexia, and/or extensive dieting). In addition, the particular types of eating problems often changed during a woman's life span. (For example, a woman might have been bulimic during adolescence and anorexic as an adult.) Among the women, 28 percent had been bulimic, 17 percent had been bulimic and anorexic, and 5 percent had been anorexic. All of the women who had been anorexic or bulimic also had a history of compulsive eating and extensive dieting. Of the women, 50 percent were compulsive eaters and dieters (39 percent) or compulsive eaters (11 percent) but had not been bulimic or anorexic.

Two-thirds of the women have had eating problems for more than half of their lives, a finding that contradicts the stereotype of eating problems as transitory. The weight fluctuation among the women varied from 16 to 160 pounds, with an average fluctuation of 74 pounds. This drastic weight change illustrates the degree to which the women adjusted to major changes in body size at least once during their lives as they lost, gained, and lost weight again. The average age of onset was 11 years old, meaning that most of the women developed eating problems prior to puberty. Almost all of the women (88 percent) consider themselves as still having a problem with eating, although the majority believe they are well on the way to recovery.

THE INTERFACE OF TRAUMA AND EATING PROBLEMS

One of the most striking findings in this study was the range of traumas the women associated with the origins of their eating problems, including racism, sexual abuse, poverty, sexism, emotional or physical abuse, heterosexism, class injuries, and acculturation.[2] The particular constellation of eating problems among the women did not vary with race, class, sexuality, or nationality. Women from various race and class backgrounds attributed the origins of their eating problems to sexual abuse, sexism, and emotional and/or physical abuse. Among some of the African-American and Latina women, eating problems were also associated with poverty, racism, and class injuries. Heterosexism was a key factor in the onset of bulimia, compulsive eating, and extensive dieting among some of the lesbians. These oppressions are not the same nor are the injuries caused by them. And certainly, there are a variety of potentially harmful ways that women respond to oppression (such as using drugs, becoming a workaholic, or committing suicide). However, for all these women, eating was a way of coping with trauma.

Sexual Abuse

Sexual abuse was the most common trauma that the women related to the origins of their eating problems. Until recently, there has been virtually no research exploring the possible relationship between these two phenomena. Since the mid-1980s, however, researchers have begun identifying connections between the two, a task that is part of a larger feminist critique of traditional psychoanalytic symptomatology (DeSalvo 1989; Herman 1981; Masson 1984). Results of a number of incidence studies indicate that between one-third and two-thirds of women who have eating problems have been abused (Oppenheimer et al. 1985; Root and Fallon 1988). In addition, a growing number of therapists and researchers have offered interpretations of the meaning and impact of eating problems for survivors of sexual abuse (Bass and Davis 1988; Goldfarb 1987; Iazzetto 1989; Swink and Leveille 1986). Kearney-Cooke (1988) identifies dieting and binging as common ways in which women cope with frequent psychological consequences of sexual abuse (such as body image disturbances, distrust of people and one's own experiences, and confusion about one's feelings). Root and Fallon (1989) specify ways that victimized women cope with assaults by binging and purging: bulimia serves many functions, including anesthetizing the negative feelings associated with victimization. Iazzetto's innovative study (1989), based on in-depth interviews and art therapy sessions, examines how a woman's relationship to her body changes as a consequence of sexual abuse. Iazzetto discovered that the process of leaving the body (through progressive phases of numbing, dissociating and denying) that often occurs during sexual abuse parallels the process of leaving the body made possible through binging.

Among the women I interviewed, 61 percent were survivors of sexual abuse (11 of the 18 women), most of whom made connections between sexual abuse and the beginning of their eating problems. Binging was the most common method of coping identified by the survivors. Binging helped women "numb out" or anesthetize their feelings. Eating sedated, alleviated anxiety, and combated loneliness. Food was something that they could trust and was accessible whenever they needed it. Antonia (a pseudonym) is an Italian-American woman who was first sexually abused by a male relative when she was four years old. Retrospectively, she knows that binging was a way she coped with the abuse. When the abuse began, and for many years subsequently, Antonia often woke up during the middle of the night with anxiety attacks or nightmares and would go straight to the kitchen cupboards to get food. Binging helped her block painful feelings because it put her back to sleep.

Like other women in the study who began binging when they were very young, Antonia was not always fully conscious as she binged. She described eating during the night as "sleep walking. It was mostly desperate—like I had to have it." Describing why she ate after waking up with nightmares, Antonia said, "What else do you do? If you don't have any coping mechanisms, you eat." She said that binging made her "disappear," which made her feel protected. Like Antonia, most of the women were sexually abused before puberty; four of them before they were five years old. Given their youth, food was the most accessible and socially acceptable drug available to them. Because all of the women endured the psychological consequences alone, it is logical that they coped with tactics they could do alone as well.

One reason Antonia binged (rather than dieted) to cope with sexual abuse is that she saw little reason to try to be the small size girls were supposed to be. Growing up as one of the only Italian Americans in what she described as a "very WASP town," Antonia felt that everything from her weight and size to having dark hair on her upper lip were physical characteristics she was supposed to hide. From a young age she knew she "never embodied the essence of the good girl. I don't like her. I have never acted like her. I can't be her. I sort of gave up." For Antonia, her body was the physical entity that signified her outsider status. When the sexual abuse occurred, Antonia felt she had lost her body. In her mind, the body she lived in after the abuse was not really hers. By the time Antonia was 11, her mother put her on diet pills. Antonia began to eat behind closed doors as she continued to cope with the psychological consequences of sexual abuse and feeling like a cultural outsider.

Extensive dieting and bulimia were also ways in which women responded to sexual abuse. Some women thought that the men had abused them because of their weight. They believed that if they were smaller, they might not have been abused. For example when Elsa, an Argentine woman, was sexually abused at the age of 11, she thought her chubby size was the reason the man was abusing her. Elsa said, "I had this notion that these old perverts liked these plump girls. You heard adults say this too. Sex and flesh being associated." Looking back on her childhood, Elsa believes she made fat the enemy partly due to the shame and guilt she felt about the incest. Her belief that fat was the source of her problems was also supported by her socialization. Raised by strict German governesses in an upper-class family, Elsa was taught that a woman's weight was a primary criterion for judging her worth. Her mother "was socially conscious of walking into places with a fat daughter and maybe people staring at her." Her father often referred to Elsa's body as "shot to hell." When asked to describe how she felt about her body when growing up, Elsa described being completely alienated from her body. She explained,

> Remember in school when they talk about the difference between body and soul? I always felt like my soul was skinny. My soul was free. My soul sort of flew. I was tied down by this big bag of rocks that was my body. I had to drag it around. It did pretty much what it wanted and I had a lot of trouble controlling it. It kept me from doing all the things that I dreamed of.

As is true for many women who have been abused, the split that Elsa described between her body and soul was an attempt to protect herself from the pain she believed her body caused her. In her mind, her fat body was what had "bashed in her dreams." Dieting became her solution, but, as is true for many women in the study, this strategy soon led to cycles of binging and weight fluctuation.

Ruthie, a Puerto Rican woman who was sexually abused from 12 until 16 years of age, described bulimia as a way she responded to sexual abuse. As a child, Ruthie liked her body. Like many Puerto Rican women of her mother's generation, Ruthie's mother did not want skinny children, interpreting that as a sign that they were sick or being fed improperly. Despite her mother's attempts to make her gain weight, Ruthie remained thin through puberty. When a male relative began sexually abusing her, Ruthie's sense of her body changed dramatically. Although she weighed only 100 pounds, she began to feel fat and thought her size was causing the abuse. She had seen a movie on television about Romans who made themselves throw up and so she began doing it, in hopes that she could look like the "little kid" she was before the abuse began. Her symbolic attempt to protect herself by purging stands in stark contrast to the psychoanalytic explanation of eating problems as an "abnormal" repudiation of sexuality. In fact, her actions and those of many other survivors indicate a girl's logical attempt to protect herself (including her sexuality) by being a size and shape that does not seem as vulnerable to sexual assault.

These women's experiences suggest many reasons why women develop eating problems as a consequence of sexual abuse. Most of the survivors "forgot" the sexual abuse after its onset and were unable to retrieve the abuse memories until many years later. With these gaps in memory, frequently they did not know why they felt ashamed, fearful, or depressed. When sexual abuse memories resurfaced in dreams, they often woke feeling upset but could not remember what they had dreamed. These free floating, unexplained feelings left the women feeling out of control and confused. Binging or focusing on maintaining a new diet were ways women distracted or appeased themselves, in turn, helping them regain a sense of control. As they grew older, they became more conscious of the consequences of these actions. Becoming angry at themselves for binging or promising themselves they would not purge again was a way to direct feelings of shame and self-hate that often accompanied the trauma.

Integral to this occurrence was a transference process in which the women displaced onto their bodies painful feelings and memories that actually derived from or were directed toward the persons who caused the abuse. Dieting became a method of trying to change the parts of their bodies they hated, a strategy that at least initially brought success as they lost weight. Purging was a way women tried to reject the body size they thought was responsible for the abuse. Throwing up in order to lose the weight they thought was making them vulnerable to the abuse was a way to try to find the body they had lost when the abuse began.

Poverty

Like sexual abuse, poverty is another injury that may make women vulnerable to eating problems. One woman I interviewed attributed her eating problems directly to the stress caused by poverty. Yolanda is a Black Cape Verdean mother who began eating compulsively when she was 27 years old. After leaving an abusive husband in her early 20s, Yolanda was forced to go on welfare. As a single mother with small children and few financial resources, she tried to support herself and her children on $539 a month. Yolanda began binging in the evenings after putting her children to bed. Eating was something she could do alone. It would calm her, help her deal with loneliness, and make her feel safe. Food was an accessible commodity that was cheap. She ate three boxes of macaroni and cheese when nothing else was available. As a single mother with little money, Yolanda felt as if her body was the only thing she had left. As she described it,

> I am here, [in my body] 'cause there is no where else for me to go. Where am I going to go? This is all I got . . .

that probably contributes to putting on so much weight cause staying in your body, in your home, in yourself, you don't go out. You aren't around other people . . . You hide and as long as you hide you don't have to face . . . nobody can see you eat. You are safe.

When she was eating, Yolanda felt a momentary reprieve from her worries. Binging not only became a logical solution because it was cheap and easy but also because she had grown up amid positive messages about eating. In her family, eating was a celebrated and joyful act. However, in adulthood, eating became a double-edged sword. While comforting her, binging also led to weight gain. During the three years Yolanda was on welfare, she gained seventy pounds.

Yolanda's story captures how poverty can be a precipitating factor in eating problems and highlights the value of understanding how class inequalities may shape women's eating problems. As a single mother, her financial constraints mirrored those of most female heads of households. The dual hazards of a race- and sex-stratified labor market further limited her options (Higginbotham 1986). In an article about Black women's health, Byllye Avery (1990) quotes a Black woman's explanation about why she eats compulsively. The woman told Avery,

I work for General Electric making batteries, and, I know it's killing me. My old man is an alcoholic. My kid's got babies. Things are not well with me. And one thing I know I can do when I come home is cook me a pot of food and sit down in front of the TV and eat it. And you can't take that away from me until you're ready to give me something in its place. (P. 7)

Like Yolanda, this woman identifies eating compulsively as a quick, accessible, and immediately satisfying way of coping with the daily stress caused by conditions she could not control. Connections between poverty and eating problems also show the limits of portraying eating problems as maladies of upper-class adolescent women.

The fact that many women use food to anesthetize themselves, rather than other drugs (even when they gained access to alcohol, marijuana, and other illegal drugs), is partly a function of gender socialization and the competing demands that women face. One of the physiological consequences of binge eating is a numbed state similar to that experienced by drinking. Troubles and tensions are covered over as a consequence of the body's defensive response to massive food intake. When food is eaten in that way, it effectively works like a drug with immediate and predictable effects. Yolanda said she binged late at night rather than getting drunk because she could still get up in the morning, get her children ready for school, and be clearheaded for the college classes she attended. By binging, she avoided the hangover or sickness that results from alcohol or illegal drugs. In this way, food was her drug of choice since it was possible for her to eat while she continued to care for her children, drive, cook, and study. Binging is also less expensive than drinking, a factor that is especially significant for poor women. Another woman I interviewed said that when her compulsive eating was at its height, she ate breakfast after rising in the morning, stopped for a snack on her way to work, ate lunch at three different cafeterias, and snacked at her desk throughout the afternoon. Yet even when her eating had become constant, she was still able to remain employed. While her patterns of eating no doubt slowed her productivity, being drunk may have slowed her to a dead stop.

Heterosexism

The life history interviews also uncovered new connections between heterosexism and eating problems. One of the most important recent feminist contributions has been identifying compulsory heterosexuality as an institution which truncates opportunities for heterosexual and lesbian women (Rich 1986). All of the women interviewed for this study, both lesbian and heterosexual, were taught that heterosexuality was compulsory, although the versions of this enforcement were shaped by race and class. Expectations about heterosexuality were partly taught through messages that girls learned about eating and their bodies. In some homes, boys were given more food than girls, especially as teenagers, based on the rationale that girls need to be thin to attract boys. As the girls approached puberty, many were told to stop being athletic, begin wearing dresses, and watch their weight. For the women who weighed more than was considered acceptable, threats about their need to diet were laced with admonitions that being fat would ensure becoming an "old maid."

While compulsory heterosexuality influenced all of the women's emerging sense of their bodies and eating patterns, the women who linked heterosexism directly to the beginning of their eating problems were those who knew they were lesbians when very young and actively resisted heterosexual norms. One working-class Jewish woman, Martha, began compulsively eating when she was 11 years old, the same year she started getting clues of her lesbian identity. In junior high school, as many of her female peers began dating boys, Martha began fantasizing about girls, which made her feel utterly alone. Confused and ashamed about her fantasies, Martha came home every day from school and binged. Binging was a way she drugged herself so that being alone was tolerable. Describing binging, she said, "It was the only thing I knew. I was looking for a comfort." Like many women, Martha binged because it softened painful feelings. Binging sedated her, lessened her anxiety, and induced sleep.

Martha's story also reveals ways that trauma can influence women's experience of their bodies. Like many other women, Martha had no sense of herself as connected to her body. When I asked Martha whether she saw herself as fat when she was growing up she said, "I didn't see myself as fat. I didn't see myself. I wasn't there. I get so sad about that because I missed so much." In the literature on eating problems, *body image* is the term that is typically used to describe a woman's experience of her body. This term connotes the act of imagining one's physical appearance. Typically, women with eating problems are assumed to have difficulties with their body image. However, the term body image does not adequately capture the complexity and range of bodily responses to trauma experienced by the women. Exposure to trauma did much more than distort the women's visual image of themselves. These traumas often jeopardized their capacity to consider themselves as having bodies at all.

Given the limited connotations of the term body image, I use the term *body consciousness* as a more useful way to understand the range of bodily responses to trauma.[3] By body consciousness I mean the ability to reside comfortably in one's body (to see oneself as embodied) and to consider one's body as connected to oneself. The disruptions to their body consciousness that the women described included leaving their bodies, making a split between their body and mind, experiencing being "in" their bodies as painful, feeling unable to control what went in and out of their bodies, hiding in one part of their bodies, or simply not seeing themselves as having bodies. Binging, dieting, or purging were common ways women responded to disruptions to their body consciousness.

Racism and Class Injuries

For some of the Latinas and African-American women, racism coupled with the stress resulting from class mobility related to the onset of their eating problems. Joselyn, an African-American woman, remembered her white grand-mother telling her she would never be as pretty as her cousins because they were lighter skinned. Her grandmother often humiliated Joselyn in front of others, as she made fun of Joselyn's body while she was naked and told her she was fat. As a young child, Joselyn began to think that although she could not change her skin color, she could at least try to be thin. When Joselyn was young, her grandmother was the only family member who objected to Joselyn's weight. However, her father also began encouraging his wife and daughter to be thin as the family's class standing began to change. When the family was working class, serving big meals, having chubby children, and keeping plenty of food in the house was a sign the family was doing well. But, as the family became mobile, Joselyn's father began insisting that Joselyn be thin. She remembered, "When my father's business began to bloom and my father was interacting more with white businessmen and seeing how they did business, suddenly thin became important. If you were a truly well-to-do family, then your family was slim and elegant."

As Joselyn's grandmother used Joselyn's body as territory for enforcing her own racism and prejudice about size, Joselyn's father used her body as the territory through which he channeled the demands he faced in the white-dominated business world. However, as Joselyn was pressured to diet, her father still served her large portions and bought treats for her and the neighborhood children. These contradictory messages made her feel confused about her body. As was true for many women in this study, Joselyn was told she was fat beginning when she was very young even though she was not overweight. And, like most of the women, Joselyn was put on diet pills and diets before even reaching puberty, beginning the cycles of dieting, compulsive eating, and bulimia.

The confusion about body size expectations that Joselyn associated with changes in class paralleled one Puerto Rican woman's association between her eating problems and the stress of assimilation as her family's class standing moved from poverty to working class. When Vera was very young, she was so thin that her mother took her to a doctor who prescribed appetite stimulants. However, by the time Vera was eight years old, her mother began trying to shame Vera into dieting. Looking back on it, Vera attributed her mother's change of heart to competition among extended family members that centered on "being white, being successful, being middle class, . . . and it was always, 'Ay Bendito. She is so fat. What happened?'"

The fact that some of the African-American and Latina women associated the ambivalent messages about food and eating to their family's class mobility and/or the demands of assimilation while none of the eight white women expressed this (including those whose class was stable and changing) suggests that the added dimension of racism was connected to the imperative to be thin. In fact, the class expectations that their parents experienced exacerbated standards about weight that they inflicted on their daughters.

EATING PROBLEMS AS SURVIVAL STRATEGIES

Feminist Theoretical Shifts

My research permits a reevaluation of many assumptions about eating problems. First, this work challenges the theoretical reliance on the culture-of-thinness model. Although all of the women I interviewed were manipulated and hurt by this imperative at some point in their lives, it is not the primary source of their problems. Even in the instances in which a culture of thinness was a precipitating factor in anorexia, bulimia, or binging, this influence occurred in concert with other oppressions.

Attributing the etiology of eating problems primarily to a woman's striving to attain a certain beauty ideal is also problematic because it labels a common way that women cope with pain as essentially appearance-based disorders. One blatant example of sexism is the notion that women's foremost worry is about their appearance. By focusing on the emphasis on slenderness, the eating problems literature falls into the same trap of assuming that the problems reflect women's "obsession" with appearance. Some women were raised in families and communities in which thinness was not considered a criterion for beauty. Yet, they still developed eating problems. Other women were taught that women should be thin, but their eating problems were not primarily in reaction to this imperative. Their eating strategies began as logical solutions to problems rather than problems themselves as they tried to cope with a variety of traumas.

Establishing links between eating problems and a range of oppressions invites a rethinking of both the groups of women who have been excluded from research and those whose lives have been the basis of theory formation. The construction of bulimia and anorexia as appearance-based disorders is rooted in a notion of femininity in which white middle- and upper-class women are portrayed as frivolous, obsessed with their bodies, and overly accepting of narrow gender roles. This portrayal fuels women's tremendous shame and guilt about eating problems—as signs of self-centered vanity. This construction of white middle- and upper-class women is intimately linked to the portrayal of working-class white women and women of color as their opposite: as somehow exempt from accepting the dominant standards of beauty or as one step away from being hungry and therefore not susceptible to eating problems. Identifying that women may binge to cope with poverty contrasts the notion that eating problems are class bound. Attending to the intricacies of race, class, sexuality, and gender pushes us to rethink the demeaning construction of middle-class femininity and establishes bulimia and anorexia as serious responses to injustices.

Understanding the link between eating problems and trauma also suggests much about treatment and prevention. Ultimately, their prevention depends not simply on individual healing but also on changing the social conditions that underlie their etiology. As Bernice Johnson Reagon sings in Sweet Honey in the Rock's song "Oughta Be a Woman," "A way outa no way is too much to ask/too much of a task for any one woman" (Reagon 1980).[4] Making it possible for women to have healthy relationships with their bodies and eating is a comprehensive task. Beginning steps in this direction include insuring that (1) girls can grow up without being sexually abused, (2) parents have adequate resources to raise their children, (3) children of color grow up free of racism, and (4) young lesbians have the chance to see their reflection in their teachers and community leaders. Ultimately, the prevention of eating problems depends on women's access to economic, cultural, racial, political, social, and sexual justice.

NOTES

1. I use the term *eating problems* as an umbrella term for one or more of the following: anorexia, bulimia, extensive dieting, or binging. I avoid using the term eating disorder because it categorizes the problems as individual pathologies, which deflects attention away from the social inequalities underlying them (Brown 1985). However, by using the term *problem* I do not wish to imply blame. In fact, throughout, I argue that the eating strategies that women develop begin as logical solutions to problems, not problems themselves.

2. By trauma I mean a violating experience that has long-term emotional, physical, and/or spiritual consequences that may have immediate or delayed effects. One reason the term *trauma* is useful conceptually is its association with the diagnostic label Post Traumatic Stress Disorder (PTSD) (American Psychological Association 1987). PTSD is one of the few clinical diagnostic categories that recognizes social problems (such as war or the Holocaust) as responsible for the symptoms identified (Trimble 1985). This concept adapts well to the feminist assertion that a woman's symptoms cannot be understood as solely individual, considered outside of her social context, or prevented without significant changes in social conditions.

3. One reason the term *consciousness* is applicable is its intellectual history as an entity that is shaped by social context and social structures (Delphy 1984; Marx 1964). This link aptly applies to how the women described their bodies because their perceptions of themselves as embodied (or not embodied) directly relate to their material conditions (living situations, financial resources, and access to social and political power).

4. Copyright © 1980. Used by permission of Songtalk Publishing.

REFERENCES

American Psychological Association. 1987. *Diagnostic and statistical manual of mental disorders.* 3rd ed. rev. Washington, DC: American Psychological Association.

Andersen, Arnold, and Andy Hay. 1985. Racial and socioeconomic influences in anorexia nervosa and bulimia. *International Journal of Eating Disorders* 4:479–87.

Arnold, Georgiana. 1990. Coming home: One Black woman's journey to health and fitness. In *The Black women's health book: Speaking for ourselves,* edited by Evelyn C. White. Seattle, WA: Seal Press.

Avery, Byllye Y. 1990. Breathing life into ourselves: The evolution of the National Black Women's Health Project. In *The Black women's health book: Speaking for ourselves,* edited by Evelyn C. White. Seattle, WA: Seal Press.

Bass, Ellen, and Laura Davis. 1988. *The courage to heal: A guide for women survivors of child sexual abuse.* New York: Harper & Row.

Brown, Laura S. 1985. Women, weight and power: Feminist theoretical and therapeutic issues. *Women and Therapy* 4:61–71.

———. 1987. Lesbians, weight and eating: New analyses and perspectives. In *Lesbian psychologies,* edited by the Boston Lesbian Psychologies Collective. Champaign: University of Illinois Press.

Chernin, Kim. 1981. *The obsession: Reflections of the tyranny of slenderness.* New York: Harper & Row.

Clarke, Cheryl. 1982. *Narratives.* New Brunswick, NJ: Sister Books.

Copeland, Paul M. 1985. Neuroendocrine aspects of eating disorders. In *Theory and treatment of anorexia nervosa and bulimia: Biomedical sociocultural and psychological perspectives,* edited by Steven Wiley Emmett. New York: Brunner/Mazel.

Delphy, Christine. 1984. *Close to home: A materialist analysis of women's oppression.* Amherst: University of Massachusetts Press.

DeSalvo, Louise. 1989. *Virginia Woolf: The impact of childhood sexual abuse on her life and work.* Boston, MA: Beacon.

Dworkin, Sari H. 1989. Not in man's image: Lesbians and the cultural oppression of body image. In *Loving boldly: Issues facing lesbians,* edited by Ester D. Rothblum and Ellen Cole. New York: Harrington Park Press.

Garfinkel, Paul E., and David M. Garner. 1982. *Anorexia nervosa: A multidimensional perspective.* New York: Brunner/Mazel.

Garner, David. 1985. Iatrogenesis in anorexia nervosa and bulimia nervosa. *International Journal of Eating Disorders* 4:701–26.

Glaser, Barney G., and Anselm L. Strauss. 1967. *The discovery of grounded theory: Strategies for qualitative research.* New York: Aldine DeGruyter.

Goldfarb, Lori. 1987. Sexual abuse antecedent to anorexia nervosa, bulimia and compulsive overeating: Three case reports. *International Journal of Eating Disorders* 6:675–80.

Gray, James, Kathryn Ford, and Lily M. Kelly. 1987. The prevalence of bulimia in a Black college population. *International Journal of Eating Disorders* 6:733–40.

Herman, Judith. 1981. *Father-daughter incest.* Cambridge, MA: Harvard University Press.

Higginbotham, Elizabeth. 1986. We were never on a pedestal: Women of color continue to struggle with poverty, racism and sexism. In *For crying out loud,* edited by Rochelle Lefkowitz and Ann Withorn. Boston: MA: Pilgrim Press.

Hsu, George. 1987. Are eating disorders becoming more common in Blacks? *International Journal of Eating Disorders* 6:113–24.

Iazzetto, Demetria. 1989. When the body is not an easy place to be: Women's sexual abuse and eating problems. Ph.D. diss., Union for Experimenting Colleges and Universities, Cincinnati, Ohio.

Kearney-Cooke, Ann. 1988. Group treatment of sexual abuse among women with eating disorders. *Women and Therapy* 7:5–21.

Marx, Karl. 1964. *The economic and philosophic manuscripts of 1844.* New York: International.

Masson, Jeffrey. 1984. *The assault on the truth: Freud's suppression of the seduction theory.* New York: Farrar, Strauss & Giroux.

Naylor, Gloria. 1985. *Linden Hills.* New York: Ticknor & Fields.

Nevo, Shoshana. 1985. Bulimic symptoms: Prevalence and the ethnic differences among college women. *International Journal of Eating Disorders* 4:151–68.

Oppenheimer, R., K. Howells, R. L. Palmer, and D. A. Chaloner. 1985. Adverse sexual experience in childhood and clinical eating disorders: A preliminary description. *Journal of Psychiatric Research* 19:357–61.

Orbach, Susie. 1978. *Fat is a feminist issue.* New York: Paddington.

———. 1985. Accepting the symptom: A feminist psychoanalytic treatment of anorexia nervosa. In *Handbook of psychotherapy for anorexia nervosa and bulimia,* edited by David M. Garner and Paul E. Garfinkel. New York: Guilford.

Powers, Retha. 1989. Fat is a Black women's issue. *Essence,* Oct., 75, 78, 134, 136.

Reagon, Bernice Johnson. 1980. Oughta be a woman. On Sweet Honey in the Rock's album, *Good News.* Music by Bernice Johnson Reagon; lyrics by June Jordan. Washington, DC: Songtalk.

Rich, Adrienne. 1986. Compulsory heterosexuality and lesbian existence. In *Blood, bread and poetry.* New York: Norton.

Root, Maria P. P., and Patricia Fallon. 1988. The incidence of victimization experiences in a bulimic sample. *Journal of Interpersonal Violence* 3:161–73.

———. 1989. Treating the victimized bulimic: The functions of binge-purge behavior. *Journal of Interpersonal Violence* 4:90–100.

Russell, Diana E. 1986. *The secret trauma: Incest in the lives of girls and women.* New York: Basic Books.

Schoenfielder, Lisa, and Barbara Wieser, eds. 1983. *Shadow on a tightrope: Writings by women about fat liberation.* Iowa City, IA: Aunt Lute Book Co.

Silber, Tomas. 1986. Anorexia nervosa in Blacks and Hispanics. *International Journal of Eating Disorders* 5:121–28.

Silberstein, Lisa, Ruth Striegel-Moore, and Judith Rodin. 1987. Feeling fat: A woman's shame. In *The role of shame in symptom formation,* edited by Helen Block Lewis. Hillsdale, NJ: Lawrence Erlbaum.

Smead, Valerie. 1984. Eating behaviors which may lead to and perpetuate anorexia nervosa, bulimarexia, and bulimia. *Women and Therapy* 3:37–49.

Spack, Norman. 1985. Medical complications of anorexia nervosa and bulimia. In *Theory and treatment of anorexia nervosa and bulimia: Biomedical sociocultural and psychological perspectives,* edited by Steven Wiley Emmett. New York: Brunner/Mazel.

Swink, Kathy, and Antoinette E. Leveille. 1986. From victim to survivor: A new look at the issues and recovery process for adult incest survivors. *Women and Therapy* 5:119–43.

Trimble, Michael. 1985. Post-traumatic stress disorder: History of a concept. In *Trauma and its wake: The study and treatment of post-traumatic stress disorder,* edited by C. R. Figley. New York: Brunner/Mazel.

What's important is what you look like. 1988. *Gay Community News,* July, 24–30.

White, Evelyn C., ed. 1990. *The Black women's health book: Speaking for ourselves.* Seattle, WA: Seal Press.

———. 1991. Unhealthy appetites. *Essence,* Sept., 28, 30.

R E A D I N G   3 7

Outcast Mothers and Surrogates: Racism and Reproductive Politics in the Nineties

ANGELA Y. DAVIS

The historical construction of women's reproductive role, which is largely synonymous with the historical failure to

Angela Y. Davis, "Outcast Mothers and Surrogates: Racism and Reproductive Politics in the Nineties" from *American Feminist Thought at Century's End: A Reader,* edited by Linda S. Kauffman. Copyright © 1993. Reprinted with the permission of Blackwell Publishers.

acknowledge the possibility of reproductive self-determination, has been informed by a peculiar constellation of racist and misogynist assumptions. These assumptions have undergone mutations even as they remain tethered to their historical origins. To explore the politics of reproduction in a contemporary context is to recognize the growing intervention of technology into the most intimate spaces of human life: from computerized bombings in the Persian

Gulf, that have taken life from thousands of children and adults as if they were nothing more than the abstract statistics of a video game, to the complex technologies awaiting women who wish to transcend biological, or socially induced infertility. I do not mean to suggest that technology is inherently oppressive. Rather, the socioeconomic conditions within which reproductive technologies are being developed, applied, and rendered accessible or inaccessible maneuver them in directions that most often maintain or deepen misogynist, anti-working class, and racist marginalization.

To the extent that fatherhood is denied as a socially significant moment in the process of biological reproduction, the politics of reproduction hinge on the social construction of motherhood. The new developments in reproductive technology have encouraged the contemporary emergence of popular attitudes—at least among the middle classes—that bear a remarkable resemblance to the nineteenth-century cult of motherhood, including the moral, legal, and political taboos it developed against abortion. While the rise of industrial capitalism led to the historical obsolescence of the domestic economy and the ideological imprisonment of (white and middle-class) women within a privatized home sphere, the late twentieth-century breakthroughs in reproductive technology are resuscitating that ideology in bizarre and contradictory ways. Women who can afford to take advantage of the new technology—who are often career women for whom motherhood is no longer a primary or exclusive vocation—now encounter a mystification of maternity emanating from the possibility of transcending biological (and socially defined) reproductive incapacity. It is as if the recognition of infertility is now a catalyst—among some groups of women—for a motherhood quest that has become more compulsive and more openly ideological than during the nineteenth century. Considering the anti-abortion campaign, it is not difficult to envision this contemporary ideological mystification of motherhood as central to the efforts to deny all women the legal rights that would help shift the politics of reproduction toward a recognition of our autonomy with respect to the biological functions of our bodies.

In the United States, the nineteenth-century cult of motherhood was complicated by a number of class- and race-based contradictions. Women who had recently immigrated from Europe were cast, like their male counterparts, into the industrial proletariat, and were therefore compelled to play economic roles that contradicted the increasing representation of women as wives/mothers. Moreover, in conflating slave motherhood and the reproduction of its labor

force, the moribund slave economy effectively denied motherhood to vast numbers of African women. My female ancestors were not led to believe that, as women, their primary vocation was motherhood. Yet slave women were imprisoned within their reproductive role as well. The same socio-historical reasons for the ideological location of European women in an increasingly obsolete domestic economy as the producers, nurturers, and rearers of children caused slave women to be valuated in accordance with their role as breeders. Of course, both motherhood, as it was ideologically constructed, and breederhood, as it historically unfolded, were contingent upon the biological birth process. However, the one presumed to capture the moral essence of womaness, while the other denied, on the basis of racist presumptions and economic necessity, the very possibility of morality and thus also participation in this motherhood cult.

During the first half of the nineteenth century, when the industrial demand for cotton led to the obsessive expansion of slavery at a time when the importation of Africans was no longer legal, the "slaveocracy" demanded of African women that they bear as many children as they were biologically capable of bearing. Thus, many women had 14, 15, 16, 17, 18, 19, 20 children. My own grandmother, whose parents were slaves, was one of 13 children.

At the same time, therefore, that nineteenth-century white women were being ideologically incarcerated within their biological reproductive role, essentialized as mothers, African women were forced to bear children, not as evidence of their role as mothers, but for the purpose of expanding the human property held by slave owners. The reproductive role imposed upon African slave women bore no relationship to a subjective project of motherhood. In fact, as Toni Morrison's novel, *Beloved,* indicates—inspired as it is by an actual historical case of a woman killing her daughter—some slave women committed infanticide as a means of resisting the enslavement of their progeny.

Slave women were *birth mothers* or *genetic mothers*—to employ terms rendered possible by the new reproductive technologies—but they possessed no legal rights as mothers of any kind. Considering the commodification of their children—and indeed, of their own persons—their status was similar to that of the contemporary *surrogate mother.* I am suggesting that the term *surrogate mother* might be invoked as a retroactive description of their status because the economic appropriation of their reproductive capacity reflected the inability of the slave economy to produce and reproduce its own laborers—a limitation with respect to the forces of economic production that is being transformed in this era of advanced capitalism by the increasing computerization and robotization of the economy.

The children of slave mothers could be sold away by their owners for business reasons or as a result of a strategy of repression. They could also be forced to give birth to children fathered by their masters, knowing full well that the white fathers would never recognize their Black children as offspring. As a consequence of the socially constructed invisibility of the white father—a pretended invisibility strangely respected by the white and Black community alike—Black children would grow up in an intimate relation to their white half-brothers and sisters, except that their biological kinship, often revealed by a visible physical resemblance, would remain shrouded in silence. That feature of slave motherhood was something about which no one could speak. Slave women who had been compelled—or had, for their own reasons, agreed—to engage in sexual intercourse with their masters would be committing the equivalent of a crime if they publicly revealed the fathers of their children.[1] These women knew that it was quite likely that their children might also be sold or brutalized or beaten by their own fathers, brothers, uncles, or nephews.

If I have lingered over what I see as some of the salient reproductive issues in African-American women's history, it is because they seem to shed light on the ideological context of contemporary technological intervention in the realm of reproduction. Within the contemporary feminist discourse about the new reproductive technologies—in vitro fertilization, surrogacy, embryo transfer, etc.—concern has been expressed about what is sometimes described as the "deconstruction of motherhood"[2] as a unified biological process. While the new technological developments have rendered the fragmentation of maternity more obvious, the economic system of slavery fundamentally relied upon alienated and fragmented maternities, as women were forced to bear children, whom masters claimed as potentially profitable labor machines. Birth mothers could not therefore expect to be mothers in the legal sense. Legally these children were chattel and therefore motherless. Slave states passed laws to the effect that children of slave women no more belonged to their biological mothers than the young of animals belonged to the females that birthed them.[3]

At the same time, slave women and particularly those who were house slaves were expected to nurture and rear and mother the children of their owners. It was not uncommon for white children of the slave-owning class to have relationships of a far greater emotional intensity with the slave women who were their "mammies" than with their own white biological mothers. We might even question the meaning of this conception of "biological motherhood" in light of the fact that the Black nurturers of these white children were frequently "wet nurses" as well. They nourished the babies in their care with the milk produced by their own hormones. It seems, therefore, that Black women were not only treated as surrogates with respect to the reproduction of slave labor, they also served as surrogate mothers for the white children of the slave-owners.

A well-known lullaby that probably originated during slavery has been recorded in some versions that powerfully reflect the consciousness of slave women who were compelled to neglect their own children, while lavishing their affection on the children of their masters. "Hushaby, / Don't you cry / Go to sleep, little baby. / And when you wake, / You shall have a cake / And all the pretty little ponies."[4]

In all likelihood, this version—or verse—was directed to the white babies, while the following one evoked the forced isolation of their own children: "Go to sleep, little baby, / When you wake / You shall have / All the mulies in the stable. / Buzzards and flies / Picking out its eyes, / Pore little baby crying, / Mamma, mamma!"[5]

A similar verse was sung to a lullaby entitled "Ole Cow": "Ole cow, ole cow, / Where is your calf? / Way down yonder in the meadow / The buzzards and the flies / A-pickin' out its eyes, / The po' little thing cried, Mammy."[6]

The economic history of African-American women—from slavery to the present—like the economic history of immigrant women, both from Europe and colonized or formerly colonized nations, reveals the persisting theme of work as household servants. Mexican women and Irish women, West Indian women and Chinese women have been compelled, by virtue of their economic standing, to function as servants for the wealthy. They have cleaned their houses and—our present concern—they have nurtured and reared their employers' babies. They have functioned as surrogate mothers. Considering this previous history, is it not possible to imagine the possibility that poor women—especially poor women of color—might be transformed into a special caste of hired pregnancy carriers? Certainly such fears are not simply the product of an itinerant imagination. In any event, whether or not such a caste of women baby-bearers eventually makes its way into history, these historical experiences constitute a socio-historical backdrop for the present debate around the new reproductive technologies. The very fact that the discussion over surrogacy

WHEN THE POLITICAL BECOMES THE PERSONAL OR AN ABORTION THAT WASN'T AN ABORTION; A RIGHT THAT HARDLY SEEMS SUCH

ELEANOR MILLER

I never thought I'd need an abortion. In 1980 we were referred to New York Hospital's Infertility Clinic. I remember Dale and I sitting in the waiting room; each man held a small container through which one could see the semen he had just collected in the bathroom. The next year we moved to Milwaukee. A lay midwife referred us to *the* infertility expert in town, one of the few physicians who would provide backup for the lay midwives who practice illegally here. Sounded like someone I would like, and I did.

He immediately noticed my congenital heart defect. No reason not to try to have a baby; we just needed to be careful. This next part of the story is a well-known one: invasive tests, temperature charts, dashes home followed by post-coital exams, clomid. Finally, in August of 1983, Samantha was born (with the crash cart outside my door in case of heart failure and intravenous antibiotics to reduce the risk of endocarditis). I was 36.

When Sam was eight months old we discovered that Dale had thyroid cancer. Given my age and history of infertility and the fact that Dale's prognosis was good, we decided that it was now or never if we wanted a second child. Radiation has a distinctive impact on male fertility, however. I remember staring at bent and pinheaded sperm through our ob/gyn's microscope. We had the same experiences we had the first time—miscarriage in my office, followed within the hour by a D&C without anesthesia in my ob/gyn's office. In 1987 Jill was born. I was very tired, but very happy.

Eleanor Miller, "When the Political Becomes the Personal or an Abortion That Wasn't an Abortion; A Right that Hardly Seems Such," *Midwest Feminist Papers* 1, New Series (1991), edited by Michael R. Hill and Mary Jo Deegan. Copyright © 1991 by Midwest Sociologists for Women in Sociology. Reprinted with the permission of *Midwest Feminist Papers*.

Given my age and health and Dale's, we were sure we didn't want any more children. Then in September of 1989, noticing that I was feeling exhausted and nauseous, I realized I was pregnant. I called Dale. He said he would be right home. After I hung up, I called my ob/gyn's office. A nurse who knew me answered. "I'm pregnant," I said. "I need. . . ." "Congratulations," says she. "No," I reply. "I want to arrange to have an abortion." She says she will have the doctor call me, nothing more.

He tells me that I am not too old to have another child. He volunteers that he could do a tubal ligation at the same time. But I'm too exhausted, I argue, and I still have a baby in diapers (not to mention that I have a good chance of soon being elected President of SWS and chair of my Department). He jokes that his wife and he will raise the child until it's three and then, becoming more serious, asks me whether I've really thought long and hard about this decision and whether I've discussed it with Dale. I can't believe this conversation. He says finally, "You know, I don't do abortions; but I will refer you to a friend I trust who does." He gives me the person's name; he's on the staff of an abortion clinic. We hang up. I feel betrayed, angry, silly. Why did I think it would be easy? Why did I trust this man?

I call the abortion clinic to set up an appointment. I notice that it is in the heart of Milwaukee's poorest, most segregated area; in fact it is the area in which I do my research. When I arrive there three days later, I'm grateful that there aren't any protesters. We park in the unpaved, litter-strewn lot beside the two-story cinder-block building that houses the abortion clinic. The first story has large aqua and orange plastic squares decorating it. There is no sign. When we enter, we approach a glass-enclosed office and I fill out a sheet that asks for basic demographic information as well as insurance information. I am then asked for $200. I begin to write a check. The receptionist looks askance. Don't I know they only accept cash? I tell her that I wasn't told. "Oh, you're Dr. So-and-so's patient; I guess it's alright." I write my check and am asked to wait in the basement of the building. I descend the stairs, holding Dale's hand.

There are four or five couples seated in orange plastic chairs, all silently staring into space or looking at a TV chained to the wall. An African-American woman is standing. She and a very young looking African-American couple are the only nonwhites in the room. With one exception, the white couples are older and appear to be married. Dale and I wait there a long time, two hours to be exact. During that time I am called to have a brief medical history taken and to have some bloodwork done. The nurse who pricks my finger to take the blood says: "I see you're a doctor; well, let's make this clear. I'll be your nurse today; you do what I say; you're my patient." I am puzzled by this obvious exercise of social control and status jockeying. I had given no indication that I thought any other situation existed. The interesting thing is that I never see her again.

I am later called into a tiny office off the small main waiting room. Here a rosy-cheeked social worker inquires as to whether I really know what I am doing and asks me whether or not my decision has been coerced. She asks me what form of birth control I had been using and looks critical when I say that I had been using none. I don't try to explain. She also asks me what sort I intend to use when I leave that day. I tell her that my husband will probably have a vasectomy, but I feel intruded upon by her questions. In fact, I hadn't thought about birth control at all, either in the past or for the future.

At about 11:00, I am ushered upstairs into a small, green room where I am asked to undress. I put on a hospital gown and a nurse helps me onto the table and into the stirrups. She turns on the vacuum aspirator; she says it would be good for me to hear what it sounds like, so as not to be alarmed later. She records my blood pressure in my chart and notes that I have been referred by Dr. So-and-so. She ventures that she is in the market for a fertility expert since she is having difficulty conceiving. I describe my ob/gyn in vaguely positive terms and then I pour out my story to her. I tell her what a cruel trick I think it is that someone

with my history should find herself pregnant. I feel human for a moment.

The doctor, pale, bespectacled, enters the room. He seems embarrassed. He says his name. He looks at my chart, puts it down and inserts the speculum. He says, "You're starting to have a spontaneous abortion; it often happens in women your age." "Look," he says to the nurse, stepping back, "see the tissue." "I am going to give you an injection of lidocaine; it will make your mouth [sic] numb." At this point the nurse took my right arm. I thought she was trying to hold my hand, but, as I groped for hers, it became clear that she was actually pinning my right arm to the table. I hear the vacuum switch on and the procedure is over in about two or three minutes. The nurse rolls me over to my left side, away from the vacuum aspirator, and tells me to bring my knees up. A brief time later, I feel something moving swiftly up my legs as she puts on my underpants to which she has attached a sanitary napkin. She tells me to dress and then leads me to the recovery room.

Three or four women are on the other cots, but most of the women who had been in the basement are in an adjoining room having soda and cookies. The nurse takes my blood pressure and massages my uterus several times. After a while she says she needs to see how much I am bleeding. I tell her I didn't think much, but she hauls me to my feet and asks me to take down my pants so she can see. While I am doing this, she holds a blanket between me and the other women. I am shocked as she goes from cot to cot doing this. She gives us instructions on aftercare and announces to the group that we should not call unless we are passing big clots or are filling, she emphasizes filling, four pads an hour. She says that we will have to listen to a talk about how to take birth control pills and participate in a question and answer period before we can be discharged. She walks us into the room where the first women to have had abortions that morning are talking, eating and reading magazines. They have apparently been detained there until all the abortions are completed. I listen to the lecture. Afterwards, there is only one question. A woman asks: "When will it be safe to lift a baby." Dale is waiting for me. He has witnessed two C-sections, but has not been allowed into the room where I have just had my D&C. Yes, somehow my abortion had been magically transformed into a D&C, at least that's how my ob/gyn subsequently refers to what happened that morning when I next meet him.

As we ride home, I feel sad and angry. The whole process has been such a degradation ceremony. I chide myself for having panicked, for trusting my infertility specialist, for not having the presence of mind to think that I would have been better off at "Bread and Roses," a feminist clinic. I am angry about the stereotypes of the abortion seeker, particularly the one of the professional

woman who is too self-absorbed to want to be bothered with children.

The next time I visit my internist, I ask him if he can recommend a gynecologist, someone who does abortions. He looks rather puzzled. I describe my experience. I make it clear that my request is a matter of politics, not immediate medical need. He replies, "Most gynecologists here don't do abortions; you know, they picket your house and things." I thought, " 'They' aren't the only ones who can picket."

tends to coincide, by virtue of corporate involvement and intervention in the new technologies, with the debate over surrogacy for profit, makes it necessary to acknowledge historical economic precedents for surrogate motherhood. Those patterns are more or less likely to persist under the impact of the technology in its market context. The commodification of reproductive technologies, and, in particular, the labor services of pregnant surrogate mothers, means that money is being made and that, therefore, someone is being exploited.

Once upon a time—and this is still the case outside the technologically advanced capitalist societies—a woman who discovered that she was infertile would have to reconcile herself to the impossibility of giving birth to her own biological offspring. She would therefore either try to create a life for herself that did not absolutely require the presence of children, or she chose to enter into a mothering relationship in other ways. There was the possibility of foster motherhood, adoptive motherhood, or play motherhood.[7] This last possibility is deeply rooted in the Black community tradition of extended families and relationships based both on biological kinship—though not necessarily biological motherhood—and on personal history, which is often as binding as biological kinship. But even within the biological network itself, relationships between, for example, an aunt and niece or nephew, in the African-American and other family traditions, might be as strong or stronger than those between a mother and daughter or son.

My own mother grew up in a family of foster parents with no siblings. Her best friend had no sisters and brothers either, so they invented a sister relation between them. Though many years passed before I became aware that they were not "really" sisters, this knowledge had no significant

impact on me: I considered my Aunt Elizabeth no less my aunt later than during the earlier years of my childhood. Because she herself had no children, her relation to me, my sister, and two brothers was one of a second mother.

If she were alive and in her childbearing years today, I wonder whether she would bemoan the fact that she lacked the financial resources to employ all the various technological means available to women who wish to reverse their infertility. I wonder if she would feel a greater compulsion to fulfill a female vocation of motherhood. While working-class women are not often in the position to explore the new technology, infertile women—or the wives/partners of infertile men—who are financially able to do so are increasingly expected to try everything. They are expected to try in vitro fertilization, embryo transplants, surrogacy. The availability of the technology further mythologizes motherhood as the true vocation of women. In fact, the new reproductive medicine sends out a message to those who are capable of receiving it: motherhood lies just beyond the next technology. The consequence is an ideological compulsion toward a palpable goal: a child one creates either via one's own reproductive activity or via someone else's.

Those who opt to employ a surrogate mother will participate in the economic as well as ideological exploitation of her services. And the woman who becomes a surrogate mother earns relatively low wages. A few years ago, the going rate was twenty thousand dollars. Considering the fact that pregnancy is a 24-hour-a-day job, what might seem like a substantial sum of money is actually not even a minimum wage. This commodification of motherhood is quite frightening in the sense that it comes forth as permission to allow women and their partners to participate in a program that is generative of life. However, it seems that what is really generated is sexism and profits.

The economic model evoked by the relationship between the surrogate mother and the woman [or man] who makes use of her services is the feudalistic bond between servant and her employer. Because domestic work has been primarily performed in the United States by women of color, native-born as well as recent immigrants (and immigrant women of European descent), elements of racism and class bias adhere to the concept of surrogate motherhood as potential historical features, even in the contemporary absence of large numbers of surrogate mothers of color.

If the emerging debate around the new reproductive technologies is presently anchored to the socioeconomic conditions of relatively affluent families, the reproductive issues most frequently associated with poor and working-class women of color revolve around the apparent proliferation of young single parents, especially in the African-American community. For the last decade or so, teenage pregnancy has been ideologically represented as one of the greatest obstacles to social progress in the most impoverished sectors of the Black community. In actuality, the *rate* of teenage pregnancy in the Black community—like that among white teenagers—has been waning for quite a number of years. According to a National Research Council study, fertility rates in 1960 were 156 births per 1,000 Black women aged 15 to 19, and 97 in 1985.[8] What distinguishes teenage pregnancy in the Black community today from its historical counterpart is the decreasing likelihood of teenage marriage. There is a constellation of reasons for the failure of young teenagers to consolidate traditional two-parent families. The most obvious one is that it rarely makes economic sense for an unemployed young woman to marry an unemployed young man. As a consequence of shop closures in industries previously accessible to young Black male workers—and the overarching deindustrialization of the economy—young men capable of contributing to the support of their children are becoming increasingly scarce. For a young woman whose pregnancy results from a relationship with an unemployed youth, it makes little sense to enter into a marriage that will probably bring in an extra adult as well as a child to be supported by her own mother/father/grandmother, etc.

The rise of single motherhood cannot be construed, however, as synonymous with the "fall" of the nuclear family within the Black community—if only because it is an extremely questionable proposition that there was such an uncontested structure as the nuclear family to begin with. Historically, family relationships within the Black community have rarely coincided with the traditional nuclear model. The nuclear family, in fact, is a relatively recent configuration, integrally connected with the development of industrial capitalism. It is a family configuration that is rapidly losing its previous, if limited, historical viability: presently, the majority of U.S. families, regardless of membership in a particular cultural or ethnic group, cannot be characterized as "nuclear" in the traditional sense. Considering the gender-based division of labor at the core of the nuclear model, even those families that consist of the mother-father-children nucleus—often popularly referred to as "nuclear families"—do not, rigorously speaking, conform to the nuclear model. The increasingly widespread phenomenon of the "working mother," as opposed to the wife/mother whose economic responsibilities are confined to the household and the children, thoroughly contradicts and renders anachronistic the nuclear family model. Not too many mothers stay at home by choice anymore; not too many mothers can afford to stay at home, unless, of course, they benefit from the class privileges that accrue to the wealthy. In other words, even for those whose historical realities were the basis of the emergence of this nuclear family model, the model is rapidly losing its ability to contain and be responsive to contemporary social/economic/psychic realities.

It angers me that such a simplistic interpretation of the material and spiritual impoverishment of the African-American community as being largely rooted in teenage pregnancy is so widely accepted. This is not to imply that teenage pregnancy is unproblematic. It is extremely problematic, but I cannot assent to the representation of teenage pregnancy as "the problem." There are reasons why young Black women become pregnant and/or desire pregnancy. I do not think I am far off-target when I point out that few young women who choose pregnancy are offered an alternative range of opportunities for self-expression and development. Are those Black teenage girls with the potential for higher education offered scholarships permitting them to study at colleges and universities like Le Moyne? Are teenagers who choose pregnancy offered even a vision of well-paying and creative jobs?

Is it really so hard to grasp why so many young women would choose motherhood? Isn't this path toward adulthood still thrust upon them by the old but persisting ideological constructions of femaleness? Doesn't motherhood still equal adult womanhood in the popular imagination? Don't the new reproductive technologies further develop this equation of womanhood and motherhood? I would venture to say that many young women make conscious decisions to bear children in order to convince themselves that they are alive and creative human beings. As a consequence of this choice, they are also characterized as immoral for not marrying the fathers of their children.

I have chosen to evoke the reproductive issue of single motherhood among teenagers in order to highlight the absurdity of locating motherhood in a transcendent space—as the anti-abortion theorists and activists do—in which involuntary motherhood is as sacred as voluntary motherhood. In this context, there is a glaring exception: motherhood among Black and Latina teens is constructed as a moral and social evil—but even so, they are denied accessible and affordable abortions. Moreover, teen mothers are ideologically assaulted because of their premature and impoverished entrance into the realm of motherhood while older, whiter, and wealthier women are coaxed to buy the technology to assist them in achieving an utterly commodified motherhood.

Further contradictions in the contemporary social compulsion toward motherhood—contradictions rooted in race and class—can be found in the persisting problem of sterilization abuse. While poor women in many states have effectively lost access to abortion, they may be sterilized with the full financial support of the government. While the "right" to opt for surgical sterilization is an important feature of women's control over the reproductive functions of their bodies, the imbalance between the difficulty of access to abortions and the ease of access to sterilization reveals the continued and tenacious insinuation of racism into the politics of reproduction. The astoundingly high—and continually mounting—statistics regarding the sterilization of Puerto Rican women expose one of the most dramatic ways in which women's bodies bear the evidence of colonization. Likewise, the bodies of vast numbers of sterilized indigenous women within the presumed borders of the U.S. bear the traces of a 500-year-old tradition of genocide. While there is as yet no evidence of large-scale sterilization of African-American and Latina teenage girls, there is documented evidence of the federal government's promotion and funding of sterilization operations for young Black girls during the 1960s and 70s. This historical precedent convinces me that it is not inappropriate to speculate about such a future possibility of preventing teenage pregnancy. Or—to engage in further speculation—of recruiting healthy young poor women, a disproportionate number of whom would probably be Black, Latina, Native American, Asian, or from the Pacific Islands, to serve as pregnancy carriers for women who can afford to purchase their services.

A majority of all women in jails and prisons are mothers and 7 to 10 percent are pregnant.[9] On the other hand, women's correctional institutions still incorporate and dramatically reveal their ideological links to the cult of motherhood. Even today, imprisoned women are labeled "deviant," not so much because of the crimes they may have committed, but rather because their attitudes and their behavior are seen as blatant contradictions of prevailing expectations—especially in the judicial and law enforcement systems—of women's place. They are mothers who have failed to find themselves in motherhood.

Since the onset of industrial capitalism, women's "deviance" has been constructed in psychological terms; the site of female incarceration has been less the prison and more the mental institution. For this reason, the population of jails and prisons is majority male and a minority female, while the reverse is the case in the mental institutions. The strategic role of domesticity in the structure and correctional goals of women's prisons revolves around the notion that to rehabilitate women, you must teach them how to be good wives and good mothers. Federal prisons such as Alderson Federal Reformatory for women in West Virginia and state institutions like the California Institute for Women and Bedford Hills in the state of New York attempt to architecturally—albeit mechanistically—evoke family life. Instead of cells there are cottages; here women have historically "learned" how to keep house, wash and iron clothes, do the dishes, etc. What bearing does this have on the politics of reproduction? I would suggest that there is something to be learned from the egregious contradiction of this emphasis on training for motherhood within a prison system that intransigently refuses to allow incarcerated women to pursue any meaningful relationship with their own children.

In the San Francisco Bay area, there are only three alternative institutions where women serving jail sentences may live with their children—the Elizabeth Fry Center, Mandela House, and Keller House. In all three places combined, there is space for about 20 to 25 women. In the meantime, thousands of women in the area suffer the threat—or reality—of having their children taken away from them and made wards of the court. Imprisoned women who admit that they have drug problems and seek to rehabilitate themselves often discover that their admissions are used as evidence of their incapacity to be good mothers. In the jails and prisons where they are incarcerated, they are presumably being taught to be good mothers, even as they are powerless to prevent the state from seizing their own children. Excepting a small minority of alternative "correctional" institutions, where social stereotypes are being questioned (although in most instances, the structure of incarceration itself is left unchallenged), the underlying agenda of this motherhood training is to turn aggressive women into submissive and dependent "mothers," whose children are destined to remain motherless.

The process through which a significant portion of the population of young Black, Latina, Native American, Asian, and Pacific women are criminalized, along with the poor European women, who, by their association with women of color are deemed criminal, hinges on a manipulation of a certain ideological representation of motherhood. A poor teenage Black or Latina girl who is a single mother is suspected of criminality simply by virtue of the fact that she is poor and has had a child "out of wedlock." This process of criminalization affects the young men in a different way—not as fathers, but rather by virtue of a more all-embracing racialization. Any young Black man can be potentially labeled as criminal: a shabby appearance is equated with drug addiction, yet an elegant and expensive self-presentation is interpreted as drug dealing. While it may appear that this process of criminalization is unrelated to the construction of the politics of reproduction, there are significant implications here for the expansion of single motherhood in Black and Latino communities. The 25 percent of African-American men in jails and prisons,[10] for example, naturally find it difficult, even in a vicarious sense, to engage in any significant parenting projects.

In pursuing a few of the ways in which racism—and class bias—inform the contemporary politics of reproduction, I am suggesting that there are numerous unexplored vantage points from which we can reconceptualize reproductive issues. It is no longer acceptable to ground an analysis of the politics of reproduction in a conceptual construction of "woman" as a sex. It is not enough to assume that female beings whose bodies are distinguished by vaginas, ovarian tubes, uteri, and other biological features related to reproduction should be able to claim such "rights" to exercise control over the processes of these organs, as the right to abortion. The social/economic/political circumstances that oppress and marginalize women of various racial, ethnic, and class backgrounds, and thus alter the impact of ideological conceptions of motherhood, cannot be ignored without affirming the same structures of domination that have led to such different—but related—politics of reproduction in the first place.

In conclusion, I will point to some of the strategic constellations that should be taken into consideration in reconceiving an agenda of reproductive rights. I do not present the following points as an exhaustive list of such goals, but rather I am trying to allude to a few of the contemporary issues requiring further theoretical examination and practical/political action. While the multiple arenas in which women's legal abortion rights are presently being assaulted and eroded can account for the foregrounding of this struggle, the failure to regard economic accessibility of birth control and abortion has equally important results in the inevitable marginalization of poor women's reproductive rights. With respect to a related issue, the "right" and access to sterilization is important, but again, it is equally important to look at those economic and ideological conditions that track some women toward sterilization, thus denying them the possibility of bearing and rearing children in numbers they themselves choose.

Although the new reproductive technologies cannot be construed as inherently affirmative or violative of women's reproductive rights, the anchoring of the technologies to the profit schemes of their producers and distributors results in a commodification of motherhood that complicates and deepens power relationships based on class and race. Yet, beneath this marriage of technology, profit, and the assertion of a historically obsolete bourgeois individualism lies the critical issue of the right to determine the character of one's family. The assault on this "right"—a term I have used throughout, which is not, however, unproblematic—is implicated in the ideological offensive against single motherhood as well as in the homophobic refusal to recognize lesbian and gay family configurations—and especially in the persisting denial of custody (even though some changes have occurred) to lesbians with children from previous heterosexual marriages. This is one of the many ways in which the present-day ideological compulsion toward motherhood that I have attempted to weave into all of my arguments further resonates. Moreover, this ideology of motherhood is wedded to an obdurate denial of the very social services women require in order to make meaningful choices to bear or not to bear children. Such services include health care—from the prenatal period to old age—child care, housing, education, jobs, and all the basic services human beings require to lead decent lives. The privatization of family responsibilities—particularly during an era when so many new family configurations are being invented that the definition of family stretches beyond its own borders—takes on increasingly reactionary implications. This is why I want to close with a point of departure: the reconceptualization of family and of reproductive rights in terms that move from the private to the public, from the individual to the social.

NOTES

1. See Harriet A. Jacobs. *Incidents in the Life of a Slave Girl.* Edited and Introduction by Jean Fagan Yellin. Cambridge, Mass.: Harvard University Press, p. 1087.

2. See Michelle Stanworth, ed. *Reproductive Technologies: Gender, Motherhood and Medicine.* Minneapolis: University of Minnesota Press, 1987.

3. See Paula Giddings. *When and Where I Enter: The Impact of Black Women on Race and Sex in America.* New York: William Morrow, 1984.

4. Dorothy Scarborough, *On the Trail of Negro Folksongs,* Hatboro, Pennsylvania: Folklore Associates, Inc, 1963. (original edition published by Harvard University Press, 1925), p. 145.

5. *Ibid.,* p. 148.

6. *Ibid.*

7. The tradition of Black women acting as "play mothers" is still a vital means of inventing kinship relations unrelated to biological origin.

8. Gerald David Jaynes and Robin M. Williams, Jr., ed. *A Common Destiny: Blacks and American Society,* Washington, D.C.: National Academy Press, 1989, p. 515.

9. See Ellen M. Barry. "Pregnant Prisoners," *Harvard Women's Law Journal,* vol. 12, 1989.

10. See Marc Mauer, "Young Black Men and the Criminal Justice System: A Growing National Problem." A Report by the Sentencing Project, 918 F Street, N.W. Suite 501, Washington, D.C. 20004, February 1990.

R E A D I N G   3 8

The Politics of Breast Cancer

SUSAN M. LOVE, M.D., with KAREN LINDSEY

If "everything is political," as they say, the politics of cancer have their roots in the 1950s. In 1952 the American Cancer Society started the Reach to Recovery program. This was a group of women helping women: survivors of breast cancer helping newly diagnosed women. Members of Reach to Recovery, all of whom had had mastectomies, would visit the patient in the hospital and reassure her that there was life after mastectomy. They were, and continue to be, a wonderful resource for women with breast cancer.

From there, support groups for women with breast cancer evolved. Women sat together and talked about their experiences and their feelings. It was tremendously helpful for these people to learn they were not alone in their feelings about a disease that was shrouded in so much mystery and fear.

Susan M. Love, M.D., with Karen Lindsey, "The Politics of Breast Cancer" from *Dr. Susan Love's Breast Book, Second Edition, Fully Revised.* Copyright © 1995, 1991, 1990 by Susan M. Love, M.D. Reprinted with the permission of Addison-Wesley Publishing Company.

All this underlined the fact that there was no psychosocial support from the medical profession—you had to get it from somewhere else. And since the disease remained one hidden from public view, there was still an aura of something shameful and disreputable about it.

The politics of breast cancer accelerated in the 1970s, when Shirley Temple Black, Betty Ford, and Happy Rockefeller told the world they had breast cancer. Their openness began to create an environment in which breast cancer could be looked at as a dangerous disease that needed to be addressed by public institutions, rather than a private and shameful secret. There was a dramatic increase in the number of women in America who got mammograms, and in the number of breast cancer cases diagnosed.

Those were the days of the one-step procedure. You'd go in for the biopsy; it would be done under general anesthetic and, if the lump was positive, your breast would be immediately removed. You'd go under the anesthetic not knowing whether you'd have a breast when you woke up. There was no psychosocial support: your doctor wouldn't talk with you beyond telling you it was cancer (if they even told you that) and they removed your breast.

In 1977 Rose Kushner, a writer with breast cancer, wrote a terribly important book, *Why Me?* It ushered in the two-step procedure. Kushner saw no reason for a woman to have to decide whether to have a mastectomy before she even knew if she had breast cancer. She argued passionately that it was important for the woman to have her biopsy, learn if she had cancer, and then, if she did, decide what route to pursue. Doctors were still working on the erroneous assumption that time was everything: if they didn't get the cancer out the instant they found it, it would spread and kill the patient. Kushner had done enough research to realize that wasn't the case—that a few weeks between diagnosis and treatment wouldn't do any medical harm, and would do a great deal of emotional good. She pushed for the two-step procedure, and her book influenced large numbers of women to demand it for themselves. She became a national figure, representing women with breast cancer on the boards designing national studies, moving closer into the realm of politics. She died of breast cancer many years later, in January 1990.

Another force on the horizon at that time was Nancy Brinker. Brinker's sister, Susan G. Komen, was diagnosed with breast cancer in 1977 and died in 1980. In 1983 Brinker founded the Susan G. Komen Breast Cancer Foundation, which is based in Dallas, Texas. Ironically, she herself got breast cancer soon afterward. Since the mid-1980s, they've been working to raise money for research. They also try to encourage funding for women to get mammography. They organize the yearly Race for the Cure, which takes place in a number of cities. Brinker's husband is a wealthy businessman, active in Republican politics, and through him she became acquainted with the Bushes, the Reagans, the Quayles, and other important Republicans whose support she was able to enlist in some of her breast-cancer work.

For a long time, that was pretty much all that was going on around breast cancer. Then in the late 1980s, almost spontaneously, in different parts of the country a number of political women's cancer groups sprang up. One was in the Boston area, started by a patient of mine, Susan Shapiro, who had breast cancer. When she was diagnosed, she began to search for anyone working on the political issues around women and cancer, and she couldn't find anything. Yet she was passionately convinced that there were political implications to cancer, and particularly to women's cancers. She wrote an article in the feminist newspaper *Sojourner,* called "Cancer as a Feminist Issue," and at the end of it she announced a meeting at the Cambridge Women's Center. A lot of women showed up, women who had been as frustrated as she by the lack of political response to their disease. They formed the Women's Community Cancer Project. Their scope was fairly broad, including all cancers that women got and the role of women as caretakers for children, spouses, and parents with cancer. Inevitably, much of the focus was on breast cancer. Shapiro died in January 1990, but the project continues to flourish.

At about the same time the Women's Community Cancer Project was beginning, another group in Oakland, California, The Women's Cancer Resource Center, started, founded by a lesbian named Jackie Winnow. It too was a political group. There was a second group in the Bay Area, Breast Cancer Action, founded by Eleanor Pred, an older woman with breast cancer who modeled her work on some AIDS activism.

In Washington, D.C., the Mary-Helen Mautner Project for Lesbians with Cancer was formed by Susan Hester after Mautner, her partner, died of breast cancer. Its purpose was to provide support for lesbians with cancer, based on the model of the AIDS buddy programs.

These four groups emerged at around the same time. There were obvious differences: in two cases, the focus was lesbians, and in two the focus was all cancers. But all were based on the premise that there were political, not just personal, aspects of cancer that affected women.

All of these groups were aware of the work the AIDS movement had been doing. For the first time we were seeing people with a killer disease aggressively demanding more money for research, changes in insurance bias, and job protection. Women with breast cancer took note of that—particularly those women who had been part of the feminist movement, and were geared, as the gay activists with AIDS were, to the idea of identifying oppression and confronting it politically.

At the time these groups were emerging, I was finishing work on the first edition of [my] book. As I went on my book tour, talking with women, I began to realize how deep women's anger was, and how ready they were to do something. The key moment for me was in Salt Lake City in June 1990, when I gave a talk for 600 women. It was the middle of the afternoon, during the week, and the audience was mostly older women. It was a pretty long talk, and at the end, I said, "We don't know the answers, and I don't know what we have to do to make President Bush wake up and do something about breast cancer. Maybe we should march topless on the White House." I was making a wisecrack, hoping to end a somber talk with a little lightness.

ASSESSING PATIENTS' SPECIAL NEEDS

SHARON DEEVEY

During the course of [my] research, I worked as a contingent staff nurse on a geropsychiatric unit in a local private hospital. One shift I was assigned to care for a 60-year-old retired nurse named Ann who had been diagnosed with depression. The psychiatrist's admitting note reported that Ann had "no family," but had lived for 35 years with a female roommate.

After I had met Ann, I returned to the nursing station and speculated quietly that this particular patient might be an older lesbian woman. The other nurses knew about my research and one of them asked, "What makes you think that?"

"Well," I said, not exactly sure myself, "because she has lived for 35 years with her roommate, and . . . she has a Gertrude Stein haircut!" How could I explain the "sense" of recognizing someone like myself?

From my research about older gay and lesbian people, I knew to avoid direct discussion of sexual orienta-

tion with older clients. Gay men and lesbian women who grew up before the Gay Liberation Movement are frequently unwilling or unable to discuss their personal lives with strangers. In the 1940s and 1950s, exposure of "homosexuality" almost guaranteed loss of family, job, and basic safety.

Ann was on suicide precautions and needed to be escorted when leaving the unit. I went with her to the laundry room, and while she washed her clothes, I chatted with her and learned something of her situation.

She had met her roommate 35 years ago when Dorie moved in next door. They'd been friends right away, had moved from the small town where they'd lived to the city of Columbus, and had helped each other through school. Ann had worked in several nursing jobs, and Dorie was a retired dietitian.

Things were hard now, Ann reported, because they could not get around much. Their younger woman friend who had been living with them had become seriously ill with cancer and had returned to her family in California. Dorie needed cataract surgery and could not see to drive. Ann had been having crying spells and angry outbursts. She had read about our special geropsychiatric unit and decided to come for help. She

---

I got a great response, and afterward women came up to me asking when the march was, how they could sign up for it, and what they could do to help organize it. I realized that, throughout the country, this issue touched all kinds of women, and that they were all fed up with the fact that this virtual epidemic was being ignored. I saw that it wasn't just in the big centers like San Francisco and Boston and Washington, D.C., where I'd expect to see political movements springing up. It was everywhere—everywhere women were ready to fight for attention to breast cancer.

I felt we needed to have some sort of national organization to give these women the hook they needed to begin organizing. I went to Washington to give a talk to the Mautner Project. Before the talk, I went out to dinner with Susan Hester, the founder of the project and two of her friends. I was talking about the thoughts I'd had after the

Salt Lake City speech. My idea was that maybe we should have a big march, and end it with the formation of a new national organization. Hester thought we needed to go about it the other way around: if we formed the organization, we could get its members to come to a big march.

When I left, I called Amy Langer, the president of NABCO, the National Association of Breast Cancer Organizations, a group dedicated to giving individuals and groups breast cancer information. I asked what she thought of the idea, and she liked it. I also contacted Nancy Brinker of the Komen Foundation.

The four of us met for breakfast in Washington on December 11, 1990, during a breast cancer event—Susan, Amy, Nancy, and I—and we discussed it further. We all were enthusiastic and the result was a planning meeting. We invited Sharon Greene, the executive director of Y-Me, a very large

spoke very quietly, rarely made eye contact, and answered little more than specifically asked. Both her answers and her guarded manner seemed to confirm my speculation about her lifestyle.

The following weekend, I was assigned to the adjoining locked adult unit. I asked the nurse in charge on the geropsychiatric unit to tell me if Ann's roommate came to visit.

A couple of hours later, the nurse came looking for me. "I think you're right about them," she said. "There's something about seeing them together. . . . Why don't you come over and talk to them during your break?"

They were sitting in the corner of the dayroom, talking quietly. Ann looked up in recognition. Her partner Dorie stood as I introduced myself. She had very short, pure white hair and startlingly blue eyes that I knew could see very little.

After a few introductory pleasantries (while I wracked my brain trying to figure out how to support these women), I said, "You seem to be very important to each other."

"Oh, yes," Dorie said. "Neither of us has any other family . . . just a nephew of mine in Cleveland."

"You need to be clear with your doctor and the nurses about that," I said. "You have the right to be treated as each other's family."

"I'm afraid someone will sneer," Dorie said, looking away. I was right. If they were just roommates they would have no reason to be afraid.

"I can't promise that everyone will understand," I answered, being intentionally vague. "This hospital generally respects what patients want, but you'll have to ask to be treated as family to each other." When I reported the conversation to Ann's primary nurse, she agreed about the importance of supporting the relationship and managing the issue sensitively.

Ann was gone the following weekend. In a team meeting, the primary nurse had mentioned the probability of Ann's lesbian sexual orientation to the other team members.

The psychiatrist was adamant. The primary nurse told me that he said no one was to discuss sex with his patient.

"I tried to convince him," she went on, "it's not about sexuality. It's about social isolation, and why Ann's so distrustful of staff, and so guarded with other patients in the dayroom. He wouldn't listen. He just kept repeating, 'no one is to discuss sex with her.' " As it turned out, Ann signed herself out of the hospital against medical advice.

It was the first time I was tempted to follow a patient home from the hospital, but I knew I could not rescue Ann and Dorie by myself. I returned with renewed determination to my research. When I am aging, or ill, and need health care, I can only hope that nurses and physicians will know more about lesbian women and treat me with the same sensitivity and respect they offer anyone else.

---

support group organization in Chicago. Then we got Ann McGuire from the Women's Community Cancer Project, and we invited Eleanor Pred from Breast Cancer Action and Kim Calder from Cancer Care and Canact from New York.

We discussed whether or not any one of the existing groups wanted to take on the political piece, and although everyone was very enthusiastic no one felt they could handle this aspect, so we decided to go for a coalition of groups. The Komen Foundation dropped out and the other groups became the planning committee for the new coalition. We set up several task forces to figure out how we'd go about it and what our goals would be. Amy Langer used NABCO's list and others threw in their lists for an invitation to an organizing meeting in May 1991. Then we called an open meeting, to be held in Washington, and wrote to every women's group we knew of.

We had no idea who'd show up. On the day of the meeting the room was packed. There were representatives from all kinds of groups: the American Cancer Society and the American Jewish Congress were there. So was the Human Rights Campaign Fund, a big gay and lesbian group. There were members of breast cancer support groups from all around the country—such as Arm in Arm from Baltimore, the Linda Creed group from Philadelphia, and Share from New York. Overall there were about 100 or so individuals representing 75 organizations. We were overwhelmed, and we started the National Breast Cancer Coalition on the spot. Out of that meeting came the first Board of the Coalition.

NABCO agreed to be the administrator of the planning committee. Its expenses would be reimbursed from the other groups. As a result Amy chaired the meetings until bylaws and officers could be chosen. A year later Fran

Visco, a lawyer from Philadelphia who had had breast cancer in her late 30s, became the first elected president. She has since taken a leave of absence from her law office and remains the president today.

From this first group of eager participants we formed a volunteer working board. Our first action, in the fall of 1991, was a project we called "Do the Write Thing." We wanted to collect and deliver to Washington 175,000 letters, representing the 175,000 women who would be diagnosed with breast cancer that year. The letters would go both to the president and to various members of Congress.

This was spring, and we were planning this for October, Breast Cancer Awareness Month. Not only did we want 175,000 letters altogether, we wanted the number from each state to match the number in that state who would get breast cancer. We managed to identify groups in each state who could work with us. In October, we ended up with 600,000 letters—it was an enormous response. We delivered them to the White House. The guards just stood there; nobody would help us lift the boxes. All these women who'd had mastectomies were lifting heavy boxes of letters onto the conveyer belt.

We were all certain that the letters would just be dumped into the shredder. To make things worse, we hardly got any media coverage, because the Clarence Thomas-Anita Hill hearings were going on. So we were afraid that our first action had been a flop. But in reality, we had succeeded in a number of ways.

For one thing, we had organized in such a way that we had a group in every state. That meant a large and potentially powerful organization. For another, even if the White House ignored us, the congresspeople didn't. When we started lobbying for increased research money the members of Congress granted us $43 million more, raising the 1993 appropriation to $132 million. That was a small triumph.

One of the things we realized, however, was that we had to do more research ourselves. When we lobbied, the congresspeople who were interested in what we had to say kept asking, "Well, how much money do you need?" And we didn't know.

We realized we had to find out, and quickly. Mary Jo Kahn from the Virginia Breast Cancer Group suggested that we ask the scientists themselves, and Amy Langer suggested we hold research hearings, which we did in February 1992. We invited scientists from around the country who studied breast cancer to come to the hearings. Since we had no money, they had to pay for their own trips. We got $10,000 from a donor in Philadelphia to fund the hearings, and there were other donations as well. We rented a hotel hall, and 15 major research scientists came. They testified about what research wasn't getting done because of lack of funding, and how much money they thought they really needed.

Those hearings went on for a day, and it was one of the first times that scientists and activists interested in breast cancer had met together. The next morning we had a congressional breakfast; many of the scientists came with us and spoke to several of the congressional representatives.

We created an interesting coalition. If the scientists alone lobby for more research money, it looks like they're doing it out of self-interest. But our involvement made it clear that this wasn't about ivory-tower research, but about work that really could save human lives.

We met again after the hearings and came up with a figure: we needed $433 million for breast cancer research. The total 1992 budget was $93 million. So we started lobbying for $300 million more, armed with our report based on the scientists' testimony.

At first the reaction was overwhelmingly negative. Everybody in Congress kept saying there was no money and it would be impossible to come up with anything like another $300 million. People kept insisting that we should reduce it; we were defeating ourselves by demanding so much. But we insisted. What we were being "greedy" for was women's lives, and we weren't willing to compromise.

The National Cancer Institute didn't initially support our efforts. For one thing, it would have embarrassed them. The Institute is bound by law to give a budget to the president every year, called the bypass budget, which is their best estimate of how much money they need. (A leftover from the Nixon administration's War on Cancer, it's called the bypass budget because it bypasses Congress and goes straight to the president.) The bypass budget had only asked for something like $197 million, so they didn't feel like they could support a new demand for $433 million more.

But we kept at it, and when the politicians told us there wasn't any more money, we said, "Well, you found money for the Savings and Loan bailout. You found money for the Gulf War. We think you can find this money too, if you really decide it's important that women are dying." We testified at the Senate, and at the House. We lobbied, we sent faxes, and we called. Eventually we got somewhere—in the fall of 1992 Senator Tom Harkin, who was very sympathetic to us because his two sisters had died of breast cancer, was the chair of the Senate Appropriations Committee in charge of NIH funding. He made sure that the budgeted amount for breast cancer spending at the NIH was $220 million. But that wasn't enough. In order to get the rest of our $433 million total he tried to put forth a transfer amendment that would move money from the Defense Department to the domestic budget. It didn't work.

But we had another advantage at this point—this was the year of the woman. Because of Anita Hill, a lot of congressmen were looking bad when it came to women's issues. They needed to spiff up their images—especially since it was an election year. They realized that breast cancer was a safe thing. There was no racial issue, no question about whether someone was telling the truth or not, no important male judge's reputation at stake—just the stark fact that women were dying. Add to this the demographics of breast cancer—it's most prevalent among white and middle- to upper-class women. These men were being asked to support their own wives, mothers, and sisters, as well as the women who are most likely to vote. So we got a lot of support from men not usually known as feminists or progressives—Arlen Specter was running radio ads in Philadelphia about how important it was to fight breast cancer. Alphonse D'Amato in New York came up with an amendment saying Congress should take 3 percent of the Defense Department's budget to give us our $300 million.

We also, of course, had the more predictable allies—Ted Kennedy held hearings in my office at the Faulkner in Boston on breast cancer research. And, of course, we had strong support from a number of congresswomen, who had their own understanding of the importance of fighting breast cancer.

Then Senator Harkin noticed that, amazingly, in the past there actually had been some money for breast cancer in the Defense Department—$25 million spent on mammogram machines for the army. At our urging he decided to try and increase that to $210 million.

The Defense Department people decided that with all these attacks on their budget, they didn't want to risk their budget being wiped out. If the money officially left their budget, they'd never get it back when they applied for the following year's budget. But if the money stayed in their budget, they could fund breast cancer research this year; and then next year, with the budget still the same or higher, they could spend that money on bombers or whatever else they decided was important. So they agreed to a bill using $210 million of defense money for breast cancer research and it passed.

About 20 senators who had voted against it left while the roll call went on. When it became clear that it was going to pass, these senators literally ran back to the room and down to the podium to change their votes. Presumably they preferred to be on the winning side. Coalition vice-

president Jane Reese Colbourne and others watched on C-SPAN as the senators did their undignified but useful turnaround. We ended up with a final vote of 89 to 4, with seven abstentions.

After all that, our victory was almost destroyed. President Bush challenged the decision because medical research funding was domestic spending and Department of Defense funding was military spending. As Jane Reese Colbourne describes it, "We ended up doing a vigil in front of the Senate while they had a meeting to determine whether we could really use that money. Senator Harkin fought for it. We were ready to call in people from Richmond and Baltimore to relieve us and keep the vigil going. Then Senator Inouye came out and told us we had the money."

So there was $210 million in the Department of Defense budget and the extra $220 million in the NCI budget. That's $430 million total. Against all odds, we had succeeded. Part of it was being in the right place at the right time. But most of it was the enormous amount of work all the women in the coalition and around the country had put in. Overnight, we had an enormous amount of clout and were well recognized for a group that had just begun.

We were ready to move on to our next step. It was one thing to raise money, but we wanted to have a say in how it was spent. We wanted women from our groups, women with breast cancer, to be involved in the decision-making panels on review boards for grants, on the National Cancer Advisory Board, and in all the decision making. We started lobbying for that, and our next major project was to deliver 2.6 million signatures to the White House in October 1993 to represent the 2.6 million women living with breast cancer at the time—1.6 million who knew they had breast cancer, and 1 million who were yet to be diagnosed. We mobilized around the country collecting signatures, and we delivered our 2.6 million signatures to President Clinton on October 18. As a measure of how far we'd gone from October 1991 when the boxes went on the conveyor belt into the shredder, this time we were welcomed in the East Room, where Fran Visco and I shared the stage with both Hillary and Bill Clinton, along with Secretary of Health and Human Services Donna Shalala. The room was filled with 200 of our people. It was an awesome moment.

And President Clinton followed up. In December we had a meeting to set national strategy—a meeting of activists, politicians, scientists, doctors, laypeople, businesspeople. We came up with a National Action Plan. In each one of the subgroups working on this plan, there was one of our activist members. We were at the table and we were changing the policy of business as usual around breast cancer.

Being with the scientists, talking and working with them, the activists were able to learn that the answers aren't always easy, that scientists have to work months and years to come up with one useful discovery. The scientists saw that the activists weren't shrill, uninformed troublemakers, but intelligent, concerned people fighting to save their own and others' lives.

Meanwhile, as in any successful movement, there's been a backlash. It's come from two places. One is from the people who have been working with breast cancer for a long time. They see the National Breast Cancer Coalition as the brash new upstart trying to shake up the status quo. And indeed we are. Nothing had changed for years, and it is time that we had some action around this issue.

There's also been a backlash from some of the scientists. They're glad for the funding, but they don't like the idea of having medical research funds earmarked for specific diseases. They point out that some of the discoveries about breast cancer have come from studying other things—which is true. One gene found in studying a rare eye cancer turned out to be present also in breast cancer. But there are an awful lot of things they've studied that haven't told us anything about breast cancer. They have this romantic notion about how only the curiosity of a scientist can bring about a medical miracle—you throw seeds into the fields and among the weeds the wildflowers will come up. And we're saying, yes, but we'll get more of the particular flowers we need if we do a little cultivation.

What it's really about is power—who gets to decide how the money is spent. Should it be decided by the taxpayer, whose money, after all, it is? Or should it be decided by the scientists in terms of their curiosity? They say, "We can't just give the money to whoever yells the loudest, and we can't politicize research and science." But research and science have always been political—it just depends on whose research and whose politics it is. Is it Nixon's war on cancer, or Jerry Lewis's Muscular Dystrophy, or the Heart Association clammering for more money and more research? What's different is that now there is a new group in the melee. And that's really what the backlash is about.

In fact, the National Breast Cancer Coalition has had a strict policy from the beginning to try not to rob one disease for another. We have always been clear that we want a bigger pie, not a bigger piece of a pie that's never been large enough in the first place. That's one of the reasons it's so important the increased funding we got this year came from the Department of Defense—not from AIDS research or asthma research or any other essential medical area.

The scientists then argue that eventually the money won't come from the military or some other budget, that it will come from some other disease research. But that "eventually" is a long way off—there's a lot of useless government spending that we can go after first.

The other argument is that the amount of money per case of cancer should be equal across all cancers. X amount of money per case of breast cancer, X amount for lung cancer. But that's too simplistic a way to measure it. The important measure is what we know about the disease. We know what causes lung cancer. But we don't know what to do about breast cancer yet. This doesn't mean the other diseases don't need money. We need to fight the tobacco industry and do better anti-smoking campaigns. But we need much more money for diseases like breast cancer, for which we don't yet have the information to get out to people.

The exciting thing is that one of the goals we had was to get researchers into the field. Generally speaking, there are only about eight centers that are specializing in breast cancer in the country.

One of the reasons we wanted the money from the Department of Defense was to attract new people, to get researchers working on new aspects of breast cancer. And it worked. With the $210 million made available by the Department of Defense, they got 2,400 grant applications. Many of these were people who had never done breast cancer research before.

And we now have representation at many of the levels at which decisions are made. Fran Visco sits as one of three members of the President's Cancer Panel. Kay Dickersin, from Arm in Arm in Maryland, was just appointed to the National Cancer Advisory Board. We were on the oversight committee for the Department of Defense money and involved in the study sections. We are forging the National Action Plan with the Department of Health and Human Services.

Our goals remain the same. We want access for all women to high-quality screening and treatment for breast cancer. The Mammography Quality Standards Act (see Chapter 10) is a first step. Health care reform will be another. We want influence for women with breast cancer. We are currently training activists to be effective advocates and contribute when they get a seat at the table. And we want research into the cause of breast cancer, how to prevent it and how to cure it. The increase in environmental research as well as basic research is in part in response to our efforts. We want more basic research, rather than focus our energies on how to treat existing disease. We need both, of course, but ultimately, the goal is to stop the cancer before a woman gets it in the first place.

I've learned through this that you really can affect how the government acts. A small group of committed people can do a lot. So few people let their feelings be known that the people who do it, and do it vociferously, get an undue amount of power. We didn't have any money—not like the gun lobby or the tobacco industry. But we organized. And now some of the groups with money started to help us— Revlon has been supporting women's lives as well as their looks. They paid for the petition campaign.

Many of the women in the coalition have never been involved in political action before, and they're finding themselves working side by side with baby boomers who marched in the '60s and learned the value of political protest—and now are confronting breast cancer, and realizing that like civil rights and war resistance and the early women's movement issues, breast cancer research needs to be fought for.

At the same time, breast cancer affects women of all ages, and all political stripes. Eighty-year-old women get breast cancer; thirty-year-old women get breast cancer. Democrats and Republicans and radicals and conservatives get breast cancer. Heterosexual and bisexual and lesbian women get breast cancer. Caucasian, African American, Hispanic, and Asian women get breast cancer.

This is an issue we can all agree on and one we have to all fight for. We can't afford to be good girls any longer. We can't let this disease pass on to another generation. Our lives and the lives of our daughters depend on it.

Last year at the Los Angeles Breast Cancer Coalition "War Mammorial" the Coalition put white plastic casts of women's torsos, 1,300 of them, on a hill. From a distance they looked like graves but up close they showed the variety of women's bodies: large breasts, small breasts, some with mastectomies and some with implants. Katie, my five-year-old daughter, was walking around trying to figure out which breasts she wanted when she grew up. Then she turned serious.

"Are these the graves of women with breast cancer?" she asked.

"No, these women are all alive," I told her. "But some women do die from breast cancer."

"Well, you're trying to stop that aren't you, Mommy?"

"Yes, Katie, I would like to stop breast cancer before you grow up."

She thought about that a minute. "What if you die first?" she asked.

"I'd like to stop breast cancer before I die," I replied. She thought again, then turned to me and said, "If there is breast cancer left after you die it is a big problem. Because I'm not going to be a breast surgeon. I'm going to be a ballerina."

Well, Katie doesn't have to worry—she can go ahead and be a ballerina. And she won't be haunted, as so many women are now, by the fear of getting breast cancer. As long as we keep fighting, the discoveries we're making, buttressed by the political activism that lets the scientists and the government know that we won't let up until we've ended breast cancer, will bring about her wish. That's what keeps me going. Twenty years from now, a comfortable retiree with no more breast cancer to worry about, I can sit in the audience waiting for the curtain to rise and my beautiful, healthy daughter to pirouette across the stage.

Violence against Women

Violence against women manifests itself in many forms. Verbal harassment, sexual imposition, sexual assault, rape, domestic battering, and lesbian bashing all contribute to a social climate that encourages women to comply with men's desires or to restrict their activities in order to avoid assault. The threat of violence against women is pervasive across cultures. Feminist analyses of violence against women focus on the extent to which violence serves as a means for the institutionalized social control of women by men. The articles in this section analyze various forms of violence against women and contrast beliefs and actualities about various kinds of male violence. Often, male-controlled ideologies encourage us to accept violence against women as either harmless or deserved. Feminist analyses take the position that this violence constitutes a system through which men frighten and therefore control and dominate women.

Sexual harassment is a form of sexual coercion that affects women's ability to function appropriately in work and academic settings. The first article in this section, " 'The Man in the Street': Why He Harasses," by Cheryl Benard and Edit Schlaffer, points out just how common harassing assaults on women are; they occur not only at work but in many public places—in coffee shops, in self-service laundries, and on the street. Benard and Schlaffer interviewed men on the streets who harassed them and found that what feminists have suggested is indeed accurate. Street harassment is not a way to flatter women but a form of male bonding through which men aggrandize their egos. Although some may consider the street harasser a minor offender, this article suggests his role as "an accomplice in the more massive forms of violence against women."

Patricia Yancey Martin and Robert A. Hummer also explore the implications of heterosexual male bonding in "Fraternities and Rape on Campus." Fraternity members' negative attitudes toward women, rigid ideas about masculinity, and pressures to demonstrate simultaneously their heterosexuality and their utter loyalty to the "brotherhood" create fraternity cultures in which men use women to demonstrate their masculinity and worth.

Pauline B. Bart and Patricia H. O'Brien make an empirical examination of women's likelihood of escaping attackers by fighting back. In "Stopping Rape: Effective Avoidance Strategies," we discover that women who resist assault escape more often than women who follow popular advice to submit to an assailant. Bart and O'Brien's research also offers an analysis of the particular strategies that women have used effectively against male assailants.

Hate crimes are crimes motivated by prejudice against particular groups. Because violence against women is so widespread, we sometimes fail to recognize it as a crime of hate. By situating the murders of women in a sexist control context in " 'Femicide': Speaking the Unspeakable," Jane Caputi and Diana E. H. Russell demonstrate that we can usefully regard such murders as crimes against women as a group, not just individual and apolitical assaults by deranged men.

Violence against women, as all these articles point out, is not simply the act of individual men against individual women. Instead, it is created and perpetuated by social institutions. The final article in this section, "Accountability or Justice? Rape as a War Crime," by Mary Ann Tetreault, documents the use of rape as "an instrument of policy" in wartime. Focusing on the Iraqi invasion of Kuwait and the war in Bosnia-Herzogovina, Tetreault examines the use of rape and charges of rape as political fodder against the enemy, the treatment of rape victims by their own communities and governments, and the responses of war crimes tribunals to rape charges. She argues that, as in other forms of rape, the shame associated with being raped prevents many women from reporting their assaults or seeking damages from war crimes tribunals.

"The Man in the Street": Why He Harasses

CHERYL BENARD and EDIT SCHLAFFER

It is a violation of my natural external freedom not to be able to go where I please, and to experience other restrictions of this kind. . . . Even though the body and life are something external, just like property, nevertheless my personality is wounded by such experiences, because my most immediate identity rests in my body.

Hegel, *Texte zur philosophischen Propaedeutik*

I am standing at Wittenbergplatz waiting for the light to turn green, in my left hand I am carrying a bag filled with groceries . . . behind me I sense the approach of two men and turn my head, at that moment the man on my left reaches for my hair which falls to my shoulders colored with henna, he runs his fingers through my hair experimentally and says to his friend: great hair. . . . An ordinary everyday experience for the colonized in a city of the First World.

Verena Stefan, *Haeutungen*

By the time we are in our twenties we have become accustomed to the laws of the street. The abrupt but regular interruptions of our daily movements have become familiar, we have acquired the habit of overhearing comments, we are graceful at dodging straying hands, we have the skill of a general in making rapid strategic evaluations, we can usually tell at a glance whether that group of young men leaning against a car door might use physical intimidation or just jokes, whispered comments, laughter, whether it's worth crossing over to the other side of the street or enough to act nonchalant and cultivate deafness. It's no longer frightening, just annoying, sometimes jolting when one is called abruptly out of a train of thought or a moment of absentmindedness. One gets used to it.

Is all of this normal, inevitable? It was a question I had stopped asking myself by the time I spent a year abroad at the university in Beirut. In the dorm I shared a room with Widad from Bahrein, an 18-year-old who wanted to be a teacher. At home, Widad always wrapped an abaya around her jeans and T-shirt when she went out of the house, and to Widad, the behavior of men on the street was news. Not yet hardened by long experience, Widad spent her first week in Beirut in tears. Sobbing with anger and confusion, she would report on the insulting and unbelievable things that had been said to her, the grabbing, the pushing, the comments, the aggressive looks, the smacking lips, the hissing in her ear. The abaya, she would conclude, has nothing to do with women. In Bahrein we wear it because of the men, someday maybe we won't have to but right now, this is how they are, and who can stand it? The final outcome, I am sorry to report, was not that Widad became hardened and militant, schooled in the martial arts and an example to us all, but that she was instrumental in organizing a group of Bahreini men, so that for the rest of the academic year the women from Bahrein moved through the city like a convoy flanked by a string of guards ready to fight at the sign of a covetous glance.

For the American women, this was an occasion to think again about the kind of world we have learned to accept as normal. On public streets, we plan our routes and our timing as if we were passing through a mine field. We are touched, harassed, commented upon in a stream of constant small-scale assaults, and in a culture which values privacy and anonymity in crowds these intimacies are considered inevitable. Secretly, women like it, popular opinion believes, and posters of men whistling after a woman are thought by advertising agencies to sell their product. Besides, popular opinion goes on to explain, women provoke it, with their fashions, their manner of walking, their behavior. These are familiar arguments; we hear them whenever the subject of violence against women comes up. There are few facts to hold up against them. Stamped as trivial, the harassment of women has received no attention from sociology, and cities that regulate almost everything from bicycles and dogs to the use of roller skates in order to keep the traffic moving have no ordinances or rules to guarantee women the right to free passage.

What kinds of men harass women, what do they think they are doing, how do women feel about it? Diaries and essays by women, and reports from other times and cultures, give some very sketchy information. For a more systematic picture, we observed the behavior of men in four cities (Berlin, Los Angeles, Rome, and Vienna) over the period of a year, allowing for differences in season, time of day, and part of town. Interviews with women provided information on how the victims feel. Some of the results were surprising and some were depressingly predictable.

That the behavior of the "man on the street" has received so little attention is odd, because it captures in quintessential, almost primordial form the combination of the ordinary and the bizarre which we have learned to regard as normal. The "man on the street" is a synonym for everyone, which in our society means every man. The behavior he casually accords to randomly passing women he has never seen before serves to identify him as a member of the ruling group, to whom the streets and the society belong. And at the same time this behavior, looked at with an analytic eye, is very peculiar. The anthropologist from outer space, that popular device for viewing the world with a bit more perspective, would be very astonished to find adult males moaning, jumping, whistling, singing, honking, winking, contorting face and body, hissing obscenities, laughing hysterically, and mumbling hoarse endearments to perfect strangers without apparent provocation. However odd, though, these single and seemingly irrational instances add up to a pattern, and the pattern spells intimidation.

Women are assigned, in this interaction, an inevitably passive part. They have a number of available responses, but their response makes little difference. A woman can ignore what she sees or hears, she can reply, she can curse, keep walking, stop, try for a disarming smile, get angry, start a discussion. What she does has little influence. A friendly answer may stop the man, or it may encourage him to further intimacies; threats and curses may silence him, or they may prompt genuine aggression. The language itself puts us at a permanent disadvantage; it is hard to exchange serious insults without using sexual putdowns that invariably go against women. And passers-by, far from supporting a woman who defends herself, will shed their former indifference to disapprove of feminine vulgarity.

It is commonly supposed that certain countries and cultures display this behavior more than others; the Mediterranean cultures, particularly, are assumed to be swarming with papagallos dedicated to the female foreign tourist. In fact, this form of male behavior is distributed quite evenly across the continents, races, and generations. The nationalist author Qasim Amin deplored the harassment of the heavily veiled Egyptian women at the turn of the century and in fact attributed masculine aggression to the veil. As a sign of women's inferior status, he argued, it encouraged men to treat them with disrespect and take liberties. This interpretation comes very close to the truth. Like other forms of sexual violence, harassment has little to do with the individual woman and nothing to do with sex; the issue is power.

Whether you wear a slit skirt or are covered from head to foot in a black chador, the message is not that you are attractive enough to make a man lose his self-control but that the public realm belongs to him and you are there by his permission as long as you follow his rules and as long as you remember your place. Badr-al-Moluk Bamdad recalls in her book on growing up in Iran that there was no way for a woman to win this game; if, in the opinion of any passing male, one's veil was not wrapped with sufficient modesty, one could be insulted, reprimanded, and threatened, while if obediently covered one would be followed and taunted by boys and young men shouting that one looked like a "black crow or an inkwell."*

Harassment of women is timeless, but the notion that women really like it and feel flattered is a refinement that has been added more recently. Women's own accounts have always shown a clear awareness of the essential hostility implied by these male attentions, even when they didn't put that awareness into the context of any more general picture of sexist structures. Descriptions have been handed down to us from many different sources. Evelyn Scott, an American

---

*Badr-al-Moluk Bamdad, *Women's Emancipation in Iran* (New York, 1977).

woman who later was to become a successful author, spent the year of 1916 in Brazil with her lover. They were poor, she was pregnant. In her diary, she wrote that, in Rio, "something objectionable always occurred" when she went outdoors unaccompanied. "Perhaps it is because I am only 20 years old," she wrote. "Perhaps it is because I am shabbily dressed. I know perfectly well that I am not particularly pretty. Inwardly shrinking and cold with an obscure fear, I make it a point to look very directly at all the men who speak to me. I want to shame them by the straightforwardness of my gaze. Perhaps I am ridiculous. If I could consider sex more factually and with less mystical solemnity I might find amusement in the stupidity of these individuals who can't be so sinister after all."*

Anger and an "obscure fear" are the most common responses of women, and those feelings are all the greater when the situation seems too intimidating to allow a reply. Pretending to have heard nothing, looking away, hoping the men will get bored and stop or will be too busy with the woman walking in front of you to attend to you are calculations that increase the impact of the experience. A 22-year-old law student remembered one pivotal incident in her life: "I was 17, and just walking around downtown with my friend Marie. Two men started talking to us, making jokes and telling us to come with them. They grabbed our arms and tried to pull us along. Marie got angry and told them to let us go. The men pushed her against a building and started shaking her and saying she was unfriendly and stuck up and should watch out. Finally they left. It was afternoon and there were a lot of people around, but nobody said anything. At the time I learned from that that it was better to ignore men who talked to you like that. If you act like you don't care, they usually let you go without any trouble. I don't think that's a very good conclusion to draw, but I still don't know how to act in situations like that without getting into trouble."

What is going on in the minds of the men who do this? Not much, judging from their difficulties in articulating their intentions. We interviewed 60 men, choosing a range of age groups out of those who addressed us on the street. (Incidentally, this was the only female response we found that genuinely and predictably disarms the harassing male, so if you want to transform a lewdly smirking man into a politely confused one within a matter of seconds you need only pull a mimeographed questionnaire out of your bag and inform him that he is part of a research project. This

method, however, is rather time-consuming.) Pressed for an explanation of their behavior, most of the men initially played it down. Boredom and a feeling of youthful camaraderie that came over them when discussing women with other men emerged as the most frequent feelings prompting harassment. The notion that women disliked this and felt infringed upon in their freedom of movement was a novel one for most men, not because they had another image of the woman's response but because they had never given it any thought at all. Only a minority, around 15%, explicitly set out to anger or humiliate their victims. This is the same group that employs graphic sexual commentary and threats. Other forms of antagonism often become mixed up with the sexual. Some migrant laborers or construction workers insult not so much the woman as the snobbish privileged class she symbolizes to them. Another minority of men believes with firm conviction that women enjoy receiving their attention. One 45-year-old construction worker portrayed himself as a kind of benefactor to womanhood and claimed to specialize in older and less attractive women to whom, he was sure, his display of sexual interest was certain to be the highlight in an otherwise drab and joyless existence. A significant group of men, around 20%, said that they would not engage in this behavior when alone, but only in the company of male friends. This supports the explanation that the harassment of women is a form of male bonding, of demonstrating solidarity and joint power.

The symbolic nature of the behavior is its most important attribute. A surprising finding was that harassment declines in the late evening and during the night, and that men are then more likely to display the kind of behavior typical of the avoidance usually shown to strangers in public or crowded situations: averting one's eyes, accelerating the pace of walking to keep a distance, etc. At first glance, this finding is surprising. It would seem that harassment would be even more effective at night, even more intimidating to the woman. Probably, this is precisely the reason it declines during the night; on a deserted street, it would be *too* effective. The woman, not merely annoyed or unnerved but genuinely alarmed, might well be driven to an "extreme" response (such as calling for help) that the good citizen would not like to have to explain. In the daytime, he takes no such risk. The age, education, and income of the man make little difference; in their street behavior, they revert to a primordially uniform condition across the lines of class and generation. Younger men tend to be more aggressive, and older men to lower their voices and whisper hastily as they pass you. Some areas are exempt altogether: small villages, where all the inhabitants know each other, and residential suburban areas.

*Mary Jane Moffat and Charlotte Painter, eds., *Revelations: Diaries of Women* (New York: Vintage, 1974), p. 100.

The genuinely *public* world is the main arena for harassment. The street, as a place where strangers encounter each other, is also the place where societies have always taken care to clearly mark the lines of order and status. It is on the streets that members of subordinate groups have to wear special clothing or identifying marks, that they must salute, take off their hat, or jump down from the sidewalk to make way for the members of the superior group. Harassment is a way of ensuring that women will not feel at ease, that they will remember their role as sexual beings available to men and not consider themselves equal citizens participating in public life. But the ritual of harassment does more than that. By its seeming harmlessness and triviality, it blurs the borders of women's right to personal integrity, and encourages men who would never commit a violent crime against a strange woman to participate in minor transgressions against her right to move freely, to choose which interactions to participate in and which people to communicate with. By making of the "man on the street," the average man, a minor sex offender, it also makes him an accomplice in the more massive forms of violence against women.

READING 40

Fraternities and Rape on Campus

PATRICIA YANCEY MARTIN and ROBERT A. HUMMER

Rapes are perpetrated on dates, at parties, in chance encounters, and in specially planned circumstances. That group structure and processes, rather than individual values or characteristics, are the impetus for many rape episodes was documented by Blanchard (1959) 30 years ago (also see Geis 1971), yet sociologists have failed to pursue this theme (for an exception, see Chancer 1987). A recent review of research (Muehlenhard and Linton 1987) on sexual violence, or rape, devotes only a few pages to the situational contexts of rape events, and these are conceptualized as potential risk factors for individuals rather than qualities of rape-prone social contexts.

Many rapes, far more than come to the public's attention, occur in fraternity houses on college and university campuses, yet little research has analyzed fraternities at American colleges and universities as rape-prone contexts (cf. Ehrhart and Sandler 1985). Most of the research on fraternities reports on samples of individual fraternity men.

One group of studies compares the values, attitudes, perceptions, family socioeconomic status, psychological traits (aggressiveness, dependence), and so on, of fraternity and nonfraternity men (Bohrnstedt 1969; Fox, Hodge, and Ward 1987; Kanin 1967; Lemire 1979; Miller 1973). A second group attempts to identify the effects of fraternity membership over time on the values, attitudes, beliefs, or moral precepts of members (Hughes and Winston 1987; Marlowe and Auvenshine 1982; Miller 1973; Wilder, Hoyt, Doren, Hauck, and Zettle 1978; Wilder, Hoyt, Surbeck, Wilder, and Carney 1986). With minor exceptions, little research addresses the group and organizational context of fraternities or the social construction of fraternity life (for exceptions, see Letchworth 1969; Longino and Kart 1973; Smith 1964).

Gary Tash, writing as an alumnus and trial attorney in his fraternity's magazine, claims that over 90 percent of all gang rapes on college campuses involve fraternity men (1988, p. 2). Tash provides no evidence to substantiate this claim, but students of violence against women have been concerned with fraternity men's frequently reported involvement in rape episodes (Adams and Abarbanel 1988). Ehrhart and Sandler (1985) identify over 50 cases of gang rapes on campus perpetrated by fraternity men, and their analysis points to many of the conditions that we discuss here. Their analysis is unique in focusing on conditions in fraternities that make gang rapes of women by fraternity men both feasible and probable. They identify excessive alcohol use, isolation from external monitoring, treatment of women as prey, use of pornography, approval of violence, and excessive concern with competition as precipitating conditions to gang rape (also see Merton 1985; Roark 1987).

The study reported here confirmed and complemented these findings by focusing on both conditions and processes. We examined dynamics associated with the social construction of fraternity life, with a focus on processes that foster the use of coercion, including rape, in fraternity men's relations with women. Our examination of men's social fraternities on college and university campuses as groups and organizations led us to conclude that fraternities are a physical and sociocultural context that encourages the sexual coercion of women. We make no claims that all fraternities are "bad" or that all fraternity men are rapists. Our observations indicated, however, that rape is especially probable in fraternities because of the kinds of organizations they are, the kinds of members they have, the practices their members engage in, and a virtual absence of university or community oversight. Analyses that lay blame for rapes by fraternity men on "peer pressure" are, we feel, overly simplistic (cf. Burkhart 1989; Walsh 1989). We suggest, rather, that fraternities create a sociocultural context in which the use of coercion in sexual relations with women is normative and in which the mechanisms to keep this pattern of behavior in check are minimal at best and absent at worst. We conclude that unless fraternities change in fundamental ways, little improvement can be expected.

METHODOLOGY

Our goal was to analyze the group and organizational practices and conditions that create in fraternities an abusive social context for women. We developed a conceptual framework from an initial case study of an alleged gang rape at Florida State University that involved four fraternity men and an 18-year-old coed. The group rape took place on the third floor of a fraternity house and ended with the "dumping" of the woman in the hallway of a neighboring fraternity house. According to newspaper accounts, the victim's blood-alcohol concentration, when she was discovered, was .349 percent, more than three times the legal limit

for automobile driving and an almost lethal amount. One law enforcement officer reported that sexual intercourse occurred during the time the victim was unconscious: "She was in a life-threatening situation" (*Tallahassee Democrat,* 1988b). When the victim was found, she was comatose and had suffered multiple scratches and abrasions. Crude words and a fraternity symbol had been written on her thighs (*Tampa Tribune,* 1988). When law enforcement officials tried to investigate the case, fraternity members refused to cooperate. This led, eventually, to a five-year ban of the fraternity from campus by the university and by the fraternity's national organization.

In trying to understand how such an event could have occurred, and how a group of over 150 members (exact figures are unknown because the fraternity refused to provide a membership roster) could hold rank, deny knowledge of the event, and allegedly lie to a grand jury, we analyzed newspaper articles about the case and conducted open-ended interviews with a variety of respondents about the case and about fraternities, rapes, alcohol use, gender relations, and sexual activities on campus. Our data included over 100 newspaper articles on the initial gang rape case; open-ended interviews with Greek (social fraternity and sorority) and non-Greek (independent) students (N = 20); university administrators (N = 8, five men, three women); and alumni advisers to Greek organizations (N = 6). Open-ended interviews were held also with judges, public and private defense attorneys, victim advocates, and state prosecutors regarding the processing of sexual assault cases. Data were analyzed using the grounded theory method (Glaser 1978; Martin and Turner 1986). In the following analysis, concepts generated from the data analysis are integrated with the literature on men's social fraternities, sexual coercion, and related issues.

FRATERNITIES AND THE SOCIAL CONSTRUCTION OF MEN AND MASCULINITY

Our research indicated that fraternities are vitally concerned—more than with anything else—with masculinity (cf. Kanin 1967). They work hard to create a macho image and context and try to avoid any suggestion of "wimpishness," effeminacy, and homosexuality. Valued members display, or are willing to go along with, a narrow conception of masculinity that stresses competition, athleticism, dominance, winning, conflict, wealth, material possessions, willingness to drink alcohol, and sexual prowess vis-à-vis women.

MEN CHANGING MEN

ROBERT L. ALLEN and PAUL KIVEL

Batterers need to be penalized for their actions, but the future safety of women and children depends on stopping the violence before it starts. With prevention in mind, Robert Allen and Paul Kivel discuss the work they do with boys and men in the Oakland Men's Project (OMP). Formed in 1979, this California-based group is a nonprofit, multiracial organization of men and women, devoted to community education and eradicating male violence, racism, and homophobia. The group has worked with thousands of boys and men. Its workshops are designed to encourage participants to examine gender roles, violence and discrimination, and alternatives to violence.

Why do men batter women? We have to discard the essay answers. Portraying batterers as ogres only serves to separate "them" from "us." But men who batter and men who don't are not all that different. Male violence is normal in our society and vast numbers of men participate. Men batter because we have been trained to; because there are few social sanctions against it; because we live in a society where the exploitation of people with less social and personal power is acceptable. In a patriarchal society, boys are taught to accept violence as a manly response to real or imagined threats, but they get little training in negotiating intimate relationships. And all too many men believe that they have the right to control or expect certain behavior from "their" women and children; many view difficulties in family relationships as a threat to their manhood, and they respond with violence.

Young people's definitions of femininity and masculinity often reflect rigid expectations of what they must live up to in order to be a "real" woman or a "real" man. Time and again we hear boys say that they are supposed to be tough, aggressive, in control, that they are not to express any feelings except anger, not to cry, and

never to ask for help. And many boys expect girls to acquiesce to men and be dependent on them.

How do boys get these ideas about male identity and manhood? Often from parents, but our whole society contributes to the process. As many as one of every six boys are sexually assaulted, and many, many more are hit, yelled at, teased, and goaded into fighting to prove they're tough. At the project, we believe that many boys become convinced that they will be violated until they learn to use force to protect themselves. Then they move to take their pain and anger out on others the way older males have done to them.

In our work we often use role play as a way of getting at some of these issues. One particularly effective exercise involves a ten-year-old and his father: the father arrives home from work and demands that the boy turn off the TV, then berates him for the messiness of his room. The boy tries to explain; the father tells him to shut up, to stop making excuses. Fueling the father's anger is the fact that he's disappointed by the boy's school report card. The father shoves the report card in his son's face and demands to know why he has gotten a "D" in math. The boy says he did his best. The father tells him that he is stupid. The boy protests and begins to stand up. The father shoves him down, saying, "Don't you dare get up in my face!" The boy is visibly upset, and begins to cry. The father explodes: "Now what? You little mama's boy! You sissy! You make me sick. When are you going to grow up and start acting like a man?"

When we do this exercise in schools, it gets the boys' undivided attention because most have experienced being humiliated by an older male. Indeed, the power of this exercise is that it is so familiar. When asked what they learned from such encounters, the boys often say things like: A man is tough. A man is in control. A man doesn't cry. A man doesn't take crap.

We write the boys' comments on a blackboard, draw a box around them, and label it the "Act Like a Man" box. We talk about how males in this culture are socialized to stay in the box. Eventually we ask: What happens if you step out of it, if you stop acting tough enough or man enough? Invariably we hear that you get called names like "fag," "queer," "mama's boy," "punk," "girl." Asked why, the boys say it's a challenge, that they're expected to fight to prove themselves. Homophobia and fear of being identified with women are powerful messages boys get from an early age, and they are expected to fight to prove that they're tough and not gay—that they're in the box.

Using exercises, like the father/son interchange, helps us examine how the male sex role often sets men up to be dominating, controlling, and abusive. We ask: How safe is it to stay in the "Act Like a Man" box? Usually, most admit that it isn't safe, because boys and men continually challenge each other to prove that they're in the box. When a boy or man is challenged, he can prove he's a man either by fighting the challenger or by finding someone "weaker"—a female or a more vulnerable male—to dominate. Hurting girls relieves any anxiety that we may not be tough enough and establishes our heterosexual credentials. It's both a sign of our interest (we're paying attention to them) and a symbol of our difference (we're in control).

Because we are taught that women are primarily sexual objects, this behavior seems perfectly natural. And many men come to believe that a woman is just another material possession. We initiate dates, pay for our time together, protect them on the streets, and often marry them. We are trained to think that in return, girls should show their appreciation by taking care of us emotionally, putting their own concerns and interests aside, and putting out sexually.

This unspoken contract is one that many heterosexual men operate by, and it often leads to the assumption that women are our dumping grounds. If we've had a hard day at work, were embarrassed or humiliated by a boss—challenged in the box—the contract leads us to believe that we can take those feelings out on "our" women, and thus regain our power. If we end up hitting her, then we have to blame her in order to deny our aggression and keep our self-esteem intact. So we say things like: She asked for it. She pushed my buttons. She deserved it.

Invariably it comes as a surprise to us that women don't meekly accept our violence. So we respond by minimizing and justifying our actions: I didn't mean it. You're too sensitive. That's the way guys are. It was just the heat of the moment.

In order to get men to take responsibility for their own actions, we have to get them to talk about what they did, and what they said, and what they felt. Making the connection between how they have been trained and hurt and how they have learned to pass that pain on by hurting women or young people is essential.

To get men to reflect on their experiences and behaviors, we use exercises we call "stand ups." We ask everyone to be silent, and then slowly pose a series of questions or statements, and ask men to stand every time one applies to them. For example, we may ask, Have you ever:

- worried you were not tough enough?
- been called a wimp, queer, or fag?
- been told to "act like a man"?
- been hit by an older man?
- been forced to fight?
- been physically injured and hid the pain?
- been sexually abused, or touched in a way you didn't like?
- used alcohol or drugs to hide your pain?
- felt like blowing yourself away?

Later in the workshop we ask, Have you ever:

- interrupted a woman by talking louder?
- made a comment in public about a woman's body?
- discussed a woman's body with another man?
- been told by a woman that she wanted more affection and less sex from you?
- used your voice or body to intimidate a woman?
- hit, slapped, shoved, or pushed a woman?
- had sex with a woman when you knew she didn't want to?

Each participant is asked to look around and see other men standing, which helps break down their sense of isolation and feelings of shame. Since we are not a therapy group, no one is questioned or confronted about his own experiences. All of our work involves challenging the notion that males are naturally abusive and that females are natural targets of male abuse. We give boys and men a way of analyzing social roles by drawing insights from their own experiences, and help them to recognize that social interactions involve making choices, that we can break free of old roles by support-ing each other in choosing alternatives to violence.

An important part of our work is getting men and boys to look at how power, inequality, and the ability to do violence to others are structured into social relation-ships in this country. We discuss how these inequalities are maintained and how violence against one targeted group encourages violence against others. This is not to excuse men's behavior; it is done in the belief that in order to make better choices, men must understand the framework of power and violence that constantly pres-sures us to be in control and on top.

There are growing numbers of men who are critical of sexism. All too often they are isolated and fearful of raising their concerns with other men because they worry about being targeted for violence. We try to help them break through the fear and reach out to other men. But we also work to get men to understand how they are damaged by sexism and how male violence against women keeps us from the collective action needed to confront racial, gender-based, and economic injustice.

For us personally this is powerful, life-changing work. We were each drawn to it because of troubling issues in our own lives: issues around our relationships with our fathers (one emotionally abusive, the other emotionally distant); relationships with women partners where we found ourselves repeating controlling, sexist behaviors that made us feel guilty, ashamed, defensive; and the fear that we might do to our children what had been done to us as children. Through the work we have discovered that many men share these concerns, but they are hesitant to talk about this with other men. Sadly, we have all learned that "real" men don't admit vulnerability. But despite their initial hesitation, many men are eager to talk about their lives, and to change the controlling and abusive behavior they've been trained to pass on. Doing this work is healing for us and for those we work with.

Men are responsible for battery and for stopping male violence. If we are to counter the myth that men's abuse of women is natural, men must challenge each other to stop the violence. We must defy notions of manhood that lead us to injure or kill those we say we love. We must confront male friends when we see them heading down the destructive path of domestic violence and urge them to get help. While it is critical that domestic violence cases be taken more seriously by the police and criminal justice system, it is equally impor-tant to examine and to change underlying social atti-tudes and practices that promote and excuse domestic violence. This is truly men's work.

Valued Qualities of Members

When fraternity members talked about the kind of pledges they prefer, a litany of stereotypical and narrowly mascu-line attributes and behaviors was recited and feminine or woman-associated qualities and behaviors were expressly denounced (cf. Merton 1985). Fraternities seek men who are "athletic," "big guys," good in intramural competition, "who can talk college sports." Males, "who are willing to drink alcohol," "who drink socially," or "who can hold their liquor" are sought. Alcohol and activities associated with the recreational use of alcohol are cornerstones of fra-ternity social life. Nondrinkers are viewed with skepticism and rarely selected for membership.*

*Recent bans by some universities on open-keg parties at fraternity houses have resulted in heavy drinking before coming to a party and an increase in drunkenness among those who attend. This may aggravate, rather than improve, the treatment of women by frater-nity men at parties.

Fraternities try to avoid "geeks," nerds, and men said to give the fraternity a "wimpy" or "gay" reputation. Art, music, and humanities majors, majors in traditional women's fields (nursing, home economics, social work, education), men with long hair, and those whose appear-ance or dress violate current norms are rejected. Clean-cut, handsome men who dress well (are clean, neat, conform-ing, fashionable) are preferred. One sorority woman com-mented that "the top ranking fraternities have the best look-ing guys."

One fraternity man, a senior, said his fraternity recruited "some big guys, very athletic" over a two-year period to help overcome its image of wimpiness. His fraternity had won the interfraternity competition for highest grade-point average several years running but was looked down on as "wimpy, dancy, even gay." With their bigger, more athletic recruits, "our reputation improved; we're a much more rec-ognized fraternity now." Thus a fraternity's reputation and status depends on members' possession of stereotypically masculine qualities. Good grades, campus leadership, and community service are "nice" but masculinity dominance—for example, in athletic events, physical size of members, athleticism of members—counts most.

Certain social skills are valued. Men are sought who "have good personalities," are friendly, and "have the ability to relate to girls" (cf. Longino and Kart 1973). One fraternity man, a junior, said: "We watch a guy [a potential pledge] talk to women . . . we want guys who can relate to girls." Assessing a pledge's ability to talk to women is, in part, a preoccupation with homosexuality and a conscious avoidance of men who seem to have effeminate manners or qualities. If a member is suspected of being gay, he is ostracized and informally drummed out of the fraternity. A fraternity with a reputation as wimpy or tolerant of gays is ridiculed and shunned by other fraternities. Militant heterosexuality is frequently used by men as a strategy to keep each other in line (Kimmel 1987).

Financial affluence or wealth, a male-associated value in American culture, is highly valued by fraternities. In accounting for why the fraternity involved in the gang rape that precipitated our research project had been recognized recently as "the best fraternity chapter in the United States," a university official said: "They were good-looking, a big fraternity, had lots of BMWs [expensive, German-made automobiles]." After the rape, newspaper stories described the fraternity members' affluence, noting the high number of members who owned expensive cars (*St. Petersburg Times*, 1988).

The Status and Norms of Pledgeship

A pledge (sometimes called an associate member) is a new recruit who occupies a trial membership status for a specific period of time. The pledge period (typically ranging from 10 to 15 weeks) gives fraternity brothers an opportunity to assess and socialize new recruits. Pledges evaluate the fraternity also and decide if they want to become brothers. The socialization experience is structured partly through assignment of a Big Brother to each pledge. Big Brothers are expected to teach pledges how to become a brother and to support them as they progress through the trial membership period. Some pledges are repelled by the pledging experience, which can entail physical abuse; harsh discipline; and demands to be subordinate, follow orders, and engage in demeaning routines and activities, similar to those used by the military to "make men out of boys" during boot camp.

Characteristics of the pledge experience are rationalized by fraternity members as necessary to help pledges unite into a group, rely on each other, and join together against outsiders. The process is highly masculinist in execution as well as conception. A willingness to submit to authority, follow orders, and do as one is told is viewed as a sign of loyalty, togetherness, and unity. Fraternity pledges who find the pledge process offensive often drop out. Some do this by openly quitting, which can subject them to ridicule by brothers and other pledges, or they may deliberately fail to make the grades necessary for initiation or transfer schools and decline to reaffiliate with the fraternity on the new campus. One fraternity pledge who quit the fraternity he had pledged described an experience during pledgeship as follows:

> This one guy was always picking on me. No matter what I did, I was wrong. One night after dinner, he and two other guys called me and two other pledges into the chapter room. He said, "Here, X, hold this 25 pound bag of ice at arms' length 'til I tell you to stop." I did it even though my arms and hands were killing me. When I asked if I could stop, he grabbed me around the throat and lifted me off the floor. I thought he would choke me to death. He cussed me and called me all kinds of names. He took one of my fingers and twisted it until it nearly broke. . . . I stayed in the fraternity for a few more days, but then I decided to quit. I hated it. Those guys are sick. They like seeing you suffer.

Fraternities' emphasis on toughness, withstanding pain and humiliation, obedience to superiors, and using physical force to obtain compliance contributes to an interpersonal style that de-emphasizes caring and sensitivity but fosters intragroup trust and loyalty. If the least macho or most critical pledges drop out, those who remain may be more receptive to, and influenced by, masculinist values and practices that encourage the use of force in sexual relations with women and the covering up of such behavior (cf. Kanin 1967).

Norms and Dynamics of Brotherhood

Brother is the status occupied by fraternity men to indicate their relations to each other and their membership in a particular fraternity organization or group. Brother is a male-specific status; only males can become brothers, although women can become "Little Sisters," a form of pseudomembership. "Becoming a brother" is a rite of passage that follows the consistent and often lengthy display by pledges of appropriately masculine qualities and behaviors. Brothers have a quasi-familial relationship with each other, are normatively said to share bonds of closeness and support, and are sharply set off from nonmembers. Brotherhood is a loosely defined term used to represent the bonds that develop among fraternity members and the obligations and expectations incumbent upon them (cf. Marlowe and Auvenshine [1982] on fraternities' failure to encourage "moral development" in freshman pledges).

Some of our respondents talked about brotherhood in almost reverential terms, viewing it as the most valuable benefit of fraternity membership. One senior, a business-school major who had been affiliated with a fairly high-status fraternity throughout four years on campus, said:

> Brotherhood spurs friendship for life, which I consider its best aspect, although I didn't see it that way when I joined. Brotherhood bonds and unites. It instills values of caring about one another, caring about community, caring about ourselves. The values and bonds [of brotherhood] continually develop over the four years [in college] while normal friendships come and go.

Despite this idealization, most aspects of fraternity practice and conception are more mundane. Brotherhood often plays itself out as an overriding concern with masculinity and, by extension, femininity. As a consequence, fraternities comprise collectivities of highly masculinized men with attitudinal qualities and behavioral norms that predispose them to sexual coercion of women (cf. Kanin 1967; Merton 1985; Rapaport and Burkhart 1984). The norms of masculinity are complemented by conceptions of women and femininity that are equally distorted and stereotyped and that may enhance the probability of women's exploitation (cf. Ehrhart and Sandler 1985; Sanday 1981, 1986).

Practices of Brotherhood

Practices associated with fraternity brotherhood that contribute to the sexual coercion of women include a preoccupation with loyalty, group protection and secrecy, use of alcohol as a weapon, involvement in violence and physical force, and an emphasis on competition and superiority.

Loyalty, Group Protection, and Secrecy Loyalty is a fraternity preoccupation. Members are reminded constantly to be loyal to the fraternity and to their brothers. Among other ways, loyalty is played out in the practices of group protection and secrecy. The fraternity must be shielded from criticism. Members are admonished to avoid getting the fraternity in trouble and to bring all problems "to the chapter" (local branch of a national social fraternity) rather than to

outsiders. Fraternities try to protect themselves from close scrutiny and criticism by the Interfraternity Council (a quasi-governing body composed of representatives from all social fraternities on campus), their fraternity's national office, university officials, law enforcement, the media, and the public. Protection of the fraternity often takes precedence over what is procedurally, ethically, or legally correct. Numerous examples were related to us of fraternity brothers' lying to outsiders to "protect the fraternity."

Group protection was observed in the alleged gang rape case with which we began our study. Except for one brother, a rapist who turned state's evidence, the entire remaining fraternity membership was accused by university and criminal justice officials of lying to protect the fraternity. Members consistently failed to cooperate even though the alleged crimes were felonies, involved only four men (two of whom were not even members of the local chapter), and the victim of the crime nearly died. According to a grand jury's findings, fraternity officers repeatedly broke appointments with law enforcement officials, refused to provide police with a list of members, and refused to cooperate with police and prosecutors investigating the case (*Florida Flambeau*, 1988).

Secrecy is a priority value and practice in fraternities, partly because full-fledged membership is premised on it (for confirmation, see Ehrhart and Sandler 1985; Longino and Kart 1973; Roark 1987). Secrecy is also a boundary-maintaining mechanism, demarcating in-group from out-group, us from them. Secret rituals, handshakes, and mottoes are revealed to pledge brothers as they are initiated into full brotherhood. Since only brothers are supposed to know a fraternity's secrets, such knowledge affirms membership in the fraternity and separates a brother from others. Extending secrecy tactics from protection of private knowledge to protection of the fraternity from criticism is a predictable development. Our interviews indicated that individual members knew the difference between right and wrong, but fraternity norms that emphasize loyalty, group protection, and secrecy often overrode standards of ethical correctness.

Alcohol as Weapon Alcohol use by fraternity men is normative. They use it on weekdays to relax after class and on weekends to "get drunk," "get crazy," and "get laid." The use of alcohol to obtain sex from women is pervasive—in other words, it is used as a weapon against sexual reluctance. According to several fraternity men whom we interviewed, alcohol is the major tool used to gain sexual mastery over women (cf. Adams and Abarbanel 1988; Ehrhart and Sandler 1985). One fraternity man, a 21-year-old senior, described alcohol use to gain sex as follows: "There are girls that you know will fuck, then some you have to put some effort into it. . . . You have to buy them drinks or find out if she's drunk enough. . . ."

A similar strategy is used collectively. A fraternity man said that at parties with Little Sisters: "We provide them with 'hunch punch' and things get wild. We get them drunk and most of the guys end up with one." " 'Hunch punch,' " he said, "is a girls' drink made up of overproof alcohol and powdered Kool-Aid, no water or anything, just ice. It's very strong. Two cups will do a number on a female." He had plans in the next academic term to surreptitiously give hunch punch to women in a "prim and proper" sorority because "having sex with prim and proper sorority girls is definitely a goal." These women are a challenge because they "won't openly consume alcohol and won't get openly drunk as hell." Their sororities have "standards committees" that forbid heavy drinking and easy sex.

In the gang rape case, our sources said that many fraternity men on campus believed the victim had a drinking problem and was thus an "easy make." According to newspaper accounts, she had been drinking alcohol on the evening she was raped; the lead assailant is alleged to have given her a bottle of wine after she arrived at his fraternity house. Portions of the rape occurred in a shower, and the victim was reportedly so drunk that her assailants had difficulty holding her in a standing position (*Tallahassee Democrat,* 1988a). While raping her, her assailants repeatedly told her they were members of another fraternity under the apparent belief that she was too drunk to know the difference. Of course, if she was too drunk to know who they were, she was too drunk to consent to sex (cf. Allgeier 1986; Tash 1988).

One respondent told us that gang rapes are wrong and can get one expelled, but he seemed to see nothing wrong in sexual coercion one-on-one. He seemed unaware that the use of alcohol to obtain sex from a woman is grounds for a claim that a rape occurred (cf. Tash 1988). Few women on campus (who also may not know these grounds) report date rapes, however; so the odds of detection and punishment are slim for fraternity men who use alcohol for "seduction" purposes (cf. Byington and Keeter 1988; Merton 1985).

Violence and Physical Force   Fraternity men have a history of violence (Ehrhart and Sandler 1985; Roark 1987). Their record of hazing, fighting, property destruction, and rape has caused them problems with insurance companies (Bradford 1986; Pressley 1987). Two university officials

told us that fraternities "are the third riskiest property to insure behind toxic waste dumps and amusement parks." Fraternities are increasingly defendants in legal actions brought by pledges subjected to hazing (Meyer 1986; Pressley 1987) and by women who were raped by one or more members. In a recent alleged gang rape incident at another Florida university, prosecutors failed to file charges but the victim filed a civil suit against the fraternity nevertheless (*Tallahassee Democrat,* 1989).

Competition and Superiority   Interfraternity rivalry fosters in-group identification and out-group hostility. Fraternities stress pride of membership and superiority over other fraternities as major goals. Interfraternity rivalries take many forms, including competition for desirable pledges, size of pledge class, size of membership, size and appearance of fraternity house, superiority in intramural sports, highest grade-point averages, giving the best parties, gaining the best or most campus leadership roles, and, of great importance, attracting and displaying "good looking women." Rivalry is particularly intense over members, intramural sports, and women (cf. Messner 1989).

FRATERNITIES' COMMODIFICATION OF WOMEN

In claiming that women are treated by fraternities as commodities, we mean that fraternities knowingly, and intentionally, *use* women for their benefit. Fraternities use women as bait for new members, as servers of brothers' needs, and as sexual prey.

Women as Bait

Fashionably attractive women help a fraternity attract new members. As one fraternity man, a junior, said, "They are good bait." Beautiful, sociable women are believed to impress the right kind of pledges and give the impression that the fraternity can deliver this type of woman to its members. Photographs of shapely, attractive coeds are printed in fraternity brochures and videotapes that are distributed and shown to potential pledges. The women pictured are often dressed in bikinis, at the beach, and are pictured hugging the brothers of the fraternity. One university official says such recruitment materials give the message: "Hey, they're here for you, you can have whatever you want," and, "we have the best looking women. Join us and you can have them too." Another commented: "Something's wrong when males join an all-male organization as the best place to meet women. It's so illogical."

Fraternities compete in promising access to beautiful women. One fraternity man, a senior, commented that "the attraction of girls [i.e., a fraternity's success in attracting women] is a big status symbol for fraternities." One university official commented that the use of women as a recruiting tool is so well entrenched that fraternities that might be willing to forgo it say they cannot afford to unless other fraternities do so as well. One fraternity man said, "Look, if we don't have Little Sisters, the fraternities that do will get all the good pledges." Another said, "We won't have as good a rush [the period during which new members are assessed and selected] if we don't have these women around."

In displaying good-looking, attractive, skimpily dressed, nubile women to potential members, fraternities implicitly, and sometimes explicitly, promise sexual access to women. One fraternity man commented that "part of what being in a fraternity is all about is the sex" and explained how his fraternity uses Little Sisters to recruit new members:

> We'll tell the sweetheart [the fraternity's term for Little Sister], "You're gorgeous; you can get him." We'll tell her to fake a scam and she'll go hang all over him during a rush party, kiss him, and he thinks he's done wonderful and wants to join. The girls think it's great too. It's flattering for them.

Women as Servers

The use of women as servers is exemplified in the Little Sister program. Little Sisters are undergraduate women who are rushed and selected in a manner parallel to the recruitment of fraternity men. They are affiliated with the fraternity in a formal but unofficial way and are able, indeed required, to wear the fraternity's Greek letters. Little Sisters are not full-fledged fraternity members, however; and fraternity national offices and most universities do not register or regulate them. Each fraternity has an officer called Little Sister Chairman who oversees their organization and activities. The Little Sisters elect officers among themselves, pay monthly dues to the fraternity, and have well-defined roles. Their dues are used to pay for the fraternity's social events, and Little Sisters are expected to attend and hostess fraternity parties and hang around the house to make it a "nice place to be." One fraternity man, a senior, described Little Sisters this way: "They are very social girls, willing to join in, be affiliated with the group, devoted

to the fraternity." Another member, a sophomore, said: "Their sole purpose is social—attend parties, attract new members, and 'take care' of the guys."

Our observations and interviews suggested that women selected by fraternities as Little Sisters are physically attractive, possess good social skills, and are willing to devote time and energy to the fraternity and its members. One undergraduate woman gave the following job description for Little Sisters to a campus newspaper:

> It's not just making appearances at all the parties but entails many more responsibilities. You're going to be expected to go to all the intramural games to cheer the brothers on, support and encourage the pledges, and just be around to bring some extra life to the house. [As a Little Sister] you have to agree to take on a new responsibility other than studying to maintain your grades and managing to keep your checkbook from bouncing. You have to make time to be a part of the fraternity and support the brothers in all they do. (*The Tomahawk,* 1988)

The title of Little Sister reflects women's subordinate status; fraternity men in a parallel role are called Big Brothers. Big Brothers assist a sorority primarily with the physical work of sorority rushes, which, compared to fraternity rushes, are more formal, structured, and intensive. Sorority rushes take place in the daytime and fraternity rushes at night so fraternity men are free to help. According to one fraternity member, Little Sister status is a benefit to women because it gives them a social outlet and "the protection of the brothers." The gender-stereotypic conceptions and obligations of these Little Sister and Big Brother statuses indicate that fraternities and sororities promote a gender hierarchy on campus that fosters subordination and dependence in women, thus encouraging sexual exploitation and the belief that it is acceptable.

Women as Sexual Prey

Little Sisters are a sexual utility. Many Little Sisters do not belong to sororities and lack peer support for refraining from unwanted sexual relations. One fraternity man (whose fraternity has 65 members and 85 Little Sisters) told us they had recruited "wholesale" in the prior year to "get lots of new women." The structural access to women that the Little Sister program provides and the absence of normative supports for refusing fraternity members' sexual advances may make women in this program particularly susceptible to coerced sexual encounters with fraternity men.

Access to women for sexual gratification is a presumed benefit of fraternity membership, promised in recruitment materials and strategies and through brothers' conversations with new recruits. One fraternity man said: "We always tell the guys that you get sex all the time, there's always new girls. . . . After I became a Greek, I found out I could be with females at will." A university official told us that, based on his observations, "no one [i.e., fraternity men] on this campus wants to have 'relationships.' They just want to have fun [i.e., sex]." Fraternity men plan and execute strategies aimed at obtaining sexual gratification, and this occurs at both individual and collective levels.

Individual strategies include getting a woman drunk and spending a great deal of money on her. As for collective strategies, most of our undergraduate interviewees agreed that fraternity parties often culminate in sex and that this outcome is planned. One fraternity man said fraternity parties often involve sex and nudity and can "turn into orgies." Orgies may be planned in advance, such as the Bowery Ball party held by one fraternity. A former fraternity member said of this party:

> The entire idea behind this is sex. Both men and women come to the party wearing little or nothing. There are pornographic pinups on the walls and usually porno movies playing on the TV. The music carries sexual overtones. . . . They just get schnockered [drunk] and, in most cases, they also get laid.

When asked about the women who come to such a party, he said: "Some Little Sisters just won't go. . . . The girls who do are looking for a good time, girls who don't know what it is, things like that."

Other respondents denied that fraternity parties are orgies but said that sex is always talked about among the brothers and they all know "who each other is doing it with." One member said that most of the time, guys have sex with their girlfriends "but with socials, girlfriends aren't allowed to come and it's their [members'] big chance [to have sex with other women]." The use of alcohol to help them get women into bed is a routine strategy at fraternity parties.

CONCLUSIONS

In general, our research indicated that the organization and membership of fraternities contribute heavily to coercive and often violent sex. Fraternity houses are occupied by

same-sex (all men) and same-age (late teens, early twenties) peers whose maturity and judgment is often less than ideal. Yet fraternity houses are private dwellings that are mostly off-limits to, and away from scrutiny of, university and community representatives, with the result that fraternity house events seldom come to the attention of outsiders. Practices associated with the social construction of fraternity brotherhood emphasize a macho conception of men and masculinity, a narrow, stereotyped conception of women and femininity, and the treatment of women as commodities. Other practices contributing to coercive sexual relations and the cover-up of rapes include excessive alcohol use, competitiveness, and normative support for deviance and secrecy (cf. Bogal-Allbritten and Allbritten 1985; Kanin 1967).

Some fraternity practices exacerbate others. Brotherhood norms require "sticking together" regardless of right or wrong; thus rape episodes are unlikely to be stopped or reported to outsiders, even when witnesses disapprove. The ability to use alcohol without scrutiny by authorities and alcohol's frequent association with violence, including sexual coercion, facilitates rape in fraternity houses. Fraternity norms that emphasize the value of maleness and masculinity over femaleness and femininity and that elevate the status of men and lower the status of women in members' eyes undermine perceptions and treatment of women as persons who deserve consideration and care (cf. Ehrhart and Sandler 1985; Merton 1985).

Androgynous men and men with a broad range of interests and attributes are lost to fraternities through their recruitment practices. Masculinity of a narrow and stereotypical type helps create attitudes, norms, and practices that predispose fraternity men to coerce women sexually, both individually and collectively (Allgeier 1986; Hood 1989; Sanday 1981, 1986). Male athletes on campus may be similarly disposed for the same reasons (Kirshenbaum 1989; Telander and Sullivan 1989).

Research into the social contexts in which rape crimes occur and the social constructions associated with these contexts illumine rape dynamics on campus. Blanchard (1959) found that group rapes almost always have a leader who pushes others into the crime. He also found that the leader's latent homosexuality, desire to show off to his peers, or fear of failing to prove himself a man are frequently an impetus. Fraternity norms and practices contribute to the approval and use of sexual coercion as an accepted tactic in relations with women. Alcohol-induced compliance is normative, whereas, presumably, use of a knife, gun, or threat of bodily harm would not be because the woman who "drinks too much" is viewed as "causing her own rape" (cf. Ehrhart and Sandler 1985).

Our research led us to conclude that fraternity norms and practices influence members to view the sexual coercion of women, which is a felony crime, as sport, a contest, or a game (cf. Sato 1988). This sport is played not between men and women but between men and men. Women are the pawns or prey in the interfraternity rivalry game; they prove that a fraternity is successful or prestigious. The use of women in this way encourages fraternity men to see women as objects and sexual coercion as sport. Today's societal norms support young women's right to engage in sex at their discretion, and coercion is unnecessary in a mutually desired encounter. However, nubile young women say they prefer to be "in a relationship" to have sex while young men say they prefer to "get laid" without a commitment (Muehlenhard and Linton 1987). These differences may reflect, in part, American puritanism and men's fears of sexual intimacy or perhaps intimacy of any kind. In a fraternity context, getting sex without giving emotionally demonstrates "cool" masculinity. More important, it poses no threat to the bonding and loyalty of the fraternity brotherhood (cf. Farr 1988). Drinking large quantities of alcohol before having sex suggests that "scoring" rather than intrinsic sexual pleasure is a primary concern of fraternity men.

Unless fraternities' composition, goals, structures, and practices change in fundamental ways, women on campus will continue to be sexual prey for fraternity men. As all-male enclaves dedicated to opposing faculty and administration and to cementing in-group ties, fraternity members eschew any hint of homosexuality. Their version of masculinity transforms women, and men with womanly characteristics, into the out-group. "Womanly men" are ostracized; feminine women are used to demonstrate members' masculinity. Encouraging renewed emphasis on their founding values (Longino and Kart 1973), service orientation and activities (Lemire 1979), or members' moral development (Marlowe and Auvenshine 1982) will have little effect on fraternities' treatment of women. A case for or against fraternities cannot be made by studying individual members. The fraternity qua group and organization is at issue. Located on campus along with many vulnerable women, embedded in a sexist society, and caught up in masculinist goals, practices, and values, fraternities' violation of women—including forcible rape—should come as no surprise.

ACKNOWLEDGMENTS

Author's note: We gratefully thank Meena Harris and Diane Mennella for assisting with data collection. The senior author thanks the graduate students in her fall 1988 graduate research methods seminar for help with developing the initial conceptual framework. Judith Lorber and two anonymous *Gender & Society* referees made numerous suggestions for improving our article and we thank them also.

REFERENCES

Allgeier, Elizabeth. 1986. "Coercive Versus Consensual Sexual Interactions." G. Stanley Hall Lecture to American Psychological Association Annual Meeting, Washington, DC, August.

Adams, Aileen and Gail Abarbanel. 1988. *Sexual Assault on Campus: What Colleges Can Do.* Santa Monica, CA: Rape Treatment Center.

Blanchard, W. H. 1959. "The Group Process in Gang Rape." *Journal of Social Psychology* 49:259–66.

Bogal-Allbritten, Rosemarie B. and William L. Allbritten. 1985. "The Hidden Victims: Courtship Violence Among College Students." *Journal of College Student Personnel* 43:201–4.

Bohrnstedt, George W. 1969. "Conservatism, Authoritarianism and Religiosity of Fraternity Pledges." *Journal of College Student Personnel* 27:36–43.

Bradford, Michael. 1986. "Tight Market Dries Up Nightlife at University." *Business Insurance* (March 2):2, 6.

Burkhart, Barry. 1989. Comments in Seminar on Acquaintance/Date Rape Prevention: A National Video Teleconference, February 2.

Burkhart, Barry R. and Annette L. Stanton. 1985. "Sexual Aggression in Acquaintance Relationships." Pp. 43–65 in *Violence in Intimate Relationships,* edited by G. Russell. Englewood Cliffs, NJ: Spectrum.

Byington, Diane B. and Karen W. Keeter. 1988. "Assessing Needs of Sexual Assault Victims on a University Campus." Pp. 23–31 in *Student Services: Responding to Issues and Challenges.* Chapel Hill: University of North Carolina Press.

Chancer, Lynn S. 1987. "New Bedford, Massachusetts, March 6, 1983–March 22, 1984: The 'Before and After' of a Group Rape." *Gender & Society* 1:239–60.

Ehrhart, Julie K. and Bernice R. Sandler. 1985. *Campus Gang Rape: Party Games?* Washington, DC: Association of American Colleges.

Farr, K. A. 1988. "Dominance Bonding Through the Good Old Boys Sociability Network." *Sex Roles* 18:259–77.

Florida Flambeau. 1988. "Pike Members Indicted in Rape." (May 19):1, 5.

Fox, Elaine, Charles Hodge, and Walter Ward. 1987. "A Comparison of Attitudes Held by Black and White Fraternity Members." *Journal of Negro Education* 56:521–34.

Geis, Gilbert. 1971. "Group Sexual Assaults." *Medical Aspects of Human Sexuality* 5:101–13.

Glaser, Barney G. 1978. *Theoretical Sensitivity: Advances in the Methodology of Grounded Theory.* Mill Valley, CA: Sociology Press.

Hood, Jane. 1989. "Why Our Society Is Rape-Prone." *New York Times,* May 16.

Hughes, Michael J. and Roger B. Winston, Jr. 1987. "Effects of Fraternity Membership on Interpersonal Values." *Journal of College Student Personnel* 45:405–11.

Kanin, Eugene J. 1967. "Reference Groups and Sex Conduct Norm Violations." *The Sociological Quarterly* 8:495–504.

Kimmel, Michael, ed. 1987. *Changing Men: New Directions in Research on Men and Masculinity.* Newbury Park, CA: Sage.

Kirshenbaum, Jerry. 1989. "Special Report, An American Disgrace: A Violent and Unprecedented Lawlessness Has Arisen Among College Athletes in all Parts of the Country." *Sports Illustrated* (February 27):16–19.

Lemire, David. 1979. "One Investigation of the Stereotypes Associated with Fraternities and Sororities." *Journal of College Student Personnel* 37:54–57.

Letchworth, G. E. 1969. "Fraternities Now and in the Future." *Journal of College Student Personnel* 10:118–22.

Longino, Charles F., Jr., and Cary S. Kart. 1973. "The College Fraternity: An Assessment of Theory and Research." *Journal of College Student Personnel* 31:118–25.

Marlowe, Anne F. and Dwight C. Auvenshine. 1982. "Greek Membership: Its Impact on the Moral Development of College Freshmen." *Journal of College Student Personnel* 40: 53–57.

Martin, Patricia Yancey and Barry A. Turner. 1986. "Grounded Theory and Organizational Research." *Journal of Applied Behavioral Science* 22:141–57.

Merton, Andrew. 1985. "On Competition and Class: Return to Brotherhood." *Ms.* (September):60–65, 121–22.

Messner, Michael. 1989. "Masculinities and Athletic Careers." *Gender & Society* 3:71–88.

Meyer, T. J. 1986. "Fight Against Hazing Rituals Rages on Campuses." *Chronicle of Higher Education* (March 12):34–36.

Miller, Leonard D. 1973. "Distinctive Characteristics of Fraternity Members." *Journal of College Student Personnel* 31:126–28.

Muehlenhard, Charlene L. and Melaney A. Linton. 1987. "Date Rape and Sexual Aggression in Dating Situations: Incidence and Risk Factors." *Journal of Counseling Psychology* 34:186–96.

Pressley, Sue Anne. 1987. "Fraternity Hell Night Still Endures." *Washington Post* (August 11):B1.

Rapaport, Karen and Barry R. Burkhart. 1984. "Personality and Attitudinal Characteristics of Sexually Coercive College Males." *Journal of Abnormal Psychology* 93:216–21.

Roark, Mary L. 1987. "Preventing Violence on College Campuses." *Journal of Counseling and Development* 65:367–70.

Sanday, Peggy Reeves. 1981. "The Socio-Cultural Context of Rape: A Cross-Cultural Study." *Journal of Social Issues* 37:5–27.

———. 1986. "Rape and the Silencing of the Feminine." Pp. 84–101 in *Rape,* edited by S. Tomaselli and R. Porter. Oxford: Basil Blackwell.

St. Petersburg Times. 1988. "A Greek Tragedy." (May 29):1F, 6F.

Sato, Ikuya. 1988. "Play Theory of Delinquency: Toward a General Theory of 'Action.'" *Symbolic Interaction* 11:191–212.

Smith, T. 1964. "Emergence and Maintenance of Fraternal Solidarity." *Pacific Sociological Review* 7:29–37.

Tallahassee Democrat. 1988a. "FSU Fraternity Brothers Charged" (April 27):1A, 12A.

———. 1988b. "FSU Interviewing Students About Alleged Rape" (April 24):1D.

———. 1989. "Woman Sues Stetson in Alleged Rape" (March 19):3B.

Tampa Tribune. 1988. "Fraternity Brothers Charged in Sexual Assault of FSU Coed." (April 27):6B.

Tash, Gary B. 1988. "Date Rape." *The Emerald of Sigma Pi Fraternity* 75(4):1–2.

Telander, Rick and Robert Sullivan. 1989. "Special Report, You Reap What You Sow." *Sports Illustrated* (February 27):20–34.

The Tomahawk. 1988. "A Look Back at Rush, A Mixture of Hard Work and Fun" (April/May):3D.

Walsh, Claire. 1989. Comments in Seminar on Acquaintance/Date Rape Prevention: A National Video Teleconference, February 2.

Wilder, David H., Arlyne E. Hoyt, Dennis M. Doren, William E. Hauck, and Robert D. Zettle. 1978. "The Impact of Fraternity and Sorority Membership on Values and Attitudes." *Journal of College Student Personnel* 36:445–49.

Wilder, David H., Arlyne E. Hoyt, Beth Shuster Surbeck, Janet C. Wilder, and Patricia Imperatrice Carney. 1986. "Greek Affiliation and Attitude Change in College Students." *Journal of College Student Personnel* 44:510–19.

Stopping Rape: Effective Avoidance Strategies

PAULINE B. BART and PATRICIA H. O'BRIEN

Try and fight him . . . it's more natural to be angry, if you let yourself feel the anger, maybe that'll give you strength . . . I used to think you could give him some kind of Jesus rap . . . I used to think you could reason 'em out of it, and talk to them like a human being, say "OK you don't want to do this, what are you doing?" . . . He seemed to listen to anger, yelling.

INTERVIEWER: What methods do you think would be ineffective, once a man tries to accost a woman?
INTERVIEWEE: Crying and pleading and begging. [Interview with a raped woman]

Women threatened with rape are in a double bind. On the one hand we are told, "Fighting back will only excite him. Fighting back will only get him angry," advice which assumes that the assailant is not already angry and that immediate retaliation is the most dangerous strategy. We are warned as well that resistance will result in serious injury, if not mutilation and death; our mangled bodies will turn up in garbage cans and under park benches.

On the other hand, rape has traditionally and legally been defined as an adult man's carnal knowledge of a woman *by force and against her will* (the man must be over fourteen and the woman must not be his wife).[1] According to this definition, it is not enough that a man used or threatened to use force for the act to be considered rape; a man can compel a woman to have sex and still not legally be acting against her will. Therefore, in order to prove legally that what happened

Pauline B. Bart and Particia H. O'Brien, "Stopping Rape: Effective Avoidance Strategies," *Signs: Journal of Women in Culture and Society* 10, no. 1 (1984). Copyright © 1984 by The University of Chicago. Reprinted with the permission of the authors and The University of Chicago Press.

was rape, the woman has to prove that it was indeed against her will. The best way to prove that she is not willing to be forced to have sex is *not* by saying "Please don't," or "I have my period." The best way to prove that the act is not mutually consensual is by physically resisting.[2] In this article we describe the strategies that have prevented rape and the conditions under which they were effective. The 1976 Queen's Bench study was the first to show that "acting like a lady" was more likely to result in rape than in rape avoidance.[3] More recently, William Sanders, Jennie McIntyre, and Richard Block and Wesley Skogan—the latter using national victimization data—have come to similar conclusions.[4] All the studies based on interviews with raped women and women who prevented their rapes, as well as Block and Skogan's work, find that active strategies, notably fighting back, are effective in rape avoidance.

Our study also addresses important theoretical issues. For many years the question whether situational or personality factors have most influence in determining behavior has been central in social psychology, with sociologists leaning toward the former and psychologists and psychiatrists toward the latter. In this study, we do not deal with personality per se, partly because we do not think there are valid and reliable ways of measuring personality in interviews. More important, we do not use personality variables because research looking at the association of personality and victimization neglects variables such as autonomy training, independence, and competence.[5]

METHODOLOGY

This report is based on an analysis of 94 interviews with women eighteen or older who had been attacked and who had either avoided being raped ($N = 51$) or been raped ($N = 43$) in the two years prior to the interview. We limited the sample to women who experienced either force or the threat of force. The interview consisted of a self-report dealing with demographic variables, and answers to unstructured and semistructured questions about situational and background factors. Because of the exploratory nature of the research, we added questions when unanticipated patterns emerged—for instance, on incest, sexual assault in childhood, or other violence in the woman's life, or on whether the woman was primarily concerned with being killed or mutilated or primarily concerned with not being raped. The first part of the interview addressed such situational variables as the presence of a weapon, the number of assailants, the response of the woman, the acts that occurred during the assault, the degree of acquaintance with the assailant. The second part dealt with background variables, with questions about a woman's sense of competence and autonomy and about her socialization as a child and an adult into a traditional female role. We asked the raped woman about how her significant others responded to the assault and about interaction with institutions such as the police, hospitals, and therapists. We also examined the negotiation process between the woman and her assailant(s) if such negotiation took place.

Eighty percent of the interviews were conducted by the principal investigator (Pauline Bart) and 20 percent by a female clinical psychologist (Marlyn Grossman). The interviews lasted from one-and-a-half to six hours, depending on the subject's desire to talk and on the history of violence in her individual life. These interviews were transcribed.

Because of the nature of our major research question, we could not obtain a random sample. Therefore, following a pretest, we launched a campaign to find respondents and recruited 94 women through newspaper ads (including major Black and Hispanic papers), press releases, public service announcements (the radio announcements were in both English and Spanish), appearances on radio and television, flyers, and contacts initiated through friendship networks of the project staff.

The resulting purposive, that is, nonrandom sample, when compared to the female population of the Chicago standard metropolitan statistical area (SMSA), which includes Cook and the surrounding counties, was disproportionately white, young, and unmarried (either single or divorced). Also none of the women who responded was engaged only in domestic labor at the time of the interview; all were either working outside the home or attending school. However, while the sample is not representative of women in the Chicago SMSA, it is not very different from the population of raped women and rape avoiders in

TABLE 1   DEMOGRAPHIC CHARACTERISTICS

	%	N
Race:		
White	81	76
Black	15	14
Hispanic	4	4
Religion:		
Protestant	38	35
Catholic	35	33
Jewish	19	18
No religion	6	. . .
Other	2	. . .
Marital status:		
Never married	58	54
Married, living with husband	15	14
Married, not living with husband	6	6
Divorced	19	18
Married, divorcing	1	. . .
Missing information	1	. . .
Education:		
High school or less	12	11
Some college	44	41
Four-year degree	19	18
Some graduate work	26	24
Occupation:		
Dependent	2	2
Homemaker	2	2
Blue-collar worker	10	9
Clerical worker	33	32
Professional	31	29
Student	9	8
Interim employment (usually student)	12	11
Missing information	1	. . .

NOTE: Interviewees ranged in age from 18 to 72. The mean age was 28.14 years.

national victimization data, except for an overrepresentation of white women (tables 1 and 2).[6] In addition to the demographic bias, the sample is shaped by the fact that the participants were volunteers.[7] A final source of possible bias in our sample was the very high proportion of women who had been raped by strangers or near strangers (approximately 80 percent).[8] An additional 10 percent were attacked by men they had met for the first time just prior to the assault.

Actually, we currently have no way of knowing what the "real" population of women who have been sexually assaulted looks like. On the one hand, rapes reported to the police are known to be gross undercounts of total rapes and

TABLE 2   COMPARISON OF DATA ON SEXUALLY ASSAULTED WOMEN

	Bart and O'Brien (N = 94) (%)	McIntyre (N = 32) (%)	Queen's Bench (N = 108) (%)	National Victimization Surveys[a] (N = approx. 22,000) (%)
Age:				
Under 25	36	66[b]	71	59
Over 35	10	. . .	7	15
Race:				
White	81	75	79	69
Nonwhite	19	. . .	21	31
Marital status:				
Single	57	68	80	58
Married	16	. . .	10	22
Separated or divorced	27	. . .	11	17
Widowed	. . .	. . .	. . .	3
Work status:				
Employed full-time	62	46	39	46
Employed part-time	13	. . .	. . .	. . .
Student	12	35	37	15
Unemployed	8	. . .	13	6
Homemaker	4	. . .	1	33
Missing information	1	. . .	. . .	. . .
Attacked by stranger	78[c]	77	81	82
Rape completed	46	60	63	33
Weapon present	46	. . .	33	40
Attacked by multiple assailants	13	14	15	16
Reported attack to police	66	. . .	. . .	56

SOURCES: Jennie J. McIntyre, "Victim Response to Rape: Alternative Outcomes" (final report to National Institute of Mental Health, grant R01MH29045); Queen's Bench Foundation, "Rape: Prevention and Resistance" (Queen's Bench Organization, 1255 Post St., San Francisco, California, 1976); Joan McDermott, "Rape Victimization in 26 American Cities" (Washington, D.C.: Department of Justice, Law Enforcement Assistance Administration, Government Printing Office, 1979).

[a] All percentages (except for the percent attacked by strangers) are calculated for attacks by strangers only.

[b] Percentage calculated for women under 26, not 25.

[c] Includes 71 percent raped by total strangers and 7 percent raped by men known by sight or met on a casual first encounter.

to involve a disproportionate number of rapes by strangers.[9] On the other hand, victimization researchers have found that some respondents fail to tell interviewers about rapes actually reported to the police.[10] The problem of defining rape adds further complications; many women who agree that they have been forced to have sex do not label the act as rape.[11]

We paid the women $25.00 for their time; moreover, all their expenses—including babysitting and travel for those who were from outside Chicago—were reimbursed. When the women telephoned us initially, we told them of the remuneration, and we asked for their own definition of the situation. Specifically, we asked them to tell us whether they had

been raped or had been attacked but had avoided being raped. In this way, the women defined themselves into the two parts of the sample: rape avoiders and raped women.

A serendipitous finding was that while there was no problem in differentiating rape from seduction, there was no hard and fast line differentiating rape from rape avoidance.[12] Since we can conceptualize rape as a continuum starting with the first approach, verbal or physical, and ending with the rapist's penetration and intercourse to orgasm, any interruption in the continuum before the rapist's orgasm could theoretically be considered an avoidance.

In order to address this issue, we examined the data in three ways: the woman's perception of herself as either a raped woman or one who had avoided rape, the nature of the acts that occurred, and the legal definition of them.[13] The acts consisted of genital intercourse, sodomy, fellatio, interfemoral penetration (the assailant masturbating himself between the woman's thighs), cunnilingus, digital penetration, fondling and touching, and kissing. The possible legal definitions coded (using Illinois statutes at that time) were rape, attempted rape, and deviant sexual assault. When we examined the relationship between self-perception and the acts that had occurred, we learned that, for the most part, the women define rape by what is done with a man's penis (genital intercourse, sodomy, fellatio), not by what is done to a woman's genitals (digital penetration, fondling and touching, cunnilingus) (see table 3).[14]

FINDINGS

Defense Strategies

When the women described their assaults, distinct types of defense techniques emerged that were classified in the following way. A woman could

1. flee or try to flee.
2. scream, yell, or talk loudly—usually in an effort to attract attention.
3. use "affective verbal" techniques such as begging and pleading with the assailant in order to gain his sympathy.
4. use "cognitive verbal" techniques, which included attempting to reason with the assailant, "conning" him, trying to make him "see her as a person," and stalling.
5. take advantage of environmental intervention—someone or something in the surroundings that intruded on the scene and either caused the assailant to stop the assault or gave her an opportunity to escape.
6. respond with physical force, the possibilities ranging from a simple push to self-defense techniques to use of a weapon.

Avoiders used a substantially greater number of strategies than raped women. All of the five respondents who employed *no* strategies were raped; these made up 11.6 percent of the raped women in the sample. Of the respondents who used only one strategy, 30 percent (13) were raped women and 18 percent (9) were avoiders. Of the respondents who used two kinds of strategies, 28 percent (12) were raped women and 29 percent (15) were avoiders. The

TABLE 3   SELF-PERCEPTION AS RAPED WOMAN OR RAPE AVOIDER, BY OCCURRENCE OF PHALLIC SEX (%)

	SELF-PERCEPTION	
	Raped Woman	Rape Avoider
Phallic sex occurred[a] (N = 45)	93	7
Phallic sex did not occur[b] (N = 49)	2	98

NOTE:—This table was constructed by Kim Scheppele.
[a]Phallic sex includes any one or any combination of the following: penile-vaginal penetration, sodomy, fellatio, interfemoral penetration, or female masturbation of assailant.
[b]Phallic sex is considered not to have occurred if only the following took place: digital penetration, cunnilingus, fondling, touching and kissing. It is considered not to have occurred as well in situations where the attack was thwarted before any overt sexual acts took place.

difference between raped women and avoiders sharply increases after this. Twenty-one percent (9) of the raped women and 35 percent (18) of the avoiders used three types of strategies; 9 percent (4) of the raped women and 18 percent (9) of the avoiders used four types of strategies. The modal number of strategies for raped women was one, while for avoiders it was three. The mean number of types of strategies for raped women was 1.86 and for avoiders was 2.53, consistent with the results reported in the Queen's Bench study.[15]

Not only did avoiders use more types of strategies, the strategies they used differed from the strategies of the raped women. Avoiders were more likely to flee or try to flee, to talk loudly or scream, to use physical force, and to be aided by environmental intervention. Raped women were more likely to plead. Both were about equally likely to use cognitive verbal techniques, the strategy most frequently used (see table 4).

Because we have qualitative data, we can also study the sequence of strategies. Our analysis took particular note of women who used physical strategies since most debates revolve around this response. Six women who stopped their rapes first used physical strategies and then yelled or screamed. Another effective sequence of strategies for women who stopped their rapes involved using cognitive verbal strategies, and when those proved ineffective, changing to physical strategies. Such strategies, then, can con-

TABLE 4   STRATEGIES OF RAPE AVOIDANCE, BY OUTCOME OF ATTACK (%)

	Raped Women (N = 43)	Rape Avoiders (N = 51)
Fled or tried to flee	9	33
Screamed	35	49
Used physical force	33	59
Used cognitive verbal strategies	72	67
Used affective verbal strategies	33	22
Benefited from environmental intervention	5	20
Used no strategy	12	. . .

vince the assailant that the woman is serious, not just feigning resistance.[16] The modal strategy for women who stopped their rapes was a combination of screaming/yelling and physical resistance. The correlation between the two strategies was +0.42 for avoiders.

Avoiding Death or Avoiding Rape

A woman's primary focus emerged during the interviews as a factor sharply differentiating raped women from rape avoiders: the women whose primary concern lay in avoiding death or mutilation have been less likely to avoid rape than those who had a gut reaction of rage and were primarily determined not to be raped. Because of the exploratory nature of this study, we were able to add a question to the interview schedule addressing this point after the pattern emerged. Twenty-eight women who were raped and 19 women who avoided rape expressed fear of death or mutilation as their foremost concern, while 3 women who were raped and 26 women who avoided rape were primarily determined not to be raped.

For example, the first woman we interviewed, a college student, was able to stop her rape even though her assailant was armed. She said, "We circled for a while; he had a knife. I was wearing some loose clothing . . . he knocked me to the ground, so he managed to get the top half of all of my clothes off and there's sort of a blank. I remember clearly wanting to fight this, not want this . . . not wanting to allow this to happen and I just thought, 'Well, I'm not going to stand for this, you know.' And I didn't. . . . He did have a knife and he did slash my coat. I didn't have any clothes on. I had an acute sense of being vigorous, stronger,

and more overpowering in myself and then there was sort of a brief flurry or something . . . or sliding away." (She had, in fact, slid away from her attacker.)

This response was surprising since we had originally thought that if there were a weapon no resistance would be possible. At the same time, the women who feared death should in no way be blamed, since descriptions of rape in the media emphasize the more lurid rape/murders and give scant attention to the women who stopped their rapes.

Psychological and Bodily Consequences of Physical Resistance

The effectiveness of using physical force to resist rape proved to be our most controversial finding, albeit one that is replicated in other studies.[17] We have suggested above that its effectiveness may lie in its communicating a clear message to the assailant, in addition to any physical injury he might receive or be in danger of receiving. Some assailants were not convinced by other strategies, presumably because they subscribed to the ideology prevalent in pornography and other media that women, whatever they might say, really want to be sexually assaulted. But what of the effect of this strategy on the women? We found that raped women who used physical strategies were less likely to be depressed than raped women who did not. The largest number of women who said they were depressed or who had symptoms of depression such as insomnia and weight loss were among those who were raped but did not use physical strategies. There was no difference in frequency of depression among women who avoided rape by fighting back and those who avoided rape without using physical strategies. Thus we can say that one of the most important functions of physical resistance is to keep women from feeling depressed even if they have been raped.[18]

If what we are tapping were merely personality differences between those who physically resisted and those who did not, then we would not find differences in depression only for those women who were raped. We think the results stem from the traditional vocabulary of motives used in our society to account for rape, a vocabulary many women have internalized.[19] In this vocabulary, rape is provoked by women through their dress, their carelessness, their foolhardiness in going to a "forbidden" place, such as a bar. Women are told, moreover, that they cannot be raped against their will—that, indeed, women really want to be raped and enjoy it. By resisting rape, however, women demonstrate to themselves and to others that this vocabulary does not apply to them. They are less likely to attribute their rape to their "personality defects"—weakness, cowardice, ineffectiveness—and thus less likely to say, "If only I had fought back it wouldn't have happened."[20] They are less likely to blame themselves and to feel depressed, more likely to gain strength from the belief that they did everything they could in that situation.

We are told that if we fight back, if we physically resist, we will pay the price through severe injury or death. This admonition is not supported by our findings or in the studies reported above. Furthermore, advising women to comply or risk injury assumes that rape in itself does not result in injury, physical as well as mental. Several women who talked to us reported serious injury from rape. One woman had a psychotic breakdown which resulted in her hospitalization. Her rapist also tore the area between her vagina and her anus so badly that it required surgical repair. In addition she became pregnant and had an abortion. Since she was not conscious during the attack, the injury did not stem from her resistance. Another contracted venereal disease, which led to pelvic inflammatory disease; she is now permanently sterile. She screamed and tried to reason with her assailant but did not resist physically.

We know that women who resist physically are more likely to avoid rape. We also know that there is little relationship between women's use of physical resistance and rapists' use of additional physical force over and above the attempted rape. True, sexual assault does not usually produce serious physical harm, while physical resistance often results in minor injuries such as bruises and scratches. Some women who used physical force were moderately or seriously injured. One such woman while arguing with her assailant, who was trying to enter her apartment, was punched in the eye and pushed into her apartment where she continued to struggle. Her screams alerted the neighbors who called the police. They arrived in time to stop the rape. A second woman screamed while being attacked in a cornfield and tried to strike her assailant. He pulled a knife, hit her twice with his fist, knocked her unconscious, and raped her. A woman who had decided to submit to rape, rather than be choked to death with a telephone cord, couldn't yield "because he was so dirty." The would-be rapist beat her, but when she yanked at his penis he hurriedly left.

Women who fought back sustained the following kinds of injuries: bruises and bite marks on the neck, soreness for a few days, strained muscles, bruises and minor cuts, more serious cuts, back injury, and aching the next morning. While we asked the women about the assailant's tactics including physical abuse, we did not systematically ask

about their own injuries and so there may have been minor injuries not reported. It is likely, however, that all the women who had serious injuries told us of them.

To judge the correlation between injury and physical resistance we must consider the interviews of the 5 women who were brutally beaten or suffered serious injury. Three were raped and 2 avoided being raped. Both avoiders' injuries resulted from their having fought back. However, for one of them, the resistance delayed the rape long enough for a train to pull into the platform where the assault was taking place, and the assailants fled. A third woman who was raped fought back even though her assailant had an ice pick as a weapon. It is unclear whether her beating was in response to her fighting back or to her screams. A raped virgin, attacked by two armed assailants, fought back and was seriously injured. But the injury was a result not of her struggle but of her seven rapes and her escape method. The last woman became sterile, as we described above.

These experiences suggest that by fighting back a woman significantly increases her chances of rape avoidance and somewhat increases her chance of rough treatment. However, not resisting is no guarantee of humane treatment.

Degree of Acquaintance with Assailant

Do women respond differently when attacked by men they know than when attacked by strangers? If so, is such difference in response associated with whether the outcome of the attack is rape or rape avoidance? Being assaulted by a stranger results in different patterns of response than does being assaulted by an acquaintance (see table 5). Both groups of women were more likely to yell or scream as well as to use both cognitive and affective verbal strategies when the assailant was a stranger than when he was someone they knew. In addition, there was environmental intervention more often among women who were not raped.

Environmental intervention, in general, occurred more frequently for women who avoided rape. In only two instances did raped women experience environmental intervention, and in both of these the assailant was a stranger. It should be noted that the mere occurrence of environmental intervention was not always sufficient to thwart attack. Sometimes the assailant(s) fled. But sometimes the woman had to be able to utilize such an opportunity in order to escape. One woman, for instance, who had been pinned against an alley wall, was able to flee when the sudden noise of a fire engine's siren caused her assailant to loosen

TABLE 5   STRATEGIES OF RAPE AVOIDANCE, BY OUTCOME OF ATTACK AND DEGREE OF ACQUAINTANCE[*]

	RAPED WOMEN (N = 43)		RAPE AVOIDERS (N = 51)	
	Known Assailant (N = 13) (%)	Stranger (N = 30) (%)	Known Assailant (N = 14) (%)	Stranger (N = 37) (%)
Fled or tried to flee	—	13.3	14.3	40.5
Screamed	23.1	40.0	42.8	51.3
Used physical force	38.5	30.0	57.1	59.5
Used cognitive verbal strategies	46.2	83.3	57.1	75.7
Used affective verbal strategies	30.7	33.3	21.4	21.6
Benefited from environmental intervention	—	6.7	21.4	18.9

[*]Percentages are based on the number of women in a given category who knew/did not know their assailant(s) and employed a particular strategy.

his grip. On another occasion a woman had negotiated with her assailant to rape her in his van rather than in the alley where he first attacked her. While walking with him to the van, she saw a strange man approach and asked him to help her. Although he never actually intervened, she used this opportunity to break away and run to a nearby tavern.

Presence of a Weapon

Conventional wisdom would suggest that the most important variable in a woman's response to attack is the assailant's possession of a weapon. And indeed, presence of a weapon does influence the outcome.[21] Of the group of women who were attacked by an unarmed assailant, 37 percent (19) were raped and 63 percent (32) avoided rape. Of the group of women who were attacked when an assailant had a weapon, when a weapon was presumed to be present, or when the assailant used a weapon to threaten or wound the woman, 56 percent (24) were raped and 44 percent (19) stopped the rape. The last point needs emphasis, however; even where there was some indication of a weapon, 44 percent of the women avoided being raped.

When the assailant had a weapon, 2 raped women fled, and 16 did not; 8 rape avoiders fled, and 6 did not. When the assailant had a weapon, 6 raped women screamed, and 12 did not; 4 avoiders screamed and 10 did not. When a weapon was present, 4 raped women used physical force, and 14 did not; 5 avoiders used that strategy, and 9 did not.

When the assailant was armed, 13 raped women and 11 avoiders used cognitive verbal strategies. Five raped women and 3 avoiders did not use such strategies. Four raped women faced with weapons used affective verbal strategies and 12 did not, while 4 avoiders used this strategy and 10 did not. Of the 5 victims who used no strategies, 3 were faced with armed assailants, and in 2 cases the assailant was not armed.

Since much of the debate about rape avoidance focuses on whether women should use physical force, it is important that one of the most striking differences between raped women and rape avoiders occurred in the case where the assailant did not have a weapon. In such situations, three-quarters (24) of the avoiders used physical strategies while one-quarter (8) did not; about half (9) of the raped women used such strategies, and about half (10) did not.

Being Attacked While Asleep

We have already seen that the most obvious situational variable, presence of a weapon, is associated with victimization rather than with avoidance. But we have also seen that even under such circumstances some women avoid rape. We will now turn to another variable that makes appropriate defense difficult and, in fact, according to Ann Burgess and Lynda Holmstrum, has particularly long-lasting effects: being attacked while asleep.[22] Two of the 5 women who were asleep used no strategies. How did the women who were not raped manage to avoid the assault? None pleaded, although all used cognitive verbal strategies. One, whom we call the "Super Negotiator," screamed, talked, and fought. Another talked, used physical force, and took advantage of environmental intervention. Their assailants were armed in both cases, and yet both women physically resisted. A third screamed and used cognitive verbal strategies, while a fourth was one of the few women who was able to avoid rape simply by persuading the man that she was not interested. The latter case is particularly striking because the assailant was later apprehended on numerous rape charges. While in prison, he wrote a letter to one of the women he raped in which he mentioned that, while he really liked her, he did not like another woman he tried to assault. We interviewed this second woman for our study. But he asked the woman to whom he wrote the letter why he was being charged with assault when he actually was raping.[23]

Two case histories give a sense of the kinds of strategies that can be employed in difficult situations. One of them involves the five-foot eight-inch tall Super Negotiator. She awoke to find herself pinned beneath the covers of her bed by a naked, armed man who was straddling her. She made an attempt to reach the phone but agreed to give up this bid for assistance in return for his removing a knife from her throat. She told the assailant she was menstruating and feigned embarrassment at the thought of removing her tampon in his presence. He agreed to allow her to go to the bathroom. However, once there, he would not allow her to close the door and scream for help. After removing her tampon, she refused to return to the bedroom, claiming that the knife, which was still in the room, frightened her. At this point, the assailant removed the knife from the nightstand and threw it down the hallway. She had attempted unsuccessfully to convince him to throw it outdoors, but he claimed that walking through the living room might cause him to be seen. Returning to the bedroom, he began to fondle her breasts and digitally penetrate her vagina. In response she feigned hysteria, in an effort to make him think that she was "going crazy." Finding this strategy unsuccessful, she asked if she could smoke some hash in order to relax. The hash pipe was big and heavy, and initially she planned on using it as a weapon; however, she was unable to work up enough nerve. After pretending to smoke for awhile, she asked if it would be all right if she went to the kitchen for a beer, as the hash had not had the desired effect. He refused and shoved her on her back on the bed. She responded by jumping and throwing him on his back, grabbing his hair and yanking his head as hard as she could over the footboard of the bed. The

assailant began to whimper. She reprimanded him for being "pushy" and for hurting her, and once again made her request for a beer and cigarette. The assailant complied, but retrieved his knife and followed her to the kitchen, pressing the knife to her back.

Once in the kitchen, she had hoped to make her escape, but she found that this was not possible. Not having any beer in the refrigerator, she successfully passed off a can of soda as a beer. As they were walking back to the bedroom she feigned anger at their return to the initial scenario— being in the bedroom with an armed man. In order to appease her, he placed the knife on the bookcase in the living room. For the first time since the start of the incident, she knew exactly where the knife was; thus, it would be accessible if she could somehow maneuver away from him. After smoking her cigarette and drinking the "beer," she clutched her stomach, pretending nausea, and ran out of the room. When he realized that she wasn't heading for the bathroom, he began to pursue her, but by this time she had reached the knife. He reached for a nearby lamp, which he intended to use as a weapon, but discovered that it was far too light to be useful. At this point she was moving toward the door and he said, "All right, that's it, I'm leaving. I was gonna try to be nice, but I'm leaving. Forget it." She ran out the back door and screamed for help. He made a couple of attempts to run out after her, but every time he did, she'd raise the knife to threaten him. Finally, he made a dash out the door, still naked from the waist down, carrying his pants. Less than a week after the attack, he parked his car behind her building after following her home from work. She flagged down a police car and he was apprehended.

Another case in which a woman was faced with seemingly impossible odds against avoiding assault involved a five-foot-ten-inch worker in a drug rehabilitation center. After completing her duties one evening, she crawled into her sleeping bag and fell asleep. Not long afterward, one of the residents came in asking for the time. In her stupor, she yelled at him and he appeared to leave. The next thing she knew "he was on top of" her with a knife pressed to her neck. Initially she froze, but then she fought him. Somehow she managed to get him off and get to the door, all the while screaming at the top of her lungs. After escaping from the room, she ran into a very large fellow female worker. Two women were too much for this assailant and he took off. Returning from the hospital, the avoider and a female companion spotted the assailant on the highway and reported his presence to the police. He was apprehended.

While both of these women were comparatively tall, we do not think it was simply their size that made the difference, although women five feet seven inches and over proved more likely to avoid rape. Rather, we suggest that short and tall women are treated differently in this society. Tall women do not have the option of being "cute" or acting helpless. They are less likely than short women to have a trained incapacity to be competent and assertive. Therefore, they are less likely to have the option of assuming the traditional "feminine" role, which rape analysts such as Susan Brownmiller and Susan Griffin suggest is conducive to being a rape victim.[24]

Much of what occurs in any assault depends on the woman's interaction with her assailant. In our interviews we discovered that women were able to negotiate parts of the scenario. Although it was difficult to avoid genital intercourse itself through negotiation, some of the women whom we interviewed were able to negotiate their way out of other sex acts after intercourse was completed; several through argument avoided sodomy, fellatio, and multiple acts of intercourse. Women also made bargains involving money or credit cards, negotiated regarding the place of assault, and modified some of the conditions of their assaults—arranged to be tied up in a more comfortable position, got assistance in walking from one place to another. The Super Negotiator superbly illustrates the range of individual negotiations.[25]

CONCLUSIONS AND POLICY IMPLICATIONS

Women who avoided rape used more kinds of strategies in response to the assault than women who were raped. They also used different strategies. Strategies associated with avoidance were fleeing or trying to flee, yelling, and using physical force. In cases where rape was avoided, there was also more likely to be environmental intervention. Women who were raped were more likely to use no strategies (no woman who avoided rape fell into this category) or to rely on affective verbal strategies. The most common strategies used were cognitive verbal—reasoning, verbally refusing, threatening, and conning. Use of such tactics, though they are frequently advised, did not differentiate raped women from those who avoided rape, and those strategies alone were rarely effective. The modal response which resulted in avoidance was a combination of yelling and using physical force. While the assailant's having a weapon made rape the more probable outcome, 37 percent of the women who avoided rape did so when the assailant was armed or claimed to be armed.

Because of the exploratory nature of the study and because ours was not a random sample, caution should be used in interpreting these results. Nonetheless, four empirical studies comparing the strategies of raped women and rape avoiders came up with similar findings. It is no accident that these findings, which suggest that women should physically resist their assailants, run counter to official ideology that women can avoid rape by behaving in ways more consonant with traditional socialization. Since rape is, after all, a paradigm of sexism in society,[26] it is not surprising that male advice to women on how to avoid rape also reflects that paradigm.

The tactics that women are usually advised to employ— verbal strategies, feigning insanity, or appealing to the assailant's humanity—are relatively ineffective. One might well conclude not only that the traditional ideology regarding rape is a form of social control over women,[27] but that traditional advice on rape avoidance also functions in this manner. This advice, when not such simple caveats about restricting one's behavior as "don't go out at night," suggests coping strategies consistent with the conventional female role, particularly use of verbal skills to manipulate the situation rather than confrontational behavior and fighting back. One police official is quoted as saying, "We recommend passive resistance, like getting a person's confidence by talking and doing what you were taught to do as girls growing up, to help resist attack."[28]

The importance of the policy implications of our study is augmented by Diana Russell and Nancy Howell's report of an intensive interview survey in San Francisco. They demonstrated the pervasiveness of the problem of sexual assault, contending "that there is at least a 26 percent probability that a woman in that city will become the victim of completed rape at some time in her life, and a 46 percent probability that she will become a victim of rape *or* attempted rape."[29] They conclude that the feminist analysis of rape, which states that sexual violence against women is endemic, is supported by research.

Feminist analysis has succeeded in making the point that rape is not a joke, that it has detrimental effects not only on the particular woman who is assaulted but on all women. For even though not all women are raped, fear of rape causes women generally to constrict their behavior.[30] Thus, it is clearly important to have data-based advice on which strategies are most effective in stopping a sexual assault. Indeed, since the National Institute of Mental Health released our findings, not only have the media been interested in disseminating our results—albeit in simplified form—but rape crisis centers and police departments have asked for our reports and papers so that they could be incorporated into their programs. We thus have the privilege of knowing that the pain our respondents endured not only during their assaults but in anticipation of their interviews, and the stress we experienced while listening to them and while analyzing the data, have not been in vain.

ACKNOWLEDGMENTS

This paper is based on research funded by the Center for the Prevention and Control of Rape of the National Institute of Mental Health, grant MH 29311-0. An earlier version was presented at the annual meetings of the American Sociological Association, New York, 1980, entitled "How to Say No to Storaska and Survive: Rape Avoidance Strategies." Frederick Storaska is the author of a book that is demeaning to women and is full of misinformation (*How to Say No to a Rapist and Survive* [New York: Random House, 1975]).

NOTES

1. Wallace D. Lok, "What Has Reform of Rape Legislation Wrought?" *Journal of Social Issues* 37, no. 4 (1981): 28–52. The Illinois sexual assault statute that went into effect in July 1984 omits the phrase "against her will." Catharine MacKinnon suggests that consent should be proven by the defense rather than disproven by the prosecution, making consent an "affirmative defense." See "Feminism, Marxism, Method, and the State: Toward Feminist Jurisprudence," *Signs: Journal of Women in Culture and Society* 8, no. 4 (1983):635–58, esp. 648, n. 29.

2. In fact, the People v. Joel Warren, 446 N.W. 2d 591, 1983, Illinois Appellate Court Fifth District (no. 82–180), reversed an original decision that found an assailant guilty of two counts of deviate sexual assault. The court reasoned that the complainant's "failure to resist when it was within her power to do so conveys the impression of consent regardless of her mental state, amounts to consent and removes from the act performed an essential element of the crime." The defendant maintained "that once complainant became aware that defendant intended to engage in sexual relations, it was incumbent upon her to resist." This decision was rendered even though the woman was five feet two inches and weighed one hundred pounds and the assailant was over six feet and weighed 185 pounds, the attack took place in an isolated area, and the woman was afraid that physically assaulting the man would anger him.

3. Queen's Bench Foundation, "Rape: Prevention and Resistance" (Queen's Bench Organization, 1255 Post St., San Francisco, 1976). See also Greer Litton Fox, "'Nice Girl': Social Control of Women through a Value Construct," *Signs* 2, no. 4(1977):805–17.

4. William B. Sanders, *Rape and Woman's Identity* (Beverly Hills, Calif.: Sage, 1980); Jennie J. McIntyre, "Victim Response to Rape: Alternative Outcomes" (final report to National Institute of Mental Health, grant R01MH29045); Richard Block and Wesley G. Skogan, "Resistance and Outcome in Robbery and Rape: Non-fatal, Stranger to Stranger Violence" (Center for Urban Affairs and Policy Research, Northwestern University, 1982).

5. Elsewhere we have addressed childhood and adult socialization as well as background and situational variables: Pauline B. Bart and Ellen Perlmutter, "Socialization and Rape Avoidance" (paper presented at the Association for Women in Psychology, Santa Monica, Calif., 1980); Bart, "A Study of Women Who Both Were Raped and Avoided Rape," *Journal of Social Issues* 37, no. 4(1981):123–37; Bart and Patricia H. O'Brien, "Stopping Rape: Strategies for Success" (Department of Psychiatry, University of Illinois at Chicago Health Sciences Center, 1983).

6. Joan McDermott, "Rape Victimization in 26 American Cities" (Washington, D.C.: Government Printing Office, 1979).

7. We attempted to allow for bias through the use of volunteers in two ways: we first asked women why they volunteered (the two primary motives proved to be altruism and catharsis, often in combination); and we then asked them where they had learned about the study. Our inquiries revealed no substantial bias from a single source.

8. While rapes reported to the police and McDermott's secondary analysis of a "representative sample of 10,000 households" also show similarly high rates of rape by strangers, other studies have found that as many as half the rapes involved assailants known to the woman: Pauline B. Bart, "Rape Doesn't End with a Kiss," *Viva*, June 1975, pp. 39–41, 100–101; Joseph J. Peters, *The Philadelphia Rape Victim Project in Forcible Rape: The Crime, the Victim, and the Offender* (New York: Columbia University Press, 1977); Menachem Amir, *Patterns of Forcible Rape* (Chicago: University of Chicago Press, 1971).

9. Bart, "Rape Doesn't End."

10. McDermott (n. 6 above).

11. Irene Hanson Frieze et al., "Psychological Factors in Violent Marriages" (Department of Psychology, University of Pittsburgh, 1979); Frieze, "Investigating the Causes and Consequences of Marital Rape," *Signs* 8, no. 3(1983):532–53.

12. It has become increasingly apparent that the concept of seduction is itself a male ideology. We have found that much, if not all, of what men perceive as seduction is in fact the result of women's having decided "to put up with it" or having planned in advance to "allow" themselves to be seduced. Bart has further refined the continuum as follows: consensual sex/altruistic sex/compliant sex/rape. In consensual sex both partners are sexually aroused. In altruistic sex the man wants sex and the woman goes along with it. When men engage in altruistic sex they use the pejorative term "mercy fucking." In complaint sex one person, usually the female, engages in the act because of the adverse consequences that follow if she doesn't, although there is no threat of force. We define rape as sexual behavior the woman engages in because of force or threat of force.

13. Pauline B. Bart and Kim Scheppele, "There Ought to Be a Law: Self-Definition and Legal Definitions of Sexual Assault" (paper presented at the meetings of the American Sociological Association, New York, 1980).

14. Kim Lane Scheppele and Pauline B. Bart, "Through Women's Eyes: Defining Danger in the Wake of Sexual Assault," *Journal of Social Issues* 39, no. 2(1983):63–80.

15. Queen's Bench Foundation (n. 3 above).

16. See Roseann Giarusso et al., "Adolescents' Cues and Signals: Sex and Assault" (paper presented at the annual meeting of the Western Psychological Association, San Diego, California, April 1979) for an analysis of the differences in the way in which males and females perceive the world.

17. Queen's Bench Foundation (n. 3 above); Sanders, McIntyre, and Block and Skogan (all n. 4 above).

18. Pauline B. Bart and Patricia H. O'Brien, "The Aftermath of Rape and Rape Avoidance: Behaviors, Attitudes, Ideologies and Response of Significant Others" (paper presented at the International Sociological Association meeting, Mexico City, August 1982).

19. Pauline B. Bart, "Social Structures and Vocabularies of Discomfort: What Happened to Female Hysteria?" *Journal of Health and Social Behavior* 9 (September 1968):188–93, esp. 189.

20. Ronnie Janoff-Bulman, "Characterological versus Behavioral Self-Blame: Inquiries into Depression and Rape," *Journal of Personality and Social Psychology* 37(1979):1798–1809.

21. This finding is also reported in McDermott (n. 6 above). According to our study, this relationship does not hold for Black women.

22. Ann Wolbert Burgess and Lynda L. Holmstrum, *Rape: Crisis and Recovery* (Bowie, Md.: Robert J. Brady, 1979).

23. Personal communication with Mary Pennington Anderson, attorney in the case.

24. Susan Brownmiller, *Against Our Will: Men, Women and Rape* (New York: Simon & Schuster, 1975); Susan Griffin, "Rape: The All-American Crime."

25. While we have been focusing on rape avoidance strategies as a way of coping with assault, there were additional ways in which women coped. Depersonalization—feeling as if it were happening to someone else, as if it were not really happening, as if one were dreaming—was a relatively common response, although, as one might expect, it was more common among raped women. Thus, 44 percent (19) of the raped women mentioned they experienced depersonalization, while 22 percent (11) of the avoiders had this response.

26. Pauline B. Bart, "Rape as a Paradigm of Sexism in Society," *Women's Studies International Quarterly* 2, no. 3(1979):347–57.

27. Stephanie Riger and Margaret T. Gordon, "The Fear of Rape: A Study in Social Control," *Journal of Social Issues* 37, no. 4(1981):71–92.

28. Quoted in Tacie Dejanikus, "New Studies Support Active Resistance to Rape," *Off Our Backs,* February 1981, pp. 9, 23.

29. Diana E. H. Russell and Nancy Howell, "The Prevalence of Rape in the United States Revisited," *Signs* 8, no. 4(1983):688–95, esp. 695.

30. Riger and Gordon (n. 27 above).

"Femicide": Speaking the Unspeakable

JANE CAPUTI and DIANA E. H. RUSSELL

Canadian novelist Margaret Atwood once asked a male friend why men feel threatened by women. He replied: "They are afraid women will laugh at them." She then asked a group of women why they feel threatened by men. They answered: "We're afraid of being killed."

However disproportionate, these fears are profoundly linked, as was demonstrated on December 6, 1989, at the University of Montreal. That day, 25-year-old combat-video aficionado Marc Lépine suited up for war and rushed the school of engineering. In one classroom, he separated the women from the men, ordered the men out, and, shouting "You're all fucking feminists," opened fire on the women. During a half-hour rampage, he killed 14 young women, wounded nine other women and four men, then turned his gun on himself. A three-page suicide note blamed all of his failures on women, whom he felt had scorned him. Also found was a hit list of 15 prominent Canadian women.

Unable to complete an application to the school of engineering, Lépine felt humiliated by women he defined as "feminists" because they had entered traditional male territory. His response to the erosion of white male exclusivity was a lethal one. It was also an eminently political one.

In the massacre's aftermath, media reports regularly denied the political nature of the crimes, citing such comments as Canadian novelist Mordecai Richler's: "It was the act of an absolutely demented man [which does not] lend itself to any explanation." This despite Lépine's clear explanation of his actions. *Whether individual hate killers are demented is beside the point.* In a racist and sexist soci-

ety, psychotics as well as so-called normals frequently act out the ubiquitous racist and misogynist attitudes they repeatedly see legitimized.

Lépine's murders were hate crimes targeting victims by gender, not race, religion, ethnicity, or sexual orientation. When racist murders—lynchings and pogroms—occur, no one wonders whether individual perpetrators are crazy or have had bad personal experiences with African Americans and Jews. Most people understand that lynchings and pogroms are motivated by political objectives: preserving white and gentile supremacy. Similarly, the aim of violence against women—conscious or not—is to preserve male supremacy.

Early feminist analysts of rape exposed the myths that it is a crime of frustrated attraction, victim provocation, or uncontrollable biological urges, perpetrated only by an aberrant fringe. Rather, rape is a direct expression of sexual politics, an assertion of masculinist norms, and a form of terrorism that preserves the gender status quo.

Like rape, the murders of women by husbands, lovers, fathers, acquaintances, and strangers are not the products of some inexplicable deviance. Murder is simply the most extreme form of sexist terrorism. A new word is needed to reflect this political understanding. We think *femicide* best describes the murders of women by men motivated by hatred, contempt, pleasure, or a sense of ownership of women. Femicide includes mutilation murder, rape murder, battery that escalates into murder; historical immolation of witches in Europe; historical and contemporary immolation of brides and widows in India; and "honor crimes" in some Latin and Middle Eastern countries, where women believed to have lost their virginity sometimes are killed by male relatives.

General male identification with killers demonstrates how rooted femicide is in sexist culture. For example, engineering student Celeste Brosseau, who had complained

Jane Caputi and Diana E. H. Russell, "'Femicide': Speaking the Unspeakable," *Ms.* 1, no. 2 (September–October 1990). Copyright © 1990 by Lang Communications, Inc. Reprinted with the permission of *Ms.*

A LETTER FROM CLAUDIA BRENNER

January 1991

Dear Friend,

On May 13, 1988, my lover, Rebecca, was murdered. I survived, with five bullet wounds.

At the trial of the attacker, it was proven that we were attacked because of who we were—two lesbians, two women living our lives and our love for each other.

There is no way to lessen the horror of that moment.

. . .

On May 13, Rebecca and I were hiking on the Appalachian trail in Adams County, Pennsylvania. At our campsite that morning, Rebecca was stopped by a man who asked her for a cigarette. He hadn't been there when we arrived at the site the previous evening, and must have arrived very late at night.

Later that day, we broke camp and continued our hike. As we checked a map at a fork in the trail, we were surprised to see the same man walking behind us. He had a rifle.

Claudia Brenner, "A Letter from Claudia Brenner." Reprinted with the permission of Claudia Brenner.

He asked us if we were lost. We said no, and turned left, onto a side trail. He continued along the main trail. The encounter made both Rebecca and me uneasy. We kept looking behind to see if the man was following us, but we never saw him again.

Late that afternoon, Rebecca and I stopped and made camp near a stream. It was a secluded spot, some distance from the trail. We ate, made love and rested.

Suddenly, there were gunshots. The shots were *so* sudden, *so* loud, *so* violent, *so* world-changing that at first I didn't even realize that they were gunshots and that we were the targets—except there was so much blood.

Because I was between the attacker and Rebecca, I was hit first. I was shot in the upper arm, twice in the neck, in the head and face. Rebecca told me to run behind a nearby tree. As she followed me, Rebecca was shot in the head and back.

The shooting finally stopped. We were both behind a large tree. In my frantic shock and fear, I didn't understand how badly hurt we were. But Rebecca had the presence of mind to tell me what to do. She told me to stop the bleeding. I believe she saved my life.

My only thought was to get us out of there and get help. I brought Rebecca her sneakers, but she couldn't see them. She was losing her vision. I tried to lift her, but she kept slumping to the ground.

---

about the sexism of the engineering faculty at the University of Alberta, was subjected to hundreds of her "fellow" students chanting "Shoot the bitch!" when she participated in an engineering society skit-night shortly after Lépine's assassinations.

The misogyny motivating violence against women also distorts press coverage of such crimes. Rape, femicide, and battery are variously ignored or sensationalized in the media, depending on the victim's race, class, and "attractiveness." Police, media, and public response to crimes against women of color, poor women, lesbian women, women working as prostitutes, and drug users, is particularly abysmal—usually apathy laced with pejorative stereotyping and victim-blaming. Moreover, public interest is dis-

proportionately focused on cases involving nonwhite assailants and white middle-class victims, such as the uproar over the 1989 Boston murder of Carol Stuart, a pregnant white woman who, her husband falsely claimed, was shot by a black robber. (She had been murdered by her affluent, white husband.)

Femicide is the ultimate end of a continuum of terror that includes rape, torture, mutilation, sexual slavery (particularly in prostitution), incestuous and extrafamilial child sexual abuse, physical and emotional battery; sexual harassment; genital mutilations (clitoridectomies, infibulations); unnecessary gynecological operations (gratuitous hysterectomies), forced heterosexuality, forced sterilization, forced motherhood (criminalizing contraception and abor-

Someplace deep within me, I began to understand how badly hurt Rebecca was. If the situation could get worse, it came with the realization that I had to go for help alone. I covered Rebecca, gave her all the first aid I could think of, and started out for help.

Before I left, Rebecca was unconscious. We never had a chance to say goodbye.

Soaked in blood, I walked on the rugged trail about two miles to a forest road. I was completely terrified that whoever had attacked us might be following and attack again. I walked on the road another two miles before I finally saw a car. I stopped the car, and the driver rushed me to the police in nearby Shippensburg.

All I could think about was Rebecca. The State Police immediately began a search for her.

That evening, I was airlifted to the Hershey Medical Center trauma unit. I had emergency surgery that night. The next day I learned that the police had found Rebecca's body. She died from the bullet wound that hit her back and exploded in her liver.

But my ordeal did not end with the horror of Rebecca's death.

The State Police caught the man who murdered Rebecca—the same man who had followed us on the trail—Stephen Roy Carr. We now know that Stephen Roy Carr stalked us, hid eighty-five feet away in the woods while we made camp, shot to kill and left us for dead.

During the legal proceedings that followed, it became clear that Carr had attacked us because we were lesbians. Carr's lawyer even implied—during the trial and the appeal—that Rebecca and I had provoked the attack.

The implication that Rebecca and I had "teased" Carr with our sexuality, and that we were responsible for this man stalking us, spying on us, and shooting to kill us was not only outrageous, it was disgusting.

Fortunately, the trial judge refused to allow this line of argument. On October 27, 1988, Stephen Roy Carr was convicted of first degree murder and later sentenced to life in prison without parole.

I survived the attack, but in the months that followed I was consumed with grief and fear. My world centered on the knowledge that Rebecca was dead and that somehow I was alive.

I had always known that the world was not a safe place for lesbians. But somehow, I believed that nothing this terrible would ever happen to me.

I believed that all I needed to do was not to look like a stereotypical lesbian and be discreet about my expressions of affection to other women. That security was shattered by the bullets. . . .

Sincerely,

Claudia Brenner

---

tion), psychosurgery, abusive medical experimentation (e.g., some efforts to create new reproductive technologies), denial of protein to women in some cultures, cosmetic surgery and other mutilations in the name of beautification. Whenever these forms of terrorism result in death, they become femicides.

Federal statistics do not reveal the scope of violence against women. Surveys by independent researchers show rates of female victimization that should shatter us all. For example, in Diana Russell's random sample survey of 930 San Francisco women: 44 percent reported being victimized by rape or attempted rape, 38 percent by child sexual abuse, 16 percent by incestuous abuse, 14 percent by wife rape, and 21 percent by marital violence.

As with rape and child sexual abuse, femicide is most likely to be perpetrated by a male family member, friend, or acquaintance. Ironically, the patriarchy's ideal domestic arrangement (heterosexual coupling) is the most potentially femicidal situation. Husbands (including common-law) account for 33 percent of all women murdered between 1976 and 1987 in the United States.

Violent crimes against women have escalated in recent decades. Some believe this increase is due to women reporting them more. But Russell's research on (largely unreported) rape, for example, establishes a dramatic escalation during the last 50 years. Although it is not yet possible to assess the number of sex murders in any given year, virtually all experts agree there has been a substantial rise

FEMICIDE: RELATED CIRCUMSTANCES
California, 1988
(Out of 689 willful femicides where related circumstances are known)

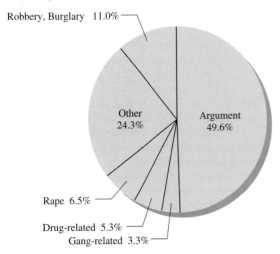

Robbery, Burglary 11.0%

Other
24.3%

Argument
49.6%

Rape 6.5%

Drug-related 5.3%

Gang-related 3.3%

Roy Norris and Lawrence Bittaker of Los Angeles raped and mutilated her with a pair of locking pliers, hit her with a sledgehammer, and jabbed her in her ear with an ice pick. The men audiotaped the torture femicide from beginning to end.

In 1987, police found three half-naked, malnourished African American women "shackled to a sewer pipe in a basement that doubled as a secret torture chamber" in the home of Gary Heidnik, a white Philadelphian; 24 pounds of human limbs were stockpiled in a freezer and other body parts were found in an oven and a stew pot.

Such atrocities also are enacted upon women by their male intimates. The case of Joel Steinberg, who murdered his adopted daughter, Lisa, and tortured his companion, Hedda Nussbaum, for years, is extreme but not unique. In 1989, a California man was sentenced to 32 years in prison for torturing his wife in a 10-hour attack. After she refused anal sex, Curtis Adams handcuffed his wife, repeatedly forced a bottle and then a broomstick into her anus, and hung her naked out the window—taking breaks to make her read Bible passages adjuring women to obey their husbands.

since the early 1960s. A surge in serial murder is recognized by criminologists to have begun in the 1950s, and has become a characteristic phenomenon of the late 20th century in the U.S. The vast majority of serial killers are white men and most of their victims are women.

We see this escalation of violence against females as part of a male backlash against feminism. This doesn't mean it's the *fault* of feminism: patriarchal culture terrorizes women whether we fight back or not. Still, when male supremacy is challenged, that terror is intensified. While women who stepped out of line in early modern Europe were tortured and killed as witches (estimates range from 200,000 to 9 million killed), today such women are regarded as cunts or bitches, deserving whatever happens to them. "Why is it wrong to get rid of some fuckin' cunts?" Kenneth Bianchi, convicted "Hillside Strangler," demanded to know. "Kill Feminist Bitches!" is a revealing graffito found on the Western Ontario campus after the Montreal massacre.

Law enforcement officials have noted the growing viciousness in slayings. Justice Department official Robert Heck said: "We've got people [sic] now killing 20 and 30 people [sic] and more, and some of them just don't kill. They torture their victims in terrible ways and mutilate them before they kill them." For example:

Teenager Shirley Ledford screamed for mercy while

MURDER: RELATIONSHIP OF VICTIM TO OFFENDER (TEXAS, 1988)

Relationship	Number	% of Total
Acquaintance	572	42.2
Stranger	250	18.5
Wife/common-law wife	89	7.3
Friend	88	5.8
Other—known to victim	68	5.8
Husband/common-law husband	55	4.1
Other family	51	3.8
Son/stepson	34	2.5
Girlfriend	33	2.4
Neighbor	28	2.1
Brother	20	1.5
Father/stepfather	18	1.3
Boyfriend	15	1.1
Ex-wife	15	1.1
Daughter/stepdaughter	11	0.8
Mother/stepmother	8	0.4
Homosexual relationship	5	0.4
Sister	5	0.4
Ex-husband	2	0.1
TOTAL	1,355	100.0

*Relationship was known in 1,355 of 2,053 murder cases.

A sense of entitlement is a major cause of sexist terrorism. Many males believe they have a right to get what they want from females. Consider the hatred exhibited in response to a trivial challenge to male dominance: female students at the University of Iowa complained about the loud stereos of male students on the floor above. A response in graffiti titled "The Top 10 Things To Do To The Bitches Below" was found in the men's bathroom and then published in the university newspaper, including exhortations to beat the women "into a bloody pulp with a sledgehammer and laugh" and instructions on "how to mutilate female genitalia with an electric trimmer, pliers, and a 'red-hot soldering iron.'" Similarly, a suggestion was made in the University of Toronto engineering students' newspaper that women "cut off their breasts if they were sick of sexual harassment."

To see where these students get such gruesome ideas, we only need look to pornography and mass media "gorenography." An FBI study of 36 sex serial killers found that pornography was ranked highest of many sexual interests by an astonishing 81 percent. Such notorious killers as Edmund Kemper (the "Coed Killer"), Ted Bundy, David Berkowitz (the "Son of Sam"), and Kenneth Bianchi and Angelo Buono (the "Hillside Stranglers") were all heavy pornography consumers. Bundy maintained that pornography "had an impact on me that was just so central to the development of the violent behavior that I engaged in." His assessment is consistent with testimony from many other sex offenders, as well as research on the effects of pornography.

Femicidal atrocity is everywhere normalized, explained as "joking," and rendered into standard fantasy fare, from comic books through Nobel prizewinning literature, box-office smashes through snuff films. Meanwhile, the FBI terms sex killings "recreational murder."

Just as many people denied the reality of the Nazi Holocaust, most people refuse to recognize the gynocidal period in which women are living—and dying—today. Some husbands and fathers act as full-time guards who threaten to kill if defied. "Dedicated Bible reader" John List was convicted this year in New Jersey for mass murder, after escaping detection for 18 years. List complained that his wife refused to attend church, an action he "knew would harm the children." His daughter wanted to pursue an acting career, making him "fearful as to what that might do to her continuing to be a Christian." In a rage over his loss of control, this godly man slaughtered his wife, daughter, mother, and two sons.

If all femicides were recognized as such and accurately counted, if the massive incidence of nonlethal sexual assaults against women and girls were taken into account, if incest and battery were recognized as torture (frequently prolonged over years), if the patriarchal home were seen as the inescapable prison it so frequently becomes, if pornography and gorenography were recognized as hate literature, then this culture might have to acknowledge that we live in the midst of a reign of sexist terror comparable in magnitude, intensity, and intent to the persecution, torture, and annihilation of women as witches from the 14th to the 17th centuries in Europe.

It is unspeakably painful for most women to think about men's violence against us, as individuals and collectively, because the violence we encounter, and the disbelief and contempt with which we are met when we do speak out, is often so traumatic and life-threatening that many of us engage in denial or repression of our experiences.

In November 1989, 28-year-old Eileen Franklin-Lipsker of Foster City, California, suddenly remembered having witnessed her father sexually abuse her eight-year-old school friend, Susan Nason, then bludgeon her to death. Twenty years later, she turned her father in to the police. Such remembrance and denunciation is the work of

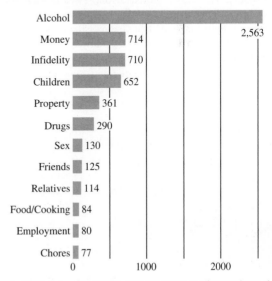

**DOMESTIC VIOLENCE:
REASONS FOR ASSAULT
Maryland, 1988**

Reason	Value
Alcohol	2,563
Money	714
Infidelity	710
Children	652
Property	361
Drugs	290
Sex	130
Friends	125
Relatives	114
Food/Cooking	84
Employment	80
Chores	77

In 1988, there were 14,521 reported incidents of spousal assault in Maryland. In 5,988 cases, reasons for the assaults were given. These are the 12 most commonly cited.

RAPE: RELATIONSHIP OF VICTIM TO OFFENDER (KANSAS, 1988)

Relationship	Number	% of Total
Acquaintance	217	28.5
Stranger	213	28.0
Friend	47	8.2
Wife/common-law wife	32	4.2
Ex-girlfriend	31	4.1
Girlfriend	19	2.5
Ex-wife	15	2.0
Daughter/stepdaughter	20	2.8
Other family/in-law	14	1.8
Sister	8	1.0
Granddaughter	2	0.3
Niece	1	0.1
Baby-sitter	1	0.1
Neighbor	1	0.1
Unknown	141	18.5
TOTAL	782	100.0

the entire feminist movement against violence against women: to disobey the fathers' commandments to forget, deny, maintain silence, and, instead, to turn in our abusive fathers, husbands, brothers, lovers, sons, friends.

The recollection and acknowledgement of history/experience that has been so profoundly repressed is what Toni Morrison in her masterpiece *Beloved* calls *rememory*. In an interview, Morrison noted that there is virtually no remembrance—no lore, songs, or dances—of the African people who died during the Middle Passage: "I suspect . . . it was not possible to survive on certain levels and dwell on it. . . . There is a necessity for remembering the horror, but . . . in a manner in which the memory is not destructive." Morrison's concept of rememory is crucial as well for all women grappling with the torment of living in a femicidal world. We too must be able to face horror in ways that do not destroy, but save us.

Canadian feminists are working to have December 6 declared a national day of remembrance for the slaughtered women. We encourage women worldwide to claim December 6 as an international day of mourning and rage, a "Rememory Day" for all women everywhere who have been victims of sexual violence.

Such rituals are modes of healing, but not cures. Feminists, collectively and internationally, must take on the task of formulating strategies of resistance as massive and formidable as the horrors that confront us.

Progressive people rightly favor an international boycott of South Africa so long as apartheid reigns; why do they/we so rarely consider the potential efficacy of boycotting violent and abusive men and *their* culture? In 1590, Iroquois women gathered in Seneca to demand the cessation of war among the nations. We must now demand an end to the global patriarchal war on women. The femicidal culture is one in which the male is worshiped. This worship is obtained through tyranny, subtle and overt, over our bruised minds, our battered and dead bodies, our co-optation into supporting even batterers, rapists, and killers. "Basically, I worshiped him," said Hedda Nussbaum. "We do not worship them . . . we do not trust them," wrote Alice Walker. In a myriad of ways, let us refuse nurture, solace, support, and approval. Let us withdraw our worship.

ACKNOWLEDGMENTS

The authors would like to thank Joan Balter, Sandy Butler, Candida Ellis, Marny Hall, and Helene Vann for their invaluable comments on this article.

READING 43

Accountability or Justice? Rape as a War Crime

MARY ANN TÉTREAULT

WARTIME RAPE AS A NORMATIVE ISSUE

Whether and how to treat rape as a war crime are complex questions. Rape is a contested issue in domestic criminal law, an assault for which the victim is blamed as much or more than the criminal—she asked for it, people say (Brownmiller 1975:373). This perversity is rationalized as the outcome of cultural traditions that associate female chastity with family honor (e.g., Peristiany 1965; Tillion 1983), and underlies some of the shame associated with being a rape victim. Shame contributes to the low likelihood that the rapist will be charged with his crime if the victim can conceal what has happened to her. Victim reluctance to suffer the social and legal repercussions of rape also shields rapists who commit their crimes during a war (e.g., Asia Watch & Physicians for Human Rights 1993:1). Even though concealment also limits the support the victim can claim from her family and friends, shame and the fear of social ostracism work for the rapist whether he is an acquaintance, a stranger, or a soldier.

But the victim is not the only person influencing the kind and amount of publicity given to rape. When rape is an instrument of policy, rapists themselves and their bureaucratic superiors publicize the act as part of the crime. Here, the purpose of rape is precisely to shame the victim, her family, and her nation, and to terrorize her entire community. "Rape [is] an act of conquest and subjugation of whole societies, involving deliberate national humiliation as a means of suppression and social control. . . ." (Makiya 1993:294). This technique is used domestically,

against ethnic minorities and opposition groups, as well as against foreign populations. Kanan Makiya notes that the government of Iraq employs "official rapists," civil servants whose job it is to rape selected Iraqi women and thus "dishonor an entire family name" (289). Other regimes, for example Jordan (Makiya 1993), Pakistan (Makiya 1993; Asia Watch 1992), Haiti (Human Rights Watch National Coalition for Haitian Refugees 1994), and India (Asia Watch & Physicians for Human Rights 1993) also rape female citizens to control dissident populations.

Rape in war is often read as the criminal—or, even worse, the inevitable—behavior of individuals (Brownmiller 1975:73). It is far more accurate to view wartime rape as an instrument of policy. Military organizations, with their hierarchical chains of command, are designed so that leaders can direct the behavior of subordinates. To argue that rapes committed by soldiers are individual acts, particularly if military rapists go uncharged and unpunished, is simply untenable (Amnesty International 1993:4). Rather, as is rape domestically when routinely performed by state employees, wartime rape is undertaken to implement strategies of genocide and terror.

Genocide, the obliteration of an enemy's social formation,[1] has been practiced since ancient times and nearly always involves the sexual violation of women (Smith 1994a). Where slavery was institutionalized—for example, in ancient Greece, Old Testament Israel, or premodern Arabia—the defeat of an enemy on his own territory resulted in killing as many men as possible, destroying the city, and capturing women and children to become concubines and slaves (Garlan 1988; Mernissi 1991; Smith 1994a).[2] This practice destroyed the enemy as an organic community.

Rape has replaced capture as the primary sexual instrument of genocide. Following the battle of Culloden in 1746,

Mary Ann Tétreault, "Accountability or Justice? Rape as a War Crime" (previously unpublished paper). Reprinted with the permission of the author.

English troops used rape to destroy the organization of Scottish tribes (clans) supporting a Stuart claimant to the throne (Brownmiller 1975:38–40). The army of Pakistan systematically raped more than 200,000 Bengali women before being routed by the Indian army in 1971 (Roy 1975); today, the Indian army uses rape against Muslim women in Kashmir (Asia Watch & Physicians for Human Rights 1993). Rape was an integral element of the genocide committed by the Nazis against the Jews and by the Khmer Rouge against other Khmer (Smith 1994b). It is used today in "ethnic cleansing" campaigns in Bosnia-Herzegovina (Amnesty International 1993; *New York Times* October 22, 1993:A4).

Wartime rape plus coerced pregnancy combine the ancient mechanism of capture with the perennial mechanism of rape to carry out another version of ethnic warfare. Women are raped repeatedly until pregnancies are confirmed and then detained until their pregnancies are too advanced for safe abortions to be performed. Reports from Bosnia indicate that this pattern was followed in camps maintained by the Bosnian Serbs (e.g., Personal Narratives 1992; Burns 1992; Lewin 1993). However, most reports from Bosnia indicate that rape victims are more likely to be killed than held to bear the children of the rapists (Amnesty International 1993:2; Burns 1993).

A similar pattern of coerced pregnancy has been reported in Rwanda, but with a twist.

[D]uring the atrocities, women of the opposite ethnic group were raped to humiliate and harm them (and they were often killed afterward). In this later phase . . . the preference was for women of the same ethnic group as the perpetrators, this time to reproduce the group. There are many stories . . . of young Tutsi women being held in Kigali by the RPF forces (mostly Tutsi) as walking wombs, where the yearnings of youth mixed with the strategies of statesmen to capture women of reproductive age—especially women of one's [own] ethnicity. . . . [I]n this case the fighting has ended up by conquering women of the same group as the soldiers (Newbury 1995).

This strategy of replenishing the group depends both on ancient beliefs that women are merely the vessels in which men breed their own descendants, and principles followed by many nation-states whereby nationality passes from father to son independently of the mother (Yuval-Davis & Anthias 1989; Tétreault & al-Mughni 1995).

Rape and the threat of rape are also terror tactics that drive people out of their homes and villages, making it eas-ier for enemy forces to extend their control over territory (Thomas & Ralph 1993). Rape is a crime against women that effectively removes male combatants from enemy ranks. The fear of rape explains why men who might otherwise remain to defend their homes will flee with their families to protect their women—and themselves: Though wartime rape of men is uncommon, it is not unknown (Tétreault 1992; Thomas & Ralph 1993; Riding 1993). Families that stay behind risk more than physical security. The rape of a family member devastates family life; those who watch feel impotent and vulnerable because they cannot protect the victims (Morton & Sangrey 1979). In cultures where shame is connected to the loss of female chastity, a raped woman is both humiliated by her attacker and rejected by family members. Indeed, rape in war, like other forms of torture, is frequently performed in front of family members to maximize its effectiveness in achieving social, emotional, and cognitive disorientation, terrorizing the community, and making it easier to control (e.g., Simons 1994; al-Mughni & al-Turkait 1994).

The unparalleled power of rape to effect or mark subjection has been exploited since ancient times. K. J. Dover (1978) notes that herms, stone markers carved to represent the face and erect penis of the god Hermes, also represented the threat of sexual retaliation against anybody encroaching on the territory of Greek property owners. The equation of penetration with subordination was so strong in ancient Athens that a man who permitted his body to be penetrated during homosexual acts risked his citizenship, while the forcible penetration of an Athenian citizen constituted the crime of hubris and required the execution of the offender to restore the victim to his former political status (103–4).

Despite the fact that both men and women can be raped, rape is overwhelmingly a crime committed by men against women. It is a crime intended to have collective and personal consequences. Rape is triggered by deep emotions and incites equally deep-seated reactions connected to the use of sexual symbolism to convey a whole range of concepts other than those dealing strictly with sexual acts. The symbolic connection between female chastity and group integrity, for example, is an important element motivating wartime rape. **Women** are living beings with personal lives and civil statuses; **woman** is the embodiment of complex constructions of community and nationality (Hunt 1984; Yuval-Davis & Anthias 1989; Mosse 1985; Theweleit 1987).

Wartime rape is a political crime against the symbol. It is a sacrilege. The group is shamed by the rape and injured as a result of the shame; however, the victim suffers both as the victim of a crime and as the scapegoat of their shame. This scapegoating has dire consequences for the sexually violated woman (Roy 1975; Brownmiller 1975; Tétreault 1992), but they are addressed—if they are addressed—as the problems of a person rather than a people. The appalling prevalence of rape in war and the even more appalling masses of evidence that it is neither inevitable nor unconnected to military strategy evoke questions about why wartime rape is personalized rather than treated as the severe human rights abuse that it is.

> Despite the pervasiveness of rape, it often has been a hidden element of war, a fact that is linked inextricably to its largely gender-specific character. The fact that the abuse is committed by men against women has contributed to its being narrowly portrayed as sexual or personal . . . a portrayal that depoliticizes sexual abuse in conflict and results in its being ignored as a war crime (Thomas & Ralph, 84).

Rape is often a prelude to murder. But whether victims live or die, rape is an engine of enormous devastation. It wreaks simultaneously physical, emotional, and psychological violence against a human being, a family, a community, and a people. It has grave physical consequences—injury, infection, pregnancy, and death (Quindlen 1993); lasting psychological consequences ranging from distaste for sexual intimacy and an impaired capacity for trust to insanity and even suicide (Hartman & Burgess 1988; Kilpatrick & Veronen 1983; Mann 1991; al-Mughni & al-Turkait 1994); and initiates a train of collective consequences that can end in the elimination of a community and its unique pattern of organized social and political life (Smith 1994a).

WARTIME RAPE AS A PRACTICAL ISSUE

In this section, I examine two contemporary cases of war in which rape was utilized strategically as part of a campaign of terror and/or genocide. These are the Iraqi invasion of Kuwait and the war in Bosnia-Herzegovina. I consider three aspects of rape as a human rights abuse: its politicization as a conflict strategy; the treatment of rape victims by families, communities, and governments; and two examples of international tribunals where victims can make claims or bring charges against rapists and those responsible for their actions.

Politicization

The politicization of rape is most likely to occur as part of an ongoing conflict, when it can motivate military and civilian populations and possibly alter the strategic balance of forces. Politicization to motivate one's own armies is clearly an incitement to retaliatory behavior against women on the "other side" (Brownmiller 1975:64–72). Here I look at cases in which parties in a conflict use charges of enemy rape to mobilize external support for their side. Paradoxically, such a strategy tends to devalue the actual suffering of victims, and is rarely pursued either to seek justice for them once the fighting is over or to hold those responsible accountable for their crimes.

Susan Brownmiller (1975) discusses the politicization of wartime rape in the context of the two world wars. During World War I, the German army was charged with the "rape of Belgium" in atrocity stories aimed at aggravating anti-German feelings among civilian populations and Allied troops. After the war, those stories were reevaluated by scholars, who concluded that they were *merely* propaganda. A numbers game ensued—*only* so many rapes had occurred, fewer than originally reported (46–48). One writer implied that allegations of rape were made for their alliterative value in French rather than because they had actually occurred (47). The initial exaggeration was used to justify this later trivialization; the reality of the rapes disappeared.

The creation of tribunals to try war criminals on the losing side following World War II led to a somewhat different result in the cases of the "rape of Nanking" and the sexual torture of Jewish women under the Nazi regime. The conquest of Nanking was marked by horrible atrocities committed by Japanese troops against the Chinese civilian population. Reports featured the trope "rape of Nanking" because it was so literally as well as figuratively true. Yet a 1938 report by a missionary group detailing the consequences of the Japanese invasion and conquest of the city "excluded rape per se" as a category of damage, despite its inclusion of many less damaging injuries (57–58).

The Tokyo war crimes tribunal did not call rape victims to testify. However, witnesses testifying to other crimes also reported on the hundreds of rapes they had seen during the carnage. From this testimony, the tribunal estimated that 20,000 rapes had occurred in Nanking during the first month of occupation alone, and that widespread rape continued to be committed, along with other crimes, "at least six weeks after the city had been taken" (cited in Brownmiller 1975:61).[3]

Adopting a "rape of Belgium/Nanking" strategy, spokespersons for the Kuwaiti government in exile, desperately aware of its dependence on external forces to liberate Kuwait, made repeated claims about Iraqi atrocities that emphasized the rape of Kuwaiti women by Iraqi soldiers during the invasion and occupation.[4] Publication of these stories in the press and on television helped to build popular sympathy in the United States and Europe for the rollback of the invasion.

After liberation, some Kuwaitis who had remained in Kuwait during the occupation questioned the motivation for this strategy and criticized its terrorizing effects on Kuwaitis living under occupation. None disputed the charge that rapes had occurred and several reported that gang rape, other forms of sexual torture, and murder were routinely inflicted on women in the Resistance unfortunate enough to have been taken captive (e.g., Tétreault 1992; al-Mughni & al-Turkait 1994). An initially classified report by U.S. army investigators released in 1993 supports the tenor of contemporary Kuwaiti allegations, though the estimates of numbers of all types of atrocities were lower than what had been alleged during the war. However, in the postliberation environment, the Kuwaiti regime was pressed by U.S. officials to minimize public comments about human rights abuses committed during the occupation to calm Kuwaitis engaged in retributory rampages against scapegoats, primarily Palestinians, accused of being collaborators (Lancaster 1993).

Unlike the Iraqi rapes of Kuwaitis which appear to have been primarily acts of terror, humiliation, and pollution (al-Mughni & al-Turkait 1994),[5] a significant number of the rapes in Bosnia-Herzegovina were committed as part of a strategy of "ethnic cleansing" intended to remove members of "ethnic" groups other than the one represented by whichever army was victorious in a particular territory. As in the case of Jewish women victimized by the Nazis, some women were taken to concentration camps and repeatedly violated; others were raped in their homes, often in front of family members. Many rape victims were also murdered (Amnesty International 1993; In re Jane Doe et al. 1993; Simons 1994; MacKinnon 1993; Lewis 1994; Coll 1994).

The organized quality of so many rapes is revealed by the sequestration of the women in camps, barracks, and motels *(New York Times* 1992) and the recording of rapes on videotape. Catherine MacKinnon (1993) equates the filming of rapes by Serbs with the expression of a culture of pornography.[6] I see this differently, as part of a propaganda campaign to influence the environment of the conflict. The films are less indicative of pornographic qualities in a particular culture than the results of a sexualization of film and video entertainment visible worldwide. The films, by their nature, get viewers' attention, but they are primarily intended to persuade. Their content depends jointly on technical capability and the government's assessment of just how much it can get away with in the process of creating and marketing its message.

The filming of the rapes is not incidental, however. It is part of the propaganda machine. According to MacKinnon, some rapes by Serb soldiers were staged to look as though they had been committed by Croatians (1993:27). Rape films are shown on Serbian television to whip up popular support for the war, and to Serb soldiers to encourage them to greater efforts (27–28). As a high school student, I watched similar (though, mercifully, far less graphic) films that had been produced during World War II by the U.S. military for the same purposes.[7] MacKinnon notes that the Nazis also made films like this and used them to produce "sexually explicit anti-Semitic hate propaganda" (30).

In this context, arguments over the pornographic value of a particular country's propaganda have the same unfortunate consequences as the personalization of wartime rape: They shift attention from the issue of wartime rape as a human rights abuse to allegations about its possible psychological causes. The exploitation of photographs and video footage of someone's rape or mutilated or dying body should qualify as a war crime, a violation of the 1949 Geneva Convention prohibiting "outrages upon personal dignity." However, this is a separate issue.

All sides in the Bosnian war have used allegations of rape to mobilize supporters, neutralize opponents, and manipulate the balance of forces in the conflict. All of them have also engaged in rape (Amnesty International 1993:3; Riding 1993:1), though the United Nations has accused only Serb commanders of committing rape and other atrocities as part of a policy of genocide (Cohen 1995:1). Even though there are vast differences in the degree of criminal culpability among the three sides fighting in Bosnia-Herzegovina, to focus on rapes by one side only makes light of the abuses of women raped by non-Serbian forces. Their attackers are virtually acquitted in the court of public opinion: One side commits war crimes while the other is only responding in kind. This is the same attitude that excused an orgy of Russian rapes of German women at the end of World War II (Brownmiller 1975:66–72; Rubin 1992). In a similarly perverse way, a focus on "cultures of pornography" attenuates the individual and collective responsibility of rapists, their commanding officers, and the political leaders who oversee and condone their actions.

The Treatment of Victims

Immediately following the liberation, the Kuwaiti government sent female military personnel to interview war victims and record their testimony. Two recorders interviewed in 1992 said that they had talked with a number of rape victims, most of whom reported aggravated circumstances. Neither was willing to report the number of rape victims she had interviewed, nor to divulge any specific information regarding any of the rapes. A clinical psychologist also refused to report the number of wartime rape victims among his patients (Tétreault 1992). A recent estimate drawn from multiple sources, including medical records, concludes that approximately 2,000 Kuwaiti women were sexually assaulted by Iraqi military personnel during the conflict (al-Mughni & al-Turkait 1994).

A mechanism for processing claims for war damages was established under UN auspices (see below), but few Kuwaiti women presented claims for damages from wartime rape. Both the discretion of medical and military officials in possession of actual data and the refusal of the women themselves to press their claims have erased rape from discussions of reparation and restitution due Kuwait from Iraq. The primary public reason given for the quiet submersion of the issue of wartime rape in Kuwait is to respect the shame of rape victims and to avoid causing them any more pain than they have suffered already. The clinical psychologist mentioned above put it this way:

> [R]ape is a social and ethical stigma for the one [raped] and for their families. Many families keep their victims locked in the house. Married victims are being divorced. Most rape victims are being treated by traditional methods, reading the Quran, or taking them to special religious people. . . . Many cases with reactive anxiety are developing severe psychotic depression—even schizophrenia. . . . Virginity is a very precious concept to a Kuwaiti (Tétreault 1992).

Here we see again the most frequently cited reasons for the nonreporting of rape: social stigma, self-blame, prevention by family members or religious counselors, fear of rejection and repudiation, and severe mental illness. This psychologist also said that he knew of cases where male family members killed rape victims or encouraged them to commit suicide; others committed suicide despite the efforts of friends and family members to stop them (Tétreault 1992). Occasional press reports told similar stories (e.g., Mann 1991). Death is the most effective silencer.

The treatment of rape victims by investigators and medical personnel was generally humane in Kuwait, including the exemplary discretion practiced by individuals collecting their testimonies. Their treatment by families and neighbors was uneven, despite widespread verbal and occasional actual support for reintegrating victims into Kuwaiti society without stigma (Tétreault 1994b; p. 301). The treatment of rape victims by the state was ambiguous. On the one hand, medical and social services were made available to rape victims as to other victims of posttraumatic stress (al-Mughni & al-Turkait 1994), while rape victims' plight was not exploited publicly as a foreign policy tool. For example, rape victims have not been featured in Kuwaiti arguments to retain UN sanctions against Iraq.[8]

On the other hand, the political value of wartime rape was not totally forgone by domestic political actors. A whispering campaign alleged that rape had been far more widespread than was reflected in official reports, and that nearly every family that had remained behind was dishonored because it harbored at least one raped woman. Some who had remained in Kuwait during the occupation were convinced that the whispering campaign was a ploy to discredit the resistance and, by implication if not inclusion, others pressing for greater democratization (Tétreault 1992). At the same time, one well-known resistance rape and murder victim, Asrir al-Qabandy, was publicly honored as a martyr for Kuwait.

Given the climate faced by raped women in similar (though far from identical) cultural circumstances, the willingness of so many women in Bosnia-Herzegovina to testify publicly to their sexual abuse by armed forces is remarkable, and the reluctance of the others is understandable. At this juncture, there is not enough information to judge how well or how poorly rape survivors are being treated by families and communities. However, there is little reason to believe that the posttraumatic treatment of Bosnian women is any less hurtful than what happened to many Kuwaiti women. Well-intentioned individuals and groups gathering evidence for future legal actions carried out their inquiries in ways that brought individual raped women to public attention. Requests that survivors "tell their stories over and over again to reporters, even if the telling was traumatic," inflicted another kind of injury (Quindlan 1993b). Some Bosnian rape victims experienced the added trauma of being interviewed on television in the course of fact-gathering expeditions, many during the extensively covered 1992 trip by a delegation from the European Community to investigate charges about rape camps and pregnancies forced on Bosnian Muslim women (Riding 1993).

The outcomes of coerced pregnancies provide evidence that the treatment of Bosnian women by their government is tainted by instrumental concerns. An unknown number of these pregnancies were terminated by abortion and others ended in the delivery and subsequent abandonment of the infants (e.g., *New York Times* January 27, 1993:A3). The Bosnian government forbade the surrender of the infants for overseas adoption, wanting them to remain Bosnians to replace in however pitifully small numbers the tens of thousands of war dead. The babies were sequestered in orphanages financed by foreign donors, while government officials continued to apply pressure on those mothers whose identities were known to accept them into homes in which husbands were unaware of their existence, much less the circumstances of their conceptions (Williams 1993).

War Crimes Tribunals

Because Iraq was not defeated by coalition forces but merely driven out of Kuwait, it was not considered possible to establish war crimes tribunals like the ones set up after World War II. However, the invasion triggered a series of resolutions in the United Nations Security Council reflecting an intention to punish Iraq for violating Kuwait's sovereignty. Significantly with respect to an innovative approach to war crimes, the resolutions created a novel set of institutions to adjudicate damage claims. The Iraqi government has so far refused to contribute actively to reparations funds to pay these damages (Crook 1993:146).[9] Even so, the claims and payment process is well under way, thanks to the availability of funds to pay damages in the form of Iraqi assets sequestered under UN-directed economic sanctions imposed on August 6, 1990. As a result, some assessment of its utility as a vehicle for bringing justice to victims can be made.

The legal foundation for Iraq's liability is Security Council Resolution 687, a comprehensive cease-fire resolution passed in April 1991 following the end of hostilities. The resolution reaffirmed Iraq's responsibility for all damages caused by its illegal invasion and occupation of Kuwait. This attribution of responsibility to the state rests on principles established under the law of war, specifically the fourth Hague Convention (1907) and its provisions regarding the conduct of war on land, their interpretation by the International Military Tribunal at Nuremberg in 1946, and their reaffirmation in the 1949 Geneva Conventions (Crook 1993:147; also Reisman & Antoniou 1994). Of particular interest for those concerned with wartime rape, under these principles, "Iraq is responsible for all acts of its armed forces in Kuwait, including acts contrary to military orders or discipline for which a state might not normally be responsible in peacetime" (Crook 1993:148). The question of whether any crime committed was "private" rather than a "war crime" thus never becomes an issue. The state is accountable in all cases.

The primary institution for collecting and assessing claims against Iraq for direct losses arising from the invasion and occupation of Kuwait is the United Nations Compensation Commission—the UNCC (Crook 1993). Created over the course of a year, the commission began sitting in July 1991, receiving its first set of claims from governments in June 1992. Governments transmitting these consolidated claims set up their own procedures to collect them. In Kuwait, the Public Authority for Assessment of Compensation for Damages Resulting from Iraqi Aggression—PAAC—was created by Amiri decree on May 27, 1991

> to serve as a national authority for Kuwaiti claims. PAAC has the responsibility to submit to the UNCC consolidated claims of Kuwaiti and certain [Gulf Cooperation Council][10] nationals, including claims of corporations and government institutions that suffered losses" (Asem & al-Mughni 1994:12).

PAAC opened five offices to process claims for compensation made under six damage categories established by the UNCC. These are claims for having had to leave Kuwait or remain out of Kuwait as a result of the invasion (category A); claims for serious personal injury or the death of a parent, spouse, or child (category B); individual claims for damages up to $100,000 (category C); individual claims for damages over $100,000 (category D); claims by corporations and other entities (category E); and claims by governments and international organizations (category F). Categories A and B carry fixed rates of compensation (Crook 1993; Asem & al-Mughni 1994).[11]

The UNCC/PAAC procedure is highly routinized, though great care is taken to protect claimants' legal rights. Claimants appear at one of the PAAC offices and fill out a form describing their injuries and losses. They must bring proof of damage such as death certificates, medical reports, receipts, statements by witnesses, and other independent corroboration. The claims are evaluated by PAAC staff members and then by a judicial committee to be sure that each meets the "threshold" standard set for each type of claim. During this process, every claim is reviewed by a lawyer. Consolidated claims are forwarded to the UNCC office in Geneva, where they are evaluated further to determine whether the claims appear to be "unauthorized, inflated or unsubstantiated." After a thorough review, a panel of commissioners recommends to the Governing Council of the UNCC the amount to be paid to each government. The Council decides how much will actually be paid (Crook 1993:153).

This streamlined procedure was directed by Decision 1 of the UNCC Governing Council and reflected the commission's desire to process small claims to compensate injured individuals, many of whom were likely to have very limited resources, as expeditiously as possible (Crook 1993:152, 154). The establishment of small fixed payments for A and B claims also makes the procedure easier on victims. The relatively small amount of the payments, given the limits of the fund available to pay them, ensures payment to a relatively large proportion of those injured; fixed payments concentrate attention on the fact of damage rather than on collateral—though important—issues such as the extent of financial losses from hasty departure and how much an individual suffered as the result of a personal injury. The inclusion of grounds such as "serious personal injury" and "mental pain and anguish" for category B claims led to a specification of the injuries that would qualify. Under Decision 3, the Governing Council listed among qualifying injuries "dismemberment, loss of use of an organ or function . . . [and] mental injury arising from sexual assault" (Crook 1993:153).

Category B payments can be supplemented by making claims under categories C and D, and here the difficulty in defining the scope of "mental pain and anguish" and therefore the extent of Iraq's liability presented problems bearing on the resolution of claims for compensation for sexual assault. Differences in "national approaches" made reaching conclusions based on anything other than what can be easily monetized—for example, losses of income or medical expenses as opposed to feelings of shame and pollution or the pain of family rejection—impossible to achieve. The potentially infinite mental anguish a victim might suffer moved the Council to establish ceilings for claims in seven categories of mental pain and anguish (Decision 8). These include a ceiling of "$5000 for each incident of sexual assault, aggravated assault or torture. Various family and overall ceilings also apply" (Crook 1993:154).[12]

Although one might contest the justice of claims limitations or outright disqualification of some categories of damage, the UNCC/PAAC model offers substantial accountability and justice to wronged individuals through a procedure that grants the maximum dignity and privacy to victims of war crimes. At the most basic level, the fundamental principle of state responsibility obviates what is a near impossibility in most instances—that is, victims having to identify particular individuals who inflicted damage on them. It is independent of the whereabouts of war criminals, a critical advantage in cases in which victims have no reason to believe the national courts of their attackers will assist them. The principles and procedures of UNCC/PAAC provide a tribunal that is especially apt for the adjudication of claims of wartime rape: The crime is defined as having been committed to implement state policy; the victim is treated as injured by state policy and not a personal attack. The relative privacy of the proceedings is an additional protection for the sensibilities of victims and their families.

The small number of Kuwaiti claims for damages due to rape, universally attributed to the shame attached to being a rape victim, could be handled differently but in a way that comports with the principles and procedures of UNCC/PAAC. The rules might accommodate a separate, yet conforming, procedure for confirming sexual assault. PAAC officials had hoped to encourage rape victims to come forward by guaranteeing them anonymity. However, only three came forward (personal communications from two PAAC staff members). Rather than requiring rape victims to present their own claims, however, medical records and records obtained by the military recorders could be used as the basis of claims of publicly unnamed persons—Jane Does and John Does—and forwarded by the responsible agencies to PAAC for review. Any money collected could be held in an escrow account from which injured individuals could apply later for their compensation. The spectacle of aged Korean women mobilizing to demonstrate against the Japanese government, and demanding compensation for sexual assaults committed during World War II,[13] demonstrates both the persistence of suffering experienced by rape victims and their greater willingness to make claims when the prospect of public shame loses its power to make them fear for their life chances.

A second strategy for adjudicating war crimes charges has been initiated in the Bosnian conflict. In Bosnia-Herzegovina, there is neither access by an international tribunal to territories and populations harboring persons accused of war crimes nor an international consensus regarding which, if any, of the belligerents is responsible for illegal acts. The ongoing nature of the conflict is a third and, perhaps in the end, the chief, obstacle to establishing anything like a satisfactory system of justice. Yet to wait for the conclusion of the conflict to move on the issue of war crimes was widely perceived as little more than an invitation for even more of them to be committed (e.g., Rubin 1992; Anthony Lewis 1994).

The ideology of ethnonationalism that shapes the discourse on the war in the former Yugoslavia is practiced as "ethnic cleansing," the elimination of persons on the basis of religion, ideology, dialect, or political allegiance from territory held by one or another victorious army. The discovery of Serb-run concentration camps in Bosnia in late summer 1992 (Engleberg 1992a–c; Crane-Engel 1994) provided evidence of genocide that were horrifyingly reminiscent of Nazi and Khmer death camps. Although the international situation remained as stalemated as ever with regard to a consensus on the war, making policy on war crimes proved to be possible though difficult.

The United Nations Security Council voted unanimously on October 6, 1992, to create a war crimes commission, the first such body to be established since World War II. The commission was charged with collecting evidence about possible atrocities committed anywhere in the former Yugoslavia and making decisions about who should be prosecuted for them (Paul Lewis 1992). Diplomats were quoted as saying that the immediate aim of the new resolution was to deter atrocities by "send[ing] a clear message that those responsible for the atrocities and gross violations . . . must be brought to justice" (A1).

Problems with the commission concept were noted immediately by international jurists. Alfred Rubin (1992:A32) criticized the injustice in the mandate of the commission, confined as it was to investigations in the former Yugoslavia: "If the tribunal is a good idea, shouldn't it be open also to complaints against Iraq . . . the Irish Republican Army and the Royal Ulster Constabulary . . . [and] the Palestine Liberation Organization?" The commission's lack of jurisdiction to investigate charges of atrocities committed by armies of nation-states in addition to insurgent groups was also noted: If the PLO, why not the Israeli army? If the IRA or the RUC, why not the British army? And if Iraq, why not the U.S. military? The Tokyo and Nuremburg tribunals were effective because they were the courts of victors; there were no victors in the former Yugoslavia—indeed, the likely winner was the primary target of the commission. Rubin concluded that the commission's flaws left deterrence through exposure as its only function.

Benjamin Ferencz (1992:A32) hoped that the commission would be just the first step toward the establishment of an international criminal court. Such an outcome would meet the objections to the commission made by Rubin and would be a permanent addition to the range of international organizations available to "enforce the rule of law." The logic of this position was compelling. In May 1993, the Security Council voted unanimously to establish a tribunal to hear charges of war crimes committed in the former Yugoslavia. U.S. delegate Madeleine K. Albright stressed during the debate that rape charges would be among those the court would hear (Paul Lewis 1993a).

The commission had begun its work without investigators of its own or even subpoena powers, having to rely on information gathered by others, chiefly governments (Robbins 1993:A8). By July 1993, a war crimes data base compiled by law students at De Paul University in Chicago had counted "some 25,000 victims of rape, torture, murder and ethnic cleansing" (A1). Despite this mounting evidence, disputes among members of the Security Council regarding the religion of a top candidate delayed the naming of the tribunal's chief prosecutor for a year. Like the eventually nominated chief prosecutor Richard Goldstone, a highly respected jurist from South Africa, none of the judges finally appointed was a Muslim.

The tribunal was not permitted to try anyone in absentia. In late 1992, a high U.S. official had accused ten Yugoslavs of being war criminals, a list including Serbian president Slobodan Milosević and Bosnian Serb leader Radovan Karadzić, persons unlikely ever to be indicted, much less brought to trial (Robbins 1993:A8). The tribunal's lack of access to top war criminals has been criticized since its inception. However, on February 13, 1995, the tribunal handed down the first indictment for genocide ever made by an international court, against Zeljko Meakić commander of the Omarska camp. The specific crimes committed under his direction include rape (Cohen 1995).

CONCLUSIONS

The repeated recurrence of wholesale rape as a strategy of conflict, together with the acute and long-lasting suffering rape inflicts on victims, support the logic and justice of treating rape as a war crime. Yet unlike other human rights abuses that inflict physical and mental harm, rape includes social opprobrium directed toward the victim as part of its repertoire of damage. This quality makes rape technically and morally difficult to prosecute successfully in domestic criminal courts. It is no less so in the context of civil or international conflict. However, the failure to prosecute offenders for wartime rape and other human rights abuses confers a kind of permission for it to continue. Ignoring rape as a war crime also has contributed to the persistent myth that rape is a crime for which the victim bears significant culpability.

It may be the similarity of rape in war to rape in domestic settings that explains the unwillingness of those responsible for charging and prosecuting offenders to treat rape the same way that other human rights abuses are treated. It is much easier to prove a case of domestic nonsexual assault in criminal court than a case of rape (Brownmiller 1975:373–74). This is not only because of men's fears that they will be falsely charged with rape but also because of the subordinate status of women and the widespread assumption that men as persons are entitled to a degree of physical dominance over women that women as persons are denied over men (Johnson 1988). Laws and customs permitting men to rape and beat their wives have no counterparts privileging violent criminal behavior by wives against husbands (Barry 1979).

The symbolic role of women and their sexual violation during war contributes to the complexity of formulating war crimes charges. At the same time the desire to avoid shame supports the privatization of rape rather than its treatment as an act of war. Still, evidence about rape contributes to charges of human rights abuses committed against civilians during a conflict. Thus, it strengthens claims for reparations and compensation or, failing that, retribution of some kind. A government's position on wartime rape depends on whether politicization is more likely than privatization to promote national interests.

The politicization of wartime rape guarantees neither consideration for the victims nor that the role of rape as a strategy of conflict will be pondered once the war is over. As the example of Nanking shows, even when evidence is overwhelming, an accounting of rapes may be omitted from assessments of damage. This lessens the likelihood that rape will appear on a list of war crimes charges or as grounds for demands for compensation to victims. Such omissions contribute to collective amnesia about the myriad specific examples of wartime rape that contradict erroneous assumptions that rape is an opportunistic crime committed by depraved or deprived individuals. This assumption feeds deeply held prejudices about the nature of rape and the relative culpability of victims and rapists.

Myths of culpability also affect the treatment of victims. Shame makes victims reluctant to press charges or demand reparations. The ostensible protectors of victims are also culpable: the family that is helpless in the face of attackers, and the state and its army whose impotence failed to shield a civilian population from atrocities. States can defend their failure to press for justice for rape victims by insisting that they are protecting the victims from further pain and harm when, in reality, leaders of nations and their armies prefer that no one remember how they failed to perform their most fundamental obligation to protect.

Ignoring rape as a war crime reinforces assumptions connected to the symbolic role of women and denies what Hannah Arendt (1965) calls their "plurality," their individual identities. It also denies them standing as injured persons before the law. When women are denied justice, rapists, their commanding officers, and their governments escape accountability. Even if rape is included as a class of war crimes, however, accountability and justice will continue to be difficult to achieve. The ability of the United Nations to develop, under UNCC, an innovative procedure that confers so much autonomy on wronged individuals depended on the decision of the UN Security Council that Iraq's invasion and occupation of Kuwait were illegal. The Security Council was the effective court for war crimes trials against Iraq. Resolutions passed by the Security Council in response to the Iraqi invasion reflected the United Nation's adjudication of the conflict. Having found Iraq guilty of the war and therefore of every crime committed in the war's prosecution, defining, collecting, and establishing the validity of individual claims for damages quickly became routine.

The drawbacks to such a procedure are also clear. Iraqi leaders from the president to field commanders escaped personal accountability for what were, after all, decisions made by people and not by an automaton—the Iraqi "state." For victims to whom "justice" includes the trial and punishment of the individuals personally responsible for breaking their bodies and ruining their lives, recognition that they were wronged and monetary compensation for the damages inflicted on them constitute incomplete rather than full justice. A second drawback is that the achievement of more than partial restitution is far from guaranteed. Iraq has so far rejected the opportunity to sell a limited amount of oil under UN supervision for humanitarian purposes, one of which is to provide money to pay damages to war crimes victims. Instead, it has flouted the Security Council's sanctions by smuggling oil out and selling it on black markets. This recalcitrance denies Iraq's responsibility for its war crimes as well as additional money to pay damage claims. A further impediment to restitution is the dependence of the replenishment of the fund on implementation by member states, some of whose interests conflict with those of war victims, once economic sanctions against Iraq are lifted. Despite these drawbacks, however, the principle of state responsibility and the procedures protecting victims that mark the operation of UNCC/PAAC are models for achieving limited but significant justice for victims of rape and other human rights abuses.

Neither accountability nor justice is an easy proposition for victims of wartime rape in Bosnia-Herzegovina. There is no international consensus on who is responsible for the conflict—whatever degree of accountability is achieved must be accumulated one defendant at a time. Unlike UNCC/PAAC, the tribunal established to try war crimes committed in the former Yugoslavia has yet to prove itself effective in achieving either accountability or justice. Under its rules, the tribunal is unlikely to indict or try those at the top of the pyramid of responsibility for policies that utilized rape as an instrument of terror and genocide, tainting the justice of trials of lower-level individuals directly involved in rape and other human rights abuses. In effect, the tribunal's necessarily retail approach to accountability reprivatizes rape and other human rights abuses as crimes committed by individuals against individuals or, at best, by a group of individuals against a helpless population.

To consider wartime rape as a human rights abuse encourages us to think about other brutal acts of war and question why so many survivors are so willing to forget them. Victims don't forget, of course, but as one moves away from the direct targets of abuse and the people who love them, shame, distaste, and denial characterize the responses of most of the rest. Much has been written about the German population and its callousness to the plight of Jews during the Nazi era. Yet people of every nationality, including Americans, dismiss human rights abuses as reasons for changing their opinions or their behavior when such actions cost money, strategic advantage, or status. Rape is more convoluted but not fundamentally different from other crimes against humanity. For every human rights abuse, accountability is too seldom demanded and justice far too rarely achieved.

ACKNOWLEDGMENTS

The author thanks Jennifer Louise Davis for her research assistance, and Martha Bailey, David Binder, Obrad Kesić, Haya al-Mughni, David Newbury, Roger Smith, Kristin Stilt, and Robin Teske for their advice and helpful comments on earlier drafts.

NOTES

1. A paradigm of genocide is developed by Helen Fein in "Defining Genocide as a Sociological Concept," *Current Sociology* 38:1 (Spring 1990), 25–30. It includes the notion of a collectivity as constituted by ideology or other forms of group identity *in addition to* ethnicity. Thus, the behavior of the Khmer Rouge in Cambodia is genocide even though the ethnic identities of killers and killed were both Khmer. Other chapters in the Fein volume discuss cases of genocide in addition to the ones noted in this text, and explore theories offering causal explanations.

2. That this practice in Greece was not confined to the Homeric period is evident in the Athenian treatment of Melos during the Peloponnesian War—see Thucydides, *The Peloponnesian War,* trans. Rex Warner (Baltimore: Penguin, 1959), 366.

3. The Nuremburg tribunal did not include rape on the list of war crimes. During the war there was no rerun in the European theater of allegations on the same level as stories of the World War I "rape of Belgium." Indeed, given both the volume of propaganda films produced by the Allies during World War II and the volume of evidence amassed afterward, contemporary charges of war crimes made against Germany during the war seem to have been vastly understated. Afterward, "sexual forms of torture, including rape, were documented at the [Nuremberg] trials" (MacKinnon 1993, 30; see also Brownmiller 1975).

4. Although most of the accusations were made on television, some also appeared in the press. See, for example, *New York Times,* December 2, 1990, 19; December 8, 1990, 8; December 16, 1990, 1. Kuwaitis whom I interviewed in 1992 said that during the war, they had heard reports that the number of Kuwaiti women raped amounted to 8,000.

5. The importance of ritual pollution to Iraqi behavior in Kuwait can be inferred from evidence other than the sexual assaults—for example, the many deposits of urine and feces on furniture, desks, documents, and other places in private homes and public buildings, and the type of vandalization of the works of Kuwaiti artists in the National Museum (Tétreault 1992).

6. "In the war crimes trials for the genocidal war against Bosnia-Herzegovina and Croatia, will those who incited to genocide through rape, sexual torture, and murder—the Serbian pornog-

raphers as well as the high policymakers and the underlings—get what they deserve (1993:30)?"

7. I recall one in particular that showed Hitler beaming down on a tableful of naked infants that the voiceover said were babies whose young, unmarried, Aryan mothers had been impregnated in special camps by German soldiers specifically selected to breed new members of the German superrace. Of all the footage that I saw, that segment, along with another from a film shot in Russia during a rout of Russian forces by German troops which featured the death of the person holding the camera, are the only ones that I remember out of the scores of hours of propaganda films that I and my classmates were subjected to in the name of social studies education at the height of the Cold War. As an adult, I would classify both of these clips as pornographic, and as powerful incitements to fear and visceral hatred.

8. The victim group that is the primary subject of Kuwaiti arguments opposing the lifting of sanctions is the several hundred Kuwaitis taken prisoner by the Iraqis and never returned.

9. Money to pay claims was to be provided by assessing Iraq a percentage of its income from oil sales but no such sales have been made to date because of continuing UN economic sanctions against Iraq (Crook 1993:144). A special procedure was established under UN Security Council Resolution 706 (August 15, 1991) authorizing the sale of $1.6 billion worth of oil over six months, with 30 percent of that to go to the fund and the rest to administrative costs and the purchase, under strict supervision, of food, medicine, and other items to meet civilian needs (146). Iraq has refused to comply with the conditions specified in the resolution.

10. The Gulf Cooperation Council is an international organization modeled after the European Community that was established in 1981. Its members are Kuwait, Saudi Arabia, Bahrain, Qatar, Oman, and the United Arab Emirates.

11. In some cases, claims for damages in excess of the limits set in categories A and B were presented as A and B claims. The additional damages were assessed for things like uncompensated medical bills. This procedure enabled small claims to be processed in the A and B categories, whose settlement was the top priority of UNCC.

12. It should be clear that mental pain and anguish were recognized as resulting from injuries other than sexual assault. Ceilings were set in other areas as well. For example, the Council approved a ceiling of $15,000 for mental pain and anguish resulting from the death of a spouse, child, or parent (Crook 1993:154).

13. These are the so-called comfort women, who were kidnapped as girls and sequestered in military brothels for the entertainment of Japanese troops. The very existence of the comfort women was denied until very recently, and their claims for reparations have so far been dismissed by the Japanese government. One reason offered for the government's refusal to admit culpability and make even token payments to the survivors is that this would amount to a very large amount of money. This by itself points up the need to institutionalize procedures for assigning responsibility and assessing damages for wartime rape as a means to limit such behavior in the future.

REFERENCES

Amnesty International. 1993. *Bosnia-Herzegovina: Rape and Sexual Abuse by Armed Forces*. New York: Amnesty International.

Arendt, Hannah. 1965. *On Revolution*. New York: Compass.

Asia Watch and the Women's Rights Project. 1992. *Double Jeopardy: Police Abuse of Women in Pakistan*. New York: Human Rights Watch.

Asia Watch and Physicians for Human Rights. 1993. *Rape in Kashmir: A Crime of War*. New York: Asia Watch.

Asem, Adel, and Haya al-Mughni. 1994. "Claiming for Compensation Through the United Nations Compensation Commission: The Case of Kuwait." Paper presented at the International Conference on the Effects of the Iraqi Aggression on Kuwait. Kuwait. April.

Bard, Morton, and Diane Sangrey. 1979. *The Crime Victim's Book*. New York: Basic Books.

Barry, Kathleen. 1979. *Female Sexual Slavery*. Englewood Cliffs, N.J.: Prentice-Hall.

Brownmiller, Susan. 1975. *Against Our Will: Men, Women and Rape*. New York: Simon and Schuster.

Burns, John F. 1992. "150 Muslims Say Serbs Raped Them in Bosnia." *New York Times* October 3:L5.

Cohen, Roger. 1993. "2 Serbs to Be Shot for Killings and Rapes." *New York Times* March 31:A6.

———. 1994. "Ex-Guard for Serbs Tells of Grisly 'Cleansing' Camp." *New York Times* August 1:A1, A8.

———. 1995. "Tribunal Charges Genocide by Serbs." *New York Times* February 14:A1–A2.

Coll, Steve. 1994. "War Crimes and Punishment: Bosnia in the Shadow of the Holocaust." *Washington Post Magazine* September 25.

Crane-Engel, Melinda. 1994. "Germany vs. Genocide." *New York Times Magazine* October 30.

Crook, John R. 1993. "The United Nations Compensation Commission—A New Structure to Enforce State Responsibility." *American Journal of International Law* 87.

In re Jane Doe et al. against Radovan Karadzic. United States District Court, Southern District of New York, Civ. 93-0878 PKL. 1993. "Complaint for Genocide: War Crimes and Crimes Against Humanity; Summary Execution; Torture; Cruel, Inhuman or Degrading Treatment; Wrongful Death; Assault and Battery; and Intentional Infliction of Emotional Harm. Class Action: Jury Trial Demand." February. "Memorandum in Support of Motion to Dismiss Before Answer." May. "Reply

Declaration of Lawrence W. Schilling in Support of Defendant's Motions to Dismiss." May. "Plaintiff's Memorandum of Points and Authorities in Opposition to Defendant's Motion to Dismiss Before Answer." August. "Plaintiffs' Sur-Reply Brief in Opposition to Defendant's Motion to Dismiss Before Answer." October.

Dover, K. J. 1978. *Greek Homosexuality.* London: Duckworth.

Engelberg, Stephen. 1992a. "Bosnians Provide Accounts of Abuse in Serbian Camps." *New York Times* August 4:A1.

———. 1992b. "Refugees from Camps Tell of Agony and Terror." *New York Times* August 7:A5.

———. 1992c. "Clearer Picture of Bosnia Camps: A Brutal Piece of a Larger Plan." *New York Times* August 16:1, 14.

Fein, Helen. 1990. "Genocide: A Sociological Perspective," *Current Sociology* 38:1 (Spring).

Ferencz, Benjamin B. Letter to the editor. *New York Times* October:A32.

Garlan, Yvon. 1988. *Slavery in Ancient Greece.* Rev. and expanded ed. Trans. Janet Lloyd. Ithaca: Cornell University Press.

Glenny, Misha. 1994. "Council of Despair." *New York Times* December 6:A15.

Hartman, Carol R., and Ann Wolbert Burgess. 1988. "Rape Trauma and Treatment of the Victim." In *Post-Traumatic Therapy and Victims of Violence.* Ed. F. M. Ochberg. New York: Brunner Mazel.

Human Rights Watch National Coalition for Haitian Refugees. 1994. *Rape in Haiti: A Weapon of Terror.* Washington, D.C.: Human Rights Watch.

Hunt, Lynn. 1984. *Politics, Culture, and Class in the French Revolution.* Berkeley: University of California Press.

Johnson, Miriam. 1988. *Strong Mothers, Weak Wives.* Berkeley: University of California Press.

Kilpatrick, Dean G., and Lois J. Veronen. 1983. "Treatment for Rape-Related Problems: Crisis Intervention Is Not Enough." In *Crisis Intervention.* Ed. L. H. Cohen, W. Claiborn, and G. Specter. New York: Human Sciences Press.

Lancaster, John. 1993. "Administration Releases Report on Iraqi War Crimes in Kuwait." *Washington Post* March 20:A18.

Lewin, Tamar. 1993. "The Balkans Rapes: A Legal Test for the Outraged." *New York Times* January 15:B15.

Lewis, Anthony. 1994. "'The Civilized World.'" *New York Times* July 1:A17.

Lewis, Paul. 1992. "U.N. Sets Up War-Crimes Panel On Charges of Balkan Atrocities." *New York Times* October 7:A1, A6.

———. 1993a. "Security Council Establishes War-Crimes Tribunal for the Balkans." *New York Times* May 26:A13.

———. 1993b. "Disputes Hamper U.N. Drive for a War Crimes Tribunal." *New York Times* September 9:A10.

———. 1994. "If There Ever Were a Nuremburg for the Former Yugoslavia. . . ." *New York Times* June 12:E7.

MacKinnon, Catherine A. 1993. "Turning Rape into Pornography: Postmodern Genocide." *Ms.* July/August.

Makiya, Kanan. 1993. *Cruelty and Silence: War, Tyranny, Uprising, and the Arab World.* New York: Norton.

Mann, Judy. 1991. "Kuwaiti Rape a Doubly Savage Crime." *Washington Post* March 29:C3.

Mernissi, Fatima. 1991. *The Veil and the Male Elite: A Feminist Interpretation of Women's Rights in Islam.* Trans. Mary Jo Lakeland. Reading, Mass.: Addison Wesley.

Mosse, George L. 1985. *Nationalism and Sexuality: Respectability and Abnormal Sexuality in Modern Europe.* New York: Howard Fertig.

Al-Mughni, Haya, and Fawzia al-Turkait. 1994. "Dealing with Trauma: Cultural Barriers to Self-Recovery: The Case of Kuwaiti Women." Paper presented at the seminar on The Effective Methods for Encountering the Psychological and the Social Effects of the Iraqi Aggression, sponsored by the Social Development Office of the Amiri Diwan. Kuwait. March.

New York Times. 1992. "Rape—And Soldiers' Morale." Editorial December 7:A18.

Newbury, David. 1995. Personal communication.

Peristiany, J. G., ed. 1965. *Honor and Shame: The Values of Mediterranean Society.* London: Weidenfeld and Nicolson.

Personal Narratives. 1992. "Rape After Rape After Rape." *New York Times* December 13:E17.

Peterson, V. Spike. 1994. "Gendered Nationalisms." *Peace Review* 6:1.

Quindlen, Anna. 1993a. "Gynocide." *New York Times* March 10:A19.

———. 1993b. "The Rescuers." *New York Times* May 5:A23.

Reisman, W. Michael, and Chris T. Antoniou, eds. 1994. *The Laws of War: A Comprehensive Collection of Primary Documents on International Laws Governing Armed Conflict.* New York: Vintage.

Riding, Alan. 1993. "European Inquiry Says Serbs' Forces Have Raped 20,000." *New York Times* January 9:1, 4.

Robbins, Carla Anne. 1993. "Balkan Judgments: World Again Confronts Moral Issues Involved in War-Crimes Trials." *Wall Street Journal* July 13:A1, A8.

Roy, K. K. 1975. "Feelings and Attitudes of Raped Women of Bangladesh Towards Military Personnel of Pakistan." In *Victimology: A New Focus,* Vol. 5, *Exploiters and Exploited: The Dynamics of Victimization.* Lexington, Mass.: D. C. Heath.

Rubin, Alfred P. Letter to the editor, *New York Times* October 23:A32.

Simons, Marlise. 1994. "Bosnian Rapes Go Untried by the U.N." *New York Times* December 7:A8.

Smith, Roger W. 1994a. "Genocide and the Politics of Rape: Historical and Psychological Perspectives." Presented at Remembering for the Future: Internation Conference on the Holocaust and Genocide. March 13–17. Berlin.

———. 1994b. "Women and Genocide: Notes on an Unwritten History." *Holocaust and Genocide Studies* 8:3 Winter.

Tétreault, Mary Ann. 1992. Interviews in Kuwait, March, September–October.

———. 1994a. Interviews in Kuwait, March.

———. 1994b. "Whose Honor? Whose Liberation? Women and the Reconstruction of Politics in Kuwait." In *Women and*

Revolution in Africa, Asia, and the New World. Ed. Mary Ann Tétreault. Columbia: University of South Carolina Press.

———, and Haya al-Mughni. 1995. "Women, Citizenship, and Nationalism in Kuwait." Paper presented at the annual meeting of the International Studies Association. February 21–25. Chicago.

Theweleit, Klaus. 1987. *Male Fantasies.* Vol. 1: *Women, Floods, Bodies, History.* Trans. Stephen Conway. Minneapolis: University of Minnesota Press.

Thomas, Dorothy Q., and Regan E. Ralph. 1993. "Rape in War: The Tradition of Impunity." *SAIS Review* 14:1. Spring.

Tillion, Germaine. 1983. *The Republic of Cousins: Women's Oppression in Mediterranean Society.* Trans. Quintin Hoare. London: Al Saqi Books.

Williams, Carol J. 1993. "Bosnia's Orphans of Rape: Innocent Legacy of Hatred." *Los Angeles Times* July 24:A1, A12.

Yuval-Davis, Nita, and Floya Anthias, eds. 1989. *Woman-Nation-State.* London: Macmillan.

P A R T F O U R

Social Change

Thus far we have emphasized the *stability* of gender inequality. We have examined how socialization, social definitions of gender, and the structure and content of all the major institutional arenas of social life converge to produce a world in which males and females are differentially valued and differentially rewarded. The forces that perpetuate gender inequality are so intricately interwoven into the social fabric and so deeply embedded in the self-concepts and personalities of individuals that to effect change is beyond the power of the individual, no matter how well-intentioned that individual may be.

Yet societies can and do *change*. Anyone who has lived through the past three decades in the United States cannot help but notice that there has been substantial change in the roles, behaviors, and consciousness of women and men. In earlier readings, we discussed some of the dynamic forces that have *unintentionally* recast gender consciousness and behavior, including technological innovations, demographic processes, and economic factors. In order to understand fully how systems of gender inequality change, it is also necessary to examine the ways that women have sought collectively and *intentionally* to reduce their disadvantage. Certainly every society or group contains individuals who are nonconformists, but significant and lasting social change is ultimately the result of collective action rather than individual action.

In Part Four, we turn our attention to women's struggle for equality in two arenas linked to the transformation of culture and social institutions in modern industrialized societies. Section Ten focuses on the politicization of gender in the state and global politics. The readings in Section Eleven document the rich history and diversity of the women's movement and demonstrate continuity and change in the history of American feminism. Understanding the part that women themselves have played in improving their status requires that we focus, on the one hand, on women's actions "within the system" through the use of conventional and orderly means and, on the other, on women's collective actions "outside the system" through the use of unconventional and disorderly means.

Politics is generally thought to refer to the institutionalized or authoritative system by which a society makes decisions, allocates power, and distributes resources. According to the traditional view, voting, campaigning, lobbying, organizational activities, office holding, and involvement in political parties are classified as politics because they take place in the context of the formal governmental structure. Feminist scholars have pointed out that the standard definition of politics is too narrow, however, for understanding women's political participation. It not only assumes a particular type of state and political system but ignores the fact that in most industrialized societies women have been denied access to the formal political process until fairly recently.

In the United States, women were not allowed to vote, hold office, or sit on juries until the first decades of the twentieth century. Even after women were enfranchised with the passage of the

Nineteenth Amendment to the U.S. Constitution in 1920, their participation in electoral politics, involvement in the major political parties, and election to public offices lagged significantly behind men's. African-American women, moreover, remained effectively disenfranchised in southern states by racist voter registration rules until the late 1960s.

It was not until a half century later in the 1970s that the gap between men's and women's party involvement and office holding began to shrink, and even today women fare better in local and state politics than in the national arena. Voting turnout differences between women and men finally disappeared in 1976. But it took until 1980 for women to use the electoral process to express their collective dissatisfaction by voting in line with their interests in women's equality, creating for the first time what has come to be known as the "gender gap."

Elections, participation in party politics, running for office, and lobbying are not, however, the only means of expressing grievances, influencing public policy, and using politics to achieve social change. Scholars have recently defined politics more broadly to include social movements, protests, and other group actions intended to influence the distribution of power and other resources in a state or community. This definition is broad enough to encompass women's long history of participation in collective action on their own behalf through the feminist movement, as well as in pursuit of other human rights causes through female reform societies, women's church groups, alternative religious societies, women's clubs, and other social movements.

Social movements can be thought of as collective attempts to bring about change. They originate outside of the established political system, are based on collective discontent, forge linkages between individuals and groups who share common concerns, and mobilize the people and resources necessary to pursue collective goals. In democratic societies, social movements and the tactics they employ—marches, boycotts, strikes, demonstrations, and protests—are a regular part of the democratic process and have proved to be an effective avenue to social change. Movements act as pressure groups on behalf of people excluded from routine decision-making processes and the dominant power structure and are a major source of new social patterns and cultural understandings.

Because participants in social movements typically challenge conventional ideas and behaviors, they are often stereotyped by the larger society as deviant and irrational and are accused of exaggerating their claims. If we take a historical perspective on social movements, we will often find, however, that today's social institution is likely to have been yesterday's social movement. Thus, scholars generally agree that social movement participants are not qualitatively different from other kinds of social actors and that their actions are governed by the same norms of rationality that underlie other groups.

Although popular opinion often presents the women's movement as a relatively recent phenomenon, its roots are well-grounded historically. Indeed, the similarities between the views of contemporary feminists and earlier feminists are remarkable. More than 200 years ago, for example, Abigail Adams gave this warning to her husband, John, when he was fashioning the Constitution of the United States:

> In the new code of laws which I suppose will be necessary for you to make, I desire you would remember the ladies and be more generous and favorable to them than your ancestors. Do not put such unlimited power in the hands of husbands. Remember, all men would be tyrants if they could. If particular care and attention is not paid to the ladies, we are determined to foment a rebellion, and will not hold ourselves bound by any laws in which we have no voice or representation.

John Adams, nonetheless, failed to take his wife's warning seriously. He urged her to be patient, noting that there were more important issues than "ladies" rights.

As this example illustrates, in the United States, as in much of the industrialized world, the history of feminist activism is long and rich. Until the past two decades, however, knowledge of the women's movement remained mostly buried. Initially most scholars studying the women's movement held that there have been two waves of feminism in the United States. The first began in the nineteenth century as a broad attack on male domination, continued for almost a century, and then died precipitously in 1920 with the passage of the suffrage amendment granting women the right to vote, which by then had become the movement's major goal. Supposedly, a forty-year lull followed before the second wave, or new feminist movement, erupted in the mid-1960s.

Recently, as a result of new research, a different interpretation of the history of the American women's movement has emerged that emphasizes the continuity and universality of women's resistance to oppression. The newer work recognizes two great waves of mass feminist activism, but also points to the survival of feminism in less highly mobilized periods. It focuses not only on the continuity of the movement but on changes in the movement's ideology, goals, constituency, tactics, and organizational style. We have, then, a long history in this society of feminist activism. At the same time, working-class women and women of color also have a long history of struggle on their own behalf, in labor unions, socialist and communist groups, women's clubs, and within churches and communities. Any analysis of contemporary feminism and the backlash against it must consider recent events in the larger context of an enduring and progressive struggle to redress gender inequality by dismantling the complex structures that are the foundation of male dominance.

The readings thus far suggest the depth, pervasiveness, and persistence of gender inequality. It is not surprising, then, that the ultimate vision of contemporary feminism is so broad as to include a fundamental restructuring of all institutions that perpetuate and sustain male dominance. Although the media have recently proclaimed the present period the "postfeminist era" and many young women disavow the feminist label, as we shall see, the women's movement is very much alive today. The contemporary movement continues to comprise many separate and diverse organizations, each with its own strategies, style, membership base, leadership, and specific goals. Feminist groups can be found within every major institution: in the professions, academia, labor, religion, politics, the arts, music, and literature. Furthermore, separate feminist groups have mobilized around practically every issue imaginable, including employment and equal pay issues, pornography, prostitution, abortion rights, health, depression, substance abuse, spirituality, disability rights, child care, nuclear power, lesbianism, incest, battering, racism, and older women's rights. Feminist groups have splintered on the basis of sexual, racial and ethnic, and class identities, so that African-American, Native American, Jewish, Cuban-American, Mexican-American, Japanese-American, Chinese-American, and lesbian women often form their own separate groups. We do not believe that this diversification indicates that the movement is about to crumble for lack of unity. Rather, because feminism permeates every facet of social life, it has a major and lasting impact not only on economic, political, and cultural institutions but also on the consciousness and lives of individual women and men.

In Part Four, we examine the diversity of women's participation in politics and the contemporary feminist movement, emphasizing the continuity and global nature of the feminist challenge as well as changes and differences in feminist goals, constituencies, and tactics. The readings document the multiple forms that feminist resistance can take, recognizing that protest can be directed at the structural, cultural, or individual level. We conclude with an overview of the American women's movement and a look to the future.

Global Politics
and the State

National governments exert wide-ranging influence on the lives of women. Government-controlled economies dictate women's wages, the prices of goods that women produce, and women's cost-of-living expenses. In market economies, federal policies on education, welfare, health, and various forms of violence against women affect women's daily lives in profound ways. Because governmental policies frequently reflect dominant sexist ideologies, they often serve to reinforce the disadvantaged position assigned to women in most countries. The state, in fact, plays a central part in maintaining a social structure of inequality between women and men (Connell, p. 509). The role of the state in perpetuating inequalities of class (through regulation of the labor market, for example) and of race (through legislative policies regarding immigration or affirmative action, for example) is widely recognized.

Feminist scholars focus on the ways that state actions and policies create and perpetuate gender categories, ideologies of women's inferiority, and differential access between women and men to valued resources and power. The state's role in upholding gender stratification, of course, is inextricably linked to its role in reinforcing race and class stratification, as the articles in this section point out.

The increasing interdependence of the world's countries means that the governmental policies restricting women's lives may reflect not only individual national cultures and economics but international politics and global economics as well. As a result, a complex web of interrelationships between states, groups within states, geography, technology, and ideologies of gender, class, race, ethnicity, and religion shapes relations between women, states, and global politics. In this section, contributors provide examples of relationships between women and the state, both in the United States and internationally, as well as demonstrations of the relationships between global politics and women's lives.

One of the major topics of analysis for feminist scholars of the state is the ways that governments regulate women's childbearing and family structures. The first reading looks at how the government regulates the lives of poor women with children. In "Surviving the Welfare System: How AFDC Recipients Make Ends Meet in Chicago," Kathryn Edin shows how AFDC payments provide too little money to support women and their children, forcing women to earn additional money by working under-the-table jobs. In contrast to the stereotypes of the lazy welfare mother, Edin shows that surviving on welfare requires hard work and ingenuity. Yet the low-wage jobs most welfare recipients are qualified for provide no better alternative. What kinds of social changes might alleviate the problems Edin describes?

Some early suffragists speculated that women's oppression by the state would end with women's access to the vote, a symbol of political participation. Yet women's suffrage did not, in fact, give women the full access to the political institution that proponents expected. In "Strangers in a Strange Land: The Gendered Experiences of Women Politicians," Abigail Halcli and Jo Reger examine the barriers to elected office that women still face in the United States and Britain. They argue that electoral politics are still pervaded by gendered assumptions and practices that serve to exclude and marginalize women. Ideologies about gender view women as unsuited for political office: Women are excluded from the political parties, networks, and funding base necessary to run for elected office, and are dismissed or discriminated against by male politicians. Nevertheless, women find ways to enter politics and transform the political institution, as Halcli and Reger document.

While Halcli and Reger examine women's resistance *within* electoral politics, the next two articles focus on women's challenges to the political institution from *outside*. Beth E. Schneider and Valerie Jenness discuss the state's expansion of control over women's sexuality in response to the AIDS epidemic in "Social Control, Civil Liberties, and Women's Sexuality." Focusing on state responses to prostitution and teenage sexuality, Schneider and Jenness show how in both cases women's control over their own sexuality has been expropriated by state authorities. Yet Schneider and Jenness also document ways that women resist such state efforts, through prostitutes' rights organizations and through young women's self-designed AIDS activism and education programs.

Emily Honig also examines women's resistance to state policy and economic constraints in "Burning Incense, Pledging Sisterhood: Communities of Women Workers in the Shanghai Cotton Mills, 1919–1949." During this time of political changes and restrictions (the Japanese occupation of China, Communist organizing, and the Chinese Civil War), women workers banded together for social and political purposes. Despite oppressive work conditions and political restrictions, women resisted by forming new communities, or sisterhoods, which in some cases led women to become activists in the Chinese Communist party. Honig's analysis demonstrates again the differences that divide women within national boundaries and the difficulties of bridging such differences in efforts to create gender-based challenges to state or capitalist oppression.

The readings in this section emphasize that despite national, ethnic, racial, and cultural differences, women around the world face various manifestations of gender inequality. The oppression of women in Third World countries is compounded, however, by the fact that wealthy countries and poor countries occupy very different positions in the global economic system. In "Our Policies, Their Consequences: Zambian Women's Lives under 'Structural Adjustment'," Amber Ault and Eve Sandberg present a case study to illustrate that the oppression of women in Third World countries is connected to the self-interested practices of wealthier countries like the United States and international agencies like the International Monetary Fund. Once again, this section returns to the question of the commonalities and differences among women. Given the disparities of wealth and power among women around the world, what do women share in common by virtue of their gender?

REFERENCE

Connell, R. W. 1990. "The state, gender, and sexual politics." *Theory and Society* 19:507–44.

Surviving the Welfare System: How AFDC Recipients Make Ends Meet in Chicago

KATHRYN EDIN

In the discourse surrounding public welfare, recipients of Aid to Families with Dependent Children (AFDC) have often been portrayed as passive dependents who rely on government handouts as their sole source of support. In this view, welfare creates dependency by discouraging people from seeking work, forcing them and their children into a permanent underclass (Mead 1989, Murray 1983, Novak 1987). During the 1980s, this image of the welfare recipient provided a rationale for state legislators to let benefit levels fall far behind inflation and prompted Congress to restrict benefits (with some exceptions) to those who can prove they are seeking work.

Those who argue that welfare engenders dependence ignore the fact that states set welfare benefits too low to live on. Because of this, recipients must work at regular or informal jobs. But they "work" the system as well: they make sure the money they earn does not come to the attention of the welfare department. They conceal outside income because if they told their caseworker they were working or receiving outside assistance, their welfare checks would soon be reduced by nearly the full amount of their earnings, leaving them as poor as before.

Using data from in-depth interviews with 50 Chicago-area welfare recipients, I show that single mothers did not receive enough money from AFDC to support their families. As a result, all the women I interviewed supplemented their checks and concealed this information from their caseworkers. Although many of these mothers had

Kathryn Edin, "Surviving the Welfare System: How AFDC Recipients Make Ends Meet in Chicago," *Social Problems* 38, no. 4 (November 1991). Copyright © 1991 by the Society for the Study of Social Problems. Reprinted with the permission of the author and University of California Press Journals.

received welfare for most of their adult lives, none liked being on welfare or having to hide outside income, though they believed their actions were economically necessary. Despite their discomfort, most mothers stayed on welfare because they could not find jobs that made them better off.

In sum, many unskilled single mothers spend much of their adult lives on welfare not because welfare warps their personalities or makes them dependent but because while welfare pays badly, low-wage jobs do not pay any better. Most welfare mothers would leave welfare for work if they could end up with significantly more disposable income as a result.

In the pages below I first describe my methods of research. Then I construct budgets of expenses and income for the mothers in my sample. There is a wide shortfall between what they spent and what they received from welfare and food stamps. Finally, I explain how these women closed this gap by relying on friends, family, absent fathers, boyfriends, and most important, by working.

METHOD

My respondents came from Cook County (Chicago and its surrounding suburbs). Cook County provides AFDC benefits that approximate the national average and has a welfare population that is quite diverse. Between 1988 and 1990, a wide variety of individuals introduced me to 59 mothers on AFDC. All but nine agreed to be interviewed for this study. These women represented 33 independent networks and resided in about one-third of Chicago's 88 community areas and five suburbs. The sample included both never-married and divorced mothers, mothers at various educational levels, mothers of black, white, Hispanic, and Asian descent, mothers living in private and public housing, mothers of different age groups, and both long-term and short-term recipients.

My sample is 46 percent African-American (as compared to roughly 40 percent of welfare recipients nationally), 38 percent non-Hispanic white (as compared to 39 percent), 10 percent Hispanic, and 6 percent Asian.[1] Because I wanted to maximize my chances of finding recipients who lived on welfare alone, I oversampled those living in public housing (42 percent as compared to 18 percent nationally) (U.S. House of Representatives 1990: 580, 586).

I conducted most of these one to three hour interviews in respondents' homes. In initial interviews, I gathered topical life histories. In subsequent interviews, I collected detailed income and expenditure data. I asked respondents to estimate income and expenditures during the previous month. I then asked how much these monthly amounts had varied over the previous 12 months. Usually, respondents had copies of phone, electric, and gas bills on hand, which they showed me. Because their budgets were tight, respondents typically knew what they spent each month. Most knew the exact cost of each food and household item they purchased and spoke at length about which stores had the lowest prices. If they could not remember how much they spent, I asked them to keep track during the next month and report back. I had respondents estimate their monthly income and expenditures at least twice and asked them to account for any discrepancies. Finally, I asked if they had made large onetime purchases during the previous year (VCRs, furniture, appliances, bicycles, etc.). Respondents generally paid for these items in monthly installments. I spread lump sum payments evenly over 12 months. I interviewed each respondent at least twice, most between three and five times. I tape-recorded, transcribed, coded, and analyzed each interview using a computer data-base program.

EXPENSES

The average woman in my sample spent $864 a month. Of this, food and housing accounted for $501. These figures appear in the first column of Table 1. The upper portion of the table is devoted to expenses and the lower portion to income. The amount of money paid for housing varied considerably depending on whether the mother lived in subsidized housing, shared housing with others, or paid the mar-

ket rate for her own apartment. Because this so heavily influenced the budgets of these women, I have broken down the sample by housing category in columns two, three, and four. Those living in private market-rate housing paid $467 for housing compared to $208 for those who doubled up and $123 for those living in subsidized housing. Those living in private and subsidized housing spent about the same amount for food ($267 and $264 respectively), but those sharing housing spent far less because most of these mothers had only one child, whereas other mothers usually had two or three.

From Table 1 we see that those living in private housing spent far less for items other than housing and food. Car payments, disposable diapers, and burial or life insurance costs (included in miscellaneous expenses) account for most of this difference. Since no privately housed mothers lived in suburbs, they did not need cars. As only a few of these mothers had infants, most did not buy diapers. Finally, these primarily white mothers did not purchase burial insurance. Most black mothers—especially those living in Chicago's dangerous housing projects—said they could not do without burial insurance, for which local morticians charged about $20 per month. If we eliminate these three items, other expenses only varied by about $20 between groups.

At the bottom of Table 1, I have calculated several overall measures of expenses compared to income. The first measure, total expenses minus welfare income, shows the net overall shortfall was $343 for all the women. However, it was $432 for women living in private housing but only $320 for those who shared housing and $276 for women living in subsidized housing.[2]

A second measure, the cost of housing and food minus total income from welfare, shows how much money these women had left over each month for all other expenses once they had paid for food and housing. Overall, there was only $10 left over once rent and food were paid for. But for women living in subsidized housing there was $119. For those sharing housing there was $52 left over. In contrast, mothers living in private housing were already $147 in debt: their total welfare benefit failed by a wide margin even to pay for their rent and food.

From this we could say that women living in private housing were $266 worse off ($147 plus $119) each month than their counterparts living in subsidized housing, even though their welfare benefits were higher ($587 versus $506 because of larger average family sizes). Mothers who share housing are $62 ($119 minus $52) worse off than

TABLE 1 BUDGETS FOR 50 CHICAGO-AREA AFDC FAMILIES BY HOUSING CATEGORY

N	All, 50	Private Housing, 17	Shared Housing, 11	Subsidized Housing, 22
Expenses				
Housing[1]	$264	$467	$208	$123
Food	$247	$267	$181	$264
Other	$353	$285	$372	$396
Phone	$28	$23	$13	$40
Check Cashing	$5	$5	$4	$6
Clothing/Shoes	$47	$39	$60	$47
School Supplies	$10	$8	$9	$12
Toiletries Cleaning	$30	$35	$31	$26
Laundry/Dry Cleaning	$32	$44	$16	$30
Transportation	$41	$39	$50	$38
Over-the-Counter Medical Costs	$13	$13	$16	$11
Time Payments[2]	$19	$22	$21	$15
Entertainment/Travel	$22	$15	$22	$28
Cigarettes/Alcohol	$27	$17	$30	$34
Lottery	$3	$5	$2	$1
Car Payments	$22	$3	$49	$24
Misc.[3]	$54	$17	$48	$85
Total Expenses	$864	$1019	$761	$782
Income				
Welfare				
AFDC	$324	$349	$287	$320
Food Stamps	$197	238	$154	$186
Income From Other Sources				
Unearned				
Friends/Family	$59	$43	$111	$45
Boyfriends	$76	$123	$18	$69
Absent Fathers	$30	$27	$37	$29
Other	$45	$70	$15	$40
Earned				
Work in the Regular Economy	$128	$88	$162	$141
Work in the Underground Economy	$38	$81	$19	$14
Total Other Sources	$376	$432	$362	$338
Total Welfare Income[4]	$521	$587	$441	$506
Total Income All Sources	$897	$1019	$803	$844
Shortfall				
Welfare Income minus Total Expenses	$343	−$432	−$320	−$276
Welfare Income minus Housing and Food	+$10	−$147	+$52	+$119
Total Income minus Total Expenses	−$33	+$0	−$42	−$62

1. Rent or mortgage, gas and electricity. Gas is the main source of heat in Chicago.
2. Most of these expenses were for furniture or household appliances.
3. This category includes expenditures for baby care (diapers), hair care, cosmetics, jewelry, expenses for special occasions (gifts and party costs), moving expenses and insurance (life and burial). Burial insurance, for example, is common in black neighborhoods, and costs about $20 per month.
4. Table has been somewhat changed from original publication, with permission of the author.

those with subsidies, but $199 ($147 plus $52) better off than those with their own market-rent apartments.

Although those paying market rents were clearly the worst off, all three categories faced the same fundamental reality—the system did not provide enough money to support a family, as several women indicated:

> I don't ever pay off all my bills, so there isn't ever anything left over. As soon as I get my check, it's gone, and I don't have anything left.

> What you have to live off isn't enough. Me myself, I just got back on, and I had been off for about six years because I was working. But having a baby I had to get back on the program. It's just not enough. You just can't live off it especially with three kids or two kids. . . . It is impossible the things you have to do, to last you 'til the next month. Me myself, I get $380 for three kids. The rent I pay is just impossible plus my other little bills.

> Oh yea. It ain't enough! It ain't enough! Get a big sign saying "That is not enough!" We want more! More! It's just not enough what we're getting.

INCOME

My sample's total income averaged $897 a month of which 58 percent, $521, came from AFDC and food stamps. Half of the remaining 42 percent came from work of various kinds and just under half from absent fathers, boyfriends, and relatives. Respondents obtained the remainder from student loans, insurance settlements, churches, and community organizations. Although no mother received income from all these sources, most combined several strategies to balance their budget. I divide these strategies in two categories: unearned and earned income.

Unearned Income

First, I discuss assistance received from others and not earned by working. This includes assistance from family, friends, boyfriends, absent fathers, churches, community organizations, student loans and grants, and legal settlements.

Assistance from Family and Friends   Nineteen recipients received contributions from family and friends. Thirteen

respondents had parents, friends, and relatives who consistently helped. For the other six, friends and family helped in emergencies and on special occasions.

Recipients felt it was unreasonable that the welfare department required them to report such assistance. Since families and friends gave support to "put food on the table" or to "pay the light bill before the electricity gets shut off," respondents maintained it was "crazy" to let welfare "take that away from us."

> A lot of people lie; I know that I have had to lie. Like that they get monies. Like my mom. If she gave me $100 to help me get through, to pay the bills that I've had overdue, or to help me get through, or whatever, I'm not going to claim that to the Public Aid!

Although respondents did not work for this assistance, they spent time and energy establishing and maintaining these relationships. Friends and relatives often pressured mothers to meet relational demands, pushed them to become self-supporting, and expected they take steps (i.e., attend educational or training programs) to achieve financial independence.

Boyfriends and Absent Fathers   Boyfriends were also a common source of unearned income. When boyfriends "lived in," mothers felt entitled to regular and substantial assistance. In my small sample, about half of the 13 live-in boyfriends worked at regular jobs. Boyfriends who worked regular jobs were a more reliable source of financial support than those who only hustled on the street or worked in illegal activities.

> It's difficult around here to find a good man. Most of them don't work. They just work the streets, you know. They just steal and deal and stuff. That kind of thing is a drag. I mean, it's very risky, and though it brings in a lot of money, eventually they're going to lose it all and you're going down with them. My first husband worked the streets, and I know now enough to stay away from that kind.

Mothers claimed they had little difficulty convincing boyfriends to assist in supporting children who were, in most cases, not their own. They had more trouble convincing absent fathers to help (see Liebow 1967:74–102). Although almost every mother sampled cooperated with government officials to establish paternity for her children, many had no court-ordered support award. Further, support orders did not guarantee payment. Even when absent fathers met their obligation, Public Aid required that support payments be made through the department. Upon receiving payment, Public Aid kept all but $50, which it "passed through" to a recipient as exempt income.

Some mothers circumvented these rules and arranged for absent fathers to pay them directly without the knowledge of the welfare department. In this way they kept the full amount. Even then, support was seldom reliable or substantial, since many of the absent fathers in question worked irregularly or for low wages, had children by other women who also needed support, or were in prison. Mothers could not count on such income, and offered this as one reason why they did not report it.

> Well, the son's father had given me a little bit of money, here and there. But I'm not going to report that: that's not a steady income. I can't rely on him.

Almost all mothers were indignant that the welfare department expected them to report such income and felt welfare officials were "cheating" when they deducted support payments from welfare checks.

Churches and Community Agencies   A few tenacious respondents "got an income" by "hitting" or "begging from" churches and community agencies. Most Chicago churches and agencies give away small amounts of food and clothing. Some also give money for specific needs, like eye-glasses or dental work.

> Two weeks before the checks come out I hit the churches. The churches will let you come the week before you are getting your check, so I hit four different churches in a week. I get about $150 worth of groceries plus they give clothes.

In Chicago, enough churches and community groups offer assistance so a recipient can receive cash and in-kind aid from several sources in a single month.

> You know, getting around and getting the car payment or insurance payment made by churches is an income too. I had to go to one church after another. I would try to remember which one I hadn't gone to and ask them. Oh gosh, I think there were three churches that gave me money to get glasses. But [I only needed one pair], so I paid my car payment and insurance too.

Student Grants and Legal Settlements   Two respondents won large cash settlements for injuries. They did not report this income to Public Aid, as they would have been cut off from all assistance until they had depleted these resources. Full-time student mothers partly relied on student loans and grants to make ends meet. By the time they paid tuition and books, they had only a few hundred dollars left per school term. Still, this extra cash was essential.

> After you pay for your books and everything you may get a refund whatever is left so I get about $200 or $300 a semester and I don't report that.

Earned Income

Just over half of those interviewed did not receive substantial outside assistance, and engaged in part-time or full-time unreported work to make ends meet. I divide earned income from unreported work into two categories: work in the regular economy and work in the underground economy.

Work in the Regular Economy   Seven mothers obtained false social security numbers and worked at regular jobs. They earned an average of $5 an hour. Mothers worked as teacher's aides, nurse's aides, fast food workers, factory workers, and secretaries. Respondents reported that obtaining false social security cards was easy:

> [You'll find welfare mothers in] any factory. They have a whole network. [False] social security cards are easy to come by—they're a dime a dozen. I could take you to a place right now to get one where I used to work. I was told many times, "Just give me $25, and I'll get you a card." [At this factory] about 25 of them was doing it, and they offered to show me. They was making $5, $6 an hour plus the welfare they was getting.

In my sample, regular jobs taken under false identities proved more reliable and profitable than off-the-books work. Respondents expressed frustration that they "had" to conceal the fact they were working regular jobs because they didn't earn enough to forgo welfare.

> [I work] at [a fast food place] for $4 an hour. It's still not enough. I wish I could go off aid and let them know that I work.

In addition to low pay, respondents cited frequent lay-offs, uncertainty over the number of hours one could work, and lack of health benefits as reasons why they could not report their work. Their claim that "everybody knows" and "everybody does it" strengthened their belief that concealment was legitimate.

Twenty-two respondents worked part-time at regular jobs or odd jobs but were paid in cash off-the-books. Jobs included bartending, catering, house cleaning, childcare, retail work, and sewing. Because these jobs paid cash, there was little chance AFDC could monitor earnings. Thus, although off-the-books jobs paid only about $3 an hour, most mothers preferred them to better paid jobs requiring social security numbers.

> I really [have] trouble claiming my work. I know and everyone else knows [about off-the-books] work where you can make cash and not tell them about it. . . . It's the only way to survive.

Some employers reportedly colluded with recipients, offering the option of cash work at a slightly lower wage.

Off-the-books jobs ranged from jobs with regular hours at a single place of employment to highly irregular neighborhood odd jobs. Many said they worked odd jobs when other more reliable strategies failed. Odd jobs offered a type of unemployment insurance to those between what respondents sometimes dubbed "real" or more regular jobs. Non-working mothers pursued odd jobs when they were between boyfriends or when a friend or relative failed to come through. Irregular jobs were also quite important to underground workers—those who made ends meet by selling sex, drugs and stolen goods—a point addressed below.

Work in the Underground Economy   Ten mothers worked in the underground economy: they engaged in activities that were against the law, in addition to violating the welfare rules. Those who sold drugs usually sold marijuana and made only a modest profit.[3] One respondent sold cocaine, but was murdered by her supplier during the course of the project because she owed him $600. Another mother said she stopped selling crack after a police officer told her the state would take custody of her children if she was caught. Some mothers fenced stolen goods, including meat, jewelry, and VCRs. The highest-paid work these women performed was selling sex, from which they earned about $40 per hour. Five mothers supplemented their welfare in this way.

To keep the frequency of their underground work to a minimum, respondents combined underground jobs with odd jobs they performed on a more routine basis.

> I might ask somebody if I could do their laundry so I could get some cigarettes, or [beg for money on the street]. I have done some of that in my day. And on a hot summer day, I might get an ounce of marijuana, roll some joints. It cost me $30, [and] I get $120 in profit. I don't do it often.

> I [buy joints wholesale] from a friend of mine and I sell them and make a profit. I do this about every other month, and I make about $150. I sell drugs, sell articles which aren't mine, pick up cans, do house chores, shovel snow, [and] cut grass.

These women did not call themselves "dealers," "fences," or "prostitutes." In fact, they distinguished themselves from "professionals," those who worked in the underground economy "for a living." Although those women who sold sex described their activities as "turning tricks," "selling ass," or "selling myself," they did not consider these activities prostitution, but rather, "a social thing," or "social prostitution." In keeping with this self-definition, they claimed they did not solicit openly or often. Most developed regular customers, often servicing only one or two for a period of time. This exclusivity lent some measure of legitimacy to the exchange of sex for money.

> I also think a lot of people have affairs with guys who will pay some of their bills. It's like a more legitimate prostitution. There is not really an exchange of money for services. It is more of a social thing. You are sleeping with this person, and in return he is taking care of a few things for you.

Informants claimed they wanted desperately to be good mothers and keep their families together. Most "professional" dealers, fences, and prostitutes they knew were not good parents to their children. Respondents believed the children of professionals were "trouble," and usually "[got] messed up at an early age." Some claimed they knew professionals who lost custody of their children through neglect or imprisonment.

Those working illegal jobs felt it was unacceptable to perform such activities unless they had exhausted all other resources and the well-being of their children was threatened.

Like if I don't have food, I have to make some extra money by turning a few tricks. I also do hair, babysitting, clean the landlord's house, laundry; . . . [from the combination of these activities] I clear close to $200 a month.

Once my bills were pretty high, and I had to pay them. So what I did was give my nephew my whole check and went in with him to get a pound of reefer. And I got my interest out of that, so I was able to pay what I had to pay.

I've sold things that wasn't mine. . . . I've stolen out of the store to feed my kids. I was sent to the court and spent a day in jail for it. The judge understood and let me out.

PASSIVE DEPENDENCY OR MAINSTREAM VALUES?

Many women on welfare told me "I never thought I'd sink so low," or "I dream of the day that I can leave welfare behind." The overwhelming majority wanted to become self-sufficient through work, and a substantial minority had tried leaving welfare for reported work, only to return to welfare when they found they could not pay their bills. Respondents disliked concealing outside income from the welfare department. In nearly every interview, women used phrases like "I had no choice" or "I was forced to" to account for their actions.

Respondents felt particularly guilty about the lies welfare "forced" them to tell to conceal outside income.

Public Aid is an agency that I believe can teach a person how to lie. If you tell them the truth, you won't get any help. But if you go down there and tell them a lie, you get help. And I can't understand it, and every woman on Public Aid will tell you the same thing. It teaches you to lie. It won't accept the truth. So when you deal with Public Aid, you have to tell them a tale.

Respondents feared they would suffer real material hardship if they didn't "beat the system."

One thing about being on AFDC . . . you have to think. You have to set up a strategy on how to beat them and not let them beat you. You know it's bad that you have to think of [a strategy] though. And yet you have to go in there and beat the system. You cannot go in there and be totally honest, because you'll lose every time.

Some feared they would go hungry, end up on the streets, or lose custody of their children. Most could not imagine living solely on welfare; no one knew anyone who did.

These mothers insisted lying was out of character for them, something which they would not do normally. One mother remarked, "Public Aid forces you into deceit and dishonesty, things you normally would not think of doing." Respondents chose between being good mothers and good citizens. In every case, concern for their children's welfare outweighed moral qualms.

[So how did you feel about having to lie?] I felt guilty. I really did. I felt I was cheating my government, but on the other hand I had to think about my family. I was not about to let my children starve or have no clothes on their backs.

The dissonance between conscience and what mothers perceived as necessary dishonesty diminished self-respect. Most respondents spoke passionately about how receiving welfare made them "feel like dirt" or "feel so ashamed I could die." Their struggle to keep their families together increased their sense on being "on the bottom."

Sometimes you get so desperate you think the only way you can make ends meet is to be a prostitute. I think that is a gut level feeling. You feel you are on the bottom anyhow.

Although recipients worried about day-to-day material survival, most viewed survival as not merely a matter of having adequate food, shelter, and clothing. They felt there were "psychological" and "social" aspects as well.

You know, we live in such a materialistic world. Our welfare babies have needs and wants too. They see other kids going to the circus, having toys and stuff like that. You gotta do what you gotta do to make your kid feel normal. There is no way you can deprive your child.

The above quote captures a common sentiment among the welfare recipients I interviewed: children need to have an occasional treat, and mothers who refuse may deprive their offspring of normalcy. On a more fundamental level, many mothers worried that if they did not provide a few extras—expensive tennis shoes, for example—their children would be tempted to sell drugs to get them.

My boy, he sees these kids that sell drugs. They can afford to buy these [tennis shoes] and he can't. So I have my little side job and [buy them for him]. You got to do it to keep them away from drugs and . . . from the streets.

The mothers themselves needed an occasional extra, too. Many women reported that by spending small amounts on cosmetics, cigarettes, alcohol, or the lottery, they could avoid feeling "like I'm not completely on the bottom," or "my life is not completely hopeless."

By setting benefits so low, welfare denies these needs and increases recipients' perceived isolation from society's mainstream. The following quote, offered by an unusually articulate respondent, reflects the commonly expressed belief that welfare fails to integrate the poor with the larger society.

I don't understand why [Public Aid is] punishing people who are poor if you want to mainstream them. If indeed, the idea is to segregate, to be biased, to create a widening gap between the haves and the have-nots, then the welfare system is working. If it is to provide basic needs, not just financial but psychological and social needs of every human being, then the system fails miserably.

WORK AND WELFARE: A DUAL DILEMMA

For the 50 Chicago-area recipients I interviewed, finding a job that paid more than welfare was nearly impossible. If welfare recipients could not live on their benefits, they could hardly live on wages resembling those benefits. Furthermore, leaving welfare has serious economic costs, since working mothers typically incur more health, transportation, and clothing expenses than their welfare counterparts.

Few of the jobs that unskilled or semi-skilled single mothers can get offer health benefits. Although Medicaid currently covers those who leave welfare for work for one year, few employers provide family coverage after that year is up. Those who qualify for coverage usually must make a co-payment they cannot afford.

They say that they want mothers to get back off the Aid and work, okay. There's a lot of mothers who want to work—okay—like me, I want to work. And then you work, [your employer] don't give you [medical insurance]. And sometimes, it depends on how much

you make, they cut off your medical card, and when you go out and get those jobs you don't make enough to pay rent, then medical and bills. Then they'll probably get laid off, or they won't like it, and then they have to start all over again and it might be months before they get their benefits going again. . . . It's just another hassle.

The added costs of health care, child care, transportation, and clothing often mean wages do not cover expenses. As a result, mothers who want to work feel they cannot.

Just looking at it doesn't make sense to have to go to a job that pays the minimum wage when you consider that $2, [per hour] goes to pay the baby-sitter so you bring home $2 and you have to put your food, medical, your rent on $2 an hour—you can't make it. So you go down to welfare because it is cheaper to live for single parents.

I have applied all over, looking for [a job]. But a lot of places that are hiring are only paying me [minimum wage], and that's not enough for me to survive. I had a chance at [a fast food] place, but I figured out how much they were paying . . . and it just wasn't enough to cover my bills.

Since most low-wage entry level workers experience periodic lay-offs, mothers feared taking a reported job: if they lost it they would have had to reapply for welfare. In Chicago, eligibles wait four to six weeks for their benefits to start. In the interim, families are left without any means of support. About one-third of those I sampled had lost low-wage jobs in the past. Some had friends and family to tide them over, but others suffered severe material hardship—an experience they did not want to repeat.

I asked respondents how much they would have to make to leave welfare altogether. Mothers said they would not take a job paying less than $7 to $10 per hour. Jobs at this wage are hard to come by, especially for women with few skills.[4]

Recipients' estimates of an adequate hourly wage agree with data from the Consumer Expenditure Survey of 1984-85, which show that single mothers who work spend about $800 more for health care, $300 more for clothing, $500 more for transportation, and $1,200 more for childcare than nonworking single mothers do. By adding these figures to the amounts privately-housed welfare mothers spent, I calculate that working mothers without housing subsidies, but with average childcare, clothing, and transportation expenses need to earn at least $14,800 per year to live as well as their welfare counterparts. Unless they too have substantial outside income, working mothers would need to earn $7.50 to $9.00 per hour to reach this amount, depending on how many hours they work (Jencks and Edin 1991). The average welfare mother cannot expect to earn much. Garfinkel and Michalopoulos (1989) estimate an average welfare mother can expect to earn $5.15 per hour (in 1989 dollars). Assuming they have average work-related expenses, this approximately equals the average welfare benefit package.

Beyond its economic costs, work has substantial non-economic costs. Few daycare centers accept newborns or children over 12, so their mothers must find alternatives. Working mothers who stay home with sick children may lose their jobs, but they cannot send sick children to daycare. Working mothers usually are not home when their school-aged children return from school. In the summer, mothers have difficulty finding responsible adults to watch their children. Unless mothers can afford after-school and summer daycare, their children forfeit adult supervision for a substantial part of each day.

In Chicago ghetto neighborhoods, unsupervised children are vulnerable to gang activity, drug use, and teen pregnancy. In my sample, one women's 12-year-old daughter was "sleeping around with a married man" while she was away at work. She found out from the man's wife, who threatened to kill her child. Another quit her job to make sure her 14-year-old son stayed in school. While she worked, her son skipped school repeatedly, ran with a dangerous gang, and was arrested for theft.

The following account reflects the frustration mothers experience when they try to function as full-time workers and mothers, especially when the resulting income is inadequate.

[Its] not worth it to go out working when you think about it, you know. It's not worth it 'cause you have kids and then they gonna be sick, and you gonna have to go to the doctor, and mainly that's why lots of mothers don't go out and get jobs because they don't think it's worth it. Going out there and working and then having a lot of problems and then can't even buy groceries and stuff like that.

DISCUSSION

The so-called "welfare trap" is not primarily one of behavioral dependency but one of economic survival. In a society where single mothers must provide financially for their children, where women are economically marginalized into unreliable jobs that pay little more than the minimum wage, where child-support is inadequate or nonexistent, and where daycare costs and health insurance (usually not provided by employers) are unaffordable for most, it should surprise no one that half the mothers supporting children on their own choose welfare over reported work.

While some argue welfare creates the very problems it tries to alleviate by setting up a system of perverse incentives that reward dependency rather than work (Mead 1989), I argue that the welfare system actually prohibits dependency by paying too little to make this possible.

The evidence presented here challenges the validity of three widely accepted stereotypes about welfare recipients: they do not work, they do not want to work, and their behaviors reflect values different from mainstream society. These findings have important implications for the debate about the underclass and current and future public policy but must be interpreted with care since the sample is not representative of mothers in other cities and states.

The obvious solution to the problem of inadequate benefits or low earnings is to increase one or the other. The expansion of AFDC benefits is politically unlikely. Since most Americans believe single mothers should work, nonworkers will always be considered outside the mainstream (Garfinkel and McLanahan 1986).

Rather than focus on expanding benefits, I suggest we insure that those who work fulltime can earn a living wage. Several leading policy analysts have proposed that we increase single mothers' income through a child support assurance system and wage supplements of various kinds (Ellwood 1988, Garfinkel 1990, Garfinkel and McLanahan 1986, Jencks and Edin 1991, Orr 1991, Wilson 1987). Any set of solutions, however, must take into account that mothers need to roughly double their current potential earnings to make work a viable alternative to welfare.

Other barriers to employment include lack of affordable child-care, insufficient health insurance coverage, and inadequate or non-existent child support payments (Danzinger and Nichols-Casebolt 1990, Glass 1990; Marshall and Marx 1991). Providing these benefits to more families would significantly lower the cost of working and facilitate the transition from welfare to self-sufficiency through work.

ACKNOWLEDGMENTS

I wish to gratefully acknowledge the help of the 50 welfare households who participated in this study, who must remain anonymous. Christopher Jencks offered invaluable assistance in every phase of this research. Malcolm Spector gave important editing assistance. Arlene Kaplan Daniels, Susan Mayer, and Timothy J. Nelson also made helpful comments. Shirlee Garcia, Sonja Grant, and Deborah Hayes assisted, with interviewing, and Julie Mittler contributed administrative support. Correspondence to Edin, 87B Wentworth Street, Charleston, SC 29401.

NOTES

1. As a white researcher, I was concerned that racial and class differences between myself and respondents might limit my interviewing effectiveness. Because of this, I hired one Hispanic and two African-American interviewers. All three were former or current welfare recipients, and after careful training they helped me contact and interview 21 of the 27 black and Hispanic respondents in the sample.

2. Benefits in Chicago are slightly higher than average: no state provides benefits generous enough to cover what the 50 Chicago-area mothers reported spending. Cook County mothers needed at least $961 in cash and food stamps to meet their monthly expenses. It is unlikely that rents in any major city average more than $100 less than in Chicago, so welfare families probably did not get by on less than $750 anywhere. In 1988, a family of three received cash and food stamps worth $750 a month in Los Angeles and San Francisco and $701 in New York City, but these cities were all more expensive than Chicago. Benefits were $699 in Detroit, $589 in Philadelphia, $491 in Atlanta, and $412 in Houston and Dallas (U.S. House of Representatives 1990). Detroit is thus the only major city where a family might have gotten by on AFDC and food stamps. Families living in low-cost rural areas of high benefit states might also get by. National figures and other small scale studies are consistent with the story of these 50 Chicago-area recipients (Edin 1989, Gardiner and Lyman 1984, Halsey, Nold, and Block 1982, Jencks and Edin 1991, Sharff 1987).

3. I asked respondents to estimate the time they spent selling drugs and stolen goods and how much they made. A simple calculation of earnings over time spent shows these jobs paid approximately the minimum-wage (from $3 to $5 an hour).

4. Approximately one-third said they would not take a job without benefits because they or their children had expensive health care needs.

REFERENCES

Danzinger, Sandra K., and Ann Nichols-Casebolt. 1990. "Child support in paternity cases." *Social Service Review* 64:458–74.

Ellwood, David T. 1988. *Poor Support: Poverty in the American Family.* New York: Basic Books.

Gardiner, John A., and Theodore R. Lyman. 1984. *The Fraud Control Game: State Responses to Fraud and Abuse in AFDC and Medicaid Programs.* Bloomington, Ind.: Indiana University Press.

Garfinkel, Irwin. 1990. "A new child support assurance system." Institute for Research on Poverty, Discussion Paper #916-90. Madison, University of Wisconsin.

Garfinkel, Irwin, and Sara McLanahan. 1986. *Single Mothers and Their Children.* Washington, D.C.: The Urban Institute.

Glass, Becky L. 1990. "Child support enforcement: An implementation analysis." *Social Service Review* 64:542–56.

Halsey, H., F. Nold, and M. Block. 1982. "AFDC: An analysis of grant overpay." Palo Alto, Calif.: Block and Nold Economic Consultants.

Jencks, Christopher, and Kathryn Edin. 1991. "Reforming welfare." In *Rethinking Social Policy,* ed. Christopher Jencks, 204–35. Cambridge, Mass.: Harvard University Press.

Liebow, Elliot. 1967. *Tally's Corner.* Boston: Little, Brown and Company.

Marshall, Nancy L., and Fern Marx. 1991. "The affordability of child care for the working poor." *Families in Society* 72:202–11.

Mead, Lawrence. 1989. "The logic of workfare: The underclass and work policy." In William Julius Williams, ed., *The Ghetto Underclass: Social Science Perspectives,* 156–69. Newbury Park, Calif.: Sage.

Michalopoulos, Charles, and Irwin Garfinkel. 1989. "Reducing welfare dependence and poverty of single mothers by means of earnings and child support: Wishful thinking and realistic possibilities." Institute for Research on Poverty, Discussion paper 882–89. Madison, University of Wisconsin.

Murray, Charles. 1984. *Losing Ground.* New York: Basic Books.

Novak, Michael. 1987. *The New Consensus on Family and Welfare.* American Enterprise Institute for Public Policy Research. Milwaukee, Wisc.: Marquette University.

Orr, Lloyd D. 1991. "Wage rate subsidies: Some new dimensions." Unpublished manuscript. Bloomington: Indiana University.

Sharff, Jagna Wojcicka. 1987. "The underground economy of neighborhood." In *Cities of the United States,* ed. Leith Mullings, 19–50. New York: Columbia University Press.

U.S. House of Representatives. 1990. "Background material and data on programs within the jurisdiction of the Committee on Ways and Means." Committee on Ways and Means. Washington, D.C.: Government Printing Office.

Wilson, William Julius. 1987. *The Truly Disadvantaged.* Chicago: University of Chicago Press.

R E A D I N G   4 5

Strangers in a Strange Land: The Gendered Experiences of Women Politicians in Britain and the United States

ABIGAIL HALCLI and JO REGER

INTRODUCTION

When Geraldine Ferraro was selected as Walter Mondale's vice presidential candidate in 1984, many political observers concluded that women had finally "made it" in American politics. Ferraro, a Democratic U.S. representative from New York, stood a chance at becoming the most visible female politician in the country and a significant player in American politics. Former Prime Minister Margaret Thatcher is also cited as a female "success" story of the 1980s. Thatcher, nicknamed the "Iron Lady" because of her powerful leadership style, governed Britain for eleven years. The achievements of these two women, along with other less prominent female politicians, stand as powerful symbols of women's growing influence in politics. However, while women in these countries are beginning to break through the barriers limiting their political roles to voters and volunteer campaign workers, they continue to be disadvantaged in politics as they are in other social institu-

Abigail Halcli and Jo Reger, "Strangers in a Strange Land: The Gendered Experiences of Women Politicians in Britain and the United States" (previously unpublished paper). Reprinted with the permission of Jo Reger.

tions. Women are still far from achieving proportionate political representation at all levels of government. Moreover, becoming a woman politician can be a difficult process and those aspiring to political careers often find the journey fraught with obstacles.

We examine the experience of being a woman politician through studies of American and British women who are active in politics at the national, state, and local levels.[1] The U.S. study draws on the experiences of nineteen feminists. The sample includes women who held elective office, were unsuccessful candidates, or had seriously considered becoming candidates. The British study is based primarily on interviews with thirteen female Members of Parliament (MPs) for the Labour party. Women from both samples discussed the processes of becoming a politician and their experiences and difficulties within political parties and government institutions in their countries.

Our studies illustrate that despite the growing numbers of women in elective office, British and American female politicians often feel like strangers in a strange land. Political institutions are gendered in that they reflect and reinforce societal gender arrangements and systems of inequality. In other words, parties and government bodies

LESBIANS CLEAR HURDLES
TO GAIN LEADERSHIP POSTS

KATHERINE BISHOP

SAN FRANCISCO, Dec. 29—After two decades of perfecting their political skills in the feminist movement and in the mainstream parties, after years of fighting for better health care programs amid the AIDS crisis, lesbians are increasingly being elected to office. And they are becoming leaders of gay organizations that have historically been run by men.

From Los Angeles to Maine, voters in the November elections showed more willingness to elect lesbians to city and state offices, often for the first time. And in large gay organizations lesbians, who were once eclipsed by gay men, are emerging in highly-visible jobs, positioning themselves as possible candidates of the future.

While it is difficult to determine numbers of lesbians in elective office around the country, five of the six acknowledged lesbians running for public office were elected in November. Their successes followed years of toiling as volunteers before conquering attitudes that have slowed the political advancement of all women.

"In part, it's a matter of the traditional issue of women thinking they have to do a lot more work before they can ask to be elected, while every man comes out of law school thinking he can be a senator," said Deborah Glick, 39 years old, who in November became the first openly gay person to be elected to the New York Assembly. Her district is in lower Manhattan.

Fading as an Issue?

Other lesbian candidates, especially those who had previously made unsuccessful attempts at elective office,

say the question of sexual orientation is fading as an issue to voters.

"Most people said, 'Thank goodness, you're not a lawyer or an incumbent,'" said Carole Migden, who with another gay woman, Roberta Achtenberg, was elected in November to the San Francisco Board of Supervisors. "Roberta and I were seen first of all as smart, capable, affirmative and new."

Dale McCormick, who became the first acknowledged lesbian to be elected to the State Senate of Maine, said she thinks lesbians have made progress in politics. Ms. McCormick, 43, the former president of the Maine Lesbian-Gay Political Alliance, said she rode her bicycle on country roads to visit 6,000 homes in her district.

"People said, 'You'll never win, you have all this political baggage, you're too outspoken,'" Ms. McCormick said, "But the voters were willing." She won in 10 of 12 towns in Southern Maine.

Agendas Were Different

The women also cite the recent support by homosexual men of lesbians in leadership roles in gay organizations as an important ingredient in their current success.

Until recently, personal and political conflicts between homosexual men and women was serious enough to drive them into separate communities. While gay men were delighting in their sexual liberation and creating their own power bases, lesbians promoted a broader feminist agenda of child custody, child care and women's health issues, often in a context of long-term partnerships.

The AIDS crisis prompted a healing of longstanding rifts that had prevented men from supporting leadership by women, they say.

"AIDS meant that suddenly there were bigger fights to fight than protecting the old boys' club and preserving the newfound network of power brokers who ran gay rights organizations," said Torie Osborn, 40. She is the first woman to serve as executive director of the Gay and Lesbian Community Services Center in Los Angeles since its founding 20 years ago. In 1985, all the women in the organization walked out for two years because the board refused to consider a woman for the position.

Many women cite Urvashi Vaid, the executive director of the 17,000-member National Gay and Lesbian Task Force in Washington, who was named "Woman of the Year" this month by The Advocate, the national news magazine for gay people. The Advocate said that for Ms. Vaid, a 32-year-old lawyer of Indian descent, to be selected to head a major lesbian and gay lobbying group "is a stunning coup for lesbians, who have been made as invisible in the gay rights movement as in mainstream society."

Homosexual men and women acknowledge that some people may believe that the current success of lesbians in leadership positions in public life is a result of the death of homosexual men from AIDS. But they reject that conclusion.

"AIDS has killed many gay men who were leaders, but it's also the case that the women have been extraordinary in the crisis," said David Scondras, a homosexual who is a member of the Boston City Council.

"Women's sense of community was touched by the horror, and it led them to fight a crusade for funding for health care and to find a cure," said Mr. Scondras, who organized the sixth annual Conference of Lesbian and Gay Elected Officials in November in Boston.

Ms. Glick agrees: "It's not simply that men are dying and now there are openings for women. It's that men are now more open to power sharing."

In November, Ms. Migden and Ms. Achtenberg were two of the first three openly gay candidates to be elected in a citywide race in San Francisco without having first been appointed to their respective offices. The third was Tom Ammiano, a teacher who was elected to the Board of Education.

Ms. Migden, 42, who serves on the State Health Commission and has headed two community mental health organizations, enters office with a strong background in Democratic Party politics. The party's San Francisco chairwoman since 1986, she was elected to the Democratic National Committee in 1988.

"There is no question the Democratic Party was a strong component of my campaign," Ms. Migden said. "I had a host of contacts and constituents that one builds up over the years."

AIDS Changes Thinking

Ms. Migden also served two terms as president of the Harvey Milk Lesbian/Gay Democratic Club here. She said her candidacy for the Board of Supervisors was backed by homosexual men as well as lesbians, in part because of her emphasis on health care issues.

"The divisions in our community began to evaporate with the AIDS emergency," she said. "There is a positive outcome of any catastrophe, and this one made gay men aware of a whole range of health care issues from medical insurance to access to specialized care that we as a society are justifiably already nervous about."

Ms. Achtenberg, a 40-year-old civil rights lawyer who headed the National Center for Lesbian Rights here, recalled that times were not always so harmonious. "The gay community has been dominated by white men, like the community at large," she said.

Health care issues are only part of the broader family agenda for lesbians. Because many are mothers, issues like affordable child care have been among their political goals, something they said also appealed to voters. Ms. Achtenberg said voters here found no dissonance in her being both a lesbian and a parent. She and her partner, Judge Mary C. Morgan of San Francisco Municipal Court, are raising a child borne by Judge Morgan. The judge, the nation's first acknowledged lesbian jurist, was appointed to the bench in 1981 by Gov. Edmund G. Brown Jr.

Ms. Vaid said openly lesbian elected officials remain a small fraction of the gay women in public service. But, she said, "voters are showing they are not going to reject you for sexual orientation if you have the background. That is huge progress for a community that has just begun to come out of hiding."

continue to operate in ways that privilege men over women. We examine how gender relations are evident in the workings of political institutions in the United States and Britain and how they shape and constrain the experiences of women politicians.

GENDERED POLITICS

Our analysis of women politicians draws upon recent theory on gender which calls attention to a *structure* of gender relations that sustains power differentials between men and women (Connell 1987). In this view, gender, like race and class, operates as a fundamental means of organizing social relations and creating "difference" among categories of people (West & Fenstermaker 1995). The behaviors, attitudes, and expectations of men and women are shaped by this structure of gender relations as they go about their daily activities. Gender arrangements are also embedded in the everyday practices and structures of social institutions, including the family, work, education, law, religion, and politics (Lorber 1994). These institutions are "gendered" in that they reproduce a system of inequality that sustains male dominance and marginalizes women.

Current research on workplaces advances our understanding of how organizations are gendered (Acker 1990; Beechy 1988; also see Mills & Tancred 1992). According to these scholars, conceiving of organizations as gender-neutral conceals the fact that their structures and practices assume a male participant. Acker (1990) identifies a "gendered substructure" within organizations that privileges male workers and masculinity. This substructure is reproduced daily in practical work activities, the division of labor and authority, and the routines and policies by which organizations are run. Workplace organizations support systems of inequality by offering male and female workers different types of rewards and opportunities.

Acker's thesis was recently illustrated in a television exposé that documented the differential treatment by employers of women and men with identical qualifications and employment backgrounds. While potential male employees were given information on a corporate management position, potential female employees were administered a typing test to determine their suitability for a secretarial position ("Primetime Live," October 7, 1993). This example shows how employers, guided by established routines of organizations and societal gender arrangements, perpetuate gender inequality in the workplace by allocating greater opportunities and privileges for men.

Political institutions are also gendered in that they reflect and maintain a system of inequality between men and women. Women in politics are often marginalized because political institutions are organized with the presumption that politicians are male. This means they operate under rules, practices, and organizational structures that sustain male privilege and limit women's access to political careers. To investigate this gendered substructure, we first explore how women seeking political careers encounter cultural and structural barriers. We then examine two ways that women politicians respond to these barriers—specifically, the ways they have organized to bypass them and how they sometimes challenge prevailing ways of "doing politics." To provide a political context for our discussion, we begin by briefly comparing British and American political systems.

POLITICS AND PARTIES IN BRITAIN AND THE UNITED STATES

The experiences of British and American women politicians are shaped by the political environments in which they operate. British politics are dominated by the Conservative and Labour parties, with the middle-of-the-road Liberal Democrats and a number of regional parties also holding some seats in Parliament. British political parties are "programmatic" in that they issue manifestos that candidates are expected to adhere to during the election and after winning a parliamentary seat. Voters therefore make choices between party programs rather than between individual candidates, although the personalities of the party leadership do figure into voters' decisions (Kavanagh 1990). The parties also control the candidate selection process for local and national elections. Therefore, potential candidates must negotiate with local party organizations to be selected as parliamentary candidates. The 651 Members of Parliament (MPs), the national legislative body, are elected from single-member constituencies (districts) by a simple plurality (winner-take-all system). Despite recent increases in the number of female parliamentarians, by 1995 only 9.5 percent of MPs were women.[2]

In the United States a system of primary elections means that in most states candidates are selected by the voters at large rather than exclusively by the party membership. Elections therefore are centered around the candidates rather than on party manifestos as they are in Britain. In addition, the federal structure of the U.S. government means political power is fragmented between local-, state-, and national-level party organizations. As a result, the Republican and Democratic parties are relatively weak political organizations compared to their British counterparts, which maintain more centralized control over party policy and candidate recruitment. The 435 members of the House of Representatives and the 100 members of the Senate are elected from single-member districts by a simple plurality, as in the British electoral system. Following the 1994 midterm elections, 10.8 percent of U.S. Representatives and 8.0 percent of senators were women.[3]

In recent years both American and British parties have shown greater interest in increasing the number of women in elective office. This concern is a response to the organized efforts of women in these countries to gain greater political representation and the belief of many party officials and strategists that women candidates attract women voters. In Britain, the Conservative party has informally encouraged more women to become candidates but is as yet unwilling to take official actions to ensure that women are selected as candidates. The Labour party, in contrast, instituted a quota system in 1993 by which 50 percent of all constituencies with vacant "safe seats" (seats traditionally held by the Labour party) and 50 percent of its most winnable marginal constituencies (competitive seats the Labour party has a fairly good chance of winning) must select female candidates for the next election. The aim of the quota system is to increase the number of female Labour MPs in the House of Common from the present thirty-nine to between eighty and ninety following the next general election.[4]

The diffusion of political power within parties in the United States makes it more difficult for them to adopt rules requiring state and local parties to nominate female candidates. However, since the 1980s both Democratic and Republican party leaders have demonstrated greater support for women's candidacies (Burrell 1993). In addition, the Democratic party has responded to demands for more equal representation of women at its nominating convention by mandating that 50 percent of delegates from each state must be female. The Republican party, like the British Conservative party, is not willing to mandate quotas, and instead allows the state parties to set their own targets for female representation at national conventions.

GENDERED BARRIERS

Geraldine Ferraro, after her 1984 vice presidential bid, coined what has been dubbed Ferraro's First Law of Gender Politics. The law, simply stated, is "it's easier for guys" (cited in Witt et al. 1994). The sentiment of Ferraro's statement is echoed by women politicians in both the United States and Britain. Female politicians face a variety of barriers resulting from women's positions in British and American societies. The gendered images, expectations, and responsibilities associated with women's traditional activities in societies often create obstacles for women interested in pursuing political careers. In this section we explore how societal images of "women" and "politicians" may keep women from seeing themselves, and being perceived by others, as potential candidates. We also examine the barriers women politicians encounter resulting from the structures, practices, and rules of political institutions that privilege masculinity and male actors.

Being a "Woman" Politician

Historically men have been expected to operate in the public sphere as breadwinners and civic leaders (Bernard 1981). Women, on the other hand, continue to be associated with the private sphere of families and domestic responsibilities, despite the fact that large numbers of British and American women work outside their homes. Women who do actively participate in public life often find themselves performing traditional activities as helpmates to men (Kessler-Harris 1981). In the political realm, this means women are more likely to be campaign volunteers than candidates. A Democratic party activist with aspirations for a state-level position recognizes that many women see themselves in the helpmate position rather than that of the potential candidate. She says:

> I go to the Democratic Party [meetings] because I realize that a political party is essential to success in your campaign. Yet you see [members of the local women's club] . . . who have been licking envelopes for thirty, forty, fifty years and just never saw themselves as the one to run for office. . . .

Because women have traditionally been positioned as auxiliaries to men in families and workplaces, they may have trouble picturing themselves as candidate material. An American woman who decided not to pursue a state level office says this about her apprehension on entering politics:

> I know how it feels to be pregnant. I know how it feels to have a baby. I do not know how it feels to be a candidate. I do not know how it feels to make that decision.

Similarly, several MPs express concern that some very talented and competent women are deterred from becoming politically active because they lack confidence in their abilities. Promoting women in politics, according to one MP, depends on "persuading women in the Party that it's quite reasonable for them to think or assume that they could do a very good job as [local] councilors or MPs." Thus societal notions of the "typical politician" are gendered, serving to dissuade women and men from supporting women's candidacies and perhaps discouraging some women from running for office.

However, gender is not the only category reflected in societal images of the typical politician. Women of color in the U.S. study must combat images of politicians as both male and white. One African-American candidate for a city council seat broke new ground simply by deciding to seek elective office. She says: "I was the first black female . . . to clearly campaign. They never saw one campaign before. . . . They were probably shocked." Another woman of color notes that though black women are "very much the backbone of the Democratic party" in her area they were not encouraged to seek elective office by party leaders. Their experiences illustrate how race and gender intertwine to create an even stronger sense of being a political "stranger."

Not only does the image of a typical politician serve to block women's access to political careers, but as women operate within male-dominated political organizations they are also made to feel different from male politicians. The women in our studies indicate that their minority status in political parties often leads to a sense of being a stranger. Due to its long-standing links with trade unions the Labour party is still perceived by many as a party run by and for working-class men (Perrigo 1995; Cockburn 1987). In fact, 61 percent of the party membership is male (Labour Party Membership Survey 1989). As a result, women in the party may feel isolated, as illustrated by the Labour MP who, after being elected for her first term in 1987, recalls feeling "completely overwhelmed" being in office at the time when just 10 percent of Labour MPs were women.

Women politicians' interactions with men also illustrate the experience of being a stranger in a male domain. An elected judge in the American sample says she confronts the daily challenge of working with male politicians who "frankly have not had any experience in dealing with women that weren't either their wife or their secretary." For some men, working with women as colleagues, rather than as subordinates, may be a bewildering experience (Kanter 1977). A newly elected councilwoman in the American study says this about her male counterparts, "They are in shock. They don't know what it is like to deal with a young woman. . . . They are just really terrified of working with me." The dilemma over her title further illustrates the masculine nature of politics. She continues, "They don't even know what to call me. . . . Is she a woman? Is she a councilman? Is she a councilmember?"

Because male privilege is maintained by differentiating between men and women, female candidates and office-holders find that their "feminine" qualities are emphasized and scrutinized. Several women in our studies report having constant attention paid to their physical appearance and feeling great pressure to put extra effort into their looks and style of dress. An American state-level politician notes she feels wearing makeup is essential to avoiding criticism about her personal appearance from party officials, political colleagues, the media, and voters. Male politicians are not subject to the same level of scrutiny with regard to their personal appearance. As one MP notes, while men are likely to get away with "a few clean shirts and some old ties," how women look may receive more attention than their political work. A first-term MP says this:

I get fed up with the times people in my constituencies say "I saw you on television last week. I've seen you in that blue suit before." Or, "Are you wearing that pink again?" And I ask "What did I say?" And sometimes they can't remember. But they remember what you were wearing. People never remember what men were wearing. They listen to them.

In addition to having their personal appearance scrutinized, women politicians, like women in other institutions, often find themselves subject to sexual innuendo and harassment. Political observers point out that women in politics have been treated two ways, either as sexual "deviants" or as available sexual partners for male politicians (Witt et al. 1994). A single, heterosexual American politician recalls a rumor about her during her first campaign:

I have no way of confirming this but at one point there were rumors being spread, particularly within the labor community, which is probably one of the more difficult for women to get through, that I had been raped and was a man-hating lesbian.

Even married women may have their sexuality called into question as a means of discrediting them as women and as politicians. Ann Richards, former governor of Texas, remembers how surprised she was to be "gay-baited" when she first ran for office. She says, "I told David [her then husband] when we started that he would hear I was sleeping with every man in Travis county. What he heard was that I was sweet on Sarah Weddington [the attorney who argued *Roe* v. *Wade* in the Supreme Court]" (Witt et al. 1994:63).

Other women who are not "gay-baited" still have experiences of being treated as "sexually available women" both in office and on the campaign trail. A male MP reports hearing other men in both the Labour and Conservative parties make comments such as "ooh, she's got great legs" about their female colleagues. Such comments may seem innocent or complimentary but they serve as a constant reminder to women that they are being judged in terms of their physical appearance and sexual desirability. The focus on women's sexuality can take the form of overtures that are meant to embarrass, degrade, and disempower women politicians. An American woman reports an incident of sexual harassment involving a male candidate that occurred while running for a city council seat. She says:

> We had this candidates' night thing and there were these two rows of chairs for the candidates to sit. . . . I come up and I say, "Can I have this seat?" [The male candidate] says to me, "Would you like to sit on my face?" It was his full page newspaper ad [on the seat], which had his big photograph. . . .

The focus on women's appearance and sexuality reinforces women's feeling of difference from male politicians. Also, having to demonstrate the propriety of their sexual behavior and dealing with sexual overtures from their male colleagues may distract women politicians from advancing in their careers and pursuing their political agendas (Witt et al. 1994).

Along with the focus on their appearance and sexuality, women report that the intense scrutiny of their political work accentuates their feelings of difference. British and American women state that this attention results in a need to prove themselves and the perception that women are being held to higher standards than their male counterparts. Many women in the Labour party report that getting selected as a parliamentary candidate is much tougher for women. According to a second-term MP, "men have managed to get selected [as candidates] just by being well thought of. . . . Because the boys supported them." Women, on the other hand, perceive that they must possess

extraordinary abilities to gain the attention of party selectors. A first-term MP notes that during the selection process female politicians are judged by a different criterion:

> So you have a woman who perhaps isn't the most brilliant performer, but certainly above average, and at least as competent as any of the men. But she will be singled out as not being up to scratch. Whereas a man doing the same job and same level of performance would not be.

Similarly, a recently elected judge in the American study remembers being informed by another female politician that she would "have to be better than the men" to succeed in her community.

Because they feel they are held to higher standards, women also report feeling additional pressure to present their ideas flawlessly. One first-term MP says:

> Sometimes women feel that in order to [participate in political debates] . . . they have to know 90 percent of all there is to know about it. Whereas men feel quite happy getting away with 30 percent.

An American politician notes that even after twenty years in her party and in elected office, she still thinks she has to work harder than her male colleagues to gain recognition for her work. She says:

> [Women] have to fight more than other people do to get some attention to basic ideas. When you put up a proposal you have to do it perfectly or else you are out. It's the demands for perfection.

Despite differences in British and American political systems, the experiences of women politicians in both countries are shaped by societal gender arrangements that make it "easier for guys" to succeed in politics. Gaining the confidence to pursue a candidacy, confronting expectations of women as helpmates or sexual objects, and being judged by higher standards are some of the barriers women politicians report in both countries. In the next section, we explore how women's opportunities are shaped by these gender arrangements as they are embedded in the practices, rules, and structures of political institutions.

Encountering Gendered Politics

While societal images that conceive of "woman" and "politician" as mutually exclusive categories contribute to women's marginalization in politics, women also encounter structural barriers to their participation in politics. These barriers result from a gendered division of labor in families and workplaces that affects women's abilities to acquire the skills, networks, funding, and partisan support necessary to pursue a political career. In addition, this gendered division of labor and associated cultural images of "appropriate" gender behavior are embedded in the very operation and practices of social institutions, including politics.

A gendered division of labor is a fundamental aspect of the structure of gender relations (Acker 1988). As women continue to be associated with the private sphere of families and households, they also shoulder a significant portion of the responsibilities necessary for its maintenance (Warde & Hetherington 1993; Coverman 1989; Hochschild 1989). Child care and domestic responsibilities may restrict women's opportunities to become involved in the same types of political activities as men. An American woman's experience illustrates this dilemma: "There is kind of an old boys network and I've never been a part of [it] . I was raising children at the time so I couldn't get involved in doing all the things that [men] do." Women in the British study also note that family responsibilities make it more difficult for Labour women to attend constituency party meetings and annual Labour party conferences. Thus, they have fewer occasions to develop the networks and political skills necessary to launch a political career.

The gendered division of labor in families is mirrored in workplaces and occupations as well and affects the routes that women and men take to political careers. In Britain, male-dominated occupations that serve as typical career routes to Parliament, including trade union official and Labour party organizer, provide a "training ground" for men to develop important political networks and skills. In the United States, professions such as law and business serve as accepted pathways to political office. Many of the women in the U.S. study, however, came to political office through feminist activism in the National Organization for Women (NOW) and other women's rights groups and express a desire to pursue certain issues such as reproductive freedom and pay equity. Though these experiences provide them with the confidence and conviction to seek elective office, this "feminist" pathway does not carry the same political accreditation and networks as more conventional career routes to political office.

Being shut out of the occupational and political networks that lead to political careers can block women's access to the financial support necessary to pursue candidacy. Because the Labour party has limited resources to aid prospective parliamentary candidates, both men and women experience financial burdens when running for office. Men, however, often have other sources of sponsorship, particularly from trade unions, which rarely sponsor women. In 1992, for example, 90 percent of all trade union–sponsored candidates were men (Emily's List U.K. 1993). Women in the American study also report difficulty getting the funds necessary to pursue a political office. After being asked by her party to be a candidate, an American woman remembers realizing that, "[the party] would never put their time and money into my campaign."

In some instances, the unwillingness of party elites to offer adequate support to female candidates is due to the fact that women are often selected or nominated for seats their party has little hope of winning. For example, though the Labour party selected 138 female candidates for the 1992 general election, 101 of them ran in "safe seats" of other parties, thus showing that few female candidates were serious contenders (Norris 1994). Until recently, most American women candidates were selected for "sacrificial" races against strong incumbents or in an area in which the opposing party was dominant (Witt et al. 1994).

Part of the reason women are not supported as viable candidates by party elites is that women's work is often seen as less skilled and less valuable than men's (Steinberg 1990; Phillips and Taylor 1980). As a member of a "female" profession, an American teacher reports feeling devalued serving on her local school board. She says of her struggles in office:

> Some of the abuse I get is not just from being a female but from being a teacher. . . . The abuse is in the form of being ignored, having your ideas undervalued, not looked at seriously.

Labour women commonly voice the sentiment that women's skills are often considered less relevant than the skills men are more likely to have developed through their occupational and political experiences. In Britain, parliamentary candidates are selected by local constituency parties. A first-term MP notes that a significant part of the selection process hinges on "whether you can make a rousing speech to the party faithful." She explains how this bias toward prospective candidates with stirring oratory abilities overlooks individuals, typically women, with equally relevant yet different types of political skills:

> Perhaps a more measured assessment of how effective you will be as a parliamentarian would be how well

organized you are, whether you are sympathetic to your constituents, whether you are able to deal with their problems. Whether you are effective on television. And lots of women have strengths in some of these other parts that are requirements[for being] a good MP but which are not given such high priority in the selection process.

Both of these accounts illustrate how the practices of politics serve to disadvantage women and privilege men by valuing certain skills and abilities over others. An American elected official recognizes this preference for masculine skills and reports using this knowledge to her advantage. She says:

> [Since in office] I have picked up definitely . . . "male traits." . . . Certain traits that are making it possible for me to succeed and be where I am."

Overcoming the lack of access to skill-building opportunities, political networks, and financial support and the devaluation of their abilities are formidable barriers to increasing female political representation. Despite these barriers, many British and American women have the conviction and experience to pursue political careers and are seeking ways to overcome these barriers. This point is illustrated by an unsuccessful parliamentary candidate who wants to run again in the next general election. She says:

> I've got the confidence. I've even got the cash (to run a campaign). . . . What I need now is a network—a strategy. I want some help with that.

In the following section we explore how female politicians in Britain and the United States come to recognize these barriers and seek ways to bypass them by organizing with other women and challenging the gendered practices of political institutions.

GENDERED RESPONSES

Developing responses to gendered barriers hinges upon women recognizing that disadvantages they experience as politicians are attributable to a masculinist political system and gender-stereotyped notions of what a "typical" politician should be. In order to identify and respond to this system of inequality, women politicians draw on their preexisting beliefs, feminist ideology, or experiences of discrimination

within politics. It is important to note that while British and U.S. politicians in our samples do share common experiences, their responses are conditioned by the distinct political environments in which they operate and their political views. As members of NOW, all the women in the U.S. study identify as feminists and women's rights activists. This provides them with a political ideology to identify obstacles as part of a cultural system that privileges men over women. While women in the British study do not necessarily embrace a feminist identity akin to that of the NOW members, most of the women interviewed nevertheless perceive British politics as favoring male politicians and a more masculine political style. This recognition allows Labour women, along with their American counterparts, to develop both individual and collective responses to the barriers blocking their pathways to political office. We focus on two of the responses running through the women's stories. First, women bypass barriers by forming their own professional organizations and informal networks. Second, women directly challenge masculinist ways of "doing politics" by trying to change practices and routines of political institutions.

Bypassing the Barriers

As the experiences described earlier illustrate, women often find it difficult to acquire the skills, networks, and partisan and financial support to launch political campaigns. A primary way in which women compensate for these barriers is to create their own sources of funding and organizational support. In recent years women in Britain and the United States have formed professional organizations and informal networks to promote women candidates at all levels of government.

In the United States, organizations such as EMILY's List (Early Money Is Like Yeast) raise money for Democratic candidates while the newly formed WISH List supports Republican candidates. In addition, the bipartisan National Women's Political Caucus sponsors training sessions to help women acquire political skills. The experience of being supported by other women and women's organizations encourages female candidates to help each other. One woman who ran a city council race reports that not only did EMILY's List help her, the organization also forwarded her request for support to another woman who sent her money. She says:

> I wrote her [the donor] a letter [and said] "You know you really taught me a wonderful lesson and I will never turn down a women's request for money who is running for office."

REINVENTING THE WHEEL

MS. MAGAZINE, GULF DISPATCH

One fateful day last November, 47 Saudi women decided to drive a few yards in their own country (see Ms.*, January/February 1991). Now we have an eyewitness/participatory report on what actually took place in Riyadh, and on the aftermath. The author, a Saudi herself, must remain anonymous for her own safety.*

3:00 P.M. Cars arrive in parking lot at Safeway supermarket on King Abdulaziz Road. Women sit beside male relatives or in the back of chauffeur-driven cars.

3:15 Fourteen women slide behind the wheels of as many cars. The men step away. Thirty-two other women join the 14, as passengers. None speak; they all move swiftly, as one black mass—wearing the traditional *gitwa* (head covering) and *abaya* (robe); all but five have their faces covered as well, with only their eyes showing.

3:22 The excitement in the air is overpowering. It is the first time the women have driven on their native soil. Furthermore, this is a country that does not favor public demonstrations of any kind, so this is a precedent. The convoy begins to move. Steady hands, heads held high.

3:25 Convoy moves out of the parking lot, turning north on King Abdulaziz Road. Some male relatives drive discreetly behind and alongside in support.

3:31 Turn west at the corner onto Mursalat Road. Two of the cars pull over by the Sheraton Hotel. People on the roads: a variety of expressions. Shock, horror, admiration. Some thumbs-up signals in encouragement, some smiles and fists held up in the air in solidarity, a few horns beeping in support.

3:35 Turn left, south on Olaya Road. Cars with curious (male) drivers begin to follow the convoy.

3:45 Another left. Four cars stopped at the traffic light are caught and pulled over by the police. The rest of the cars continue.

3:48 Back onto King Abdulaziz Road. En masse they decide to make the round one more time.

3:53 Stopped by police at the traffic light in front of the mosque. Afternoon prayers have just ended. The police don't know what to do. One officer leaves to call his superiors for instruction. They in turn call City Hall.

3:55 The imam of the mosque comes out to ask the police about the situation, then goes back in. Within minutes, about 30 *mutawa* (fundamentalists) emerge, screaming epithets: "Whores! Prostitutes! Sinners!" They surround the cars and pound on the windows and doors. The women sit silently inside.

4:00 The police move in. They ask the women what they think they are doing. "Driving," is the simple reply. "Why?" "In time of war mobilization and national emergency we need to, for the safety of our families." The police seem strangely awed, filled with respect. More *mutawa* appear, screaming and cursing, demanding that the women be taken to their own (religious) prisons. The police refuse, saying this is a secular matter.

4:30 The eight cars and the other two cars are allowed to drive to where the other four cars are parked. Now numbering well over 50, the *mutawa* follow, becoming more abusive. The women no longer answer questions; they sit with the car windows rolled up while the fundamentalists surround and batter the cars.

5:15 Finally, a policeman takes the wheel of each car, with a *mutawa* sitting alongside him, haranguing the women. Only one carful of women refuses to permit the *mutawa* inside. The cars are driven to the Olaya police station, and the women are told to enter. They refuse to do so until a government representative is present.

5:50 The women are finally escorted into the police station. Seven *mutawa* insist on entering, and only after repeated requests by the police that they leave do they comply. The questioning begins.

Q: "Did your husbands or fathers or brothers know you were planning to do this?" A: "Does it matter?" Q: "Is this demonstration politically motivated?" A: "Why, no, it is a matter of safety during a time of national crisis." The women are polite and peaceable, courteous in giving the necessary information. One woman, assumed to be the ringleader, is taken to another room and questioned intensely. The other women chant, "We want her back with us. She is not our leader. This is a collective act." She is brought back, but later again sequestered for more interrogation. This continues for at least three hours.

9:30 Some of the husbands of the women appear. They are told to wait in an adjoining room.

12 MIDNIGHT Interrogation of the men begins—about a half hour each.

1:00 A.M. A government representative appears. The male relatives are urged to sign a document declaring that the women will never again participate in such an action, will never again drive or even speak of this matter, under threat of punishment or imprisonment. Only then will the women be released.

2:30 All the male relatives comply except one, who refuses as a matter of principle. Finally, so much pressure is put on him that he signs. Another male relative is so angered at his wife that he refuses to come to the police station at all; at last he too appears and complies. One of the women is single; her father is dead, and her brothers are in another city. Since she is not permitted to sign for herself, she names a male friend who appears to sign for her, so that she can be released. (Later, this man is harassed and called a criminal for having helped.)

3:30 The entire group is finally permitted to leave the police station and go to their homes.

The Next Day

Handwritten copies of "police reports" (bearing no official stamps) appear as leaflets; these are distributed in government offices, pasted or nailed to the walls of public buildings, left on the front windows of cars, passed out in the streets. These so-called reports claim that the women in the driving demonstration were wearing shorts; that they hurled insults at religious men and condemned the government. Included in the allegations: the women were sluts; their husbands were secularist, Westernized, communist pimps. . . .

Aftermath

The women and their families have been ceaselessly harassed, threatened, cursed—by telephone, mail, and in person. Some of the women are educators; their university offices were broken into and ransacked by fundamentalist students who believed the allegations. . . . The women have been fired from or suspended from their jobs, and they (and their husbands) are banned from traveling abroad. . . .

Postscript

January 15: Today I rang up my neighborhood civil defense office. I said that my brother is in the army, my father is dead, and my driver is too scared to drive me anywhere—he wants to stay in his room or go back to the Philippines right away. I told the civil defense office that I need tape and plastic to seal the windows against possible chemical warfare. I need bread and bottled water and basic supplies. May I have special dispensation to drive in this emergency?

"No," was the reply, "Call 999 emergency and they will bring you what you need." I called. They gave me another number. I have been trying to get through to this other number now for days. The line is continually busy.

Late January

We are at war.

In the midst of all this horror and uncertainty, last night a group of *mutawa* climbed over a fence to throw stones through the windows of the home of one of the women. They shouted threats for an hour before departing.

In a time of national crisis, they have nothing better to do than terrorize women?

She now reports that she divides her salary into three accounts: one to finance her reelection campaign, the second for her retirement, and the third to help other women launch campaigns.

For women in the U.S. study, their feminism and organizational affiliations also serve as an important resource base. Many of the women credit NOW with not only inspiring their goal to obtain public office but also with making it a reality. Several candidates report working on other women's campaigns in order to gain political skills and experience. One woman, inspired to run because of a speech by former NOW president Eleanor Smeal, recalls thinking this about her work as a campaign volunteer for a female candidate:

> [I decided] this is the campaign where I'm going to go and I'm going to learn how it is to run a campaign. . . . I said "Look, I want to know everything there is to know." . . . I just sucked it all in.

Women in the U.S. study also report using their NOW involvement as an opportunity to learn skills necessary to being a politician. One woman recalls the political education she received from working with NOW for the passage of the Equal Rights Amendment (ERA). She says:

> Through working for the Equal Rights Amendment you get a lot of skills like how to petition, how to leaflet, how to go door-to-door, how to present yourself, how to present your issue, how to stay focused. Those are all things that we used for the ERA campaign and they clearly could be used for a political campaign.

Several American politicians also report drawing on NOW's membership as an important source of volunteer labor and support while running for office. A candidate who mounted a state-level campaign recalls the varied tasks performed by other NOW members during her campaign. She says:

> They constantly staffed my phones. They constantly did lit[erature] drops. They worked the polls on election day. They were constantly there. Their members were graphic artists who designed logos for me. . . . I met a woman who started cutting my hair. . . . She did a lot of little, funny, odd crazy things for me in terms of just helping me get through the physical part of [running] .

Her experience illustrates that in addition to supplying financial assistance and volunteer labor, American women assist female candidates through more informal means such as providing encouragement and moral support. A politician in the American sample, for example, says she openly encourages other women to pursue political office. After winning a spot in the local government, this respondent reports approaching other prominent women in her community and saying, "You'd make a great council member. Run against me, run for office. I'll help you. I'll tell you every trick I have." As her statement illustrates, many women believe that increasing the number of female politicians will improve working conditions and raise the level of acceptance for all women in politics.

In Britain, women active in the Labour party have also created political organizations to help women launch parliamentary careers. The Labour Women's Network, founded in 1988, sponsors seminars and workshops to provide prospective candidates with training in public speaking and media skills, instructions on writing a curriculum vitae for a selection committee, and information about public policies. This network also sponsors social events "to enable women to build up networking links" (Labour Women's Network, no date). In addition, EMILY's List U.K., modeled after its American counterpart, was organized in 1993 to encourage women to donate money to help Labour women launch political careers. The money raised is used to offset the costs of training, traveling, and child care, and even to help women buy a "professional" wardrobe. The skills training, networking functions, and financial assistance provided by these organizations are important ways that women have organized to provide other women with opportunities to overcome the disadvantages that may result from lack of involvement in, or exclusion from, the occupational and political networks that lead to political careers.

As members of the same political party, the women in the British sample draw on their sisters in the Labour party as an important source of political advice and social support. One MP discusses how Labour women in Parliament have formed an informal support system:

> . . . Tomorrow night all the [Labour] women MP's are going out for a meal together. It's unheard of to be so social. It's very noticeable. And the men that are coming in don't have that same kind of support. So once [women] do get here there is a wonderful sort of support system.

As her comment indicates, an important strategy for Labour women is to create support mechanisms to help them manage their minority status in Parliament.

From forming professional political organizations to raise campaign funds to providing volunteer labor and emotional support, the women in our studies recognize the barriers embedded in political institutions and find ways to bypass them. Organizing with other women, as these accounts indicate, enables women politicians to create opportunities both for themselves and for other aspiring candidates. In the following section we address a second way in which women respond to barriers by examining how they seek to change political practices and structures that disadvantage women.

Challenging Gendered Politics

Dorothy Smith (1990) asserts that for a "gender revolution" to happen, women need to recognize and challenge the ways that social institutions operate. This idea is echoed by many of the women in our studies, who see themselves as directly challenging the gendered barriers and practices of political institutions. For women in the U.S. sample, this challenge takes the form of presenting a visible female presence in government. As Labour MPs, the women in the British sample have the opportunity to join collectively to challenge the ingrained gender biases of Parliament and the Labour party.

Working for Visibility   For many women in the U.S. study, getting women into public office is the focus of their challenge to the barriers set before them. Three of the women report how being selected as delegates to the 1980 Democratic Convention gave them their first exposure to how women could be a more visible part of national level politics. The push to see more women in office was elevated to a national debate in 1991 when the televised Clarence Thomas–Anita Hill sexual harassment hearings drew public attention to the predominantly white male composition of the U.S. Senate and its masculinized style of procedure. A woman who was campaigning for a local office during the hearings recalls a conversation she had with a voter:

> I remember this one old gentleman telling me, "You know, I'm going to vote for every woman on the ballot. . . . I think we need to kick all the guys out and bring in a whole bunch of new women in there."

Taking advantage of the backlash from the Thomas–Hill hearings, organizations such as NOW have actively promoted women as political outsiders who are "different" and better than many male politicians. This strategy can be effective because of the structure of the U.S. political system, where running as a political outsider can make the most of the weak party system and candidate-focused elections. American women report being inspired to run by NOW's slogan, "Elect a Woman for a Change," a phrase which refers not only to the need for a visible female presence in government but also to the idea that women represent a new and positive influence on the political arena. A city councilwoman echoes many of the U.S. women's sentiments when she notes the difference between male and female politicians. She says:

> I think most women are in politics with the idea of doing specific things. It's not been the power trip for women that it is for a lot of men. I mean just to win, just to be there, just to have this position is a goal in itself for some men.

American respondents see the presence of women in political office as a necessary step in transforming politics. One respondent bluntly summarizes why women should become candidates by saying, "Because it makes changes. It's the only way you can make a change." Another American woman, observing the political scene in her district, remarks, "I can't understand why there isn't any woman up there who will run against him. Even if she loses . . . then she's bringing some sort of an awareness, an education process to the district."

Once elected, women see their presence in terms of a challenge to the prevailing gender order. One U.S. politician reflects on her struggles in office and concludes:

> It's tough finding myself dealing with all these huge male egos and they don't want to listen to me but they have to because I'm there. They're stuck with me for a two-year term and . . . bit by bit I am going to peck away at that."

As the statements of women in the American study illustrate, they feel their presence in office challenges cultural notions of what a politician should be. In addition, women politicians believe they are in a position to transform political institutions and policies. Through these responses they work to dismantle some of the barriers to female political participation and encourage other women to pursue public office.

Changing Institutions   Like their American counterparts, women politicians in the British study recognize that increasing women's visibility in elective office is essential to transforming politics. As MPs, most of the women studied are also actively involved in the process of creating a more "woman friendly" space in an institution long the exclusive domain of men. For example, Labour women challenge government institutions by attacking such seemingly harmless practices as the sitting hours of Parliament. Parliament is routinely in session until the late hours of the evening. This tradition clearly presents difficulties for anyone with family responsibilities, and may discourage people, particularly women with children, from seeking a seat. For these reasons, women Labour MPs have taken the reform of parliamentary sitting hours as one of their main objectives. A first-term MP talks about how this issue affects male and female MPs alike:

> [A reform in sitting hours] will actually probably make a lot of the male MPs better family people. Because here we are talking about making policies for families, yet most people here abandon their families from Monday to Friday. And they appear to boast about it and think it's part of being an MP.

Another significant way in which party members have sought to create more opportunities for women is by agitating for fundamental changes in the rules and operation of the Labour party. In 1993 pro-woman forces were successful in getting the party to support women's quotas for parliamentary candidates for the next general election to ensure women's increased representation. The quota system is a divisive issue among party members and Labour officials and they are still uncertain as to how the system will be enforced. Nevertheless, the knowledge that the party has committed itself to greater representation of women creates a sense of opportunity among many of the Labour women interviewed. Several MPs comment that women in the party are close to reaching a "critical mass" that will force greater recognition of women's agendas in national political debates. Party officials hope that these dramatic changes in party rules will promote the idea that "Labour is truly the party for women" and encourage British women to vote Labour in the next general election.

Whether they are working for a more visible female presence in government or challenging the rules and routines of parties and political institutions, most of the women in both countries found ways to respond to experiences of exclusion and discrimination. These women challenge cultural and structural barriers to female political participation by pooling their resources and encouraging other women to pursue political careers. As more women become involved in national, state, and local politics, they also have greater opportunities to challenge the political policies and practices that disadvantage women in all spheres of social life.

CONCLUSION

The stories of British and American women politicians illustrate how distinctions between "masculine" and "feminine" become institutionalized and have far-reaching effects. Masculine privilege is evident in the images of the typical politician and in the practices, rules, and values embedded in political institutions. The experiences of female politicians in both countries illustrate how women find themselves sanctioned for their appearance, sexuality, family responsibilities, and occupations and skills. By meeting the institutionalized code of gender expectations for appropriate feminine behavior, women find themselves disadvantaged when they "travel" into an arena designated for men—in this case, electoral politics.

Our studies also illustrate how British and American women often come to recognize that they are disadvantaged by cultural and structural barriers to female political participation. Though their responses to these barriers vary due to social and political contexts, women in both countries confront these gendered obstacles by working to create greater opportunities for women in politics. By increasing women's visibility and working to change the system from within, women continue to increase their political power and challenge the structure of gender relations that hinders their ambitions. Revealing how institutions are gendered can help people to understand more completely how male dominance is replicated, sustained, and challenged in our societies.

ACKNOWLEDGMENTS

The authors gratefully acknowledge the contributions and support of Melinda Goldner, Murray Low, Gail McGuire, Verta Taylor, and Nancy Whittier.

NOTES

1. Jo Reger's (1992) study of female politicians in the United States was conducted over a nine-month period in 1991–1992. It is based on interviews with nineteen members of the National Organization for Women (NOW) in the Midwest. NOW is a large, liberal feminist organization operating at the national and grassroots levels. Of the nineteen women interviewed, seventeen were Democrats, one was a Republican, and one was a member of a local third-party committee. Eight women held political office at the time of the interview. Including those that ran again and were not elected, a total of seven unsuccessful attempts were made for office. Three women had seriously considered races and decided not to run.

The sample of female Labour party politicians draws upon a larger research project of Abigail Halcli's exploring the relationship between the British women's movement and Labour party. This research was conducted in Britain during a five-month period in 1994. Thirteen of the thirty-six female Labour members of Parliament (MPs) who held office at this time were interviewed for this study. This paper also incorporates data from interviews with an unsuccessful female parliamentary candidate who hopes to run again in the next general election and a male MP.

2. Of the sixty-one female members of Parliament thirty-nine are Labour, nineteen are Conservatives, three are Liberal Democrats, and one is from the regional Scottish Nationalist party.

3. Of the forty-seven female U.S. representatives, seventeen are Republicans and thirty are Democrats. Of the eight senators, three are Republicans and five are Democrats.

4. As this paper was going to publication, new Labour party leader Tony Blair announced that quotas for female parliamentary candidates will be abandoned following the next general election, which is expected to occur in 1997. The party is currently undergoing rapid change in all areas of public policy, thus making it difficult to evaluate the potential impact of this particular policy at this time.

REFERENCES

Acker, Joan. 1990. "Hierarchies, jobs, bodies: A theory of gendered organizations." *Gender and Society* 4:139–58.

———. 1988. "Class, gender, and the relations of distribution." *Signs* 13:473–97.

Beechy, Virginia. 1988. "Rethinking the definition of work." Pp. 45–62 in *Feminization of the Labour Force: Paradoxes and Promises,* edited by Jane Jenson, Elisabeth Hagen, and Ceallaigh Reddy. New York: Oxford University Press.

Bernard, Jessie. 1981. "The good provider role." *American Psychologist* 38:1–12.

Burrell, Barbara. 1993. "Party decline, party transformation and gender politics: the USA." Pp. 291–308 in *Gender and Party Politics.* London: Sage.

Cockburn, Cynthia. 1987. *Women, Trade Unions, and Political Parties.* Fabian Research Series 349. London: College Hill Press Limited.

Connell, R. W. 1987. *Gender and Power.* Stanford, CA.: Stanford University Press.

Emily's List U.K. 1993. "Seats for Labour women." Pamphlet.

Hochschild, Arlie. 1989. *The Second Shift.* New York: Viking.

Kanter, Rosabeth Moss. 1977. *Men and Women of the Corporation.* New York: Basic Books.

Kavanagh, David. 1990. *British Politics: Continuities and Change.* Oxford, England: Oxford University Press.

Kessler-Harris, Alice. *Women Have Always Worked.* New York: McGraw-Hill.

Labour Women's Network. No date. "Labour women's network." Pamphlet.

Lorber, Judith. 1994. *Paradoxes of Gender.* New Haven, Conn.: Yale University Press.

Mills, Albert J., and Peta Tancred. 1992. *Gendering Organizational Analysis.* London: Sage.

Norris, Pippa. 1994. "Labour party quotas for women." Pp. 167–80 in *British Elections and Parties Yearbook 1994,* edited by David Broughton, David M. Farrell, David Denver, and Colin Rallings. London: Frank Cass.

Perrigo, Sarah. 1995. "Gender struggles in the British Labour party from 1979 to 1995." *Party Politics* 1:407–17.

PrimeTime Live, ABC. "The Fairer Sex?" October 7, 1993.

Reger, Joanne E. 1992. "Equality through the ballot box: An examination of social movement community, identity, and structure." Unpublished Master's thesis. Ohio State University.

Smith, Dorothy. 1990. *Conceptual Practices of Power: A Feminist Sociology of Knowledge.* Boston: Northeastern University Press.

Warde, Alan, and Kevin Hetherington. 1993. "A changing domestic division of labour? Issues of measurement and interpretation." *Work, Employment and Society* 7:23–45.

West, Candace, and Sarah Fenstermaker. 1995. "Doing difference." *Gender and Society* 9:8–37.

Witt, Linda, Karen M. Paget, and Glenna Matthews. 1994. *Running as a Woman: Gender and Power in American Politics.* New York: Free Press.

READING 46

Social Control, Civil Liberties, and Women's Sexuality

BETH E. SCHNEIDER and VALERIE JENNESS

"Crises and disasters have always held a special fascination for social scientists, at least in part because they expose the fundamental assumptions, institutional arrangements, social linkages, and cleavages that are normally implicit in the social order."[1] The AIDS epidemic is no exception. The biological and medical imperatives associated with HIV have been effectively translated into a moral panic.[2] This panic has in turn uncovered significant social processes and arrangements related to sexuality, gender, and social control.

Not surprisingly, the AIDS epidemic has brought with it repetitive calls that "somebody do something." Historically, epidemics typically evoke demands for some form of managerial response and some mobilized effort to control identifiable, projected, and even unknown hazards.[3] In particular, epidemics inspire new public policy, as well as the reform of extant public policy. Again, the AIDS epidemic has proven to be no exception.

In this paper we focus on several public responses that have emerged purportedly to assist in the control of "the AIDS problem." Specifically, we focus on those responses that have consequences for the expansion of social control mechanisms and the potential denial of civil liberties. Although the AIDS epidemic in the United States has touched every segment of society, it is increasingly becoming an illness of women, as well as of racial, ethnic, and sexual minorities. There is no reason to presume that this trend will reverse as the epidemic continues through the nineties and into the next century.[4] Thus, our overarching

concern is with how public policy responses to the multitude of threats born of AIDS are structured by gender and sexuality.

The AIDS epidemic has inspired and justified interventionist policies on the part of the state to regulate not only the exchange of bodily fluids, but the social organization of gender and sexuality as well. To illustrate, we focus on public policy surrounding prostitutes and sex education for adolescents, both of which have consequences for the civil liberties of girls and women and the social control of female sexuality through the reinforcement of notions of "good girls" and "bad girls." This particular comparison permits an examination of the complexity of state responses to AIDS and illustrates differing strategies of social control undertaken by two institutions: the legal and the educational.

Some public policies implicitly or explicitly seek to control sexuality and gender; these are our concern in the remainder of the chapter. Different laws and other forms of public policy inspired by the AIDS epidemic operate to interrupt, forbid, and often punish the existence or enactment of particular sexualities. We examine two quite divergent cases—policy surrounding prostitutes in the United States and the policy and practice of AIDS education—for what each reveals about the social control of female sexuality through the construction of "good girls" and "bad girls." We conclude with a discussion of the role that law and other forms of public policy play in redefining social control in general and, more specifically, privacy in light of the "AIDS crisis." We consider what places, spaces, and matters remain private and thus outside the purview of the state, for girls and young women, as well as how processes of protection, intrusion, and redefinition are bound by and reflect the fact that AIDS is structured by race, class, gender, and sexuality.[5]

THE AIDS EPIDEMIC AS A DISEASE AND AS A MORAL PANIC

The evolution of AIDS resembles the social construction of such diseases as leprosy, syphilis, tuberculosis, and cholera.[6] In each of these epidemics, the evolution and consequences of the disease were tied not only to its biological characteristics, but also to the socially constructed meanings attached to the disease. From the beginning, many interested parties, including some units of the state, have sought to make their interpretations of HIV and AIDS dominant. Scientists, physicians, afflicted groups, government agencies, religious officials, politicians, social workers, and other claims makers concerned with the disease have been and continue to be quick to formulate and disseminate interpretations of the disease.[7]

The melange of meanings surrounding the AIDS epidemic has merged to produce a "moral panic." In simplest terms, a moral panic can be thought of as a widespread feeling on the part of the public—or some relevant public—that something is terribly wrong in society because of the moral failure of a specific group of individuals. The result is that a subpopulation is defined as the enemy. Cohen describes the evolution and consequences of a moral panic:

> A condition, episode, person or group of persons emerges to become defined as a threat to societal values and interests: Its nature is presented in a stylized and stereotypic fashion by the mass media; moral barricades are manned by editors, bishops, politicians, and other right-thinking people; socially accredited experts pronounce their diagnoses and solutions; ways of coping evolve, or (more often) are resorted to. . . . Sometimes the panic passes over and is forgotten, except in folklore or collective memory; at other times it has more serious and long-lasting repercussions and might produce such changes as those in legal and social policy.[8]

Such "changes as those in legal and social policy" are necessarily intertwined with the negotiation of power and morality and, by extension, are consequential for major societal processes of social change.

Moral panics are inevitably linked to, and thus consequential for, formal systems of social control. They explicitly or implicitly challenge existing systems of control by defining them as failing or defunct. The consequence is that mandates for reform in legal and social policy are rendered timely and legitimate. Wars, epidemics, and other such moral panic-generating events have, at different points in history, served to justify the expansion of old or the introduction of new mechanisms of social control. These emergent forms of social control often constitute significant incursions on the rights of individuals or groups.

Calls for reform in legal and social policy that are consequential for individual civil liberties are especially pronounced when moral panics are tied, in some real or imagined way, to issues of sexuality.[9] Gayle Rubin, for example, has argued that "it is precisely at times such as these [the era of AIDS], when we live with the possibility of unthinkable destruction, that people are likely to become dangerously crazed about sexuality."[10] As a consequence, regulations emerge to control public and private spaces associated with sexuality and eroticism (such as attempts to close bathhouses frequented by gay men or refusal to perform abortions for HIV-positive women).

The AIDS crisis has generated contemporary discourses in which the social conditions attached to the epidemic serve to rationalize formal and informal social control mechanisms on sexuality and gender, ostensibly in the name of safeguarding the public's health. But this has not been done without historical precedent and without overcoming material and symbolic obstacles.

In an effort to make sense of the variety of ways in which history, culture, and politics frame responses to AIDS, Moerkerk and Aggleton[11] identify four overall approaches that nations in Europe have taken to deal with AIDS. Three of these approaches—the pragmatic, the political, and the biomedical—have particular relevance for our understanding of the mechanisms put in place in the United States to manage female prostitutes and to educate female adolescents. The *pragmatic response* emphasizes provision of crucial education and information, whatever that might be for a group of people, and the need to protect the afflicted. It relies on a cultural consensus and avoids coercive forms of social control. In contrast, the *political response* is based in judgment of what is politically possible and consistent with the beliefs of the nation's leadership. It relies on the law to regulate behavior, and consequently it interprets AIDS prevention as a mechanism for producing behavior it considers desirable. The *biomedical response* is limited; it relies exclusively on medical personnel to determine policy and shows little interest in the involvement of affected groups. As our analyses indicate, each response, often in combination with others, is evident in the United States, especially in the control of young women by educational and legal institutions.

PUBLIC HEALTH AND CIVIL LIBERTIES: A DIFFICULT DILEMMA

The extension of formal social control mechanisms by the state is not done automatically in times of epidemics because, as Brandt has documented, epidemics marshal two sets of values that are "highly prized by our culture": the fundamental civil liberties of the individual and the role of the state in assuring public welfare.[12] From a public policy point of view, individual civil liberties and public health concerns are generally conceived as values in competition with each other. There is a tension between the extension of social control in the name of "protecting public health" and the prohibition of such extension in the name of "preserving individual civil liberties," especially those related to notions of "privacy" as an aspect of personal liberty protected by the Fourth and Fourteenth Amendments of the U.S. Constitution.[13]

This tension is especially pronounced in situations or contexts where sexuality is salient. For example, the state still interferes in the practice of homosexual sodomy and other sexual acts. However, after providing an extensive review of relevant legislation at state and federal levels, Stoddard and Rieman conclude that, under recent Supreme Court decisions, the right to privacy has effectively precluded or sharply limited governmental interference with some personal decisions surrounding sexuality (such as the use of contraception or access to abortion). They warn that this trend is open to reversal in light of the many hazards posed by AIDS: "the government undoubtedly could treat persons who carry the HIV differently from others for some reasons."[14] The same holds for people who are "at risk" for HIV or presumed to be carriers of the virus. Indeed, everything from tattooing on the buttocks to more drastic segregation measures, such as forced quarantining, have been proposed, entertained, and occasionally adopted.[15] As a result, over the course of the epidemic, the rights of the individual have not invariably prevailed and privacy has, at least from a policy point of view, been redefined.[16]

Although it is clear that prostitutes, frequently considered women in need of control, have been particularly susceptible to constraints on their civil liberties, children are rarely understood in these terms. Children's civil liberties are effectively unacknowledged. Indeed, the treatment of children, especially their education and protection, rests far less securely on any right to privacy. Children and adolescents often need, by law, their parents' permission for most of what adults take for granted as sexual—to receive contraceptive devices at school, to attend sex education classes, to seek an abortion. Familial and educational institutions exercise physical and legal control over how young people learn about sexuality and gender. Schools are social control mechanisms that reinforce patriarchal relations of male domination and female submission. In the face of the AIDS epidemic, the ideological apparatus of schools extends social control over its charges by framing, constraining, and ultimately censoring what is thought about AIDS and how it comes to be understood.

PRIVATE SPACES, PUBLIC INTRUSIONS: THE CASE OF PROSTITUTION

There has been a virtual explosion in the formulation of policy designed to control the spread of HIV and the people who are infected. Laws have been passed by the U.S. Congress and state legislatures; the courts have issued various pronouncements; and businesses, government agencies, prisons, schools, hospitals, and other such public settings have developed workplace policy. Policy proposals with implications for civil liberties in general and privacy in particular include, but certainly are not limited to requiring blood screening of prisoners or military recruits; banning people with AIDS from being restaurant workers; prohibiting seropositive persons from donating blood; closing gay bathhouses; banning homosexual sodomy; quarantining "suspect" groups, especially prostitutes; dismissing from federal jobs employees suspected of being seropositive; and refusing to care for or provide shelter for PWAs.[17] This list, of course, is not exhaustive of the measures that have been proposed or implemented to control AIDS by restricting liberty and, in some cases, redefining privacy. (In this volume, see the chapters by Hunter and Pies for other examples directly relevant to women's lives.)

Throughout the AIDS epidemic, calls for mass and mandatory testing have been put forth. Initial calls for mass testing and an administrative system developed around testing were expanded in a context of considerable ambiguity over test accuracy, counseling procedures, and the relationship between knowledge of test results and behavior or attitudes. Moreover, these calls seem to point in the direction of quarantining and other forms of detention.[18] However, such calls for testing are not equally applicable to all citizens. They have selectively targeted specific groups—usually gay men, intravenous drug users, prisoners, immigrants, pregnant women, and sex workers.

Implicating Female Prostitutes in AIDS

Stereotypes about women—especially African-American women, pregnant women, and female prostitutes—have been infused with policy proposals. Perhaps the most obvious case of social and legal policy embedded in gender and sexuality is that surrounding sex work. From the beginning, legislation supporting forced quarantining, reporting, screening, and prosecution of sex workers has been proposed and adopted. The biological characteristics of AIDS, combined with the way in which the disease has been socially constructed, almost guaranteed that prostitutes would be implicated in the social problem of AIDS. In an article entitled "Prostitutes and AIDS: Public Policy Issues," Cohen, Alexander, and Wofsy concluded that "prostitutes have often been held responsible for the spread of AIDS into the heterosexual population in this country."[19] This is not surprising given that AIDS has been conceived of primarily as a sexually transmitted disease and was, at least originally, connected with "promiscuous" sex and "deviant" lifestyles.[20] The historical association of prostitution with venereal disease, unfettered sex, and moral unworthiness remains strong.[21] The prostitute is either dangerous, bad, or both. In short, the historical and contemporary context within which female prostitutes have operated ensured that they would be implicated in the AIDS epidemic, even prior to epidemiological evidence justifying such a focus.[22]

As early as 1984, medical authorities were investigating the possibility that prostitutes could spread AIDS into the heterosexual population. Meanwhile, the media continued to spread suspicion about prostitution as an avenue of transmission for the disease. For example, on an episode of the nationally televised "Geraldo Show" entitled "Have Prostitutes Become the New Typhoid Marys?" the host offered the following introduction to millions of viewers:

> The world's oldest profession may very well have become among its deadliest. A recent study backed by the federal Centers for Disease Control found that one third of New York's prostitutes now carry the AIDS virus. If this study mirrors the national trend, then the implications are as grim as they are clear. Sleeping with a prostitute may have become a fatal attraction. . . . A quick trick may cost you $20, but you may be paying for it with the rest of your life.[23]

Supporting Rivera's introduction, a New York-based AIDS counselor appearing on the show argued:

> A high percentage of prostitutes infected with HIV pass it on to their sexual partners who are johns or the tricks, a lot of whom are married or have sex with a straight woman. I think this is how the AIDS epidemic is passed into the heterosexual population.[24]

He argued further that working prostitutes testing positive for HIV are guilty of manslaughter and/or attempted murder. In a relatively short period of time, claims like this became commonplace. Moreover, claims focusing on prostitution were and still are focused on female prostitutes to the exclusion of male prostitutes, and on female prostitutes but not their customers.

Legislation as Social Control

Like the media, legislators have turned their attention to female prostitution as an avenue of transmission. In the name of preventing HIV transmission, legislation that intrudes into private, consensual sexual relations has sprung up around the country. A number of proposals have been introduced and adopted that, in one way or another, make it a crime for someone who is antibody positive to engage in sex with anyone else, regardless of the degree to which the behavior is mutually voluntary, the use of condoms, and the failure of the uninfected participant to test seropositive.[25] Luxenburg and Guild have shown that, as early as 1987, more than 140 AIDS-specific laws had been passed across the United States. Approximately a dozen of these criminalized the act of *exposing* another individual to the HIV. In addition to the emergence of new legislation, jurisdictions that have no AIDS-specific criminal laws have begun to rely on traditional criminal laws (attempted murder, aggravated assault, and the like) to prosecute HIV-positive individuals who engage in behaviors that put seronegatives at risk for acquiring the HIV infection—even when the risky contact is conscious and voluntary on the part of the seronegatives.

The introduction of AIDS-related legislation has posed a significant legal threat to female prostitutes. Many governmental and medical establishments have reacted to AIDS with calls for increased regulation of prostitution in the form of registration, mandatory AIDS testing, and prison sentences for those carrying antibodies to the virus.[26] In the mid-eighties and into the nineties, many states considered legislation requiring arrested prostitutes to be tested for HIV infection. By 1988, some states had introduced and passed legislation requiring mandatory testing of arrested prostitutes. Georgia, Florida, Utah, and

Nevada were among the first states to legislate the forcible testing of arrested prostitutes; those who test positive can then be subject to arrest on felony charges. These mandatory testing laws in effect create a state registry of infected prostitutes, while the felony charges could create a quarantine situation if prostitutes are kept in isolation while awaiting trial.

Coinciding with the introduction of this legislation, many judges and district attorneys began contemplating and occasionally charging arrested prostitutes who tested positive for HIV with attempted manslaughter and murder. In July 1990, for example, an Oakland, California, prostitute was arrested after *Newsweek* ran a photo of her and quoted her saying that she contracted the deadly virus from contaminated needles but continued to engage in prostitution. According to newspaper reports, Oakland police asked a judge to force the woman to be tested for HIV and pressured the district attorney's office to pursue an attempted manslaughter charge if she tested positive. The arresting officer stated, "I think her actions, with the knowledge that if you're going to get AIDS you're going to die, is a malicious act akin to firing into a crowd or at a passing bus."[27] Although the judge denied the charge, the woman was held for a number of days while the possibility was contemplated. As another example, in Orlando, Florida, an HIV-infected prostitute was charged with manslaughter even though she used a condom with all of her clients and despite the finding that all of her clients who had been tested were negative.[28]

In essence, the AIDS epidemic has led to increased social control of prostitutes, especially in the form of repressive legislation and increasingly punitive legal sanctions. Such changes reflect the commonly held belief that prostitutes constitute a "vector of transmission" for AIDS into the heterosexual population; thus, legislation and increased legal sanctions have been pursued in the name of controlling the spread of AIDS. Female, not male, prostitutes are arrested, even though male prostitutes are much more likely to be infected.[29] Social policy continues to be used to enforce select moral positions[30]—in this case, the control of female rather than male sexuality. Such laws effectively constitute a social x-ray, one that classifies individuals as mainstream or peripheral, normal or deviant.

Resistance

Some have suggested that the introduction and implementation of AIDS-related statutes and "enhanced penalties" is merely an attempt to mollify public fear of AIDS spreading into the "population at large."[31] Whatever the state's intention, this testing of certain special groups without consent, at both the state and the federal level, has not gone uncontested.[32] The existence of resistance underscores the control of women's sexuality; it is a sign that women are directly experiencing either the reality or the threat of constraints on their sexual practice.

In order to resist the scapegoating of prostitutes, COYOTE and other U.S. prostitute advocacy groups, using scientific studies and research to lend legitimacy to their assessment, went public with two main arguments: (1) that the rate of HIV infection among prostitutes, compared to that among other identifiable groups, is relatively low; and (2) that, regardless of infection rates, it is a violation of prostitutes' civil rights to selectively impose mandatory testing on prostitutes if they are arrested. Additionally, they publicly and persistently explained that sex workers are not at risk for AIDS because of sex work per se. As the codirector of the International Committee for Prostitute Rights explained in the late 1980s:

> They [prostitutes] are demanding the same medical confidentiality and choice as other citizens. . . . They are contesting policies which separate them from other sexually active people, emphasizing that charging money for sex does not transmit disease.[33]

An editorial on this issue by COYOTE's media liaison argues a kind of prostitute exceptionalism:

> Many readers are well aware that prostitutes practice safe sex techniques, using condoms for oral services as well as intercourse, and quite often restricting their activities to manual gratification. Many prostitutes emphasize massage, still others combine fantasy stimulation (S&M, etc.) with minimal physical contact. There is much a "working girl" can do to assure her health and the health of her clients, and we have done it. Most of us followed safe sex practices long before the onset of this epidemic.[34]

These assertions suggest that what separates prostitutes from women in general is higher rates of condom use. In essence, these sex work organizations hold that sex work per se is not responsible for the spread of HIV; viruses do not discriminate between those who exchange money for sex and those who do not. When prostitutes are infected, intravenous drug use is the primary cause.

In promoting the notion that prostitutes do not represent a pool of contagion, COYOTE and other sex worker groups regularly distributed public announcements and issued press releases; attended local, state, national, and international conferences on AIDS; and staged protests to oppose legislation requiring the mandatory testing of prostitutes. At legislative hearings they protested mandatory testing of prostitutes for HIV on the grounds that selective testing is discriminatory and a violation of individuals'—in this case prostitutes'—civil rights.

The AIDS epidemic poses a multitude of threats for prostitutes, their organizations, and their movement to decriminalize and legitimate prostitution. It has siphoned personnel and resources from sex work organizations; organizational agendas and activities have shifted in response to the way in which AIDS has been constructed as a social problem implicating sex workers.

But, at the same time, the AIDS epidemic has served to legitimate prostitutes' rights organizations. It has provided prostitutes and their advocates with financial, rhetorical, and institutional resources. The AIDS epidemic has also brought public officials and prostitutes' rights organizations together in direct and indirect ways. As a result of concern over the spread of AIDS into the heterosexual population, government agencies such as state legislatures, the Centers for Disease Control, and local departments of health have turned to prostitutes' rights organizations for assistance.

Those concerned with halting the spread of AIDS have enlisted the help of prostitutes in investigating the role of prostitution in the spread of the disease. For example, COYOTE applied for and received funds to begin an AIDS prevention project for prostitutes. This new entity, the California Prostitutes Education Program (CAL-PEP) is, as its statement of purpose reads:

> an education project developed by members of COYOTE, the prostitutes' rights advocacy organization, to provide educational programs for prostitutes and the interested public on various aspects of prostitution. Our first project is an AIDS prevention project designed and implemented by prostitutes, ex-prostitutes, and prostitutes' rights advocates to help prostitutes to protect themselves and their clients from AIDS.

CAL-PEP outreach workers go into the stroll districts where street prostitutes work and distribute condoms, spermicides, bleach bottles, and educational materials, and talk to prostitutes about how they can work safely. CAL-PEP outreach workers take a van into the stroll districts, and the prostitutes are invited to come into the van, which is fully equipped with HIV-prevention items, to rest and to talk about how to keep themselves and their clients free of AIDS. In addition, CAL-PEP sponsors support groups and monthly workshops in a hotel room in the stroll district for prostitutes and their regular customers, safe-sex workshops at the county jail, and other programs. (See the interview with Gloria Lockett in this volume.)

This is obviously an outcome replete with contradictions. The state is not dealing with the problem of AIDS and prostitutes in a singular and consistent fashion. It has utilized what Moerkerk and Aggleton call the pragmatic and political responses. Prostitutes are scapegoats and criminals, but also allies with a unique constituency to educate. Women leaders of these organizations, which in certain ways have been made stronger by the struggle around legal control and HIV prevention work, are nevertheless forced to sustain political work at odds with their original intention to free prostitutes from surveillance by health and legal authorities and promote a less constrained sexuality.

SEX EDUCATION: TO BE OR NOT TO BE, AND IN WHAT FORM?

Unlike prostitutes, other young women face a different set of social control mechanisms. Adolescent girls, even from the most privileged backgrounds, do not have the freedom and resources to organize on their own behalf, and rarely do they have strong advocates. Their families and schools, the primary socializing institutions of children, exercise physical and legal control over what and how they learn about sexuality and accomplish gender. In the face of the AIDS epidemic, the ideological apparatus of schools, which contributes to the perpetuation of race and gender inequality, extends social control over its charges by framing, constraining, and in fact censoring what is thought about AIDS and how it comes to be understood. In that process, it specifies some of the parameters of female sexuality.

Sex education is the vehicle through which children and adolescents learn some portion of what they know about HIV/AIDS, and that learning has not been accomplished (when it has occurred at all) unproblematically. Prevention and control of the spread of HIV requires discussions of sexual and drug-using activities, and sex/health education is a primary institution through which youth are advised whether, as well as how and when, to be sexual beings. In the process, it cues them to what is "safer," "safe," and "risky sex."

Schools respond to AIDS with a hybrid of the political, pragmatic, and biomedical approaches. An examination of how these programs come about in schools reveals a systematic preoccupation with heterosexuality and with the social control of young women's sexuality. These are evident in the multiple discourses of community political struggles over the control of the schools' curricula and over the specific content of prevention materials. Some of these extensions of social control are patently obvious, while others are more implicit. Their limitations are revealed whenever they are resisted, when teenagers provide education for each other in the form of theater, make their own AIDS videos, or join with groups like ACT-UP in the distribution of condoms.

Community Struggles, Social Control, and Censorship

AIDS education for young people was initially proposed in a climate of fear that reflected deep social and cultural anxieties about the disease and its transmissibility. Most importantly, homosexuality and its central symbolic attachment to AIDS rendered particularly problematic the matter of the structure and the content of AIDS education in the public schools.[35] School officials anticipated controversy as parents considered the prospects of such programs for their children. The expectations of trouble were not without cause: legislators were publicly unwilling to support mandatory AIDS education packages for children, teachers harbored memories of painful struggles to introduce sex education, and all school administrators wanted to avoid antagonizing community groups who oppose homosexuality and birth control and favor either no sex education programs or teaching of traditional values about sex.[36]

There has not been a consensus about the need for AIDS education programs (nor about their specific content) in the public schools. By the mid-1980s, the Christian Right's campaign to gain control of the nation's school boards was underway. Among the issues around which its efforts to gain control revolve are bilingual education, the teaching of evolution, affirmative action, and the existence or form of AIDS education and condom distribution. For the last decade, conservative parents have been particularly active in banning books and other materials they found offensive.[37] In the 1992–1993 New York City struggle over school board membership, traditional values groups, reaching out to the Latino community—usually one of their targets—argued that the city, through its "elite" school board (and its approval of condom distribution and its Rainbow curriculum), intended to turn their children into homosexuals.[38]

This sort of censorship has a chilling effect on the search by women, including young women, to understand their own sexuality. While early twentieth-century censorship shielded women from knowledge of birth control, the current round is preoccupied with gay and lesbian depictions and expressions of women's rebellion.

In spite of the real and anticipated trouble, most school systems have offered some form of AIDS education to their students. They have engaged in complicated debates and a variety of institutional maneuvers to structure a nonproblematic AIDS education curriculum.[39] A recent study by the Sex Information and Education Council of the U.S. reported that, although every state in 1993 required or recommended AIDS education, students were getting incomplete information from unprepared teachers. Only 11 states provided "balanced information about safe sex" and numerous states prohibited any discussion of homosexuality. Their summary suggests that only three states provided good programs that provided more than biological information, explained sexual orientation, and discussed a range of safe-sex behaviors and strategies.[40]

Our study of a school system in California reveals a variety of these maneuvers, "deflection strategies" taken by accident or design to reduce the probability of criticism and interference.[41] These strategies include special parental permission forms, preview nights for parents, integration of the AIDS materials into already-existing curricula, cooptation of potential student and parent troublemakers, utilizing the "objective" approach in presentations, and avoiding all discussion of homosexuality. Each strategy enhances the influence of parents and diminishes accordingly the power and participation of students. It is the last two strategies that deserve more detailed attention here since they serve very directly to shape the contours and content of the materials presented to young women.

Gender and the Biomedical Model in Sex Education

The discourses of expertise position recipients of educational messages in a way that disables their ability to actually apply information to their lives, and leaves them liable for failing to have understood that they were to have appropriately responded to the "danger" of AIDS.[42]

The dominant view of adolescents' sex education and sexuality, heavily influenced by the fields of medicine and psychology, has shaped HIV prevention practice. Adolescents are often understood as "other," as strange beings, with those from racial/ethnic groups viewed as particularly so. The fields of medicine and psychology put forward essentially deterministic models of social behavior that are simply not flexible enough to capture the variation and dynamism of sexuality and social interaction. The supposedly value-free behaviorism that provides information about anatomy, reproductive physiology, contraception, and a limited variety of sexual practices assumes that scientific knowledge about sexuality is nonjudgmental and can be used easily by students in making their own choices about sexual behavior. It conveys the message that heterosexual intercourse is normal behavior that can be engaged in responsibly and calmly with the use of contraception and abortions when birth control fails.

This approach is, or should be, unsatisfactory to feminist parents, educators, and young women themselves. We believe that the limits of the debate about what students should and should not have is premised on the view that they are not capable of critical thinking, emotional self-discipline, and intellectual self-direction. It isolates sexuality from other social relations. It focuses on organs or viruses with little link to humans' relationships to one another or the historical context. It tends to ignore the continued, persistent discrepancies between young women and men regarding attitudes toward birth control, sex, and relationships. As research on classroom interaction continues to indicate, male domination is uncritically accepted as natural, as an important topic but never as one requiring critical discussion or presented as in any way problematic.[43] Hence, most of these efforts ignore the unequal power relations between men and women that structure heterosexuality.

Moreover, the models utilized in public health campaigns teach biomedical safe sex guidelines as the basis of individuals' everyday behavior. But neither of the two prevailing models deals directly with common-sense knowledge about AIDS and its relationship to AIDS prevention. And it is how these youth understand AIDS that is crucial to what they do. For example, Maticka-Tyndale's study shows gender differences in the ways in which young women and men assess the risk of intercourse based on their views of its consequences. As she describes it:

For women, coitus, even before AIDS, carried a variety of risks; they commonly cited both risks of pregnancy and emotional hurt. Relative to other risks, HIV was the least likely to occur . . . For men, the experience of coitus generally lacked any prior sense of risk. Lacking a concept of risky coitus, men spoke of risk by ranking coitus against other sexual activities [such as anal intercourse].[44]

Finally, in high schools AIDS is seen as an aspect of health and family services, not as a political or historical matter. Public policy issues and historical debates are typically not discussed. Students consequently are shielded from an understanding of what is controversial in what they may be learning or doing and from a more conscious understanding of the political significance of condoms, contraception, and sex. The passive, "objective" stance of most education prevents the expression of opposing or alternative perspectives. The family life-planning classes, though the site of whatever sex education is offered in California high schools, emphasize pregnancy and disease. They are not about sex; indeed, they de-eroticize sexuality. When schools avoid presenting alternative perspectives, including those that incorporate a discussion of eroticism and pleasure, they continue to perpetuate existing class, race, gender, and sexuality hierarchies.

Nevertheless, adolescents have learned the public health information presented to them. Considerable research over the last five years has confidently concluded that adolescents have high levels of knowledge about AIDS and can voice the biomedical position about the role of condoms in AIDS prevention.[45] However, numerous studies show that the major rule they follow to prevent HIV infection is to try not to have sexual intercourse (unprotected and protected) with an infected partner, a determination requiring trust in a specific partner and/or strong faith in one's own ability to judge people based on reputation or appearance.

Gender differences in sexual scripts are also evident. Trust means something different for women and men. Young women expect young men to disclose prior risky sexual activities; men expect that women with whom they are sexual have had no prior sexual activities.[46] That is, they expect them to be "good girls." Since condoms are still seen as primarily for contraception, there are serious gender differences in the ways women and men approach the introduction of condoms. Women, presumed to be using contraception, may be queried about their lack of other birth control and/or about their own or their partners' infection status. Men may introduce condoms in the guise of protecting their partner and in fact be protecting themselves. Young heterosexual women, similar to older women who have been studied in efforts to improve AIDS interventions, fear the regular use of condoms as an insult to their male partner. Most couples—prostitutes with boyfriends included—determine a point in their relationship when they stop using condoms, a point representing deepening trust and commitment. Indeed, the decision to use safe sex is based on perceived HIV status of the partner or on quality of feelings. (For further discussion of these issues in this volume, see the chapter by Sosnowitz.)[47]

AIDS Videos and Social Control

Videos are a major educational tool through which adults bring children AIDS education. In many school systems, a video with an hour or two of discussion may be all the AIDS education students receive.[48] In the best situations, the program around AIDS takes several days, speakers from Planned Parenthood or the local AIDS project appear, and students get to role-play some of what they have learned. But these elaborations on a basic program are rare. The package as a whole usually fosters heterosexism, and every point in the process has its gendered content or outcome.

An examination of four of the commonly used videos available to high schools in the district we studied indicates the variety of ways in which gender inequality and gender difference is reproduced. When given a choice from among these videos, parents tend to select the ones produced by the Red Cross, "A Letter from Brian, and Don't Forget Sherrie," targeted primarily to white students, and "Don't Forget Sherrie," targeted to their African-Americans counterparts.[49] In each, a young woman or man learns that a former sex partner is HIV-infected and near death. The friends of the just-notified teenager try to figure out what all of them should think and do about their future sexual or drug use behavior in light of the information that one of them might be infected. The two videos carry a long disclaimer on a black screen:

> [This video deals] with teens and others discussing sexual activity and AIDS prevention in frank terms. The film deals with the threat of the disease, AIDS, for teenagers, and how they can avoid getting the disease.

It is followed by the American Red Cross position: Abstinence is highly recommended for young single teenagers, and education regarding sex should be provided within the family with supplementary materials from the schools and community organizations. "Sex education should be based on religious, ethical, legal, and moral foundations."

"Sex, Drugs, and HIV" takes a less apologetic and fearful approach. This video uses popular music, an actress familiar to young people, and an interracial cast. It is divided into three parts: "Relax, AIDS is Hard to Get," a section intended to overcome myths about mosquitoes, touching, and other forms of casual contact; "You Can Get AIDS By Sharing Needles," a brief section whose sole point is that shooting drugs is bad, "so don't shoot up"; and a last section, "AIDS Can Be a Sexually Transmitted Disease."

Each of the videos talks about the "facts" or the "truth" about AIDS. "Sex, Drugs, and HIV," a 19-minute video, goes so far as to conclude with "That's it. That's all you need to know." This is not only simplistic, it is misleading. Most videos take approximately one minute to explain that "AIDS is caused by a virus," one that infects a person and causes the failure of the immune system. And in most videos one confident speaker or the narrator refers to AIDS as a fatal disease.

Even though videos try to use the language of the teenagers to whom they are geared, the language is not believable in its description of risk behaviors. Not only do young girls and boys not use the same language to talk about sex, virtually none call their own practices vaginal, oral, or anal intercourse. Typically only penile-vaginal intercourse "counts" as "going all the way." This is particularly problematic for AIDS education. As Melese-d'Hospital found in her study with adolescents, many are staying "virgins" as a means to avoid HIV. However, the meaning of virginity, what it includes and what it does not, is consequential. The concept is a marker for what is acceptable sexual behavior. For young women, virginity was "located in the vagina" and related to pregnancy, a greater and more visible concern to them than HIV.[50]

Even in those videos that move away from simply telling the facts to more emotion-laden interactions, it is highly unusual to find serious interaction between males and females: males talk to males, females talk to females. "Sex, Drugs, and HIV" has two such scenes. Three girls are stretching in a gymnasium. They are talking about true love, about whether to have sex, about which birth control to use. One suggests that her friend, who has never before had intercourse, should use the pill; the third counters that pills do not protect against disease or AIDS. The young woman without the experience of vaginal intercourse is convinced to use a condom but worries about being rejected. The friend with the handy condom responds: "Sit and talk to him. He cares about you. . . . If you can't talk to him about birth control, you shouldn't have sex with him. . . . If you're not sure you want to have sex, you should wait." This enactment, one of the best of its kind in this genre, ignores any direct acknowledgment of the normative context of gender inequality and gendered differences in knowledge about sex.

Conversation among the males in both "Sex, Drugs, and HIV" and "A Letter from Brian" show young men trying to persuade one another to use condoms, with one attempting to best the others by claiming always to have used them. This is a positive and important effort to change the norms of the group. Yet it does not deal directly with the variety of myths surrounding condom use or the interactional and emotional matters at stake in sexual encounters.

The videos are not sex-positive. No other sexual practices are discussed, though adolescents engage in a great many other activities. Consistent with the political approach to the control of AIDS, as described in the Moerkerk and Appleton study, no acknowledgment is made of the possibility of same-sex experience or of the existence of gay and lesbian students. And, in these and other videos, vague use is made of such terms as *love, respect, commitment* and *monogamy* without any attempt to operationalize them or recognize their multiple meanings. Adolescents are treated as if they are one group, in spite of the strong evidence of diverse and overlapping communities of youth even within similar schools and neighborhoods.[51]

As many women involved in AIDS prevention work have already noted, women are expected to take responsibility for what happens sexually. Many of the videos are addressed to young women, even when they aren't explicitly targeted to them. For example, in the "Brian" video, the U.S. surgeon general offers this confusing statement:

> There is another way where you don't need to worry about condoms and that's to have a mutually faithful relationship. In other words, find someone worthy of your love and respect. Give that person both and expect the same from him and remain as faithful to him as he is to you. [If you do this] you will never have to read about AIDS again in your life because it doesn't apply to you.

Aside from the head-in-the-sand attitude, the use of the male pronoun implies that women are the only ones likely to be "good," that they have the burden to make men safe in any relational or sexual situation, and that monogamy protects.

Finally, there are the absences. These videos ignore entrenched fears about homosexuals or unconscious fears about death, though these can surely be said to frame the reception of the facts of AIDS education. With the exception of "Sex, Drugs, and HIV," neither compassion nor "complicity with discrimination"[52] are taught in these and most other HIV-prevention videos. Hence, the strategies of deflection used to shape the content, particularly the avoidance of discussion of homosexuality, highlight the hidden curriculum of schools in their transmission of dominant values and beliefs about heterosexuality. Students are sheltered from the controversial nature of the material presented to them and subsequently rendered politically ignorant.

Working from a feminist framework, a good sex education program would not be simply biological; it would be a political program to change gender relations, free women from emotionally and physically debilitating inequality, and foster positive values about sex. If social relations are bad, so are sexual ones. This kind of sex education would provide what young women need: lessons that women are not just victims of sexuality, that they can construct their own sexual identities and pleasures. This would require a significant restructuring not only of the substance of AIDS education, but also of the organizations responsible for delivering it—the schools. This is no small feat, in that it requires greater recognition of institutionalized gender inequality, including that which is routinely affirmed in the classroom.

Although this sort of sex/AIDS education is not available in any complete form anywhere, some student initiatives are moving in this direction. Students often perceive that part of adults' interest in AIDS education is its potential for containing adolescent sexuality.[53] Young women have been integrally involved in, if not actually leaders of, a number of innovative, usually nonschool-based AIDS prevention programs, such as theater groups supported by local Planned Parenthood organizations and off-campus condom distribution efforts initiated by ACT-UP. At the college level, young women are the major players in most AIDS education efforts.

DISCUSSION

While the cultural and economic implications of the AIDS epidemic are certainly far reaching, so are the consequences for the social organization of sex and gender. Through a logic born of the current epidemic, forms of regulatory intervention that might in other circumstances appear excessive can now be justified in the name of prevention. Such justifications are embedded in, and seemingly cannot be divorced from, larger social systems of gender and sexuality.

The social organization of gender and sexuality is policed by laws and public policy that oversee and regulate our sexual desires, exchanges, images, and identities.[54] The AIDS epidemic strengthens, in legal and educational discourses, the rationale for the extension of social control. Though the special treatment of prostitutes and HIV education of young women in schools may seem wildly divergent, each helps shape the contours of female sexuality, in efforts to contain the "bad girl" and to construct the "good" one. Whether through limits on mutually contracted sex by prostitutes or through limits on balanced information on safe sex for young women, the state is interrupting and forbidding certain sexual practices.

Yet, these processes are not consistent or unidirectional. The combination of political and pragmatic approaches to prostitutes by public health and legal institutions expands social control while legitimizing and in some ways normalizing the existence of prostitutes' organizations. To the extent that prostitutes are organized and in charge of their own HIV education, they are positioned to shape, if not to transform, their own sexuality in their own terms. Still, regulation of this always-suspect group of women continues.

Young women face a different, seemingly more constrained, situation. Schools are forced to confront their own failure to educate, as the rate of new infection in women and adolescents increases in the United States. Because of their use of three approaches to HIV prevention (political, pragmatic, and biomedical), the schools are faced with a continuing series of contradictions. They are the locus of community struggles over the nature and meaning of sexuality. For them, virtually every effort to educate, even in the simple case of supplying just the biological facts, results in challenges to their program, from both interested parties who want more and from those who want less.

Since young women in school are not in charge of their education and are politically disenfranchised, they have severe limits on their privacy and virtually no cultural permission to construct their own sexuality in their own terms. The protection of their "innocence" through the narrowness of the programs presented to them offers some, but rather limited, access to a fuller knowledge of sexuality and the range of sexual options a young woman might have. Moreover, while the few most expansive programs recognize young women as sexual actors and no longer force them to be chaste and modest, almost all still enforce a femininity centered in presumed heterosexuality in appearance and practice.

It is certainly possible that this crisis has the potential for the adoption of a more positive approach to the sexual in talk and in practice. Nevertheless, it will require the leadership of women of all ages, of all cultural and economic backgrounds, with strong feminist motivations, to counter the emergent forms of social control. Such controls do not stop or slow the epidemic and constitute incursions on the rights of individual and specific groups of women.

NOTES

1. Susan Shapiro, "Policing Trust," in *Private Policing,* ed. Clifford D. Shearing and Philip C. Stenning (Newbury Park, Calif.: Sage, 1987), 194–220.

2. Watney (p. 43) argues that "we are not, in fact, living through a distinct, coherent and progressing 'moral panic' about AIDS. Rather, we are witnessing the latest variation in the spectacle of the defensive ideological rearguard action which has been mounted on behalf of the 'family' for more than a century." Simon Watney, *Policing Desire: Pornography, AIDS, and the Media* (Minneapolis: University of Minnesota Press, 1987).

3. Allan Brandt, *No Magic Bullet: A Social History of Venereal Disease in the United States Since 1880* (New York: Oxford University Press, 1985); Linda Singer, *Erotic Welfare: Sexual Theory and Politics in the Age of Epidemic* (New York: Routledge, 1993). See also Susan Sontag, *Illness as Metaphor* (New York: Vintage, 1977) and *AIDS and Its Metaphors* (New York: Farrar, Straus and Giroux, 1988).

4. William Darrow, "AIDS: Socioepidemiologic Responses to an Epidemic," in *AIDS and the Social Sciences: Common Threads,* ed. Richard Ulack and William F. Skinner (Lexington: University of Kentucky Press, 1991), 83–99; Samuel V. Duh, *Blacks and AIDS: Causes and Origins* (Newbury Park, Calif.: Sage, 1991); Nan D. Hunter, "Complications of Gender: Women and HIV Disease," in *AIDS Agenda: Emerging Issues in Civil Rights,* ed. Nan D. Hunter and William B. Rubenstein (New York: The New Press, 1992), 5–39; Beth E. Schneider, "Women, Children, and AIDS: Research Suggestions," in *AIDS and the Social Sciences: Common Threads,* ed. Richard Ulack and William F. Skinner (Lexington: University of Kentucky Press, 1991), 134–148; Beth E. Schneider, "AIDS and Class, Gender, and Race Relations," in *The Social Context of AIDS,* ed. Joan Huber and Beth E. Schneider (Newbury Park, Calif.: Sage, 1992), 19–43.

5. Duh; Hunter; Schneider 1991, 1992; also Richard Ulack and William F. Skinner, eds., *AIDS and the Social Sciences:*

Common Threads (Lexington: University of Kentucky Press, 1991).

6. The history of epidemics is vast. Some of the books and articles most frequently used in discussions of AIDS include, in addition to Brandt 1975, Sontag 1977, and Sontag 1988. Charles E. Rosenberg, *The Cholera Years* (Chicago: University of Chicago Press, 1962) and William H. McNeill, *Plagues and Peoples* (Garden City: Anchor Books, 1976). See also, Elizabeth Fee and Daniel M. Fox, eds., *AIDS: The Burdens of History* (Berkeley: University of California Press, 1988) and Ilse J. Volinn, "Health Professionals as Stigmatizers and Destigmatizers of Diseases: Alcoholism and Leprosy as Examples," *Social Science and Medicine* 17(1983): 385–393.

7. In addition to Watney, see Virginia Berridge, "AIDS: History and Contemporary History," in *The Time of AIDS: Social Analysis, Theory, and Method,* ed. Gilbert Herdt and Shirley Lindenbaum (Newbury Park, Calif.: Sage, 1992), 41–64 and Cindy Patton, *Inventing AIDS* (New York: Routledge, 1990).

8. Nachman Ben-Yehuda, *The Politics and Morality of Deviance: Moral Panics, Drug Abuse, Deviant Science, and Reversed Stigmatization* (New York: State University of New York Press, 1990); Stanley Cohen, *Folk Devils and Moral Panics* (London: MacGibbon and Kee, 1972).

9. Brandt, Singer.

10. Gayle Rubin, "Thinking Sex: Notes for a Radical Theory of the Politics of Sexuality," in *Pleasure and Danger: Exploring Female Sexuality,* ed. Carole S. Vance (Boston: Routledge and Kegan Paul, 1984).

11. Peter Aggleton, Peter Davies and Graham Hart (eds.), *AIDS: Individual, Cultural and Policy Dimensions* (London: The Falmer Press, 1990), 181–190.

12. Brandt, 195.

13. Larry Gostin, ed., *Civil Liberties in Conflict* (New York: Routledge, 1988); Joel Feinberg, "Harmless Immoralities' and Offensive Nuisances," in *AIDS: Ethics and Public Policy,* ed. Christine Pierce and Donald VandeVeer (Belmont, Calif.: Wadsworth, 1988), 92–102; Thomas B. Stoddard and Walter Rieman, "AIDS and the Rights of the Individual: Toward a More Sophisticated Understanding of Discrimination," in *A Disease of Society: Cultural and Institutional Responses to AIDS,* ed. Dorothy Nelkin, David P. Willis, and Scott V. Parris (Cambridge: Cambridge University Press, 1991), 241–271.

14. Ibid.

15. William Buckley, "Identify All the Carriers," *The New York Times,* 18 March 1986, p. 26; Ronald Elsberry, "AIDS Quarantining in England and the United States," *Hastings International and Comparative Law Journal* 10 (1986): 113–126; Mark H. Jackson, "The Criminalization of HIV," in *AIDS Agenda: Emerging Issues in Civil Rights,* ed. Nan D. Hunter and William B. Rubenstein (New York: The New Press, 1992), 239–270.

16. Privacy encompasses "those places, spaces and matters upon or into which others may not intrude without the consent of the person or organization to whom they are designated as belonging" (p. 20); Albert J. Reiss, Jr., "The Legitimacy of Intrusion Into

Private Space," in *Private Policing,* ed. Clifford D. Shearing and Philip C. Stenning (Newbury Park, Calif.: Sage, 1988), 19–44.

17. Jackson; Pierce and Vande Veer.

18. Buckley; Elsberry; Jackson; Stoddard and Rieman.

19. Judith Cohen, Priscilla Alexander, and Constance Wofsy, "Prostitutes and AIDS: Public Policy Issues," *AIDS & Public Policy Journal* 3(1988):16–22.

20. Edward Albert, "Illness and/or Deviance: The Response of the Press to Acquired Immunodeficiency Syndrome," in *The Social Dimensions of AIDS: Method and Theory,* ed. Douglas A. Feldman and Tom Johnson (New York: Praeger, 1986), 163–178; Edward Albert, "AIDS and the Press: The Creation and Transformation of a Social Problem," in *Images of Issues; Typifying Contemporary Social Problems,* ed. Joel Best (New York: Aldine De Gruyter Press, 1989), 39–54. See also, Ann Giudici Fettner and William Check, *The Truth About AIDS: The Evolution of an Epidemic* (New York: Holt, 1985); Randy Shilts, *And the Band Played On* (New York: St. Martin's Press, 1988); Harry Schwartz, "AIDS and the Media," in *Science in the Streets* (New York: Priority Press, 1984).

21. For an historical overview see, in addition to Brandt 1985, Beth Bergman, "AIDS, Prostitution, and the Use of Historical Stereotypes to Legislate Sexuality," *The John Marshall Law Review* 211 (1988):777–830; Barbara Hobson, *Uneasy Virtue: The Politics of Prostitution and the American Reform Tradition* (New York: Basic Books, 1987); Gail Pheterson, *The Whore Stigma: Female Dishonor and Male Unworthiness* (The Netherlands: Dutch Ministry of Social Affairs and Employment, 1986); Gail Sheehy, "The Economics of Prostitution: Who Profits? Who Pays?" in *Sexual Deviance and Sexual Deviants,* ed. Erich Goode and Richard Troiden (New York: William Morrow, 1974), 110–123.

22. Darrow; Joan Luxenburg and Thomas Guild, "Prostitutes and AIDS: What Is All the Fuss About" (Paper presented at the annual meetings of the American Society of Criminology in New Orleans, LA., 1992); Valerie Jenness, *Making It Work: The Contemporary Prostitutes' Rights Movement in Perspective* (New York: Aldine de Gruyter, 1993).

23. Geraldo Rivera, "Are Prostitutes the New Typhoid Mary's?" The Geraldo Show, 1989, Fox Headquarters, 10201 Pico Boulevard, Los Angeles, California.

24. John Cristallo, "Are Prostitutes the New Typhoid Mary's?" The Geraldo Show, 1989, Fox Headquarters, 10201 Pico Boulevard, Los Angeles, California.

25. Jackson; Luxenburg and Guild, 1992; Joan Luxenburg and Thomas Guild, "Coercion, Criminal Sanctions and AIDS" (Paper presented at the annual meetings of the Society for the Study of Social Problems, Washington, D.C., 1990).

26. This parallels what happened to prostitutes in the first half of the twentieth century when "physicians and social reformers associated venereal disease, almost exclusively, with the vast population of prostitutes in American cities" (Brandt, p. 31). Perceived threats like these led to the increased social control of prostitution, primarily in the form of state regulation.

27. "No Murder-Try Case for Addicted Hooker," *Sacramento Bee,* 18 July 1990, p. B7.

28. Priscilla Alexander, "A Chronology of Sorts," personal files, 1988.

29. Darrow, p. 94. He observes, "To date, no HIV infections in female prostitutes or their clients can be directly linked to sexual exposure."

30. Lord Patrick Devlin, "Morals and the Criminal Law," in *Pierce and Vande Veer*, 77–86.

31. Carol Leigh, "AIDS: No Reason For A Witchhunt," *Oakland Tribune*, (17 August 1987), p. 1; Carol Leigh, "Further Violations Of Our Rights," in *AIDS Cultural Analysis, Cultural Activism*, ed. Douglas Crimp (Cambridge, MA: The MIT Press, 1988), an October book, 177–181.

32. Stoddard and Reiman, 264.

33. Gail Pheterson, *A Vindication of the Rights of Whores* (Seattle: Seal Press, 1989), 28.

34. Leigh 1987, 1.

35. Dennis Altman, *AIDS in the Mind of America* (New York: Anchor, 1987); Paula A. Treichler, "AIDS, Homophobia, and Biomedical Discourse: An Epidemic of Signification," in *AIDS: Cultural Analysis, Cultural Activism*, ed. D. Crimp (Cambridge, Mass.: MIT Press, 1988), 31–70.

36. Beth E. Schneider, Valerie Jenness, and Sarah Fenstermaker, "Deflecting Trouble: The Introduction of AIDS Education in the Public Schools" (Presented at the annual meetings of the Society for the Study of Social Problems, 1991).

37. Michael Granberry, "Besieged by Book Banners," *Los Angeles Times*, (10 May 1993), p. 1ff.

38. Donna Minkowitz, "Wrong Side of the Rainbow," *The Nation*, (28 June, 1993), pp. 901–904.

39. Douglas Kirby, "School-Based Prevention Programs: Design, Evaluation, and Effectiveness," in *Adolescents and AIDS: A Generation in Jeopardy*, ed. Ralph DiClemente, (Newbury Park, Calif.: Sage, 1992); David C. Sloane and Beverlie Conant Sloane, "AIDS in Schools: A Comprehensive Initiative," *McGill Journal of Education* 25 (1990): 205–228.

40. John Gallagher, "Why Johnny Can't Be Safe," *The Advocate* 631, (15 June 1993), pp. 46–47.

41. Schneider, Jenness, and Fenstermaker.

42. Patton, 99.

43. Susan Russell, "The Hidden Curriculum of School: Reproducing Gender and Class Hierarchies," in *Feminism and Political Economy: Women's Work, Women's Struggles*, ed. H. J. Marmey and M. Luxton (Toronto: Methuen, 1987).

44. Eleanor Maticka-Tyndale, "Social Construction of HIV Transmission and Prevention Among Heterosexual Young Adults," *Social Problems* 39 (1992):238–252.

45. DiClemente, 1992.

46. Maticka-Tyndale.

47. For additional consideration of these issues, see ACT-UP/New York Women and AIDS Book Group, *Women, AIDS and Activism* (Boston: South End Press, 1990); Laurie Wermuth, Jennifer Ham, and Rebecca L. Robbins, "Women Don't Wear Condoms: AIDS Risk Among Sexual Partners of IV Drug Users," in *The Social Context of AIDS*, ed. Joan Huber and Beth E. Schneider (Newbury Park, Calif.: Sage, 1992), 72–94.

48. Kirby.

49. These videos were produced in 1988. "Sex, Drugs and HIV," referred to in a later discussion, was produced in 1990 after complaints by parents resulted in revisions to an earlier version, "Sex, Drugs and AIDS."

50. Isabelle Melese-d'Hospital, "Still a Virgin: Adolescent Social Constructions of Sexuality and HIV Prevention Education" (Paper presented at the annual meetings of the American Sociological Association, Miami, 1993).

51. Benjamin P. Bowser and Gina M. Wingood, "Community Based HIV-Prevention Programs for Adolescents," in DiClemente.

52. Patton 1990, 108.

53. Sloane and Conant Sloane; Schneider, Jenness, and Fenstermaker.

54. Singer; Watney. See also Jeffrey Weeks, *Sexuality and Its Discontents: Meanings, Myths & Modern Sexualities* (New York: Routledge, Kegan Paul, 1985).

Burning Incense, Pledging Sisterhood: Communities of Women Workers in the Shanghai Cotton Mills, 1919–1949

EMILY HONIG

When we swore sisterhood we would go to a temple and burn incense. Everyone would have to make a pledge. We pledged to be loyal through life and death. And if someone was halfhearted in their loyalty, then we prayed that when they got on a boat, that boat would turn over.

A woman who worked in the Shanghai cotton mills in the 1920s

During the thirty years between the end of World War I and Liberation in 1949, it was common for women who worked in the cotton mills of Shanghai to form sisterhood societies (*jiemei hui*). After working together for several years, six to ten women would formalize their relationship with one another by pledging sisterhood. Sometimes this simply involved going to a restaurant, eating a meal together, drinking a cup of "one-heart wine," and toasting their loyalty to one another. Because large numbers of women workers were Buddhists, it was more common for those forming sisterhoods to go to a Buddhist temple, burn incense before the statue of a deity, and pledge to be loyal to one another "through life and death."

Once they had formed a sisterhood, the members would call each other by kinship terms based on their age: the oldest was "Big Sister," the next oldest "Second Sister," and so

Emily Honig, "Burning Incense, Pledging Sisterhood: Communities of Women Workers in the Shanghai Cotton Mills, 1919–1949," *Signs: Journal of Women in Culture and Society* 10, no. 4 (1985). Copyright © 1985 by The University of Chicago. Reprinted with the permission of the author and The University of Chicago Press.

forth. Often members of the sisterhoods contributed money to buy a cloth in order to make each member an identical Chinese-style, long blue cotton gown. They wore the gowns when they went out together to express their unity.[1]

Women displayed their loyalty to one another both inside and outside the mills. Members of sisterhoods walked together to work in order to protect each other from hoodlums on the street. During the twelve-hour shifts they worked in the factory, one woman would do the work of two while the other ate lunch, went to the bathroom, or hid in a yard bin to take a nap. They defended each other if a male worker or overseer threatened one of them. Often the sisterhoods functioned as an economic mutual aid society: in order to avoid borrowing from "stamp-money lenders" who charged over 100 percent in interest, women paid a monthly "sisterhood fee." Then if one of the members faced an extraordinary expense such as a wedding, a funeral, or an illness, she could draw on this fund.[2] Members of sisterhoods socialized together: they would get together at one member's house to chat on Sundays, to go window-shopping, or to hear performances of local opera, a favorite form of entertainment among women workers in Shanghai.

These sisterhoods are scarcely mentioned in contemporary surveys of working-class life in Shanghai. This is not because those conducting the surveys failed to observe and record the conditions of women cotton-mill workers, whose number represented over one-third of the ranks of the famed Shanghai proletariat.[3] Historians have used these contemporary records to describe the transformation of women workers from passive, ever-suffering victims of industrial poverty to heroines of the organized labor movement and, in some cases, to class-conscious revolutionaries.

The interviews I conducted with women who had worked in Shanghai cotton mills during the three decades before 1949 suggest that the majority of women working in Shanghai were not lonely, isolated individuals; but neither were they members of trade unions, political organizations, or the Chinese Communist Party (CCP).[4] They survived by forming ties with other women workers who helped and protected them. These informal groups in time formalized as sisterhoods.

Although all women can recall in great detail the ways in which they depended on each other, questions about the sisterhoods provoked a number of seemingly contradictory answers. Some said that only women who had worked for many years pledged sisterhood, while others disdainfully described the sisterhoods as a phenomenon most prevalent among young women workers who liked to go out shopping, dress up, and hear local opera. Some said they were hoodlum organizations, while others insisted they were formed by women who wanted to protect themselves against hoodlums. Some remembered that only the most ideologically "backward" women pledged sisterhood, while others said the sisterhoods had been organized by the CCP. And finally, there were women who, when asked about the sisterhoods, exclaimed, "We women mill workers—we *all* used to pledge sisterhood!"

This variety of explanations suggests that there was no single type of sisterhood, that sisterhoods were formed for a host of reasons, and that they engaged in many different kinds of activities. There were some sisterhoods, however, that encompassed all these contradictory aspects, and one purpose of this article is to explain this phenomenon.

The major focus of this article, though, is to evaluate the significance of the sisterhoods. It would be tempting when studying these organizations formed by women workers, largely to serve the needs of women workers, to assume that they represent members' development of a consciousness as women and as workers. By looking more closely at these sisterhoods—at the women who formed them and at their activities—this article will suggest that associations constituted solely of workers are not necessarily an expression of working-class consciousness and that neither are autonomous women's groups inherently an expression of female consciousness. When examined in their cultural and historical context, working women's organizations, such as the Chinese sisterhoods, may as easily confirm and perpetuate traditional social relationships as challenge them.

WHO ARE OUR SISTERS?

In order to understand the development of sisterhoods, we must first look at the conditions inside the cotton mills and working-class districts that made it necessary for women workers to depend on one another. It was this need for mutual aid that led to the development of a sense of community among women workers and, ultimately, to the sisterhoods.

The daily work routine in the mills—if women had adhered to the rules—would have been grueling. They were required to work twelve-hour shifts with only a ten-minute break for lunch. Even while they ate, the machines continued to run. But women did not passively accept these rules. They often made work-sharing arrangements with those who labored beside them. "Those who got along well," a worker named Gu Lianying recalled, "one would help the other work, so that the other could eat." If a woman was exhausted and wanted to sleep for a few hours, another worker watched her machine and woke her up when the overseer made his rounds through the workshop. Sometimes women had to leave the mill for several hours to take care of a child. Since requesting formal permission would have jeopardized their jobs, they instead asked a friend to guard their machine while they were gone.

The world outside the mills was equally threatening, and women were compelled to help each other if they were to survive. Local toughs—many of whom belonged to Shanghai's powerful gang organizations—gathered at the mill gates, then flirted with and even pursued women walking home from work. On payday they seized women's wages, and on ordinary days they collected some cash by engaging in an activity called "stripping a sheep"—robbing a woman of her clothes, which they then sold.[5] While sexual abuse by male hoodlums was the most common problem, women mill workers had reason to be equally fearful of female gangsters, who specialized in the lucrative business of kidnapping young girls for sale to brothels or as future daughters-in-law.[6] All women workers had family members or friends who had been raped, beaten, or kidnapped by neighborhood hoodlums. For protection they almost always walked to and from the mills in groups—accompanied by parents when they were young and by siblings and neighbors as they grew older.

Part of the experience of growing up in the mills, for girls who had begun working when they were ten or eleven, was developing a network of "sisters" on whom they could depend for both help and protection. "We younger workers would not help each other in the workshop," one woman recalled, "but when I was older, I also had 'little sisters.' Then when I would eat, one of them would tend my machine. It was the girls in the lane next to me—we would help each other. This started when I was about fifteen." As women developed such relationships in the mills, they began to socialize with these other women workers as well. "After working a long time, then you'd start to have friends," the same woman continued. "And on Sundays, if you had time, you could go visit their house. Maybe that started when I was seventeen or eighteen. All of my friends then were cotton-mill workers." These relationships often continued after women were married. "We used to love to go see Subei operas," Chen Zhaodi recalled. "We would go in the evening, from seven to eleven. We almost never went with our husbands or children. It was usually some of us women who worked together who would go. But I would not tell my family where I was going. My mother-in-law would never have let me go. I just went secretly, with my 'sisters.'"

These relationships often remained casual, but frequently they were formalized as sisterhoods. One woman described this process: "Originally we would go to work together, and leave work together, because then it was not good to walk alone. After a while we would get to know each other. Then, if I thought that person was very decent, I would say to her, 'Why don't we pledge loyalty? Then if you have some problems I'll help you, and if I have some problems you can help me.'" It was at this point that they would go to a Buddhist temple and burn incense to establish their sisterhood. Women who pledged sisterhood were thus formalizing relationships with people outside their families as they began to perceive the women with whom they worked in the factory as their sisters.

This does not mean, however, that individual women perceived *all* other women mill workers, or even all other women who worked in the same mill, as potential sisters. In fact, most of the relationships of work sharing and mutual assistance that I have described were based on traditional connections between those from the same native place. In order to understand the nature of communities formed by women workers—and ultimately the nature of the sisterhoods—we must look briefly at the workers' origins and the extent to which their native place determined their experience in Shanghai, both inside and outside the mills.

Although some women who worked in the cotton mills were natives of Shanghai, throughout this thirty-year period the overwhelming majority of women came from rural villages in the provinces of Jiangsu and Zhejiang. (Shanghai is located at the southeastern corner of Jiangsu, on the border of Zhejiang.) They came from villages with almost every kind of economy imaginable—from places that relied on salt production to ones that depended on rice cultivation to ones where cotton was the major crop, from areas where handicraft industries such as silk or cotton spinning and weaving were a vital part of the peasant household economy to ones where handicrafts were almost nonexistent. They came from locales where foot-binding was still common in the 1930s as well as from places where the practice had long since ceased.

The villages from which women came can be roughly divided into two groups: those located in Subei, the part of Jiangsu Province north of the Yangzi River, and those located in the Jiangnan, the area south of the river. (The Yangzi River flows just north of Shanghai.) The Jiangnan has historically been one of the richest agricultural areas in China. Although no systematic research has considered the role of women in the rural economy, it appears that most peasant women in this area engaged in handicraft work. The places in the Jiangnan from which the mill workers came, such as Wuxi and Changzhou, had also exported many mill owners and technicians to Shanghai.

Subei was a much poorer area. Handicraft industries were less developed than in the south, and most peasant women played an active role in agricultural work. Throughout the early twentieth century vast numbers of families fled villages in the north that had been devastated by floods. Ever since that time, refugees from northern Jiangsu had performed the coolie jobs—such as collecting night soil and pulling rickshaws—that locals considered too demeaning to do themselves.[7]

These basic differences in the rural economies north and south of the river were replicated and perpetuated in the mills of Shanghai. In general, women from Subei, considered strong, robust, and accustomed to dirt, were channeled into the mill workshops, where the labor was most arduous and dirty. Often they did the jobs that in earlier stages of industrialization had been performed by male workers and that women from Shanghai proper or from villages of Jiangnan were not willing to do. Women from Jiangnan concentrated in the workshops where the labor was lighter and better paying. They also had the possibility of being promoted to supervisory positions.

Individual departments in the cotton mills were usually staffed by workers from a particular village.[8] This does not appear to have been the result of a management strategy to create divisions in the labor force, even though it had that effect. Hiring in the Shanghai mills was not controlled by a central personnel office but rather was the prerogative of the "Number Ones" (forewomen) in the workshops, and women secured jobs by dint of their "connections" with a Number One. When women who had migrated from the countryside arrived in Shanghai in search of work, they sought out people from their hometown who could introduce them to a Number One, usually someone from the same town. People from the same native place considered it their duty to help others from their district.[9]

The cotton mills were the only enterprise in Shanghai that brought several thousand women of disparate origins together under one roof. But they did not necessarily provide a setting where traditional patterns of localism were dissolved. Women from the same village were likely to be employed in the same workshop, surrounded by relatives and neighbors who came from their town, shared their customs, and spoke their particular dialect of Chinese. Furthermore, in the course of a working day, women had little reason to leave their workshop and have contact with women from others.

This localism pervaded the lives of women outside the mills as well. They usually lived in neighborhoods where people from their hometown had gathered.[10] Their hairstyles and eating habits often reflected the traditions of their native villages, and, as Chen Zhaodi observed:

> People from each place had different styles of dress. People from Subei liked to wear red, brightly colored clothes. People from Wuxi, Changzhou, and Tongzhou had their own looms, so they wore clothing they had woven themselves. They had little square scarves they would wrap on their heads. They also had long aprons. People from Nantong liked to wear long aprons. People from Yangzhou liked to dress up their hair. They would wear a bun. People from Changzhou and Wuxi liked to wear hairpins.

When they socialized on Sundays or holidays, they almost always did so with friends from their native place. Women from Zhejiang socialized with relatives and other people from Zhejiang and "did not bother too much with other people." When attending performances of local opera, Subei women went to theaters where they could hear Yangzhou opera, women from Wuxi went to hear Wuxi opera, and those from Zhejiang attended performances of Shaoxing (a city in Zhejiang) opera. When they married, their spouses were inevitably from the same district.

Place of origin was the major way in which women perceived themselves as similar to or different from others. Their attitude toward women from other villages was indifferent, at best, and sometimes overtly hostile. Women from Shanghai and from villages in the Jiangnan were contemptuous of women from Subei and often swore at them, "You Jiangbei swine!" It was not unheard of for a Subei woman to dump a bucket of night soil on the head of a fellow worker from Jiangnan or to shove a woman from Jiangnan into one of the rivers or canals that crisscrossed Shanghai.[11] Regional animosity—often the cause of bloody battles between male laborers—was also expressed by women who worked in the mills.[12]

When women pledged sisterhood, they were perpetuating both intraregional bonds and interregional divisions. No systematic information about the membership of sisterhoods is available. Yet based on what we know about patterns of migration to and settlement in Shanghai and about hiring practices, which usually resulted in concentrations of people from the same village in particular workshops, it seems safe to assume that, when women pledged sisterhood, it was with women from the same village. This is confirmed by the comment of a woman from Wuxi who, when asked whether she had ever joined a sisterhood, replied, "There was no one else in my workshop from Wuxi, so with whom could I pledge sisterhood?"

Thus the sisterhoods were not organizations that drew and bonded all women workers together. The women who joined them by no means perceived themselves as sisters to all women who shared their predicament. The important commonality was a shared native place. Yet the sisterhoods involved something more than traditional relationships. It is important to remember that new workers did not have a group of sisters on whom they could depend. To some degree the relationships embodied in the sisterhoods were ones that developed during the time women worked in the mills, and in that sense they were indeed a product of factory life.

SISTERS, NOT BROTHERS

Even if women in the Shanghai cotton mills did not perceive themselves as sisters to all women workers, they did indeed enter into formal organizations with some of their fellow laborers. They could have simply continued to help each other at work, walk with one another to and from the mill, and socialize together without bothering to go to Buddhist temples, burn incense, and pledge sisterhood. Thus we must return to the question, What does it mean that women mill workers formed autonomous female organizations?

Before confronting this question, I must point out that there is some evidence that the sisterhoods were not exclusively female. In describing the sisterhoods, one woman explained, "When ten of us women workers pledged sisterhood, we usually included one male worker and two or three tough women workers. Otherwise our group would not have power for defense." That this was not an atypical situation is suggested by a similar phenomenon among prostitutes in Shanghai. "Wild chickens," the lowest class of prostitutes in Shanghai, and the only ones who went out onto the streets to attract customers, also formed sisterhood societies. Their sisterhoods are described as consisting of nine prostitutes plus one male, usually a petty gangster who had connections with the local police, who was supposed to help protect the women if anyone tried to abuse them while they were out at night.[13]

Unfortunately, we do not know if the practice of including men in the sisterhoods of women mill workers was widespread. Nor do we know what role the men played. It is possible, for example, that they were part of the sisterhood simply to give physical protection when necessary but did not participate in the other functions of the sisterhood such as work sharing, providing economic mutual aid, and socializing.

While the evidence of men's inclusion in the sisterhoods is perplexing, what we know about male membership at this point is not enough to negate our consideration of the sisterhoods as organizations formed primarily for and by women. This is confirmed by the simultaneous existence of "brotherhoods" among male workers in the mills. Groups of eight to ten male workers pledged loyalty to each other by burning incense, and members of brotherhoods referred to each other as "Oldest Brother," "Second Brother," and so forth. If women did not intend to form separate, autonomous organizations, then why did they not form "brother-sister societies" or simply "workerhoods"? The answer to this question, I would argue, is found in the historical and cultural context in which sisterhoods developed.

During the three decades before Liberation, it was socially acceptable for women to participate in activities or associations with other women but not with men. This was a reality that even radical organizers in the CCP—who would have preferred to develop organizations that included both men and women—had to accept in order to mobilize women. "Although I am an extreme supporter of the belief that men and women should study together," Xiang Jingyu, head of the Women's Bureau of the CCP, wrote in 1924, "when it comes to establishing workers' schools, I am an absolute advocate of male and female separatism. . . . It is only by setting up schools especially for women that women will be willing to come, and that their fathers and husbands will be willing to let them come and study."[14] That year, the first Party-sponsored workers' schools were established in one of Shanghai's cotton-mill districts: one for men and one for women.[15] A year later Xiang Jingyu extended this principle to unions, suggesting

that, in order to attract female members, there would have to be separate unions for women.[16] As late as 1941, when the Party was trying to organize underground during the Japanese occupation, the person responsible for organizing in the cotton mills lamented that it was still necessary to establish separate Party branches for women workers.[17]

In this context, forming a mixed-gender group may have presented a more profound challenge to traditional social relationships than forming a women's organization. Or, more modestly put, establishing a women's association and calling it a sisterhood did not necessarily indicate that women desired autonomy from men. In Shanghai (and in most of China) separate female organizations were traditional, not radical.

This does not mean, however, that the formation of autonomous women's groups was inherently conservative. It would have been equally possible for women to have established organizations that expressed their determination to challenge the existing social order. This is in fact what happened in the Canton delta during the late nineteenth and early twentieth centuries, according to Marjorie Topley. Many peasant women in this area, who played a critical role in sericulture, formed sisterhoods to resist marriage. Groups of women pledged loyalty to one another before a deity in a Buddhist temple and made vows never to marry. This was possible because they could support themselves through the wages they earned as silk workers.[18]

Although women in the Shanghai mills, like peasant women in Canton, enjoyed independent incomes, there is little similarity between the two types of sisterhoods besides the name and ceremony of pledging loyalty. The women in Shanghai were not coming together to demand change in their status either as women or as workers. The majority of women who joined sisterhoods in Shanghai accepted what they probably considered to be their fate: they would work twelve hours a day in a mill only to return home to face the task of maintaining a household; they were vulnerable to sexual abuse by overseers inside the mills and thugs on the streets; they would marry the person who had been chosen for them by their parents, often when they were only children. The purpose of the sisterhoods was not to advocate change or express resistance but simply to help each other survive within the context of traditional social relationships.

Sisterhoods were not the only associations women workers formed to ensure their survival in Shanghai. To protect themselves from the wrath of the Number Ones in the mills and from attacks by hoodlums outside, many women workers also "pledged godmothers" (*bai ganniang*). "For protection from the gangs, you could make arrangements with one gang member," Zhu Fanu recalled. "Male workers would find a male gang leader, and women workers would find a woman. This was called pledging a godmother. When you found the person who would protect you, you would send her presents. Then if another gangster ever bothered you, you could go tell your godmother, and she would take care of you, because she had power." Often women mill workers pledged loyalty to the Number One in their workshop as their godmother. Most of the Number Ones not only had the power commensurate with their position in the mills but also were members of the gangs (or were married to gang members) and therefore were influential in the neighborhood as well. With such godmothers, women workers had protection both on and off the job.

Like pledging sisterhood, pledging loyalty to a godmother also involved a ceremony: burning incense, kneeling, and reciting a vow in front of an altar. Once a woman had a godmother, she was expected to demonstrate her appreciation by periodically sending gifts, preferably cash. Whenever the godmother had a pretext—such as a birthday or holiday—she would send invitations to all her "godchildren" to partake in a celebration (chi jiu). "You had to go, and when you went, you had to send them money. That was the main purpose," one worker commented.

Sometimes the distinction between pledging sisterhoods and pledging a godmother blurred. While individual women may have chosen either to pledge sisterhood or to pledge a godmother, some may have pledged both. More important, there is some evidence that the two practices sometimes merged—that some sisterhoods included a godmother. One woman, for example, described the sisterhoods as including "one male and two or three tough women." More compelling evidence comes from a description of organizing strategies developed by the CCP during the Anti-Japanese War (1937–45). According to this account, the Party, in an attempt to adapt organizational forms familiar to women workers, established sisterhoods that included several ordinary mill workers, a woman who was a Number One, and an older woman who was married to a gang leader.[19] In these cases women of different ages and of different status in the mill were bonded together in the sisterhoods.

This information affects how we ultimately assess the relationships among the members of sisterhoods. The term "sisterhood" usually evokes the notion of equality, and it is appealing to think of the associations as ones composed of women who saw themselves as sisters, hence equals. Even if these "hybrid" sisterhoods were the exception, not the rule, they caution us not to assume uncritically that sisterhoods are egalitarian organizations.

SISTERS IN REVOLUTION

Although the sisterhoods were not self-consciously political, they often took actions that had political implications. This was particularly evident when groups of sisters, banding together to protect one member, opposed—or even physically attacked—their employers. "One time a girl worker was being harassed by an overseer," one woman remembered. "She told us sisters, and we all attacked that overseer and beat him up." Sometimes their commitment to mutual protection put them in strikelike situations. If a Number One threatened to fire a woman who belonged to a sisterhood, her sisters would refuse to work until the Number One revoked her threat. These were common, spontaneous incidents, but it does not require much stretch of the imagination to recognize how these loyalties might be appropriated in an organized labor movement. If one member of a sisterhood shut off the motor of her spinning frame or loom as part of a strike, her sisters could be expected to shut off their machines too, even if for no reason other than personal loyalty.

The most vivid example of how the sisterhoods were used to advocate principles very different from those that characterized their original purpose comes from CCP actions during the Anti-Japanese War and during the Civil War from 1946 to 1949. The political situation during both conflicts made only the most covert means of organizing possible, and Party members began to pay closer attention to preexisting social networks among workers, such as sisterhoods, viewing them as potentially revolutionary organizations. In one of the only available reports on this phenomenon, the Party in 1941 instructed local organizers:

> Because of the subjective and objective circumstances of women's lives, they must often help each other. In order to prevent strangers from flirting with them, or thieves from trying to take away their wages, they often walk together. On their time off, when they go buy things, they also usually go in groups of seven or eight. In all of these groups there is always one or two people who are at the center. If we can attract them, then it is easy to attract the others in their group. More and more of these groups are developing in the areas occupied by the Japanese, where women want to protect themselves. So, it is not just important to unite with these elements in struggle, but also important to do this in their everyday organizations.[20]

Thus, instead of encouraging the members of sisterhoods to read progressive literature, to participate in discussions of the workers' movement, or to go to secret screenings of Russian movies, organizers initially went shopping with their "sisters" or played in parks with them. "First we just tried to develop friendships," a woman who was active in the Party underground in the late 1930s and 1940s recalled, "and then later we could talk about the conditions of women workers."

In some cases Party activists did not simply join sisterhoods that already existed but actually began forming sisterhoods themselves. In order to do so, however, they had to adhere to the practices that made pledging sisterhood meaningful to ordinary women workers, no matter how far they may have diverged from the principles upheld by the Party. Thus, when the CCP formed sisterhoods, the Party activists had to go along with the other members to a Buddhist temple, where they all burned incense, knelt in front of a statue of a deity, and took oaths to "be loyal to each other through life and death."[21]

If these new sisterhoods differed from the traditional ones, the differences were small, almost imperceptible. At the Da Kang mill, for instance, after a group of women pledged such a Party-supported sisterhood, they each contributed a small sum of money to buy a piece of white cloth. They cut the cloth into squares, sewed handkerchiefs, and on each one embroidered the words "working together with one heart." Each member of the sisterhood kept a handkerchief as a souvenir.[22] While members of traditional sisterhoods occasionally made identical gowns—or may even have made identical handkerchiefs—to symbolize their relationship, they were not likely to have expressed their common interests as workers as did the new sisters with their embroidered emblem.

Similarly, it had always been common for members of sisterhoods to get together on Sundays, to go out window-shopping, or to go to a park. Party members encouraged and participated in these activities and gradually introduced new dimensions. When they went to parks, for example,

Party members spent part of the time telling their sisters about the progress women had made through the Russian Revolution and about the work of the CCP in Yanan.[23] Women who were sympathetic to these ideas were enlisted by the Party organizers to attend schools for women workers run by the YWCA.[24] Some eventually joined the CCP themselves.[25]

This strategy was apparently successful, for during the Civil War, unprecedented numbers of women workers continuously participated in strikes, for the first time demanding and winning benefits specifically for women, such as maternity leave and nurseries. For some women, the potential for the development of worker and female solidarity that had been inherent in the sisterhoods was finally realized.

CONCLUSION

The significance of the sisterhoods, then, is that they indicate the ways in which women were not passive victims of industrial poverty. They demonstrate women's resistance to unbearably long work hours, beatings by overseers, and physical abuse by neighborhood gangsters. They also characterize the communities formed by women workers in Shanghai—communities in which women drew on traditional social relationships to survive in a new, unfamiliar, and threatening environment. The Shanghai sisterhoods suggest that organizations formed by women workers are not necessarily expressions of working-class or feminist consciousness. And once formed, the sisterhoods did not inevitably lead their members to see that by acting collectively they could change their circumstances. Nevertheless, the sisterhoods do provide a critical link in the story of how some women became revolutionaries. It was only when Communist Party organizers burned incense and pledged sisterhood that women workers, as sisters, became active participants in the Chinese revolution.

NOTES

1. Materials provided by the Institute for Historical Research, Shanghai Academy of Social Sciences. These materials include unpublished factory histories, transcripts of interviews, and accounts of strikes collected as part of an effort undertaken in the 1950s to chronicle the history of the pre-Liberation labor movement in Shanghai. The documents are not labeled or cataloged. Further information about these materials can be obtained by contacting me [at Yale University].

2. Cora Deng, "The Economic Status of Women in Industry in China, with Special Reference to a Group in Shanghai" (M.A. thesis, New York University, 1941), p. 73.

3. In 1929, when the industry was close to its peak of development, there were sixty-one cotton mills in Shanghai, employing 110,882 workers. Of these, 84,270 (76 percent) were women (Shanghai Bureau of Social Affairs, *Wages and Hours of Labor, Greater Shanghai, 1929* [Shanghai, 1929]). Throughout the period

from World War I through Liberation in 1949, Shanghai was the largest industrial center in China, and the cotton industry was Shanghai's major industry.

4. I conducted these interviews during two research trips to Shanghai. Under the auspices of the Committee on Scholarly Communication with the People's Republic of China and the Social Science Research Council, I was an exchange scholar at Fudan University in Shanghai from 1979 to 1981. I returned to conduct follow-up research in September and October of 1982. The interviews with women workers were almost all arranged by Fudan University and usually took place at the cotton mills. I interviewed approximately fifty women. Often these interviews were set up as "round-table discussions," in which I questioned four or five women during a single three-hour session. There was almost no opportunity to conduct follow-up interviews with individual women. Unless otherwise cited, all quotations in the text are from these interviews.

5. For a discussion of these problems, see Liu Ta-chun, *The Growth and Industrialization of Shanghai* (Shanghai: China Institute of Pacific Relations, 1936), p. 169; and Shanghai shehui kexueyuan, jingji yanjiusuo (Institute for Economic Research, Shanghai Academy of Social Sciences), ed., *Shanghai penghuqude bianyi* (Changes in the squatter settlements of Shanghai) (Shanghai: Shanghai renmin chubanshe, 1965), p. 24.

6. Mary Ninde Gamewell, *Gateway to China: Pictures of Shanghai* (New York: Fleming H. Revell Co., 1916), p. 210. See also *Shanghai heimo yiqian zhong* (A thousand kinds of shady plots in Shanghai) (Shanghai: Shanghai chunming shudian yinxing, 1939), pp. 1–31

7. For a more detailed discussion of the workers' origins, see Emily Honig, "Women Cotton Mill Workers in Shanghai, 1919–1949" (Ph.D. diss., Stanford University, 1982).

8. See, e.g., Zhongguo fangzhi jianshe gongsi (China Textile Reconstruction Corp.), *Shanghai dishisi fangzhichang sanshiwu-niande gongzuo nianbao* (Yearly report on the work at the Shanghai Number Fourteen Textile Mill, 1946) (Shanghai, 1946), pp. 63–65. See also *Xin qingnian* (New youth) (Beijing), vol. 7, no. 6 (May 1920). This segregation of workers by place of origin is also documented by the retirement cards from one of the largest cotton mills in Shanghai. These cards—filled out when a worker retires—are part of the personnel records at each mill. They indicate the worker's name, place and date of birth, and work history.

9. For a more extensive discussion of hiring practices in the cotton mills, see Honig, pp. 95–104. See also Jean Chesneaux, *The Chinese Labor Movement, 1919–1927* (Stanford, Calif.: Stanford University Press, 1968). These patterns of people from the same hometown helping each other are not unique to workers. See, e.g., Susan Mann Jones, "The Ningpo Pang and Financial Power at Shanghai," in *The Chinese City between Two Worlds,* ed. Mark Elvin and G. W. Skinner (Stanford, Calif.: Stanford University Press, 1974), pp. 73–96.

10. This observation is based on interviews as well as on Herbert Lamson, "The Problem of Housing for Workers in China," *Chinese Economic Journal* 11, no. 2 (August 1932):139–62.

11. *Shen Bao* (The Huangpu Daily) (Shanghai) (May 6, 1924).

12. For a discussion of regional rivalries in Shanghai, see Chesneaux, p. 123; and Leung Yuen Sang, "Regional Rivalry in Mid-Nineteenth Century Shanghai: Cantonese vs Ningpo Men." *Ch'ing shih wen-t'i* 4, no. 8 (December 1982):29–50.

13. Materials provided by the Institute for Historical Research, Shanghai Academy of Social Sciences. The source does not explain the relationship of the men to the sisterhoods of prostitutes. Since the men who acted as pimps are discussed in a separate section of the article, it seems safe to assume that these men were not pimps.

14. *Xiang Jingyu wenji* (The collected works of Xiang Jingyu) (Changsha: Hunan renmin chubanshe, 1980), pp. 146–47.

15. Shanghai shehui kexueyuan lishi yanjiusuo (Institute for Historical Research, Shanghai Academy of Social Sciences), ed., *Wusa yundong shiliao* (Historical materials on the May Thirtieth Movement) (Shanghai: Shanghai renmin chubanshe, 1981), 1:270.

16. *Xiang Jingyu wenji,* p. 216.

17. Materials provided by the Institute for Historical Research, Shanghai Academy of Social Sciences.

18. Marjorie Topley, "Marriage Resistance in Rural Kwangtung," in *Women in Chinese Society,* ed. Margery Wolf and Roxane Witke (Stanford, Calif.: Stanford University Press, 1975), pp. 67–68.

19. Materials provided by the Institute for Historical Research, Shanghai Academy of Social Sciences.

20. Ma Chunji, "Shanghai nugong gongzuo baogao" (Report on work among women workers in Shanghai) (Yanan, 1941), reprinted by Zhonghua quanguo zonggonghui ziliaoshi (Materials Department of the All-China Federation of Labor) (1954).

21. Materials provided by the Institute for Historical Research, Shanghai Academy of Social Sciences.

22. Ibid.

23. Ibid.

24. Tang Guifen, "Huxi shachang gongren douzhengde gaikuang" (General conditions of the cotton workers' struggle in western Shanghai), in *Shanghai gongren yundong lishi ziliao* (Materials on the history of the Shanghai workers' movement) (Shanghai, 1956, mimeographed). Starting in the 1920s, the YWCA operated a number of night schools for women industrial workers. Ostensibly the schools taught literacy, but they were known for teaching women workers to understand their position in the social and economic system. They also taught women skills, such as public speaking, that were useful in labor organizing. By the 1940s, the CCP began using the schools to organize women workers, and many teachers in them were Party members (interview with Cora Deng, Shanghai, 1980; Robin Porter, "The Christian Conscience and Industrial Welfare in China, 1919–1941" [Ph.D. diss., University of Montreal, 1977]; Wang Zhijin et al., "Huiyi Shanghai nuqingnianhuide nugong yexiao" [Recalling the YWCA night schools for women workers in Shanghai], *Shanghai wenshi ziliao xuanji* [Selected materials on Shanghai culture and history], no. 5 [Shanghai, 1979], pp. 83–93).

25. Shanghai gongren yundong shiliao weiyuanhui (Shanghai Labor History Committee), ed., *Shanghai guomian shichang gongren douzheng lishi ziliao* (Materials on the history of the workers' struggles at the Number Ten Textile Mill in Shanghai) (Shanghai, 1954, mimeographed).

ACKNOWLEDGMENTS

I would like to thank Margery Wolf, Lisa Rofel, and Marilyn Young for discussions of the ideas developed in this article as well as for comments on earlier drafts.

R E A D I N G   4 8

Our Policies, Their Consequences: Zambian Women's Lives under "Structural Adjustment"

AMBER AULT and EVE SANDBERG

Women around the globe share many concerns, including meeting basic subsistence needs, improving the prevention and treatment of diseases like AIDS, providing for reproductive health and freedom, reducing infant mortality and childhood illness, preventing violence against women, ensuring gender equity in labor, law, and education, and increasing women's ability to exercise sexual self-determination. Because wealthy countries and poor countries occupy very different positions in the global economic system, however, the social, economic, and political oppression experienced by women of poor countries differs in form from that experienced by women in wealthy countries. Furthermore, the oppression of women in Third World countries does not exist in a vacuum that begins and ends at national borders. Indeed, much of the poverty, discrimination, disease, and violence experienced by Third World women results from the exploitation of their countries by

Amber Ault and Eve Sandberg, "Our Policies, Their Consequences: Zambian Women's Lives under 'Structural Adjustments'." Reprinted with the permission of the authors.

wealthier countries and the international organizations that they control. As feminist scholars and activists in wealthy Western countries, we must educate ourselves about our roles in supporting the systems of domination which perpetuate the exploitation of women elsewhere.

We do not argue that all women in industrialized nations enjoy vast, substantial advantages over all women in Third World countries. Indeed, many women in the United States live in extreme poverty, without decent housing, steady health care, stable employment, or any assurance of personal safety, while some women in poor nations enjoy relatively high standards of living. Nonetheless, because wealthy Western countries benefit from the labor of exploited Third World workers, Western feminists need to understand the roles their governments play in women's oppression in other countries.

In this brief report, we use a case study to demonstrate how the self-interested practices of wealthier countries in one international organization exacerbate and sometimes create the oppression of Third World women as women, citizens, and workers. To explicate the connections between the United States government, one powerful international organization, and the lives of women in Third World countries, we recount the impact of an International Monetary Fund (IMF) Structural Adjustment Program in the African country of Zambia.

The International Monetary Fund constitutes an international agency designed to promote a stable world economy. As part of its mission, it provides loans to countries with failing economies. Capital for such loans comes from deposits made by the countries participating in the International Monetary Fund. The conditions each borrowing country must meet to secure a loan are contingent on the ultimate approval by the Board of Directors of the Fund, which includes representatives of the member states, whose votes are weighted relative to their countries' financial contributions; wealthy nations like the United States make large contributions and therefore enjoy great influence over the contingencies attached to loans the agency makes, as well as its policies and actions. Not surprisingly, the terms of loans to Third World countries reflect the economic and political interests and values of the world's wealthiest nations.

The "Structural Adjustment Program" constitutes one kind of loan package managed by this organization. The International Monetary Fund makes financial assistance to Third World countries contingent upon borrower countries' willingness to make significant adjustments in their economic systems. The adjustments required by the International Monetary Fund reflect Western capitalist economic ideologies. In addition, they often reflect a disregard for the structural, cultural, social, and technological features of the borrowing country. As a result, Structural Adjustment Programs administered by the International Monetary Fund frequently result in dramatic and devastating changes in the countries that adopt them. Nonetheless, because the International Monetary Fund constitutes one of the few sources of loan capital to which an indebted country can turn, countries suffering severe economic difficulty often accept the terms of Structural Adjustment Programs.

Such was the case of Zambia, a Black-governed country in South-Central Africa that implemented an IMF Structural Adjustment Program in October, 1985 and wrestled with it in various forms until its termination in May, 1987. Before we describe the policies and outcomes of the Structural Adjustment Program in Zambia, we offer a brief description of some features of the country, so that readers may more fully grasp the ramifications of the program on the lives of citizens in general and women in particular.

At the time it instituted its IMF Structural Adjustment Program, Zambia reported that its population numbered about 6.7 million citizens. About 3.81 million Zambians over the age of 11 were working or actively seeking work, but only about 71% of these people could find jobs. While some urban Zambian women worked as teachers, nurses, secretaries, and waitresses, many more were self-employed as food sellers, street vendors, and charcoal producers, or in other jobs in the "informal sector"; in rural areas, women usually worked as farmers.

Then, as now, Zambia imported many goods. Government controls on foreign exchange rates held in check the cost to consumers of food and other goods imported by retailers before the implementation of the Structural Adjustment Program. Such controls helped to allow families in both urban and rural areas to meet their basic subsistence needs, and were especially beneficial for women upon whom rests most of the responsibility of supporting the family.

Other government policies and programs helped to make life in Zambia manageable for its citizens before the Structural Adjustment Program. For example, the Zambian government made heavily subsidized health care available to all citizens, and ensured access to basic education. Zambian governmental policies also kept domestic tensions in check by equitably distributing government-subsidized resources to the four separate geographic areas occupied by the country's four major ethnic groups.

Before it would disburse a loan to Zambia, the IMF required the Zambian government to promise to make major changes in the structure of its economy. According to the IMF, the required changes would allow the country to participate more successfully in the world market and, as a result, would allow it to repay its loan. Although many of the wealthy countries with controlling interests in the IMF do not have balanced national budgets, the IMF's Structural Adjustment Program packages are designed around the idea that Third World countries should achieve balanced budgets, and that they should do this in part by suspending support to domestic programs.

The International Monetary Fund required Zambia to devalue its currency, discontinue its subsidization of food, health, and education, suspend social welfare programs, lay-off federal employees, and turn its attention to both diversifying and increasing its exports for international markets. The result: a socio-economic nightmare for the country's people. The changes required by the IMF produced widespread unemployment; inflation of astronomical proportions; the suspension of the education of many people, especially girls; a dramatic decrease in access to health care; an increase in violence; conflict between the country's ethnic groups; and increased class stratification. While these problems affected most citizens, they made life especially arduous for women.

Over night, the devaluation of Zambian currency and the suspension of government subsidies on imported goods produced massive inflation. The consumer prices of domestically produced products and services, including health care, school fees, and transportation, rose by 50%; the prices of many imported goods doubled. Women and girls were especially hard-hit by inflation. For example, because women are primarily responsible for feeding and clothing their children, the dramatic increases in the cost of food and household goods took a great toll on their limited incomes; with the increase in household expenses, and the end of nationally subsidized health care and education, medicine and schooling became increasingly beyond the means of most families. As a result, families made difficult decisions about who would receive the benefit of increasingly limited resources, and those decisions reflected entrenched patriarchal values. In the case of education, for example, families often reverted to traditions that promoted the education of male children over that of girls.

Sudden, massive unemployment exacerbated the problems resulting from inflation. The IMF required the Zambian government to lay-off scores of government workers as a means of reducing expenditures. As a result of reduced consumer spending, private businesses and industry also let large numbers of workers go. In both spheres, women suffered great losses because their positions were frequently regarded as the most expendable. Joblessness, coupled with inflation, left Zambians destitute; sexist social structures disadvantaged women, even relative to men who were suffering greatly.

For example, while the inflated price of gasoline made the cost of public transportation beyond most citizens' means and forced those who retained jobs to walk long distances to and from work, after-work hours were very different for men and women. Because they are responsible for feeding their families, many women had to extend their days with either extra income-producing activities or by obtaining land on which to create family gardens. Women's "double burden" of work and child-care became even greater under the hardships of the Structural Adjustment Program.

Women also suffered directly at the hands of men as a result of the social stress the country experienced during the Structural Adjustment Program. Men, pressed to their limits, took advantage of women's resources and patriarchal social structures which allowed them to succeed in

such efforts. For example, one woman farmer interviewed recounted how her brother had stolen from her: their father had willed them an ox to share, and every year she and her brother took turns using the animal to plough their fields; in the first year of the Structural Adjustment Program, the brother took the ox, refused to return it, and rented it to others for extra income, saying that his family could not survive if he did otherwise; the woman, in turn, could not plant enough to feed her family that year, and since customary law in the area did not recognize women's right to property, had no recourse. Such situations were not uncommon.

Nor was physical violence. In the years of the Structural Adjustment Program, the rate of violent crime in Zambia rose sharply. Women's increased activity away from home, as a result of their need to have extra income-generating activities, made them increasingly vulnerable to attack; women walking to and from work or their gardens, often distant from their homes, were fearful of being assaulted. At home, too, people were wary. One interviewee described how she and her husband took turns staying awake at night to protect themselves from prospective robbers.

These problems were further exacerbated by increasing conflict between groups in Zambia. As a result of IMF conditions, the government suspended its policy of distributing agricultural resources equitably throughout the country. Some areas of the country began to receive more and better supplies, setting the stage for conflicts between the ethnic groups living in different geographic regions. The Structural Adjustment Program also indirectly produced increased stratification among the country's women: those women farmers who happened to live along the country's supply roads received many more resources than those who lived in remote territories. While such women were among the few to benefit financially from the Structural Adjustment Program in Zambia, their prosperity rested on the deprivation of others.

Clearly, the imposition of the conditions of the IMF Structural Adjustment Program in Zambia wreaked havoc on the lives of the country's people. Similar IMF Structural Adjustment Programs throughout the Third World have produced equally devastating effects. We note that some IMF Structural Adjustment Programs in other impoverished countries have included a feature missing from the Zambian program: special encouragement for multinational corporations to promote exports. The mistreatment of women workers by such corporations has been well documented by other feminist scholars. (Nash and Fernandez-Kelly, 1983; Fuentes and Ehrenreich, 1983; Ward, 1990)

A small number of women entrepreneurs benefit from the free-market conditions created by IMF adjustment programs, and some women find empowerment and forge coalitions with other women in their efforts to resist the hardships the programs impose. Generally, however, throughout the Third World, people suffer greatly as a result of the conditions their governments must accept in order to procure loans designed to relieve the economic instability of their countries.

As voting members in the IMF, western governments, including that of the United States, condone and encourage the policies that so disrupt the lives of so many millions in Third World states. The United Nations Economic Social and Cultural Organization (UNESCO) and the United Nations Africa Economic Committee (UNAEC) have criticized the extraordinary toll that citizens in Third World states, especially women, are paying for their governments' Structural Adjustment Programs. In the 1990s, other organizations and individual citizens in Western countries are also attempting to alter IMF policies. The Development Gap, for example, a Washington, D.C. based non-governmental organization concerned primarily with the environment, began a campaign in 1991 to urge the U.S. Congress to use the U.S. voting position in the International Monetary Fund to alter IMF Structural Adjustment Programs.

Western feminists can join or initiate efforts to alter the IMF's programs. Women from wealthy countries must recognize our collaboration in the global system that oppresses women. As citizens of the countries intimately involved with the implementation of international policies which foster the exploitation of women in the Third World, we can seek to change the system. Indeed, we must: to fail to act on behalf of the women suffering as a result of our government's involvement in the IMF is to perpetuate the oppression of others, even as we seek to relieve our own.

REFERENCES

Fuentes, Annette and Ehrenreich, Barbara, eds.: *Women in the Global Factory.* Boston: South End Press, 1983.

Nash, June and Fernandez-Kelly, Patricia, eds.: *Women, Men, and the International Division of Labor.* Albany: State University of New York Press, 1983.

Ward, Kathryn, ed.: *Women Workers and Global Restructuring.* Ithaca: Cornell University Press, 1990.

Social Protest and the Feminist Movement

Throughout *Feminist Frontiers IV* we have begun to understand the breadth and magnitude of the social forces working to disadvantage women. Socialization, the organization of social institutions, and social and economic policies all come together to hinder women's full political participation, self-determination, economic security, and even health and safety.

Despite the ubiquitous nature of sexism, racism, classism, nationalism, homophobia, and the other forms of prejudice embedded in our social institutions, women resist. As we have seen, women often fight to undermine the forces of oppression in individual ways. Women also come together to take collective action to pursue social change. This section explores contemporary feminist movements, noting that feminist issues are different in particular cultural and historical contexts.

Women's resistance has a long history and has taken many different forms. In "Black Club Women and the Creation of the National Association of Colored Women" Stephanie Shaw documents African-American women's tradition of organizing against racism and sexism. The National Association of Colored Women, which served as the preeminent African-American organization during the late 1800s and early 1900s, built on existing community institutions and stressed "self-determination, self-improvement, and community development." The women Shaw writes about would not, by and large, have

called themselves "feminist," because that term was appropriated by white activists of the time. Nevertheless, their resistance is central to a history of women's movements.

Also important to the history of women's movements is an understanding of the effects of feminist organizing on women's everyday lives. Judith Stacey examines the relationship between the feminist movement, the transition to a service-oriented economy, and women's strategies for managing their daily lives in "Postindustrial Conditions and Postfeminist Consciousness in the Silicon Valley." Stacey asserts that the feminist movement may have served as unwitting midwife to the birth of new family and work situations that, ironically, perpetuate gender stratification and limit possibilities for feminist consciousness and practice.

What constitutes feminist resistance, and what feminist priorities should be, is not always clear-cut. Myra Marx Ferree discusses the construction of very different definitions of feminism by women in the former East and West Germanies, in "Patriarchies and Feminisms: The Two Women's Movements of Post-Unification Germany." Ferree argues that women in the two Germanies experienced patriarchy in vastly different ways: While women in West Germany were economically dependent on their husbands, women in East Germany were dependent on the State. As a result of these different experiences, feminists from West Germany tended to focus on the oppressive aspects of private family relationships, while those from East Germany emphasized the role of public policy and the State in women's oppression. Neither side is "right," Ferree suggests. Instead, we need to understand "feminism as intrinsically multiple in its analyses and emphases."

Despite continuing gender stratification, women's movements have produced important changes in women's lives and in social institutions. As feminist gains and policies became institutionalized, social change and women's resistance often occurred within workplaces and established institutions. The abortion and women's health clinic that Wendy Simonds analyzes in "Feminism on the Job: Confronting Opposition in Abortion Work" is a well-established feminist organization that operates within an often hostile environment. Workers in the clinic must cope with both the emotionally difficult work of providing abortions and a constant barrage of antiabortion protest. They do so, Simonds argues, by interpreting their experiences in feminist terms. Simonds' article gives us a sense of the daily struggles and rewards of feminist resistance at the grassroots.

In the anthology's final reading, Verta Taylor and Nancy Whittier present an overview of the multiple forms of the feminist movement from its emergence in the 1960s to the present. Their article, "The New Feminist Movement," traces three stages in the contemporary women's movement: the period of resurgence, 1966–1971; the feminist heyday, 1972–1982; and the period of abeyance, 1983 through the present. Taylor and Whittier discuss the transformations and ideologies driving each state and, in contrast to other descriptions of the 1980s and 1990s as a "postfeminist era," suggest that the women's movement continues in the 1990s, taking a new focus and new strategies for change. Feminism, in short, has a long and continuous past and strong prospects for the future. As women's movements enter the twenty-first century, they are becoming more diverse than ever and hold great promise for transforming the lives of both women and men for the better. As you finish reading *Feminist Frontiers IV,* what changes would you like to see in the gender system?

Black Club Women and the Creation of the National Association of Colored Women

STEPHANIE J. SHAW

Much of what we know about black club women has been explained in the context of the creation of the National Association of Colored Women (NACW).[1] This scholarship often links black club women's activities to the most immediate and most obvious stimuli—the rising tide of Jim Crowism, the increase in lynching and other acts of mob violence, the vile verbal and literary attacks on the character of black women, and the general deterioration of race relations throughout the nation.[2] Historian Rayford Logan referred to these decades at the end of the nineteenth century as "the Nadir" in the history of American race relations.[3]

Club women themselves spoke out and wrote enough to suggest that those problems were important catalysts for their activism. Late-nineteenth-century journalist, community activist, and club leader Ida B. Wells Barnett launched her antilynching crusade not simply after the brutal killing of her good friend, Thomas Moss, but also after her thorough investigation of lynching incidents concluded that the recent increase in lynching was carefully and deliberately orchestrated in response to black economic gains and political potential. Mary Church Terrell added the abuse of vagrancy laws, the convict lease system, and peonage to the increasing threats to black life and security. Prominent turn-of-the-century Virginia club woman Janie Porter Barrett summarized the feelings of sympathetic contemporary observers (and recent scholars) when she wrote: "No one can deny that the Negro race is going through the most trying period of its history. Truly these are days when we are 'being tried as by fire.' "[4]

Stephanie J. Shaw, "Black Club Women and the Creation of the National Association of Colored Women," *Journal of Women's History* 3, no. 2 (Fall 1991). Copyright © 1991 by Indiana University Press. Reprinted with the permission of the publishers.

Considering the evidence that black club women left, it is not difficult to see why current-day scholars interpret the organization of the NACW as a response to these bad conditions. But such a conclusion ignores considerable evidence that reveals the obvious flaw in the interpretation. According to historian Willie Mae Coleman, the Colored Women's League, formed in Washington, D.C., in 1892, was a coalition of 113 organizations. The more nationally oriented National Federation of Afro-American Women, formed in 1895, represented the combination of 85 organizations.[5] When these two federations combined in 1896 to form the NACW, the impetus and inclination for black women to form a collective was more than a few years old. In fact, it predated the so-called nadir of African-American history by generations.

The purpose of this article is to formulate a new interpretation of the creation of the national black women's club coalition of the 1890s—one that points to the internal traditions of the African-American community rather than activities in the white community. Numerous factors suggest the need for the alternative view. First, the history of "voluntary associations" among African-Americans indicates a historical legacy of collective consciousness and mutual associations. Second, individual histories of diverse club women reveal early lessons in racial consciousness and community commitment. And third, the work of organized black women before the formation of the NACW was no different from the activities of club women after the creation of the NACW. Altogether, the founding of the NACW did not mark the beginning of the important organized work of black women against racism, sexism, and their effects, as earlier studies imply. Instead, the creation of the national organization represents another step in an internal historical process of encouraging and supporting self-determination, self-improvement, and community development.

At least as early as the advent of American slavery, African-Americans consistently demonstrated inclinations toward community consciousness and collective activity. Historians of the antebellum South, slavery, and slave culture inform us that even under slavery, black men and women operated as a community within a community in which both personal and social identities developed and helped to ameliorate the harsh conditions of their enforced bondage.[6] Slaves often acted together in rebellion, or colluded afterwards to protect those implicated in acts of resistance.[7] Plantation childcare situations, the forced secrecy surrounding organized religious ceremonies, and the potential for and actual loss of blood family members continually encouraged the development of group consciousness.[8] Folk tales provided lessons in group survival and examples of community ethics.[9] Historian Lawrence Levine writes that the most enduring characteristic of slave songs was their group nature. While they often functioned to set the pace of work for slaves, in improvised verses, one gang member might chastise another for not carrying his/her burden of the work. Structurally, through lining-out and call-and-response forms, the songs allowed a slave "at one and the same time to preserve his voice as a distinct entity and to blend it with those of his fellows."[10] Slaves in All Saints Parish, South Carolina, even imposed "a cooperative work ethos upon the highly individualist task system" of work which their owners used in an attempt to regulate their labor. Slaves adapted the labor system proposed by their masters and overseers "to their own sense of appropriateness" as they worked the crop in a row, hoeing and moving across the field synchronously to the rhythm of a work song.[11] Historian Deborah Gray White notes that slave women developed a network within the slave community that was supportive, empowering, and instrumental to their survival.[12]

Within the non-slave population of the antebellum period, the associations of individuals could take on more structure. They abounded in the North and South as benevolent and beneficial societies and intellectual and community uplift groups, among others. The Free African Society, formed in Philadelphia in 1787 by Richard Allen and Absolom Jones, is best known for the creation of the African Methodist Episcopal Church. From its inception, however, The Free African Society was also a mutual-aid society. The Female Benevolent Society of St. Thomas took over the organization in 1793, and two years later the all-male African Friendly Society of St. Thomas joined the

women. The Daughters of Africa, which existed as early as 1821, was a mutual-aid organization of approximately 200 black working-class women. Members bought groceries and supplies for the needy, paid sick benefits, and lent money to society members in emergency situations. One scholar estimates that by 1850 there were at least 200 black mutual-aid societies in the country's major cities, with a total of 13,000 to 15,000 members.[13] This estimate is undoubtedly conservative, for in 1838 there were 119 such organizations with 7,372 members in Philadelphia alone.[14]

African-American women worked for self-improvement and racial advancement in a variety of settings during the antebellum period. Historian Linda Perkins writes that "the threads that held together the organizational as well as individual pursuits . . . were those of 'duty' and 'obligation' to the race. The concept of racial obligation was intimately linked with the concept of racial 'uplift' and 'elevation.'" Perkins notes the efforts of the Colored Female Produce Society, formed in 1831, to boycott slave-made products. Members of the Boston-based Afri-American Female Intelligence Society used their collected dues to buy newspapers and books and to rent a reading room. Also, members of at least one year were eligible for illness benefits. One reporter claimed that the Ohio Ladies Education Society had, by 1840, done " 'more towards the establishment of schools for the education of colored people . . . in Ohio than any other organized group.' "[15]

When slavery ended, African-Americans had considerable experience operating mutual associations, and carrying those practices through the Reconstruction period ensured future survival. Greater physical mobility, the tremendously unstable economy, and a determination to be free and independent of whites continued to encourage mutual associations. Historian Armstead Robinson writes that during the Reconstruction period, black men and women began to develop "their communal infrastructure."[16] To that end, among the many associations created during this period were agricultural societies concerned with planting, harvesting, contracting labor, and homesteading; savings and loan associations; insurance companies; trade unions; fire departments; burial, literary, social, educational, and business societies; and many others.[17] Even the educational institutions developed among former slaves during this period focused not simply on schooling the individual but on the educational needs and interests of the group in tandem.[18] Taken to the extreme, all-black towns formed in the south and west during and immediately after the Reconstruction period were radical and ultimate examples of mutual associations.[19]

Although Federal Reconstruction organizations and institutions eventually collapsed, black self-help groups continued to thrive, and black women's activities were prominent. The Daughters of Zion, founded in 1867 in Memphis, Tennessee, was a church-affiliated group that served the same purpose that the earlier associations and later women's clubs served—individual and community self-help and uplift. With over 300 members at one time, the group organized relief efforts after the war, employed a physician to care for congregation members, and worked in various other public health and education activities.[20] Mary Prout founded The Independent Order of St. Luke (IOSL) in 1867. The Order began as a traditional beneficial society for women, and later admitted men. Under the subsequent leadership of Maggie Lena Walker, the organization flourished financially and grew to 100,000 members in 28 states. Walker also devised the plans for the St. Luke Penny Savings Bank, a major financial institution that came about as a result of community cooperation. And once in place, the bank fostered that tradition by becoming a symbol of accomplishment, a source of pride, and a facilitator of community development. Walker credited her success not simply to her own abilities but also to "the strength of the St. Luke collective as a whole and . . . the special strengths and talents of the inner core of the St. Luke women in particular." She linked black women as individuals to the advancement of the group by encouraging them to work to improve conditions of the home, community, and race.[21]

The details of Elsa Barkley Brown's study of Maggie Lena Walker indicate that the development of community consciousness and social responsibility was not accidental but a consequence of deliberate processes. Among black women in general, a variety of individuals participated in those processes. For example, if Clara Jones, a prominent Detroit librarian and clubwoman, had not heard it before, when she was preparing to leave home to attend college in the late 1920s, her grandfather, a former slave, reminded her: "You're going to get your education, and it's not yours. You're doing it for your people."[22] Jones later characterized her family as "a fiercely education-conscious family." And she added that "it was accepted that my four brothers and sisters and . . . [I] would all go to college to help our race. That was the way everyone thought in those days."[23]

Janie Porter Barrett's community activism is well known, but rarely do we get a glimpse of aspects of her early life that might help to explain her activism. Born in 1870, Barrett founded the Locust Street Settlement House in Hampton, Virginia, and the Peak Turnout, Virginia, Home for Delinquent Girls (later called the Girls' Industrial

School). Her mother worked as a nurse for a wealthy white family, and she reared Janie in their home. Janie's mother apparently accepted her employer's educating Janie along with the white children of the family, but she left her position when the white woman of the house announced that she wanted to become Janie's legal guardian and send her to a northern white school for more education. Historian Tullia Brown Hamilton notes that the employer expected Janie to pass for white while attending the school. After quitting her job, Janie's mother sent her daughter to Hampton Institute instead. Obviously, Barrett's mother wanted to have control over her daughter's education, but we can also speculate about Barrett's mother's race consciousness. That is, it was not only unacceptable for her child to pass for white, but it was also important for Barrett to go to a black school. Not surprisingly, because of her upbringing in the comfortable white household, Barrett found the living conditions at Hampton in the 1880s to be very disappointing. After all, she had always enjoyed having a room that "was daintily furnished, and . . . surroundings [that] bespoke refinement and ease." Evidently, the white household did not foster the development of any realistic racial identity either. But Hampton could and did remedy that. Barrett wrote that when she first arrived at Hampton, she got tired of being drilled on her "duties to the race." She noted that she always woke up happy on Sundays, because on Sundays, she said, "I didn't have to do a single thing for my race." But students and faculty at Hampton succeeded at making Barrett more socially responsible and racially conscious. And when she created the Locust Street Settlement House in 1890—six years before the formation of the NACW and 18 years before the creation of the Virginia Federation of Colored Women's Clubs (VFCWC)—she used money that she and her husband intended to use to install indoor plumbing in their home.[24]

Twenty-five years later, Barrett, a well-seasoned community activist, had held offices in the NACW and the VFCWC and was launching her project to create a home for delinquent black girls in Virginia. When Margaret Murray Washington, a principal at Tuskegee Institute and the wife of Booker T. Washington, offered her a principalship at Tuskegee Institute, Barrett wrote to Hollis Frissell (then president of Hampton Institute) that "Washington's letter makes me wish that I could be in two places at once. I should be glad to serve at Tuskegee, but I know I am going where I am needed [most?] and though this undertaking is most difficult, it isn't impossible, and if the friends will stand by me, this Home School will be, in time, a tremendous power for good." In fact, the home school became a model program, set up on the cottage plan and the honor system, with the VFCWC as one of its major financial supporters.[25]

Ida B. Wells (Barnett) was born a slave in Holly Springs, Mississippi, in 1862, of parents who insisted on educating their children, and some of Wells's first teachers were individuals who came to Holly Springs specifically to aid the recently freed men and women. Wells eventually left her hometown to continue her education, but after her parents died during the yellow fever epidemic of 1878, she and her surviving siblings immediately came under the guardianship of the Masons, a fraternal society of which her father was a member. Such fraternal societies traditionally assumed the responsibility for the surviving dependents of deceased members. While it is unlikely that this incident alone caused Wells to become an activist, surely the lesson in social responsibility was not lost. Within a short time, she became very active in civil rights causes. In 1884 she successfully sued the Chesapeake and Ohio Railroad for not allowing her to ride in a first-class car for which she had a ticket, but a higher court overturned the decision. Before the reversal occurred, railroad company lawyers offered Wells money to settle the case out of court, but she turned down their offers, dismissing the possibility of an individual payoff while pushing for a larger victory for the race. By the 1890s her articles on educational conditions for black residents in Memphis resulted in her being fired from her teaching position. More scathing pieces on lynching resulted in her fleeing for her life.[26] While she lived in exile, other black club women helped to support and protect her.[27] Wells wrote that most of the trouble she encountered with whites resulted from her actions on behalf of the race. But she said she owed it to herself and her race to tell the truth about white racism.[28]

Jane Edna Hunter, born in 1882 on a South Carolina plantation, grew up in a household with her parents that at one time also enjoyed the presence of her grandmother and great grandmother, both of whom were former slaves. Her parents appreciated the value of formal education but apparently could neither assume the right nor afford the privilege; Hunter worked her way through school. At the end of one summer of employment, because she needed all of her earnings to obtain school necessities, a friend agreed to purchase her return train ticket. When at the last minute it became apparent that the person who had offered to purchase the ticket would not follow through, the 20 or so proud friends and neighbors who gathered at the train station to see her off began to put together their change, ulti-

mately collecting enough money for her ticket and fifty cents to spare.[29]

Hunter eventually finished secondary and nursing school, but when she relocated to Cleveland in 1905, she did not easily find housing or work. She had no family and few friends in that city, and the first place she lived turned out to be a residence for prostitutes. As soon as she established herself favorably in housing and in work, she and a few friends met to form the Working Girl's Home Association to build a home for "the poor motherless daughters of the race." The women who formed this voluntary association pledged to contribute five cents a week and committed themselves to recruiting new members. The first home opened in 1911. After the second facility opened in 1917, Hunter tried to explain her motivation:

> There was something . . . [that] kept urging and making me less content with what I was doing and calling me into a broader service. . . . Then the thought came to me that there were other girls who had come to Cleveland, perhaps under similar circumstances as myself and were strangers and alone and were meeting with the same difficulties and hardships in trying to establish themselves in a large city.

The Working Girl's Home Association proved to be a successful venture and its residence grew from a 23-room facility to a 72-room facility in 1917. By 1928 the institution had 135 bedrooms, 4 parlors, 6 clubrooms, a cafeteria, and a beauty salon.[30]

The creation of the Working Girl's Home Association represented a traditional response to a particular problem in that the black community historically turned to voluntary associations to resolve internal problems. But Jane Edna Hunter's organization also represented what was new about many of the black women's associations (more often called leagues or clubs after 1890) formed around this time. It was a voluntary association, but the women who came together to form the association did not share the common local history that the earlier church and/or community society members shared. Hunter and many of her colleagues were relative newcomers to Cleveland. In general, the origins of the membership of the late-nineteenth to early-twentieth century women's clubs were often different in this substantial way. These women were not necessarily total strangers to one another, but they were quite often newcomers to the geographic locales where they became prominently associated with club work.

Records of the Federation of Colored Women's Clubs of Colorado, for example, indicate that many of its members were not natives of Colorado. Gertrude Ross, who held numerous offices beginning in 1911, was from Illinois. Ruth Howard, one of Denver's most active residents, came to Colorado from Texas. Elizabeth Ensley, the founder of the Federation in 1903, came from Massachusetts by way of Washington, D.C., and Mississippi. Among the many other examples, Bettey Wilkins, a member of several federated clubs in Colorado, came from Ohio.[31]

The few published accounts of black women's clubs suggest the same. Elizabeth Lindsay Davis provides brief biographical sketches of 71 Illinois club women in her book on the state federation. She notes the birth place and location of the club work for 39 of the women (54%). Only one of the women was active in club work in the place where she was born.[32] Delilah Beasley's 1919 work on black pioneers in California explicitly identifies 19 women who were members of clubs, at least 14 of whom were migrants to California.[33]

Tullia Brown Hamilton studied the leadership of the NACW and detailed similar statistics. Out of 108 women, Hamilton determined the birth places of 70. Approximately half of that number were born in the antebellum slave states (while over 90% of the general population was born and still lived there in the 1890s), and of that number born in the south, 65% settled in the north or west after some migration within the south. Hamilton also concluded that even among northern club women, "in all likelihood [they] migrated to other areas of the North, West, or even the South before settling down."[34]

To be sure, because of turn-of-the-century migration patterns, many African-Americans in the urban areas where clubs proliferated had migrated there.[35] More important, the clubs allowed women who had left their original communities to continue to associate with one another for individual and collective advancement as earlier mutual associations had. Significantly, the diverse geographic origins of the residents now meant that "the community" was no longer local; it had national roots. And so to effectively address the concerns of the members, the club network and many club activities became national.[36]

The 25 members of the Willing Worker's Club of Stamford, Connecticut, gave $2,000 to "needy causes throughout the city" between 1901 and 1907. The Art and Study Club of Moline, Illinois, enumerated among its functions visiting the sick and clothing the poor. Members of the Adelphi Club of St. Paul, Minnesota, read race literature, supported two elderly women, took fruit and magazines to city hospitals, gave food baskets to the needy on Easter and Thanksgiving, took clothes to a local orphanage,

and supported a South Carolina kindergarten. Black club women in Boston supported a kindergarten in Atlanta, Georgia. Although charters, bylaws, and objectives are not available for most turn-of-the-century clubs, the actions of members of many of them suggest that they also believed in a stated aim of the Neighborhood Union of Atlanta, Georgia: "to develop group consciousness and mass movements."[37]

Supporting the less able and improving standards of living meant providing services normally supported by local governments through public taxes. But providing these services pushed the activities of these women beyond traditional "charity work" and, in fact, represented community development. Charleston, South Carolina, club woman Susan Dart Butler operated a library for African-Americans in a building owned by her father and stocked primarily with his books. Local black club women helped to maintain the facility until it became too expensive for them to operate. At that point, Butler leased it to the city for one dollar a year on the condition that public officials maintain it as a black library. Black club women in Atlanta, Georgia, helped the Neighborhood Union to establish and maintain a public health clinic for black residents. They eventually leased it to the city, also, and thereby forced the public support that similar clinics in the white community always enjoyed. In both instances, the women ultimately donated the facilities to the city.[38]

In Delaware, Texas, Arkansas, West Virginia, Florida, Virginia, and Alabama the state federations of colored women's clubs created institutions for sheltering black juvenile delinquents who would otherwise have suffered incarceration with adult prison populations. In Missouri, Texas, North Carolina, Mississippi, Florida, Virginia, Alabama, Georgia, South Carolina, and Louisiana, black club women funded, built, and maintained public health clinics and/or hospitals.[39] Club women also created homes for black working women in such urban areas as Cleveland, Chicago, New York, Newark, Boston, Little Rock, and Kansas City (Missouri). The Neighborhood Union House was a model settlement house that groups throughout the country sought to emulate. Other prominent settlements created by club women included the Locust Street Settlement in Hampton, Virginia, the Phillis Wheatley in Cleveland, and the Russel Plantation Settlement and the Calhoun Settlement in rural Alabama. In all of the former confederate states, in midwestern states including Kansas, Indiana, Ohio, Illinois, Minnesota, and in numerous northern and western states, black club women built, supported, and/or managed nursery schools and kindergartens, orphan-

BLACK WOMEN AS DO-ERS:
THE SOCIAL RESPONSIBILITY OF BLACK WOMEN

JOYCE A. LADNER

When I think of social responsibility, I think of Bill and Camille Cosby, whose gift of $20 million to Spelman College is one of the most extraordinary examples of duty and commitment and faith and hope for Black women. When I think of the social responsibility of Black women, I think of the generations of our foremothers and forefathers who instilled within us the idea and value that it is our duty to help those in need. I think about the women who have gone before us who although poor, understood that the only way they could assure progress for the race would be through the dint of their own efforts. I think of Harriet Tubman who risked her life while helping other Blacks escape to freedom, because she understood the importance of duty. I think of Sojourner Truth who understood that it was she who had to take responsibility for interpreting the plaintive cries for freedom of enslaved Blacks. I think of Ida B. Wells Barnett, who took the responsibility to advocate against lynching. I think of Anna Julia Cooper who knew she had to take responsibility to educate Black youths. I think of Mary Church Terrell who understood the relationship between advocacy and race. I think of Mary McLeod Bethune who took up the mantle of responsibility to educate, to advocate, to lobby, to pester—because she knew that if she didn't, there would be few others who could.

When I think of social responsibility, I think of Zola Jackson, my first teacher in Hattiesburg, Mississippi, who believed every child has something to give, and that it is up to us to help them to develop. I think of Ruby Doris Robinson, a Spelman student who was one of the founders of the Student Nonviolent Coordinating Committee— who spent weeks in jail, who was a tireless organizer, strategist and leader within the civil rights movement. Ruby D., who walked this campus, sat in these classrooms, and left her indomitable courage and relentless efforts to bring equality to Blacks—here on this campus to

Joyce Ladner, "Black Women as Do-ers: The Social Resposibility of Black Women," *Sage* 6 (Summer 1989). Copyright © 1989 by Sage Publications, Inc. Reprinted with permission of the publishers.

be passed on to another generation. And yes, I think of Fannie Lou Hamer, the short, stout woman from the Delta of Mississippi, who stands alone as the voice and spirit of grassroots social change in America. I think of Ella Jo Baker, the spirited civil rights activist who had the moral courage to try to change America. I think of Mother Hale, the Harlem woman who soothes the cries of babies born addicted to drugs; I think of the Black woman who operates "Grandma's House" in Washington, D.C., where Black babies born with AIDS are given a chance to grow and develop, to play and to be normal, for whatever period they live. Ruby Doris Robinson once sat here in Sisters Chapel, pondering the relationship between education and social responsibility. In a real sense, it was her model that women of my generation, women of Johnnetta Cole's generation, followed in defining ourselves, defining our sense of duty and obligation.

The women I have talked about inherited a noble tradition for being "do-ers"; that is, they were brought up to believe they could do anything. They were taught that they had to learn to be flexible, they had to learn to wash, cook, sew, get an education, raise children, work in their churches and clubs, establish orphanages, relief societies, become presidents of colleges, start colleges, and everything else that needed to be done.

Being a "do-er" was normal and expected. Being a "do-er" meant that you saw what had to be done, and you simply went out and tried to do it. No task was too small, no reward too minimal to do what had to be done. All around us the idea was hammered into our heads that social responsibility was a normal part of life—it was not something that was tucked off to the side as a special volunteer activity. It was part of the way you defined your identity, your sense of purpose, your values, your reason for being. Our religious upbringing reinforced this concept of obligation, this sense of helping the needy, giving something back to the community, or in the words of my mother, "earning your space in the world."

What does all of this mean today? How do we, how should we, define social responsibility? How do we get more women involved? How do we pass these values and this sense of duty on to the next generation, especially at a time when the tasks before us seem impossible?

Our communities are so fragmented, our families are under such stress and many poor families are suffering the effects of such acute crisis and devastation that it is easy to become discouraged—it is easy to think that there is nothing we can do to help people who have such tremendous need. Over the past twenty years Black families have experienced a record number of problems. Since 1960 we have seen the number of Black families become so fractured that today, 52 percent are headed by women. The majority of children in such families are living in poverty. Black infant mortality rates continue to increase, as the gap between Blacks and whites widens.

The school drop-out rate continues to increase. The numbers of homeless individuals and families (600,000 to 3 million) escalate by the day. Blacks now have a disproportionate number of the AIDS cases. Teenage pregnancy continues to be a huge problem with Black women becoming grandmothers as young as 24 years old. The rates of child abuse and neglect escalate, especially among drug addicted mothers and teenage mothers. Crime and violence have torn many communities apart, undermining stable neighborhoods where people are now afraid for their safety. And drugs have come to symbolize a modern day plague—a plague in its seriousness and its proportions. In Washington, D.C., drug-related violence has caused almost three-hundred deaths this year. Most of them involve young Black men in their late teens and early twenties—young Black men who are cut down in the prime of their lives—long before they have had the opportunity to become husbands, fathers, workers in productive jobs, and socially responsible citizens. More enter prison than enter college each year. A similar pattern has developed among young Black women, whose futures are just as dim, who see their prospects for a bright future with a college degree, a good career, a good marriage with children—as something that is absolutely impossible. They don't value life very much because they don't feel they will live very long.

What do we do? How do we intervene? How do we help these young people to get off their destructive courses? How do we help to restore a sense of normalcy to our communities so that elderly men and women can walk the streets safely? How do we keep children in school long enough to graduate? How do we stop chil-dren from having children? How do we inspire hope and trust, and a desire to achieve? Whose responsibility is it to do these things?

I do not pretend to have the answers to all these questions. I do know that if we fail to act, if we fail to try to find solutions to these problems, we will have failed the sense of mission and the sense of history that our foremothers charted for us. We will have failed to be this generation of "do-ers," a generation that is blessed with more wealth, more education, more skills than any before us. It is our obligation to become involved. It is our obligation to teach this sense of responsibility to solve problems to the young women who are now entering adulthood. It is our responsibility to use our social and civic clubs, our professional organizations, our churches, our workplaces—and everywhere else—to organize for change. Black women need to establish a National Corps of 'Do-ers', an army of concerned citizens who can reclaim our legacy and chart new courses in these seemingly impossible muddy waters.

There are no easy answers; there are no magical and quick-fix solutions to these extraordinary problems. One might ask, why do WE have to assume the responsibility to fix the problems of others? Why shouldn't the Federal government, or the people themselves, fix their own problems. *We* have to fix them because no one else is trying to do it. *We* have to fix them because we care. *We* have to help to fix them because they are also our problems. *We* have to be concerned about drugs and child care because these are problems that also affect middle class kids. *We* have to fix them because we have to insure that there will be a wholesome and healthy generation of young Black people to take over the reins after we have stepped aside. *We* have to fix them because, in my mother's words, *we* have to earn our space in this world.

Whether we are aerospace engineers, social workers, professors, day care providers, or homemakers, we have to take up the do-er mantle of our heritage of social responsibility, for there is no contradiction between being a good and competent professional and a "do-er."

The voice of Ruby Doris Robinson, my friend Ruby D., speaks softly, gently but firmly as she, like Meridian, the heroine of the Alice Walker novel, by the same name, guides us toward regeneration and renewal as we go forth in our challenging tasks—as we become the do-ers in the spirit of our foremothers.

ages, and homes for the black elderly. The White Rose Home in New York gained a national reputation for its work to protect black women migrants from the south. Altogether, the work of black club women on behalf of the race involved a broad range of activities. And even when their activities seemed explicitly directed to the benefit of women—as with the effort for women's suffrage and work with the YWCA movement—or some other less race-specific topic, they understood the consequences of all such work in terms of improving conditions for the race.[40]

The activities of NACW affiliates did not differ dramatically from earlier association activities. Club women provided aid to people in the community at large and therefore worked as the old benevolent societies worked. They provided emergency support for members and therefore functioned as the old mutual aid/beneficial associations functioned. And they worked for self-improvement and community uplift as both benevolent and beneficial societies of an earlier period had. But the NACW was different from those earlier associations not only in that it was a national black women's collective, but also, it was the country's leading national race organization—predating the creation of the NAACP by 15 years. Even after the founding of the NAACP, the NACW remained, for some time, the leading black national organization working for the individual and collective advancement of African Americans, because the NAACP remained controlled by whites for many years.

Self-help and racial uplift were always important objectives of black women's public activism, but the focal points of the activism did change over time. In earlier decades, the shared conditions of slavery and the limited mobility that slaves enjoyed restricted their associations to groups that included but went beyond the "family" to embrace the whole slave community. Except for the anti-slavery societies, associations of free blacks in the antebellum period maintained a local orientation as well. In the post-emancipation period, black women's organizations abounded, and many, like the ISOL, eventually had national connections. But the voluntary associations formed by club women around the turn of the century embraced

local women with shared traditions and outlooks who were often no longer from the same families, churches, neighborhoods, or even regions. And not only did that aspect of diversity not preclude their organizing, but it encouraged the creation of a national structure to perpetuate the historical traditions of self-help, community development, and racial uplift despite the demographic shifts in progress.

If the formation of black women's clubs represents but one phase in a long history of group identification and mutual association, then the formation of the NACW represents not only the broadening base, vision, and abilities of black club women, but also another logical step in the effort to maintain and/or improve important historical mechanisms for racial self-help. Through this newly rationalized and nationalized structure, black women could speak more profoundly about problems specific to them as black women and problems that affected them as they affected the race. There is no need to defend black club women against charges of imitating white women (the General Federation of Women's Clubs) or compensating for exclusion by the white women. African-American women's tradition of mutual association predated the GFWC by many years. And black women were reformers long before the Progressive Era. It is equally inappropriate to interpret the creation of the national coalition of African-American women's clubs as a response to the contemporary attacks on black female morality. Such attacks undoubtedly gave the organizers an important "cause" that could evoke an immediate response from the black community. But those attacks rested on an historical tradition, too, and at best the attacks only became more public and more frequent at this time. White society had always maintained that black people were immoral and evil; black slavery itself had been rationalized through this explanation.[41] The formation of the NACW represented no psycho-social shift in the women's personal identities or in their social, political, and economic agendas. Rather, it was simply a new national voice through which black club women could continue the struggle to improve their personal lives and the general standard of life in the ever-broadening communities of which they were a part.

NOTES

1. See for examples, Ruby M. Kendricks, " 'They Also Serve': The National Association of Colored Women, Inc.," *Negro History Bulletin* 42 (March 1954): 171-75; Tullia Kay Brown Hamilton, "The National Association of Colored Women, 1896-1920" (Ph.D.

diss., Emory University, 1978); Angela Y. Davis, *Women, Race and Class* (New York: Random House, 1983), 127-36. Activities of church and civic groups not associated with the NACW are included in Gerda Lerner's "Early Community Work of Black Club

Women," *Journal of Negro History* 59 (April 1974): 158-62; and throughout Dorothy C. Salem's "To Better Our World: Black Women in Organized Reform, 1890-1920" (Ph.D. diss., Kent State University, 1986). The most recent treatment of black women's organized self-help efforts is Anne Firor Scott, "Most Invisible of All: Black Women's Voluntary Associations," *Journal of Southern History* 56 (February 1990):3-22.

2. See Cynthia Neverdon-Morton, *Afro-American Women of the South and the Advancement of the Race, 1895-1925* (Knoxville: University of Tennessee Press, 1989), 191-201. And see local and state studies, including Darlene Clark Hine, *When the Truth is Told: A History of Black Women's Culture and Community in Indiana, 1875-1950* (Indianapolis: National Council of Negro Women, 1981); Marilyn Dell Brady, "Kansas Federation of Colored Women's Clubs: 1900-1930," *Kansas History: A Journal of the Central Plains 9* (Spring 1986): 19-30; Erlene Stetson, "Black Feminism in Indiana, 1893-1933," *Phylon* 64 (December 1983): 292-98; Earline Rae Ferguson, "The Woman's Improvement Club of Indianapolis: Black Women Pioneers in Tuberculosis Work, 1903-1933," *Indiana Magazine of History* 84 (September 1988): 237-61; Wilson Jeremiah Moses, "Domestic Feminism, Conservatism, Sex Roles, and Black Women's Clubs, 1893-1896," *Journal of Social and Behavioral Sciences* 24 (Fall 1987): 166-177. When historians discuss the attacks on black female morality as the most important reason for organizing the NACW, they usually point to the infamous James Jacks letter, in which he charged that all black women were prostitutes, liars, and thieves. Maude Thomas Jenkins, in "The History of the Black Woman's Club Movement in America" (Ed.D. diss., Columbia University Teacher's College, 1984), does explore the complex range of issues that crystallized and encouraged the formation of the NACW. She also links black women's associations in general to an African tradition of mutual aid.

3. See Rayford Logan, *The Negro in American Life and Thought: The Nadir, 1877-1901* (New York: Dial Press, 1954). The revised version of this book was published with the title, *The Betrayal of the Negro.*

4. Alfreda E. Duster, ed., *Crusade for Justice: The Autobiography of Ida B. Wells-Barnett* (Chicago: University of Chicago Press, 1968), 47-52; Ida B. Wells, *Southern Horrors: Lynch Law in all its Phases* (New York: New York Age Print, 1892); and *A Red Record: Tabulated Statistics and Alleged Causes of Lynchings in the United States, 1892-1893-1894* (Chicago: Donohue and Henneberry Press, 1895); Mary Church Terrell, "Lynching From a Negro's Point of View," *North American Review* 178 (June 1904): 853-68; Janie Porter Barrett, *Locust Street Social Settlement: Founded and Managed by Colored* (Hampton, Va.: Hampton Normal and Agricultural Institute, 1912), 19 in the Harris and Janie Porter Barrett Collection, Huntington Library Archives, Hampton University, Hampton, Va.

5. Willie Mae Coleman, "Keeping the Faith and Disturbing the Peace. Black Women: From Anti-Slavery to Women's Suffrage" (Ph.D. diss., University of California-Irvine, 1982), 75.

6. See, for examples, Sterling Stuckey, "Through the Prism of Folklore: The Black Ethos in Slavery," *The Massachusetts Review* 9 (Summer 1968): 417-37; John Blassingame, *The Slave Community* (New York: Oxford University Press, 1972); George Rawick, *From Sundown to Sun Up* (Westport, Conn.: Greenwood Publishing Co., 1972); Eugene Genovese, *Roll, Jordan, Roll: The World the Slaves Made* (New York: Pantheon Books, 1974); Herbert G. Gutman, *The Black Family in Slavery and Freedom, 1750-1925* (New York: Vintage Books, 1976).

7. See Angela Davis, "Reflections on the Black Woman's Role in the Community of Slaves," *The Black Scholar* 2 (December 1971): 2-15; Allan Kulikoff, *Tobacco and Slaves: The Development of Southern Cultures in the Chesapeake, 1680-1800* (Chapel Hill: University of North Carolina Press, 1986), 343-44; Herbert Aptheker, *American Negro Slave Revolts* (New York: Columbia University Press, 1943); and see note 6 above.

8. Orville Vernon Burton, *"In my Father's House are Many Mansions:" Family and Community in Edgeville, S.C.* (Chapel Hill: University of North Carolina Press, 1985), 164-65; Allan Kulikoff, *Tobacco and Slaves,* 345-51; Albert J. Raboteau, *Slave Religion: The "Invisible Institution" in the Antebellum South* (Oxford: Oxford University Press, 1978); Norrece T. Jones, Jr., *Born a Child of Freedom Yet a Slave: Mechanisms of Control and Strategies of Resistance in Antebellum South Carolina* (Hanover: University Press of New England, 1990).

9. Sterling Stuckey, "Through the Prism of Folklore"; Lawrence Levine, *Black Culture and Black Consciousness: Afro-American Folk Thought From Slavery to Freedom* (New York: Oxford University Press, 1977), 81-135; John Blassingame, *The Slave Community,* 127-30.

10. Lawrence Levine, *Black Culture and Black Consciousness,* 6, 7, 10, 33-34; Albert Raboteau, *Slave Religion,* 243-45.

11. Charles Joyner, *Down by the Riverside; A South Carolina Slave Community* (Urbana: University of Illinois Press, 1984), 58-59.

12. Deborah Gray White, *Ar'n't I a Woman: Female Slaves in the Plantation South* (New York: W. W. Norton & Co., 1985), 119-141.

13. Leonard P. Curry, *The Free Black in Urban America, 1800-1850* (Chicago: University of Chicago Press, 1981), 197-214; Dorothy Sterling, ed., *We Are Your Sisters: Black Women in the Nineteenth Century* (New York: W. W. Norton & Co., 1984), 104-07. See also Philip S. Foner, *History of Black Americans: From Africa to the Emergence of the Cotton Kingdom* (Westport, Conn.: Greenwood Press, 1975), 555-78; Herbert Aptheker, *A Documentary History of the Negro People in the U.S.,* 3 vols. (New York: Citadel Press, 1951, 1973, 1974), *passim;* Dorothy Porter, "The Organized Educational Activities of Negro Literary Societies, 1828-1846," *Journal of Negro Education* 6 (October 1936): 555-576; Julie Winch, *Philadelphia's Black Elite: Activism, Accommodation, and the Struggle for Autonomy, 1787-1848* (Philadelphia: Temple University Press, 1988), 5-15.

14. Leonard P. Curry, *The Free Black in Urban America,* 202. An 1835 issue of *Niles Register* estimated that Baltimore had 35-40 black mutual-aid societies. Curry's estimate of 200 groups is baffling considering that he cites the individual statistics for Baltimore and Philadelphia.

15. Linda Perkins, "Black Women and Racial 'Uplift' Prior to Emancipation," in *The Black Woman Cross Culturally,* ed. Filomina Chioma Steady (Cambridge: Schenkman Publishing Co., 1981), 317-334.

16. Armstead Robinson, "Plans Dat Comed From God: Institution Building and the Emergence of Black Leadership in Reconstruction Memphis," in *Towards a New South? Studies in Post-Civil War Southern Communities,* ed. Orville Burton and Robert G. McMath (Westport, Conn.: Greenwood Press, 1982), 71-102.

17. See W. E. B. DuBois, ed., *Some Efforts of American Negroes for their Own Social Betterment* (Atlanta: Atlanta University Press, 1898); Guy B. Johnson, "Some Factors in the Development of Negro Social Institutions in the United States," *American Journal of Sociology* 30 (November 1934): 329-337; Inabel Burns Lindsay, "Some Contributions of Negroes to Welfare Services, 1865-1900," *Journal of Negro Education* 25 (Winter 1956): 18; Joel Williamson, *After Slavery: The Negro in South Carolina During Reconstruction, 1861-1877* (Chapel Hill: University of North Carolina Press, 1965), 321-23; Vernon Lane Wharton, *The Negro in Mississippi, 1865-1890* (Chapel Hill: University of North Carolina Press, 1947; reprint, New York: Harper & Row, 1965), 270-73; Peter Rachleff, *Black Labor in Richmond, 1865-1890* (Urbana: University of Illinois Press, 1989), *passim;* Elsa Barkley Brown, "Womanist Consciousness: Maggie Lena Walker and the Independent Order of St. Luke," *Signs: Journal of Women in Culture and Society* 14 (Spring 1989): 610-633. A scrap of paper dated 1898 in the Harris and Janie Porter Barrett collection at Hampton notes the creation of The People's Building and Loan Association of Hampton, Virginia in 1889. The note claims that by 1898, the organization had loaned over $140,000 to members, earned over $30,000 in dividends, and helped stockholders purchase 250 houses.

18. See James D. Anderson, *The Education of Blacks in the South, 1860-1935* (Chapel Hill: University of North Carolina Press, 1988).

19. For examples of studies on black towns, see Nell Irvin Painter, *The Exodusters: Black Migration to Kansas After Reconstruction* (New York: Alfred A. Knopf, 1977); Kenneth M. Hamilton, *Black Towns and Profit: Promotion and Early Development in the Trans-Appalachian West* (Urbana: University of Illinois Press, 1990).

20. Kathleen C. Berkeley, " 'Colored Ladies also Contributed': Black Women's Activities from Benevolence to Social Welfare, 1866-1896," in *The Web of Southern Social Relations: Women, Family, and Education,* ed. Walter J. Fraser, Jr., R. Frank Saunders, Jr., and Jon L. Wakelyn (Athens: University of Georgia Press, 1985), 180-82.

21. Benjamin [Griffith] Brawley, *Negro Builders and Heroes* (Chapel Hill: University of North Carolina Press, 1937), 267-70; Elsa Barkley Brown, "Womanist Consciousness," 616-17.

22. See Mary Brinkerhoff, "Books, Blacks Beautiful to Her," *Dallas Morning News,* 23 July 1971, in vertical files, Biographical-women, "Clara Jones," Walter P. Reuther Archives of Labor

History and Urban Affairs, Wayne State University, Detroit. (Hereafter cited as Labor Archives.)

23. Robert Kraus, "Black Library Chief Bears No Scars After Squabble," Detroit *Free Press,* February 18, 1971 in vertical files, Labor Archives; Maggie Kennedy, "A Librarian Who Speaks Her Mind," *Dallas Times Herald,* October 21, 1976, in 1970-76 Clippings box, Clara Jones Papers, Black Librarians' Archives, North Carolina Central University School of Library Science, Durham. Interestingly, when Jones read Joel Chandler Harris's Uncle Remus stories as an adult, she recognized them as stories she had heard all her life, but she was appalled by what she characterized as the "injected" racism. In their original form, the stories often included themes of collective consciousness.

24. Florence Lattimore, *A Palace of Delight (The Locust Street Settlement for Negroes at Hampton, Virginia)* (Hampton, Va: Hampton Normal and Agricultural Institute, 1915), 4-8; Sadie Iola Daniel, *Women Builders* (Washington, D.C.: Associated Publishers, 1970), 54-61; Tullia Brown Hamilton, "The National Association of Colored Women," 140.

25. "Virginia State Federation of Colored Women's Clubs: Its Origin and Objectives," and Edna M. Colson, "The Petersburg Women's Council," typescripts, Virginia Federation of Colored Women's Clubs Papers, Johnson Memorial Library Special Collections, Virginia State University, Petersburg, VA; William Anthony Aery, "Helping Wayward Girls: Virginia's Pioneer Work," *Southern Workman* 44 (November 1915): 598-604; Esther F. Brown, "Social Settlement Work in Hampton," *Southern Workman* 33 (July 1904): 393-96; Janie Porter Barrett to Dr. [Hollis P.] Frissell, December 25, 1915, Harris and Janie Porter Barrett Collection. Cited in full in note 4.

26. Alfreda M. Duster, *Crusade for Justice,* xiv-xix, 5, 15-20.

27. See Dorothy Salem, "To Better Our World: Black Women and Organized Reform," 24-25.

28. Alfreda M. Duster, *Crusade for Justice,* 69, 93. Wells-Barnett dedicated her autobiography to "our youth [who] are entitled to the facts of race history which only the participants can give." *Ibid.,* 5.

29. Adrienne Lash Jones, "Jane Edna Hunter: A Case Study of Black Leadership, 1910-1950" (Ph.D. diss., Case Western Reserve University, 1983), 49-64. Also note that black community residents of Norfolk, Virginia, were so proud of Lula McNeil and so optimistic about her potential for the community that, after she graduated at the top of the first graduating class of the first black high school in that city they all contributed money for educating her further at the state normal school. After graduation, she taught school for awhile and later returned to nursing school and became a public health nurse. See Lula Catherine McNeil interview transcript, Black Nurses Archives, Hampton University, Hampton, Va.

30. Adrienne Lash Jones, "Jane Edna Hunter," 93-100; Mayme V. Holmes, "The Story of the Phillis Wheatley Association of Cleveland," *Southern Workman* 57 (October 1928): 399-401; Jane E. Hunter, "Phyllis [sic] Wheatley Association of Cleveland: An Institution Devoted to Better, Brighter Girls, Happier, Heartier Women," The Competitor 1 (March 1920): 52-54.

31. Minutes of the Federation of Colored Women's Clubs of Colorado, June 28, 1911; June 13, 1917; June 9, 1920; June 14-17, 1932; June 11-13, 1946; "Autobiography of Mrs. Hattie Taylor"; "Biography of Mrs. Elizabeth Ensley, Founder of the State Federation of Colored Women's Clubs"; and "Biography of Betty Wilkins," in the Records of the Federation of Colored Women's Clubs of Colorado, Western History Division, Denver Public Library, Denver.

32. Elizabeth L. Davis, *The Story of the Illinois Federation of Colored Women's Clubs* (n.p.,n.d.), esp. chapter 6, "Who's Who," in the Henry P. Slaughter Collection, Woodruff Library, Atlanta University Center Archives, Atlanta.

33. Delilah L. Beasley, *The Negro Trail Blazers of California* (Los Angeles: Times Mirror Printing, 1919), esp. chapter 13, "Distinguished Women."

34. See Tullia Brown Hamilton, "The National Association of Colored Women," 39-53.

35. Hamilton notes that 42 of the 59 clubs represented at the first NACW Convention in Nashville in 1897 were from urban areas. *Ibid.,* 55.

36. This is not to suggest that the "communications revolution" under way at the time had no impact on these women's efforts to create a national organization.

37. W. E. B. DuBois, *Efforts at Social Betterment Among Negro Americans,* 45-50; Elizabeth Lindsay Davis, *The Story of the Illinois Federation of Colored Women Clubs,* 6-10; Dorothy Salem, "To Better Our World," 155; "Neighborhood Union's Aim Granted By the Laws of Georgia Under the Charter of the State of Georgia," box 3, f. 1931, Neighborhood Union Collection, Atlanta University Center Archives, Atlanta.

38. Ethel Evangeline Martin Bolden, "Susan Dart Butler: Pioneer Librarian," (M.A. thesis, Atlanta University, 1959); Jacqueline Anne Rouse, *Lugenia Burns Hope: Black Southern Reformer* (Athens: University of Georgia Press, 1989), 71-73; Cynthia Neverdon-Morton, *Afro-American Women of the South and the Advancement of the Race,* 159-161. Janie Porter Barrett also eventually turned over the Industrial School to the State of Virginia.

39. Untitled typescript [a history of the Virginia State Federation of Colored Women's Clubs], 2-3 and Edna M. Colson,

"The Petersburg Women's Council," typescript, The Virginia Federation of Colored Women's Club Papers; Frances Reynolds Keyser, "Florida Federation of Colored Women's Clubs Establish a Home for Delinquent Girls," *The Competitor* 3 (May 1921): 34; Dorothy Salem, "To Better Our World," 124-209; Tullia Brown Hamilton, "The National Association of Colored Women," 72, 76.

40. Dorothy Salem, *Ibid;* Paula Giddings, *When and Where I Enter: The Impact of Black Women on Race and Sex in America* (New York: William Morrow & Co., 1984), 135; isolated papers of the Kansas City, Mo., Federation of Colored Women's Clubs, b. 28-4, f. 96, Frederick Douglass Collection, Moorland-Spingarn Research Center, Howard University, Washington, D.C.; "The History of the Cincinnati Federation of Colored Women's Clubs (1904-1952)," typescript, Mirriam Hamilton Spotts Papers, Amistad Research Center, Tulane University, New Orleans; William Anthony Aery, "Helping Wayward Girls"; Pitt Dillingham, "Black Belt Settlement Work," *Southern Workman* 31 (July 1902): 383-388 and (August 1902): 437-444; Jane E. Hunter, "Phyllis [sic] Wheatley Association of Cleveland"; Mrs. Laurence C. Jones, "Mississippi's Bright Club Fields," *The Competitor* 3 (May 1921): 27-28; Mayme Holmes, "The Story of the Phillis Wheatley Association of Cleveland, Ohio." Almost every issue of *Woman's Era* and *National Notes* includes details of similar activities for NACW affiliates throughout the country. On suffrage and interracial cooperation, see Jane Olcott, *The Work of Colored Women* (New York: War Work Council, National Board of the YMCA, 1919), issued by the Colored Work Committee; Cynthia Neverdon-Morton, "The Black Women's Struggle for Equality in the South, 1895-1925," in *The Afro-American Woman: Struggles and Images,* ed. Sharon Harley and Rosalyn Terborg-Penn (Port Washington, N.Y.: Kennikat Press, 1978), 43-57; and Rosalyn Terborg-Penn, "Discontented Black Feminist: Prelude and Postscript to the Passage of the Nineteenth Amendment," in *Decades of Discontent: The Women's Movement,* 1920-1940, ed. Lois Scharf and Joan M. Jenson (Westport, Conn: Greenwood Press, 1983), 261-78.

41. See discussions on origins of American racism in Winthrop Jordan, *White Over Black: American Attitudes Toward the Negro, 1550-1812* (New York: Oxford University Press, 1974), or the abridged version, *The White Man's Burden.*

Postindustrial Conditions and Postfeminist Consciousness in the Silicon Valley

JUDITH STACEY

When I moved here, there were orchards all around, and now there are integrated-circuit manufacturing plants all around. . . . That's been the thrill, because I've been part of it, and it's the most exciting time in the history of the world, I think. And the center of it is here in Silicon Valley.

> *Female engineer at Hewlett Packard, quoted in* San Jose Mercury News, *February 19, 1985*

During the past three decades profound changes in the organization of family, work, and gender have occurred in the United States, coincident with the rise of second wave feminism.* Feminist scholars have demonstrated that an important relationship exists between the development of the earlier feminist movement and that of capitalist industrialization in the West. In the United States, for example, the disintegration of the agrarian family economy and the reorganization of family, work, and gender relationships that took place during the nineteenth century provided the major impetus for the birth of

American feminism.[1] Although the more recent history of feminism and social change is equally intimate, it has received far less attention.

This essay explores a number of connections between the recent transition to an emergent "postindustrial" stage of capitalist development and the simultaneous rise and decline of a militant and radical phase of feminism in the US.[2] First I reflect on an ironic role second-wave feminism has played as an unwitting midwife to the massive social transformations of work and family life that have occurred in the post-World War II era. Secondly I draw from my field research on family life in California's "Silicon Valley"—a veritable postindustrial hothouse—to illustrate some of the effects of this ironic collaboration in fostering emergent forms of "postfeminist" consciousness.

Let me begin, however, by explaining my use of the troubling term "postfeminist," a concept offensive to many feminists who believe that the media coined it simply "to give sexism a subtler name."[3] Whatever the media's motives, I find the concept useful in describing the gender consciousness and the family and work strategies of many contemporary women. I view the term postfeminist as analogous to "postrevolutionary" and use it not to indicate the death of the women's movement, but to describe the simultaneous incorporation, revision, and depoliticization of many of the central goals of second wave feminism.[4] I believe postfeminism is distinct from antifeminism and sexism, for it aptly describes the consciousness and strategies increasing numbers of women have developed in response to the new difficulties and opportunities of postindustrial society. In this sense the diffusion of postfeminist consciousness signifies both the

---

*By "second wave" feminism I refer to the resurgence of feminist politics and ideology that began in the mid-1960s, peaked in the early 1970s, and has been a major focus of social and political backlash since the late 1970s.

Judith Stacey, "Postindustrial Conditions and Postfeminist Consciousness in the Silicon Valley," *Socialist Review* 17 (November–December 1987). Copyright © 1987 by the Center for Social Research and Education. Reprinted by permission.

achievements of, and challenges for, modern feminist politics.

FEMINISM AS MIDWIFE TO POSTINDUSTRIAL SOCIETY

Hindsight allows us to see how feminist ideology helped legitimate the massive structural changes in American work and family that invisibly accompanied the transition to postindustrial society in the 1960s and early 1970s.[5] I believe this period of postindustrialization should be read as the unmaking of a gender order rooted in the modern nuclear family system, the family of male breadwinner, female homemaker and dependent children that was grounded in the male family wage and stable marriage, at least for the majority of white working class and middle class families. Family and work relations in the emergent postindustrial order, by contrast, have been transformed by the staggering escalation of divorce rates and women's participation in paid work. As the US changed from having an industrial to a "service" dominated occupational structure,[6] unprecedented percentages of women entered the labor force and the halls of academe, while unprecedented percentages of marriages entered the divorce courts.[7] Unstable, and often incompatible, work and family conditions have become the postindustrial norm as working class occupations become increasingly "feminized."

This process generated an extreme disjuncture between the dominant cultural ideology of domesticity, an ideology that became particularly strident in the 1950s, and the simultaneous decline in the significance placed on marriage and motherhood and the rise of women's employment.

The gap between the ideology of domesticity and the increasingly nondomestic character of women's lives helped generate feminist consciousness in the 1960s. As that consciousness developed, women launched an assault on traditional domesticity, an assault, that is, on a declining institution and culture.* Therefore this feminist movement was backward looking in its critique, and unwittingly forward looking (but not to the future of our fantasies) in its effects.

---

* Betty Friedan's *The Feminine Mystique* was one of the earliest, most successful polemical examples of this assault.

Feminism developed a devastating critique of the stultifying, infantilizing, and exploitative effects of female domesticity on women, especially of the sort available to classes that could afford an economically dependent housewife. Although the institutions of domesticity and its male beneficiaries were the intended targets of our critique, most housewives felt themselves on the defensive. Feminist criticism helped undermine and delegitimize the flagging but still celebrated nuclear family and helped promote the newly normative double-income (with shifting personnel) middle- and working-class families. We also provided ideological support for the sharp rise of single mother families generated by the soaring divorce rates.[8] Today fewer than 10 percent of families in the US consist of a male breadwinner, a female housewife, and their dependent children.[9]

Millions of women have derived enormous, tangible benefits from these changes in occupational patterns and family life and from the ways in which feminist ideology encouraged women to initiate and cope with these changes. Yet it is also true that since the mid-1970s, when the contours of the new postindustrial society began to be clear, economic and personal life has worsened for many groups of women, perhaps for the majority. The emerging shape of postindustrial society seems to have the following, rather disturbing characteristics: As unionized occupations and real wages decline throughout the economy, women are becoming the postindustrial "proletariat," performing the majority of "working-class," low-skilled, low-paying jobs.[10] Because the overall percentage of jobs that are secure and well-paying has declined rapidly, increasing numbers of men are unemployed or underemployed. Yet the majority of white, male workers still labors at jobs that are highly skilled and comparatively well-paid.[11] Family instability is endemic with devastating economic effects on many women, as the "feminization of poverty" literature has made clear.[12] Increasing percentages of women are rearing children by themselves, generally with minimal economic contributions from former husbands and fathers.[13] Yet rising numbers of those single mothers who work full time, year-round do not earn wages sufficient to lift their families above the official poverty line.[14]

In the emerging class structure, marriage is becoming a major axis of stratification because it structures access to a second income. The married female as "secondary" wage-earner lifts a former working-class or middle-class family into comparative affluence, while the loss or lack of access to a male income can force women and their children into

ECOFEMINISM: ANIMA, ANIMUS, ANIMAL

CAROL J. ADAMS

Feminists, building on women's experiences, have emphasized such values as connectedness, responsibility, attentive love, an embodied ethic incorporating body-mediated knowledge. If we were to touch, hear, and see animals whom we eat, wear, or otherwise use, we might replace current exploitation with a respectful relationship.

Notions of human nature exaggerate differences and minimize similarities between the other animals and ourselves. We talk about animals as if we were not animals ourselves. This permits humans in the United States alone to imprison almost six billion animals in intensive farming systems that violate the animals' basic physical and behavioral needs; to tolerate the killing of as many as three animals a second in laboratories; to purchase fur garments that require the suffering and death of at least 70 million animals each year; to hunt and kill 200 million animals annually for "sport"; and to exhibit millions of animals in circuses, rodeos, and zoos, where they endure boredom, mistreatment, lack of privacy, and deprivation of their natural environment.

Parallels between women's experiences and those of other animals have been made repeatedly in feminist literature and theory. Animals are meat, experimental guinea pigs, and objectified bodies; women are treated like meat, guinea pigs, and objectified bodies. We see pornographic pictures of "beaver hunters" who "bag" a woman, or of women put through meat grinders. Batterers have forced their victims to watch the killing of a favorite animal. Sexually abused children are sometimes threatened with a pet's death to ensure their compliance. "Why Can't This Veal Calf Walk?" by performance artist Karen Finley is a poem about rape and incest. (Well, why can't she or he walk? Kept in small crates, "veal" calves are unable to turn around, since exercise would increase muscle development, toughen the flesh, and slow weight gain. Standing on slatted floors causes a constant strain. Diarrhea, resulting from an improper diet that fosters anemia to produce pale flesh, causes the slats to become slippery; the calves often fall, getting leg injuries. When taken to be slaughtered, many can hardly walk.)

Raised in enclosed, darkened, or dimly lit buildings, other intensively farmed animals fare as poorly, their lives characterized by little extraneous stimuli, restricted movement, no freedom to choose social interactions, intense and unpleasant fumes, and ingestion of subtherapeutic doses of antibiotics (50 percent of the antibiotics in the U.S. go to livestock). Hens are kept as many as five to a cage with dimensions only slightly larger than this magazine. When being cooked in an oven, the chicken has four times more space than when she was alive.

Many feminists have noted that women's oppression and animal exploitation are interrelated. Rosemary Ruether has established a connection between the domestication of animals, the development of urban centers, the creation of slavery, and the inequality of the sexes. Some anthropologists correlate male domination with hunting economies. One ecofeminist, Sally Abbott, speculates that patriarchal religion resulted from the guilt of consuming animals. Another, Elizabeth Fisher, proposes that the breeding of animals suggested ways to control women's reproductivity. Gena Corea shows how embryo transfer was applied to women after being developed in the cattle industry. Andrée Collard and others argue that the beast slain in hero mythologies represents the once powerful goddess.

Feminist philosophers have exposed the methodology of science as arising from and valorizing human male (usually white, heterosexual, and upper-class) experience. They say that how science defines or selects research problems, how it defines *why* these are problems, how it designs experiments, constructs and confers meaning—all aspects of science also used to defend animal experimentation—are sexist, racist, homophobic, and classist. Animal rights adds speciesism to this analysis.

Yet for many, feminism and animal rights are antithetical, partly because of approaches adopted by the animal rights movement. Who isn't offended by a poster of a woman that declares, "It takes up to 40 dumb animals to make a fur coat. But only one to wear it"? Why have farm animals—who represent at least 90 percent of the exploited animals—not been the focus of animal activism, rather than such women-identified consumer objects as cosmetics and furs? No law requires the testing of cosmetics on animals, and so, like fur, cosmetics are equated with vanity, and are seen as more expendable than animal foods. Furthermore, women are seen as more caring about animals. The animal rights movement seems to sense that women will identify with the exploited animal because of our own exploitation.

Some feminists fear that animal rights would set a precedent for the rights of fetuses. Ironically, antiabortionists agree, assailing activists for caring about animals but not fetuses. But it is disingenuous to compare a fetus with a living, breathing animal. A fetus has potential interests; an animal has actual interests. Speciesism is perhaps nowhere more pronounced than in the protestation about the fate of the human conceptus, while the sentience of other animals is declared morally irrelevant because they are not human. Some antiabortionists define meaningful life so broadly as to encompass a newly fertilized egg, yet so narrowly that fully grown animals with well-developed nervous systems and social sensibilities are excluded. Extending the feminist understanding of reproductive freedom, we see that both women and other female animals experience enforced pregnancies.

Animal rights is charged with being antihuman. (This is reminiscent of "antimen" charges against feminists.) It is convenient to divide the issue of animal rights from human rights issues, to complain that we are concerned about animals when humans are starving. But this division is perpetuated out of ignorance; animal agriculture greatly *contributes* to the devastation of the environment and to inequity in food distribution. Frances Moore Lappé describes how half of all water consumed in the United States, much of it from unrenewable resources, is used for crops fed to livestock. More than 50 percent of water pollution is due to wastes from the livestock industry (including manure, eroded soil, and synthetic pesticides and fertilizers). "Meat"

production also places demands on energy sources: the 500 calories of food energy from one pound of cooked "steak" requires 20,000 calories of fossil fuel. Some environmentalists argue that 40 percent of our imported oil requirements would be cut if we switched to a vegetarian diet (because of the energy used in growing food for animals, keeping them alive, killing them, and processing their bodies). Livestock are responsible for 85 percent of topsoil erosion, and methane gas, much of it being emitted by cows being raised to be our food, accounts for at least 20 percent of the human contribution to the greenhouse effect.

Actually, animal *exploitation* is antihuman. In positing animal suffering as essential to human progress and conceptualizing morality so that this suffering is deemed irrelevant, a deformed definition of humanity prevails. Besides environmental degradation, many human illnesses are linked to eating animals (on a pure vegetarian diet the risk of death by heart attack is reduced from 50 percent to 4 percent, and the risk of breast and ovarian cancer is three times lower). Animal research now wastes billions of tax dollars yielding misleading results because it fails to use models that could produce information more quickly, more reliably, and for less cost than animal "models."

Charges that animal rights is antihuman really mean: "The animal rights movement is against what I am doing and so is against me." If animal rights arguments are persuasive, personal change becomes necessary. As with feminism, if you accept the arguments, the consequences are immediate. You can't go on living the way you have, for suddenly you understand your complicity with an immense amount of exploitation. This can be very discomforting if you enjoy eating or wearing dead animals, or accept the premises of animal experimentation.

I know: that described me. For the first half of my life I ate animals and benefited in other ways from their exploitation. But feminism predisposed me to wonder if this was right or necessary. It equipped me to challenge language that removes agency and cloaks violence: "Someone kills animals so I can eat their corpses as meat" becomes "animals are killed to be eaten as meat," then "animals are meat," and finally "meat animals," thus "meat." Something *we do to animals* has become instead something that is a part of animals' nature, and we lose consideration of our role entirely. Alice Walker regained understanding of this role through a horse, recalling that "human animals and nonhuman animals can communicate quite well," and perceiving in eating "steak," "I am eating misery."

If the model for humanity was, say, a vegetarian feminist, rather than a male meat eater, our idea of human nature would be fundamentally challenged—ani-mals would be seen as kin, not as prey, "models," or "animal machines"; *we* would be seen as radically in relationship with these kin, not as predators, experi-menters, or owners. Reconstructing human nature as feminists includes examining how we as humans inter-act with the nonhuman world. Animal rights is not anti-human; it is antipatriarchal.

poverty.[15] In short, the drastic increase in female employ-ment during the past several decades has meant lots more work for mother, but with very unevenly distributed eco-nomic benefits and only a slight improvement in relative income differentials between women and men.[16]

This massive rise in female employment also produces a scarcely visible, but portentous social effect through the drastic decline in the potential pool of female volunteers, typically from the middle class, who have sustained much of family and community life in the United States since the nineteenth century. The result of this decline may be a gen-eral deterioration of domesticity and social housekeeping that, in turn, is fueling reactionary nostalgia for traditional family life among leftists and feminists as well as among right wing forces.[17]

In light of these developments, many women (and men) have been susceptible to the appeals of the antifeminist backlash, and especially to profamily ideologies. Because of its powerful and highly visible critique of traditional domesticity, and because of the sensationalized way the media disseminated this critique, feminism has taken most of the heat for family and social crises that have attended the transition from an industrial to a postindustrial order in the US. Despite efforts by feminists like Barbara Ehrenreich to portray men as the real family deserters, many continue to blame feminism for general decline of domesticity and nurturance within families and communi-ties.[18] Feminism serves as a symbolic lightning rod for the widespread nostalgia and longing for "lost" intimacy and security that presently pervades social and political culture in the United States.[19] Not by accident do 1950s fashions and symbols dominate popular culture in the 1980s.

It is in this context, I believe, that we can best under-stand why during the late 1970s and the 1980s, even many feminists began to retreat from the radical critique of con-ventional family life of the early second wave.[20] The past decade, during which postindustrial social patterns became firmly established, has been marked instead by the emer-gence of various forms of postfeminist consciousness and family strategies.

FAMILY AND WORK IN THE SILICON VALLEY

Material from my current study of family and work expe-rience in California's "Silicon Valley" highlights a num-ber of features of postindustrial society and several of the diverse postfeminist strategies that contemporary women have devised to cope with them. After briefly describing the major postindustrial contours of the region, I will draw from my fieldwork to illustrate some of these strate-gies.

As the birthplace and international headquarters of the electronics industry, the "Silicon Valley"—Santa Clara County, California—is popularly perceived as representing the vanguard of postindustrialism. Until the early 1950s the region was a sparsely populated agricultural area, one of the major fruit baskets in the United States. But in the three decades since the electronics industry developed there, its population has grown by 350 percent and its economy, ecology, and social structure have been dramatically trans-formed.[21]

During this period, electronics, the vanguard post-industrial industry, feminized (and "minoritized") its pro-duction work force. In the 1950s and 1960s, when the industry was young, most of its production workers were men, for whom there were significant opportunities for advancement into technical and, at times, engineering ranks even for those with very limited schooling. But as the industry matured, it turned increasingly to female, eth-nic minority, and recent migrant workers to fill production positions that offered fewer and fewer advancement opportunities.[22] By the late 1970s, the industry's occupational structure was crudely stratified by gender, as well as by race and ethnicity. At the top was an unusually high proportion (25 percent) of the most highly educated and highly paid salaried employees in any industry—the engineers and professionals employed in research and design. As in traditional industries, the vast majority were white males (89 percent males, 89 percent non-Hispanic whites). At the bottom, however, were the women, three-fourths of the very poorly paid assembly workers and operatives who performed the tedious, often health-threatening work assigned to 45 percent of the employees. In between were the moderately well-paid technicians and craft workers, also primarily Anglo males, but into whose ranks women and Asians were making gradual inroads.[23]

In the heady days of technological triumph and economic expansion, when the Silicon Valley was widely portrayed as the mecca of the new intellectual entrepreneurs and as a land where factories resembled college campuses, its public officials also liked to describe it as a feminist capital. Indeed San Jose, the county seat, had a feminist mayor in the late 1970s and was one of the first public employers in the nation to implement a comparable worth standard of pay for city employees.

What is less widely known is that the area is also the site of a significant degree of family turbulence. Much of the data on local family change represent an exaggeration of national and even California trends, which tend to be more extreme than the national averages. For example, whereas the national divorce rate has doubled since 1960, in Santa Clara County it nearly tripled so that by 1977, divorces exceeded marriages. Likewise the percentage of "non-family households" grew faster than in the nation, and abortion rates were one and one-half times the national figures. And although the percent of single-parent households was not quite as high as in the US as a whole, the rate of increase has been far more rapid.[24] Thus the coincidence of path-breaking changes in both economic and family patterns makes the Silicon Valley an ideal site for examining women's responses to these transformations.

During the past three years I have conducted intermittent fieldwork in the Valley concentrating on an in-depth study of two kinship networks of people, which mainly consist of non-ethnic caucasians who have lived in the region during the period of postindustrialization. My key informant in each network is a white woman now in her late forties who married in the 1950s and became a homemaker for a white man who was to benefit from the unusual electronics industry opportunities of the 1960s. Both of

these marriages and careers proved to be highly turbulent, however, and in response both women and several of their daughters have devised a variety of postfeminist survival strategies. At first glance their strategies appear to represent a simple retreat from feminism, but closer study has convinced me that these women are selectively blending and adapting certain feminist ideas to traditional and modern family and work strategies. Vignettes from their family histories suggest the texture and purpose of such strategies as well as important generational variations.

PATHS TO POSTFEMINISM

Let me first introduce Pam, currently a staff analyst in a municipal agency.* We became friendly in 1984 when I was interviewing clients at a feminist-inspired social service program where Pam was then an administrator. From various informal conversations, lunches, and observations of her work goals and relations, I had pegged Pam as a slightly cynical divorcee who came to feminist consciousness through divorce and a women's reentry program at a local community college. I had learned that Pam's first husband Don, to whom she was married for twelve years and with whom she had three children, was one of those white male electronics industry success stories. A telephone repair worker with an interest in drafting when they married, Don entered the electronics industry in the early 1960s and proceeded to work and job-hop his way up to a career as a packaging engineer, a position which currently earns him $50,000 annually.

I had heard too that Don's route to success had been arduous and stormy, entailing numerous setbacks, failures, and lay-offs, and requiring such extraordinary work hours that Don totally neglected Pam and their children. This and other problems led to Pam's divorce fifteen years ago, resulting in the normative female impoverishment. Pam became a single mother on welfare, continued her schooling (eventually through the master's level), developed feminist consciousness, experimented with sexual freedom, cohabited with a couple of lovers, and began to develop an administrative career in social services. Before the 1984 election Pam made many scornful remarks about Reagan, Reaganomics, and the military build-up. Therefore, I was quite surprised when, four months after meeting Pam, I learned that she was now married to Al, a construction

---

* I have given pseudonyms to all the individuals described in this essay.

worker with whom she earlier had cohabited. I also learned that they both were recent converts to charismatic, evangelical Christianity, and that they were participating in Christian marriage counseling to improve their relationship. Pam had been separated from, but was on a friendly basis with her second husband, Al, when he had an automobile accident followed by a dramatic conversion experience. Al "accepted Jesus into his life," and Pam suddenly accepted Al and Jesus back into hers.

Pam acknowledges the paradoxes and contradictions of her participation in "Christian marriage"* and Christian marriage counseling, based, as they are, on patriarchal doctrines. Pam, however, credits the conversion experience and the counseling with helping her achieve a more intimate, positive marital relationship than she had experienced before. The conversion, she claims, changed Al from a defensive, uncommunicative, withholding male into a less guarded, more trusting, loving, and committed mate.[†] Although Pam and Al's marriage is not as communicative, nurturant, and intimate as Pam would like, she believes their shared faith is leading them in this direction. And she believes that "if you can work out that kind of relationship, then who would care who's in charge, because it's such a total wonderful relationship?" Moreover, Pam cedes Al dominance only in the "spiritual realm"; financially, occupationally, interpersonally, and politically, she retains strong independence, or even control.

Pam's selective adaptation and blending of feminist and fundamentalist ideologies first struck me as rather unique as well as extremely contradictory. I have gradually learned, however, that a significant tendency in contemporary fundamentalist thought incorporates some feminist criticisms of patriarchal men and marriage into its activism in support of patriarchal profamilialism. Quite a few evangelical ministers urge Christian wives to make strong emotional demands on their husbands for communication, commitment, and nurturance within the framework of patriarchal marriage, and they actively counsel Christian husbands to meet these demands.[25]

Feminism served Pam well as an aid for leaving her unsatisfactory first marriage and for building a career and sense of individual identity. But Pam failed to form successful, satisfying, intimate relationships to replace her marriage. Struggling alone with the emotional and social crises to which two of her three children were prone, Pam describes herself as desperately unhappy much of the time. Although Pam received support from several intense friendships with women, neither this nor feminism seemed to offer her sufficient solace or direction. Her retreat from feminism and her construction of an extreme form of postfeminist consciousness took place in this context.

Dotty Lewison, one of the key informants in the other kinship network I studied, has a more complex story. I first sought out Dotty because of her early experience in electronics assembly work and because of her intact thirty-year marriage to Lou Lewison, another white male electronics industry success story. Dotty had been a teenager in 1954 when she met and married Lou, a sailor who had dropped out of school in the ninth grade. Although Dotty primarily had been a homemaker for Lou and the five children she bore at two-year intervals during her first decade of marriage, she also had made occasional forays into the world of paid work, including one two-year stint in the late 1950s assembling semiconductors. But Dotty neither perceived nor desired significant opportunities for personal advancement in electronics or any occupation at that time. Instead several years later she pushed Lou to enter the industry. This proved to be a successful strategy for *family* economic mobility, although one which was to have contradictory effects on their marital and family relationships as well as on Dotty's personal achievement goals. With his mechanical aptitude and naval background, Lou was able to receive on-the-job training and advance to the position of line maintenance engineer. Then, as Lou told me, "the companies didn't have many choices. No one even knew what a circuit looked like. . . . [But] you can't find many engineers starting out now who don't enter with degrees . . . because the companies have a lot more choices now."

When I first arrived at the Lewison's modest, cluttered, tract home, Dotty was opening a delivery from a local gadgets sale. A "knick-knack junkie" by her own description, Dot unpacked various porcelain figures and a new, gilded Bible. My social prejudices cued me to expect Dot to hold somewhat conservative and antifeminist views, but I was wrong again. She reported a long history of community and feminist activism, including work in the anti-battering movement. And she still expressed some support for feminism, "depending," she said, "on what you mean by feminism."

Later I learned that Dotty's intact marriage had been broken by numerous short-term separations, and one of two year's duration that almost became permanent. During that

---

* Pam, like many evangelical and fundamentalist Christians, uses the term "Christian" to designate only born-again Christians.
[†] Al, as well as Pam's children, agrees with this description.

separation Dot too was a welfare mother, who hated being on welfare, and who had a serious live-in love affair. Dot does not repudiate very many of her former feminist ideas, but she has not been active since the late 1970s. She specifically distances herself from the "militant man-hating types."

Dotty is a feisty, assertive woman who had protofeminist views long before she (or most of us) had heard of the women's liberation movement. Yet for twenty years, Dotty tolerated a marriage in which she and her husband fought violently. Her children were battered, sometimes seriously, most often by Lou, but occasionally by Dotty as well. Before I learned about the violence, Dotty and Lou both led me to believe that their near-divorce in the mid-1970s was caused by Lou's workaholism as an upwardly mobile employee in the electronics industry. They spoke of the twelve- to fourteen-hour days and the frequent three-day shifts that led Lou to neglect his family completely. Later I came to understand the dynamic relationships between that workaholicism and their marital hostilities. Dotty had become a feminist and community activist by then, involved in antibattering work and many other community issues. Partly due to her involvement with feminism (again, some of it encountered in a college women's reentry program), Dotty was beginning to shift the balance of power in her marriage. In this situation, I suspect Lou's escape into work was experienced more as relief than neglect on all sides. Although now Dotty blames the work demands of the electronics industry for Lou's heart disease and his early death last year at the age of 52, at the time Lou's absence from the family gave Dotty the "space" to develop her strength and the willingness to assume the serious economic and emotional risks of divorce and an impoverished life as a single-parent.

Dotty kicked Lou out, although she did not file for divorce. Two years later she took him back, but only after his nearly fatal, and permanently disabling, heart attack, and after her live-in lover left her. Even then she took him back on her own rather harsh terms. She was to have total independence with her time and relationships. Despite the economic inequality between them, Dotty now held the undeniable emotional balance of power in the relationship, but only because she had proven she could survive impoverishment and live without Lou. And, of course, Lou's disability contributed to the restructuring of the division of labor and power in their household. Lou did most of the housework and gardening, while Dotty participated in the paid labor force. Nonetheless, Dotty remained economi-

cally dependent on Lou, and she regrets her limited career options. Indeed this was one crucial factor in her decision to resume her marriage with Lou.

By the late 1970s Dotty was no longer active in feminist or community causes. She says she "got burned out" and "turned off by the 'all men are evil' kind of thinking." More importantly, I believe, Dotty's life stage and circumstances had changed so that she did not feel she needed or benefited from feminism any more. In the mid-1970s, she "needed to have my stamp validated," to be reassured that her rebellious and assertive feelings and her struggles to reform her marriage were legitimate. But, partly due to the feminist-assisted success of those struggles, Dotty came to feel less need for reassurance from feminists. Dotty also finds she has no room for feminism today. She is "too tired, there's too much other shit to deal with." These days she has been trying to maintain her precarious hold on her underpaid job at a cable television service, while heroically struggling to cope with the truly staggering series of family tragedies that befell the Lewisons this year. Lou and two of the adult Lewison children died and one son spent four months in prison. Under these circumstances Dotty too has found more comfort from organized religion than from feminism. After the death of their first son, Dotty and Lou left a spiritualist church they had been attending and returned to the neighborhood Methodist church in which Dotty once had been active. Since Lou's death last fall, Dotty's oldest daughter Lyn and Dotty's mother have joined her in attending this church regularly.

Parallels and idiosyncracies in the life histories just described illustrate some of the complex, reciprocal effects of the family and work dynamics and gender consciousness that I have been observing in the Silicon Valley. Pam and Dotty both were young when they married. They both entered their marriages with conventional "Parsonsian" gender expectations about family and work responsibilities and "roles." For a significant period of time, they and their husbands conformed to the then culturally prescribed pattern of "instrumental" male breadwinner and "expressive" female housewife/mother. Assuming primary responsibility for rearing the children they began to bear immediately after marriage, Pam and Dotty supported their husbands' successful efforts to develop middle to upper-middle class careers as electronics engineers. In the process, both men became workaholics, increasingly uninvolved with their families.

As their marriages deteriorated, both Pam and Dotty enrolled in a women's reentry program where they were

"I'M NOT A FEMINIST, BUT I PLAY ONE ON TV"

SUSAN FALUDI

According to the latest lifestyle headlines and talk-show sound bites, from *USA Today* to *Good Morning America,* we are witnessing the birth of a new wave of feminism. It's "like a second revolution in the women's movement," the Washington *Times* enthused, referring us to one of the nouveau revolution's adherents, who "compares her position with the 1970s feminists who burned their bras." The neo-rebel tells the *Times,* "I feel the same as I did when I was 19 years old during the women's liberation movement"; she confides she even had a 1970s-style "'click' moment" of feminist revelation.

The evidence for what the Washington *Times* calls "a nationwide trend"? New "feminist" organizations called the Women's Freedom Network, the Independent Women's Forum (IWF), and the Network for Empowering Women (or NEW, which, to hear its organizers tell it, will soon be displacing NOW). New inspirational "feminist" tracts like *Who Stole Feminism?* and *Feminism Without Illusions.* New "feminist" voices from a younger generation, like Katie Roiphe, author of *The Morning After: Sex, Fear, and Feminism,* and Rene Denfeld, author of *The New Victorians: A Young Woman's Challenge to the Old Feminist Order.* And members of a new "feminist" intelligentsia like philosophy professor Christina Hoff Sommers, hailed in the Boston *Globe's* headlines as A REBEL IN THE SISTERHOOD WHO WANTS TO RESCUE FEMINISM FROM ITS "HIJACKERS."

That feminist leaders don't seem to be embracing these new reinforcements does give the trend's reporters pause—but only momentarily. Feminist standoffishness must just be jealousy—or, as the Chicago *Tribune* put it, "sibling rivalry."

But big-sister envy is not the problem here. . . .

What is being celebrated is no natural birth of a movement—and the press that originated the celebration is no benign midwife. It would be more accurate to describe this drama as a media-assisted invasion of the body of the women's movement: the Invasion of the Feminist Snatchers, intent on repopulating the ranks with Pod Feminists. In this artificially engineered reproduction effort, the press has figured twice: the right-wing media have played the part of mad-scientist obstetrician-cum-spin doctor, bankrolling, publishing, and grooming their pod women for delivery to a wider world of media consumption. And the mainstream media have played the role of trend-hungry pack-journalism suckers; in their eagerness to jump on the latest bandwagon, they have gladly accepted the faux feminists' credentials without inspection.

If journalists were to investigate, they would find the "new" feminist movement to possess few adherents but much armament in the way of smoke and mirrors. The memberships of such groups as NEW are each in the low to mid three-digits, compared with NOW's 250,000. And they wouldn't find these women out on the hustings, in the streets, guarding a family planning clinic from antiabortionist attacks, or lending a hand at a battered women's shelter. Instead, if the media were to take a closer look, they would find a handful of "feminist" writers and public speakers who do no writing, speaking, organizing, or activism on behalf of women's equality at all. A review of their published writings unearths not one example of a profeminist article or book.

They define themselves as "dissenters" within the feminist ranks, but they never joined feminism in the first place; they have met each other mingling at conservative academic gatherings (like the "anti-P.C." National Association of Scholars) and conservative Washington networking circuits, not the feminist trenches of pro-choice demonstrations and clerical unionizing meetings. They define themselves as politically diverse, but the leadership of the Women's Freedom Network, the IWF, and NEW is overwhelmingly rightward leaning. And when one looks back at where these women were launched as writers, it is, over and over, conservative antifeminist journals like *National Review* and *Commentary,* or the, of late, feminist-bashing pages of *The New Republic.* They define themselves as representing "the average woman," but they are privileged women who rarely stray from their ivory-tower or inside-the-Beltway circles; they are in touch with "the average woman" only to the extent that such a phrase is a code word to signal that they themselves are white and middle- or upper-class. And their opposition to government assistance for women who need help with child care, education, basic shelter, and nutrition betrays a lack of concern, and a buried well of racially charged and class-biased ill will toward women who don't fit the narrow confines of their "average woman." They define themselves as feminists, but their dismissive-to-outright-hostile attitudes toward feminist issues—from sexual harassment to domestic violence to rape to pay equity to child care to welfare rights—locate them firmly on the antifeminist side of the ledger.

Yet their rallying cry—or more precisely, their resting cry, their call to disarm—appeals to some women for its comforting message of female victory and success. Christina Hoff Sommers, author of *Who Stole Feminism?*, and her pod sisters—columnist Cathy Young; history professor and *Feminism Without Illusions* author Elizabeth Fox-Genovese; former *New Republic* writer Karen Lehrman; and writer Katie Roiphe, who, as a graduate student at Princeton, brought us *The Morning After*, to name the prime anointed media stars—maintain that sufficient progress has been made and that now should be a time of back-patting and "reconciliation" with men. Their conferences aren't planning sessions to advance women's rights; they are well-heeled business-card-swapping events where conservative luminaries speak from the podium about how feminism has gone too far—and how women should quit pressing for their rights and start defending men's. Women shouldn't try to spark social change; rather, as the Women's Freedom Network's mission statement asserts, "male and female roles should be allowed to evolve naturally"—that is, without a political shove in a feminist direction. Of course, as the most casual student of women's history could tell you, allowing gender roles to evolve "naturally," without the aid of political agitation, means allowing gender roles to evolve not at all.

Theirs is a beguiling line of argument because it is (a) positive, in a rah-rah "Year of the Woman" way, and (b) nonthreatening. NEW, et al., aren't encouraging women to pursue social change, and they certainly aren't asking men to change. It is no-risk feminism for a fearful age: just post your achievements, make nice with men, and call it a day. The Power of Positive Thinking will take care of the rest. . . . Their brand of feminism doesn't appear to run deeper than a surface gimmick to get airtime. Maybe their slogan should be "I'm not a feminist, but I play one on TV."

The precursor to the pods, the mother of all "I'm feminist, but . . ." declaimers, is that made-for-TV antifeminist feminist Camille Paglia. . . . Paglia's tactic of labeling herself a "feminist, but . . ." has been followed, without the wit, by a small cast of media stars who emerged in the early nineties. Most prominent is Sommers, who says she's a feminist, but . . . has mass-marketed her belief that feminists should just shut up now because women have pretty much attained equal opportunity and anyone who claims otherwise is a liar and a whiner. Joining her in deputy status is Roiphe, who calls herself a feminist, but . . . has peddled the idea that acquaintance rape is really a minor problem that feminists have exaggerated all out of proportion. Then there's Cathy Young, who says she's a feminist, but . . . has convicted feminist leaders on the false charge of having crowned Lorena Bobbitt as Feminist of the Year. And there's Elizabeth Fox-Genovese, who says she is a feminist, but . . . was most eager last year to testify in court (and later, at greater length, in the conservative *National Review*) against women's admission to the Citadel, the state-supported all-male military academy in South Carolina. There's Karen Lehrman, a journalist and author of a forthcoming book on what she calls "postideological feminism" (whuh?), who says she's a feminist, but . . . has tarred all of feminist scholarship with her sneering accounts of a few instances of excessive touchy-feeliness and self-involvement in the women's studies classroom.

The cherry-picking of "feminist excesses" is a favored strategy—and an effective one, because there *are* some feminists (particularly on campus, where many of the pod feminists reside) who say "all men" are creeps, or who jump down your throat for less than perfectly P.C. terminology, or who get mortally offended over minor slights, or who want to "share" tedious personal revelations in the classroom. Surely one can always find psychobabble and navel-gazing in an undergraduate population . . . or even in gatherings like, ahem, the pod feminists' "International Gender

Reconciliation Conference" last September, which offered such sessions as "Looking at Yourself," "Women's Wounds," "Emotional Support," and even a "Healing Break." Every movement with a membership larger than ten will have such folks, but the women's movement has consistently been tarred in the press for the overzealous or dippy remarks of a very few. The media have exploited these "excesses," distorting them into an emblematic portrait of the movement. And so, when the pod feminists come along and decry such behavior, it rings true for many readers and viewers who get their portrait of the women's movement from the media—and hence have come to believe that feminism is, in fact, overpopulated by shrieking ninnies. . . .

In *The Grounding of Modern Feminism*, historian Nancy Cott recounts how a group of women writers got together and produced a journal that proclaimed, in words that echo the position of the Women's Freedom Network, "We're interested in people now—not in men and women." These writers wanted to drop gender analysis and make nice with men. They had a name for their new posture: "postfeminist." The year was 1919. As Cott observes about the career women of the post–World War I era: "Professional women . . . might enthusiastically support equality of opportunity and yet frown on feminism. Among ambitious young careerists who intended to seize the main chance and relied on advancing by their individual talents, feminism was a 'term of opprobrium,' journalist Dorothy Dunbar Bromley found in 1927.". . .

Soon after the emergence of the second wave of the women's movement in the early seventies, Madison Avenue sought to convince women that they could attain feminist objectives via the markeplace. They could achieve the right independent lifestyle and "have it all" if they bought the right products, drank the right diet drinks, smoked the right cigarettes. Feminism, reinterpreted by advertising's creative directors, was simply a form of narcissism that could be sated in the shopping mall and the mirrors of mass media. The pod feminists of the nineties, in a sense, embody that seventies consumerist reinterpretation of feminism. By posing for the TV cameras with their "postideological" message that women have "made it" and can relax, they have become the nineties real-life equivalents of the blissed-out fashion models adorning the old Virginia Slims ads. They, too, gaze into the camera lens and congratulate themselves for having "Come a Long Way, Baby." This is Madison Avenue-hatched "feminist" celebrity come home to roost on the editorial pages: in place of rights, we'll give you a makeover and your moment in the klieg-light sun. But it is a promise that leads nowhere, as the pseudofeminists may discover when the ever-restless media move on in search of new spectacles.

Like the seedless pods of that B-grade horror film, the pod feminists are incapable of bringing new life to the women's movement. Theirs will always be a stillborn form of feminism, because it is an ideology that will not and does not want to generate political, social, or economic change. The pods do not look forward to creating a better future, only inward to the further adulation of self as this year's "most talked-about" model. No matter how many times they replicate themselves on the television screen, they will never produce a world that is wider or fairer for their sex.

affected profoundly by feminist courses. Eventually both women left their husbands and became welfare mothers, an experience each of them found to be both liberating and debilitating. Each experienced an initial "feminist high," a sense of enormous exhilaration and strength in her new independent circumstances. One divorced her husband, developed a viable career, experimented with the single life, and gradually became desperately unhappy. The other did not develop a career, lost her lover, and only then decided to take back her newly disabled husband (with his pension). Their rather different experiences with failed intimacy and their different occupational resources, I believe, help explain their diverse postfeminist strategies.

POSTFEMINIST DAUGHTERS

Between them Pam and Dotty had five daughters who, reckoning by the calendar, were members of the quintessential postfeminist generation.[26] (One died recently at the age of twenty-six; the surviving four range in age from twenty-three to thirty-one.) To varying degrees, all of the daughters have distanced themselves from feminist identity and ideology, in some cases in conscious reaction against what they regard as the excesses of their mothers' earlier feminist views. At the same time, however, most of the daughters have semiconsciously incorporated feminist principles into their expectations and strategies for family and work. A brief description of the family and work histories and gender consciousness of Dotty's and Pam's oldest, and most professionally successful daughters illustrates this depoliticized incorporation of feminist thought.

Pam's oldest daughter Lanny is twenty-three. Like Dotty's oldest daughter Lyn, she is a designer-drafter who received her initial training in a feminist-inspired skills program. She is now in her second marriage, with one child from each marriage. Lanny dropped out of high school and at seventeen married a truck driver who moves electronics equipment, and who she describes as addicted to drugs and totally uncommunicative. Staying home with their baby, she found herself isolated and unbearably lonely. Pam encouraged Lanny's entry into a drafting course sponsored by a county agency, and Lanny soon found ready employment in electronics via various temporary agencies.[27] After she discovered her husband's narcotics addiction and convinced him to enter a residential detox program, Lanny spent a brief period as a welfare mother. Although she hated drafting, she job-shopped frequently to raise her income sufficiently to support herself and her daughter. She was earning 14 dollars an hour, without benefits, in 1985 when she met her present husband, Ken, at one of these jobs where he worked as an expediter in the purchasing department for eight dollars an hour until a recent lay-off.

Lanny does not consider herself a feminist and has never been active or interested in politics. She also hates her work, but has no desire to be a homemaker and is perfectly willing to support her husband if he wants to stay home and take care of the children, or if, as they hope, she can afford to send him back to engineering school. She would like to become an interior designer.

Although Lanny started out in a rather traditional working-class marriage, she is an authentic postfeminist. She was not able to tolerate the isolation, boredom and emotional deprivation of that traditional marriage. Lanny's goals are to combine marriage to a nurturant, communicative, coparenting man (the way she perceives Ken) with full-time work at a job she truly enjoys. There is an ease to Lanny's attitudes about the gender division of labor at home and at work, and about gender norms more generally that is decidedly postfeminist. These are not political issues

to Lanny, nor even conscious points of personal struggle. She did actively reject her traditionally gendered first marriage, but without conceptualizing it that way. Lanny takes for granted the right to be flexible about family and work priorities. Remarkably, Ken appears to be equally flexible and equally oblivious to feminist influences on his notably enlightened attitudes.

The postfeminism of Dotty's oldest daughter Lyn, however, represents a somewhat more conscious and ambivalent response to feminism. Like Lanny, Lyn was a high school drop-out who took a variety of low-wage service sector jobs. But, unlike Lanny, the father of her child with whom she cohabited left during her pregnancy, making Lyn an unwed welfare mother. Lyn got off welfare by moonlighting at an electronics security job while developing her successful career in drafting. She is now a hybrid designer at one of the world's major semiconductor companies. Unlike Lanny, Lyn loves her work in drafting, although she is constantly anxious, exhausted, and deeply frustrated by the extreme demands, stress, and unpredictability of her working conditions, and by their incompatibility with her needs as a single mother. There have been long periods when Lyn hardly saw her son and depended upon her parents and friends to fill in as babysitters.

Lyn's desire for a father for her son was a major motive for her brief marriage to a man who quickly abused her. She has lived alone with her son since she divorced her husband five years ago. Although Lyn is proud and fiercely independent, during the past two years she has somewhat ambivalently pursued a marital commitment from her somewhat resistant boyfriend, Tom. Tom, like Lanny's husband Ken, appears both unthreatened by Lyn's greater career drive and income and quite flexible about gender norms generally. He, however, seems much less willing or able than Ken to commit himself to the long-term responsibilities of marriage and parenthood.

Lyn is aware of sex discrimination at work and of issues of gender injustice generally and will occasionally challenge these by herself. Yet more explicitly than Lanny, Lyn distances herself from a feminist identity which she regards as an unnecessarily hostile and occasionally petty one: "I do not feel like a feminist, because to me my mother is a perfect feminist. . . . If someone asks her to make coffee, she first has to determine if it is because she is a woman." Upon reflection Lyn acknowledges that it is the word "feminist" that she does not like, "because of the way I was brought up with it. It meant slapping people in the face with it. . . . I do what I think is right, and if I am asked, I tell them why. . . . Honestly I guess I am a very strong feminist, but I don't have to beat people with it."

I consider Lyn a stronger postfeminist than feminist because of her thoroughly individual and depoliticized relationship to feminist issues. She cannot imagine being active politically on any issue, not even one like battering which she experienced: "I leave them for people like my mother who can make issues out of that, because I don't see it that way. I'll help the neighbor next door whose husband is beating her to death . . . but I do it my way. My way is not in a public form. I am very different from my mother." Equally postfeminist are the ways Lyn fails both to credit feminist struggles for the career opportunities for women she has grown up taking for granted, or to blame sexism or corporation for the male-oriented work schedules and demands that jeopardize her family needs. For example, she would like to have a second child, but accepts the "fact" that a second child does not fit with a successful career. Lyn shares Lanny's postfeminist expectations for family and work, that is, the desire to combine marriage to a communicative, egalitarian man with motherhood and a successful, engaging career. While Lanny has achieved more of the former, Lyn has more of the latter.

The emergent relationships between postindustrialism, family turbulence and postfeminism are nuanced and dynamic. Crisis in the family, as manifested in escalating rates of divorce and single-mother households, contributes both to the peculiar gender stratification of this postindustrial workforce, and to a limited potential for feminist consciousness. Marital instability continually refuels a large, cheap female labor pool which underwrites the feminization of both the postindustrial proletariat and of poverty.[28] But this crudely gender-stratified and male-oriented occupational structure helps to further destabilize gender relationships and family life. Moreover, the skewed wages and salaries available to white men help to inflate housing costs for everyone, thereby contributing to the rapid erosion of the working class breadwinner and the family wage.[29]

One consequence of family instability in such an environment seems to have been an initial openness on the part of many women, like Dotty and Pam, to feminist ideas. Feminism served many mothers of the postfeminist generation well as an ideology for easing the transition from an unhappy, 1950s-style marriage and for providing support for efforts to develop independent career goals. Neither feminism nor other progressive movements have been as successful, however, in addressing either the structural inequalities of postindustrial occupational structure, or the individualist, fast-track culture that makes all too difficult the formation of stable intimate relations on an egalitarian, or, for that matter, any other basis. Organized religion, and particularly evangelical groups, may offer more effective support to troubled family relationships in these circumstances.

I believe this explains the attractiveness of various kinds of postfeminist ideologies and strategies for achieving intimacy, or for just surviving in a profoundly insecure milieu. Postfeminist strategies correspond to different generational and individual experiences of feminism as well as postindustrial family and work conditions. For many women of the "mother" generation, feminism has become as much a burden as a means of support. Where once it helped them to reform or leave unsatisfactory relationships, now it can intensify the pain and difficulty of the compromises most women must make in order to mediate the destructive effects of postindustrial society on family and personal relationships. Too seldom today can women find committed mates, let alone those who also would pass feminist muster.

Perhaps this helps to account for Pam's simultaneous turn to religion and her subtle adaptation of patriarchal, evangelical Christian forms to feminist ends and for Dotty's return to, but also reform of, a previously unsatisfactory marriage coupled with her shift from political engagement to paid work and organized religion. In a general climate and stage of their lives characterized by diminished expectations, both seek support for the compromises with and commitments to family and work they have chosen to make, rather than for greater achievement or independence. Without repudiating feminism, both Dotty and Pam have distanced themselves from feminist identity or activism. On the other hand, their postfeminist, oldest daughters take for granted the gains in female career opportunities and male participation in child rearing and domestic work for which feminists of their mothers' generation struggled. Lanny and Lyn do not conceptualize their troubling postindustrial work and family problems in political terms. To them feminism and politics appear irrelevant or threatening.

These diverse forms of postfeminism, I believe, are semiconscious responses to feminism's unwitting role as midwife to the new family and work conditions in postindustrial America. Some versions are more reactionary, some more progressive, but all, I believe, differ from *anti*feminism. They represent women's attempts to both retain and depoliticize the egalitarian family and work ideals of the second wave. This is an inherently contradictory project, and one that presents feminists with an enigmatic dilemma. Is it possible to devise a personal politics that respects the political and personal anxieties and the exhaustion of women contending with the destabilized family and work conditions of the postindustrial era? To do so without succumbing to conservative nostalgia for patriarchal familial and religious forms is a central challenge for contemporary feminism.

ACKNOWLEDGMENTS

I wish to thank Linda Gordon, Carole Joffe, David Plotke, Rayna Rapp, and Barrie Thorne for their challenging and supportive responses to earlier drafts of this article.

NOTES

1. Historians have argued that the establishment of separate spheres for the sexes had as one of its paradoxical consequences the development of feminist consciousness and activity. See, for example, Nancy Cott, *The Bonds of Womanhood: "Woman's Sphere" in New England, 1750–1835,* (New Haven: Yale University Press, 1976); Mary Ryan, *Womanhood in America* (New York: Franklin Watts, 1983). There were similar developments in Europe. By contrast, feminism has been weak in most preindustrial and "underdeveloped" societies, including even revolutionary societies with explicit commitments to gender equality.

2. As with the term "postfeminist," which I discuss below, I use the term "postindustrial" with trepidation as it carries a great deal of ideological charge. I use it here exclusively in a descriptive sense to designate a form and period of capitalist social organization in which traditional industrial occupations supply a small minority of jobs to the labor force, and the vast majority of workers labor in varieties of clerical, sales, and service positions. Daniel Bell claims to have formulated the theme of postindustrial society in 1962 in an essay, "The Post-Industrial Society." See his *The Coming of Post-Industrial Society. A Venture in Social Forecasting* (New York: Basic Books, 1973), p. 145.

3. Thus Geneva Overholser concludes a *New York Times* editorial opinion titled "What 'Post-Feminism' Really Means," 19 September 1986, p. 30.

4. My appreciation to Steven Buechler for first suggesting this analogy to me.

5. For an analogous argument about the relationship between feminism and deindustrialization in modern England, see Juliet Mitchell, "Reflections on Twenty Years of Feminism," in *What is Feminism?,* Juliet Mitchell and Ann Oakley, eds. (Oxford: Basil Blackwell, 1986), pp. 34–48.

6. There is considerable debate among economists concerning the accuracy of labeling the US as a service economy. For example, see Richard Walker's challenge to this characterization, "Is There a Service Economy? The Changing Capitalist Division of Labor," *Science & Society* 49, no. 1 (Spring 1985):42–83. The debate involves the politics of semantics. Few disagree, however, that significant occupational changes have occurred in the past few decades, or that these involve the decline of unions and real wages and the rise of female employment. For a synthetic analysis of occupational trends, see Bennett Harrison and Barry Bluestone, "The Dark Side of Labor Market 'Flexibility': Falling Wages and Growing Income Inequality in America," International Labor Office, File IL02 (June 1987).

7. Labor force participation rates for women increased steadily but slowly between 1900 and 1940, climbing from 20.5 percent to 25.4 percent. However, this pattern accelerated rapidly in the post-1940 period. In 1950 29 percent of women 14 years and older were in the labor force; in 1960 this percentage grew to 34.5 percent; in 1984 63 percent of all women ages 18–64 were in the labor force. See, Valerie Kincade Oppenheimer, *The Female Labor Force in the United States,* Population Monograph Series, No. 5, Institute of International Studies, University of California, Berkeley, 1970; and Barbara F. Reskin and Heidi I. Hartmann, eds., *Women's Work, Men's Work* (Washington, D.C.: National Academy Press, 1986). The dramatic rise in female enrollment in colleges occurred in the 1960s and 70s, rising from 38 to 48 percent of enrollees between 1960 and 1979. Rosalind Petchesky, *Abortion and Woman's Choice* (Boston: Northeastern University Press, 1984), US marriage rates peaked at 16.4 per 1,000 people in 1946, declined sharply to 9.9 in 1952, and have fluctuated around 10 ever since, while divorce rates have increased steadily to 5.0 in 1985. National Center for Health Statistics, Annual Summary of Births, Marriages, Divorces and Deaths, *Monthly Vital Statistics Reports.* More significantly, the age of women at their first marriage has risen and their rate of marriage has declined steadily since 1960. Fertility rates peaked at 3.6 per 1000 women during the famous mid-1950s baby boom and declined steadily thereafter

to 1.8 in 1976. See Petchesky, *Abortion and Women's Choice,* pp. 103–107. Even more striking are the rising proportions of women who never marry or bear children. The cohort of women born between 1935–39 had the lowest rate of childlessness in the twentieth century—10 percent. The Census Bureau projects a childless rate of 20–25 percent, however, for women born in the 1960s, and it estimates that 40 percent of college-educated women born in this decade never will bear children. "The Birth Question," *USA Today,* 28 February 1986, p. 1.

8. In 1960 one out of every eleven children lived with only one parent, but by 1986 one out of four children lived in a single-parent household, and 90 percent of these lived with their mothers. Tim Schreiner, "US Family Eroding, Says Census Bureau," *San Francisco Chronicle,* 10 December 1986.

9. "A Mother's Choice," *Newsweek,* 31 March 1986, p. 47.

10. See Harrison and Bluestone, "Dark Side of Labor Market 'Flexibility'."

11. These are among the findings of a study that attempted to operationalize Marxist criteria for assigning class categories to workers in the US. Even though the study excluded housewives from its sample, it found "that the majority of the working class in the United States consists of women (53.6 percent)." See, Erik Olin Wright, et al., "The American Class Structure," *American Sociological Review* 47 (December 1982), p. 22. For additional data on female occupational patterns and earnings and an astute analysis of the paradoxical relationship between female employment and poverty, see Joan Smith, "The Paradox of Women's Poverty: Wage-Earning Women and Economic Transformation," *Signs* 10, no. 2 (Winter 1984).

12. The concept "feminization of poverty" also misrepresents significant features of contemporary poverty, particularly the worsening conditions for minority men. See Pamela Sparr, "Reevaluating Feminist Economics: 'Feminization of Poverty' Ignores Key Issues," and Linda Burnham, "Has Poverty Been Feminized in Black America?" in Rochelle Lefkowitz and Ann Withorn, eds., *For Crying Out Loud: Women and Poverty in the United States* (New York: The Pilgrim Press, 1986).

13. As the much publicized findings from Lenore Weitzman's study of no-fault divorce in California underscore. In the first year after divorce women and minor children in their care suffer a 73 percent decline in their standard of living while husbands enjoy a 42 percent gain. *The Divorce Revolution: The Unexpected Social and Economic Consequences for Women and Children in America,* Lenore J. Weitzman (New York: Free Press, 1985). For a qualitative study which focuses on the plight of divorced, single mothers, see Terry Arendell, *Mothers and Divorce: Legal, Economic, and Social Dilemmas* (Berkeley: University of California Press, 1986).

14. In 1980, households headed by fully employed women had a poverty rate almost three times greater than husband-wife households and twice that of households headed by unmarried men. The number of female-headed families doubled between 1970 and 1980. By 1981, women headed almost one fifth of all families with minor children. Smith, "Paradox of Women's Poverty," p. 291.

15. Households with working wives accounted for 60 percent of all family income in 1985, which made it possible for 65 percent of all families to earn more than $25,000 per year, compared with only 28 percent of families who achieved comparable incomes 20 years ago. In 1981 the median earnings of full-time year-round women workers was $12,001, 59 percent of the $20,260 that men earned. That year married women contributed a median of 26.7 percent of family income. The lower the family's annual income, however, the higher the proportion contributed by women. Paradoxically, however, there is an inverse relationship between family income and the percentage of wives working. See *The Working Woman: A Progress Report* (Washington D.C.: The Conference Board, 1985), and Reskin and Hartmann, *Women's Work, Men's Work,* p. 4. The combined effects of these trends are acute for black women, for whom astronomical divorce rates have overwhelmed the effects of their relative gains in earnings, forcing them increasingly into poverty. For data see US Department of Labor, *Time of Change: 1983 Handbook on Women Workers* (Washington D.C.: Dept. of Labor, Women's Bureau Bulletin 298, 1983), p. 29; Paula Giddings, *When and Where I Enter: The Impact of Black Women on Race and Sex in America* (Toronto: Bantam Books, 1985), p. 353.

16. For a more optimistic evaluation of the economic and social effects of these changes on women, see Heidi I. Hartmann, "Changes in Women's Economic and Family Roles in Post World War II United States," in Lourdes Beneria and Catherine Stimpson, eds., *Women, Households, and Structural Transformation* (New Brunswick: Rutgers University Press, 1987).

17. It seems plausible that there has been a concomitant decline in political activism as well. Note, for example, the stark contrast in the amount of time available for politics for women active on opposing sides of the abortion controversy. In a recent study of this conflict, most of the antiabortion activists were housewives who spent at least thirty hours per week on antichoice politics, whereas most of the prochoice activists were career women, few of whom spent more than five hours per week on this issue. See Kristin Luker, *Abortion & the Politics of Motherhood* (Berkeley and Los Angeles: University of California Press, 1984). Although there are problems with Luker's prochoice sample that may exaggerate its career and income levels, it seems unlikely that the contrast is spurious.

18. Barbara Ehrenreich, *The Hearts of Men: American Dreams and the Flight from Commitment* (Garden City: Anchor Press/Doubleday, 1983).

19. Christopher Lasch has made a sideline industry out of this sort of attack on feminists. For some of his most recent polemics on this subject, see "What's Wrong with the Right?" *Tikkun* 1, no. 1 (1986); and "Why the Left Has No Future," *Tikkun* 1, no. 2 (1986). The latter was his response to critics of the former, including Lillian Rubin's "A Feminist Response to Lasch." The most comprehensive and popular recent book to scapegoat feminism in this way is probably Sylvia Ann Hewlett's, *A Lesser Life: The Myth of Women's Liberation in America* (New York: William Morrow, 1986). For a critical discussion of this book that does not

deny the power of its approach, see Deborah Rosenfelt and Judith Stacey, "Second Thoughts on the Second Wave," *Feminist Studies* 13, no. 2 (Summer 1987).

20. The most conspicuous representatives of this backlash within feminist thought are Betty Friedan, Jean Bethke Elshtain, and Germaine Greer. For critical discussions of their writings see my "Are Feminists Afraid to Leave Home? The Challenge of Conservative Pro-family Feminism," in Juliet Mitchell & Ann Oakley, eds., *What is Feminism?* (London: Basil Blackwell 1986), and Zillah Eisenstein, *Feminism and Sexual Equality: Crisis in Liberal America* (New York: Monthly Review Press, 1984).

21. The county population grew from 290,547 in 1950 to 1,295,071 in 1980. US Bureau of the Census. *Census of Population: 1950,* Vol. 2, *Characteristics of the Population* pt. 5, California, 1952; and *Census of Population: 1980* Vol. I. *Characteristics of the Population, General Population Characteristics,* pt. 6, California, 1982.

22. For data and a superb ethnographic and analytical account of this transition, see John Frederick Keller, "The Production Worker in Electronics: Industrialization and Labor Development in California's Santa Clara Valley," (Ph.D. dissertation, University of Michigan, 1981).

23. For data on the occupational structure of the electronics industry, see Keller, "Production Worker in Electronics;" Marcie Axelrad, *Profile of the Electronics Workforce in the Santa Clara Valley* (San Jose: Project on Health and Safety in Electronics, 1979); Lennie Siegel and Herb Borock, "Background Report on Silicon Valley," prepared for the US Commission on Civil Rights (Mountain View, CA: Pacific Studies Center, 1982).

24. For the data on divorce rates and household composition for Santa Clara County in comparison with California and the US as a whole, see Bureau of the Census, *Census of Population,* 1960, 1970, and 1980. During the 1970s Santa Clara County recorded 660 abortions for every 1000 births, compared with a statewide average of 489.5 and a ratio of less than 400 for the nation. See Bureau of the Census, *Statistical Abstract of the United States,* 1981.

25. The most influential representative of this tendency may be James Dobson, founder and president of Focus on the Family, "a nonprofit corporation dedicated to the preservation of the home." Focus produces a radio talk show on family issues aired as much as three times daily on hundreds of Christian stations throughout the US and abroad. The organization also produces and distributes Christian films, tapes, and audio-cassettes on family topics. Dobson, who served on the recent Meese Commission on Pornography, has also authored scores of advice books and pamphlets on family and personal relationships, most of which advocate the doctrine of "tough love." The uneasy fusion of patriarchal and feminist thought is marked in his advice book on marital crisis, *Love Must Be Tough* (Waco, Texas: Word Books, 1983). For a discussion of the infusion of the female sexual revolution into fundamentalist culture, see Barbara Ehrenreich, Elizabeth Hess, and Gloria Jacobs, *Re-Making Love: The Feminization of Sex* (New York: Anchor Press, 1986), chapter 5.

26. Indeed the first media use of the term "postfeminist" to catch my attention was in the title of an essay about women in their late twenties. Susan Bolotin, "Voices From the Post-Feminist Generation," *New York Times Magazine,* 17 October 1982.

27. The very concept of "temporary" employment is being reshaped by postindustrial labor practices. High tech industries in the Silicon Valley make increasing use of temporary agencies to provide "flexible staffing" and to cut employee benefits. In 1985 one of every 200 workers in the US was a "temp," but one of 60 workers in the Silicon Valley held a "temporary" job. See David Beers, " 'Temps': A High-Tech's Ace in The Hole," *San Bernardino Sun,* 28 May 1985.

28. Nor are the effects of the relationship between marital instability, female production work, and poverty confined to the US. As many have noted, in the postindustrial economy, women work on a "global assembly line." Maria Patricia Fernandez-Kelly discusses the effects of these international processes on Mexican women who work in electronics and garment factories on the Mexican-US border in "Mexican Border Industrialization, Female Labor Force Participation, and Migration," in June Nash and Maria Patricia Fernandez-Kelly, eds., *Women, Men, and the International Division of Labor,* (Albany: SUNY Press, 1983), pp. 205–223.

29. More work needs to be done on ways in which the practice of one pattern of family life by some constrains options for others. The most obvious of the asymmetrical relationships among family patterns available to different social classes today is that between affluent dual-career couples and the poorly-paid women who provide the child care and domestic services upon which their egalitarian marriages depend. For a valuable study of the former, see Rosanna Hertz, *More Equal Than Others: Women and Men in Dual-Career Marriages* (Berkeley: University of California Press, 1986). For a sensitive analysis of other kinds of unanticipated feedback effects of the electronics industry on the social ecology of the Silicon Valley, see AnnaLee Saxenian, "Silicon Chips and Spacial Structure: the Industrial Basis of Urbanization in Santa Clara County, California," (Masters thesis, University of California Berkeley, 1980).

Patriarchies and Feminisms: The Two Women's Movements of Post-Unification Germany

MYRA MARX FERREE

In the nearly five years that have passed since the Berlin Wall was opened with such hope and joy, there have been many accounts of enormous problems in the now-unified Germany. Unemployment and anomie in the East (ex-GDR), higher taxes and greater competition in the West, and a resurgent racism in both parts have tempered the mood of celebration. Although many foretold the costs, particularly for women, the extent of these problems has been sobering for all. The phrase "women are the losers of the unification" has become virtually a cliché; moreover, it does reflect reality. Women's official unemployment rate (over 20 percent is twice as high as men's, rises in the cost of living and the end to subsidies for basic goods have widened the gap in standards of living, leaving those with lower incomes (often women) relatively worse off, and benefits such as child care leaves and kindergarten subsidies have been slashed (Bialas and Ettl 1993). In addition, the change in abortion law has cost ex-GDR women their previous right to abortion on demand in the first trimester.

In this painful situation, feminists both East and West have actively drawn attention to women's problems, but have found it surprisingly difficult to establish a common ground from which to combat such issues. This article attempts to analyze certain aspects of the problems of mutual understanding that have arisen between East and West German feminists in particular and East and West German women more generally. I argue that some of these tensions and incomprehensions have their roots in the dif-

ferent structures of state policy and in the resulting differences in women's experiences and collective identities in the two postwar Germanies. In this sense, the conflicts between East and West feminists can be understood as a specific case of a more general problem of feminist identity. Other conflicts over feminist identity—such as those between White and Black feminists[1] in the United States or between First and Third World feminists globally—both illuminate and are illuminated by consideration of the dynamics of this specific case.

I suggest that these broad conflicts over interpretations of feminism are often rooted in different experiences of women with the state. States and state policies play a major role in systematically shaping women's experiences of paid work, marriage, and motherhood. Their effects may be seen in part in the interpretations of oppression and freedom that women construct based on personal and deeply felt experiences.

It is important to clarify at the outset that I am not arguing for a simplistic translation of women's experience into the politics of feminism in general or in either part of Germany specifically. In Germany, both before and after unification, there has been a complex process of debate both among feminists and between feminists and others that has contributed to shaping the understanding of the kinds of goals the women's movement stands for and of the appropriate means with which to accomplish those goals (Hampele 1991; Gerhard et al. 1990). In each locus of debate there arose what I call a "collective self-representation" of feminism, that is, a shared and yet personal sense of the meaning of a feminist collective identity. Such a collective identity links an interpretation of the past (women's experiences) to an interpretation of the future (women's aspirations). Collective identity is thus neither simply a reflection of past experience nor independent of it, but an actively constructed interpretation of shared history (Melucci 1988; Taylor and Whittier 1992).

Such feminist collective self-representation is different in important ways in each part of Germany; some of these differences arise from the nature of women's experiences with patriarchy when there were still two different countries. At the root, each system was organized around a fundamentally different sort of patriarchy. Following the lead offered by some feminist theorists of the welfare state (Siim 1987; Brown 1987; Jonasdottir and Jones 1988; Sassoon 1987), I distinguish between what has been called public and private patriarchy. At an abstract level, most analysts of gender oppression would agree that patriarchal power is both private and public and that both intrafamilial relations and state politics are arenas in which women's subordination is constructed and male domination is exercised on a daily basis. At a practical level, however, one or the other form of patriarchy may dominate certain women's concrete experiences and thus carry a disproportionate weight in the explanations of oppression and aspirations for freedom that these women develop for themselves. Such collective explanations and aspirations are invoked whenever women refer to themselves as "feminist." Jane Mansbridge (1994) calls this the "street theory" of feminism and I refer to it as their collective self-representation.

My core argument is that at least two such practical feminisms arose in postwar East and West Germany. Each reflected women's efforts to interpret experiences that were fundamentally different because each was predominantly structured by a different type of patriarchial state system: East Germany reflected principles of public patriarchy and West Germany those of private patriarchy. Because of this, mutual incomprehension, misunderstanding, and recriminations have become commonplace among feminists in unified Germany (Holland-Cunz 1990; Helwerth and Schwarz 1993; Rohnstock 1994). Even when there is a shared self-identification as "feminist," there are often different interpretations of what this term means. Some of the sources of these unanticipated communication difficulties are in the experiences of domination, competition, or recrimination in the period after unification; while these are also important, they are not my focus here (see Ferree 1992 for a fuller examination of these issues). In this article, I limit my discussion to factors that were already present before the Wall fell, problems that arise from the specific structures of state policy in each country, and the resulting differences in women's experiences and collective self-representations.

THE TWO GERMANIES AND THEIR POLICIES

The distinction between public and private patriarchy rests fundamentally on the role of the state as either supplanting or supporting the conventional authority and practical power of the individual male as household head. The state socialism of East Germany (German Democratic Republic, GDR) supplanted the individual male head and thus embodied principles of public patriarchy; the state policies undergirding the social market economy of West Germany (Federal Republic of Germany, FRG) are, in contrast, strongly oriented to sustaining private patriarchy. The issue defining this distinction is *not* whether the state is more or less influential in women's lives, but rather the nature of the effects that it strives for and accomplishes.

In the GDR, state policy tended to diminish the dependence of women on individual husbands and fathers, but it enhanced the dependence of women as mothers on the state (Ferree 1993; Bastian, Labsch, and Müller 1990). In the FRG, state policy instead followed the principle of subsidiarity and actively encouraged private dependencies. In particular, the state had a mandate to preserve "the" family, which it defined primarily as the husband-wife relationship as a context in which children can be raised (Moeller 1993; Ostner 1994). Thus, overall, the nature of the state's role in public patriarchy was to emphasize the *direct* relationship of mothers to the state; the nature of the state's role in private patriarchy was to encourage wives' dependence on husbands and children's on parents. In turn, this means that in public patriarchy women experienced their oppression as *mothers* and as more directly connected to the activities of the state as patriarch; in private patriarchy, women experienced their oppression as *wives* and as more directly connected to their individual dependence on their spouses.

To make these abstractions more concrete, compare the nature of women's ordinary life experiences in the two systems. In the former GDR, approximately one-third of all babies were born out-of-wedlock, and virtually all women were in the labor force and worked essentially full-time jobs, where they earned on average 40 percent of the family income. Out-of-home child care for children under three and kindergartens and after-school care for older children were universally available at low cost (which, incidentally, is an exception among socialist as well as nonsocialist countries). State subsidies for child care, rent, and other basic necessities reduced differences in the standards of living between single mothers and two-parent, two-income families. Divorce was easy to obtain; women were more often the ones who petitioned for divorce; and the divorce rate was the highest in the world.[2] Dependence on an individual husband appears to have been reduced to a minimum.

In the FRG, by contrast, 90 percent of babies were born within marriages. Living together was not uncommon, but when the baby arrived, so did marriage (87 percent of cohabiting relationships were childless compared to 18 percent of marriages). Having a child was structurally inconsistent with holding a full-time job, given the short and irregular school hours and scarcity of child care for preschool children. There were child care places for less than 5 percent of the children under three years of age. This incompatibility forced women to choose between having a baby or having a job. Of women aged 30 to 50, only one-third had full-time jobs; on the other hand, fully 15 percent of women aged 40–50 remained childless. A majority of employed mothers interrupted their careers for at least six years; even mothers of older children (15 years and older) were less likely than nonmothers to be in the labor force at all, not even considering the reductions they faced in the hours they worked or the status of their jobs. Given their restricted labor force participation, it is not surprising that West German women provided on average only 18 percent of the family income and that the majority of employed women did not earn enough to support themselves independently, let alone raise a child. Tax subsidies such as income splitting further widened the gulf between the standard of living of two-parent families and single mothers; if a mother was confronted with the choice of keeping her job or keeping her marriage, the economic incentives strongly favored the latter.[3] Dependence on an individual husband was thus strongly institutionalized.

These differences are well-known. The way they play themselves out in feminist identity and analysis is less obvious. There are several distinct areas where I think the differences between public and private patriarchy, and thus the structurally different experiences of dependency and oppression, were expressed in the specifics of feminist consciousness and politics before unification and which still carry a residue into current interactions.

FEMINIST IDENTITY AND THE STRUCTURES OF EXPERIENCE

The most central difference relevant for feminism may be how women's identities are shaped in relation to the dominant form of patriarchy in general and how patriarchy has been institutionalized in particular. In West Germany, there was a conceptual package invoked by the phrase "wife-mother": these two roles were inseparably bundled together. This conceptualization has not carried over easily to the eastern part of unified Germany where motherhood was not bound so structurally to wifehood. Thinking about mothers in the FRG shaded easily into imagining them only as wives; one needed to specify "single mother" and, in doing so, one invoked the image of mothers who were politically and culturally deviant as well as impoverished. In the East, the imagery of single mother was not so necessary: women were mothers and workers and they may or may not have chosen to be or stay married. Being unmarried and a mother was not an identity that carried a connotation of victimhood, deviance, or struggle.

The imagery of "woman" was more shaped by the wife role in the West; the "conventional" picture of womanhood was structured in terms of a woman's tenuous connection to the labor force, her need to attend to her appearance and to the care of the household, and to be sexually attractive to and able to depend on an individual man. Women's magazines instructed their readers in how they could achieve the current style of satisfying their husband's needs. Identity was expressed in "lifestyle," which for most women meant the nature of their consumer activities and personal appearances.

For East Germans, the conventional woman was not at the disposal of an individual man but instrumentalized by the state as patriarch. The image of woman was thus the "worker-mother" who contributed both reproductive and productive labor to a collectively male-defined state. The concept of worker-mother appears to have been as much a self-evident package as the West's concept of wife-mother; the ability to combine paid employment and motherhood was not questioned any more in the East than the ability to combine wife and mother roles was in the West. In both the conventional image and the self-understanding of GDR women, wifehood was much less salient than the role of worker. Not only did the GDR woman's constant work at home and in the labor force take precedence over her appearance or the appearance of her home in others' perceptions of her, but she identified her children and her job, not her spouse or her home, as her achievements. Consumption was a chore, not a means to identity and self-expression. That this was an issue of identity, not merely deprivation of consumer goods, is suggested by the collapse of Western-style women's magazines in ex-GDR markets; indeed, the West German firm that bought the largest existing women's magazine in the GDR and tried to use it to market "glamour" to women in eastern Germany largely failed to attract an audience. Within a year the magazine ceased publication.

The exaggerations and stereotypes of each version of womanhood are distorted reflections of the differently organized patriarchal demands: on the one hand, the wife of leisure working on her appearance and waiting for her husband to come home; on the other, the single working mother who has the support of the state in attending to all of her responsibilities. Note that from each side, the dependency of the other woman is idealized; husbands support "their" wives, the state supports "its" mothers, and neither patriarch supposedly asks for anything in return. Envy of the "ease" and generous support offered to women in the other way of life is a theme that was used politically on both sides of the Wall. From inside either public or private patriarchy, it was never so simple, of course. The price for each of these "privileged" ways of life was more evident to the women paying it than to the women whose personal experiences were with patriarchy of a different sort.

In reality, neither public nor private patriarchy constitutes liberation for women, but each tends to shift the focus of women's attention to different aspects of their oppression. In the context of private patriarchy, the family, sexuality, and marital relations are initially at the forefront of theorizing (Janssen-Jurreit 1976; Millett 1970; Friedan 1963). The initial feminist idea is that if relationships between men and women as individuals could be put on a different footing, it would lead to structural change and vice versa—the structural changes that are sought are those that would change the balance of power within familial relationships. Power relationships within the family are often problematized and are seen as "spilling over" into the rest of social organization. In fact, rejecting marriage and seeking full-time employment, in the context of private patriarchy, are ways for women to challenge the status quo—to struggle against the individualized dependency prescribed by gender norms and almost invisibly upheld by state policy.

In the context of public patriarchy, the role of public policy and the state is more immediately central and obvious. The male domination of political decision-making in all areas, the role of the state as the "guardian" who speaks for women rather than allowing them to speak for themselves, and the felt absence of collective political voice are all aspects of the sense of powerlessness that are directly evident in the experience of women's subordination by collective rather than by individual male power. Power relations within the family, if problematized at all, are seen as stemming from more fundamental policies and decisions taken at the public political level. Private relationships—

whether lesbian or heterosexual—are experienced as irrelevant or secondary in comparison (e.g., Merkel et al. 1990; Kahlau 1990; Hampele 1991). The common theme of feminist critiques is that women are "instrumentalized" by the state and that such state power must be challenged.

Neither of these experientially grounded perceptions is wholly wrong. Both the family and the state are arenas in which women's power and self-determination are restricted and where efforts to reconstitute social relations along less patriarchal lines are essential to the feminist project. Both forms of patriarchal organization, however, tend to encourage a distinctively one-sided form of analysis, because each type of model "fits" and explains certain gut-level experiences of oppression better. What is particularly instructive, albeit painful, is the collision between these two understandings.

THE DOUBLE VISION OF FEMINISM

Unlike the other Eastern European countries, the GDR in the 1980s had a slowly emerging feminist movement that became mobilized during the course of the transition and played an active political role in the process of Germany's restructuring. This movement was largely demobilized as the reform of the GDR was transformed into its absorption into the Federal Republic (Ferree 1994). In West Germany, there had been an active autonomous feminist movement and a variety of local feminist projects since the early 1970s (Ferree 1987). Each of these two differently grounded feminist identities that arose in these differently organized social contexts have been forced by unification now to share the same political space. Each has a tendency to disparage the degree of feminist understanding of the other with terms such as backward, hypocritical, arrogant, atheoretical, callous, naive, hypersensitive, know-it-all (Rohnstock 1994). The charges and countercharges go on and on and are unfortunately cast primarily in terms of the individual or collective personalities of the "other." Such attempts to define "better" and "worse" feminists, and in the process to defend one's own version of feminism as "more true," ultimately founder on the reality of difference.

This reality is that the contexts of public and private patriarchy and separate national experiences, which were independently theorized and from which two different women's movements emerged at two different times, are in practice differing organizations of oppression. What "feels true" as a collective self-representation has to resonate with each woman's experience of her own oppression to be

JUDAISM, MASCULINITY, AND FEMINISM

MICHAEL S. KIMMEL

In the late 1960s, I organized and participated in several large demonstrations against the war in Vietnam. Early on—it must have been 1967 or so—over 10,000 of us were marching down Fifth Avenue in New York urging the withdrawal of all U.S. troops. As we approached one corner, I noticed a small but vocal group of counter-demonstrators, waving American flags and shouting patriotic slogans. "Go back to Russia!" one yelled. Never being particularly shy, I tried to engage him. "It's my duty as an American to oppose policies I disagree with. This is patriotism!" I answered. "Drop dead, you commie Jew fag!" was his reply.

Although I tried not to show it, I was shaken by his accusation, perplexed and disturbed by the glib association of communism, Judaism, and homosexuality. "Only one out of three," I can say to myself now, "is not especially perceptive." But yet something disturbing remains about that linking of political, religious, and sexual orientations. What links them, I think, is a popular perception that each is not quite a man, that each is less than a man. And while recent developments may belie this simplistic formulation, there is, I believe, a kernel of truth to the epithet, a small piece I want to claim, not as vicious smear, but proudly. I believe that my Judaism did directly contribute to my activism against that terrible war, just as it currently provides the foundation for my participation in the struggle against sexism.

What I want to explore here are some of the ways in which my Jewishness has contributed to becoming an anti-sexist man, working to make this world a safe environment for women (and men) to fully express their humanness. Let me be clear that I speak from a cultural heritage of Eastern European Jewry, transmuted by three generations of life in the United States. I speak of the culture of Judaism's effect on me as an American Jew, not from either doctrinal considerations—we all know the theological contradictions of a biblical reverence for

Michael S. Kimmel, "Judaism, Masculinity, and Feminism," *Changing Men* (Summer/Fall 1987). Copyright © 1987. Reprinted with the permission of *Changing Men*.

women, and prayers that thank God for not being born one—nor from an analysis of the politics of nation states. My perspective says nothing of Middle-Eastern machismo; I speak of Jewish culture in the diaspora, not of Israeli politics.

The historical experience of Jews has three elements that I believe have contributed to this participation in feminist politics. First, historically, the Jew is an *outsider*. Wherever the Jew has gone, he or she has been outside the seat of power, excluded from privilege. The Jew is the symbolic "other," not unlike the symbolic "otherness" of women, gays, racial and ethnic minorities, the elderly and the physically challenged. To be marginalized allows one to see the center more clearly than those who are in it, and presents grounds for alliances among marginal groups.

But the American Jew, the former immigrant, is "other" in another way, one common to many ethnic immigrants to the United States. Jewish culture is, after all, seen as an ethnic culture, which allows it to be more oppressive and emotionally rich than the bland norm. Like other ethnic subgroups, Jews have been characterized as emotional, nurturing, caring. Jewish men hug and kiss, cry and laugh. A little too much. A little too loudly. Like ethnics.

Historically, the Jewish man has been seen as less than masculine, often as a direct outgrowth of this emotional "respond-ability." The historical consequences of centuries of laws against Jews, of anti-Semitic oppression, are a cultural identity and even a self-perception as "less than men," who are too weak, too fragile, too frightened to care for our own. The cruel irony of ethnic oppression is that our rich heritage is stolen from us, and then we are blamed for having no rich heritage. In this, again, the Jew shares this self-perception with other oppressed groups who, rendered virtually helpless by an infantilizing oppression, are further victimized by the accusation that they are, in fact, infants and require the beneficence of the oppressor. One example of this cultural self-hatred can be found in the comments of Freud's colleague and friend Weininger (a Jew) who argued that "the Jew is saturated with femininity. The most feminine Aryan is more masculine than the most manly Jew. The Jew lacks the good breeding that is based upon respect for one's own individuality as well as the individuality of others."

But, again, Jews are also "less than men" for a specific reason as well. The traditional emphasis on literacy in Jewish culture contributes in a very special way. In my family, at least, to be learned, literate, a rabbi, was the highest aspiration one could possibly have. In a culture characterized by love of learning, literacy may be a mark of dignity. But currently in the United States literacy is a cultural liability. Americans contrast egghead intellectuals, divorced from the real world, with men of action—instinctual, passionate, fierce, and masculine. Senator Albert Beveridge of Indiana counseled in his 1906 volume *Young Man and the World* (a turn of the century version of *Real Men Don't Eat Quiche*) to "avoid books, in fact, avoid all artificial learning, for the forefathers put America on the right path by learning from completely natural experience." Family, church and synagogue, and schoolroom were cast as the enervating domains of women, sapping masculine vigor.

Now don't get me wrong. The Jewish emphasis on literacy, on mind over body, does not exempt Jewish men from sexist behavior. Far from it. While many Jewish men avoid the Scylla of a boisterous and physically harassing misogyny, we can often dash ourselves against the Charybdis of a male intellectual intimidation of others. "Men with the properly sanctioned educational credentials in our society," writes Harry Brod, "are trained to impose our opinions on others, whether asked for or not, with an air of supreme self-confidence and aggressive self-assurance." It's as if the world were only waiting for our word. In fact, Brod notes, "many of us have developed mannerisms that function to intimidate those customarily denied access to higher educational institutions, especially women."[1] And yet, despite this, the Jewish emphasis on literacy has branded us, in the eyes of the world, less than "real" men.

Finally, the historical experience of Jews centers around, hinges upon our sense of morality, our ethical imperatives. The preservation of a moral code, the commandment to live ethically, is the primary responsibility of each Jew, male or female. Here, let me relate another personal story. Like many other Jews, I grew up with the words "Never Again" ringing in my ears, branded indelibly in my consciousness. For me they implied a certain moral responsibility to bear witness, to remember—to place my body, visibly, on the side of justice. This moral responsibility inspired my participation in the anti-war movement, and my active resistance of the draft *as a Jew.* I remember family dinners in front of the CBS Evening News, watching Walter Cronkite recite the daily tragedy of the war in Vietnam. "Never again," I said to myself, crying myself to sleep after watching napalm fall on Vietnamese villagers. Isn't this the brutal terror we have sworn ourselves to preventing when we utter those two words? When I allowed myself to feel the pain of those people, there was no longer a choice; there was, instead, a moral imperative to speak out, to attempt to end that war as quickly as possible.

In the past few years, I've become aware of another war. I met and spoke with women who had been raped, raped by their lovers, husbands, and fathers, women who had been beaten by those husbands and lovers. Some were even Jewish women. All those same words—Never Again—flashed across my mind like a neon meteor lighting up the darkened consciousness.

Hearing that pain and that anger prompted the same moral imperative. We Jews say "Never Again" to the systematic horror of the Holocaust, to the cruel war against the Vietnamese, to Central American death squads. And we must say it against this war waged against women in our society, against rape and battery.

So in a sense, I see my Judaism as reminding me every day of that moral responsibility, the *special* ethical imperative that my life, as a Jew, gives to me. Our history indicates how we have been excluded from power, but also, as men, we have been privileged by another power. Our Judaism impels us to stand against any power that is illegitimately constituted because we know only too well the consequences of that power. Our ethical vision demands equality and justice, and its achievement is our historical mission.

NOTE

1. Harry Brod, "Justice and a Male Feminist" in *The Jewish Newspaper* (Los Angeles) June 6, 1985, p. 6.

accepted, and that feeling of authenticity varies based on the fundamental political structuring of personal experience. Given such different ways of structuring experience in public and private patriarchy, what "feels true" to a woman raised in one system will likely "feel alien" to a woman whose identity has been formed in the other. Because an authentic feminist politics has to "feel true," it cannot—and should not—aspire to universal priorities or any single dimension of "correctness." Although sustaining a view of feminism as intrinsically multiple in its analyses and emphases is difficult, such pluralism enriches and strengthens feminist practice.

This indicates the need to preserve as much as possible the perspective that arose out of the experience of public patriarchy in the GDR—not only for the insights it already generated into the contradictions and identity processes of such a system for women, but also because it continues to offer valuable insight into features of private patriarchy that women who live under it might otherwise tend to take for granted and allow to become theoretically invisible. Moreover, the comparison suggests the extent of analytical problems that women in eastern Germany will have to overcome as they attempt to grapple with understanding the costs and benefits of the new, imposed status of dependent wife.

Contrasts such as these help to expose the experiential preconditions of feminist theorizing and thus broaden and differentiate theories. Western European and North American feminists have already learned much from such critical contrasts drawn by women in Third World countries and from the differences in experience and interpretation between women of dominant and subordinate ethnic and racial groups in the industrialized countries. The common ethnicity and developed industrial economies that existed on both sides of the Wall may have made German feminists underestimate the difficulties of communication and the gulf in experience and identity that was still to be bridged when the Wall fell. The sheer unexpectedness of such fundamental differences blocked many attempts to listen to and learn from theory grounded in a significantly different structuring of women's lives. Nonetheless, the contrast between public and private patriarchy now being painfully articulated in both parts of Germany is worth attending to, rather than wishing away, because it may bind together a number of common experiences across specific situations.

One of the most interesting of these potential analogies is the way in which Black feminist thought has also attempted to come to terms with the greater significance of public patriarchy in African American women's lives than in the lives of White American women. Using such an analogy should not be interpreted to suggest that African American women's experience with a racist state is in any way identical to East German women's experience in the GDR, but rather to indicate that some of the elements that define public patriarchy, especially the direct relation of mothers to the state, may be responsible for observed similarities in identity and perspective that would otherwise be very surprising. Thus, despite dramatic differences in economic opportunity, family poverty, and social devaluation, among many other things, there are some points where African American feminist thought touches closely on issues that women in eastern Germany have also been attempting to express (the best summary of the diverse insights from Black feminist thought is Collins [1990]). Such surprising commonalities need some explanation. One possibility is that they reflect some general characteristics of difference between public and private patriarchy.

First, there has been a tendency for feminists in eastern Germany to talk more positively about the family and to see a challenge for feminism in integrating men more fully into family life. In comparison to women under private patriarchy, they did not see men's exclusion from the family as offering a good in itself nor did they define single parenting as freedom from male oppression—but they were also not so willing to marry, unless men met their expectations for family participation (e.g., Rohnstock 1994). Men's relationship to children was something that women valued and that the state ignored and actively marginalized. These are experiences on which African American feminists have also had to insist and about which White feminists have been skeptical (Collins 1990).

The experience of family as a support system in opposition to the culture at large, of withdrawal into the family as a form of privacy from the state, is another theme that presents family in a positive light in African American feminist writing; it is also echoed in some of the descriptions of the role of the family in state socialism in East Germany and elsewhere (e.g., Einhorn 1993; Funk and Mueller 1993). Because private patriarchy has not been so dominant in the experience of Black women or women in East Germany, it may be easier for them to imagine bringing men more centrally into families, without conceding patriarchal authority to them, than it is for many White American women or West German feminists. It seems at least possible that political practices that simply exclude men, as if changing them were either irrelevant or impossible, do not make nearly as much sense from a vantage point of public patriarchy as they do for women whose experiences have been more shaped by domination by individual men.

Second, women's labor force participation is easy to connect to women's liberation in the context of private patriarchy since the extent of women's earnings are in practice directly related to their independence from individual husbands. This link is more problematic in public patriarchy, since women's labor is expected—even demanded—in the paid labor force as well as in unpaid domestic chores. For African American feminists and feminists in East Germany, paid employment has provided a self-evident part of their identity as well as a burden—but it is hard to confuse it with "emancipation." The conditions of their integration into the paid labor force (e.g., ongoing discrimination), rather than the fact of employment itself, tend to draw theoretical attention and need more explanation.

For many feminists in West Germany, labor market discrimination has clearly been a problem but one that apparently could be explained by women's frequent and extensive exclusion from the labor force in whole or in part when they have children. From this perspective, marginality rather than discrimination is the problem and creating compatibility between paid employment and motherhood is the solution; from a perspective of public patriarchy, the issue is the conditions under which such compatibility has already been produced and why and how women are made to pay for it. Such ongoing discrimination needs explanation in terms of something other than women's intermittent labor force participation.

For women in eastern Germany, paid employment is certainly no longer self-evident. Thus, answering the question of what this growing exclusion from the labor force means is an entirely new issue, not a standard part of their feminist repertoire of self-understandings. As long as permanent or quasi-permanent exclusion was simply inconceivable, it did not need to be theorized as a source of oppression. For women under public patriarchy, the idea of paid employment as somehow "an expression" of feminism did not make much sense, yet it was also not experienced as irrelevant to a feminist agenda. It was more the invisible precondition of experience and selfhood, parallel almost to the way literacy is taken for granted in industrialized countries.[4]

Third, within a framework of public patriarchy, it makes little sense to talk about doing politics that remains "autonomous" by virtue of keeping its hands out of the affairs of government for fear of being coopted. Such a claim to autonomy has been a popular position among feminists in West Germany, albeit a stance that has been losing some support in recent years (Ferree 1987). Insofar as it is the state that is directly usurping the right of women to speak for themselves, as in public patriarchy, there is little alternative to pragmatically challenging this "guardianship" head-on. This means that women can and must find practical ways to restructure the state in less patriarchal ways. This concern with making policy and holding political office makes much less experiential sense to women in private patriarchy, who perceive their lives as being more directly shaped by nonstate actors and by cultural norms and expectations that are not formally enacted into law. Within the context of private patriarchy, the role of the state is more indirect and thus less visible, and the more obvious targets for action seem both more diffuse and more personalized. To those accustomed to public patriarchy, this focus can look like too much concern with symbolic issues, such as language, that are "trivial" compared to direct confrontations with policymakers.

For women who have lived under public patriarchy, the direct tie experienced between mothers and the state means that the state cannot so easily be felt as remote and irrelevant. The specific demands leveled at the state will vary by political context, of course. U.S. women of color have pointed particularly to the significance of welfare levels, access to health insurance, and affordable housing as feminist issues of great and burning relevance to their daily lives, and they have directed attention to state policy in these areas which White feminists have more easily overlooked. Women in eastern Germany have raised issues such as public child care, the anti-discrimination law, and representation in state and national politics higher on the feminist agenda in the post-unification state by highlighting the immediacy of their impact. While feminist practice in West Germany even before unification had increasingly emphasized the importance of such state policies, this concern has been greatly accelerated by unification and its aftermath. It remains to be seen whether a national feminist organization aimed at influencing federal policy, such as originally favored by feminists in eastern Germany, will ultimately emerge as well.

CONCLUSION

The experience of family, paid employment, and state politics shows certain common threads between feminist concerns in East Germany and those raised by some women of color in the United States. These commonalities in theorizing and in critiques of pseudo-universalized theories that fail to reflect their experiences suggest that some common explanation might be sought. Such an explanation may rest in the different purposes that state intervention serves in public and private patriarchy. It is not a question of quantitative differences in the degree of state activism or state determination of people's life chances overall, but rather of the qualitative differences in the ends that such state intervention serves: either supporting the authority and power of an individual husband as patriarch or undermining it in favor of the collective authority of the male-dominated state for the benefit of men as a group.

As more Eastern European feminists find a voice with which to articulate their concerns, we may find that their collective self-representation of feminism, structured by their experiences of public patriarchy, may be even more different from the feminism arising from private patriarchy than is now apparently the case in unified Germany. What some have advanced as the reasons why there is "no women's movement" in Eastern Europe may yet become explanations for why the feminism that emerges there will take a distinctive form (Tatur 1992).

The experiences of the feminism articulated from "the other side" as not "really" being feminism, according to the standards of one's own collective self-representation, have contributed to the disillusionment and discouragement of both sides. The early efforts to deny differences, pointing instead to the always present indisputable commonalities, have over the course of the past five years largely been abandoned. The many practical experiences

German feminists have had in conferences, workshops, meetings, and projects have provided ample evidence of difference. The model of public and private patriarchy outlined here suggests that the tensions and resentments that often accompany such expressions of difference are built up not just from political competition over scarce resources, new hierarchical relationships, and personal failures of empathy and understanding in the current crisis—important as such experiences have been—but also from threats to the collective self-representation of feminism itself. These varying self-representations may contain a large structural component reflecting the differently organized forms of patriarchy that women experienced. Thus, different aspects of feminist politics can "feel true" to women on each side of the now-crumbled Wall, and feminist authenticity for each set of women pushes them to reject and criticize claims that express understandings of what "women" are and need that are not validated by their own experiences.

Ultimately, however, the reality of such diversity in women's experiences—not just in their interpretations of them—demands a definition of feminism that encompasses difference. What is now so often expressed as "better" and "worse" versions of feminism in Germany should not be understood so much as matters of women being naive or antimale or careerist or statist—in other words, not as expressions of deficiencies of feminist analysis—but rather as reflections of the differences in the organization of patriarchy and of women's lives. Theorizing difference in this context takes on a new meaning and a new urgency.

NOTES

An earlier version of this article was presented at the conference "Crossing Borders," Stockholm, Sweden, May 1994. The research for this article was conducted with the support of research fellowship 3-53621 from the German Marshall fund of the United States and by a Provost's Award from University of Connecticut Research Foundation. The article has benefited from the comments of many of the conference participants. Still earlier versions benefited from comments and suggestions from Christine Bose, Lisa D. Brush, Irene Dölling, Christel Eckart, Jo Freeman, Ute Gerhard, Carol Hagemann-White, Eva Maleck-Lewy, Natalie Sokoloff, Verta Taylor, Wayne Villemez, Lise Vogel, Jane Wilkie, and Brigitte Young. My thanks to them, even though I (perversely) do not accept all the arguments they have offered.

1. Black and White are used here as political terms and thus capitalized.

2. For details and statistics on the status of women in the DDR, see Einhorn (1993); Helwig and Nickel (1993); Maier (1992). For a history of policy that discusses its objectives and how it has secured these outcomes, see Penrose (1990).

3. For more extensive and detailed data on the status of women in the preunification Federal Republic of Germany, see Helwig and Nickel (1993); Maier (1992); Kolinsky (1989). For a history of policy that suggests how these outcomes were sought and institutionalized, see Moeller (1993) and Ostner (1994).

4. For differences in specific attitudes and experiences relating to paid work and family relations, see Institut für Demoskopie

(1993). As one illustration of the substantial gulf in expectations between East and West, consider the level of agreement with the statement "an employed mother can give a child just as much warmth and security as a mother who does not have a job." While 66 percent of East Germans agreed, only 39 percent of West Germans did. In this regard, it is the East Germans who are closer to the European average (61 percent agreement).

REFERENCES

Bastian, Katrin, Evi Labsch, and Sylvia Müller. 1990. "Zur situation von Frauen als Arbeitskraft in der Geschichte der DDR." Originally published in *Zaunreiterin* (Leipzig), reprinted in *Streit* 2:59–67.

Bialas, Christiana, and Wilfried Ettl. 1993. "Wirtschaftliche Lage, soziale Differenzierung und Probleme der Interessenorganisation in den neuen Bundesländern." *Soziale Welt* 44, no. 1:52–75.

Brown, Carol. 1987. "The New Patriarchy." Pp. 137–60 in *Hidden Aspects of Women's Work,* ed. Christine Bose, Roslyn Feldberg, and Natalie Sokoloff. New York: Praeger.

Collins, Patricia Hill. 1990. *Black Feminist Thought.* Boston: Unwin Hyman.

Einhorn, Barbara. 1993. *Cinderella Goes to Market: Citizenship, Gender, and Women's Movements in East Central Europe.* New York: Verso.

Ferree, Myra Marx. 1987. "Equality and Autonomy: Feminist Politics in the United States and West Germany." Pp. 172–95 in *The Women's Movements of the United States and Western Europe,* ed. Mary Katzenstein and Carol McClurg Mueller. Philadelphia, Pa.: Temple University Press.

———. 1992. "The Wall Remaining: Two Women's Movements in a Single German State." Paper presented at conference on German Unification, Western European Studies Program, Notre Dame University, South Bend, Ind.

———. 1993. "The Rise and Fall of 'Mommy Politics': Feminism and Unification in (East) Germany." *Feminist Studies* 19:89–115.

———. 1994. "'The Time of Chaos Was the Best': The Mobilization and Demobilization of a Women's Movement in East Germany." *Gender and Society* 8, no. 4.

Friedan, Betty. 1963. *The Feminine Mystique.* New York: Dell.

Funk, Nanette, and Magda Mueller, eds. 1993. *Gender Politics and Post-communism.* New York: Routledge.

Gerhard, Ute, Metchthild Jansen, Andrea Maihofer, Pia Schmid, Irmgard Schultz, eds. 1990. *Differenz und Gleichheit.* Frankfurt a/M: Ulrike Helmer Verlag.

Hampele, Anne. 1991. "Der unabhängige Frauenverband." Pp. 221–82 in *Von der Illegalität ins Parlament,* ed. Helmut Müller-Enbergs, Marianne Schulz, and Jan Wielgohs. Berlin: LinksDruck Verlag.

———. 1993. "'Arbeit mit, plane mit, regiere mit': Zur politischen Partizipation von Frauen in der DDR." Pp. 281–320 in *Frauen in Deutschland, 1945–1992,* ed. Gisela Helwig and Hildegard Maria Nickel. Bonn: Bundeszentral für politische Bildung.

Hampele, Anne, Helwerth Ulrike, and Gislinde Schwarz. 1993. "Drei Jahre nach der Wende: Zum Stand der Ost-West-Beziehungen in der Frauenbewegung," Paper presented at the Goethe Institute, New York.

Helwig, Gisela, and Hildegard Maria Nickel, eds. 1993. *Frauen in Deutschland, 1945–1992.* Band 318, Studien zur Geschichte und Politik. Bonn: Bundeszentrale fúr politische Bildung.

Holland-Cunz, Barbara. 1990. "Bemerkungen zur Lage der deutsch-deutschen Frauenbewegung." *Links* Sept.: 35–39.

Institut für Demoskopie Allensbach. 1993. *Frauen in Deutschland: Lebensverhältnisse, Lebensstile, und Zukunftserwartungen.* Köln: Bund Verlag.

Janssen-Jurreit, Marielouise. 1976. *Sexismus.* München: Carl Hanser Verlag.

Jonasdottir, Anna, and Kathleen B. Jones, eds. 1988. *The Political Interests of Gender: Developing Theory and Research with a Feminist Face.* London: Sage.

Kahlau, Cordula, ed. 1990. *Aufbruch! Frauenbewegung in der DDR.* Munich: Frauenoffensive.

Kolinsky, Eva. 1989. *Women in West Germany: Life, Work, and Politics.* Oxford: Berg.

Maier, Friederike. 1992. "Frauenerwerbstätigkeit in der DDR und BRD: Germeinsamkeiten und Unterschiede." Pp. 23–35 in *Ein Deutschland—Zwei Patriarchate?,* ed. Gudrun-Axeli Knapp and Ursula Müller. Bielefeld: University of Bielefeld.

Mansbridge, Jane. 1995. "What is Feminism?" In *Feminist Organizations: Harvest of the New Women's Movement,* ed. Myra Marx Ferree and Patricia Yancey Martin. Philadelphia, Pa.: Temple University Press.

Melucci, Alberto. 1988. "Getting Involved: Identity and Mobilization in Social Movements." Pp. 329–48 in *From Structure to Action: Comparing Social Movement Research across Cultures,* ed. Bert Klandermans, Hanspeter Kriesi, and Sidney Tarrow. Greenwich, Conn.: JAI Press.

Merkel, Ina, Eva Schäfer, Sünne Andresen, Frigga Haug, Kornelia Hauser, Jutta Meyer-Siebart, Eva Stäbler, and Ellen Woll, eds. 1990. *Ohne Frauen ist kein Staat zu machen.* Hamburg: Argument Verlag.

Millett, Kate. 1970. *Sexual Politics.* Garden City, N.Y.: Doubleday.

Moeller, Robert. 1993. *Protecting Motherhood: Women and the Family in the Politics of Postwar West Germany.* Berkeley: University of California Press.

Ostner, Ilona. 1994. "Back to the Fifties: Gender and Welfare in Unified Germany." *Social Politics: International Studies in Gender, State, and Society* 1, no. 1:32–59.

Penrose, Virginia. 1990. "Vierzig Jahre SED-Frauenpolitik: Ziele, Strategien, Ergebnisse." *IFG: Frauenforschung* 4:60–77.

Rohnstock, Katrin. 1994. *Stiefschwestern: Was Ost-Frauen und West-Frauen voneinander denken.* Frankfurt a/M: Fischer.

Sassoon, Anne Showstack, ed. 1987. *Women and the State: The Shifting Boundaries between Public and Private.* London: Hutchinson.

Siim, Birte. 1987. "The Scandinavian Welfare States: Toward Sexual Equality or a New Kind of Male Domination?" *Acta Sociologica* 3/4:255–70.

Tatur, Melanie. 1992. "Why Is There No Women's Movement in Eastern Europe?" Pp. 61–75 in *Democracy and Civil Society in Eastern Europe,* ed. P. G. Lewis. London: Macmillan.

Taylor, Verta, and Nancy Whittier. 1992. "Collective Identity in Social Movement Communities: Lesbian Feminist Mobilization." Pp. 104–30 in *Frontiers of Social Movement Theory,* ed. Aldon Morris and Carol McClurg Mueller. New Haven, Conn.: Yale University Press.

R E A D I N G   5 2

Feminism on the Job: Confronting Opposition in Abortion Work

WENDY SIMONDS

This essay explores ways in which feminism is conceived of and acted upon in the work lives of women. With the goal of illustrating how feminist identity and practice are constructed on the job, I show how abortion workers in a private nonprofit abortion clinic in the southeastern United States build feminist methods of thought and action through their encounters with antifeminist, anti-abortion opposition. Workers deal intermittently with anti-abortion protesters and continually worry about restrictive legislation, potential dismantling of procreative rights for women, and the attitudes that foster these threats. Staff members must negotiate the ambivalence and emotional stress involved in providing abortion in a hostile environment, and confront a moral minefield of anti-abortion rhetoric to arrive at feminist "truths" that support abortion. In this context, workers' activities appear both as *feminist* work and as *defensive* practice. My investigation fits into feminist sociological

Wendy Simonds, "Feminism on the Job: Confronting Opposition in Abortion Work: from *Feminist Organizations: Harvest of the New Women's Movement*, edited by Myra Marx Ferree and Patricia Yancey Martin. Copyright © 1995 by Temple University. Reprinted with the permission of Temple University.

attempts to uncover how personal views about abortion and feminism are shaped by social forces (e.g., Freeman 1975; S. Evans 1979; Luker 1984; Echols 1989; Ginsburg 1989; Martin 1989), as well as into a tradition of ethnographies of controversial, service-providing, "dirty" workplaces (e.g., Ball 1967; Hughes 1971; Walsh 1974; Lipsky 1980; Detlefs 1984; Joffe 1986; Simonds 1991).

In 1976, a small group of women in a moderate-sized city in the Southeast organized around their interest in the women's health care movement and formed a self-help group, which shortly became The Womancare Center (TWC, a pseudonym). TWC began as a nonprofit collective but gradually expanded into a clearly delineated hierarchy, though it remains a nonprofit organization. TWC has moved in and out of debt over the years and by 1992 had an annual budget of over $2 million. Approximately 90 percent of its income comes from abortions. In 1991, TWC performed an average of seventy abortions each week while serving an average total of 189 clients weekly. Since the mid-1980s TWC has been targeted by anti-abortion protesters and, beginning in 1988, by members of Operation Rescue (OR).

At this writing, TWC staff numbers forty-five workers: three upper-level managers (two of the original founders hold the positions of executive director and clinic coordinator, and the director of administrative services joined the center two years after its founding), one director of development, seven administrative workers (two work part time), one health educator, one lab technician, six nurses (five work part time), three doctors (two work part time), four supervisors, and nineteen health workers (four work part time). The staff ranges in age from the early twenties to the early fifties; most health workers and supervisors are under thirty. The top three administrators are White and heterosexual; eleven of the staff are African American (two administrative workers, six health workers, the lab technician, one supervisor, and one of the per diem physicians), and one is Latina (a health worker). Approximately one-fourth of TWC staff members are lesbian.

Between April 1992 and December 1993, I spent one-half to one day each week as a participant-observer at TWC. In addition, I conducted interviews with twenty-nine TWC workers between fall 1990 and fall 1992. Each interview took place in private and lasted one to three hours; all but one were tape-recorded. I asked each respondent to describe her history at the center and as a feminist, the ups and downs of her work, her views about the workings of the organization, and her feelings about the current and future politics surrounding abortion in the United States.

The interviews defy neat categorization and, often, even comparison with one another, because the macro- and micro-level circumstances under which they occurred were not the same. Interview transcripts seem to impose an artificial sense of closure on each woman's views, yet public events continually transform the conditions of each participant's work and thus her experience and evaluation of it. Over the course of the interview project, anti-abortion protests diminished locally, so workers' direct experience with anti-abortion attitudes at TWC lessened. At the same time, ironically, legislative restrictions on abortion increased both locally and nationally. A parental notification bill has gone into effect in TWC's state. The Supreme Court's Webster decision of July 1989, making legislative decisions about abortion a state matter, was backed by the Casey decision of June 1992, which upheld most proposed state restrictions on abortion as constitutional. As the potential for a democratic presidential victory grew, however, TWC workers spoke more optimistically about the future of abortion rights. At this writing, workers are guardedly optimistic that the Clinton administration's commitment to abortion rights may translate into legislative changes that reverse the conservative trend of the Reagan-Bush years.

ARRIVING AT FEMINIST TRUTHS

TWC workers develop a conception of what it means to be feminist through their experiences as workers in the organization. The clinic encourages each woman to adopt a conceptualization of abortion that explicitly counters the fetishizing and sanctification of the fetus promoted by anti-abortionists (called "antis" by clinic staff), and to challenge the medical profession's common portrayal of women and fetuses as antagonistic entities (Rothman 1986, 1989; Petchesky 1987).

From what TWC workers told me, the events that are most capable of both challenging *and* affirming their commitment to procreative freedom are second trimester abortions. Several workers related that they were disturbed by their initial exposure to late abortions. One supervisor describes using a sonogram to assist a physician during a late abortion: "The first time I did a sono throughout a whole D & E, and the doctor did this thing: he wanted to wait until the fetus was dead, so he ripped . . . through the placenta and got the cord and waited—we all waited—on the sono until the heart stopped beating. It was *gross*. That upset me, you know." Though she found the procedure unpleasant, she asserted that she saw the clinic's decision to extend abortion services to women who are up to twenty-six weeks pregnant as a "*good* thing." The availability of D & E (dilation and evacuation) abortions at TWC means that clients can avoid referral to another area clinic for induction abortions, which are much more painful procedures (because labor is actually induced). The supervisor also affirmed her support for women's having late abortions, despite her "gut" response of disgust, saying, "You have your reality check if . . . you talk to these women, and you find out why they're having [abortions] . . . and you go, 'you know, I know why I'm doing it.'"

Several TWC workers called working in the sterile room (where fetal tissue is weighed, evaluated, and packed for disposal) during late abortions their least favorite part of their jobs. Many of the health workers acknowledge that they experience second trimester sterile room work as more difficult than first trimester sterile room work for several reasons: the fetuses are larger and "look like babies," especially if they come out whole, which is more likely in later abortions; the fetal tissue is very warm and "feels creepy"; and there is much more blood.

For a few health workers, working in the sterile room remains a problematic part of their jobs, but most strive to resolve their negative feelings with the feminist ideology of the self-help movement: they deliberately focus on the women they know they are helping and speak about their empathy with these women's experiences. Even in empathy, however, there often remains a sense of distance. In the words of one TWC health worker, "My experience with women who are having D & E's is they're—I hate to generalize, but . . . most of them have lives that are so out of control and tornado-ish, and in a whirlwind. And they experience themselves as victims." She sees her role as enabling women to take control over one crucial event in their lives. Another says: "I remind myself that it's not me" having a late abortion.

In an effort to protect themselves from emotional overload, TWC women shield themselves from the pain they see in their clients' lives and in their abortion experiences. A third woman discusses her ambivalence about late abortions by imagining what would happen if a hypothetical second trimester client did not abort: "I think of the big picture, that this woman knows what she has to do. She knows that she can't take care of this baby. . . . Sterile room and late D & E's, though, sometimes make me feel sad, because . . . [the fetuses] look like little babies. But I always just have to put it in the proper perspective, that . . . it could have been here [born] , and still you would feel sad when you saw the news report about that baby on TV." The bottom line, for this woman and her co-workers, is that no one should have an unwanted child. Though they may wish to distance themselves from their clients' distress or "whirlwind" lives, they repeatedly express their understanding of every woman's struggle to have children only when she feels the time and circumstances are right.

When I first began interviewing TWC workers, my sense was that several women *confessed* their unease over sterile room work in a way that indicated they would not openly talk about such responses on the job. When I began doing ethnographic work, however, I found that this was no secret. Health workers speak openly about their feelings about handling fetal tissue, and everyone knows who likes or dislikes sterile room work. The reticence I encountered early on was, I think, an uneasiness about discussing the issue with an outsider. Uncomfortable responses to aborted fetuses are, after all, what anti-abortion activists hope for and seek to encourage.

Workers discussed ways in which they had attempted to share with other people, both on and off the job, their views about how important procreative rights are, but they tended to avoid talking about their work in superficial social situations. Many participants told stories about how discussing their work off the job could mean instant arguments, unpleasantness, broken or strained relationships. According

to one worker, "Even the clients look at you and go . . . 'thank you so much—I don't know how you can *do* this.' "

TWC's director, focusing on the aborting woman rather than the abortion worker, elaborated on the theme of abortion as stigmatized: "I think that the anti-abortion people have been very successful in making the public view women who receive abortions in a bad light, and also make the women themselves feel really guilty. I think that's been something that's remarkably different here in our clients over the past thirteen years. . . . Women are still getting abortions, but they feel a lot worse about it." In the 1970s, she explained, because the right to abortion was newly won, "everybody who came for an abortion knew somebody who had had an illegal abortion, or they themselves had had an illegal abortion; [women] were just really *happy* to be able to have an abortion with more dignity." Now, she said, young women do not confront the dangers of illegal abortion, but they do experience the wrath and determination of anti-abortionists. Women "are bombarded everywhere they go with this message: *'abortion's murder.'* They hear it in school; they see it on TV; they get it in church. Their own lives are less significant than the lives [*sic*] of the fetus in the way that abortion's being debated now." Because of the prevalence of antiabortion rhetoric, she believes clients do not see having an abortion as exercising a crucial right but, rather, experience it as a deviant act to undo a personal failure.

One TWC worker articulated the belief that maintaining a veil of secrecy around abortion helps to perpetuate stigmatization: "We do everything that we can to retain confidentiality. We treat the woman like no one in her life knows that she's having an abortion. . . . And if they knew, we assume they would, like, totally ostracize her or kill her, you know. We . . . really go about taking confidentiality so seriously. And I think on the one hand, that's really good that we respect that. But on the other hand, we're just perpetuating this myth. And we're perpetuating this shame about abortion." In her view, the pro-choice movement's focus on the right to privacy, along with the inequitable gender relations concealed in such a focus (cf. MacKinnon 1983), contributes to a silencing of women's voices.

TWC workers talked at length about how anti-abortionists' activities, rhetoric, and visual props had worked to stifle any *honest* public discussion of abortion, a discussion they see as essential to continued procreative freedom. One worker said, "I think that legal changes [prohibiting or restricting abortion] will be a lot easier if people are afraid to talk, or don't know that they *can* talk" about abortion.

Another woman described the closeting of abortion as a failure of the pro-choice movement, resulting from feminists' reluctance to address the emotional issues that abortion evokes for many people:

> The reason why . . . we've been falling back in terms of abortion rights is because we haven't been talking about abortion. . . . We've been so afraid to dialogue honestly about it, that when we talk abortion . . . it's like this constitutional right. We talk about it as, you know, "what can we do to help?" You know, you go and you write your congressman a letter. . . . We have our armor on, like we're ready for this battle. . . . We've just been on the defensive so long that we haven't changed the language about abortion. . . . We still say "products of conception." Well, why don't we say it looks like—you know, a twenty-week fetus looks like a baby. Why can't we say that in public? Because that's what the *antis* say, you know. But you know, it's pretty much true, and you'd better say it. . . . The antis have this one extremist language, and then the pro-choice movement has this other extremist language, and there are all these people in the middle and they don't believe either one.

Most participants attribute the infusion of anti-abortion sentiment into public consciousness to the persistence and aggressiveness of the antis, whose views are bolstered by conservative, misogynist politics, rather than to feminists' reticence about abortion. Many workers feel resentment that pro-choice activism does not seem to be "taking" the way it once did, and they do not understand how society can remain apathetic. They believe the American public does not understand the centrality of abortion's importance to women's freedom. As one TWC employee eloquently stated: "Part of what abortion is about is a woman's *wholeness* . . . And *that's* what's at stake. It's not just having a cannula put in your uterus. It's whether the world has enough room for you."

CONFRONTING THE OPPOSITION IN PERSON

I asked participants to tell me about their interaction with anti-abortion protesters and its effects on their work. Confrontations with antis make evident to workers the fact that abortion rights are threatened. Participants frequently said they felt deeply frightened about the future.

Their fears are informed by TWC's history. Anti-abortion demonstrators picketed the clinic sporadically dur-

ing the mid-1980s. During the summer of 1988, Operation Rescue (OR) staged "rescues" at most abortion clinics in the city, and because of its avowed feminist stance, TWC was a favorite target. Despite a city injunction barring many of the group's more assaultive tactics, OR protesters continue to demonstrate at city clinics (though no longer on a regular basis or in great numbers at TWC) and routinely disobey the injunction.

When hundreds of antis arrived from out of state in 1988, their mission was to shut the city's clinics down. Fortunately, workers say, OR communicated its mission to the police. Until this point, the city police had been uninterested in the upcoming protests and refused to promise clinics that they would become actively involved. Once it became clear that OR was coming, TWC's executive director recounted,

> I met with other providers and the police to try to start up preparation. . . . The police's response was: "Well, just shut down to avoid confrontation." And we were adamant that there was no way that we were going to shut down, and that was never going to be an acceptable solution for us . . . [and] we demanded that they protect . . . us. At first, I'd say the police were pretty reluctant to agree that it was really any danger. And then Operation Rescue met with the police and were very arrogant—as they always are—and just told the police: "We don't care about your protest area. We don't care what you say. We're coming to town to break the law." So the police all of a sudden thought, "Well, maybe these clinics have something to say here."

OR's bragging about its plans seemed to awaken the sensibilities of the police. They vowed to prevent OR from breaking the law, and since that time, police have been allies of TWC. Clinic workers recognize that this relationship is a fragile one; they often talk about how strange it has been to come to see police as allies and about what it would be like to be working against the police to provide abortion.

Employees who were present during the 1988 protests remember those months as a long and seemingly neverending nightmare. Many say that at the time they thought their work was like what war must be like for soldiers. A few TWC women described the OR blockades as also exciting or wonderful because of the unexpected consequences of enduring the intense ordeal: they say it brought the staff together as a group and gave them a sense of daily accomplishment when the antis were unable to shut the clinic down. In the words of one participant: "Nothing in the history of the health center had drawn all of the staff together like being under the assault of anti-abortionists. You know, it was the one thing that we could all bond on, 'cause you know there are a lot of divisions at the health center. . . . And it was really like we drew together and we fought them off, you know? Everyone was just so committed to winning that battle."

For women who have remained at TWC since 1988, working through the experience of OR blockades strengthened their commitment to providing abortion. But in the six months after the summer when TWC was heavily targeted by OR, eleven clinic workers quit. Though none said the experience was their reason for leaving, the clinic director said she was sure that OR's attack was the impetus.

In *The Managed Heart* (1983), Arlie Hochschild contrasts the occupations of flight attendant and bill collector to demonstrate the types of emotional labor expected of workers. In this case, TWC employees performed emotional work across the spectrum, being called upon to demonstrate empathy and nurturance to their clients and with each other, yet at the same time to appear controlled, united, and assertive in the face of the enemy. Sandra Morgen (1983) writes about a case study she conducted in a feminist health center where emotions acted as "filter" for ideology in the day-to-day running of the clinic. The reverse is true as well: ideology also filters emotion. TWC women spoke repeatedly of not wanting to let the antis see how they felt, telling how they often resisted displaying their anger and fear because they worried that, unleashed, these emotions could become uncontrollable. One woman described the inner turmoil the activities of the protesters evoked for her:

> This one night . . . I'd walked a client up to her car, and it was like the end of the night. . . . And I walked over the hill . . . and there they were. And I just had this, like, *panic,* you know? This complete . . . feeling of panic. And I was just *over* it that night, just totally over it. Like they had gotten under my skin, and that was absolutely the worst thing. . . . I remember those nights, I would just get in the car and get on the Interstate, and I'd roll up my windows and just scream. Just scream. You know, you do this whole job of like, protecting the clients—but who's protecting you?. . . . I mean, it's just like this bully in the classroom; you don't want to let them know that they're bothering you. You know, don't—don't cry in front of the bully.

Managing anger remains a constant challenge for TWC workers, especially because antis are a forceful reminder that women are not safe or secure in the public realm. TWC women repeatedly likened the antis' treatment of women (themselves and clients) to sexual assault or rape. But participants also repeatedly express their belief that the antis are entitled to their views, however distasteful, untruthful, or dangerous clinic workers may find them to be. They say they object not to the views of the antis so much as to their hostile treatment of women. As one worker said: "I can really respect the other side of the issue . . . because I was in that dilemma myself [of feeling anti-abortion sentiments]. And it's not like I can't see the other side. It's just when they lose that rational ability to think and talk about it, and it becomes this other, just obsessive thing that they're doing. . . . Just crazy, and *scary* crazy." As participants reiterate their belief that anti-abortionists are entitled to believe anything, however warped, they also come down against the moral relativism that undergirds their own abstract notion of free speech. TWC women are angry at *both* the substance of the antis' views and the tactics they use to make their views known. They are enraged that the antis remain impervious to feminist truths while workers feel perpetually vulnerable to antis' attacks.

TWC workers are all subject to antis' verbal harassment because until they are recognized as staff, they are considered by OR members to be potential clients. Once the antis learn who workers are, their assault changes but does not end. The litany addressed to staff members ranges from vehement accusations ("Murderer!" "Baby killer!") to a more plaintive rhetorical interrogation: "Why do you want to kill babies?" "Why don't you get another job?" The antis also employ religious scripts similar to the ones they use with clients, telling staff members they will "burn in hell" or, alternatively, adopting a friendlier tone and claiming to "pray for" workers' souls.

The antis reserve a specialized script for minority women; according to one worker the protesters, who are overwhelmingly White, attempt to engage with African American women by focusing on their race:

> Well, being a Black woman, the way the protesters handle me, I think, is a little different . . . from the way they handle other women . . . who are not of color. They tend to use my history to try to slash out at me. . . . They always say things like, "The Reverend Dr. Martin Luther King would be very upset because you're creating genocide on your people." . . . They try to make me feel responsible for my whole race of people, as

opposed to things that they would say to a woman who's not of color. . . . I don't know if they think that women of color don't care about what happens to themselves, but [they think] we care more about what happens to our people. So they . . . try to lay a bigger realm of guilt on me. . . . If I go in there and have an abortion, I'm gonna just stop the whole Black race. And that's basically how they say it.

Another African American worker relates a similar experience: an anti singled her out, saying, " 'See those two little Black boys over there? Their mother didn't have abortions.' And I can't tell you on how many levels I was enraged by that statement."

Black and White workers alike believe antis are so ignorant that they have no idea they are being racist in such encounters but, rather, seem to feel that particularized treatment demonstrates a sensitivity to issues of race. But this specialized rhetoric, like the antis' assaults in general, works only to infuriate staff members; in fact, many women say they feel such impassioned hatred toward the antis that their feelings themselves become stressful, and they talk about their attempts to gain control of emotions that seem overwhelming. In the words of one TWC worker: "It's disgusting. You feel soiled and gross and emotionally raped that you've been made to feel this way. It makes you face a lot of things about yourself—that we're not, you know, intrinsically all that different. I mean, that same kind of gross disgusting stuff that they feel is what I felt for them at that moment, . . . I was capable of that same kind of hatred."

TWC workers say they dislike responding with such hatred toward other human beings, especially other women. (Roughly half of the demonstrators I've observed are women, but most of the leaders are men.) Hatred does not play a part in the feminist ideals these women believe in; hatred in feminist and pro-choice rhetoric, they say, is really the other side's forte. Hatred for the antis feels productive at times only in the sense that it seems a step above hopelessness. Hatred infused by anger takes energy and becomes emotionally exhausting, adding insult to injury, because the women already experience their work as draining. Yet anger fuels motivation, even as it frustrates it. Workers struggle to hold on to their anger without letting it overwhelm them or make them feel guilty. The woman just quoted elaborated on the positive aspects of anger and animosity, even visceral hatred, but talked in a circle, ending as she began with unresolved ambivalence: "You just have to get comfortable allowing yourself to feel it. Women are

just, you know, we're not allowed to be angry. We're not allowed to be bitchy. We're not allowed. And allowing yourself to do it, and feel it, as long as you don't act on it [is necessary]. . . . As long as I don't act on the feeling of wanting to tear one of their limbs off and beat them to death with it, you know? As long as . . . I don't level a good drop-kick to their head, you know? . . . Who wants to feel that kind of anger and gross disgusting stuff?"

This woman, like many of her co-workers, at once feels entitled to, resents, and regrets her own anger. Although TWC women believe their anger is justified, they know that in our culture women's anger is considered unseemly. They find few ways to demonstrate their anger productively and no way to purge themselves of it absolutely. They speak of attempts they made to "deal with" anger and hatred, both through the tight-knit community of TWC and alone, both by confronting the antis and by ignoring them.

Most say that though they may have interacted with antis at first, they found there was little to be gained from any interaction. They explain their efforts to ignore the protesters as an attempt to preserve their own well-being. Workers describe their attempts to communicate or to achieve common ground with the antis as ineffectual. Most interchanges become sarcastic or angry on one or both sides. One woman, an actively religious Christian, described the "last" time she had spoken to the antis:

It was the feast of St. Mary. . . . So I had left work and gone to church during lunch and then I was on my way back in. And it was these assholes out front again, talking to me. . . . "Oh, if you *only knew* how much Jesus loves you." And I said, "I am *sick* of your arrogance! You don't *own* God! And it may interest you to know that I just got back from church," and I *wanted* to say, "—so fuck off!" . . . They said something like, "You may *think* that you know Jesus, and dah dah dah," and I just kept walking at that point. Because I wasn't there to dialogue with them. I just needed to tell them that they don't own God. And even though they couldn't *hear* that from me, I still just wanted to say it, even though I knew it wouldn't make any difference. So it made a difference to me.

Despite their beliefs that the attacks on them are ungrounded and ridiculous, workers still feel accused, and feeling accused makes them want to respond. Though workers usually described ignoring the antis as a position of strength, they also expressed ambivalence, as with their anger and hatred. TWC workers feel that if they ignore antis' provocations, their stance may be mistaken for passivity, as if they have no words with which to fight. And thus, they explain that ignoring the protesters, though sensible, may not always be what they do. A few workers said they continued to engage in conversations with the antis in order to let off steam.

More commonly, clinic workers joke loudly with each other or with clinic escorts. Sometimes they comment on the antis' paraphernalia: "Oh, you brought my favorite sign today!" or, about the little plastic fetuses antis often hold in the palms of their hands during prayers: "Wouldn't they make nice earrings!" The women mentioned collectively engineered jokes made at the expense of the antis as the most productive means of retaliation. Their favorite began one day when, after several hours of protesting, only a handful of antis remained outside the building, all of them men. One of the clinic workers brought out a ruler and a large handprinted sign that read "Small Penis Contest," and posed next to the group of men while another took pictures. Mimicking the protesters' wielding of signs and their shaming techniques greatly amused clinic workers. But although incidents like this one help to diffuse the hostility the staff feels and to reinforce a sense of solidarity against the enemy, they are not enough so long as the antis and the threat they represent remain.

All workers, however remote their job responsibilities are from the performance of abortions, have been subjected to shouted insults or affronts, bomb threats, and vandalism both of the clinic and of their personal property. Many participants spoke of their attempts to protect themselves from this sort of invasive assault: some have unlisted phone numbers; some say they avoid discussing their work with people they don't know well; most describe being more attentive to who is around them when they are out alone, especially in transit between work and home.

FEMINISM AND (F)UTILITY

Interaction with anti-abortionists strengthens the determination of TWC staff to preserve procreative freedom, and has made those who stayed after 1988 feel more committed to their work. But this interaction also makes workers feel marginalized *because* they are feminist. Even though most people are not members of OR, or even anti-choice, TWC staff see the antiabortion movement's rhetoric and stance as having made an indelible mark on mainstream Americans' thinking.

Already, anti-abortion activities have resulted in the curtailment of abortion services across the country and enormous cuts in both public funding (Medicaid now covers abortions in only a handful of states as a result of the 1976 Hyde Amendment) and private support. Susan Faludi gives evidence of this trend: "In 1988, United Way stopped funding Planned Parenthood, and in 1990, under pressure from the Christian Action Council, AT&T cut off its contributions, too (after twenty-five years), claiming that shareholders had objected to the agency's association with abortion—even though 94 percent of its shareholders had voted in favor of funding Planned Parenthood" (1991, 418). TWC women have plenty of evidence of the danger to women's procreative freedom, including the imposition of restrictions such as parental notification, parental consent, and waiting periods in various states; the reduction of Title X funds during the 1980s (Wattleton 1990, 269); dramatic increases in clinic bombings, bomb threats, and vandalism in the mid-1980s (Staggenborg 1991) and again in the early 1990s; and a dearth of doctors who are willing to perform abortions. TWC women's direct contact with antis makes them profoundly aware of the danger women face, danger they feel the general public does not perceive or does not care about *because* it accepts anti-abortionists' terms for framing the debate over abortion.

Participants share a core ambivalence about the future: their cynicism, anxiety, and sense of futility about the "chipping away" of procreative freedom coexist with an optimism that the feminist conception of women's "wholeness" will prevail. TWC workers' experiences during the conservative era of the 1980s fuel resistance, even as they result in emotional exhaustion. A new—or revived—radicalism burgeons in these women's outrage as they struggle to attain emotional equilibrium. They question the effectiveness of democratic means of achieving political change but want to believe that the democratic process works. They are ambivalent about the liberal ideology that frames the legal right both to abortion and to freedom of speech, torn because of their belief in feminist absolutes that attest to women's integrity and worth. Their radicalism is tempered by their feelings of powerlessness and vulnerability; they know that, practically, daily survival must take precedence over revolutionary ideological change. TWC workers' contact with anti-abortion opposition has taught them that frustration, ambivalence, anger, and commitment are all integral to feminist work in an antifeminist environment.

REFERENCES

Ball, Donald. 1967. "An Abortion Clinic Ethnography." *Social Problems* 14 (Winter): 293–301.

Detlefs, Malinda. 1984. "Abortion Counseling: A Description of the Current Status of the Occupation Reported by Seventeen Abortion Counselors in Metropolitan New York." Master's thesis, City University of New York.

Echols, Alice. 1989. *Daring to Be Bad: Radical Feminism in America, 1967–1975.* Minneapolis: University of Minnesota Press.

Evans, Sara. 1979. *Personal Politics: The Roots of Women's Liberation in the Civil Rights Movement and the New Left.* New York: Random House.

Faludi, Susan. 1991. *Backlash: The Undeclared War against American Women.* New York: Crown.

Freeman, Jo. 1975. *The Politics of Women's Liberation: A Case Study of an Emerging Social Movement and Its Relation to the Policy Process.* New York: David McKay.

Ginsburg, Faye D. 1989. *Contested Lives: The Abortion Debate in an American Community.* Berkeley: University of California Press.

Hochschild, Arlie. 1983. *The Managed Heart: Commercialization of Human Feeling.* Berkeley: University of California Press.

Hughes, Everett C. 1971. *The Sociological Eye.* Chicago: Aldine.

Joffe, Carole. 1986. *The Regulation of Sexuality: Experiences of Family Planning Workers.* Philadelphia: Temple University Press.

Lipsky, Michael. 1980. *Street-Level Bureaucracy: Dilemmas of the Individual in Public Services.* New York: Russell Sage Foundation.

Luker, Kristin. 1984. *Abortion and the Politics of Motherhood.* Berkeley: University of California Press.

MacKinnon, Catherine. 1983. "The Male Ideology of Privacy: A Feminist Perspective on the Right to Abortion." *Radical America* 17(4):23–35.

Martin, Patricia Yancey. 1989. "The Moral Politics of Organizations: Reflections of an Unlikely Feminist." *Journal of Applied Behavioral Science* 25(4):451–20.

Morgen, Sandra. 1983. "Towards a Politics of 'Feelings': Beyond the Dialectic of Thought and Action." *Women's Studies* 10:203–23.

Petchesky, Rosalind Pollack. 1987. "Fetal Images: The Power of Visual Culture in the Politics of Reproduction." *Feminist Studies* 13 (Summer):263–92.

Rothman, Barbara Katz. 1986. *The Tentative Pregnancy: Prenatal Diagnosis and the Future of Motherhood.* New York: Viking.

———. 1989. *Recreating Motherhood: Ideology and Technology in a Patriarchal Society.* New York: Norton.

Simonds, Wendy. 1991. "At an Impasse: Inside an Abortion Clinic." *Current Research on Occupations and Professions* 6:99–115.

Staggenborg, Suzanne. 1991. *The Pro-Choice Movement: Organization and Activism in the Abortion Conflict.* New York: Oxford University Press.

Walsh, Edward. 1974. "Garbage Collecting: Stigmatized Work and Self-Esteem." In *Humanizing the Workplace,* ed. R. Fairfield, 181–94. New York: Prometheus Books.

Wattleton, Faye. 1990. "Teenage Pregnancies and the Recriminalization of Abortions." *American Journal of Public Health* 80(March):269–70.

READING 53

The New Feminist Movement

VERTA TAYLOR and NANCY WHITTIER

Popular authors and scholars alike have described the 1980s and 90s as a "post-feminist" era of political apathy during which former feminists traded their political ideals for career mobility and Cuisinarts, and younger women single-mindedly pursued career goals and viewed feminism as an anachronism. While there is a kernel of truth to these stereotypes, by and large they fail to recognize the continuity of the women's movement. Although feminism has changed form in the late 1980s and 90s, neither the movement nor the injustices that produced it have vanished. Of all the manifestations of social activism in the 1960s, feminism is one of the few that continued to flourish in the 1970s and 80s and remains active in the 1990s. Yet few authors have studied the women's movement of the late 1980s and 90s, and the transformations that the movement has undergone in recent years have not been documented. We attempt here to trace the ideology and structure of the most recent wave of the American women's movement into the 1990s, using existing studies and our own research to outline the movement's primary characteristics and changes from the 1960s to the present.

From a social movement perspective, women in the United States have always had sufficient grievances to create the context for feminist activity. Indeed, instances of collective action on the part of women abound in history, especially if one includes female reform societies, women's church groups, alternative religious societies, and women's clubs. However, collective activity on the part of women directed specifically toward improving their own status has flourished primarily in periods of generalized social upheaval, when sensitivity to moral injustice, discrimination, and social inequality has been widespread in the society as a whole (Chafe 1977). The first wave of feminism in

this country grew out of the abolitionist struggle of the 1830s and peaked during an era of social reform in the 1890s, and the contemporary movement emerged out of the general social discontent of the 1960s. Although the women's movement did not die between these periods of heightened activism, it varied greatly in form and intensity.

Structural conditions underlie the emergence of protest (Oppenheimer 1973; Huber & Spitze 1983; Chafetz & Dworkin 1986). Chafetz and Dworkin (1986), for example, propose that as industrialization and urbanization bring greater education for women, expanding public roles create role and status conflicts for middle class women, who then develop the discontent and gender consciousness necessary for a women's movement. The changing shape and size of women's movements depend on the opportunities for women to organize on their own behalf, the resources available to them, and their collective identity and interpretation of their grievances. All of these vary for different groups of women and at different times and places (West & Blumberg 1990). Thus, it is to be expected that the ideology, structure, and strategies adopted by the women's movement are quite different depending on when, where, and by what groups of women it is organized.

Most scholarly analyses of the women's movement of the late 1960s—the "new feminist movement"—divide it into two wings, with origins in the grievances and pre-existing organizations of two groups of women: older professional women who formed bureaucratic organizations with a liberal ideology, and younger women from the civil rights and New Left movements who formed small collective organizations with radical ideology (Freeman 1975; Cassell 1977; Ferree & Hess 1985; Buechler 1990).

The organizations and ideologies developed by these two factions have not, however, remained separate and distinct since the 1970s. Our analysis divides the contemporary wave of feminist activism into three stages: resurgence

Verta Taylor and Nancy Whittier, "The New Feminist Movement." Reprinted with the permission of the authors.

(1966–1971), the feminist heyday (1972–1982), and abeyance (1983–1991).

Scholars generally mark the feminist resurgence with the founding of the National Organization for Women (NOW) in 1966 (Buechler 1990; Ryan 1992). During the resurgence period, the movement established itself, forming organizations and ideologies and moving into the public eye. We place the end of this stage in 1971. By this time, major segments of feminism had crystallized: liberal feminism with the formation of groups such as NOW, the Women's Equity Action League (WEAL) in 1967, and the National Women's Political Caucus (NWPC) in 1971; radical feminism and socialist feminism with the development of consciousness raising groups, theory groups, and small action groups such as Redstockings and the Feminists in 1969; and lesbian feminism with the establishment of groups such as Radicalesbians in 1970 and the Furies (initially called "Those Women") in 1971 (Echols 1989).

The year 1972 was pivotal both for the movement's success and for its opposition. The Equal Rights Amendment (ERA) passed the Congress and Phyllis Schafly launched her first attacks, signifying the transition to a second phase of feminist activism that lasted until the defeat of the ERA in 1982 (Mansbridge 1986). While some authors argue that this period saw a decline in the women's movement and a retreat from radicalism (Echols 1989), we think it should be considered the movement's heyday because the feminist revolution seemed to be on the move. The campaign to ratify the ERA in the states brought mass mobilization, fostering female solidarity and enlisting women into feminism, women's studies programs were introduced on college campuses, the number and variety of feminist organizations proliferated, and the movement entered the political arena and encountered active opposition (Matthews & DeHart 1990; Ryan 1992). Not only did feminism flourish in the ratification campaign but it spread into the political mainstream while radical and lesbian feminist organizing heightened outside it.

Following the ERA's defeat in 1982, we argue that the women's movement has entered a period of abeyance, in which it has developed new structural forms in order to survive a shrinking membership and an increasingly nonreceptive environment. The 1980s saw a turning away from the values of equality, human rights, and social justice and even a deliberate backlash against the feminist momentum of the 1970s (O'Reilly, 1980; Yankelovich 1981). Rights won by feminists in the 1960s and 70s—from affirmative action to legal abortion—have been under siege throughout the 1980s and 90s.

Yet in the United States, the feminist challenge lives on. The 1980s and 90s are not the first hostile period in which feminism has endured. In the period following World War II, when strict gender roles and social and political conservatism flourished, the women's movement adopted a tight-knit abeyance structure that enabled it to survive (Rupp & Taylor 1987; Taylor 1989). The so-called "postfeminist" era of the 1980s and 90s no more marks the death of the women's movement than did the 1950s. In fact, although the women's movement of the 1990s takes a different form than it did twenty years earlier, it remains vital and influential.

IDEOLOGY

While ideas do not necessarily cause social movements, ideology is a central component in the life of any social movement. The new feminist movement, like most social movements, is not ideologically monolithic. In the 1970s, it was commonplace to characterize the women's movement as consisting of three ideological strands: liberal feminism, socialist feminism, and radical feminism (Ryan 1989; Buechler 1990). Feminist ideology today continues to be a mix of several orientations that differ in the scope of change sought, the extent to which gender inequality is linked to other systems of domination, especially class, race/ethnicity, and sexuality, and the significance attributed to gender differences. Our analysis here explores the diversity of feminism by focusing on the evolution of the dominant ideologies that have motivated participants in the two major branches of the new feminist movement from its inception, liberal feminism and radical feminism.

The first wave of the women's movement was by and large a liberal feminist reform movement. It asked for equality within the existing social structure and, indeed, in many ways functioned like other reform movements to reaffirm existing values within the society (Ferree & Hess 1985). Nineteenth-century feminists believed that if they obtained the right to an education, the right to own property, the right to vote, employment rights—in other words, equal civil rights under the law—they would attain equality with men.

The basic ideas identified with contemporary liberal or "mainstream" feminism have changed little since their formulation in the nineteenth century when they seemed progressive, even radical (Eisenstein 1981). Contemporary liberal feminist ideology holds that women lack power simply because we are not, as women, allowed equal opportunity

BLACK STUDENTS WHO REJECT FEMINISM

bell hooks

Recently I stood in a crowded auditorium talking about the ways feminist thinking had changed my life, naming the joy I experience in the feminist movement. When I finished, the only black female student who rose to speak gave an impassioned diatribe against feminism, insisting that it could not meet "our" needs because it was only about the needs of white women, with whom black women had nothing in common. I was stunned. My presence as a black woman academic celebrating the power of feminist thought and practice had in no way challenged her to rethink her ideas about feminism. Indeed, her gaze was not on me but on some imagined group of white women who were making a feminist movement that had nothing to do with her. Nothing I had said had shifted that gaze.

This experience troubled me greatly. Even though feminist scholars like me have worked to create an inclusive feminist movement, one that acknowledges the importance of race and embraces black perspectives, many of today's black students seem to reject the entire idea of feminism.

Most young black females learn to be suspicious and critical of feminist thinking long before they have any clear understanding of its theory and politics. From the mass media and such unlikely sources as black male rap stars, they learn that feminism only serves white women and that "dissin'" it will win them points with just about anybody, particularly sexist black men. Just as some black males hold on to macho stereotypes about maleness as a way of one-upping white men, whom they characterize as wimpy, some young black females feel that they finally can one-up white girls by insisting that they are already "real" women, taking care of business, with no need of feminism. These young women are more likely to have read what the rapper Ice T has to say about feminism, in his collection of essays *The Ice Opinion,* than they are to have read a feminist book.

bell hooks, "Black Students Who Reject Feminism" *The Chronicle of Higher Education* (July 13, 1994): A44. Copyright © 1994. Reprinted with the permission of the author.

Without saying where his understanding of feminism comes from, Ice T asserts: "I don't believe the conflict with feminists is between feminists and men. I think the real controversy is between feminists and other feminists." His attitude conveys the message that there is a problem with feminism itself.

Given that such attitudes reflect a broad suspicion of feminism in our culture, it is not surprising that when black female college students challenge sexism, many want to do so outside the framework of feminist politics. Many of these students call themselves "womanists," as opposed to feminists (even though the writer Alice Walker defined "womanism" as synonymous with feminism). Without rigorously engaging feminist thought, they insist that racial separatism works best. This attitude is dangerous. It not only erases the reality of common female experience as a basis for academic study; it also constructs a framework in which differences cannot be examined comparatively.

Some of the students who reject feminism have taken women's-studies classes in which the professor and most of the students have been white. The black students have been disappointed to find little discussion of how sexism affects male and female roles in black culture. In such classrooms, black students often feel that their perspectives are devalued and their voices silenced, until the rare moment when they may be asked to speak as the "expert" on race.

Furthermore, they encounter a substantial body of work that is racially biased, often written from a standpoint that ignores black women's experiences and thus reinforces white supremacist thinking by viewing white women's experiences as the universal standard for evaluating gender status and identity.

Although I and other progressive feminist thinkers, both women of color and white women, acknowledge the biases in some feminist work, we nevertheless still urge all women and men to study feminist thought. We believe that it is especially crucial for black females to be active in producing and analyzing feminist theory and feminist politics. When black students refuse to engage feminist thinking, they deny themselves full understanding of a broad base of knowledge that is needed for their intellectual growth and development. Women and men cannot create unbiased scholarship—or even challenge sexism in the workplace and in other aspects of their daily lives—without an understanding of feminist thought grounded in historical knowledge of gender relations and in theoretical arguments.

The notion that black folks have nothing to learn from scholarship that may reflect racial or racist biases is dangerous. It promotes closed-mindedness and a narrow understanding of knowledge to hold that "race" is such an overwhelming concept that it negates the validity of *any* insights contained in a work that may have some racist or sexist aspects. Students may believe that rejecting, without serious critical inquiry, any body of knowledge that emerges from a "racist" source is a form of political resistance, a challenge to mainstream ways of knowing. This may be especially true of black students who embrace neonationalist conceptions of black identity. Actually, such actions promote a cultural narcissism that mirrors the narcissism in Eurocentric thinking that ignored black perspectives in the first place.

Separatism of any kind promotes marginalization of those unwilling to grapple with the whole body of knowledge and creative works available to others. This is true of black students who do not want to read works by white writers, of female students of any race who do not want to read books written by men, and of white students who only want to read works by white thinkers. When the issue is learning, racial separatism of any kind reinforces the dangerous notion that it is acceptable for one group to distort ideas to perpetuate its own specific interests and biases. The dangers are apparent when we remember that it has taken years to undo the racist and sexist scientific scholarship that once held that women were biologically inferior to men and blacks were inferior to whites.

The hostility to feminism that we see among many black college students today is part of a backlash that includes a strand of Afrocentric thinking that incorporates rigid gender roles supposedly drawn from ancient Africa. Dismissing feminism in this way allows students to ignore the ways that feminist thinking enriches and expands our understanding of black experience. Black female thinkers have continually challenged biases

within mainstream feminist scholarship, insisting that race be recognized as a crucial factor shaping identity.

In the last five years, our work, along with that of other women of color, has pushed feminist thinking to grow and change. For example, feminism began with the premise that women were not part of the work force and would be liberated when they joined it. But when we saw that black women had always worked—without necessarily breaking away from male domination or altering their own ideas of appropriate female behavior—we realized that work was not the only key to improving women's lives. The tremendous revolution in feminist theory generated by collective recognition of the significance of race shows that white supremacist thinking and the racist biases it stems from are not absolute but can be documented and then changed in the face of persuasive evidence.

Although the struggle of progressive feminists to challenge biases continues, our students need to understand that many feminist thinkers have broadened their perspectives. Such openness to learning and to critical inquiry is essential to academic study and to the promotion and preservation of intellectual life.

We must continually remind students in the classroom that expression of different opinions and dissenting ideas affirms the intellectual process. We should forcefully explain that our role is not to teach them to think as we do but rather to teach them, by example, the importance of taking a stance that is rooted in rigorous engagement with the full range of ideas about a topic.

In learning communities from grade school to college, everyone, especially those of us from marginalized groups, must critically resist any thinking that encourages us to close our minds and hearts. We must constructively confront our differences. Through interaction, questioning, and rigorous exchange of ideas, we learn to be more responsive to the actual world of diversity that we encounter, in one way or another, every day of our lives.

We are rarely able to interact only with folks like ourselves, who think as we do. No matter how much some of us deny this reality and long for the safety and familiarity of sameness, inclusive ways of knowing and living offer us the only true way to emancipate ourselves from the divisions that limit our minds and imaginations.

to compete and succeed in the male-dominated economic and political arenas but, instead, are relegated to the subordinate world of home, domestic labor, motherhood, and family. Its major strategy for change is to gain legal and economic equalities and to obtain access to elite positions in the workplace and in politics while, at the same time, making up for the fact that women's starting place in the "race of life" is unequal to men's (Eisenstein 1981). Thus, liberal feminists tend to place as much emphasis on changing individual women as they do on changing society. For instance, teaching women managerial skills or instructing rape victims in "survival" strategies strikes a blow at gender social definitions that channel women into traditionally feminine occupations or passive behaviors that make them easy targets of male aggression. Liberal feminists likewise tend to define patriarchy in individualistic rather than structural terms—as a problem of certain men oppressing certain women, for example (Friedan 1963).

In sum, the liberal concept of equality involves equality under the law, in the workplace, and in the public arena, and fails to recognize how deeply women's inequality is rooted in their responsibility for the care of children and the home (Hartmann 1981; Huber & Spitze 1983), their dependence on men in the context of traditional heterosexual marriage (Rich 1980), and in men's use of their dominant status to preserve male advantage by establishing the rules that distribute rewards (Reskin 1988). As several scholars have recently noted, liberal feminism ironically provided ideological support through the 1970s and 80s for the massive transformation in work and family life that was occurring as the United States underwent the transition to a postindustrial order (Mitchell 1986; Stacey 1987). By urging women to enter the workplace and adopt a male orientation, the equal opportunity approach to feminism unwittingly contributed to a host of problems that further disadvantaged women, especially working-class women and women of color, including the rise in divorce rates, the "feminization" of working-class occupations, and the devaluation of motherhood and traditionally-female characteristics (Gordon 1991).

Radical feminist ideology dates to Simone de Beauvoir's early 1950s theory of "sex class," which was developed further in the late 1960s among small groups of radical women who fought the subordination of women's liberation within the New Left, and which flourished in the feminist movement in the 1970s (Beauvior 1952; Firestone 1970; Millett 1971; Atkinson 1974; Rubin 1975; Rich 1976, 1980; Griffin 1978; Daly 1978; Eisenstein 1978; Hartmann 1981; Frye 1983; Hartsock 1983; MacKinnon

1983). The radical approach recognizes women's identity and subordination as a "sex class," views gender as the primary contradiction and foundation for the unequal distribution of a society's rewards and privileges, and recasts relations between women and men in political terms (Echols 1989). Defining women as a "sex class" means no longer treating patriarchy in individual terms but acknowledging the social and structural nature of women's subordination. Radical feminists hold that in all societies, institutions and social patterns are structured to maintain and perpetuate gender inequality and that female disadvantage permeates virtually all aspects of sociocultural and personal life. Further, through the gender division of labor, social institutions are linked so that male superiority depends upon female subordination (Acker 1980; Hartmann 1981; Chafetz 1990). In the United States, as in most industrialized societies, power, prestige, and wealth accrue to those who control the distribution of resources outside the home in the economic and political spheres. The sexual division of labor that assigns childcare and domestic responsibilities to women not only ensures gender inequality in the family system but perpetuates male advantage in political and economic institutions as well.

In contrast to the liberal position, radical feminists do not deny that men are privileged as men and that they benefit as a group from their privilege—not just in the public arena but also in relation to housework, reproduction, sexuality, and marriage. Rather, they view patriarchy as a system of power that structures and sustains male advantage in every sphere of life, in economic, political, and family institutions, in the realms of religion, law, science and medicine, and in the interactions of everyday life. To unravel the complex structure on which gender inequality rests requires, from a radical feminist perspective, a fundamental transformation of all institutions in society and the existing relations among them. To meet this challenge, radical feminists have formulated influential critiques of the family, marriage, love, motherhood, heterosexuality, rape, battering, and other forms of sexual violence, capitalism, the medicalization of childbirth, reproductive policies, the media, science, language and culture, the beauty industry, politics and the law, and technology and its impact on the environment. Thus, radical feminism is a transformational politics engaged in a fight against female disadvantage and the masculinization of culture. Its ultimate vision is revolutionary in scope: a fundamentally new social order that eliminates the sex-class system and replaces it with new ways of defining and structuring experience.

Central to the development of radical feminist ideology was the strategy of forming small groups for the purpose of "consciousness-raising." Pioneered initially among New Left women, consciousness raising can be understood as a kind of conversion in which women come to view experiences previously thought of as personal and individual, such as sexual exploitation or employment discrimination, as social problems that are the result of gender inequality and sexism. Because it enables women to view the "personal as political," for most women, consciousness-raising is an identity-altering experience. Becoming a feminist can transform a woman's entire self-concept and way of life: her biography, appearance, beliefs, behavior, and relationships (Cassell 1977).

A major consequence of the strategy of seeing the personal as political is that, ideologically, the new feminist movement has become increasingly more radical in the decades since its inception. By the mid-1970s, the distinction between liberal and radical feminism was becoming less clear (Carden 1978; Whittier 1995). Ideological shift took place at both the individual and organizational levels. Participation in liberal feminist reform and service organizations working on such "women's issues" as rape, battering, abortion, legal and employment discrimination, and women's health problems raised women's consciousness, increased their feminist activism, and contributed to their radicalization as they came to see connections between these issues and the larger system of gender inequality (Schlesinger & Bart 1983; Sparks 1979). Women were also radicalized by working through their own personal experiences. Whether through sexual harassment, divorce, rape, abortion, incest, alcoholism, drug addiction, depression, or discrimination in the workplace, women have become aware of the political rather than the personal nature of their problems (Huber 1973; Keuck 1980; Klein 1984).

Radicalization has also occurred at the group level. By the end of the 1970s, liberal feminist organizations, such as the National Organization for Women (NOW), the Women's Equity Action League, the Women's Legal Defense Fund, and the National Abortion Rights Action League, which had been pursuing equality within the law, began to adopt strategies and goals consistent with a more radical stance. NOW included in its 1979 objectives not only such legal strategies as the Equal Rights Amendment (ERA) and reproductive choice, but broader issues such as the threat of nuclear energy to the survival of the species, lesbian and gay rights, homemakers' rights, the exploitation of women in the home, sex-segregation in the workplace, and the influence of corporate, patriarchal, and hierarchical

models of organization on the activities and strategies of NOW (Eisenstein 1981). If there is a single objective that reflected the extent to which the dichotomy between liberal and radical feminism had blurred by the 1980s, it was the Equal Rights Amendment. Although the ERA asked for equality for women within the existing legal and economic structure, it was based on the fact that women are discriminated against as a "sex class" (Mansbridge 1986). Recognizing the radical potential of feminism, sociologist Jessie Bernard in 1975 described the "restructuring of sex roles as no less epochal than the restructuring of the class system which was one of the first consequences of the industrial revolution."

By the 1980s, feminism had become, as activist and writer Charlotte Bunch (1987) put it, more than just a "laundry list of women's issues" or areas for social reform. Neither was feminism merely a constituency of women. There were and always will be women organized against feminism (Marshall 1984). Rather, feminism was becoming a transformational politics, a comprehensive ideology that addressed nearly every social issue, from international peace and the economic policy of the United States to animal rights. It is precisely because feminist ideology has become a tool for linking such a wide range of social issues and multiple forms of domination that it poses such a fundamental challenge to the established order. The belief in woman's right to control her body that underlies the campaign for reproductive rights, for example, raises the questions not only of rape, incest, battering, and sexual harassment, but also of job safety, environmental illness, chemical dumping, nuclear proliferation, the exporting of unsafe drugs and food additives banned in the U.S. to the Third World, and world hunger.

Radical feminism is premised on the belief that there are underlying or "essential" differences between women and men. Early radical feminists sought equality by striving to eradicate gender differentiation (Echols 1989). More recently, lesbian feminists have pursued an end to gender inequality by celebrating or affirming femaleness and glorifying that which is different or "special" about women. Even though most radical feminists believe that women's differences are socially constructed as a result of gender stratification and socialization, the notion of "woman" as a social category mobilized women to organize on behalf of common issues during the height of the new feminist movement. Beginning in the mid-1980s, with the defeat of the unifying issue of the ERA and the growing diversification of the movement, radical feminism entered a new stage of "deconstructing" the term "woman." Shifting the emphasis away from gender oppression, women of color, Jewish women, lesbians, and working class women challenged radical feminists' idea of a "sex class" that implied a distinctive and essential female condition. In reality, women are distributed throughout all social classes, racial and ethnic groupings, sexual communities, subcultures, and religions. Thus, disadvantage for women varies and is multidimensional. The recognition that the circumstances of women's oppression differ has given way to a new feminist paradigm that views race, class, gender, ethnicity, and sexuality as interlocking systems of oppression, forming what Patricia Hill-Collins (1990) refers to as a "matrix of domination." Pointing out that the unity on which feminism has been based is largely a white middle-class heterosexual unity, much of contemporary feminist ideology focuses on women's differences from one another as a way of seeing the connections among as well as the additive effects of multiple systems of domination (Hill-Collins 1990).

Some scholars have charged that focusing on women's differences has resulted in the demise of radical feminism and a retreat into "identity politics" (Echols 1989) and that ideological debates among feminists have undermined the unity of the movement (Ryan 1989). To the contrary, we think that by linking the oppression of women to other systems of human domination, such as race and ethnicity, class, sexuality, religion, and subcultural differences, contemporary radical feminism poses a fundamentally more radical critique of society predicated on resisting all forms of human domination at every level of exchange, whether individual, cultural, or structural. In some ways, as an ideology feminism has come full circle; by focusing on women's differences based on race, class, and sexuality, it is renewing its alliance with other movements for human rights from which it has emerged in this country and around the world. While the feminists of the late 1960s and the 1970s viewed the "woman problem" primarily from the perspective of the wrongs that have been done to women and the discrimination we have borne, feminists now are asking a much larger question: How can United States society be changed according to feminist principles so that it is just and fair for all people regardless of sex, race, class, sexual orientation, or any other social characteristic?

Although the new feminist movement appears to be moving toward an increasingly radical position ideologically, ideas alone are an incomplete explanation of either the direction or the consequences of a social movement (Marx & Wood, 1975; McCarthy & Zald 1977). Much depends on a movement's structure, as well as on the larger political context.

STRUCTURE

Social movements do not generally have a single, central organization or unified direction. Rather, the structure of any general and broad-based social movement is more diffuse—composed of a number of relatively independent organizations that differ in ideology, structure, goals, and tactics—is characterized by decentralized leadership, and is loosely connected by multiple and overlapping memberships, friendship networks, and cooperation in working toward common goals (Gerlach & Hine 1970). The organizational structure of the new feminist movement has conformed to this model from its beginnings (Freeman 1975; Cassell 1977). While the movement as a whole is characterized by a decentralized structure, the various organizations that comprise it vary widely in structure. The diversity of feminist organizational forms reflects both ideological differences and, as Freeman (1979) points out, the movement's diverse membership base (for example, differences in members' prior organizational expertise, experience in other movements, expectations, social status, age or generation, and relations with different target groups).

There have been two main types of organizational structure in the new feminist movement since its resurgence, reflecting the two main sources of feminist organizing in the late 1960s: bureaucratically structured movement organizations with hierarchical leadership and democratic decision-making procedures, such as the National Organization for Women (NOW); and smaller collectively structured groups that formed a more diffuse social movement community held together by a feminist political culture. It is important to recognize, however, that while these two strands emerged separately, they have not remained distinct and opposed to each other. On the contrary, the two structures have converged as bureaucratic organizations adopted some of the innovations of collectivism, and feminist collectives became more formally structured (Staggenborg 1988, 1989; Martin 1990; Ryan 1992; Whittier 1995). In addition, many individual activists are involved in a variety of organizations with differing structures.

The bureaucratically structured and professionalized movement organizations initially adopted by liberal groups such as NOW were well suited to work within the similarly-structured political arena and to members' previous experience in professional organizations. The structures that radical feminist groups initially adopted, on the other hand, built on their prior involvement experiences in the New Left (Evans 1979). Collectivist organizations grew from radical feminists' attempt to structure relations among members, processes of decision making, and group leadership in a way that reflected or prefigured the values and goals of the movement (Rothschild-Whitt 1979; Breines 1982). Put differently, the belief that "the personal is political" dictated collective structure. Feminist collectivist organizations made decisions by consensus, rotated leadership and other tasks among members, and shared skills to avoid hierarchy and specialization. As Jo Freeman (1972/3) and others have noted, such groups often failed to meet their ideals and did, in fact, spawn unacknowledged hierarchies. Nevertheless, the conscious effort to build a feminist collective structure has had a lasting impact on the women's movement and has led to the growth of what Steven Buechler (1990), in a study of women's movements in the United States, calls a social movement community.

Buechler proposes that movements consist not only of formal organizations, but that they also include more informally organized communities, made up of networks of people who share the movement's political goals and outlook and work toward common aims. The collectivist branch of the women's movement initially sparked the growth of a feminist social movement community in which alternative structures guided by a distinctively feminist women's culture flourished—including bookstores, theater groups, music collectives, poetry groups, art collectives, publishing and recording companies, spirituality groups, vacation resorts, self-help groups, and a variety of feminist-run businesses. This "women's culture," though it includes feminists of diverse political persuasions, has been largely maintained by lesbian feminists in the 1980s and 90s. It nurtures a feminist collective identity that is important to the survival of the women's movement as a whole (Taylor & Whittier 1992).

Both bureaucratic organizations working within mainstream politics and the alternative feminist culture have expanded since the movement's emergence in the 1960s. Following 1972, the scope of feminist goals broadened as the ideology of the movement as a whole grew more radical, and the decentralized structure of the movement made it possible for feminist groups to proliferate. Feminism flourished throughout the 1970s, and the issue of gender took center stage in American politics and in other arenas. Membership in NOW reached 250,000 in 1982, an increase from 35,000 in the mid-70s (Ryan 1992), and uncounted numbers of small independent feminist groups formed in cities and towns across the country. Structural distinctions between the bureaucratic and collectivist branches of the movement diminished along with ideological distinctions, as small and large groups alike became institutionalized,

and the thriving women's movement community drew participants from both traditions of feminist activism. As a result of feminist values of egalitarianism and avoidance of hierarchy, organizations such as NOW and the National Abortion Rights Action League (NARAL) incorporated some of the innovations of collectivism, including CR groups, modified consensus decision-making, and the use of direct action tactics and civil disobedience. A host of structural variations emerged, including formally-structured groups that use consensus decision-making, organizations with deliberately democratic structures, and groups that officially operate by majority-rule democracy but in practice make most decisions by consensus (Tierney 1982; Staggenborg 1988, 1989; Martin 1990; Ryan 1992; Taylor forthcoming). At the same time, feminist collectives shifted their focus from consciousness-raising and radical feminist critique to the development of feminist self-help and service organizations, such as rape crisis centers, shelters for battered women (Tierney 1982), job training programs for displaced homemakers, lesbian peer counseling groups, support for single mothers, and the presentation of women's theatrical and musical productions. At the same time, many feminist collectives revised their structure to depend less on consensus decision making, and permit specialization of skills. In short, some groups that identified themselves as part of the radical branch of the movement assumed a more reform-oriented stance and adopted relatively institutionalized structures and strategies for change.

During the period from 1972 to 1982, the campaign for ratification of the ERA, the struggle to win and maintain abortion rights, and the candidacies of women for political office galvanized feminists of diverse persuasions into cooperation with one another. Coalition efforts brought notable successes in the early 1970s. The ERA passed through Congress in 1972 and was ratified by 22 states within the first year, and the Supreme Court handed down the Roe v. Wade decision in 1973 legalizing abortion. In the late 1970s, more bureaucratically structured organizations such as NOW, the National Women's Political Caucus (NWPC), and NARAL came to function as interest groups aligned with the Democratic party. The culmination of this trend was the nomination of a woman, Geraldine Ferraro, for vice president, on the Democratic ticket in 1984, as the Democratic party sought the endorsement of feminist groups (Klein 1984; Mueller 1987; Frankovic 1988). The necessity of working as an interest group on Capitol Hill brought further structural developments to this wing of the movement, with the creation of Political Action Committees, the adoption of mass mailing techniques to gain supporters and contributors, and the further professionalization of movement organizations (Boles 1991; Staggenborg 1991; Ryan 1992).

Institutionalization and professionalization were not limited to liberal feminist groups. Even groups that developed out of the radical branch have gained access to the established political structure and won support for their goals. Feminist anti-rape groups, for example, have received financial support from government agencies and private foundations to provide rape-prevention and treatment services in public schools and universities. The widespread acceptance of the feminist analysis of rape as an act of violence and power rather than a strictly sexual act further attests to the impact of the feminist anti-rape movement. Likewise, the movement to provide shelters for battered women has grown from a small group of radical feminists to a project supported by such agencies as the United Way and, in some states, by a tax on marriage licenses (Tierney 1982). In addition, the movement to integrate feminist research and study into the academy has led to the establishment of women's studies programs at most colleges and universities and the proliferation of journals dealing with women and feminism. The distinction between "working outside the system" and "working within the system," so important in the late 1960s, no longer has the same significance.

The women's movement community also became institutionalized and flourished in the late 1970s and 1980s. National cultural events such as the Michigan Womyn's Music Festival, which draws from between 5,000 and 10,000 women annually, and a multitude of local events such as "Take Back the Night" marches against rape, feminist concerts, lesbian writers' workshops, and conferences on topics ranging from feminist spirituality to substance abuse, proliferated. As the liberal branch of the women's movement retreated from protest and disruptive tactics and focused instead on actions within the political arena, the network of feminist counter-institutions grew more elaborate. It is within the structure of the women's movement community that the ideologies and goals of radical feminism and lesbian feminism have continued to flourish (Taylor & Whittier 1992).

The women's movement remained relatively homogenous in terms of race, class, and ethnicity throughout the 1970s and 1980s. Although individual women of color and working-class women had participated in the founding of NOW and in the early protests against sexism in the civil rights movement, the women's movement attracted primarily white middle-class women. Buechler (1990) proposes

that because white middle-class women are oppressed on the basis of gender and not on the basis of class or race, they are the most likely to be drawn to a movement that focuses on eliminating sexism. Certainly, it is not that women of color and working class or poor women experience no oppression as women or oppose feminist goals. A 1989 *New York Times*/CBS News poll, for example, showed that, while only 64% of white women saw a need for a women's movement, 85% of African American women and 76% of Hispanic women thought the women's movement was needed (Sapiro 1991). Yet the feminist movement has remained predominantly white both because of the continuation of its tradition of defining its goals with an eye to the concerns of white middle-class women and because black women and other women of color place a priority on working with men of their own communities to advance their collective interests. Independent organizing by women of color did occur during the 1970s, and when African American activists in the women's movement formed the National Black Feminist Organization in 1973 it grew to a membership of 1,000 within its first year (Deckard 1983). Several anthologies of feminist writings by women of color in the early 1980s called attention to the ways in which white-dominated feminist organizations continued to marginalize and overlook women of color, despite increased rhetorical commitment to anti-racism (Moraga & Anzaldúa 1981; Hull, Scott, & Smith 1982; Smith 1983). In response, women of color have persistently formed active caucuses within predominantly white feminist organizations, such as the National Women's Studies Association, to work against racism within the women's movement. Likewise, Jewish women, who had historically played important roles within the women's movement, began to organize their own groups and speak out against anti-Semitism within the movement (Beck 1980; Bulkin, Pratt, & Smith 1984).

Although the class bias of the women's movement has made working-class and poor women unlikely to participate in sizable numbers, class boundaries have been more permeable than race boundaries (Buechler 1990). Union women played a significant role in the formation of NOW in 1966; they supported the fledgling organization by providing office space and clerical services until the group's endorsement of the ERA in 1967 forced the women of the United Auto Workers, an organization that at the time opposed the ERA, to withdraw such support. Women committed to both feminism and the union movement eventually formed their own organization, the Coalition of Labor Union Women (CLUW) in 1974 (Balser 1987). CLUW claimed 16,000 members by 1982 and had made progress in its fight to win AFL-CIO support for feminist issues. While the women's movement had been criticized in the early 1980s for neglecting issues relevant to working women (Hewlett 1986), working-class and middle-class feminists cooperated throughout the 80s on issues of economics and childcare such as comparable worth, daycare tax credits, and parental leave (Gelb & Paley 1982). The basic class and race composition of the movement may have changed little throughout the 70s and 80s, but feminists began to recognize the need to expand the definition of "women's issues" to include problems of central concern to women of color, working-class and poor women, and lesbian women. In sum, as Buechler (1990:158) puts it, the new feminist awareness of race and class means that "a movement that began as unconsciously class-bound and race-bound has now become consciously class-bound and race-bound."

The fact that collective action by the women's movement has both created new institutions and moved into almost every major institution of our society suggests that the feminist challenge has had a significant impact on every facet of social life and on the lives of many individuals as well. However, in direct proportion to the successes of the women's movement, a countermovement has developed that has successfully reversed some feminist gains, stalled progress on others, and has changed the face of the women's movement.

FROM HEYDAY TO ABEYANCE

The early 1980s saw a rapid decrease in the number of feminist organizations and a transformation in the form and activities of the women's movement. In part, this was a response to the successes of the New Right: so powerful were antifeminist sentiments and forces that members of a major political party, the Republican party, were elected in 1980 on a platform developed explicitly to "put women back in their place." After forty years of faithful support of the ERA, the Republican party dropped it from its platform, called for a constitutional amendment to ban abortion, and aligned itself with the economic and social policies of the New Right. After the election of the conservative Reagan administration in 1980, federal funds and grants were rarely available to feminist service organizations, and because other social service organizations were also hard hit by budget cuts, competition increased for relatively scarce money from private foundations. As a result, many feminist

programs such as rape crisis centers, shelters for battered women, and job training programs were forced to close or limit their services.

The failure of the ERA in 1982 seemed to reflect the changed political climate, setting the stage for other setbacks throughout the 1980s. Abortion rights, won in 1973 with the Supreme Court's decision in Roe v. Wade, were reduced in 1989 by the Supreme Court's decision in Webster v. Reproductive Services permitting states to enact restrictions on abortion (Staggenborg 1991:137–8). Following the Webster decision, state governments enacted increasingly tight restrictions on abortion, ranging from "informed consent" laws that required a waiting period before women could have abortions, to parental consent laws for underage women, to outright bans on abortion unless the mother's life was in danger. In 1991, the Supreme Court further limited abortion rights by ruling that federally-funded family planning clinics could be barred from providing information on abortion. The anti-abortion movement also escalated and hardened its tactics in the late 80s: it bombed abortion clinics, picketed doctors who performed abortions, and attempted to dissuade women entering clinics from having abortions (Staggenborg 1991).

Further, Women's Studies programs in colleges and universities, which had been established in the 1970s in response to feminist agitation, have come under attack by conservatives in the late 1980s and early 90s. A backlash against "multiculturalism" and "political correctness" in academia seeks to restore the traditional academic focus on the "great thinkers" of Western European thought, and thus to maintain the primacy of white, male perspectives and experiences. Women's Studies, Black Studies, Latin American Studies, Lesbian and Gay Studies, and other curricula that focus on minority perspectives, diversity, or oppression are ridiculed for, as a critical article in *New York* magazine put it, "their conviction that Western culture and American society are thoroughly and hopelessly racist, sexist, oppressive" (Taylor 1991:34) and for their preoccupation with such "insignificant" questions as the terminology used to refer to ethnic groups, or the relationship between subtle coercion in heterosexual relations and date rape (Will 1991).

The women's movement has suffered not only from opposition, but also from its apparent success. Overt opposition to the feminist movement had been muted in the mid- to late 1970s. Elites in politics, education, and industry gave the appearance of supporting feminist aims through largely ineffectual affirmative action programs and the appointment of a few token women to high positions in

HELPING OURSELVES TO REVOLUTION

GLORIA STEINEM

For the past year, I've been traveling around this country talking to women in shopping malls and bookstores, school gyms and community centers, universities and living rooms—learning that there's a great impatience out there to put the internal and the external together into one revolutionary whole.

I stumbled on this by writing what I was experiencing: the need to connect self-authority to standing up to authority, self-esteem to revolution. Unexpectedly, the book struck a chord that was both wide and deep. It was as if two great movements of our time, those for social justice and for self-realization, were halves of a whole just waiting to come together. And as if the feminist movement that pioneered the connection between the personal and the political had been under such political pressure for so long that the personal part of the equation had been neglected—and had left a deep longing.

Of course, there was also resistance to bringing up the personal; a fear that it would be energy taken away from the political. This isn't surprising given the either/or culture we live in, not to mention the cases in which turning inward really *is* hiding out. But the truth is that once we get out of "either/or" thinking and into an "and" state of mind, we can combine what we've learned about political effectiveness *and* inner growth over the last 25 years, and inspire a response from women that is beyond anything I've witnessed since the movement's early years.

When this second wave was beginning, small-group feminism was more natural because that's what we usually were: a few "crazy" women in each town who met in living rooms, coffee shops, and church basements. As Ann Forer, Carol Hanisch, Kathie Sarachild, the small group then known as Redstockings, and other pioneers of consciousness-raising demonstrated in the late 1960s, this method that paralleled the "testifying" meeting of the civil rights movement and the "speaking bitterness" meetings of the Chinese Cultural Revolution allowed

the truth of feelings and experiences to lead to theory and to action.

I remember meetings about which we never said, "Oh, god, I have to go to another meeting"—because they were the highlight of our week. We brought our problems and experiences, from what to do about a racist/sexist boss to tensions with mothers and lovers; we went around the room with serious personal themes and also with outrageous jokes; we talked about sex with an honesty I'd never heard before; we really *listened* to each other for clues to our mutual welfare; and we unearthed archaeological fragments of our lives that were parts of a political pattern. Those insights led to actions and speakouts that turned shared experiences into public issues.

But as the tasks got bigger and a feminist analysis grew more widespread, there was also a need for bigger groups that could handle larger numbers and more sustained projects. Gradually, volunteers were joined by salaried staffs, there were phone bills and office rents to pay, and the schedule of the outside world—whether it was a meeting of a professional psychiatric organization where patient abuse was finally discussed, or a vote on abortion or gay rights in the state legislature—began to create our schedules for us. Larger organizations were a sign of energy and success, yet in the process of forming them, the free-form small group of the past was largely displaced.

When I began in the late 1970s to ask women at movement gatherings if they had ever experienced a small-group, consciousness-raising process, only about a tenth said they had. When I asked how many still had any similar group as a regular part of their lives, even fewer said yes. By the end of the 1980s, there were almost no yeses to the first question, and a grab bag of answers to the second—from large networks of professional women to small groups of old friends who met for lunch—but little that consciously linked personal affect to political cause—or vice versa.

Those early consciousness-raising groups left ongoing legacies, and personal truth-telling as a path to social change is the most important and enduring one.

Since the 1970s, an ever-increasing number of women, both in and outside the movement, have caught this contagious spirit, and have told their own stories of sexual abuse as children, violence from men in their own households—and much more. Once you've heard someone else tell an experience that is like yours, it exerts an irresistible pull. Just look at the fallout from Anita Hill's testimony.

Yet in the 1980s when women's chain reaction of truth-telling was rising to nationwide visibility in incest survivor conferences and TV talk shows, most movement groups—thanks to the antiequality backlash launched by the Reagan and Bush administrations—were stretched to the breaking point just trying to hang on to past gains, and to defend against efforts to demonize feminism.

So, with no movement place to go, our exponential truth-telling led mostly to support groups and therapists for women with resources, and renewed silence, passivity, and despair for those without. It also swelled the ranks of free 12-step programs, whose (mostly male) meetings for alcohol and drug addiction were joined by (mostly female) groups for "codependency" and eating disorders. Though such programs saved many women's lives by understanding the healing power of personal stories, they remained so apolitical that "codependent" was used to describe what is really just a well-socialized woman, and men in groups who sexually hit on women were common enough to be called "13-steppers." As Wendy Kaminer argues in *I'm Dysfunctional, You're Dysfunctional* (Addison-Wesley), if you imagine the 12-step instruction to admit that you're powerless and submit to a higher power as a political slogan, the dangers of this movement are clear. Even as we criticize this model of permanent personal illness, however, we must admit that there was no free, accessible feminist alternative. There still isn't.

That's a brief history of how we got here, but the "here" is a place of increasing danger and lost opportunities. I've talked to hundreds of women with one of the country's most common problems—having a full-time job inside the home as well as outside it—yet they lacked the sense of mutual entitlement to imagine a world in which men were equal parents, or even picked up their own socks; much less to demand a national system of child care. I've met smart and brave women in the all-black housing project of a midwestern city, sin-gle mothers trying to survive on welfare, who see their neighbors as sister victims, not as potential supporters, because they believe the women's movement is for any women but them. I've met equally smart and brave young white mothers in southern suburbs who go to the shopping mall with their babies and sit on benches for hours because it's their only chance to see other adults. In city offices, I've met women executives who feel so needy of their bosses' approval, and have so little experience of female support, that they don't share vital information with their women coworkers. And there are also a lot of activists who are constantly on the edge of burnout, with no system of personal support or political renewal. . . .

So here is my proposal for a goal by the year 2000: *A nationwide system of small groups of women who support each other personally and act politically.* It doesn't matter whether we call them testifying or soul sessions as in the civil rights movement; consciousness-raising or rap groups as in early feminism; covens, quilting bees, or women's circles as in women's history; or councils of grandmothers, "speaking bitterness" groups, or revolutionary cells as in diverse cultures. The crucial thing is that they are free, no bigger than an extended family, personal/political—and everywhere. . . .

A nationwide contagion of such groups within this decade isn't as big an order as it may seem. A few women have had versions of such groups in their lives for many years, and are walking testimonials to how important they are in growing personally and staying effective politically. Others have started women's reading clubs that are really consciousness-raising groups in disguise, albeit with less activism, or professional networks that provide workplace support, even if they're too big to be personal.

If you are still skeptical about women's longing for community, consider the 1992 Women's Voices project, a nationwide public opinion poll on women's attitudes about their lives that was commissioned by the Ms. Foundation for Women and the Center for Policy Alternatives, and conducted by a multiracial, bipartisan, multicultural team. "Strategically," the poll concluded, "the women's movement needs to organize locally where women live their lives, and where women see themselves most likely to want to be active." This local emphasis becomes even more important for women at lower income levels, or within less powerful racial and ethnic groups. More than half of all women were active in local parent, community, and religious organizations—all bodies in which women are more the source of support than the subject of it.

Do you still believe that women's groups are a luxury only some women can afford? Or that taking time for ourselves and making a psychic/political family is just one more obligation? Or an impossible dream?

I think the hundreds of women's stories I've listened to in the past year would convince you otherwise. In rural Oklahoma, a school superintendent said only meeting privately with other women helped her confront religious groups trying to retain corporal punishment in schools. In the rarefied air of Aspen, a therapist told me only meeting regularly with a group of women as equals had helped her take care of herself

and take on the politics of her profession—in spite of her years of training.

This message of need for small continuing groups has been so clear that I've come to wonder about the price we've paid for neglecting it. In a landmark new book, *Trauma and Recovery* (Basic Books), Judith Herman . . . quotes Virginia Woolf's words of more than 50 years ago: "The public and private worlds are inseparably connected . . . the tyrannies and servilities of one are the tyrannies and servilities of the other." Yet as we came to know only long after her death, there were secrets of childhood sexual abuse Woolf couldn't write about, much less make part of a larger movement. What if she had lived in a time when she had the personal/political support of other women?

She deserved that support—and so do we.

their respective areas. Meanwhile, the popular image of feminism advanced by the mass media suggested that the women's movement had won its goals, making feminism an anachronism. Despite the real-life difficulties women encountered trying to balance paid employment and a "second shift" of housework and childcare (Hochschild 1989), the image of the working woman became the feminine ideal. The public discourse implied that since women had already achieved equality with men, they no longer needed a protest movement, unless they happened to be lesbians and man haters. Both popular and scholarly writers, in short, declared the 1980s and 90s a "post-feminist" era.

In addition to external obstacles, the movement's shift from heyday to abeyance has been marked by internal divisions and conflict. Some scholars have argued that these internal factors are largely responsible for the decline of mass feminist activism. Alice Echols (1989), tracing the demise of radical feminism, contends that when feminist ideology began to emphasize the essentialist nature of sex differences in the early 1970s, idealizing the feminine and denigrating the masculine, the women's movement lost its radical potential and impetus. In her view, the move toward building an alternative feminist culture represented a feminist retreat from confronting and changing social institutions. In a similar vein, Barbara Ryan (1989) argues that internal debates over the correctness of competing feminist theories and the political implications of personal choices—which she terms "ideological purity"—along with

the rise of lesbian feminism and its emphasis on separatism and criticism of men and heterosexual relationships, tore the women's movement apart. It cannot be disputed that the task of building a movement of such a diverse group of women has proven difficult and has, at times, distracted activists from the important work of confronting social institutions.

As feminists increasingly question the notion of women as a unified sex class, the emphasis on women's differences from each other has sometimes fragmented the movement. Identity politics, then, has been both a strength of the women's movement and an obstacle, as women with different allegiances struggle to find common ground. Battles over heterosexism, homophobia, and lesbianism strained the women's movement in the 1970s and early 80s, but during the late 1980s and 90s, it was the issues of race and racism that most divided the movement. Major organizations such as the National Women's Studies Association (NWSA) were split by accusations of racism leveled by women of color caucuses and the defensive reactions of white women (Ruby et al. 1990). Participants at the first national lesbian conference held in Atlanta in 1991 decided that they were unable to found a national lesbian organization because lesbians' differences from each other made it difficult to find common ground (Sharon et al. 1991). Other differences among women have also become points of contention: fat women, disabled women, women with environmental illnesses, old women, young women, women with seizure disorders, women confronting substance abuse, and numerous other groups have met at conferences, proposed their own agendas, and demanded changes in policies and culture at feminist events in order to accommodate their needs and prevent their oppression (see Sharon et al. 1991 for a sample account of such proceedings). While some scholars argue that such debates are counterproductive and divisive (Ryan 1989, 1992), others point out that the problem that divides the movement is racism itself, not the criticism of it (Smith 1983; Hill-Collins 1990). Because the women's movement has been based on the common identity of "woman," it faces difficult and far-reaching challenges as it attempts to recognize differences and divisions among women.

We are suggesting here that the women's movement of the late 1980s and 90s is in abeyance. Verta Taylor (1989), building on research on the women's movement of the 1950s (Rupp & Taylor 1987), suggests that movements adopt abeyance structures in order to survive in hostile political climates. Movements in abeyance are in a "holding pattern," during which activists from an earlier period maintain the ideology and structural base of the movement, but few new recruits join. A movement in abeyance is primarily oriented toward maintaining itself rather than confronting the established order directly. Focusing on building an alternative culture, for example, is a means of surviving when external resources are not available and the political structure is not amenable to challenge. The structure of the women's movement has changed as mass mobilization and confrontation of the social system have declined. Nevertheless, feminist resistance continues in different forms. Patricia Hill-Collins suggests that resistance can occur at three levels: the individual level of consciousness, the cultural level, and the social structural level (1990:227). This conceptualization allows us to recognize that protest takes many forms and to acknowledge the role of social movements in changing consciousness and culture.

The women's movement has sought to make profound changes in the lives of women. At the level of consciousness and individual actions, women who were active in the women's movement of the 1960s and 70s have continued to shape their lives around their feminist beliefs in the 1980s and 90s, even when they are not involved in organized feminist activity. For example, many feminists hold jobs in government, social service organizations, or Women's Studies and other academic programs that allow them to incorporate their political goals into their work, and continue to choose leisure activities, significant relationships, and dress and presentation of self that are consistent with

feminist ideology (Whittier 1995). The consciousness and lives of women who do not identify as feminist have also been altered by the women's movement. In a study of gender and family life in the Silicon Valley of California [see Reading 52, pages 519 to 532], Judith Stacey (1987) argues that in the 1980s some women have incorporated portions of feminism into family and work structures that are otherwise traditional, combining a feminist emphasis on developing satisfying careers, sharing household work with husbands, and increasing men's emotional expressiveness, with fundamentalist Christianity and its focus on the importance of the family. In short, even some segments of fundamentalist Christianity have adopted elements of the feminist critique of men's absence from families and lack of emotional expression, and are encouraging men to broaden their gender roles. In an example of these changes, President George Bush received applause when he broke masculine conventions and wept as he spoke to a Southern Baptist conference about his emotional decision to send troops to the Persian Gulf war (*Columbus Dispatch,* 6/7/91:2A). While many feminists may not rejoice at such changes in traditional religion, it is nevertheless apparent that the effects of the women's movement stretch far beyond policies and practices that are explicitly labeled feminist.

At the cultural level, the feminist social movement community has continued to thrive into the 1990s, with such events as, for example, an "annual multicultural multiracial conference on aging" for lesbians (*Off Our Backs* 1991:12), feminist cruises, several annual women's music festivals and a women's comedy festival in different parts of the country. Gatherings and conferences in 1990 included groups such as Jewish lesbian daughters of holocaust survivors, women motorcyclists, fat dykes, practitioners of Diannic Wicca, Asian lesbians, practitioners of herbal medicine, and survivors of incest. Newsletters and publications exist for groups including women recovering from addictions, women's music professionals and fans, lesbian separatists, disabled lesbians, lesbian couples, feminists interested in sadomasochism, feminists opposed to pornography, and a multitude of others. The growth of the feminist community underscores the flowering of lesbian feminism in the late 1980s and 90s. A wide variety of lesbian and lesbian feminist books and anthologies have been published on topics ranging from lesbian feminist ethics, to separatism, to sexuality, to commitment ceremonies for lesbian couples (see, for example, Hoagland 1988, Hoagland & Penelope 1988, Loulan 1990, Butler 1990), reflecting diverse perspectives that have been hotly debated in the pages of lesbian publications and at conferences and festivals. For example, a series of letters to the editor in a national lesbian newsletter argued over the correct lesbian feminist response to lesbians serving in the armed forces in the Persian Gulf War: some readers held that the war was a manifestation of patriarchy and that lesbians in the military should not be celebrated; others argued that lesbian soldiers should be supported because they are lesbians in a homophobic institution, regardless of support or opposition to the war; still others argued that the Gulf War was justified and that lesbian servicewomen should be celebrated for their patriotic service (*Lesbian Connection* 1991). Clearly, the task of building a community based on the identity "lesbian" has proven complex, if not impossible. Nevertheless, the institutional structure of the social movement community has continued to expand, and within the community feminists construct and reinforce a collective identity based on opposition to dominant conceptions of women and lesbians (Taylor & Whittier 1992).

At the social structural level, the feminist movement has not been unresponsive to the conservative backlash. In fact, the gains of the New Right in the late 1980s sparked some of the largest feminist demonstrations and actions in years. In April, 1989, NOW and abortion rights groups organized a national demonstration in Washington, DC, that drew between 300,000 and 600,000 women and men to protest restrictions on abortion. Additional national and local demonstrations followed, and pro-choice activists organized electoral lobbying, defense of abortion clinics, and conferences, and attempted to form coalitions across racial and ethnic lines and among women of different ages (Staggenborg 1991; Ryan 1992). The National Abortion Rights Action League (NARAL) experienced a growth in membership from 200,000 in 1989 to 400,000 in 1990 (Staggenborg 1991: 138), and membership in NOW also continued to grow in the late 1980s and 90s after a decline in the early 1980s, with a membership of 250,000 in 1989. In addition, a wide variety of feminist organizations continue to pursue social change at state and local levels (Ferree & Martin 1995).

The women's movement has also had a substantial impact on other social movements of the 1980s and 90s. Movements such as the gay and lesbian movement, AIDS movement, recovery from addictions, New Age spirituality, and the animal rights movement have been profoundly influenced by feminist values and ideology, including the emphasis on collective structure and consensus, the notion of the personal as political, goddess-worship, and the critique of patriarchal mistreatment of animals and ecological resources. The women's movement also trained a large

number of feminist activists in the 1970s, particularly lesbians, who have participated in new social movements and integrated feminism into them (Cavin 1990; Whittier 1995). For example, the gay and lesbian movement has begun expanding its health concerns to include breast cancer as well as AIDS and has adopted strategies of the feminist anti-rape movement to confront violence against gays and lesbians. The recovery movement discusses the ways that gender socialization makes women co-dependent. Many women's self-help groups, such as the postpartum depression movement, sprung directly out of the early women's health movement and continue to model support groups on feminist consciousness-raising groups. In addition, feminists have renewed coalitions with the peace, environmental, socialist, anti-U.S. intervention in Latin America and anti-apartheid movements, transforming these movements both by forming separate feminist organizations that address these issues and by moving into mixed-sex organizations (Whittier 1995). In a sense the women's movement has come full circle, re-joining the 1990s versions of the movements that composed the New Left in the 1960s when feminists split off to form a separate women's movement.

Given the scope and size of women's movement activity in the late 1980s and 90s, why do we argue that the movement is in abeyance? We think that, although the movement may resurge in the mid 1990s, the level of mass mobilization and confrontation of the social structural system clearly declined following 1982. Because feminism in the late 80s and 90s is focused more on consciousness and culture and has established roots in other social movements of the period, feminist protest is less visible than it was during the heyday of the women's movement. Notably, in keeping with the patterns that characterize movements in abeyance (Taylor 1989), the most active feminists in the late 1980s and 90s have been women who became involved with the movement during the late 1960s and 1970s, were transformed by their involvement, and formed a lasting commitment to feminist goals. Despite support for feminist goals, many young women do not identify themselves as feminists, apparently because the identity of feminist is stigmatized. A feminist is seen as someone who deviates from gender norms by being unattractive, aggressive, hostile to men, opposed to marriage and motherhood, lesbian, and seeking to imitate men (Schneider 1988, Dill unpublished). Despite the gains made by women in some areas, gender norms are still so rigid and deeply internalized that they successfully deter many women who otherwise support the feminist agenda from participating in the movement.

Yet, some younger women have joined the women's movement in the late 1980s and 90s despite the risks entailed in identifying with a stigmatized and unpopular cause. In a study of young feminist activists in the 1990s, Kim Dill has found that a new generation of women has been recruited to feminism primarily through Women's Studies courses and through the transmission of feminism from mothers to daughters (unpublished). In short, the institutionalized gains of the heyday of feminist activism in the 1970s are enabling the women's movement to survive and to spread its ideology to new recruits.

The history of the women's movement, and its present survival despite the challenges it has confronted from within its own ranks and from a conservative political climate, suggest that because feminism is a response to the fundamental social cleavage of gender it will continue to exist (Taylor & Rupp 1993). As one generation of feminists fades from the scene with its ultimate goals unrealized, another takes up the challenge (Rossi 1982). But each new generation of feminists does not simply carry on where the previous generation left off. Rather, it speaks for itself and defines its own objectives and strategies, often to the dismay and disapproval of feminists from earlier generations. The activism of a new generation of feminists may take the form of distributing condoms and dental dams to women for AIDS prevention, or organizing "Kiss-Ins" with Queer Nation, or organizing a "warm line" for women suffering postpartum depression (Taylor forthcoming), or sponsoring recycling drives. While earlier generations of activists may not view such endeavors as feminist, as Myra Ferree and Beth Hess (1985:182) point out, "feminism is not simply a form of received wisdom" but something that evolves with each new cycle of feminist activism. Both continuity and change, then, will characterize the feminism of the twenty-first century.

ACKNOWLEDGMENTS

We would like to thank Leila Rupp and Kate Weigand for their insightful contributions, careful readings of earlier drafts of this paper, and steadfast support.

REFERENCES

Acker, J. 1980. "Women and stratification: A review of recent literature." *Contemporary Sociology* 9:25–35.

Atkinson, T. G. 1974. *Amazon odyssey.* New York: Links.

Balser, Diane. 1987. *Sisterhood and solidarity: Feminism and labor in modern times.* Boston: South End Press.

Beauvoir, S. de. 1952. *The second sex.* New York: Bantam.

Beck, E. T. 1980. *Nice Jewish girls: A lesbian anthology.* Watertown, MA: Persephone.

Boles, Janet. 1979. *The politics of the equal rights amendment.* New York: Longman.

Breines, 1982. *Community and organization in the New Left, 1962–68.* New York: Praeger.

Buechler, Steven M. 1990. *Women's movements in the United States.* New Brunswick, NJ: Rutgers.

Bulkin, Elly, Minnie Bruce Pratt, and Barbara Smith. 1984. *Yours in struggle: Three feminist perspectives on anti-Semitism and racism.* New York: Long Haul Press.

Bunch, C. 1987. *Passionate politics.* New York: St. Martin's.

Butler, Becky. 1991. *Ceremonies of the heart: Celebrating lesbian unions.* Seattle, WA: The Seal Press.

Carden, Maren. 1978. "The proliferation of a social movement." Pp. 179–196 in *Research in social movements, conflict, and change,* vol. 1, edited by Louis Kriesberg. Greenwich, CT: JAI Press.

Cassell, J. 1977. *A group called women: Sisterhood and symbolism in the feminist movement.* New York: David McKay.

Cavin, Susan. 1990. "The invisible army of women: Lesbian social protests, 1969–88." Pp. 321–332 in *Women and social protest,* edited by Guida West and Rhoda Blumberg. New York: Oxford University Press.

Chafe, W. H. 1977. *Women and equality: Changing patterns in American culture.* New York: Oxford University Press.

Chafetz, Janet and Gary Dworkin. 1986. *Female revolt.* Totowa, NJ: Rowman and Allenheld.

Chafetz, Janet. 1990. *Gender equity: An integrated theory of stability and change.* Newbury Park, CA: Sage.

Columbus Dispatch. 1991. "Bush cries as he tells Baptists of his prayers, tears before war." Friday, June 7: 2A.

Daly, Mary. 1978. *Gyn/ecology.* Boston: Beacon.

Deckard, Barbara Sinclair. 1983. *The women's movement.* New York: Harper and Row.

Dill, Kim. Unpublished. "Feminism in the nineties: The influence of collective identity and community on young feminist activists." Master's thesis, The Ohio State University, 1991.

Echols, Alice. 1989. *Daring to be bad: Radical feminism in America 1967–1975.* Minneapolis: University of Minnesota Press.

Eisenstein, Z. 1981. *The radical future of liberal feminism.* New York: Longman.

Evans, Sarah. 1979. *Personal politics.* New York: Knopf.

Ferree, Myra Marx, and Beth B. Hess. 1985. *Controversy and coalition: The new feminist movement.* Boston: Twayne.

——— and Patricia Yancey Martin. 1995. *Feminist Organizations: Harvest of the New Women's Movement.* Philadelphia: Temple University Press.

Firestone, S. 1970. *The dialectic of sex.* New York: William Morrow.

Frankovic, Kathleen A. "The Ferraro factor: The women's movement, the polls, and the press." Pp. 102–123 in *The politics of the gender gap: The social construction of political influence,* edited by Carol M. Mueller. Newbury Park, CA: Sage.

Freeman, Jo. 1972/3. "The tyranny of structurelessness." *Berkeley Journal of Sociology* 17:151–164.

——— . 1975. *The politics of women's liberation.* New York: David McKay.

——— . 1979. "Resource mobilization and strategy: A model for analyzing social movement organization actions." Pp. 167–89 in *The dynamics of social movements,* edited by M. N. Zald and J. D. McCarthy. Cambridge, MA: Winthrop.

Friedan, B. 1963. *The feminine mystique.* New York: Norton.

Frye, Marilyn. 1983. *The politics of reality: Essays in feminist theory.* Trumansburg, NY: Crossing Press.

Gelb, Joyce and Marian Lief Paley. 1982. *Women and public policy.* Princeton: Princeton University Press.

Gerlach, L. P., and V. H. Hine. 1970. *People, power, change: Movements of social transformation.* Indianapolis: Bobbs-Merrill.

Gordon, Suzanne. *Prisoners of men's dreams.* New York: Little, Brown.

Griffin, S. 1978. *Women and nature.* New York: Harper & Row.

Hartmann, H. 1981. "The family as the locus of gender, class, and political struggle: The example of housework." *Signs* 6 (Spring):366–94.

Hartsock, N.C.M. 1983. *Money, sex, and power: Toward a feminist historical materialism.* New York: Longman.

Hewlett, Sylvia. 1987. *A lesser life.* New York: Morrow.

Hill-Collins, Patricia. 1990. *Black feminist thought.* Boston: Unwin Hyman.

Hoagland, Sarah Lucia. 1988. *Lesbian ethics: Toward new value.* Palo Alto, CA: Institute of Lesbian Studies.

——— and Julia Penelope, eds. 1988. *For lesbians only.* London: Onlywomen Press.

Hochschild, Arlie. 1989. *The second shift.* New York: Avon.

Huber, J. 1973. "From sugar and spice to professor." In *Academic women on the move,* edited by A. S. Rossi and A. Calderwood. New York: Russell Sage Foundation.

Hull, Gloria T., Patricia Bell Scott, and Barbara Smith. 1982. *But some of us are brave: Black women's studies.* New York: The Feminist Press.

Keuck, D. 1980. "Community action to prevent rape." A class presentation in Sociology of Women course, Ohio State University, Columbus.

Klein, Ethel. 1984. *Gender politics.* Cambridge, MA: Harvard University Press.

Lesbian connection 1991. Vols. 13 and 14. Lansing, MI: Ambitious Amazons.

Loulan, JoAnn. 1990. *The lesbian erotic dance.* San Francisco: Spinsters Book Company.

McCarthy, J. D., and M. N. Zald. 1977. "Resource mobilization and social movements: A partial theory." *American Journal of Sociology* 82 (May):1212–1239.

MacKinnon, C. A. 1983. "Feminism, Marxism, method, and the state: Toward feminist jurisprudence." *Signs* 8(4):635–58.

Mansbridge, Jane. 1986. *Why we lost the ERA.* Chicago: University of Chicago Press.

Marshall, S. 1984. "Keep us on the pedestal: Women against feminism in twentieth-century America." Pp. 568–81 in *Women: A feminist perspective,* edited by Jo Freeman. Palo Alto: Mayfield.

Martin, Patricia Yancey. 1990. "Rethinking feminist organizations." *Gender and Society* 4(2):182–206.

Marx, G. T., and J. L. Wood. 1975. "Strands of theory and research in collective behavior." Pp. 363–428 in *Annual review of sociology,* vol. 1, edited by A. Inkeles, J. Coleman, and N. Smelser.

Mathews, Donald G. and Jane Sherron DeHart. 1990. *Sex, gender, and the politics of ERA: A state and the nation.* New York: Oxford.

Millett, K. 1971. *Sexual politics.* New York: Avon.

Mitchell, Juliet. 1986. "Reflections on twenty years of feminism." Pp. 34–48 in *What is feminism?* edited by Juliet Mitchell and Ann Oakley. Oxford: Basil Blackwell.

Moraga, Cherrie, and Gloria Anzaldúa. 1981. *This bridge called my back: Writings by radical women of color.* Watertown, MA: Persephone.

Mueller, Carol McClurg. 1987. "Collective consciousness, identity transformation, and the rise of women in public office in the United States." Pp. 89–108 in *The women's movement of the United States and Western Europe,* edited by M. F. Katzenstein and C. M. Mueller. Philadelphia: Temple University Press.

O'Reilly, J. 1980. "To fight them, we've got to understand what they're saying." *Savvy,* October.

Off Our Backs 1991. "Passages 7—Beyond the barriers." Vol. 21(6):12.

Oppenheimer, Valerie Kincade. 1973. "Demographic influence on female employment and the status of women." Pp. 184–199 in *Changing women in a changing society,* edited by Joan Huber. Chicago: University of Chicago Press.

Reskin, Barbara. 1988. "Bringing the men back in: Sex differentiation and the devaluation of women's work." *Gender and Society* 2:58–81.

Rich, Adrienne. 1976. *Of woman born.* New York: Norton.

———. 1980. "Compulsory heterosexuality and lesbian existence." *Signs* 5:631–60.

Rossi, A. S. 1982. *Feminists in politics.* New York: Academic Press.

Rothschild-Whitt, Joyce. 1979. "The collectivist organization: An alternative to rational-bureaucratic models." *American Sociological Review* 44:509–527.

Rubin, G. 1975. "The traffic in women: Notes on the 'political economy' of sex." In *Toward an anthropology of women,* edited by Rayne Reiter. New York: Monthly Review Press.

Ruby, Jennie, Farar Elliott, and Carol Anne Douglas. 1990. "The National Women's Studies Association conference." *Off Our Backs* 20(8).

Rupp, Leila J. and Verta Taylor. 1987. *Survival in the doldrums: The American women's rights movement, 1945 to 1960s.* New York: Oxford University Press.

———. Unpublished. "Women's culture and the persisting women's movement." Paper presented at the Annual Meeting of the American Sociological Association, Washington, DC, August, 12, 1990.

Ryan, Barbara. 1989. "Ideological purity and feminism: The U.S. women's movement from 1966 to 1975." *Gender and Society* 3:239–257.

———. 1992. *Feminism and the women's movement.* New York: Routledge.

Sapiro, V. 1991. In *The annals of the American Academy of Political and Social Science* 515 (May), edited by Janet Boles.

Schlesinger, M. B., and P. Bart. "Collective work and self-identity: The effect of working in a feminist illegal abortion collective." In *Feminist frontiers,* edited by L. Richardson and V. Taylor. Reading, MA: Addison-Wesley.

Schneider, Beth. 1988. "Political generations in the contemporary women's movement." *Sociological Inquiry* 58:4–21.

Sharon, Tanya, Farar Elliott, and Cecile Latham. 1991. "The National Lesbian Conference: For, by and about lesbians." *Off Our Backs* 21(6):1–4, 18–23.

Smith, Barbara. 1983. *Home girls: A black feminist anthology.* New York: Kitchen Table Women of Color Press.

Sparks, C. H. 1979. "Program evaluation of a community rape prevention program." Ph.D. diss., Ohio State University, Columbus.

Stacey, Judith. 1987. "Sexism by a subtler name? Postindustrial conditions and postfeminist consciousness." *Socialist Review* 17(6).

Staggenborg, Suzanne. 1988. "The consequences of professionalization and formalization in the pro-choice movement." *American Sociological Review* 53:585–606.

———. 1989. "Stability and innovation in the women's movement: A comparison of two movement organizations." *Social Problems* 36:75–92.

———. 1991. *The pro-choice movement.* New York: Oxford University Press.

Taylor, John, 1991. "Are you politically correct?" *New York Magazine.* January 21:33–40.

Taylor, Verta. 1989. "Social movement continuity: The women's movement in abeyance." *American Sociological Review* 54:761–775.

———. Forthcoming. Rock-a-by Baby: Feminism, Self-Help, and Postpartum Depression. New York: Routledge.

——— and Leila Rupp. 1993. "Women's Culture and Lesbian Feminist Activism: A Reconsideration of Cultural Feminism." *Signs* 19:32–61.

——— and Nancy Whittier. Forthcoming. "Collective identity in social movement communities: Lesbian feminist mobilization." In *Frontiers of social movement theory,* edited by Aldon Morris and Carol Mueller. New Haven, CT: Yale University Press.

Tierney, K. J. 1982. "The battered women movement and the creation of the wife beating problem." *Social Problems* 29:207–20.

West, Guida and Rhoda Lois Blumberg. 1990. *Women and social protest.* New York: Oxford University Press.

Whittier, Nancy E. 1995. *Feminist Generations: The Persistence of the Radical Women's Movement.* Philadelphia: Temple University Press.

Will, George F. 1991. "Yes, teach complete history, but curriculums of group grievances are divisive." *Philadelphia Inquirer,* Monday, July 15.

Yankelovich, D. 1981. *New rules.* New York: Random House.